Transition Planning for Secondary Students with Disabilities

Robert W. Flexer

Kent State University
Kent, Ohio

Thomas J. Simmons

University of Louisville
Louisville, Kentucky

Pamela Luft

Kent State University
Kent, Ohio

Robert M. Baer

Kent State University
Kent, Ohio

Merrill
Prentice Hall

Upper Saddle River, New Jersey
Columbus, Ohio

Library of Congress Cataloging-in-Publication Data

Transition planning for secondary students with disabilities / Robert Flexer . . . [et al.].

    p. cm.

   Includes bibliographical references and index.

   ISBN 0-13-020572-9

   1. Handicapped youth—Education (Secondary)—United States.   2. Handicapped youth—Vocational education—United States.   3. Handicapped students—Services for—United States.   4. School-to-work transition—United States.   I. Flexer, Robert W.

LC4031.T733 2001

371.9'0473'0973—dc21

00-060692

Vice President and Publisher: Jeffery W. Johnston
Executive Editor: Ann Castel Davis
Editorial Assistant: Pat Grogg
Production Editor: Sheryl Glicker Langner
Production Management: Larry Goldberg, Carlisle Publishers Services
Design Coordinator: Diane Lorenzo
Cover Designer: Linda Fares
Cover art: Image Bank
Production Manager: Laura Messerly
Director of Marketing: Kevin Flanagan
Marketing Manager: Amy June
Marketing Services Manager: Krista Groshong

This book was set in Novarese by Carlisle Communications, Ltd. It was printed and bound by R.R. Donnelley & Sons Company. The cover was printed by Phoenix Color Corp.

Photo Credits: p. 439 by Gary Harwook / Kent State University. All other photos by Center for Innovation in Transition and Employment.

Merrill
Prentice Hall

10 9 8 7 6 5 4 3 2 1
ISBN 0-13-020572-9

Contributors

Robert Baer, Ph.D.
Kent State University
Kent, OH

Debra Bauder, Ph.D.
University of Louisville
Louisville, KY

Greg Clary, M.Ed.
Clarion University
Clarion, PA

Bryan Cook, Ph.D.
Kent State University
Kent, OH

Lysandra Cook, M.Ed.
Kent State University
Kent, OH

Randall L. De Pry, Ph.D.
University of Colorado at Colorado
    Springs
Colorado Springs, CO

Robert Flexer, Ph.D.
Kent State University
Kent, OH

Penny Griffith, Ph.D.
Kent State University
Kent, OH

Deborah Headman, M.Ed.
Polaris Joint Vocational School
Middleburg Heights, OH

Jackie June, M.Ed.
Jefferson County Schools
Louisville, KY

James Knoll, Ph.D.
Morehead State University
Morehead, KY

Lynn Koch, Ph.D.
Kent State University
Kent, OH

Janice Kreiner, M.Ed.
Baldwin-Wallace College
Berea, OH

James Krouse, Ph.D.
Clarion University
Clarion, PA

Preston Lewis, M.Ed.
Division of Exceptional Children
    Services
Frankfort, KY

Pamela Luft, Ph.D.
Kent State University
Kent, OH

Laura Huber Marshall, M.A.
University of Colorado at Colorado
    Springs
Colorado Springs, CO

James Martin, Ph.D.
University of Colorado at Colorado
    Springs
Colorado Springs, CO

Rachel McMahan, M.Ed.
Kent State University
Kent, OH

Patrick O'Connor, Ph.D.
Kent State University
Kent, OH

Phillip Rumrill, Ph.D.
Kent State University
Kent, OH

Richard Sabousky, Ph.D.
Clarion University
Oil City, PA

Thomas Simmons, Ph.D.
University of Louisville
Louisville, KY

Joyce Strand, Ph.D.
Notherns State University
Aberdeen, SD

Melody Tankersley, Ph.D.
Kent State University
Kent, OH

Cynthia Trevino, M.A.
Rutland City Schools
Rutland, VT

Lisa Turner, Ph.D.
Clarion University
Clarion, PA

Deborah Durham Webster, M.Ed.
Kent State University
Kent, OH

Barry Whaley, Ph.D.
Community Employment, Inc.
Louisville, KY

Carolyn Wheeler, Ph.D.
Interdisciplinary Human Development
    Institute
Lexington, KY

Preface

For each individual student, with a disability or not, school is a transitional experience. Each year of high school forms a foundation for the next, culminating in graduation. Another transitional experience is offered up to students the day after high school—be it work or further education. From a transition perspective, high school should be enjoyed for what it is. Nonetheless, beyond the meaning of the everyday learning and living, all students, on varying timetables and with individual urgency, take on a future orientation during the high school years. Looming in the background is the question: What am I going to do after high school? High school programs and transition activities are steppingstones to the future. Their importance directly relates to the degree to which they constitute learning and experiences that reflect movement toward or clarity about the student's transition goals after high school.

For students to have an investment in their education, meaningful participation in the "right" programs is essential. If students cannot say to themselves, "I'm going somewhere, and this is the way or path to my goals," disengagement is inevitable. Access to the full range of high school programs and individualized and varied work-based learning is essential. Again the student must be able to "walk through the door" and be free to participate in the programs of their choice that relate to their goals. This process needs to deal with any adjustments, adaptations, or auxiliary aids and services necessary for the student to perform within the program or work setting. Access is necessary to realize the benefits of participation in regular education, vocational education, and school-to-work programs. *Transition Planning for Secondary Students with Disabilities* describes the varied transition needs of students and the myriad options and career paths potentially available.

Section I: Transition Foundations

Section I provides the broad background required to understand the complex developmental and educational process that takes place from early adolescence through young adulthood. In Chapter 1 (History and Transition Legislation), the evolution of transition law and policy is traced within a framework of the maturing disability rights movement and transition initiatives. The requirements and the need for transition services are no longer debatable. A clear direction for individualized services within an interdisciplinary and coordinated system emerges from the vast literature and comprehensive legislation on transition practices.

The models and best practices, which have been developed over the roughly 50 years of the modern era, are described in Chapter 2 (Transition Models and Best Practices). Models are described that delineate the major components of transition, are related to the essential elements, and then are fleshed out in a description of "best practices" that have emerged from the literature. A theoretical base of career development is provided in Chapter 3 (Career Development: Theories for Transition Planning) so that the individual developmental and educational needs of students are understood.

Planning is central to transition and enables the needs and preferences of students to be the beginning point of the transition process. A career development framework enables the transition team to view the student as evolving and maturing. Career development is a general approach for fitting the students' transition goals within high school programs and preparation options.

The roles of both school and postschool professionals functioning within a team process are explored and outlined in Chapter 4 (Transition Collaborators). Major responsibilities and contributions to the transition process are described for both disability professionals and generic educators and service providers. Coordinated activities among diverse programs and discipline approaches are needed to meet transition needs across the diverse populations of special education students. In Chapter 5 (Multicultural Competence in Transition Planning Processes) the changing composition of the special education student is described from a multicultural viewpoint. In order to engage the student and family in the transition process, the transition team needs to understand the value base, beliefs, and structures of students and families in their natural environments.

Section II: Career and Transition Services

Section II moves from the foundations of transition addressed in Section I to its programmatic implementation. The five chapters in this section provide the application of career theory to career and vocational education and curriculum development, and the implementation of these programs through valid assessment and effective instruction. Assessment practices are used to monitor and evaluate these programs to ensure success, and instruction and the use of technology guarantees access to these programs as well as a full range of optimizing life and career opportunities.

Chapter 6 (Career and Vocational Education) summarizes the concepts and principles of career education and their integration with vocational education as the student begins the final steps of the high school segment of preparation for a career. It describes several examples of career and vocational programs used in schools to prepare students with disabilities for adult living. Chapter 7 (Transition Assessment and Postschool Outcomes) describes basic assessment practices and processes which are at the heart of special education eligibility as well as appropriate program selection and ongoing monitoring which ensures optimal learning and skill acquisition for the student.

Chapter 8 (Curriculum Development and Transition) provides background in curriculum development across a range of content area choices. The IEP team and teachers must make choices that implement career and vocational preparation, in conjunction with other content and skill areas that prepare the student for his or her individually chosen transition outcomes. When these choices are integrated and assembled across the student's profile of educational and transition strengths and needs, they become a curriculum.

Chapter 9 (Instructional Strategies) describes the instructional strategies that are used to provide the student with the knowledge and skills in career and vocational education and across his or her full educational curriculum. Assessment practices are used to ensure that these strategies and classroom management practices are effective in promoting student learning and development, and that they lead to the achievement of desired transition outcomes.

Chapter 10 (The Role of Technology in Transition Planning) describes several of the technologies available that allow students to access the full range of curricular and postschool options that lead to a quality adult life. It provides team members with the processes needed for investigating and making decisions about technology and assistive devices that will lead to long-term satisfaction and use.

Section III: Transition Planning

Section III moves from a discussion of programs in rehabilitation and special, general, and vocational education to a discussion of how these programs can be integrated into transition planning and program development for youth with disabilities. These four chapters can be viewed as a technical manual that describes how to weave policy, best practices, and myriad programs and services into transition activities that promote student self-determination, effective transition planning, service coordination, and family involvement.

Chapter 11 (Participatory Decision-Making: Innovative Practices That Increase Student Self-Determination) provides an overview of self-determination and related curriculum. It presents an in-depth look at how students move from passive spectators to involved decision-makers and a step-by-step process for supporting students in this process. It discusses one self-determination curriculum in detail so that the reader can become familiar with how these instruments work, and it provides an overview of other self-determination instruments.

Chapter 12 (Transition Planning) provides an overview of policy related to transition planning and discusses some common myths in regard to transition planning. It then moves the reader through the process of developing a transition planning process, preplanning for the IEP meeting, conducting that meeting, and evaluating progress. Chapter 12 also provides a case study that demonstrates this process and answers questions that parents frequently ask. (A glossary of terms commonly used in transition planning can be found in Appendix D at the back of the the book.)

Chapter 13 (Coordinating Transition Services) talks about transition service coordination from both an individual and systemic perspective. It examines state-of-the-art case management and service coordination models and discusses some of the barriers to applying these in a highly bureaucratic and fragmented transition system. Chapter 13 then looks at the major goals of transition coordination and discusses how the transition coordinator can address these goals through specific transition activities. It concludes with an extensive case study that demonstrates these concepts. (A sample blanket release of information and member agreement are shown in Appendix E. A self-survey of transition practices can be found in Appendix F.)

Chapter 14 (Family Involvement) discusses the role of the family in transition and provides an overview of best practices. It looks at practices that are conducive to family involvement and examines families' transition concerns and barriers to family involvement. This chapter includes a number of case studies drawn from the authors' experience that illustrate some of these principles and concepts. It concludes with a discussion of interventions and strategies that can facilitate family involvement.

Section IV: Postschool and Community Environments

Section IV concretizes the issues of employment, postsecondary education, recreation and leisure, and independent living. These four domains of postsecondary experience have been discussed at length in the prior sections regarding the execution of planning and the formulation of future goals, educational preparation, collaborative enterprises, and joint programmatic efforts. In keeping with the design of this book, the authors of this section explore programs and services that generally exist in postschool settings. In Chapter 15 (Transition to Employment) the authors discuss various issues around work, sheltered work, and the need for good planning and training in real-life situations. Chapter 16 (Postsecondary Programs and Career Paths) provides a wealth of knowledge about issues surrounding admissions, participation, and the need for understanding one's own needs when entering these demanding environments. Chapter 17 (Recreation and Leisure in the Community) provides a view of recreation services and their role in independence. This chapter discusses roles and responsibilities along with various perspectives on how recreation and leisure programs operate.

Finally, Chapter 18 (My Home: Developing Skills and Supports for Adult Living) provides information regarding the history and issues related to living on your own. Like Chapter 1, the final chapter details a policy history, but, in this instance, more specifically to the independent living and self-advocacy movements. The need for partnership and empowerment are consistent themes for creating supports and services that maximize independence and community integration. Issues discussed in Chapter 18 include transition to independence, supported living, and personal assistance programs. The chapter concludes with a discussion of independent living skills.

This section is filled with information that will expand understanding of transition issues after students leave school and explore issues that most educators do not think about. The authors feel that these future environments have a very important role, and they often require a special effort by transition teams. Communication and interaction among team members in future environments enhance the goal-setting process and help students "keep their eye on the ball."

To the Reader

The purpose of *Transition Planning for Secondary Students with Disabilities* is to provide a comprehensive yet practical text for advanced students at the undergraduate level and students at the graduate level from the diverse fields that contribute to the transition process. School-based teachers from regular, vocational, and special education and other professionals, including psychologists, related services professionals, and guidance coun-

selors, also would benefit from reading this text—especially if they are in the process of establishing or improving interdisciplinary and collaborative transition services. Families and a variety of postschool service providers (e.g., rehabilitation counselor and case managers) would also benefit from the broad framework and specific examples that illustrate the varied educational, career, and personal issues that arise in students' transition to postschool life.

This book, like the transition process, was developed through a team approach. The four authors have over 100 years of combined experience in transition in a variety of settings, working with varied populations of students with disabilities. Recognizing our limitations, we went to yet other individuals for specific chapters because of the contributing authors' unique qualifications. As you might guess, we found it very hard to synchronize our schedules and had many disagreements about the organization and content of this book. However, in the process, we learned a great deal about each other and eventually settled on a framework that guided the text's organization. On the whole, we believe that the book and chapters weave the conceptual framework that is necessary to understand what comprises quality transition services—education and services that support students in the transition process as they pursue their life's dream.

The reader's understanding of transition is built on a structure comprised of four *essential elements*. Every recomme nded practice can be analyzed through this framework. The reader is continuously brought back to the four basic questions raised by the *essential elements*.

1. Is there meaningful student involvement?
2. Are student goals directed toward postschool outcomes shared by the student and their family and team?
3. Are all team members working in a coordinated fashion in relation to the students' goals?
4. Are the education and transition services

promoting movement toward the students' accomplishing their goals?

The application of the *essential elements* provides a test of transition services both for individual students and across all school and postschool services. Transition is treated in a generalized way by cross-categorical, practical, and real transition examples.

Acknowledgments

For 20 years, the Center for Innovation in Transition and Employment at Kent State University has had as its mission supporting the efforts of people with disabilities in realizing quality in their lives. In developing programs to prepare transition professionals and to reach out to schools and communities, innumerable individuals have had an impact on our programs. We hope that they gained insight and useful skills for supporting students. The first author, there from the start, will be indebted forever to his three friends, coauthors, and colleagues for all they have taught him. All the authors thank all of the students with disabilities who contributed so much to us personally and professionally. Likewise, all the Kent State University students and professionals trained in transition at the Center, families of students with disabilities, and Center collaborators who have contributed to our efforts need to be acknowledged for the important lessons they have taught us. All of these individuals with whom we have interacted provided the "data" and stories upon which this book is based. These relationships brought much joy and will endure into the future. Our profession is about caring, commitment, and trust. The authors hope that this book with serve you, the reader, in the same way that all our associations have enhanced us as people. We would like to thank our spouses, Carol, Debbie, Drew, and Judy, whose love and appreciation of us provided much of the "staying power" on this journey. We would like to thank Sherrie Blalock, especially, who kept us organized and provided timely assistance in all phases of preparation of this book.

Large projects such as a book always involve innumerable individuals who give their time to make the book the best possible product it can be. We are very thankful and indebted to individuals at Merrill and Carlisle Publishers Services who have supported us in a thoughtful, kind way—Ann Davis, Sheryl Langner, and Larry Goldberg. The individuals who reviewed the book provided an invaluable service to us by suggesting improvements. We would like to thank these individuals: Brent A. Askvig, Minot State University (ND); Rhonda S. Black, University of Hawaii at Manoa; Ruth M. Buehler, Millersville University (PA); Patricia M. Carlson, Iowa State University; Nikki Cvetkovic, Hiram College (OH); Nola McKee Leggett, Southern Illinios University at Carbondale; Kathy Peca, Eastern New Mexico University; and James Yanok, Ohio University.

Robert Flexer
Thomas Simmons
Pamela Luft
Robert Baer

Discover the Companion Website Accompanying This Book

The Prentice Hall Companion Website: A Virtual Learning Environment

Technology is a constantly growing and changing aspect of our field that is creating a need for content and resources. To address this emerging need, Prentice Hall has developed an online learning environment for students and professors alike—Companion Websites—to support our textbooks.

In creating a Companion Website, our goal is to build on and enhance what the textbook already offers. For this reason, the content for each user-friendly website is organized by topic and provides the professor and student with a variety of meaningful resources. Common features of a Companion Website include:

For the Professor—

Every Companion Website integrates **Syllabus Manager**™, an online syllabus creation and management utility.

- **Syllabus Manager**™ provides you, the instructor, with an easy, step-by-step process to create and revise syllabi, with direct links into Companion Website and other online content without having to learn HTML.
- Students may logon to your syllabus during any study session. All they need to know is the web address for the Companion Website and the password you've assigned to your syllabus.
- After you have created a syllabus using **Syllabus Manager**™, students may enter the syllabus for their course section from any point in the Companion Website.
- Class dates are highlighted in white and assignment due dates appear in blue. Clicking on a date, the student is shown the list of activities for the assignment. The activities for each assignment are linked directly to actual content, saving time for students.
- Adding assignments consists of clicking on the desired due date, then filling in the details of the assignment—name of the assignment, instructions, and whether or not it is a one-time or repeating assignment.
- In addition, links to other activities can be created easily. If the activity is online, a URL can be entered in the space provided, and it will be linked automatically in the final syllabus.
- Your completed syllabus is hosted on our servers, allowing convenient updates from any computer on the Internet. Changes you make to your syllabus are immediately available to your students at their next logon.

For the Student—

- **Topic Overviews**—outline key concepts in topic areas
- **Electronic Bluebook**—send homework or essays directly to your instructor's email with this paperless form
- **Message Board**—serves as a virtual bulletin board to post—or respond to—questions or comments to/from a national audience
- **Web Destinations**—links to www sites that relate to each topic area
- **Professional Organizations**—links to organizations that relate to topic areas
- **Additional Resources**—access to topic-specific content that enhances material found in the text

To take advantage of these and other resources, please visit the *Transition Planning for Secondary Students with Disabilities* Companion Website at

www.prenhall.com/flexer

Contents

Section I
Transition Foundations   1

1

History and Transition Legislation   2
Robert W. Flexer

Definitions and Essential Elements of Transition   3

IDEA-Mandated Transition Services   3

Division on Career Development and Transition Definition   4

The Essential Elements of Transition   5

A Transition Law Framework   7

Policy and Social Foundations Through the 1960s   8

The Development of Societal Values   8

Legislation of the 1960s   11

Policy Foundation and Legislation of the 1970s   12

Precursors of the Disability Rights Movement   12

Legislation of the 1970s   14

Legislation of the 1980s   19

Special Education and Vocational Education Legislation   20

Employment and Training Programs   22

Rehabilitation and Developmental Disability Legislation   22

Transition-Related Legislation of the 1990s   23

Americans with Disabilities Act   23

Access and Accommodation   25

Rehabilitation Act Amendments of 1992 and 1998 and Work Force Investment Act of 1998   26

Goals 2000, School to Work Opportunity Act, and the 1990 and 1998 Carl D. Perkins Act Amendments   27

IDEA of 1990 and 1997   30

IDEA 1990   30

IDEA of 1997   31

Conclusion   32

2

Transition Models and Best Practices   38
Robert W. Flexer, Rachel K. McMahan, and Robert Baer

Early Transition Models   39

Work-Study Programs   39

The Career Education Initiative   41

Models of Transition in the 1980s   42

Will's Bridges Model   42

Halpern's Alternative to the Bridges Model   43

Linkages in Transition Systems   44

Work Preparation Models   45

Emerging Models of the 1990s   48

Quality-of-Life Focus on Transition   48

Kohler's Model   49

Siegel's Model   51

Problems in Defining "Best
Practices" in Transition   54

Best Practices in Transition   56

Self-Determination   57

Ecological Approaches   59

Individualized Backward Planning   60

Service Coordination   61

Community Experiences   62

Access and Accommodation Technologies
and Related Services   64

Supports for Postsecondary Education   65

Family Involvement   66

Systems Change Strategies   67

Conclusion   68

3

Career Development: Theories for Transition Planning   69

Pamela Luft and Lynn C. Koch

Overview   70

The Relationship of Career Development to
Transition Planning   71

Additional Goals of Transition Planning   73

Careers for Individuals with Disabilities   75

Theories of Career Development   76

Structural Theories   79

Developmental Theories   79

Work-Adjustment Theories   80

Krumboltz's Social Learning Theory   81

**Models for Applying Career Development
Theories to Students with Disabilities   82**

Ecological Model of Career Development   83

Framework for Linking Career
Theory and Practice   85

**The Career Development of Students
with Disabilities   89**

Conclusion   92

4

Transition Collaborators   95

Thomas Simmons, Jackie June, and Robert W. Flexer

Key Concepts in Transition Collaboration   96

The Interface of Transition Collaboration   97

Transition Disciplines   98

Team Models   100

Transition Roles   102

Transition Coordinator   102

Transition Collaborator Responsibilities   102

School-Based Programs and Services   104

Special Education Teacher   104

Related Service Providers   107

Academic and Technical Content Teachers   107

Administrators   108

**Public Sector Support Services
Collaborator   109**

Federal/State Vocational
Rehabilitation Program   109

Federal/State Employment Training   110

Long-Term Support Agencies   111

**Postschool Education and Training
Service Collaborators   113**

**Case Study of an Interagency
Agreement   113**

Collaboration and Group Process   114

Stages of Team Development   115

Additional Aspects of Group Dynamics   116

Transition Team Processes   117

Students' Needs, Interests, and
Preferences   117

Outcome-Oriented Process   117

Interagency Responsibilities and Linkages   118

Movement from School to
Postschool Activities   118

Conclusion   118

5

Multicultural Competence in Transition Planning Processes   120

Pamela Luft

Overview of Culture   121

Our Diverse Country   121

American Cultural Forces   122

Defining Cultural Competence   124

Multicultural Issues for Transition   124

Cultural Diversity in Special Education   126

Special Education Placement Patterns   126

Institutionalized Cultural Values   128

Cross-Cultural Concerns for Transition Professionals   129

Status Issues of Families   131

The Impact of Cultural Difference on Transition Mandates   132

Contrasting Transition Values   133

Negotiating Multicultural Differences   137

Negotiating Transition Mandates   147

Providing Culturally Competent Transition Planning Services   154

Professional and In-Service Training   156

Strategies for Supporting Minority Parents   157

Comprehensive Cultural Training   157

Conclusion   158

Section II
Career and Transition Services   161

6

Career and Vocational Education   162

Pamela Luft, Lynn C. Koch, Deborah Headman, and Patrick O'Connor

Overview   163

Definitions of Career and Vocational Education   163

Historical Influences and Legislative Mandates   165

Career and Vocational Education Programs   166

Career and Vocational Education Models   166

Stages of Career and Vocational Education   171

Foundational Skills and Attitudes   173

Integrating Academic and Career Skills   174

Academic Skill Development   174

Classroom-Based Career Development   176

Community-Based Career Experiences   177

Career Planning Strategies   179

Monitoring Career Development Processes   181

Monitoring the Student   182

Monitoring Potential Work and Living Environments   182

Monitoring Congruence Between the Student and Potential Work and Living Environments   184

Career-Specific Vocational Preparation   185

Labor Market Trends and Forces of Change   186

The Structure of Vocational Education   187

Types of Vocational Programs   187

Interfacing Vocational Education with Transition Planning   188

Initiating a Career: Placement and Linkages   189

Job-Seeking Interventions   189

Community Linkages   190

Maintaining and Advancing in Careers   192

Supported Employment   193

Career Maintenance Clubs   194

Accommodations Planning   194

The Portfolio as a Career Maintenance Strategy   195

Conclusion   195

7

Transition Assessment and Postschool Outcomes 197

Robert W. Flexer and Pamela Luft

Overview of Transition Assessment 199
Characteristics of Transition Assessment 199
Defining Transition Domains 201
IDEA Requirements 203
Functional Assessments 205

Formal Transition Assessments 206
General Skills Test 207
Current and Future Working Environments 208
Current and Future Living Environments 209
Current and Future Personal-Social Environments 209
Academic Assessment 210

Informal Transition Assessments 211
Student School Records 213
Curriculum-Based Assessment 213
Criterion-Referenced Assessment 214
Portfolio Assessment 214
Surveys and Interviews 215
Situational Assessments 216
Work Samples 220
Behavioral Assessment 220
Appropriate Use of Tests 221

Interdisciplinary Assessment Processes 223
Collaborative Processes 223
Comprehensive Transition Planning 224

Conclusion 225

8

Curriculum Development and Transition 227

James Krouse and Richard Sabousky

Overview of Curriculum 228

Definition of Curriculum 228
Academic, Vocational, and Functional Curricula 230
Fads in Special Education 231

General Education Curriculum 231
Existing Instructional Systems 231
State Standards and Curriculum 231

Social Skills 236

Functional Skills 238
Functional Curricular Models 239
Major Components of a Functional Curriculum 240

Functional Curriculum and Transition 244
Functional Curriculum Considerations 244
Barriers to Curriculum Development 245

Conclusion 245

9

Instructional Strategies 247

Bryan G. Cook, Cindy Trevino, Lysandra Cook, and Melody Tankersly

Effective Teaching 248
Learning Time 249
Review and Preview 250
Demonstration 251
Practice 251
Accountability and Assessment 253
Behavior 253
Application of Effective Teaching Literature to Students with Disabilities 256
Application of Effective Teaching Literature to Transition Curricula 257

Complementary Instructional Techniques 258
Cooperative Learning 258
Self-Monitoring 261
Community-Based Instruction 263

Conclusion 271

10

The Role of Technology in Transition Planning   272

Deborah Bauder and Preston Lewis

The Importance of Technology   273

    Legislation and Definitions   273

    Examples of Assistive Technology   274

Application of Technology   276

Barriers to Implementation of Assistive Technology   281

    Lack of Professional Development or Teacher Training   286

    Assistive Technology Support Services Not Always School Based   286

    Need for Follow-Up Services   287

    Inability to Evaluate Assistive Technology before Purchase   287

    Lack of Parent Knowledge of Assistive Technology   287

Technology and Transition   288

Technology, Transition, and IDEA Principles   290

    Students' Needs, Interests, and Preferences   290

    Outcome-Oriented Process   291

    Movement from School to Postschool Settings   292

    Interagency Responsibilities   293

Role of Technology in Postschool Environments   294

    Work Environments   295

    Community Environments   297

    Recreational and Leisure   297

    Travel   298

    Home   299

Conclusion   299

Section III
Transition Planning   303

11

Participatory Decision-Making: Innovative Practices That Increase Student Self-Determination   304

James E. Martin, Laura Huber Marshall, and Randall L. De Pry

Self-Determination: The Basic Facts   305

    The Choice Strand   305

    The Goal Setting and Attainment Strand   307

    Which Strand?   307

    Self-Determination Components   308

    The Importance of Self-Determination   310

    Federal Laws, Regulations, and State Practice   310

Infusion of Self-Determination into the IEP   311

    Establishing Self-Determination as an IEP Need Area   312

    Standard-Referenced IEPs   315

Teaching Self-Determination and Creating Participatory Decision-Making Opportunities   316

    The ChoiceMaker Series   316

    Teaching and Creating Opportunities for Choosing Goals   318

    Teaching and Creating Opportunities for Expressing Goals   322

    Teaching and Creating Opportunities for Attaining Goals   324

    Impact of Take Action Lessons   325

    Teaching and Creating Opportunities for Students with Severe Needs   326

Student-Directed Functional Assessment and
   Behavior Support Planning   330

   Traditional Approach   330

   Student-Directed Functional Assessment
   and Behavior Support Planning   330

   Opportunity for Participatory Decision Making   331

Conclusion   331

12

Transition Planning   333

Robert Baer

Transition Planning and the IDEA
   of 1990 and 1997   334

   IDEA Regulations Pertaining to Determining
   Student Needs, Interests, and Preferences   337

   IDEA Regulations Pertaining to Outcome-
   Oriented Transition Planning   337

   IDEA Regulations Pertaining to Developing a
   Coordinated Set of Activities   337

   IDEA Regulations Pertaining to Promoting
   Student Movement to Postschool Activities   338

   Common Myths in Regard to IDEA Transition
   Policy Implementation   338

   Myth One: There Is One Transition Planning
   Process for All Students   338

   Myth Two: Transition Planning Occurs Only
   in the IEP/Transition Meeting   338

   Myth Three: Transition Plans
   Cover One Year   339

   Myth Four: Transition Teams Meet
   Only Annually   339

Preparing for the Transition Meeting   339

   Choosing Transition Planning Processes   339

   Time Lines for Transition Planning   341

   Forming the Transition Planning Team   341

   Transition Assessments   344

   Transition Service Options   347

   Backward Planning   348

   Preparing for Student and Family Led
   IEP/Transition Meetings   349

Implementing the Transition Plan   349

   Writing the Statement of Needed Transition
   Services into the IEP   349

   Assessing Transition Progress
   Using a Career Portfolio   350

   A Case Study on Transition Planning   352

   Writing IEP Goals for Transition Services   356

Questions Families Frequently Ask   359

Conclusion   362

13

Coordinating Transition
Services   364

Robert Baer and Phillip Rumrill

Service Coordination: A Brief History   365

Goals of Transition Service Coordination   367

   Student-Focused Planning   367

   Planning   368

   Student Development   374

   Family Involvement   376

   Collaboration   376

   Development of Program Attributes
   and Structures   379

A Case Study in Transition Service
   Coordination   381

Conclusion   384

14

Family Involvement   386

Lisa Turner

History of Family Involvement   389

Parent Involvement in the IEP Process   389

   Passive participation   389

   Lack of Equal Status in Decision Making   389

   Types of Parent Participation/Interaction   390

   Lack of IEP Efficacy   390

   Minimal Roles in the Planning Process   391

Need for Parent Training   391

Parent Involvement in Transition Planning   392

Parents as Key Component in
Transition Planning Process   392

Limited Research Substantiating
Parent Involvement   392

Empirically Substantiated Positive
Parent Effect on Outcome   393

Empirically Substantiated Parent
Involvement as a Recommended Practice   393

Parents' Desire for More Involvement   394

Lack of Information Provided to Parents   394

Students' Perspectives   395

Parent Roles and Responsibilities   396

Parental Expectations   396

Transition Team Membership   396

Transition Planning Roles
and Responsibilities   397

Attributes of Parents   397

Family Functions   397

Cultural and Linguistic Differences   398

Strategies for Family Involvement   399

Guidelines for Parent Participation   399

Need for Parent Education/Training   399

Need for Specific Knowledge Regarding
Outcome Areas and Service Options   401

Preplanning Opportunities   401

Effective Method to Increase Active
Parent Participation   401

Informing Parents Regarding Legal Rights   402

Legislative Guidelines for Parent Involvement
in Shared Decision Making   403

Parent as Advocate   404

Professionals as Advocates   405

Social Support Mechanisms   406

School Initiated Training for Parents   406

Provision of Community Experiences   406

Information Regarding Adult
Service Programs   407

Parent-to-Parent Support Groups   407

Professional Regard for Parents   408

Conclusion   413

Section IV
Postschool and
Community Environment 415

15 _____

Transition to Employment   416

Thomas J. Simmons and Barry Whaley

**Four IDEA Principles and
Relation to Employment**   417

Postschool Employment Agencies   418

Vocational Rehabilitation Agency   419

Developmental Disabilities Agencies   422

Mental Health Agency   423

State Bureau of Employment Services   424

Work Force Investment Act   425

**Employment and Employer Involvement,
Models and Practices**   425

Why Real Jobs?   426

Supported Employment   428

Four Features of Supported Employment   429

**Social Welfare, Social Entitlements,
and Work Incentives**   435

Social Security/Disability Insurance   435

Supplemental Security Insurance   435

Additional Work Incentives   435

Services and Agency Delivery Matrix   436

Conclusion   436

16 _____

Postsecondary Education
and Career Paths   439

*Deborah Durham Webster, Greg Clary,
and Penny L. Griffith*

Why Go to College?   440

Secondary and Postsecondary Programs   441

Participation and Outcomes in
Postsecondary Programs   441

Types of Postsecondary Programs   443

High School versus Postsecondary
Environments   445

Disability Support Services in
Postsecondary Settings   451

College Climate   452

Four Essential Elements of Transition   456

Determining Students' Needs and Interests   457

**Identifying Goals and Preparing Students
for Postsecondary Outcomes**   460

Interagency Responsibility and Linkages   464

Promoting Positive Postsecondary
Outcomes   464

**Enhancing Participation in
Postsecondary Education**   468

Social Aspects of a Postsecondary
Education   468

First-Generation College Students   469

Rural Students   469

Specialized Programs   470

Conclusion   471

17

Recreation and Leisure in the Community   474

Joyce Strand and Janice Kreiner

**Community Participation, Recreation
and Leisure**   476

Transition Needs   476

Health and Wellness   477

Community-Based Programs   478

Essential Elements of Transition   479

Students' Needs, Interests, and Preferences   480

Outcome-Oriented Process   481

Interagency Responsibility or Linkages   484

Movement from School to
Postschool Activities   486

Leisure Program Options   487

Specific Programs   487

Implementation of Leisure Programs   489

Transition Coordination for
Recreation and Leisure   489

Roles and Responsibilities   491

Individualized Leisure Planning
and Supports   493

Assessment   495

Leisure Assessment Instruments   495

Leisure Skills, Age Appropriateness,
and Safety   497

Conclusion   497

18

My Home: Developing Skills and Supports for Adult Living   499

James A. Knoll and Carolyn Bardwell Wheeler

**The Parental Perspective: Life Is More
Than a Job**   500

**The Personal Perspective:
Young and Restless**   501

Transition to a New Vision   503

From Placements to People   504

Relocation   504

Renovation   505

Revisioning   509

Living in My Own Home   510

Supported Living   511

Current Challenges   513

Access to Supported Living   514

One State's Approach to Supported Living   515

Personal Assistance Services   519

Access to Personal Assistance Services   520

Transition to Interdependent
  Life as an Adult 523
  Vision 524
  Skills 526
  Resources 528
  Supports 534
Conclusion 536

Appendixes   541

A

Self-Evaluation Strategies to
Assist in Examining Cultural
Beliefs and Multicultural
Compentence   542

B

Relationships with
Minority Families   543

C

Life-Centered Career
Education Transition Model
and Competencies   544

D

Glossary of Terms Commonly
Used in Transition Planning   548

E

Sample Blanket Release of
Information and Member
Agreement   555

F

Self-Survey of Transition
Practices   559

References   571
Name Index   605
Subject Index   614

Note: Every effort has been made to provide accurate and current Internet information in this book. However, the Internet and information posted on it are constantly changing, so it is inevitable that some of the Internet addresses listed in this textbook will change.

Section I

Transition Foundations

1 History and Transition Legislation

2 Transition Models and Best Practices

3 Career Development: Theories for Transition Planning

4 Transition Collaborators

5 Multicultural Competence in Transition Planning Processes

1

History and Transition Legislation

Robert W. Flexer

LEARNING OBJECTIVES

The objectives of this chapter are:

1. Define transition as outlined in the IDEA of 1997.

2. Explain the disability policy background for each period of legislation.

3. Describe the basic principles and provisions of transition and related legislation for each period.

4. Explain how legislation in different areas is coordinated and what this means.

5. Describe changes in transition focus across the periods of legislation.

Transition services for youth with disabilities became official policy in secondary special education with the passage of the Individuals with Disabilities Education Act (IDEA) of 1990. A specific component of IDEA related to the incorporation of transition services into the Individualized Education Program (IEP). These requirements directly addressed the fundamental purpose of secondary education preparation for life. Moreover, this mandated planning process also emphasized student, family, and professional attention to the challenges, uncertainties, and promises of making the transition to adulthood.

Educationally, the high school transition period for all students concerns the future. During high school, students gain renewed intensity and interest in issues of identity and independence as they progress to graduation. The high school years can be viewed as stepping-stones into the future and a protracted and structured period for students to sharpen their postschool goals and to test themselves through a variety of experiences.

Quality transition programs that can engage youth during the adolescent period were the added focus of the IDEA amendments (P.L. 105-17) in 1997. Embedded in these requirements is the availability of a full range of preparation programs and experiences and access to all the academic and career possibilities within the high school program. Goals 2000: Educate America Act of 1994 (P.L. 103-227) requires standards-based, quality education for all students and stipulates that qualified youths with disabilities should have the opportunity for meaningful participation in programs of choice in general education. Vocational education programs, Carl D. Perkins Act of 1998 (P.L. 105-800), have the potential to bring out special talents and to provide challenges to students in order to motivate them toward high skill careers and jobs. The School to Work Opportunity Act (STWOA) of 1994 (P.L. 103-239) provides experiences in transition programs for students that may result in discovery of unknown career paths.

Access to programs for career enhancement and personal growth applies from the elementary through the postsecondary levels and to all types of disabilities. Because students with disabilities are very individual, and, as a group, represent a full range in their needs, preferences, and abilities, it is necessary that opportunities within all school programs be accessible to qualified youth. The laws and policy framework for transition provides guidance to transition teams to get students into the right programs.

The purpose of this chapter is to provide the social, policy, and legislative context from which transition requirements developed. Initially in this chapter, transition is defined. Then four periods of policy and legislation are described: up to the 1960s and the 1970s, 1980s, and 1990s. For each period, background information and specific laws are provided, including how the policy framework fits into general developments in the disability field. Requirements for transition in special education are obviously important but other laws are also critical (e.g., vocational education and rehabilitation), which address transition in relation to employment, community adjustment, and secondary and postsecondary education.

Definitions and Essential Elements of Transition

IDEA-Mandated Transition Services

The Individuals with Disabilities Education Act (IDEA) of 1997 definition of transition services reads:

> The term "transition services" means a coordinated set of activities for a student, with a disability, that: (A) is designed within an outcome-oriented process, that promotes movement from school to post-school activities, including postsecondary education, vocational training, integrated employment (including supported employment), continuing and adult education, adult services, independent living, or community participation; (B) is based on the

student's needs, taking into account the student's preferences and interests; (C) includes instruction, *related services*, community experiences, the development of employment and other post-school objectives, and, when appropriate, acquisition of daily living skills and functional vocational evaluation (section 602).

This book is developed around what the authors call essential elements. The term "essential elements" was chosen because they should be true of any transition service or program and because they provide a common ground between the legal requirements for transition and empirically supported practices. From the IDEA definition of "transition services," a possible way to break down sequentially essential elements is that services must be (1) based on student needs, taking into account the students' preferences and interests, (2) designed within an outcome-oriented process, (3) a coordinated set of activities, and (4) able to promote movement from school to postschool activities.

Critical Point   The essential elements spell out a framework to meet transition requirements. They serve as the starting point to determine effective transition services.

By using a framework of essential elements, this book intends to provide an integrated view of transition. *Transition services* across various middle school, secondary, and postsecondary programs need to be viewed longitudinally and holistically, including the domains of community life and employment. The design and implementation of transition services foster positive postschool outcomes when individualization and interdisciplinary service delivery are utilized. The *essential elements* address how to educate and support individual students working toward their future with service delivery based on educators, youth and families, and communities working in partnership. Therefore, transition services should be student oriented and directed (i.e., based on students' needs, taking into account students' preferences and inter-

ests), focused on the future (i.e., designed within an outcome-oriented process), delivered consistently by both transition and school staff (i.e., used a coordinated set of activities), and tracked and monitored in relation to student goals (i.e., promote movement from school to postschool activities).

Division on Career Development and Transition Definition

The Division of Career Development and Transition (DCDT) of the Council for Exceptional Children is the primary professional group of transition service providers within special education. DCDT provided a definition of transition which reflects professional consensus. The DCDT definition contains descriptions of what needs to be the focus for secondary special education and transition and career education services. It describes the major implications for a transition IEP (an IEP for middle and secondary-age youth with disabilities) and the essential elements. Briefly, a long-range outcome-oriented process leading to self-determined goals and interdisciplinary transition services is advocated.

Transition, as defined by DCDT,: refers to a change in status from behaving primarily as a student to assuming emergent adult roles in the community. These roles include having employment, participating in postsecondary education, maintaining a home, becoming appropriately involved in the community, and experiencing satisfactory personal and social relationships [*designed within an outcome-orientated process*]. The process of enhancing transition involves the participation and coordination of school programs, adult agency services, and natural supports within the community [*using a set of coordinated activities*]. The foundations for transition should be laid during the elementary and middle school years, guided by the broad concept of career development [*promote movement from school to postschool activities*]. Transition planning should begin no later than age 14, and students should be encouraged, to the full extent of their capabilities, to assume a maximum amount of responsibility for such planning [*based on their needs, taking into account the students' preferences and interests*] (Halpern, 1994 p.117).

The Essential Elements of Transition

The IEP in special education is the cornerstone for providing education to students with disabilities. The plan takes into account all the needs of the student and specifies how both to deliver education and to be responsible for that education. Secondary special education and transition is also primarily concerned with appropriate and effective IEPs for youth in middle school and high school and in postsecondary and community settings. Further, IDEA of 1990 emphasizes high school linkages to postschool activities, whereas IDEA of 1997 added middle school linkages to the high school program. Whereas the elementary-age student's IEP deals with a curriculum based on moving to the next grade, the transition IEP considers relating instructional activities to an outcome more than one year into the future.

The *essential elements* of transition apply to all levels of school (elementary through postsecondary) and to all types of disabilities. The variations in transition by age group are a function of the student growing older, being more mature, and being more capable. The differences by disabilities are found in the implementation of specific transition strategies. As always, transition services like the IEP are based on the unique needs of the student.

Comprehensive longitudinal transition needs are shown in Figure 1–1. From Figure 1–1, transition foci and needs range from fairly broad to more specific when comparing elementary to secondary levels. For example, the needs of elementary students revolve around understanding the nature of work, whereas high school students focus preparation on performance in postschool settings. At the middle school and

early high school levels, exploration of needs and preferences is important in contrast to the later high school level when students are testing specific goals through experiences and activities. Although the focus and needs in transition are different depending on the age of the student, the refinement of student needs and preferences requires an outcome orientation and coordination of services to enhance movement toward long-range outcomes. The outcome orientation and coordination requirements of the essential elements become more critical for secondary students because transition goals become more specific and there is less time to develop linkages with postschool service providers.

The transition focus by level and the transition needs listed in Figure 1–1 are pertinent regardless of the type of disability. The transition focus of employability and independent living at the elementary level is relevant to students with mild to moderate disabilities and to those with severe disabilities. At the middle school level, students with mild to moderate disabilities will be examining vocational, college preparatory, and school-to-work options in light of their goals and support needs. Students with severe disabilities will be exploring a variety of community environments as the focus for their high school program. As students progress to high school, goals, supports, and linkages will vary by their unique needs and preferences. Students with mild to moderate disabilities may be looking toward postsecondary education, whereas students with severe disabilities may be planning and preparing for a community job.

Basing services on student needs and taking into account the students' interests and preferences indicate that transition planning and activities should involve the student to the maximum extent possible with attention given to increasing self-understanding and self-determination. To be outcome oriented, transition planning should reflect the goals which

Primary Level: Grades Grades 1–4

Focus

Employability and independent living skills and attitudes.

Needs

1. Develop positive work habits.
2. Appreciate all types of work.
3. Develop an understanding of how to cope with disability.

Middle School: Grades 5–8

Focus

Career exploration and transition planning relative to course of study.

Needs

1. Understand relationship of school to work.
2. Understand interests, preferences, aptitudes.
3. Understand work, education, independent living, and community options.
4. Determine a general course of secondary study.
5. Identify needed accommodations and supports for secondary education.
6. Specify transition services needed to participate in desired course of study by no later than age 14.

Four Essential Elements

1. **Student needs and preferences:** Transition planning and activities should involve the student in a meaningful way.
2. **Outcome oriented:** Transition services should result in development of postschool goals.
3. **Coordinated set of activities:** Transition services should involve teamwork and communication among school and postschool professionals and the student and family.
4. **Promote movement to postsecondary environments:** Transition services should result in progress toward postschool goals.

High School: Grades 9–10

Focus

Career exploration and transition.

Needs

1. Develop meaningful and realistic postsecondary goals.
2. Develop work, education, residential, and community participation skills and supports relevant to goals.
3. Learn to manage disability technology and request accommodations.

High School: Grades 11 and up

Focus

Transition and overlap into postsecondary environments desired by the student.

Needs

1. Test goals through experiences and activities.
2. Secure options for postsecondary education and/or employment.
3. Develop residential and community participation supports and contacts.
4. Develop linkages with adult services.
5. Empower families to function in adult service environments.

FIGURE 1–1
Essential Elements: Focus and Needs

express the student's desired future postschool environments and lifestyle. Coordinated activities and teamwork are required to meet the diverse education and support implied by the transition needs and being prepared for adult life. Progress at each level and for each need for each individual student ensures educational continuity and should be documented, ensuring that needs are met in an effective fashion and promote movement from school and to postschool activities.

The thread over time is a concern about outcomes; that is, what happens to students when they graduate. Transition efforts over the last 15 years have provided many positive demonstrations for the group of students who have fared well in postschool life, while follow-up studies have documented that many students did not make a successful transition and are floundering (Blackorby & Wagner, 1996). Therefore, the transition movement must continue to emphasize the centrality of the planning process and the delivery of proven transition programs to youth who need them. Accomplishing these goals will require developing, implementing, and evaluating effective transition practices; that is, addressing needs beyond the academic and increasing the relevance and usefulness of high school programs in general. By following the essential elements outlined in this book, individual students and school programs will enhance, in general, the quality and effectiveness of secondary education.

Critical Point   Effective transition services include programs that are (1) based on student need and preference, (2) outcome oriented, (3) a coordinated set of activities, and (4) promote movement from a school to a postschool setting.

Transition services should be developed and implemented from an informed perspective. Having provided a description of the elements and their foci at various school levels, the following section provides an overview of specific laws and policy, as well as legal requirements related to transition services.

A Transition Law Framework

Transition activities are based on the laws on special education, rehabilitation, vocational education, ongoing lifelong supports, higher education, employment and training, and general education. Legislation within each area has provisions to protect the rights of persons with disabilities. For example, because vocational education is a delivery system dealing with preparation for and entry into employment, programs and services within vocational education are important to students with disabilities in order to attain transition. Vocational education law provides assurances that youth with disabilities will have access to the range and variety of program options where appropriate (i.e., if qualified). Moreover, although transition services for students with disabilities are not referenced in the vocational education legislation, supplemental aids and services can be provided through IDEA to support participation and program completion. Understanding the unique provisions of legislation and how they are related to transition requirements is part of what transition teams need to know in their role in service coordination.

Critical Point   The essential elements of needs and preferences and postschool goals may require programs outside the purview of special education requiring coordination among special education, regular education, and postschool service providers.

Some transition-related legislation deals with laws that fall into the rehabilitation and the ongoing supports domains, a major service delivery system for postschool services and supports for students who are in transition. A major shift in the status of students in moving to adulthood is that supports and services go from being an entitlement to being based on eligibility criteria. This means that these students may or may not receive services, depending on whether they meet specified criteria. The kind of disability and its severity in some instances constitute the criteria of eligibility.

Rehabilitation services are those that are provided under rehabilitation legislation and deal with supports and services for entry or reentry into the labor market and meet the rehabilitation needs and goals of those found eligible. Generally, a service is viewed as a one-time investment to move an individual into a new or improved role and status (e.g., employment versus unemployment). Thus, rehabilitation services are often referred to as time-limited services.

Other legislation dealing with adults and students who are in transition are adult/postschool services that are assumed to be ongoing. Eligibility in these agencies has criteria related to the severity of disability and the need for long-term, ongoing support (in many instances, for the person's lifetime). Still other services and supports are provided primarily only to enable participation and access, not to meet specific disability needs for individuals, such as services that are part of postsecondary education or general community services like employment and training programs.

In the legislation which follows, laws fall into one of three categories: (1) Students with disabilities in special education have an entitlement to an education through age 21. (2) As adults, they must meet specific criteria and must be found to be eligible in order to receive specialized services. (3) Both in schools and communities, programs and activities are required to be accessible and not to discriminate against people with disabilities.

In the following sections, groups of laws are broken into four time periods. Through the 1960s, national interest in disability issues developed. During the 1970s, a foundation for a delivery system was laid down, whereas the 1980s dealt with refinements of transition systems and expansion of services to all youth regardless of disability. With the 1990s, consolidation and cooperative models were outlined in laws to provide mandated transition services and a coordinated system of services.

Policy and Social Foundations Through the 1960s

The Development of Societal Values

Early Values and Cultural Approaches

Modern concepts of disability can be traced back to the Elizabethan Poor Laws in seventeenth-century England that differentiated between the deserving and undeserving poor. The undeserving poor were seen as living in poverty as a result of poor moral character and, therefore, were expected to work and "pull themselves up by the bootstraps." In contrast, the deserving poor, primarily the "crippled," the blind, and orphans were responded to with charity (Macklesprang & Salsgiver, 1996) and were usually not expected to work. Persons with disabilities had been seen as both the deserving and undeserving poor, depending on the type of disability. This notion of charity had its drawbacks, for both persons considered as deserving and those who were not. When seen as deserving, persons with disabilities were patronized and not expected to work or contribute. When seen as undeserving, they faced unemployment and servitude or a life of crime and imprisonment. This concept can be viewed as underlying much of Western society's response to disability to the present day. For example, a deserving person with blindness receives much higher benefits than persons with emotional disturbances and addictions, who may face the same options as their English predecessors.

Wolfensberger in 1972 provided one of the seminal works on cultural or historical models of disability. The thesis behind historical models of disability is that the concept and value assigned to disability (perception) subsequently plays out in how people with disabilities are treated by society and social institutions. The models described how, at various times in history, people with disabilities have been treated as less than human "at worst, or charitable cases, at best." See Table 1–1.

TABLE 1–1

Sociohistorical Deviancy Role Perceptions and Resultant Service and Staffing Models

Role Perception	Service Model	Staff Model

Subhuman:
  Animal
  Vegetable
  Insensate object
	Neglect, custody, destruction	Catcher, attendant, caretaker, keeper, gardener, exterminator

Menace, or object of dread	Punitive or detentive segregation, or destruction	Guard, attendant, exterminator
Object of ridicule	Exhibition	Entertainer
Object of pity	Protection from demands	Member of religious bodies, charitable individual
Burden of charity	Industrial habilitation	Trainer, disciplinarian, work master
Holy innocent	Protection from evil	Member of religious bodies, charitable individual
Eternal child	Nurturant shelter	Parent
Sick person	Medical	Physician, nurse, therapist

Source: From Overview of normalization, by W. Wolfensberger in *Normalization, social Integration, and community services,* Flynn, R. J. & Nitsch, K. E. (Eds.), 1980, Table 2, p. 10, Chap. 1. Reprinted with permission.

The power in models is that they filter the perception of individuals through disability and place individuality in the background. Several examples that extended to the more modern period in the history of human services are:

- Institutional exposés like Willowbrook, portrayed in *Christmas in Purgatory* (Blatt, 1966) and reported by Geraldo Rivera, demonstrated that in the 1970s people with severe and profound mental retardation were still abused and lived in horrific conditions.
- Children with more severe disabilities were excluded from public school until 1975.
- Day activity centers served people with mental retardation but provided little meaningful activity and were separated from the community in the 1970s.

Early Rehabilitation Influences

Early in this century, the evolution of the concept of disability was influenced by the emergence of rehabilitation services. This was an outgrowth of medical and technical progress in World War I. In 1917, the Smith-Hughes Act (P.L. 64-347) provided government support for this notion of disability by providing rehabilitation services for disabled World War I veterans. The Smith-Sears Act (P.L. 65-178) in 1918 embodied both a notion of charity and rehabilitation by caring for veterans as deserving and by rehabilitating them to meet employer needs through vocational education and early forms of disability technology. This concept had an earlier analogue in the development of institutions for persons with mental retardation, where children and adults with disabilities were sent to large state schools for rehabilitation and training. Two years later, in 1920, the Smith-Fess Act (P.L. 66-236) was established by the Federal Board of Vocational Education and offered vocational training (e.g., in the form of guidance, occupational adjustment, and placement) for civilians who had become disabled while engaged in civil employment. This early rehabilitation legislation focused on the correction of individual deficits, not on social change. These early twentieth-century roots of American concepts of disability can still be seen in the philosophy and strategies of many current disability professions, including rehabilitation, vocational education, and special education (DeStefano & Snauwaert, 1989).

Critical Point   Early professional concepts and service models of disability were influenced greatly by cultural meanings. These societal influences are still in evidence today.

Legislation from 1917 to 1943, the period between the "two great" wars (World War I and World War II), dealt with fairly limited populations and a more limited service delivery system. Legislation during this period dealt primarily with the support and training of disabled veterans and civil service (government) employees. In 1943, the Barden-LaFollete Act (P.L. 77-113) was passed to provide vocational training and retraining to civilians other than those who were government workers. Besides retraining or training for employment within limits set by the individual's disability, needed medical services such as examinations, surgery, and prosthetic and orthotic devices that were essential to becoming employed were included as rehabilitation services under the program. In principle, rehabilitation services were expanded to include people with mental retardation and those with mental illness, although no *funded* services were provided. It was not until 1954 (with the Vocational Rehabilitation amendments P.L. 83-565) that funding for expansion of vocational and rehabilitation programs and research and professional training became available. These monies did not make work-study, sheltered workshops, and job placement services generally available to all people with disabilities in all states. They were "seed" monies for the establishment of pilot programs and the building of capacity of states and local programs to make the services part of an overall system.

Development of Advocacy Organizations
Rehabilitation services were gradually extended to more persons as technologies improved; however, persons with severe disabilities continued to be seen as charity cases with nothing to con-

tribute to society. In 1950, a challenge to this concept came from the National Association for Retarded Children (now known as the ARC), an organization formed by parents. Initially, the ARC and other parent organizations (such as United Cerebral Palsy) set out to fund and create skill development programs and activities for children and adults with severe disabilities (e.g., moderate to severe mental retardation, cerebral palsy, autism, and other developmental disabilities). Early childhood programs and special schools were established for children who were excluded from school, and sheltered employment and day activity centers were established for adults. Parent information and support were a cornerstone for these organizations which supported countless families in facing a challenge few professionals understood or had resources to deal with (Turnbull & Turnbull, 1990).

Critical Point   The first national attention to disability issues stemmed from efforts by family-based advocacy organizations.

Numerous advocacy organizations, many aligned along disability lines and comprised of parents of children with disabilities and sometimes professionals, were the early stimulus for community and societal awareness of needs for special education and rehabilitation services. The 1960s were a period of emerging visibility of disability issues and the first national commitment of the government to persons with disabilities and their needs, hopes, and desires. The Kennedy administration stressed a new program of public welfare, service, and training, rather than prolonged dependence resulting from the absence of community and educational programs. This national commitment, attention, and awareness are embodied in the recommendation of the first President's Panel on Mental Retardation (see Table 1–2). These recommendations have stood the test of time and are as relevant today as they were almost 40 years ago. The language may be somewhat different but the values and concepts underlying the recommen-

TABLE 1–2

President's Panel on Mental Retardation:
1962 Recommendations

- The establishment of research centers for the study of retardation, its causes, and especially its prevention
- The improvement of welfare, health, and general social conditions of all the people, particularly those in the greatest need
- Improved educational programs and availability of appropriate education for all; the extension of the definition of education beyond the academics
- The training of professional and service personnel to work in all aspects of retardation, particularly at the leadership level
- The development of comprehensive, community-centered services on a continuum to meet all types of needs

Source: From President's panel on mental retardation (1962). A Proposed Program for National Action to Combat Mental Retardation. Washington, D.C.: U.S. Government Printing Office.

dations remain central currently in efforts to improve the quality of services and outcomes for persons with disabilities.

Legislation of the 1960s

The legislation in the 1960s also reflected interest by the federal government in the needs of children with disabilities. In 1965, P.L. 89-313, amendments to Title I of the Elementary and Secondary Education Act (ESEA), provided support for education of children with disabilities in state-operated schools and hospitals. In 1966, the amendments of ESEA (P.L. 89-750) changed the focus of grants from state-operated schools and hospitals to serving children with disabilities in the local schools. It also called for state plans on needs and priorities of children with disabilities and set up the Bureau for Education of Handicapped Children, whose function was to administer all federal authorities for the education of children with disabilities. In 1968, the first federal government legislation specifically addressing the needs of children with disabilities was the Handicapped Children Early Education Assistance Act, P.L. 90-583. This act established experimental demonstration centers for the education of preschool children with disabilities. The 1960s were a period in which there was a growing federal interest in the needs of children with disabilities on a national level, which was stimulated in part by the development of the President's Panel in 1962.

Other legislative authorities were created which had specific provision for meeting the needs of children and adults with disabilities. The Vocational Education Act of 1963 (P.L. 88-210) had provisions for the development of vocational programs for disadvantaged populations and students with disabilities. (Funding was not provided for students with disabilities until 1968 when the Vocational Education Act amendments authorized and set aside up to 10% of funding for education and services to students with disabilities.) The rehabilitation amendments of 1967 created new programs for recruitment and training of rehabilitation service providers and funded rehabilitation services and research at much higher levels. An example of this expansion is the development of work-study programs, a program of work experiences and functional academics and life skills developed originally for persons with mild mental retardation. In 1969, 37 directors of vocational rehabilitation services reported a total of 1,344 cooperative agreements with special education nationwide. A total of 96,604 secondary students with mental retardation were served in these programs (State Agency Exchange, 1969).

Critical Point   The beginnings of federal laws in the 1960s laid a foundation to meet the national need in disability services. This was the governmental response to meet the needs of unserved persons with disabilities.

Developmental disabilities and mental health legislation also expanded during this era. The legislation sharpened the definitions, eligibility, and scope of services for these two populations. For example, the Mental Retardation and Facilities and Construction Act of 1963 (P.L. 88-164) established, for the first time, a federal priority to meet a national need for persons with mental retardation. A framework was set up to define the need and subsequently to develop a national framework for service delivery. Monies became available to states and community agencies to establish community-based services with government support.

This legislation was an important beginning in defining functional needs in major life activities and a comprehensive system (across life domains) for individuals who may need assistance/ongoing support throughout their lifetime. At this time, people with moderate to profound mental retardation or other significant disabilities of childhood who lived in the community were virtually unserved and identified as in need of comprehensive life-span services and supports. Special education, vocational education, rehabilitation, developmental disability, and mental health legislation outlined some basic service needs and funded the beginning of a federal-state-local service system.

Critical Point   The period from 1915 to 1945 focused on support and training for veterans with disabilities and marked the beginning of a federal government role. The period from 1945 to 1968 saw expansion of training and rehabilitation for the whole population of persons with disabilities and the emergence of a disability policy and a larger government role.

Summary
From 1917 to 1945, the primary federal role was rehabilitation for veterans with disabilities and the development of vocational education alternatives in public schools. Beginning in the late 1950s and continuing into the 1960s, legislation was passed for special education, special needs vocational education, statewide rehabilitation

programs, and a developmental disability and mental health service system. This was the beginning of disability policy development and a federal government role in the education and rehabilitation of people with disabilities. Table 1–3 compares and contrasts the federal role in disability services through the 1960s.

Policy Foundation and Legislation of the 1970s

Precursors of the Disability Rights Movement

PARC v. *Commonwealth of Pennsylvania*, 1972
While continuing to provide community services, the ARC expanded its advocacy role into the political arena in the 1970s. Students with severe disabilities, particularly those with more severe mental retardation, were excluded from public school in most states by law so that in the 1970s the Pennsylvania ARC (PARC) filed a class action suit. This suit demanded public education for all children regardless of disability under the argument that their rights to education could not be taken away without due process of law (PARC v. *Commonwealth of Pennsylvania*, 1972), and won the case. This class action suit was instrumental in creating the structure of the Education of All Handicapped Children Act (P.L. 94-142) in 1975.

Critical Point   Legislation mandating education for students with disabilities and establishing an appropriate education as a right was accomplished as a result of parental efforts. Parents and families knew all too well the impact of children and youth being excluded from education or inappropriately served.

Independent Living Movement
While parents and families were advocating for children and some adults with disabilities, adults with physical and sensory disabilities began advocating for themselves. In Berkley, CA. a small group of young adults challenged the

TABLE 1–3

Legislation Prior to and during the 1960s

1917–1945

Focus on support and training for disabled veterans
Beginnings of a federal government role:

- 1917 Smith-Hughes Act (P.L. 64-347): Provided for vocational rehabilitation and employment for veterans with disabilities and vocational education
- 1918 Smith-Sears Act (P.L. 65-178): Provided additional support for veterans with disabilities
- 1920 Smith-Fess Act (P.L. 66-236): Provided funding for vocational training for civilians with disabilities who worked in federal civil service jobs
- 1943 Barden-LaFollette Act (P.L. 77-113): Provided for vocational rehabilitation for all civilians with physical disabilities and mental retardation

1945–1968

Expansion of training and rehabilitation for the whole population of persons with disabilities
Emergence of disability policy and federal government role:

- 1954 Vocational Rehabilitation amendments (P.L. 83-565): Provided funding for research and training of professionals and for expanding and improving rehabilitation
- 1963 Vocational Education Act (P.L. 88-210): Provided for expansion of vocational programs and services for person with disabilities
- 1966 Elementary and Secondary Education Act amendments (P.L. 89-750): Provided for support of state programs of special education and created federal Bureau of Education of the Handicapped
- 1968 Vocational Education amendments (P.L. 90-576): Established set-aside of basic state funding for special populations (10% for students with disabilities and 15% for students with academic and economic disadvantages)
- 1967 Vocational Rehabilitation amendments (P.L. 90-99): Provided increased funding for rehabilitation, research, demonstration, and training projects
- 1968 Vocational Rehabilitation amendments (P.L. 90-391): Provided increased funding for rehabilitation, research, demonstration, and training projects
- 1963 Mental Retardation and Facilities and Construction Act (P.L. 88-164): Provided funding for creation of community-based programs for people with mental retardation

Source: Adapted from School-to-work transition: Overview of disability legislation by R. A. Stodden in *Beyond high school: transition from school to work,* Rusch, F. R. & Chadsey, J. G. (Eds.), 1998, Wadsworth Publishing Company.

University of California to make its programs and education accessible to persons with physical disabilities. This resulted in the "independent living movement," which emphasized that community participation and access to social institutions were the right of *all* citizens, including persons with disabilities.

With leadership from a variety of advocacy groups, the Rehabilitation Act of 1973 (P.L. 93-112) was passed and considered a major victory for disability advocates. Passage of the Rehabilitation Act of 1973 (P.L. 102-569) mandated equal access for persons with disabilities to all federally funded programs. However, the implementation of this law was hindered because the government did not write regulations. Five years later, in 1978, advocates and persons with disabilities had to stage a sit-in at the office of the cabinet secretary and in regional offices of the U.S. Department of Health, Education, and Welfare to spur the government into promulgating the needed regulations. This bureaucratic stonewalling was typical of the battles that disability movements faced in affirming the rights of people with disabilities.

Critical Point   Legislation mandating access to employment, postsecondary education, and the community was achieved by coalitions, including persons with disabilities.

People First

The 1970s also were a period for self-advocacy for other disability groups. The origins of People First, the self-advocacy organization of people with mental retardation, is a case in point and a poignant story. Because of cognitive limitations, persons with mental retardation were not being heard, except through their parents. A group of these individuals came together in Oregon to tell professionals what they wanted from their programs. Accounts of the meeting describe a young woman standing up and saying, "We want to be people first!" This sparked a movement in the disability community that persons with disabilities should be referred to and treated as "persons first." People First challenged society and professionals to attach primary attention to "personhood" and to view disability as only a part of a whole person, not the defining characteristic (Perske, 1973).

The "people first movement" led to a change in thinking and talking about persons with disabilities. Professional and social discourse about persons with disabilities began to discard terms such as, "retardate," "cripple," and "the disabled." Person-first language and disability etiquette has been characterized as political correctness, but respect was seen as very important in increasing the presence and participation of people with disabilities. Person-first language conveys respect for the person with a disability by:

1. Recognizing a person's right to self-esteem
2. Recognizing a person's right to be thought of as a person first and foremost in word and in thought (in other words, the person is "first a person" and second a person with a disability)
3. Accurately describing a person without being judgmental (i.e., just as it is not always necessary to convey the color of a person's hair, it is also not always necessary to mention that a person has a disability). Table 1–4 provides both an overview of some issues that are important in interacting with people with disabilities and some useful guidelines to personal and professional behavior. Person-first language should generally be used in talking about persons with disabilities unless they request otherwise. It may also be necessary to educate others (e.g., send guidelines to the media) so that they can support social behaviors that show respect for persons with disabilities.

Critical Point   People with mental retardation directly experience the rejection and fear resulting from others who define them only through the label of their disability.

Legislation in the 1970s

During the period of the 1970s, legislation was expanded in education (e.g., special education, career education, and vocational education) and in adult services and postschool supports. Cross-references to requirements in special education were made in vocational education legislation. Interagency cooperation was more clearly outlined within rehabilitation and developmental disability and mental health legislation and between education and rehabilitation. Interagency cooperation was a requirement in all the legislation with the goal that services would be coordinated among the systems and that professional training and interaction would reflect common philosophies, goals, and commitments within a teamwork and interdisciplinary framework.

School-Based Legislation of 1970s

During the 1970s, special education and vocational education were the most closely tied to-

TABLE 1–4

Person-First Language Suggestions

- Refer to people first and disability second.
- Avoid the use of terms which equate a person with his or her disability (i.e., the "quadriplegic" or "epileptic"; instead, use the person with a seizure disorder or the person with quadriplegia).
- Use adjectives which do not have negative connotations (i.e., "stricken," "afflicted," "victim," or "crippled").
- Use the words "typical" and "normal" appropriately (i.e., in comparison to people without disabilities, people with disabilities are "atypical," but the term "abnormal" conveys inaccurate, negative meanings).
- Focus on what a person with disabilities *can do* rather than what they cannot do.
- Avoid describing persons as having disabilities when it is not pertinent to the conversation.
- Avoid sensationalizing or implying that superhuman qualities are possessed by persons with disabilities (persons with disabilities have the same range of talents and successes as others; to sensationalize their accomplishments implies that they must overcompensate to succeed—most need only a regular effort when they have equal access and reasonable accommodations with which to accomplish their work).
- Avoid using words associated with disability in a manner which has negative connotations (i.e., terms such as "deaf and dumb," "retarded," or "spastic" evoke negative images and are easily replaced by accurate descriptions).
- Avoid the use of terms such as "wheelchair bound" or "confined to a wheelchair" (persons who *use wheelchairs* view them as most people view cars, as tools which enable freedom and independence, not traps! It is inappropriate to associate wheelchairs with helplessness and dependence and to treat wheelchairs as an extension of personal space; to lean or hang on it is like leaning or hanging on the person using the wheelchair).

Source: Adapted from class materials "Disability Policy," developed by Deborah Durhan Webster, Kent State University, 1999.

gether. Coordinated changes were made in the special education and vocational education legislation. The Education for All Handicapped Children Act of 1975 (P.L. 95-142) mandated multifactored evaluations (MFE) every 3 years, parental right to due process, free appropriate public education (FAPE), least restrictive environment (LRE), and the Individualized Education Program (IEP), which were the cornerstones of special education (343 F Suppl. 279 CED, PA, 1972). The IEP could now include career and vocational objectives for youth with disabilities. The education amendments of 1976 (P.L. 94-482) coordinated the state plans of special education and vocational education and established priority for access to regular vocational education. Assurances that the full range of vocational options are accessible was an important requirement in state plans for vocational education. IEPs and the possible need for voca-

tional teacher participation were mentioned in this legislation. The teaming of vocational and special education instructional staff was expected for participation in regular vocational education. Thus, many states developed a continuum of vocational education services for students with disabilities.

In 1977, the concept of career education was put into legislation and introduced as "the totality of experiences through which one learns about and prepares to engage in work as part of his or her way of living" (Hoyt, 1977). States were to implement programs on:

a. encompassing the total curriculum of the school and providing a unified approach to education for life

b. encouraging all members of the community to share responsibility for learning within classrooms, homes, private and public agencies, and the employment community

c.   providing for career awareness, exploration, and preparation at all levels and ages

d.   encouraging all teachers to review their subject matter for its career implications.

Special educators increased their career education emphasis because of its functional and skill orientation and as a method to link academic and vocational preparation (Clark, 1979). Career education, although legislated, was passed under a sunshine provision; when the act expired in 1982 so too did funding to states for career education efforts. Nonetheless, the concept and structure to bring career education into the overall school curriculum was implemented in various ways and has left some structures that still exist in schools today. These changes most notably can be seen in counseling and guidance, special education, and vocational education. In fact, the School to Work Opportunity Act of 1994 is a belated federal initiative and successor to the Career Education Implementation Incentive Act of 1977.

Critical Point   The common underpinnings of special education, vocational education, and career education were established through legislation. Preparation beyond academic subjects and career and personal development became important goals of public education.

Rehabilitation Act of 1973

Historically, the Rehabilitation Act of 1973 is of great importance for several reasons. First, the act was completely rewritten and was a "new" law (rehabilitation legislation prior to 1973 consisted of amendments to the Barden-LaFollete Act of 1943). Second, the 1973 act was also a reflection of comprehensive and functional service delivery as was other legislation (e.g., developmental disability legislation). Third, most importantly, with passage of the Rehabilitation Act of 1973, Congress for the first time officially enacted a law on disability rights.

The act had three important provisions. First, rehabilitation programs in the states were to give priority to persons with the most severe disabilities. Because many of these people did not receive services, Congress stated that people with severe disabilities should have the opportunity to receive services in order to become employed. This was the beginning of an ongoing trend in service delivery which highlights insufficient resources to meet the need.

Second, independent living services were included as a Title—a section of the law to cover those kinds of services. Independent living programs emphasized two major points: (1) Living in the community and getting help with activities of daily living was as important as working. The underlying principle was that the act should deal with the whole person and all the domains of living in the community. (2) Independent living made it necessary that the client or consumer of services should have considerable input and control over what services are provided and how they are delivered.

The third area of the Rehabilitation Act was rights. Of particular importance was section 504, the nondiscrimination requirements pertaining to people with disabilities. Section 504 reads:

> No otherwise qualified person with a disability in the United States . . . shall, solely on the basis of disability, be denied access to, or the benefits of, or be subjected to discrimination under any program or activity provided by any institution receiving federal financial assistance or under any program or activity conducted by any Executive Agency or by the U.S. Postal Service (29 U.S.C. • 794).

Critical Point   Independent living services and priority for persons with severe disabilities through the Rehabilitation Act of 1973 broadened the concept of rehabilitation beyond simple employment processes and addressed the role of environments and societal attitudes as handicapping factors.

Use of the terms *otherwise qualified* persons with disabilities requires that we define a person with a disability first. A "person with a disability" means anyone with a physical or mental impairment that interferes with at least one major life

TABLE 1–5

Subpart E of Section 504

104.41   Applies to recipients of federal funds
104.42   Admissions and recruitment
• May not limit the number of persons admitted
• Nondiscriminatory criteria and test
• May not make preadmission inquiry
104.43   Treatment of students; general
• Covers overall and general discrimination
• Operates programs in most integrated settings
104.44   Academic adjustment
• Modification to requirements to include qualified persons
• Does not apply to essential requirements
• Course examinations should reflect achievement, not disability
• Auxiliary aids must be provided to ensure access (i.e., for students with impaired sensory, manual, or speaking skills)
104.45, .46, .47
• Also covered are housing, financial and employment assistance, and nonacademic services

Source: Adapted from Section 504 of Rehabilitation Act of 1973, 29 U.S.C. § 794 *et seq.*, subpart E.

activity (e.g., employment, independent living, etc.). "Otherwise qualified" means that the person meets the requirements for skills, abilities, degrees, and training for gaining entrance into, for example, school or a job (DuBow, Geer, & Strauss, 1992). This indicates that people with disabilities must be evaluated on their qualifications and not on their disability. When a person has a disability, it is important that he or she know and meet the qualifications for gaining entrance into the program of choice.

"Solely by reason . . . disabilities, be excluded . . . denied or subjected" means just what it says. Disability in and of itself cannot be a determinant in decisions by schools, employers, and others. More often, when a disability presents a barrier in a given environment, like a classroom, there are ways to alter the environment so that the person can perform or participate. Besides banning discrimination, this part of the definition affirms that participation must be meaningful and that the person with a disability has some opportunity to benefit from the activity or program. Persons with disabilities need to have access to activities that

are important to functioning within a particular environment so that they can perform and compete on the same level as others.

Critical Point   The Rehabilitation Act established both basic rights of persons with disabilities and the importance of community integration and inclusion in employment, housing, and postsecondary education.

"Any program or activity . . . receiving federal financial assistance" includes all aspects of programs and institutions, including education, employment, housing, transportation, and so on. For postsecondary education, this includes almost all types of schools, public and private, because most students receive money from the federal government. Colleges and universities and other postsecondary programs must not discriminate in the recruitment, admission, or treatment of students under section 504 of the Rehabilitation Act. Under subpart E of section 504, qualified students with documented disabilities may request modifications, accommodations, or auxiliary aids that will enable them to participate in and benefit from programs and activities (see Table 1–5).

A major theme throughout rehabilitation and special education legislation during the 1970s is that the person with a disability has a central role in the accommodation process. That is, there are many responsibilities that go along with exercising one's right. Moreover, without participation, the development of workable accommodations is unlikely. Therefore, the student needs to understand the educational implications of disability and educate and inform others. All these skills then are applied in transition and career planning in the student's educational program in high school and beyond.

Developmental Disability and Mental Health Legislation

The field of developmental disabilities is perhaps unique in that its origins can be traced to an act of Congress. As the mental retardation legislation of the 1960s was expiring, leaders and advocacy groups grasped the opportunity to expand the previous laws to benefit not only individuals who were mentally retarded but also disability groups whose impairments were developmental in nature and who had similar service needs. Consequently, P.L. 91-517, the Developmental Disabilities Services Facilities Construction Act of 1970, was enacted and included persons who were mentally retarded and also persons who were affected by cerebral palsy, epilepsy, and other neurological conditions found to be closely related to mental retardation or to require comprehensive services similar to those required by individuals with mental retardation.

Two important background factors were related to these changes. One was the desire to focus on the developmental aspects of these conditions. Developmental disabilities result in impairment to a broader range of functions, which in turn affect the acquisition of basic life skills, while the word "developmental" also reduces the stigmatizing effect of the mental retardation label. The second factor concerned the chronicity of conditions considered to be devel-

opmental disabilities and the need for extended services. Clearly, the intent of the earlier laws was to serve those who have substantial unmet needs (Lubin, Jacobson, & Kiely, 1982; Summers, 1981).

Critical Point The developmental disability legislation established that some disabilities will require services and support throughout the person's lifetime. Substantial impairments were tied to the concept of major life activities such as employment, independent living, and so on.

However, since many persons who are most in need still were not receiving services after passage of the 1970 act, P.L. 95-602, in 1978, dropped the specification of categories of disability in favor of reference only to substantial impairment. Public Law 95–602, Rehabilitation, Comprehensive Services, and Developmental Disability amendments of 1978, defined developmental disability as:

> a severe, chronic disability of a person which:
>
> A. is attributable to mental or physical impairment, or combination of mental and physical impairments;
>
> B. is manifested before the person attains age twenty-two;
>
> C. is likely to continue indefinitely;
>
> D. results in substantial functional limitations in three or more of the following areas of major life activity:
>
>   (i) self-care,
>
>   (ii) receptive and expressive language,
>
>   (iii) learning,
>
>   (iv) mobility,
>
>   (v) self-direction,
>
>   (vi) capacity for independent living, and
>
>   (vii) economic self-sufficiency.
>
> E. reflects the person's need for a combination and sequence of special, interdisciplinary, or generic care, treatment, or other services which are individually planned and coordinated.

As can be seen from the definition, five guidelines were utilized in framing the definition: etiology, age of onset, chronicity, need for extended services, and substantial impairment (Lubin et al., 1982). The duration and degree of impairment (both within and across major life activities) certainly suggests that developmental disabilities would meet most other definitions of severe disability. Indeed, historically, developmental disability was designated as severe because this population is less vocal, subject to less visible improvement, and more expensive to service, which often leads to lack of service in the rehabilitation system. Further implications of the definition are that comprehensive, coordinated lifelong management of services will be required to meet the needs of the person with a developmental disability.

Critical Point   The rights of school-age children with disabilities were protected as well as the right to access for persons with disabilities in the general population. In the 1970s, legislation established the main parts that are needed for a coordinated service system to meet the needs of transition students and adults.

Summary

Table 1–6 shows the legislative progression through the 1970s. The focus during this period was on appropriate education for special education youth and access and accommodation for all persons with disabilities, including adults. On the special education side, all students were to be provided with a free appropriate public education (FAPE) at no expense to parents and a program that meets the unique needs of each student (i.e., IEP). This was to include vocational education for secondary-age students. The focus on career education brought special and regular education closer together after years of separation. The career development and outcome orientation of the 1970s addressed education beyond pure academics needed by all students. Rehabilitation and developmental disability and mental health legislation provided guidelines for definitions and service systems for children and adults with the most severe disabilities, those historically underserved. Further, integration and participation in

TABLE 1–6

Legislation During the 1970s

Ensured rights to appropriate education and access for persons with disabilities in general Established service system supported by federal government:
- 1970 Developmental Disabilities and Bill of Rights Act of 1970: Provided support to states' creation of a developmental disabilities service system—emphasized long-term support
- 1973 Rehabilitation Act (sections 503 and 504) (P.L. 93-112): Funded independent living centers, prioritized rehabilitation of persons with the most severe disabilities, provided protection from discrimination
- 1973 Comprehensive Employment and Training Act (P.L. 93-203): Provided manpower services to raise employment levels of unemployed, unskilled youth and adults
- 1975 Education of Handicapped Children Act (P.L. 94-142): Partially funded a free appropriate public education (FAPE) in the least restrictive environment; included vocational education
- 1976 Vocational Education amendments (P.L. 94-482): Emphasized access to regular vocational education and development of new vocational programs; funded vocational assessment and support services for students with special needs

Source: Adapted from School-to-work transition: Overview of disability legislation, by R. A. Stodden in *Beyond High School: Transition from School to Work,* Rusch, F. R. & Chadsey, J. G. (Eds.), 1998, Wadsworth Publishing Company.

the mainstream of schools and communities and society was central to all the disability legislation while, for the first time, rights for people with disabilities were spelled out, for both school-age children and youth and adults.

Legislation of the 1980s

Whereas legislation of the 1970s laid a foundation for special education and a service system for adults with disabilities, the 1980s were a period of consolidation and further coordination among legislative acts. Further clarification was given as to how an appropriate education was to be provided within vocational education by the Carl D. Perkins Vocational Education and Technology Act of 1984 (P.L. 98-210). Within the rehabilitation system, the Rehabilitation Act amendments of 1986 (P.L. 99-506) provided a specific program and service structure (i.e., supported employment) to serve individuals with the most severe disabilities. This period, known for the legislative activity of the 99th Congress, was particularly targeted toward issues surrounding employment rates of persons with disabilities (e.g., disincentives to employment such as the loss of social security benefits).

Special Education and Vocational Education Legislation

With P.L. 94-142 in 1975, the field of special education became a federal-state-local system for delivery of special education. With a new structure in place to serve students, a variety of programs emerged to research and evaluate services and education. One aspect of this activity was a reemergence of follow-up studies. (Through the 1950s and 1960s follow-up studies were conducted to evaluate work study and by and large found some benefit in these programs.) The follow-up studies of the 1970s and early 1980s provided a picture of the status of graduates of special education, although somewhat cloudy. The consensus, which emerged from the transition field, was that some students benefited from secondary special education but for a vast majority of students, postschool outcomes were not positive (e.g., Hasazi, Gordon, & Roe, 1985; Wehman, Kregel, & Barcus, 1985). Unemployment, low wages, low-level jobs, lack of postsecondary education, and lack of community participation and independent living were descriptive of large numbers of students with disabilities.

Special Education

As a result of concern generated by these outcomes within professional and advocacy organizations, the 1983 amendments to the Education of Handicapped Children Act (P.L. 98-199) included section 626 on secondary education and transition and a federal initiative was launched. Substantial discretionary programs were implemented for the purpose of researching the transition process and provided demonstration and capacity-building activities to improve transition services in the state and local education agencies. Table 1–7 lists the numerous kinds of grant activities supported by section 626 (secondary education and transition services for handicapped youth) and subsequent amendments in 1986. A perusal of the list is quite informative in identifying factors related to postschool success. For one, secondary education improvements were addressed through projects on direct transition services, community-based education and services, cooperative models, job training, self-determination, and local education agency capacity to deliver transition services among others. Moreover, research and demonstration activities in the postschool arena were also funded for follow-up/follow-along systems, special populations, and postsecondary supports and education.

The funding of the National Longitudinal Study of Transition was noteworthy. This study followed school graduates 2 and 5 years out of school. It provided a picture of outcomes for a national representative sample of all disability categories as well as a view of the nature and type of transition services received in high school. Part of the study addressed the impact of programs—the relation of programs to outcomes. The study provided a baseline of national transition effectiveness in the mid-1980s. The results of this national study are discussed in more detail in Chapter 2.

Critical Point   In the 1980s, the federal initiative on transition brought national attention to the needs of secondary youth with disabilities.

TABLE 1–7

Goals of 15 Federal Grant Competitions Funded Since 1983

- Demonstrate innovative approaches to transition using direct service delivery.
- Support new model demonstration projects that link transitioning individuals to community-based training programs and services.
- Stimulate higher education (e.g., postsecondary, vocational, technical, continuing, or adult education) possibilities for persons with mild disabilities.
- Focus on special adaptations of postsecondary services/career placement.
- Design, implement, and disseminate practices that facilitate the transition of youth with severe disabilities into employment.
- Support projects that develop and establish exemplary school-community models for specific vocational training and job placement.
- Design cooperative models (state or local education agency) that facilitate effective planning to meet employment needs of exiting students with disabilities.
- Support projects designed to plan and develop cooperative models for activities among SEAs (state education agencies) or LEAs (local education agencies) and adult service agencies.
- Identify the skills and characteristics necessary for self-determination, as well as the in-school and out-of-school experiences that lead to development of self-determination.
- Identify job-related training needed by secondary students with mild handicaps.
- Support research projects on effective strategies to provide transitional services to youths with disabilities, ages 16 through 21, from one or more of the following special populations: Adjudicated youths, youths with severe emotional disturbances, or youths with severe physical disabilities (including traumatic brain injury).
- Support projects that enhance the capacity of local educational agencies by promoting implementation of proven transition models, or selecting components of these models, in multiple school districts within a state based on specific needs.
- Encourage follow-up and follow-along studies to document the impact of transition services and to revise program options based on analysis of outcome data.
- Assist youth with handicaps and their families in identifying, accessing, and using formal and informal networks to obtain needed supports and services to maximize independence in adult life.
- Identify factors that facilitate student involvement in the transition planning process and to develop national dissemination of effective interventions and strategies.

Source: From Emerging Transition Best Practices, by Rusch, F. R. & Miller, D. M. in *Beyond High School: Transition from School to Work,* F. R. Rusch & J. G. Chadsey (Eds.), 1998, p. 47. Copyright 1998. Reprinted with permission of Wadsworth, a division of Thomson Learning. Fax 800-730-2215.

Vocational Education

The strengthening of transition services for youth with disabilities was also an important component of the Carl D. Perkins Vocational Education Act of 1984 (P.L. 98-524). The emphasis in this act was to assure access to quality vocational education programs and the expansion of set-aside use. In 1984, the Carl D. Perkins Vocational and Technical Education Act was passed with the following intent:

. . . assure that individuals who are inadequately served under vocational education programs are assured access to quality vocational education programs, especially individuals who are disadvantaged, who are disabled, men and women who are entering non-traditional occupations, adults who are in need of training and retraining, individuals with limited English proficiency, and individuals who are incarcerated in correctional institutions (P.L. 98-524, 98, Stat. 2435).

Access was viewed as critical to youth preparing for the transition from secondary education to work environments in their local communities. Youth who were identified as disabled and disadvantaged were now required to receive vocational assessment, counseling, support, and transition services; IEPs were to include vocational goals; vocational education in the least restrictive environment was reemphasized; and state and local education agencies were to coordinate vocational education programs with requirements under P.L. 94-142 and amendments. Underlying all these legal requirements and assurances is the question of students enrolling in and completing vocational education. The test of effectiveness of vocational education mandates was determined through the national assessment of vocational education: By and large, vocational education was serving students with special needs except (1) Students with disabilities were still underserved and (2) access to regular vocational education was still an issue.

Critical Point   The development of transition models and practices and the expansion of transition services resulted in greater numbers of students receiving a broader array of secondary options.

Employment and Training Programs

Within the U.S. Department of Labor, programs were also developing in a way that required more coordination with education legislation. From the programs of the 1970s (e.g., Comprehensive Employment and Training Act, CETA) in which federal employment and training programs were consolidated, the Job Training and Partnership Act (JTPA) (P.L. 97-300) emerged in 1982, providing significant funding for job training and placement programs directly benefiting youth with disabilities. With CETA and JTPA, the needs and unemployment of both youth and adults were addressed, providing occupational skills to those who were not able to contribute to the nation's economy.

Rehabilitation and Developmental Disability Legislation

The rehabilitation legislation of the 1980s again took on the rehabilitation service needs of the most severely disabled. "Supported employment" was defined as paid employment in integrated real-work situations in which one must work at least 20 hours a week (P.L. 99-506). The significance of these amendments was that supported employment was to be a regular case service like other services and that interagency cooperation was required between rehabilitation services and adult service agencies that were to provide extended services and the long-term support implicit in service need definitions of persons with severe disabilities. There were corresponding changes in developmental disabilities legislation and mental health legislation to be consistent with delivery of employment and other services.

Critical Point   Supported employment was a major postschool rehabilitation and adult service legislated for students with severe disabilities.

Summary

The 1980s were a period of legislation which focused on coordination among the various legislative authorities. As already pointed out, the 99th Congress attempted to update and revise legislation in rehabilitation, developmental disabilities, income maintenance and health programs, and employer incentives in order to improve the employment prospects of persons with disabilities. As shown in Table 1–8, major amendments or new bills were passed across every disability-specific and transition-related area. The 1980s could be considered the period of federal initiative. As you will see, federal initiatives do not equate with quality transition programs in every community. Nonetheless, during the 1980s, a general framework tying together all the relevant legislation was established; issues of capacity were identified; and programs were put into place.

TABLE 1–8

Legislation during the 1980s

Authorized funds to develop transition models and practices
Provided further clarifications of rights, reinforced coordination of legislation across transition and related areas, and expanded service eligibility

- 1982 Job Training Partnership Act (P.L. 97-300): Provided significant funding for job placement and training programs directly benefiting youth with disabilities
- 1983 Individuals with Disabilities Education Act (P.L. 98-199): Provided finds for grants to demonstrate support and coordination among educators and adult service programs to foster transition to postschool settings
- 1984 Carl D. Perkins Vocational Education Act (P.L. 88-210): Set aside funds to facilitate equal access to full range of vocational education activities through supplemental services; includes vocational education in IEPs
- 1986 Rehabilitation Act amendments of 1986 (P.L. 99-506): Provided definition and funding for supported employment
- 1984 Developmental Disabilities amendments of 1984 (P.L. 98-527): Defined supported employment and emphasized productivity and participation in the community

Source: Adapted from School-to-work transition: Overview of disability policy, by R. A. Stodden in *Beyond high school: Transition from school to work*, Rusch, F. R., & Chadsey, J. G., 1998, Wadsworth Publishing Company.

Transition-Related Legislation of the 1990s

As of this writing, the 1990s have come to an end and we are embarking on the "new millennium." The 1990s, therefore, define how far transition has come in the twentieth century. Like all previous decades, the 1990s had its ups and downs. The century started with the Americans with Disabilities Act (ADA) and new special education legislation (i.e., the IDEA). The rights of people with disabilities in all segments of society were affirmed and given protection by federal law: In other words, constitutional rights were reaffirmed. Also, in 1990, the IDEA mandated transition services as part of the IEP. Full participation and equal opportunity marked the beginning of the decade. These two pieces of legislation represent the culmination of the disability rights movement and the transition movement. Advocacy and professional groups truly became part of a national movement, which no longer viewed disability and the service system as charity.

Americans with Disabilities Act

In 1990, the ADA was passed into law and signed by President Bush. The ADA was designed to be comprehensive and to cover all aspects of rights within all areas of citizen participation. It is overarching; that is, it provides organizing principles from previous laws and a standard for measuring policies on how to implement the law (West, 1991). The ADA deals more with breadth than with new concepts. Before the ADA, only federal contractors and recipients of federal funds were required not to discriminate against people with disabilities. Now, the private sector must comply with a comprehensive disability antidiscrimination mandate.

Principles of The Americans with Disabilities Act

The ADA sends "a message about what society's attitude should be toward persons with disabilities: respect, inclusion, and support" (West, 1991, p. xviii). Of course, attitudes cannot be mandated. A corollary to this principle is that legislation about rights is based on values, not on knowledge. This can be tricky, however, because values are very broad statements about beliefs and have importance in both the group and individual context. Respect, in part, means that people without disabilities view disability as a unique characteristic without devaluing the person. The disability is part of the identity and self-concept of the person. Disability is a natural way in which persons differ from each other. Inclusion and support mean that society values the contributions and participation of people with disabilities. The goal of inclusion is to create an experience that is a *meaningful, equal opportunity* for the person with a disability. Because the social and physical environment can create barriers and prohibit meaningful involvement, accommodations are required in order to provide a means of participation for people with disabilities. The value is that society should make that extra effort to include *everyone*. The "accommodation" imperative means that a fair society would make experiences accessible while the inclusion ethic deals with the value that society wants to give everyone an equal opportunity (West, 1991).

Critical Point   Respect, inclusion, and support are the philosophical and value base of the ADA. Interaction and communication on equal ground are necessary to create positive attitudes.

Rights *Covered by the* ADA

The ADA is organized into five sections called "Titles." As pointed out, the ADA covers aspects of living and participating in community life that have not already been covered by other laws, reinforces standards in applying the law, and generalizes rights protections to the private as opposed to only public or publicly supported activities. In the ADA law, the major entities covered are (1) private employers who do not receive federal money; (2) state and local government agencies; (3) public accommodations (e.g., restaurants, hotels, and theaters); and (4) telephone companies (for "functionally" equivalent relay services: TTY). The fifth title covers miscellaneous areas. These titles of the ADA require

that reasonable accommodations (employment) be made and that other entities, activities, and programs be made accessible (e.g., government agencies and public accommodations).

Critical Point   An important precept of the ADA is "qualified person with a disability." The definition of "qualified" includes accommodation: an alternative manner to accomplish tasks or activities.

Title I of the ADA prohibits an employer from discriminating against a qualified individual with a disability in the following areas: (1) job application procedures; (2) hiring; (3) discharge; (4) compensation; (5) advancement; and (6) any other terms, conditions, and privileges of employment. Under the ADA, a qualified individual is one who, with or without reasonable accommodations, is able to perform the essential functions of the job. "Essential functions" are those duties of a job that are basic—not marginal—to the position (DuBow et al., 1992). For example, in many jobs, answering the telephone is listed as a qualification when, in fact, it is not essential to the job. This requirement would tend to screen out, unnecessarily, hard-of-hearing people who could not answer the telephone. Reasonable accommodations can be a variety of strategies to enable the hard-of-hearing person to perform the essential functions of a job (i.e., modifications, adjustments, or technology). The employer is exempt from providing accommodations if they are too expensive or difficult (undue hardship).

Title II of the ADA requires all state and local government agencies to make all their services accessible to individuals with disabilities. It also requires public transportation agencies to be accessible. State and local governments must ensure effective communication with individuals with disabilities. For persons with vision, hearing, or speech impairments, appropriate auxiliary aids or services are often needed for effective communication. Agencies and services should publicize how to request special services. Auxiliary aids include qualified interpreters, assistive listening devices, real-time recorders, television captioning and decoders, TTYs, videotext displays, readers, taped texts, and large print materials. The important point is that the activity, service, or program must be made accessible so that persons with disabilities can use and benefit from the activity and achieve meaningful participation. The person's expressed choice of auxiliary aids or services should be given primary consideration. Nonetheless, the public entity has the final decision on how accommodations are provided.

Title III of the ADA provides people with disabilities with rights to equal access to public accommodations. Title III covers many places, such as hotels, theaters, restaurants, doctors' and lawyers' offices, retail stores, banks, museums, parks, libraries, day care centers, and private schools. Again, auxiliary aids and services must be provided to ensure meaningful access. *Title* IV requires telephone companies to provide both local and long-distance telecommunications relay services across the nation.

Critical Point Accommodations require a two-way communication and problem-solving process.

Access and Accommodation

If disability happens to present a barrier to meaningful participation in a program, then the question becomes how the barriers of disability can be accommodated for successful performance in the program. Sometimes access deals with being able to participate (e.g., have an elevator for persons who use wheelchairs to get to the second floor chemistry lab and accessible to lab facilities). At other times, it deals with individual accommodations that are needed in order for the student to meet the performance requirements of the program (e.g., physical assistance to do experiments or assistive technology devices). The features of buildings are necessary to provide access to programs, activities, and services. Without consideration or

thought of the design stage to address access to the building and locations within the building, persons using wheelchairs would be excluded. Without individual accommodations, a student who has a mobility impairment may not be able to participate in the activities of the program.

To provide access for persons with disabilities, it is necessary to define (1) the important performance requirements and desired outcomes, (2) how a specific disability presents barriers to participation (i.e., define the problem), and (3) what assistance in the broadest sense is needed to circumvent barriers and/or to provide alternatives so that access is possible (i.e., solve the problem). Access, generally, views a disability or impairment in an interactive manner with the environment. It is implied that some environmental adaptation allows participation. If the input or process of the activity is not changed/modified, the person with the disability cannot participate. The access approach focuses equally on the manner in which programs and activities are available, as well as on a person's disability that presents barriers to participation.

People with disabilities share the common experience of (1) barriers created by impairments and (2) environmental barriers that make participation in activities difficult. For example, people who are hard-of-hearing cannot access spoken communication under unamplified conditions in a classroom. Someone who uses a wheelchair cannot gain entry into classrooms that are in an inaccessible building. Without enlarged print, people who are visually impaired do not have access to printed material. Without taped texts, the person with a learning disability may not have access to reading material for classes. In all cases, disability and environments interact in a manner that prevents participation, but the specific barriers, even for two people with the same disability, can be quite different.

Within the same group, however, individual experiences can vary and needs for accommodation can vary in different situations. For example, a person who is hard-of-hearing needs amplification to gain access to spoken communication, whereas a person who is deaf and uses sign language needs visual communication in order to have access. Even within the same group, individual experiences can vary and needs for accommodation can be different in different situations. This diversity and the unique situations of individual persons with disabilities means that individual situations and preferences need to be accommodated for in addition to general accessibility.

Rehabilitation Act Amendments of 1992 and 1998 and Work Force Investment Act of 1998

Rehabilitation Act Amendments of 1992
Whereas the ADA established a new paradigm for disability and the rightful place of persons in society, the Rehabilitation Act of 1992 further reinforced the ADA precepts and addressed, specifically, accessibility and responsiveness to the needs and goals of the customers of vocational rehabilitation. Several parts of the Rehabilitation Act of 1992 illustrate connections to IDEA and ADA. The following are some highlights of the Rehabilitation Act amendments of 1992:

1. The statement of purpose of the bill notes that, "disability is a natural part of the human experience and in no way diminishes the right of individuals to live independently; enjoy self-determination; make choices; contribute to society; pursue meaningful careers. . ." This bill further embraces principles of "equality of opportunity, full inclusion and integration in society, employment, independent living and economic and social self-sufficiency."
2. Presumption of employability: "Individuals with disabilities, including the most severe disabilities, are generally presumed to be capable of engaging in gainful employment."
3. Use of appropriate existing data and information provided by other agencies and individuals and their families is required "to

the maximum extent appropriate" as "a primary source" to determine eligibility and "for choosing rehabilitation goals, objectives and services."

4. Individualized written rehabilitation plan (IWRP): New language requires the "IWRP to complete an assessment for determining . . . vocational rehabilitation needs. . ." Changes to the IWRP also ensure personal choice in the development of the plan, including "a statement by the individual, in the words of the individual. . ." on how he or she was involved in the process.
5. Title I services: Services available under Title I include personal assistance services, transition services, and supported employment services.
6. Use of natural supports: Families and natural supports can play an important role in the success of a vocational rehabilitation program, if the individual with a disability requests, desires, or needs such supports.

Rehabilitation Act Amendments of 1998
These rehabilitation amendments are part of the Work Force Investment Act (WIA) of 1998 (P.L. 105-220). The inclusion of rehabilitation legislation within workforce development reflects an attempt to integrate employment and training programs on a federal, state, and local level. WIA is a comprehensive job-training bill that consolidates over 45 previous federally funded programs. The intent of the bill is to simplify the worker-training system. More emphasis on meeting skill shortages in the labor market and career individualization are prominent features. Therefore, local needs of business and individual needs and preferences of those served will be the major factors which determine what education and services are provided and how the delivery system is set up.

Three block grants to states will be used as the major funding mechanism in the WIA: adult employment and training, disadvantaged youth employment and training, adult education and family literacy. Under Title I, workforce invest-ment systems with state and local boards will be established, along with a "one-stop" delivery sys-tem. Youth councils will be set up as a subgroup of local boards. Accountability systems and stan-dards are part of the requirements of local boards to ensure that consumer needs are met.

Title IV of WIA contains the 1998 amendments to the Rehabilitation Act of 1973, as amended. The amendments were a bipartisan consensus with emphasis on increasing opportunities to prepare for, secure, maintain, and regain em-ployment. Informed choice and a "fair shot" at rehabilitation to employment are hallmarks of the new amendments. A "fair shot" includes pro-visions for presumptive eligibility in cases which historically were determined ineligible because of the severity of the disability (IWRP is now des-ignated as the Individual program of employ-ment). At the other end of the continuum, other individuals with rehabilitation needs, who are not served because of the order of selection (ser-vices provided to the most severely disabled), will now have available a referral and informa-tion system designed to assist them in obtaining an appropriate service within the workforce in-vestment system or other community service.

Critical Point   The Rehabilitation Act amendments reflect a customer focus. Programs and service design must reflect a partnership and joint decision making.

Goals 2000, School to Work Opportunity Act, and the 1990 and 1998 Carl D. Perkins Act Amendments

Reform of the public education system has been a "hot topic" of discussion, on and off, since the early 1980s. Regular and vocational education are important because many students with dis-abilities receive their education within these two systems. Access to the education and curricu-lum in these systems in many instances consti-tutes an appropriate education for students and reflects transition services that students need to make movement toward their postschool goals.

Career programs often are an appropriate education.

IDEA has been aligned more with what is pro-vided in general education. The generic systems, in coordination with special education transi-tion, meets the requirement for a coordinated set of activities. There are numerous ways to identify how provisions of vocational education, regular education, and school to work line up with what is meant by a statement of needed transition services as provided within the IEP with the IDEA legislation.

Goals 2000: *Educate America Act of* 1994 (P.L 103–227)

This legislation provided a framework for restruc-turing education based on national goals—in essence, the act was about educational reform. Reform is concerned with the outcomes of edu-cation and how these outcomes are affected by education, curriculum, and school structure. The goals to be used as the framework were:

1. *School readiness*: All students will come to school ready to learn.
2. *School completion*: The high school gradua-tion rate will be at least 90%.
3. *Student achievement and citizenship*: Students will demonstrate competencies and mas-tery over challenging subject matter, includ-ing the ability to use their minds in order to

be prepared for responsible citizenship, further learning, and productive employment in our current and future economy.

4. *Teacher education and professional development*: The nation's teaching force will have access to programs in order to support continuing improvement of professional skills and acquisition of the knowledge and skills needed to instruct and prepare all American students for the next century.

5. *Mathematics and science*: American students will be first in the world in mathematics and science.

6. *Adult literacy and lifelong learning*: Every American adult will be literate, will possess the knowledge and skills necessary to compete in a global economy, and will exercise the rights and responsibilities of citizenship.

7. *Safe schools*: Every school in the United States will be free of drugs, violence, and unauthorized presence of firearms and alcohol, which will result in a disciplined environment conducive to learning.

8. *Parental participation*: Every school will promote partnerships that will increase parental involvement and participation in promoting the social, emotional, and academic growth of children.

Numerous benefits for the transition arena can be drawn from the implications of national goals. Since students with disabilities have higher dropout rates than the general student population, the goal of high school completion could have tremendous benefit to transition students if accomplished. This is especially so for students with behavior disorders who drop out at a 40% rate (Blackorby & Wagner, 1996). High academic achievement and lifelong learning and productive employment will enhance transition goals for students which reflect high expectations, meaningful career goals, and participation in the economy in high skill, high-paying jobs (goals 3 and 6). Partnering with parents has been a keystone of transition services since the very

earliest efforts to work with high school youth in order to achieve adult success. Even the teacher education and professional development goal has transition implications, that is, preparing students for the future. This requires working with youth so that they can define and envision their own and their communitie's future.

School to Work Opportunity Act of 1994 (P.L. 103-239)

Transition is the underlying and defining principle in the School to Work Opportunity Act (STWOA) of 1994 (P.L. 103-239). This act calls on states to plan and implement transition systems that will enable all youth to make the transition from school to postschool environments. The components and expected outcomes of statewide school-to-work systems include provision (1) to enable all youth to acquire the skills and knowledge necessary to make the transition smoothly from school to work or further education and training, (2) to impact the preparation of all youth for a first job toward a career and to increase opportunities for further education, (3) to expand ways through which school- and work-based learning can be integrated, and (4) to link occupational and academic learning and to strengthen the linkage between secondary and postsecondary education (Norman & Bourexis, 1995).

All these provisions are consistent with and reinforce special education transition requirements. Again, there is emphasis on outcomes, career development and education, and education and training beyond high school. The whole point here, is that preparation for life and career after school must begin when the student is still in high school. This preparation must and can be integrated with academic core subject learning necessary for further education in postsecondary programs.

Indeed, two of the purposes of STWOA are (1) "to build on promising school-to-work

TABLE 1–9

Carl D. Perkins Vocational and Applied Technology Education Act of 1990

Criteria for services and activities for individuals who are members of special populations—required assurances:

- Equal access to *recruitment, enrollment,* and *placement activities*
- Equal access to the full range of vocational education programs available
- Provision of vocational education in the *least restrictive* environment
- Vocational planning for individuals with disabilities coordinated by representatives of *vocational education, special education,* and *state vocational rehabilitation agencies*
- Vocational education monitored for students with disabilities to ensure consistency with their IEP
- Notification to members of special populations and their parents at *least one year prior to eligibility, including information about specific courses, services, employment opportunities, and job placement*
- Assistance with transitional service requirements for individuals with disabilities
- Provision of supplementary services, including such things as curriculum modification, equipment modification, classroom modification, supportive personnel, and instructional aids and devices
- Provision of guidance, counseling, and career development activities by professionally trained counselors and teachers
- Provision of counseling and instructional services designed to *facilitate the transition from school to postschool employment and career opportunities.*

Source: From Carl D. Perkins Vocational and Applied Technology Education Act. (1990) Pub. L. No. 101–392, 104, Stat. 756.

activities, such as tech-prep education, career academies, school-to-apprenticeship programs, cooperative education, youth apprenticeship, school-sponsored enterprises" and (2) "to improve the knowledge and skills of youths by integrating academic and occupational learning, and building effective linkages between secondary and postsecondary education" (p. 5). As with prior education-for-work legislation, STWOA addresses the need for all students to have access to programs and specifically mentions individuals with disabilities, low-achieving youth, school dropouts, and those from disadvantaged or diverse racial, ethnic, or cultural backgrounds (Kochar & West, 1995). It is interesting to note that some of the practices used in vocational special education for the past 20 years, such as career awareness and exploration activities; exposing students to broad career opportunities; and matching students' interests, goals, strengths, and abilities with program options, are highlighted in STWOA.

Perkins Act

The 1990 Carl D. Perkins amendments had two major themes:

1. To improve the quality of vocational education programs
2. To provide supplemental services to special populations

The 1990 amendments moved away from traditional job skills orientation to integrating vocational and academic skills training; focused more on poor districts and reform issues; and restructured the state-local administration, with local schools getting involved in reform and states developing standards. Apprenticeships were emphasized and tech-prep came into existence. Special funding set-asides for special populations were eliminated. Nonetheless, as shown in Table 1–9 the Perkins Act of 1990 had numerous provisions that addressed transition issues for students with disabilities.

The 1998 Carl D. Perkins Act amendments represent many consistencies with the 1990 act but also include provisions which will present challenges to the vocational education system. As Kimberly Green, the executive director of the National Association of State Directors of Vocational Education, said: "Legislators want vocational education graduates on the same level as someone who goes through regular academics so that students are just as prepared and have as many options as a person who is college bound." There are no longer any set-asides for special populations, giving schools more control over how they spend funds but now schools have to set and meet performance standards. The bill did not include school-to-work requirements but that does not mean that existing school-to-work systems will not be coordinated with vocational education systems. Tech-prep came out strong in the bill. There are longer reauthorization periods, not year to year, and separate funding streams have been set up for tech-prep.

The 1990s were a period when transition was introduced to the general field of special education through legislation. National policy debates, federal initiatives, and intense interdisciplinary activity took place for the few years leading up to IDEA. At the same time, more attention was paid to the lack of participation in the economy and career satisfaction by adults with disabilities. Legislation emphasized employment, needs of the labor market, and efficiency issues in the delivery of services.

Critical Point   The reinforcement of how special education fit within the general education system and coordination among all the federal laws was a goal of the overall federal initiatives and the transition movement in the 1990s.

IDEA of 1990 and 1997

IDEA 1990

The Individuals with Disabilities Education Act of 1990 (P.L. 101-476) provided for an FAPE to students with disabilities. Besides rights protections, laws provide programs and services to assist people with disabilities. Although P.L. 94-142

(Education of All Handicapped Children Act) was the first federal law mandating special education, it also reinforced that education was a right for students with disabilities in a fundamental way (constitutionally) as well as a right, as defined for all students. Prior to 1975, some students with disabilities may have been excluded from school. With IDEA 1990, like P.L. 94-142, education was to be appropriate to the individual needs of the students and it must be received with peers to the maximum extent possible.

IDEA 1990 provided the basic definition of transition services in use today. Under P.L. 101-476, the term "transition services" means a coordinated set of activities for a student with a disability that is designed within an outcome-oriented process. The activities were to promote movement from school to postschool activities, including postsecondary education, vocational training, integrated (including supported employment), continuing and adult education, adult services, independent living, or community participation. Based on the individual student's needs, taking into account the student's preferences and interests, transition services included instruction, related services, community experiences, the development of employment and other postschool adult living objectives at a minimum, and, when appropriate, acquisition of daily living skills and functional vocational evaluation.

In this book, these mandated services are framed in a functional way and also are related to proven practices in the literature to flush out further what a transition system may look like in high schools and the postschool environment. The essential elements put the requirements in a logical order. By starting the framework with needs and preferences and the outcome orientation, this text highlights the importance of involving the student and looking to the future and transition goals as the distinctive features of the high school transition. As the DCDT definition emphasizes, the high school transition is a status change, which is of extreme significance as a life stage—moving from school and being a student to becoming an adult with rights and responsibilities and the need to find one's place in the community and society. Transition also has unique coordination features with major linkages during the middle, high school, and post high school periods. Moreover, the essential elements demand that the high school curriculum and transition services directly connect to the students' postschool transition goals, which brings the process back to the beginning.

Identified transition services are to be incorporated into the IEP. This has to be done by including the necessary transition services within the IEP. Of great significance to IEP development is that, with high school students, an outcome-oriented process is required based on the student's expressed goals for postschool activities. IEPs for high school students are not bound anymore to a single school year framework. Also, the coordinated activities and process for transition planning must address movement from school to postschool, specifically referencing the discussion to what students want in employment, college, services from community agencies, vocational training, continuing and adult education, independent living, and community participation. Movement toward postschool activities implies that the students' goals are addressed in a systematic way from year to year during the final years of formal secondary education: Progress toward postschool goals are tracked over this entire period with built-in accountability.

In addressing the requirement of an outcome-oriented process, there are several general types of activities in developing and implementing IEPs that meet these requirements. In conducting transition planning in an outcome-oriented process directed by meaningful postsecondary goals, students should include such activities as career exploration and job shadowing that relate to their goals. As students progress toward completion of high school, postschool goals should become more clearly stated in the IEP. In promoting movement to postschool activities, IEPs should make referrals to adult service agencies

two or more years before graduation while providing exposure to desired postschool settings (e.g., colleges, businesses, and other community settings). In basing the coordinated activities on individual students' needs, preferences, and interests, personal future planning, student surveys, career inventories, and counseling, IEPs can have some positive impact on student empowerment in goal setting and involvement in the planning process.

The coordinated set of activities intends to be inclusive of all available and possible activities that will address the students' goals. Instruction is classroom or community curriculum that is designed to teach skills relative to work, postsecondary education, independent living, and community participation. The inclusion of related services indicates that they may be necessary to implement transition services and activities (e.g., transportation to a work experience; speech language and audiology, physical and occupational therapy, psychological and counseling services). Community experiences should be provided to allow the student to try out or become established in work, education, independent living, and community participation roles. The development of employment and other postschool adult living objectives include activities and experiences to help the student develop or refine postschool goals. Activities within transition services can also include the acquisition of daily living skills and functional vocational evaluation.

Critical Point Transition, as defined by IDEA 1990, mandated the incorporation of transition services into the IEP. The focus, then, must be on students' postschool goals, with all activities in the IEP supporting the acquisition of those goals.

IDEA of 1997

IDEA of 1997 incorporated several broad policy shifts reflecting major changes in the way that persons with disabilities would receive an education (Stodden, 1998). One change from earlier special education legislation and IDEA of 1997 is that special education will focus on educational and transition results rather than on the process, steps, and procedures to implement programs. This shift represents an increasing focus on what happens to students when they exit the educational system and their quality of life and success in postschool environments. Specifically, this focus needs to be the framework in the design of individual transition services and to be educationally accountable for the general population of students with disabilities. This attempts to address the generally unfavorable outcomes for students documented in follow-up studies and is reflective and consistent with general educational reform.

Another change from earlier legislation and the present IDEA is that of greater attention to the general educational curriculum framework in assessment processes and planning and instructional activities when compared to the past. Special education needs to make larger efforts in ensuring participation of children with disabilities in statewide performance tests and accountability systems. Within the IEP, annual instructional goals must be referenced to the general education curriculum. With a greater mixing of general and special education instruction, participation in inclusive programs and the variety of curricula available in regular education will require participation of general and vocational education teachers in the IEP process.

Finally, changes reflect more emphasis on how assessment and planning have an impact on the results of instruction. Improvement in results from adaptations and supports in the general education curriculum will take precedence over the past practices focusing on disability categories and remediation models.

With IDEA 1997, related services are also available so that students can participate in and benefit from education and what takes place in the classroom and community settings. Students should be able to compete equally with students

without disabilities. Impairments or lack of technology to enhance learning environments may *not* be used as a reason for excluding students from the classes and curricula of their choice. Disability rights have to do with contributing to, participating in, and benefiting from activities in all aspects of community living, citizenship, and the pursuit of personal and career goals. Education is a basic right under the U.S. Constitution because without education one can neither fully exercise other rights nor realize the benefits of citizenship.

With IDEA 1997, there were a variety of wording changes to several major sections. Noteworthy in the purposes section (601) was the addition of "prepare them for employment and independence," an outcome orientation, to the endurance of FAPE. The limitations of FAPE for incarcerated youth with disabilities was spelled out for the first time. Participation in assessments (section 612), composition of state advisory panels, local funding for service coordination and interagency cooperation and personnel training, and transfer of rights to students at the age of majority represented some broad changes that were new to IDEA 1997. See Table 1–10 for a comparison of IDEA 1990 and 1997.

Critical Point Legislative changes in IDEA 1997 changed the focus of special education from process and procedures to accountability in educational and transition postschool outcomes. Additionally, there is greater focus on the general education curriculum assessment processes and planning and instructional activities within the IEP.

Conclusion

The IDEA of 1990 and 1997 ushered in a period of transition that (1) broadened the definition of transition services, (2) focused on self-determination, and (3) required alignment of special education and transition services with the regular education curriculum. The IDEA of 1990 regulations broadened the definition of transition services beyond linkages to include (1) instruction, (2) community

TABLE 1–10

Comparison of the Transition Requirements of the IDEA of 1990 and 1997

Transition and the IDEA of 1990	Transition and the IDEA of 1997
Definition of Transition The term "transition services" means a coordinated set of activities for a student, designed within an outcome-oriented process, that promotes movement from school to post-school activities, including postsecondary education, vocational training, integrated employment (including supported employment), continuing an adult education, adult services, independent living, or community participation. The coordinated set of activities described in paragraph (a) of this section must be based on the student's needs, taking into account the student's preferences and interests, and shall include (i) instruction, (ii) community experiences, (iii) the development of employment and other post-school objectives, and (iv) when appropriate, acquistion of daily living skills and functional vocational evaluation (20 U.S.C. 1401 (19)).	**Definition of Transition** The term "transition services" means a coordinated set of activities for a student with a disability that (A) is designed within an outcome-oriented process, that promotes movement from school to post-school activities, including postsecondary education, vocational training, integrated employment (including supported employment), continuing and adult education, adult services, independent living, or community participation; (B) is based on the student's needs, taking into account the student's preferences and interests; (C) includes instruction, related services, community experiences, the development of employment and other post-school objectives, and, when appropriate, acquisition of daily living skills and functional vocational evaluation (Section 602).
Transition Statement and the IEP The term "individualized education program" means a written statement for each child with a disability . . . which statement shall include: (C) a statement of needed transition services for students beginning no later than age 16 and annually thereafter (and, when determined appropriate for the individual, beginning at age 14 or younger), including, when appropriate, a statement of the interagency responsibilities or linkages (or both) before the student leaves the school setting (20 U.S.C. 1401 (2)).	**Transition Statement and the IEP** (vii)(I) beginning at age 14, and updated annually, a statement of the transition service needs of the child . . . that focuses on the child's courses of study (such as participation in advanced-placement courses or a vocational education program); (II) beginning at age 16 (or younger, if determined appropriate by the IEP Team), a statement of needed transition services for the child, including, when appropriate, a statement of the interagency responsibilities or any needed linkages; (III) beginning at least one year before the child reaches the age of majority under State law, a statement that the child has been informed of his or her rights under this title that will transfer to the child . . . on reaching the age of majority under 615 (m) Section 614(d).

Individualized Education Program
a. Definition:
    (1) IEP is a written statement developed by a representative of LEA or IEU who is qualified to provide or supervise specialized instruction to meet the unique needs of children with disabilities, teacher, parents, and when appropriate the child;
	Individualized Education Programs
	a. Contents of the IEP-current law with the following additional statements:
	    (1) Present level of educational performance, including
	        (a) how the child's disability affects involvement and progress in general curriculum; or,

continued

TABLE 1–10 *continued*

Transition and the IDEA of 1990	Transition and the IDEA of 1997

(2) IEP shall include statements of . . .
  (a) present levels of educational performance;
  (b) annual goals, including short-term objectives;
  (c) specific educational services to be provided and extent to which child will participate in regular educational programs;
  (d) needed transition services for students, beginning no later than age 16, including as appropriate interagency responsibilities or linkages;
  (e) projected "start" date and duration of service; and,
  (f) objective criteria and evaluation procedures, and schedule for determining at least annually whether objectives are being met.
b. LEA or IEU must provide assurance that will establish or revise an IEP for each eligible child at the beginning of each school year, and will review and revise, if necessary, at least annually. (Section 602 (a)(20); 614 (a)(5)).
	(b) for preschoolers, how disability affects participation in appropriate activities;
	(2) Special education & related services and supplementary aids & service to be provided and program modifications or supports provided for personnel . . . to advance appropriately toward attaining annual goals;
	  (b) to be involved and progress in general curriculum and to participate in extracurricular and other nonacademic activities; explanation of extent to which child will not participate in regular class;
	(2) Any individual modifications needed for student to participate in State and district-wide assessments; and if child will not participate in general assessments, why assessment is not appropriate and how child will be assessed;
	(3) Frequency and location of services and modifications;
	(4) Beginning at age 14, transition service needs focusing on child's course of study;
	(5) Beginning at least one year before child reaches age of majority; information regarding rights transferred on reaching age of majority; and,
	(6) How child's progress toward annual goals will be measured, and how parents will be regularly informed of progress.
	b. IEP Team—current law with following additions:
	  (1) At least one regular education teacher if child is or might be participating in regular education environment;
	  (2) At least one special education teacher;
	  (3) LEA representative knowledgeable about general curriculum and about availability of LEA resources;
	  (4) Individual who can interpret evaluation results; and,
	  (5) At parents' or LEA's discretion, other individuals with knowledge/expertise about the child, including related services personnel. (Section 614 (d)).

TABLE 1–10 *concluded*

Transition and the IDEA of 1990	Transition and the IDEA of 1997
Participation in Assessments Not addressed in the IDEA of 1990	**Participation in Assessments** (A) IN GENERAL—Children with disabilities are included in general State and district-wide assessment programs, with appropriate accommodations where necessary. As appropriate the State or local education agency— (I) develops guidelines for the participation of children with disabilities in alternate assessments for those children who cannot participate in State and district-wide assessment programs; and (ii) develops and, beginning not later than July 1, 2000, conducts those assessments (Section 612) (a) (17).
Transfer of Rights at the Age of Majority Not addressed in the IDEA of 1990	**Transfer of Rights at the Age of Majority** . . . when a child with a disability reaches the age of majority under State law (except for a child with a disability who has been determined to be incompetent under State law)— (A) the public agency shall provide any notice required by this section to both the individual and the parents; (B) all other rights accorded to parents under this part transfer to the child; (C) the agency shall notify the individual and the parents of the transfer of rights . . . (2) . . . a child who has not been determined to be incompetent, but who is determined not to have the ability to provide informed consent with respect to the educational program of the child, the State shall establish procedures for appointing the parent of the child, or if the parent is not available, another appropriate individual, to represent the education interests of the child throughout the period of eligibility of the child under this part (Section 615).

experiences, (3) development of employment and other postschool adult living objectives, (4) daily living skills, and (5) functional vocational evaluation [§ 300.347 (b) (2)]. The IDEA of 1997 further broadened the definition of transition services by adding "related services" to the list of recognized transition services [§ 300.327 (b)].

The IDEA of 1990 also supported student self-determination by requiring that students be invited to IEP meetings in which transition is discussed and by requiring provision of services related to the development of employment and other postschool adult living objectives. The IDEA of 1997 broadened support for self-determination by making it necessary to notify students and families of the transfer of IDEA rights when the student reaches the age of majority [§ 300.347 (c)].

The 1997 reauthorization of the IDEA promoted alignment of special education with regular education curriculum and educational reform initiatives (sections 612 and 613), mandated initiation of transition planning by no later than age 14 (section 614), required better integration of transition services into other aspects of the student's educational program (section 614), and mandated evaluating outcomes as a means of promoting program improvement (section 612).

The IDEA of 1997 emphasized that special education students should be involved in school reform initiatives. Two school reform initiatives were to have a major impact on how transition was implemented in the 1990s—the School to Work Opportunity Act and the Goals 2000 Educate America Act. Goals 2000 shifted the educational focus from outcomes-based education to standards-based education, thereby seriously undermining the parallel functional curricula used by many transition programs. The IDEA of 1997 reinforced Goals 2000 by making it necessary that special education be designed to teach the same skills and competencies as regular education and by requiring participation of all students with disabilities in general statewide and districtwide assessments [§ 300.347 (a) (5)].

The School to Work Opportunity Act (STWOA) of 1994 introduced transition as a major initiative for *all students* by promoting the development of career paths, applied academic courses, workforce experiences, and partnerships with community colleges and 4-year institutions to align high school and postsecondary curricula. STWOA reforms were an effort to develop curricula and activities within general education that supported career education, especially for students who were not bound for typical 4-year liberal arts education. School-to-work reforms were implemented in many different ways at the local level (Benz & Kochar, 1996; Stodden, 1998). Surveys of state school-to-work opportunity sys-

tems identified several indicators of effective practice, including (1) establishing partnerships with schools/businesses, (2) using transition specialists to assist partners in program development, (3) promoting student self-determination, (4) focusing on long-term outcomes, (5) setting high standards, and (6) developing social and interpersonal skills of students (School-to-Work Information Center, 1996). The IDEA of 1997 linked with school to work (STW) by requiring transition services that focused on a particular course of study by age 14 [§300.347 (b)(2)].

The 1990s represented an era in which transition was defined and mandated in special education legislation. It was also a period of intense debate of disability policy. IDEA of 1990 required a statement of needed transitions no later than age 16 and at 14 if appropriate. The basic requirements and definition of transition was set out in IDEA of 1990. Coordinated activities necessitated interdisciplinary services reflecting regular, vocational, and special education while closer connections between secondary and postschool education and services were needed. This coordination pointed toward more communication and cooperation among all segments of transition, disability, and general education systems up through college and other postsecondary education. An outcome-oriented process must be set up in which students set goals, and progress and movement toward those goals are monitored. Transition required looking at the entire period of education from middle school through postsecondary education and employment in order to establish a career path that is based on the student's needs, preferences, and interests.

Study Questions

1. What are the differences between disability services as an entitlement versus based on eligibility?
2. Why is disability considered a rights issue?
3. Why is disability and disability policy generally misunderstood by the general public?
4. Why is access and accommodation important in vocational and regular education and postsecondary education?

5. How would you characterize disability policy and services in the 1960s?
6. How would you characterize disability policy and services in the 1970s and 1980s?
7. How would you characterize disability policy and services in the 1990s?
8. What were the changes in emphasis in legislation among the 1960s and 1970s and 1980s?
9. What were the changes in emphasis in legislation between the 1970s and 1980s and 1990s?
10. Why is general education and disability legislation other than special education (SPED) important to transition and IDEA requirements?
11. What were changes in transition with IDEA of 1990?
12. What were changes in transition from IDEA of 1990 to IDEA of 1997?

Web Sites

Facts about School-to-Work Transition:
http://TheArc.org/faqs/transit.html

National Information Center for Children and Youth with Disabilities:
http://www.nichy.org

National School-to-Work Office:
http://www.stw.ed.gov/

National Transition Alliance for Youth with Disabilities:
http://www.dssc.org/nta/html/index_2.htm

Office of Special Education Programs Outcome Data:
http://www.ed.gov/pubs/OSEP95AnlRpt/ch3a.html

School-to-Work Site Devoted to Students with Disabilities:
http://www.ici.coled.umn.edu/schooltowork/default.html

Thomas:
http://Thomas.loc.gov/

2

Transition Models and Best Practices

Robert W. Flexer
Rachel K. McMahan
Robert Baer

The objectives of this chapter are:

1. Know the history of practices to help youth with disabilities in the transition to adulthood.

2. Understand how transition history shaped transition policy.

3. Identify problems in defining the "best practice" in transition for youth with disabilities.

4. Know the nine best practices in transition.

Transition models date back to the 1930s when special educators began to realize that a strictly academic curriculum was not sufficient to meet the needs of students with mild mental retardation. During this period, some states developed functional curricula; and educators, in urban areas in particular, advocated for curriculum change, reflecting a life skills and a vocational approach to special education for secondary youth (see Clark & Kolstoe, 1995 and Neubert, 1997 for a more thorough discussion). Clearly implied in these efforts was direct teaching of skills needed for successful adult functioning. Numerous follow-up studies spanning a 20-year period documented the effectiveness of this functional life skills approach to secondary curriculum for students with mild mental retardation (see Cobb, 1972).

The life skills approach ushered in a renewed interest in serving greater numbers of students with mental retardation. Similarly, a functional and job skills approach was implemented in the early work-study programs in the late 1950s (e.g., Frey & Kolstoe, 1965). Since earlier efforts at transition, various models, approaches, and perspectives have been proposed and implemented with varying degrees of success in meeting the needs of youth with disabilities. There are both general models which have applicability across disability groups and specific models which provide more detail for service provision for specific groups. In all of these models, a multitude of transition services and methods have been proposed to focus transition teams on student involvement, outcome orientation, coordinated services, and promoting movement to postschool activities.

As Halpern (1992b) pointed out, transition programs may be "old wine in new bottles." In a classic article in 1992, Halpern reviewed the 25-year history of transition models and concluded that transition models have matured. He also noted that new approaches are variations of the "tried and true" approaches of the past. As in all

of special education, transition advocates need to be aware of the dangers of the "band wagon" effect, that is, adopting something because it is new and is marketed as the "silver bullet." As consumers of transition literature and developers of transition services, transition teams can serve their students better if they are informed and intelligent in the selection of transition methods and are accountable in assessing the impact of their teaching and service coordination.

The previous chapter focused on the history of social concepts of disability and how those ideas shaped disability legislation and current transition policies. Chapter 1 introduced four essential elements of transition services as defined in the Individuals with Disabilities Education Acts (IDEA) of 1990 and 1997. These elements require services to be (1) based on student needs, taking into account interests and preferences, (2) outcome-oriented, (3) a coordinated set of activities, and (4) designed to promote movement from school to postschool settings. This chapter is designed to provide a framework for using these four essential elements in order to organize and evaluate transition practices that are considered the "best practice" by policymakers, advocates, and researchers. It starts with a history of transition and describes how early transition research and practice led to the four essential elements of transition services in the IDEA. This chapter then provides a discussion of nine transition practices that are generally seen as the "best practices" by policymakers, advocates, and researchers.

Early Transition Models

Work-Study Programs

Before transition became part of the language of secondary special education, several program initiatives were put forward as meeting some of the needs of youth as they prepared for transition into adult roles. Halpern (1992) suggested that the concept of transition originated from work-study and career education programs of the 1960s and 1970s. The work-study model emerged in the late 1950s as a collaboration between public schools and local offices of state rehabilitation agencies. Work-study programs provided integrated academic, social, and vocational curriculum coupled with community work experiences to prepare youth with mild disabilities, mostly mental retardation, for productive community adjustment. Halpern (1992) noted that these programs had many elements in common with transition programs, including a focus on vocational instruction, community experiences, and formal linkages with rehabilitation services. Work study was also the first example of collaboration in which there was formal interagency cooperation.

Like many transition models, work study was an initiative of the federal government, in this case through vocational rehabilitation legislation. As vocational rehabilitation became a federal–state partnership (i.e., federal money being matched by state money), various populations of people with disabilities were identified as in need of rehabilitation and employment-related services. Students with mild mental retardation in high school were targeted as such a group. The work-study program had many features in common with the transition practices of today. They were as follows:

1. *Part-time work experiences were combined with part-time school with credit* toward graduation for work experience. Community employment was legitimized as part of the curriculum and recognized for its educational value. Work-adjustment classes and functional academics were correlated with work experience to aid students in adapting and problem solving in the work site and in the community.
2. *The classroom teacher as a work coordinator* along with the rehabilitation counselor worked as a team reflecting an interdisciplinary approach. The employment orientation of vocational rehabilitation became part of the school program; students became clients of vocational rehabilitation and were eligible for all the services of the agency.
3. *Interagency agreements* were utilized to increase resources for work-based learning and rehabilitation services. Thousands of students with mild mental retardation became clients of the state rehabilitation agency while preparing for the transition to successful employment. In most states, there were agreements between local schools and the rehabilitation agency in many communities: Local offices of vocational rehabilitation, in some instances, had counselors who were assigned exclusively to serving schools.

Through work-study programs, thousands of students with mild mental retardation became clients of the state rehabilitation agency while making the transition to successful employment. Although it held great promise, the work-study cooperative arrangement with rehabilitation services lasted little more than a decade. Halpern (1992) suggested that the collaboration between schools and state rehabilitation programs was undermined by both funding mechanisms and the "similar benefits" requirement of the 1973 amendments to the Vocational Rehabilitation Act. The funding mechanism used to support work-study programs included the use of teachers' salaries as an "in-kind" match. Using teachers, however, required that they be supervised by certified rehabilitation personnel, an arrangement that was not agreeable to school principals. But the ultimate demise of rehabilitation-funded work-study programs was due in large part to the passage of Public Law (P.L.) 94-142 in 1975. This legislation was interpreted as passing the responsibility for work study to schools as part of the requirement that they provide "free appropriate public education" (FAPE). This made it difficult for rehabilitation agencies to justify purchasing work-study services from schools since they were now considered the schools' responsibility (Halpern, 1992b).

Work-study programs have continued to operate in most states. Frequently, there is a staff person who is funded and assigned to implement a schoolwide work-study program. In the current service picture, work-study program services are provided to students with learning disabilities and behavior disorders in addition to students with mild mental retardation. Having some kind of work experience while in high school is related to better postschool outcomes for some students (Hasazi, Gordon, & Roe, 1985; Stanford Research Institute [SRI] International, 1990). Students learn the basic skills required in all work settings and may make valuable contacts that often lead to employment after graduation. Work-experience programs also provide students with real-life experiences that can make education more relevant and contribute to their staying in school (SRI International, 1990).

Critical Point   Work-study programs emerged during the 1960s to serve students with mild mental retardation in the high schools. State rehabilitation programs and the high schools worked collaboratively to provide employment training experiences. Although these cooperative agreements no longer exist, most states have work-study programs to serve high school students with learning disabilities, emotional and behavioral disorders, and mild mental retardation.

The Career Education Initiative

Career education, a second precursor to transition, emerged in the 1970s and was established in 1977 with passage of P.L. 95-207, the Career Education Implementation Incentive Act. Halpern (1992) said this initiative could be seen as an extension of the earlier work-study movement. He noted that unlike work-study programs, career education programs included all ages and types of students and focused on broader goals than work-study programs. How-

Work experience is vital to career education programs.

ever, the career education movement had to rely on local efforts when the Career Education Implementation Incentive Act expired in 1982.

Although the Career Education Implementation Incentive Act expired in 1982, career education in special education continued to be a central theme and an integral approach to transition. Added emphasis was placed on elementary and middle school as a foundation for the development of career maturity and life skills. With attention to career awareness and exploration, elementary and middle school programs were developed to increase students' self-understanding and skills and competencies related to occupation, interpersonal, domestic, and community curricular domains. At the same time, community-based instructional programs were being developed from a framework of the criterion of ultimate function (Brown et al., 1979). Students with severe disabilities, in particular, were instructed in community environments where they would eventually function as adults.

Critical Point   The career education programs differed from work-study programs in that they included students of all ages (with and without disabilities). The goals of this movement were broader than work study because elementary and middle school students were targeted for career awareness and exploration.

Models of Transition in the 1980s

Will's Bridges Model

Follow-up studies through the 1970s documented that many students were preparing for the transition from high school with poor outcomes (e.g., Hasazi, Gordon, & Roe, 1985). This, coupled with the repeal of the Career Education Act (P.L. 95-207), underscored the need for more effective approaches to direct youth with disabilities to meaningful postschool outcomes. In 1984, Madeleine Will, a conservative parent advocate and assistant secretary of the Office of Special Education and Rehabilitation Services (OSERS) within the U.S. Department of Education, proposed a model for transition from school to work that emphasized "bridges" or linkages between school and postschool environments (Will, 1984). For the first time in the history of special education, transition became a set of activities recognized by the federal government that should be provided by schools.

Will's model focused on employment and conceptualized transition as three bridges to employment: (1) transition without special services (e.g., postsecondary education), (2) transition with time-limited services (e.g., vocational rehabilitation), and (3) transition with ongoing services (e.g., supported employment). The basic concept behind her model was that secondary and postsecondary environments for youth with disabilities needed to be connected by services and supports that overlapped. Will's model highlighted the need for collaboration between special educators and adult service providers, as well as regular educators, employers, and families. Her model recognized the fact that special educators and adult service providers often labored under differing assumptions about whom was to be served, what types of services should be available, and who was responsible (DeStefano & Snauwaert, 1989) (see Figure 2–1).

This "bridges" concept of transition was narrower in focus than either the work-study or career education movements (Halpern, 1992). It

FIGURE 2–1
OSERS Transition Model, 1984

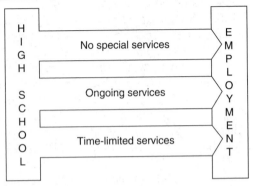

Source: From OSERS programming for the transition of youth with disabilities: Bridges from school to working life, by M. Will, 1984, U.S. Office of Education.

focused totally on employment through generic, time-limited, or ongoing interventions. The "bridges" model suggested that some students would only need generic services (such as postsecondary education) to make the transition to employment. Others would need time-limited interventions such as vocational rehabilitation, and some would need ongoing support to maintain employment (e.g., supported employment). Although Will (1984) did not dismiss the importance of the residential, social, and interpersonal domains, she saw their importance only in relation to obtaining employment and enjoying its benefits.

Critical Point The "bridges" model emerged in a time when transition did not exist in special education. Will believed that in order for students to be successful upon graduation, they must be directly linked to adult service employment and training opportunities while still in high school.

Will's model suggested that it was a natural extension of the interagency cooperation focus of the earlier work-study models. Edgar (1987) indicated that the problem for students with disabilities who were leaving the school environment was that more services and supports were needed. This assumption was based on data

FIGURE 2–2
Halpern's Revised Transition Model, 1985

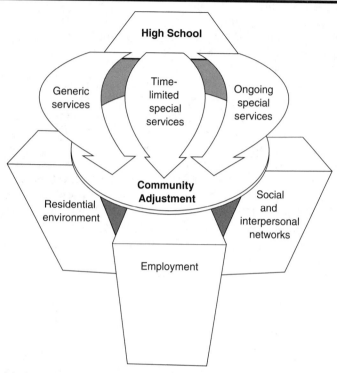

Source: From Transition: A look at the foundations, by A. S. Halpern, *Exceptional Children, 51* (6), 1985, p. 481. Copyright (1985) by the Council for Exceptional Children. Reprinted with permission.

from follow-up studies showing that students with disabilities were in great need of postschool services and supports. According to Edgar (1987), systems change would be required in order to create a variety of services that are needed for there to be services for bridges.

Halpern's Alternative to the Bridges Model

Halpern's model challenged Will's total focus on employment. His research showed that employment was not the sole factor in quality of life, and that the residential and interpersonal domains must be considered (Halpern, 1985). Halpern proposed that community adjustment

should be the broader outcome toward which transition services should be directed. He developed a model that focused on three "pillars" of community adjustment: employment, residential environments, and social and interpersonal networks. According to Halpern (1985), transition programs were needed to build each of these pillars in order to affect the overall quality of life and community adjustment for students with disabilities (see Figure 2–2).

Like Will, Halpern addressed the bridges aspect of transition, relabeling what Will referred to as "no services" as "generic services." He noted that these generic services were important to many students with disabilities, including postsecondary programs and employment and training programs. Also, a variety of social welfare and community programs, which served specific functions, were available to persons without disabilities. Halpern (1985) suggested that although these generic services did not provide any disability-specific services, they were often necessary to help students achieve quality of life after graduation and that such services should benefit persons with disabilities as they would other individuals. Halpern's model emphasized that transition was more than simply the process of the school's handing off the student. It was closer to a career education model that prepared and linked students to postsecondary environments (Halpern, 1992). Halpern's model was largely adopted as the basis for defining transition services in IDEA, leading to independent living and community participation, in addition to work and education (Johnson & Rusch, 1993).

Critical Point Whereas the "bridges" model focused on employment, Halpern looked at the broader issue of "quality of life." He expanded Will's model to include residential environments and social and interpersonal networks, in addition to employment. Halpern believed that all three "pillars" must be addressed to enhance the student's overall community adjustment.

Linkages in Transition Systems

Rehabilitation, special education, and vocational education linkages were addressed in the 1980s with a great deal of transition legislation and research. While transition was emerging in special education, it was developing in a parallel but often contradictory manner in the rehabilitation and vocational education disciplines (Szymanski, Hanley-Maxwell, & Asselin, 1990). As noted earlier, the "similar benefits" clause of the Rehabilitation Act of 1973 (P.L. 93-112) led to considerable problems in developing the linkages that were critical to early work-study programs. Additionally, DeStefano and Snauwaert (1989) noted that the service philosophies un-

derlying special education and rehabilitation were often at odds; that is, special education centered on equity and entitlement in services and rehabilitation services concentrated on efficiency and eligibility. They suggested that this value conflict impeded the transition initiative by creating inconsistencies and cross purposes in the system serving students with disabilities. Advocates coined this move from special education entitlements to rehabilitation services as a "transition to uncertainty" (Ward & Halloran, 1989) and "rights roulette" (Turnbull, Turnbull, Bronicki, Summers, & Roeder-Gordon, 1989).

Parallel and often discrepant transition initiatives also developed in the field of vocational education. The education amendments of 1976 (P.L. 94-486) set aside 10% of each state's federal vocational education grant for youth with disabilities. However, little was done to coordinate services between vocational education and the other transition disciplines until the 1990 Carl D. Perkins Vocational and Applied Technology Education Act mandated coordination among vocational education, state rehabilitation agencies, and special education. Despite this mandate, Lombard, Hazelkorn, and Neubert (1992) found little mention of vocational services in the IEPs of students with disabilities in vocational programs.

In the 1980s, OSERS began to focus on interagency agreements to bring together the three transition disciplines of vocational education, special education, and rehabilitation. Heal, Copher, and Rusch (1990) studied the characteristics and perceived value of these agreements in 29 demonstration projects. They found that although several agencies were involved (average 3.93 per agreement), less than half of them (i.e., 11) involved vocational education. Heal et al. (1990) also found that interagency agreements did little to address the problem of fragmented transition services. Generally, the respective agencies invested minimal time and resources and typically focused on information and referral (Heal et al., 1990).

Critical Point Linkages among special education, vocational education, and rehabilitation were not easy to develop because the underlying service philosophies were conflicting. During the 1980s, OSERS focused on developing interagency agreements to bring the three disciplines together in order to work in a more collaborative manner.

Work Preparation Models

Two specific transition approaches emerged during the "bridges" period, including (1) special needs vocational education and (2) community-based vocational training. Special needs vocational education grew out of the legislation that set aside monies to serve special populations (such as students with disabilities) and to serve primarily students with mild to moderate disabilities. Community-based vocational training and supported employment programs resulted from rehabilitation and ongoing support legislation to assist students with severe disabilities. Special needs vocational education was designed to provide adapted and modified occupational specific programs with supplemental services to serve students with mental retardation, learning disabilities, behavioral disorders, and sensory and physical impairments. Community-based vocational training (e.g., supported employment, on-the-job training services, and community-based instruction) was initiated while students were still in high school. Before graduation, students were placed in a permanent job with the plan that community agencies would take over support and case management services after the student graduated (Wehman, Kregal, & Barcus, 1985).

The special needs vocational model required that students with disabilities obtain access to all forms of vocational education that was critical to their career path. Figure 2–3 shows one model for providing access to vocational and career education developed by the Ohio Department of Vocational Education. At the first level, students could be served in any regular vocational program with

appropriate accommodations. Other students may require adaptations or adjustments in the program, such as specialized instruction and other support services to enable them to succeed. In other instances, curriculum modifications may be necessary for student success. Finally, some students may need segregated programs offering a fairly focused curriculum for a narrower range of skills and possible future job positions. In other instances, a totally alternative program, such as supported employment, may be the most appropriate to meet the needs of students for vocational education.

Wehman's vocational transition model (Wehman et al., 1985) was an example of a work preparation model where special education, vocational education, and rehabilitation were linked to support transition for students with severe disabilities (see Figure 2–4). The principles of Wehman's model were:

1. Members of the multiple disciplines and service delivery systems must participate.
2. Parent involvement is essential.
3. Vocational transition planning must occur well before 21 years of age.
4. The process must be planned and systematic.
5. The vocational service provided must be [of] a quality nature (p. 26).

Wehman's model required movement through the three stages of school instruction, planning for the transition process, and placement into meaningful employment. The first stage is important because instruction in the public school can be the foundation for later services and planning. School instruction should include (1) a functional curriculum, (2) services delivered in integrated school environments, and (3) community-based activities to enhance the student's ability to apply functional academics. The second stage involves the planning process. Students and their families are at the core of transition planning. Support services, beyond the public school, must also be involved in the planning process to help identify all potential postsecondary outcomes for the students. The planning process must be individualized to

FIGURE 2–3
A Continuum of Vocational Placement Options for Students with Disabilities

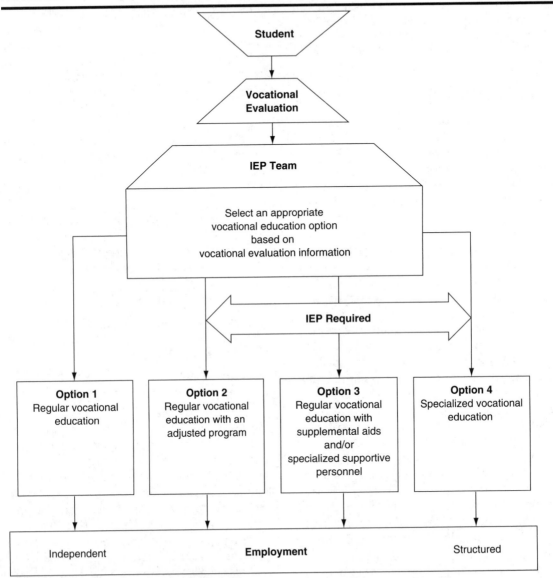

Source: From *Vocational Education for Ohio's Handicapped Children,* by Ohio Division of Career and Vocational Education, N.D.

FIGURE 2–4

Three-Stage Vocational Transition Model for Youth with Disabilities

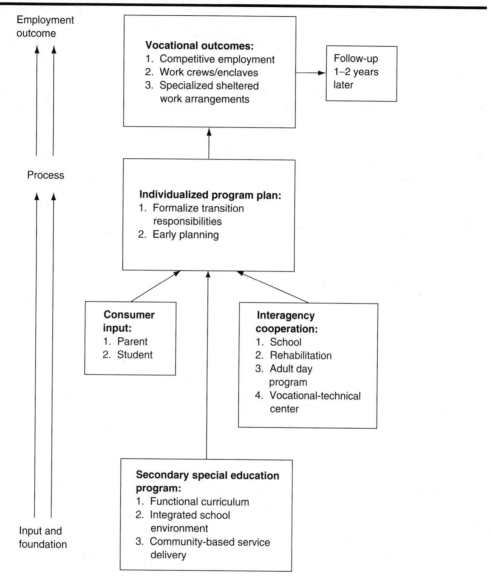

Source: From School to work: A vocational transition model, by P. Wehman, J. Kregel, & J. M. Barcus, *Exceptional Children, 52* (1), 1985, 28. Copyright (1985) by the Council for Exceptional Children. Reprinted with permission.

specify the skills needed by students and the various transition services that are necessary to be successful. The final stage of Wehman's model is the vocational outcome of competitive employment, supported employment, or specialized sheltered work. Wehman and his colleagues stated that students should be placed before leaving the school environment in order to make the transition smooth to adulthood (Wehman, et al., 1985).

Critical Point   Ohio's special needs vocational model offers a continuum of four options to meet the needs of students with disabilities in work preparation programs. Wehman's model focuses on students with severe disabilities who are in need of community-based vocational training through the stages of school instruction, transition planning, and job placement.

Emerging Models in the 1990s

Quality-of-Life Focus on Transition

A widespread concern about quality-of-life outcomes drove the IDEA focus on outcome-oriented planning for students with disabilities. Bowe (1992) observed that after $20 billion in funding each year for special education and $2 billion for rehabilitation, more than 8 million persons with disabilities were on supplementary security income (SSI) or social security disability insurance (SSDI), with total assistance costing more than $290 billion annually. The national transition longitudinal study of more than 8,000 special education students found that 3 to 5 years after graduation only 43.5% of graduates were working full time and only 36.9% were taking any postsecondary courses (SRI International, 1992). Stanford Research Institute (SRI) International determined that youth with disabilities who became employed tended to go into low wage, low status jobs, with few opportunities for advancement. In 1990, the President's Committee on Employment of Persons with Disabilities reported that 63% of male and

72% of female adults with disabilities were unemployed nationally.

Student outcomes regarding independent living and community participation were equally discouraging (SRI International). One of the reasons for poor postsecondary outcomes was the lack of outcome orientation in the development of IEPs. Woolcock, Stodden, and Bisconver (1992) noted that, "without an understanding of the rationale or solid basis for decisions about a student's future, the process of transition decision making often lacks direction and validity" (p. 236). Studies of students in vocational education found that half or less had vocational goals on their IEPs (Krom & Prater, 1993; Lombard, Hazelkorn, & Neubert, 1992), and vocational assessment was provided to small percentages of students.

In the 1980s, quality of life became a critical component of transition because individuals with disabilities had a high likelihood of living in poverty, being victims of crime, and having health and medical care concerns (West, 1991). For advocates, quality of life was often seen as a function of values or fundamental beliefs about transition outcomes. It encompassed questions such as, "What quality-of-life perspectives underly our professional philosophy, our society, and the individuals and the families we are serving?" Goode (1990) summarized the criteria needed for a complete picture of quality of life:

> When an individual, with or without disabilities is able to meet important needs in major life settings (work, school, home, community) while also satisfying the normative expectations that others hold for him or her in those settings, he or she is more likely to experience a high quality of life (p. 46).

Halpern, Doren, and Benz (1993) discovered that outcomes and student goals were not driving instruction. He concluded that the field was still deficient in what was taught, how it was taught, and where it was taught. Halpern established an analysis framework for the secondary foundation to transition. He analyzed 41 outcome studies for

TABLE 2–1

Quality-of-Life Domains and Desired Postschool Outcomes

Physical and material well-being:
- Physical and mental health
- Food, clothing, and lodging
- Financial security
- Safety from harm

Performance of adult roles:
- Mobility and community access
- Vocation, career, employment
- Leisure and recreation
- Personal relationships and social networks
- Educational attainment
- Spiritual fulfillment
- Citizenship (e.g., voting)
- Social responsibility (e.g., does not break laws)

Personal fulfillment:
- Happiness
- Satisfaction
- Sense of general well-being

Source: From Quality of life as a conceptual framework for evaluating transition outcomes, by A. S. Halpern, *Exceptional Children, 59* (6), 1985, p. 491. Copyright (1985) by the Council for Exceptional Children. Reprinted with permission.

students with disabilities to see how researchers measured transition quality-of-life outcome. He found a primary focus on education and employment, a minor focus on social networks and relationships, and none on personal fulfillment. Halpern's analysis led him to expand his notion of quality of life to include three quality-of-life domains: (1) physical and material well-being, (2) performance of adult roles, and (3) personal fulfillment. These quality of life and related concepts are presented in Table 2–1.

Johnson and Rusch (1993) noted that during the 1980s several other transition models emerged that focused on transition more broadly than the bridges models. These included the career education models such as the life-centered career education model (Clark & Kolstoe, 1995),

the life-planning program model (Schumaker, Hazel, & Deshler, 1985), the independent living and community adjustment model (Halpern, 1985), and person-centered planning models such as personal futures planning (Mount & Zwernick, 1988). The career education models were a natural extension of earlier career education movements and person-centered planning models drew heavily on ecological psychology approaches.

Critical Point   Quality-of-life issues still persist today based on poor outcomes in all domains of life for students with disabilities. Transition programs must: (1) be based on student needs and preferences, (2) be outcome-oriented, (3) be a coordinated set of activities, and (4) promote movement to postsecondary settings to affect positively the overall quality of life for students with disabilities.

Kohler's Model

Kohler (1998) offered an infusion-based career education model called a "transition perspective of education." Kohler's model emphasized the importance of a broad view of what education is or should be and delineated a taxonomy or description for transition planning and services that included (1) student-focused planning, (2) family involvement, (3) program structure and attributes, (4) interagency collaboration, and (5) student development (see Figure 2–5). This approach emphasized that transition is another facet of education and the importance of a broad view of what education should be. Kohler also delineated a taxonomy or description for transition planning and services which suggested that transition was the way to look at education. According to Kohler, the most frequently asked questions on transition planning are what, who, and how in services development and implementation. Kohler emphasized three major activities that provide a framework for her model:

- Postschool goals are identified based on student abilities, needs, interests, and preferences.

FIGURE 2–5
Emerging Model of Transition Practices

Source: From Implementing a transition perspective, by P. D. Kohler in *Beyond high school: Transition from school to work,* Rusch, F. R. & Chadsey, J. G. (Eds.), p. 208. Copyright 1998. Reprinted with permission of Wadsworth Publishing, a division of Thomson Learning. FAX 800-730-2215.

- Instructional activities and educational experiences are developed to prepare students for their postschool goals.
- A variety of individuals, including the student, work together to identify and develop the goals and activities.

An outcome-oriented planning process is at the core of transition planning and reinforces the need for individualization. This shift in paradigm structure focuses on the students' abilities, desires, and the various options available to them in the future. The five categories of Kohler's model define the transition perspective as tasks that must be performed in order to promote a transition-focused education. The first category, *student-focused planning,* includes (1) IEP development, (2) student participation, and (3) planning strategies. Student participation is inherently important in individualized planning because the IEP is the main vehicle in determining appropriate goals, objectives, and services. Second, *student development*, includes (1) life skills instruction, (2) employability skills instruction, (3) career and vocational curricula, (4) structured work experiences, (5) assessment, and (6) support services. Schools must provide options in which students can learn the skills necessary to become successful participants of society. Instruction must also be provided in a number of different settings to enhance the generalization of skill acquisition. Kohler (1998) emphasizes that schools should: (1) provide academic and vocational instruction through a number of curricular options, (2) identify and provide supports to facilitate learning by all students, (3) conduct and utilize assessment related to instructional planning, and (4) provide structured work experiences where needed.

Third, *interagency and interdisciplinary collaboration* encompasses the collaborative framework as well as collaborative service delivery. The lack of collaboration and cooperation can often create barriers to programming for students with disabilities. Interagency transition teams that include key stakeholders (e.g., parents, students, employers, and service providers) can often (1) eliminate service gaps, (2) avoid service duplication, (3) increase efficient use of resources, (4) reduce territorial issues, and (5) create holistic planning and service delivery. Participants of interagency transition teams can increase their personal knowledge about other delivery systems, create contacts with those systems, and work collaboratively to work out resource problems through cooperative agreements. "Establishing methods of communication among providers is a key practice in developing [a] collaborative framework" (Kohler, 1998 p.186). The process of creating a means to address problems, to share information, and to identify solutions enables all professionals (i.e., school,

agency, and community-based) to coordinate their efforts to maximize resources.

Fourth, *family involvement* includes participation, empowerment, and training. Students and their families are participating more in the planning process, yet, they still may feel uncomfortable to be active participants in the whole process for several reasons: (1) understanding the assessments, (2) ambiguity and confusion of requirements and practices of professionals, (3) lack of familiarity with all professionals, (4) jargon, and (5) primary domination of meetings by transition professionals.

The final category of Kohler's taxonomy, *program structures and attributes*, looks at the service system and the corresponding philosophy, policies, planning procedures, evaluation methods, resource allocations, and human resource development. In many instances, the way in which school and adult service delivery systems are managed is not conducive to implementing transition. Educational programs must look at postschool goals and provide a variety of curricular options. School systems dedicated to improving transition services must have (1) systematic community involvement in the development of educational options, (2) community-based learning opportunities, (3) systematic inclusion of students in the social life of the school, and (4) increased expectations related to skills, values, and outcomes for all students.

Siegel's Model

Siegel (1998) proposed an infusion career education model of transition with a heavy emphasis on integrating transition with school-to-work programs. In this approach the collective educational experiences of students should answer three basic questions:

1. Who am I?
2. What is my community?
3. How do I engage in a meaningful way?

TABLE 2–2

Siegel's Five Intensity Levels of Transition

Youth	Service Needs	STW System Should Provide . . .
Level 5: Low-achieving or with significant disabilities and/or at high risk of chronic unemployment/illegitimate career paths	Early intervention; immersion programs; intensive follow-along services	Middle school-initiated programs; job corps; conservation corps; supported employment; model community programs; new and experimental models under the Americorps and other initiatives
Level 4: Low to average achievers; at risk of dropping out, school failure, illegitimate career paths; need all of level 3, but with more intensity	Early interventions; supervised work-experience internships; paced training options; assistance with college education; intensive follow-along services	Intensified community-based agencies and programs; new and innovative school programs; new and innovative vocational rehabilitation and other state/regional programs
Level 3: Low to average achievers; some college-bound; lower socioeconomic status; need reasonable opportunities and career counseling; advocacy and some monitoring	Early interventions; monitored work-experience internships; paced training options; assistance with college education	Vocational/special education co-operatives, tech-prep; existing community-based agency programs; school district; Private Industry Council; adult education; community and technical colleges
Level 2: Average to high achievers; some college-bound; more from a low socioeconomic status; lack only reasonable job opportunities	Job and job-training opportunities; unsupervised work-experience internships; targeted college scholarships and options	Tech-prep, private sector; school district; academies; adult education, community college, college and university
Level 1: Average to high achievers; many college-bound; average to high SES; have social and professional connections	Existing college and employment options	Tech-prep, existing education and employment institutions

Source: From Foundations for a school-to-work system that serves all students by S. Siegel in *Beyond high school: Transition from school-to-work* by Rusch, F. R. and Chadsey, J. G., 1998, p. 154. Copyright 1998. Reprinted with permission of Wadsworth Publishing, a division of Thomson Learning. Fax 800-730-2215.

In Siegel's multiple-option school-to-work system, students have the flexibility to adjust their individualized program as their interests and needs change over time. Career pathways consist of course work clustered in five or six career areas (e.g., communication and arts; marketing and business; health occupations; and human services). A career application context for an entire curriculum allows students to shape their course of study in a way that is meaningful to them. For an integrated pathway serving all levels of students, pathways must be broadly defined (e.g., an introduction to health occupations course may serve future surgeons, students interested in obtaining a nursing license, or students who may be projecting career interests in volunteer or entry-level work in a hospital). Table 2–2 shows Siegel's intensity level model of transition. Students may use combinations of levels, going back and forth between levels depending on need.

Siegal's model of multiple options in a school-to-work system consists of five levels of transition services. These levels differ by the intensity of student need. The level is not determined by a student's disability label but rather by his or her individualized need to participate with other students and to become independent after graduation. Siegel's levels are not intended to be used as a tracking system. They are multiple options that students can utilize depending on their individual needs at a given time and can use in a combination of levels to become successful in the future.

Level 5, *services for youth at the greatest risk of unemployment and marginalization*, offers the most intense supports. The students most often served by this level include (1) those students with the most significant and profound disabilities, (2) those students with excessive and challenging behaviors who may have been adjudicated or at great risk for adjudication, and (3) those students with the most serious conduct and behavioral disorders that may not have been identified as having a disability. Services may include supported employment for students with the most severe disabilities and very individualized programming for students at risk for adjudication. Programming for students with behavioral and/or conduct disorders may encompass day treatment; residential services; and, in most severe cases, immersion programs to remove students from their typical environments and to give them 24-hour services to support more intensive needs. Level 4 transition services, *services for youth at moderate risk of unemployment and underemployment*, are for students who exhibit one or more of the following characteristics: (1) are at risk for dropping out of school, (2) are failing in school, (3) are academically behind, (4) have mild learning/emotional disabilities, (5) have been arrested one or two times, (6) have had mild drug involvement, (7) are parenting, or (8) are a sex minority. Programs that benefit this group of students include vocational preparation programs, job shadowing, supervised work

experiences, classes that support work experiences, and peer supports.

Level 3, *services for students in need of state-of-the-art education for careers*, focuses on students who are achieving at low or average academic levels. These students may be from lower-income families and have a mild disability. The more accommodating schools may handle students with these needs easily. Level 2, *services for youth in need of career opportunities*, is for average to high achievers. Many of these students are from lower-income families and require structured career education programs to achieve postsecondary success. Most school districts have many career training opportunities for their students but discrepancies in funding exist across districts, making some programs better than others. The final, least intrusive level of transition services, *services for all students, including high achieving, high-income youth*, is for average to high academically achieving students who tend to be college bound.

Siegel's levels of transition services focus on individualized programming for all students, which is the primary goal of the special education law and the school-to-work initiative. "Individualization is one of the subtleties of exemplary educational practices, and has been the foundation of special education for over 30 years" (Siegel, 1998, p. 166). Levels 4 and 5 of Siegel's transition services do not exist in many systems, yet they are the most needed in school districts because of high dropout rates and poor graduation outcomes for students with significant disabilities. Many educational systems do not have the money, staff, training, and time to individualize the programming of the students who do not fit into the already existing service system. Transition services must look at the student as the center of individualized program development in order to ensure postgraduation success.

Critical Point   Kohler's transition perspective of education describes transition planning in a broad context and emphasizes the need for outcome-oriented planning and individualization. Siegel's model of multiple options offers varying service intensity levels in which students can participate depending on their interests and needs at the time.

Problems in Defining "Best Practices" in Transition

In the 1980s, research on the best practices in transition yielded up to 12 criteria for model transition programs. However, Kohler (1993) found that only four best practices were well-supported by empirical research. These were parent involvement, vocational training, paid work, and social skills training. Research on demonstration projects also suggested areas of the best practice in transition. These included interagency cooperation, effective placement techniques, systems change strategies, coordinated needs assessment, outreach, and barrier resolution (Johnson & Rusch, 1993). Research on transition projects funded by OSERS suggested that vocational assessment, prevocational and vocational classes, on-campus work experience, placement, and orientation to adult agencies were typical approaches used by model transition programs (Heal, Copher, & Rusch, 1990). A meta-analysis of transition practices by Phelps and Hanley-Maxwell (1997) found two transition practices as universally supported by research: (1) functional curriculum and (2) school-supervised work experiences. In their study, vocational education was strongly but not universally supported (Phelps & Hanley-Maxwell, 1997).

Baer, Simmons, and Flexer (1996) surveyed Ohio's special education supervisors and administrators, work-study coordinators, vocational special education coordinators, and school psychologists to determine statewide implementation of IDEA transition mandates and four other best practices in transition. The best practices were identified and recommended by the Ohio Futures Forum: Goal 4 Committee on Transition (Ohio Department of Education, 1990). These practices included (1) follow-up studies on students who have exited special education, (2) interagency transition teams, (3) parent/student involvement, and (4) employer involvement. The committee found that reported compliance with IDEA transition mandates was the highest in areas related to procedural issues. In addition, it was determined that policy compliance scores were higher for those respondents who reported the use of interagency transition teams.

In 1998, the statewide cross-training team of project L.I.F.E. (linkages for individual and family empowerment), Ohio's 5-year systems change grant, and Kent State University's Transition Center cooperatively adapted the Johnson, Sharpe, and Sinclair (1997) study, which used a national survey on the implementation of the IDEA transition requirements. This Ohio survey updated Johnson's policy compliance portion to include 1997 IDEA amendments and added a section on the best practices. The best practices were derived from Johnson's survey, research, and findings of project L.I.F.E. Students, parents, educators, and adult service professionals were surveyed on issues concerning policy compliance and the best practice in transition. Like Baer et al. (1996), this survey found that the respondents self-reported that they were in compliance with the law; however, many of the best practices that were indicators of policy compliance had low percentages of use in transition programs. For example, it was reported that 76.4% of the students participated in their IEP meetings, yet the main opportunity for students to enhance their decision-making skills was through being interviewed about their future goals by a transition professional (77.5%), whereas using person-centered planning strategies was least likely to occur. Another example indicated that 83.4% of parents participated in the IEP meeting in which transition was discussed; yet the most likely method to involve and empower families in the planning process was the use of parent mentors (29.1%). Although this indicated that students and parents are participating in the IEP meetings where transition is discussed, it is not clear to what extent they are participating. Students and families may be present at the meetings, but they are not always comfortable and knowledgeable enough to provide input and leadership. Student and parent involvement in transition planning has increased over time in Ohio, but training and strategies need to be developed in order to enhance the relationships better. When asked about the training of students, families, and professionals concerning transition, the most likely strategy was the use of local interagency transition teams to provide cross-training. However, a low percentage of teams used this strategy (24.2%). It was also found that having a local interagency transition team was a strong predictor of policy compliance and overall the best practice used in transition services (McMahan & Baer, 1999).

As Paula Kohler noted, "transition planning means different things to different people" (Kohler, 1998, p. 180). Some see transition narrowly as a process of linking traditional education, rehabilitation, and vocational services to promote postsecondary outcomes, whereas others see it as fundamentally restructuring the core of education (Kohler, 1998; Stodden & Leake, 1994). Distilling principles of the best practice from transition research can, therefore, be hampered by differing assumptions about the purpose of education.

Critical Point   Infusing the best practice into existing practice creates many issues concerning the foundation of education.

Halloran (1993) and Wehman (1996) identified several issues that needed to be addressed to define the best practice in transition. Browning (1997) summarized these issues in the form of the following questions:

1. To what extent is the field truly ready to shift from teacher/service provider control to that of student recipient control?

2. Should the type and range of opportunities for choice-making be contingent on the student's cognitive level?
3. Should all students be subjected to the same curriculum?
4. How much curriculum will need to be devoted to functional life skills?
5. Does career education aid or hinder mainstreaming or inclusive education efforts?
6. How can the system devote students' teen years helping them to prepare for successful postschool outcomes when, in fact, continued needed services are not readily available to them once they exit school?
7. Should all students be required to meet minimum competency standards to qualify for a high school diploma?
8. Are the current trends and issues in educational reform increasing the dropout rate?
9. How aligned are public policies truly when:
    a. Students cannot become employed after graduation without fear of losing important benefits.
    b. So many disincentives to work exist in federal programs.
    c. Disagreement exists between regular and special educators on the meaning of inclusion, "all means all," and benefits and costs to disabled and nonabled students for either a separate system or a merged system?

The authors cannot fully answer these questions. As Kaufmann (1999) noted, when selecting rules for any type of practice, professionals must consider the fact that:

(a) We need different rules for different purposes, since no single set of rules is a fully satisfactory guide to all aspects of living; (b) all rules are grounded in values and we must specify the values of our rules; (c) the origins and appropriate application of particular rules are often misunderstood; (d) personal experience and popularity of ideas are often unreliable guides to rule making; and (e) all truths are tentative . . . (p. 266).

As Stodden and Leake (1994) noted, the process of importing and adapting the best practices in transition may be more exportable than the practice itself. This is because the transition best practice is defined by unique cultural, community, policy, and individual characteristics. Consequently, the transition best practice can be adapted to (1) the policies governing education and rehabilitation, (2) the community and postsecondary environments that the student will be entering, and (3) the needs of the individual and the family.

"Postschool environments" are rapidly evolving, creating changing economic, independent living, and community involvement demands on individuals with disabilities and their families. As more students with disabilities enter postsecondary education, transition practices emerge that address the needs of increasing numbers of students with disabilities entering 2- and 4- year programs. As adult service providers shift toward emphasizing supported employment approaches, transition programs for youth with severe disabilities must provide a greater emphasis on provision of technology and work experiences that lead to supported employment.

Education and rehabilitation policy impacts the transition best practice from another side. Special education, regular education, vocational education, and rehabilitation policy, as embodied in the four essential elements of transition presented in Chapter 1, define how transition is characterized and how it will be researched. As IDEA requires greater alignment with regular education curriculum, transition programs based on specialized curriculum will be less likely considered as the best practice. Additionally, political concerns are likely to shape how transition services will be defined by policy in the future.

The political climate of the late 1990s has been characterized by Stodden (1998) as including (1) downsizing, (2) cost reduction, (3) consolidation, (4) use of generic services, and (5) cost benefit. It can be anticipated that research and practice in transition will be im-

pacted by these policy trends by (1) becoming increasingly consolidated with regular, vocational, and classroom special education programs; (2) becoming more focused on outcomes rather than on processes, and (3) being less specialized to disability populations.

The individual with a disability and the family are at the core of transition. However, their access to the transition best practices are to a large extent mediated by policy concerns. Policy related to transition can be seen as both a support and a barrier to student and family access to the best practices in transition (Stowitschek & Kelso, 1989). On the one hand, education and rehabilitation transition policies can assure access to some transition practices. On the other hand, however, transition policy may have the effect of screening out other best practices in transition. For example, IDEA's requirement that transition curriculum be aligned with regular education curriculum may screen out or create logistical problems in adopting career education approaches at some schools.

Best Practices in Transition

Although the authors are reluctant to endorse any transition practice as being good for all students all of the time, it is possible to establish some general principles that should be considered in the adoption of any transition practice. Wehman (1996) lists nine guiding principles for transition implementation: (1) self-determination, (2) support focus, (3) family and student attitudes, (4) person-centered planning, (5) secondary curriculum reform, (6) inclusion, (7) career development, (8) longitudinal curriculum, and (9) business connections and alliances.

Kohler (1993) conducted a review of literature to determine what transition best practices were well-supported by research. She determined that vocational training, parent involvement, interagency collaboration, and service delivery were strongly supported. She also found support for (1) social skills training, (2) paid work experience, (3) individualized transition planning, (4) transition and career planning within the IEP, (5) focus on integrated employment, and (6) functional community-referenced curricula.

Policymakers have also defined the transition best practice in establishing goals for transition grant competitions. Since 1983, these goals have included (1) community-based training, (2) postsecondary education, (3) career placement, (4) vocational training, (5) job placement, (6) cooperative planning, (7) self-determination, (8) follow-up of graduates, (9) use of formal and informal supports, (10) student involvement, and (11) assistive technology (Rusch & Millar, 1998).

A review of transition policy and research shows some areas of disagreement about the best practice in transition for youth with disabilities (Kohler, 1993; Phelps & Hanley-Maxwell, 1997). However, the following list provides some common themes and related concepts which have been identified by advocates, researchers, and policymakers as principles of the best practice in transition:

1. Student self-determination (social skills training)
2. Ecological approaches (use of formal and informal supports)
3. Individualized backward planning
4. Service coordination (interagency collaboration)
5. Community experiences (paid work experiences)
6. Access and accommodation technologies (assistive technology)
7. Supports for postsecondary education (postsecondary education)
8. Systems change strategies (vocational career education, secondary curricular reform, and inclusion)
9. Family involvement (parent involvement)

Self-Determination

With the arrival of self-advocacy movements such as People First and the "independent living center movement" in the 1970s and 1980s, the discussion of disability began to focus on self-determination and individual fulfillment. This expanded the notion of quality of life that stressed individual decision making and control of programs that provided services to persons with disabilities. Starting with the nondiscrimination provisions of the Rehabilitation Act of 1973 (P.L. 93–112) and culminating in the Americans with Disabilities Act of 1990 (P.L. 101–336), advocates defined self-determination as a right rather than as something earned through rehabilitation. This movement was, in part, a response to the fact that social programs were not delivering on their promises to make persons with disabilities "ready" to assume valued adult roles and employment (e.g., segregated schools and sheltered workshops).

Student self-determination further emerged in the 1990s as a principle for effective transition programs. While Nirje (1972) addressed self-determination in the context of normalization, "this seed did not blossom" (Browning, 1997, p. 44) until 1992 with the federal initiative on self-determination. OSERS funded projects across the country to develop self-determination assessments and curricula for students with disabilities. Some efforts dealt with the fundamental psychological and emotional development of students, whereas other curricula focused on specific programs for student involvement in setting goals and participating in their own IEPs. As Wehmeyer (1993) concluded, "students with disabilities must be allowed to assume greater control over and responsibility for educational and transition planning and to be involved in selecting and prioritizing goals and objectives" (p. 144). The self-determination movement required a tremendous shift in the way transition planning and services were delivered and reflected in the IDEA of the 1997 requirement that students with disabilities should be informed that IDEA rights transfer to them upon reaching the age of majority.

Wehmeyer et al. (1998) provided a synthesized definition of "self-determination" as a combination of skills, knowledge, and beliefs that enable a person to engage in goal-directed, self-regulated, autonomous behavior. An understanding of one's strengths and limitations together with a belief in oneself as capable and effective are essential to self-determination. When acting from these skills and attitudes, individuals are able to take control of their lives and to assume the role of successful adults. Wehmeyer et al. (1998) further developed this concept by developing a secondary curriculum that considered student needs in the areas of (1) self-awareness, (2) decision making, (3) self-advocacy, and (4) goal expression and exploration.

Self-determination can be seen from several perspectives, including empowerment, self-advocacy training, and sensitivity to values. Knowlton, Turnbull, Backus, and Turnbull (1988) asserted "a fundamental aspect of the transition into adulthood involves increasing the exercise of direct consent in making decisions about one's own life within one's inherent capacities and means and consistent with one's values and preferences" (p. 61). Ward (1988) suggested that self-determination needs to address both individual attitudes and abilities. Woolcock, Stodden, and Bisconer (1992) noted that "transition is a highly value-driven process in which the values of educational personnel are coordinated with the values of the student's family and, most importantly, the values of the student who is about to enter adulthood" (p. 236).

Critical Point Wehmeyer defined self-determination as a combination of skills, knowledge, and beliefs that enable a person to engage in goal-directed, self-regulated, autonomous behavior. For people to be self-determined, they must understand their strength and limitations and view themselves as individuals with the ability to take control of their lives and to assume adult roles.

Practical Implications

There have been practical as well as philosophical reasons for involving students in transition planning. Studies show that students with dis-

abilities or family-friend networks play major roles in finding employment and achieving independence (Halpern, Doren, & Benz, 1993; Haring, Lovette, & Smith, 1990; Hasazi et al., 1985, Scuccimarra & Speece, 1990; SRI International, 1992). Across all these studies, less than 25% of the jobs that were found for students resulted from school/agency contacts or efforts.

To be involved in the planning and education, students with disabilities must learn the meaning of their disability and identify how to overcome, circumvent, or deal with disability-related barriers. Studies have shown that an awareness of one's disability was characteristic of both students who succeeded in college and good employees (Dalke, 1993). For students to have this understanding, there is the need for related services and learning specialists (e.g., audiology, physical therapy, behavior management) who can explain the impact of the student's disability to him or her. For students with disabilities, questions need to be answered, such as knowledge of exactly what their disability is, how their disability is tested, what test results document their disability, and how the results of diagnostic test information can be interpreted meaningfully.

Also included in self-understanding for students is knowledge of the technology and strategies that provide both access to their strengths and a compensation for barriers presented by their disability. It is important for students to focus on the critical role of requesting and obtaining appropriate education, support, and technology. This includes knowledge about the specifics of their needed technology, its use, and their explanation of these to individuals with whom they come in contact. Developing independence and a sense of worth requires emotional growth and coming to terms with their disability, over and over again with each new transition and environment. Plans made without the student's input and lack of involvement in the design of transition activities will result in educational goals that do not address what students want in the future. Consequently, students will have little investment in their education and will put a minimal effort toward achieving those goals.

Ecological Approaches

Ecological approaches provide opportunities to learn and perform in a variety of environments. By assessing and training in settings with varying demands and requirements, students learn about their abilities, talents, and interests in a real-life context. Ecological approaches place student goals in relation to specific present and future environments (Syzmanski, 1998). An ecological framework is crucial (1) to focus transition curriculum, (2) to develop a variety of formal and informal (natural) supports, (3) to provide experience in a variety of environments, and (4) to instill consistency in performance across varied environments.

Lou Brown's model of curriculum development had a strong ecological focus and was the first model to make a significant departure from more clinically oriented developmental approaches (Snell, 1983). In his model, Brown defined the four ecological domains—domestic, leisure-recreation, community, and vocational (Brown et al., 1979). He recommended that all four domains be assessed for individual students for both current and future natural environments. These four domains or environments could then be broken into subenvironments for each student through the development of an ecological inventory of where the student went each day and where he or she could go in the future. Each of these environments was then surveyed for relevant activities performed there. Activities are then broken down into teachable units and instructional programs are developed to teach the identified skills.

Ecological approaches to transition were supported by Halpern's model of transition. The initial "bridges to employment" model of transition, although defining it as concerned only with the ecological domain of employment, redefined the purpose of special education as an outcome rather than as an activity. In the intervening years since the bridges model of transition, the transition initiative has become ecologically broader, both in scope and duration. The IDEA of 1990 (P.L. 101-476) identified adult living and community participation as transition outcomes, and the IDEA of 1997 (P.L. 105-17) extended transition to the student's course of study. Increasingly, ecological lifespan approaches were being discussed as the most effective way to conceptualize transition (Syzmanski, 1998). The age at which transition services are begun extended downward from age 16 and younger in 1990 to age 14 and younger in 1997. Repetto and Correa (1996) even proposed integrating the concepts of early childhood transition, middle school transition, secondary transition, and adult transition.

Critical Point   An ecological approach to transition provides opportunities for students to learn in a variety of environments. By assessing and training in different environments, students are able to develop their abilities, talents, and interests in a real-life context.

Practical Implications

From an ecological perspective, *transition* is defined as an interactive process that requires the school to become involved with the current and future environments of students with disabilities. In this process, teachers and students learn (1) what is expected of them, (2) what goals they hope to achieve, (3) how they will negotiate their disability in the context of expectations, and (4) the process of planning. For many students with disabilities this will require teachers to become much more involved with their communities and families. Teachers, parents, adult service providers, employers, and friends need to be enlisted to provide training opportunities that support and assist students in learning skills, cultivating supports, and developing transition goals. Through ecological approaches, transition planning becomes more relevant and culturally sensitive, and provides more individualized and focused options. This in turn enhances individual

FIGURE 2–6
Relationship of Outcomes to Individualized Transition Plan and Individualized Education Program

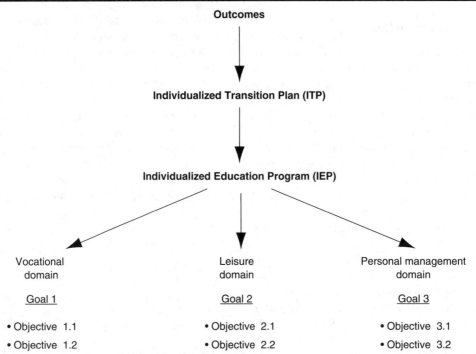

Source: From Outcome-based school-to-work transition planning for students with disabilities, by D. Steere, R. Wood, E. Panscofar, & J. Butterworth. *Career Development for Exceptional Individuals, 13* (1), 1990, p. 67. Copyright (1990) by The Council for Exceptional Children. Reprinted with permission.

opportunities and the capacity of educators to help bring about meaningful outcomes.

Individualized Backward Planning

Even for students with transition plans as part of their IEP, research showed very little orientation to postsecondary outcomes. Lombard et al. (1992) examined IEP transition plans for students with disabilities and found that only 18% of students with learning disabilities, 17% of students with emotional disturbances, and 21% of students with mild mental retardation had any postschool transition goals. This research validated concerns expressed by Stowitschek and Kelso (1989), who warned that transition planners may fall into the same traps as IEP planners.

These traps included irrelevant activities, low-quality goals, and infeasible strategies (Gallivan-Fenlon, 1994; Grigal, Test, Beattic, & Wood, 1997). In response to these problems, user-friendly planning approaches began to be put forward in the late 1980s. Although organized in many formats, these approaches would generally be referred to as person-centered planning (Pumpian et al., 1992). Steere, Wood, Panscofar, and Butterworth (1990) described a model using "backward planning," where personal goals drove the development of the transition plan which in turn drove annual goals in the IEP (see Figure 2–6).

Practical Implications

This research suggests that transition planning requires a method of planning that starts with the student's future (postschool) goals and works backward to the present. This is a difficult process since many students and families have only been able to focus on current issues and stressors. They often ask, "How will we get through the next year?" or "What seems to be the *best* available program in the high school program?" For professionals this creates a strong incentive to deal with current issues. Consequently, extra effort and new ways of relating to education are required to carry out transition planning successfully. Person-centered planning provides the greatest promise in this area.

Transition planning requires that the student and the transition team consider what the student wants to do after high school. The transition planning process must be very open, nonjudgmental, and student focused. Person-centered planning promotes this by addressing not only *what* outcomes the student desires (going to college or employment) but also *why* the student desires these outcomes. It helps the student to focus on the future and to delineate his or her strengths, talents, and interests. Person-centered planning also helps students to visualize themselves doing something meaningful and fulfilling. The principles of person-centered planning suggest that a plan about a person's future ecologies (e.g., work, education, living, and community environments) must begin with the person's understanding of him- or herself and what the plan is about.

Critical Point   It is important that transition planning be postschool oriented because the students' individualized programming must reflect their preferences for adult life. The process of backward planning involves helping students to focus on their future and working backward to ensure that their years of transition programming reflect their desires for adult life.

Brainstorming is a key beginning to help students describe themselves and their future. An outcome orientation requires communication and consensus. Team members must come to

their own understanding of the students' goals, engage in collaboration and sharing, and all of them must be in agreement. Because the team plan outlines how the students will pursue their goals, team members must be in communication about how (in what context) they know the students. These diverse and varied viewpoints are necessary to get a complete picture of the individuals. The brainstorming process should be positive, that is, focus on the students' desired future and capabilities. In subsequent steps and stages in the process, reality testing should take place as the students and team members gain greater understanding of the students' goals.

Service Coordination

The problem of integrating services in a transition system that was really a nonsystem was discussed by a number of authors. Ward and Halloran (1989) suggested that there was a serious discrepancy between the entitlement philosophy of school programs and the availability of adult services. Szymanski et al. (1990) noted that differences between state and local special education programs and state and local vocational rehabilitation programs were rooted in history, definitions of disability, funding differences, and differences in evaluation standards. Kochar and Deschamps (1992) maintained that vocational and special education policies were often at odds in assuring services for learners with special needs, and Kortering and Edgar (1988) emphasized the need for more cooperation between special education and vocational rehabilitation. To address these needs, authors of the best practice have recommended the development of school-interagency transition teams to develop channels of communication and to "iron out" policy differences (Everson, 1990; Halpern, 1992b; Heal et al., 1990; Phelps & Maddy-Bernstein, 1992; Wehman, 1990; Wehman, Moon, Everson, Wood, & Barcus, 1988).

These authors also saw the involvement of employers and other community members as an important function of transition teams. Wehman (1990) stated that a school-business linkage was a critical element of a successful transition program. Rhodes, Sandow, Mank, Buckley, and Albin (1991) indicated that activities involving employers would be the major source of growth for training in a future in which special education and adult service budgets were expected to show little or no growth. Rhodes et al. (1991) noted that employer resources already dwarfed those that were available through special education and rehabilitation. Phelps and Maddy-Bernstein (1992) found that the benefits of business-education partnerships included additional resources, employment opportunities, increased personal attention, improved facilities, and better teacher morale.

Critical Point   Interagency transition teams should include students, parents, educators, adult service professionals, employers, and community service agencies. These teams can provide a point of reference for information sharing and problem solving among transition service providers.

Practical Implications
The practical implications of this research suggest that generic and special services in the transition plan must be understood by the student, family, and team members. Transition services provide direction and motivation for completion of goals on the IEP and heighten efforts and performance both in and out of the classroom. The focus in coordinating services is on identifying specific needs and finding the "right" service to meet the need. Students have the right to all available resources and must be knowledgeable and willing to work with team members in accessing needed services.

Once there is agreement on the student's future goals, professionals and the family must work in a united manner to support the student in taking action in reference to those goals. Coordination speaks to all parts of the transition plan to be consistent with each other. Regular and special education staff need to work in con-cert to help the student achieve his or her programs of choice. The regular education teacher has to be clear about *what* the student must achieve in the program, whereas the special educator must obtain necessary adaptations and accommodations and work with the regular teacher to use them. Educators must also communicate with representatives of postschool environments and adult service professionals to convey the direction of the students' transition plan and how the high school program connects to the students' desired postschool environments.

Whether the students desire employment or postsecondary programs, high school programs should provide the knowledge, attitudes, and skills to perform, grow, and learn how to learn. Work and education beyond high school provides paths to the realization of personal goals relating to both starting out in life and changing the course in life. The purpose of transition planning is to help students get into postschool environments that are "right" for them and equip them to succeed in their chosen endeavors. Students need to learn about and take control of their lives and the critical planning and preparation processes. Involvement in the planning and preparation of activities is time well spent because students enter life with those tools needed to get the best start possible.

Community Experiences

Community experiences have been found to be critical for youth with disabilities in transition to postschool activities. Research showed a strong correlation between community experiences and postsecondary employment. SRI International (1990) determined that students who had work experience as part of a vocational education program experienced 13.9% better employment outcomes. Wehman (1990) also noted that community work experiences provided students with exposure to social situations and natural contingencies that are unavailable in the school

Students learn about career interests through community experiences.

setting. Unfortunately, researchers found that many special educators remained committed to training in classroom settings (Lynch & Beare, 1990; Stowitschek & Kelso, 1989). The IDEA mandate, therefore, was necessary to move many special educators away from an excessive focus on remedial programs and academics in the classroom to a community-based approach.

Community experiences were also seen as critical to the development of career maturity. Rojewski (1993) determined that students with disabilities were less able than typical students to identify career options due to limited experiences and opportunities. Additionally, Lombard et al. (1992) found that less than one-fifth of the transition-age students they surveyed had any postsecondary transition goals on the IEP. Community experiences (e.g., career exploration, job shadowing, and community work experiences) were found to be significantly related to career maturity and postschool outcomes for youth

with disabilities (Gill & Edgar, 1990; Halpern et al., 1993; SRI International, 1990; Storey & Mank, 1989; Wehman, Kregel, & Barcus, 1985). Community experiences have also been identified as critical to the acquisition of daily living and social skills (Halpern, 1985; Johnson & Rusch, 1993).

Community experiences have been generally supported as the best practice in functional vocational assessment. Research indicates that standardized assessment procedures often lack validity for students with disabilities because they do not consider the effects of supports, technology, and training on student performance (Menchetti & Piland, 1998). Hagner and Dileo (1993) point out that standardized assessment procedures may have little use for students with severe disabilities since they lack the pressures, clues, sights, and sounds of the environments where students will have to perform. These researchers advocate strongly for the use of situational assessments, or assessments that are conducted in the actual environments in which the student is expected to perform.

Critical Point   Community experiences are important for students with disabilities because exposure to social situations and natural settings enhances the transition to postschool activities. Community experiences are critical to the acquisition of work skills and daily living and social skills.

Practical Implications

Students with disabilities need help in exploring work, living, and community participation opportunities in the community. This can include school-supervised work experiences. The Bureau of Vocational Rehabilitation or the school can provide job coaches for students with intense support needs while they are still in high school. School districts may choose to hire their own job coaches or to use vocational rehabilitation services for eligible students. It is important to establish eligibility and to involve adult service providers in transition planning, if they are providing or paying for job coaches.

Community experiences should not be limited to work, however. Research indicates that students with disabilities may become more isolated as they grow older. Due to lack of mobility, income, and social networks, students with disabilities may have difficulty in making safe choices regarding friends and in meeting appropriate people to assure a good adult quality of life. Membership in religious/cultural affiliations (e.g., church or synagogue), clubs, and recreational programs provide natural and ongoing support networks that can assist persons with disabilities in maintaining friendships throughout their life.

Access and Accommodation Technologies and Related Services

Access and accommodation for youth with disabilities imply a particularly broad range of specialized assessment perspectives and related services (e.g., audiology, ophthalmology, orientation and mobility training, speech-language pathology, physical therapy, rehabilitation engineering, ergonometrics, and job carving) which require interdisciplinary collaboration (Cavalier & Brown, 1998). Additionally, persons with access and accommodation needs often require the assistance of paraprofessionals and other assistive personnel (Salzberg & Morgan, 1995). Even for persons with mild disabilities, Behrmann (1994) identified seven areas of assistive technology application that may be essential in achieving positive educational, employment, and independent living outcomes. These include (1) organizational technologies (e.g., computers and electronic organizers), (2) note-taking technologies (e.g., optical character recognition, microcassette recorders, videotapes and CDs, and voice synthesizers), (3) writing assistance (e.g., grammar/spell-checkers, and macros), (4) productivity (e.g., personal digital assistants, calculators, and software), (5) access to reference materials (e.g., telecommunication networks and multimedia), (6) cognitive assistance (e.g., computer

tutorials and multimedia), and (7) materials modification (e.g., instructional software).

Access and accommodation also imply the ability to integrate individual assistive technologies with the many technologies used in employment, educational, and independent living environments (Blackhurst, 1997). It is estimated that 75% of jobs will involve the use of computers by the year 2000 (Bender, Richmond, & Pinson-Millburn, 1985 cited in Sowers & Powers, 1995). These technologies include telephone technologies, environmental controls, robotics, constructed devices, and other adaptive strategies (Sowers, & Powers, 1995). Technology is also an important consideration in educational, independent living options, and community activities of persons with disabilities. Educational forms of assistive technology include electric page turners, books on tape, software and computers, orthotics, FM systems, prosthetic devices, and augmentative communication devices. Independent living technology includes ambulation devices, switches, environmental controls, postural supports, wheelchairs, assisted driving devices, telecommunication devices, warning systems, audiovisual media, closed caption decoders, and augmentative communication. Community participation and recreation technology include switches, Velcro grips, and equipment adaptations.

Critical Point   Access to services requires appropriate assessment and a selection of technologies to enhance the individual's participation in education, employment, and living environments.

Practical Implications

Access and accommodation technology is a concept based on some basic principles and values that span the major legislation pertaining to transition in regular, vocational, and special education, and in rehabilitation. All the education-related acts emphasize the need to evaluate the individual's qualifications aside from disability in relation to the important performance requirements or outcomes for a given program. Access concerns meaningful participation in activities and programs. It is the central idea embedded in the requirements of the Americans with Disabilities Act (ADA) and section 504 of the Rehabilitation Act of 1973 and its amendments.

Determining student accommodations in career programs involves a process that requires communication among team members, who need to understand a student's future goals and the current year's transition activities. Interdisciplinary communication is needed whereby team members have gained knowledge of and respect for the expertise of one another. In the case of access to the general curriculum, the regular education teacher needs to articulate and make clear the curriculum and the classroom philosophy and environment. The special education teacher needs to provide a framework and rationale for individualization and curriculum adaptation within the framework of the regular classroom. The student in question must be able to explain his or her disability and how accommodations are designed to provide an opportunity to participate and complete requirements within the class. The student gains an ability to play this role in the process because the process has provided the problem-solving experiences, framework, and practice in being adept at requesting. Requesting accommodations and explaining the reasons they are necessary in the context of one's disability is a lifelong skill that a student will use and is fundamental to education across the life span in the domain of self-understanding and communication.

Supports for Postsecondary Education

Postsecondary education has been a rapidly growing target of transition programs for youth with disabilities. There are four major types of postsecondary education: (1) vocational/technical schools, (2) community colleges (2-year), (3) liberal arts colleges, and (4) state universities.

Students with disabilities have been attending postsecondary education programs and their numbers steadily grew through the 1990s. SRI International (1992) found that 4.2% of special education graduates enrolled in 4-year colleges 3 to 5 years after graduation, 15.9% enrolled in vocational schools, and 15.9% enrolled in 2-year colleges (i.e., 11.8%). In 1998, federal statistics indicated that 10.5% of all postsecondary students had disabilities which represented an increase from 8.8% in 1988 and 2.6% in 1978 (Gajar, 1998).

The research on the best practice in helping youth with disabilities in the transition to postsecondary education has been limited to date. However, Dalke & Schmitt (1987) have laid down several principles for transition programs serving youth who are planning to enter postsecondary education (cited in Gajar, 1998). These include:

1. Provision of educational experiences similar to those in postsecondary education
2. Identification of strengths and needs relative to higher education settings.
3. Provide experiences where students with disabilities are outside their familiar support system of family, friends, and teachers.
4. Provide students the opportunity to practice self-advocacy.
5. Familiarize students with the physical environments of postsecondary education.
6. Familiarize students with campus and community supports available to students.
7. Provide [students] instruction related to study skills, time management, test-taking, and library use.
8. Provide [students] direct instruction in academic areas such as reading, writing, and mathematics.
9. Provide staff with formal and informal performance data.

Practical Implications
Postsecondary options should be explored early in high school to select the proper course work

and to choose a postsecondary program that provides the services and supports that the student will need after graduation. Every postsecondary program has academic requirements that must be met, although state universities and community colleges often have remedial programs for students who have had difficulty in general areas of course work such as mathematics and English. The student should receive training in asking for the necessary accommodations and supports and should visit and/or audit classes from desired schools (Turner, 1996).

Critical Point   Access to postsecondary environments require careful coordination of transition services early in the student's secondary program.

Family Involvement

The best practice in transition must also address the concerns of the family. McNair and Rusch (1991) noted that 63% of the parents they interviewed had a plan for what their child should be doing once school was completed. SRI International (1990) found that parents and guardians had definite expectations about postschool activities of youth with disabilities, with 84% expecting their children to be working in a paying job and 78% expecting them to live independently. SRI International (1992) determined that 55% of the youth with disabilities whom they surveyed continued to live with their parents 3 to 5 years after graduation and that parents found jobs for 11.3% of them 3 to 5 years after graduation. Scuccimarra and Speece (1990) and Halpern et al. (1993) found that parents located jobs for 25 to 30% of the graduating youth they surveyed.

Students with disabilities reported that parents and families were their most important supporters (Morningstar, Turnbull, & Turnbull, 1996). Outcome studies showed that after graduation from high school, the family was often the only consistent source of support for students with disabilities (Hanley-Maxwell, Pogloff, & Whitney-Thomas, 1998). Ecological approaches address these multicultural issues, family background,

and the students' community context in which the students are engaged in the process of transition.

Despite the important role parents played in shaping student career goals and outcomes, they continued to be largely underinvolved in transition planning. McNair and Rusch (1991) found in a study involving 200 parents of transition-age students that nearly 70% desired involvement in transition programs, while only 30% experienced involvement. McNair and Rusch also found that parents wanted to be involved in finding job placements and community-living arrangements more often than they were afforded the opportunity to do so.

Parental lack of information was another concern in regard to student and parent self-determination. McDonnell, Wilcox, Boles, and Bellamy (1985) determined that only 32% of parents they surveyed reported receiving any information about adult services from school personnel. Carney and Orelove (1988) noted that parental influence toward community integration depended on parents beliefs about both their children's needs and capabilities and the availability and appropriateness of community services. They found that parental ability to make informed decisions related to six factors: (1) knowledge of the range of options, (2) ability to evaluate options, (3) knowledge of the child's skill, (4) knowledge of the child's preferences, (5) knowledge of how to get services, and (6) knowledge of how to advocate for services that are not available (Carney & Orelove, 1988).

Critical Point   Parents continue to be largely underinvolved in transition planning. Following graduation from high school, large numbers of students with disabilities continue to live with their parents, and parents are the ones who often find them jobs.

Practical Implications
The best practices relative to family involvement must address these issues. Hanley-Maxwell, Pogoloff, and Whitney-Thomas (1998) outline the four best practices in family involvement relative to transition planning. These are:

1. Reciprocal family education
2. Cultural sensitivity
3. Personal futures planning
4. Longitudinal involvement in transition planning

Systems Change Strategies

Researchers, advocates, and policymakers have recognized systems change as an essential strategy for capacity building in transition (Halpern, Benz, & Lindstrom, 1992). It can take place from either the "bottom-up" or the "top down." Major systems change efforts in transition were funded by the federal government and OSERS, who awarded grants to states in order to create structural changes in the statewide system of transition services. Two basic objectives had to be met by states in order to receive these grants:

1. To increase the availability, access, and quality of transition assistance through the development and improvement of policies, procedures, systems, and other mechanisms for youth with disabilities and their families as those youth prepare for and enter adult life.
2. To create incentives for the implementation of lasting statewide system changes in the transition of students with disabilities to postsecondary training, education, and employment (p. 66290).

The program was initiated in 1991; all states have received grants; and most have concluded their 5-year projects. The results of these projects highlighted what became the central themes of policy debates leading up to IDEA of 1997. Issues relating to how to serve all students in one overall system and at the same time to design individual programs are the challenges that emerged from system change efforts and found expression in IDEA of 1997.

During the same time period that state system issues were being addressed, local transition issues were also a focus of systems change efforts. Based on approaches developed through the discretionary programs funded by section 626 of the Education for All Handicapped Children EHCA

Act amendments in 1983, community transition teams were developed as a mechanism to meet transition needs comprehensively on the local level. Members of core transition teams (Wehman et. al. 1988) consisted of a full array of people who had a stake in outcomes for secondary students with disabilities. Local or community transition teams pooled their efforts in identifying and meeting needs at the local level. Inherent in the continued functioning and success of such teams has been skills related to teamwork and group processes.

Practical Implications
Often the system of educational and adult services present transition barriers that cannot be addressed at the individual level. To deal with these issues, the transition service coordinator must be aware of exemplary transition practices and be able to mobilize transition stakeholders toward incorporating these practices in the school. The school-level interagency transition team can be an effective way of doing this. Transition system issues that may be addressed by the schoolwide transition team include:

- Development of accommodations and procedures for proficiency testing of students with disabilities
- Adoption of person-centered IEP planning approaches
- Definition of graduation requirements for students with severe disabilities
- Cross-training for students, parents, and professionals
- Strategies to empower youth with disabilities and their families
- Development of linkages with providers of career opportunities for students with disabilities

The membership of the school-level interagency transition team should include all transition stakeholders, consisting of families, adult service providers, administrators, educators, employers, and transition specialists. The makeup of the team may vary from meeting to meeting depending on the students or on the issues to be discussed.

Conclusion

Transition policy and practice is a dynamic concept that has changed along with beliefs about the best practice in education. Its early roots can be traced to work-study and career education programs. It has evolved from the narrowly focused bridges model of Madeline Will (1984) to the broadly defined transition education models of Kohler (1998). Defining the best models and practice for transition remains difficult because of the interaction of local variables, including divergent concepts of education, different needs of individuals with disabilities, and the changing environments that youth with disabilities are likely to be entering in the future. The authors present factors where these transition practices are contingent upon postsecondary environments, transition and education policy, and individual needs, interests, and preferences. In the remainder of this book, the authors will provide the readers with a basic understanding of the aforementioned transition best practices from these three perspectives. While transition concepts continue to evolve, some general principles of the transition best practice are widely held by educators, advocates, and policymakers. The authors presents nine practices for transition that have wide support from advocates, policymakers, and researchers.

Study Questions

1. What were the main models through the 1980s that form today's concept of transition?
2. What are the major differences between Will's and Halpern's models of transition?
3. Why was the work-study movement started and what services were added to improve transition?
4. Name two best practices in transition and discuss how they are related to postsecondary outcomes, transition policy, and individual/family needs.
5. How is self-determination addressed in the IDEA of 1990 and 1997?
6. How is service coordination addressed in the IDEA of 1990 and 1997?
7. How is family involvement addressed in the IDEA of 1990 and 1997?
8. How does the IDEA of 1990 and 1997 support ecological approaches?
9. How has alignment of transition curriculum and regular education curriculum helped and hampered the implementation of career education approaches to transition?
10. How is the School to Work Opportunity Act similar to transition?

Web Sites

California School-to-Work Interagency Transition Partnership:
http://www.sna.com/switp/

Models of Transition for At-Risk Students:
http://www.ed.gov/databases/ERIC_Digests/ed321158.html

National Center to Improve Practice:
http://www.ncip.org

National Transition Alliance Model Programs:
http://www.dssc.org/nta

Sample High School Programs:
http://www.oursc.k12.ar.us/coop/dept/techprep.html

http://www.regiononline.com/~lvbep/

The Transition Center Project:
http://tac.elps.vt.edu/htmldocs/transition/html

3

Career Development: Theories for Transition Planning

Pamela Luft
Lynn C. Koch

LEARNING OBJECTIVES

The objectives of this chapter are:

1. Explain how career development theories influence the identification of the student's needs, interests, and preferences in terms of choosing and initiating a career path.

2. Explain how career development theories impact the development of linkages and relationships with students and families, and with other agencies and community services, and the types of relationships that are emphasized within a given theory.

3. Explain how career development theories influence planning for movement from school to postschool activities regarding

important variables to consider and relationships to build.

4. Explain how use of a particular theory impacts the choice of tools and strategies for career decisions at exploratory, experiential, and work skill acquisition stages of career growth.

5. Describe the major differences among structural, developmental, work-adjustment, and learning theories.

6. Describe the differences between using the ecological model and the linking framework for making eclectic, theory-based choices to address students' needs and goals.

Aperson's pursuit of a particular career path is the result of multiple life experiences and influences that begin in childhood, and continue throughout his or her working years and beyond (Hershenson & Szymanski, 1992; Super, 1990). These same factors influence the choices made by students with disabilities and their families in terms of how competent and capable they view themselves to be, what goals and options seem the most realistic, and what barriers or needs must be overcome in order to implement these choices and goals. The student's, the family's, and society's beliefs about these goals and their implementation will be important factors that impact the student's career development and adult roles.

The previous two chapters have described the legislative and historical background that had led to the ways by which transition planning is done today. This chapter provides similar foundational information about theoretical approaches for making choices about careers. The planning and implementation of a specific career choice often has significant impacts across other transition domain areas, including independent living and community participation, socialization, and recreation (cf. Will, 1984; Wehman & Kregel, 1985). One's career also remains an important defining characteristic of successful attainment of American adulthood and, therefore, remains central to much of transition planning.

The information in this chapter provides a background in several theoretical models. A team's choice among career theories will influence the types of information the team gathers about a student and the related intervention strategies it uses to promote career development. In addition, several of these theories have been applied and translated into assessments, curriculum planning programs, intervention strategies, and transition planning processes that can be found in a number of later chapters and particularly in Chapters 6, 7, and 8.

Overview

This chapter defines career development as a lifetime process of growth that results in some type of work. When done as a formalized, curricular-based, and systematic program of training, this is typically referred to as career education (Clark & Kolstoe, 1994). However, career development is much broader than school-based learning, and in many ways begins in infancy with the child's first attempts at understanding the world (Brown & Brooks, 1984, Hershenson & Szymanski, 1992; Super, 1990). The family's responses to, and values about, work and working as well as the neighborhood's and the community's perceptions of work, all become part of the child's conceptions regarding a potential career. The school also transmits values about working, and furthermore, it evaluates the child's successes and failures in comparison to other children. All these fundamental experiences with values, attitudes, habits, human relationships, and learning about caring for oneself and one's belongings occur long before the initiation of formal programs that address work and possible career choices (Clark & Kolstoe, 1994).

An individual's career development is a lifetime process that encompasses the growth and change process of childhood, the formal career education in school, and the maturational processes that continue throughout a person's working adulthood and into retirement (Brown & Brooks, 1984; Super, 1990). This perspective is important because it allows students with disabilities the time and types of experiences they need to help them make choices that meet their needs, preferences, and abilities. An ecological perspective responds to needs and circumstances that change over time, with transition goals that change as society becomes more accessible and supportive and the student becomes more mature and self-aware.

Critical Point: Viewing career development from a life-span perspective allows students with disabilities multiple opportunities and extended time lines to move into fulfilling life and employment roles.

An important precept of career decision making is that individuals need opportunities to try various types of work in order to make a meaningful decision about their preferences. Particularly for students with disabilities, the transition team may need to provide experiences they did not have during their earlier development. Students may have had little or no exposure to work environments, expectations, and "work culture" as a result of physical or attitudinal barriers and other reasons related to their disability (Clark & Kolstoe, 1994; Hershenson & Szymanski, 1992). The team will need to ensure that students are exposed to a variety of work environments and work settings and the range of tasks within each. This lack of exposure includes years of overhearing adults discuss their own work and what it means to them, so that the students may need a greater number of these experiences in order to understand themselves and to integrate successfully into the world of work. The team will need to collect information about the students' responses to these experiences and to help the students apply their responses to career choice preferences.

The type of information collected about the student and the timing and manner in which career decisions are made often vary greatly depending on the theory of career development that underlies many of the curricula and assessments that may be used by the team. Savickas (1996) recommends this knowledge to optimize career planning. Each theory focuses on specific aspects of the career development process and the resulting tests and career instruments reflect this focus. Depending on the needs and issues of the student, a particular theory may not match well with these issues, and as a result, their related instruments and interventions will not always be successful or helpful (Savickas, 1996).

The transition team faces choosing among an array of popular and well-recognized assessments and strategies, only some of which will best help any particular student. Team members with an understanding of basic career theories and their application to individuals with disabilities will be better prepared for making these choices and, as a result, implementing a transition plan that leads to a successful career. This chapter reviews an array of theories and their application to transition planning. Descriptions of each theory will end with a summary of their perspective on the student and work environment, and with a list of related instruments. The next section describes career development in terms of transition planning mandates as a background for the theories.

The Relationship of Career Development to Transition Planning

Students with disabilities are likely to experience highly unique career development paths. This is due to the impact of disability on their lives, the reaction of others to their disabilities and how capable these others view them to be, and the presence of physical or societal barriers that reduce their access to equal opportunities and experiences with work-related activities (Clark & Kolstoe, 1994; Hershenson & Szymanski, 1992; Szymanski & Hershenson, 1998). The way that these affect the students' perceptions of their work abilities and limitations can have a dramatic impact on their vision of adulthood and life goals, and ultimately, on all other aspects of transition planning.

Supporting the student's needs, interests, and preferences is basic to career development and career choice. The student's developmental trajectory or path at any one point in time includes the sum of all work-related experiences and values up to that point. These affect the student's interests and preferences, and particularly, their beliefs regarding what is or is not possible for their career path. The transition team must ensure that the student and his or her family has sufficient background and experience as to what is currently possible and provide opportunities that broaden perceptions that have been significantly limited. The increased accessibility guaranteed under the Americans with Disabilities Act (ADA) and the increasing willingness of society to include persons with significant disabilities provides new options that were not available only a few years ago. New assistive devices and the rapid growth in technology are continually changing previous conceptions of "accessibility." The team can expect new career avenues to open that should be considered when designing exploratory career experiences.

Identifying the Student's Needs, Interests, and Preferences

During the student's career exploration and early training experiences, the team should gather data on the student's needs, interests, and preferences. Many of the interest, aptitude, and readiness tools are based on theoretical frameworks (from theories of career development) that view the individual, the environment, and his or her interaction in specific ways (Savickas, 1996). What may have worked well with one particular student may not be successful with another student. In addition, because these assessment tools can only sample limited portions of work-related behaviors, the team must be aware that some results may be inaccurate representations of the student's true abilities in a real environment. An instrument's expectations about prior experiences with work and work settings also will influence the results.

Several new assessment processes may assist the team in developing an accurate profile of the student's transition strengths and needs (see Chapter 7). Situational assessments are used to observe the student in work or community environments to identify those settings in which he or she is most likely to be successful and satisfied (Sitlington, 1996). Career portfolios and other types of authentic assessments can be used with paper/pencil and interview assessments to confirm potential career and lifestyle preferences. A typical combination of these assessments could include observational measures of the student's performance in various work sites, at home performing chores and self-care tasks, and in the community or at school interacting with friends and engaging in hobbies. Videotapes are a powerful tool for documenting skills over a period of several years and across several settings and can be convincing evidence in a career portfolio for potential employers (cf. Sarkees-Wircenski & Wircenski, 1994).

Planning for Future Environments

Well-planned career development experiences should result in a positive career and life outcome. Transition represents a new aspect of responsibility for school personnel that moves beyond graduation. The team members must plan for a smooth movement into postschool environments whether they include employment, postsecondary training at a technical or vocational program, a 4-year college program, or supported living and employment activities. Yet, career development goes beyond immediate postschool planning and should address long-term adult outcomes of career and life roles. Many career theories now take a life-span approach to making career decisions.

The anticipated outcome of all career development and transition planning is that students ultimately will engage in some type of work as part of achieving a satisfying adulthood. Plans should address multiple postschool environments if these plans need to identify and prepare for full-time work through skill training and work experiences within the school, and then for part-time work with continued skill refinement through on-the-job training in the community. For other students, more extensive career exploration and readiness experiences may require additional work site and skill training preparation that extends for several years after leaving high school.

Once again, this emphasizes the unique nature of career development for many students with disabilities and the flexibility that the transition team will need in addressing these potentially vast differences. The team needs to determine the types and depth of experiences needed that will optimize the student's career development and provide the greatest likelihood of success. The ways in which this outcome is accomplished can vary greatly among individuals, depending on the interests and preferences, as well as on the supports that are available or must be developed. A limited local job market and poor economic stability in an area may require modifying student preferences. Training opportunities through adult agencies and the availability of support through employment specialists or job coaches may also vary and impact the entry path that the student may take into a particular career.

Coordinated Interagency Responsibilities or Linkages
These are a very important aspect in ensuring that anticipated employment outcomes are, in fact, achieved. The existing linkages and cooperative agreements between the school and community agencies may fit the outcome needs of one student. However, the transition team may need to develop new relationships that provide access to additional training and support services that allow for career development in the preferred field of another student. For example, a student may have a strong interest in working with animals. If no specific school-based training is available in this field, the team will need to develop some trial training and work experiences with local pet groomers or pet stores in the area, in addition to supportive school and classroom-based skill training.

Critical Point: Career development theory is an important element in the team's successful compliance with fulfilling transition planning requirements.

Additional Goals of Transition Planning
Throughout the team's planning with the student and his or her family, it is important to build a career path that will be motivating and

engaging for many years into adulthood. Such a path also should lead to what the student considers an optimal *quality of life*. These concerns are addressed in the lifelong aspects of many theories of career development. Although these issues extend beyond the responsibility of the planning team, the decisions and choices about how the team views the student's early aspects of his or her career development path will have lifetime effects. A motivating and successful career path will have a direct impact on the student's basic quality of life. The difficulty for the team is that motivation, fulfillment, and even quality of life are highly individualized in nature.

Career development theories also define these issues differently. Some focus narrowly on a single career choice that occurs during young adulthood (Brown, 1996; Hershenson & Szymanski, 1992). These seem to imply that this single choice is the most significant element leading to an optimal quality of life. Other theories take a broader perspective that include opportunities for many decisions that impact a career, such as marriage, children, community and leisure activities, and so on. These broader models tend to view choices as occurring throughout a lifetime made according to changing development and needs, and responding to influences from other life roles and responsibilities; suggesting that quality of life is a lifelong process that grows and changes with one's life needs. The choice of perspective taken by the transition team will impact how members define quality of life and work to implement it through the various assessment and planning tasks.

Self-determination and *self-advocacy* are important to career development as a means of actualizing one's lifetime career goals. Theories that focus on the adjustment processes between the worker and his or her work site will view entry into a career as beginning a process that may require periodic assessment of oneself and the environment for "fit" and mutual satisfaction. Self-determination and self-advocacy will be needed to ensure continued satisfaction across any theory as individual and/or work site needs change. Within the broader career theories, self-determination and self-advocacy necessary in any one aspect of an individual's life may affect one's career and require parallel self-advocacy and change. Regardless of the model chosen, team members should prepare students to view their increasing career maturity and experience as an employment advantage and as deserving of the same opportunities for career advancement and growth as would be granted to coworkers and peers. Self-advocacy and self-determination will be important in ensuring that these equal opportunities occur.

Family involvement in career decision making and planning is critical; families are important sources of support as the student moves into the world of work. Although transition planning is focused on the student's needs, interests, and preferences, the preferences of the family cannot be ignored. Their support of career opportunities often is a critical factor to the success of the plan or program (Siegel et al., 1993). In addition, the family's involvement in the career development process can be very helpful to the team by providing access to the student's informal network of support: visits to parents' or relatives' places of work, visits to friends and neighbors at their work sites, and encouragement through optimistic determination to pursue their child's preferred career choice. A family with a rich supply of employment contacts through friends and relatives can significantly expand a team's resources for trial work opportunities.

Many of the life-span and developmental career theories use ecological approaches to assess the broad range of factors that interact in the work environment and to assure job maintenance after initial placement has been made. Theories using a more narrow approach may still specify a range of factors, within certain parameters of focus, that must be identified and addressed. *Ecological assessments* are important to the team, and may raise issues that are not addressed in a more narrowly focused theory. For example, not only the physi-

cal environment and barriers can present problems not specified in the theory (i.e., many do not specifically address disabilities), but the work culture and climate of the employees and their relationships with each other can have subtle, long-term impacts on the work success of a student with disabilities. In contrast, a student who is physically comfortable in the work environment and who feels psychologically accepted and emotionally supported by his or her coworkers has a much greater chance of maintaining and advancing in a career. Ecological assessments of the student's current work exploration or training sites, and of potential future sites, provide the team with important information for planning continued career development activities (cf. Hanley-Maxwell & Szymanski, 1992). An accumulation of these assessments can identify patterns regarding factors that are important to a particular student's success, for example, finding someone who shares a hobby or current interest or someone who is willing to be a mentor or "buddy."

Successful collaboration among team members is critical to achieving maximal transition planning outcomes (Gajar, Goodman, & McAfee, 1993; Sitlington et al., 1997). Successful career development requires involvement of key individuals across all the student's important environments. As the student moves into greater community participation and work, including and welcoming employers, supervisors, and coworkers into the team process can greatly contribute to his or her career success. The addition of these individuals and other community members who may form part of the family's informal support network can greatly increase developmental opportunities for the student and information for more realistic outcome planning. The information that these individuals gain from the meetings will in turn assist them in working better with the student. Including these individuals during school-based transition planning can greatly assist the student and his or her family in leaving school with a network of support to address the potential adult-based career development decisions and issues that arise, and can help adult agency personnel to provide continuous, high-quality services.

In summary, career development is a core aspect of transition planning processes that contributes to the successful functioning of the four essential elements and the additional core concepts that comprise exemplary planning practices. The theoretical framework that guides a team's perspectives will influence how each of these elements and concepts is implemented. These theories can be recognized as influencing much of transition planning and the remainder of this book, as explained in the next section.

Careers for Individuals with Disabilities

Work is a highly valued activity in the American society. In fact, not only does it provide economic support, but it also has a major impact on one's social status and self-image (Szymanski & Hershenson, 1998). Unfortunately, people with disabilities often encounter obstacles to participation in the workforce. Recent statistics indicate that, despite the fact that almost 80% of people with disabilities in the United States report a preference for working, approximately 76% are unemployed (LaPlante, Kennedy, Kaye, & Wenger, 1997). Hagner and colleagues (1996) point to several interrelated factors that contribute to the high employment rate among people with disabilities:

(1) discrimination in employment and other aspects of life,
(2) practical difficulties (e.g., transportation, non-traditional means of communication) that make it difficult to seek employment,
(3) limited access to the "hidden job market" and those jobs not advertised by formal means, and
(4) employer presumptions about the characteristics and abilities of qualified job applicants.

All four of these factors create difficulties that go beyond the acquisition of needed skills and abilities. Often transition teams do not address these less obvious employment problems. In addition, obstacles are also frequently encountered when individuals with disabilities attempt to maintain a certain position or advance in their employment. In fact, employed people with disabilities often experience career patterns that consist primarily of movement from one entry-level job to another, with extended periods of unemployment in between jobs (Roessler & Bolton, 1985).

Critical Point: Individuals with disabilities have high rates of unemployment and underemployment. The use of a career development theory that helps the team to identify and address important career issues will help to improve these employment statistics.

Individuals with disabilities face a number of deterrents to their continued working. Factors such as physical and attitudinal barriers within the work site, health insurance issues, and work disincentives inherent in the social security system (which provides important medical insurance coverage when one is *not* working, in addition to basic subsistence support) can function as deterrents to career maintenance and the person's motivation to stay with an earlier job choice.

In many instances, problems with initially securing and then maintaining or advancing in a particular company or career path can originate in the school years. In their review of research on postschool outcomes, Hanley-Maxwell, Szymanski, and Owens-Johnson (1998) found that students with disabilities have the following difficulties:

(1) are at least twice as likely as their non-disabled peers to drop out of school;
(2) experience high rates of unemployment regardless of whether or not they graduate from high school;
(3) are less likely than their nondisabled peers to participate in postsecondary educational programs;

(4) receive low wages when they do obtain employment; and

(5) experience difficulties in other areas of their lives such as independent living and relationshipbuilding.

The authors attribute these poor outcomes to a variety of factors that include the method of school leaving (lower rates of graduation), special education placement, type of disability, a low percentage of time spent in regular classrooms, limited vocational experiences, and lack of employment during high school. In addition, they have limited exposure to the variety of employment options available and, therefore, have restricted opportunities to develop generalizable work skills that could enhance their performance across a variety of jobs.

These factors are identified as major career development concerns for students with disabilities (Conyers, Szymanski, & Koch, 1998; Luft & Koch, 1998). They also have significant impact on transition planning issues. Linkages with other agencies are critical in creating successful movement into postsecondary settings and in ensuring that the independent living issues are resolved. For example, a student living in a group home may have significant constraints placed upon working hours and transportation. Frequently, staff are not scheduled during daytime hours to supervise or monitor residents or to provide support services. Another important concern for transition teams is that the research on postschool outcomes has "consistently supported the critical connection between high school employment and postschool employment" (Hanley-Maxwell et al., 1998, p. 152). Unfortunately, few high school students with disabilities have opportunities to work part-time or during the summers.

The issues summarized earlier underscore the need to incorporate experientially based career planning activities into the curricula of students with disabilities. The Individuals with Disabilities Education Act (IDEA) emphasizes the importance of addressing this need in the school environment, with the new amendments emphasizing this through planning that is mandated to begin at age 14. Theories of career development provide a description of the experiences, attitudes, values, and competencies that individuals need in order to choose and maintain a satisfying and optimal career path. Many of these aspects may be missing or poorly developed in students with disabilities, particularly if they have had few work-related opportunities or limited exposure to the world of work prior to their transition plan. The next section describes several theories of career development to help transition professionals better understand the various career needs of transition-age students and provide suggestions that can lead to optimal career paths.

Theories of Career Development

Although many career development theories have been generated in the past 70 years, no universal, all-encompassing definition of career development can be offered in this chapter, due to the highly individualized nature of this long-term and complex process. Career development has alternately been described as the "lifelong process of getting ready to choose, choosing, and typically continuing to make choices from occupations available in our society" (Brown & Brooks, 1984, p. ix) and, more broadly, as "the total constellation of psychological, sociological, educational, physical, economic, and chance factors that combine to shape the career of any given individual over the life span" (Herr & Cramer, 1992, p. 27). "Career" itself is also a complex term that cannot be easily defined. Perhaps the most useful way to conceptualize this construct is to view it as the combination of all life roles (e.g., child, student, volunteer, worker, leisurite, parent, teacher, and mentor) that the individual assumes at various stages of his or her life (Wolffe, 1997). This definition allows the

Career development is a lifelong process.

transition team to examine all possible roles that a student may wish to undertake and to use these multiple aspects of their future adulthood as the basis for comprehensive transition plan development. These multiple roles can be used to support an optimal career plan rather than compete with or contradict this plan.

Many of the career theories reviewed in this chapter and used in transition services and vocational rehabilitation counseling have been adopted from career and vocational studies done with people *without* disabilities. These theories bring insights about careers in general, but also can lead to difficulties, particularly in their lack of attention to the unique experiences and abilities of people with disabilities (Hershenson & Szymanski, 1992). These theories also assume several different perspectives in examining the workers they describe. An important distinction between these theories is in those that describe occupational choice versus career development, and work adjustment. Hershenson and Szymanski define these three key differentiating concepts as follows:

(a) *occupational choice*: the process of choosing a specific job at one point in time,

(b) *career development*: the developmental processes of one's lifelong sequence of occupationally relevant choices and behaviors,

(c) *work adjustment*: adjustment to the work process itself, independent of the occupation in which it is performed (Hershenson & Szymanski, 1992, p. 274).

At one time, career counselors believed that young adults made one occupational choice prior to entering the workforce, which remained intact and unchanged throughout their lifetime. Current studies of adult work patterns show that workers make multiple job changes during their work career, a trend that continues to grow. The Bureau of Labor Statistics (1992) reported that an employee typically remains with a particular employer for a median of 4.5 years. Students with disabilities should be allowed the same opportunities for job change and should not be "stuck" in a position that they do not enjoy, or find challenging and rewarding (Pumpian, Fisher, Certo, & Smalley, 1997). The transition team needs to view job changes and even "negative" work experiences as part of the important learning opportunities that allow more realistic choices and that will lead to jobs that better fit a student's needs and abilities.

Critical Point: Individuals with disabilities should have the same opportunities to change jobs and careers that individuals without disabilities have.

The recognition that all workers are likely to change jobs has influenced career theories. Theories of *occupational choice* examine those personal and situational factors that lead to a satisfactory job choice. Many of these theories now allow this choice to occur at various times during a person's working life. *Career development* theories examine lifelong work patterns and change, often examining the impact and interrelationships of multiple life roles with those of just being a worker. They identify several areas of growth and change that occur in an individual's life and can lead to changes in other areas. *Work-adjustment* theories examine conditions within both the worker and the work environment that support a good "match." Several theories were developed specifically to address the unique needs and coping strategies of individuals with disabilities that were often not addressed in theories of occupational choice or career development (Szymanski, Hershenson, Enright, & Ettinger, 1996).

Across these three categories, some of these theories have been used and tested for several decades and others are much newer with less data on their usage and outcomes. These three categories have changed as theories have continued to be used and modified to accommodate differences in lifestyles and social conditions. In addition, new theories have emerged as the field's understanding of careers and adulthood has evolved. The transition team needs to note that each theory attempts to provide a distinctive organization and meaning to this highly complex process; that is, each offers its own unique perspective on those factors that lead to the greatest success, or to the greatest impediments to optimal career development. The theories also tend to define "success" differently: Some focus only on the individual, others focus on the balance between the individual and the environment, and still others focus on multiple interrelationships and factors. Some of the differences in the theories are a result of the variety of their originating disciplines: counseling, organizational psychology, sociology, and business, to name a few (Szymanski, Fernandez, Koch, & Merz, 1996). Transition team members should select the theory that best describes the needs and concerns of the student first and then identify related and appropriate assessment instruments later. When using newer theories, teams may find that many related assessment instruments do not as yet exist.

Critical Point: Each career development theory views the individual, the environment, and critical factors differently. "Successful" career development is also defined uniquely.

The variety of theories are best understood by using some type of organizing system. Wolffe (1997) categorizes theories as being either "structural" or "developmental," categories that are used in this chapter to describe these two major differentiating types. In addition to these two major categories, a number of work-adjustment and social learning theories have some important applications they can provide to further understand the career development of students with disabilities (Szymanski, et al., 1996). Examples of each of these types of theories will be described subsequently. When available, the section will list some of the assessment and career instruments that have been developed to implement these theories.

CASE STUDY A

Michael is a relatively physically active, 18-year-old male who enjoys sports. He has a moderate cognitive delay and suspected ADHD, which makes him highly distractible with a short attention span. He communicates best nonverbally with strangers and has approximately 50 spoken words that are understood by family and friends. However, he frequently forgets to use his communication book when with others and easily becomes angered and frustrated when he is not understood. Michael can be physically aggressive at times, although he is small and thin for his age with a low tolerance for lifting or strength-based activities. He has expressed strong interests in working in an autobody shop and is involved with activities with his family that support this interest.

CASE STUDY B

Paulina is a 15-year-old-female who has just entered high school. She has a mild to moderate cognitive delay with moderate vision loss and moderate/severe bilateral hearing loss. She wears glasses but needs nonglare lighting and high contrast work papers. Her hearing aids frequently bother her (she complains of headaches) but when she takes them out, she hears very few environmental sounds and no speech. She has a spoken functional vocabulary that is adequate for simple tasks and does not use sign language. Paulina has not had any work exposure, partly because the prior principal believed she would be a safety hazard.

Structural Theories

Structural theories emphasize the correspondence or "match" between individuals and work environments. They focus on the concept of appropriate *occupational choice* as leading to a satisfactory career. Structural theories date back to the early 1900s when Parsons introduced the idea of matching client attributes or traits (e.g., aptitudes, abilities, interests, and functional limitations) to workplace demands (Wolffe, 1997). Parson's model became known as the trait-factor approach and is still used extensively in modern career counseling and vocational rehabilitation practice (Szymanski, et al., 1996; Wolffe, 1997). His theory examines occupational choice and three variables that are key to this decision:

(a) the individual—aptitudes, abilities, interests, ambitions, resources, and limitations;

(b) the occupation—requirements, conditions of success, advantages and disadvantages, compensations, opportunities, and prospects; and

(c) the relationship between these two groups of factors (Brown & Brooks, 1996; Crites, 1981; Szymanski, et al., 1996).

More recent theories have incorporated constructs of midlife career change as well as multiple and lifelong factors impacting individuals and society, and have given increasing attention to diverse groups (Brown & Brooks, 1990). These theories view the individual and the environment as a set of variables which should be as similar to each other as possible in order to ensure job success.

One of the most prominent structural theorists today is John Holland. Holland's (1992) theory of career development categorizes personality into six general types with six corresponding work environments: realistic, investigative, artistic, social, enterprising, and conventional (abbreviated as RIASEC). Although most people have a dominant personality type, their personalities typically fit into two or three types. Combinations of three personality types are used by Holland in his career assessment instruments to characterize the individual's typical personality and to identify congruent occupational matches. These instruments include the *Self-Directed Search* (Holland, Fritzsche, & Powell, 1994) and the *Vocational Preference Inventory* (Holland, 1985). Holland proposed a three-step process: (1) to identify individual traits according to the six personality types, (2) to classify the work environment by type, and (3) to match the two sets of factors as a basis for establishing congruency and a series of success and satisfaction cycles (Brown, 1990; Spokane, 1996). Personalities and environments also vary along the attributes of consistency, differentiation, identification of strength, congruence, and consistency between the person and the environment. The six personality factors (RIASEC) should match with work environment type in order to establish congruency and satisfaction.

CASE STUDY

Examine the prior experiential and life opportunity histories of the two students. How would these contribute to, or serve as barriers to, using this career theory?

Developmental Theories

The developmental theories focus on life-span stages and their impact on career development and view occupational choice as one aspect of a person's work life, in contrast to the structural theories. They focus on the concept of *career development* as the result of lifelong work patterns, change, and the positive interrelationships between the elements of a person's life as leading to a fulfilling career and life. Super (1990) provides one of the more comprehensive and well-known theories. He defines occupational choice as the implementation of self-concepts that unfolds across a lifetime (Brown & Brooks, 1996;

Super, Savickas, & Super, 1996). His life-span, life-space approach identifies roles (e.g., child, student, leisurite, citizen, worker, and home-maker) and life stages across time (i.e., growth, exploration, establishment, maintenance, and disengagement). This time dimension used a developmental perspective to address how people change and make transitions as they prepare for, engage in, and reflect upon their life roles, and particularly, their work role (Super et al., 1996; Super, 1984, 1990).

Super (1990) also investigated a number of career patterns and worked to define the concept of career maturity. Since the 1970s, the theory increasingly has addressed changing women's roles, ethnicity, and cultural context (Szymanski, Hershenson et al., 1996). This theory views the person as encompassing multiple roles and stages with change inherent in every transition. The work environment is less well-specified but the ability to cope with environmental demands increases with experience; this is called "career maturity." Related instruments include the *Career Development Inventory* (Super, Thompson, Lindeman, Joordan, & Myers, 1981) and the *Career Maturity Index* (Super, 1974).

CASE STUDY

What characteristics of each of the two students might be the most important considerations in planning a career path using this theory? What type of experiences or interventions might be suggested using this approach?

Work-Adjustment Theories

Minnesota Theory of Work Adjustment

The initial work for this theory was borne out of a focus on persons with disabilities through the Department of Vocational Rehabilitation and the University of Minnesota (Dawis & Lofquist, 1984; Hershenson & Szymanski, 1992). The framework consciously focused on work adjustment and work behavior rather than on occupational

choice or career development models because of concerns with adequately addressing the unique life circumstances that disability status and experience often brings (Hershenson & Szymanski, 1992). This and other theories of work adjustment focus on the concept of identifying factors of the worker and the environment that lead to meeting the needs and requirements of each. The Minnesota Theory of Work Adjustment identifies *work personality* as an important characteristic of each individual that contributes to work satisfaction. It consists of needs that the worker expects to have fulfilled on the job and the specific abilities that he or she possesses to perform required duties. The workplace is described in terms of its ability requirements and its potential to meet a worker's needs. *Work adjustment* is defined as the interaction of two sets of indicators, "satisfaction" and "satisfactoriness." *Satisfaction* relates to the overall work conditions and to various aspects of the individual's work environment, as well as to the fulfillment of personal aspirations and expectations. *Satisfactoriness* is indicated by the individual's productivity, efficiency, and his or her evaluation by supervisors, coworkers, and the company (Dawis, 1996; Dawis & Lofquist, 1984; Lofquist & Dawis, 1969; Szymanski et al., 1996). Job tenure is a job function of satisfactoriness and satisfaction. This theory views the person and the environment as each presenting factors that lead to satisfaction/satisfactoriness when matched.

CASE STUDY

How would this theory describe the work personality of each of the two students? What type of work-adjustment factors would be important considerations that could lead to satisfaction and satisfactoriness?

Hershenson's Theory of Work Adjustment

This theory combines aspects of an individual's career development path with his or her work adjustment by focusing on two essential elements: the person and the person's environment (Hershenson & Szymanski, 1992; Szymanski, et al., 1996). It tends to combine the two concepts of lifelong accumulation of roles and interrelated factors, with meeting mutual needs across the worker and the work environment. The personal aspects consist of three domains. Work personality is the first domain, consisting of a person's self-concept as a worker and his or her motivation for work. Work competencies is the second domain, consisting of work habits, physical and mental skills for work, and work-related interpersonal skills. Appropriate and clear work goals is the third domain. The interaction of these three personal domains and the work environment leads to work adjustment. Work adjustment also consists of three individual components: task performance, work-role behavior, and work satisfaction. Hershenson describes the three personal domains as developing during certain focal periods, with continued development throughout a person's work career.

The three personal domains are accorded certain dominant developmental time periods. Work personality develops primarily during preschool and is influenced by the family. Work competencies develop during school years and are modified in response to successes and failures in that environment. Work goals are influenced by peer and other reference groups as the individual prepares to leave school and to begin working. This theory views the person as a set of interrelated and interdependent factors or domains. Successful adjustment occurs when these factors and the individual's work components interact successfully with the environment. Hershenson and colleagues have developed several self-rating and observer ratings to assist with evaluating these domains (Hershenson & Szymanski, 1992).

CASE STUDY

Across the three personal domains, at which stage does each student appear to be primarily developing? How would you describe the work personality, work competencies, and work goals for each student? For which domain do you need more information? For which domain would you want to develop additional work-life experiences or opportunities?

Krumboltz's Social Learning Theory

The application of the social learning theory to career decision making has its roots in the work of Bandura. It is also based on elements of the reinforcement theory, classical behaviorism, and cognitive information processing (Mitchell & Krumboltz, 1996). Krumboltz's theory of career decision making explains the origins of a person's career choice and then applies learning theory aspects during career counseling and in terms of suggested interventions (Mitchell & Krumboltz, 1996). This theory is less easily classified by major concept (i.e., occupational choice, career development, or work adjustment), but its lifelong growth and learning focus would tend to place the theory in a more developmental category.

This theory proposes two major types of learning experiences that result in individually based behavioral and cognitive skills and preferences. Instrumental learning experiences occur when an individual is positively reinforced or punished for behaviors. For example, a student does poorly in assigned household chores and is scolded and reprimanded. Associative learning experiences occur when the individual associates some previously affectively neutral event or stimulus with an emotionally laden stimulus. The student is doing the laundry and opens the washer during its cycle and is sprayed with warm water. This recalls an episode when the student spilled boiling water on himself, and thereafter he is very afraid of doing the laundry. Both of these instrumental and associative learning experiences occur through direct experience with reinforcing or punishing events. Associative learning may also occur indirectly through vicarious learning experiences in which the individual watches someone else performing a task, and then does it successfully on his or her own (Mitchell & Krumboltz, 1996).

This theory uses instrumental and associative learning experiences to explain why people enter particular programs or occupations, why they express preferences, and why they may change their preferences at selected points in their lives. In addition, four categories of factors influence career decision-making paths, which include (1) genetic endowment and special abilities, (2) environmental conditions and events, (3) learning experiences, and (4) task approach skills. These four factors interact in infinite ways to form a set of beliefs (Mitchell & Krumboltz, 1990, 1996). Individuals develop self-observation generalizations that assess their own performances, and worldview generalizations that predict certain expectations about the future. Faulty self-observations, generalizations, or inaccurate interpretations of environmental conditions can lead to a variety of problems in career decision making. The theory suggests strategies for modifying and correcting these perceptions.

This theory sees the career counselor as a professional who promotes client learning and thereby assumes the roles of educator, coach, or mentor depending on the situation (Mitchell & Krumboltz, 1996). The theory also supports counselors' addressing current career trends that go beyond an individual's occupational choice. This may require the counseling to expand an individual's capabilities and interests beyond existing characteristics and to include preparing for changing work tasks and empowering the individual to take action. This theory views the individual as changing through learning with change viewed as potentially continuous, within the appropriate learning environment.

CASE STUDY

How would you describe Michael's work preference in terms of this learning theory? How would you describe Paulina's lack of a preference? Do either one show some potentially faulty beliefs about themselves or the world? What types of interventions and experiences would this theory suggest as the next steps for the students?

The theories previously described represent a range of those presently used in transition and vocational rehabilitation or career counseling services. Each theory views students and their interaction with the work and adult world somewhat uniquely. A challenge for practitioners has been how to choose the theory that best addresses an individual's needs, particularly when the individual is still developing, growing, and changing according to the person's needs, abilities, and preferences. The next section describes two methods that comprehensively organize career theories for better professional decision making.

Models for Applying Career Development Theories to Students with Disabilities

Although numerous career development theories have been formulated and tested over the years, no single theory, in and of itself, adequately explains the career development of people with (or even without) disabilities (Szymanski, et al., 1996; Wolffe, 1997). People with disabilities represent a large and heterogeneous group. The diversity of their abilities and limitations, supportive or limiting life experiences, as well as gender, cultural, and the myriad of other unique factors limits the degree to which any single theory is applicable or nonapplicable to their unique situations (Szymanski, et al., 1996). Furthermore, the nature of a person's disability cannot reliably predict how that individual will proceed through the career development process: Two individuals with the same disability may have extremely different life experiences and career concerns. In addition, disability can pose a risk factor to the career development process to which every family, neighborhood, and community respond differently.

Experiences associated with the early onset of disability may result in career development barriers for students with disabilities (Szymanski & Hershenson, 1998). Functional limitations, for example, may restrict the child's ability to participate in important activities that contribute information about life and work capabilities (e.g., play, chores, extracurricular activities, and after-school jobs). These are also important in that such experiences facilitate the development of the student's occupational interests, career decision-making skills, work competencies, and a positive occupational self-concept (Conyers, Koch, & Szymanski, 1998). Furthermore, the expectations of parents, teachers, service providers, and employers can serve either to impede (i.e., if expectations are too low) or promote (i.e., if expectations are appropriately high) the development of a healthy self-concept and appropriate career aspirations.

Many of these unique life experiences are not taken into account in existing career theories. However, a professional may be able to adapt a particular theory to a student if these considerations are added and appropriate modifications are made. Changes made to any of the procedures (such as allowing more time or providing certain prompts) or instrument items (such as providing alternative and more familiar choices that are within the student's experience) when using normed assessment instruments, if available, will, of course, impact their interpretation. Many of these theories require the transition team to provide additional considerations of critical factors, including the role of reasonable accommodations and newly developed technology, in addition to the student's potentially limited work-related learning experiences. Consideration of these factors can greatly expand a student's possible career options and the usefulness of these career theories (Szymanski & Hershenson, 1998).

The proliferation of these theories has led some practitioners to search for convergence among the theories. Some of this has resulted from the tension between career theorists and practitioners (Savickas, 1996). In many instances, practitioners have had to focus more on getting results with their clients and feel disenchanted with theory. The result has been two major efforts to integrate theory across the variety of concerns and issues presented by individuals, in an effective manner that assists practitioners with appropriate, theory-based service delivery (Szymanski, et al., 1996). Each of the two models allows practitioners to work across several theories using an integrated and comprehensive theoretical framework, which leads to specific interventions according to the unique issues of the individual. The hope is that the specific insights and strategies provided across this range of theories will better serve the range of individuals. These models make this array of theories usable for practitioners.

Ecological Model of Career Development

Szymanski et al. (1996) developed an ecological model to organize the various career development theories and to aid in designing individualized career planning interventions. Their model proposes five groups of factors or constructs: individual, contextual, mediating, work environment, and outcome. These constructs interact to enhance and/or impede the career development process of people with disabilities (Szymanski & Parker, 1996; Szymanski, et al., 1996). These constructs are described in Table 3–1.

This theoretical framework has been used to integrate a number of career theories into one model, including theories developed by Hershenson and Szymanski (1992), Holland (1992), Krumboltz (1988), Super (1990), and the Minnesota theory of work adjustment (Szymanski & Parker, 1996; Szymanski, et al., 1996). This can help transition teams in making decisions about how to address the career and adult-living needs of students, some of which can be quite complex. The model is helpful also in ensuring that the team takes into account the myriad of influencing factors and events that have impacted the student to date and will continue to do so throughout his or her career. Reviewing the

TABLE 3–1

Five Constructs Used with the Ecological Model of Career Development

---

Individual factors: The physical and psychological attributes of the person such as race, gender, interests, and physical and mental abilities

Contextual factors: All aspects of the individual's situation that are external to the person, such as socio-economic status, family, educational opportunities, and relevant legislation (e.g., the ADA)

Mediating factors: The individual, societal, and environmental beliefs that influence how each person perceives his or her relationship with the world.

   Individual mediating factors include self-concept, work personality, self-efficacy, outcome expectations, and adjustment to disability.

   Societal mediating factors include cultural or structural beliefs about community, spirituality, religion, gender, and disability. Also included in this grouping of factors are racism, discrimination, limited opportunity structures, and disability and gender-role stereotypes.

   Environmental mediating factors are beliefs (e.g., outcome expectations, worldview generalizations) that affect how the individual interacts with his or her surroundings.

Work environment factors: All aspects of the work setting, such as task requirements, reinforcement systems, and organizational culture.

Outcome factors: The results of the interaction of all the factors to include states or behaviors, such as job satisfaction, job satisfactoriness, tenure, productivity, and competitiveness.

Source: The table is based on the work of Szymanski & Hershenson, 1998. Career development of people with disabilities: An ecological model in Szymanski, E. M. & Parker, R. M. (Eds.), *Work and disability: Issues and strategies in career development and job development* (pp. 79–126). Austin, TX: PRO-ED.

framework annually can help to address new factors that have arisen and that are now important in order for the student to achieve his or her preferred career and life outcomes. The ecological framework can help the team to target specific areas for assessment and to identify possible career development interventions.

Critical Point: Career development is the result of multiple sets of factors (or constructs) and processes.

Szymanski and Hershenson (1998) expanded their original model to include six interrelated career development processes: congruence, decision making, development, socialization, allocation, and chance. These are described in Table 3–2

The five groups of *constructs* assist the team in identifying considerations to address in order to ensure comprehensive planning across all major life issues. The six *processes* describe mechanisms by which the constructs can be ad-

dressed. Table 3–3 uses the constructs and processes to provide a series of related questions and suggested interventions for each construct and process. Table 3–2 addresses many of the unique characteristics and limitations that students with disabilities may face and identifies how the transition team can deal with each one.

The use of this model can assure the transition team that major issues are not neglected when planning across the complicated issues of achieving adulthood.

CASE STUDY

How would you describe Michael and Paulina in terms of the five constructs: individual, contextual, mediating, work environment, and outcome? Which of the six developmental processes have been most important for each student so far: congruence, deci-

TABLE 3–2

The Six Interrelated Career Development Processes Impacting the Ecological Model of Career Development

Congruence: The degree of match or mismatch between individuals and the environments in which they live and work. The process of congruence is particularly important to the career development of students with disabilities and one that is often a target of interventions, such as reasonable accommodations and assistive technology.

Decision making: Occurs within the context of career development and is the process of exploring the various work alternatives available in society and then formulating a vocational decision. This process is also a common target of intervention among students with disabilities, particularly those who have had limited exposure to different career options and/or restricted opportunities to learn and practice decision-making skills. Interventions include activities such as decision-making training, job shadowing, and trial work experiences.

Developmental processes: The "systematic changes over time, which are interwoven with characteristics and perceptions of the individual" (p. 354). Parents and teachers should use these processes by encouraging children and adolescents with disabilities to become involved in play, chores, and other activities that introduce them to new interests in order to enhance the development of work personality and work competencies.

Socialization: The process whereby people learn various life roles (e.g., student, worker, parent, and citizen). Students with disabilities may be socialized to assume a "sick" or "disabled" role if parents and teachers do not work to empower them and emphasize self-determination.

Allocation: The process whereby "societal gatekeepers (i.e., parents, teachers, vocational counselors, school administrators, and personnel directors) use external criteria to channel people into or exclude them from specific directions" (p. 354). Special education placement is an allocation process by its very nature and may restrict career options for students with disabilities; thus, "periodic self-assessment is an important professional responsibility for [educators] seeking to empower rather than disempower" (p. 362).

Chance: Unforeseen events or encounters that can have a strong impact on career development. Educators, parents, and service providers can facilitate positive career development experiences for students with disabilities by teaching them how to cope with negative chance events and to take advantage of positive opportunities that unexpectedly present themselves.

Source: The table is based on the work of Szymanski & Hershenson, 1998. Career development of people with disabilities: An ecological model in Szymanski, E. M. & Parker, R. M. (Eds.), *Work and disability: Issues and strategies in career development and job development* (pp. 79–126). Austin, TX: PRO-ED.

sion making, development, socialization, allocation, or chance? Which interventions do you suggest as the most important at this point for each student?

Framework for Linking Career Theory and Practice

A second comprehensive career development framework was developed by Savickas (1996) based on his work as a practitioner and a desire to use multiple theories in order to best meet the needs of individual clients. The framework

serves as a problem-solving model to determine which of the theories and interventions best address a particular individual's issues. For example, a team may try to learn about a particular student's career needs by using several career assessments but may find that the results are not particularly helpful in planning for interventions. This linking framework presents a decision tree across the diverse repertoire of possible intervention techniques and theories. Savickas (1996) poses six types of career questions based on the individual's needs that correspond to

TABLE 3–3

Assessment Questions and Interventions for the Ecological Model of Career Development

Questions	Possible Interventions
Individual constructs	
What are current abilities, interests, and limitations?	Active involvement in self-assessment
How are these perceived by the student and family?	Career portfolio
What skills have been learned as a result of education or work experience?	Career portfolio
What values are considered important to career planning by the student and family?	Career portfolio
Has the student had sufficient experiences to foster interest development?	Volunteer and paid work experience
How can individual abilities be enhanced?	Skill training, further education, job supports
How can limitations be lessened?	Assistive technology, job accommodations
Contextual constructs	
How have family background and neighborhood influenced perception of opportunities and responsibilities?	Work role models, mentors, chores, and work experience
How has education facilitated or impeded realization of potential?	Remedial education
What are the financial incentives or disincentives perceived by the individual and family as associated with work?	Inclusion of financial considerations in career planning
Mediating constructs	
How does the student perceive her or his work-related abilities?	Career counseling, successful work experiences
What outcomes does the student expect from employment preparation or rehabilitation?	Appropriate role models, mentors
What are the student's abilities in career planning?	Career classes and workshops, career counseling
What are the student's and family's cultural and religious beliefs that relate to education and work?	Culturally sensitive career planning, culturally sensitive career portfolios
How has the student been impacted by discrimination or stereotypes?	Advocacy
Environmental constructs	
How physically accessible are various target environments?	Consultation on barrier removal, assistive technology, job accommodation, consideration of alternate environments
What is the organizational culture of the target work environment? Does the student understand how to get along in such a culture?	Job analysis, social skills training
How has the student gotten along in previous work or school environments?	Social skills training, job coaching
What are the tasks of the environment?	Job analysis
What are the reinforcements?	Job analysis, planning for career advancement

Questions	Possible Interventions
Outcome constructs	
How well do the student's skills and behaviors meet the requirements of possible work environments?	Additional training, on-the-job training, social skills training
How well do the reinforcements of the work environment meet the student's needs?	Additional training for career advancement, possible job change
Has the student experienced job-related stress?	Stress reduction techniques, wellness planning, encouragement to use social support, leisure and lifestyle planning
How well is the student equipped to cope with job-related stress?	
Congruence or correspondence processes	
Is the student aware of potential job accommodations or assistive devices? Have other possibilities been considered?	Discussion and exploration of accommodation possibilities and assistive devices
Have ability scores been lowered by problems of construct validity?	Ecological or qualitative approaches to measurement
Is self-efficacy limiting the types of occupations considered?	Enrichment experiences, role models
Decision-making processes	
What are the cultural practices of the student and her or his family relating to decision making and independence?	Incorporate the student's culture into interventions and goals, involve family members, if appropriate
What are the student's skills and experiences related to making choices or decisions?	Decision-making training, assistance with identifying alternatives and making choices, multiple trial work experiences
Developmental processes	
Has disability limited developmental experiences?	Longitudinal approach to career planning, cautious approach to interpretation of interest measures
Has social skill development been limited?	Social skills training
Has work personality and work competency development been impeded?	Chores, supervised work experiences
Socialization processes	
How have socialization processes affected the student's current role and consideration of future roles?	Role models, psychoeducational interventions
Allocation processes	
Have opportunities been limited by gatekeeping functions in education, rehabilitation, or other service delivery systems?	Remedial education, mentoring, recruitment programs
Do the requirements or processes of current service delivery programs restrict options, create dependency, or otherwise disempower?	Program evaluation, capacity-building interventions
Chance processes	
Is the student prepared to recognize and capitalize on chance opportunities?	Career planning workshops, career portfolios

Source: Based on Career development of people with disabilities by E. M. Szymanski & D. B. Hershenson in Parkes, R. M. & Szymanski, E. M. (Eds.), *Rehabilitation counseling: Basics and beyond* (pp. 366–369). Copyright (1998) by Pro-Ed. Reprinted with permission.

TABLE 3–4

Framework for Linking Career Theory and Practice

Question	Career Intervention Problem	Career Service
Who am I?	Career self	Career counseling
How can work help me to grow as a person?	Drives (fulfilling needs)	Career therapy
How do I shape my career?	Career attitudes, beliefs, and competencies	Career education
What shall I choose?	Vocational self	Vocational guidance
How can I do better?	Occupational stimuli and vocational responses	Position coaching
How do I get a position?	Life roles: work, friends, love	Occupational placement

Source: The table is based on the work of Savickas, 1996. A framework for linking career theory and practice, in *Handbook of career counseling theory and practice,* by M. L. Savickas and W. B. Walsh, Palo Alto, CA: Davies-Black Publishing.

specific interventions and career services that best meet these needs. These are shown in Table 3–4.

The first step in using this framework is to assess the student's career issues according to these six questions. This is an important step because the nature of the student's issue should be determined prior to beginning a series of assessments and measurements (Savickas, 1996). These instruments are designed to collect more detailed information needed to design an intervention and transition plan and are only useful when the nature of the problem is first made clear.

Critical Point: Not all career assessments address all issues, so it is important for the team to have a general understanding of the student's career issues first in order to choose the assessments and interventions that are most appropriate.

Based on the students' particular issues, the initial determination to be made by the team or career counselor is whether or not the students are ready for vocational guidance and have a clear vocational identity. For example, if the students are able to describe in some manner their interests, abilities, values, and life goals, then they are ready to begin identifying and exploring vocational possibilities. If they cannot do so, the team can focus on obstacles or issues that are preventing this from occurring. This might include self-concept difficulties, delayed career development, or motivational difficulties. These latter issues are represented in the career self, drives, or career attitudes—the first three rows of Table 3–4.

Students with a clear identity but having some remaining concerns or confusions about how to achieve this vocational identity suggest issues with achieving a good fit between themselves and their work environment (will they be satisfied and fulfilled, will they succeed and fit-in?). These are represented by one of the remaining three rows of Table 3–4 (how to actualize their vocational selves, how to make better decisions and vocational responses, and how to move into a position of choice). The team or career counselor can get additional information by asking the students about their school and work experiences, their perceptions of their successes and frustrations, and desires to improve or change their current position. These answers can help to identify an area of further focus and intervention.

As a result of identifying which of the six questions best represents the students' issues, the team can select a theory that addresses these concerns. Each theory suggests general interventions and strategies and the more developed theories will provide assessment instruments. For example, a student who is unable to describe his or her career beliefs and values may benefit from taking the *Career Maturity Inventory* (Crites, 1978) and examining the results with a career counselor. A student who has a strong vocational identity but is unsure of which career to choose could use the *Self-Directed Search* (Holland, 1985). A list of theories, related instruments (where available and appropriate), and suggested interventions is described in Table 3–5, based on the six guiding questions (Savickas, 1996).

Instruments and assessments that are suggested for several of the questions are good starting points for data gathering and discussion between the transition team (or career counselor) and the student. They can lead to further experiences and interventions to reaffirm and develop indicated preferences. Those questions with no specified instruments tend to rely upon interaction-based approaches and interventions. For example, questions that reflect concerns about environmental fit and interrelationships between the individual and the environment may be addressed by Super's (1990) life career rainbow model and concepts of role salience that can affect the individual. Krumboltz's (1979) social learning theory may help to examine and address the individual's perceptions and beliefs about his or her relationships with the world. In other cases, educational and vocational experiences and programs are needed to help the person learn necessary work skills and competencies. The linking framework can be a useful tool for the team in identifying a primary issue and in selecting the appropriate vocational instruments and/or interventions that best reflect these issues.

CASE STUDY

Which career question best captures the primary issues of Michael and Paulina? What instruments, strategies, and interventions are suggested?

The Career Development of Students with Disabilities

The career theories described earlier offer a variety of perspectives that can be useful to the transition team for facilitating educational experiences that enhance the career development of students with disabilities. The individual career theories provide unique perspectives for working with students and their families. The two comprehensive models provide a way to organize across multiple theories for working with a student: The ecological model provides a structure for developing a comprehensive profile of multiple factors, and the linking framework provides a structure for giving assistance to the student that links with specific theories and intervention strategies.

Although this chapter's description is much too brief to suggest detailed decision-making and intervention planning, this background can help transition team members to be better prepared in determining the most relevant aspects of a student's career development that must be addressed, and to suggest some possible theories and approaches for doing so. The career development theory that the team uses will form much of the basis for later transition planning: It establishes the priorities for issues that should be addressed first, suggesting a perspective to take when viewing the multiple aspects of making a student successful in the workplace. The theoretical approach (or use of an eclectic approach) also will suggest assessments and interventions which the transition team will use for collecting further data about current and potential future environments in order to develop a student profile. It is recommended that the team also undertake regular and ongoing ecological assessments that can be important in tracking aspects of a students career development and maturity.

A tool that can be helpful in tracking career planning information has been developed by several states. This tool is the Individualized

TABLE 3–5

Interventions for the Career Framework

Question	Characteristics of the Individual	Theoretical Models	Career Interventions
Who am I?	Not yet able to articulate self-concepts and wants help in exploring who he or she is and the life goals he or she should pursue	*Focus:* Career patterns and self-exploration *Theories:* Brown and Brooks (1991), Savickas (1989), Super (1954) *Instruments: Career Development Inventory* (Super, Thompson, Lindeman, Joordan, & Myers, 1981), *Career Maturity Inventory* (Crites, 1978), *Career Beliefs Inventory* (Krumboltz, 1988)	*Strategies:* Focus on self-awareness and values with assistance in reflecting upon patterns in his or her life; self-exploration to clarify values and life issues *Interventions:* Self-exploration and values clarification to heighten self-awareness and to increase self-esteem, and elaboration of self-concepts through introspection
How can work help me to grow as a person?	Has significant problems in formulating an integrated and coherent self-concept; he or she wants help in overcoming barriers and conditions that frustrate gratification of his or her needs; tends to feel insecure and often has been discouraged by life experiences	*Focus:* Personal adjustment counseling *Theories:* Blustein (1987), Blustein & Spengler (1995), Meara & Patton (1994), Subich (1993) *Instruments: Vocational Apperception Test* (Ammons, Butler, & Herzog, 1950), card sorts (Slaney & McKinnon-Slaney, 1990)	*Strategies:* Address excessive indecisiveness, anxiety, and conflicts that thwart efforts to form a coherent self-concept and adaptive lifestyle; some benefit from modifying typical reactions to situations *Interventions:* Therapy to work through traumatic experiences, to increase sense of self-worth, and to cope with problematic situations and significant others
How do I shape my career?	Has confusion about careers, he or she wants help in understanding vocational developmental tasks; has issues dealing with career attitudes, beliefs, and competencies	*Focus:* Developmental and educational concepts *Theories:* Blocher (1974), Hoyt (1975), Ivey (1986), Super (1974)	*Strategies:* Educational interventions that emphasize self-control and concentrate on developing adaptive attitudes toward and competencies for designing and managing their own careers; strengthening of self-efficacy and decision-making competencies *Interventions:* Deliberate psychological education and counseling to orient toward developmental tasks and to foster competencies leading to task mastery

Question	Characteristics of the Individual	Theoretical Models	Career Interventions
What shall I choose?	Possesses a clear vocational identity but he or she wants help in identifying occupational alternatives	*Focus:* Personality and work setting congruence *Theories:* Holland (1985), Katz (1993), Lofquist & Dawis (1991) *Instruments: Self-Directed Search* (Holland, 1985), *Strong Interest Inventory* (Harmon, Hansen, Borgen, & Hammer, 1994)	*Strategies:* Guidance that translates self-concepts into congruent occupations; exploring matches between self-concept and jobs *Interventions:* Administration and interpretation of interest inventories and ability tests, providing educational and vocational information, prompting exploratory behavior, and identifying career fields for consideration
How can I do better?	Encounters problems in meeting educational or vocational position's demands regarding adaptation to life roles, he or she wants to increase his or her success and satisfaction with work roles	*Focus:* Establishing and adjusting to a career *Theories:* Carden (1990), Dix & Savickas (1995), Hall (1987), Lofquist & Dawis (1969), Savickas (1991)	*Strategies:* Can benefit from strategizing how to get ahead and to get along; emphasize adaptations that improve the fit between the individual and the position through learning about organizational culture, position requirements, and coworkers *Interventions:* Clarify problems, identify relevant attitudes and behaviors, and rehearse and implement new attitudes and behaviors
How do I get a position?	Knows his or her preferred occupation; has made a choice and a commitment; has concerns with the world of work and related behaviors	*Focus:* Successful career placement *Theories:* Herr, Rayman, & Garis (1993), Shingleton & Fitzpatrick (1985), Stevens (1973)	*Strategies:* Reduce job search anxiety, increase assertiveness, encourage exploratory behavior, and increase social skills and self-presentation behavior *Interventions:* Skill training, information gathering, writing résumés, networking, searching for opportunities, and preparing for interviews

Source: The table is based on the work of Savickas, 1996. A framework for linking career theory and practice, in *Handbook of career counseling theory and practice,* by M. L. Savickas and W. B. Walsh, Palo Alto, CA: Davies-Black Publishing.

Career Plan, which accompanies the Individualized Education Program (IEP) and the Individualized Transition Plan (ITP) documents and focuses on gathering and recording career-specific information (cf. Ohio Rehabilitation Services, 1997). The purpose of this Individualized Career Plan (ICP) is to identify the student's career and educational goals and the steps that will need to be taken in order for the student to achieve her or his goals. The transition team develops the ICP by working with the student to determine where he or she hopes to be after high school graduation and by analyzing the student's career goals in terms of skill and training requirements (Simmons & Baer, 1996). Skill and training requirements are then broken down into action steps (e.g., course work, trial work experiences, and extracurricular activities) to be taken by the student prior to leaving school. This can be a very useful tool for including the detail necessary to prepare the student for achieving his or her ultimate career goal. The individualized career planning document includes the following items:

(1) a specification of career goal(s),
(2) a statement reflecting upon how the student's current interests, knowledge, and skills support career goal(s),
(3) an explanation of the additional skills and knowledge that the student will need to achieve his or her career goal(s),
(4) a listing of educational activities through which additional skills and knowledge can be developed, and
(5) a description of additional certification and/or specialized training that the student will need to achieve his or her career goal(s) (Ohio Rehabilitation Services Commission, 1997).

Because their career plans are likely to change over time, students should be given opportunities to review and revise their plans on, at least, an annual basis. Table 3–6 gives an example of a career plan for Michael, one of the two students with disabilities who is described in this chapter. Such a career plan is helpful in documenting

plans and achievements across several years as the student completes a variety of work and career experiences.

CASE STUDY

Develop an individualized career plan for Paulina. Because she has not indicated any preferences, no specific work goal can be identified. However, you can begin by thinking about the type and setting of work that might seem appropriate to the team members and the family—would it be full-time or part-time, community-based, and so on? Certain aspects of certification and higher-level training cannot be specified until an area is determined. However, if community employment is the goal, there may be issues of raising her performance to competitive levels for quality and quantity that may require extended or intensive training.

Conclusion

Career development begins at birth and continues until death. A variety of theories have been developed to explain this complicated process. Most of these theories can be categorized as either structural (i.e., those concerned with identifying individual traits and corresponding work environments) or developmental (i.e., those that view career development as constituting different stages), learning-based, or focusing on work-adjustment processes. Career development theories have been criticized as being limited in their application to understanding the concerns of people with disabilities. It may be more important to view career development as an intricate and highly individualized process that cannot be adequately explained by any single theory.

Two models were presented that are organized to represent multiple theories. Transition teams can use these models to assess the career development needs of our students from an ecological perspective, taking into consideration the multiple factors and processes that interact to shape each student's unique experiences. The

TABLE 3–6

Individualized Career Plan

ICP Elements	ICP for Michael, Sophomore Year
1. A specification of career goals	Michael will work full time in an autobody repair shop doing detailing and assisting with painting preparation.
2. A statement reflecting upon how the student's current interests, knowledge, and skills support career goals	Michael collects magazine pictures of cars, talks about cars frequently in conversation, particularly their colors and special paint designs. He enjoys helping his father and brothers to clean, wax, and polish their cars and volunteers to help. He is quite insistent that when he works, he does not just clean but that he is involved in painting.
3. An explanation of the additional skills and knowledge that the student needs to achieve his or her career goals	Michael needs to develop competitive-level and consistent detailing work competencies. He has the requisite initial skills but becomes distracted and loses his place in the process, and he is slower than desired. He needs near 100% cleaning and work accuracy for paint preparation work. He may need to adjust to wearing a mask. Michael needs to learn ways of expressing his frustration with communication. Identifying a work "buddy" whom he trusts may help. The environment is somewhat tolerant of physical displays of anger but it must be "appropriate" to the situation.
4. A listing of educational activities through which additional skills and knowledge can be developed	Michael will enroll in the autobody course at the vocational school when he is eligible next year, as a junior. As a sophomore, he will get a part-time job at a detailing shop on weekends and during the summer. As a senior, his training will continue to become more community-based and lead to part-time employment in an autobody shop. He will be encouraged to maintain his detailing job, if possible. This will provide him a "backup" position and serve to strengthen his résumé.
5. A description of additional certification and/or specialized training that the student will need to achieve his or her career goals	Michael needs to pass the autobody course and to receive a certificate in order to work as a painter. This may not be realistic given his distractibility and poor physical strength (regarding a 40-hour workweek with the equipment). It is more realistic that he assist with painting preparation and continue as a detailer, with increasing involvement in specific painting operations as he shows that he is capable.

Source: The individualized career plan (ICP) elements are based on the work of Ohio Rehabilitation Services Commission, 1997.

transition teams also can use a linking framework to assist them in choosing a particular issue for focus and the appropriate, related career interventions.

An understanding of theoretical career models and their related assessment instruments and intervention strategies will lead to a choice that best meets the student's needs. This will lead to a better understanding of how the different theoretical perspectives define career development issues, and how these perspectives have been incorporated into the array of transition practices and programs that now exist. Understanding these options, team members can design individualized career and transition plans that optimize the development of students with disabilities and lead them to a satisfying and fulfilling adulthood.

Study Questions

1. You are a member of a transition team that is collecting data on the needs, interests, and preferences of a student. How can use of the different theories of career development impact the collection of these data?

2. Choose three of the career development theories from this chapter, one structural, one developmental, and one learning or work-adjustment theory. Identify the perspective that each theory takes in defining key elements of the individual, the workplace, and the interaction between the two. From these differences in perspective, determine and compare the important interagency linkages that should be developed for each theory.

3. Compare these same three theories in terms of planning for a student's movement from school to postschool environments. Based on their perspective of the individual, the workplace, and their interaction, how do they differ in supportive movement to postschool environments? How are they similar?

4. For each of the three previous theories, determine how they would integrate into the ecological model and into the linking framework.

5. Use the ecological model and the linking framework to identify strategies for each that would support a student who is (a) entering a work exploration experience (observing a series of work sites spending 2 weeks at each site), (b) beginning a job try-out/job shadowing experience (spending one month working/following a worker in each of several work sites), and (c) beginning a part-time community work experience in an area of his or her preference.

Web Sites

Career Development Competencies at Turner Tech:
http://www.flstw.fsu.edu/online74/instrategies.htm

Career Development Information: North Salem High School Career Services:
http://www.teleport.com./,kcaldwel/index.shtml

High School School-To-Work/Career Development Needs: Sharing Success Programs:
http://www.sharingsuccess.org/code/wsr/stw_hs.html

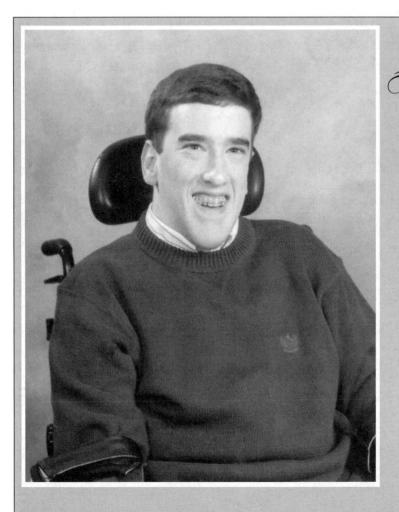

4

Transition Collaborators

Thomas Simmons
Jackie June
Robert W. Flexer

The objectives for this chapter are:

1. Describe various professional and agency services and practices and how different disciplines impact transition outcomes.

2. Describe the stages of group process and transition team activities that might be used to facilitate transition team outcomes.

3. Describe how the roles and responsibilities of LEA members of the transition team vary and foster positive outcomes.

4. Describe the roles of adult services and postschool professionals and how services vary and foster positive outcomes.

Chapters 1, 2, and 3 set out the legal requirements for transition, described the service delivery system of transition, and delineated some of the "best practices" in transition. These topics provided the policy and practice context in which transition planning, services, and secondary education are implemented. This chapter describes the professionals, agencies, and team processes involved in transition. Each professional and agency within the individual transition plan team needs to provide support to the student and family in clarifying and refining postschool goals within the outcome-oriented process. This includes the contributions made to the team, such as resources and experience, by persons from a variety of disciplines. The coordinated activities refer to services delivered each year that culminate in students achieving their postschool goals. The functioning of the transition team has a great bearing on students making progress each year. The team contributions, both individually and collectively, should promote movement toward the students' postschool goals.

Key Concepts in Transition Collaboration

Collaboration and consultation among school and a variety of postschool educators and service providers are required under the IDEA of 1997 (Eber, Nelson, & Miles, 1997). Eber et al. (1997) suggested a "wraparound" approach and comprehensive services to facilitate the success of the student in community and school programs. They further described the broad range of skills required of transition professionals and came to the conclusion that individual personnel alone cannot accomplish the requisite desired transition outcomes. DeFur and Taymans (1995) highlighted the need for significant degrees of communication, coordination, and collaboration among vocational rehabilitation, vocational education, and special education programs and staff.

Team development and its utilization within a transition services framework provide the opportunity and context for transition collaboration. As collaborators, team members develop shared values, develop appreciation of unique team member contributions, and derive student- and family-driven transition goals that are consensually developed by the team (see Everson & Guillory, 1998). By clarifying who should be involved and their responsibilities, transition teams will be enabled to coordinate and utilize effectively the myriad of programs and services available in schools and the community.

The *essential element* of a coordinated set of activities relates directly to the need for interdisciplinary approaches. Coordinated activities come into play in meeting the IEP requirement that consensus be obtained from a multidisciplinary team. Moreover, transition requirements add players from postschool agencies and environments to the team. The uncertainty of the future of the student makes the role and participation of these additional team members tenuous and ambiguous at times. For example, although many students may benefit from vocational rehabilitation, few of them will actually receive services because need for the service alone is not the only criterion for eligibility. Similar challenges exist for access to secondary options such as vocational education and school-to-work programs.

Critical Point Transition planning involves the collaboration of many professionals and agencies with different philosophies, service delivery approaches, and legal frameworks.

When transition needs of students are identified, questions of availability and access to an appropriate service usually arise. Often possible options lie in interdisciplinary team functioning. Developing and implementing IEPs based on consensual goal development and interdisciplinary education and services remain both the ideal and the challenge in special education as well as in transition.

The delivery of transition services can be viewed as occurring on three levels. Transition services can be viewed programmatically at a federal-, state-, and local-level system. Policies and funds flow from one level to the next within corresponding and mutually supporting structures.

Working from the federal structure, statewide and local interagency teams need to be established in order to make transition services accessible and to address barriers. Individual transition teams are another level at which groups of professionals work with students and families in obtaining transition services. Team processes are what the three groups have in common, as well as meeting transition needs through establishing joint values and common goals. An understanding of collaboration processes of transition teams is facilitated by a foundation in:

1. Individual agencies and their underlying structure of similarities and differences
2. Individual professionals and their underlying structure of similarities and differences
3. Team models

The Interface of Transition Collaboration

Integrated services that incorporate the education and expertise of special education, rehabilitation, and vocational education are necessary to meet the comprehensive needs presented by the diverse populations of students with disabilities. All three transition systems are needed, but how they fit together and meet the needs of students in a unified manner requires a working framework among all three respective systems. An understanding of the relationships among the three systems is necessary to develop such a working framework, which is sometimes referred to as the "interface."

Syzmanski, Hanley-Maxwell, and Asselin (1992) described the interrelationships among special education, vocational rehabilitation, and vocational education as being imperfect and frequently working against one another during these most important stages of the transition process. In general, the history and emphasis of the three delivery systems share similar concerns and emphasis on education and counseling processes. Although complementary, the three systems have distinct features as well. Syzmanski et al. (1992) described this interface as follows:

> The three service delivery systems share many common concerns. Specifically, special education and vocational education share concerns for education; special education and vocational rehabilitation specialize in serving people with disabilities; and vocational education and vocational rehabilitation share interests in employment preparation. Nonetheless, these service delivery systems are administered by separate federal agencies, which may or may not facilitate coordinated efforts (p. 165). (See Table 4–1.)

Syzmanski et al. (1992) provided a chronology of the service delivery system interface too. Indicative of the lack of systems interface is the lack of coordination and separate administration. Contradictions grow from these mismatches between systems. One example is the "cessation of matching funds for work study programs on the one hand and the simultaneous promotion of collaboration for transition on the other"(Syzmanski et al., 1992, p. 169). Although issues and programs have changed since Syzmanski published her research in 1992, significant differences persist. Examples of these discrepancies include distinctive definitions of severe disabilities for each system; lack of consistency in cooperative efforts between rehabilitation and vocational education; completely different administrative organizations; no more set-aside monies for students with disabilities in vocational education; and, in many cases, lack

TABLE 4–1

Service Delivery System Differences among Vocational Rehabilitation, Special Education, and Vocational Education

Category of Difference	Vocational Rehabilitation	Special Education	Vocational Education
Legislation	Rehab Act	IDEA	Perkins Act
Administration	Office of Special Education and Rehabilitative Services, Rehabilitation Services Administration	Office of Special Education and Rehabilitative Services, Office of Special Education Programs	Office of Vocational and Adult Education
Funding	75% federal, 25% state; no local funds	Federal, state, and local; largest share local and state	Federal, state, and local; largest share local and state
Eligibility	Disability, and potential to benefit	Disability, need for special education services	Attendance
Populations served	Adults and adolescents with disabilities	Persons with disabilities from birth through age 21	Adolescents and adults
Scope of services	Range of services for employment and independent living	Range of special education and related services	Vocational assessment, vocational instruction
Service mechanism	District vocational rehabilitation offices/rehabilitation counselors	Local school districts/special education teachers and related service personnel	Local school districts, Postsecondary programs/teachers, etc.
Evaluation	Numbers rehabilitated; percents with severe disabilities	Compliance with law; service in least restrictive environment	Number of students served
Personnel qualifications	Relevant education in counseling	Usually certified to teach	Usually certified to teach

Source: Adapted from Szymanski, E. M., Hanley-Maxwell, C., Asselin, S. B. Systems interface: Vocational rehabilitation, special education, and vocational education. In *Transition from school to adult Life: models, linkages, and policy* by Rusch, F. R., Destefano, L., Chadsey-Rusch, Phelps, L. A., Szymanski, E. (1992). Sycamore Publishing Company; Sycamore, IL. Reprinted with permission.

of emphasis on employment outcomes for special education.

Transition Disciplines

The process of collaboration in transition involves a variety of professionals from diverse fields and a number of "service delivery systems." The three concepts of field, professions, and systems are distinctive yet related. For example, concepts of field and professional identity correspond to a service system. A given field and professional identity (e.g., rehabilitation and rehabilitation counseling) are tied to a given service system (e.g., a federal-state program of rehabilitation).

The association between the field of study and the profession is also evident in special education and vocational education. Special education and special education teachers are concerned with the delivery of education to students with disabilities within a federal-state-local system of public and private schools. Vocational education and vocational education teachers are concerned with the delivery of specific occupational education to adults and high school students within a federal-state-local system in varied settings. The correspondence of services is the system interface, whereas the interaction of the professionals is an interdisciplinary process. Special education and rehabilitation and vocational education are described as the transition disciplines, with corresponding professional identities and scope of practice and service delivery systems.

Critical Point Three important transition disciplines are typically involved in transition planning for youth with disabilities: vocational education, special education, and rehabilitation.

Scope of Practice of Rehabilitation Counseling

Rehabilitation counselors have a field of study that is based in counseling practices and is applied to issues of instilling or restoring function and performance for persons with disabilities in major life activities. The federal-state vocational rehabilitation (VR) system provides services to eligible persons with disabilities to become employed and to live independently. Qualified rehabilitation counselors are the professionals who are at the direct service level in the VR system, however, rehabilitation counselors can apply their practice in any environment or programs where persons with disabilities are in the process of treatment, recovery, rehabilitation, integration, or reintegration into work and community roles.

Vocational educators have a field of study that is based on teaching occupational skill development and academics as they apply to particular vocational programs. Vocational educators also can provide a wealth of information, counseling, and assessments pertaining to careers, in addition to apprenticeships or other community-based work training. Vocational educators are concerned with addressing both social and work-related skills and behaviors, as well as the self-determination skills that are vital to the success of all students.

Scope of Practice of Vocational and Special Education

Secondary special educators have a field of study that is based on teaching individual students with disabilities specific skills, such as those involved in self-determination; social skills; learning strategies; and, where appropriate, academic content. They also must have an understanding of all the aspects involved in transition planning, including coordinating assessments, setting and evaluating IEP/ITP (individualized transition plan) goals and objectives, collaborating with the student, their families and communities, and other appropriate service providers, both within and outside the school, to ensure a smooth transition to adulthood.

Interdisciplinary Identity

Although professional identities for different professionals vary, they also share similarities in their scope of practice. Rehabilitation counselors and special educators both have expertise in disability, but special educators focus on instruction and school settings, whereas rehabilitation counselors focus on counseling and postschool settings. Given the overlap yet distinctive backgrounds and expertise, transition collaboration requires that all team members:

1. Can function in an interdisciplinary context
2. Are grounded in their own discipline (e.g., special education)
3. Can collaborate with other transition disciplines

An interdisciplinary transition identity requires that team members understand their own roles and contributions in relation to all other team members, whereas all members understand their own contribution to student transition development.

The professionals who work in the three transition systems are partly defined by the characteristics of the system in which they work. Vocational educators focus on occupational preparation; special educators emphasize transition skill instruction; and rehabilitation counselors use counseling and coordination as a primary means of delivering transition services. To promote movement toward student goals, the broad background and specialized skills appropriate to transition services must be applied in a team context in which all members speak the same language, share the same assumptions and beliefs, and draw from a common culture (Flexer, Simmons, & Tankersley, 1997).

Team Models

Transition is a process that calls for both a common frame of reference and some transition-specific aspects for assessment and planning with students and families. Interdisciplinary assessment and planning, called for in IDEA (Individuals with Disabilities Education Act), requires a communication process that generates common themes or topics that take into account unique perspectives. Stated another way, teamwork requires that the student and family-generated transition goals should be the common base from which professional contributions are made and communication takes place. It is also a set of rules by which contributions are noted and differences are resolved.

Everson and Guillory (1998) defined the concept of the collaborative interagency team as "a group of individuals representing multiple and diverse agencies and organizations who come together to address a common need and agree to pursue a common goal" (p. 301). Mattessich

Teamwork is critical for coordinated services.

and Monisey (1992) emphasized the importance of mutual goals, shared roles, joint ownership, and shared resources. For sharing to happen, the interactions and communication among team members require that they leave the comfort of their discipline or program/agency and make a commitment to teaching and learning with each other (Varney, 1989). All points of view should be represented in teamwork since each member has a unique contribution to make. Team development process is discussed later in the chapter.

An overview of team models used in the field illustrates these major points about teamwork. Table 4–2 provides an overview of the similarities and differences in types of teams. Multidisciplinary approaches are characterized by each professional discipline providing its assessments and recommended programs independent of each other. In the interdisciplinary model, team members provide contributions to the team based on their professional perspective by providing inputs regarding appropriate goals and services. This type of communication links each professional's assessments to a common goal and facilitates communication and synthesis of the information. However, individual professional recommendations are generally not linked to each other in service delivery.

In contrast, a transdisciplinary model includes all the aspects of multi- and interdiscipli-

TABLE 4–2

Comparison of Service Models

Multidisciplinary	Interdisciplinary	Transdisciplinary
Participation of the student is limited to a professional-student relationship.	*Participation* of the student is as a member of a team.	*Participation* of the student is as a member of a team.
Assessment is done or interpreted by the professional seeing the individual student.	*Assessment* is based on needs and preferences as seen by the student and each team member, including nonprofessionals.	*Assessment* is based on needs and preferences, as seen by the student and each team member, including nonprofessionals.
Planning is confined to organization of individual treatments provided by the professionals.	*Planning* is based on functional needs within professions, coordinated to obtain outcomes desired by the student and the family.	*Planning* is based on functional needs and preferences, across disciplines, in which activities are shared to obtain outcomes.
Implementation consists of a series of individual treatments.	*Implementation* consists of services and activities coordinated by the transition coordinator.	*Implementation* consists of services and activities collaboratively provided by professionals and team members.
Evaluation is based on progress in regard to year-to-year goals.	*Evaluation* is based on progress toward individual postsecondary goals set by the team and the student.	*Evaluation* is based on progress in achieving the student's total quality of life before and after graduation.

Source: Adapted from An interdisciplinary approach to rehabilitation, by R. P. Baer, G. Goebel, & R. W. Flexer. In R. W. Flexer & P. L. Solomon, *Psychiatric rehabilitation in practice.* Boston: Andover Publishers.

nary approaches with the added benefit that the programs for students share a commonality. The individualized plan is integrated and there is a sharing of program implementation among professions. As such, they are capable of crossing the boundary of their professional identity and of entering the domain of practice of other professionals. Transdisciplinary communication also requires that programs and services are integrated and reinforced, and support each other.

Critical Point   Typically, services to youth with disabilities are provided through a multidisciplinary approach, when interdisciplinary or transdisciplinary approaches might better meet their needs.

Role expansion and role release are the key concepts in understanding how teams achieve a high level of sharing and interdependence. As an

example, consider the roles of the vocational and special education teachers, the guidance counselor, and the rehabilitation counselor. The special education teacher could provide adapted instructional strategies to support performance as required in a vocational program taught by the vocational teacher. The rehabilitation counselor could assess the student in actual or simulated work environments, which could provide information on accommodated performance related to the vocational program. The guidance counselor could provide career assessments to determine if interests and abilities match the jobs and requirements that correspond to careers represented by occupations being prepared for in the vocational program. The level of sharing is such that the implementation of the vocational program is dependent on the expertise of the special education teacher and is necessary for the vocational teacher to instruct the student. The expertise of the guidance counselor and the rehabilitation counselor provides a validity check that shows how to accommodate for the vocational skills learned in the vocational program that will allow performance in the future available work/job environments.

Transition Roles

Transition Coordinator

The transition plan process and the coordinated set of activities suggest a role for transition coordination. *Transition coordination* requires that program development and monitoring be provided across all the components of the transition plan. Numerous individual team members and programs may be part of the transition plan. With so many players and programs, oversight and coordination are necessary in order to achieve consistency in program implementation. Kohler (1998) identified the need for a transition coordinator/specialist role. She argued that one person was needed to be responsible for linking the services and instruction with broader program issues of schools and community. The transition coordinator role provides a professional that fosters the collaboration, coordination, and communication discussed thus far.

Kohler (1998) further delineated the specific activities subsumed under the role of the transition coordinator/specialist. Under the categories of student-focused planning and student development, she emphasized the need for work experiences and referral to adult service agencies. The transition specialist has key responsibilities for coordinated planning and services, including chairing an interagency coordinating team and ensuring coordinated student assessments. The transition coordinator serves as the resource and training consultant for all team members including the family. Because transi-

tion goes well beyond activities in the classroom, the coordinator is required to keep the diverse activities of the team on a straight course regarding transition plans and schoolwide transition initiatives.

Critical Point The roles of transition coordinators transcend the typical role of the special education teacher and include collaboration and systems change activities.

Asselin, Todd-Allan, and deFur (1998) studied the activities of transition coordinators in Virginia. The outcome of that study corresponded very closely to the outcome of Kohler's study. The various responsibilities that transition staff reported are shown in Table 4–3. A perusal of the roles and responsibilities shows primary responsibilities as including: (1) development of individual student transition plans, (2) development of linkages both within and outside the school, (3) resource development, (4) evaluation, and (5) team education activities.

A transition coordinator role or function shows the major activities involved in developing a coordinated set of activities for students with disabilities. This role draws upon the strengths and contributions of each system and professional expertise for a coordinated effort to effect a meaningful array of transition services. The transition coordinator provides leadership to guide the team and the family/student to accomplish appropriate outcomes. The transition coordinator should be an individual who can organize and facilitate meetings, provide direction for transition programs, and be able to lead and train a variety of professionals in performing the respective aspects of their tasks.

Transition Collaborator Responsibilities

School collaborators are important for all the services and program options included in the student's transition plan. Staff involvement ranges from those who directly deliver instruction and services (e.g., teachers) to those who

TABLE 4–3

Transition Coordinator/Specialist Roles and Responsibilities

I. Intraschool Linkages
   A. Disseminate transition information.
   B. Present in-service training.
   C. Assist families.
   D. Facilitate communication between special education and vocational education teachers.
   E. Facilitate appropriate referrals to school-based programs.
   F. Provide technical assistance to school staff.
   G. Coordinate work/training activities with core content curriculum.

II. Interagency/Business Linkages
   A. Refer students with disabilities to DVR starting at age 16.
   B. Identify, establish, maintain linkages with community agencies (DVR, supported employment agencies), colleges, and businesses.
   C. Educate agencies/schools about programs and procedures.
   D. Facilitate referrals.

III. Assessment and Career Counseling
   A. Identify/refer students for vocational assessment.
   B. Facilitate implementation of recommendations from reports.
   C. Coordinate the development of career awareness and exploration activities as part of the career counseling process.
   D. Collaborate with guidance for student participation in career/job fairs.
   E. Oversee the development of postsecondary employment or training plans.

IV. Transition Planning
   A. Identify transition services provided by community agencies.
   B. Attend/participate in team and IEP/ITP meetings.
   C. Assist in planning/placement decisions.
   D. Help to identify appropriate assistive technology.
   E. Monitor adherence to federal laws.

V. Education and Community Training
   A. Promote self-advocacy.
      1. Develop activities.
      2. Coordinate training for special education teachers.
      3. Train students.
   B. Coordinate school and community work-based learning opportunities.
   C. Examine/identify postsecondary training and education options.
   D. Conduct various tours of employment/training options.

VI. Family Support and Resources
   A. Inform parents/families of community resources/services.
   B. Develop and provide parent training.
   C. Assist families in "navigating the system"/accessing services.
   D. Counsel parents regarding parent/student changing roles.

VII. Public Relations
   A. Disseminate information to employers/parents.
   B. Provide awareness events.
   C. Develop business partnerships (e.g., guest speakers, field trips, and mentorship programs).
   D. Promote work-based learning opportunities.

VIII. Program Evaluation
   A. Carry out needs assessment.
   B. Identify gaps in transition services.
   C. Conduct follow-up study on students who exit the program.
   D. Complete monthly/annual reports.

Source: From Asselin, S. B., Todd-Allen, M., & deFur, S. Transition coordinators: Define yourselves. *Teaching Exceptional Children,* January/February, 1998, 30(3), p. 14. Copyright 1998 by Council for Exceptional Children. Reprinted with permission.

are responsible for program development schoolwide (e.g., administrators). Various staff work together to meet all the transition needs at the high school level. DeFur and Patton (1999) describe the many areas of expertise within schools that are relevant to transition. They point out that the transition resources and expertise of school professionals often are overlooked because of the emphasis on interagency collaboration with adult services.

School-Based Programs and Services

High schools have evolved to be places where many diverse programs and services are delivered, and for transition programs, they have become integral to the successful delivery of services to students with disabilities (Wehman, 1992). Today, the school is a place for academics, recreation, athletics, and all sorts of programs that benefit students and society. In order to accomplish the broad goals of schools, school personnel need to demonstrate a diverse array of skills and expertise to enable effective program implementation. Transition from school to postschool environments has become one of those "hot-button" issues that schools have become responsible for implementing (Wehman, 1992). Transition involves a diverse array of issues and activities requiring skills and knowledge that a single individual cannot accomplish or demonstrate. Consequently, a significant level of division of labor is necessary when organizing the efforts to help students with disabilities from high school to post high school independence.

The roles that teachers play can vary widely depending on the school district and staffing issues within that district (deFur & Taymans, 1995). Syzmanski, Hanley-Maxwell, and Asselin (1992) have pointed out the various critical skills and roles that professionals should have in their repertoire in order to implement transition prac-

tices. Syzmanski et al. (1992) indicated that collaboration, professional role exchange, and other collaborative skills were critical for transition programs to succeed. Further, Foley and Mundschenck (1997) reported that secondary education professionals expressed that lack of collaboration with other professionals and knowledge about community-based services seems to detract from successful transition. An understanding of various roles and responsibilities of team members provides a foundation for determining school-based personnel's competencies and type of involvement in the implementation of transition services for students with disabilities.

Critical Point Secondary educators often lack knowledge of community services and collaboration strategies that are critical to transition.

Special Education Teacher

Because special education teachers work with students with disabilities on a day-to-day basis, they may understand the specific needs of individual students more completely than counselors, school administrators, or community service providers. Also, because special education teachers may provide team leadership, it is essential that they have an understanding of all the aspects of the transition process including community resources. In order to increase systematic transition planning for students with disabilities (June & Kelley, 1998), teachers are needed who are well-versed in these transition functions.

Integration of Students with Nondisabled Peers
Special education teachers need to work with content teachers in order to develop a plan for increasing the number of collaborative courses taught within the school. This is obviously based on individual student need as reflected in the IEP. However, often the best places for special education students to receive grade-level core-content concepts and socialization skills are in

Various educators work as a team in transition services.

the regular classroom where appropriate accommodations are provided. Teachers can further foster integration by:

- Scheduling students with disabilities in regular classes
- Assisting regular education teachers in understanding and implementing specially designed instruction
- Encouraging participation of students with disabilities in extracurricular and daily social/leisure activities.

Community-Based Education

Community-based education (CBE) allows a student to have hands-on experiences in (1) employment, (2) recreation/leisure, (3) postschool adult living, (4) community functioning (e.g., accessing community resources, such as medical, travel, safety, banking, etc.). Addressing these domains is important for students who have difficulty generalizing information. Furthermore, special education's responsibility is to develop appropriate community sites in these domains by assessing students' needs.

Drop-Out Prevention Activities

A team effort is needed to work with students who are at high risk of dropping out of school. "Dropping out" is not a single decision for stu-

dents; it is a process that grows over time as students move to the margins of the school environment and experience less and less success. Students who drop out are not able to complete their transition plans and leave school with little or no support in making a successful transition to adult life.

Two activities, specific to the teacher, are working with the student to improve his or her participation in class and community activities and facilitating the parents' involvement. Specifically, the special education teacher should:

1. Identify students at risk.
2. Increase parental involvement.
3. Provide for personal futures by planning meetings, when appropriate.
4. Provide support information to students, parents, and school personnel; provide weekly checks on emotional well-being, academic involvement, and attendance.
5. Create a positive reward system; provide social skills training for students to acquire and practice appropriate behavior.
6. Provide conflict prevention and resolution skills in the classroom and community work; refer students as needed to alternate programs offered by the school district and/or community agencies.
7. Connect students to a peer mentor or adult mentors.

Transition Planning

Special education teachers need to ensure that students with disabilities are provided career assessments by the eighth grade and again during sophomore and junior years. Career assessment centers may provide evaluations for regular education students and for students who have a "mild disability." Students with more significant cognitive disabilities require assessment through a functional approach that includes vocational, recreation, and community-related environments.

The special education teacher's responsibility is to explain the results of these assessments to students and parents. The information gained from these assessments should be embedded into the curriculum, helping students to explore all aspects of specific career interests, as well as to expand possible career choices. This can be done in a variety of ways, including (1) providing speakers from different career clusters, (2) taking students to potential job sites for job exploration, and (3) providing mentoring/shadowing experiences. If vocational or technical education is appropriate, the special education teacher has the responsibility to collaborate with the vocational and technical education teachers to develop accommodations and the specially designed instruction needed to help a particular student succeed.

Critical Point   Special educators need to work with other professionals to pull together the expertise to make transition planning successful.

As students move into the upper grades in high school, the special education teacher needs to take the lead in the discussion of postsecondary options and the required steps to get there. This starts by further developing student IEP/ITP goals for competitive or supported employment in integrated, community work environments and/or postsecondary education. To support this effort, the special education teacher should provide self-advocacy strategies needed for students to access successfully postsecondary education. Self-advocacy training can begin as early as the fifth grade (Wehmeyer, 1998).

Parent Involvement
Active parent involvement is a key component in addressing factors that relate to dropping out of school. Parents are often unsure of how to be involved in schools as their children get older. Although they may not show it, students want and need the support of their parents as they make decisions about their life after high school. Special education teachers can help parents to un-

derstand how important their involvement is and to provide strategies for staying involved. This should include:

1. Informing parents about conferences, workshops, speakers, and so on that help to inform parents of transition issues, services, and agencies
2. Providing information explaining transition; involving parents in transition planning throughout the year, including helping to complete their child's IEP/ITP
3. Teleconferencing with parents who are unable to attend meetings; inviting parents to observe student work sites and travel training in the community
4. Collaborating with parents and community agencies/resources to provide a smooth transition to postschool adult life.

Involving the Student in the Transition Process
The special education teacher is responsible for working with the other members of the transition team to develop an appropriate IEP and transition plans. This includes the most important collaborator: the student. Simply inviting the student to the IEP/ITP meeting is not enough. The special education teacher's responsibility is to help students develop self-advocacy strategies that enable them to become active participants in the transition process, including their own IEP/ITP meetings.

Involving students in planning and increasing their sense of responsibility for education and outcomes are among the most important tasks of the special education teacher. Wehmeyer (1998) suggested two methods of involving students in the transition process. First, students can be provided transition planning activities. Second, students may increase their involvement and advocacy for themselves within the transition planning and implementation process.

The transition team uses input from all team members, assessments, current progress data, parent and student surveys, career inventories, and/or functional vocational assessments to outline the student's present level of performance. With this information, the IEP team develops the student's ITP with appropriate goals and objectives listed on the IEP. The implementation of the IEP/ITP is the responsibility of all the participants listed, which can include special education teachers, academic and technical teachers, related service providers, adult service representatives, job trainers, counselors, and/or school administrators.

Critical Point   Student self-determination and family involvement are critical to student success after graduation.

Related Service Providers

There are many different kinds of related service professionals. Those involved in transition may include speech and language therapists, occupational therapists, physical therapists, assistive technology liaisons, orientation and mobility teachers, audiologists, interpreters, and rehabilitation counselors. In the past, many of these services have been provided as pull-out programs. As students become actively involved in the transition process, it is essential that the related service personnel work with students within the environments in which they will be living, working, and playing. People involved with a particular student must understand and support this method of instruction. For example, it is obvious that a student receiving speech therapy will benefit from learning how to be understood at his or her job site. A collaborative effort among the speech pathologist, the job trainer or special education teacher, and the employer may make the difference between a successful job placement and a failure.

Critical Point   Related service providers *must* become involved in transition planning and assess and provide interventions in a variety of student environments.

Related service providers form an integral part of the transition team, providing information on the

student's strengths, essential instruction in areas of need, and critical resources for overcoming the barriers that students with disabilities often encounter. The aforementioned related service providers are self-explanatory in terms of the types of services provided (e.g., speech therapy, i.e., a speech clinician providing interventions that are intended to improve the student's speech production).

However, increasingly incorporating interventions within school and community environments requires that activities performed are the base of the intervention. Services may be integrated into the setting in order to reduce the discrepancy of the student's performance with working peers or to allow learning to occur with little if any disruption to the daily work routine. Consequently, related services must be developed so that the intervention is easily implemented and effectively integrated into the teachers' or coworkers' daily routines.

Much of the input provided by related services personnel provided in the transition meeting will be consultative in nature. However, the related services specialists also may (1) provide services during times of the day that the student is away from the workplace; (2) provide technical assistance to the individual providing the one-on-one training to the student; or, in some circumstance, (3) on the job, demonstrate the necessary training techniques to the direct service provider or coworker. Any of the preceding strategies would have to be implemented based on the needs of the student and the availability or freedom in the workplace.

Academic and Technical Content Teachers

Content teachers (academic and technical) have the responsibility to work with special education teachers in order to provide students with disabilities content by using appropriate accommodations, such as the utilization of assistive technology, and/or specially designed instruction. This content, as required by the new IDEA

TABLE 4–4

Administrator Roles and Responsibilities

- Provide professional development training on transition, school to work, and available community resources for the special education department.
- Support collaboration among special education, academic, and vocational/technical teachers.
- Include in the master schedule career development courses that provide CBE/Co-op for credit for students with disabilities taking into consideration the need for extended time in the community.
- Encourage CBE certification of all special education teachers.
- Schedule students (i.e., special education and regular education) through technical exploratory rotations.
- Assure that staff incorporates transition planning throughout the student's high school career.
- Call parents to schedule IEP/ITP meetings in order to arrange a mutually agreed upon time.
- Provide student counseling to decrease drop-out rate.
- Provide flexible scheduling and support for students at risk of dropping out or reentering school.
- Assure that community agency representatives are invited to transition meetings.
- Meet with transition resource teacher regularly to monitor progress in transition planning for the school.

Source: From June, J., & Kelley, Y. (1998). *Quality indicators handbook.* Louisville, KY: Jefferson County Public Schools.

rules and guidelines, helps students to develop the skills required for them to live, work, and play as independently as possible in their transition into adult life. Content teachers working with students with disabilities should be active members of the student's transition team. By playing an active part in a student's transition meeting, content teachers will increase their understanding of transition and provide valuable insight into the student's strengths and abilities. They also bring a network of community resources that may provide a linkage necessary for the student's successful transition to adult life.

Administrators

School administrators are the leaders who set the tone in their building. In a research report, *Assessing the Impact of High School Restructuring in Kentucky*, the Kentucky Institute for Education Research reports, "principals are the most critical variable in the successful implementation of new ideas and innovations." Administrators provide the vision and support necessary to develop innovative programming for students with disabilities.

To facilitate the practice of state-of-the-art transition, administrators must create a positive environment and provide leadership. Review Table 4–4 for a listing of "actions" that are the responsibilities of administrators providing the vision of quality transition planning (June & Kelley, 1998).

Peter Senge (a noted author in the area of organizational theory and practice) suggests that effective organizations are those that learn (Senge, 1990). Furthermore, learning organizations are those entities that are effective in "Systems Thinking, Personal Mastery, Mental Models, Building a Shared Vision, and Team Learning." In general, these five components can be represented functionally by showing that the organization and all of its members develop a vision, develop methods for accomplishing this mission, maintain data on implementation variables, and make changes in procedures and practices to accomplish the joint vision (Senge, 1990).

Following this model, the building administrator must demonstrate integrative and leadership capabilities (Wehman & Revell, 1997). The principal should develop a process for jointly facilitating a philosophy and "tenor" for the school. Regularly scheduled meetings should occur that enable the staff to express their concerns and work on improved coordination and communication. School/teacher/staff professional development should evolve around the development of effective skills for the community. Extra planning time and in-service training should be provided that fosters the goals of transition. Further, data should be collected ascertaining accomplishments. Finally, changes should be implemented in practice that would support achieving outcomes of improved transition practice.

Critical Point   Regular educators, content specialists, and administrators must become involved in transition planning to assure student access to a desired course of study and required curriculum.

Public Sector Support Services Collaborators

The public sector (governmental agencies and not-for-profit community organizations) can provide a significant amount of assistance regarding the transition needs of students with disabilities. The primary agencies that should be considered in the transition process are:

1. The state departments of vocational rehabilitation
2. The Bureau of Employment Services
3. The job training partnership program (a subagency under the Workforce Development Act)
4. The regional adult mental retardation and developmental disabilities provider
5. The regional mental health provider

Federal/State Vocational Rehabilitation Program

The state agencies of vocational rehabilitation services are available throughout the United States and its territories. The program was originally developed in 1917 (as a result of the Smith-Hughes Act, P.L. 64-347) to address the employment needs of military personnel who acquired disabilities during World War I (Stodden, 1998). The agency evolved over the years and now provides services to all individuals with disabilities who are impaired enough to restrict their ability to be employed. Vocational rehabilitation (VR) agencies, which have different names in different states, are funded via federal and state dollars. At the federal level, the Rehabilitation Services Administration provides oversight and funding for all the state agencies. Furthermore, the federal agency provides these funds to states in a matching process in which the state must match approximately $25 for every $75 the federal VR agency provides to the state. The total amount that a state can receive is dependent on a number of factors, including population size, relative poverty rates, and other characteristics along with the total dollars offered by the state for the match. Some states do not "draw down" all their potential federal dollars because state VR programs do not offer enough state money for the match.

In general, Stodden (1998) has indicated that the VR legislation provided for the development of the following:

- Funding for rehabilitation, research, demonstration, and training projects
- Creation of programs for the recruitment and training of rehabilitation service providers
- Authorization of funds for vocational and rehabilitation programs for persons with disabilities
- A mandate that various public and private agencies and businesses provide affirmative action and accommodations for qualified persons with disabilities
- Development of individualized employment programs for all qualified participants

Acceptance for services from the state VR agency, as it is with almost all adult human service agencies, is not guaranteed. State VR agencies follow a process in which all applicants must meet specific criteria to be accepted for receiving services. These are (1) having a physical or mental disability that is expected to last longer than 12 months and (2) this disability results in a substantial impediment to becoming employed. In addition, since the state VR money is not able to serve all people with disabilities, the agency is required to develop a set of criteria which focuses on admitting those individuals with disabilities who are the most severe and who meet certain individualized state needs. This individualized differentiated criterion is called the "order of selection."

Critical Point Vocational rehabilitation providers may have differing definitions of disability and typically are only able to serve a fraction of the students who are eligible for services.

In general, counselors who oversee the provision of services represent the VR agency. The VR counselor conducts interviews, helps to develop an individual plan of employment, provides oversight of financial expenditures for services, and provides counseling. The VR agency provides a variety of services. Although VR and the VR counselor operate differently in each state, the services that are offered and coordinated by the counselor include vocational assessments, career/rehabilitation counseling, job preparation activities, job development, assistive technology and devices, follow-up services, and postemployment services. Other services that a counselor may coordinate include driver's license training, college tuition, and treatment for physical or mental health issues. In coordinating these services, the VR counselor must assure that the services provided be related to an eventual outcome of improving the likelihood of employment.

In accessing VR services, the counselor facilitates the referral process of the individual with a disability. This can take place by either self-referral or another individual. In any case, the individual with the disability (or his or her legal representative) must work with the counselor in completing an application, participating in testing, and transmitting necessary documentation of the disability. The primary method for acquiring the services once accepted for participation is through the development of the Individualized Plan for Employment (IPE). This is coauthored by a VR counselor and the individual.

To enable the VR system to work effectively with the public school, school personnel should make initial contacts, indicating the need for their (the VR agency's personnel) participation. Generally, VR has indicated that 2 years prior to graduation is an optimal time for contact and referral. This contact, however, changes based on the severity and the rehabilitation needs of the individual. In some cases, a VR counselor may not be able to participate in every IEP meeting where transition services are discussed. However, the VR counselor should be able to participate via providing written recommendation, verbal communication to the IEP team leader, or in some other manner.

Critical Point Due to large caseloads carried by vocational rehabilitation counselors, it is important to use their time wisely and to use flexible means for them to provide input.

The VR agency and counselor should be able to make available a significant amount of help in meeting the employment needs of the individual and in many cases providing primary resources for achieving the eventual job outcome. As was indicated, the VR counselor is able to provide many resources in order to help the individual attain employment. In most cases, the transition services provided to the individual with a disability are purchased by the VR agency. Consequently, there will be a need to involve the services and professional(s) purchased by the VR counselor to train or facilitate the career development activities of students with disabilities.

Federal/State Employment Training

Another agency that should be included in the development of transition programs regarding employment is the particular state's employment and training programs (ETP). The federal conduit for this agency is the U.S. Department of Labor (DOL). Again, this agency exists in every state and is titled differently depending on the state. The federal and state agencies generally have oversight of the country's labor laws regarding health and safety, equal employment, labor relations, and employee benefits along with assisting in the job-seeking process. Each state's employment and training system is designed to assist all people who are unemployed to become employed. As with the VR agency, an individual can access the ETP agency's services through a counselor. Employment service counselors are generally able to provide résumé development assistance and job leads. The counselors also may provide access to testing services and other training programs depending on how the services have evolved within the state. The counselor generally does participate in transition meetings. They will, however, work with the VR counselor to coordinate employment-related benefits, such as targeted jobs tax credits (to be described in a later chapter), and other incentives that might facilitate employers hiring individuals with disabilities.

The former Job Training Partnership Act (JTPA) agencies within each community are another employment service provider. JTPA is now an agency generally subordinate to the Workforce Development Act agency. The JTPA programs are still being offered; however, in most locations, they are now called workforce services, career one-stop shops, or some other related term. In any event, the services that can be accessed are those that should be taken advantage of when planning for the development of transition services.

JTPA programs are typically focused on providing services to persons with low socioeconomic status or those who are too disadvantaged to become employed. As with the other agencies, a counselor is the conduit by which services are acquired. The services provided range from skill training to employment readiness training and

General Equivalency Diploma (GED) training. In general, the agency functions much like the VR programs in that they fund other agencies or programs that provide those needed services. The general method of distributing funds is through grants to existing agencies or service providers. The potential grantee must submit a proposal that substantiates the need and validates the proposed method. In many cases, the grantee is reimbursed for services rendered or for the accomplishment of their proposed objectives. These same agencies may still operate in communities but under the authority of the Workforce Investment Act.

Critical Point   Employment training programs typically focus on students and adults from low-income families but may serve students with disabilities under some conditions.

Long-Term Support Agencies

Final groups of agencies that are potential collaborators in the transition process include regional mental health and developmental disability (MH/DD) service providers. These two agencies will be covered together because in many locations the agencies are one and the same. Additionally, the two agencies are funded and function, in most cases, in the same manner. The state and regional MH/DD agencies generally receive money from both state and federal funds. In some states, the MH/DD agencies have the authority to collect local taxes. Each agency has a target population for which the agency must provide services and specific guidelines for determining an individual's eligibility. In any case, these agencies are generally not-for-profit. They function by either providing community services or funding other not-for-profit agencies to perform these duties.

In recent years, MH/DD agencies contracted with managed care agencies to provide mental and physical health services to qualifying clients. The types of services that are funded by MH/DD programs include (but are not limited to) employment programs, a range of independent to more closely supervised living programs, case management, counseling and advocacy programs, physical or mental health services, and, potentially, legal assistance. Furthermore, the services that are provided to the eligible participants of the MH/DD agencies can be provided from the moment of eligibility until noneligibility or death. Consequently, a student may have been receiving services since birth.

The MH agency generally deals with people who have significant and persistent mental health problems, such as obsessive-compulsive disorder, schizophrenia, bipolar disorder, and so on. The participants of which the services are provided or funded by the MH agency are usually diagnosed with such disorders by a medical doctor or a psychiatrist and are provided services based on their needs. The range of transition services that would be provided by the MH agency would be case management, housing/independent living, job placement or employment programs, and counseling/drug management services.

The student with mental health issues should have a counselor/case manager assigned to him or her. This individual should participate in the planning of his or her transition services. One could expect that the case manager would participate in most if not the entire IEP/ITP meeting. Additionally, the case manager should provide liaison services with other agencies such as VR or JTPA. The case manager has broad responsibilities with regard to the student with mental health issues. However, the case manager does not have legal guardianship or any specific ability to cause or force the student to perform certain activities. The services that are provided by the MH agency, and additionally for the DD agency, are generally voluntary. In any case, if the student has potential mental health problems, the local MH agency should be contacted and a request made to include a representative who is involved with the student's mental health services.

Critical Point   Mental health agencies typically provide services through the counselor or mental health professional who is providing mental health services.

The DD agency operates much like the MH agency. Eligibility is determined through a variety of assessments, however, the primary determination of eligibility is whether the student has significant impairments in three or more of the seven major life activities (e.g., communication, independent living, employment, self-direction, mobility, learning, and self-care). These disabilities should be the result of a physical or mental impairment that occurred before age 22 and are expected to continue indefinitely (Beirne-Smith, Ittenbach, & Patton, 1998). The DD agency is responsible for determining eligibility and should be an active participant in determining goals and services. In many cases, the DD agency will have supported employment programs and/or will provide ongoing support services to enable access to funding from VR for supported employment. Other services that the DD agency may provide or coordinate are independent living, group homes, and so on. Historically, DD agencies ran or, at the very least, funded sheltered employment programs. Thus, for individuals whose families truly want a sheltered employment setting, the DD agency is usually the agency to contact.

Both the MH and DD agencies should be contacted as soon as the school is aware or considers that the student should be eligible for either agency's services. Remember that persons who have a behavior disorder do not necessarily qualify for MH services. Additionally, eligibility for both these programs is limited and the majority of the students served by special education (i.e., students with learning disabilities and many with behavior disorders) do not qualify. School representatives can improve the chances of a student's acceptance by providing full documentation of the student's disabilities and behavioral tendencies when a release of information is requested by the MH/DD agency. Additionally, any classroom behavioral notes or intervention data also may be useful.

Critical Point   Developmental disability (DD) agencies typically serve students with the most severe disabilities although some services (e.g., case management) may be available to students and adults with milder developmental disabilities.

Postschool Education and Training Service Collaborators

Collaborators from postsecondary programs include people from vocational/technical schools, community colleges, and universities (Gajar, 1998). Training services collaborators could include apprentice programs provided by unions or trade associations and job-readiness training programs. Based on the student's interests and preferences, the placement and IEP teams are the ones to decide which, if any, of these programs will meet the needs of the student. The next step is to allow the student and his or her parents to explore the opportunities and requirements that appropriate programs can provide. This can be done by building the exploration into the student's curriculum, building self-advocacy skills and having the student and parents begin making contacts with postschool collaborators, and/or by inviting these collaborators to the next transition planning meeting.

Critical Point   Postsecondary education and training programs should be involved in the development of transition programs at schools and, in some cases, be invited to individual IEP meetings.

All postsecondary institutions receiving federal funds must provide services and accommodations for students with disabilities (Osborne, 1996). Many community colleges and universities have disability centers that provide these services. However, a major difference exists between the services provided at the high school level and those provided in colleges and universities. In most cases, the postsecondary education institution does not provide services unless the service is requested.

There is a need for students with disabilities to be able to ask for accommodations. To assure that the student with a disability is capable of maintaining academic performance, the student must demonstrate a significant amount of independence and assertiveness. Thus, after high school, the student should be able (1) to contact the postsecondary institution's office of disability services, (2) to provide appropriate documentation (usually the latest psychological tests and/or IEP), (3) to maintain records that certify the student's disability and his or her needed accommodations, and (4) to advocate for oneself. Obviously, in order for students with disabilities to be successful at the college and university level, they must have strong self-advocacy strategies and skills. The special education teacher begins to build these skills as early as elementary school. If students with disabilities leave high school without strong self-advocacy skills, the chances of their success in all aspects of adult life are greatly diminished.

Critical Point   Students with disabilities need to learn to advocate for themselves before they leave high school because after graduation, unless the students ask for services, there is no requirement to provide them.

Case Study of an Interagency Agreement

The training of students with disabilities in high school can begin with postsecondary education and training programs while the student is still in high school. Developing such a program takes creativity and planning for the collaborators from each of the institutions involved. An example of such a program is the Steps Toward Educational Progress (STEP) project in Louisville, KY (Simmons, 1996). People with disabilities are now working in all kinds of businesses, receiving at least minimum wage and often higher. This change has come from the support of job trainers, as well as employment agencies. However, planning for these transition supports must start early. As students, parents, and teachers begin to map out future employment goals, it is essential that collaborators from agencies providing support after high school should be active participants in the transition planning process. Together this team delineates the skills needed in the future and begins to build them into the goals and objectives of the student's IEP/ITP. In order to achieve these goals and objectives, additional support may be required.

In the state of Kentucky, the collaboration between the Department of Vocational Rehabilitation (DVR) and local school districts has developed a program entitled the community-based work transition program (CBWTP). The program is collaboratively funded by DVR and local school districts. The schools that opt into the program must provide a 25% match to draw down the 75% VR dollars. The CBWTP provides job trainers for students during their last 2 years in school. Job trainers work with local school staff in assessing each student's interests and in placing each student in several different evaluation sites. This gives the student and job trainer an opportunity to see actually what the requirements of specific jobs are compared with the student's individual interests and abilities. After determining an appropriate job match by the student, parent, special education teacher, job trainer, rehabilitation counselor, and employer, the student is placed in the job and the training component of the CBWTP begins. The goal of this program is for the student to be placed in a permanent job by the time he or she graduates from high school. This level of support is required for many students to be successful after they leave high school.

For other students, additional supports are needed. This is often provided through supported employment agencies. Job coaches or trainers provide ongoing long-term support. These agencies work with employers either to provide additional support required for success in jobs currently available or to help "carve out"

a job to meet the specific needs of the client while still filling a need of the business. The goal of supported employment agencies is to find a good match between the client and the job that allows the job coach to pull away slowly while building as much independence as possible for the client.

However, some people with the most severe disabilities require even more support. A few school districts around the country have risen to this challenge, developing community-training programs for students. The difficulty with these programs is developing long-term plans that will support the student throughout the student's adult life. Few supported employment agencies have the necessary resources to support people with significant levels of support. At this level, support requires a strong collaborative effort.

Collaboration and Group Process

Collaboration and team development are critical to the development of appropriate transition services for youth with disabilities (Baer, Simmons, Flexer, & Martonyi, 1994). Transition team members must be familiar with methods of facilitating various group activities and individual discipline contributions. Improving transition services and outcomes for youth with disabilities are dependent on the members functioning as a team. Effective transition collaboration has its foundation in the ability of groups to work effectively together (Everson & Guillory, 1998).

Smith, Belcher, and Juhrs (1995) describe an example of a highly collaborative and coordinated program in their book, A *Guide to Successful Employment for Individuals with Autism*. Various activities are required to support a person with severe impairments in an employment setting, and integral to this process is the development of collaborative activities with employers, coworkers, and families. While Smith et al. (1995) describe a program for adults with autism, the same collaborative issues face all students with severe disabilities who are preparing for transition from school to postschool environments. Hughes et al. (1998a) also supported this emphasis on collaboration in her review of transition practices for youth with disabilities.

In order to achieve effective team efforts, Baer, Goebel, and Flexer (1993) and Everson and Guillory (1998) cite effective strategies to effect organizing structures of teams by utilizing effective team management. Baer et al. (1993) have indicated that the "key concepts behind developing the individual's plan are participant-defined preferences (team development), appropriate goals (leadership and participation), and discipline contributions (group dynamics)" (p. 68). Critical to the development of professional contributions and appropriate outcome development is the need to follow and understand the "proper functions of a team, state of team development, and group dynamics" (Baer et al., 1993).

Critical Point Transition coordinators need group process skills to facilitate collaboration among transition stakeholders.

Although proper team functioning can vary from one team to another, certainly the ideal outcome for transition planning is the facilitation of a successful transition of the student with a disability. Baer et al. (1993) suggest that a significant level of ambiguity can exist when team members represent a variety of perspectives and professional groups. Further, because not all team members may support the successful transition of the student as their utmost focus, team members may be performing the function of a "foil" within the process. In general, however, the team approach provides for facilitating a broader array of ideas and coordinated activities that are of greater benefit than planning individually (Baer et al., 1993; Everson & Guillory, 1998). Three interlocking aspects of team life are needed: gaining a sense of shared responsibility, moving toward consensus, and harnessing the team's resources to solve a problem (Baer et al., 1993).

Stages of Team Development

Tuckman and Jenson (1977) assert that all groups go through five predictable stages of development: forming, storming, norming, performing, and adjourning. The initial stage, *forming*, involves all the initial aspects of uncertainty and uneasiness of getting to know unfamiliar people. Within that process, the individual is exploring personalities, organizing and confirming membership (Everson & Guillory, 1998). Although the forming stage could take a varying length of time, Everson and Rachal (1996) found that this stage required approximately four meetings to finalize.

Following the initial forming stage, the team begins the storming phase in which the team reacts to the task (Baer et al., 1993). In the *storming* stage, the team commences to question the reality of the situation and asks a variety of questions surrounding the issue of authority, task appropriateness, values, procedures, and so on. In some respect, the storming phase provides for a significant level of dissonance that can lead to the bonding and formational structure for the next stage of development.

Critical Point Team process develops in five stages: forming, storming, norming, performing, and adjourning.

The *norming* stage is marked by the development of a mission or structure for accomplishing a task (Everson & Guillory, 1998). Within this stage, the participants develop guidelines and strategies to accomplish the outcome. During the *performing* stage, the team members implement, monitor, and evaluate the team's effectiveness (Everson, & Guillory, 1998). Further, the team members should be developing alternative strategies for accomplishing the task confronting them. Finally, Tuckman and Jensen (1977) indicate that *adjourning* is the next and final stage of team development. During this stage, the team focuses on the accomplished tasks and a reorientation to differing relationships and participants begin to focus on other activities that they must accomplish.

Baer et al. (1993) stress that forming the team and focusing on the task are two pillars of team success. The majority of energy should be centered on these two activities. Furthermore, Baer and his colleagues suggest that each member of the team has different responsibilities and the members must maintain focusing on the outcomes at hand. Baer et al. (1993) also suggest that, "Team members who have an understanding of the tasks of the team, and who are comfortable with its interpersonal context, are now able to improvise both individually and as a group" (p. 73).

Team Decision Making

In every team, there must be a leader with others providing support and resources to enable the tasks to be achieved. The transition team consists of several different members who have different perspectives and approaches. With differing viewpoints, a potential exists for conflict and focus on attaining different outcomes. The team must learn how to develop a consensus that meets the individual's needs and preferences. This consensus should be obtained by functionally addressing these differences. Leadership is necessary to address these many obstacles. Baer and his colleagues suggest that leadership must be provided by someone who not only has been accepted in a leadership role but who also has the knowledge and understanding to facilitate the overall effectiveness of the team (Baer et al., 1993).

The degree of involvement in team decision making contributes to the individual team member's commitment regarding the implementation of the activities (Baer et al., 1993). Such things as member's contributions and participation are factors that improve the likelihood that each member understands and executes expected tasks.

Whoever leads the team also is a factor regarding the follow-through of activities (Baer et al., 1993). Due to their expertise or status, leaders are strong influences on group behavior (Thibaut & Kelley, 1959). In fact, the perception of knowledge or understanding can motivate team membership to achieve goals (Everson & Rachal, 1996). Everson and Rachal (1996) found that if the student with the disability and his family lead the team, the team would be more likely to achieve change.

Critical Point   For every team, issues such as leadership, time of involvement, and skill of the team members affect the outcome.

Additional Aspects of Group Dynamics

One should be aware of more than the role aspect of team membership to understand group dynamics. Members participate based on their ability to contribute and their understanding of the goals of the team. However, other issues related to sharing information or the methods utilized in making decisions are just as important as understanding leadership (Baer et al., 1993). Strategies such as *clarifying, questioning, restating, summarizing,* or *questioning* may be used to facilitate the team process.

Other issues may arise regarding various roles that different members may take. Some examples of roles include:

- Energizer (someone who attempts to motivate others), aggressor (someone who may be overly motivated to finish the task)
- Self-confessor (someone who expresses personal problems within the meeting)
- Recognition-seeker (someone who may exaggerate or express themselves too long), dominator (someone who interrupts or controls the meeting)
- Blocker (someone who disagrees with everything) (Baer et al., 1993).

One or more members of the team may assume each of these roles. The membership may assume different roles within the same meeting or series of meetings. The participants or leader must recognize these different roles and facilitate the situation to enable positive outcomes to be accomplished.

Critical Point   Various team roles may interfere or support the development of a successful conclusion to a team outcome.

Transition Team Processes

It is essential that the transition team develop a complete understanding of the student's life with respect to the student's needs, interests, and preferences. Further, individual team members can have a significant role in developing a knowledge base that helps to identify goals and steps in order to achieve them. The four *essential elements* indicate how agencies, their personnel, and school staff can help to develop transition services within a team context.

Students' Needs, Interests, and Preferences

Transition teams need to start the planning process from the point of view of the student and his or her family and the vision that he or she has. Needs, interests, and preferences of individual students can be relatively simple or very complex depending on the accommodations indicated by the disability and the intensity and scope of supports available from friends, family, and professionals. Getting a true understanding of a student's needs, interests, and preferences begins by obtaining information from the student, the family, friends, educators, and community service providers involved in the student's life. All team members have information, experience, or perspectives that will shed some light on the needs, interests, and preferences of the individual. In order to gain a full knowledge of the possibilities of a student's future, it may be necessary to contact other community agencies such as recreation groups with programs that provide services presently. In addition, neighbors or friends may be able to provide insights into the student's functional skills and community environments. Pulling these pieces together begins to "paint the picture" of the individual needs of a particular student. Omitting any one of these pieces or viewing them separately will give a limited view of a student's future possibilities.

Critical Point   The transition coordinator must be able to bring leadership and group process skills to assure that transition teams focus on the postsecondary goals rather than on the limitations of individual students.

When transition is under discussion, the student should always be an active participant in the team process. It is essential that the transition team develop the individual transition plan with the student and his or her family based on the student's interests and preferences. Students and families should be involved in the selection and interpretation of vocational and career assessments. Career inventories, functional vocational assessments, surveys, interviews, data collected from the classroom, job sites, and community-based instruction reflect upon interests when they have direct meaning to the student and the family. Within the transition process, a variety of agencies or school programs may be able to pay for or facilitate job shadowing, to coordinate a volunteer job, or even to provide paid experiences to improve outcomes in employment. A group of team members might pull together to provide facilities and programs for independent living. The parents may be able to provide facilitation of obtaining driver's training or other legal aspects of the transition process. The best conceived transition plan would fail if the student and his or her family have not been actively involved in its development with the student's interests and preferences acting as a guide every step of the way. In the final analysis, many agencies and professionals may be involved in facilitating effective transition programs and services.

Outcome-Oriented Process

The foundation for many skills in achieving independence begins developing at a very young age. With transition goals and objectives building on one another, previous goals and activities determine how successful the student will be at achieving the next steps in the transition process. Each collaborator plays an important part in this process and the team members' responsibility is to make sure that the outcomes are achieved. Collaborators within this process should provide an accurate picture of required adult and real-world skills and needed outcomes. Further, although vocational training and employment are considered important, we must not exclude the domains of community participation and postsecondary education (Grigal, Test, Beattie, & Wood, 1997).

Interagency Responsibilities and Linkages

The responsibilities of collaborating agencies and school programs in this process can vary widely. As the student progresses through the transition process, the student's transition planning team is required to consider if interagency linkages are required, which agencies should be involved, and when these linkages should be created. Potential collaborating agencies should be invited to transition planning meetings to discuss the ITP and how the individual agency can help to meet the specific needs of the student. This should be documented on the IEP/ITP. Further, if in fact an agency is not providing what the agency had indicated it would provide, the ITP team must reconvene and determine the degree to which the outcome is important and, depending on the importance, determine other methods for achieving the goal or activity. This could mean polling the members of the team, asking for other strategies or other resources. For instance, parents may be able to pay for or facilitate the driver's education training if the school or agency has dropped the class. In any event, the team should redress the issues that were stated in the ITP but are not being achieved.

Movement from School to Postschool Activities

A collaborative effort between all people involved in a student's life (e.g., the student, family, friends, secondary and postsecondary educators, and community service agencies) is essential at this critical point in the transition process. This is a process, however, not a senior year activity. This collaborative effort will not work if it has not evolved over a period of time. The team should build upon a variety of group and process-oriented practices to facilitate the development of postsecondary outcomes (Baer, Simmons, & Flexer, 1996). The focus of the team should be on the student's development and awareness of needed skills, the parents' understanding of those skills, the student's and parents' ability to access community resources, the ability to self-advocate for the student's needs, and the development of relationships with key people in community agencies. If the preceding components are present, along with a well-developed and implemented transition plan that has been outcome based, focusing on the student's needs, interests, and preferences, with active interagency involvement, then the transition from school to postschool activities will be smooth and successful.

Conclusion

A variety of professionals and agencies may be involved in transition planning and services. Each member of the transition team has unique expertise and professional skills that can be applied in the transition process. School-based collaborators need to work together so that education and transition services are effective and relate to the student's goals. General, vocational, career, and transition curricula are delivered in a coordinated manner in high school programs by special, related services, vocational, and regular educators with the support of administrators. Postschool collaborators are involved in the transition process for their contributions regarding future environments. When they contribute to the knowledge of future participation and goal development, they are in a position to provide continuity and to take satisfaction when students achieve the transition to postschool activities. Of utmost importance is that resources of team members should be brought out in support of the student-family determined goals. To accomplish this, the team members must apply their energies in a consistent direction and in a coordinated manner. The team process applied to develop the goal consensus is a prerequisite to transition services that promote movement toward student goals. Knowing the contributions and roles of each team member is necessary for all team members by allowing a given team member to make his or her own contribution consistent with other team members. Skills of team membership and, in some cases, team leadership, is requisite for team cohesion: the process underlying goal consensus and productive team interactions.

Study Questions

1. Who should be involved in the ITP team? Name at least five examples.
2. What is accomplished during the norming stage of the group process?
3. What types of services can a person with a disability receive from a vocational rehabilitation counselor?
4. What is the final phase of groups and what should one do or facilitate within this phase?
5. At what point should a student be referred to adult services?
6. How should related services be included in the transition programming for students with disabilities?
7. Is employment the only goal on which the team should focus regarding postsecondary settings?
8. What are the skills that the transition facilitator should exhibit?
9. How can the building administrator of a school facilitate or hinder transition practices?
10. What are some of the components of a learning organization?

5

Multicultural Competence in Transition Planning Processes

Pamela Luft

The objectives for this chapter are:

1. Describe at least two major reasons that transition team members can expect to work with culturally different families and students.

2. Describe some of the major differences between identified U.S./American beliefs and values and minority group beliefs and values in the areas of worldview, personal identity, disability, and relationships.

3. Describe how cultural differences between team members may impact team processes for identifying and addressing the student's needs, interests, and preferences in the transition process.

4. Describe cultural differences that impact goal-setting and outcome-oriented processes of transition planning, including movement from school to postschool activities.

5. Describe potential conflicts in developing participatory decision making with families who are not acculturated into the American interaction style (e.g., represent culturally different groups) and culturally competent and appropriate approaches to support such decision making.

6. Describe strategies for preparing staff and families in culturally competent interaction processes.

This chapter addresses the impact of cultural difference between families and other transition team members. Many legal mandates and transition components described in Chapter 1 are based on American cultural beliefs about disability, optimal outcomes for all people, and how best to achieve these outcomes. These are not shared by all cultures, thereby impacting some of the basic precepts of transition planning.

This chapter builds upon the foundations of transition described in the first four chapters. Transition legislation and historical processes represent accomplishments supported by the majority of American society. For those who do not represent this sector of society, these accomplishments often have unanticipated and less positive impacts. Many transition models and the systems organized within schools and agencies to provide these services and models do not assist personnel in recognizing and addressing the unique needs and concerns of these families and children. Theoretical frameworks in career development and transition often underrepresent minority and diverse ethnic groups.

The overview section describes the four essential elements and related concepts of transition in terms of potential cultural differences. The next section describes patterns of special education placement and population demographics of the United States that make it likely that transition team members will work with families who are culturally different from themselves. This multicultural perspective will be important for later chapters that describe these services in more detail, including career and vocational planning (Chapter 6), transition assessment (Chapter 7), curriculum development (Chapter 8), and instruction (Chapter 9), as well as the later sections of the book that describe programs and their implementation. This chapter then continues with a description of key values and beliefs of several major cultural groups and contrasting values that may present barriers to effective transition planning and delivery of

services. The chapter concludes with suggestions for training personnel and parents and for effective cross-cultural team interactions.

Overview of Culture

Our Diverse Country

The United States has been the home of immigrant peoples from around the world since its inception. The Statue of Liberty serves as a symbol of this welcome to people across the globe. The United States often prides itself on being an international refuge and a great "melting pot" of these diverse cultures and ethnicities, embracing these differences as contributing to the strength of its citizens and its mission (DeVillar, 1994; Hanson, 1998a). However, it is an ongoing challenge to meet this national ideal, requiring tolerance and understanding in order to live harmoniously together. Creating a united nation of citizens from a mixture of many different people, cultures, and ethnicities has not always succeeded. Episodes of ethnic violence and intolerance that erupt periodically are not easily resolved.

The difficulties of cultural pluralism and tolerance for diversity arise from our nature as people: We have an instinctive preference for cultural homogeneity in our daily lives (Brislin, 1993; Green, 1999). We wish to be with, and interact with, others who are like us: They make us feel comfortable, we understand them, and we associate easily because they share our general lifestyle and beliefs. Our national ideals for diversity can create both personal and professional conflicts; often it becomes a struggle to understand and interact with people who may have significantly different practices and beliefs from our own. As the United States continues to become increasingly diverse, we have an increased likelihood of working with and living near those who are culturally different from ourselves. Learning about these differences and how we may better mediate between our own beliefs and those that are highly dissimilar will help us to become more personally comfortable and understanding. In addition, as professionals we have an obligation to provide quality services to all our students, families, and clients. Often we are most effective with those who are culturally similar to ourselves. Becoming culturally competent will allow us to provide better services to everyone.

The difficulty with learning about culture is that it remains largely invisible. Culture consists of the "ideals, values, and assumptions about life that are widely shared among people and that guide specific behaviors" (Brislin, 1993, p. 4). However, ideals and assumptions remain largely internalized until called upon to guide their behavior. When values are not challenged, there are no visible behaviors that lead us to think about or remember the value. For example, cleanliness and personal hygiene habits generally are not an issue in our daily life until challenged by a person who, through physical appearance or smell, does not meet expected cultural standards (Brislin, 1993). At that point, the typical response is to "protect" the cultural value and to reaffirm how important it is; in this case, how much "better" people are when they practice regular and thorough hygiene (e.g., they will experience negative consequences at work, socially, to their health, etc.).

Critical Point: Our own cultural beliefs and values are generally invisible to us until they are challenged.

Another difficulty with examining culture is that we are socialized into our culture as children, guided into a particular set of behaviors and beliefs without considering them (Brislin, 1993; Lewis, 1997). The early nature of these experiences make it difficult to distance ourselves enough to analyze them. People who share the same culture also rarely discuss their values and assumptions, adding to their hidden nature. For example, only when democratic processes are challenged or struggling (as in the violence in East Timor after voting to become independent)

might Americans discuss related cultural values and assumptions within the United States that appear *not* to be present in Indonesia, and that represent a functioning democracy.

The hidden and deeply internalized nature of culture creates difficulties for us as transition team members working with families and students who are culturally different from ourselves. When a cross-cultural interaction becomes unsatisfactory, our own cultural values usually are not obvious enough to state them clearly and to ask the other person to do the same, in an effort to begin negotiating a mutual compromise. In fact, people often find violations of their culture to be emotionally upsetting and remember them vividly (Brislin, 1993).

Learning about cultural differences has been found to decrease negative emotional responses and discomfort when faced with a culturally conflicting situation. Families and clients also are able to sense that we are working to create a comfortable and positive interaction climate (Brislin, 1993). Cross-cultural knowledge and skills allow us to feel more relaxed in these situations and better able to establish open and trusting relationships with culturally different families, leading to more collaborative interactions and effective transition planning for all team members.

American Cultural Forces

Learning about culture is accomplished through socialization, and society plays an important part in determining and guiding this process. Societies, by nature, impact how interactions are structured and certain processes or tasks are organized (e.g., making decisions and solving problems) (Brislin, 1993; Lewis, 1997). This organization usually results in allowing more power to a few individuals who assume leadership roles, creating differences in personal status. Status differences are, thus, a normal aspect of social interaction between people. These differences also occur whenever members of two cultural groups meet: One culture will dominate, resulting in a high-status versus lower-status interaction (Althen, 1988; Green, 1999; Hanson; 1998a). Maintaining equality between diverse people and diverse cultures is not typical of societies. Those individuals who better represent the leadership characteristics of the dominant culture are accorded increased status and social power. As a result, they are likely to have increased opportunities for achievement and success.

Because of the U.S'. diverse immigrant background, one might assume that there is no single set of cultural beliefs and values that predominate and that relationships between people could, therefore, be more equalized than in other countries. The United States does provide unique opportunities for change in social status and is less socially structured than several other countries (Brislin, 1993). However, researchers have indeed identified a mainstream culture that has evolved with time and which predominates over most of the business and governing functions of this country (Brookhiser, 1991; Dunn & Griggs, 1995; Green, 1999; Hammond & Morrison, 1996; Hanson, 1998a; Harry, 1992a; Hobbs, 1975; McPhatter, 1997; Pinderhughes, 1995). Many of these beliefs and values were brought to the United States with the pilgrim and Protestant immigrants, and impacted by pioneer movements into the largely unknown territories. These beliefs are reflected in a number of national expectations, including hard work, personal independence, self-reliance, delaying gratification (i.e., work first and play later), efficient use of time and energy (i.e., being on time, not wasting time or energy), as well as direct discussion of problems and efficient problem solving, and moral and honest interpersonal behavior.

Today, the predominant ideas, values, and standards for behaviors within American culture are primarily reflected in the lifestyle of the white, middle and upper-middle class (Althen, 1988; Dunn & Griggs, 1995; Green, 1999; Hanson,

1998a; Harry, 1992a; McPhatter, 1997; Pinderhughes, 1995). The middle class holds the majority of powerful positions in this country and uses its class-based power to influence these processes: Its tax base supports the country; it lobbies for changes in laws; it serves on public school boards, which decide curriculum and teaching practices; it provides the majority of civil servants, such as police, teachers, government workers, and so on. The more we subscribe to, or represent these values, the more easily we are able to assume important social or governing roles in this country. Individuals who are perceived as being "different" and not subscribing to these values usually have much greater difficulty in achieving equal levels of social and other power. For example, parents who are middle or upper-middle class have been found to be more successful in creating genuinely individualized IEPs for their child that represent a broader range of options than typically made available to minority and lower- or working-class parents (Lareau, 1989; Lynch & Stein 1987; Mehan, Hertweck, & Meihls, 1986). One of the reasons this occurs is that middle- and upper-middle-class parents interact more easily with school and agency staff; and when individuals feel more comfortable with each other and share the same basic values, their interactions tend to be much more successful.

Critical Point Those who represent a national or ethnic "ideal" tend to have the most prestige and power; those who are further from this ideal are frequently marginalized, with decreased power over their own lives.

Demographic trends indicate growing ethnic and linguistic diversity in this country. It is very likely that professionals will work with families who are ethnically different from themselves, and despite potential difficulties in working with them, will be responsible to provide equal levels of services. Therefore, it is increasingly important that we learn how to interact effectively with a range of families from a variety of cultural groups. The variety of immigrant groups entering our country guarantees that we will know little or nothing about some of these families and that some will represent values and beliefs that are quite different from our own. Learning skills of cultural competence will be important for all public school, agency personnel, and anyone who provides public services. Professionals themselves who are ethnic minorities or recent immigrants can provide important strategies in developing bicultural/bilingual competencies but are not necessarily experts in the wide variety of minority cultures (Luft, 1995). In fact, no one person can be equally knowledgeable about the current range of cultures living in, and moving into, the United States.

Defining Cultural Competence

As professionals, we are likely to experience profound impacts that result from working with ethnically different students and families who envision transition planning very differently from us. *Multiculturalism* is a concept used in this chapter that recognizes the diversity of cultures and ethnicities within the people of our schools and public services, and competencies in diverse cultures are important for professionals in these services. Professionals who learn the understandings, concepts, and strategies that support "cultural pluralism" will be better able to develop harmonious coexistence among the different cultures with whom they work (Green, 1999).

Multicultural understandings, concepts, and strategies provide a base from which to develop the *cultural competence* needed to function as a responsible and accountable professional in today's world. Cultural competence has been variously defined by several authors (Green, 1999; Lynch, 1998b). It begins with an understanding of, and respect for, cultures and ethnic backgrounds and their impact on ourselves and others. This chapter does not provide a single set of skills or knowledge for working across all

cultures because "culture" and "competence" vary with the situation and those people involved (Green, 1999; Lynch, 1998b). Instead, learnings in *cultural competence* support the reader's acquisition of, "the ability of service providers to respond optimally to all children, understanding both the richness and the limitations of the sociocultural contexts in which children and families as well as the service providers themselves, may be operating" (Barrera & Kramer, 1997, p. 217). This chapter describes central beliefs and values of several cultural groups. It also includes information about interacting across cultures and general strategies for being alert to, and flexible in responding to, potential cultural differences.

Critical Point   Cultural competence is built upon an understanding of, and respect for, the many different cultures of the world. It leads to the ability to respond in optimal ways with all children and their families, within both the richness and limitations of our current sociocultural environments.

Multicultural Issues for Transition

Legislation and policy are formalized expressions of societal and cultural ideals and values. The IDEA's four *essential elements* of transition represent a number of these values. The first *essential element*—consideration of the student's needs, interests, and preferences—mandates that the transition team individually assess the students' preferences for their future career and lifestyle. In the United States, an important cultural value is that of being independent and self-reliant as a means of achieving personal and social success (Althen, 1988; Dunn & Griggs, 1995; Green, 1999; Hammond & Morrison, 1996; Hanson, 1998a; Harry, 1992a; Hobbs, 1975; McPhatter, 1997; Pinderhughes, 1995). However, a number of other cultures place greater value on belonging to a group and do not prefer to be highly independent or self-reliant (Chan, 1998a; Hanson, 1998a; Harry, 1992a; Joe & Malach, 1998; Lynch, 1998b; Pinderhughes, 1995; Zuniga,

1998). These cultures believe that the needs, interests, and preferences of the group (e.g., the extended family, the neighborhood, the community, or the tribe) are more important than those of the individual. Some may not accept the notion of "student choice" but, rather, that the group's needs should be addressed before those of an individual (i.e., if the group is functioning effectively, then the individual's needs will be met). As professionals, we need to know how to negotiate such differences in culturally competent ways so that our families can participate as equal partners and meet the goals for their child, and we are able to satisfy the legal mandates for transition planning as well.

The second *essential element* of transition planning is an outcome-oriented process. This also varies greatly by culture and ethnicity. For example, many people who are acculturated into the American value system (are accepting of these values) are likely to have personal goals for earning more money (we value financial success), buying a nicer car or home (accumulate material possessions) and having important or successful friends (social status) as ways to improve our quality of life. Achieving these things leaves us feeling successful and content. As transition team members, these same values may result in finding a particular student a well-paying job, teaching her or him how to seek raises or better paying positions within the company, and making friends with key coworkers and supervisors. In contrast, the student's family members may prefer that she or he live and work within the family or community (value on being with the group) and remain loyal to people in the community (personal worth gained through being honorable, respectful, and loyal) who were helpful in the past. This is considered far more important than social status, increased salary, or a satisfying job (Harry, 1992a, 1992b; Turnbull, 1993; Turnbull, Barber, Kerns, & Behr, 1995). Therefore, the family's goal may be for their child to live at home because of her or his disability and to take a low-paying job with a long-time family friend.

The third *essential element* of transition planning is coordinated interagency responsibilities or linkages. School personnel are mandated to invite individuals from adult service agencies and other community service organizations who are currently assisting the student and family, or who are expected to provide services after the student leaves school. Families may not believe that these various external agencies are important, or they may prefer to accept what the family and community can provide with regard to the child's future adult needs. Some cultural groups have great difficulty in seeking help or in disclosing a need for help from others. They may not feel comfortable with a large group of individuals ("outsiders") discussing theirs or their child's "needs." Some families may feel very stigmatized by having a child in special education and it may be difficult for them to attend IEP/ITP meetings in general.

The fourth *essential element* of transition is movement from school to postschool activities and is similar to the second essential element, outcome-based planning. As certified and licensed professionals, many of us have been taught to support high expectations for young adults moving into adult roles and responsibilities; we are encouraged to have strong ideals for their achieving optimal and fulfilling lives. These same hopes and ideals may not be shared or accepted by the family. For example, some cultures view having single, unmarried children living outside the home as indicative of parental dysfunction and failure (Turnbull et al., 1995). Other families may expect all income earned by unmarried children to be given to the parents, without question, in loyalty to the group that has the responsibility for providing for their needs. These values are likely to conflict with typical transition goals of independent living and self-support from salaried work.

Students with disabilities always need the support of their families and communities as they move into adulthood, and parent involvement remains a critical element in transition success

(Salembier & Furney, 1997). We must be mindful not to create situations that will lead to conflict between students and their families. Careful planning and mutually agreed upon goals are very important in many of these cross-cultural situations.

Mandates for transition planning processes represent culturally defined beliefs about desired outcomes and reflect upon many hidden American cultural values. Schools and agencies are organized to implement these values as representing mainstream society's beliefs. Many transition practices presume a certain vision for achieving a high-quality life and for becoming self-determined and self-advocating future adults. Cultures that value group harmony and identity (through family, community, tribe, etc.) may not believe that their child needs to develop independent decision-making or advocacy skills. Such cultures have great faith in the group's ability to respond to the needs of the individual (middle-class Americans have much more faith in the individual's ability to take care of him- or herself). The family may not agree with team members regarding a variety of transition activities and view the team's suggestions as undermining their family and community harmony.

Critical Point   Legislated and mandated transition practices often represent beliefs and values of mainstream society more than they represent those of diverse cultures. Professionals need cultural competence in successfully negotiating between these mandates and ethnically diverse families.

These types of examples describe cultural differences that can occur between transition team members and ethnically diverse families. This chapter alone cannot provide sufficient information about the multitude of cultural differences that you may face, and much of this cross-cultural learning will have to occur elsewhere. This includes a personal and professional commitment to interact openly with minority staff and families in seeking information about, and ways of, resolving potentially conflictual values and beliefs. However, the information about differ-

ent cultures provided here will sensitize you to noticing when teams are experiencing cultural difficulties or conflicts, so that you and your other team members (including the family) can address these difficulties and reduce what can otherwise become ongoing, and increasing levels of cultural discomfort and conflict. This next section describes some of the particular needs for becoming culturally competent in special education and transition planning as preparation for examining aspects of cultural difference.

Cultural Diversity in Special Education

Many of us have entered special education and disability services because we enjoy helping others who have special challenges. However, the history of our profession has not been completely altruistic. The structure of special education programs has resulted in minorities being consistently overreferred to programs and overrepresented in classes in comparison to their proportions within the larger society (Sarason & Doris, 1979). The first compulsory education laws passed during the 1880s and early 1900s were attempts to socialize immigrant Catholic children in what was a traditionally Protestant country (Hobbs, 1975). Special education programs at this time were used to classify and segregate immigrant Irish, Italians, Hungarians, Germans, Russians, and other groups and to isolate them from the more established American children (Sarason & Doris, 1979). Intelligence tests were used to show that these children were inferior and needed special classroom placement; we realize now that these tests and their procedures were highly biased.

Special Education Placement Patterns

Current special education legislation describes appropriate referral and assessment processes for determining that students are eligible for placement into special education programs.

These are critical aspects for ensuring that proper services are provided to all children. The danger of biased procedures continues and, therefore, Public Law (P.L.) 94-142 and IDEA (Individuals with Disabilities Education Act) require special education placement to be based on multiple measures (not just on one test). In addition, all assessments must be done in the child's primary language or mode of communication, administered by trained personnel, and each must test specific areas of educational need (Turnbull, 1993; van Keulen, Weddington, & DeBose, 1998). At least one person on the multidisciplinary team must have knowledge in the area of the suspected disability.

The U.S. Department of Education Office for Civil Rights has monitored ethnic proportions in special education classes since P.L. 94-142; however, results continue to show biased procedures. Records show (U.S. Department of Education, 1987) that twice as many African-American students were placed in classes for mild mental retardation, and 1.5 times as many were placed in classes for severe behavior disorders. Latino students in Texas were categorized with learning disabilities at a rate of 315%, according to their population (Holtzman, 1986). More recent data (U.S. Dept. of Educ., 1994, 1997) still include high placement rates for Native American and Latino students in all classes designated for students with mental retardation. In summary, despite mandates for fair assessment processes, minority students continue to be placed into special education programs at a higher than expected rate (Burnette, 1998; Greenberg, 1986; Harry, 1992a; Markowitz, 1996; Reschly, 1997; Russo & Talbert-Johnson, 1997; Sarason & Doris, 1979; U.S. Dept. of Educ., Office of Civil Rights, 1987, 1994, 1997).

This situation may worsen in the future if professionals are not better prepared to work with cultural and linguistic minorities. Demographic trends predict white student enrollment to decline and proportions of nonwhite students to increase (Bose, 1996; Garcia & Yates, 1986; Knopp & Otuya, 1995; Wald, 1996). By the year 2000, minority children will constitute one-third of all children, and by 2030, they are expected to be 41% of the child population (van Keulen et al., 1998). These figures suggest that large numbers of students will be at risk of being placed in special education (Greenberg, 1986). Because of differences in behavioral and personal interaction styles and in learning styles (global and holistic versus linear and analytic), and as a result of bilingual communication, needs may be misinterpreted as evidence of a disability (Burnette, 1998; Turnbull, 1993). Few school professionals are trained to provide multicultural special education assessments or classroom interventions (Burnette, 1998; Obiakor & Utley, 1996; Talbert-Johnson, 1998). Consequently, referral teams rarely examine classrooms or schools for cultural factors that may contribute to the child's difficulties or consider culturally specific attributes and skills that the child is able to perform successfully (Burnette, 1998; Cummins, 1986; Obiakor & Utley, 1996; Simich-Dudgeon, 1986; Willig, 1986).

Critical Point   Lack of cultural competence in identifying and assessing ethnically diverse children who demonstrate authentic disabilities continues to lead to high rates of referral and placement in special education programs.

Transition team members rely upon a variety of assessment processes to identify transition strengths, needs, interests, and preferences (further described in Chapter 7). Design of tests that are culturally neutral has been extremely challenging and difficult, with accurate and culturally fair testing difficulties still unresolved (cf. Markowitz, 1996; Reschly, 1997; Russo & Talbert-Johnson, 1997; U.S. Dept. of Educ., 1987, 1994, 1997). Transition team members must be very cautious about the accuracy and interpretation of these tests when making decisions about appropriate futures for culturally and linguistically different students. Assessment items may need

TABLE 5–1

Suggestions for Modifying Assessments with Culturally Different Students

Modification of the item stimulus

1. Repeat the instructions using different words, repeat them more often than recommended, or use sign language.
2. Change the pronunciation of words to reflect the child's culture.
3. Use different pictures when getting unexpected responses; use more culturally appropriate pictures as needed.
4. Modify item wording, probe for related responses, and include additional items to give the student every opportunity to respond.
5. Allow the parents or a trusted adult to administer test items.
6. Administer only a portion of the test; complete the testing in several sessions.

Modification of the item response requirements

1. Allow more time than recommended by the test.
2. Accept responses that are different from allowable responses but that are appropriate for the child's language or culture.
3. Allow the student to change responses.
4. Allow the student to clarify responses and ask questions.
5. Allow the student to respond using sign language, a foreign language, or a gesture.

Scoring

1. When altering a standardized test in any way, this must be described in the report and with the results of the testing; be certain to include this.
2. Do not use the modified results to present normed scores, percentiles, or grade equivalents; changes in assessment procedures always impact normed scoring procedures.
3. Use the modified results to explain your findings and results in terms of the student's abilities; this may have helped you to learn that the student possesses certain skills or knowledge that were masked by cultural differences, and explain how these modifications helped you to learn these things.

Source: Adapted from Keitel M. A. Kopala M., & Adamson W. S. (1996); Ethical issues in multicultural assessment. In Suzuki, L. A., Miller, P. J. & Ponterotto, J. G. (Eds.). *Handbook of multicultural assessment* (pp. 29–48) San Francisco: Jossey-Bass; and van Keulen, J. E., Weddington, G. T., & Du Bose, C. E. (1998), *Speech, language, learning and the African-American child.*   Boston: Allyn & Bacon, pp. 123–125.

to be modified both when presenting the item (the stimulus) and with the required responses from the student. Culturally appropriate interaction styles can greatly impact on how well children understand directions for each task and their ability to respond to specified testing protocol. Table 5–1 provides suggestions that may be helpful to the transition team in addressing these issues (Keitel, Kopala, & Adamson, 1996; van Keulen et al., 1998).

Institutionalized Cultural Values

An important aspect of understanding the interrelationships between culture and the special education system must include an understanding of how cultural values are organized and maintained. A society's organizations and governmental patterns are important structures that are designed to implement the core values and beliefs of that culture. Our public agencies, including public schools and adult service organizations, support many of our American cultural values (Brislin, 1993). In addition, although education in this country has been a means for ensuring literate and democratic citizens, we have seen that the public schools also have served a purpose of enculturating immigrant children into U.S. beliefs and values (Sarason & Doris, 1979; Turnbull, 1993). Schools are very powerful socializing agents with an obligation to conform to the wishes of their community. For example, when asked to identify the most important things for children to learn in preschool, 80% of Japanese listed sympathy, empathy, and concern for others. Only 39% of Americans and 20% of Chinese listed these items as the most important (Tobin, Wu, & Davidson as cited in Brislin, 1993). The social learnings that occur in schools can create significant difficulties for culturally different students and families.

Interaction style differences can create some of the most profound cross-cultural difficulties that occur frequently in schools. For example, during a classroom debate, African-American students tend to respond in an animated, interpersonal, challenging, and high-spirited manner (van Keulen et al., 1998). White students tend to be relatively low-keyed, dispassionate, impersonal, and nonchallenging. African-American students view persuasion as a time to challenge and do not see these behaviors as antagonistic. However, white American culture teaches that debates should be without strong emotion or personal challenge and both teachers and white students may misinterpret the African-American students' behaviors as hostile. Van Keulen et al. (1998, pp. 210–211) describe how public schools frequently create difficulties for culturally different students:

> Traditionally, American schools perpetuate cultural discontinuity for students from different cultures by promoting only those perspectives, values, beliefs, attitudes, and traditions of European American culture . . . . Cultural clashes occur when school administrators, teachers, and other

school personnel from the American mainstream culture do not recognize or acknowledge the cultures and languages of their students as valid and legitimate.

As professionals, we need to understand that the public schools and agencies for which we work are organized to support mainstream American beliefs and values. Families and students may already have experienced cultural barriers and conflicts during referral and assessment processes; during classroom interactions and activities; and in their previous communications with teaching, administrative, and agency personnel. They may feel limited trust for professionals, as a result. The general lack of cultural training for many public service professionals means that the reader may be one of the few transition team members with information and strategies for negotiating these types of difficulties.

Critical Point   Ethnically diverse families and children may have had poor prior experiences with professionals who did not recognize or value their cultural differences. They may have difficulties trusting and communicating with the team until members demonstrate their cultural competence and sensitivity.

Cross-Cultural Concerns for Transition Professionals

The high rate of minority group presence in special education classes means that transition teams are likely to work with families who are culturally different (Wald, 1996). The demographics of personnel in education and other public services (e.g., counselors, social workers, etc.) show a likelihood of being white, middle class, and female (Burnette, 1998; Eubanks, 1996; Moores, 1996). Proportionally fewer members of minority groups become special educators and the number of African-American personnel is expected to continue to decline (Sexton, Lobman, Constans, Snyder, & Ernest, 1997). The result is that few students of color or who are male can expect to have teachers of similar backgrounds (Knopp & Otuya, 1995; Simpson, 1997).

A critical difficulty with delivering cross-cultural services is that professionals may not be able to evaluate accurately the quality of their services when working with culturally different families. Perceptions of services and family satisfaction often are gauged through culturally based behaviors. For example, family members may smile, greet, and interact with team members pleasantly and appear to have few questions or concerns. However, this may not reflect satisfaction with services. A comparison of African-American and Caucasian early intervention specialists found that the Caucasian personnel rated their services to African-American parents higher than did their African-American peers (Sexton et al., 1997), including:

1. openness to input from parents,
2. establishing positive relationships with parents,
3. actively encouraging parents to be involved in their children's program, and
4. services were a positive experience for children and their families.

The difficulty in accurately assessing our own cross-cultural effectiveness as professionals is compounded by frequent lack of training in this area (Markowitz, 1996). Families may have a limited understanding of American organizations and related cultural values, particularly if they are recent immigrants, compounding the nature of cross-cultural difficulties.

Assimilation and Acculturation of American Values.
Professionals who work with and study immigrant people often view them in terms of steps they have made toward "assimilation" or "acculturation" (Green, 1999; Lynch, 1998a; Joe & Malach, 1998). These steps categorize individuals in terms of their acceptance of the dominant cultural characteristics of a particular society, in contrast with those who retain their native language and habits (considered to be "traditional"). Green (1999) proposes an alternative view that defines the entire concept of ethnicity as a perspective about oneself and others that

shifts and changes with time. His work shows that the degree to which people are acculturated is "situational" rather than absolute and is modified to suit the needs of various types of cross-cultural encounters. For example, a family may adhere to ethnic patterns while in their community by celebrating festivals, eating traditional foods, and socializing with others; however, they may accept the dominant culture's standards about work, housing, and traumatic health care (Green, 1999; Hanson, 1998a).

This definition coincides with the ecological approach used in this book (described in Chapter 1) and the fact that transition processes are impacted by multiple factors. Ethnicity and acculturation are similarly affected by influences of the community around an individual, including the relationship between the particular minority and majority culture and each person's own changing needs over time. This view allows family members to become increasingly bicultural, according to situation demands. Thus, they can retain traditional values that they believe are important, but they also can learn to use IEP/ITP meetings in a more "Americanized" way to support their child's development. This view also allows professionals to support families who may wish to learn specific skills that will increase their sense of success at these meetings, without having to address the entire "acculturation" process that families are facing.

Another important concept regarding acculturation is that, as successful students and (future) professionals, we ourselves have assimilated certain American values. These values have led to our academic success and admittance into programs and schools. For example, we have developed abilities leading to individual achievement, competing for high grades, test-taking skills, hard work, and delaying gratification (in terms of salary and free time). We have become socialized and acculturated "into the profession" and into a specific segment of the working American population, regardless of whether we were born into middle- or upper-middle-class families, lower- or working-class families, or are members of ethnic minority communities. Some of us, as a result of assimilating these American professional values, may even experience a form of "culture shock" when returning to visit our families or hometowns (Lynch, 1998a). Our schools and universities have been powerful acculturating forces.

Our professions also require advanced levels of education in order to deliver services. This education and professional status results in increased social and economic power in this country. We are viewed by others as having this power, whether or not we always agree with this perception. This becomes important when we interact with families who have less education and who may be ethnic minorities: That is, we are likely to have a higher social status than they do (Green, 1999).

Personal and Professional Power

The issues of interpersonal power, status, and resulting conflicts are frequently uncomfortable topics to address (i.e., this also is an American cultural value, in that certain topics are considered "private"). This may be particularly true for those who are white and middle or upper-middle class: it is difficult to be seen as "oppressors" who unfairly wield this inherited social power and status. Yet, studies of status and narratives from those who are nonwhite indicate that white people in the United States *do* have increased power (Green, 1999; van Keulen et al., 1998). The same accomplishments by an ethnic minority are likely to have been much more difficult and viewed less favorably by others in society: They probably were told in a variety of ways that they did not belong, would never be successful, and were wasting their time and money in attempting this goal (Green, 1999). Willis (1998, p. 184) states the following:

> In general, white people have trouble relating to this because they have never experienced discrimination on the basis of the color of their skin. Many white people feel that African Americans are overly

sensitive and that they imagine slights and offenses and too often see racism where none exists. Many African Americans have tried to explain to white friends and colleagues the validity of their sensitivity to racism as an adaptation and survival strategy.

When we meet with families and other team members, our ethnicity and cultural heritage signal important social status attributes. We must recognize and accept how this is perceived by others and how it influences our own perceptions. In turn, a family's perceived social status is equally impacted by these attributes, which can affect transition planning and participatory decision-making processes. The greater the difference in status is between team members and families, the more difficult it will be to develop genuine participation (cf. Friend & Cook, 1990).

Critical Point As successful professionals, we all have assimilated certain American cultural values. Our success and achievement has led to an increase in perceived status. We must be aware of how families may view us and use our professional "power" judiciously.

Status Issues of Families

Several of the important characteristics of status in the United States have been described in terms of how they impact professionals. For many families with whom we will work, race, education, economic levels, and having a child with a disability interact in potentially detrimental ways. These aspects and their effects on families are described subsequently.

Definitions of Race

Public schools and service organizations frequently classify students and clients based on racial categories. However, the definition of *race* is not a scientifically valid concept (Green, 1999; Pollitzer, 1994). The "races" of today did not exist 10,000 years ago, and they cannot be objectively defined or consistently measured. No one can be categorized as a member of any particular "race" because of skin pigmentation or characteristics of their nose, eyes, or hair (Green, 1999). Instead, scientists identify "gene pools" with the understanding that intermarriage makes clear distinctions difficult and that these pools change over time (Pollitzer, 1994).

As professionals, we must be alert to interactions and judgments based on racial aspects of students and families. Specifically, characteristics such as degrees of "color" may be viewed with importance with an underlying presumption that certain other characteristics, such as being "white," is superior (Harry, 1992a; Turnbull, 1993). Negative stereotyping of families may be based on racial characteristics presumed to be associated with their home environments and readiness to provide "appropriate" nurturing to their children (Harry, 1992a, 1992b, 1992c; Willis, 1998).

Economic and Educational Status
Although not true of all families, statistics show that many minority and immigrant families live in the lower-income brackets of this country, and minorities continue to be overrepresented in this country's poorest groups (Dennis & Giangreco, 1996; Fujiura & Yamaki, 1997; Harry, 1992a; Janesick, 1995; Miller & Roby, 1970; Rose, 1972). For example, 31% of African Americans, 26% of Hispanics, and 10% of white Americans lived below the poverty level in 1989. Immigrants who do not move into an existing and well-established support system can experience lower social status as a result of being a minority, which can result in poorer income potential. Families who struggle with both language and cultural barriers also are likely to have poor wages and limited employment opportunities.

Although social movements of the 1960s raised social consciousness in general, ethnicity and lower socioeconomic status interact and continue to be viewed negatively. Poor people are historically viewed as having a distinctly different and "deficient" value system (Miller & Roby, 1970; Rose, 1972). They may be treated more negatively despite having similar income

or educational levels. Families who are poor often are more dependent on government programs but also are less likely to have the interpersonal and linguistic skills of middle-class and better educated persons that could help them to manage these bureaucratic, organizational systems. Thus, they are poor and need help but are less likely to have the skills to use these support systems effectively in their lives.

Impacts of Disability
The addition of a child with a disability greatly exacerbates a family's difficulties and the associated medical and other costs that are likely to increase the family's stress and to stretch their limited employment and financial resources to the maximum (Westling & Fox, 2000). The interaction of ethnicity, lower-income and educational levels, and having a child with a disability increases the likelihood that these families will have to deal with American institutions but that these will be unsatisfactory (Fujiura & Yamaki, 1997). In terms of receiving special education services, research has shown that minority families are less likely to get appropriate IEP services (Harry, 1992a; Lareau, 1989). Parents whose values differ from those of school personnel often find themselves alienated and ignored because of their beliefs (Gault, 1989).

The Impact of Cultural Difference on Transition Mandates

Public Law 94-142 and IDEA provide parents with substantial safeguards against authoritarian and unilateral decision making by the school through mandates for participatory decision making and due process (Turnbull, 1993). However, parents with an inadequate understanding of English and American culture and less than middle-class social status are likely to feel powerless to use these rights. For the parents to proceed with a formal appeal and hearing process is to subscribe to American beliefs and values that this is an appropriate method and will be successful for them in resolving an IEP disagreement or in addressing racial or other types of discrimination.

Even if these families received translated documents that they understood, several cultures would not support openly confrontational or adversarial action by parents. These cultures hold professionals in very high esteem and, in particular, teachers and healers (Lynch, 1998a). They would not openly contradict an opinion of an educator, let alone file for due process. This has tremendous implications for IEP and transition planning processes; families are expected to be actively involved in the planning process. Participatory decision making presumes that families will personally be involved in discussions on appropriate goals, placements, and progress. Yet, families from several of these cultural groups do not believe it is their role to be assertive or talkative participants in developing or evaluating services. Some also may find it upsetting and embarrassing to be asked directly to state their concerns and priorities.

Table 5–2 describes some typical U.S./American characteristics and contrasting cultural characteristics that impact interactions and, therefore, transition team processes. As the table shows, some expectations about our place in the world, our ability to control our future, our way of viewing time and interpersonal relationships, and our family structure are widely variable depending on our culture of origin. Knowledge of interaction preferences and styles can greatly enhance our professional effectiveness. However, realization of the tremendous impact that behavior can have on those who are culturally different is likely to increase one's anxiety at first and lead to some awkwardness (Brislin, 1993). This will decrease with time and additional cross-cultural opportunities as the information becomes more integrated into one's behavioral repertoire.

Contrasting Transition Values

In addition to the interaction differences in Table 5–2, a number of ideals, values, and beliefs mandated and expected in the transition planning process can lead to cultural conflicts. The following section describes some of these key contrasts to alert you to potential difficulties.

Contrasting Values of Identity

Several cultures emphasize group identity rather than individualism, which can significantly impact family expectations for adulthood. The child's future roles may be defined as his or her place within the family structure. The family also may disagree with, or see as destructive and undermining, transition team goals to develop their child's independence, self-reliance, and abilities to make his or her own decisions and choices. Several cultures have very different values about young adult independence from parents with age expectations that are both younger and older than typical American youths.

Contrasting Views of Disability

In the United States, we tend to believe in a "medical model" for identifying and addressing differences among people (discussed in Chapter 2). This has resulted in an ever-growing list that is increasingly specialized in nature (Ysseldyke, Algozzine, & Thurlow, 1992). Not all cultures recognize the variety and number of disabilities as we do in the United States. For example, some cultures focus only on obvious physical or mental disabilities (Harry, 1992a; Zuniga, 1998). Many mild disability categories reflect upon what other cultures see as part of normal child behavior and development. Families may have great difficulty in understanding why their child is being identified as "problematic" and placed in specialized programming. Their religious or cultural beliefs may result in much less of an urgency for intervention planning and remediation because it is their "fate" or a result of God's plan.

In terms of transition planning outcomes, the family may be completely committed to allowing

TABLE 5–2

Key Cultural Differences between U.S. American and Other Cultural Groups

Cultural Characteristic	U.S/American Cultural Value	Culturally Contrasting Value
Cooperation versus competition	Society (and public schools) encourage doing better than others as proof of mastery; games are based on having a winner and loser, winners in a variety of activities are regularly rewarded.	Cooperative societies work together to achieve a mutual goal; children may be taught to wait until everyone has finished so that no one is embarrassed; individual achievement is likely to be less motivating in comparison to roles as family member and group or community pride.
Individual versus family or group orientation	Standard value on small, nuclear family units with little reliance on the extended family. Use of professional assistance and services when issues cannot be resolved within the nuclear family unit.	Importance of extended family or group and blood kinship lineage, with respect for elders and ancestors. Child's achievement (or disability) may reflect upon the entire family. Family and group identity may be of primary importance and contribute to the family's reputation, status, cohesiveness, and sense of collective (group) responsibility.
Time orientation	Time is measured and used efficiently; punctuality is expected and rewarded. People wear watches and professionals use appointment calendars; wasting time or lateness is viewed negatively. Monochronic orientation for doing one thing at a time—for example, "business before pleasure," and students work without talking or distractions.	Time is "given" in many other parts of the world and is generously shared; quality of interpersonal relationships takes priority. Polychronic time orientation handling several interactions and activities simultaneously, encouraging business and pleasurable activities together; appear to have several individuals talking at the same time with intermittent listening, laughing, and commenting.
Gender roles and responsibilities	Traditional nuclear family remains the ideal with a working father and stay-at-home mother who cares for the family's emotional and physical needs; this is responding to increased single-parent homes and working mothers with greater role and gender flexibility.	Some cultures have strict gender-based roles with pampering of young males and girls caring for younger siblings, with home responsibilities and limited independence. Some discourage conversations between children/adults, or males/females until appropriate times. Some groups have highly adaptable family roles among parents, extended family, and older children.

their child with a significant disability to remain at home under their protection and love. For a child with a mild disability, the family may believe that the school's elaborate transition plans are unnecessary and that their child will be a successful adult within the community and its support system. Families may not view transition planning as important because they do not foresee a future that is problematic or believe that the family or community structures will provide the

Cultural Characteristic	U.S/American Cultural Value	Culturally Constrasting Value
Interaction style	Tendency to be direct with a topic, factual and impersonal. There is an expectation to identify and address difficulties and conflicts directly, including expression of related concerns and use of a highly verbal style. Laughing and giggling are expressions of enjoyment. Typically, focus on one topic or activity at a time. Americans tend to prefer more interaction space than many Latinos, southern Europeans, and Middle Easterners; less than African Americans and Asians.	May use indirect means to address a topic with requirements to begin serious discussions with initial, interpersonal, and social interactions. May use a more emotive style or an unobtrusive, nonemotive interaction style depending on group. Status, authority, and roles of interaction partners may be very important and dictate specific styles. Southeast Asians may see laughing and giggling as a sign of extreme embarrassment or discomfort. Loud talking or personal contact may be rude or offensive; others see it as natural expression and friendliness. May be comfortable with multiple conversations simultaneously. Interpersonal space preferences vary widely with culture.
Fate versus individual	There is very little that cannot be controlled—cars, services, utilities, or medical interventions. Emphasis is on individual rights and responsibilities, self-determination and autonomy. Is rewarded for taking care of one's own needs independently.	May believe that control lies outside the individual, with external forces largely responsible for what happens to people. Value on harmonious existence with surroundings and circumstances. May feel responsibility toward oneself as is reflected in terms of family and group roles, not through own achievements.

Source: This table is based on Chan (1998a, 1998b), Green (1999), Hanson (1998b), Harry (1992a, 1992b, 1992c), Joe and Malach (1998), Lynch (1998a, 1998b), Sharifzadeh (1998), van Keulen et al. (1998), and Willis (1998).

necessary support. Others believe that the disability reflects poorly upon the family and they are very uncomfortable discussing these issues in the detail that Americans prefer.

Contrasting Values for Family Relationships
American families remained focused on the nuclear family as the center of all primary relationships. Other cultures that utilize wide kinship or community webs may not view parents as the primary decisionmakers or caretakers. These parents may even view their signatures on

IEP/ITP documents as meaningless because they lack the formal approval of their extended family or community group. Child-rearing practices may not focus greatly on independence and self-reliance as measured by development milestones that include the age at walking, talking, and toilet training (i.e., these are often viewed as a critical event by both American professionals and parents). In many Asian cultures, young children are not diapered but are expected to relieve themselves freely and are washed as needed. Older children and adults may feed young children for an extended period because caring for a younger child, or also a child with a disability, is not viewed as a burden (Lynch, 1998a). These are viewed as part of the normal interdependence (versus American independence) of family members on each other.

This can impact transition planning in that parents and family members may not be able to provide information about the age at which children attained certain developmental milestones or how much they participate in certain activities "independently." These "American" attainments are not seen as important and family members simply may not remember when and if they occur. Other important relationship characteristics are the strict status, gender, or age roles and restrictions which may conflict with typical transition practices that place adolescents in independent trial work and self-care situations.

Table 5–3 lists some key aspects of transition planning and their impact on families. The table also suggests potential negative impacts when professionals are unaware of the impact of their own values and behaviors and ways to resolve some of these differences. For example, schools and agencies often schedule IEP/ITP meetings in one-hour blocks to promote efficiency and rational decision making, with little time spent in building a relationship with family members. Schools may not invite key family or community decisionmakers, which can confuse and insult them.

Without cross-cultural training, families and professionals may become increasingly confused and distrustful of each other and initial barriers are likely to become more solidified as each responds in culturally appropriate, but cross-culturally offensive, ways. Minority families may withdraw out of respect or to allow the school to save face, or they take steps within their own family or community that address their child's issues that are very different from school expectations. Schools, however, are expecting them to comply with the signed documents (Harry, 1992a). Families may be puzzled and hurt that school personnel spend so little time establishing relationships with the extended family and their community as well, which would demonstrate their commitment to a genuine understanding of their child. They may interpret meetings based on rapid decision making and problem resolution as rude, overbearing, and controlling (Harry, 1992a).

From the educators' perspectives, their painstaking planning and efforts to achieve critical outcomes that they believe are vital to the child's success may be met with a lack of family enthusiasm or outright neglect. School personnel may conclude that the family does not participate or cooperate with these plans because they are either unable or unwilling to do so. They may be judged as "bad parents," who lack both caring and commitment to their child (Harry, 1992a, 1992b, 1992c). When schools believe families are uncooperative or incapable of providing what was promised, they often limit the information and choices presented to parents (Lynch & Stein, 1987; Mehan et al., 1986). Across 12 studies, Harry (1992a) found that minority parents were less involved and less informed, and parents felt that the professionals implicitly or explicitly discouraged their participation.

The previous sections have described some key cultural and status variables that impact interactions and, ultimately, transition team processes with culturally different families. The process of becoming culturally competent starts with a clear understanding of one's own beliefs and values and an acknowledgment that they will differ from those of others (Dennis & Giangreco, 1996; Fradd & Weismantel, 1989; Hanson & Carta, 1996; Harry, 1992a; Lynch, 1998a). This includes becoming aware of one's own personal levels of acculturation and the impact of cultural learning on one's personal and professional behaviors and expectations.

Special education and transition services have growing needs for culturally competent personnel. As professionals in these fields,

TABLE 5–3

Potential Impacts and Resolution of Cultural Differences

	ITP Legislative Mandates and Practices	Contrasting Cultural Values	Results of Unresolved Conflicts	Culturally Competent Responses
Goals of the IEP/ITP planning processes	Identify student's skills, needs, preferences, achievement levels. Identify goals and plan steps to achieve desired outcomes.	Contribute to group and family needs, and listen to others. Build relationships that value communication, harmony, and personal/family honor.	Schools limit the information or choices given to families. Families are offended that key members are excluded from meetings. Families may not voice concerns out of respect or due to status differences.	Be alert to goal and outcome differences; begin with personal interactions (visiting). Establish a trusting relationship with family (regarding cultural preferences for formal/informal, gender, and role-consciousness).
Transition outcomes for students	To develop independence, self-reliance, assertiveness, and economic success for work, ability to live alone (with minimal support), and satisfying leisure activities.	To develop group interdependence, social harmony, and extended support networks that contribute to the family and community. To develop noncompetitive attributes and skills with a focus on relationships and respect for others.	Schools judge families as unable or unwilling to work toward critical goals. Families withdraw or "ignore" advice from school; may not attend future meetings.	Gradually begin to solicit from family members their description of preferred adult outcomes (in a culturally appropriate manner). Negotiate differences by suggesting a variety of alternatives and explain rationale for professional suggestions in a culturally appropriate way.

we can expect to work with an increasing number of families and students who are culturally different from ourselves. The next section adds culturally specific details that build upon key contrasting values presented in the previous sections and tables. The comparison of these descriptions with (1) our own personal beliefs and values and (2) the values frequently supported in the public and agency organizations where we work (or hope to work) will lead to a broader understanding and sensitivity to the reasons for the cross-

cultural difficulties that may arise between professionals and families.

Negotiating Multicultural Differences

An important aspect of becoming culturally competent is to interact with culturally different individuals. A book cannot provide the range of experiences that explore the realities and implications of these statements. Green (1999) recommends using a cultural guide with frequent visits to ethnic communities and interactions with minority individuals in order to become culturally competent. Some of this learning can occur through honest and open communication with families; however, they should not be placed in a role of becoming the primary source of cross-cultural teaching.

The descriptions of cultural groups cannot address the range of variability that exists within each group nor represent the individual beliefs and values which may be quite different from that of the "normative group." Identification of the cultural group creates bonds between people and can be an important source of identity (Hanson, 1998a). It also can be used negatively when associating certain traits rigidly, according to culture, which results in stereotyping (Green, 1999; Hanson, 1998a). As mentioned earlier, families also may subscribe to these values in varying degrees depending on the specific nature of the situation.

A family's affiliation with their cultural group may change with their acculturation into American lifestyles. This will depend on a number of factors described earlier, including if they live within a strong minority community, if they have American relatives nearby, if they had previous exposure to American cultural values, if they are recent immigrants, and if they desire to accept American values. A family's level of acculturation also may change over time and between generations. The child may have different perspectives on the American lifestyle in comparison to their parents or extended family members. These perspectives may change as the child develops and has either positive or negative interactions with American cultural values. The transition team will need to know how the family interprets and reinterprets adulthood for their child in terms of these ongoing bicultural issues (Harry, 1992a).

American Values and Beliefs

Some American cultural values were described earlier. Additional ones include industry, success and achievement, civic-mindedness, usefulness, individualism and personal choice, self-reliance and independence from others, privacy, equality, informality, future orientation and progress, and a focus on efficient management (Brookhiser, 1991; Hammond & Morrison, 1996; Hobbs, 1975; Stewart, Danielian, & Festes, 1969). These translate into behaviors such as keeping busy, setting personal goals, reading self-help books (i.e., independent self-improvement), rating importance and giving time according to immediate "relevance," expecting meetings to follow an agenda and a time schedule, successfully competing against others (for individual honors, grades, salaries, etc.), addressing problems succinctly and rationally, and using day planners to maintain organization and efficiency (scheduling leisure and family activities as well as professional meetings and appointments, leisure should be goal oriented to achieve fitness or health). A fuller description across several characteristics is provided in Table 5–4.

Native American Values and Beliefs

These groups in the United States include 517 separate tribes or nations with over 150 languages. There is tremendous diversity and cultural differences that exist particularly among the Navajo, Eskimo, and Cherokee peoples (Dunn & Griggs, 1995). General tribal interests and life pathways often are similar although tribal customs, languages, and life practices frequently are unique (Hanson, 1998b). The descriptions in Table 5–5 represent the more common values across this variation.

The existence of these peoples has been significantly influenced by life on the reservation, although more than one-half do not live there. Levels of affiliation with tribal members and traditions may vary greatly, however they may continue to provide a strong level of personal and cultural identification. Much of the Native American culture of today is impacted by adaptive and acculturation strategies from three centuries of contact with a highly dissimilar and

TABLE 5–4

U.S. American Cultural Values and Behaviors

Worldview

1. Judeo-Christian, Protestant, and Anglo-Saxon tradition with a belief in the ability to dominate nature (e.g., self-reliance and independence), strong values on individual direction, determination, independence, autonomy, equality among individuals, patriotism, self-discipline, thrift, honesty, and respect for elders. Strong protection of the individual's right to practice or not practice the religion of one's choice; practices are centered on life events (e.g., marriage and death) and otherwise, religious life is not prominently displayed.

2. A focus on big accomplishments and heroic status, overcoming adversity on one's own, and accomplishing goals without depending on others. Highly valued for the ability to change and improve oneself regardless of background: This is accomplished through achievement, action, work, and materialism (i.e., work orientation focuses on acquisition of material possessions). Attention is given to what one "does" (rather than who one's family "is"). Highly active and achievement-oriented lifestyle, even in leisure. Has a strong belief that the future, change, and progress are beneficial.

Life satisfaction

3. Self-fulfillment and self-worth are achieved through hard work and overcoming personal or societal obstacles, mastery over nature and the environment, and moral living. Evidence of achievement is often measured through accumulation of social status, income, education, and material possessions.

Family structure

4. Loyalty to the nuclear family with recent broadening of this definition to include nonmarried adults, single-parent families, and extended family groups (although these other members are usually called "relatives" rather than family). Upon reaching adulthood, responsibilities to family of origin are reduced to focus on developing one's own family.

5. A tendency for "child-centeredness" with active schedules for children. Childrearing focuses on independence, freedom, assertiveness, equality, self-help, and self-directedness; this translates into separate bedrooms for children and emphasis on achieving developmental milestones for independence (e.g., toilet training, feeding, chores, decision making, part-time work, owning a car). There is a belief in educating all children to the fullest extent as creating a better future for the family and society.

Interaction style

6. A preference for informality, directness, and assertiveness. This is seen in casual dress, use of slang, and an open and friendly style even with strangers. There is a tendency to be forthright about many matters, including serious issues (but less so about personal topics).

7. Time efficiency and organization are highly valued; time must be used well and saved. Fast-food restaurants represent this through focusing on efficiency rather than on the "process" of eating. Meetings should have posted agendas and scheduled items; professionals use "personal calendars" to maximize efficiency for all significant events (e.g., appointments, meetings, family gatherings and events, leisure and recreation).

Medical and disability perspectives

8. A fascination with high technology regarding equipment and diagnostic or treatment procedures (also supporting beliefs in the "medical model," efficiency, and progress). A strong conviction that accurate and specific diagnosis will lead to a cure with an emphasis on prevention through distribution of information and regular, scheduled care. Reliance upon a trained "expert" to give qualified advice with compliance from the patient.

9. Disability occurs as the result of causal agents (e.g., genetics, environmental agents, and disease); if the impact of these causal agents cannot be remedied, the individual with a disability should work to overcome obstacles and adversity (e.g., heroic status of Helen Keller).

Source: Compiled from Althen, 1988; Brookhiser, 1991; Dunn & Griggs, 1995; Hammond & Morrison, 1996; Hanson, 1998b; Harry, 1992a; and Hobbs, 1975.

TABLE 5–5

Native American Peoples' Cultural Values and Behaviors

Worldview

1. The spiritual God is viewed as positive, benevolent, and an integral part of daily living; the self is part of the interconnections between all living and nonliving things and their function and place in the universe. A holistic view of living and emphasis on the interrelatedness of spirit and body (contrasts with the Judeo-Christian role of humanity's role to dominate nature and all other life forms).

2. Admired personality traits include bravery, patience, honesty, respect for others, controlled emotions, and self-respect. Wealth is defined by one's cultural knowledge and role in the tribe/nation with teachings to respect the land and forbid desecration of ancestral lands. Ceremonies and rituals ensure harmony and protection of the land.

Life satisfaction

3. Living in harmony with the universe through respecting all of nature as part of daily existence. A belief that events occur as part of the natural order of life and one must learn to live with and accept both the good and the bad.

Family structure

4. Family includes extended family members and tribal members who may have primary caretaking responsibilities rather than biological parents; grandparents may assume care so that parents can be employed. In some tribes, uncles rather than grandfathers provide most of the discipline while grandfathers provide spiritual guidance and teaching; some have informal adoption processes. Parents may seek the advice of older family members and elders who are valued for age and life experiences. Elders are respected but relationships are egalitarian, nonjudgmental, and noncompetitive; there is some suspicion of outsiders.

5. Children are viewed as complete (rather than immature) beings at birth and given early responsibilities to contribute to the group. They often become self-sufficient at an earlier age (e.g., dressing, chores, left or sent alone, care of younger sibling), with a focus on the adult-centered world and praise for adultlike behaviors. They are disciplined through use of admonitions and advising rather than force or scolding; shaming or threats of punishment by supernatural powers are more common (the earlier independence than in mainstream U.S. culture and flexible kinship networks is sometimes misinterpreted as parental neglect).

somewhat hostile U.S. government, lifestyle philosophy, and social organization. Native Americans live in most major U.S. cities and although many are part of mainstream society, many also retain their traditional beliefs and values to some degree. The Bureau of Indian Affairs continues to exert a strong influence and exists as a separate governmental body in the United States (Hanson, 1998b; Joe & Malchi, 1998).

Wide cultural belief and value differences exist between Native American people and U.S./American perspectives on relationships with and dominance over nature, paths to harmonious lifestyles, family structure, childrearing, interaction and communication, and causation of disabil-

ities. This can lead to profound differences in goals of transition planning and what constitutes an optimal adult lifestyle. American values of directness and efficiency in communication with meetings that follow a time line and agenda can have very negative implications for developing trust, communication, and participatory decision making.

African-American Values and Beliefs

This group includes people from West Africa, the Caribbean, and those who have lived in the United States for many generations, resulting in many different cultural patterns, lifestyles, and beliefs. As a whole, these people have distinct patterns of thinking, feeling, and acting, some of which have

---

Interaction style

6. Cultural values stress cooperation, interdependence, interpersonal relationships, group living, sharing, and helping others (potential discomfort in competitive situations and competing for top grades). Group consensus is used for important decision making, with sufficient time (sometimes hours) allowed to examine an issue until consensus is reached.

7. Less verbal and direct than U.S. culture with a tradition of noninterference in the affairs of others; they do not impose themselves or their views on others unless asked. Interactions have a low-keyed and slower-paced style without attempts to exert dominance over others, gaze too directly, or draw undue attention to oneself or others. Use of a general pattern of addressing others rather than individuals, few interruptions, tendency for long pauses and silence with culturally distinctive ways of regulating interaction (contrasts with U.S. patterns of gaining attention, speaking more loudly, nodding or gazing directly at speaker, nodding and vocalizing "hmmm" or "yes"). Humor and "joking" are very important aspects of life.

8. Time is measured by natural phenomena—phases of the moon, the changing seasons, the rise and fall of tides, and the movements of the sun; this includes a focus on seasons and tribal customs (e.g., "naming ceremony" or puberty ceremonies) rather than child's developmental milestones (first words, first steps, etc.), resulting in possibly incomplete data on school forms. The focus is on present time and present needs (contrasts with future orientation in U.S. culture) and time is seen as "flexible."

Medical and disability perspectives

9. Interconnections among mind, body, and spirit lead to health and wellness as reflecting harmony or disharmony; natural unwellness is caused by the violation of a sacred or tribal taboo, and unnatural unwellness caused by power of evil. The Indian Health Service is the primary health care provider, although the incidence of poverty leads to poor medical care and health. Acceptance of authority decisions related to children is shown with respect and silence.

10. Some illness and misfortunes may be attributed to natural or supernatural causes; for example, parents told of a genetic disorder would understand "how" this occurred but may use cultural resources to understand "why" it occurred—the result of breaking a cultural taboo. The parents may use native healers or traditional ceremonies prior to seeing health care workers or consenting to other interventions. Western medical explanations may cause conflicts regarding spiritual dimensions of disability, and most Native American languages do not have words for the various disabilities.

Source: Compiled from Dunn & Griggs, 1995; Green, 1999; Harry, 1992a; Joe & Malach, 1998.

---

developed as an adaptation to discrimination and their history of slavery. The family, marriage, and kinship bonds are extremely important and the impacts of slavery on relationships can still be seen. African-American family members may or may not live together (this has been misinterpreted by American culture as instability within the nuclear family). However, great value is placed on the extended family and blood relatives with strong kinship networks which include multigenerational social networks for relatives, friends, and neighbors (see Table 5–6).

Family remains the source of their culture, providing socialization and guidance with a great value on communication. There is value placed on group effort given to common interests, with some expectation that private gain will be shared in a reasonable measure with the larger community. The family provides members with a sense of who they are, including their relationship with the dominant white culture. Family structure is significantly impacted by socioeconomic class (lower versus middle or upper class) and rural versus urban location. There

TABLE 5–6

African-American Families' Cultural Values and Behaviors

Worldview
  1. Values of collective responsibility and kinship obligation that extends into the larger community, including frequent fosterage of children and informal adoption, strong work orientation with a tradition of working wives, adaptable family roles with egalitarian patterns, high achievement orientation, and religious orientation. Many tend to be bicultural and code-switch according to the situation, particularly as they attain higher levels of education and social status. This group is sharply aware of mainstream prejudice toward their culture with marked distrust of mainstream society.
  2. Much of the cultural patterns have their roots in West Africa, with a strong religious orientation and an emphasis on feelings and interpersonal relationships. These traditions were nearly obliterated; most are now Protestant but with an emphasis on group solidarity and collectivity, with spontaneous and emotive qualities contrasting with U.S. formal style and emphasis on private spiritual life; increasing numbers practice Islam. Spiritual resources of the community have a strong impact.

Life satisfaction
  3. Contribution to the family and community with a value on wide relationship networks with the family; families support attaining potential through education, life skills, and personal competence with education seen as the means for withstanding change. Strong spiritual values combine with the strong role of the church in the community; traditionally, the church has been the place where members learned leadership and organizational skills that lead to betterment of life for all community members.

Family structure
  4. Blood relatives and close friends are very important; "family" are those who feel they belong to each other although they may or may not live in the same house. Young children may be cared for by older women or children when biological parents have limited time or direct involvement. Family is seen as a source of strength, resilience, socialization, guidance, and inspiration.
  5. Children are seen as the future with the need to feel loved and that they belong. They need adult protection and guidance, and all responsible adults in the community contribute to their education and discipline. Children tend to be restrained among strangers, with touching reserved for family and close friends (may be offended when teachers touch them).

is comparatively high unemployment, which impacts families in terms of health and poverty despite a higher rate of working mothers than found among many white Americans. Family structure is more flexible with collective responsibility and the sharing of child care across family and community relationships. The American meeting and communication styles that focus on direct, assertive, and nonemotive recitation of "facts" with an expectation of timely decision making can negatively impact effective collaborative planning. In addition, if the team is primarily white, the family may be suspicious and challenge opinions and educational options recommended by the team

Latino Peoples' Values and Beliefs

Latinos include people from Mexico, Puerto Rico, Cuba, and Central and South America, with specific cultural characteristics that are unique to each geographic area. Puerto Ricans are the second largest Latino group in the United States (Mexicans are the largest), with Central and South Americans the fastest growing group. Cubans tend to have more economic success; Central Americans immigrate for job opportunities but experience greater levels of poverty. Family commitment is of paramount importance to all, including loyalty to family, a strong family support system, and a view that the child reflects upon the honor of the family (see Table 5–7).

6. Acculturation has diluted the importance of older adults, although there is still a high value on respecting and obeying elders (spoken to with titles and respect: "Ma'am" or "Sir"). They are perceived as having wisdom and hindsight, and oldest family members may have a special status with God; they value obedience to parents and to older siblings.

Interaction style

7. Interaction is based on informality, expressiveness, with a strong emphasis on a sense of peoplehood; use of facial gestures and nonverbal communication styles vary from U.S. style. Verbal and musical communication is highly valued. Humor is used to interpret the world with value on the act of telling; ordinary conversations contain metaphors, descriptors, and body and motion to illustrate points. There is a tendency to rely more upon inferential learning, view things in their entirety (holistically), focus on people and not on objects, and be more approximate with space, time, and numbers.

Medical and disability perspectives

8. There are varying beliefs impacted by social class; those with strong ties to the rural South may prefer holistic, natural approaches and high-technology medical care for trauma situations; those who live in poverty or working but poor may wait for illness before seeking assistance. Middle-class members tend to subscribe more to Western traditions.

9. Disability may be interpreted in fatalistic and/or religious ways as bad luck or misfortune, or the result of misdeeds by parents and punishment for disobeying God, the work of the devil, or to evil spirits; variation occurs with social class. Mothers tend to experience less emotional distress and self-sacrifice and fathers have less denial about the disability than other cultures. There is less prejudice toward people with disabilities and many communities have incorporated these individuals into all aspects of their lives.

10. Parents are suspicious of the overreferrral of African Americans for mild disabilities and the frequently poor diagnosis and treatment processes by mental health professionals. They often are distrustful of school officials and mainstream authority figures.

Source: Compiled from Dunn & Griggs, 1995; Harry, 1992a; Willis, 1998.

There may be a strongly hierarchical order among siblings with a duty to care for members who have a disability, are ill, or are elderly.

Ethnic networks and supports are very important for teaching families about resources, procedures, and mechanisms of organizations in the United States. This is especially important for Latino women when they no longer have family or community networks from home; the barrio church often provides important sources of help. Many communities offer support groups for parents with some of the more common disabilities (e.g., cerebral palsy or Down syndrome).

Strong cultural differences with American values may occur in terms of the strong focus on the family and community for a sense of identity and appropriate life roles (gender and age-specific). Planning processes are influenced by interaction styles that expect attention to group issues and familial well-being more than to individuals within the group. Relationships are very important with development of related personal values of trustworthiness, loyalty, and respect.

Asian-American Values and Beliefs

An older term "Asian-Pacific Americans," has been separated to differentiate between the many widely varying beliefs and values (Pacific Island Americans are described separately). Asian Americans include ethnic groups that originate from

TABLE 5–7

Latino Families' Cultural Values and Behaviors

Worldview
1. Values include spirituality, dignity of each individual, and respect for authority figures. Beliefs in the importance of procreation, human dignity, service to others, and morality are based on Catholic ideology interwoven with native Central and South American views of the universe; there is a growing influence from Protestantism and religion is important to most families. There is a sense of obligation to ancestors and elders and respect to this hierarchy, including obedience and reverence.
2. Family loyalty is very important with a collective orientation that supports family and community life; identity and cooperation with the group or family are important values (versus U.S. emphasis on individualism). Godparents are important and may participate in special training or care for the child. There is value in being a good mother or parent, a caring and compassionate person, and moral and religious. The strong family identity leads children to adopt their parents' religious and political beliefs, occupational preferences, and philosophical lifestyle.

Life satisfaction
3. Strong value is on respect, dignity, personalism, honor, and trust with explicit deference from one person to another; such a person is considered to be "well brought-up" or "well-educated" (United States gives respect based on professionalism, possession of specific skills regardless of personal characteristics). Being a good parent, family member, and contributing to the community are important.

Family structure
4. The concept of "familia" includes immediate and extended family; family and relatives are more important than friends. Needs of the individual are secondary to the needs of the family; children who work give this money to their parents. Family reputation is a central consideration and means of identification with the community (U.S. culture focuses on the preeminence and separateness of self).
5. Clearly defined roles of ultimate patriarchal authority with male supremacy, maternal submissiveness, and strict sex-role delineations with childrearing as the exclusive domain of mothers. Men remain the primary provider; if a man is unable to obtain work and his wife works outside the home, he may lose face, self-esteem, and respect, impacting his marriage and interaction with other family members. Mothers play the major spiritual role in the family, and siblings have authority and responsibility according to their age. Male adolescents have earlier independence than American boys; girls are protected and their freedom often is restricted.

east Asia—China, Japan, and Korea—Southeast Asia—Burma, Cambodia, Indonesia, Laos, Malaysia, the Philippines, Singapore, Thailand, and Vietnam—and south Asia—India, Pakistan, Sri Lanka, Bangladesh, Bhutan, and Nepal (Chan, 1998a; Dunn & Griggs, 1995). Although several Asian-American groups are known for their industriousness and economic success, refugees (e.g., from Cambodia, Laos, and Vietnam) tend to have high rates of unemployment and low wages.

These diverse groups represent a variety of religions, beliefs, and lifestyles. Hindus believe in reincarnation, a respect for all living things, and the worship of many gods. Muslims believe in one God and strive to live in accord with the five pillars of their religion, including daily confessions of faith, praying five times daily, charity to those less fortunate, fasting during the ninth month, and a pilgrimage to Mecca at least once during their lifetime. The majority from Southeast Asia practice Buddhism, which believes in peace, harmony, strong family commitment, nonmaterialism, and the avoidance of extremes. Those from east Asia practice either Confucianism, Taoism, or Shintoism, which follow a set of ethical standards, including obedience to authority, honesty,

6. Marriage is for the purpose of having children; parent-child relationships are more important than the marital relationship. Parents are nurturing, permissive, and indulgent with young children; they have a relaxed attitude toward attainment of early skills or development milestones, with a focus on interdependence among family members. Discipline practices of a "well-educated" child include adherence to convention, respect for authority, identity with the family, and respect for elders.

Interaction style

7. Strong sex roles define males as dominant and the strong provider, with the female perceived as being nurturing, submissive, and self-sacrificing. "Machismo" is aligned with the concept of chivalry, gallant, courteous, charitable, and courageous. These roles often are weakened as family members become more highly educated.

8. Greater trust in people results in discomfort with "systems" that work too well; these are seen as too "impersonal" (The United States has more confidence in efficient organizations than in people). They are highly sensitive to interpersonal relationships and communication, including nonverbal cues. The power of social class and the relative immobility of status in native countries can strongly influence immigrants; social class is associated with lighter skin and European features, but there is a belief that such disadvantages can be offset through education or money.

Medical and disability perspectives

9. Caribbean peoples have added Catholicism with African-based beliefs, including folk healing in a variety of forms; Mexico provides traditional Indian folk-healing beliefs. Class issues are important; use of natural healers is often for poorer families who are unable to afford Western treatments. Families may see a traditional healer for a second opinion.

10. The birth of a child with a disability can be interpreted as an act of a punishing God, a curse from someone, the effects of an evil spirit (child may wear amulets), or the result of the pregnant mother being careless with sharp objects. Fatalistic views see life as laden with tragedy that one must accept. Those who are middle class or more educated may have a more Western view; however, asking for "cures" from God may remain.

11. Severe disability may be difficult to accept because of familialism and stigma: Children may be hidden. Mild disabilities may not be accepted or recognized especially if the child meets culturally appropriate norms. Those believing in folk medicine may accept severe disability as an "act of God." Families may allow special treatment for children with a disability, which can include a lack of discipline or making no demands on them.

Source: Compiled from Dunn & Griggs, 1995; Harry, 1992a; Skinner, Bailey, Correa, & Rodriguez, 1999; Zuniga, 1998.

kindness, and respect for elders. Refugee groups may retain stronger tribal beliefs such as spiritualist and animist practices.

All these religions share deference to authority, emotional restraint, specified roles defined in paternalism (i.e., men and elders enjoy greater status than women and children); a hierarchical, extended family orientation; interdependence; harmony with nature; and commitment to learning and academic achievement. Although these groups are primarily and strongly patriarchal in their families, there are several strong matriarchal groups (see Table 5–8).

Wide differences with American culture occur in religious practices and worldviews, including peace and harmony (nondominance over nature and others), strong family commitment which extends to previous generations, and strong social roles and proscribed relationships. These impact interaction and often conflict with American preferences for communication that is flexible in role, informal, assertive, and direct.

TABLE 5–8

Asian-American Families' Cultural Values and Behaviors

Worldview
1. There is a strong sense of collectivism and harmony (versus Western individualism and competition) based on their religious orientations. They may have a fatalistic life orientation shown by acceptance of one's fate and maintenance of inner strength and dignity. Strong values for responsibility, hard work, self-sacrifice (spiritual, emotional, material, and physical), modesty and humility, a reluctance for confrontation or self-promotion, indirectness in expressing feelings, aversion to share personal information outside the family, and comfort with structured social roles (may be uncomfortable with ambiguous/flexible social roles that are more typical of U.S. mainstream interactions).

Life satisfaction
2. Religious beliefs promote social order through individual virtues that follow reciprocal social obligations, rules of propriety, loyalty, cooperation, harmony, and benevolence (versus U.S. competition, autonomy, self-reliance, and flexible social roles). Social order includes strong values for family and links to ancestors.
3. The individual strives to achieve harmony personally, interpersonally, and with nature by focusing on each situation separately. Individuals often seek oneness with the group and being in step with others, neither ahead nor behind.
4. There is a reverence and status conferred on teachers and scholarship; children are ingrained with a lifelong respect for knowledge, wisdom, intelligence, and love of learning.

Family structure
5. Family is the most basic social institution, including the immediate family (husband, wife, unmarried children, and sons' wives and children) and extended family (family, close relatives sharing the same family name, and ancestors). The immediate family has well-defined, highly interdependent roles within a patriarchal structure. Gender roles may vary; however, men often have ultimate authority and women have authority for household affairs. Sons are more valued than daughters; they carry the family name and care for parents when they become old. Daughters are raised to marry and join another family; the wife accumulates power when she produces a son and becomes a mother-in-law. The strongest family ties are between parent and child rather than between spouses; parents are prepared to sacrifice personal needs in serving the interests of their children.
6. Individual behavior reflects on the family; a child's actions contribute to family pride, or to severe punishment and loss of face. There is strict parental authority with personal accountability and responsibility for the child's behavior. Parents assume primary responsibility for ensuring that children receive

Pacific Island-American Values and Beliefs

This group includes the Pacific Rim islands (people from the Philippines, Indonesia, and Polynesian islands of Hawaii, Samoa, and native New Zealanders) as a separate cultural group. Indonesia is strongly influenced by Muslim and Asian religions; however, there also is a strong Christian presence. For example, Filipinos are primarily Catholic and Hawaiians are strongly Christian (Chan, 1998b; Mokuau & Tauili'ili, 1998). The Christian religions emphasize brotherly love, justice, and charity as strong values. The influence of

Asian religious beliefs encourage obedience to authority, honesty, kindness, and respect for elders with strong links to ancestors. There is a tendency toward paternalism in certain cultures, although Polynesian cultures have strong matriarchal structures (see Table 5–9). The influence of native folk beliefs and Asian religions provide the most contrasting cultural differences in social structure and child-rearing practices when doing transition planning.

Filipinos tend to be highly educated with professional backgrounds but experience underem-

---

appropriate guidance and have a good education; parents' self-esteem may be tied to the academic success of their children in a highly competitive educational system. Children fulfill their obligation to the family through academic achievement which brings honor to the family and enhanced social status from their economic well-being.

7. Childrearing shows tolerance and permissiveness; parents immediately gratify the infant's early dependency needs. Mothers and infants have close physical contact and infants are carried much of the time. Preschool begins a transition between indulgence to discipline and education; older siblings are often responsible for care of younger siblings and are expected to model adultlike behaviors through strict obedience and unquestioned parental authority. There may be a distrust of outsiders, including restricting a child's social interactions to selected role models; children typically leave the home at older ages than American norms.

Interaction style

8. Asian groups tend to avoid direct confrontation, conform to rules of propriety, and "give face" or recognition and respect to others; this translates into verbal, social, and emotional restraint and consistent use of politeness, tact, modesty, self-control, and gentleness in interpersonal relations.

Medical and disability perspectives

9. There is considerable variation among the groups, with many families adopting a pluralistic blend of health care systems, including Chinese, folk medicine, and Western medical practices. Southeast Asians often believe in the supernatural cause of illness, particularly for mental illness. Bodily health is viewed as the balance between mind and body and there may be a reluctance to seek outside assistance, including many refugees who seek professional help only in extreme circumstances despite tremendous previous stress.

10. The most severe disabilities are traditionally viewed with considerable stigma, often due to beliefs about retribution for sins of ancestors/parents, possession by evil spirits, specific behaviors of the mother during her pregnancy, and an imbalance of physiological functions. All may bring shame to the family (with a stigma for needing/seeking outside help) compounded by the child's inability to demonstrate occupational or academic achievement. Parents may be highly tolerant of deviant behavior in young children and reluctant to admit an inability to cope or seek professional help; persistent psychosocial or learning difficulties at school can lead to a sense of severe parental inadequacy.

Source: Compiled from Chan, 1998a; Dunn & Griggs, 1995; Harry, 1992a.

ployment when their professional training is not recognized in the United States. Native Hawaiian and Somoan families value education but economic and social factors have led to a lower success rate.

Negotiating Transition Mandates

These descriptions of cultural groups and your growing awareness of your own culturally based beliefs and values will make you more sensitive and alert to difficulties that result from unspoken cultural expectations. For example, culturally different families who do not attend a particular meeting, who make minimal if any efforts to discuss or participate in setting goals for their child, or who fail to follow through with written plans may need culturally appropriate assistance.

The required transition procedures and documents presume knowledge and comfort with typical American values and assumptions: ITPs (Individualized Transition Plans) are individually focused on developing independence; they require

TABLE 5–9

Pacific Island-American Peoples' Cultural Values and Behaviors

Worldview
1. The Asian and Catholic traditions support a strong focus on family; it is their source of personal identity as well as emotional and material support. Their sense of patience, determination, responsibility, hard work, and self-sacrifice, modesty, and humility also supports Christian traditions. Native Hawaiian and Somoan groups have a growing appreciation of their native beliefs in spirituality and their connection to the spiritual world.

Life satisfaction
2. A value for fitting in with the family and the group, and following rules of propriety with respect to others. They possess a sense of endurance with a fatalistic life orientation toward unalterable conditions and acceptance of one's fate. They have a strong reverence for, and status conferred on, teachers and scholarship. Filipinos value education and professional preparation highly; Filipino women have the highest percentage of participation in the U.S. labor force among all Asian-American groups and earn more than the U.S. median.

Family structure
3. Family is very important, including the extended family (such as the family and close relatives sharing the same family name and ancestors). An individual's primary duty and commitment is to the family and to those who are successful and share their money and material belongings, often purchasing things for others before themselves. There is a mixture of patriarchal societies although the immediate family gives greater rights and responsibilities to women than in many other Asian countries; these families are generally more egalitarian with recognition of matrilineal lineage with Filipino women controlling family finances. Decision making occurs within the group with older extended family members solicited for advice. Native Hawaiian and Somoan families combine strong family loyalties with ties to their land.

only the parents to attend; the signatures are considered legally binding; and parents are expected to participate in meetings as equal partners. The transition team will likely need to serve as cultural mediators in order to ensure that transition mandates are satisfied and that family goals also are met.

One of the most important aspects of collaborative planning is to begin with shared goals and values (Friend & Cook, 1990). Transition team members need to understand the particular beliefs and values of the family and how they define their child's ultimate adult outcomes. From this, the team will be able to move into developing mutual goals and values and to begin transition program development and implementation. Soliciting family input on these outcomes and goals is most successful when done in a culturally supportive manner rather than the typically "direct" and efficient American style. Initially, culturally

different interaction styles may seem awkward and uncomfortable, and the family's response may be difficult to gauge. As trust and comfort develops between all members, the process will become increasingly easier.

Supporting Family Participation

As a mandate for transition planning, this is an important aspect of transition team processes that may require flexibility and perseverance to achieve. Information concerning parental rights as well as program and placement options must begin from what the family currently understands about these issues, relative to their values and beliefs. Sharing this information may require more than one visit and a period of time that begins with culturally appropriate "visiting" and getting to know each other. Of most importance is that team members learn to be sensitive to cultural dissonances and when communica-

4. Authority in Filipino societies is earned through social class or professional status and is accompanied by many privileges; however, these individuals have a responsibility to support and assist others and to maintain the harmony of the group. Within families, status is given through age, with more responsibility given to older siblings. All seek to maintain smooth interpersonal relations and good feelings through avoiding conflict and confrontation, yielding to group opinion, and avoiding "loss of face" and shame. Joy, humor, flexibility, creativity, adaptability, respect, and dignity for others are important aspects of family life.

5. Child-rearing responsibilities may be shared among relatives, such as godparents, with some surrogate parenting roles assumed by landlords and employers. Divorce is prohibited in Filipino societies except for Muslims. Child discipline occurs through persuading the child rather than by imposing authority, with greater indulgence given to young children.

Medical and disability perspectives

6. There is a variation of beliefs according to religious orientation. Folk and native beliefs may see illness as caused by God or external powers, which need to be appeased. There may be a blending of Western health care practices with folk medicine traditions with a belief that God or spirits are working through hospitals and doctors. Exposure, access to, and acceptance of Western medical practices influence beliefs and care in conjunction with Christian traditions.

7. Disability may be viewed as divine or external punishment for sins or moral transgressions. Asian beliefs about stigma and the child may also influence family perceptions.

Source: Compiled from Chan, 1998b; Dunn & Griggs, 1995; Mokuau & Tauili'ili, 1998.

tion appears to break down or expectations are widely discrepant, they stop the meeting process to begin probing "gently" in order to ascertain potential cultural conflicts.

Once the team has obtained a fairly comprehensive description of the family's vision, it can begin to establish mutual goals. This vision should include, as much as possible, if and where their child will work, live, and participate in leisure and recreational activities, and with whom. Some of these may be very different from the team's vision because of views of disability, gender, or family honor. A good point to begin negotiations may be to present a potential alternative outcomes. Using this procedure, the team members usually need to present the rationale for these outcomes in terms of the benefit to the child and family/community (i.e., from their cultural perspectives) and why they feel this is a good alternative (i.e., it is the best practice because it complies with the legal mandates, which are considered important). An alternative is to

agree on some initial steps rather than ask the family to agree to an entire program. This may help the family to see the benefits to themselves, their community, and their child that they at first may have had difficulty envisioning. Developing consensus on aspects of this vision can lead to further consensus later.

Team members must guard against a temptation to present only one, optimal "American" set of adult outcomes as the complete transition program. This can be particularly challenging if the family has difficulty expressing their goals (long-term planning is not an activity valued by all cultures [Lewis, 1997]) or is reticent in discussing these topics. Unfortunately, the family may not be able to express this directly to team members and may see this type of discussion as pushy and overbearing, further reducing their willingness to participate in decision making.

Some cultural and family groups will need more time to make decisions than is typical for American IEP/ITP meetings. If they need to share meeting suggestions with their larger community group or particular leaders who are not present, the meeting may have to be continued later. This can present a problem for the team, particularly with some school administrators who prefer not to end a meeting without a parental signature. This type of "American" pressure also must be negotiated carefully, supporting the need for comprehensive multicultural training that addresses all levels of personnel.

Supporting Student Participation
Mandates to address the student's needs, preferences, and interests can be seen as undermining and insensitive to proscribed social and family order in other cultures. The team must use considerable delicacy in balancing the student's desires with the family and community needs for cultures that place greater value on the family and community identity. The team can use information about the acculturation levels of the family members, including the student, to help evaluate whether significant differences are present concerning specific transition outcomes. It is helpful to remember that acculturation can vary across work, living, socialization, and recreational areas so that there can be strong family consensus on some, if not all, aspects. Students can feel highly supported by and comfortable with their culture and community and have interests and preferences that align closely with their family's interests and preferences. Those aspects that do not align so closely can be negotiated on a step-by-step process, thus allowing all team and family members (including the student) to feel comfortable with this new bicultural situation. For example, if a student wishes to work outside the community in a position different from that envisioned by their family, the team can negotiate for trial work in a similar position inside the community or for a more comfortable type of position outside the community. Both the family and student can learn about how comfortable they are, or are not with this type of placement. It also is typical of adolescents to require

a number of trial learning experiences before being able to make realistic decisions about their future.

Another potentially conflictual aspect of transition planning is the need for individually based interest and choice assessments that lead to better student decision making. It is important to explain these types of activities and the rationale for doing so to the family. The team may wish to assign activities and exercises to be carried out jointly with the family so that the child is not placed in a position of engaging in activities that could create difficulties or conflicts at home or with the community. Balancing family, student, and legal issues can be extremely delicate. At no point does the team wish to set up the student for increased family conflict nor to support increased acculturation that may lead to such conflicts. Most young adults require some, if not extensive, cooperation from their family and community to complete the process of becoming successful adults, long after the transition team has relinquished responsibility. Again, the team may need to identify a series of steps that both the parent and student can agree upon, as well as other team members, that can be used to test everyone's comfort level in achieving specific paths toward adulthood. Likewise, the team should work to support both the student and family members and avoid being placed in a position of mediating an escalating conflict. This latter situation is not dissimilar to what can occur between any teenager and his or her parents. Having appropriate cultural knowledge and background can help to avoid additional pitfalls offered by bicultural and acculturation issues. A summary of these issues are organized into five steps and appear in Table 5–10.

This one chapter cannot cover the complexity of cross-cultural interpersonal interactions and the flexibility and creativity that may be required. Table 5–11 provides some additional interaction suggestions that may be helpful and organized according to different phases of the meeting process.

TABLE 5–10

Negotiating the Transition Planning Process

Step 1: Begin with the family's current understandings and perceptions. The descriptions of cultural values and the team's assessment of the family's acculturation in terms of transition planning and their child's future provide a basis for opening discussions about transition planning. Information about the nature of transition mandates and the laws should be provided using culturally based values and explanations and not depend on written descriptions and pamphlets. Move to having the family describe their goals for their child as adults (some cultures are much less future oriented, which may pose a challenge: Focusing on specific aspects of work and living arrangements may help).

Step 2: Address culturally different goal areas. Use information from the previous step to identify areas in which the family's and the mandates or team members' perceptions differ significantly. Determine as a team the type of compromises that will satisfy these differences. Offer a range of acceptable alternatives to the family and allow time to build consensus, as is appropriate. Some families may need to discuss things among themselves or to confer with members who are not present. Try to allow this as a possibility with an agreement from team members about a future meeting time and the specific issues to be decided. Discussions about independence and individually determined needs, interests, and preferences can be problematic. Focusing on specific acceptable aspects of work, living, or recreation/leisure can address these same issues in a potentially less direct manner. Issues of self-advocacy, self-determination, or related quality-of-life issues can also be more effectively addressed in terms of specific situations where you believe the student needs these skills in order to succeed.

Step 3: Use trial experiences to gather additional information. A series of steps can help family and team members to learn whether or not certain settings and tasks are acceptable and successful. Family members may be unsure of certain transition experiences but are willing to let their child try them out. The students also need to learn how comfortable they are in these settings, and the team needs to evaluate the impact of settings and tasks on the student and family. This can provide a compromise to a previously rejected or unacceptable option. The team must be careful not to be overly pushy, however. Families often need time to adjust to new conditions and expectations. The results of these trials will be useful in moving forward with these goals or in refocusing on another acceptable alternative.

Step 4: Focus on building relationships with family members. Development of a caring, trusting relationship with family members is important and often valued more heavily than in American culture. Transition planning meetings will continue for several years, allowing team members time to develop this relationship. At times, the quality of the relationship may be a more important long-term goal than pushing the family into a current ITP with which they are uncomfortable. The team may need to adjust "participation" in order to solicit their responses and opinions in a way that is appropriate for them. Families who expect the school to make all such decisions unilaterally may need time to adjust to their new roles. The time spent initially on building a relationship is likely to create an atmosphere in which mediating differences becomes much easier.

Step 5: Use culturally competent interaction styles and behaviors as much as possible. With families who are culturally different from ourselves and whose interaction styles are significantly different, we may not be able to modify our learned behavioral patterns easily. Demonstrating respect and positive regard for the family will still be recognized and appreciated. As we become more culturally competent and more comfortable with the family, we may be better able to evaluate accurately their satisfaction with our services.

TABLE 5–11

Additional Suggestions for Transition Team Members

Preparing for the meeting

1. Recognize how the family's culture addresses disability: This may include beliefs about "sickness" versus wellness, typical versus atypical behavior, as well as etiology, symptomatology, and treatment methods.

2. Identify who the important members are of the family group: Include all in important meetings.

3. If a problem is identified, recognize the culturally based resolutions that may be expected: Religious or community assistance can be important factors; learn how they solve problems within their own communities and what may be the expected outcomes.

Planning the meeting

4. Ask parents whom they want to include in meetings; capitalize on kinship bonds with families, including extended families in interventions if they are responsible for child care. Direct communication to the entire group when extended family members attend.

5. Several ethnic groups view professionals as authority figures and deserving of unquestioned respect. Some expect directive, structured approaches with specific advice and recommendations; families take a "dependent" orientation of deference and noninterference. Legal mandates for participatory decision making and parental rights may confuse families and leave them feeling very uncomfortable with these "collaborative" practices, which can seem alien and threatening. Family members who disagree with professional decisions may be culturally uncomfortable with expressing this out of respect; instead, they may emotionally withdraw or not follow through with what they "agreed" to do in formal IEP/ITP documents. Plan for ways to address these issues if they arise.

6. Public disclosure of disabilities is extremely difficult for some cultures and may be considered a betrayal of family loyalty or trust. The concept of face-saving is very important in nearly all relationships with Asian-American families in order to protect their dignity, honor, and self-respect. Consider how to present information and discussion to a full team of individuals and still demonstrate respect of the family's privacy concerns.

7. Always offer a skilled interpreter for families who use English as a second language and discuss the choice of an interpreter with the family (Asian-American families may prefer to use an English-speaking family member or a known interpreter whom they trust). Prepare families with the discussion topics and, if you must, ask a lot of questions. Allow them to discuss issues with other family members and give them time to think or discuss something before responding.

8. Do not assume that families are always literate in their native language; assess their education levels and class status as well as you can so that you can evaluate ways to best assist them.

9. For Latino families, you may need to address issues of illegal immigration and, out of respect, most professionals prefer to use the term "undocumented immigrants", let families know that you are not bound to inform the Immigration and Naturalization Service (*La Migra*).

10. Be aware of family resources; they may agree with plans but be embarrassed to admit that they have no transportation to follow through, or may not know how to negotiate freeway and highway systems. They may not know of certain agencies or services that you refer to, so always check with them before assuming that they know.

11. Each cultural group has unique ways of defining adulthood and "independence." Be sensitive to unique definitions with transition planning and realize that some families will view unmarried children, and particularly daughters, working and living independently as signs of family "failure" or dysfunction. Parental and family views need to be carefully negotiated when the child is more acculturated and has different adult goals than those of his or her family. Remember that in many cultures there may be strong,

hierarchichal patterns for decision making; asking the student only what he or she prefers may place them in a difficult and conflictual situation with their family.

12. Be prepared for families who have firmly proscribed interaction and behavioral patterns according to age, gender, and social status. They may be highly uncomfortable with the informal and egalitarian approach typical of U.S. interactions. Use a more polite and formal manner as is appropriate and focus on communication that is more personal (rather than "factual" and "informative") to increase the family's comfort level. Realize that many ethnic groups also have a much more flexible perspective about time so that scheduled meetings and services are likely to need greater flexibility than the typical U.S. goal of "efficiency."

During the meeting

13. Show respect by listening to the family/group's ideas by acknowledging their concerns and feelings and include all interested family members. Address family members formally with titles and last names until given permission to be more informal.

14. Take time to learn the communication style preferences of the family. For example, Native American communities often require a reserved and quiet approach until they feel comfortable, which includes long periods of silence and talking slowly. Asian/Pacific Island-American families require a development of "trust" and tend to view outsiders with suspicion. African-American families may challenge and distrust opinions of white professionals. Latino families believe general interest in the entire family is important before focusing on an individual member (e.g., the child).

15. Take time for "small talk" and visiting when beginning each meeting; proceed at a pace that is comfortable for the Native American family and that allows plenty of time for Latino families, each of whom may interpret a "hurried" atmosphere as giving them less respect or concern. Establish well-defined roles and clear communication with Asian-American families about what is being requested of them and what services can be offered.

16. Spend time with all families, establishing personal rapport to allow for discussion about information that may be tangential or unrelated to the referring problems—sensitivity to face-saving needs, showing an interest in the extended family group, and use of indirect discussion approaches are culturally important. Demonstrate attention to small and important details of their lives and show interest and concern in their comfort, general health, and well-being. This indicates that you are a caring professional and can help in gaining their trust and confidence.

17. Use culturally competent ways to show respect for authority, including making appropriate use of nodding, avoiding eye contact, refraining from asking questions or making desires explicit. Chinese and other Asian groups avoid hugging, backslapping, and handshakes; Muslims and Middle Easterners view use of the left hand to touch another person or object as inappropriate. Behaviors interpreted as being "rude," "pushy," or improper can lead to families' reluctance to continue to meet, to seek explanations of services and policies, or to clarify communications and explanations despite their great need or desire for this information.

18. Ask families if they have planned activities or events which might interfere with scheduled evaluations or interventions. Also, ask if this information can be shared with other team/school members, and if so, how this can best be done; be careful about violating different perceptions of privacy.

19. Do not be embarrassed to admit that you know little or nothing about the family's culture (the variety of distinct immigrant groups makes it impossible to be knowledgeable about all groups). Take time to know the individual family's circumstances, education and social status levels, and exposure to American culture. Work on creating an atmosphere in which the family members can let you know if you do or say something culturally inappropriate (i.e., they will appreciate sincere efforts in most cases).

20. Explain all time lines and time limitations to families that you or the team are unable to change (i.e., try to allow flexibility whenever possible). Let them know the reasons for these and what the options are. Make sure the families know if a decision must be made by a certain date.

TABLE 5–11

(Concluded)

21. Be sensitive to acculturation processes that may create distress in families; the second generation often becomes increasingly bilingual and bicultural, with resulting changes in authority patterns, acceptance of outside assistance or advice, and differing views about disability and appropriate interventions. Typical IEP/ITP procedures often support directness that may be alienating and offensive to cultures that require reticence, modesty, or privacy in these matters.

After the meeting

22. Family members may display gratitude for help from those in "superior" (i.e., professional) positions through gift giving, invitations to dinner or family celebrations, and other expressions of appreciation that support building a longer term relationship; some have a strong sense of "debt" or duty to those who have helped them. Refusal to accept gifts, favors, or invitations may be construed as rejection and failure to "give face" and require great tact and sensitivity.

23. Families should be given opportunities to talk to other parents who have children with special needs and especially so if they are members of their same ethnic group and social class; offer this more than once because families need time to feel ready.

24. Use informal and community support networks (e.g., church, neighbors, and friends) whenever possible (i.e., this may be a particularly helpful and welcome resource for African-American and Latino families). Use formal and informal communication networks to assist in work with Asian-Pacific-American and Native American families, including use of respected third parties or identified community leaders. Learn and use information about how each community may prefer to examine available options and to solve problems.

Source: Compiled from Chan, 1998a, 1998b; Correa, 1989; Gault, 1989; Hanson, 1998a; 1998b; Harry, 1992a, 1992b, 1992c; Joe & Malach, 1998; Lynch, 1998a, 1998b; Mokuau & Tauili'ili, 1998; Pinderhughes, 1995; Sharifzedeh, 1998; Stewart, Danielian, & Festes, 1969; Turnbull et al., 1995; van Keulen et al., 1998; Willis, 1998; & Zuniga, 1998.

Even when using effective and culturally competent strategies, families may not be used to or prepared for the decisions they are being asked to make. It will require effort from all team members to support families in ways that allow them to adjust to these tasks. Each member has an individual responsibility to increase his or her cultural competence in order to provide effective and appropriate services. However, you may be faced with the task of working with other professionals who are not culturally sensitive or competent. The growing numbers of culturally different students, families, and agency clients may lead your workplace to address this issue through a training or in-service program. You may be called upon to provide input and assistance in planning this program.

Some of these issues and strategies are described in the next section.

Providing Culturally Competent Transition Planning Services

School and agency personnel have great needs for information about, and access to, culturally competent practices (Burnette, 1998; Markowitz, 1996; Obiakor & Utley, 1996). The first and most important step, as described earlier, is to be aware of one's own values and cultural beliefs. From there, team members must then become committed to an ongoing process of learning about the other culture(s). Although some of this can occur through reading and studying other

TABLE 5–12

Becoming a Culturally Competent Professional

Steps to develop cultural competence

1. Background preparation: Read descriptions in journals, make a series of visits to the community to learn about the social interactions and characteristics and the resources that are available.

2. Use of cultural guides: These are ordinary people who may or may not be community leaders but who can articulate what is going on around them.

3. Participant observation: This is a long-term commitment to learning in detail about the life of a community with minimal intrusion into the day-to-day activities of the residents by participating in community activities with simultaneous observation of all interactions and details about community life.

Questions to ask in evaluating your cultural competence

1. How much personal and social time do I spend with people who are culturally similar to or different from me?

2. When I am with culturally different people, do I reflect upon my own cultural preferences or do I spend time openly learning about the unique aspects of another person's culture?

3. How comfortable am I in immersion experiences, especially where I am in a numerical minority?

4. How much time do I spend engaged in cross-cultural professional exchanges?

5. How much work have I actually done to increase my knowledge and understanding of culturally and ethnically district groups?

6. What is my commitment to becoming culturally competent? What personal and professional sacrifices am I willing to make?

7. To what extent have I nondefensively extended myself in approaching professional colleagues with the goal of bridging cultural differences?

Source: Adapted from Green, J. N. (1999) *Cultural awareness in human services: A multi-ethnic approach* . Boston: Allyn & Bacon, p. 76.

cultures, personal involvement is critical to becoming truly competent. A survey of 100 Southwest U.S. rural school administrators identified (1) involvement with parents and (2) an understanding of the cultural and linguistic background of the family as key professional competencies (Rodriquez, 1994). It is significant to note that personal involvement was listed as the first important competence. Although relationships with families is not typical of American values (the medical model believes that noninvolvement maintains objectivity and, therefore, greater accuracy in diagnosis and treatment), several cultures consider this essential to receiving satisfactory services from professionals.

Several authors suggest ways to become culturally competent. Green (1999) suggests a three-step plan that includes background readings and research but also depends on personal interactions through the use of a chosen cultural guide and frequent visits into the community (see Table 5–12). Pinderhughes (1995) also suggests a model for cultural competence and adds important elements of being comfortable with difference, willing to change previously held ideas, and flexible with one's own thinking and behavior. Among the most difficult aspects of this type of learning is that of personal discomfort, which can arise when confronting oneself with difference and a need to change. Green (1999, see Table 5–13) provides a number of issues and questions to consider while developing cultural competence. Appendixes A and B provide additional questions and considerations that support

TABLE 5–13

Models of Cultural Competence

Minimal components of a cultural competence model
1. Awareness of self-limitations (including one's own cultural beliefs and preferences)
2. Interest in cultural differences (willingness to examine own and others' beliefs)
3. Systematic learning style (to examine differences and increase cultural knowledge)
4. Utilization of cultural resources (those typically found in the ethnic communities)
5. Engagement with diversity (personal involvement with others)

Characteristics of cultural competence
1. Respect for others, including the ability to perceive individuals and families through their own cultural lens
2. Knowledge of specific beliefs and values that are characteristic of the person or family's community
3. Personal comfort with existing differences and values
4. A willingness to change previously held ideas
5. The ability to be flexible and adapt one's thinking and behavior to novel settings
6. The skill of sorting through diverse information about a community to understand how it might apply to particular individuals or families

---

Sources: Green, J. W. (1991) and Pinderhughes, E. (1998). *Cultural awareness in human services: A multi-ethnic approach.* Boston: Allyn & Bacon, p. 87; Empowering diverse populations: family practice in the 21st century *Families in Society, 76,* 131–140.

additional self-reflection upon some of the many issues that impact cross-cultural effectiveness.

This chapter strongly recommends development of a trusting relationship with a member of the ethnic or cultural minority to serve as a cultural guide. This person can be a very useful source of support in becoming culturally competent and can assist in facing difficult or confusing issues that cannot always be addressed directly with families or other team members. This person should be competent, both as a member of a minority group and one who is articulate and knowledgeable about his or her own culture.

Parents also are a potential source of cultural expertise (Brame, 1995; Harry, 1992a); however, this is best done outside the IEP/ITP meeting. They can serve as important members of advisory groups and can assist with training. Minority school personnel as well can provide valuable information and experiences, including strategies for successfully balancing two or more

cultures (Harry, 1992a; Obiakor & Utley, 1996). However, they cannot be expected to know about the range of cultures within an area (Luft, 1995). Each locale may have highly specific immigrant populations with distinct cultural values that are unknown to nonmembers. Parents and community leaders would function as the best resource, particularly in these instances (Harry, 1992a).

Professional and In-Service Training

School- and agency-based in-services and workshops provide an important starting place for improving cultural competence; however, they are not sufficient unless continuous and ongoing, with mechanisms that allow for feedback and evaluation (Green, 1999; Hanson, 1998a). Typically, in-services and workshops are designed to address one or a series of narrow topics through informal or formal training programs. Often they have little or no sufficient follow-through and re-inforcement of learnings in order to achieve significant change.

A more complete planning process would include schoolwide and agencywide planning and potential restructuring to address multicultural issues and needs for all staff and key personnel (Fradd and Weismantel, 1989). Frequently, multiple processes and organizational procedures may create cultural barriers that are best addressed in a comprehensive manner. This approach is most successful when it aligns with, or is used to redefine a school's or agency's vision in conjunction with identifying related organizational needs and resources.

An organizationwide program is the best means for addressing issues of cultural competence across the range of personnel that can interact with culturally different families and clients. Professionals need information about cross-cultural interaction styles, culturally fair assessment and referral/eligibility processes, identifying and building upon cultural strengths and resources in carrying out IEP/ITP plans, and developing appropriate staff expectations regarding students and families (cf. Markowitz, 1996; Obiakor & Utley, 1996). Other support personnel often are used to make contacts, set up appointments and meetings, or solicit information to be used in files and they also need information on appropriate interaction styles. Each school or agency consists of unique cultural strengths, needs, and challenges that are best incorporated in and addressed through this type of program.

Strategies for Supporting Minority Parents

When meeting with family members, team members must be very sensitive to issues of family resources and time availability. Not all families have cars for transportation or have work schedules that can accommodate typical meeting times and schedules (Brame, 1995). This is true for many families, regardless of ethnicity. Lynch and Stein (1987) also found that 54% of minority families were unable to attend their last school meeting because of work, time, transportation, or child-care conflicts. Teams may want to consider holding meetings in the family's home and in the evenings or weekends as a way to reduce some of these barriers, and to show their commitment to learning about the family and supporting their involvement in their child's education (Brame, 1995; Lynch & Stein, 1987). Such an arrangement would not be appropriate for all cultural groups, and team members must meet with the comfort level of the family.

Another important resource for providing training, advocacy assistance, and increased participation in educational planning is the use of peer parent groups. These have proven to be a highly effective means because families often feel more comfortable in learning from each other and through the social ties they form (Dybwad, 1989; Harry, 1992a; Gliedman & Roth, 1980). This is especially true if the peer parent groups are of the same cultural group and social/educational status. Transition team members also can be included in family groups and can provide important assistance and liaison support.

Comprehensive Cultural Training

Minority families may wish to benefit from the resources and support of schools and agencies in learning to better understand American culture and services. A combination of professional and family training could offer an effective way to develop and support cultural competence for all team members including parents (Correa, 1989). Family members could be included with the organization's training plans to serve as individual cultural guides, to serve on professional development planning groups in order to provide comprehensive training to both staff and families, and to help ensure ongoing feedback between parents and professionals to assure mutual trust and communication. This type of inclusive and comprehensive training would include all key stakeholder individuals who are involved in educational and transition service planning to develop the cross-cultural skills needed to work effectively with each other.

Regardless of the particular approach used to increase multicultural understanding, both parents and school personnel need basic information and assistance in becoming culturally competent (Brame, 1995; Burnette, 1998). For parents, this includes information about the special education system and transition planning processes, as well as support from peers. Transition team members need specific information about cultural values, their impact on transition planning, and skills for mediating between conflicting values and beliefs that meet professional and legal obligations. An important consideration in planning multicultural training programs is that program administrators themselves may not have an extensive background. A survey of 30 special education administrators in Ohio showed that although most believed that teachers should participate in multicultural education training, only 4 of the 30 had received any such formal training (Ford, 1992). It can, in fact, be left to individual members of schools and agencies to raise issues about the need for cultural competence and to assist in assuring comprehensive and appropriate planning and training procedures.

Conclusion

The cultural understandings described in this chapter impact cross-cultural relationships that go far beyond transition and IEP planning meetings. In fact, the need for cultural competence impacts all aspects of family and student interaction. Every conversation with the child or his or her parents, every note, telephone call, written report, and meeting convey beliefs and opinions, many of which unintentionally convey culturally based expectations. The team should be aware of potential differences in learning styles that can impact the effectiveness of instructional training programs that have been selected to implement transition plans. Many classroom instructional tasks expect analytical and cause-effect thinking which differ from cultures that support global and holistic perspectives (for information about culturally different learning styles, see Dunn & Griggs, 1995).

The steps toward becoming culturally competent are gradual and require time and perseverance. Each of us must learn to recognize the power of our own cultural beliefs and values and to understand the ways in which these differ from the families with whom we work. These differences frequently include race, educational level, economic level, and social status. The process of learning about culture requires being flexibile, having a willingness to abandon previous ways of thinking, and becoming culturally challenged through interacting with those who are different from you by visiting their communities and reading and studying about these differences. Although we are likely to feel awkward at first, our positive intentions may allow us to become increasingly comfortable and effective.

Our skills in cross-cultural interaction may become increasingly important with the continuing immigration and changing demographics of the United States. Many families with whom we will work have neither the language skills nor the cultural competence to interact effectively with American institutions. The unique adult-focused and outcome-oriented nature of transition planning and its requirements for participatory decision making create a situation that can lead to substantial cultural barriers and conflicts between families and transition team members. The current lack of cross-cultural expertise in many schools and agencies makes the skills we acquire even more valuable.

This chapter has provided a starting point with information and insights for improving cross-cultural transition planning and team interactions. This is a time of opportunity and change, with U.S. public services becoming more willing to recognize cultural difference as an area of need. Readers of this book may become the few members of their workplace with a background in cultural competence. Those who continue to develop their competence can play an important role in seeing that all members of the transition planning team, and the workplace, have the necessary knowledge and skills to provide high-quality and effective services.

CASE STUDY INTRODUCTION

Asian-Pacific Americans represent one of the largest current groups of immigrant peoples in the United States (Chan, 1998a, 1998b). Examine your cultural competence by planning how you would work with these two students and their families.

CASE STUDY A

Tru Lang is a 15-year-old Vietnamese student who has a visual impairment and mild/moderate developmental delays. He once showed you a scar on his chest that he said was from a camp. You know that as a child he spent some time in a war orphans camp separated from his parents and had moved to the United States to stay with an uncle. He was reunited with his parents and siblings when they were able to leave Vietnam a few years later. He is very outgoing and animated, with strong vocational interests in working outdoors. He seems very interested in being like other American teenagers. You know little about his family at this point but believe that his uncle and aunt lived here for several years and may be important acculturating factors and bicultural interpreters for the family.

CASE STUDY B

Crystal is a 17-year-old Cambodian girl who lives with her family, which includes an older sister. She has developmental disabilities and had little or no language until she entered school here at age 11. You know little about the family and they have not shared much in past interactions or in school records. You have been told that her "parents" are really her aunt and uncle although it is her real sister. She and her sister were able to escape but you believe that her real parents were killed. You do not know whether or not she and her sister witnessed this. Crystal, like her family, expresses little about herself or her activities. Although her name is Americanized, she does not seem to have strong desires to act like other American teenagers. She does not have strong friendships with the other students (girls or boys) and does not talk much about the TV shows she watches. Only occasionally have you seen her express strong anger, which surprised you, perhaps as the result of someone doing something culturally offensive to her. Crystal has done job shadowing and trial work experiences across the major occupational categories, but it has been difficult for you and the other team members to get a strong sense of any of her preferences. She is a very compliant and pleasant student to work with in other ways; however, it is becoming important for her to make a vocational choice soon.

Study Questions

1. What are the reasons and processes that lead to overrepresentation of minority students in special education programs? From your experience in schools and agencies, what could you do as an individual that would help to correct these tendencies?
2. What are the major differences among white, middle-, and upper-middle-class values and minority group beliefs and values in the areas of identity, disability, and relationships? What are your beliefs and values, and how closely do they align with the majority of American values?
3. How can team processes accommodate culturally different families in terms of (a) determining student needs and preferences, (b) setting goals, (c) determining appropriate outcome-oriented processes, and (d) in moving from school to postschool activities? What can you do as an individual team member to encourage greater accommodation?

4. A family does not speak during the annual IEP/ITP meeting and even does not respond to direct questions from team members. What are (a) some of the culturally appropriate reasons that this family might not do so and (b) how would you approach the family to support their greater participation in a future meeting?

5. One of the interagency members of your transition team has a very directive approach that you believe is causing the family to withdraw emotionally from the team. This agency member has informed you that the family is poor, a minority, and, therefore, uncaring and uninterested. You disagree with this conclusion. How would you approach this person and provide information about cultural differences?

6. Your principal/supervisor has asked you to help plan a program to increase cultural sensitivity and appropriateness in your school/agency. How would you begin such a program, whom would you include in the planning process, and what would be your specific outcomes of this training?

Web Sites

Council for Exceptional Children:
http://www.cec.sped.org

    Division for Culturally and Linguistic Diverse Exceptional Learners
    Standing Committee on Ethnic and Multicultural Concerns

Diverse and Ethnic Studies: Virtual Community:
http://www.public.iastate.edu/~savega.divweb2.htm

Ethnic Studies at USC:
http://www.usc.edu/isd/archives/ethnicstudies/

Resources for Research on Ethnic Studies
National Association for Ethnic Studies:
http://www.ksu.ksu.edu/ameth/naes/naes.htm

    Annual Conference
    Ethnic Studies Programs
    Ethnic Web Sites
    Journals and News Sources
    Libraries, Universities, and Research Centers

SECTION II

Career and Transition Services

6   Career and Vocational Education

7   Transition Assessment and Postschool Outcomes

8   Curriculum Development and Transition

9   Instructional Strategies

10   The Role of Technology in Transition Planning

6

Career and Vocational Education

Pamela Luft
Lynn C. Koch
Deborah Headman
Patrick O'Connor

LEARNING OBJECTIVES

The objectives of this chapter are:

1. Describe the relationship between career education and vocational education and how to integrate each into the transition planning process.

2. Describe the four stages of career education development.

3. Describe the foundational and prevocational skills and their impact on later career choices.

4. Describe work-site experiences and career planning strategies and how they support successful transition planning.

5. Describe appropriate monitoring strategies for use with the student and potential work sites.

6. Describe strategies for initiating, maintaining, and advancing a career.

Career and vocational education represent two of the most important training avenues through which students with disabilities acquire transition preparation. If either programming or planning in these areas is poorly done, students are unlikely to acquire the knowledge, skills, and work competency levels that will allow them to obtain and keep a job in the community. Without the income that work provides and the opportunity to share in this central activity of American adulthood, the lifestyle and satisfaction of students preparing for transition is likely to be substantially compromised.

This chapter describes career education and vocational education programs to prepare educators and transition team members facing the task of preparing a student for the comprehensive roles of adulthood. The resulting plan must begin with the *student's needs, interests, and preferences* in order to ensure that the career the student chooses will continue to interest and challenge him or her well into adulthood. All related career and vocational planning should focus on the student's preferred career goal and employment *outcome*. The team needs to determine an optimal series of instructional and training programs that moves the student from *school and into postschool environments*. In addition to classroom-based instruction, students also need work experiences in the community that progress from part-time to full-time employment after graduation. Establishing community-based training and linking this with classroom instruction requires ongoing collaborative *interagency linkages*, and may benefit from collaboration with a variety of other community service agencies in order to meet the students' needs. The IDEA requirements are important elements of a successful career and vocational program. In addition, career and vocational education provide critical learning experiences that contribute to a student's self-knowledge regarding work and adulthood. A well-planned set of learnings builds the student's self-confidence and pro-

vides opportunities to develop self-determination and self-advocacy, which will contribute to the ultimate outcome of a high-quality and satisfactory life.

The information presented in this chapter builds upon the theoretical models of career development presented in Chapter 3 and describes their implementation through career and vocational education concepts and curricula. Thorough and ongoing assessment (Chapter 7) allows the team to evaluate and monitor a student's career and vocational growth, to integrate appropriately other content areas into a comprehensive curriculum (Chapter 8), and to select instructional approaches that will lead to maximal success (Chapter 9). Later chapters will extend career and vocational development concepts when describing the transition process for moving into employment (Chapter 15) and postsecondary programs (Chapter 16).

Overview

Definitions of Career and Vocational Education

Career and vocational education represent the instructional paths that will lead students with disabilities into successful employment. Because employment plays such a central role in adulthood and can be a significant source for developing independence and community involvement, team members need to become familiar with its structures and organization. Whereas vocational education provides skill and knowledge preparation for employment, career education prepares a student for a lifetime of work and adult roles. These two programs have significant overlap, which has led to some confusion about the differences between the two programs (Clark & Kolstoe, 1994).

Career education has been defined in contradictory ways, including (1) a narrow program that imitates vocational education, (2) a program for students in nonacademic tracks of postschool preparation, and (3) a broad program that prepares all students for the various life roles they will assume as adults in society (Clark & Kolstoe, 1994). Teams may encounter one or all of these definitions in their work. This broad perspective was introduced by Sidney Marland in 1971 when he was the U.S. Commissioner of Education, defining it as *learning about living* as well as *earning a living* (Brolin, 1997; Clark & Kolstoe, 1994). Kokaska and Brolin (1985) later expanded it as follows: "Career education is the process of systematically coordinating all school, family, and community components together to facilitate each individual's potential to economic, social, and personal fulfillment" (Kokaska & Brolin, 1985, p. 43).

Current definitions continue to favor a comprehensive, life-span approach which is similar to the perspective taken by life-span career development theories. Using a life-span perspective, a student with a disability would be assisted by the team in selecting a job based on current interests and abilities. In addition, the team would help the student to integrate this career choice with other lifestyle choices for independent living, community participation and leisure activities, and long-term interest in continuing his or her training and education, career advancement, and parenting roles.

In contrast, vocational education is that critical portion of job-related academic and work skills that moves a student who has made a career choice and makes him or her "job ready." It forms a critical preparation stage that occurs just prior to a student beginning his or her work career. Typically, vocational education programs provide:

1. preparation for jobs requiring less than a baccalaureate degree;

2. activities and experiences whereby one learns to assume a primary work role;

3. an emphasis on skill development or specific job preparation;

4. a focus of attention at the upper-middle grades, senior high, and two-year postsecondary levels; and

5. a program, rather than an educational philosophy, with the major goal being gainful employment (Meers, 1987, p. 22).

Career education programs provide a general background in preparation for employment and adulthood and assist in making appropriate choices. Vocational education programs provide specific skill and competency preparation sequences that are needed for students after they have selected a particular career path and vocation. Several of the life-span career education programs described in this chapter incorporated aspects of vocational education. During some aspects of the student's overall career development, there may be some overlap between general career learning and specific job-skill instruction. Students with disabilities may make a selection of a career, begin skill training, and determine that this initial choice is no longer appropriate (this also is true of students without disabilities). In such cases, the team will need to provide additional experiences to help the student make a more satisfying choice. Teams may have students who move between introductory career and vocational experiences for some time before making a final selection. This can be challenging to transition team members in that career research suggests that the transition age is a time of relative career instability for all adolescents, regardless of the presence of a disability (Super, 1990; Pumpian, Fisher, Certo, & Smalley, 1997). Students are likely to need assistance in making a job or career move, and doing so in a positive manner (Luft, 1999; Wehmeyer, 1993). The team provides a critical guiding role in using the sometimes multiple career trials of students as an opportunity to learn about themselves and their abilities. They may need to be creative in using both career and vocational education resources to meet student needs.

This next section provides a brief historical and legislative review of specific contributions to career and vocational education. The chapter then describes several career and vocational education programs. It uses these programs to explain career development processes for students, how academic and employment learnings are best integrated, and suggest strategies for monitoring this development. Next, the chapter describes the final career preparation processes and how students' careers can be initiated, maintained, and advanced.

Historical Influences and Legislative Mandates

As you have seen in Chapters 1 and 2, the historical background of today's programs has molded them into what they currently are, and what they are not. It is interesting to note that career education was first identified as a successful means for teaching skills to children with mental retardation in the 1940s and continued to be used primarily with special education students for quite some time (Clark & Kolstoe, 1994). In 1965, Kolstoe and Frey described a work-preparation curriculum identifying needed job performance skills as well as academic, personal, and social skills that are important to a satisfying lifestyle, suggesting a broader application for all persons (Clark & Kolstoe, 1994). During this time, career education became defined as a effective program to help students without disabilities attain better employment outcomes.

Although career and vocational education has been funded since The Vocational Education Act of 1963, monetary support for students with disabilities has been limited to approximately 10% with the Act Amendments of 1968, 1976, and the Carl D. Perkins Vocational Education Act of 1984 (P.L. 98-524) (Clark & Kolstoe, 1994; Maddy-Bernstein, 1997; Wermuth, 1991). The reauthorization of the Carl D. Perkins Vocational and Applied Technology Education Act of 1990 (P.L. 101-392) was passed to remedy difficulties from the prior legislation, to strengthen career and vocational offerings made available to special education students, and to provide for equitable participation. Vocational educators also

must now assist in fulfilling transition requirements under the IDEA (Individuals with Disabilities Education Act). Access to programs is further ensured by mandates for supplemental services, including curriculum changes, equipment modification, classroom redesign, supportive personnel, instructional aids and devices, guidance, counseling, and career planning. All career development activities must use participatory decision-making procedures that include students, parents, teachers, and other concerned area residents who also support IDEA processes (American Vocational Association, 1990; Maddy-Bernstein, 1997; Wermuth, 1991).

Critical Point   Vocational education programs must be accessible to students with special needs and must provide supplemental services to ensure that this occurs.

The School-to-Work Opportunities Act of 1994 (STWOA, P.L. 103-239) does not have specific special education requirements. However, states must plan for and implement systems that support *all* youths in moving into employment. The result is that special education students have increased opportunities for community-based work and training experiences through these statewide school-to-work systems (Stodden, 1998). Now transition teams no longer are limited to reliance upon special education teachers to organize and implement work experiences and apprenticeships in the community. STWOA programs are to provide students with the skills and knowledge necessary to make the transition smoothly from school to work, with placement in an entry-level position that leads to a career or to options for further education (Cobb & Neubert, 1998; Siegel, 1998).

This legislation, in conjunction with the ADA (Americans with Disabilities Act) guarantees of accessibility to community sites, now allows the transition team to assist the student in planning a career that encompasses a much more equitable range of training and employment placement opportunities. The next section provides an overview of several career and vocational education programs before moving into a fuller description of the processes that end with beginning and advancing within a career. The new opportunities provided through Carl Perkins, STWOA, and ADA are an important part of these developmental processes.

Career and Vocational Education Programs

The interest in career education for students with disabilities that began in the 1940s has led to a number of career education curriculum programs and models that are used today. What began as efforts to increase the benefits of this preparation in terms of career earnings has led to support for current broad-based and comprehensive programs in order to address the current, lifelong, and comprehensive definitions (Anderson & Strathe, 1987; Clark & Kolstoe, 1994; Wehman, 1996). These programs should be examined carefully for their appropriateness to the special needs of students with disabilities. The team may need to investigate options for modifying training sequences and adapting processes that best accomplish desired goals for the individual student. This is necessary because the career development experiences for a student with disabilities may be quite different from what has been described in any particular program.

The decisions that have led to our current career choice began when we were young children, overhearing our parents and other adults talking about work, learning about people who lived and worked in our communities, seeing and hearing advertisements about work, and thinking about what we wanted to be when we grew up. Students with disabilities may not have had many of these experiences, or may have been informed in any number of verbal and nonverbal ways that "work" was not something they would be able to do.

Critical Point   Students with disabilities often require additional exploratory career experiences to compensate for a lack of exposure when they were younger.

This lack of work-related exposure results in adolescents who may face transition planning with little or no "incidental" background knowledge of what work entails and what their potential work interests may be. They may have been sheltered from learning about work values and behaviors and not included in the comments of teachers and other adults comparing their personality traits to certain work expectations and careers. The foundations for values about work, the desire to work, and work ethics that support job acquisition and maintenance are formed in these early, incidental learning experiences (Hershenson & Szymanski, 1992; Szymanski & Hershenson, 1998).

The transition team may need to provide a series of direct learning experiences to replace these traditional early learning opportunities. A comprehensive career education program is likely to specify some of these early learnings, but the team will also need to monitor the student's progress throughout his or her career and vocational education program for potential gaps or misunderstandings about these basic values.

Career and Vocational Education Models

The first two models describe processes of comprehensive, life-span career education. Both have been developed quite extensively by their authors and will be explained in some detail. The remaining models will be described in less detail and include both career and vocational education programming. These will provide some sense of the range of programs available.

The Life-Centered Career Education model (LCCE) by Brolin and Kokaska (Brolin, 1989, 1996, 1997; Kokaska & Brolin, 1985) is a very broad model that has remained one of the most popular over time (Wehman, 1996). It integrates career education into the regular education curriculum using a three-dimensional model of

TABLE 6–1

Life-Centered Career Education Competencies

Curriculum Area	Competency
Daily living skills	1. Managing personal finances
	2. Selecting and managing a household
	3. Caring for personal needs
	4. Raising children and meeting marriage responsibilities
	5. Buying, preparing, and consuming food
	6. Buying and caring for clothing
	7. Exhibiting responsible citizenship
	8. Utilizing recreational facilities and engaging in leisure
	9. Getting around the community
Personal-social skills	10. Achieving self-awareness
	11. Aquiring self-confidence
	12. Achieving socially responsible behavior—community
	13. Maintaining good interpersonal skills
	14. Achieving independence
	15. Making adequate decisions
	16. Communicating with others
Occupational guidance and preparation	17. Knowing and exploring occupational possibilities
	18. Selecting and planning occupational choices
	19. Exhibiting appropriate work habits and behaviors
	20. Seeking, securing, and maintaining employment
	21. Exhibiting sufficient physical-manual skills
	22. Obtaining specific occupational skills

Sources: From Brolin, 1989, 1996, 1997; Kabaska & Brolin, 1985.

competencies across (1) four interrelated stages of career development; (2) key environments of school, family, and community; and (3) 22 basic life-centered competencies with 97 subcompetencies (Brolin, 1996; Clark & Kolstoe, 1994). Table 6–1 provides a list of the 22 life-centered competencies across the three curriculum domain areas: Daily Living Skills, Personal-Social Skills, and Occupational Guidance and Preparation. (Appendix A shows the three domains and the relationship between the 22 competencies and the 97 subcompetencies, and the integration of career and regular education.)

The 22 competencies provide a comprehensive preparation for future life roles. As seen in Table 6–1, students learn about personal finance and household management, marriage and rais-

ing children, personal responsibility and citizenship, self-awareness and self-confidence, independence and decision making, as well as employment preparation skills of knowing and planning for occupational choices, exhibiting appropriate habits and behaviors, obtaining skills, and securing employment (Brolin, 1995). This program has developed numerous supportive materials for instruction, with 400 instructional objectives across the 97 subcompetencies. These are further organized for teaching with 472 lesson plans for the Daily Living Skills domain, 370 lesson plans for the Personal-Social domain, and 286 lesson plans for the Occupational domain.

This career education program spans kindergarten through postsecondary experiences across stages of career awareness, career exploration, career preparation, and career assimilation (Brolin, 1995). The lesson plans address the first three levels of career stages, those that are primarily school-based. In addition, the plans are taught across three major instructional settings—school, home, and community—thereby ensuring that all major potential future environments have been addressed. The program also includes a curriculum guide (e.g., Conceptual Model—Set of Standards), assessment materials (e.g., Knowledge Battery, Performance Battery, Competency Units, and Self-Determination Scale), and staff training materials (e.g., Academy on LCCE, Video Training Program, and Distance Learning Program)(Brolin, 1989, 1992a, 1992b, 1992c, 1992d, 1993, 1996; Sumner & Fritts, 1997). The On-Site Implementation/Technical Assistance lists over 100 materials and their publishers, according to competency and subcompetency (Brolin, 1995, pp. 479–492). The comprehensive nature of this program, its integration of special and regular education programs, and its extensive support materials make this a viable choice for the transition team. However, the team must also make sure that this or any such program matches well with the particular strengths and needs of the student and will provide instructional experiences that indeed lead to his or her preferred transition outcomes.

CASE STUDY A

Ronald has moderate mental retardation as a result of phenylketonuria (PKU) that was not identified until his second foster home placement, when he was 6 years old. His mother abandoned him at 3 months of age, possibly due to her drug addiction. He also has a mild hearing loss and difficulty with anger and impulsivity. His foster parents and elementary teachers agreed that the LCCE would provide Ronald with opportunities to begin learning important daily living, personal-social, and occupational skills. His foster parents found him to enjoy most chores around the home, although they had to monitor him regularly, at first to make sure that he completed tasks. At school, he focused on anger and self-management

strategies. By the end of elementary school, he no longer was threatening others but would still occasionally break small items. Ronald's teacher had him visit workers in the school and learn about the kind of tasks they did.

The School-Based Career Development and Transition Education Model (Clark & Kolstoe, 1994) is a curriculum developed from a variation of a model proposed by Marland. Wehman (1996) reviews this as an excellent model for planning services for offering options across a range of disabilities, beginning at prekindergarten levels with the acquisition of basic job and daily living skills. Figure 6–1 shows how this model integrates the range of abilities across the life span.

This program is unique for specifying a range of possible secondary school options, including cooperative education, work evaluation, and technical education. Its postschool options consist of community rehabilitation facilities, vocational training, community or technical college, and 4-year college and graduate levels of training. The program identifies specific employment outcomes at various stages of the development process: entry-level jobs, semiskilled or specialized jobs, specialized or technical jobs, and professional or managerial jobs. The life-span nature of this program includes an ongoing option for adult and continuing education, and adult service agencies.

The childhood years (i.e., prekindergarten through grade 8) focus on four domain areas, consisting of (1) values, attitudes, and habits; (2) human relationships; (3) occupational information; and (4) acquisition of job and daily living skills. The program provides further guidance on addressing specific disabilities, ethnic diversity, appropriate assessment, instructional methods and materials, and prevocational and occupational programming (Clark & Kolstoe, 1994). The program supports information describing career guidance and counseling processes and strategies

FIGURE 6–1

A School-Based Career Development and Transition Education Model for Adolescents with Disabilities

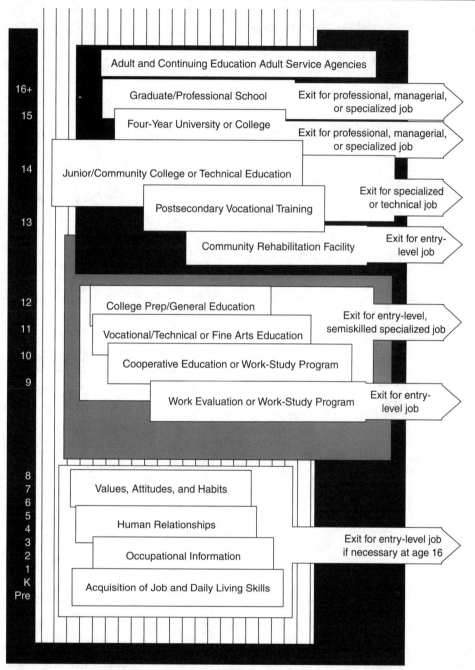

Source: From Clark, G. M., & Kolstoe, O. P. (1995). *Career development and transition education.* Copyright (1995) by Allyn & Bacon, Reprinted with permission.

for interagency linkages. The types of transition processes and employment outcomes addressed in this program make it an important option to consider with particular relevance for students to match with the identified employment outcomes.

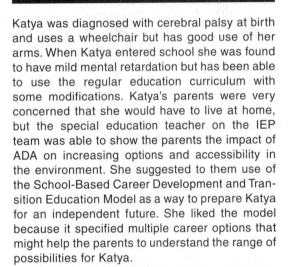

CASE STUDY B

Katya was diagnosed with cerebral palsy at birth and uses a wheelchair but has good use of her arms. When Katya entered school she was found to have mild mental retardation but has been able to use the regular education curriculum with some modifications. Katya's parents were very concerned that she would have to live at home, but the special education teacher on the IEP team was able to show the parents the impact of ADA on increasing options and accessibility in the environment. She suggested to them use of the School-Based Career Development and Transition Education Model as a way to prepare Katya for an independent future. She liked the model because it specified multiple career options that might help the parents to understand the range of possibilities for Katya.

The remaining two programs are somewhat older and focus on a more focused skill development model, closer to vocational education than the current life-span career education models described earlier. The Experience-Based Career Education (EBCE, 1976; Larson, 1981) model was developed using a cooperative education model. A series of different community sites provided for training as an extension of the special education classroom (Anderson & Strathe, 1987). EBCE can be used particularly as an exploratory experience to teach about work with students working as volunteers without pay. Work sites are changed according to student needs and interests to give them exposure to work environments and experience with a variety of work cultures. The cooperative education

model also can be an important part of vocational skills development. STWOA programs can expand such a program and lead from part-time school-initiated work experiences described here to entry-level employment positions in the community.

Farren, Gray, and Kaye (1984) developed a mentoring model with businesses that also would integrate well with STWOA. This program identifies business mentors to act as sponsors, teachers, coaches, and other role models as needed by the student and his or her environment. Mentoring is used to facilitate the move from career exploration into vocational preparation and can assist the team and the student in making informed career choices. This model provides the student with fairly specific learning experiences related to an identified occupation through advice and coaching (Anderson & Strathe, 1987).

CASE STUDIES A AND B

Neither Ronald's nor Katya's IEP teams felt that a community or mentoring work model was appropriate at this time but let the parents know that these or other vocationally oriented programs might be recommended by the ITP teams when the students were older.

The four program models described earlier provide the team with information about a variety of available resources, one of which may meet the specific and unique needs of the student. Career and vocational educators or specialists, or career guidance counselors may provide additional program suggestions, if needed. In any case, the descriptions provided in this chapter are too brief to allow detailed planning or decision making and will require further reading and investigation. An important beginning point in implementing any program is an understanding of the developmental processes associated with career and vocational education and appropriately applying these to the transition student with disabilities. This next section describes a series of stages of career education.

Stages of Career and Vocational Education

The developmental career development theories describe stages of career development across the life span. Similarly, life-span career education programs describe age, and stage-related experiences and processes that students will have in developing a career. A comprehensive career and vocational education program will provide differentiated experiences that promote career readiness and maturity. Preschool learning experiences often begin with learning basic life roles and responsibilities and early identification of work, such as the difference between "work" and "play" (Brolin, 1993, 1996; Clark & Kolstoe, 1994). Early experiences address many of the foundational work values and personality traits that combine to form a work personality and identity. Formal career and vocational experiences often are begun in middle school or in late elementary school.

During late middle school and early high school, most career education programs begin exposing students to a variety of careers and work settings. It is this type of career programming that is specified in the IDEA 1997 Amendments and must begin at age 14. Individual work experiences are typically of short duration across a semester or a year. They provide information regarding the student's initial preferences as well as their success in integrating into these particular environments. Based on this experiential foundation, the student then begins a program of specific curricular offerings to build existing interests and preferences into the necessary skills and attitudes that will lead to lifelong success. Career course work continues to further refine work habits and attitudes and pro-

vides specific skills in interviewing, job seeking, and job maintenance. At some point during this sequence, the student begins job-specific skill training and work trials in the community.

The LCCE describes four developmental stages: career awareness, career exploration, career preparation, and career assimilation as shown in Table 6–2 (Brolin, 1995, 1996). For students with disabilities, these stages are identified as beginning earlier and lasting longer; all stages can begin after birth and continue well into adulthood. *Career awareness* is emphasized with elementary school experiences with basic home and health care, developing a sense of self-worth and confidence, and developing positive attitudes about work. These reflect introductory goals across the three curriculum domains of the LCCE, Daily Living Skills, Personal-Social Skills, and Occupational Guidance and Preparation (also see Table 6–1 and Appendix A). Although earlier than mandated transition team involvement, the school should monitor the attainment of these basic competencies and record potential preferences, interests, and skills in these areas.

Career Exploration

Career exploration begins in elementary school but becomes the focus in middle school levels. Students begin to investigate their own unique abilities, needs, and interests in terms of work, leisure, recreation, and other potential life roles. They should be given greater opportunities to develop independence, particularly in Daily Living and Personal-Social Skills areas. Occupational skills development should include investigation of career clusters and some trial experiences, at both on- and off-site locations. The transition team will be formed during the later portion of this stage. It should collect prior interests and needs information and continue to track responses to career and living experiences. Evidence of patterns of preference can help the team to work with the student in later identifying a potentially valid career choice (Brolin, 1996).

TABLE 6–2

LCCE Stages of Career Development

Stage	Description
Career awareness	Begins in elementary levels to provide awareness of the existence of work (paid and unpaid), workers, and how the student will fit into a work-oriented society; this relates to self-awareness developing at this stage.
Career exploration	Emphasized at the middle school level to help students explore their interests and ability in relation to lifestyle and occupations; students examine their own unique abilities and needs, have hands-on experiences, and engage in several community-based experiences.
Career preparation	Emphasized at the high school level to provide for career decision making and skill acquisition; students should be able to identify their specific interests and aptitudes and the type of lifestyle that will meet these characteristics.
Career assimilation	The transition of students into postsecondary training and community-adjustment situations; students should be able to engage in satisfying avocational, family, and civic/volunteer work activities as well as paid employment; continuing education and follow-up services will be needed.

Source: From Brolin, D. E. (1995). *Life centered career education.* Upper Saddle River, NJ: Merril/Prentice Hall

Career Preparation

Career preparation is the focus of high school years, particularly for those who are not planning to attend postsecondary training. During high school, the team needs to ensure attainment of required competencies across the 22 strands within the three curriculum domain areas. All team members will likely need to be involved in investigating and determining competency levels across the school, home, and community environments. Students who have acquired the necessary work values and attitudes can begin the selection process for an appropriate career area. Teams who can show evidence of a relatively stable set of career preferences collected across several prior years of introductory and trial experiences can have some confidence that this is an appropriate career choice.

Career Assimilation

Career assimilation occurs during the high school or postsecondary years depending on the student's readiness for this stage. Experiences often include work experience in the preferred

career, beginning with part-time and moving into full-time employment. It is important that students be placed in an authentic job and are expected to function as real workers, even if they are not paid wages at this point. Students also should assume adultlike roles in Daily Living and Personal-Social Skills domains as much as possible. This allows the team to evaluate realistically the students' potential for meeting transition outcomes prior to their leaving school.

The school-based transition team's functions often end before the student has been entirely assimilated into a strong and stable career path. This leaves the community adult service providers with the responsibility to continue the work. The transition team may wish to do end-stage planning prior to the student's exit from school. In some cases, team members may be willing and interested in continuing to meet with adult services as student advocates. This can help to provide important continuity and further bridge the movement from school-based entitlement services to community-based eligibility services (described in Chapter 2).

Foundational Skills and Attitudes

Several authors do not describe a stage-based developmental sequence but, instead, identify basic elements that each student must have in order to have a satisfying career and lifestyle. Clark and Kolstoe's (1994) School-Based Career Development curriculum, described earlier, identifies several of these foundational areas. These are identified in the lower four boxes of Figure 6–1 in this chapter. The authors recommend that these be systematically addressed across every career or vocational program available to students with disabilities.

Critical Point The development of foundational skills and attitudes are critical to the employment success of every worker, regardless of disability.

The first area is identified as *values, attitudes, and habits*. Although this can be a sensitive topic for instruction, Clark and Kolstoe (1994) believe that values are the foundation of codes of conduct, preferences, beliefs, and processes that guide all decision making. They suggest that team members seek a consensus of values that they consider to be important and plan instructional activities accordingly. The process of identifying and agreeing upon specific values can be especially important when transition team members do not share the same ethnicity or social class as the student and family.

The next foundational skill area is *human relationships*. This area should address topics of differentness and the rejection often associated with disability and prepare students to deal with both acceptance or rejection. Communication with others should include how to address ignorance, naivete, or oppressive attitudes in those without disabilities. Specific training is also needed in how to create and maintain positive relationships, and social learning activities should not occur just in the classroom or at home but should include peers at school and adults and other peers in the community.

The area of *occupational information* should include all aspects of the world of work that are important to the student's future success. This includes information about occupational roles, occupational vocabulary, occupational alternatives, and information related to realities of the world of work. Occupational roles include those as producer/worker such as volunteerism, roles at home, and those as a consumer. For students with disabilities, realistic options and alternatives must be provided with sensitivity to their self-esteem but that are honest in addressing some of the less positive realities of work (Clark & Kolstoe, 1994).

Job and daily living skills are critical aspects of being judged a competent adult despite having appropriate values, attitudes, and habits; or good relationship skills. Failure to acquire many of these competencies cannot be isolated from failure in the work environment. For example, similar skills are needed for using break time appropriately and for making good leisure-time decisions; for following work safety and performance rules and for following community or state laws. Students need instruction in assuming increasing amounts of responsibility in job roles as they get older and in addressing the complexities of adding daily living responsibilities to their job roles.

Hershenson (Hershenson & Szymanski, 1992; Szymanski & Hershenson, 1998) has identified foundational skills as three separate but interrelated domains that correspond to his career development theory described earlier in Chapter 3. The development of these skills and attitudes begins at birth and continues throughout the child's formal and informal schooling. Hershenson identifies the first, *work personality*, as the person's self-concept as a worker and his or her motivation for work. This develops primarily during preschool and is highly influenced by family. Students with disabilities may have a very vague and undifferentiated work personality. Some may not view themselves as able to work and, therefore, have little initial motivation or interest in doing so.

The second domain consists of *work competencies* which are comprised of work habits, physical and mental skills for work, and work-related interpersonal skills. These competencies are developed more in relationship to school experiences and successes. For example, students without disabilities are often rewarded for doing well in certain tasks. Teachers and classmates may even suggest that they have certain traits that would lead to success in specific career areas. Students without disabilities are unlikely to have equivalent experiences with school success. They may have few of the work habits or interpersonal skills that are basic to engaging in a successful career.

The third domain is *appropriate and clear work goals*. Work goals develop later and are influenced by peer and other reference groups as the individual prepares to leave school and to begin working (Hershenson & Szymanski, 1992; Szymanski & Hershenson, 1998). Students with disabilities who have had few prior opportunities to develop a work personality and work competencies are unlikely to be able to set appropriate work goals. Their peers may, or may not, be positive influences in their lives, or they may have few opportunities for work-related interactions. Peers may have naive or inaccurate perceptions of a student's true abilities, particularly if he or she needs technology or an assistive device.

CASE STUDY B

Katya's IEP team began integrating basic foundational skills into her classwork and at home. Katya was somewhat shy, so the regular classroom teacher helped to identify two classmates who showed some interest in her. Katya's parents agreed to invite one of these girls to their home once a month. They also began identifying movie theaters and recreation centers that were accessible. Both the teacher and Katya's parents began talking to her about work and work expectations to build her confidence as a future worker. The team developed a list of people who worked in wheelchairs to act as po-

tential role models. The O.T. (Occupational Therapist) helped the parents to identify personal hygiene and home chores that Katya could do independently. The parents began working on the easier of these tasks and sought periodic input from the O.T. on Katya's progress.

The student's growth toward increasing career maturity occurs through developmental stages and by acquiring important foundational skills and attitudes. The transition team will be instrumental in ensuring that basic career and vocational requirements are met before placing the student in job settings. Although employment specialists can develop compensatory measures or negotiate modified job responsibilities that allow the student to be successfully employed, a student who lacks a strong sense of work ethics and positive attitudes and habits cannot be easily accommodated. These foundational characteristics make a worker with a disability a valuable and contributing member of any employment site.

Integrating Academic and Career Skills

Academic Skill Development

The team needs to monitor both school-based academic and career/vocational skills to gather important information about the student's acquisition of basic foundational and career skills. For example, the team will want to track the acquisition of important work and daily living skills, such as self-monitoring for speed and quality of work, ability to accept feedback and work with peers/coworkers and supervisors/teachers, and ability to follow procedures and rules. Many of these skills are taught through daily school practices addressing attendance and timeliness, following schedules and routine, working with others, and accepting feed-

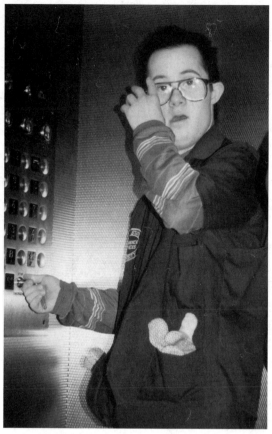

Students learn functional academic skills in the community.

tion outcomes and how these can be best attained. For students continuing on to postsecondary education, particularly in a 2- or 4-year-college program, high-level academic skills will be a requirement. The students should be placed in inclusive settings and be able to demonstrate success in an academic-based program. The team also needs to plan for meeting academic entrance requirements for college entrance and for possible professional licensure or certification. Some vocational-technical programs require specific documented ability levels. Although these may be primarily skill-based, a certain level of academic skills also may be required in the licensure process. Teams must assess whether or not the student can realistically meet these expectations, and plan accordingly. At some point, teams may wish to include representatives from postsecondary institutions and professional licensure groups to ensure that they are addressing all key requirements.

Most high schools offer an academic program that prepares students for postsecondary opportunities and the team members should familiarize themselves with the curriculum offerings as well as the various vocational-technical training, Tech-Prep, and 2 + 2 programs (linking high school with advanced community college placement), which are potential options for students. STWOA provides important linking opportunities for business/employment and academic classwork. The team should investigate the state and local plan for opportunities that will support the student's transition outcome. If the student's academic teachers are not involved in a project linked with business (which offers reciprocal instruction of academic and work-site skills), the team may wish to include the teacher in transition meetings so that she or he can plan instruction that more closely reflects the student's career future.

For students who are following a special education and functionally-based academic curriculum, instruction is likely to have a more direct relationship with career and vocational courses.

back. However, students with disabilities often do not generalize from one situation or setting to another (Westling & Fox, 2000). The team needs to examine these skills in each of the specific work environments into which the student is to be placed, especially during early career exploration and preparation activities. The LCCE (Brolin, 1995) and School-Based Career Development (Clark & Kolstoe, 1994) programs can assist in coordinating these multiple personal, career, vocational, and academic aspects of transition planning.

Another important function of the team is to determine the extent to which academic skills are important to the student's preferred transi-

For example, in language arts class, students may be practicing vocabulary from their work sites, refining interaction and communication skills used with coworkers and supervisors, and practicing with forms for self-evaluating their work preferences and performance. In math class, they may sum and average their self-evaluation forms and practice fractions when measuring (1/2, 1/3, 1/4 cup). In science class, they may practice safety rules and procedures for their job, master hygienic procedures used in a restaurant kitchen, or learn how to apply and work with different cleaning chemicals.

Basic literacy and mathematics skills often are considered very important to getting a job; however, students with significant disabilities may not be able to acquire these skills beyond functional levels. The team may need to identify creative ways to support students in work-related use of these skills. Employment specialists can also be important resources in developing job-related adaptations and modifications and in identifying important aspects of jobs that the student *can* do well without being highly literate.

CASE STUDY B

Katya's IEP team ensured that she had some career awareness instruction during elementary school. When she entered middle school, the IEP team provided all her teachers with a list of foundational skills on which she was working. Katya was getting mostly "Bs" and "Cs" in her academic classes and the IEP team believed this provided a good program for her. During eighth grade, Katya's IEP team enrolled her in a career exploration course that visited workers in the community and included activities about work values and habits, and about occupational clusters.

For students at these levels, acquisition of foundational interpersonal and daily living skills become more important aspects of their personal repertoire of skills. Functional competen-

cies may include academic skills, such as reading basic directional words, telling time, and following directions, as well as life skills, such as selecting and buying goods, maintaining a healthy body, following directions, and abiding by designated rules and laws. These competencies undergird many of life's experiences and failure to acquire them often cannot be isolated from a person's success or failure in the world of work (Clark & Kolstoe, 1994). In fact, these are critical skills that should be acquired by all students, with or without a disability. The transition team may need to ensure that academic students also know these more functional competencies (e.g., the 22 LCCE competencies).

Classroom-Based Career Development

Functional academic and regular academic courses can, and should, include many work-related literacy and mathematics skills that students need for successful work. However, not all important information can be covered through academic courses only. All students will need career classes of some type to complete their preparation. These classes should occur at varying levels in a student's career development to reflect the necessary and relevant information at each stage. During *career awareness* and *exploration* phases, classes should focus on the values, attitudes, and habits that comprise a valued employee. They may include investigations into different career domains and encourage students to indicate initial career preferences. These classes should be integrated with career exploration experiences and job shadowing, which the students also are having, and focus on related terminology and important job and daily living skills that contribute to successful work evaluations and performance.

During the *career preparation* stage, classes should focus on aptitude and interest descriptions that match with the student's career preferences. Instruction should address specific terminology and concepts that relate to employment, such as payroll, deduction, taxes, social security, benefits, and the like, according to the student's academic skill levels. The class should include important interpersonal skills, including interviewing, accepting feedback from coworkers and supervisors, maintaining good relationships with coworkers and supervisors, and terminating employment appropriately.

Classes during the *career assimilation* stage may take on a different format. Students may spend much of their day at the work setting and some may be in a postsecondary environment. Course issues would consist of job tenure and maintenance skills, negotiating and resolving interpersonal issues, and the implementation of self-advocacy and self-determination skills for advancement and ultimate career and life satisfaction. Rather than be scheduled as a typical class, these courses may be organized in the form of a job club that meets at the school site, an adult agency, or at a convenient community facility.

Long-term job tenure often can be a problem for young adults with disabilities, which is frequently complicated by time-limited adult services support. For example, a young adult with a disability who experiences increasingly hostile interpersonal interactions from a coworker may find this situation building to a crisis one year after being hired. However, at that time, he or she may not be receiving ongoing support services that could help to provide strategies to resolve this issue. Instead, the young adult may feel forced to quit or may erupt in an emotional display that leads to a forced resignation. Typically, vocational rehabilitation services end within 60 to 90 days of being hired and supported employment may not be continued if the individual is able to complete job tasks successfully. Long-term problems that develop slowly are not addressed successfully by this type of service delivery (Pumpian & Fisher, 1993; Pumpian et al., 1997). Ongoing job clubs can be used successfully to provide peer support to address difficult situations as well as trained professional guidance, assistance, and monitoring.

Critical Point   Individuals with disabilities will frequently need information, strategies, and support to maintain employment, often because they have lacked access to this information and support while growing up.

Community-Based Career Experiences

At some point in the student's career and vocational development, he or she will need to leave the school and venture into the community. This begins an important career preparation stage in which the student moves beyond familiar environments of home and school to learn about the expectations, behaviors, communication styles, and ethics of the world of work. IDEA and STWOA have both identified communities as important training arenas, and the ADA has made many of these community sites accessible. As a result, classes at all levels of career education development are being held in relevant community sites.

Community-Based Instruction
Community-based instruction (CBI) has provided schools with unlimited opportunities to teach students the necessary skills for adulthood, including many of the skills identified in the career programs described earlier. Use of the community is particularly important because some career skills cannot be taught effectively in school-based programming. These include mobility in the community and transportation skills; using community facilities such as stores, laundromats, and public services; learning to care for and maintain personal living space; developing hobbies and recreational and social interaction skills; and using workplace skills related to employment. Because students with disabilities have difficulty in generalizing from one setting to another (Wehman, 1996; Westling & Fox, 2000), classroom-based instruction often is not sufficient. The community provides an important setting for practicing skills in the environments where students will be when they are living and working in the community.

Community-based instruction also offers individuals the potential for social and personal fulfillment and participation in productive living and work-related activities. In some instances, and depending on the age of the students, leaving the school grounds is not always possible or practical. Creative teachers can identify sites and tasks within the school or on the grounds that can approximate natural community environments (Wehman, 1996). In-school classroom and work experiences should supplement or prepare students for off-site experiences. They can provide students with opportunities to learn initial skills and preferences and foundational skills related to vocational strength and weaknesses, work condition likes and dislikes, and the means that aid them to be their most productive worker. Schools frequently offer a number of potential vocational training avenues (e.g., office work, filing, custodial, and food service). But it is not realistic to expect all students to enjoy or benefit from working in the cafeteria, for example, just because it is easy to schedule and the staff are amenable to student workers. When the student is ready to move into the community, the team must be committed to find ways to allow this to occur.

Community-based career exploration activities may be the student's first experience away from the school site. These activities often begin in middle school and become increasingly focused on one preferred career domain as the student matures (Brolin, 1995). Early experiences usually involve visiting a variety of job sites. They may include job-shadowing experiences in which a student observes and follows a worker as he or she goes about his or her job tasks. At the high school levels, CBI often is more focused at providing specific work-adjustment or vocational skill development. These experiences function best when used as an extension of the classroom educational program and can be supplemented by classroom activities. Extension school-based activities can also include business or work simulations in which the students create a business and assume various roles to "run" this company.

As these experiences accumulate, students are able to start developing preferences regarding short- and long-term career objectives. An example of such a program is the Cooperative Transitional Program (CTSP) offered at Kent State University (KSU). This program provides career exploration and job skills training to youths with disabilities at various sites on the KSU campus (Flexer, Simmons, & Tankersley, 1997). Graduate students who are studying to become transition specialists provide the coordination of services and the worksite-training. The youths participating in the program "try out" different job categories (e.g., clerical, food service, indoor and outdoor maintenance, library, bus maintenance and mechanics, mail sorting and delivery, and inventory and stock audits) at job sites such as at the bookstore, library, cafeterias, residence halls, groundskeeping department, transportation services, supply center, administrative offices, and the food court. After participating in these various work experience activities, students are better equipped to make realistic decisions and to state preferences regarding long-term job placements.

Wehman (1996) suggests a number of principles be followed when planning community-based instruction, as presented in Table 6–3. As with all other educational programs, community-based work experiences should be individualized for the student and should be part of a plan that leads to a realistic and preferred career outcome.

An additional caution for professionals developing community work experiences is that they must structure them in line with the U.S. Department of Labor, Fair Labor Standards Act. This Act allows students with disabilities to participate as a "trainee" in unpaid community-based experiences pertaining to school vocational goals. Each of the six criteria presented in Table 6–4 must be met in order for a student to be considered a "trainee."

TABLE 6–3

Planning Strategies for Community-Based
Instruction

1. Individualized and person-centered approach: This tenet requires the development of a specialized set of instructional objectives that are particularly suited to a student's needs and based on the student's desired outcomes.
2. Functional or practical curriculum: The design of subject matter should promote the student's competence at home and in the community.
3. Adaptive curriculum: The course of study should be modified to the specific goals, needs and desires, and capabilities of individual students.
4. Ecologically oriented: A high priority should be placed on skills needed for the activities students want to perform in their major living environments upon leaving high school.

Source: From Wehman, P. (1996). *Life beyond the classroom: Transition strategies for young people with disabilities* (2nd edition). Baltimore: Paul H. Brookes.

TABLE 6–4

Criteria for "Trainee" Status under the U.S.
Department of Labor, Fair Labor Standards Act

1. The trainining, even though it includes the actual operation of a business facility, is similar to that which would be given in a vocational school.
2. The training is for the benefit of the trainees or students, not the business.
3. The trainees or students do not displace regular employees, but work under close supervision.
4. The business providing the training derives no immediate advantage from the activities of the trainees or students, and on occasion business operations may actually be impeded.
5. The trainees or students are not necessarily entitled to a job at the conclusion of the training period.
6. The business and the trainees or students understand that the trainees or students are not entitled to wages for the period of time spent in community-based vocational instruction.

Source: Fair Labor Standards Act.

Career Planning Strategies

The transition team needs to document career planning and curriculum decisions, beginning at age 14, that comply with the 1997 IDEA amendments. The team may wish to use a strategy that is more career-specific than the IEP (which focuses on educational goals) or the ITP (Individualized Transition Plan, which identifies needs across all transition life domains).

Individualized Career Plan

The individualized career plan (ICP) was developed to accompany other planning documents such as the IEP and the ITP and is used in conjunction with identifying the student's career and educational goals. In developing the ICP, the transition team works with the student to determine what he or she hopes to do after high

school graduation and analyzes the student's career goals in terms of skill and training requirements (Simmons & Baer, 1996). All skill and training requirements are broken down into action steps (e.g., course work, trial work experiences, and extracurricular activities), which are to be completed by the student before graduation. Table 6–5 lists the elements of the ICP planning document.

Using the ICP, the team would meet with the student beginning at age 14, assist him or her in identifying a career goal area (or career domain, if a specific career cannot be identified) (step 1). The team would then describe what the student has done or experienced that leads to his or her current interests, knowledge, and skills (step 2). The team would identify some skills and knowledge areas that the student will

TABLE 6–5

Elements of the Individualized Career Planning (ICP) Document

The ICP planning document should include the following:

1. A specification of career goal(s)
2. A statement reflecting upon how the student's current interests, knowledge, and skills support career goal(s)
3. An explanation of the additional skills and knowledge that the student will need to achieve his or her career goal(s)
4. A listing of educational activities through which additional skills and knowledge can be developed
5. A description of additional certification and/or specialized training that the student will need to achieve his or her career goal(s)

Source: From Ohio Rehabilitation Services Commission. (1997). *Transition guidelines and best practices.* Columbus, OH: RSC Office of Public Information.

need. If the student has only selected a domain area, the team will list knowledge and skills that are typically expected across the domain (step 3). Next, the team will identify course work, training opportunities, or life experiences that will lead the student to the next developmental step in his or her career path. Additional job shadowing and exploration across the domain will help the student and team to identify continued interest in the domain and a potential career path in which the student shows increased interest (step 4). The last step is to list the certification and specialized training for this career path. For the student who has selected only a domain, a general description of potential certification and specialization can help the student and team to determine realistic options (step 5).

Because their career plans are likely to change with experience and maturity, students should be given opportunities to review and revise their plans at least annually. The plans should become increasingly focused and specific in identifying a career goal and in documenting the student's interests, knowledge, and skills that support this goal. Systematic exposure to work-related in-school and community-based experiences should lead to an increasingly explicit ICP.

Career Portfolios

Career portfolios are another tool used in career planning to guide the student and the transition team in decision making and goal setting. They also provide a means for monitoring the student's progress toward reaching his or her career objectives. Because portfolios are highly individualized, they also empower students to control the decision making and career planning processes (Koch & Johnston-Rodriguez, 1997).

Ideally, the student determines the design, organization, and contents of the portfolio, with the transition team contributing guidance as needed. Work samples (e.g., products, photos of products, etc.) included in the portfolio should comprise only the best representations of the student's knowledge and skills. As the student improves his or her abilities and gains new experiences, portfolio samples must be updated so that the portfolio is always current (Koch & Johnston-Rodriguez, 1997). Examples of items that also could be incorporated into a career portfolio include the ICPs, informational interview reports, corrected class assignments, lists of competencies mastered in after-school jobs or trial work experiences, copies of awards, photographs or written descriptions of projects completed in vocational classes, copies of vocational certificates (e.g., CPR, Red Cross, and baby-sitting), and letters of recommendation from teachers or employers. A video work sample of the student successfully performing and interacting on the job site can also be a powerful tool (Sarkees-Wircenski & Wircenski, 1994). For students with limited communication skills or for employers or coworkers who are skeptical, this can be a very powerful and convincing tool demonstrating the student's work abilities.

The academic, classroom-based, and community-based instructional program that the team designs in conjunction with the student forms the basis for the student's career development during his or her school years. The use of a career and vocational education program can help the transition team to ensure that instructional activities and community experiences complement and build upon each other. Community participation experiences are vital to helping students learn the skill and attitude expectations of the environments of their futures. However, CBI should be included only as part of a coordinated set of activities which move students toward the realization of their desired goals. Using the full range of home, school, and community environments allows the team to provide students with the widest range of potential training environments.

Varied experiences help students with their career interests.

CASE STUDY A

Ronald received career awareness information for the remainder of his elementary school years. During middle school, his IEP team integrated functional academics with an employment focus in conjunction with the LCCE. Ronald turned 14 during seventh grade and his IEP/ITP team agreed to begin a 2-year sequence of job shadowing across career clusters. Ronald also would begin self-evaluating his own responses to the job shadowing and learn to accumulate these responses to help him select preferred options. He began saving these forms with pictures of the preferred job sites in his ICP. The special education teacher began taking students into the community to teach transportation, shopping, and laundry skills.

Another important part of the team's functioning is to accumulate information about the student's interests, needs, and preferences in response to these classroom and community experiences. A number of tools and strategies can help the team systematically to record these data. Others, such as the use of a career portfolio, are emerging alternative assessment formats that have been used very effectively for transition planning. This next section addresses the identification and collection of this information.

Monitoring Career Development Processes

Successful career planning requires both self-awareness and an understanding of the world of work. An important part of this is the transition team's involvement in collecting information that will support the student and team in making appropriate decisions about realistic outcomes. Students also need to be actively involved, according to their abilities, in gathering information about their interests and abilities, in learning about the labor market, in setting short-term and long-term career goals, and in formulating plans for achieving their goals (Szymanski, Hershenson,

Enright, & Ettinger, 1996). Teams will need to provide varying levels of support in assisting the students with these tasks.

The transition team members may want to discuss the type of information they wish to collect with a vocational evaluator. The evaluator also can suggest a number of assessment strategies as well as instruments and tests. A number of these are described in detail in Chapter 7. The suggestions made in this chapter are related to specific aspects of career development and vocational education as part of the ongoing monitoring of the student's growth and maturity. Ongoing monitoring is an important strategy in identifying student interests and preferences and change with time and as a result of their career education experiences.

Monitoring the Student

Career-related information about the student should be compiled from a variety of sources, including interviews, interest inventories and aptitude tests, work samples, vocational assessment, and portfolio assessment. *Interest inventories and aptitude tests* are important sources of information about student interests, preferences, and skills. Inventories provide a range of career options for students to choose from and define a profile of career characteristics that represent the student's pattern of choices. The use of these inventories in conjunction with related classroom activities will help the students to become more self-aware. Aptitude tests are designed to predict vocational success or occupational readiness. Those most commonly given in prevocational or vocational training programs are those tests that examine manual skill and dexterity (Clark & Kolstoe, 1994).

Work Samples
Work samples provide important information about the student's performance under real-life work circumstances using accurate and reliable observation techniques. Work samples are work situations that are similar to or that reproduce tasks required on a real job. High school special education and special needs vocational education programs are increasingly relying upon work samples (Clark & Kolstoe, 1994). They can provide important information about work behaviors, interpersonal skills, attitudes, and vocational potential (Gajar, Goodman, & McAffee, 1993; Luft, 1999; Sitlington, 1996).

Curriculum-Based Vocational Assessment
Curriculum-based vocational assessment is an approach that emerged as an effort to improve evaluation relevancy to students and their environments (Gajar et al., 1993; Luft, 1999; Sitlington, 1996). Information is collected directly on the students while they are enrolled in vocational-technical education or other training programs, using identified curriculum goals and standards (Clark & Kolstoe, 1999). This can be particularly helpful to teams who need periodic feedback about a student's success in a particular class or vocational program.

Portfolio Assessment
Portfolio assessment is a collection of work and can be part of the student's career portfolio. The portfolio documents the student's career interests, academic accomplishments, and vocational skills and was reviewed earlier as a strategy for career planning. As an assessment tool, the portfolio is an extremely valuable tool for assessing the student's progress at developing career-related competencies. Sarkees-Wircenski and Wircenski (1994) described a project in which specific competencies (e.g., employability skills, work-related social skills, self-help skills, generalizable skills, and job-specific skills) that are necessary for successful postschool outcomes were documented using career portfolios.

Monitoring Potential Work and Living Environments

Information about potential work environments should examine the tasks involved in occupations of potential interest, the skills and worker characteristics that are required, and the availability of local job opportunities within occupational categories. State and local job classification resources, job analyses, informational interviews, and job shadowing all can provide information about potential jobs to students and team members. National resources include the U.S. Department of Labor (DOL) with three widely used resources: the *Dictionary of Occupational Titles*, The *Guide for Occupational Exploration*, and the *Occupational Outlook Handbook* (Wolffe, 1997).

State and local resources provide information that is sensitive to local market conditions and employment availability (Patterson, 1996). Chambers of commerce provide listings of major employers in the community and how many workers they employ in various positions. State employment service agencies develop reports on current and projected labor market trends within different counties. Many states have Career Information Delivery Systems (CIDS) that can be accessed through computer-based systems to learn about the availability of employment and educational and training opportunities.

The preceding organizations and resources provide basic job descriptions and availability data. However, the team will need to do a *job analysis* to gather more detailed information about a specific position in order to match the student's skills and interests (Patterson, 1996). Most job analyses are conducted either to learn more about specific jobs for future placements or to gather information with a particular student in mind (Patterson, 1996). In the context of students with disabilities, the job analysis is conducted by the work-study coordinator, the special education teacher, or the transition specialist who is concerned primarily with identifying both the essential functions of the position and what kind of accommodations may be possible (Rumrill & Koch, 1998). Information is gathered about both the work performed (e.g., specific job tasks, work materials, products pro-

TABLE 6–6

Steps the Student Takes to Conduct an Informational Interview

1. Schedule an appointment with someone working in the occupation of interest.
2. Develop a list of questions to guide the interview.
3. Conduct the interview and record interview information.
4. If possible, get a brief tour of the business.
5. Send a thank you note to the interviewee

duced or services provided) and required worker characteristics (e.g., general educational development, specific vocational preparation; aptitudes, temperaments, interest areas, physical demands, environmental conditions; and U.S. DOL, 1991). In many cases, the job analyst also conducts a *task analysis* which involves breaking down and analyzing jobs according to their specific tasks. The series of tasks is used for identifying instructional strategies to use with the student or can be used to identify key tasks that need to be modified or adapted. *The Revised Handbook for Analyzing Jobs* (U.S. DOL, 1991) and *Job Analysis and the* ADA: A *Step-by-Step Guide* (Blackwell, Conrad, & Weed, 1992) offer helpful guidelines for conducting job analyses.

The *informational interview* is a strategy that students can use to collect a detailed, up-to-date and personalized perspective on a specific occupation. In this strategy, the student conducts an interview of a potential job site (which also supports self-determination and empowerment strategies). Table 6–6 identifies the steps that a student should take in conducting such an interview.

The list of questions that guide the interview should focus on educational or training requirements, employment outlook, description of a typical day, likes and dislikes about the occupation, appropriate training programs, salary ranges, advice for those interested in pursuing the occupation, and related occupations. Transition team members or teachers can assist the student by providing guidelines for conducting such interviews.

Job shadowing can be considered an expansion of the informational interview. Used in this way, job shadowing is the process of observing an employee at the work site as he or she performs his or her job. This type of career exploration activity enables students with disabilities to acquire first-hand knowledge about what specific tasks and worker skill requirements are involved in any given job. Job shadowing typically involves observing the worker for a period of up to a day. Job shadowing opportunities can be organized and scheduled by guidance counselors, work-study coordinators, family members, transition team members, or the students themselves. Prior to the actual event, the student should be provided with guidance regarding what types of observations to make and questions to ask the employer.

Many of these work-focused monitoring procedures can be applied to potential living settings. For example, it is important for the team to do a "job" analysis of a possible apartment living situation or to analyze a club or team that a student may want to join. The analysis identifies essential functions and expectations and may include a task analysis for specific or complex tasks. The student might want to do an informational interview as well. A "shadowing" experience of an activity or potential hobby may help the student to better decide if this is truly within his or her interests.

Monitoring Congruence Between the Student and Potential Work and Living Environments

The team will want to use information collected about the student and about the environments in order to determine if they match or "fit." Once this has been determined, the team will want to collect ongoing information about the contin-

ued appropriateness of this match and identify any difficulties. Interventions such as situational assessments and trial work experiences provide opportunities for team members (1) to observe directly how students function in different work situations, (2) to determine the appropriateness of different occupations and living environments, (3) to identify optimal conditions for student success, and (4) to evaluate the effectiveness of different adaptation or accommodation strategies.

A *situational assessment* is a means of evaluating student/environment "fit" through direct observation of students in actual or simulated work or living situations. Valuable information about the student's general employability skills and adaptive work behaviors (e.g., task performance, ability to follow directions, grooming, punctuality, openness to constructive criticism, social skills, and reinforcer needs) is gathered by using the situational assessment approach (Chan et al., 1997; Power, 1991). This approach has the added advantage of providing students with the opportunity to learn and practice the role of worker (Taylor, 1997). In addition, students can be introduced to self-assessment strategies and checklists to monitor their own reactions (see Martin, chapter 11). Typically, information is collected over an extended period of time (e.g., several weeks) during which the evaluator observes and evaluates the student as he or she performs job tasks and interacts with other employees. Rating and evaluation forms are used to gather and report assessment information that is then used by the transition team to assist the student with career planning. Situational assessments can also be performed in the student's current and future living environments to determine "fit" and readiness for these experiences.

Situational assessments examine isolated environments and settings. When collected over the range of potential environments, they are known as *ecological assessments*. They are particularly useful for transition teams in planning across comprehensive lifestyle choices. Ecological assessments are a means for systematically collecting information about the multiple environments in which the student functions and is expected to function in the future, the key individuals within each environment, and the interrelationships among the student, the key other people, and the environment. The team can use this information to acquire an in-depth understanding of (1) the student, (2) the potential work and living environments, and (3) the congruence between the student and these potential environments (Parker & Schaller, 1996). The ecological approach is an ongoing process during which the student's performance is "monitored and assessed under changing conditions and challenges of new situations" (Chan et al., 1997). The ongoing aspect allows teams to track students' development, including ways in which they may change and modify their career and adult life goals in response to experiences that they have had.

CASE STUDY B

Katya completed her career exploration class with a love of computer work. In high school, her guidance counselor gave her several interest inventories which confirmed that office work was a preferred option. The IEP/ITP team placed her in a business course and she did well in learning word processing and data entry. Her parents were not sure she could perform for a full day because she complained of fatigue when using the computer at home.

CASE STUDY A

Ronald completed his career exploration activities with a preference for both groundskeeping and stocking/warehouse work. He made videos of himself working in both settings to show potential work experience employers. The high school IEP/ITP team had a diagnostician do some nonverbal inter-

est inventories, which were not conclusive and no strong pattern emerged. The team determined to begin an extended part-time work experience with one-quarter each semester devoted to each of his preferred activities. His foster parents felt it was important for Ronald to experience daily work in groundskeeping (outside) when it was both hot and cold. This was somewhat difficult to schedule with employers, who prefer a continuous schedule, but the team found two who would agree. An employment professional did a job and task analysis at each site and began training Ronald during his ninth grade year for the next year. He also continued to work on the LCCE competencies.

Thus far, we have addressed career and vocational programs with a focus on foundational career development processes. These have addressed career stages and programs, school-based and community-based experiences, and strategies for monitoring the student's development to assure appropriate decision making. If the team has followed these processes conscientiously, the student will arrive at a point where his or her career choice is both stable and realistic. At this time, the student enters into more intensive vocational preparation in preparing for leaving school and entering the world of work. This is described in the next section.

Career-Specific Vocational Preparation

Although a comprehensive career education program contains aspects of vocational education, transition teams typically find that initiating a vocational education program involves collaborating with a new set of personnel and program structures that are distinct from those in regular or special education. All three programs (i.e., regular, special, and vocational education) may be located within the same high school building, but they operate under distinct educational guidelines, legislative mandates, and procedures within the overall public school structure. This section describes some unique structures of vocational education.

The benefits to students who enroll in their programs largely result from vocational education's unique workplace focus. Research has shown vocational education to lead to increased postschool success of students with disabilities (Patton et al, 1996; Wagner, Newman, & Shaver, 1989). For example, a student may have well-defined interests and developed adequate abilities for daily living and personal-social skills. However, without specific and competitive levels of employment skills and knowledge, it will be extremely difficult for him or her to get a job.

Formal vocational education consists of educational programs at secondary, postsecondary, and adult levels. It is specifically designed to prepare future workers and to improve the quality of the existing workforce. Programs are commonly found as part of offerings in comprehensive high schools, in vocational high schools, and in vocational centers (Cobb & Neubert, 1998). High school programs typically prepare new workers for specific occupations within an assortment of industries, such as health care, business, and manufacturing. Many high school students also take vocational education courses to learn a specific skill, such as word processing, or to explore a career area, such as health care.

Vocational programming at the postsecondary and adult levels includes trade schools and technical and community colleges. These programs have purposes similar to high school programming but with more emphasis on specific skill training and upgrading. Many of them, especially in community colleges, include basic academic instruction in addition to technical and trade-school training. Both community college programs and vocational centers require a certain level of academic preparation, including graduation from high school and academic Carnegie units (Cobb & Neubert, 1998).

Students in special education are guaranteed access to high school vocational programs under Carl Perkins and STWOA (Cobb & Neubert, 1998). Opportunities at the postsecondary level are generally based on meeting program eligibility requirements although programs cannot discriminate or fail to make accommodations due to disability. It is important for team members to help the student with admissions requirements and procedures if he or she plans to continue his or her education after high school. The team should include members from potential postsecondary or vocational-technical training facilities prior to graduation in order to address graduation and eligibility issues prior to the student's making application.

Labor Market Trends and Forces of Change

Vocational education's focus on preparing future workers makes it highly responsive to societal and economic forces and needs. Three major trends have impacted and continue to impact program offerings and entrance/exit requirements. The student and transition team must also be prepared to address potential changes in market demand and requirements that may well occur in the years when transition planning first begins at age 14, and until the student leaves school, possibly at age 21 or 22. Forces in *technology, industrialization, and automation* have led to new occupations and training needs and eliminated some occupations and displaced workers. Tremendous technological change in recent years has impacted postsecondary and adult vocational programming, leading the student and team to focus on upgrading skills and preparing workers for future careers. The team must be prepared for increasing automation of the repetitive tasks to eliminate the job for which students with significant disabilities are often trained. *Demographic changes* have resulted in higher percentages of women, minorities, and youths and adults with disabilities participating in the workforce. Vocational programs have made curricular and delivery changes, including use of instructional materials that are gender neutral and equipment that accommodates individuals with disabilities. However, students with significant disabilities who do not have the required academic background are unlikely to find a technological or assistive device that will allow entry into all employment programs. The third force, *work processes*, refers to the methods, tasks, and job duties needed to perform work, including the tasks and systems for manufacturing products and delivering services. These processes also are influenced by the characteristics of those doing the work and have changed dramatically, in some instances, when an employee has a disability. The nature of work processes has been identified as increasingly important. The SCANS (1992, June) report identified competencies in allocating resources, in acquiring and evaluating information, and in utilizing interpersonal collaboration as some of the important processes in today's workplace.

The Structure of Vocational Education

The delivery of vocational programming is organized around several operational principles that shape the programs. Programs tend to be *occupationally specific* and taken after students have completed general interest or career exploration programs. Students enroll in order to prepare for a specific occupation by learning the tasks and duties that are necessary to be a competent, employable worker in a specific occupation or industry. Programs are also *experience-based* with a focus on real-world experience that is incorporated into virtually all aspects. Vocational teachers must have successful work experience in a specific occupation to become licensed to teach. Curriculum development occurs in conjunction with business and professional organization expectations. Students get experience through laboratory work, internships, and work experiences, which are coordinated with classroom instruction. A *real-world focus* prepares the student, as closely as possible, in an actual work

setting. Students use the actual tools, equipment, and processes employed in the occupation. In some cases, instruction will include performing authentic work. A cosmetology student, for example, will perform services for customers as part of the program under supervision by the vocational instructor.

The fourth principle is *three-dimensional learning*. This consists of (1) a cognitive or knowledge component, including specific terms, concepts, and information related to a specific occupation; (2) a psychomotor dimension in which there must be skill proficiency; and (3) an attitudinal or affective dimension that is associated with the occupation. Vocational education programs blend these three dimensions into one comprehensive learning experience. The cognitive dimension occurs in a traditional classroom setting. Application occurs in a laboratory or actual work setting. These two settings foster learning in the third or attitudinal dimension, which are strengthened by cocurricular involvement in student organizations. Each vocational program includes organizations such as Distribution Education Clubs of America (DECA), Vocational Industrial Clubs of America (VICA), Future Farmers of America (FFA), and Business Professionals of America. These student organizations foster personal and social development as they relate to specific occupations or industries.

For students with disabilities, it is likely that they will need additional and longer experiences to develop the same level of competency as their peers. The team may need to negotiate with vocational programs for opportunities to repeat, or to extend, course work in another way. Students also may not be able to acquire all the academic and cognitive content normally associated with a program and may need assistance from the team in negotiating more realistic alternatives.

Types of Vocational Programs

A number of vocational programs exist to prepare and upgrade workers for virtually all industries.

TABLE 6–7

Vocational Programs That Represent Vocational Education

1. *Agricultural education:* Includes occupations in horticulture, agribusiness, selected food and crop production industries.
2. *Business education:* Focuses on secretarial, administrative, office and business management occupations.
3. *Marketing education:* Includes occupations in retailing, marketing, merchandising, and services, such as real estate, hospitality, and financial.
4. *Family and consumer sciences:* Prepare workers for occupations in the consumer and homemaking occupations, such as day care, lodging, and food service.
5. *Trade and industrial education:* Includes a wide range of occupations in the trades such as graphic arts, metalworking, automotive technology, and manufacturing.
6. *Health occupations:* Focus on preparation for careers in nursing, medical and dental assisting, nurse aid, radiology, and other medical occupations.
7. *Technology education:* Prepares students to work in a wide assortment of technical occupations related to manufacturing, construction, transportation, and other industries.

Table 6–7 describes programs that represent the majority of instructional programs offered through vocational education. The two areas with the largest vocational student enrollment are trade and industrial education and family/consumer sciences.

Transition team members need to become familiar with the range of businesses available in the area, both large and small, their resiliency to economic hardship, and the opportunities for internal job advancement when helping the student to choose a viable and lifelong career path. Another consideration is the adaptations of the vocational education curriculum that may be necessary for the student to be successful. And although Carl Perkins guarantees curricular and supportive adaptations, the team must keep in mind the real-world standards that a student may still need to meet.

The choice of an appropriate program of vocational education and the modification strategies that are best for a specific program involve judgments about the skill readiness of the student and market conditions that may not be within the expertise or experience of educators, vocational rehabilitation counselors, or parents. The active participation of vocational educators in this phase of transition planning becomes particularly critical for ensuring that a student will, indeed, be job ready by the time of graduation or program completion. Vocational educators have become increasingly important partners in this process.

Interfacing Vocational Education with Transition Planning

Federal legislation (e.g., IDEA, ADA, Carl Perkins, STWOA) and workforce changes (i.e., increased the number of individuals with disabilities) has led to a closer alignment among vocational education, special education, and vocational rehabilitation. Professional preparation of vocational educators now includes course work on working with students who have disabilities and special needs. Vocational educators typically have participated in staff development programming to learn about transition planning, adapting their programs for special needs students, and mandates for compliance with legal mandates. The National Association for Vocational Education Special Needs Personnel (NAVESNP) was formed in the 1970s and the Special Needs Division (SND) of the American Vocational Association (AVA) also works to support vocational special needs personnel in terms of cooperation, coordination, and enhanced communication between professionals (West & Meers 1992). These two professional organizations help to support collaboration that results in better vocational outcomes for students with disabilities.

CASE STUDY A

Ronald completed high school and was not eligible for postsecondary training. His part-time work experience led him to choose warehouse/stocking as his preferred employment option. He continued to work in this position through high school. Unfortunately, the employer had to lay off several workers because of local economic conditions and was not able to hire Ronald when he graduated. Ronald's independent living skills were much improved but he was not ready to live independently. His vocational counselor suggested a supported living apartment where Ronald would live with one roommate and a supervisor would make daily checks on them.

CASE STUDY B

Katya enrolled in a program for business education taught at the county vocational technical high school. She was very nervous about changing environments and her IEP/ITP team scheduled several preliminary visits to show her where the accessible entrances and facilities were located. The team knew that Katya might not be able to develop competitive level skills, and this was the case. After graduation she met the entrance requirements for the local community college and continued to work on her skills there. The vocational rehabilitation counselor attended the last 2 years of IEP/ITP meetings in the high school and continued to work with Katya while she attended community college. Katya was given the options of possibly job sharing with another worker to split business productivity requirements, or having an employment specialist do job development/job carving to identify a position that would take advantage of her typing and data entry skills but would not overtire her. Katya was living at home but had asked her counselor about independent living options available to her after she finished school.

Initiating a Career: Placement and Linkages

At this point, the transition team has overseen their student's successful acquisition of daily living, personal-social, initial career skills, and the recent completion of a vocational education program. The student has effectively concluded school and community-based work experiences to include part-time work in his or her chosen career. The next step becomes placement in a full-time job in the community. This is a pivotal time for the student and the transition team, when the results of all previous training and experience are evaluated by the "real-world" community. This process initiates a critical aspect of career and vocational education programming: getting and keeping a job.

Job-Seeking Interventions

If the student has completed the vocational education program to industry and community standards, business contacts through vocational educators, guidance counselors, and friends and family may be very successful in locating a job. However, if the student has not been able to meet all these standards, he or she still has valuable employment and interpersonal skills that he or she can contribute to the workplace. In these instances, the team may use a placement specialist who will consider ways to modify and adapt jobs to fit the student's ability levels to find an employment position for the student. *Job development* is an important strategy used by employment professionals when a student's needs and abilities do not correspond to a currently available job. Yet, the professional may have observed that certain tasks remain uncompleted and are negatively impacting the overall performance of the organization. In this case, the professional negotiates with the employer and supervisor to create a position that meets both the student's and the organization's needs. Examples include assigning a person to focus only on mail services, filing, or reporting tasks. *Job carving* is similar, in that it creates a position that meets the needs of both the individual and the organization. The difference is that the employment professional may accumulate parts of several job descriptions to fit the abilities of an individual and simultaneously increase organizational efficiency. Again, having one person assigned to mailroom tasks frees up several other individuals to focus on doing clerical tasks that needed to be completed in addition to sorting and delivering mail.

While the professional is preparing to make a placement, the student also can be participating in the job search process. Many curricula are available that provide instruction on specific job-seeking skills, such as securing leads, filling out applications, and interviewing. These commercially available tools can be adopted or adapted to meet the needs of students within a particular school or classroom. *Job clubs* also are a useful strategy that empower the student to develop job-seeking skills. It utilizes a small group format to provide counselor support, encouragement from other club members, and prospective job leads to people who are actively seeking employment (Azrin & Philip, 1979). Job seekers meet in groups of 8 to 12 every day for about 2½ hours until employment is secured. The job club method emphasizes group support to club members as they cultivate and follow up on job leads. Lesson plans and standardized scripts for obtaining leads and employment interviews are incorporated into club activities.

The traditional job club approach described earlier can be adapted to meet the specific needs of students in transition. Lindstrom, Benz, and Johnson (1996) describe a job club model for special education students between the ages of 16 and 21 who are either actively seeking employment or who are already employed. The emphasis of this model is on preparing students for "the transition from the structure of the school environment to the unpredictable and often confusing adult world" (Lindstrom et al., 1996, p. 19). Thus, the primary objective is to teach students how to set both short- and long-term career and independent living goals. Job club meeting sessions might include a structured activity to teach or practice specific job-seeking skills as well as time for each student to set and report on individual goals. Small rewards (e.g, a gift certificate, or a free movie pass) might also be given to students who meet their weekly goals. Job clubs may consist only of special education students or could include a combination of students with and without disabilities.

Community Linkages

As transition team members work with the student to explore different employment options, it is especially important to establish community linkages with informal, professional, and employer contacts. Students also must be assisted with establishing their own "professional board of directors" (Hecklinger & Black, 1991). This "board" is essentially a listing of people who can provide advice and encouragement to the student as she or he conducts a job search. The board may include family members, close friends, counselors, teachers, and so on. New members can be added as the student confronts new challenges in the job search process. Students can invite members to participate in transition team meetings (if they are not already doing so), or they may prefer to seek out support from board members on an as-needed basis. The transition team can assist the student with selecting members for his or her board of directors. Educators may be familiar with similar "team" approaches, including "Circles of Support," "Circles of Friends," and other team planning strategies (Forest & Lusthaus, 1989; Forest & Pearpoint, 1993; Forest, Pearpoint & Snow, 1993; Pearpoint, 1990).

Professional Linkages

Professional linkages are very important to the transition team in accessing a range of services that the student may need. The team members are likely to need an ongoing network of community and business links to apprise them of market conditions and fluctuations, and of employers who are supportive of hiring individuals with disabilities. Vocational rehabilitation counselors need linkages with the variety of adult service providers, including private practice and nonprofit community organizations. A broad network of these linkages increases the range of support services that a counselor can provide to any one individual. Some of these linkages may become important members of the student's "board of directors," "Circle of Support," or other planning teams.

Employer Linkages

Employer linkages are critical to making appropriate job placements that meet the needs of the students. School systems may wish to institute a central clearinghouse for job referrals to support all the transition-age students (Baer, Martonyi, Simmons, Flexer, & Goebel, 1994). Establishing these linkages can occur through job fairs held at high schools and at postsecondary institutions. They also can be developed through community service agencies, including Chambers of Commerce, Private Industry Councils, and service organizations such as the Kiwanis. Employer advisory boards can be an important means to gain input from local employers about how to better utilize vocational programs for students with disabilities as a labor resource. (Baer et al., 1994). Once linkages are established, maintaining ongoing relationships with employers is an important tool to the transition team and to vocational professionals. The team may wish to consider asking the student's employer and/or supervisor to attend meetings that plan to address current and future employment issues.

Mentoring programs are another strategy for preparing students for the world of work that de-

TABLE 6–8

Important Components of a Placement Plan

---

1. The target occupation and alternative occupations
2. A brief statement of the skills and abilities the student has to offer an employer
3. An assessment of the student's need for job-seeking skills training
4. Consideration of job search needs such as transportation and interview attire
5. The cooperation of the student's family
6. Likely job accommodations and modifications (e.g., instructional strategies that might be needed at the job site)
7. A list of potential job search leads
8. Assignment of respective student and transition team member job search responsibilities
9. A timetable for conducting the job search

Source: From Flexer, D. W., Simmons, T. J., & Tankensley, M. (1997). Graduate interdisciplinary transition training at Kent State University. *Journal of Vocational Rehabilitation, 8,* 183–195.

pend on quality employer linkages. A mentoring type of program was reviewed earlier in the chapter, which was developed by Farren et al. (1984). Their model used business mentors to act as sponsors, teachers, coaches, and other roles as needed by the student and the environment. Mentoring can facilitate the move from career exploration into preparation and can assist in making informed career choices (Anderson & Strathe, 1987).

Once the student is ready to pursue employment, he or she should focus on developing a specific plan for securing a job. Table 6–8 presents a useful tool that assists the team and job placement personnel with this process. This *Individualized Placement Plan* (IPP) can be used as an extension of the ITP and the Individualized Career Plan (ICP) for structuring both the job search and the student's initial placement at the work site.

TABLE 6–9

Steps to Follow to Maintain Job Placement

1. Respective student and job coach responsibilities
2. Specific accommodations and supports that the student will need in order to maintain employment
3. Other job-related needs (e.g., work schedule, on-going medical care, job orientation) and how these will be addressed
4. Methods for assisting students to develop natural supports (establish relationships with supervisors and coworkers)
5. Anticipated career maintenance needs and agency providers

Source: From Flexer, D. W., Simmons, T. J., & Tankensley, M. (1997). Graduate interdisciplinary transition training at Kent State University. *Journal of Vocational Rehabilitation, 8,* 183–195.

Placement planning involves the "preparation of the youth with disabilities and development of plans for initial instruction and supports that the youths may need in order to be successful at their job site" (Flexer et al., 1997).

Once the student has secured employment, the team should identify any other supports and resources that will contribute to ongoing job success. For example, if the student is unable to perform a job independently and at competitive business standards, vocational rehabilitation may hire a job coach or employment specialist to assist the student. This support may be ongoing or time-limited, depending on the extent and nature of the student's disabilities. These programs are known as supported employment and will be described in more detail later. The team should identify both the student's and job coach's roles and move the student into using increasing amounts of natural supports within the work environment. Whether or not the student uses supported employment, the team should develop a list of steps to ensure that the student will be able to maintain the job. These are identified in Table 6–9

CASE STUDY A

Ronald's vocational counselor hired an employment specialist to find another position. She located several part-time positions but many of the full-time positions required some warehouse shipping/receiving work and Ronald's literacy skills were not sufficient. When she located a position in a large Sam's store, it was across town. The bus route involved a transfer which was difficult for Ronald to learn. On two occasions he got lost but had a wallet identification card which he showed to a bus driver. The job, however, was a good match for Ronald. The store did not require stocking and display of individual items. Ronald could stock the items by matching the labels on the boxes. His employment specialist developed a card that enabled Ronald to track which items belonged in which aisles.

CASE STUDY B

Katya completed her community college and moved into an accessible apartment with a cousin. Her vocational counselor found her a part-time job and continued to look for an arrangement that could be full time. Katya found the daily work environment to be challenging despite her preparation in school. When she became overly tired, she was likely to get sick and have to miss 1 to 2 days of work.

Maintaining and Advancing in Careers

Once the student has secured a job, the team still has responsibilities to ensure that the student can keep the job and has the skills and potential to seek promotion. *Career maintenance* refers to the ability to sustain, advance in, and change one's career, as desired. Students need job retention skills and may need skills in managing future career transitions, a particularly important skill given the unpredictability of today's labor market.

Trends such as the globalization of the economy, rapid advances in technology, the automation of industry, and corporate downsizing require all workers, regardless of their disability status, to anticipate proactively and prepare for disruptions in their careers (Ryan, 1995).

Career maintenance strategies are particularly important to young adults with disabilities. Once they have a job, they may have little or no contact with school-based personnel and may have graduated from school. The direct responsibility of the transition team ends at this point. In most cases, students are unlikely to have regular classes or support to help them sustain and keep a job after the initial novelty of work has expired.

The transition team can play a key role in providing critical skills in the area of career maintenance during their school program. Interventions that are designed specifically to assist students with developing job retention skills include supported employment, career maintenance clubs, and accommodations planning strategies. Career portfolios can be used to help students develop the skills necessary to advance in their employment and to manage career changes.

Supported Employment

Supported employment is "a job placement and training model designed to prepare people with severe disabilities for competitive employment in regular community settings" (Reed & Rumrill, 1997, p. 238). It evolved in the 1970s as a model that leads to community-based employment after students leave high school. Its key feature is the provision of ongoing support services to assist the individual with job retention. Ongoing support is typically provided by the job coach or employment specialist who is responsible for the duties listed in Table 6–10. Job coaches should begin to "fade" (gradually reduce the amount of support they offer) from the work site as natural supports begin to increase in the supervision of the supported employee.

TABLE 6–10

Ongoing Support Services Provided by the Job Coach

1. Providing on-site vocational training to the supported employee
2. Assisting the employer with restructuring job duties
3. Supervising and evaluating the supported employee's work performance
4. Ensuring that the supported employee completes job tasks accurately and in a timely manner
5. Helping the supported employee to develop independence and natural supports (coworkers who informally provide job coaching)
6. Providing follow-along services on an as-needed basis

Source: From Flexer et al. (1997).

Supported employment services consist of four basic approaches: individual placement, clustered placement, mobile work crew, and entrepreneurial (Hanley-Maxwell, Szymanski, & Owens-Johnson, 1998; Reed & Rumrill, 1997). *Individual placement*, viewed as the most inclusive of the four approaches, involves matching the strengths, interests, and needs of a specific student with the requirements of a specific job. Utilizing the individual placement approach, the job coach tailors training and support to the individual needs of the student. *Clustered placement*, also referred to as enclaves, consists of a small group of three to ten supported employees who are collectively trained at a specific place of employment. In this approach, the job coach functions as a supervisor of the entire group. *Mobile work crews* consist of a group of supported employees who perform contracted work (e.g., janitorial service, landscaping, and delivery services) for different businesses. Again, the job coach functions as a supervisor of the entire group. *Entrepreneurial* approaches involve the creation of a small business for the specific purpose of employing supported workers. The approach is integrated in that workers without disabilities are also hired. Although students may start out working in a group placement, the goal is for them to move eventually into an individual placement. This approach also can assist the transition team in realistically considering work preferences for which the student does not initially meet competitive work standards or needs ongoing supervision for specific aspects of a job.

Career Maintenance Clubs

Another effective strategy for addressing the career maintenance concerns of students with disabilities is the career maintenance club (Rumrill & Koch, 1998). Expanding on the job club approach, the career maintenance club utilizes a small group format to address the issues that students with disabilities confront in attempting to keep and advance in their jobs. Whereas job clubs emphasize ongoing support to students participating in a job search, career maintenance clubs emphasize ongoing support to students who have already secured employment but need additional assistance in order to keep their jobs.

Group members meet weekly or biweekly to address career maintenance concerns, such as initial adjustment to a new job, employer expectations, appropriate work habits, problem solving, time management, social skills, coworker attitudes, transportation issues, and reasonable accommodations. Meeting agendas and group activities can be structured to address both general topics and individual concerns. Role play can be incorporated into the meetings to provide opportunities for students to practice their career maintenance skills (e.g., assertiveness, communication, and self-assessment) and to receive constructive feedback from other group members. Of course, ongoing support from both the group facilitator and student members is the most critical factor in the success of the career

maintenance club, regardless of how the meetings and activities are structured.

Accommodations Planning

As students with disabilities begin to explore career goals with transition team members and to examine issues related to career maintenance, they must incorporate consideration of job accommodations into their planning. Roessler and Rumrill (1995) identified three accommodations planning steps that can be completed by employees with disabilities to increase their job retention potential. These steps meet the requirements of the Americans with Disabilities Act (ADA) and include (1) identify barriers and accommodations strategies, (2) initiate requests with the employer for reasonable accommodations, and (3) implement, in collaboration with the employer, accommodations to remove or minimize barriers to job retention.

In order to accomplish these steps, students and/or their advocates must possess accurate information about their legal rights under the ADA and be able to communicate their needs assertively to employers. The transition team plays a central role in assisting students to access information about their legal protections, to develop skills at disclosing disability-related information to employers, to identify their accommodation needs, and to request and implement accommodations (Luft & Koch, 1998). Career classes or job-seeking skills workshops, in which role-playing activities and videotaping are used to facilitate the development of these competencies, provide ideal scenarios for addressing these important topics. As transition team members work together to foresee and proactively plan for the student's future accommodation needs, they must "understand the impact of the [student's disability] in the high school setting" and "be able to visualize its potential impact in the post-secondary setting" (Edelman, Schuyler, & White, 1998, p. 8).

CASE STUDY B

Katya decided to join a job maintenance club to help her learn to better gauge her health needs. She also learned some assertiveness and was able to talk to others about barriers she encountered in the environment. After 1½ years, Katya was hired full time at her job. The employment specialist realized there were places in the office that became backed up (e.g., mailroom, and filing end-of-month reports). This gave Katya a break from typing and the office made sure that the mail work and filing was accessible to her. A few years later, Katya asked her boss if she could get training to learn the network systems software packages that she saw the office managers using. The boss was reluctant at first and unsure whether she would be successful. She got some books and showed them to her boss to convince him of her sincere interest. Katya knows that she may not become an office manager but this will allow her to increase her skills and work abilities, and probably qualify for a raise.

The Portfolio as a Career Maintenance Strategy

In addition to its utility as an assessment, planning, and placement tool, the career portfolio helps students to prepare for future career transitions (Koch & Johnston-Rodriguez, 1997). As they approach graduation, students should be encouraged to explore career maintenance and advancement issues (e.g., preparing for the transition to adult services and changing labor market trends and pursuant implications for career planning, future career goals, other life goals, plans for continuing education, and resources for confronting future career challenges) and to incorporate samples (e.g., phone lists of adult service providers, labor market surveys, career maintenance and advancement plans, and application packets for postsecondary training programs) that address these issues in their career portfolios (Rumrill & Koch, 1998). Career classes, career maintenance clubs, and individ-

ual counseling sessions all provide meaningful forums for exploring career maintenance concerns with students and for offering instruction on how to use their portfolios to self-assess and enhance their career maintenance skills.

CASE STUDY A

Ronald worked at Sam's for several years before a coworker took an interest in him and the two began to do weight lifting together at a gym. Ronald's increased strength was a substantial asset in his work: It enabled him to work faster and to lift heavy boxes with greater ease. His boss noticed this (with some encouragement from the coworker) and Ronald got a raise that year. This recognition led the boss to realize that Ronald got along very well with the other workers and had an excellent attendance record. Ronald and his foster family were delighted when he received the "employee of the month" award.

Conclusion

Students with disabilities and their families need the combined expertise of the entire transition planning team in order to prepare adequately for adulthood. The unique and often limited early career experiences of these students require experiences that build awareness of the variety and number of employment positions open to persons with disabilities. The team may need to spend considerable energies in educating the student, the family, and the community on these potential positions. The student is likely to need a wide range of exploratory career experiences that will help him or her to decide on their ultimate career preferences.

Career opportunities have greatly expanded as a result of the ADA and the transition legislation that supports long-term planning. In addition, new technologies continue to open new employment avenues and to increase the equal access students with disabilities have to these jobs. All members of the team need to update themselves continually on these technologies and the latest accommodations in order to ensure the widest potential job market (Luft, Rumrill, & Snyder, in press). The expertise of the vocational educator is becoming increasingly important in ensuring that accommodations provide more than "passing" levels of skill and that the student is truly marketable.

A number of career education and vocational education curricula are available that assist the team in compiling a comprehensive educational plan of activities and experiences. This chapter also has presented instructional activities and community experiences that are integral to a successful transition plan in which a student is able to obtain and maintain a job. The quality and extent of these activities and experiences provide the background and learning opportunities upon which the student depends for the rest of his or her adult life. The role of the transition team members and their ability to collaborate effectively with each other remains of vital importance.

Study Questions

1. You are trying to explain the differences between career education and vocational education programs to the parents and relatives of a student with disabilities. Describe what you would say and include some examples of each. How would you change what you say to address programs that are appropriate for a student with mild disabilities who plans to attend postsecondary training? For a student with significant cognitive disabilities? For a student with multiple cognitive, physical, and sensory disabilities? For an ethnically diverse family?

2. You are describing the four stages of career education to the same family. Give examples of what kinds of activities their child would be involved.

3. You need to develop interventions that address foundational or prevocational skills for a student. Would you choose the LCCE (Brolin, 1995) or The School-Based Career Development and Transition Education Model (Clark & Kolstoe, 1994), and why? Would the ability levels of your student impact your decision: Why or why not?

4. You are working with a student who is ready to begin some community-based experiences. Describe how you would implement two of the work-site experiences and two of the career planning strategies with this student.

5. Your transition team is trying to decide between using the LCCE and the School-Based Career Development programs. How would you explain the advantages and disadvantages of each?

6. Your team has realized that it needs a systematic plan for gathering and keeping information about the student's work-site experiences (from question 4). Design a plan for collecting the information and describe how it can be used for later transition planning.

7. You are addressing the family from questions 1 and 2 on some fears they have about their child's success in the workplace, specifically in making an appropriate placement and then implementing career maintenance strategies. How would you explain your plans for implementing these aspects?

Web Sites

Career Education Association:
http://www.c-e-a.org/index.html

National Center for Research in Vocational Education 1988–1999:
http://vocserve.berkeley.edu/

National Centre for Vocational Education Research, Ltd.:
http://www.ncver.edu.au/ncver.htm

National Network for Curriculum Coordination in Vocational and Technical Education (NNCCVTE):
http://www.ed.gov/pubs/TeachersGuide/nnccvte.html

Office of Postsecondary Education:
http://www.ed.gov/offices/OPE

Office of Vocational and Adult Education:
http://www.ed.gov/offices/OVAE

7

Transition Assessment and Postschool Outcomes

Robert W. Flexer
Pamela Luft

The objectives of this chapter are:

1. Explain the major similarities and differences between special education assessment and transition assessment.

2. Describe the types of skills that are tested in each of the three transition domains: current and future work, living, and personal-social areas.

3. Explain the purpose and contributions of formal (standardized) and informal tests (nonstandardized) in transition assessment. Describe the kinds of information each test can provide to support compre-

hensive data gathering, and describe the advantages and disadvantages with each test.

4. Describe how functional or ecological assessments can be used in each of the three areas of transition assessment and give examples.

5. Describe how academic performance assessment can be assessed for both high- and low-achieving students, and what this information can contribute to transition planning.

6. Explain your preferred choice in the process of assessment planning and decision making for transition teams.

Chapter 6, "Career and Vocational Education," presented various options and approaches to preparing for life after high school. Educational programs and career experiences provide foundational competencies and specific skills to embark on a career path. In this planning context, transition assessments are important for student and team discussions in selecting and modifying career paths during and after high school. They also provide important data in supporting the student in successful completion of programs. Information obtained through transition assessments is especially critical to the *essential element* of *determining needs, interests, and preferences.* The student's and team's understanding of his or her abilities and needs in relation to career and vocational programs, postschool options, and independent living capabilities and preferences are directly related to the quality and completeness of assessment data. In order to develop career and other postschool living goals through an *outcome-oriented process*, specific assessment data are needed on how the student responds to school and community environments that are important to his or her transition goals. Assessments also can provide a communication and monitoring function for the *coordination of transition* activities between programs and adult agencies. They provide a test of whether transition activities are actually *promoting movement* toward the student's goals.

Assessment for transition shares several features with assessments for special education. Transition assessments, like special education assessments, may be conducted in order to determine eligibility in programs (e.g., for certain educational or training programs) and to help the student and the transition or IEP (Individual Education Program) team select appropriate courses and programs and test the effectiveness of the programs and courses that have been selected. Transition assessments differ in their focus on the skills and knowledge that the students will need as adults. This often includes

areas that schools have not previously addressed in much depth, such as independent living and community-based skills.

Transition assessments are critical for students and transition team members to understand the students' needs and abilities and their potential to pursue the educational and transition options they prefer. All team members must agree on the adult goals for the students that are implemented based on a related set of assessments. The resulting assessment data provide the information resources the team needs to build a successful and realistic transition plan that will achieve the desired goals.

Assessment provides the informational framework from which all later transition planning occurs. Therefore, it is critical that testing results are as accurate as possible and are comprehensive in addressing all areas that will be important to the students' adult life. Assessment results should be synthesized into a clear transition profile of the student that all team members can understand. From the many tests that are available, team members will have to choose those that best assess according to the student's desired transition goals and that provide technically adequate assessment data. Team members need to feel confident that results are valid and reliable and accurately reflect the student's current abilities and future potentials. The quality of the assessment process will be reflected in the quality of the resulting transition plans and ultimately, the student's successful movement into adulthood.

Critical Point   The transition profile should synthesize all assessment results in a comprehensive manner to depict accurately the student's abilities, interests, and needs. The transition team must choose assessments that will provide technically sound data to promote the student toward his or her postsecondary goals.

When assessments are appropriate for the student and used effectively by the team, they can promote interdisciplinary communication between team members and help the student to learn more about him- or herself. Assessments that measure student progress toward goals can help team members to provide the necessary supports and services or to fade these supports as the student becomes more independent.

This chapter provides an overview of assessments for transition with a description of the major types of assessments that are important to transition planning. The chapter begins with the purposes of assessment data as they pertain to the decision-making process and IDEA (Individuals with Disabilities Education Act) requirements. The various types of assessments are classified according to formal and informal transition measurement tools with descriptions and examples. The concluding section presents several suggestions for managing the assessment and decision-making processes that an interdisciplinary transition team may choose to use.

Overview of Transition Assessment

Transition assessment is ultimately about the gathering and use of information that will lead to implementation of the student's transition goals. Because achieving adulthood is a long-term process, assessment and transition planning take place beginning with middle school and continuing through the postschool years. Longitudinally, transition assessment begins with career exploration, identifying lifestyle preferences and abilities, and with the establishment of a foundation in the variety of life skills needed for successful adulthood. Assessment processes provide an ongoing means to document and track the student's development of abilities and levels of performance for all areas of transition. Accurate assessments are reflected in the quality of related IEP objectives and transition planning, leading to achievement of desired outcomes. Sitlington, Neubert, Begun, Lombard, and Le Contea (1996, p. 3) state that transition assessments "should provide the foundation for the

transition process" including the information from which the team will identify the student's specific preferences, strengths, and needs. The transition team needs to have familiarity with a range of assessment methods and transition assessment instruments because of:

- The multiple domains that represent transition to adulthood
- The multiple purposes that the transition team must accommodate in meeting a student's lifestyle preferences
- The variety of individual needs and abilities the team will address across a group of transitioning students.

This section is organized to provide a foundation in transition assessment practices which are critical for team members. Definitions and purposes will provide familiarity with the variety of assessment approaches that have been developed from several professional disciplines. The breadth of transition domains requires an equal breadth of measurement such that no one perspective or professional discipline can provide a comprehensive profile of an individual student. This range is described in terms of definitions of transition domains. IDEA guidelines provide the legislative context in which team members will conduct and interpret transition assessments. The assessments are classified and described within a broad framework to enable the reader to understand better the differences between types of specific transition assessments.

Characteristics of Transition Assessment

Assessment can be defined as the gathering of information for purposes of planning, instruction, or placement to aid in individual decision making (Taylor, 2000). All transition team members will be involved in gathering this information and all may assist in performing assessments. This includes the special education teacher, school psychologists, therapists, counselors, and other specialists (e.g., diagnosticians, speech therapists, occupational therapists, and physical therapists) who are typically involved in IEP planning. For transition planning, this list will expand to include personnel from rehabilitation counseling, health or mental health services, colleges or universities, developmental disability services, social security administration, and other assistance or employment services depending on the student's potential future (Halpern, 1994; Sitlington et al., 1996). Particularly in rural communities, paraprofessionals, concerned business leaders, church representatives, or civic group representatives who assist with transition goal implementation may be involved in the transition and, therefore, in the assessment process. They can be important sources of information about the student and the community's resources and support (Bickford & Sheldon, 1989; Luft, Rumrill, & Snyder-Marks, in press).

Transition assessment uses some of the same tests as those used for IEP development. However, the broad scope of adulthood requires some unique approaches and perspectives as well. One of the most important aspects of the assessment process is that it should be ongoing and continuous. Adolescent and young adult students are experiencing tremendous developmental changes. These changes, the impact of their peers, and their learning from transition activities and experiences will clarify and change their values and preferences over time. As the student and the team learn more about these abilities and preferences, they may decide to alter and modify the student's adult outcomes. Ongoing evaluation is vital to ensuring that final adult plans represent the accumulation of the student's growth, education, and experiences before leaving high school.

A second important aspect of transition assessment is that it should have a clearly specified purpose. Whereas special education eligibility testing covers broad general areas of achievement, performance, and behavior, transition assessment must address abilities and needs related to specific, individualized adult outcomes. General ability and behavior tests provide important background information, but in order to select potentially successful outcomes, the team needs data regarding the student's success with specific tasks in actual environments. The team needs to assess the student's success in the environments that reflect his or her lifestyle preferences and abilities. Clear identification and specification of the areas in which the team needs information and those persons who can contribute this information will greatly assist the team in developing a comprehensive and realistic transition profile.

A third important aspect of transition assessment is that it should be individualized. The variety of needs and abilities, of career and lifestyle preferences, and of the pace of developmental and program-based changes that students experience require that team members individually select the types of assessments that are most relevant and appropriate. Some newer assessment processes are less formalized and allow for the creation of alternative formats. These may be useful and contribute more detailed information about the student's success in an environment and with a particular set of tasks. This results in a highly individualized assessment process and choice of tests.

A fourth important aspect is the effective summarization and integration of the assessment results into a comprehensive, accurate, and realistic transition profile. Transition assessment involves more than administering, scoring, and reporting tests and results. It involves careful analysis of the assessment results that lead to functional, relevant, appropriate recommendations and decisions. The integration of the results into a complete understanding of the student and the analysis of this profile are difficult and complex aspects of the team's task.

Critical Point Transition assessments are ongoing, specific, and individualized according to the students' goals and programs. A comprehensive profile can validate needs and preferences and reflects the team's developed "picture" of the students.

The diverse domains of transition and the unique needs of each student may require evaluations that are unfamiliar to some or all team members. Yet, transition planning remains most effective when all members understand these results sufficiently to be able to contribute their own analyses and interpretations, respectively. This includes the student and family. It is particularly important that the student, at a minimum, has some recognition of how these assessments contribute to knowing about him- or herself. The task of summarizing and compiling a transition profile is challenging, but when done effectively, it ensures that all team members are equally involved in developing and supporting the resulting plan.

Defining Transition Domains

Transition planning and IEP planning are integrated and reflective of each other. Therefore, transition assessment will be related to IEP planning processes. IEP assessments for current level of functioning and for making instructional decisions are part of the overall transition assessment process. The CEC Division of Career Development and Transition (DCDT) reinforces this relationship and defines the important areas of transition assessment as follows:

> Transition assessment is the on-going process of collecting data on the individual's needs, preferences, and interests as they relate to the demands of current and future working, living, and personal social environments. Assessment data serve as the common thread in the transition process and form the basis for defining goals and services, to be included in the individualized education program (IEP) (Sitlington, Neubert, & Le Conte, 1997, pp. 70–71).

This definition categorizes transition assessment into three broad areas of current and future environments for the student. This chapter uses this definition of the transition domains to

describe types of transition testing. Each type is briefly described next.

Current and Future Working Environments

Work and career assessments use approaches that are based in theories of career development (discussed in Chapter 3) and include both career assessment and vocational evaluation. They provide information on work and career interests for exploration and lead, ultimately, to career selection. Career assessment concerns lifelong career development along a series of stages of career development and maturity. Assessments may focus on general abilities and interests, for example, in early stages, or may examine specific aptitudes and career attitudes needed for success in later stages.

Vocational assessment deals with the role of the worker and demands of the workplace. When testing no longer focuses on a general career area but narrows into a specific job type, it usually is called *vocational assessment*. The Interdisciplinary Council on Vocational Evaluation and Assessment describes the vocational evaluation/assessment process as comprising:

> Services to measure, observe, and document an individual's interests, values, temperaments, work-related behaviors, aptitudes and skills, physical capacities, learning style, and training needs (Smith, Lombard, Neubert, LeConte, Rothenbacher & Sitlington, 1996, p. 74).

These tests focus on work-related characteristics and aptitudes of the student, representing finite vocational and work-oriented approaches (Le Conte, 1999, p. 393). Areas vary with the individual in order to identify special aptitudes and special needs, work habits and behaviors, personal and social skills needed for work, values and attitudes toward work, work tolerance and work adjustment, physical abilities, and dexterity.

Critical Point Career assessments look at the life span as a series of stages toward career maturity and measure abilities and interests. Vocational assessments focus on the worker and the demands of various workplace environments and measure work-related aptitudes and characteristics of the student.

Current and Future Living Environments

This second category of transition assessment is extremely broad and variable, depending on the student's lifestyle preferences and potential for independence. The transition team would use assessments in this area to ensure that the student has developed a range of necessary self-care and management skills. When independence is limited, students should have skills that allow a maximum sense of independence and choice within a supported living environment. Some skills that the team may need to assess include basic health and hygiene, medical and dental, home care, safety and community survival skills, and self-advocacy. Some students may need to learn community travel and transportation skills, shopping, cooking, housecleaning, and money management depending on their current and anticipated levels of independence.

The family or student's group home staff can be extremely helpful in providing information about current levels of performance in these areas. Developmental disability agency staff members may be able to begin processes associated with supported living options as well. All of these individuals can help to define what they believe are realistic future alternatives and the ongoing monitoring and support that may be needed as the student moves into adulthood. This area of transition is less well defined by testing and assessment instruments; therefore, including the individuals who can assist with gathering relevant data is very important.

Critical Point   Assessments for living environments are not well defined; therefore, family and/or support staff involvement is crucial to identify accurately areas of ability, preference, and need.

Current and Future Personal-Social Environments

This third and final category of transition is another area that is highly dependent on the potential and preferences of the student. For example, most students will have desires for friendships, but the number of friends they need in order to feel satisfied may vary greatly. Certain routine environments, such as work and their neighborhood, may be arenas in which they have a strong need to belong; or some may be happy to have a few friends outside these environments whom they see regularly.

Some students may wish to marry and have children of their own. The team will need to address dating, sexuality, child care, and possibly, sexual vulnerability in the community while dating. Hobbies and community participation, including sports teams or interest groups, are skills that the team also should support according to the student's preferences. In addition, friendship, dating, marital, and parenting skills are areas where there are few assessments. Teams will need to rely upon gathering information from the student and those individuals who know the student best.

Team members who see the student regularly—parents, teachers, group home staff, coaches—will have valuable perspectives on the student's current abilities in making, maintaining, and, when necessary, ending relationships and friendships with others. The involvement of all important community members on the team can greatly assist in addressing all important transition areas and in better predicting future needs and potential environments.

A unique aspect of this area is its influence on success in the two other transition areas. The team may have to address social skill needs in work and in community living environments as well. A number of assessments address behavioral and interaction aspects of personal-social skills that the team may find helpful. The team may need to develop an integrated assessment approach that identifies related strengths and needs across all three domains with an intervention plan that addresses all simultaneously.

Table 7–1 summarizes some major purposes of career and transition assessment. For work, living, and personal-social current and future environments, the various purposes give rise to

TABLE 7–1

Purposes for Transition Assessment

Category	Description
Determination of development in working, living, and personal/ social environments	To find out where the student stands in terms of: awareness, orientation, exploration, preparation, placement, or growth/maintenance. Appropriate for middle school/early junior high and beyond (Neubert, 1985).
Measurement	To identify abilities, interests, capabilities, strengths, needs, potentials, behaviors, and preferences within the areas of personal-social, functional-academic, community-independent living, employment and employability areas. Initial testing appropriate for middle school; more involved analyses appropriate for high school and beyond (Neubert, 1986).
Prediction	To match an individual's preferences and abilities with appropriate program options. Appropriate for high school (Neubert, 1985).
Prescription	To identify strengths and needs and to recommend types of adaptive techniques and/or accommodation strategies that will lead to improved performance. Appropriate for high school and young adults and beyond (Neubert, 1985).
Exploration	To "try out" different tasks or activities and to determine how preferences match abilities for program options and postschool outcomes. Appropriate for high school and young adults (Neubert, 1985).
Skill development	To implement the techniques or strategies that will help a student to explore performance requirements. Appropriate for high school and beyond (Le Conte, 1986).
Advocacy	To develop a profile to help students, their families, and others identify concrete ways to assist students in achieving their goals. Appropriate for high school and beyond (Le Conte, 1986).

Sources: Adapted from National Information Center for Children and Youths with Disabilities (NICCYD). (1990). *Vocational assessment: A guide for parents and professionals,* Washington, D.C.: NICCYD.

specific questions that the team will address in planning with the student and family. The assessments made to answer the questions provide the inputs in profile development.

Critical Point Current and future environments, based on student and family preferences require very specific information which addresses how students function in specific environments.

IDEA Requirements

Well-done and appropriate assessments are the basis for all successful special education and transition programming. In order to ensure appropriate testing practices, IDEA ad-

dressed assessment in both 1990 and 1997. The IDEA of 1990 required IEP assessments to be unbiased and given in the native language of the student. In addition, placement in special education could not be based on any single test or instrument but must include multiple assessments across more than one environment (Turnbull, 1993). This is known as a multifactored evaluation.

Transition assessments must follow these same guidelines. In addition, the IDEA of 1997 represented a significant shift in assessment processes. It included a greater emphasis on informal assessments that examined the student's performance in specific environments according

TABLE 7–2

New IDEA Requirements For Assessment and Evaluation

Use a variety of assessment tools and strategies to gather relevant functional and developmental information, including information provided by the parent, that may assist in determining whether the child has a disability and the contents of the child's Individualized Educational Program. Include information related to child's involvement in the general curriculum or, for preschool children, participation in appropriate activities. Other requirements are as follows:
- Increased emphasis on functional and developmental information
- Specific requirement that information from parents is included in the evaluation process
- Results are to be used for determining eligibility for special education services and in developing the child's IEP
- Eligibility determination and IEP development
- Provide information about how the student can best succeed in the general education classroom

Source: Drawn from Taylor, R. L. (2000). *Assessment of exceptional students: Educational and psychological procedures,* Needham Heights, MA: Allyn & Bacon.

to each environment's expectations. In contrast, formal assessments tend to be given under strict, neutral conditions; that is, often in a room without distractions, following a standard set of directions, using paper and pencil, or copying or manipulating objects or tools.

Informal assessments allow the team to examine the student's behavior within the variety of environments that are natural to the individual's life, including the anticipated future environments (Sitlington et al., 1996). Formal tests can provide important general information but are usually isolated from critical environmental contexts that frequently either support or create barriers for the student. The greater emphasis on informal assessments also allows greater participation from students and parents in the assessment process because these assessments can be more individualized to better fit their current preferences and visions of possible futures.

Critical Point The use of both informal and formal assessments provides the transition team with a holistic view of the student. Informal assessments allow for more variability across environments to create a realistic picture of the student's abilities.

An additional aspect of IDEA 1997 that the transition team needs to address is the extent to which the student should be integrated into the general education curriculum and classroom as part of the IEP plan. The 1997 Amendments emphasize placement with peers, and if the team does not feel this is appropriate, then it provides a statement as to why this is so.

This issue is very important in terms of the preferences of the student and family. Team members may hold contradictory views in terms of what constitutes "normal peers." Some may believe that integration into a work and community environment with typical adult coworkers represents the ultimate goal of transition and integration and, thus, complies with IDEA. Others may believe that work and community training is "atypical" for most high school students and, thus, represents a "handicapping" placement that contradicts the IDEA. The preferences of the student and family are probably the best gauge of what is most appropriate. Table 7–2 summarizes some specific IDEA requirements pertaining to transition assessment.

TABLE 7–3

Characteristics and Example of a Functional Assessment

Characteristics
- Practical, real-world skills
- Specific individual functioning in specific environment
- Focuses on supporting learning/performance
- Assesses performance progress

Using a laundromat
- Compare students' performance with typical customer
- Identify skills that help performance:
  - Watch clock
- Identify distracters that hinder performance:
  - Watch others or television
- Identify reminders that work:
  - Using picture cue cards
  - Going with a supportive neighbor
  - Setting a timer
- Identify checkpoints for monitoring:
  - Keep checking sorting because colors and whites are still being mixed

Functional Assessments

The assessments that provide information that is directly related to a student's transition outcomes are sometimes called *functional assessments*. The student's performance or behavior is measured in a specific environment. The standard or criterion of the performance is established to meet that level which is required for success/achievement within that setting. This level is compared to the individual's performance within this setting. Functional assessments are emphasized within the new recommendations by IDEA 1997. Sitlington et al. (1996) suggest their greater use in place of standardized paper-and-pencil assessment.

Gaylord-Ross and Browder (1991) contended that although functional assessment has been defined broadly, it has some of the following characteristics: (1) focuses on practical, independent living/work skills that enable the person to survive and succeed in the real world; (2) has an ecological emphasis that looks to the individual functioning in his or her surrounding en-

vironment; (3) examines the process of learning and performance; (4) suggests intervention techniques that may be successful; and (5) specifies ongoing monitoring procedures that can evaluate performance progress (p. 45). Table 7–3 provides an example of a functional assessment.

Functional assessments can be either formal or informal assessment tools. Regardless of their respective unique features, functional assessment requires a relationship between data and the decision-making process about the student's transition services, whether the data are for curriculum, program, or community-based instruction. They are functional in providing information directly related to current or future environments (e.g., regular or special classes, or community, work, or home settings), tasks (basic work literacy, home care and personal hygiene, soldering integrated circuits onto the mother board), and behaviors (adhering to medical restrictions, following safety precautions, and taking the correct bus). These assessments also should relate directly to the student's transition outcomes. Functional testing more often may use informal procedures. Grade equivalent scores from standardized tests are rarely "functional" because neither work, living, nor personal-social domains require a specific grade level of attainment. However, if a student wishes to apply for vocational or postsecondary programs, grade equivalent scores may be a requirement for certain programs and, therefore, become functional in their impact on future environments or some accommodation to reading if the student has the required conceptual skills.

Ecological assessments may be "functional" and directly related to transition outcomes. They are used to assess all aspects (e.g., people, places, and things) and interrelationships among these elements within a particular environment that impact a student's performance. Important aspects can include environmental conditions (e.g., heat, light, indoors/outdoors, proximity of others, number of coworkers, size and condition of building, etc.), relationships with others (e.g., impact of the student on coworkers and supervisors, quality of mutual interactions, acceptance and mutual regard, abilities to give and take feedback, etc.), and performance accommodations/adaptations. The assessment examines the interactive and mutual nature of these relationships and their impacts to evaluate the student's success in meeting both formal and informal expectations within the setting.

A team may use a functional assessment to determine employment positions that are most likely to lead to success within a particular preferred career area for a student: The evaluator observes in order to determine if the student performs at adequate levels and is able to integrate socially and personally in the work environment. When preparing to seek a specific job, the team may ask for an ecological evaluation at a specific company to ensure that the physical conditions and coworkers/supervisors at that company are compatible with and supportive of the student's needs. Teams will choose to use each assessment to meet their specific needs for information.

Critical Point   Functional assessments can be formal or informal. They tend to focus on practical skills, compare student's performance in different environments, examine the process of learning and performance, and specify evaluation procedures to determine progress.

Summary

Transition assessment processes are broadly inclusive of competencies that are needed for adulthood. These competencies can be categorized into three main areas: current and future work, living, and personal-social domains. The team chooses among a range of formal and informal assessments, including functional and ecological assessments. These provide both general and specific data that are used in planning for desired transition outcomes. The nature of transition assessments means that it must be ongoing, have a specific purpose, and should be individualized and effectively summarized.

The assessment process begins with consensus among team members on a student's potential future. They use this to identify the kinds of information that are necessary to assemble a comprehensive transition profile of the student. From this, the team shapes future transition potentials by matching interests and talents with potential job requirements and career profiles, lifestyles and living arrangements, and community participation and socialization opportunities. The next section further describes the types of tests that the team uses in gathering the required information to create the transition profile.

Formal Transition Assessments

Assessments can be classified into two general categories: formal and informal. Standardized or *formal assessments* are designed for the purpose of determining a person's relative standing within a group for a general trait or characteristic. Typical examples include intelligence tests (i.e., we calculate a number that compares the student's ability to learn with others of the same age) and achievement tests (i.e., we give a grade equivalent or stanine score that ranks the student's progress compared with others of the same age or grade). Standardized assessments follow formal procedures that were used for developing the test and must be used in giving and interpreting their results. The ability of these tests to compare one individual with another depends on this consistent administration and interpretation. Some tests require prior training with strict rules on who can be assessors.

In addition to intelligence tests and achievement tests, special education and transition programs often use formal adaptive behavior scales, personality tests and vocational and career aptitudes, interests, worker characteristics, and occupational skills tests for evaluating student ability and progress. Some newer transition tests are being developed that are designed to assess one's knowledge and skills specifically required in community functioning. It has been long recognized that standardized tests give a limited view of the individual (e.g., a focus on deficits) and are not perfectly reliable and valid, particularly for individuals with disabilities. However, there are certain qualities and circumstances that make standardized tests valuable.

Formal, standardized tests go through a development process that strengthens their reliability and validity and allows them to make comparisons between individuals. Reliability refers to stability of scores. For example, a student taking a social skills test should get approximately the same score if he or she takes it again (of course, we hope that training and practice might raise any areas of need). Validity means that a test accurately measures what it is intended to assess. For example, if the results of a vocational abilities test shows an aptitude in a particular career area, the student will also demonstrate those aptitudes successfully in a work situation. The difficulty for students with disabilities is that few are included in most test

development or in the norming processes that establish the comparison scales. In addition, students who need specific accommodations or who do poorly on certain types of tests (e.g., those that are timed or require transferring answers onto a standardized "bubble" test form) are not likely to perform in ways that represent their true abilities. These comparisons with other students can provide some useful, general information for the team. However, for more specific information about a student's potential in specific environments, the team should combine formal test results with those from informal tests. When both sets of results identify patterns of behavior or gaps and needs for programs, the team can be fairly certain that these are trustworthy and accurate results. Any one test, whether formal or informal, should never be used as the sole indicator of success or difficulty experienced by a student.

Critical Point Formal assessments tend to be standardized and measure a student's skills relative to a norm group of their "peers." These tests have formal procedures for administration and evaluation of the results.

General Skills Tests

A number of instruments provide general assessments of transition skills that can help the team to identify broad strength and need areas. Adaptive behavior scales often are used in multifactored assessments and typically request individuals who know the student well (e.g., teachers, parents, etc.) to rate the individual on the skills required for functioning in the community or school. An example is the *American Association on Mental Retardation* (AAMR) *Adaptive Behavior Scales*. Teachers and parents rate the student's abilities across a number of life-skill areas (e.g., basic academics, self-care, meals, and hygiene). Results provide an age-normed score with 100 as the "average." The *Vineland Adaptive Behavior Scales* is another commonly used instrument with a similar format.

Halpern (1996) developed the *Transition Skills Inventory*, which is completed by the student, parent, and teacher. The skills inventory consists of four broad areas and their respective subdomains, including the following areas:

(a) Personal life: communication with other people, relating to authorities, relating to peers, responsibility, solving problems, controlling anger, personal safety;

(b) Jobs: knowing about jobs, finding a job, skills on the job;

(c) Education and training: reading, writing, math; and

(d) Living on your own: self-care, nutrition and fitness, money management, home management, community and leisure activities.

The inventory uses a self-report student form in conjunction with forms for parents and teachers. This helps students to learn about their interests, strengths, and weaknesses and then to use the information obtained to make important decisions that affect their lives. Students can use this to enhance their self-evaluation as a foundation for greater participation with the team in developing their transition plans.

The *Transition Planning Inventory* (Clark & Patton, 1997) is designed to help its user identify and comprehensively plan for the student's transition needs. The instrument assesses employment, education, daily living, leisure, health, self-determination, communication, and interpersonal relationships. There are three forms completed by the school, home, and students. There are over 600 transition goals that are correlated with transition planning statements. Together, these results can assist the team in integrating perspectives from several people regarding the student's needs, preferences, and interests.

Some transition assessments have a more narrow focus. The *Social and Prevocational Information Battery* (SPIB) (Halpern & Irvin, 1986) assesses knowledge of skills and competencies for the vocational and community adjustment of students with mental retardation. The nine subtests examine knowledge of job search skills, job-related behavior, banking, budgeting, purchasing, home management, health care, hygiene and grooming, and functional signs. The battery is intended primarily for junior and senior high school levels and consists mostly of true-false, orally administered items. One important note for team members is that students who have difficulty responding to questions asked in this manner may not give reliable answers.

Current and Future Working Environments

The area of work has been fairly well developed for formal assessment through career counseling and vocational rehabilitation programs. Assessment often begins with identification of career interests. The *Becker Reading-Free Interest Survey*, *Career Development Inventory* (CDI), *Career Maturity Inventory* (CMI), *Knowledge Of The World Of Work Scale*, *Kuder Vocational Preference Record*, *Reading-Free Vocational Interest Inventory*, *Self-Directed Search*, and *The Wide-Range Interest And Opinion Test* (WRIOT) all provide for some aspects of interest assessment. Additional information about these and other instruments listed in this chapter can help team members to evaluate which, if any, are appropriate for their student (see Clark & Kolstoe, 1990; Gajar et al., 1993; Kokaska & Brolin, 1985; Linn & Destefano, 1986; Luft, 1999; Sitlington et al., 1996).

Another well-developed area of assessment is work skill and aptitude measurement. Some of these instruments are the *Bennett Hand-Tool Dexterity Test*, *Differential Aptitude Test* (Dat), *Macquarrie Test For Mechanical Ability*, *Minnesota Spatial Relations Test*, and *Purdue Pegboard Test* (Clark & Kolstoe, 1990; Gajar et al., 1993; Kokaska & Brolin, 1985; Linn & Destefano, 1986; Luft, 1999; Sitlington et al., 1996). The team may want to consult with a vocational evaluator in order to select specific tests that best assess a student's skills in a particular area.

Use of work samples is another popular format that was developed by rehabilitation and vocational education to examine work tasks and performance variables. A work sample is "a well-defined work activity involving tasks, materials and tools that are identical or similar to those in an actual job or cluster of jobs. Work samples are used to assess a persons vocational aptitudes, work characteristics, and vocational interests," (VEWWA, 1988, p. 16). Because a work sample approximates an actual job, the evaluator can observe actual work behavior in a controlled situation (usually a testing room or classroom). Commonly used examples include *Apticom*, *McCarron-Dial Work Evaluation System*, *Singer Vocational Evaluation System*, and *Valpar Work Sample* (Clark & Kolstoe, 1990; Gajar et al., 1993; Kokaska & Brolin, 1985; Linn & Destefano, 1986; Luft, 1999; Sitlington et al., 1996). These typically involve asking the students to perform certain specific tasks which are evaluated for speed, accuracy, quantity, and quality.

These formal and standardized work samples, like other standardized measures (e.g.; intelligence tests, adaptive behavior scales, and the others described earlier), do not predict job success perfectly because they are based on performance of job tasks that only resemble actual jobs and do not occur in a real work environment with typical distractions and conditions. They continue to be used as a means of identifying a student's relative areas of strengths. Although it can change their interpretation and scoring, some experienced evaluators choose to modify these assessments to learn valuable information about a student's rate of learning these tasks, responsiveness to suggestions, and related work behaviors. This can provide helpful information to the team when standardized scores are not necessary.

Current and Future Living Environments

This area has fewer standardized measures although a number of instruments recently have been developed that assess aspects of this broad domain. The ARC's *Self-Determination Scale* (Wehmeyer, 1995b; Wehmeyer & Kelchner, 1995)

is a formal assessment that is a student self-report instrument designed for use with adolescents with cognitive disabilities, including mild mental retardation and learning disabilities. Through this instrument, students can evaluate their own beliefs about themselves and their self-determination skills or needs, and can assess their progress.

Another important area to assess is whether students have sufficient survival skills to live safely and happily. Several instruments that assess general areas of survival skills include the *Independent Living Behavior Checklist*, the *Street Survival Skills Questionnaire*, and the *Test for Everyday Living*. These typically use an interview or survey format (Clark & Kolstoe, 1990; Gajar et al., 1993; Kokaska & Brolin, 1985; Linn & Destefano, 1986; Sitlington et al., 1996). A student's satisfaction is the ultimate measure of transition success. Although there are few such instruments as yet, an additional assessment is the *Lifestyle Satisfaction Scale*, which might provide some useful information for the team.

Survival skill needs may have related effects on personal-social skills and skills needed for work (Menchetti, Rusch, & Owens, 1983; Rusch, 1979). A key feature of survival skill measurement is that the instruments should have social validity and should meet the expectations and beliefs of the community and environments in which the student will live, work, and play. The team may need to interpret some of these standardized tests cautiously; conditions vary considerably between urban, suburban, and rural settings as well as across ethnicity and social class. What meets the expectations of one community may violate those in another community.

Current and Future Personal-Social Environments

Abilities or needs in this domain can greatly impact the other two transition domains. An inability to form satisfactory relationships can lead to unacceptable behaviors in any environment, ranging from social withdrawal to aggression and

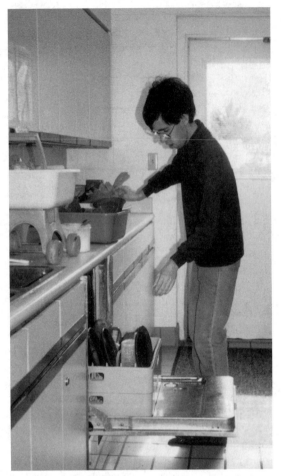

Daily living skills are an important transition curriculum.

violence toward others. Not many formal assessments address formation of friendships and dating/marital relationships, but they do address more general social abilities. Some of these assessments include the *Progress Assessment Chart of Social and Personal Development*, *Social and Prevocational Information Battery*, *Waksman Social Skills Rating Form*, and the *Leisure Time Activities Scale* (Clark & Kolstoe, 1990; Gajar et al., 1993; Kokaska & Brolin, 1985; Linn & Destefano, 1986; Sitlington et al., 1996).

An assessment that combines work with social skills is the *Test of Interpersonal Competency for Em-*

ployment (TICE). This is a 61-item survival skill measure that has been validated in terms of important skills that are specific to job tenure (Foss, Cheney, & Bullis, 1986). The student's competence is evaluated in terms of responding to criticisms/corrections, following instructions, and requesting assistance from supervisors; working cooperatively, responding to teasing/provocation, and coping with personal problems as coworker issues. The instrument accompanies a comprehensive training curriculum (Foss & Vilhauer, 1986) so that need areas can be efficiently addressed.

Academic Assessment

Although it is not one of the three transition domains defined by DCDT, transition teams have to do some academic assessment for students with disabilities. However, the extent to which the team addresses academic outcomes will depend on the student's academic potential and career/lifestyle preferences. The *Adult Basic Literacy Assessment*, *Brigance Diagnostic Inventory of Essential Skills*, *and Wide Range Achievement Test* (WRAT) are several general academic tests that can be used to assess basic competencies. The team must also realize that not all students are able to achieve these levels, in which case accommodations and alternative performance options will need to be investigated.

For some students, postschool transition preferences may include 2- or 4-year-college or postgraduate and professional training. For other students, postsecondary education will involve further development of transition skills. For many of these individuals with disabilities, there is a need to provide a broader array of experiences and opportunities for attainment of academic skills to allow access to more challenging and advanced jobs (High School/High Tech, 1999). The team members will need to emphasize and build upon these students' academic performance to ensure their success in postsecondary settings.

Although it is normal for all students to be assessed in the realm of academic performance, much of those assessments are more closely allied with classroom curriculum and activities. They may not address the individual student's projected needs in postsecondary environments (Thurlow & Elliott, 1998). Academic assessment for transition purposes must focus specifically on those academic skills that will provide the foundation needed for success in postsecondary education and community and work life. Students who plan to live and work independently in the community also need job-related academic skills as well as functional and survival skills in communication (either written or oral), math, science, social studies, and government/civics. They must be able to budget their income and to balance their checkbook, as well as, for example, to read directions on cleaning products and recipes. Their adult goals will determine the extent and nature of the academic testing that the team needs to pursue.

Ysseldyke and his colleagues (Ysseldyke, Thurlow, & Erickson, 1994: Ysseldyke, Thurlow, & Gillian, 1993: Thurlow & Elliott, 1998) have outlined a comprehensive set of evaluation standards for students from preschool to postschool levels. Each level describes direct indicators of academic assessments, including communication competence, problem solving, basic math, and reading and writing skills. The team can match the student's academic needs with transition-related experiences that will further reinforce these skills through application to realistic problems. For instance, if a student's goal was to attend a postsecondary technical school and to become a construction worker foreman, academic assessment might show weaknesses in understanding and calculating angles (related to calculating roof pitch angles). The team could include specific academic goals in math in conjunction with real-life training in building a roof.

Many academic tests use formal and standardized procedures although informal procedures also can provide valuable information. Students who wish to enter academically focused postsecondary programs need to develop abilities to take general achievement tests. In addition, they should consider participating in mandatory statewide testing, which is required of regular education students in many states. IDEA requires that students with disabilities should be part of the system of assessment and accountability that is part of school improvement and reform efforts, unless they choose not to do so. The type of high school diploma a student receives may depend on his or her ability to take and score well on achievement and state proficiency tests. An academic diploma is increasingly important for assuring entry into postsecondary training facilities. The team may need to be creative devising appropriate accommodations and methods to ensure that this testing reflects the student's actual skills and accomplishments.

Table 7–4 shows the general categories of standardized tests and possible accommodations. Accommodations are necessary in many instances to allow the true abilities of the student to be determined. Because of the technical issues of test standardization, the interpretation of the test results is unclear. Tests taken with accommodations are under different conditions so that comparing scores with others (e.g., norm group) is not valid.

Informal Transition Assessments

In the early 1980s, contemporary and functional assessment emerged as an alternative approach to supplement limitations of formal, standardized tests of student characteristics and abilities (Halpern & Fuhrer, 1984). IDEA 1997 emphasizes the use of functional, informal assessment because of these types of weaknesses: "the relevance of traditional intelligence, personality, and neuropsychological instruments and their

TABLE 7–4

Transition-Related Large-Scale Standardized Tests and Accommodations

Types of tests/examinations

Proficiency: Measures on accomplishment of standard curriculum, knowledge, and/or performance in academic subjects at different grade levels

Graduation: Measures on attainment of certain levels of competence to receive a regular diploma

General education development: Tests on meeting high school level requirements in reading, mathematics, writing, social studies, and science in lieu of a diploma

Entrance: Tests on level of preparation for college course work (e.g., ACT, SAT) or graduate/professional school level work (GRE, LSAT, etc.)

Credential: Tests to determine proficiency preparation to enter a line of work/occupation (e.g., BAR, medical boards, teacher license exams, etc.)

Types of accommodations
- Increased time
- Different setting
- Different response types (e.g., oral versus written)
- Revised formats (e.g., enlarged print)

From: Drawn from Thurlow, M. & Elliott, J. (1998). Student assessment and evaluation. In Rusch, J. R. & Chadsey, J. G. (Eds.), *Beyond high school: Transition from school to work* (pp. 265–296), New York: Wadsworth Publishing Company.

respective results to the pragmatic educational, work, and community adjustment focus of rehabilitation programs is unclear at best, and may be totally unrelated to the rehabilitation process" (Bullis, Kosko, Waintrup, Kelley, & Issacson, 1994, p. 9).

Informal assessments are used to determine what the students' needs, interests, and preferences are and how well they are progressing in reaching their transition and IEP goals. Informal assessments also can be functional to determine performance on some specific task directly relevant to the educational program of the student. The student's performance or behavior is measured in a specific environment, for example, the classroom or community setting. The standard or criterion of performance is what in fact is required for success/achievement within that setting, in comparison to the individuals' own performance.

One important concern is the potential lack of validity and reliability of informal assessments; in other words, are they really testing what is desired (and not other irrelevant but

obscure factors), and, are the results reliable (e.g., if different people are observed over several weeks, would the results be the same?) Clark (1996) identified some conditions for determination of valid nonstandardized assessments. He believed that the team's agreement that an assessment is an accurate reflection of a student provides some face validity for an informal assessment. When these results are supported by what is already known (e.g., other informal assessments or formal assessments), then the results may be considered affirmed and useful for program planning.

Informal assessments are a vital complement to standardized test results in transition planning by providing examples of specific successes, strengths, and needs in relation to transition planning and IEP outcomes. Because informal assessments do not meet the technical standards of formal tests, describing how the information was obtained, providing caveats and limitations in their interpretation, and examining the assessments as a whole and among several sources (e.g., different team members in different situations) become very important. Nonetheless, because informal assessments occur in specific environments, their results provide authentic information about how the student performs in these environments and their needs for training, resources, and accommodations in order to be successful. Informal assessments include several types of formats that address all three transition domains depending on the setting in which they are used. Several are described next.

Critical Point   Informal assessments are emphasized in IDEA 1997 to supplement the use of standardized tests. Informal assessments provide detailed information on a student's specific successes, strengths, and needs that are directly related to his or her transition and IEP outcomes.

Student School Records

As a preliminary step in developing and updating the students' transition IEP, the cumulative record can be a source of past behavior, attitudes, and performance. School grades, special services, attendance records, performance on group tests, and other information are contained in the student's permanent record. Checklists and anecdotal notes on teacher perceptions of classroom behavior and performance also may be helpful. In particular, patterns of special needs, growth, and development may be detected over time if several teachers noted the same issues from year to year. Since the manner in which information was collected is not known nor are the conditions at the particular time periods, the reviewer of records must be careful not to base their current evaluation primarily on past observations.

Curriculum-Based Assessment

One of the most common alternatives to traditional measurement is curriculum-based assessment. These measures assess a student's progress through a particular curriculum, either academic or vocational. Some better curriculum-based assessments also use a criterion-referenced mea-

sure that sets a standard reflecting real-world expectations (e.g., the driver's education curriculum expects the same driving and testing performance as found on the state exams).

These assessments are based on the specific activities and objectives within the curriculum, making it a highly accurate test of the student's progress in the program. This type of test was developed because many standardized tests were far removed from the activities of daily instruction and, therefore, were not an accurate measure of "progress" in that program. Curriculum-based assessment also allows for an analysis of content or skills to be completed so that these can be broken down into smaller curriculum objectives or tasks as needed to promote student success.

These assessments require that the student should be taught from an existing curriculum program. Although IDEA 1997 strongly encourages inclusion of all special education students in the regular curriculum, for some students this may not be practical, or may not meet with some of the transition outcomes that are determined to be important by the team. In these cases, curriculum-based assessment may not be practical. However, students enrolled in vocational training programs can be evaluated using curriculum-based vocational assessment which documents their progress within the training program and ultimately, toward achieving industry-level skills. Case Study A provides an example of a curriculum-based assessment strategy for vocational school settings.

CASE STUDY A

Curriculum-Based Assessment in a Welding Program

A tenth grade student is enrolled in a welding program. The vocational and special education teacher develop curriculum-based measures in order to determine the student's progress and instructional needs in completing the program. The tasks and activities in performing the welding operations are broken down to assess student learning (e.g., a competency checklist). Additional tests or ratings are developed to measure student interest and motivation, the ability to use equipment and tools in the program, and the ability to communicate with the instructor and other students. In the process of assessing and teaching, the two teachers devise any instructional or equipment accommodations/adaptations that are required for the student to perform welding operations and related or academic tasks. The student and the two teachers are in regular communication while the student progresses through the program.

Source: Adapted from Sitlington, Neubert, Begun, Lombard, and Le Conte 1996.

The comprehensive *Life-Centered Career Education* curriculum program includes a related assessment program and employs a criterion-referenced measurement (Brolin, 1992a, 1992b; Brolin, 1995; Bucher & Brolin, 1987). This comprehensive curriculum is designed to prepare students with disabilities with the important skills needed to function successfully as productive workers in the home and community (described previously in Chapter 6). The three accompanying curriculum-based measures are the LCCE knowledge battery, LCCE performance battery, and competency rating scale. Collectively, these criterion measures make it possible to evaluate the knowledge and skills to determine individually appropriate instructional goals in 22 competency areas and 97 subcompetencies related to the areas of daily living skills, personal-social skills, and occupational and preparation skills.

Criterion-Referenced Assessment

A criterion-referenced standard is used to evaluate mastery with either formal or informal assessments for instruction on objectives and skills. For some work-related and community tasks, there may be specific industry, union, or site-based standards of production quality and quantity that the student must meet. These are

examples of socially validated external criteria which the team will want to follow. Formal assessments including many statewide proficiency tests often use criteria to establish categories of attainment.

School programs typically use criteria in an informal way to measure attainment of IEP and instructional objectives. Some of these standards are arbitrary (e.g., is 70 or 80% an appropriate measure of what is "good" for any particular student?) and others are based on common-sense and safety. For example, skills in crossing the street should be mastered at 100%; defining mastery at 80% means that in one out of five times the student will be in danger, an unacceptable level of error in this case. The team should ensure that objectives and programs that use criterion-based assessment reflect upon community and real-world standards as much as possible.

Portfolio Assessment

In some areas of academic performance, a portfolio has been developed to assess student performance. In fact, many institutions of higher education are using portfolios as a means for partial evaluation of a student before receiving a bachelor's degree (Karp & Stroble, 1999; Winograd & Gaskin, 1992). The portfolio assessment process is the accumulation of work in the various academic and performance areas to represent the achievement of students. Thurlow and Elliott (1998) have indicated that the purpose of such a process is to document the student's work, to provide knowledge beyond that of standardized assessments and grading processes, and to provide an accountability of educational performance. The portfolio method also has disadvantages in terms of being subjective, difficult for the student who needs a lot of structure, time-consuming, and difficult for establishing reliability and validity. These issues can be addressed particularly if the team knows of specific performance or behavioral standards that are required in a work or community situation. The portfolio can be used as an alternative way of documenting the student's ability to perform at these levels.

Critical Point   The portfolio assessment provides an alternative means to evaluate a student's work and improvement over time. The portfolio can include assessment information related to academic performance, job-related skills, independent living, and social skills.

Portfolio assessment with regular and special education students uses student performances (or products) that display accomplishments and improvement over time (Airasian, 1994). Various types of student information or experiences can be included that range from academic to career development to job and community preparation. Through portfolios a very individual record of the student's growth and development and performance in specific contexts can be recorded, making it somewhat unique (Carey, 1994). Sarkees-Wircenski & Wircenski (1994) recommend portfolio assessment as a good tool for documenting a variety of transition competencies and for directly involving the student in the assessment process. They suggest using videotapes to record students who are successfully performing a variety of tasks. This can be very convincing to a prospective employer or community individual who might not be able to see a student's potential. These types of career or transition portfolios can reflect upon progress over time in critical areas such as:

- Employability skills
- Work-related social skills
- Self-help/independent living skills
- Generalization skills
- Job-specific skills
- Home management
- Independent travel
- Safety and survival skills

Surveys and Interviews

Surveys and interviews are an effective means of gathering information directly from the student and others who are involved with the student in important settings. These individuals include parents, work supervisors and coworkers, group home staff, transportation staff, and a variety of community persons and friends. The team may need to seek out some of these individuals for their help in identifying either factors and conditions that lead to the student's success, or that create barriers.

Interviews are generally conducted face to face or by telephone. Surveys can be either self-administered or completed orally. The value of this method is that the information is obtained directly from the source. Students are the best source for their likes, dislikes, and other transition-related preferences; employers, supervisors, and coworkers are the best sources for what is important in the work environment and how students are performing; parents and families have a unique perspective on the student and their own views on the student's personality and developmental history; and friends and community members have information about interests and participation in other environments.

A number of the instruments listed previously in the formal testing section utilize an interview or survey format. These differ from informal procedures and often include scoring procedures that are based on asking the full set of questions, which are asked in the manner described in a manual.

With informal interviews and surveys, the team members may decide that certain types of information that have not been gathered by other methods are needed and so they design questions to solicit this information. It is important that when creating such an instrument the questions should be relevant, clear, and well designed. Team members may want to have their interview or survey reviewed by several other individuals to ensure its effectiveness. Also, consideration must be given as to how the respondent will answer; that is, yes-no, multiple-choice, or an open-ended format. Students may have difficulty with certain types of questions and answers, requiring that the linguistic structure and conceptual complexity be controlled. In addition, there are dangers with self-report formats because people, for example, may answer in ways that they believe will please the committee or put the student or themselves in the best light. Answers may be well-intentioned but not entirely factual; therefore, it is best to compare interview and survey responses across several individuals to find a consensus. Figure 7–1 provides a sample of a needs and preferences survey.

Situational Assessments

The primary purpose of *situational assessment* is to observe, record, and interpret a student's general work behavior and adaptation in a specific work or community setting. The assessment provides a measure of the overall behaviors of the student and also provides the opportunity to observe the student's reaction to specific environments. The student and the team member conducting the assessment can learn information on a wide range of behaviors that are important to the student's transition goals.

The open nature of this type of assessment requires that the team provides the assessor with a specific list of behaviors to observe. The team may want information on general interaction or performance in global, descriptive forms. If the team wishes the observer to note specific types of behaviors or responses, it will need to provide specific definitions and examples of what to observe in order that this is clear. Some examples of types of observational goals include:

- Getting along with coworkers
- Accepting criticism
- Following directions
- Punctuality and attendance
- Greeting known neighbors in apartment building and stores
- Crossing streets safely
- Waiting for change when paying for items

Situational assessments can be used across a variety of settings. They also can be used in school to create "simulations" of community environments as a type of training assessment. Their usefulness is in being able to identify variables that may be problematic to the student and those that support their success. When done well (accurate observations of specific behaviors and conditions) by a number of persons who have the same conclusions, these are a useful tool in helping to select potentially successful future environments. See Case Study B for a sample of a situational assessment.

CASE STUDY B

Sample Situational Assessment for Middle School Student

An eighth-grade student is placed in the library for an in-school work situational assessment. The purpose of the assessment is for career exploration and observation of the individual's work and social skills. The librarian and teacher determine that the student will check out books, return books to shelves, and repair torn and damaged books. Over a three-week period the special education teacher observes the student's social interactions at the checkout desk, ability to catalog books alphabetically and numerically, and ability to work independently repairing books on an intermittent basis. The librarian agrees to supplement these data with information concerning the student's interest level, attention to task, and social interaction. At the end of the situational assessment period, the librarian, teacher, and student discuss the student's interest level, attention to task, and social interaction as well as the student's strengths, needs, and interests noted throughout the assessment. Additional in-school work sites are then discussed and compared in order to further the career exploration process.

Source: Adapted from Sitlington, Neubert, Begun, Lombard, & Le Conte, 1996.

FIGURE 7–1
Transition Needs and Preferences Survey

This survey is designed to help the school determine what type of experiences and education you will need to prepare for life after graduation from high school. It will be used to develop a long-range plan (or transition plan) which will be discussed at the next IEP meeting.

PLEASE ANSWER THE FOLLOWING QUESTIONS BASED ON WHAT YOU KNOW ABOUT YOURSELF (OR THE STUDENT, IF FILLED OUT BY A PARENT/GUARDIAN)

Student Name: Parent/Guardian:

Student Age: Today's Date:

1. What kind of work or education do you hope to see yourself in after graduation from high school?

Full-Time	Part-time	
❏	❏	University or College - *academically oriented four-year program*
❏	❏	Community/ Technical Colleges - *technical/paraprofessional training*
❏	❏	Adult Vocational Education - *advanced job training (e.g., secretary)*
❏	❏	Military Service - *Army, Navy, Air Force, Coast Guard, Marines, etc.*
❏	❏	Competitive Employment - *a job trained by employer (or job coach)*
❏	❏	Supported Employment - *a job with training then support from job coach*
❏	❏	Sheltered Employment - *low-pay work activities and training*
❏	❏	Other

2. What age do you want to exit school?   18   19   20   21   22

3. Is there a job or hobbies you enjoyed or that you are currently interested in? If so, specify:

4. Where do you hope to ultimately live as an adult?

   ❏   Independently in a home or apartment - *generally requires more than minimum wage*

   ❏   Independently in subsidized housing - *usually requires minimum wage or higher income*

   ❏   Wheelchair-accessible housing - *ability to live on own or with personal care attendant*

   ❏   Supported living - *staff assist a few hours per day with cooking, shopping, budgeting etc.*

   ❏   Group home/foster care - *staff provide 24 hour care and help in self-care, health, etc.*

   ❏   With parents or relatives - *sometimes with help of support staff or Medicaid services.*

   ❏   Other _____

5. Is there a neighborhood, city, or locality you hope to live in?

6. What types of community participation do you hope will be available to you as an adult? (check all that apply)

   ❏   Clubs or groups that meet to talk about a common interest (e.g., computers, astronomy)

   ❏   Specify, if possible _____

continued

FIGURE 7–1
(Continued)

- ❏ Community recreational activities (e.g., YMCA, Community Centers, out with friends)

  Specify, if possible _____

- ❏ Religious and cultural activities (e.g., church, synagogue, temple, study groups)

  Specify, if possible _____

- ❏ Transportation for work and leisure activities (e.g., car, bus, friends, parents, bicycle)

  Specify type(s) and for what purpose _____

- ❏ Continuing education (e.g., computers, cooking, sewing, home repair)

  Specify, if possible _____

- ❏ Political participation (e.g., voting, involvement in political groups)

  Specify type of participation if possible _____

- ❏ Other/ Comments: _____

STUDENT NAME: _____ PAGE 2

7. *Check any of the following services that you feel would be helpful to you in achieving your goals.*

❏ Interest Inventories (e.g., OASYS)	❏ Entrance Exam Training (e.g., SAT)
❏ In-School Job Placement	❏ Job Shadowing (i.e., observing a job)
❏ Work Adjustment Training	❏ Guidance Counseling
❏ Community Work Experience	❏ Vocational Education
❏ Summer Jobs	❏ College Experience
❏ Other/Comments:	

FIGURE 7–1
(Concluded)

- ❏ Transportation and Driver Education
- ❏ Consumer Sciences/Home Economics
- ❏ Money Management Training
- ❏ Sewing and Clothing Care Training
- ❏ Other/Comments:

- ❏ Training in Handling Emergencies
- ❏ Training in Cooking and Nutrition
- ❏ Home Repair and Maintenance Training
- ❏ First Aid Training

- ❏ Language and Hearing Services
- ❏ Accommodations and Technology
- ❏ Relationships and Marriage
- ❏ Psychology, Social Work, Psychiatry
- ❏ Other/Comments:

- ❏ Occupational or Physical Therapy
- ❏ Self-Advocacy Training
- ❏ Vocational Rehabilitation
- ❏ Community Awareness Activities

- ❏ *Evaluation(s) (Specify Type Needed):*
- ❏ Referrals (Specify to Whom):
- ❏ *Are You Currently Receiving Rehabilitation Services from Any other Agency? If so, Specify:*

Work Samples

Work samples were described earlier in terms of formalized assessments. When they are developed or modified to accommodate specific work settings, specific student needs, and strengths or to evaluate a specific school or vocational program, they become informal assessments. These measures screen for relevant aptitudes, sample specific components of programs, and identify subsequent assessments that may be more specific. An additional variation to work samples is to build in a teaching component so that rate and style of learning in relationship to specific work tasks are noted. These types of work samples can serve as a basis to match compatibility of student aptitudes and training program requirements or to determine training and accommodation needs within a specific program. A *Consumer's Guide* discusses and analyzes 30 work sample systems (Brown, McDaniel, Couch, & McClanahan, 1994) and is a good resource for general and specific issues of work sample batteries.

Behavioral Assessment

Behavior assessment is used to assess functional relationships between training and observed behavior. Many of these processes are based on the use of applied behavioral analysis to identify and examine thoroughly factors that are contributing to the existence of certain behaviors. Although this process is quite detailed and deserving of separate study, a brief summary will be included here.

Observation and documentation of behaviors is the basis for much of our work with students with disabilities, with written goals and objectives that are observable and measurable. Many techniques described here can be applied to the range of student behaviors (e.g., improving quantity or quality of work products and improving quality of hygiene practices) and are not limited to undesirable interpersonal behaviors.

Five major recording procedures are employed in behavior assessment. *Anecdotal recording* is for the purpose of identifying a behavior and its antecedent events, and reinforcing consequences. The behavior must be specifically defined so that all observers know exactly what to measure. For example, a "tantrum" must be defined as the exact series of behaviors that a student demonstrates so that if she just stamps her feet or engages in one aspect but not the full tantrum episode, this can be accurately noted (When more is known about the behavior, the staff may choose to watch for "early" signs, which have been shown to indicate that a tantrum will soon begin; however, initial observations must first identify all aspects of a sequence.)

Antecedent events are those incidents that happen right before the behavior. They suggest possible causes or triggers and, thus, they are important. The consequences are events that happen immediately after the behavior, such as "time-out," lots of attention from other students and adults, and so on. The following example is based in a case presented by Browning (1997). Through this analysis, an intervention program can be designed around the behavior under consideration: "When Bill has a tantrum at his work site, what occurs immediately prior to that outburst, and what happens immediately following it?" The analysis may show that Bill becomes angered by a certain coworker who won't talk with him (because the coworker is focusing on his work), and the tantrum gives Bill considerable attention from others, which reassures him that he is "likable." Another explanation (depending on which antecedents and consequences are found to be related) is that Bill becomes bored with work (he becomes increasingly agitated, makes increasing attempts to talk with others, or asks to go to the restroom) and the tantrum removes him from the workstation and also reduces the amount of work he has to do!

Observers can use one or more ways to count how often and at what times the target behaviors occur. *Event recording* assesses the frequency in which the event occurs: "How often does Bill have tantrums on the job-training site?" *Time sampling* is for the purpose of determining the time period in which the behavior occurs: "Do Bill's outbursts seem to happen in the early mornings/late afternoons, beginning or end of week, when few or many work peers are around?" *Interval recording* is an observation period that is divided into a number of equal time intervals in which the presence or absence of the behavior (activities) is recorded, especially when the behavior is relatively frequent. Finally, *duration recording* refers to the length of time that the behavior (activities) occurs. "How long do Bill's tantrums last?" All these types of measurements help to identify specific conditions that lead to the behavior, prolong it, and lead to its happening again. The type of recording depends on whether the behavior occurs frequently or infrequently, or if time-related patterns are suspected. Observing periodic tantrums, how often Bill stopped working to try to talk with a coworker, or how often and long he engaged in "off-task" behaviors would be measured using different techniques.

These observational techniques are used to identify a pattern of behavior and then to document behavioral changes. First, behavioral assessment is used to establish a "baseline" of measurement prior to any training or intervention. This establishes the type, rate, and frequency of the behavior under "typical" conditions. Powell et al. (1991) refer to this baseline assessment as "a process of obtaining information about the worker's current ability to complete an activity before any instruction" (p. 64). From this baseline pattern, the team can gauge if and how much change, if any, has occurred as a result of instruction or intervention.

The area of behavioral change is extremely complex and the team may need to consult a specialist. Improving behavior does not merely consist of reducing or eliminating problematic behaviors but also must teach appropriate replacements. For example, a team may feel successful in reducing Bill's frequency and duration of tantrums. However, this will be short lived if they realize a few weeks later that he has now become increasingly physically violent with training staff and coworkers.

When done consistently and conscientiously, behavioral assessment and management is an important informal assessment tool. It can be used across the range of transition settings to meet the requirements of a variety of work, independent living, and personal-social environments. Powell et al. (1991) provide a practical step-by-step guide for conducting baseline assessments on individuals for supported employment training.

Appropriate Use of Tests

When using any type of assessment instrument, whether a formal device to collect general information or an informal instrument that the team has developed and reviewed to assemble a more complete transition profile of the student, one must follow the intended purposes, technical considerations, and interpretation guidelines. Formal and standardized assessments usually provide this information and expect evaluators to adhere to it. Any change means that the results will not be comparable and the interpretation will need to be modified; the standard interpretation of scores may not be possible.

Informal assessments will not have these guidelines, so the purposes, technical considerations, and interpretation must be carefully determined. Teams who construct their own instruments need to spend time ensuring as much validity and reliability as possible. A more specific set of guidelines for method selection was provided by Sitlington, et al. (1997), as shown in Table 7–5. These authors reinforce the need for ongoing evaluation that samples behavior across multiple settings, using several assessors and different methods or instruments. All assessments must be appropriate to the individual and accommodate learning, linguistic, cultural, and technology/assistive device needs.

TABLE 7–5

Guidelines for Transition Assessment Processes

- Assessment methods must be tailored to the types of information needed and the decisions to be made regarding transition planning and various postsecondary outcomes.
- Specific methods selected must be appropriate for the learning characteristics of the individual, including cultural and linguistic differences.
- Assessment methods must incorporate assistive technology or accommodations that will allow an individual to demonstrate his or her abilities and potential.
- Assessment methods must occur in environments that resemble actual vocational training, employment, independent living, or community environments.
- Assessment methods must produce outcomes that contribute to ongoing development, planning, and implementation of "next steps" in the individual's transition process.
- Assessment methods must be varied and include a sequence of activities that sample an individual's behavior and skills over time.
- Assessment data must be verified by more than one method and by more than one person.
- Assessment data must be synthesized and interpreted to individuals with disabilities, their families, and transition team members.

Source: From Sitlington, C. L., Neubert, D. A., & LeConte, P. J. (1997). Transition assessment: The position of the division on career development and transition. *CDEI, 19,* 69–79.

The results must be reported and synthesized into a format that all team members can understand in order to maximize their usefulness in planning.

Critical Point   Informal assessments do not have the strict guidelines for administration and evaluation—like the formal assessments. It is very important for transition teams to identify the behavioral goals for assessment as well as the method of data collection to ensure valid results.

In summary, there are a variety of formal and informal assessments that transition teams will use when planning and conducting a series of transition assessments. Tests should be selected based on their ability to provide information that the team needs in relation to potential transition outcomes. Teams may need to ask the advice of diagnosticians in making these choices. Diagnosticians (or school psychologists) may be the only persons who are qualified to give certain types of formal assessments.

When the assessments have been completed, the accumulated results should be synthesized and compiled into a transition profile. This will ensure that team members have a comprehensive understanding of the student's needs, strengths, and preferences and that there are no additional knowledge gaps. This synthesis must be done in a manner that is clear to the student, the parents, and all team members. The assessment results form the basis for all later transition planning and determination of appropriate outcomes and therefore, must be done carefully and used conscientiously.

The assessments that the team chooses to use will have both benefits and drawbacks to consider. Formal assessments provide comparative information but may not measure important specific aspects of performance. Informal assessments may require much more time to develop, use, and interpret but can provide setting-specific information concerning the student's performance. Table 7–6 provides a comparison of types of formal and informal assessments that may be used in secondary special education.

TABLE 7.6

Formal and Informal Transition Assessments

Formal	Informal
• Intelligence, achievement, adaptive behavior • Aptitudes, interests, values, personality • Motivation and affective factors • Work samples • Transition-adaptive behavior assessments • Criterion-referenced • Transition assessments • Norm-referenced transition assessments	• Situational or observational learning styles assessment; • Curriculum-based assessments from courses; • Observational reports from teachers, employers, and parents/guardians; • Situational assessments in home, community, and work settings; • Environmental assessments (specific to student's placement options); • Personal-future planning activities/procedures; • Structured interviews with students; • Structured interviews with parents/guardians/advocates/peers; • Adaptive, behavioral, or functional skill inventories/checklists; • Social histories; • Rating scales of employability, independent living, and personal-social skills; • Applied technology/vocational educational prerequisite skills assessments; and • General physical examinations.

Source: Adapted from Clark, G. M. (1996) Transition planning assessment for secondary-level students with learning disabilities. *Journal of Learning Disabilities, 29*(1), 79-92.

Interdisciplinary Assessment Processes

Collaborative Processes

The process of identifying assessment needs, carrying out the assessments, interpreting the results and compiling them into a succinct profile, and reassessing the information gathered for accuracy, relevancy, and completeness is a very complex task. One important characteristic that makes this process successful is the development of collaborative relationships among team members (Gajar et al., 1993). A trusting and open relationship will allow the many professional disciplines and community representatives that may be present, including the student, parents, and interested neighbors and friends, to share their perceptions and to participate in providing support and services in planning and achieving transition outcomes.

The amount and variety of information collected across types of instruments and observers/assessors may be difficult to summarize and synthesize. Results may be contradictory or raise additional questions. Team members may be unfamiliar with or doubtful about some types of testing. Establishing and maintaining open communication will allow issues and questions to be addressed early and while there is still time to explore alternatives.

Transition planning includes multiple outcomes.

Comprehensive Transition Planning

One strategy that may help the team to synthesize assessment data and to prioritize the results into achievable goals is by using a comprehensive planning format. A number of authors have developed holistic procedures to promote comprehensive and cohesive transition planning. Three such programs include the following:

1. *Personal Futures Planning* (Mount, 1989, 1992; O'Brien, 1987): This program determines activities, supports, and next steps needed.
2. *McGill Action Planning System* (MAPS; Forest & Pearpoint, 1993; Pearpoint, 1990): Identifies "dreams" and "nightmares," strengths and needs for planning.
3. *Circles of Support* (Forest & Lusthaus, 1989; Forest, Pearpoint & Snow, 1993; Pearpoint, 1993): Identifies abilities, strategies, and commitments among nonpaid supportive peers or colleagues related to an individual's needs.

All these techniques involve collaboration between professional and community individuals who begin

with conceptualizing present and/or future life goals for the student. These may best suit transition teams who prefer open-ended and highly individualized approaches. The benefit gained is from the supportive networks that are developed through this process and that can continue well beyond the end of the student's schooling. However, not all agencies and individuals will be equally accepting of a highly student-centered approach (Luft, Rumrill, & Snyder-Marks, in press).

Several curriculum-based transition programs also include frameworks that assist with assembling comprehensive assessment data. The Brolin (1993, 1996) LCCE curriculum described earlier provides detailed and comprehensive curricular planning across 22 domain areas. The Ysseldyke and Thurlow (1994) curriculum and assessment program is similarly detailed and comprehensive. Its goal of ensuring productive and participating students regardless of the presence of a disability may be well suited for students in inclusive settings. Teams who use a process approach may prefer this. A curriculum guide by Kohler (1996) provides a comprehensive delineation of elements needed for transition success. Teams who prefer a detailed product focus for planning may wish to use this program.

When teams do not choose to use a comprehensive planning tool, they may wish to make checklists of services, providers, and specific transition goals with more specificity across the three broad transition domains. Wehman, Moon, Everson, Wood, and Barcus (1988) recommend a detailed listing for assessing the student's needs in the following areas: (1) employment, (2) vocational education/training, (3) postsecondary education, (4) financial/income needs, (5) independent living, (6) transportation/ mobility, (7) social relationships, (8) recreation/ leisure, (9) health/safety, and (10) self-advocacy/ future planning.

The task of identifying, carrying out, and synthesizing comprehensive assessment and planning is highly complex. In addition to using one of the comprehensive planning strategies described earlier, the team may need to establish a proce-

TABLE 7–7

Steps To Ensure Comprehensive Transition Assessment

1. Determine a shared vision of the student's potential future. Use this to identify areas for gathering data.
2. Review past records and existing information for transition-related information. Identify and confirm areas in which additional information is needed.
3. Identify potential formal and informal assessments that can be used for each area above. Use a comprehensive planning or curriculum program, or checklist across the domains of work, living, personal-social current and future environments to ensure coverage of all important areas.
4. Contact diagnosticians and specialized assessors for recommendations on current and additional instruments, if needed. Create additional informal assessments (with assistance/advice from specialists).
5. Schedule formal assessments to be given by qualified evaluators and informal assessments that occur across the student's multiple settings. Present scores and interpretations in written form and discuss with the team. Ensure that all members understand results and their implications regarding potential outcomes and goals.
6. Assemble all assessment information into a comprehensive and clear transition profile.
7. Assess profile for additional information gaps or when information is insufficient, retest and reevaluate contradictory results. Use consensus to reestablish/confirm a shared vision of the student's future.
8. Schedule ongoing assessments, particularly in areas where the student is receiving training or intervention procedures to ensure that the program is successful and that the student is achieving desired short-term goals. Monitor areas that are subject to change as a result of growth and development, maturing interests, and life experiences.
9. Periodically, reevaluate ongoing assessments to ensure their continued usefulness. Examine new procedures and formats if they seem more appropriate.
10. Periodically, reexamine team membership to include additional members who can contribute new information as the student's transition training settings change. Examine the effectiveness of team processes to maintain open, positive communication among members. Make adjustments to assimilate new and changing membership.

dure to ensure that all aspects of the assessment process have been observed. Such a process should include the steps described in Table 7–7.

Use of a comprehensive planning guide or a task-focused process with checklists such as described earlier can assist the team in determining and coordinating the assessment, data synthesis, and needs-prioritizing processes. However, for some students, this is likely to necessitate moving beyond current models and requiring ingenuity and creativity from team members (Luft, 1999). Much success of the assessment and transition planning processes depend on the dedication and motivation of the team to meet challenges and to design appropriate solutions.

Conclusion

Transition is a process in special education that combines a common frame of reference with transition-specific requirements for assessment and planning with students and families. Interdisciplinary assessment and planning requirements use student and family-generated transition goals to form a framework for consensus-based planning with professional and community individuals. Assessment processes provide the informational foundations upon which these interdisciplinary processes operate in planning and implementing transition goals.

The multiple-step process that comprises transition assessment processes results in a comprehensive transition profile of needs, strengths, and preferences of the student that is updated and evaluated in an ongoing manner. Transition assessment provides information and data on the important planning, curriculum, and instructional decisions needed by youth with disabilities, their teachers, and other members of their teams. These assessments consist of both standardized (formal) and non-standardized (informal) assessments that provide the variety of information that the team will need in completing its tasks. Ongoing assessments are needed to modify goals as a result of growth, training, and experience; and to choose programs and guide program and service delivery so that students are supported for success. Interdisciplinary and team process are necessary for effective communication and for ensuring consensus throughout the assessment and planning processes. When effectively and conscientiously carried out, team members will have confidence that their resulting transition plans are based on accurate and reliable data and are likely to lead to the student's successful movement into adulthood.

Study Questions

1. Describe the similarities and differences between special education assessments and transition assessments.

2. What are the three transition domains and the skills tested in each area?
3. Describe the purpose of formal and informal assessments.
4. What kind of information do formal and informal assessments provide?
5. What are the advantages and disadvantages in using formal and informal assessments?
6. What types of information can be gained from the use of functional or ecological assessments?
7. How can academic assessments be used to complement informal assessments?
8. What is the purpose of the comprehensive transition planning approach to informal assessment development?
9. In your opinion, what is the best method of assessment in transition?

Web Sites

Vocational Tests:
http://www.crc.ufl.edu/choosing_using.html

Assessing Students for Workplace Readiness:
http://vocserve.berkeley.edu/centerFocus/cf15.html

Vocational Evaluation and Work Adjustment Association:
http://www.vewaa.org

Curriculum Development and Transition

James Krouse
Richard Sabousky

LEARNING OBJECTIVES

The objectives of this chapter are:

1. Describe how curriculum planning promotes postsecondary outcomes for students with disabilities.

2. Describe several principles for establishing a functional curriculum that is referenced to the general curriculum for all students.

3. Identify methods for infusing functional curriculum into the general curriculum.

4. Provide examples of the importance of the interaction between community-based and classroom instruction.

5. Identify barriers to effective curricular design and implementation.

The last chapter covered assessment and how to identify student postsecondary goals, desired course of study, and needed transition services. This chapter examines how to use this information from the perspective of curriculum development in transition. It covers essential element one—*determining student needs, interests, and preferences*—in the section on "negotiating goals" where the student's goals are set during the Individualized Education Program (IEP) meeting in which transition is discussed. Essential element two—*Outcome-Oriented Process*—and essential element three—*Coordinated Set of Activities*—are discussed in the sections on academics and functional curricula. Finally, essential element four—*Promoting Movement to Postschool Settings*—is discussed in the section on major elements of functional curricula, where the authors discuss the activities that educators must complete to ensure students can meet the needs of their selected postschool environments.

Due to the growing interest and the recent mandate to aid the transition of youth with disabilities to postsecondary settings, various curricular models have emerged to facilitate this process. These models provide professionals with a structure to develop curricula that promote transition. However, even with such tools, it should be remembered that special education teachers typically create the curriculum for their classes (Stowitschek & Kelso, 1989). Additionally, no single curriculum will be appropriate for all students in all schools. Thus, the professional must have knowledge of all phases of curriculum development, implementation, evaluation, and the design of effective programs. As Hanley-Maxwell and Collet-Klingenberg (1994) indicated:

> It is important to note specifically that because of the varied entry skill level of each student, the varied interest of each student and his/her family and community, the varied outcomes desired by the student and his/her family, the varied family perspectives, and the varied community demands, there is no curriculum that can meet the transition needs of all students (p. 30).

This chapter describes important considerations for creating a curriculum and the perspective required for promoting transition from school to postschool outcomes. The chapter describes curriculum development from the perspective of promoting individualized postsecondary outcomes. Traditional notions of a curriculum based on disability or the expectations of the teacher to promote yearly success can be barriers to an effective curriculum design for transition. The selection of curricular material has to be expanded to plan for outcomes that are more than a year and sometimes years away. Such a perspective is not easy.

In order to monitor movement toward goals, backward planning is required. With backward planning, educators start from the student's desired goals and plan backward to the student's current level of functioning. Regardless of the activities identified for a particular student, curricular selections have to be made from all possible areas for instruction. The discussion of the variety of curricular choices focuses upon the following areas: (1) academic, (2) social, (3) functional (including community-based and vocational), and (4) the need for combinations of activities from each to promote the transition from the school to the community for students with disabilities.

Overview of Curriculum

Definition of Curriculum

In discussions concerning curriculum, there are varied opinions and perspectives. Some professionals view curriculum as little more than a set of books from which teachers teach; others identify curriculum as being completely separate from instruction; still others only recognize an academic focus to curriculum. In the literature, there are various definitions of curriculum.

Doll (1964) described curriculum as changing "from content courses of study and lists of subjects and courses to all the experiences that are of-

FIGURE 8–1
Transition Curricular Areas

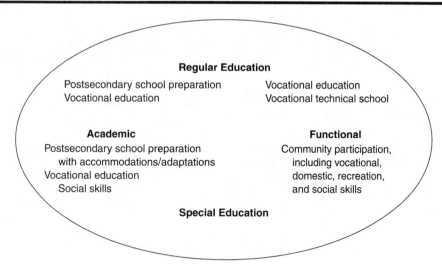

Source: From Finch and Crunkilton (1993).

fered to learners under the auspices or direction of the school" (p. 15). According to Berman and Roderick (1977),"Curriculum development . . . consists of establishing a view of man and ascertaining what school can do to help persons achieve the qualities inherent in this view" (p. 118). Armstrong (1990) indicates that curriculum is "a master plan for selecting and organizing learning experiences for the purpose of changing and developing learners' behaviors and insights" (p. 4).

Although different in their definitions, one common theme is that the central focus of the curriculum is the student. The student is the recipient of all planned experiences in school and also the experiences outside the typical curriculum such as vocational organizations, clubs, sports, band, and drama. Curriculum, then, must be examined through the lens of the broadest goals for education.

According to Finch and Crunkilton (1993), the basic goals of education are "education for life, and education for earning a living" (p. 8). Although broad and generic, it is this frame of reference that drives curricular development for transition. For students being served

through education, education for life and education for earning a living are not mutually exclusive; in fact, these must be considered in harmony. Personal attributes also contribute significantly to success in postsecondary environments. For example, researchers have found that individuals with disabilities typically lose their jobs for social reasons rather than for job performance reasons (Rusch, Mithaug, & Flexer, 1986). In addition, the postsecondary school success of individuals with learning disabilities has been related to the student's ability to be a self-advocate (Durlak, Rose, & Bursuck, 1994).

Critical Point   Curriculum for students with disabilities must include a life skills approach that addresses functional and social skills as well as academics.

Curriculum content will be viewed as existing on a continuum from a functional perspective to an academic one. Each of these quadrants represents a particular perspective from which to view curriculum development. Figure 8–1 shows how both regular and special educators have addressed curriculum along this continuum.

Academic, Vocational, and Functional Curricula

An *academic* high school curriculum typically prepares students for postsecondary education, with higher percentages of students without disabilities now attending colleges. However, students with disabilities also are attending and including postsecondary education goals in their transition plans. In a review of transition plans, Grigal, Test, Beattie, and Wood (1997) found that about 31% of the transition plans they reviewed contained postsecondary school outcomes. Therefore, although postsecondary preparation is typically structured within regular education, the special education program needs to consider the skills and activities that students with disabilities need to be successful in these postsecondary environments, making this preparation a part of the special education curriculum.

Vocational education developed in response to identified needs by employers. It may be part of either an academic or a functional curricular focus. The workplace is constantly changing and creating new challenges in the preparation of workers, and it is becoming increasingly difficult to separate the technical skills from academic skills. Therefore, many curriculum planners are integrating both academic and vocational curricula (Finch & Crunkilton, 1993). Students involved in this type of preparation receive training in either their home high school or a vocational technical school for part of the day. Grigal et al. (1997) identified vocational training as the outcome most often identified on transition plans for students with disabilities. Thus, although typically existing through regular education, special education needs to ensure accommodations within these programs to allow access to vocational education for students with disabilities.

The functional curriculum is specifically designed to lead to a successful adulthood but without a primary focus upon academic skills.

McDonnell, Wilcox, & Hardman (1991) asserted, "it [functional curriculum] must support student learning that leads to success in home, work and community environments" (p. 50). In this context, the special educator is the facilitator of various activities across multiple environments and professional agencies. In more than half the transition plans reviewed by Grigal et al. (1997), adult services participation and independent living were indicated as goals for optimizing adult success.

There is considerable overlap between the regular curriculum and special education curriculum areas, especially for transition. Special educators hold the primary responsibility for programs toward meeting IEP goals in all the areas identified earlier, yet few have such a comprehensive training. In studies, most special educators reported that they received their curriculum training on the job (Sands, Adams, & Stout, 1995). The most important characteristic of a special education teacher may be the philosophy that supports opportunities across both functional and academic curricula to students with disabilities. No single educator or professional can be an expert in all the preceding areas. However, specific skills allow the special educator to be successful in managing the educational plan. This includes the ability to work as part of a team to develop the curriculum and goal outcomes for students. Teachers need to develop a vision that all students can be successful and that they should have access to all the curricular areas. When academic and functional curricula are well integrated into an educational plan that addresses adulthood, the resulting curriculum will have a truly functional perspective.

Critical Point A functional curriculum requires a collaborative approach, where the student's entire education experience is directed toward postschool success.

A transition perspective takes a long-range outcome-oriented view. This is in contrast with strictly developmental and readiness approaches that focus upon learning the next steps. The outcome-oriented approach helps to ensure a functional perspective. It has been suggested that "the framework that guides the content of classroom instruction is determined primarily by teacher judgment and secondarily by the IEP" (Sands et al., 1995, p. 77). Using the IEP as a planning document provides a way to determine if the activities for the day's instruction facilitate the desired outcomes for students. For example, a functionally driven IEP ensures that objectives concerning a student's reading ability have a bearing on the student's desired postsecondary environments.

Fads in Special Education

If there has been one consistent theme throughout the history of special education, it may well be the proclivity of the field readily to adopt new practices in the absence of data that attest to their efficacy. Reliance upon fads and "reforms" has often adversely affected curricular decisions. As Grossen (1996) succinctly stated:

> Unlike most other fields of scientific inquiry, education places extraordinary emphasis on the new and the novel. Believing that the most recent theory—at whatever level of research—is also the most important, educational leaders may lose sight of the value of seminal research and proven practices. (p. 22)

It is often difficult for practitioners to resist the latest educational trend. Sometimes this is due to pressure from the community. In the not so distant past, educators could generally rely upon articulated official position papers from professional organizations to guide their practice (e.g., The Board of Trustees of the Council for Learning Disabilities, 1986). However, this may not be the case today. For example, facilitated communication has been disclaimed by a number of professional organizations (e.g., the Academy of Child and Adolescent Psychiatry,

the American Association of Mental Retardation, the American Academy of Pediatrics, the American Psychological Association, and the American Speech-Hearing-Language Association), whereas the PA-TASH organization (1994) has urged full support of the technique.

Critical Point Educators need to examine research to validate curricular approaches that may be popular but not substantial.

Clearly, the guiding principle in curriculum design is for teachers to consider carefully the social and philosophical positions and empirical evidence for new techniques. This does not imply blind adherence to the status quo as some (e.g., Haskew & Donnellan, 1992) may suggest. Rather, it is incumbent upon special educators to base curricular decisions on data, not on dogma.

General Education Curriculum

Existing Instructional Systems

Fortunately, practitioners do not need to rely upon fads or intuition for guidance in the development of effective academic curriculum. Instead, research results from the past 30 years have explicitly addressed the topics of what particular behaviors characterize effective teachers and what elements of curriculum design are essential to maximize student achievement. Although every question has certainly not been answered, some defensible suggestions can be made based on this research.

The *Nineteenth Annual Report to Congress on the Implementation of the* IDEA (1997) recommended that students be taught by using explicit instruction. "Students are provided with models of appropriate methods for solving problems or explaining relationships, are supported amply during the stages of the learning process, and are provided with adequate practice" (section III, p. 60).

As Gersten, Woodward, & Darch (1986) state, "despite the importance and consistency of research findings derived from the perspective of direct instruction research (e.g., Rosenshine, 1986), this characterization of direct instruction may be too restrictive because it concentrates too heavily on *how* to teach and too little on *what* to teach." In contrast, "Direct Instruction" as conceptualized by (Englemann, Adams & Engle-mann, 1996) concentrates attention on the explicit design of curricular materials. For cur-riculum issues, the Direct Instruction system may be helpful to teachers because it both pro-vides direct and practical implications regarding curriculum design, delivery, and evaluation and has a research base of support.

Adams and Englemann (1996) suggest that a common misconception of Direct Instruction is that it is merely teacher-directed instruction and, as such, represents the opposite of ap-proaches such as discovery learning or open classrooms. They stress that Direct Instruction is not synonymous with the more typical proce-dures of teacher-directed instruction. Lecture, for example, may be used in teacher-directed in-struction, but it does not reflect Direct Instruc-tion practices (Ellis & Fouts, 1997). Gersten, Carnine, and White (1984) note that several components of Direct Instruction are common to many behavioral approaches: systematic use of reinforcement, use of mastery learning, con-tinuous monitoring of student progress, use of task analysis, and sequential teaching of preskills. However, they note that the major dif-ference between Direct Instruction and other be-havioral models is the amount of attention devoted to antecedent control, including the ex-act nature of the instructional materials to be used and exactly how teachers present material and word their questions.

Perhaps the most fundamental tenet of Direct Instruction is that faulty instructional systems, "not deficits in students," account for much of the failure seen in schools (Gersten, Carnine, & Woodward, 1987). As such, Direct Instruction re-flects upon a very optimistic position: What we as teachers do can make a significant difference in achievement of our students. Becker and Car-

nine (1982, p. 170) and Englemann, Becker, Car-nine, and Gersten (1988, p. 303) have suggested that there are two major rules of Direct Instruc-tion: "The first rule might be termed beat the clock or teach more in less time. The second rule is control of the details of what happens." At first glance, these appear relatively simple but this is not the case. To accomplish these goals, Di-rect Instruction offers a "complex way of looking at all aspects of instruction, from classroom or-ganization and management to the quality of student-teacher interactions, the design of cur-riculum materials, and the nature of in-service training" (Gersten et al., 1987, p. 48).

Becker and Carnine (1982) summarized the ma-jor features of the model. The Direct Instruction program provided (1) aides who were taught to function fully as teachers to increase the amount of student-teacher interaction time, (2) activities to increase academic engaged time, (3) programs that were already developed which focused upon development of general case strategies, (4) appro-priate teacher training in the use of the techniques of Direct Instruction, (5) daily lesson scripts that told the teacher exactly what to say and do, (6) procedures to monitor student and teacher progress, and (7) supervisors who spent at least 75% of their time directly working with teachers and aides in classrooms.

Many specific instructional procedures were developed through research on Direct Instruction. Englemann et al. developed the basic approach (controlled teacher presentations, structured task sequences, use of scripted formats, etc.) and con-tracted with Science Research Associates (SRA) to make the programs publicly available. Since that time, a number of Direct Instruction programs have become available in the areas of reading, language arts, spelling, handwriting, science, so-cial studies, mathematics, and creative writing.

State Standards and Curriculum

The IDEA of 1997 requires that curricula for spe-cial education students be referenced to general education standards. Typically, secondary curriculum has focused upon college preparation, as evidenced by the number of course requirements (e.g., algebra) that in some cases have limited applicability for youth who are entering employment or vocational training after graduation.

In response to a school reform mandate (Kentucky Education Reform Act, [KERA], 1990), the Kentucky Department of Education developed a set of academic standards that are designed to be outcome oriented and applicable to all students, including students with disabilities (Kleinert, Kearns, & Kennedy, 1997). Kentucky is one example of a state that has derived outcomes and learner expectations to provide guidelines for curriculum on a statewide basis. In many states, teachers and school districts base their curriculum on guidelines developed at the state level.

In the Kentucky Department of Education Futures Curriculum, academic standards are related to specific learning goals relative to competencies that all students will need as adults. These learning goals are organized into six general categories: (1) basic communication and math skills, (2) core concepts and principles, (3) self-sufficiency, (4) responsible group membership, (5) thinking and problem solving, and (6) integration of knowledge. Within each of these areas, curriculum is organized according to outcome-oriented principles (Kentucky Council on Postsecondary Education, 1999). Table 8–1 provides an overview of curriculum objectives developed for all students in Kentucky. The Kentucky curriculum standards are broad and related to both general standards and the information needed by students relative to their individual course of study.

Critical Point   It is important to understand the general education curriculum and how it can be used to promote the transition of students with disabilities.

For students with disabilities, the special education teacher is in control of how instructional content is tied to educational standards for individual students. To deliver meaningful content, an instructional match must be maintained between the student's skills, needs, interests, and preferences and the curriculum. Typically, this refers to a sequence of prerequisite skills and background knowledge; however, the special education teacher needs also to consider other factors, such as characteristics of the learner, desired postsecondary outcomes, and use of supports and accommodations. The maintenance of the instructional match is accomplished through ongoing assessment and this matching process drives curricular choices concerned with instructional content (Mercer & Mercer, 1998; Rivera & Smith, 1997).

Regular education curriculum adaptation may be difficult when standards are based on "pencil-and-paper" criteria that are not relevant to a student's postsecondary outcomes. However, by using the student's needs and desired postsecondary outcomes, teachers are able to identify appropriate content. For example, the English requirement of the general education curriculum becomes relevant to a person with a severe disability when it is applied to the types of words that he or she encounters in the community, at home, and on the job. The following case study suggests how general education curriculum content can be adapted to a person with a severe disability.

CASE STUDY A

A special education teacher is team teaching a mathematics class with a general education teacher. One student, with a developmental disability, has an interest in working as a cook after graduation. The goal of the general education mathematics program is for students to understand and apply mathematical procedures. The student in question has been unsuccessful in comprehending and solving word problems. The special education teacher was able to adapt the lesson to the student's needs by providing a hand calculator and using problems related to measuring and adapting

TABLE 8–1

Kentucky State Learner Objectives

Goal 1. Basic Math and Communication Skills

1. *Accessing sources of information and ideas:* Students use reference tools such as dictionaries, almanacs, encyclopedias, and computer reference programs and research tools.
2. *Reading:* Students make sense of the variety of materials they read.
3. *Observing:* Students make sense of the various things they observe.
4. *Listening:* Students make sense of the various messages to which they listen.
5. *Computing:* Students use mathematical ideas and procedures to communicate, reason, and solve problems.
6. *Classifying:* Students organize information through development and use of classification rules.
7. *Writing:* Students write using appropriate forms, conventions, and styles to communicate ideas and information to different audiences for different purposes.
8. *Speaking:* Students speak using appropriate forms, conventions, and styles to communicate ideas and information to different audiences for different purposes.
9. *Movement:* Students make sense and communicate ideas with movement.
10. *Using electronic technology:* Students use computers and other kinds of technology to collect, organize, and communicate information and ideas.

Goal 2. Core Concepts and Principles

1. *Nature of scientific activity:* Students understand the scientific way of thinking and working, and use those methods to solve real-life problems.
2. *Number concepts:* Students understand number concepts and use numbers appropriately and accurately.
3. *Mathematical procedures:* Students understand various mathematical procedures and use them appropriately and accurately.
4. *Democratic principles:* Students understand the democratic principles of justice, equality, responsibility, and freedom and apply them to real-life situations.
5. *Structure and function of political systems:* Students can accurately describe various forms of government and analyze issues that relate to the rights and responsibilities of citizens in a democracy.
6. *Structure and function of social systems:* Students observe, analyze, and interpret human behaviors, social groupings, and institutions to better understand people and the relationships among individuals and among groups.
7. *Cultural diversity:* Students interact effectively and work cooperatively with the many ethnic and cultural groups of our nation and world.
8. *Family life and parenting:* Students demonstrate skills that promote individual well-being and healthy family relationships.
9. *Consumerism:* Students evaluate consumer products and services and make effective consumer decisions.
10. *Community health systems:* Students demonstrate the skills to evaluate and use services and resources available in their community.
11. *Career path:* Students use strategies for choosing and preparing for a career.
12. *Employability attributes:* Students demonstrate skills and work habits that lead to success in future schooling and work.
13. *Postsecondary opportunities search (jobs, school, military):* Students demonstrate skills such as interviewing, writing résumés, and completing applications that are needed to be accepted into college or other postsecondary training or to get a job.

Goal 3. Self-Sufficiency (This goal is not included in the state's academic assessment program.)
   1. *Positive self-concept:* Students demonstrate positive growth in self-concept through appropriate tasks or projects.
   2. *Healthy lifestyle:* Students demonstrate the ability to maintain a healthy lifestyle.
   3. *Adaptability and flexibility:* Students demonstrate the ability to be adaptable and flexible through appropriate tasks or projects.
   4. *Resourcefulness and creativity:* Students demonstrate the ability to be resourceful and creative.
   5. *Self-control and self-discipline:* Students demonstrate self-control and self-discipline.
   6. *Ethical values:* Students demonstrate the ability to make decisions based on ethical values.
   7. *Independent learning:* Students demonstrate the ability to learn on one's own.

Goal 4. Responsible Group Membership (This goal is not included in the state's academic assessment program.)
   1. *Interpersonal skills:* Students shall develop their abilities to become responsible members of a family, work group, or community including demonstrating effectiveness in community service.
   2. *Productive team membership:* Students use productive team member skills.
   3. *Consistent, responsive, and caring behavior:* Students individually demonstrate consistent, responsive, and caring behavior.
   4. *Rights and responsibilities for self and others:* Students demonstrate the ability to accept the rights and responsibilities for self and others.
   5. *Multicultural and worldview:* Students demonstrate an understanding of, appreciation for, and sensitivity to a multicultural view and worldview.
   6. *Open mind to alternative perspectives:* Students demonstrate an open mind to alternative perspectives.

Goal 5. Thinking and Problem Solving
   1. *Critical thinking:* Students use critical thinking skills, such as analyzing, prioritizing, categorizing, evaluating, and comparing to solve a variety of problems in real-life situations.
   2. *Conceptualizing:* Students organize information to develop or change their understanding of a concept.
   3. *Creative thinking:* Students use creative thinking skills to develop or invent novel, constructive ideas or products.
   4. *Decision making:* Students use a decision-making process to make informed decisions among options.
   5. *Problem solving:* Students use problem-solving processes to develop solutions to relatively complex problems.

Goal 6. Integration of Knowledge
   1. *Applying multiple perspectives:* Students connect knowledge and experiences from different subject areas.
   2. *Developing new knowledge:* Students use what they already know to acquire new knowledge, develop new skills, or interpret new experiences.
   3. *Expanding existing knowledge:* Students expand their understanding of existing knowledge by making connections with new knowledge, skills, and experiences.

Source: From *Futures: Your guide to life after high school,* Kentucky Council on Postsecondary Education.

recipes, a skill that this student is capable of accomplishing.

Unfortunately, the more the general education curriculum focuses upon specific competencies (e.g., understanding classical literature), the harder it becomes to develop instructional materials that promote both classroom and transitional competencies for students with disabilities. In this regard, transition stakeholders need to collaborate with advocates of school reform to promote more inclusive general education standards such as those defined by Kentucky's Education Reform Act.

Critical Point Curriculum content should be relevant to both the student's current level of functioning and his or her postsecondary goals.

Social Skills

The development and validation of effective techniques for promoting the acquisition, maintenance, and generalization of social skills will impact nearly all future adult roles and settings. As Schloss, Smith, and Schloss (1995) noted, social skills are more reliable predictors of adult adjustment than either intelligence or academic achievement. Additionally, deficits in social skills have been more highly correlated with lower achievement levels and to problems with maintaining employment than to deficiencies in specific job-related skills.

Historically, one approach toward improving social skills was based on the premise that deficiencies in self-concept are root problems. Providing a warm, accepting situation in which students can openly express their emotions would, it was thought, improve self-concept, which would be reflected in improved social behavior. As Kauffman (1997) points out, however, it is probably the other way around: Improvements in self-concept follow improvements in actual behavior.

Numerous definitions of the term "social skills" have been offered (Cartledge & Milburn, 1986; Gresham, 1986; McFall, 1982; Walker, Colvin, & Ramsey, 1995). Most definitions reflect either an emphasis on overall social competence or an emphasis on specific social responses. This distinction is important because it directly impacts assessment and curricular decisions. Social competence refers to the "overall, summative judgment that key social agents (parents, teachers, peers) make regarding the social effectiveness of one's behavior" (Walker et al., 1995, p. 7). The definition of Cartledge and Milburn (1986, p. 7) reflects this approach: "learned behaviors that enable a person to interact in ways that elicit positive responses and assist in avoiding negative responses."

Schloss and Smith (1998) noted that definitions based on evaluating overall social competence are difficult to translate directly into statements of behavioral objectives. They do not lend themselves to precise measurement as do definitions based on specific responses and, as a result, provide less direct evaluation data. On the other hand, Strain, Odom, and McConnell (1984) have questioned what they termed the "individual specific" skill deficit approach to assessment of social behavior. They offer three compelling arguments in support of their position. First, the skill deficit approach assumes that the absence of a particular social behavior implies the lack of skill. They argue that it is also necessary to examine the environmental context to determine conditions that sustain the problem. Second, Strain et al. argue that the individual-specific approach focuses too heavily upon the target child rather than upon the behavior of the peer group. To improve social interaction most effectively, it is necessary to alter the behavior of all parties involved. Third, because the individual-specific approach emphasizes discrete behaviors, it can dampen the level of reciprocal exchanges that occur.

The following case study shows an application of a social competence approach to developing curriculum.

TABLE 8–2

Lesson for Direct Instruction of Social Skills

Review	"Last week we practiced the appropriate way to have eye contact with someone during a conversation. Can you *all* turn to your neighbor on your left and show me *appropriate eye contact?* [Signal.] Good, everyone seems to remember that appropriate eye contact means holding your head up and looking at your partner directly in the eyes."
Goal statement and teacher presentation	"Today we are going to practice identifying the appropriate tone to use during conversations. Watch the video monitor while I play some examples for you. [Video presents several examples of "This is an appropriate tone of voice" and several nonexamples (i.e., "This is *not* an appropriate tone of voice.")] Remember, an appropriate tone of voice is not too loud or too soft, and it is interpreted as one in which you are interested in speaking with your partner." [Show several additional examples and nonexamples.]
Guided practice	"Now, we are going to select the examples that show us an appropriate tone of voice. [Turn on video for additional examples and nonexamples.] Is this appropriate? [Signal.]" [Provide corrective feedback as necessary throughout the presentation of several instances and noninstances.]
Independent practice	[Student continues with similar activity that requires individual responding on paper.]
Formative evaluation	[Teacher uses a similar practice activity but collects examples to grade and score later.]

Source: From *Effective Instruction for Special Education* (2nd ed., p. 311), by M. A. Mastropieri and T. E. Scruggs, 1994. Austin, TX: PRO-ED. Reprinted with permission.

CASE STUDY B

John exhibited attention-seeking behaviors that were socially unacceptable. He frequently called out at inappropriate times and would stand uncomfortably close to people from whom he was seeking attention. Reinforcement of quiet and in-seat behaviors was having no apparent impact on John's behavior.

After consultation with a behavior specialist, it was determined that John's behavior resulted from a lack of social skills relative to obtaining attention and conversing with others. A social skills curriculum was designed to teach John appropriate ways of interacting and seeking behavior. These included starting interactions using socially appropriate greetings, listening and responding to others, and reading about current events in order to have things to talk about. John was then reinforced with attention for any of these behaviors while inappropriate attention-seeking was simply ignored.

As a result of this social competence approach, John began to elicit more favorable responses from others who began naturally to reinforce his behavior as his inappropriate behaviors subsided. It was eventually possible to phase out all planned reinforcers in favor of natural reinforcers.

Literature on teacher effectiveness and direct instruction offer practitioners empirically defensible strategies to teach social skills. Mastropieri and Scruggs (1994) provide an excellent model to follow. As they note, students must be able ultimately to demonstrate the ability to apply the various social skills that are directly taught. Consequently, they must be able to discriminate situations which call for specific skills from those which do not, recall the steps that are necessary to perform the skill, and successfully demonstrate the skill in a variety of environments. Table 8–2 is a sample lesson plan for teaching the social skill of identifying the appropriate tone of voice to be used during conversational speech.

The lesson uses Direct Instruction which begins with a review of previously covered material. Homework assignments also are reviewed at this point. New material is introduced by the teacher who explicitly states the goals and objectives of the lesson. Teachers, then, supply examples and nonexamples of appropriate responding. Guided practice provides all students with opportunities to develop proficiencies in the skill. Correct responses are reinforced and corrective feedback is provided for errors. Once students demonstrate competent performance, independent practice activities are conducted which address generalization issues. Weekly and monthly reviews are provided to ensure maintenance of behavioral improvement. Formative evaluations are conducted both to monitor student progress and to provide feedback to the teacher in order to evaluate the lesson and to alter the next lesson accordingly. An additional suggestion that Mastropieri and Scruggs (1994) recommend to promote socially significant generalization is to include "on-the-spot" instruction for social skills. Similar to what Walker et al. (1995) termed "opportunistic teaching," this strategy is used to prompt, coach, shape, praise successful use, or correct inappropriate use of the skills taught as they occur within the context of natural settings. Thus, the initial structured lesson is generalized to important postschool environments.

Another teacher-managed instructional option is use of commercially available social skills curricula. A number of such packages exist; for example, PEERS, *program for establishing effective relationship skills* (Hops et al., 1978); *Skill streaming the adolescent* (Goldstein, Sprafkin, Gershaw, & Klein, 1980); SCIPPY, *Social Competence Intervention Package for Preschool Youngsters* (Day, Powell, & Stowitschek, 1980); ASSET, A *Social Skills Program for Adolescents* (Hazel, Schumaker, Sherman, & Sheldon-Wildgen, 1982); ACCEPTS, A *Children's Curriculum for Effective Peer and Teacher Skills* (Walker et al., 1983); *Getting

Along with Others (Jackson, Jackson, & Monroe, 1983); *Skill Streaming the Elementary Child* (McGinnis, Goldstein, Sprafkin, & Gershaw, 1984); CLASS, *Contingencies for Learning Academic and Social Skills* (Hops & Walker, 1988); and RECESS, A *program for reducing negative-aggressive behavior* (Walker, Hops, & Greenwood, 1993). Before adopting any packaged program, the reader should ask:

1. Does the program promote both the acquisition of socially valid target behaviors and the development of overall social competence?
2. Does the program take into account the distinction between skill and performance deficits in its assessment and instructional procedures?
3. What does the research suggest regarding the instructional design and efficacy of the program?
4. Does the program provide clear, explicit directions to teachers?
5. Are socially competent peers involved in the program?
6. Does the program have sufficient flexibility to be tailored to the unique needs of individual students?

Critical Point   Students with disabilities may need social skills curriculum, but it is important to teach these skills in a way that promotes social competence and involves everyone in their environment.

Functional Skills

Some students require a curriculum that has a functional approach. "A functional approach is when instruction is directed toward the acquisition of those basic behaviors required for daily existence" (Snell, 1981, p. 532). Instructional areas may include, but are not limited to, vocational, domestic, recreation, personal skills, and

Curriculum standards focus on adult outcomes.

certain academic skills. If we subscribe to the notion that at least some academic success is required for daily existence, then it should not be excluded from a functional curriculum. Instruction using a functional curriculum can be delivered in various locations, including community environments.

The decision to use a functional curriculum orientation should not be based on disability type but, rather, on how the curriculum can best support the identified postschool outcomes for the particular student (Edgar & Polloway, 1994; Hanley-Maxwell & Collet-Klingenberg, 1994). A functional curriculum approach is often referred to as a top-down model because it requires instruction to begin with identifying the terminal behaviors that the student should be able to complete. For example, teaching a student to diagram a sentence may be a legitimate objective for some students; however, if the goal is to increase the student's ability to participate in a vocational, domestic, personal, or recreational activity, then diagramming sentences is not relevant.

The functional curricular content areas do not exist independently. Although they may be specific to one setting, they frequently have overlapping impacts on various environments in which the student currently participates (or will

participate in the future). For example, proper grooming is not a vocationally specific skill but is an issue in the vocational and employment setting.

Functional Curricular Models

In the examination of various materials on curricula, a number of functional models have been identified. The following are some examples. The Ecological Inventory developed by Brown, Branston, Hamre-Nietupski, Pumpian, Certo, and Gruenewald (1979) is a functional curriculum approach that examines specific environments, the demands of those environments, and instructional responses required to function in those environments. The specific domains described in this model are domestic domain, leisure-recreational domain, community domain, and vocational domain. Task analysis is used to guide instruction in achieving terminal behaviors that minimize discrepancies between the skills of the student and the demands of the environment.

The teaching of functional academics has been described in A *Functional Curriculum for Teaching Students with Disabilities* (Vallentutti, Bender, & Sims-Tucker, 1996). In this text, a functional approach is described for teaching reading, writing, and mathematics. IMPACT: A *Functional Curriculum Handbook for Students with Moderate to Severe Disabilities* (Neel & Billingsley, 1989) is also a guide for developing a functional curriculum. It is divided into two types of inventories, *Impact Environmental Inventory for the Home and Community*, and *Impact Environmental Inventory for School and Community* Activities. It presents "an instructional system that teaches skills in context so that the child's performance will be brought under the control of natural cues and consequences" (p. 6). The *Life-Centered Career Education Curriculum* (LCCE) (Brolin, 1995) provides competencies that are required for adult adjustment, including academic curricular competencies, school, family and community experiences, and stages of career development (as described in Chapter 6). This program is designed to complement and integrate with the regular education curriculum to provide a comprehensive curriculum.

> The LCCE competency-based approach does not advocate the elimination of current [regular education] courses or a significant change in the structure of education. Instead it recommends that educators change the focus of instructional content to meet the career development needs of students and for the family and community resources to become an integral part of the educational process (Brolin, 1995 p. 88).

It is beyond the scope of this chapter to do a critical analysis of the many commercially available functional curriculum programs. Generally, no one list of identified behaviors, skills, or activities meet the needs of all students since transition curriculum planning must truly be individualized. In order to accomplish this task, a functional curriculum should be designed for each student based on his or her own unique needs, interests, and preferences. Programs must be designed for students, rather than limiting students to choices available in existing programs. For each student, the curriculum should take into account the skills needed for community living, vocational activities, academic activities, social activities, and any other activities that the student requires to move into adulthood.

As previously noted, functional curriculums should be used in conjuction with the general education curriculum. Many functional curricula (e.g., LCCE) are designed to be infused into the general curriculum. This is important because students with disabilities otherwise may be forced to choose between academic course work leading to a diploma and functional course work leading to success after graduation.

Because functional instruction is broad and deals with all aspects of preparation for adult functioning, a variety of programs can poten-

tially be involved in some aspect of a student's transition program. These include vocational education, regular education, and school-to-work programs for career preparation. This very pervasiveness of functional curriculum is at times problematic.

Cronin and Patton (1993) identify three approaches to including functional curriculum in secondary education: infusion, augmentation, and course work. The infusion of functional curriculum requires integrating content (life skills) into existing courses. The augmentation approach dedicates portions of existing courses to life skills instruction. The course work approach develops whole courses for a specific or range of life skills topics. Implementation of functional curriculum must be correlated with regular curriculum and typically requires that special and regular education teachers work together. Moreover, it is critical to tie functional curriculum to individual student goals (An example of approaches to including functional curriculum in general education curriculum is provided in Table 8–3.)

Critical Point   Functional curriculum should be infused into the general curriculum whenever possible. It should be provided as augmentation to existing classes or in addition to existing classes only when it has a very high priority.

Major Components of a Functional Curriculum

The major components of a functional curriculum are (1) identifying functional activities for instruction across all domains, (2) establishing priorities for instruction (Wehman, Moon, Everson, Wood, & Barcus, 1988), and (3) deciding where the instruction should take place.

Identifying Activities

Wehman et al. (1988, p. 138) provide the basic procedures for determining the functional activities for instruction:

TABLE 8–3

Organizing Information/Skills Content

Approach	Example
Infusion approach: Integrating life skills into existing courses	Including activities on record-keeping systems to manage family finances in consumer math course
Augmentation approach: Adding units on life skills topics	Adding a unit on financial implications of dating to consumer math course
Course work approach: Developing a specific or series of life skills course(s)	Organizing life skills topics in general by domain (e.g., family and employment) or by subject (e.g., real-world math)

Source: From Browning (1997).

1. Select a broad curriculum domain category (i.e., recreation, community, vocational, and domestic) to be analyzed.
2. Identify a list of environments within the home, school, and community settings where students may perform activities related to the identified domain category.
3. Identify additional environments by surveying other professionals, the parents, and the students.
4. Observe these identified environments and list those skills that are essential for competence in each environment.
5. Verify the list of skills with other professionals and with parents.
6. Repeat this process for all domain categories.
7. Review and revise as needed (with a minimum of one review annually).

It is important that the activities chosen for instruction have some type of validity. Social validity ensures that the activities have value for both the learner and those in the learner's surroundings. Kazdin (1989) described two social validation procedures: "One procedure compares the level of the client's behavior with that of his or her peers or others who are considered to be functioning adequately in their environment" (p. 101). This is often called a normative comparison. It allows the educator to compare the activities to be taught with the demands of the environments currently under consideration. If the behavior is performed and re-

quired of others, then the activity is probably appropriate. "Another method of evaluating the importance of behavior change is to have the level of behavior judged by people who interact with the client [student] or who are in a special position to do so by virtue of their expertise" (p. 101). If it is possible for these people to identify improvements or development of new behaviors (activities), then these changes have been meaningful. If the student's ability to participate in more activities in the identified environment has been enhanced, then chances for greater independence and community participation also are enhanced.

Prioritizing Activities

After identifying the variety of instructional domains and activities for a student's curriculum, educators need to prioritize these activities to ensure teaching those that are the most important. Wehman et al. (1988, p. 139) provided guidelines for establishing priorities for instruction:

1. Identify, with the student and her or his family, the student's performance in each of the transition domain categories. Then, identify desired relevant future environments in which it is projected that the student will be functioning.
2. Identify activities and skills relevant to the student's current environment; identify skills that are necessary to function in projected future environments.

3. Review all relevant current and future activities and indicate those activities that occur in two or more domains and are age-appropriate.
4. List these activities from the most to the least frequent in occurrence.
5. From this list, identify those activities that are crucial for the student's safety. Next, identify those activities that are critical for functioning independently in the identified future environments.
6. Select for immediate instruction:
   a. Those activities that are essential to the student's safety within current environments
   b. Those activities that the student must perform frequently in order to function independently within her or his current and identified future environments
7. Select remaining objectives from the list of activities. (step 4)

The following case study illustrates this principle for the domain of independent living.

CASE STUDY C

Susan's goal was to live in an apartment with friends after graduation. She currently lives with her parents and knows how to respond in emergency situations, for example what to do in the case of a fire and how to ask her parents for help. She has no budgeting, cooking skills, or ability to use a phone book. She has some vacuuming, cleaning, and dishwashing skills but requires some prompting.

Of these behaviors, it was determined that cooking, phone use, vacuuming, cleaning, and dishwashing were the skills that Susan would perform most frequently in her new environments. Phone use and fire safety skills were considered the most critical for safety, and cooking, cleaning, lunch packing, and dishwashing were considered critical to independence. Home repair and budgeting were lower frequency behaviors and less critical to independence since they could be provided by the landlord and social service agencies.

Because phone use was a skill that was critical for Susan's safety in her current environment when her parents were away, this was chosen as the highest priority for instruction. It was determined that Susan did not need to use a phone book since a programmable phone could contain all phone numbers she would routinely need as well as in the case of an emergency. Use of a programmable phone was, therefore, taught first.

Because cooking and lunch packing were two behaviors that Susan would need daily to live in an apartment, they were taught next. Because Susan could not read a recipe, the teacher used a microwave oven and illustrated instructions for menu planning. Susan continued to learn the remaining skills based on the prioritized list.

Negotiating Goals

The previous selection process is done with the transition team and often is referred to as the negotiating of goals (Ryndak & Alper, 1996). Since many professionals serve on the multidisciplinary team, the varying perspectives of each member, including parents and students, also are taken into account in identifying goals for the IEP. The interactions during these negotiations are very important.

Parents and students often have different perspectives concerning curricular issues. Malian and Love (1998) found that, "The majority of parents reported that their student had not received enough instruction in the following: reading, math, writing, handling money, problem-solving, exploring different types of jobs, and looking for jobs" (p. 5). Students had a different perspective, "On the other hand, the majority of students reported they had received 'just the right' amount of instruction in reading, math, writing, problem solving, how to look for a job, and transportation" (p. 5). Interestingly, both parents and students reported that more instruction was required in the areas of "handling money and exploring different jobs" (p. 5). Although they may not always agree with each other, parents and students must have input in the curriculum to retain an ecologically valid orientation for transition team processes. Negotiating these types of differences can be difficult. In a survey of professionals, Defur and Taymans (1995) found that the use of effective interpersonal skills was the highest ranked competency transition specialists should have.

In some cases youth with disabilities may continue to disagree with their family or guardian regarding curriculum or guidance and support that they need. In these situations, it may be necessary to mediate by providing the youth and their family with additional information or experience in regard to curriculum choices or by scheduling follow-up meetings involving guidance counselors or service providers. In the few instances where youth/family consensus cannot be reached, it may be necessary to follow the wishes of the family while supporting the student before the age of majority, and vice versa, after the age of majority.

Instructional Setting

The next decision to be made is where instruction should take place. Instruction can take place in the classroom, the vocational-technical school, or the community environment where the student ultimately will need his or her skills. The notion of "classroom" may reflect any of the school programs in which a student with disabilities may participate. A regular classroom, special education classroom, or a vocational-technical classroom or shop, could all be settings to teach activities based on a functional curriculum. For example, a student being trained to work in a future vocational environment consisting of a quick lube oil change garage may participate in the automotive trades shop class. The student would receive training in oil changes and chassis lubrication in the class. Support may be provided by the special education teacher in the form of techniques, prompts, or social skills but the regular instructor would provide the technical content.

Another example is the Wild Dream Team (Dunn, 1995). The State College Area School District in Pennsylvania places students into community living situations to allow them opportunities to learn all activities required for living in the community. This program addresses curricular areas, including cooking, cleaning, and interpersonal skills that are required to live in an apartment in the community.

Community-based training allows individuals with disabilities the opportunity for learning and practicing skills under the conditions that they will experience as adults. There are some skills that can only be taught in natural environments (Ryndak & Alper, 1996). Skills such as operating machinery to satisfy a vocational goal or street crossing can be extremely difficult if not impossible to simulate. Therefore, "the value of community-based design is that it provides instruction in natural settings, eliminating many of the problems students encounter attempting to generalize what they have learned in a classroom situation to the real world" (Patton & Polloway, 1990, p. 241).

Critical Point Functional curriculum needs to be socially valid, age-appropriate, and provided in real-life settings whenever possible.

Classroom instruction can also be used to support community-based instruction under a number of conditions. "The first is when training in the actual performance setting cannot be structured to provide the number of training trials that will be necessary to ensure the student's mastery of a difficult step" (McDonnell et al., 1991, pp. 117–118). Students may require the opportunity to practice a skill more than natural environments will allow. For example, the mail only comes once a day. A student working at sorting mail may need more practice on that task than on the one occasion when it occurs in the natural environment. Second, certain academic skills may need to be infused into the activities that students are learning in community-based settings (Edgar & Polloway, 1994). The classroom allows the educator to provide instruction of the skill to be mastered and later to direct its use in the actual setting.

Critical Point   Functional skills may be taught in a classroom setting and then generalized to the actual environments in which they are needed.

Functional Curriculum and Transition

A functional curriculum and the use of community-based instruction have been demonstrated in the literature to be effective for learning various skills (e.g., Simmons & Flexer, 1992; Snell & Browder, 1986; Phillips, Reid, Korabek, & Hursch, 1988). The benefits of using functional curricula as a base for transition include:

1. The curriculum is based on functional and age-appropriate skills needed by the student in a number of school and nonschool settings within the community (Ryndak & Alper, 1996, p. 24).
2. Many skills taught are performed by people who do not have disabilities which supports the validity of the skill (Ryndak & Alper, 1996, p. 24).
3. It provides for activity instruction that supports all the transition areas regardless of disability.
4. It allows for teacher flexibility in the infusion of academics and functional adult skills.

Although attractive, this type of curriculum also has its disadvantages:

1. It may require a substantial reallocation of school resources, such as arranging transportation to community-based training sites.
2. The selection of goals and objectives may be *arbitrary* since the selection process is somewhat *subjective* (Ryndak & Alper, 1996).
3. There is lack of empirical evidence in the literature to support a functional curriculum for the specific transition outcomes.

Functional Curriculum Considerations

Even with the disadvantages just described, the utilization of a functional curriculum is important for students with disabilities. The selection of goals and the education of students across all the domains relevant to their adult outcomes is critical. For example, Rylance (1997) found that, "the absence of vocational education during high school served as a predictor of dropping out for high school youths with SED [Serious Emotional Disturbance]" (p. 14). For students planning to attend postsecondary settings, Halpern, Yovanoff, Doren, and Benz (1995) found that transition programming needed to be comprehensive and functional:

> Our measures pertaining to instruction and instructional outcomes examined five instructional domains: reading, writing, math, problem solving, and getting along with other people. . . . The implications are fairly straightforward: We should attend to these five curricular domains during high school if our goal is to enhance participation in postsecondary education. (p. 162)

Addressing all curricular areas ensures that students with learning disabilities, for example, will receive the instruction they should in academic curricular content, as well as in life skills or other needed functional skills. Addressing their needs based only on an academic remediation strategy may not account for other types of activities they will need to perform as adults (Sitlington, 1996). In fact, a curriculum will be functional only in relation to the student for whom it is designed in taking into account their complete needs: academics, social skills, vocational training, preparation for postsecondary education, community living, and ability to utilize community resources. Addressing all curricular areas leads to the development of a curriculum that meets the needs of all students with disabilities in facilitating their transition from school to adult life.

Barriers to Curriculum Development

There are some identifiable barriers to developing an effective curriculum for young adults with disabilities. These barriers are not insurmountable, but they must be considered by the teacher in program design. Zigmond and Miller (1992) labeled the issue of "environmental press against academic content" (p. 25). This issue describes the classroom environment as being nonacademic because of the remedial activities which predominate in resource programs leading to a sense of purposelessness that pervaded much of the academic work. A second barrier is the requirement of P.L. 105–17 (IDEA 1997) to link the annual goals of students to the general curriculum. For students with severe needs, this may not be practical. The educator may spend much of his or her time trying to relate certain specific personal goals, such as dressing, to the general curriculum. A third barrier can be the education reform inclusion movements that are currently under way, leading to unquestioning placement of students in a regular education classroom setting. Neubert (1997) writes:

> Often educational reform vs. functional movements are in direct conflict with what we know works best for students with disabilities in terms of functional skill instruction, and vocational training in the community. Other students with disabilities and their families may choose to participate in inclusive academic classrooms, thus forfeiting some instruction in functional, vocational, and self-determination skills (p. 14).

The special educator may find him- or herself in the position of negotiating or balancing functional outcomes for students and for issues of inclusion. Halpern et al. (1995), in a study of identifying predictors of postsecondary participation concluded:

> Inclusive instruction did not contribute to participation in postsecondary education. In other words, the mere presence of high school students with disabilities in integrated classrooms had no apparent impact on the probability of their participation in postsecondary education. At the very least, this must raise the question about the present efficacy of inclusionary instruction at the high school level, if participation in postsecondary education is regarded as a desired outcome of inclusionary instruction. (p. 162)

The reform movements that increase the standards in the regular classroom also may be a barrier to appropriate curriculum design. Rylance (1997) states that the push for absolute standards of achievement may have precipitated an increase in the drop-out rate among younger students with SED. If students are not in school, they cannot benefit from a curriculum regardless of how good it may be. Inclusion and a quality transition curriculum are not mutually exclusive; however, creative planning is required to achieve success in both areas (Clark, 1994).

Critical Point   Educational reform efforts to raise academic standards may result in a general education environment that is hostile to delivery of functional curriculum and detrimental to inclusion of students with disabilities.

Conclusion

Curriculum design for transition requires the development of skills and activities from all curricular domains to ensure preparation for movement into adulthood. The regular as well as special education components of curriculum contain important areas from which transition activities should be developed depending on the needs, interests, and abilities of the student. The educator has to be able to make functionally based decisions concerning what is in the curriculum for each student while assuring that these decisions are congruent with the general education curriculum. The development of functional curriculum requires careful selection of activities that are designed to promote movement to postsecondary environment. It also requires establishing priorities because there is not enough time to teach students all topics and skills in academic, social, and functional curricula. Finally, it is important to determine where and how the content will be delivered since content may be relevant to a student only if it is delivered in socially valid settings.

Study Questions

1. Describe three issues that must be considered in the development of a curriculum for an individual student with a disability.
2. Discuss how you would develop a curriculum for a youth with a developmental disability who has an interest in working in a clerical setting.

3. Describe three approaches to providing functional curriculum in postsecondary settings.
4. Provide some examples of how functional curriculum can be infused into English, mathematics, and social studies.
5. Discuss some of the barriers to providing functional transition-related curriculum in a general education setting.

Web Sites

Kentucky Department of Education:
http://www.kde.state.ky.us

Math Resource for People with Disabilities:
http://form.swartmore.edu/social/math.disabled.html

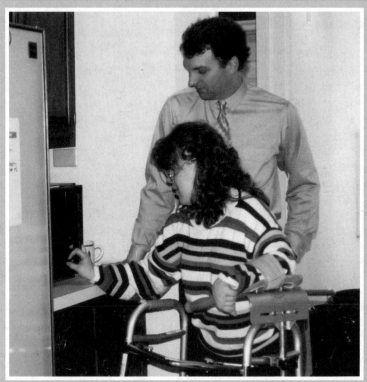

9

Instructional Strategies

Bryan G. Cook
Cindy Trevino
Lysandra Cook
Melody Tankersley

LEARNING OBJECTIVES

The objectives of this chapter are:

1. Describe the components of effective instruction.
2. Describe the components of effective behavior management.
3. Explain how effective instruction and behavior management interact or relate.
4. Explain how effective instruction and behavior management strategies can be applied in both classroom and nonclassroom settings.
5. Describe the components and benefits of cooperative learning, self-monitoring, and community-based instruction.

Instruction is not unique to teaching or schools. Parents, for example, frequently employ purposeful behaviors that result in their children learning something. I remember my mother spending days and days modeling and practicing how to tie my shoes with me (successfully so, I am proud to say). That was instruction. Instruction also can be delivered by oneself, by a classmate, by a stranger, and so on, and can be received by adults, children, and animals—essentially anyone who has the capacity to learn. In this chapter, we focus on the instruction provided by teachers to students whose ultimate achievement goal is successful transition to adult roles and outcomes. Chapters 7 and 8 covered issues related to assessment and curriculum, respectively. This chapter focuses on instruction, which is closely interrelated to both curriculum and assessment. Assessment serves as the foundation (to determine at what level to instruct students appropriately) and evaluation of instruction. Instruction is also the vehicle through which students are taught their curriculum. Instruction is defined in this chapter as purposeful behaviors resulting in the achievement of learning goals.

Instruction forms the basis for assisting students in achieving their transition goals. It is the means whereby the student's needs, interests, and preferences become successful transition outcomes. The four essential elements of transition are addressed throughout the chapter. Specifically, determining the student's needs, interests, and preferences is important in planning for effective instruction, especially community-based instruction. Instruction, particularly for transition students, is an outcome-driven process. Outcomes are frequently assessed as part of effective instruction and used to engender accountability as well as plan for subsequent instruction. Effective instruction and behavior management also entail coordination of a wide array of activities and components, as described throughout the chapter. Finally, all the instructional techniques described in this chapter have

as their ultimate goal successful movement to postschool settings and life.

This chapter provides the methods for implementing the earlier chapters in this section. It is through effective instruction that career and vocational education goals become the work careers and life skills of successful adulthood. The particular curriculum or body of content area knowledge contributes to the student's movement into adulthood through learning and instruction. Assessment provides the gauge for where and when to begin and end instruction as well as ongoing information about student progress. The next chapter addresses technology, increasing the instructional opportunities available to students, particularly those with physical and sensory disabilities.

Given the central role of instruction to teachers and teaching, it is surprising that we often disagree on what constitutes effective instruction, and frequently feel at a loss on how to instruct effectively many of our students. Fortunately, we have access to a body of literature that identifies instructional behaviors that have been empirically associated with effective teaching and high student achievement (see Brophy & Good, 1986; Doyle, 1986; Englert, Mariage, & Tarrant, 1992; Mastropieri & Scruggs, 1987; Rosenshine & Stevens, 1986 for reviews of this literature). The first section of this chapter provides an overview of what research has shown to be effective teaching. The second section of the chapter presents an additional specific strategy in each of the three curricular domains relevant to transition defined in Chapter 8 (i.e., academics, social skills/behavior, and vocational/domestic/leisure skills) to complement the general model of effective instruction introduced in the previous section.

Effective Teaching

In a school context, instruction is what teachers do to enable their students to achieve their school-related

TABLE 9–1

Summary of Effective Teaching Techniques

- Maximize learning time.
- Use brisk pacing and avoid downtime.
- Review previous instruction.
- Preview instruction.
- Demonstrate skills directly and clearly.
- Break down curriculum into manageable "chunks."
- Use guided practice to ensure that students are practicing skills correctly.
- Ask lots of questions during guided practice.
- Move onto independent practice when students are performing at a high rate of accuracy.
- If students do not perform accurately, provide further directed prompts or reteach at a later time.
- Independent practice should be completed with few or no errors.
- Provide material that is not boring, but with which students experience a great deal of success.
- Frequently assess to maintain student accountability.
- Display "withitness" by always knowing what is going on in instructional environment.
- Frequently circulate around and scan instructional environment.
- Quickly and accurately reprimand misbehavior
- Consistently recognize appropriate behavior
- Do not concentrate solely on an individual or small group in a large group setting.
- Simultaneously attend to and monitor more than one activity (overlapping)
- Address minor misbehaviors with brief and personal interventions.
- Use established classroom rules and procedures to deal with problem behaviors.
- Clearly state rules and directions.
- Rehearse what rules mean.
- Spend lots of time teaching rules during the beginning of instructional term.

goals. The practice of instructing students is probably the most central component, or essence, of what we think of as teaching. What do teachers do? They instruct their students. Without implementing effective instructional procedures, teachers are allowing their students to achieve at a lower level than possible and simply are not doing a good job of teaching. Knowledge and implementation of effective instructional practices makes the difference between laypeople attempting to impart information to children and professional teachers who are able to address a range of learners' needs in a manner that, although never guaranteeing success, is most likely to produce appropriate outcomes that enhance the quality of the student's present and future lives.

How teachers present instruction and manage their classrooms do matter. Research has shown that effective teachers, in whose class-rooms students learn more, tend to act in particular ways. Table 9–1 presents a summary of some of the most important facets of instruction that characterize effective teachers, which are described in the next section of this chapter.

Learning Time

There appear to be two underlying and related themes regarding the instruction of effective teachers: (1) They allocate a lot of time for students to learn and (2) they make the time allocated to learning productive. Thus, the first axiom of effective teaching is to devote as much time as possible to the learning goals you want students to attain (see Brophy & Good, 1986). Yearly, monthly, daily, and specific lesson plans should, of course, reflect this time commitment.

However, planning does not necessarily correspond to the reality of classroom activity. For example, a teacher may plan to devote an hour of each day in a particular week for instructing students on balancing a checkbook. However, because math comes right after lunch in this class, instruction seldom begins until at least 5 minutes after the bell, as the students seem to need some time to "settle down." Students also consistently ask to get a drink of water ("I was running around in the sun all lunch period") and to go to the bathroom ("I just drank a ton of water"). There is also a lot of time devoted every day to getting out materials and to dealing with inappropriate behavior. In order to get ready for the next lesson, the teacher usually asks students to pack up 5 minutes before the end of the hour. In all, students may average 35 to 40 minutes a day, rather than an hour, engaged in active learning regarding how to balance a checkbook. In contrast to this scenario, effective teachers not only allocate as much time as possible to learning goals, but also clearly communicate that engaging in academic learning is the primary role of teachers and students and that classroom time will be spent accordingly (Brophy & Good, 1986). Effective teachers also manage their classrooms, starting on the very first day of school to set the tone for the remainder of the school year so that inappropriate behaviors and interruptions, which detract from time devoted to achieving learning goals, are kept to a minimum (Brophy & Good, 1986; Doyle, 1986; see later discussions on classroom management).

The remainder of this chapter consists of techniques that have been shown to make the time that teachers devote to their learning goals effective and productive (i.e., time that results in high achievement of goals). For example, throughout their instruction, effective teachers use a brisk pace (Brophy & Good, 1986). Although effective teachers are careful not to move too fast so that students are left behind (they ascertain this through careful monitoring and checking for understanding),

they do not spend more time than is necessary on any topic and avoid "downtime" in which no active learning is taking place. In this way, they are able to cover more with the time they have allotted for learning and students are apt to be more attentive and less bored, making them more effective learners. By adhering to the following descriptions of essential components of effective instruction, teachers are more likely to utilize effectively the large amount of time allotted to instruction, which in all probability will result in achievement of learning goals. It should be noted that these are not particularly novel approaches to teaching. All teachers engage in these behaviors to some degree. However, as Rosenshine and Stevens (1986) noted, effective teachers—whose students' achievement is higher—engage in them all the time.

Review and Preview

People learn better when they can integrate the material they are learning with previous knowledge. Therefore, effective teachers review previous learning that is relevant to the material to be covered (Rosenshine & Stevens, 1986). By conducting such a review, effective teachers also are successfully able to determine if students have retained the knowledge that is necessary to learn the material successfully. For example, when teaching a lesson on making change from a dollar, the instructor would have to determine if students had mastered the value of the various coins with which they will be working by having students demonstrate how much pennies, nickels, dimes, and quarters are worth. If they have not mastered prerequisite skills, it would be necessary to reteach them. In addition, by reviewing previously learned relevant material, students are prompted to recall the skills that they will need to master the new task. Further, students are provided a context for situating the new knowledge in their memory, which will make it easier for them to remember and use in the future. Students are also more apt to encode appropriately or learn new material if they are told what they are going to learn in advance. Because effective teachers preview their instruction (e.g., by giving an overview of the content, sequence, and objectives of the lesson; by putting an outline of the main ideas on the board or on an overhead), students can know what to expect in the forthcoming lesson and begin the process of contextualizing the instruction with previous skills, knowledge, and experience (Rosenshine & Stevens, 1986). Teachers often can explicitly combine the review and preview process to start instruction by guiding students to see the relationship between the reviewed and previewed material.

Demonstration

After reviewing relevant, previously learned material and previewing the content of forthcoming instruction, effective teachers demonstrate and explicitly teach the new skill, technique, or activity (Rosenshine & Stevens, 1986). Teachers should not leave students guessing about what is the correct way to do something if they want students to learn quickly and efficiently. When teaching rules and important concepts, effective teachers repeat information and are extremely direct and clear in their presentation. For example, when teaching rules regarding interacting with coworkers on a job site, an effective teacher might instruct students not to say anything audible to other workers when they are not on a break, rather than using vague terms or phrases such as "you all need to behave" (see Brophy & Good, 1986). While modeling, teachers should "think out loud" to demonstrate to students the thought processes involved in correctly completing the task at hand. When appropriate (e.g., when teaching social skills or more abstract concepts), teachers also may provide nonexamples. For example, after showing students the correct way to raise their hand to be called on during group instruction, the teacher may give nonex-

amples, such as raising one's hand no higher than one's head, or raising one's hand while simultaneously blurting out a question or response. Teachers should be careful not to "overload" students during demonstration. Students frequently will not be able to digest a great deal of new information presented in rapid sequence. Instead, effective teachers break the curriculum down into small steps and take adequate time to teach each specific skill (Brophy & Good, 1986). Illustrative of the importance of demonstration in the teaching sequence, Evertson, Emmer, Clements, Sanford, Worsham, and Williams (1980) reported that the more effective teachers in their investigation demonstrated, lectured, or discussed lessons with their class for approximately 23 minutes per day, whereas the less effective teachers did so for approximately 11 minutes.

Practice

After students have been provided with models or demonstrations, effective teachers lead students in guided practice of the new skill, technique, or activity (Rosenshine & Stevens, 1986). The purpose of guided practice is to allow students to work through the problems or tasks in a more or less errorless fashion. That is, teachers use prompts or guide students through the activity so that students are engaging in the skill themselves but are practicing how to do it correctly. While engaging in guided practice, effective teachers ask a high number of questions. For example, the most effective teacher in a study conducted by Evertson, Anderson, Anderson, and Brophy (1980) asked 24 questions during the average math lesson. Alternatively, the least effective teacher asked less than 9 questions during an average math lesson. It is also important to note that the more effective teachers asked three times more process questions (e.g., "Explain why you answered that way?") than their less effective peers (Evertson et al., 1980). As with demonstrations, questions should be clear and direct. Even if students are unable to answer the question correctly, they should know what is being asked (Brophy & Good, 1986). In this way, the information obtained by teachers from questioning represents student knowledge and understanding of content, not misunderstanding of the question. Asking questions, particularly process questions, not only stimulates student thinking but serves as a check for understanding as well. Effective teachers also have students demonstrate that they can successfully complete and understand the new task or skill before moving on to independent practice. Just asking if everyone understands is not typically sufficient. Students may not be willing to indicate publicly that they cannot do the work, and some students may believe that they can do the work when they actually cannot. As a rule of thumb, Brophy (1980) suggested that students should not be given independent work until they are performing tasks with at least 80% accuracy.

When students do not understand what is being taught and are not performing tasks with adequate accuracy, effective teachers have two primary options (Rosenshine & Stevens, 1986). They may provide prompts or hints to guide students to the correct answer or procedure. Often this type of prompting is precisely the feedback that students need during guided practice and should be the teachers' first response to misunderstanding. Prompting can be as simple as rewording a question in a guiding manner (Brophy & Good, 1986) or pointing out a specific area on which the student needs to concentrate. However, if prompting does not quickly result in increased comprehension, it will be necessary to go back and reteach the skill at a later time. (Extensive individualized prompting/teaching is not advisable at this stage of instruction in a group setting because it refocuses instruction away from other learners, breaks the flow of the lesson, and decreases the monitoring and circulation of the teacher, thereby adding to classroom management problems; see subsequent

discussion on classroom management.) It is also important to remember to provide brief and specific positive feedback to students who answer correctly and to reinforce the new skill for those students whose response was accurate but hesitant by explaining what they did correctly (Rosenshine & Stevens, 1986).

After students have demonstrated that they understand the material and can correctly perform it, effective teachers have students practice independently. Independent work is not a time for students to learn new material. Indeed, Brophy and Good (1986) suggested that the work selected for independent practice should enable students to approach a 100% rate of accuracy. This time is for students to develop speed and automaticity with work at which they have already shown themselves to be successful. By developing automaticity, or "overlearning" their work, students will not only become more proficient in a particular task or operation, but also will be able to apply that skill more adeptly to future work, which requires the current skill as a prerequisite. For example, much of higher and functional math would be very difficult without overlearning one's times tables. Similarly, successful job interviewing is unlikely if one has not mastered basic social skills such as eye contact and appropriate greetings. Independent practice should begin under the supervision of a teacher (often students can do the first few items together with the teacher), who, when the practice is occurring in their presence, is consistently monitoring students' work to make sure that they are practicing the skill correctly. After some level of mastery is attained, independent practice outside the supervision of a teacher is a good idea to facilitate mastery and overlearning.

During both guided and independent practice, research has shown that student achievement is correlated with the number of correct responses (see Rosenshine & Stevens, 1986, for a review). Quite simply, the more students work on a skill, technique, or activity, the better they achieve it, as long as they are practicing it correctly. It is, therefore, important to maintain a balance somewhere between boring students with work that they have already mastered and giving them work that is too difficult for them and at which they will not be successful. In addition, note that Evertson (1982) found that low-achieving students performed better in classes taught by teachers who spent relatively more time in guided practice and less time focused upon demonstrations and independent practice. It appears that teachers often assume that low-achieving students, including students with disabilities, are ready to profit from independent work before they actually are.

Accountability and Assessment

Effective teachers also enhance students' achievement by making them accountable for their work. Students feel compelled to complete their work because they know that it will be assessed and they will receive prompt feedback on it (Brophy & Good, 1986). Effective teachers also use frequent measures of students' work (e.g., curriculum-based measurement, Deno, 1985; Fuchs, 1993; also see Chapter 7) to gauge the progress of their students and to assess the effectiveness of their instruction. Teachers can effectively assess instruction in the beginning of a subsequent lesson during the review of previously learned relevant material. Effective teachers also provide periodic reviews of important skills and concepts to enhance overlearning and to assess whether students have retained their learning or whether reteaching some or all the concepts or skills is necessary.

Behavior

Behavior of students is an important outcome for students in its own right—indeed, there are curricula and instructional methods focused solely upon behavior—and because appropriate behavior allows students to be engaged in active learning. Alternatively, if a student is engaged in inappropriate behavior (e.g., talking to coworkers), it is impossible actively to learn the instruction being presented. As is the case for other pedagogical outcomes, teachers make a great deal of difference in whether or not students behave appropriately. For example, Kounin (1983) reported that the rate of task involvement for students attending the class of the most effective teacher in his study was 98.7%. Students who were in the class of the least effective classroom manager were on task for only 25% of the time, due to the inordinate amount of time spent dealing with and attempting to curtail inappropriate behavior.

Withitness

So, what does the literature tell us about how to be effective behavior managers? One of the key concepts associated with effective classroom management is "withitness" (Kounin, 1970). Teachers who circulate around the learning environment and constantly monitor the activity and behavior of their students have an accurate perception of what is going on (Doyle, 1986). Beyond accurately perceiving classroom activity, "with-it" teachers must also communicate to students that they constantly know what is going on in their learning environment. Students, then, do not feel that they can "get away" with misbehavior, and the incidence of inappropriate behavior, therefore, is reduced (leaving more time to concentrate on the intended content of instruction). Kounin (1970) reported that teachers exhibit withitness to students by responding to misbehavior with prompt and accurate reprimands. In this way, appropriate behavior is encouraged because students feel that when they engage in inappropriate behavior, they will quickly be caught and reprimanded, and when they are engaging in appropriate behavior, there is little or no chance that they will be unfairly reprimanded. Emmer, Evertson, and Anderson (1980) and Evertson and Emmer (1982) reported that with-it teachers also frequently and accurately noted the occurrence of appropriate student behavior, thus providing incentive for appropriate behavior and further increasing students' perceptions that the teacher knows what is going on. One other thing that beginning teachers can do to facilitate "withitness" is to focus upon monitoring and scanning the activity of the whole group with which they are working. Spending extended time concentrating solely on one individual or small group of students in a large group environment means that the teacher is not aware of what most students are doing, inviting opportunities for unrecognized and unreprimanded misbehavior. It also appears that simply commenting on events that are occurring in the classroom likewise demonstrates to students that teachers are "with-it" (Doyle, 1984).

Overlapping

"Overlapping" (Kounin, 1970), or attending to more than one event or activity at the same time, is another key concept associated with maintaining withitness. There are many occasions in which the teacher's attention is temporarily drawn away from the larger group of students (e.g., helping a struggling student, talking to a supervisor who drops by). Effective teachers are able to attend to such specific concerns while remaining keenly aware of what the rest of their students are doing. One way to facilitate overlapping is to arrange strategically the instructional environment. For example, if the teacher anticipates doing work or talking with individual students while the rest of the class is engaged in work, she should situate herself so that she can see all or most of the learning environment when talking with the student. It is important to communicate to students that although the teacher is engaged in another activity, he or she is still actively monitoring the learning environment and students are not able to "get away" with inappropriate or off-task behavior. Not surprisingly, then, effective managers often are reported by students to have eyes in the back of their heads.

Responding to Behavior

From the very first day of instruction, effective behavior managers respond consistently to appropriate and inappropriate behavior. They do not discipline only some students on a sporadic basis. Such an inconsistent pattern of discipline encourages inappropriate behavior by sending the message to students that they will "get away" with misbehavior as often, or more often, than they will be disciplined for it. Effective behavior managers also make sure to acknowledge consistently (although not constantly) appropriate behavior. In instructional environments where behavior management is effectively used and facilitates students' achievement of their goals, disruptive behavior is quickly stopped. In other words, teachers do not just take action once a behavior has become extreme, but, because they are consistently aware of what is going on, they are frequently able to recognize misbehavior in its earlier stages and to stop it before a major disruption occurs (Doyle, 1986). For example, if a teacher notices that a student is lightly kicking the seat in front of him during the bus ride to a job site, it is best to address this behavior immediately even though the problem is not particularly severe. If ignored, the teacher allows for the possibility that the behavior will lead to stronger, more frequent combative acts and/or a confrontation with another passenger.

Effective teachers respond to the majority of misbehavior (which is recognized early and, therefore, is usually a relatively minor disturbance) by brief and personal interventions that do not significantly disrupt the flow or focus of instruction. For example, misbehavior often can be curtailed by the teacher simply by moving closer to the student and making eye contact. Teachers also may make a brief comment that often includes directions for appropriate behavior (e.g., "Shhh, put your hand up if you want to say something"; Doyle, 1986, p. 421). Doyle (1986) noted that these types of interventions do not invite dialogue with students about misbehavior, which would shift the focus to behavior rather than to learning. It should also be noted that students being focused upon their work is a prerequisite for the success of this type of intervention. If students are unruly and unfocused to begin with, addressing any particular behavior only allows the teacher to return to the unruly and unfocused environment that engendered misbehavior in the first place. For example, Kounin (1983; cited in Doyle, 1986) reported that the least successful teacher in his sample attempted to stop misbehavior an incredible 986 times a day. However, without an effective and focused instructional environment, the interventions were obviously unsuccessful judging by their frequency and a student on-task rate of 25%.

Students with and without disabilities present behaviors from time to time that will not be curtailed by the unobtrusive type of interventions that were discussed earlier. When a misbehavior is intense and does not respond to initial attempts to intervene, the effective teacher should make use of other resources and techniques. Although beyond the scope of this chapter, it is recommended that teachers analyze and manipulate the antecedents and consequences of problematic behaviors and implement one of a host of empirically validated interventions associated with the field of applied behavioral analysis (see Alberto & Troutman, 1995).

Rules and Clarity of Directions

Effective behavior managers also use established rules and procedures to deal with disruptive behavior (Doyle, 1986). That is, they do not delve into the causes or explanations of disruptive behavior. Students become aware that the rules have meaning when they are used as the primary standard against which behavior is being evaluated. Effective classroom managers also state rules and directions for daily tasks and assignments with great clarity and directness. As is the case for academic learning, students are less likely to follow behavioral management rules and directions if they are not entirely sure what exactly the rules mean for them in terms of

their behavior. For example, instead of teaching students to "work hard" (a vague term which may mean different things to different people) on their job sites, effective teachers may teach students to perform their tasks proficiently while not talking or taking prolonged unscheduled breaks.

Effective behavior managers at the junior high school level have been found to differ from those at the elementary level in that the latter spent more time teaching and rehearsing rules (Evertson & Emmer, 1982). This appears logical because older students may be assumed to understand and be familiar with typical rules. However, it may not always be safely assumed that all students will adequately understand what all rules mean and how they are applied, particularly students with disabilities. Therefore, effective managers of secondary students who often exhibit problem behaviors, such as students with disabilities, may be wise to teach and rehearse rules and procedures deliberately in the very first days of the school year and to remind students of these rules and procedures throughout the first weeks of instruction (see Emmer et al., 1980).

Pacing and Accountability

Brisk pacing of instruction that includes a variety of tasks which are challenging to students (but are not too difficult so as to engender frustration and acting out) has behavioral as well as learning benefits (Doyle, 1986; Evertson & Emmer, 1982). In this way, students are not bored and looking to act out as a means to keep themselves entertained. Additionally, in effectively managed instructional environments, all students participate and are held accountable so that they never have the opportunity to disengage from instruction and to act out (see Kounin, 1970). In a classroom context, students often are asked to respond in chorus, and a with-it teacher is able to tell who is and who is not following the lesson. Students also may be called upon without previous warning to encourage accountability. However, care must be taken so that students do not feel that they are being called upon to embarrass them when they do not know the answer even if they were paying attention. Students with low academic self-esteem or ability should only be called upon in front of the entire class when the teacher feels that they can respond correctly if they have been following the lesson.

Transitions

The transition from one lesson or activity to another is critical to effective behavior management because the transition sets the tone for upcoming instruction. Effective managers clearly delineate transitions and move quickly through them. Less effective managers tend to blend activities together, and it is difficult to differentiate the transition period from the ends and beginnings of activities together. They also fail to monitor students closely during transitions (encouraging misbehavior which may frequently spill into the next class activity) and take a long time to work their way through transitions (Doyle, 1986). For example, when making the transition from a lesson in functional math to instruction in social skills, an effective teacher clearly announces the end of the functional math lesson, has students turn in assignments and put materials away, then regains the attention of all students and announces the beginning of social skills instruction.

Importance of the Beginning of the School Year

It appears to be extremely important to establish patterns of appropriate behavior by enacting and ingraining rules and procedures in the first few days of the school year (Doyle, 1986). Effective managers often spend an inordinate amount of time during the first week focused upon rules and procedures rather than upon academics (Evertson & Emmer, 1982). By rigorously instilling rules and procedures in the first days of the year, effective managers have more time to focus upon academics throughout the

remainder of the school year. Although content learning is sometimes not the focus of these first days of the school year for effective managers, these teachers always provide students with planned activities in which to occupy them. The message is sent that students are to be actively engaged in learning and not free to idle away time. Additionally, even the instruction regarding rules and procedures often is presented in the style of a lesson, and students are held accountable for their learning, further reinforcing the message of an active learning environment. After the very first days of the school year (once class rules and procedures have been mastered), effective junior high school teachers changed the focus of instruction to the curriculum while continuing to monitor behavior closely and quickly to stop misbehavior (Evertson & Emmer, 1982). Ineffective managers spend a great deal of time focusing the whole class upon misbehavior throughout the year, thereby sending the message that learning is not of utmost importance and can be avoided by misbehavior.

Application of Effective Teaching Literature to Students with Disabilities

The research summarized earlier was primarily conducted on nondisabled students in general education classrooms. However, Ysseldyke and Algozzine (1995) noted that these same instructional principles are theoretically appropriate for students with disabilities and are used to form recommendations about the instruction of students with disabilities (see also Bickel & Bickel, 1986; Englert et al., 1992; Mastropieri & Scruggs, 1987). Moreover, Rosenshine and Stevens (1986) indicated that these instructional procedures appear to work better for "slower" (p. 378) or lower-achieving students, such as those with disabilities. Indeed, empirical investigations have consistently shown that effective teaching techniques are associated with higher achievement among students with disabilities as well. For example, Englert (1983) reported that more effective special education teachers (in whose classrooms students with disabilities achieved at a higher level) presented information at a quicker rate, broke material into smaller pieces and conducted shorter lessons, asked questions that more often were answered correctly by students, simply told students the correct answer if they answered a question incorrectly less frequently (effective teachers prompt or guide students to the correct answer or engage in reteaching), and had fewer instances of misbehavior in their classrooms. Larrivee (1986) similarly found that 15 effective teaching behaviors significantly related to the achievement of students with and without disabilities in mainstreamed classrooms. Examples of these effective teaching behaviors include frequent positive feedback to students, sustained feedback to students who respond incorrectly, asking questions that students answered correctly, giving assignments at which students were successful, efficient use of classroom time, little noninstructional or transition time, infrequent need to discipline students, and low rate of student off-task behavior. Finally, Sindelar, Smith, Harriman, Hale, and Wilson (1986) reported that the effective practices of providing directed instruction and teacher questioning were the best predictors of the achievement of students with learning disabilities and mild mental retardation.

Application of Effective Teaching Literature to Transition Curricula

The research on effective teaching has typically used academic achievement and classroom behavior as their outcome variables. In one sense, this is extremely relevant for students for whom transition is an important concern. Achieving highly and behaving appropriately in school will serve these students well when they enter the world of work. However, it might seem that other outcomes of concern to those of us interested in

transition (e.g., job skills) could not be effectively taught using the principles reviewed earlier. Yet, just as these techniques have been shown to apply to students with disabilities although the research was conducted with nondisabled students, the principles of effective teaching can be applied to any situation in which one wishes to teach something new to a student, including outcomes such as job skills.

Let us turn to an example to illustrate how effective teaching techniques can be applied to teaching a student how to bus tables. First, sufficient time must be allocated to teach the student actively (whom we will call Bobby) how to bus a table. We cannot assume that Bobby knows how to because he has gone to restaurants before or that he will "pick it up" in the course of observing others do it at his new job site. Although the instructor is engaged in teaching Bobby how to bus tables, the two of them do not socialize much or get distracted by the customers, they are focused upon achieving the learning goal of successfully busing tables. The instructor should preview what Bobby is going to learn today (e.g., how to clear the dirty dishes from the table and take them to the dishwasher) and review what he learned previously (e.g., how to tell when to clear a table, where the container for carrying dirty dishes is located, and where to put dishes for the dishwasher to clean). The instructor would then demonstrate the task a few times to Bobby, clearly delineating the specific steps involved in clearing a table (e.g., locate a dirty and unoccupied table, get the container for dirty dishes, carefully place all dishes in the container, carry the container to the dishwashing station, unload all dirty dishes), and perhaps talk through each activity as Bobby completes it. Thus, the instructor provides a description and demonstration of the procedure at the same time.

Depending on the functional level of the student, each of these components may be taught separately, and the instructor would be careful not to overload Bobby with too much information or too many tasks. The instructor should then ask Bobby to practice the skill with the assistance or guidance of the instructor. Bobby also might be asked questions on what to do next at each stage of the task. When the instructor has determined that Bobby is performing the task correctly almost all the time, Bobby is ready to practice on his own. While Bobby is performing his task, he needs to know that he is accountable for his work (e.g., Bobby may not keep the job if he does not perform adequately) and that his work will be systematically assessed. While supervising Bobby at his work site, an instructor should demonstrate withitness and overlapping to let Bobby know that he cannot "get away" with inappropriate behavior or inattention to his work. Because it is frequently not possible, and probably not desirable, to have an instructor or supervisor present every moment at every work site once the student has mastered the skills of the job, there must be close and open communication with the manager of the business so that the student is aware that the instructor still knows what is going on at the work site.

Complementary Instructional Techniques

The remainder of the chapter provides brief overviews of three specific instructional techniques: cooperative learning, self-monitoring, and community-based instruction. These techniques may be used within the framework of the effective teaching practices identified earlier to enhance the educational opportunities for transition students in the respective curricular domains of academics, behavior and social skills, and vocational and transition skills. Although these techniques are respectively associated with improved outcomes in each curricular area discussed in Chapter 8, they in no way are intended to represent a complete repertoire of techniques that are sufficient for effective instruction.

Cooperative Learning

As the name implies, *cooperative learning* is a general term that encompasses a number of more specific strategies in which the teacher structures the class so that students work together to achieve a shared goal. In addition to the physical proximity and interaction of students, cooperative learning is unique in that students are accountable for the whole group's achievement, not solely the individual's own. The positive achievement effects of cooperative learning have been found across grade levels. Moreover, high, average, and low achievers have all been found to benefit from cooperative learning. Other positive outcomes associated with cooperative learning include increased self-esteem, positive intergroup relationships, acceptance of special education students, increased positive attitudes toward school, and increased ability to work cooperatively (see Slavin, 1991, for a review of this research). Cooperative learning is especially suited to heterogeneous and inclusive classrooms because it encourages socialization and learning among students of various academic abilities, disabling conditions, and racial and ethnic backgrounds (King-Sears, 1997; Putnam, 1998; Sharon, 1980). Rosenshine and Stevens (1986) suggested that cooperative learning can be an important facet of effective instruction because it gives students an opportunity for extended practice with new ideas or techniques which facilitates overlearning and automaticity.

Required Elements of Cooperative Learning
Although there are a variety of group configurations from which a teacher can choose, depending on their objectives, two elements must be present to reap the full benefits of cooperative learning: *group goals* and *individual accountability* (Slavin, 1991). Having group goals means that the success of the group is dependent on all members learning the objectives being taught. If the goal of the group was to just turn in a complete and correct worksheet, the highest achiever in

the group might do all the work while the lower-achieving group members (typically including students with disabilities) do and learn nothing. The task of the group, then, must be for all members of the group to learn something, not just to complete an assignment or project. To ensure that group goals are met, the related concept of individual accountability is applied. Individual accountability implies that the success of the group is dependent on the individual learning of every member. In this way, students are not allowed to rely solely upon the output of other members of the group. The assessment component of the lesson, therefore, must be set up by the teacher to assess the learning of individuals, not merely task completion. This may be as simple as monitoring the groups or by having individual assessments after lesson completion. If rewards are used, the group reward also may be based on each individual group member attaining predetermined criteria.

The two elements of group goals and individual accountability must be intertwined to make cooperative learning effective. When the group perceives that all members learning is the objective rather than any particular assignment or project, real cooperation and interdependence will develop. When learning is the ultimate goal, students engage in meaningful discourse, including explanations of concepts and skills rather than simply ensuring that every member has the right answer. It has been shown that achievement gains in cooperative learning depend on students giving and receiving elaborate explanations of concepts and skills and that answers without explanations are negatively related to achievement gain (Webb, 1985). One way to ensure that group goals and individual accountability are built into a cooperative lesson plan is by structuring an assessment to measure individual growth, yet base the grade on the average gain of the group. Thus, individual accountability and group goals are simultaneously fostered.

Team-building activities are completed before students begin working together and regular discussions regarding how the group is working together are incorporated. One example of a team-building activity which raises students' awareness of the value of working together is to present students in academic and inclusive settings with pictures of a high number of randomly grouped objects for about 10 seconds. During the first trials, students try to memorize as many objects as they can on their own. Students, then, are put into groups and encouraged to develop strategies for working together (e.g., each student is responsible for memorizing items in a particular quadrant of the picture) to identify more objects than they could when working independently. Students in a functionally based program can be given separate steps so that when put together in the correct order (they must work together and share in order to accomplish this), it shows them how to do a specific task, for example, their weekly laundry.

Roles

When first introducing cooperative learning to a group of students, the teacher will find it beneficial to assign students to teams and roles to students. Each member should be given a role that accents the student's strength, both to increase self-esteem and to show other members that everyone has a strength and can contribute to the success of the team. Roles assigned may vary depending on the nature of the assignment. These are some of the most common roles utilized in cooperative learning:

- *Recorder* is responsible for recording (through writing or drawing pictures) the ideas and responses of the group.
- *Reporter* reports back to the class at large to summarize the group's activities or findings.
- *Runner* collects needed supplies and often is the only member who is allowed to get out of his or her seat.

- *Encourager* is responsible for praising the efforts of group members and for keeping the team moving in a positive direction (the encourager can also be assigned as the one member who can raise his or her hand to elicit help from the teacher once all members agree that outside help is needed).

It may be necessary to give specific instruction to students on how to perform each role and ensure that the group is rewarded based on each member performing his or her role, and not solely because the assignment was completed.

Configurations of Cooperative Learning

Three basic forms of cooperative learning are group project, jigsaw, and peer teaching. In each of these formats, there is wide teacher discretion in terms of how groups are formed, how learning is assessed, and for what duration the groups work together. When first implementing cooperative learning, the teacher should take the lead in setting up teams, lessons, and assessments to ensure the highest degree of success and the greatest amount of cooperative interdependence. By facilitating success in students' beginning efforts with cooperative learning, teachers are likely to engender a feeling of comfort with the new class structure, which will result in greater productivity and success in subsequent time spent in cooperative learning.

As the name suggests, in the group project format, students are assigned to four or five member teams which pool their knowledge and skills to create one project or to complete one assignment as a group. The group's praise, reward, and evaluation are based on the one-group product. This format is easily adapted and can fit a variety of academic or social objectives. The task also can be expanded to include academic-based research teams where larger research projects are broken up and each member is responsible for a particular part. For example, in an assignment to complete a biography of a famous person, each group member can be re-

sponsible for researching a different aspect of that person's life (e.g., childhood, major contributions, and later years). Students then work together to combine the separate sections into a comprehensive project. Assessment can take the form of academic games or tournaments (i.e., spelling bees) in which the whole group generates the answer.

In the *jigsaw* format, students are broken into teams of four to six members. Each member of the team is given different information on which the entire team must eventually demonstrate mastery. The group splits up and individuals meet with members of other teams whom have been given the same material in "expert groups." The students become experts on their material in these groups. They then return to their original team and each member teaches his or her material to the team. Next, the team is assessed on all the material. The only way for a student to have all the necessary information is to listen carefully to and ask appropriate questions of their teammates. Jigsaw cooperative learning is a very efficient method for learning from a text. For example, a chapter can be divided into segments among students. In a functional lesson on meal preparation, each student can receive instruction regarding one aspect of preparing a meal (e.g., setting the table, cooking the rice, making the salad, oven-frying the chicken, and baking a box cake, which they teach to the rest of their group). Each student is individually assessed on all the information. Jigsaw is also a good method to use when first introducing cooperative learning to the class because each member's value as a resource for the team is readily apparent.

In *peer teaching*, one student tutors or assists another in mastering a new skill. Peer teaching is most appropriate for specific skill instruction, with a student who has demonstrated mastery in a particular area explaining and practicing that specific skill to a peer (Schniedwind & Salend, 1987). The tutor must be well versed in the subject and socially adept. Once implemented, a teacher must monitor to ensure that peer teaching is socially and academically beneficial for both students. Teachers must be aware that the tutoring students may begin to take on a dominant or overly nurturing role toward the peer whom they are tutoring. Peer teaching should not result in peers thinking less of the student being tutored or in decreased self-esteem for that individual. Teachers must also train the tutors for the specific task at hand, which may take some students out of class time, depending on the tutoring task. However, because using peers to teach higher-order or difficult skills would typically involve a great deal of time for training and would be more effectively taught by a trained teacher, peer teaching should probably involve practicing skills in a simple and repetitive manner that requires little training (e.g., using flashcards to master times tables). It also may be necessary to elicit support from other teachers if tutors or tutees are coming from other programs or grade levels. It should be noted that cross-age peer teaching has been shown to be most beneficial for the outcomes of students with disabilities when they serve as the tutors for younger children rather than as the recipients of tutoring (Elbaum, Vaughn, Hughes, & Moody, 1999).

Self-Monitoring

Self-monitoring refers to the strategy of observing and assessing one's own behavior and recording its occurrence or nonoccurrence. It usually involves specific procedures for teaching students how to use the technique. Often students monitor the occurrence of their behavior when presented with a cue, such as a prerecorded tone, that prompts them to assess the occurrence of the target behavior. Once students hear the cue, they are to record its occurrence. Students typically record the occurrence of their target behaviors by marking a tally or checking a yes/no sheet. For example, a teacher may wish to target increasing the rate at which

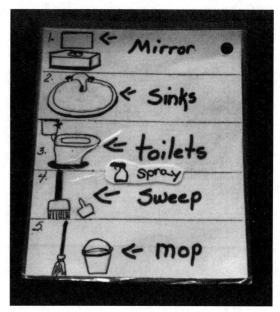

A picture task analysis supports task independence.

a student smiles on a job site. A tape recorder is placed behind the counter where the student works and emits a periodic tone. Each time this cue is emitted, the student assesses whether or not he or she is smiling and records a plus (smiling) or a minus (not smiling) on a prepared check sheet. These two acts, (1) observing and assessing the occurrence of the behavior and (2) recording the occurrence of the behavior, promote students' abilities for taking responsibility for their own behavior. Students, therefore, learn to act as observers of their own behavior. This self-observation often results in the natural occurrence of the behavior changing; behaviors that are undesirable often decrease and behaviors that are desirable often increase. Although researchers are not certain why self-monitoring helps students to change their behavior, they believe that by drawing attention to the presence or absence of the behavior, students are more aware of what they are doing and can begin to regulate their behavior.

Rationale for Self-Monitoring

Many teaching and management procedures used in school and community settings require considerable time and effort on the part of the instructor to design, implement, and assess. Because of such reliance upon the instructor, some learned skills are not readily generalizable; that is, students may depend on the presence or actions of the instructor to initiate or follow through with the skill. For example, a student working in a video store as a rental clerk may greet customers appropriately when his or her instructor is overseeing the task and rewarding appropriate greeting. However, when the instructor is not present, the student says nothing at all when customers approach him or her. In this example, the teacher has become a cue to remind the student to greet customers appropriately. Unfortunately, few environments consistently provide natural cues to help remind students to engage in appropriate behaviors or tasks. Therefore, students need a way to remind themselves. To help students rely less upon others to provide cues and to develop control over their own behavior, many authorities recommend teaching self-management techniques (see Cooper, Heron, & Heward, 1987, for a discussion).

Self-management techniques are those that emphasize internalization of behavioral responsibility and the use of specific self-guided strategies aimed at increasing appropriate social, behavioral, and academic skills. Internalization of behavioral responsibility is an aspect of intervention that is frequently overlooked when teaching children and youth with disabilities. Consequently, students often do not learn how to manage their own behavior but, instead, they learn that those in authority will provide that management. Self-management techniques allow students to shift this focus from external to internal control, thereby encouraging behaviors such as problem solving, self-regulation, reflective thought, and metacognitive skills. One particular form of self-management, self-monitoring, has been shown to

be very successful for helping students to change their behavior.

Components of Self-Monitoring

The procedures for teaching self-monitoring have varied across programs. Most training programs, however, have included components of direct instruction, cueing, and matching. Direct instruction techniques are used to help the student distinguish episodes of the desired behavior from episodes of undesirable behaviors. The teacher may model examples and nonexamples of the desired behavior and have the student practice the desired behavior. Such instructional procedures help to ensure that the student knows how and when to perform the behavior and to be accurate in recording the occurrence of the behavior. The skills targeted for self-monitoring should reflect the student's needs regarding successful educational and social functioning. Care must be taken when instructing students in these techniques to ensure that they comprehend the procedures, the targeted behavior, and the purpose of engaging in self-monitoring.

Although many different signals have been used to prompt recording of the behavior (e.g., tape-recorded segments of music as in Shapiro, McGonigle, & Ollendick, 1980; kitchen timer as in Workman, Helton, & Watson, 1982), the cue that has been used in most studies is a tape-recorded tone. For example, Hallahan, Lloyd, Kosiewicz, Kauffman, and Graves (1979) used a prerecorded cassette tape that emitted short beeps at irregular intervals (ranging from 15 to 90 seconds between beeps, with an average time of 45 seconds). The tones signal the student to assess his or her behavior and to record whether the target behavior occurred. Regardless of the type of signal used, the cue to assess and record has been found to be an important component to maintaining high student performance during self-monitoring (Heins, Lloyd, & Hallahan, 1986).

Another component that is used during training has been matching. *Matching* is when the teacher and the student compare their judgments about the occurrence of the behavior. Periodically, the teacher may record the occurrence of the student's behavior at the same time that the student self-records. At the end of the self-monitoring procedure, the student and the teacher may compare their judgments on the occurrence of the target behavior. Although the judgments may not agree totally (many students overestimate the occurrence of their positive behaviors), high agreement typically signifies that the student is following the self-monitoring procedures accurately. Conversely, if agreement is not strong, the teacher may need to reteach the procedures so that the student is assessing the behavior at the appropriate times, as well as recording the occurrence of the behavior reliably.

Benefits and Applications of Self-Monitoring

Self-monitoring has numerous benefits for students as well as for teachers. Students have the opportunity to take responsibility for their behavior and to become less dependent on teacher directions. This helps students to generalize their behavior to new situations and promotes the likelihood of students performing the behavior throughout the course of their lives. Therefore, self-monitoring can help to promote self-sufficiency without requiring supervision of others. Furthermore, when students are engaged in self-monitoring of their behavior, teachers do not need to monitor the behavior or intervene in other ways that might be more intrusive or time-consuming. This means that teachers can spend more time teaching new skills rather than managing behavior or helping students to remember to engage in a specific task.

Self-monitoring programs have been shown to be very effective for improving many behaviors associated with success in and out of schools for a variety of students across the age span and in a variety of placement options. For example, numerous studies have shown that self-monitoring has been effective for increasing students' attention to task (e.g., Blick & Test,

1987; McLaughlin, 1983), academic productivity (e.g., Maag, Reid, & DiGangi, 1993; McLaughlin, 1983), and academic accuracy (e.g., Maag et al., 1993). Self-monitoring also has been shown to decrease specific undesirable behaviors, such as out-of-seat behavior (e.g., Sugai & Rowe, 1984), and to increase social skills behaviors (e.g., Kiburz, Miller, & Morrow, 1985). Self-monitoring techniques have also been successfully introduced in vocational settings (e.g., Warrenfeltz et al., 1981). It also can be introduced into the special education classroom and then generalized into the regular education class or job site so that no additional time is needed in new placements to learn the procedures (see Lloyd, Landrum, & Hallahan 1991, for an example of a self-monitoring training program).

Although self-monitoring has been shown to be quite effective as an independent intervention, it also has been shown to work well in combination with other management programs, such as token economies or contracts (Lloyd & Landrum, 1990) or charting (DiGangi, Maag, & Rutherford, 1991). For example, a contract can be written stipulating that the student will be rewarded—with, for example, free time to play basketball with a friend and with the teacher after school—when the student's self-recording of a particular behavior agrees with the teacher's recording at a predetermined level (e.g., at least 90% of the time) and that occurrence of the desirable behavior (e.g., being in one's seat during math period) meets the criterion level (e.g., 95%).

Community-Based Instruction

Community-based job training is a viable means of providing effective instruction for students involved in the transition from school to work. By receiving training in the community, particularly if training begins at an early age and progresses throughout the student's school years, the student will be better prepared to meet the social and work demands required in

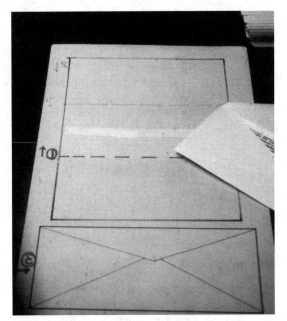

Redundancy cue for folding increases independent task performance.

the workplace. Community-based instruction, then, deserves the same attention to use of effective teaching principles as do academic instruction and classroom management. Too often students are placed in the community without effective supports and training, which leads to less than desirable outcomes. By using the effective teaching practices described earlier in this chapter, the transition team can help to assure an efficient and effective community-based experience.

Rationale for Community-Based Instruction

The rationale for community-based instruction is to ensure that the task on which the student is being trained is functional in a natural setting. Community instruction provides for social interactions with community members and opportunities to learn and practice skills, such as time management, public transportation, and grooming, which are not typically available in the school setting. Generalization of skills is more likely to occur when the antecedents and

consequences for the behaviors are more natural to the environments into which the student will be placed during the transition process (Stainback, Stainback, Nietupski, & Hamre-Nietupski, 1986). For example, if a student desires to hold a job as a rental clerk in a video store in the future, he or she will be best prepared for that job by training and acquiring skills as a rental clerk at a video store rather than in a classroom setting. In addition, by providing students with options that connect to life outside the school, students are more likely to be motivated to do well and to stay in school.

Locations of Community-Based Instruction

Community-based instruction can take many forms based on the student's identified transition goals. It may be a job-shadowing experience to broaden career knowledge, a job exploration experience, or an actual job. It can be visitations to college admissions offices, meetings with the financial aid office at a technical school, or visiting an apartment rental office to discuss leases. Locations of classrooms for transition-aged students may be at local college campuses and in house/apartment settings where students can be responsible for daily living chores, such as grocery buying, meal preparation, budgeting, and home maintenance. When classes take on a much more traditional form, community-based programming may be, in the form of experiences outside the school day or in the summer (Hagner & Sande, 1998).

Preparation for Community-Based Job Training

Careful attention is required prior to placement in a job setting. This is the time to use the transition documentation that has been compiled, including the student's needs and preferences form and any vocational evaluations or career assessment tools (see Chapter 7). This information should be the foundation for any planned experiences. Some students may have a clear direction as to their postsecondary goals and their experiences can be focused upon their stated preferences. Others may need a variety of short-term experiences to help them identify their interests.

The teacher can be helpful by using other resources within the school system and community to help identify potential placement sites for students. By working with the work-study coordinator, adult agency personnel, and business partners, the teacher can develop a job bank and share this resource with the transition team. A *job bank* is a listing of potential employers as well as the type of work experiences that may be available at the site. After a site is identified, the next step is to conduct an analysis of the work and environmental-social demands. Both explicit and implicit demands of the site are important to record as people are often fired for not fitting into the social fabric of a site. It may be helpful to use a form similar to the one in Figure 9–1 to compile information about the job site to match students to jobs that meet both their interests and abilities.

With the job-site analysis and information about the student, a match can be made which will allow the student to gain needed experience in a setting conducive to his or her needs and interests. Depending on the purpose of the training in the setting, the teacher/work-study coordinator or the student will approach the site about the possibility of using it for job skills training. Under the Fair Labor Standards Act (1985), caution must be taken in setting up an unpaid experience to assure that the student is not seen as an employee (see description in Chapter 6). This means that both the student and employer understand that the purpose of employment is for training and, thus, the student is not entitled to wages, the student may not displace other employees or benefit the employer, and the student is not entitled to a job at the completion of the experience.

Staffing at community sites is a major concern. Teachers must be resourceful in identifying possible sources for supervision. Existing school staff often are available, including paraprofessionals, team teaching partners, volunteers, and peers. Related service providers such as occupational therapists may be willing to do integrated therapy at the work site. Although individual placements are desirable, it is often necessary to group students at a site that has several jobs to be learned. Frequently, teachers take their classes to sites such as shopping malls or college campuses in which a variety of work experiences are available.

How to transport students is another concern. Ideally, public transportation such as buses should be used, as these are most likely to benefit the student after leaving high school. When these are not convenient or are unavailable, school vehicles such as vans or buses, individual teachers' cars, parents, or community civic groups may be able to provide needed transportation (Wehman, 1996).

Once the arrangements have been made and students are scheduled to complete specific job tasks, some sort of assessment should take place to identify needed areas for instruction. An effective evaluation and teaching tool is the task analysis (see Salend, 1994). To conduct a *task analysis*, the job trainer should observe a coworker doing the task and record each discrete behavior that occurs. The instructor can use this to teach the specific behaviors that the student must be able to perform to complete the task successfully. Task analyses can be quite detailed. For example, Snell (1987) identified 14 steps involved in hand washing, including these separate aspects of rinsing: "put hands under water," "rinse palm of hands (until all visible suds are removed)," and "rinse back of hands (until all visible suds are removed)" (p. 75). The needs of the student and the complexity of the task will dictate the extent to which a task needs to be broken down. For instance, a fairly proficient student may use the task analysis primarily to guide them in the proper sequencing of specific behaviors which they have already mastered or may require only a few number of general steps specified (using the preceding

FIGURE 9–1

Kent State University Cooperative Transitional Services Program Job Analysis/Requirements

Adapted from Virginia Commonwealth University

Job Title: _____   Job Site: _____

Job Site Supervisor Name: _____   Phone: _____

Transition Coordinator Name: _____   Date: _____

1. Hours Needed	Weekend work	Morning work	Evening work	Part-time work	Full-time work

Comments:

2. Training Location	On public/ accessible route	Off public/ accessible route			

Comments:

3. Street Crossing	None	Two-lane with light	Two-lane without light	Four-lane with light	Four-lane without light

Comments:

4. Employer Attitude	Supportive of workers with disabilities	Supportive with reservations	Indifferent toward workers with disabilities	Negative toward workers with disabilities	

Comments:

5. Job Financial Requirements	Paid position	Possible paid position	Nonpaid position		

Comments:

6. Physical Mobility	Sit or stand in one area	Stairs and/or minor obstacles	Full physical abilities needed		

Comments:

7. Strength Required	Very light work (4–5 lbs.)	Light work (10–20 lbs.)	Average work (30–40 lbs.)	Heavy work (50 + lbs.)	

Comments:

8. Endurance	Work < 2 hours with no break	Work 2–3 hours with no break	Work 4–5 hours with no break	Work 4 + hours with no break	

Comments:

9. Orienting	Small area only	One room	Several rooms	Building wide	Building and grounds

Comments:

10. Appearance Requirements	Appearance of little importance	Cleanliness required	Neat and clean required	Appearance very important	

Comments:

11. Communication Required	None/minimal	Key words and signs needed	Unclear speech accepted	Clear signing required	Clear speech required

Comments:

12. Social Interactions	Interaction not required	Appropriate responses only	Infrequent instructions	Frequent instructions	

Comments:

13. Behavior Acceptance Range	Many behaviors accepted	Few behaviors accepted	No unusual behaviors accepted		

Comments:

14. Initiative/ Motivation	Staff will prompt to next task	Volunteering helpful	Initiation of work required		

Comments:

15. Attention to Task/ Perseverance	Frequent prompts available	Intermittent prompts/ high supervision	Intermittent prompts/ low supervision	Infrequent prompts/ low supervision	

Comments:

16. Reinforcement Available	Frequent reinforcement available	Reinforcement daily	Reinforcement weekly	Minimal reinforcement	Paycheck only

Comments:

17. Sequencing	One task performed at a time	2–3 task changes	4–6 task changes	7 or more task changes	

Comments:

18. Work Rate	Slow	Average-steady pace	Above average/ sometimes fast	Continual fast pace	

Comments:

19. Discrimination Skills	No need to distinguish between work supplies	Must distinguish between supplies with external cue	Must distinguish between work supplies		

Comments:

20. Time Awareness	Time factors not important	Must identify meals/ breaks, etc.	Must tell time with cue	Must tell time to hour	Must tell time to minute

Comments:

21. Functional Reading	None required	Sight words and symbols	Simple reading required	Fluent reading required	

Comments:

22. Alphabetization	None required	To first letter	To second letter	All letters	Letters and numbers

Comments:

23. Functional Math	None required	Simple counting subtraction	Simple addition/	Complex computations	Cash register use

Comments:

Attach job description if available.

List job duties of position (sequentially if possible):

1. _____
2. _____
3. _____
4. _____
5. _____
6. _____
7. _____
8. _____
9. _____
10. _____

Source: From Cooperative Transition Services Program, Center for Innovation in Transition and Employment, Kent State University.

example, simply list "rinse hands"). A student with more severe disabilities or less job experience alternatively may need each step broken down into its most basic components.

Job-Skills Training

After the task analysis is completed, it is useful to assess the student to identify the skills he or she already has and those that must be taught. Two methods to take baseline data include the single opportunity method and the multiple opportunity method (Snell, 1983). Before any instruction occurs, the teacher can ask the student to do the task. The teacher records correct and incorrect subtasks on the analysis sheet until the student stops doing the task or displays inappropriate behavior. The teacher does not prompt or assist the student in any way. This is called a "baseline."

An alternative method allows the teacher to intervene when the student gets to a point where he or she cannot continue. The teacher will do the next task without comment and give the student the opportunity to continue from that point. This continues until the task is completed. It is particularly useful for complex tasks in which the student may be able to do later steps, such as mop, but perhaps unable to mix the cleaning solution. The teacher can also note when prompts or cues allow the student to complete the task. Doing these assessments over time also will help to evaluate the student's progress and the effectiveness of the teaching. Figure 9–2 presents an example of an ongoing task analysis to evaluate a student's progress toward the goal of appropriate work preparation.

With this information, the teacher can now devise a plan using effective teaching practices to begin training and the specific skills to be taught. Dependent on the results, the teacher may want to utilize forward chaining, backward chaining, or whole sequence instruction (see Snell, 1983). In *forward chaining*, the trainer begins by teaching the first skill and then works on each successive skill as mastery is achieved, continuing to practice from the beginning of the chain of skills. With the

example of teaching mopping, the teacher would begin with how to mix the cleaning solution, then move to how to mop, and so on. *Backward chaining* is useful for students who know the last part of the skill but may not know the earlier steps. With the mopping example, the teacher could begin with the last step—the mopping—and then teach the skills, one at a time, prior to the mopping (ending each lesson with mopping) until the entire task is learned. With *whole sequence instruction*, the teacher would work on the whole task each time rather than on teaching isolated skills in order to allow the student to understand how things work together. In some cases, this may be a more natural and quicker method for teaching.

To teach a skill, a hierarchy of prompts may be used to help the student demonstrate the correct behavior. It is usually desirable to begin with the least intrusive prompt and what is most natural for use in the work or community site. Types of prompts from the least intrusive to the most intrusive (Wehman, 1996) include:

- *Verbal prompts*, in which the job trainer talks the student through a task or prompts to continue the task. The task analysis is used to make sure the prompt is short, direct, and necessary. This is the method used by most people and thus is seen as natural.

- *Gestures*, such as pointing or use of manual communication, which can accompany verbal direction or be used by itself.

- *Modeling*, which can be done by either the job trainer or the coworkers. If possible, this should take place next to the worker, as confusion can take place in translating a mirrorlike position.

- *Physical*, which includes the job trainer using hand over hand instruction.

Teachers should utilize sequentially more intrusive prompts only when the less intrusive alternative was unsuccessful in enabling the student to complete the task successfully. After initial skill acquisition, attention needs to be paid to fading the level of prompting. Teachers should begin to use less intrusive prompts as soon as possible, with the eventual goal of allowing the student to self-monitor his or her own behavior.

FIGURE 9–2A
Cooperative Transitional Services Program Task Analysis

*When interpreting the graph, bear in mind that some days (like 9/26) did not have all steps included—e.g., there was no one around who could find a new time card, soap was missing, etc.

Name: _____   Job Site: _A LaCavle_
Instructional Strategy: _Verbal_   Terminal Behavior: _Work Prep_

Legend for graphing: % of prompts (I, R, V, M, P, N)

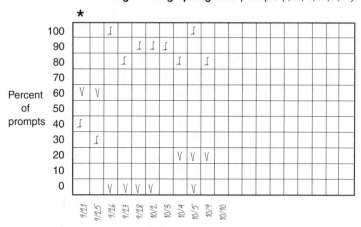

Steps of tasks:

Walk to card holder	−	V	V	V	V	I	V	V	V	V	I	I								
Select correct card	+	I	N/A	I	I	I	N/A	V	V	I	N/A	V								
Place card in machine	+	I	N/A	I	I	I	N/A	I	I	I	I	I								
Remove card from machine	+	I	N/A	I	I	I	N/A	I	I	I	I	I								
Return card to original slot in folder	−	V	N/A	I	V	I	N/A	V	I	V	V	I								
Walk to cooler	−	V	V	I	I	V	I	V	V	I	I	I								
Open and put lunch bag inside	+	I	I	I	I	I	I	I	I	I	I	I								
Close door securely	−	I	V	I	I	I	I	I	I	I	I	I								
Walk to office	−	V	V	I	I	I	I	I	I	I	I	I								
Take off coat	+	I	V	N/A	N/A	I	I	I	N/A	N/A	N/A	N/A								
Hang coat on coat rack	−	V	V	N/A	N/A	V	I	I	N/A	N/A	N/A	N/A								

9/19/95 9/21/95 9/25/95 9/26/95 9/27/95 9/28/95 10/2/95 10/3/95 10/4/95 10/5/95 10/9/95 10/10/95

Date of trials:
(every day after initial)

Initial test:
(first time job is done)

- -

Legend of prompts:

I = Independent	R = Redundancy cue	V = Verbal prompt
M = Model prompt	P = Physical prompt	N = No response

Source: Figure 9–2A and 9–2B from Cooperative Transition Service Program, Center for Innovation in Transition and Employment, Kent State University.

FIGURE 9–2B
Cooperative Transitional Services Program Task Analysis

*When interpreting the graph, bear in mind that some days (like 9/26) did not have all steps included—e.g., there was no one around who could find a new time card, soap was missing, etc.

Legend of prompts:

I = Independent	R = Redundancy cue	V = Verbal prompt
M = Model prompt	P = Physical prompt	N = No response

Steps of tasks:

Step		9/19	9/21	9/25	9/26	9/27	9/28	10/2	10/3	10/4	10/5	10/9	10/10
Collect hat and soap on shelf		V	V	I	I	I	I	I	I	I	I	I	
Walk to laundry room	−	V	V	V	V	V	V	V	V	V	V	V	
Put on apron	+	I	V	I	I	I	I	I	I	I	I		
Pick up towel	−	V	I	N/A	V	N/A	I	N/A	I	I	I	I	
Walk to sink area	−	V	V	V	V	V	V	V	V	V	V	V	
Pick up metal pot	−	V	V	I	V	I	I	I	I	I	V	I	
Put soap in pot	−	V	I	N/A	V	I	I	I	I	I	V	V	
Add water	+	I	I	I	N/A	I	I	I	I	I	I	I	
Swish vigorously		−	V	V	I	I	I	I	I	I	I	I	I
Walk to kitchen door	−	V	I	V	I	I	I	I	I	I	I		
Exit kitchen into serving area	+	I	V	I	I	I	I	I	I	I	I		
Walk into dining room	−	V	I	I	I	I	I	I	I	I	I		

Other types of instruction are specific to the task. For instance, telling time is a skill frequently required by students at job sites, as it may be necessary for a student to identify times to go on break, eat lunch, clock out, or change tasks. This can be accommodated for students in a number of ways, including alarms on clocks, picture cue cards to match with a clock, or having a coworker on a similar schedule prompt the student. Other techniques specific to a particular job may involve a great deal of creativity. For example, a student who vacuums an area needs to be sure to vacuum the entire area systematically and not just where he or she sees dirt. The job trainer can sprinkle baking soda, or teach the student to sprinkle baking soda, over the entire carpet to help the student discriminate what has and has not been vacuumed. For students who have trouble remembering total task sequencing, a written or picture list may be posted for the student to utilize when completing the task. This is also useful for a skill that a student will not be using on a regular basis.

In addition to the instruction that teachers provide, it also is important to get input from the employer and the coworkers as their perspective may be critical in the continuing success of the student in an employment site. Often educators are unaware of the unique needs associated with an employment site and may fail to recognize issues that arise at the site. By using both written checklists, which are completed weekly or biweekly, and personal contact, the employer can contribute to the training of the student. The employer must feel comfortable in reporting both positive and negative aspects about the student's performance. It is especially useful if the employer can talk directly to the student about expectations and, after the initial stage, can provide typical consequences to the student.

Occasionally, despite the efforts to train a student on a job, success does not happen. It is important to remember that lack of success is not always because of poor training. Frequently it is simply a mismatch between a student's skills and interests and a particular job or job site that engenders success or failure. When a student is not successful at a particular job, we must remember that another placement may yield differing results and should be attempted. Failure can provide an important opportunity for the entire team, including the student, to learn about his or her needs and abilities.

Conclusion

Kauffman (1999) recently stated that if we, as educators, particularly special educators, do not continually seek to identify and use effective instructional techniques, then we should get out of the business of education. Whether we are delivering academic instruction in a general education classroom, social skills instruction in a special classroom, or teaching job skills in the community, we should always strive to use the instructional techniques that are most likely to result in students achieving their goals. The general model of effective teaching described early in the chapter can serve as a general guide for teachers to teach their students effectively, regardless of the disability status of the student or specific content and location of the lesson. These general principles, however, can only serve as a framework for effective instruction. Specific techniques and content vary depending on the needs and goals of the student as well as on the instructional environment. By incorporating instructional techniques such as cooperative learning, self-monitoring, and community-based instruction into their effective teaching, teachers can optimize the transition experiences of students with a variety of disabilities.

Study Questions

1. Assume that you are a teacher of students with disabilities who are involved in transition. A new colleague who is experiencing difficulties in classroom instruction comes to you for advice. How would you make a convincing argument regarding why and how he or she should consider using effective instructional and behavior management techniques?
2. Now assume that the same colleague is subsequently required to teach his or her students in a community-based program and is worried that he or she does not know anything about teaching in this environment. What argument would you make that effective teaching strategies should be used in community-based settings, such as a job site?
3. One of the biggest problems in teaching is how to address simultaneously a variety of needs. How do the use of the strategies discussed in this chapter allow you (a) to attend to more than one student at a time? and (b) to address students' learning and behavior goals simultaneously?
4. Suppose that you are using cooperative learning and self-monitoring as well as community-based instruction in your teaching. How could you infuse in these methods the effective teaching strategies discussed in the first half of the chapter?
5. How might using effective teaching strategies, cooperative learning, self-monitoring, and community-based instruction help students to prepare for a successful transition into adult roles?

Web Sites

Effective Teaching:
www.cec.sped.org/conv/zigmund.html

curry.edschool.virginia.edu/go/cise/ose/information/interventions.html

Cooperative Learning:
www.cde.ca.gov/iasa/cooplrng.html

www.ascd.org/services/eric/ericcoo.html

Self-Monitoring:
tor-pw1.netcom.ca/~rinholms/selfmon.htm

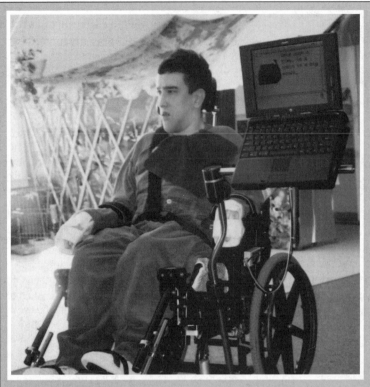

10

The Role of Technology in Transition Planning

Deborah Bauder
Preston Lewis

LEARNING OBJECTIVES

The objectives of this chapter are:

1. Understand the role that technology plays in an individual's life.

2. Explain the differences of assistive technology, rehabilitation technology, and rehabilitation engineering.

3. Identify the key elements in process for determining a person's technology needs.

4. Identify categories of assistive technology.

5. Discuss the purpose and functions of devices found within various assistive technology categories.

6. Identify some of the barriers associated with the planning and implementation of assistive technology.

7. Understand legislative requirements regarding transition and the role of technology and assistive technology.

8. Understand the outcome-oriented process in using technology as a tool for effective instruction or learning.

9. Understand the process of how interagency agreements are determined through the transition process.

10. Identify considerations for the use of technology/assistive technology in work environments, community environments, and postsecondary environments.

For many students with disabilities, the principles found within the Individual with Disabilities Education Act (IDEA) cannot be meaningfully addressed without adequate consideration of students' needs in relation to technology. For many students, access to assistive technology will be inherent to their basic ability to function, especially in terms of having basic receptive and expressive communication or access to school and natural environments and environmental control. Other students with mild disabilities may not have severe physical or mental limitations that depend on technology usage for performance. However, for most, if not all, students with disabilities, some level of competency in computer usage will be requisite to both school and transition success.

Many chapters in this text have provided in-depth information about transition from theoretical models to best practices in transition planning, community participation, and career development. This chapter looks at a different aspect, in that it discusses how technology can benefit individuals with disabilities throughout their educational, vocational, and postsecondary activities. An underlying premise of this chapter is the belief that technology should be considered as a tool through which individuals may achieve their goals. Another tenet of this chapter is that all students have a right to use technology to improve, remediate, or compensate for their functional abilities (Bowser & Reed, 1995) in the process of achieving such goals.

However, although the use of technology has become a necessity for individuals with disabilities to have access to and to participate in daily activities throughout their environment, there are many factors that need to be considered in relation to its use. Therefore, the focus of this chapter revolves around the application of technology, primarily assistive technology, and its role as it pertains to a student's secondary and postsecondary activities (e.g., school, recreation, and community participation).

The Importance of Technology

Technology has come to play an increasingly important role in the lives of all individuals. In every aspect of life (e.g., work, recreation, and school), individuals use technology as an effective way to meet the demands of their environment (Behrmann, 1984; Blackhurst & Hofmeister, 1980; Derer, Polsgrove, & Rieth, 1996). For example, every day in some way a person uses technology as a means to perform a function within his or her environment, whether it is to turn on a television using a remote control or to purchase a soft drink from a soda machine. In each instance, technology plays a role for one's convenience, efficiency, or increased effectiveness.

However, some individuals with disabilities frequently encounter difficulties meeting environmental demands. Therefore, assistive or adaptive technology may need to be used for an individual with a disability to perform or function within his or her environment. With the support of technology, specifically assistive technology (AT), individuals are able to communicate more effectively, control their environment, or achieve greater mobility (Blackhurst & Shuping, 1990; Raskind, 1997/1998). Research has demonstrated that the use of technology, including assistive and adaptive devices, can improve an individual's level of functioning (Berliss, Borden, & Vanderheiden, 1989; Blackhurst & Shuping, 1990; Raskind, 1997/1998).

Legislation and Definitions

The benefits of AT were recognized by Congress in 1988 when it passed the *Technology-Related Assistance for Individuals with Disabilities Act* (known as the Tech Act) (P.L. 100-407) and an AT device was defined as: "any item, piece of equipment, or product system whether acquired off the shelf, modified or customized that is used to increase, maintain, or improve functional capabilities of individuals with disabilities" (P.L. 100-457, section

1401 (a) (25)). However, it is important to realize that AT is not solely under the domain of devices or adaptive equipment.

An equal and important part under the AT umbrella also is service. An AT service is defined as "any service that directly assists a child with a disability in the selection, acquisition, or use of an assistive technology device" (IDEA, P.L. 105-17, section 1401 (a) (26)). Examples of an AT service include:

> (a) the evaluation of the needs of a child with a disability, including a functional evaluation of the child in the child's customary environment; (b) purchasing, leasing, or otherwise providing for the acquisition of assistive technology devices by children with disabilities; (c) selecting, designing, fitting, customizing, adapting, applying, maintaining, repairing or replacing of assistive technology devices; (d) coordinating other therapies, interventions, or services with assistive technology devices, such as those associated with existing education and rehabilitation plans and programs; (e) training assistance for a child with or, if appropriate, that child's family; and (f) training or technical assistance for professionals (including individuals providing education or rehabilitation services), employers, or other individuals who provide services to employ, or are otherwise substantially involved in the major life functions of children with disabilities (IDEA, P.L. 105-17, section 1401, (a) (26)).

As an individual transitions from school to postsecondary activities, AT terminology changes to "rehabilitation technology." With the passage of the Rehabilitation Act Amendments of 1992 (P.L. 102-569), AT devices and AT services are now included as part of rehabilitation technology. *Rehabilitation Technology* is defined as "the systematic application of technologies, engineering methodologies, or scientific principles by individuals with disabilities in areas including education, rehabilitation, employment, transportation, independent living, and recreation" (P.L. 102-569). It should be noted that the term "rehabilitation technology" includes reha-

bilitation engineering, AT devices, and AT services. (P.L. 102-569).

The reason that these terms and their respective definitions are important for professionals, parents, and students to understand is that they are referred to in planning meetings. Also, in essence, AT and rehabilitation technology refer to the same types of technology. The difference between them is in which service provider arena they are used. For example, in a transition meeting, a vocational rehabilitation counselor may refer to rehabilitation technology, whereas a special education teacher may refer to AT. Both individuals are discussing the same type of technology but are using different terminology.

Examples of Assistive Technology

Substantial progress has been made in the development of AT devices, including adaptations to existing products and devices. Such devices and adaptations increase the involvement of individuals in programs and activities, such as education, rehabilitation and training, employment, residential living, independent living, recreation, and other aspects of daily living. There are literally thousands of AT devices that allow individuals to accomplish many tasks. For example, for individuals with physical impairments, there are devices that can facilitate movements, such as a walker, a switch, or a wheelchair (Fielder, 1996; Weber & Demchak, 1996). Other types of devices bridge the gap of communication for individuals with speech or language impairments through the use of an augmentative or alternate communication system (AAC) (Blackstone, 1992). Additional types of communication devices include Braille and speech synthesis for individuals with visual impairments (Brown, 1992; Lazzaro, 1996). Also, some types of AT devices provide additional learning opportunities for individuals with mild or moderate mental disabilities (Wehmeyer, 1998).

Assistive technology is a huge umbrella under which a vast number of devices may be found. To a novice or beginning service provider, the thought

TABLE 10–1

Examples of Assistive Technology by Functional Categories

Functional Category	Assistive Technology Example
Existence. Technology that provides assistance in basic function areas needed to sustain life	Respirators, feeding devices, and adapted potty chairs
Communication. Primarily consists of augmentative and alternative communication systems, alternative communication (AAC) Augmentative/alternative communication refers to any technique to enhance or augment communication	Gestures, sign language, nonelectronic augmentative communication systems (e.g., dial scans, communication boards), voice output communication aids, tactile speech aides, visual doorbells, alert and alarm systems
Body support, protection, and positioning. Devices that provide stabilization, body support, or protection to the body	Braces, crutches, standers, walkers, splints
Travel and Mobility. Devices that help a person move about, either horizontally or vertically	Wheelchair, lifts, and electronic travel aids (ETA) with obstacle detection indicators. Adapted buses and vans
Environmental interaction. Devices and accessories designed to assist a person perform daily living skills, both indoors and outdoors	Environmental controls that activate appliances such as telephones, lights, TV, and blenders
Education and transition. Devices that support the educational and vocational needs	Computer-assisted instruction software, work-site adaptations, such as electric staplers, switch-activated filing systems, and adjustable desks
Sports, fitness, and recreation. Assistive technology that promotes participation in individual or group sports, play activities, hobbies, and crafts	Bowling ball chutes, audible baseballs, adapted recreational snow equipment (e.g., adapted ski poles and adapted sleds)

of AT can, at best, seem overwhelming. To help individuals better understand AT devices, seven major functional areas have been developed and include (1) existence; (2) communication; (3) travel and mobility; (4) body support, protection, and positioning; (5) environmental interaction; (6) education and transition; and (7) sports, fitness, and recreation (Blackhurst, Bausch, Bell, Burleson, Cooper, Gassaway, McCrary, & Zabala, 1999). Descriptions of the functional categories are provided in light of possible AT devices and services are displayed in Table 10–1.

It should be noted that embedded within each of these categories are levels of technology

device sophistication, including no technology, low technology, medium technology to high or advanced technology (Blackhurst & Cross, 1993; Blackhurst, 1997). Therefore, AT can be as simple as a pencil grip or as complex as a computer with voice activation capabilities.

In addition, it is important to understand the implications of the continuum of AT from low technology solutions through high technology solutions. A general principle is that the lowest level of technology that will meet the individual's needs should be considered first. Generally, individuals with disabilities want what will be the most useful for them in providing greater access to their environment, (i.e., school, home, and community). The latest, most expensive device is not necessarily the most appropriate or may not meet the needs of an individual. However, the level of sophistication of the device is determined by the needs of the individual.

Specific examples of AT adaptations are provided in Figure 10–1. These examples are categorized by functional areas. It should be noted that this list in not exhaustive but merely provides possibilities of the types of AT that might be available to an individual. For further assistance in ascertaining the types of AT that are available, an individual should turn to resources such as AbleData (www. abledata.com) or the Closing the Gap Resource Guide (www.closingthegap.com) or search the Internet using keywords, such as "assistive technology." A listing of AT web sites is provided at the end of the chapter.

Application of Technology

It is impossible for any single individual to be an expert (Holder-Brown & Parette, 1992) in all types of AT. Therefore, the appropriate identification and implementation of AT usually relies upon the knowledge of several disciplines (Holder-Brown & Parette, 1992), including occupational therapists, special education teachers, speech and language pathologists, and physical therapists (Zabala, 1994). A team approach is necessary because of both the number of factors and the possible complexity involved in the delivery of AT systems to an individual (Parette, Hourcade, & VanBiervliet, 1996). Underlying the need for a multidisciplinary or transdisciplinary approach to an AT selection is the realization that service providers are required to have a wide variety of skills (Reed, 1997; Zabala, 1994).

The process in the selection of AT starts with the assessment process. Several models (e.g., Blackhurst & Cross, 1993; Reed, 1997; Zabala, 1994) have been developed to assist evaluation teams to determine AT devices for individuals.

The three important characteristics that are embedded within all assessment models are (1) the environmental demands placed on an individual; (2) the individuals' needs, abilities, and preferences (Chambers, 1997); and (3) the technology characteristics (Thorkildsen, 1994).

As an example, Blackhurst (1997) illustrated how assessment can be accomplished through the use of the *unifying functional model* (see Figure 10–2). The key elements to this model include environment and context, functional demands, exploration of options, personal perceptions, personal resources, external supports, functional response, personal changes, and evaluation and feedback (see Blackhurst & Cross, 1993; Blackhurst 1997 for further information). The goal of this model is to address a person's functional responses in light of their environmental demands (Blackhurst, 1997). Using this model as a process for decision making, a school team would be able to make judgments about the use of technology based on a student's functions in response to academic demands as well as to community and vocational demands (Blackhurst, 1997). (See Example A.)

A school-based assessment team may be able to assess what is or is not working for a student and determine how AT can be applied to evaluate whether specific AT devices and services are necessary to meet the specific needs of a child (Reed, 1997; Scherer, 1997). However, the IEP (Individualized Education Program) team may determine that they do not possess knowledge of resources or do not have knowledge to evaluate AT needs (Chambers, 1997). In these situations, the team would seek additional support from individuals with the level of knowledge or resources necessary to assist the team in evaluating a child's specific educational needs for AT. Additionally, an evaluation to determine appropriate AT should be done in a variety of environments to determine the impact on school activities across curriculum areas, in vocational sites, and in community and home settings (Bauder, et. al., 1997).

FIGURE 10–1

Examples of Assistive Technology by Functional Domain

Functional Category	Examples

Physical functioning
(includes vision, hearing)
	Braille' n Speak 2000
	  (Blazie Engineering)
	  Web site: www.blazie. com
	FM Auditory Training Systems
	  (Phonic Ear)
	  Web site: www.phonicear.com
	Wobble Switch
	  (Enabling Devices)
	  Web site: www.enablingdevices.com
	Big Red Switch
	  (AbleNet)
	  Web site: www.ablenetinc.com
	Page Turner
	  (Zygo, Inc.)
	  Web site: www.zygo-usa.com
	Dragon Naturally Speaking
	  (Dragon Systems, Inc.)
	  Web site: www.dragonsys.com/
	Intellikeys Keyboard
	  (Intellitools, Inc.)
	  Web site: www.intellitools.com/

Communication functioning	Big Mac
	  (AbleNet)
	  Web site: www.ablenetinc.com
	Cheap Talk 4
	  (Enabling Devices)
	  Web site:www.enablingdevices.com
	Boardmaker
	  (Mayer-Johnson)
	  Web site: www.mayerjohnson.com/
	Dynavox
	  (DynaVox Systems, Inc.)
	  Web site: www.dynavoxsys.com

Cognitive functioning	Early Learning Software
	  (Marblesoft)
	  Web site: www.marblesoft.com

Social competence	TeleTrainer
	  (Qualtek)
	  Web site: www.qualtek.com
	Palm Pilot
	  (3Com Corporation)

(continued)

FIGURE 10–1
(Concluded)

Functional Category	Examples

Academic performance	Write Out Loud
	  (Don Johnston, Inc.)
	  Web site: www.donjohnston.com
	Co:Writer
	  (Don Johnston, Inc.)
	  Web site: www.donjohnston.com
	AlphaSmart 2000
	  (Intelligent Peripheral Devices, Inc.)
	  Web site: www.alphasmart.com
	Quicktionary Reading Pen
	  (Seiko Instruments)
	  Web site: www.readingpen.com

Vocational functioning	Motorized Easel
	  (Extensions for Independence)
	  Web site: www.mouthstick.net
	Electric Stapler
	  (various vendors)
	Braille Rulers
	  (American Printing House)
	  Web site: www.aph.org
	Talking Clock Calculator
	  (LS & S)
	  Web site: www.lssgroup.com

Recreation and leisure functioning	Pinochle Large Print
	  (The Lighthouse)
	  Web site: www.lighthouse.org
	TV/VCR/Cable Remote
	  (Enabling Devices)
	  Web site: www.enablingdevices.com
	Velcro Tic Tac Toe
	  (Dragonfly Toys)
	  Web site: www.dragonflytoys.com
	Battery Power Card Shuffler
	  (Dragonfly Toys)
	  Web site: www.dragonflytoys.com
	Mono-ski
	  (Groves Innovations)
	  Web site: www.sitski.com/grove.html

Example

A

Functional Model

Environment and context: Completing written tasks at job site

Functional demands: Uses left hand, poor fine motor control

Explore options: Adapted pencil grips, ergonomic pens, and writing cuff

Personal perceptions: Prefers to work independently and does not want accommodation to "single him out" or to make him look "different"

Personal resources: Willing to try adaptations in order to complete written tasks in a more timely manner

External supports: Occupational therapist available for consultation

Functional response: Weighted ergonomic pen and clipboard

Personal changes: Accommodation provided support for individual to complete job tasks. Individual satisfied that accommodation did not make him look or act different in order to complete written tasks

Evaluation and feedback: Follow-up by occupational therapist to review accommodations and to determine the need for other solutions if warranted

Critical Point   The 1997 reauthorization of IDEA (P.L. 105-17) specifies that all children who are identified as having special education needs must be considered for assistive technology.

Critical Point   *Question:* Who should be considered for assistive technology?

Answer: The initial issue is one of consideration. All children eligible and receiving specially designed instruction through an IEP must be considered for assistive technology.

The team documents whether or not a child is in need of assistive technology by considering (a) what specific tasks the student is not able to do or participate in because of the disability or suspected disability,(b) what has been tried to enable the student to complete the task or to participate, and (c) if a particular strategy or modification enables the student to complete the task or participate within the least restrictive environment.

It is believed that many school personnel are not sufficiently familiar with AT to use it effectively (Sax, Pumpian, & Fisher, 1997). Coupled with the unfamiliarity of AT, school personnel and service providers often encounter many issues and misconceptions regarding the provision of AT that may hinder the potential of the use of AT to aid children with disabilities in meeting their educational outcomes (Lee, 1995).

These issues may directly impact service providers, families, and student attitudes toward AT and can become invisible barriers to the successful acquisition and use of AT in the home, work, school, or community (Burkhead, Sampson, McMahon, 1986; Lee, 1997).

Scherer and Galvin (1996) outline some misconceptions that service providers and school personnel may have about AT. These misconceptions and corresponding realities are displayed in Table 10–2.

Furthermore, the determination of the type of AT that would be beneficial must be determined on the basis of an individual's needs and educational goals and not the technological whim of the moment. Assistive technology embraces a wide range of equipment that one might consider. Therefore, in order to make informed decisions, one should seek out information from many sources and resources. Table 10–3 is an example of an AT consideration form that might help to facilitate discussion and determination if a student needs an AT assessment during an IEP meeting.

There are many sources of information regarding AT, including HyperAble DATA (Trace, 1996), Closing the Gap Resource Guide, Alliance for Technology Access Centers, and local AT centers to name a few of the available resources.

FIGURE 10–2
Unifying Functional Model

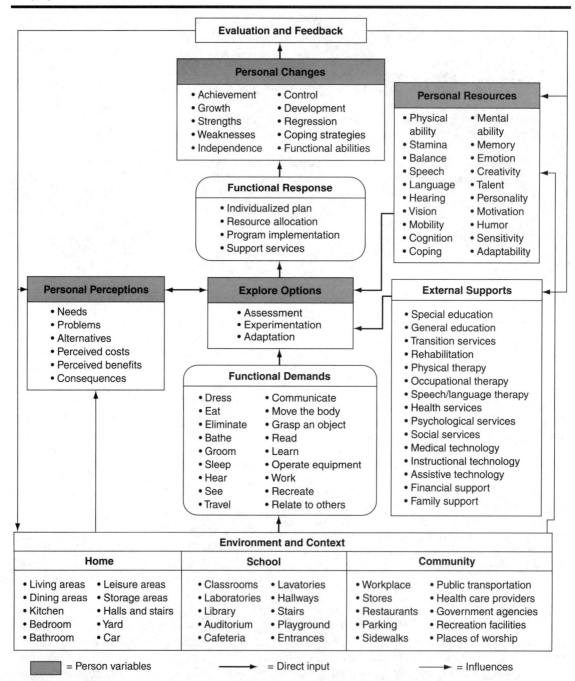

Source: A Framework for Aligning Technology with Transition Competencies by A. E. Blackhurst, E. A. Lahm, E. M. Harrison, N. G. Chandler, *Career Development for Exceptional Individuals*, 22, 1999. p. 159. Copyright 1999 by the Council for Exeptional Children, reprinted with permission.

TABLE 10–2

Assistive Technology Misconceptions and Realities

Misconception	Reality
1. AT is the "be all and end all."	AT is only a tool. It is not the solution to address all of a person's needs.
2. AT is complicated and expensive.	Some AT devices are complicated and expensive. However, there are many devices that might address the same need that are low tech and inexpensive. AT devices can be categorized according to a continuum of no tech, low tech, medium tech, and high tech.
3. Persons with the same disability benefit from using the same devices.	Determination of AT for an individual is highly individualized. It is necessary to match the needs of a person with the characteristics of AT that will provide the most benefit.
4. Professionals are the best source of information about AT.	There are many sources of information about AT, including web sites, vendors, journals, AT consultants. Note that no one person can be an expert in all aspects of AT.
5. AT product descriptions are always accurate and helpful.	Not all product descriptions are accurate and helpful. That is one good reason that a person should try out a device prior to purchase.
6. A user's AT requirements only need to be assessed once.	AT is dynamic and requires reevaluation. This might be due to an individual reaching development, milestones, or the development of a better AT device.
7. AT devices will always be used.	It is inappropriate to use some AT devices in certain environments, such as using an electronic device while taking a bath.
8. People with disabilities want the latest, most expensive devices.	The important concept here is not the device in itself, rather, what will facilitate or compensate one's functional ability. In other words, what can I use in a user-friendly way that will help me to conduct or accomplish my task.
9. AT is a luxury.	For some individuals, AT is a necessity. It helps individuals to function within their environments.

Source: From Scherer and Galvin, 1996).

Barriers to Implementation of Assistive Technology

For successful implementation of assistive technology, many factors must be considered. If these factors are not addressed, then they become barriers to the implementation of AT. This section reviews fundamental barriers to the successful implementation of technology. Following this overview of barriers, Table 10–4 addresses each barrier and lists possible solutions.

TABLE 10–3

Assistive Technology Consideration Guide for IEP Teams

Student:	Date of Birth:	Current Date:
Contact or Location:		
Persons participating in consideration:		

This student's IEP team considers the assistive technology needs of this student in accordance with the provisions of the Individuals with Disabilities Education Act. Consideration of this student's possible need for assistive technology is directly related to the implementation of this student's IEP, which is directly related to the provision of a free appropriate public education (FAPE).

1. In the first column, review each domain. Considering this student's IEP, in the second column identify areas of concern and related tasks that this student needs to be able to do that would be difficult or impossible to do without assistance.

2. *If there are no areas of concern, proceed to step #9.*

3. If concerns are identified, place a check in each appropriate box in column 2 and briefly describe the expected task. Document only those tasks relevant to the student's IEP and successful participation in various environments.

4. For each task listed, determine if the student is currently able to complete designated tasks with special strategies, accommodations, or modifications. Is the student currently using any assistive technology tools, or has the student used assistive technology tools in the past? If yes, describe in column (A).

5. Determine if there are any continuing barriers that the student encounters when attempting a task? If yes, complete column (B).

6. Consider whether the use of new or additional assistive technology would: (a) help the student perform this task with more ease or efficiency in the least restrictive environment, or (b) perform the task successfully with less personal assistance. If yes, indicate in column (C).

7. If members of the IEP team are not familiar with assistive technology tools that could address remaining barriers or need additional assistance, indicate in column (C) that further investigation is necessary in this area.

8. Use the information that has been entered while completing steps 1 through 6 to complete #9.

Domains Relating to the Student's IEP.	Area of Concern / Task	Consider all environments in which the IEP is to be implemented.		
		(A) Describe the special strategies, accommodations, and tools that are currently being used to remove barriers to the task for this student.	(B) Are there continuing barriers that the student encounters when attempting this task? If so, describe.	(C) Describe new or additional assistive technology to be tried, or indicate a need for further investigation. Consult AT specialist.
Physical: Vision, hearing, health, motor abilities, speech mechanism	□ Vision			
	□ Hearing			

Domains Relating to the Student's IEP.	Area of Concern / Task	(A) Describe the special strategies, accommodations, and tools that are currently being used to remove barriers to the task for this student.	(B) Are there continuing barriers that the student encounters when attempting this task? If so, describe.	(C) Describe new or additional assistive technology to be tried, or indicate a need for further investigation. Consult AT specialist.
	☐ Positioning / Seating			
	☐ Mobility			
	☐ Mechanics of writing			
	☐ Computer access			
Communication: Speech sound production and use, receptive and expressive language, voice, fluency, augmentative, and alternative communication.	☐ Communication			
Cognitive: An appraisal of aptitude and mental processes by which an individual applies knowledge, thinks and solves problems.	☐ Learning and studying			
Social competence: Adaptive behaviors and social skills which enable a child or youth to meet environmental demands and to assume responsibility for his own and other's welfare.	☐			

continued

283

TABLE 10–3

Assistive Technology Consideration Guide for IEP Teams (*continued*)

Domains Relating to the Student's IEP.	Area of Concern / Task	(A) Describe the special strategies, accommodations, and tools that are currently being used to remove barriers to the task for this student.	(B) Are there continuing barriers that the student encounters when attempting this task? If so, describe.	(C) Describe new or additional assistive technology to be tried, or indicate a need for further investigation. Consult AT specialist.
Academic performance: Basic and content reading; reading comprehension; mathematics calculation, reasoning and application; written expression; oral expression; listening comprehension; learning preference; learning style, strategies; effect of the disability on acquisition, development, mastery, and applications of academic skills.	☐ Reading			
	☐ Math			
	☐ Composing written material			
Vocational functioning: General work behaviors; following directions; working independently or with job supports; job preferences or interests; dexterity; abilities; interpersonal relationships and socialization; related work skills.	☐			
Recreation / leisure functioning: Free time, maintenance of physical fitness, use of generic community recreation facilities and resources, and degree of social involvement.	☐			
Environmental functioning: Relationship with family; relationship with peers; family's dominant language; cultural influences; expectations of the parents for the child or youth in the home, school, and community environments; services received in the community; economic influences.	☐ Activities of daily living (ADLs)			
	☐ Environmental control			

9. **Summary of the Consideration** of this student's possible need for assistive technology services. If the IEP team has determined that a need exists, describe what will be provided (more specific assessment of need for assistive technology; existing tools, adaptation or modification of existing tools; additional tools; technical assistance on device operation or use, or training of student, staff, or family).

Consideration Summary	Agree. Describe.	Disagree. Describe.
Student's needs are currently being met. Assistive technology is not necessary at this time.		
Assistive technology devices/services are required by this student and will be used for designated tasks in customary instructional environments. (Specify in the IEP.)		
Assistive technology devices/services are of potential benefit to the student and will be included in extended trials. (Specify in the IEP.)		
Further investigation/assessment is necessary to determine what assistive technology devices and services may be required. (Specify in the IEP.)		

List AT devices and services to be provided. Include those currently used successfully and those to be tried or added.	Responsible Parties	Initiation	Duration

NOTES:

Source: Denham, A P., & Zabala, J. S. (1999). Assistive technology consideration guide for IEP teams [Adapted from Georgia AT Project (GPAT), Wisconsin AT Initiative (WATI), Kentucky AT Guidelines, and the SETT Framework]. For more information or to provide feedback, contact by e-mail: *denham@ntr.net or zabala@technologist.com*

Lack of Professional Development or Teacher Training

There is a lack of technology training for both regular education and special education teachers on how to determine which devices are the most appropriate for each child's needs and how to use technology within classroom instruction (Bauder, 1999; Behrmann, McCallen, & Morrissette, 1993). The need for training in the use of AT is a widespread problem of national interest and concern (Blackhurst & Morse, 1996).

In order for students with disabilities to realize the benefits of using AT, it is necessary to have knowledgeable special education teachers. Without trained teachers, the awareness, selection, and implementation of AT are, at best, ineffectual. The need for providing AT training programs for professionals is critical.

Although teachers express concerns about lack of training in order to implement AT (Scott, 1997), there also appears to be a perceived lack of need to be proficient in the application of AT by special education teachers (Cross et al., 1996). If professionals do not seek and/or are not provided the professional development necessary to know what types of AT exists and how it can be used to improve instruction for all students, then too many scenarios may occur in which the transition and IEP team meet the process requirements of IDEA but sorely neglect to fulfill the spirit or the original intent of this federal act.

Assistive Technology Support Services Not Always School Based

The AT support services available to teachers often are not available within their school building or, for that matter, school district. This can create difficulties in obtaining technical assistance, feedback, and troubleshooting assistance when it is needed (Parette & VanBiervliet, 1991). Since technology support is not usually available within a school district, educators and children may need to travel to a regional AT service agency to obtain AT assessments and recommendations for individual children. Although this is one way to provide this needed AT service, it defeats the principle of providing an ecological evaluation. A problem with this provision is the time and cost factors. In some situations, students may have to travel long distances to reach an AT service provider. For some students, such a trip is difficult and the likelihood of obtaining accurate information is questionable. Of course, there is the reverse possibility, that is, contracting with an AT specialist who drives to the school. With this scenario, the cost of travel time and consultant fees may be expensive. Another drawback of hiring a consultant is that it defeats one of the principles of AT assessment: using a multidisciplinary team approach.

There are some promising possibilities to rectifying some AT application issues. The use of videoconferencing may close the gap between distance and available expertise. The Kentucky Department of Education, Division of Exceptional Children, is presently investigating the potential of conducting AT assessments through this technology medium. Videoconferencing is presently used in schools to provide students with educational opportunities that the students otherwise would not have. For example, videoconferencing events with zoos and museums are available to any school within the United States.

The use of videoconferencing in education for professional development training and AT assessment is a relatively new concept, which is based on the telemedicine model. Within this model, medical experts can help medical personnel across the county to diagnose individual medical conditions, to review patient information, to provide on-line consultations, and to provide trainings using a camera with audio capability connected to a telephone line. The use of videoconferencing technologies is in its infancy but has the potential to assist students with disabilities, not only with their AT needs, but also with other identified needs, and holds great promise with the assistance it could make accessible from experts around the country.

It should be noted that there are AT centers throughout the country. See the Alliance for Technology Access web page for a list of AT centers (www.ata.org) or contact your state's tech act project for information about available AT service agencies. A listing of personnel at each state tech act project can be found at the RESNA web site: www.resna.org/taproject.

Need for Follow-Up Services

Continual AT support services are rarely available to provide follow-up and to reassess AT needs of children with disabilities. As children develop, their AT needs change. As an individual gains skills and/or reaches developmental milestones, it is important to realize that there will be a need to reassess the child's development and AT requirements. A previously recommended device may no longer meet those requirements. Therefore, AT assessment should be considered as ongoing processes rather than as one-time events (Bauder et al., 1997).

Inability to Evaluate Assistive Technology before Purchase

As with any product, descriptions and claims about the use of, or effectiveness of, a particular device are not always accurate. Therefore, it is strongly encouraged that before purchasing a device, one should try to obtain the device through a loan. Through trial use, one can determine if the device is appropriate for an individual. Additionally, the cost of AT and the inability to evaluate the effectiveness of AT devices before purchasing them creates financial difficulties for districts. Often, devices are purchased based on recommendations of a brief AT assessment performed through a technology center or vendor without the opportunity to test its effectiveness over a period of time.

It should be noted that nearly one-third of all purchased AT devices were reported to be abandoned (Phillips, 1991), most often during the first year after they were recommended (Scherer, 1991). Reasons consumers gave for not using AT were that (1) they did not improve independent functioning; (2) servicing and repair were too difficult to obtain or too expensive; and (3) the device was too difficult to use, was unreliable, or required too much assistance from another person (Phillips, 1992; Blackstone, 1992). Therefore, when considering technology, one should be cognizant of potential factors that might impede its usage.

Lack of Parent Knowledge of Assistive Technology

Families and staff encounter a variety of obstacles in obtaining, implementing, and maintaining AT for their children (Parette, Brotherson, Hourcade, & Bradley, 1996). Parents often are unaware of how to use AT devices, how to obtain AT devices for home use, or how the devices are used at school (Parette, 1999). Therefore, the use of AT is frequently limited to use in school because parents do not have the necessary information to use it in the home (Parette & Hourcade, 1997; Parette, 1999).

As stated by one parent,

> Technology has been an important contributor to the partnership of families and professionals moving along the road toward accessibility and acceptance.
>
> Technology has modified environments, helped to make our children more versatile. Parents and helping professionals sometimes feel old and tired from the struggles we have won and the trials we have left to go. Technology, though, seems always new, always adapting, always searching for a new solution to an old problem. Technology has often served us well by bringing the world to our children and our children out into the world. As our children are more integrated, as their horizons expand, technology becomes ever more important, playing a larger part in our lives.

TABLE 10–4

Barriers and Solutions to AT Implementation

Barrier	Solution(s)
Lack of professional development or teacher training	*District Level:* 1. Conduct a training needs assessment. 2. Provide school personnel with brief informational sheets on various aspects of AT. 3. Develop short (20 to 30 minutes) training opportunities that could be provided during lunch times, before school, or after school. 4. Develop training that specifically addresses current needs of school personnel. 5. Develop strategies to identify when and how to consider AT during and after ARC meeting. 6. Obtain videos about AT. *State Level:* 1. Conduct a training needs assessment. 2. Develop a statewide training plan. 3. Consider training initiatives for the development of local assistive technology teams. 4. Develop mechanisms that provide teachers with information without requiring attendance and time away from classroom. 5. Consider the use of distance and web-based training initiatives. 6. Consider the need for AT teacher certification endorsement initiatives.

Additionally, family values and parental views of the student impact on acquisition and implementation of AT and can be fundamentally different from the professionals' viewpoints (Parette, Brotherson, Hourcade, & Bradley, 1996; Todis & Walker, 1993). Thus, it is important that school personnel and parents work together when exploring potential AT solutions. (See Table 10–4.)

Technology and Transition

Successful transition from school to postschool settings is based on the premise that the student has been taught what he or she needs to know in order to meet the demands of adult environments. For many persons with disabilities, it is not only having learned what they need to know, but also having the tools, such as AT, to be able to use what they know. Therefore, as a transition plan is developed, the need or revision of technology should be included as part of a student's short- and long-term goals.

However, the incorporation of technology within transition plans is not always considered a need or preference. Since the implementation of IDEA, technology advances have increased the potential for integrating children with disabilities into general education programs and for expanding their participation in these and other settings (Bauder et al., 1997). Although the

TABLE 10–4

(Concluded)

AT support services are not always school based and lack follow-up services	*District:* 1. Survey for qualified personnel within region. 2. Identify AT resources available within community. 3. Develop a network of AT professionals within state. 4. Invest financial resources to train school personnel. 5 Develop local AT team. 6. Investigate videoconferencing possibilities.
Inability to evaluate AT before purchase	*District:* 1. Develop a district AT Inventory. 2. Identify AT lending libraries within region. 3. Identify AT lending libraries with state. 4. Collaborate with other school districts or cooperatives and develop a regional AT lending library. 5. Identify vendors that lend equipment.
Lack of parent knowledge of AT	1. Develop information sheets on various aspects of AT. 2. Provide parents with video about AT. 3. Invite parents to trainings on specific equipment related to their child's use. 4. Videotape how to use specific equipment related to their child's use. 5. Encourage parent participation in the identification of AT.

growth in technology assistance, use, and application appears to have been rapid (Thorkildsen, 1994), there continues to be little information describing how technology is integrated into the full range of school-related activities. Because of this lack of information, issues have arisen with regard to the use and effectiveness of AT for individuals in reaching their goals or educational outcomes.

One must realize that when determining the appropriate AT, each situation is highly individualized and all relevant information must be obtained in order to decide what device or service will meet an individual's needs (Esposito & Campbell, 1993; Inge & Shepard, 1995). The application of AT involves awareness (Chambers,

1997; Lahm, 1989); assessment (e.g., Blackhurst & Cross, 1993; Reed, 1997; Scherer, 1997; Zabala, 1994); identification of appropriate solutions, training (Bauder, Lewis, & Whitlock, 1996; Wisniewski & Sedlak, 1992), and practice with inclusion of skilled professionals from multiple disciplines.

There is a critical factor in that professionals need to understand the possibilities of the use of technology and to be able to apply that information at IEP and transition planning meetings. Some AT transition issues are clearly a part of what needs to be addressed in an interagency transition planning meeting where the student's transition plan (i.e., IEP statement of transition services) is completed along with specifics of each agency's responsibilities in the process. Some agencies that may be involved are Vocational Rehabilitation (VR), employment services, postsecondary education staff (e.g., technical school, community college, and university). Some of these technology concerns cannot be adequately met without some opportunity to work with the student, their parents, and others in targeting the community, vocational, home, and leisure sites that the student has listed on his or her transition plan, and then looking at each site in terms of the use of current AT. Examination of these situational needs also could lead to identification of an AT which is presently not being used by the student but that will be essential to the student's successful transition to a particular setting (e.g., work site modifications needed for specific jobs).

Technology, Transition, and IDEA Principles

The four principles found in IDEA regarding transition include (1) students' needs, interests, and preferences; (2) outcome-oriented process; (3) interagency responsibility or linkages; and (4) movement from school to postschool activities. Each of these principles will be discussed in relationship to the role of technology.

Students' Needs, Interests, and Preferences

An aspect of the use of technology and transition revolves around IDEA regarding students participation in the development and implementation of their transition plan and its incorporation in the IEP. There may be times when students are unable to participate or communicate their preferences or ideas in the planning of a transition plan. For example, the need for technology is for an individual to participate in events throughout his or her environment on a daily basis as well as for achieving one's IEP goals. A case in point, a 21 year old with cerebral palsy was in her last year of school. Her transition plan had evidence of three previous years of her presence and attention to her postschool goals and needs. In the section of her transition plan addressing postschool outcomes, her transition plan stated, "undecided." So, here was an individual ready to exit the school system and there was no visible plan for her successful transition to anything other than sitting at home, with the premise being that she and the family were "undecided." Although this has tremendous implications for some liability on the part of the school district for a basic failure to provide career exploration and other instructional activities related to development of postschool goals tied to student needs, preference, and interests, her case was further complicated by the fact that she had not yet been provided a viable means of communication. Her most reliable communication method continued to be gestural combined with the use of guttural sounds, primarily being interpreted by her most familiar family members.

The point is, how can one even begin to express needs, interests, and preferences if that person has not yet been provided the basic tool of functional communication? This places considerable emphasis on the need for the IEP team to ensure that efforts are made to meet IDEA requirements for participation in the transition and IEP process, the professionals involved must be certain that the student has not only been given the instructional and vocational services that are fundamental to successful transition, but also the AT that fully supports the student's realization of his or her academic and employment potential.

The student in question had been referred for an AT evaluation; however, ironically, this motion had been delayed by the speech pathologist contending it would yield no new information. So, we have an individual who was attending her annual IEP meetings with no means, verbally or otherwise, to communicate her thoughts or preferences; and as a result, it was concluded she was "undecided." Although this is a gross example of the system not fulfilling its responsibility to IDEA transition requirements, the example also demonstrates a failure to meet adequately standards for minimal consideration of student needs in terms of his or her communication disability and the need for AT service. This situation is further compounded by the fact that the professionals involved believed that they had met the requirements of the student's participation because of her attendance at all IEP and transition planning meetings. Obviously, the student's physical presence at the meetings without the tools or technology to communicate meaningfully does not meet the basic requirements of IEP development. If there is an IEP team that is unable to perceive the most obvious technology needs in relation to instruction and transition, what faith can we have of teams dealing any more appropriately with students who have milder disabilities?

For the most part, though, this type of situation goes beyond the implications for professional development and training needed for professionals to make knowledgeable decisions. Training is ineffective without being predicated on a value system that pursues transition planning with the mindset that even the most involved students *all* have needs, interests, and preferences. Supporting students in attaining their dreams requires exhaustive and innovative efforts to use all the tools at our disposal to help them realize their goals. This is invariably inhibited or denied when we approach IDEA requirements as "process" requirements rather than viewing IDEA also as an increased "expectation" for students with disabilities to benefit from their school experience, which builds to attaining an adult lifestyle of choice, not of limited circumstance.

We can embark on massive professional development initiatives designed to raise the awareness and skill levels of educators serving students with disabilities, but practices will not change until we change both values and skills (Derer, Polsgrove, & Rieth, 1996; Johnson & Guy, 1997). As set forth at a TASH meeting by Colleen Wieck, some look at abilities of persons with disabilities to learn and say, "I'll believe it when I see it," but as Ms. Wieck pointedly noted, "you can only see it when you believe it." The provision of technology as a tool for persons with disabilities to communicate, access and use environments, and for instruction, can be the most significant catalyst to transition success for many individuals with disabilities.

Outcome-Oriented Process

When focusing upon an "outcome-oriented process," we need to know what specific outcomes we are focusing upon that pertain uniquely to the student in question. In transition planning, typically the focus is upon outcomes related to employment and/or continuing education, residential, and recreational choices.

If we look at technology in relation to the ability to communicate, access, and use natural environments and/or for effective instruction and learning, then connections of AT to potential outcomes begin to present themselves. In terms of communication, it may be related to looking at the communicative needs in the targeted postschool environments as well as looking at the nature of the communication technology that is most likely to be conducive to successful functioning in that setting. For employment, it may mean that we need to do some situational assessments for determining vocational needs of students with disabilities (Meers, 1992; Rudrud, Ziarnik, Bernstein, & Ferrara, 1984). The same can be said of students with physical disabilities who benefit as well from an ecological approach to employment. Providing high school students with physical disabilities real-work experiences and concurrent access to AT assessment may significantly increase their options to enter successfully the competitive job market after graduation.

Ultimately, incorporating comprehensive AT assessment in the overall vocational evaluation process may eliminate many barriers in determining a student's preferences, aptitudes, and potentials with regard to employment (Behrmann & Schepis, 1994). For many students, until we know the exact communicative and environmental demands of the actual vocational settings of choice, we do not know what form of AT is needed or how to program it to match the environment(s). Just for purposes of career exploration and work-based learning alone, all students, including students with disabilities, can benefit from real-work experiences prior to exiting school.

Another major point that pertains to the outcome-oriented process is technology used as a tool for effective instruction or learning. The amendments to IDEA of 1997 specify that beginning at age 14 there is to be a statement of transition services under the applicable components of the IEP that focuses on the child's course of study. There are at least two critical issues when IEP teams look at the student's course of study: (1) the use of computers or other technologies as an accommodation for learning and (2) the growing expectation of computer literacy in the job market. In addition, there are new requirements regarding evidence in the IEP of the child's involvement and progress in the general curriculum. Also, states are required to establish goals for the performance of children with disabilities and how these goals are consistent with other goals and standards for all children. For many states, this results in an increased emphasis on students with disabilities being able to meet the content standards of the general curriculum versus their being taught on a separate or "watered-down" curriculum (Ellis, 1997).

Students with disabilities are dropping out of school at an alarmingly high rate, and if content standards and requirements increase, this will only increase student frustrations and tendency to leave school early. A major key will be the ex-amination of technology as a form of specially designed instruction that in some way needs to be a part of every student's IEP. For example, at the 1994 conference of the Council for Exceptional Children, Lahm and Morrissette, (1994) outlined seven areas of instruction where AT could assist students with mild disabilities. These areas include organization, writing assistance, productivity, access to reference materials, cognitive assistance, and materials modification. Each of these areas has implications for various forms of computer software and hardware that need to be available for student use. This is not to say that every student needs to have a personal computer as a form of AT on their IEP, but if students are to meet the increasing performance demands for graduation, then computers must be accessible to all students with disabilities and should be located where learning takes place, that is, in the classroom, not in a laboratory (Behrmann, 1994).

The second point is that, over the next decade it is estimated that up to 75% of all employment will involve the use of computers (Bender et. al., 1995). Many jobs and tasks that once required skills that were difficult for persons to perform are now computerized (Sowers, 1991). All students, including those with disabilities, must have a course of study that includes basic computer literacy in order to compete in the job market of the future. In addition, the computer itself can serve as an accommodation that allows the student with a disability to perform parts of job tasks that once were dependent on higher level skills (e, g., inventory, filing, pricing, etc.).

Movement from School to Postschool Settings

Reference was made earlier to the use of AT for a variety of purposes (i.e., communication, environmental access or control, or for instruction). When students are in school, we have a fairly good opportunity to look at students' needs in relation to their use of AT supports for success in the school setting, although admittedly most schools are only beginning to understand the breadth of technology that exists and how to use it.

When a student exits school, he or she hopefully will spend the day in a diverse number of settings, whether for continued schooling, employment, recreation, or leisure and chores at home. Except for the home setting, most of these adult settings will be somewhat new to the student, and it will take time for them to understand and learn what they must do to benefit most from the experiences gained in each new setting. This is where possibly the AT that was most useful in school is not so well adapted to the new environments of adulthood.

This places the critical emphasis on opportunity for the student to explore and experience these settings as much as possible before exiting school in order to determine if the communicative, environmental, or instructional technology that he or she uses is best fitted to the adult environments. This must be more than "exposure"; it should allow the students to spend some meaningful time in the settings so that they can truly grasp the realities and requirements of these novel environments. Only by an experiential approach to transition that minimizes the difference between the last day of school and the first day of adulthood can the student and his or her transition team adequately anticipate the unique AT supports and services that may be needed.

Robert Williams (1991) provided a view of AT that might help us to understand better how it could change during transition. Williams (1991) stated that:

> We must come to view assistive technology as being like art in at least one very critical respect. Its beauty and power lies not in the hands of its inventors or innovators. Rather, its real beauty and power to transform our lives lies in the eyes of the beholders, in the eyes of those of us who actually choose to use and depend on it to get on with the act of living our lives as we see fit (p. 9).

His statement points out that the best transition plan possible for movement from school to postschool activities cannot be determined by the professionals but is defined by the individuals and their families actually "living their lives" in the real contexts of their potential adulthood prior to exiting school. Otherwise, we relegate ourselves to a "guessing game" of what the student's needs will be without the experiential information to make valid decisions through transition planning.

Interagency Responsibilities

Interagency responsibility in relation to AT must be clear if a student is to have the technological supports often essential for postschool success. One of the most frequent issues regarding transition and the use of AT comes from the fact that when a student has AT included in his or her IEP, then this technology has been purchased by local, state, or federal funds. The AT cannot just follow the individual into postschool settings without some agreement for transfer of ownership from the school agency to a postschool agency, or preferably to the individual him- or herself.

If the AT has been purchased through a medicaid reimbursement process, then it becomes the property of the individual, and the need is for examining a postschool agency (e.g., Vocational Rehabilitation) for assistance with maintenance or evaluation of the continued appropriateness of the device for certain environments, such as an employment setting. If the AT has not become the property of the individual, then the transition interagency responsibilities must include a plan for how the AT supports can be picked up by an adult service agency who subsequently pays the school to provide them to the individual beyond graduation. There may already be interagency agreements in place at the state or local level that establish the procedures for this transfer of AT, or they may need to be developed to assure equity and accountability in this process.

An interagency matter to be resolved, though, may relate to the fact that once the students exit school, there are a variety of environments in which they will need to utilize their AT. For instance, if a student uses an augmentative communication system, then most likely this will need to be available for use in the workplace, home, and community. The rehabilitation agency may be able to support access to this AT in the workplace or for continued schooling but may not be able to finance its use in the home and community. So, there may be another agency, such as developmental disabilities services or even a community civic organization, that can help to offset hardware or software costs for applications in these other settings. However, if these details of interagency responsibility are not dealt with prior to the student's exiting school, then it becomes much more difficult to reconvene the transition team to devise a plan of action.

During transition, AT issues related to equipment, training, and successful implementation should be planned for in terms of:

- How this technology will relate to transition success (e.g., use of a communication device that needs to be tailored to performance in a school or in a job setting, etc.)?
- How the technology will be able to follow the student from each school setting and then to postschool settings?
- How will financing be arranged (e.g., selling device to another agency, Medicaid reimbursement, interagency agreement, employer support, status of any maintenance agreements, etc.)?
- What will be the continued appropriateness of the technology for use in the student's school or postschool settings (e.g., device may be too stigmatizing to student, device may not be mobile enough for job requirements, student may need new or different device, etc.)?
- What training will be needed and who will do it for those who will be supporting the stu-

dent in the school or the postschool settings and how to connect them to the training source (e.g., need for directions from an AT specialist, OT/PT, or SLP)?

The IEP team needs to provide documentation of considering the necessity for AT for each student with a disability based on its relation to implementation of the IEP. If AT has been an identified need for any student of high school age, there should be a plan for how the technology will be handled during this process of planning for transition to life after school as outlined in the following checklist:

- Has the IEP been kept updated as individual goals are met?
- Have school representatives talked with students and parents about vocational, postsecondary education, or adult living opportunities?
- Has assistive technology (AT) been considered in the child's IEPs and transition plans?
- Are students provided exposure to specific jobs and places of employment?
- Is there a representative who can help to take advantage of available resources, employment, and postsecondary education and opportunities?
- Have state and federal laws that offer assistance in training, rehabilitation, and eventual employment been utilized?
- Have issues of AT and work-site modifications been addressed with potential employers?
- Is there a process for how AT devices will transfer to and/or be purchased by another agency to support postsecondary activities?

Role of Technology in Postschool Environments

This chapter has provided information about technology, from its definition to consideration and implementation factors. Through this discussion, AT application factors have also been presented. However, one area that has not been reviewed is the role of technology in postschool activities or environments. The role of technology will be discussed in light of work and community environments.

It should be noted that the individual transition planning (ITP) team needs to consider all aspects of an individual's life from high school to adulthood, understanding what technology might be required as part of the job and what modifications or adaptations, including determination of the AT, must be part of the planning process (Fisher & Gardner, 1999).

One also needs to have a sense of what aspects of postschool environments relate to technology. By looking at each postschool setting in which the person needs to function and evaluating the nature and needs of the individual for AT that is unique to each of those environments, an interagency team can more clearly sort out what and how each agency should contribute its resources to assure access by the individual to the proper AT for each desired setting.

Work Environments

A person with a disability may require a high-tech or low-tech accommodation in order to perform tasks that comprise a specific job. The accommodation should be directly related to an essential job function and lead to an increase in the productivity of the worker. The ecological inventory approach to assessing learning needs is an authentic assessment procedure which allows for identifying the specific skills required in a work setting in order to meet expected performance demands. Once an ecological inventory has been completed, a student repertoire inventory can provide an accurate measure of the student's existing performance against the skills identified in the ecological inventory (Falvey, Brown, Lyon, Baumgart, & Schroeder, 1980). The student repertoire inventory tells us specifically what the student can and cannot do, which results in a discrepancy analysis of the student's performance in the real-work setting. From this,

we can develop an adaptation hypothesis, which may well lead us to identify the way in which AT can bridge the gap between current performance and expected performance of specific work skills.

An example is a student that wanted to work in a grocery store in the produce section and needed to learn how to weigh out 10-pound bags of onions to within a tenth of a pound and to put these bags out for purchase. The student had a mental disability that prevented his understanding of how to use decimals, so an adaptation was needed to allow for successful performance. The student's job coach suggested a simple assistive device after conducting an ecological inventory and discrepancy analysis of the skills that the student was unable to perform in the sequence of bagging onions. The student was able to "eyeball" the amount of onions to go into the bag within half a pound by having a completed model for comparison. Then, the student was given a picture of a bag of onions, with an arrow pointing in the bag for numbers on the scale's digital readout that were between 9.5, 9.6, 9.7, and 9.8. There was a picture of an arrow going out of the bag for numbers that were 10.2, 10.3. 10.4, and so on. Therefore, since the student could use this adaptive device of a visual guide for when to add or take out onions to get within one-tenth of a 10-pound measure, he was able to complete a task successfully, which, on the surface, seemed insurmountable because of his cognitive disability. It was solely a matter of identifying what the student could not do and using creative ingenuity to develop the assistive device that circumvented the need for skills that were not in the student's repertoire.

Sowers and Powers (1991) outlined three phases of workplace adaptations that need to be considered when analyzing a work site: (1) initial design prior to an individual's job start, (2) intensive adaptation during the first month, and (3) ongoing adaptation refinement in response to problems or job changes. The employer as well as the employee should be active in each phase, thereby providing a stakeholder relationship.

During the first phase, an analysis regarding the accessibility of the work site and each of the tasks that the individual must perform is conducted. During this phase, it is important to identify the elements that would influence accessibility or job performance (Sowers, 1995). At this stage, the employment team needs to brainstorm possible solutions to overcome possible accessibility or job performance difficulties. Furthermore, the employer must agree to the specific adaptations that are necessary for a person to gain access to the work site as well as the modifications that need to be made in order for the prospective employee to perform in his or her job. According to Sowers (1995), it is critical not to overadapt, in that adaptation should only be considered when, "it is clear that a person could not learn to perform a job or component of a job without any adaptations" (p. 172).

When analyzing a job, one usually may find several solutions or adaptations. Consideration of adaptations that would be the least intrusive in the workplace and yet assist the individual in performing the job tasks should be made. The least intrusive approach affects not only the employee, but also lessens the impact that the potential adaptation might have upon coworkers. Cost also is always a factor. Although some experts in the field recommend applying the least expensive device, this viewpoint is shortsighted. The same concepts used when determining the AT through a student's IEP/ITP apply to analyzing the work site and determining appropriate adaptations or modifications for an individual to complete the tasks required for that job. First, one must identify what the individual's functional abilities are, and what functional areas need some type of assistance in order to complete the necessary tasks. Then, the next step is to match the individual's needs with the required tasks. By conducting this type of analysis, a more successful employment placement will likely occur.

The second phase encompasses intensive design/adaptations. During this phase, once the tasks have been identified that need to be adapted, it is necessary to try out the various adaptations/modifications. One must understand that this phase is important, trial use to ascertain if the AT meets the needs of the individual in performing the job is essential. This, then, leads into the third phase, which is referred to as "design refinement." Applying various modifications will provide all concerned individuals with important information, as well as determine if further adaptations are needed, if the adaptations provide the necessary support, or if other solutions should be determined.

These three phases can be applied not only to analyzing potential work sites, but also to community-based instruction activities as well as to vocational education programs. The key is to look at the overall picture of the demands that will be required in order for an individual to function within the selected environment. From this analysis, one should determine possible solutions that could include commercially made adaptations, low-tech modifications, adaptation of an existing device or implement, or whether fabrication of a device or implement is needed. It is best to try the solution out, and then determine if it meets the employers and employee's needs and if not, to try other solutions. There often are many possible solutions to meet any one need an individual might have in order to perform a job successfully.

Lastly, a widely held belief of employers is that accommodations are expensive, but as shown by the earlier examples, some of the simplest solutions are the best solutions. Research on job accommodations (Pati & Morrison 1982; Hendricks & Hirsh, 1991; Job Accommodation Network, 1987) has indicated that the accommodations usually cost $500 or less. In a follow-up study conducted by the Job Accommodation Network (1994), regarding the cost of work-site adaptations/modifications, in 19% of the cases, the accommodation had no dollar cost, 49% cost less than $500, and 14% cost more than $2,000.

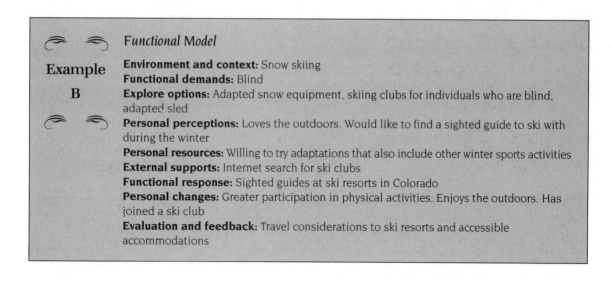

Functional Model

Example

B

Environment and context: Snow skiing

Functional demands: Blind

Explore options: Adapted snow equipment, skiing clubs for individuals who are blind, adapted sled

Personal perceptions: Loves the outdoors. Would like to find a sighted guide to ski with during the winter

Personal resources: Willing to try adaptations that also include other winter sports activities

External supports: Internet search for ski clubs

Functional response: Sighted guides at ski resorts in Colorado

Personal changes: Greater participation in physical activities. Enjoys the outdoors. Has joined a ski club

Evaluation and feedback: Travel considerations to ski resorts and accessible accommodations

Community Environments

Assistive technology solutions should also be considered in the variety of community environments where an individual might participate in activities, including recreational and leisure facilities and public facilities, such as libraries, courthouses, shopping malls, and even homes. Each environment may place a different functional demand on an individual with a disability to participate.

Community environments can be approached in the same manner as work environments in the use of authentic assessment strategies to determine what performance-based demand requires an adaptation. For instance, a skill that often challenges students with more severe disabilities in community environments is knowing how to deal with the proper amount of change to put in a vending machine to purchase a snack or a soft drink. One strategy is the provision of coin cards that provide a picture or a soft drink or similar item and then having a picture of three quarters so that the student can see how much money it takes to buy a particular item merely by matching to the sample. Another way is just to show the student how to put in one dollar bill, which is the amount that most items will cost, or somewhat less, so

that there is no real need to understand fully how to count change. Just teaching the student how to retrieve any change that comes out of the machine is sufficient for that task.

The rest of this chapter focuses upon three areas: recreation and leisure, travel, and home environments. Transition teams often overlook these environments. However, each of these areas is important to an individual. Through the use of technology, one has greater access for participation as well as for the potential of greater independence.

Recreational and Leisure

According to Moon, Hart, Komissar, and Friedlander (1995), recreational and leisure activities can include almost anything and may fall into the following classifications: "(a) physical, cultural, or social, (b) indoor or outdoor, (c) spectator or participant, (d) formal or informal, (e) independent, cooperative or competitive or (f) sports, games, hobbies" (p. 188). Assistive technology within this environment might include adapted easels, adapted skin-diving equipment, beeper balls, adapted sport wheelchairs, and switch-activated potter's wheels to name just a few.

Once a determination of an individual's preferences, likes and dislikes, has been conducted, then there is the process of matching the AT with the individual's needs and the activities that are being pursued. For example, a student who is blind has indicated that he wants to snow ski. If we use the functional model, then the analysis may be outlined as shown in Example B.

So far, the discussion has centered on the types of devices that might be used in order for an individual to participate. However, there are other considerations that should be made. For example, modification of the activity: Will rules need to be changed? If the activity is a team sport, how will accommodations affect the other members? Would the accommodations create other barriers to participation? These are all important factors that must be considered. Additionally, one very important factor involves the accessibility to the program or sports facility.

The Americans with Disabilities Act (ADA) (P.L. 101-336) contains standards in which a public building, such as a restaurant, sports facilities, shopping malls, and the like, must abide by in order to allow all individuals access to that particular facility (Moon et al., 1995). Sometimes this might include physical modifications, such as building a ramp, providing a bowling ball chute at a bowling alley, or providing audio description services for theatrical events or museum tours. Other examples might include accessible seating for individuals who use a wheelchair so that they can attend movies or sporting events. Therefore, the role of technology is expanded to include not only one's individual needs but also the needs of others.

Travel

Although not a community environment, travel considerations should be determined in order to allow all individuals the ability to move from one community environment to another. Of course, basic travel modes include walking and driving. Travel aids are available for both types of modes.

For example, a travel aid for an individual who is blind or visually impaired might be a long cane or a guide dog. Newer technologies being introduced include electronic travel devices. Some of these devices emit ultrasound waves and an individual listens through earphones to detect echoes that obstacles may make (Leventhal, 1996). Additionally, there are devices that use satellites to help an individual maneuver in both walking in towns and cities. This type of technology is also installed in automobiles.

Of course, automobiles are modified in many ways, again depending on the needs of the individual with a disability. For example, vans can be fitted with many types of lifts. Steering wheels can be adapted with special implements that allow easy turning of the wheel without moving one's arms. Gas pedals and brakes can be adjusted, by either raising, lowering, adjusting the amount of pressure needed to activate the vehicle, or hand controls can be installed to allow an individual to accelerate or stop (Langone, 2000).

Another aspect of travel involves other modes of transportation, such as trains, subways, public buses, and airplanes. Accessible travel for public transportation is also required under the ADA. For example, today many subway systems are accessible to individuals who use a wheelchair. Some subway systems have an accessible entrance or elevator for entry. The doors are opened wide enough and there are places within the subway train to accommodate a wheelchair.

The need for accessible transportation is particularly critical for an individual to be able to travel to his or her place of work, as well as to get to various community environments. This need for accessible transportation is confounded for many in rural areas. Although there are more accessible transportation venues within metropolitan areas, that is not the case for many people living in rural communities. Therefore, brainstorming possible modes of transportation and determining how an individual might get from one place to the next may be challenging. For example, a young man with physical disabilities lived out of town on a farm. He was able to obtain a full-time job in town; however, he had no means of accessible transportation. It was imperative during his transition meeting to suggest ideas about how he could keep his job and yet not move from his residence after graduating from high school. One idea that the team came up with included adapting a golf cart. This idea was a possibility; however, there were concerns about the winter months. It was decided that a rehabilitation engineer could help to adapt a golf cart including winterizing the vehicle.

Home

Within the home environment, the most typical type of AT often is called daily living aids (DLAs). These devices are usually low tech in nature and are used by all individuals. Some DLAs have a specific purpose (Cook & Hussey, 1995), such as a specially designed cutting board that allows one to cut food or to butter bread with one hand.

However, there are many types of DLAs, for example, self-care aids. Types of equipment found within this group include food preparations, dressing, and hygiene aids (Cook & Hussey, 1995). Adapted silverware, drinking aides, plates with enlarged rims, adapted button hooks, talking thermometers, zipper pulls, adapted shaving equipment, modified toothbrush handles, gripping cuffs for brooms and mops, and long-handled reaching devices are but a few examples of DLAs.

Additionally, there are DLAs that allow individuals to control their environment, such as talking alarm clocks, shake awake alarm clocks, voice-activated control units, environmental control units, and remote control units, which also are types of aids that help people with disabilities to be more independent and self-sufficient within their home environment. Many control units increase the ability to access and monitor appliances, heating and cooling units, and phones.

Conclusion

Various issues and strategies have been identified in this chapter for using AT to contribute to a student's successful transition. As a result, a better understanding of the role that technology plays in one's life is a key point. Each day, month, and year, the society's use of technology increases by leaps and bounds. However, certain misconceptions remain about the use of technology by individuals with disabilities. Efforts to dispel this misconception are essential. Training professionals about the many types of AT, its uses, and the potential positive outcomes that might help to facilitate its use is crucial if individuals with disabilities are to be given the opportunity to profit from its use. Although there are legislative acts that encourage the consideration of AT, only through increased efforts to train professionals and parents will the use of AT be realized for students within our schools.

It is also important to note that technology does not just encompass the use of computers; rather, technology is a continuum of low-tech to high-tech solutions. The exciting aspect of all of this is the fact that the possibilities are endless as to how technology might be used. The possibilities can only be limited by one's imagination. Also, many barriers are decreasing, and as a result, individuals potentially have greater opportunities for participation or access to activities, work environments, and public facilities. No longer should individuals with disabilities not be afforded opportunities that were once only available to their nondisabled peers.

However, technology is not a panacea: Only through careful consideration, assessment, and ongoing follow-up will technologys assist individuals to achieve their education and transition goals. Technology for technology sake is not the answer: Only through purposeful observation, analysis, and opportunities to try out various devices prior to the final selection will the potential of technology be realized. Central to the successful application of technology during the transition years is developing a clear vision of the student's lifestyle of choice. From this vision, we must not judge whether or not their dreams are attainable but should challenge ourselves to combine our most creative thoughts and knowledge with the use of technology to help the student make his or her dreams a reality.

Study Questions

1. What is the definition of assistive technology (AT) and rehabilitation technology? What are the commonalities and differences between these two types of technology?
2. Identify the categories of AT, and provide examples of devices that might be found within each category.
3. Identify the three important characteristics that always should be considered when determining the need for the use of AT.
4. Discuss the importance of a multidisciplinary team when determining an individual's needs for AT.
5. Discuss how technology may relate to an individual's transition success (e.g., use of a communication device that needs to be tailored to performance in a school or job setting, etc.)
6. Describe the roles, constraints, and perspectives of the stakeholders during a transition meeting regarding the identification and implementation of AT.
7. Discuss some of the issues of how AT might be addressed in an individual's work, community, and/or postsecondary environments.
8. Describe a process as to how AT devices will be transferred to and/or purchased by another agency to support postsecondary activities?
9. For successful implementation of AT, many factors come into play. Discuss these factors in light of how they might affect the outcome of an individual's transition meeting.
10. Identify some of the barriers that might prevent an individual from obtaining or using AT in the school, work, or community.

Web Sites

ABLEDATA—A searchable database of products, devices, and information on assistive technology-related items that puts assistive technology at one's fingertips:
www.abledata.com

Alliance for Technology—The alliance for technology access (ATA) is a network of community-based resource centers dedicated to provide information and to support services to children and adults with disabilities, and to increase their use of standard, assistive, and information technologies:
www.ataccess.org/

CAST—Center for Applied Special Technology provides opportunities for individuals with disabilities through the development and innovative uses of technology:
http://www.cast.org/

Closing the Gap—Closing the Gap is an internationally recognized source for information on innovative applications of computer technology in special education and rehabilitation:
www.closingthegap.com

EASI (Equal Access to Software and Information)—EASI's mission is to serve as a resource to the education community by providing information and guidance in the area of access-to-information technologies by individuals with disabilities:
http://www.rit.edu/~easi/

Disability Resources, Inc.—Information about legal rights, financial resources, assistive technology, employment opportunities, housing modifications, and educational options, transportation and mobility services:
http://www.disabilityresources.org

Giant Disability Resource Page—Independence, Inc. in collaboration with the Northeast (Kansas) Assistive Technology Site (NEAT) has created a resource page of links to Disability Related and Assistive Technology Sites on the World Wide Web:
lawrence.ks.us/~indepinc/ability.html

Job Accommodation Network—The Job Accommodation Network (JAN) is an international toll-free consulting service that provides information about job accommodations and the employability of people with disabilities. JAN also provides information regarding the Americans with Disabilities Act (ADA):

janweb.icdi.wvu.edu

RESNA's World Wide Web—Assistive Technology Resources
Links to Assistive Tech Act Projects and other assistive tech-related web sites:

www.resna.org/taproject

The Trace Center—This site includes links to Trace Program Areas; Project Descriptions, Services, and Contact Information; Trace Publications and Media Catalog Online; Designing an Accessible World; and a Cooperative Electronic Library:

trace.wisc.edu

SECTION III

Transition Planning

11   Participatory Decision-Making: Innovative Practices that Increase Student Self-Determination

12   Transition Planning

13   Coordinating Transition Services

14   Family Involvement

11

Participatory Decision-Making

Innovative Practices that Increase Student Self-Determination

James E. Martin
Laura Huber Marshall
Randall L. De Pry

Your life is the sum result of all the choices you make, both consciously and unconsciously. If you can control the process of choosing, you can take control of all aspects of your life. You can find the freedom that comes from being in charge of yourself.

—Robert F. Bennett

The previous chapters described the systems and programs designed to help youth in the transition to adulthood and were primarily concerned with developing effective transition programs and services. This chapter addresses the issue of how these systems and programs can be brought under the control of the individuals they are designed to serve. The authors describe self-determination as both a means and an outcome of the transition process. It is described as a means of addressing the essential transition elements of (1) determining the student's needs, interests, and preferences; (2) coordinating activities; and (3) promoting movement from school to postschool environments. Self-determination also is described as both a means of addressing the essential element of developing an outcome-oriented process and a critical outcome of the transition process itself (Halloran, 1993).

Educators increase students' self-determination by teaching skills and by providing participatory decision-making opportunities where students practice what they have learned. Many typical school functions do not allow student participatory decision making. However, by looking at these typical functions with a self-determination outcome in mind, what are mundane become innovative teaching opportunities: ones that enable students to become participatory decisionmakers. As students become participatory decisionmakers, they put into practice their learned self-determination skills.

Critical Point Self-determination must be infused into the teaching process.

Four scenarios shown in Table 11–1 depict how typical school functions convert into innovative opportunities to learn self-determination skills. These examples and nonexamples provide a glimpse into what is possible. Our field is just now beginning to realize the numerous opportunities that exist to teach self-determination every day by converting typical teacher-directed school functions into participatory decision-making opportunities.

Self-Determination: The Basic Facts

Since the late 1960s, our professional literature has discussed self-determination. Over time, self-determination conceptualizations split into two strands: (1) the choice strand and (2) the goal setting and attainment strand.

The Choice Strand

The earliest, and a few modern self-determination definitions, cluster into the choice definitional strand. Within these conceptualizations, choice becomes a right that people with disabilities exercise (Ippoliti, Peppey, & Depoy, 1994). Self-determination begins with choice and motivates action. A few of these definitions include:

Nirje (1972): Self-determination is a critical component of the normalization principle. Choices, wishes, and aspirations of people with disabilities must be considered when actions affect them.

Deci and Ryan (1985): Self-determination is the capacity of individuals to choose and then have these choices be the driving force behind their action. Individuals are self-determined to the extent that they freely choose their behaviors (Deci & Ryan, 1994).

Wehmeyer (1992, 1994): Self-determination refers to the attitudes and abilities required to act as the primary causal agent in one's own life and to make choices regarding one's actions free from undue external influence.

The trend in special education is toward greater involvement of students in their own education by providing them opportunities to make their own choices (Smith, 1994). Opportunities to engage first in simple, then increasingly

TABLE 11–1

Case Scenarios

Scenario	Typical Functions	Innovative Opportunities
Scenario 1: The IEP Meeting	The special education teacher invites a student to his IEP meeting, but he is not provided with any instruction about the IEP or what to do at the meeting. The student does not want to attend and does not come to school the day of his meeting. Teachers, support staff, and parents talk about the student's interests, skills, needs, and last year's IEP goal performance. They make plans for this year without any direct student input.	Prior to the IEP meeting, Sean learns about the IEP, the meeting, and prepares a script of what to do and say. During the meeting, Sean actively participates and even directs part of *his* IEP meeting. He begins by stating the purpose, introduces everyone, talks about his interests, skills, and how he did on accomplishing last year's IEP goals. He asks for teacher and parent support to accomplish his goals.
Scenario 2: IEP Goal Attainment	The special education teacher assumes responsibility for attaining the IEP goals. The teacher builds supports, implements strategies, and collects data. The student does not know her IEP goals or how she is progressing toward accomplishing them.	Bekah shares the responsibility for attaining her IEP goals. The teacher educates Bekah on how to accomplish her goals. Each week Bekah completes a plan to accomplish a portion of her goals and then evaluates the success of her plan at the end of the week.
Scenario 3: Course Scheduling	The special education team determines what classes students take for the next semester. The team considers their perception of student skills, limits, and interests in building the student schedule.	Students build their own schedule in consultation with their teachers. Students learn what classroom characteristics they like and learn their school skills and limits. The students next consider their needs and goals, then match their interests, skills, and limits to required and optional courses.
Scenario 4: Functional Assessment	The special education team conducts a functional assessment in reaction to a persistent behavior problem, then develops a behavior support plan.	Sean actively participates in the functional assessment process, helps to analyze and interpret data, and develops a support plan in collaboration with the team. Sean shares responsibility in accomplishing the goals of his behavior support plan.

complex choice making must be infused throughout students' education (Winup, 1994). When educators provide individuals choice-making opportunities, students express their individuality, and teachers show that they value and respect their students (Coupe-O'Kane,

Porter, & Taylor, 1994). Belief in choice making impacts practice, as the following three examples demonstrate. First, when teachers provide students task choice opportunities, disruptive behavior significantly decreases and learning increases (Munk & Repp, 1994). Second, when students are given a choice of vocational tasks, their productivity increases (Mithaug & Mar, 1980). Third, when students read text materials that interest them, the students comprehend and enjoy the task better than with material they do not enjoy (Ryan, Connell, & Plant, 1990).

Critical Point   Self-determination practices improve learning and productivity because students are engaged in tasks they have chosen and are meaningful to them.

Special educators said in a statewide survey that they consider choice as the primary self-determination strategy. When asked what strategies constitute self-determination, 91% of the special education teachers identified choice making (Agran, Snow, & Swaner, 1999). They identified goal setting as the second ranked strategy.

The Goal Setting and Attainment Strand

This second self-determination strand includes choice but emphasizes goal setting and the goal attainment process. Ward (1994), who champions this view, wrote that the optimal outcome of the self-determination process is setting a goal and achieving it. A few of the goal attainment definitions include:

- Ward (1988): Self-determined individuals define goals for themselves and take the initiative in achieving those goals.
- Martin, Huber Marshall, and Maxson (1993): Self-determined individuals know what they want and how to get it. From an awareness of personal needs, self-determined individuals set goals, then they doggedly pursue *their* goals. This involves asserting *their* presence, making *their* needs known, evaluating progress toward meeting *their* goals, adjusting *their* performance as needed, and creating unique approaches to solve problems.
- Wolman, Campeau, DuBois, Mithaug, and Stolarski (1994): Self-determined individuals know and can express their own needs, interests, and abilities. They set appropriate goals,

make choices and plans in pursuit of their goals, and make adjustments as needed to achieve their goals.
- Field and Hoffman (1994, 1995): A self-determined person defines and achieves their goals from a base of knowing and valuing themselves.
- Wehmeyer, Palmer, Agran, Mithaug, and Martin (in press): Self-determination consists of the set of skills that are needed to act on a person's environment to achieve goals that satisfy one's needs and interests.

Critical Point   Goal attainment strategies are critical in ensuring that students with disabilities are truly self-determined.

When goal attainment defines self-determination, certain practices result. Martin and Huber Marshall (1995) indicated that students should identify their needs and interests across different transition domains; establish goals that match their interests, skills, and limits; develop a plan to accomplish their goals; evaluate their progress toward meeting their goals, and make adjustments in their support, strategies, or goals. An opportunity for this to occur, for example, exists within the IEP process: getting ready for the meeting, the meeting itself, and the subsequent goal attainment process. When typical school functions change to become participatory decision-making opportunities, students actively participate as an equal team member to help establish goals.

Which Strand?

Just having the opportunity to make choices and decisions does not ensure that a person will be self-determined (Wehmeyer, 1997, p. 36). Self-determined individuals *choose* goals that match their interests, skills, and limits (Martin & Huber Marshall, 1995). The goal attainment strand includes choice but goes much further. Goal attainment strategies empower individuals to achieve their choices (Wehmeyer, Agran, & Hughes, 1998).

TABLE 11–2

ChoiceMaker Self-Determination Constructs

1. *Self-awareness:*	Identify needs; identify interests; identify and understand strengths
	Identify and understand limitations; identify own values
2. *Self-advocacy:*	Assertively state wants and needs; assertively state rights; determine needed supports
	Pursue needed support; obtain and evaluate needed support; conduct own affairs
3. *Self-efficacy:*	Expects to obtain goals
4. *Decision making:*	Assess situation demands; set goals; set standards
	Identify information to make decisions; consider past solutions for new situation; generate new creative solutions
	Consider options; choose best option; develop plan
5. *Independent performance:*	Initiate tasks on time; complete tasks on time; use self-management strategies
	Perform tasks to standards; follow through on own plan
6. *Self-evaluation:*	Monitor task performance; compare performance to standards; evaluate effectiveness of self-management strategies
	Determine if plan completed and goal met
7. *Adjustment:*	Change goals; change standards; change plan
	Change strategies; change support; persistently adjust
	Use environmental feedback to aid adjustment

Source: Adapted from a table originally published in: Martin, J. E., & Marshall, L. H. (1996a). ChoiceMaker: Infusing self-determination instruction into the IEP and transition process. In Sands, D. J. & Wehmeyer, M. L. (Eds.), *Self-determination across the life span* (pp. 215–236). Baltimore: Paul H. Brookes. Used with permission from University Technology Corp.

We consider the goal attainment strand as the most important for students in transition because it includes choice yet emphasizes goal setting and attainment.

Self-Determination Components

Martin and Huber Marshall (1996a) interviewed adults with disabilities, parents of children with disabilities, conducted a multidiscipline literature review, and undertook a national survey to determine a set of self-determination skills. This resulted in seven self-determination constructs (see Table 11–2). These include (1) self-awareness, (2) self-advocacy, (3) self-efficacy, (4) decision making, (5) independent performance, (6) self-evaluation, and (7) adjustment. These seven constructs breakdown into 37 additional components.

Other goal attainment definitions of self-determination include similar conceptualizations. These definitions consider goal setting, planning, evaluation, and adjustment as central components. Field and Hoffman (1994) developed a self-determination model consisting of five areas: (1) know yourself, (2) value yourself, (3) plan, (4) act, and (5) experience outcomes and learn. Mithaug, Wehmeyer, Agran, Martin, and Palmer's (1998) self-determination learning model poses questions that students ask, then answer across three phases: (1) setting learning goals, (2) constructing a learning plan, and (3) adjusting behaviors. The Mithaug et al. (1998) model also provides teacher objectives to facilitate answering the questions. We present these questions and selected teacher objectives in Table 11–3.

TABLE 11–3

Self-Determination Learning Model

Phase 1: Setting a Learning Goal

Student Questions

- What do I want to learn?
- What do I know about it now?
- What must change to learn what I do not know?
- What can I do to produce that change?

Selected Teacher Objectives

- Enable student to identify specific strengths and instructional needs in a specific area.
- Enable student to evaluate and communicate preferences, interests, beliefs, and values that relate to this area.
- Assist student to gather information about opportunities and barriers in physical and social environment.
- Teach student to prioritize need.
- Teach student to state a goal and identify criteria for achieving that goal.

Phase 2: Constructing a Learning Plan

Student Questions

- What can I do now to change what I do not know?
- What will prevent me from taking action now to produce that change?
- What can I do to remove these obstacles?
- When will I take action and remove these obstacles?

Selected Teacher Objectives

- Enable student to self-evaluate progress toward goal achievement.
- Enable student to determine plan of action to bridge gap between self-evaluated current status and self-identified goal status.
- Enable student to identify most appropriate instructional strategies.
- Enable student to identify and implement strategies to overcome barriers and obstacles.
- Support student to implement student-directed learning strategies.
- Enable student to determine schedule for action plan.
- Enable student to self-monitor progress on implementing action plan.

Phase 3: Adjusting Behaviors

Student Questions

- What actions have I taken?
- What obstacles have been removed?
- What has changed about what I do not know?
- Do I know what I want to know?

Selected Teacher Objectives

- Enable student to self-evaluate progress toward goal.
- Collaborate with student to identify if action plan is adequate or inadequate given revised goal.
- Assist student in deciding if goal remains the same or changes.
- Assist student to change action plan if necessary.

Source: Excerpts taken from Mithaug, D. E., Wehmeyer, M. L., Agran, M., Martin, J. E., & Palmer, S. (1998). The self-determined learning model of instruction. In Wehmeyer, M. L. & Sands, D. J. (Eds.), *Making it happen: Student involvement in education planning, decision making, and instruction* (pp. 299–328). Baltimore: Paul H. Brookes.

The Importance of Self-Determination

A growing number of studies indicate the positive impact of self-determination skills upon postschool outcomes. Wehmeyer and Schwartz (1997) collected self-determination measures on students with learning disabilities and mental retardation prior to their exiting from high school. After leaving high school, the former students who had higher levels of self-determination while in high school had higher employment rates than those who had lower self-determination scores.

Critical Point   Self-determination has been linked to better postschool outcomes for persons with disabilities.

Gerber, Ginsberg, and Reiff (1992) interviewed a group of adults, who were identified as learning disabled during their school years, to determine why some were successful and others were not. They found that successful individuals with learning disabilities had:

- Control of their lives and surroundings
- A desire to succeed
- Well-thought-out goals
- Persistence
- Adapted to their environment
- Built a social support network that facilitated their success

After conducting the interviews, Gerber et al. (1992) realized that successful individuals decided, long before they became successful, that they would be successful. The authors concluded that successful adults with severe learning disabilities wanted to succeed, set achievable goals, and confronted their learning disability so that appropriate measures could be taken to increase the likelihood of success. One highly successful young man explained it like this: "Successful people have a plan. You have to have a plan, goals, strategy, otherwise you are flying through the clouds and then you hit the mountain" (Gerber et al., 1992, p. 480). These findings, when combined

with what we know from other disciplines, strongly suggest the beneficial outcome of increased self-determination skills (Martin & Huber Marshall, 1995). In part because of these results, federal disability law codified self-determination practices.

Federal Laws, Regulations, and State Practice

Federal special education legislation and regulations include four explicit self-determination statements designed to teach crucial self-determination skills and to provide student participatory decision-making opportunities. First, the Individuals with Disabilities Education Act (IDEA) mandates that secondary transition-aged students be invited to attend their IEP meeting. Second, IEP transition goals and activities must be based on *student* needs, interests, and preferences. The spirit of IDEA implies that students of transition age, with support from the IEP team, should determine and implement their own goals, objectives, and activities based on *self-perceived* needs, preferences, and interests—not simply those expressed by parents and educators. Third, with the Rehabilitation Act amendments of 1992 (P.L. 102-569), the U.S. Congress declared that the presence of a disability does not diminish the rights of individuals to enjoy self-determination. Fourth, the Rehabilitation Act mandates that all programs and activities funded by the federal and state offices of vocational rehabilitation must promote the principles of self-determination.

Critical Point   The IDEA and the Rehabilitation and Vocational Education Act amendments specifically address self-determination.

State Practice

Each state must minimally implement its special education practices to match the expectations established in the federal laws and regulations. States, however, may exceed the federal minimum requirements. The transition vision of the Ohio Department of Education, Division of Special Education, for example, implements the spirit of the law. Special education practice in Ohio could satisfy the minimum requirements by inviting only students to their IEP meetings but, instead, students are expected to be present at their IEP meeting and to participate actively in the planning and implementation of their transition to adult life educational program (Ohio Department of Education, Division of Special Education, 1999). To this end, special education transition practice in Ohio:

- Expects students to lead their own IEP meetings
- Expects students to describe and discuss their postsecondary transition goals
- Teaches students about their transition process
- Expects students to develop postsecondary goals based on their interests and preferences

To document this transition vision, Ohio school districts must report the number of student-led IEP meetings, documentation of efforts to develop postsecondary goals based on student interest and preferences, the number of students who discuss their postsecondary goals, and a listing of the programs or strategies used to educate students about transition.

Going beyond IDEA's minimum requirement of inviting students to participate in their IEP meetings is not unique to Ohio. The Iowa Department of Education (1998) believes that prior to the IEP meeting, students in transition need instruction in the IEP process and their role in the meeting. IEP team members all share an equal responsibility in facilitating the active participation of individuals with disabilities in their meeting. The country of Wales in the United Kingdom also believes that students need to become involved in the development of their own IEP. The Welsh Code of Special Education Practice mandates that a student's transition plan should answer several questions, including (1) What information do young people need in order to make informed choices? (2) How can

young people be encouraged to contribute to their own transition plan and make positive decisions about the future? (Welsh Office, Department of Education, 1994, p. 118).

Infusion of Self-Determination into the IEP

Self-determination skills make a difference in the postschool outcomes of people with disabilities. Unfortunately, students with disabilities possess far fewer self-determination skills than do secondary students who do not have an IEP (Wolman et al., 1994). Only a few IEPs include self-determination goals, even though teachers value self-determination skills. For students to learn and use self-determination behaviors in their everyday life, self-determination skills must be taught and opportunities provided for students to practice self-determined behaviors.

Critical Point   States and local education agencies need to go beyond the minimum requirements for self-determination established by federal legislation.

Educational practice appears to reflect this view. Agran et al.'s (1999) survey of special education teachers found that 77% considered self-determination as an important curricular area, with only 3% of the teachers rating self-determination as a low priority. However, a discrepancy exists between the teachers' expressed importance and their inclusion of self-determination into most of the IEPs they write. The Utah teachers said that:

- 14% include self-determination skills on most IEPs
- 61% include self-determination skills on some IEPs
- 25% include self-determination on few or no IEPs

What can be done to create more of a match between the perceived importance and the inclusion of self-determination goals into students' IEPs? One answer to this question begins with considering self-determination as a need to be discussed at the IEP meeting.

Establishing Self-Determination as an IEP Need Area

Educators and parents must consider self-determination as an educational necessity, one to be pursued as seriously and systematically as any other skill area we value (Agran et al., 1999, p. 301). The route to making self-determination an educational necessity begins with establishing its need in the IEP's present level of performance section (Sale & Martin, 1997). Assessments, either formal or informal, typically document the present level of performance and establish the need. Self-determination assessment tools may assist with this process.

Self-Determination Assessment

Three published self-determination assessments may help to determine students' self-determination strengths and needs. These include The ARC's *Self-Determination Scale* (Wehmeyer & Kelchner, 1995) the *Self-Determination Knowledge Scale* (Hoffman, Field, & Sawilowsky, 1996); and the *ChoiceMaker Self-Determination Assessment* (Martin & Huber Marshall, 1996b). Each tool provides a unique perspective and reports the results in different ways (see Field, Martin, Miller, Ward, & Wehmeyer, 1998; Sale & Martin, 1997 for detailed descriptions of the three assessments). The *ChoiceMaker Self-Determination Assessment* singularly produces suggested IEP goals and objectives.

The *ChoiceMaker Assessment*, as a curriculum-referenced assessment, matches the ChoiceMaker curriculum (see Table 11–4). It consists of 54 items that evaluate student self-determination skills and the opportunities at school to exercise these skills. The *ChoiceMaker Assessment* contains three sections: choosing goals, expressing goals, and taking action. The "choosing goals" section assesses goal setting based on students' knowledge of their interests, skills, and limits across school, employment, and post high school education domains. The "expressing goals" section assesses students' participation and leadership in IEP meetings.

The "take action" section measures students' goal attainment skills (see Table 11–4 for sample questions).

Teachers evaluate each of the 54 items using a 5-point scale across both the student skills and opportunities at school columns. The raw scores for each of the three sections are summed, graphed, and compared to the total points available to find the percent of available self-determination skills and opportunities. Items assessed as zero, one, or two become possible IEP goals and objectives.

Case Study

Zeke, a 14-year-old high school student, lives in Colorado and receives special education services due to the impact his learning disability and emotional problems have upon his educational performance. The special education team at Zeke's high school believes in teaching self-determination skills and in providing many opportunities to practice learned self-determination skills. In preparation for Zeke's first high school IEP meeting, Mrs. Gomez and Zeke jointly complete the ChoiceMaker assessment to document his present level of educational performance.

Zeke's ChoiceMaker assessment profile (see Figure 11–1) shows that Zeke's high school provides 33% of the choosing goal opportunities, 100% of the expressing goals opportunities, and 99% of the taking action opportunities. Zeke's skill profile depicts low and variable self-determination levels: a 30% choosing goals skills level, a 10% expressing goals skill level, and a 38% taking action skills level. The skill levels differ significantly from the opportunities provided by his high school program.

Critical Point Self-determination should be measured in terms of choosing goals, expressing goals, and taking action.

In preparing for Zeke's annual IEP review meeting, Mrs. Gomez writes the results of her assessment into the IEP form's transition present

TABLE 11–4

Sample ChoiceMaker Assessment's Expressing Goals Questions

	Student Skills					Opportunity at School				
Section 2: Expressing Goals	(Does the student do this?)					(Does school provide structured time?)				
E. *Student Leading Meeting*—Does the student:	(not at all)				(100%)	(not at all)				(100%)
E1. Begin meeting and introduce participants?	0	1	2	3	4	0	1	2	3	4
E2. Review past goals and performance?	0	1	2	3	4	0	1	2	3	4
E3. Ask questions if student does not understand something?	0	1	2	3	4	0	1	2	3	4
E4. Ask for feedback from group members?	0	1	2	3	4	0	1	2	3	4
E5. Deal with differences in opinion?	0	1	2	3	4	0	1	2	3	4
E6. Close meeting by summarizing decisions?	0	1	2	3	4	0	1	2	3	4
				Subtotal ___					Subtotal ___	
F. *Student Reporting*—Does the student:										
F1. Express interests.	0	1	2	3	4	0	1	2	3	4
F2. Express skills and limits.	0	1	2	3	4	0	1	2	3	4
F3. Express options and goals.	0	1	2	3	4	0	1	2	3	4
				Subtotal ___					Subtotal ___	
				TOTAL (E + F) ___					TOTAL (E + F) ___	

Source: Excerpt taken from: Martin, J. E. & Marshall, L. H. (1996b). *ChoiceMaker self-determination assessment.* Longmont, CO: Sopris West. © 1997 University of Colorado. Used with permission from University Technology Corp.

FIGURE 11–1
ChoiceMaker Assessment Profile

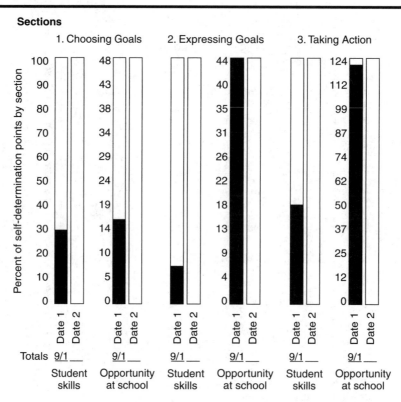

level of educational performance and needs section (see Table 11–5). She then sends a copy of her self-determination assessment and a draft present level of performance section home for Zeke and his parents to review and discuss prior to the IEP meeting.

At the IEP meeting, Zeke (with coaching by Mrs. Gomez) showed the team his self-determination assessment profile, then described his strengths and a few of the self-determination skills he has not yet mastered. Mrs. Gomez then reviewed the school's self-determination expectations. The team realized a large discrepancy existed between Zeke's current performance and the expectations to engage in self-determination activities. Zeke and the team decided his self-determination needs included:

- Choosing education, employment, and personal goals based on an understanding of his skills and limits
- Learning to lead his educational meetings
- Learning the goal attainment skills needed to take action on his IEP goals

Mrs. Gomez wrote these into Zeke's "transition need" section of his IEP, referenced them to Colorado's academic standards and access skills, and then wrote a self-determination IEP goal and related objectives:

Goal   Within the next 20 weeks, Zeke will increase self-determination skills to an average of 83%.

This goal references Reading, Writing, and Speaking Academic Standard 2 (Students write and speak for a variety of purposes and audiences), and Colorado Access

TABLE 11–5

ChoiceMaker Lesson Matrix

Section	Goals	Lessons	Students
Choosing Goals	A. Student understanding B. Student interests C. Student skills and limits D. Student goals	• Choosing employment goals • Choosing personal matters goals • Choosing education goals	• Middle and high school general education students • Middle and high school students with an IEP and mild to moderate learning and behavior problems
Expressing Goals	E. Student leading meeting F. Student reporting	• Self-directed IEP	• Middle and high school students with an IEP and mild to moderate learning and behavior problems
Taking Action	G. Student plan H. Student action I. Student evaluation J. Student adjustment	• Take action	• Middle and high school general education students • Middle and high school students with an IEP and mild to moderate learning and behavior problems

Source: Adapted from a table originally published in: Martin, J. E., Marshall, L. H., Maxson, L., & Jerman, P. (1996c). *Self-directed IEP.* Longmont, CO: Sopris West. Used with permission from University Technology Corp.

Skills 1 (communication), 2 (decision-making), and 3 (self-determination).

Objectives

1. Within the next 10 weeks, Zeke will increase taking action skills to 90% as measured by the ChoiceMaker self-determination assessment.
2. In the next 15 weeks, Zeke will increase choosing goals to 70% as measured by the Choice-Maker self-determination assessment.
3. Within the next 20 weeks, Zeke will increase expressing goals skills to 90% as measured by the ChoiceMaker self-determination assessment.

Standard-Referenced IEPs

IDEA 1997 requires students to participate to the greatest extent possible in their school's general education curriculum. The Colorado Department of Education (1998), for example, believes that academic standards define the general education curriculum, and IEPs must reference these academic standards. The standards establish benchmarks that delineate by grade level student outcomes across academic content, including math, social studies, civics, and science (see web site listing at the end of this chapter to obtain Colorado's academic standards).

For many students of transition age in Colorado, an IEP goal referenced to academic standards alone may be insufficient since they also may need skills to access the community. Access skills enable students to master specific academic content standards and life outcomes, including career goals and community participation (Colorado Dept. of Educ., 1998). From the identified areas of need, IEP teams develop academic standard and access skill-referenced goals. Many states use the term "expanded standards" to represent what the Colorado Department of Education calls access skills (S. Bechard, personal communication, September 29, 1999).

Critical Point Self-determination and community access skill should be addressed in IEPs along with academics.

Colorado's access skills include eight domains: (1) communication and basic language skills; (2) decision making and problem solving; (3) self-determination; (4) physical functions; (5) inter/intrapersonal; (6) organization; (7) technology; and (8) career development and workplace competencies. Each domain consists of several subdomains. Decision making, for example, includes:

- Setting goals to plan for action
- Self-monitoring
- Advocating for self and needs

The self-determination domain consists of four subdivisions, each of which breaks down into additional skills:

- Self-awareness
- Self-advocacy
- Self-management
- Decision making and goal setting

The workplace competencies domain divides into five subdomains with, goal setting and goal attainment prominent in two of these.

Combined, the Colorado access skills and the academic standards include all the self-determination competencies assessed by the ChoiceMaker assessment. Clearly, the Colorado Department of Education considers self-determination as a crucial set of skills. In Colorado, students' IEPs may contain goals that are referenced to academic standards, access skills, or both (Bechard, 1999).

Teaching Self-Determination and Creating Participatory Decision-Making Opportunities

Once self-determination goals are written into the IEP, special education teachers need to make teaching self-determination skills a priority. Teachers may develop their own lessons, or choose to use, or modify, already developed lesson packages in order to teach self-determination skills to their students. (See Field et al., 1998 for a review of numerous self-determination lesson packages.) Teachers across the country use the ChoiceMaker self-determination instructional packages to teach basic self-determination skills and to practice learned self-determination behaviors.

The ChoiceMaker Series

The ChoiceMaker series consists of the *Choice-Maker Self-determination Assessment* and six instructional packages. The instructional packages include:

- *Choosing employment goals* (Huber Marshall, Martin, Maxson, & Jerman, 1997)
- *Choosing education goals* (Martin, Hughes, Huber Marshall, Jerman, & Maxson, 1999)
- *Choosing personal goals* (Huber Marshall, Martin, Hughes, Jerman, & Maxson, 1999)
- *Self-directed IEP* (Martin, Huber Marshall, Maxson, & Jerman, 1996c).
- *Take action: Making goals happen* (Huber Marshall, Martin, Maxson, Hughes, Miller, McGill, & Jerman, 1999).
- *Choose and take action* (Martin, Huber Marshall, Wray, O'Brien, & Snyder, submitted for publication)

Each instructional package teaches specific goals and objectives of the ChoiceMaker curriculum (see Table 11–5). The ChoiceMaker curriculum, which operationalizes the self-determination constructs identified in Table 11–1, contains three strands, nine broad teaching goals, and 54 objectives.

Development of the ChoiceMaker Lesson Packages (see Table 11–6)

The development of each lesson package followed the same process. A team of University of Colorado faculty, public school special educators and administrators, parents, students with an IEP, and adults with disabilities jointly

TABLE 11–6

ChoiceMaker Self-Determination Curriculum Matrix

Sections	Teaching Goals	Teaching Objectives							
1: Choosing Goals (through school and community experience)	A. *Student interests*	A1. Express *education* interests	A2. Express *employment* interests	A3. Express *personal* interests	A4. Express *daily living, housing, and community* interests				
	B. *Student skills and limits*	B1. Express *education* skills and limits	B2. Express *employment* skills and limits	B3. Express *personal* skills and limits	B4. Express *daily living and community* skills and limits				
	C. *Student goals*	C1. Indicate options and choose *education* goals	C2. Indicate options and choose *employment* goals	C3. Indicate options and choose *personal* goals	C4. Indicate options and choose *daily living, housing, and community* goals				
2: Expressing Goals	D. *Student leading meeting*	D1. Begin meeting by stating purpose	D2. Introduce participants	D3. Review past goals and performance	D4. Ask for feedback	D5. Ask questions if don't understand	D6. Deal with differences in opinion	D7. State needed support	D8. Close meeting by summarizing decision
	E. *Student reporting*	E1. Express interests (from A1–A4)	E2. Express skills and limits (from B1–B4)	E3. Express options and goals (from C1–C4)					
3: Taking Action	F. *Student plan*	F1. Break general goals into specific goals that can be completed now	F2. Establish *standard* for specific goals	F3. Determine how to get *feedback* from environment	F4. Determine *motivation* to complete specific goals	F5. Determine *strategies* for completing specific goals	F6. Determine *support* needed to complete specific goals	F7. Prioritize and *schedule* to complete specific goals	F8. Express *belief* that goals can be obtained
	G. *Student action*	G1. Record or report performance	G2. Perform specific goals to *standard*	G3. Obtain *feedback* on performance	G4. *Motivate* self to complete specific goals	G5. Use *strategies* to perform specific goals	G6. Obtain *support* needed	G7. Follow *schedule*	
	H. *Student evaluation*	H1. Determine if goals are achieved	H2. Compare performance to *standards*	H3. Evaluate *feedback*	H4. Evaluate *motivation*	H5. Evaluate effectiveness of *strategies*	H6. Evaluate *support* used	H7. Evaluate *schedule*	H8. Evaluate *belief*
	I. *Student adjustment*	I1. Adjust goals if necessary	I2. Adjust or repeat goal *standards*	I3. Adjust or repeat method for *feedback*	I4. Adjust or repeat *motivation*	I5. Adjust or repeat *strategies*	I6. Adjust or repeat	I7. Adjust or repeat *schedule*	I8. Adjust or repeat *belief* that goals can be obtained

Source: Adapted from a table originally published in: Martin, J. E., Marshall, L. H., Maxson, L., & Jerman (1996c). *Self-directed IEP.* Longmont, CO: Sopris West. © 1996 University of Colorado. Used with permission from University Technology Corp.

Self-determined choices enhance postschool outcomes.

worked on conceptualizing, writing, and field-testing the materials. The development teams wrote the lessons to attain specific ChoiceMaker goals and objectives. The teams repeatedly took the draft lessons into middle and high school programs to field-test. Feedback from the teachers and students resulted in numerous revisions. Other educators, then, conducted rigorous studies to demonstrate the programs' effectiveness. We will describe the results of these studies when we explain each lesson package.

Critical Point   ChoiceMaker was developed and field-tested in collaboration with educators, students, adults with disabilities, and parents.

Use of the ChoiceMaker Lesson Packages

Each ChoiceMaker lesson package may be infused into existing educational programs. Because the *choosing goals* and *taking action* materials are compatible with middle and high school content area courses, they may be used for general education students *and* with students who have an IEP. The *self-directed* IEP materials, which teach the *expressing goal* section of the curriculum, are designed for students with an IEP. The *choose and take action* multimedia software package teaches essential self-determination skills and

vocational choice making to students and adults who cannot read and who have more severe cognitive disabilities. All other ChoiceMaker lesson packages teach students who have at least minimal reading and writing skills.

Teaching and Creating Opportunities for Choosing Goals

The choosing goals section of the *ChoiceMaker curriculum* provides students the skills and knowledge needed to express their interests, skills, limits, and goals across different transition areas. The choosing goals lesson packages include *choosing employment goals*, *choosing education goals*, and *choosing personal goals*. As exemplars of the choosing goals lesson packages, in this section, we review the general choosing goals process and samples from the *choosing employment goals* lesson package. We then briefly describe the *choosing education goals* and *choosing personal goals* instructional packages.

Choosing Goals Process

Each of the choosing goals lesson packages includes methodology for students to determine quickly their goals across transition areas. A student video included in each of the three lesson packages, entitled *Choosing Goals to Plan Your Life*, introduces the choosing goals process by showing actual high school students learning and using the choosing goals process.

After watching the video and completing the choosing goals lessons, students complete a choosing general goals worksheet. Figure 11–2 presents a sample section of a choosing general goals worksheet from the *choosing employment goals* lesson package for a high school student who wants to work as an autobody repairman. After the student knows how to complete the form, he simply reads each question and writes in his answer. If he does not know the answer, then that becomes his goal. In this example, Cal does not know the requirements to become an autobody repairman. So, learning the requirements to be

FIGURE 11–2
Choosing General Goals

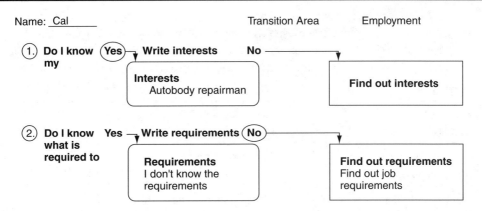

Source: Excerpt taken from: Huber Marshall, L., Martin, J., Maxson, L., & Jerman, P. (1997). *Choosing employment goals.* Longmont, CO: Sopris West. @ 1997 University of Colorado. Used with permission from University Technology Corp.

an autobody repairman becomes his goal. Once completed, students may use the form for discussions in their transition class, with their parents, or in their IEP meeting. If students do not know their goals, the lesson packages teach students to identify their goals based on an understanding of their interests, skills, and limits.

Choosing Employment Goals
The ChoiceMaker curriculum objectives (see Table 11–2) addressed by *choosing employment goals* are:

   Objective A2. Express employment interests.
   Objective B2. Express employment skills and limits.
   Objective C2. Indicate options and choose employment goals.

The *choosing employment goals* lesson sequence is flexible and designed to be mixed and matched with the content and opportunities of existing school curriculum, classes, and schedules.
   The lesson activities, which take place at community job sites and in the classroom,

teach students to reflect upon their experiences, draw conclusions about themselves, and learn about community opportunities. Students collect and assimilate this information over time so that they can make informed career decisions. The *choosing employment goals* lesson package consists of three parts: (1) choosing general goals lessons (discussed earlier), (2) experience-based lessons, and (3) dream job lessons.

Experience-Based Lessons. Teachers use these lessons and materials with students who are involved in on-the-job activities through work study, on-the-job training, volunteering, or in an after school job. These lessons teach students to draw meaningful conclusions about their interests, skills, and limits based on their own work experience.
   Students learn the job characteristics and job duties they like by completing the *Job Characteristics I Like Worksheet* (see Figure 11–3) and *Job Duties I Like Student Worksheet* process. To examine their on-the-job skills and limits they complete a *Work, Social, and Personal Skills* (see Figure 11–4), and a *Job Duties—How I Did* process. When done

FIGURE 11–3
Job Characteristics I Like Worksheet

Name: _____   *Job Site* _____   *Date:* _____

Directions: WHAT I LIKE column: Circle the job characteristic that you like best in each box.

WHAT IS HERE column: Circle the job characteristic in each box that best describes what is at this job.

MATCHES column: Circle YES if the first two columns are the same. Circle NO if they are not.

	What I Like	What Is Here	Matches	
1.	Work alone Lots of people around	Work alone Lots of people around	Yes	No
2.	Quiet workplace Noisy workplace	Quiet workplace Noisy workplace	Yes	No
3.	Work close to home Distance to job doesn't matter	Work close to home Distance to job doesn't matter	Yes	No
4.	Weekdays only Weekends too	Weekdays only Weekends too	Yes	No
5.	Easy job Challenging job	Easy job Challenging job	Yes	No

Source: Excerpt taken from: Marshall, L. H., Martin, J. E., Maxson, L., & Jerman, P. (1997). *Choosing employment goals.* Longmont, CO: Sopris West Publishers. © 1997 University of Colorado. Used with permission from University Technology Corp.

repeatedly across time, the results yield a self-directed vocational profile that may be shared with others (see Figure 11–5). Students save their results to develop a self-directed vocational portfolio, which they can show at their IEP meeting to add data to the IEP's present level of performance section.

Dream Job Lessons. With the dream job lessons, students in a general education academic or a transition class gather information about a variety of jobs, then research those they think they would like. Students determine how their interests, skills, and limits match those jobs. The lessons may be used sequentially or separately. There are four lessons in the dream job section: (1) job clusters, (2) dream job research, (3) dream job interviews (see Table 12), and (4) dream job shadowing.

Choosing Education Goals

The *choosing education goals* lesson package teaches students to choose high school and post-secondary education goals that match their interests, skills, limits, and available opportunities. The *ChoiceMaker self-determination transition curriculum* objectives addressed by the *choosing education goals* lessons include:

Objective A1. Express education interests.

Objective B1. Express education skills and limits.

Objective C1. Indicate options and choose education goals.

The choosing education goals lesson activities all take place in the classroom. The lessons teach students to reflect upon their experiences, draw conclusions about themselves, and learn

FIGURE 11–4
Work, Social, and Personal Skills Student's Worksheet

How I Did column: Circle 3, 2, or 1 whichever best describes your performance.

Supervisor Thinks column: From the *Work, Social, and Personal Skills Supervisor Worksheet,* copy the numbers that your supervisor chose to describe your performance.

Matches column: Circle Yes if yours and your supervisor's evaluations are the same. If they are not the same, circle No.

Skills	How I Did		Supervisor Thinks		Comments	Matches	
1. Follows company rules	Very good	3	Very good	3		Yes	No
	OK	2	OK	2			
	Needs improvement	1	Needs improvement	1			
2. Comes to work on time or calls if late or absent	Very good	3	Very good	3		Yes	No
	OK	2	OK	2			
	Needs improvement	1	Needs improvement	1			
Social							
8. Talks the right amount	Very good	3	Very good	3		Yes	No
	OK	2	OK	2			
	Needs improvement	1	Needs improvement	1			
9. Behaves appropriately	Very good	3	Very good	3		Yes	No
	OK	2	OK	2			
	Needs improvement	1	Needs improvement	1			
Personal							
12. Works independently	Very good	3	Very good	3		Yes	No
	OK	2	OK	2			
	Needs improvement	1	Needs improvement	1			
13. Good grooming	Very good	3	Very good	3		Yes	No
	OK	2	OK	2			
	Needs improvement	1	Needs improvement	1			

Source: Excerpt taken from: Marshall, L. H., Martin, J. E., Maxson, L., & Jerman, P. (1997). *Choosing employment goals.* Longmont, CO: Sopris West Publishers. © 1997 University of Colorado. Used with permission from University Technology Corp.

about education opportunities. Students will collect and assimilate this information over time to make informed decisions about their secondary and postsecondary education plans.

While using the choosing education goals lessons, students complete a variety of activities that are designed to help them:

- Determine what students hope to do at different stages of their lives.
- Identify the school subjects that students like.
- Complete a personalized graduation checklist.
- Develop an individualized education performance summary.

- Learn postsecondary education terminology.
- Complete study habits, work habits, and academic skills self-assessment.
- Maintain a study habits log.
- Develop an individualized postsecondary education options information table.
- Choose secondary and postsecondary education goals.

Choosing Personal Goals

The *choosing personal goals* lesson package teaches students how to develop satisfying personal lives and how to spend their free time in safe,

FIGURE 11–5
Job Characteristics I Like Graph

	Characteristics	Times I chose each characteristic
1.	Work alone	
	Lots of people around	
2.	Quiet workplace	
	Noisy workplace	
3.	Weekdays only	
	Weekends too	
4.	Easy job	
	Challenging job	
5.	Dress up for work	
	Do not dress up	
	Wear a uniform	

Source: Excerpt taken from: Marshall, L. H., Martin, J. E., Maxson, L., & Jerman, P. (1997). *Choosing employment goals.* Longmont, CO: Sopris West Publishers. © 1997 University of Colorado. Used with permission from University Technology Corp.

legal, and healthy ways. The ChoiceMaker self-determination transition curriculum objectives addressed in the lessons include:

Objective A3.   Express personal interests.

Objective B4.   Express personal skills and limits.

Objective C5.   Express options and choose personal goals.

While using the choosing personal goals lessons, students complete a variety of activities designed to help them:

- Consider how they interact with other people.
- Evaluate the interactions of the groups in which they are involved.
- Identify the activities they do in their free time to further their relationships, hobbies, talents, recreation; or health and wellness.
- Decide if they would like to make changes in the way they interact with people or in the activities they do and identify ways to make those changes.

- Investigate activities, events, and services that are available in the community or school that can help them to make those changes (e.g. classes, clubs, teams, art groups or activities, sports, counseling, and community events).
- Consider their interests, skills, and limits in relation to the opportunities and choose personal goals of activities they want to try.
- Try their chosen activity and evaluate the results.

Summary
Once students identify their goals based on an understanding of their interests, skills, and limits, they then need the skills to express their goals at their IEP meeting.

Teaching and Creating Opportunities for Expressing Goals

Powers (1997) discovered that if students attend their IEP meetings with no prior instruction in what to do, they did not enjoy their IEP meetings and they did not understand the language or the meeting's purpose. She also found that students (and parents) believed that IEP team members did not talk to the student or ask for student input. Martin, Huber Marshall, and Sale (1999) conducted a survey of almost 1,770 IEP team members who attended middle and high school meetings over a 3-year period. They found that when students attend their meetings, the students talked less and understood less about the reason for the meeting than did all other participants.

Critical Point Students' presence at the IEP meeting is not enough. They must learn their role and how to participate meaningfully.

Presence at the IEP meeting without knowledge of the process and skills in what to do achieves very little. Clearly, to make student-directed IEPs a meaningful education experience, students should learn their role in the IEP process and what they can do to become a meaningful part of that process.

The expressing goals section of the Choice-Maker curriculum provides students the skills and knowledge needed to become actively involved in and to direct their own IEP meeting. While at the meeting, the students learn how to discuss their interests, skills, limits, and goals across different transition areas.

Five available lesson packages help educators to teach students the skills required to participate in and direct their own IEP meetings. These include the *Self-Advocacy Strategy for Education and Transition Planning* (Van Reusen, Bos, Schumaker, & Deshler, 1994); *Whose Future Is It Anyway?* (Wehmeyer & Kelchner, 1995); *A Student's Guide to the* IEP (McGahee-Kovac, 1995); *Next Steps* (Halpern, Herr, Wolf, Lawson, Doren, & Johnson, 1997); and the *Self-Directed* IEP (Martin, Huber Marshall, Maxson, & Jerman, 1996c). The *Self-Directed* IEP specifically teaches students to attain the expressing goals section of the ChoiceMaker curriculum.

The Self-Directed IEP

The *self-directed* IEP teaches students to become active participants in their IEP meetings and to chair the meetings to the best extent of their ability. It teaches students the two goals and 11 objectives that are crucial for student involvement in their own education planning process (see Table 11–2). Through the use of the self-directed IEP materials, role-play practice prior to the meeting, and participatation in their actual meeting, students learn the leadership skills that they need to manage their IEP meeting. The Self-directed IEP contains several different instructional materials. These include:

- *Self-Directed* IEP *in Action video* (7 minutes). This video shows students with different disabilities using the self-directed IEP lessons in their classes and talking about their experiences. This video is used to introduce the self-directed IEP to students, parents, teachers, and administrators.
- *Self-Directed* IEP *Video* (17 minutes). This video shows a student, named Zeke, using each of the 11 steps to lead his IEP meeting while describing the process to a younger, reluctant friend. Zeke's meeting provides a model for each of the 11 steps needed to lead an IEP meeting (see Table 11–7). The meeting depicted in the video shows an ideal meeting, in which the student viewers focus upon the steps that are necessary to lead an IEP meeting.
- *Teacher's Manual.* This book provides background information, detailed lesson plans, and a teacher answer key to the quizzes and activities. Lessons include a variety of activities to teach each step, including a mnemonic learning strategy, vocabulary-building exercises, role-playing, discussion, and brief reading and writing activities. The lessons are all presented in a model, lead, test approach.
- *Student Workbook.* This consumable workbook provides students an opportunity to apply each step to their own IEP. A script, summarizing all the steps, is completed at the end of

TABLE 11–7

Eleven steps to the Self-Directed IEP

1.	Begin the meeting by stating the purpose.
2.	Introduce everyone.
3.	Review past goals and performance.
4.	Ask for others' feedback.
5.	State your school and transition goals.
6.	Ask questions if you do not understand.
7.	Deal with differences in opinion.
8.	State what support you will need.
9.	Summarize your goals.
10.	Close the meeting by thanking everyone.
11.	Work on IEP goals all year.

Source: Excerpt taken from: Martin, J. E., Marshall, L. H., Maxson, L., & Jerman, P. (1996c). *Self-directed IEP.* Longmont, CO: Sopris West Publishers. © 1997 University of Colorado. Used with permission from University Technology Corp.

the lessons for students to use at their IEP meeting.

Instructional Considerations

The IEP is the one unique aspect that defines special education. If educators and families are serious about involving students in their IEP process, then students must be taught their role. This means that even in fully included schools, students who have an IEP must receive instruction about the IEP process and their role in it.

The self-directed IEP contains 11 sequential lessons that can be taught in six to ten 45-minute sessions. The lessons may be taught in a resource room, study skills class, or other settings. To teach students who are fully included in general education classes may involve meeting with individuals or with a group during study hall or other convenient times. The lessons also may be taught in an elective class.

Impact of the Self-Directed IEP

Sweeney (1996) undertook a pre-post-controlled group study to measure the impact of the *self-directed*

IEP upon Florida high school students with learning disabilities and mental retardation. In comparison to the students in the control group who did not receive instruction, Sweeney (1996) found that the students who completed the self-directed IEP lessons:

- Attended more of the IEP staffings
- Had more parents attend IEP staffings
- Talked more about their interests
- Shared more of their dreams for the future
- Talked more about the job they wanted
- Felt like they were the boss of their IEP meeting
- Felt more confident in reaching their IEP goals

Likewise, Snyder and Shapiro (1997) found in their study that the self-directed IEP is an effective method to teach adolescent students with emotional and behavior problems the skills needed to direct their own IEP meeting. Bedore-Bideaux (1998) studied the self-directed IEP with high school students who had learning disabilities. She found that the self-directed IEP produced significant changes in the quantity and quality of goal development and IEP leadership.

Summary

The goals and objectives are the most important instructional outcome of the IEP meeting. In a self-directed IEP meeting students play a major role in determining the goals. But after the meeting, how are the goals attained? Typically, goal attainment becomes an educator's duty. However, do educators need to be the only people responsible for goal attainment? What about the student?

Teaching and Creating Opportunities for Attaining Goals

Currently, special education teachers feel it is their responsibility to attain students' IEP goals. However, is this really the best education practice? To us, something is wrong with a practice in which the student is absolved of any goal attainment responsibility. After all, whose education is it, and whose goals are on the IEP? If goal attainment is the most important part of being self-determined, then why are students not more responsible for their own goals? Are educators really acting in the student's best interest if teachers carry the entire burden of responsibility for goal attainment?

We do not think so. We believe that students should have at least equal, if not greater, responsibility for achieving their own IEP goals. Our dream is that once the IEP meeting is concluded, the goal attainment process begins. Our dream is for students to meet weekly with their teachers in order to develop plans to achieve their own IEP goals, after evaluating the progress they made the previous week in achieving the past week's plans. We cannot think of a better way to make the IEP process a student-centered, living document. *Take Action: Making Goals Happen* is the ChoiceMaker instructional program that teaches goal attainment.

Critical Point It is believed that students should take as much responsibility as possible for their own IEP goals.

Take Action Overview

The *take action* lesson package teaches students a simple, yet effective goal attainment process. As with the other ChoiceMaker lesson packages, this lesson package is introduced with a student-oriented video demonstrating the take action concepts. Take action lessons teach students to plan how they will attain their goal by deciding (1) a standard for goal performance, (2) a means to get performance feedback, (3) what motivates them to do it, (4) the strategies they will use, (5) needed supports, and (6) schedules. This leads to student action, evaluation, and adjustment. These lessons can be applied to any goal or project and, thus, are excellent for use in content classes.

Take Action Lessons

By using a model-lead-test approach, the *take action* lessons systematically teach students an easy and effective goal attainment process. Here we discuss four lessons:

- *Lesson 1.* Introduces the *take action* process for accomplishing goals. Students watch the 10-minute take action video, which shows students developing plans and working on attaining their own goals. The students in the video assisted in writing and creating the video. The goals you see them working on in the video use goals from their own lives. Introduced in this lesson are the four major parts of the take action process: plan, act, evaluate, and adjust.
- *Lesson 2.* This lesson begins the process of teaching students how to break long-term goals into short-term objectives. To do this, students participate in an example process showing what a student must do to get her driver's license.
- *Lesson 3.* Students are introduced to plan making. Here they learn the parts of a plan that is needed to attain their goal. Hands-on activities are used to demonstrate each plan part. One of the concluding activities is for students to match the question being asked to the correct part of the plan (see Figure 11–6).
- *Lesson 6.* Students learn the importance of evaluation and adjustment to goal attainment. They examine the evaluation and adjustments of earlier plans.
- *Remaining lessons.* The remaining lessons teach students how to develop their own plans for sample goals, then for their own goals. The last lesson teaches students how to use the take action goal attainment process in other settings, and with a wide range of goals.

Impact of Take Action Lessons

German, Martin, Huber Marshall, and Sale (in press) undertook a study to determine the

FIGURE 11–6
Take Action Review

Name _____   Date _____

Find the question that explains each part of a plan. Write it under the correct part of the plan.

Questions

| How will I get information on my performance? | What help do I need? | When will I do it? | What will I be satisfied with? | What methods should I use? | Why do I want to do this? |

Parts of a Plan

Standard	Motivation	Strategy	Schedule	Support	Feedback

Source: Excerpt from: Marshall, L. H., Martin, J. E., Maxson, L. M., Miller, T. L., McGill, T., Hughes, W. M., & Jerman, P. A. (in press). *Taking action.* Longmont, CO: Sopris West, Inc. © 1997 University of Colorado. Used with permission from University Technology Corp.

effectiveness of take action in teaching goal attainment to six students with mild to moderate mental retardation. After completing the take action lessons, all the students had significant increases in the attainment of specific daily goals. The students went from achieving 0 to 25% of their daily goals during baseline to 80 to 100% after instruction in the take action lessons.

Teaching and Creating Opportunities for Students with Severe Needs

Most available lesson packages teach self-determination skills to students with mild learning and emotional challenges. Only a few materials exist to help educators teach self-determination skills to students with more severe cognitive needs (Field et al. 1998). Martin, Mithaug, Oliphint, and Husch (in press) with their self-directed supported employment methodology, use illustrations to develop a self-directed vocational assessment and to establish self-directed goal attainment (see Figure 11–7). The *choose and take action* multimedia teaches students and adults with moderate to severe cognitive disabilities self-determination skills. When using the software program, students watch video segments, select a job that matches their interests, try the selected job at a community site, evaluate the experience, and then make new choices based on what they learned.

The choose and take action instructional activities are designed to teach students numerous self-determination skills, including:

- Choosing from a variety of work options
- Planning whether they want to watch or do the activity

FIGURE 11–7
Characteristics I Like Versus Here Form-B

Name				Date	Job Site		Page 1 of 2
What I Like before work					What Is Here after work		
Circle what you like. *Star top 10 √4 most preferred					Circle what is here		Matches

		*	√				
Work alone	Work with lots of people	✗(star)	√	Work alone	Work with lots of people		Y (N)
Quiet workplace	Loud workplace			Quiet workplace	Loud workplace		Y (N)
Part time	Full time	✗(star)		Part time	Full time		Y (N)
Weekdays only	Weekends too			Weekdays only	Weekends too		Y (N)
Hard job	Easy job			Hard job	Easy job		(Y) N
Inside	Outside	✗(star)		Inside	Outside		Y (N)
Few rules	Lots of rules	✗(star)	√	Few rules	Lots of rules		Y (N)
Standing up	Sitting down	✗(star)		Standing up	Sitting down		Y (N)
Work mornings	Work afternoons			Work mornings	Work afternoons		(Y) N

Source: Excerpt from: Martin, J. E., Mithaug, D. E., Oliphint, J. V., & Husch, J. (in press). *ChoiceMaker employment: A self-determination transition and supported employment handbook.* Baltimore: Paul H. Brookes.

- Completing the plan in the community setting
- Evaluating what they liked and did not like about the setting, activity, and work-site characteristics, and how the students did while they were at the setting
- Using the information gained in the experience to make the next choice

The choose and take action software also introduces students to a variety of job and career possibilities and teaches them to identify what is most important to them about a job: the setting, the activity, or the characteristics.

Target Population
Choose and Take Action is designed for students and adults with disabilities who are unable to read and write. The characteristics of students for whom this program will work the best include:

- Students with moderate to significant cognitive needs
- Students who have difficulty getting information from print
- Students who can attend to a computer screen
- Students who can follow simple verbal instructions
- Students in middle and high school
- Students with limited work experience

How It Was Developed
The development of the choose and take action software program involved numerous steps. First, a group of teachers, adult-service-supported employment personnel, former students with a disability, parents, advocates for students with disabilities, and University of Colorado faculty met to brainstorm. The group identified critical self-determination skills. Next, a project advisory panel (made up of transition specialists, teachers, former students, parents, agency and university personnel, and school administrators) voted on the relative importance of each skill area. Third, the development team along with representatives from three states spent sev-

eral days creating a rough draft of the software specifications and functions. Fourth, the advisory panel reviewed and finalized the software plan. Fifth, the software plan underwent a nationwide social validation process. Experts in transition, self-determination, employment for individuals with disabilities, individuals with disabilities, and parents reviewed the plan. Then, the comments and suggestions were incorporated into the software and lessons. Sixth, the software and lessons underwent extensive field-testing in four states, with their findings incorporated into the final product

The Choose and Take Action Cycle
The *choose and take action* cycle includes four steps. Students complete the first two cycle steps, choice making and plan development, in one session.

Step 1: Choice Making. During choice making, students view pairs of randomly presented videos showing different employment settings, activities, and job characteristics. From each pair, students select the one they like the best. After they have viewed all the videos once, the ones they chose the first time are paired and the students choose again. This continues until students choose one final video option to try. Then, students develop a plan.

Step 2: Plan. During the plan part of the program, students determine if they want to *watch* someone do the activity at their selected setting or if they want actually *to do* the activity. Printed plans are produced and shown with pictures that students chose: the setting, activity, two characteristics, and whether they want to watch or do the activities. The evaluation questions regarding these choices are also printed on the plan.

Step 3: Try It. Based on the plan, the student goes into the community to "try it" at the chosen setting. Students will interact with the workers at the site as much as possible as they watch or do the activity.

TABLE 11–8

List of Setting, Activities, and Characteristics Included in the Video Clips

Settings	Activities	Characteristics
Auto dealer/mechanic	Assemble and disassemble	Spacious
Construction site	Bag items and bring in carts	Cozy space
Factory	Bus tables	Noisy
Florist/Green house/Nursery	Care for animals	Quiet
Grocery store	Care for people	Inside
Hospital/Nursing home	Care for plants	Outside
Hotel	Heavy cleaning	Wear own clothes
Janitorial service	Laundry	Wear a uniform
Landscape/Outdoor maintenance	Light cleaning	Many people
Office	Move materials	Few people
Restaurant	Filing	Messy
Retail	Paperwork	Clean
School/child care	Stock shelves	
Vet office/Kennel/Grooming	Wash dishes	
	Yard work	

Step 4: Evaluate. Students, with the instructor's guidance, evaluate the experience, then they enter that information into the computer.

With each step, the teacher provides only instruction that the students require to complete the step independently. Of course, an educator will need to arrange the detail involved in visiting a "try-it" site. The *choose and take action* software is designed for students with limited work experience; therefore, it is critical for students to complete the process a number of times in order to try many different things.

Video clips

The software contains 31, 20-second video clips, across 14 employment settings and 15 activities. Twelve characteristics, each shown at least four times, are also included in the 31 video clips. Each video clip shows an employment setting, an entry-level activity, and two characteristics of the job. For each setting, there are two or three video clips showing a different activity, and each activity is shown in at least two settings.

The teacher may limit the number of video clips that a student will see in one session. The settings and activities shown in the video clips represent entry-level jobs and cover most job categories in the Department of Labor's *Occupational Outlook Handbook*. The jobs represent opportunities that are available in most communities. See Table 11-8 for a listing of video settings, activities, and characteristics.

Importance of Try-It

Students in the target population may have difficulty generalizing from what is depicted in the video to a real setting. The videos give more information than a text or pictured version of an employment interest inventory, but they still do not exactly replicate the community settings students will visit. Students must go to the settings and try it to make their choices meaningful.

Reports

The software records students' choices throughout the program and creates reports indicating the students' choices in the choose, plan, and evaluate sections. There is also a place for instructors to record their observations and notes about the students' experiences and their discussions. Students will be able to graph their results on simple bar graphs. The reports and graphs will help students and the IEP teams to see the students' emerging interests and skill trends. These reports, including the instructor's evaluations and observations, may be included in a student portfolio. This provides information about students' preferences for IEP meetings and vocational assessments. This will give students a starting place for employment decision making.

Summary

The choose and take action lesson package infuses the best of what is known about teaching self-determination with available technology. The use of interactive video software provides an additional means for students with severe needs to show teachers what they want.

Student-Directed Functional Assessment and Behavior Support Planning

Students with emotional and behavioral disorders (EBD) present a challenge to the transition process. Data from the U.S. Department of Education (1994) indicates that both in-school and postschool outcomes for these students are extremely poor. For example, students with EBD have the lowest graduation rate of all students with disabilities, the highest drop-out rate, and a high rate of contact with the criminal justice system. Innovative practice for students with behavioral challenges provides the opportunity to combine self-determination instruction *and* effective behavioral support planning. The following examples show what we mean.

Traditional Approach

William, a 12th grade student at a local high school, acts out chronically at his community-based vocational placement. The teaching team decides that a functional assessment is needed, and they spend several hours collecting data and observing William across settings using both indirect and direct functional assessment methodologies. Upon completion of the functional assessment, the team convenes and develops a behavior support plan outlining a replacement response and teaching strategies to establish new and more appropriate behavior. After 3 weeks of implementing the support plan, the team becomes frustrated: William's acting-out has actually increased.

Student-Directed Functional Assessment and Behavior Support Planning

William's teaching team is more concerned than ever about William's increased chronic acting-out at his community-based vocational placement. This time, rather than using a traditional teacher-directed functional assessment, they involve William. The team meets with William over a morning snack to determine his beliefs regarding the problem behavior. William talks about his behavior at the vocational setting. With this new information, the team, with William as an equal member, conducts indirect and direct functional assessments. The collected data identify the perceived function or purpose of William's problem behavior. Following the functional assessment, William leads his behavior support planning meeting and shares what he learned with the teaching team. During the meeting, he identifies his interests, skills, and goals. The teaching team (with William as an equal member) writes a behavior support plan with instructional and support strategies and environmental modifications to help William learn a new replacement response to his acting-out behavior. The behavior support plan is also incorporated into William's IEP.

Data are collected for several weeks by the teaching team *and* William. After 3 weeks, the data clearly show that the problem behavior has decreased and William's replacement behavior is demonstrated consistently at his vocational placement.

Opportunity for Participatory Decision Making

O'Neill et al. (1997) writes that a functional assessment is an information gathering process that includes an analysis of the person's schedule, activity patterns, curricula, staff support, and physical environment, as well as the observation of the person's behavior in the targeted setting. When collected, this information provides alternatives to the behavioral problem. Many educators complete the functional assessment process without direct student input. However, there is an alternative.

Critical Point   Students can participate in functionally assessing their own behaviors and in developing intervention strategies.

Student-directed functional assessment and student-directed behavior support planning involve the student as an equal member of the teaching team. We believe that the student has the right and is the best person to speak about his or her needs, interests, schedules, activities, curricula, problem settings, and intervention strategies (see Kern, Dunlap, Clarke, & Childs, 1994; O'Neill et al., 1997). As students learn self-determination skills, they can become an increasingly effective member of the teaching team. Students that participate in their behavior support planning process will (1) *choose goals*—identify needs and interest based on the functional assessment, (2) *express goals*—lead the behavior support planning meeting which results in the development of a behavior support plan, and

(3) *take action*—implement their behavior support plan, evaluate progress toward goal attainment, and make adjustments to their plan as needed.

Conclusion

Self-determination skills contribute to a successful transition. Since most students with an IEP lack well-developed self-determination skills, teaching these skills must become a priority in the transition process. For this to occur, self-determination must be considered as a transition need. Once the need becomes established, self-determination teaching goals detail what must be taught. Educators, then, must teach students self-determination skills and provide opportunities for students to practice and generalize their learned skills.

Study Questions

1. You are a member of a high school IEP team and believe that self-determination skills need to be taught to your students. How will you include self-determination in the IEP process?
2. From your knowledge of what takes place in secondary programs, identify at least three different ways that each self-determination concept depicted in Table 11–1 can be taught and practiced by students with high incidence disabilities.
3. Write a letter to your Congress representative detailing how IDEA needs to be modified when the act is again authorized to make its self-determination emphasis even stronger than it is today.
4. Your team has a budget of $1,800 to purchase new materials. Go to the web sites of different educational publishing houses and build a purchase request document to submit to your principal. Include a description of the material, its use, how it will help to meet your students' IEP goals, and purchasing information. (See the list of web sites at the end of the chapter.)
5. Using your state's academic standards, write a standards-referenced IEP goal and objectives to teach a self-determination construct from Table 11–1.

Web Sites

Colorado's academic standards:
www.cde.state.co.us/cdedepcom/stanbrowser.htm

Selected list of publishers that distribute self-determination materials:
Sopris West for ChoiceMaker materials:
www.sopriswest.com

Pro-Ed (see books and materials):
http://www.proedinc.com/

Council for Exceptional Children
http://www.cec.sped.org/

Self-Determination Synthesis Project Homepage:
http://www.uncc.edu/sdsp/

12

Transition Planning

Robert Baer

LEARNING OBJECTIVES

The objectives of this chapter are:

1. Develop a general concept of transition planning as it relates to youth with disabilities and the Individuals with Disabilities Act (IDEA) of 1990 and 1997.

2. Identify some common myths about transition planning that have emerged since it has become IDEA policy.

3. Understand the process of preparing for the IEP/transition meeting and the many models, assessments, and considerations that must be addressed before the actual meeting occurs.

4. Understand the process of implementing the transition plan from the development of the IEP/transition plan to the assessment of progress.

5. Develop a general understanding of common questions that may be asked by families in the development and implementation of the transition plan.

Chapter 11 discussed transition planning from the perspective of student self-determination. This chapter examines transition planning from the perspective of the educator who is responsible for creating a choice-rich and supportive environment for individual students in transition. This chapter provides a blueprint for combining the previously discussed transition policy, the best practice, and self-determination strategies into a comprehensive process known as "transition planning." Specifically, this chapter describes a step-by-step method for developing an individualized transition planning process that involves students and their families in (1) the determination of their needs, interests, and preferences, (2) the creation of an outcome-oriented transition process, (3) the development of a coordinated set of transition activities, and (4) the promotion of student movement to desired postsecondary settings.

Transition Planning and the IDEA of 1990 and 1997

The Individuals with Disabilities Education Act of 1990 (IDEA; Pub. L. No. 101-476) mandated transition planning in response to studies that showed poor postsecondary outcomes for students graduating with IEPs (Hasazi, Gordon, & Roe, 1985; SRI International, 1990). The "statement of needed transition services" in the IEP (also known as the individual transition plan or ITP) was designed to improve postsecondary outcomes by assuring that students' IEPs supported their postsecondary goals." The IDEA of 1990 was the first piece of legislation to mandate transition planning by requiring a statement of needed transition services in the IEP for students no later than age 16 and annually thereafter.

The IDEA of 1997 (P.L. 105-17) extended the notion of transition services to include the transition into a high school course of study related to students' individual career interests. It mandated that by no later than age 14, student IEPs (individualized education programs) must specify transition services that are necessary for them to participate in their *desired course of study* (e.g., vocational education or college preparation). This provision was added in order to deal with the concern that students with disabilities often were unable to access educational and vocational programs related to their transition goals. In promulgating regulations for the IDEA of 1997, the committee noted, "the IEP provisions added by P.L. 105-17 are intended to provide greater access by children with disabilities to the general curriculum and to educational reforms [such as school-to-work programs] . . ." (p. 55091).

Critical Point The IDEA of 1990 and 1997 mandated transition planning for all students with IEPs, at first aged 16 or younger, and now aged 14 years or younger.

Table 12–1 outlines and compares the major transition provisions of the IDEA of 1990 and 1997. This table shows that policymakers see transition services as moving in the direction of career education, participation in standards-based reforms (i.e., state and districtwide assessments), and greater student self-determination, especially after the age of majority.

The IDEA of 1990 and 1997 promoted four major criteria for designing transition services. First, they must be based on students' needs, taking into account their preferences and interests. Second, they must be developed through an outcome-oriented process and identify a series of steps toward reaching students desired employment and adult living goals. Third, transition services must be a coordinated set of activities encompassing a broad range of services and supports, including those provided by the school, the family, the community, the adult service system, and the postsecondary environments. Finally, they must be designed to promote student movement from school to

TABLE 12–1

Comparison of the Transition Requirements of the IDEA of 1990 and 1997

Transition and the IDEA of 1990	Transition and the IDEA of 1997
Definition of Transition	**Definition of Transition**
The term "transition services" means a coordinated set of activities for a student, designed within an outcome-oriented process, that promotes movement from school to postschool activities, including postsecondary education, vocational training, integrated employment (including supported employment), continuing and adult education, adult services, independent living, or community participation. The coordinated set of activities described in paragraph (a) of this section must be based on the student's needs, taking into account the student's preferences and interests, and shall include (I) instruction, (ii) community experiences, (iii) the development of employment and other postschool objectives, and (iv) when appropriate, acquisition of daily living skills and functional vocational evaluation (20 U.S.C. 1401 (19)).	The term "transition services" means a coordinated set of activities for a student, with a disability that - (A) is designed within an outcome-oriented process, that promotes movement from school to postschool activities, including postsecondary education, vocational training, integrated employment (including supported employment), continuing and adult education, adult services, independent living, or community participation; (B) is based on the student's needs, taking into account the student's preferences and interests; (C) includes instruction, related services, community experiences, the development of employment and other postschool objectives, and, when appropriate, acquisition of daily living skills and functional vocational evaluation (section 602).
Transition Statement and the IEP	**Transition Statement and the IEP**
The term "individualized education program" means a written statement for each child with a disability . . . which statement shall include: (C) a statement of needed transition services for students beginning no later than age 16 and annually thereafter (and, when determined appropriate for the individual, beginning at age 14 or younger), including, when appropriate, a statement of the interagency responsibilities of linkages (or both) before the student leaves the school setting (20 U.S.C. 1401 (2)).	(vii) (I) beginning at age 14, and updated annually, a statement of the transition service needs of the child . . . that focuses on the child's courses of study (such as participation in advanced-placement courses or a vocational education program); (II) beginning at age 16 (or younger, if determined appropriate by the IEP Team), a statement of needed transition services for the child, including, when appropriate, a statement of the interagency responsibilities or any needed linkages; (III) beginning at least one year before the child reaches the age of majority under state law, a statement that the child has been informed of his or her rights under this title that will transfer to the child . . . on reaching the age of majority under 615 (m) (section 614 (d)).

(continued)

335

TABLE 12–1

(Concluded)

Transition and the IDEA of 1990	Transition and the IDEA of 1997
Participation in Assessments	**Participation in Assessments**
Not addressed in the IDEA of 1990	(A) In General—Children with disabilities are included in general State and districtwide assessment programs, with appropriate accommodations where necessary. As appropriate, the state or local education agency— (I) develops guidelines for the participation of children with disabilities in alternate assessments for those children who cannot participate in state and districtwide assessment programs; and (ii) develops and beginning not later than July 1, 2000, conduct those assessments (section 612 (a) (17)) .
Transfer of Rights at the Age of Majority	**Transfer of Rights at the Age of Majority**
Not addressed in the IDEA of 1990	. . . when a child with a disability reaches the age of majority under state law (except for a child with a disability who has been determined to be incompetent under state law)— (A) the public agency shall provide any notice required by this section to both the individual and the parents; (B) all other rights accorded to parents under this part transfer to the child; (C) the agency shall notify the individual and the parents of the transfer of rights . . . (2) . . . a child who has not been determined to be incompetent, but who is determined not to have the ability to provide informed consent with respect to the educational program of the child, the state shall establish procedures for appointing the parent of the child, or if the parent is not available, another appropriate individual, to represent the education interests of the child throughout the period of eligibility of the child under this part (section 615).

Sources: The Individuals with Disabilities Education Act of 1990 and the Individuals with Disabilities Education Act of 1997; Pub. L. 101-476 and Pub. L. 107-17, respectively.

postschool activities by developing bridges of generic, time-limited, and ongoing supports that extend into early adulthood (Will, 1984).

IDEA Regulations Pertaining to Determining Student Needs, Interests, and Preferences

The IDEA of 1990 resulted in a number of federal regulations relative to assuring the consideration of student needs, interests, and preferences in transition planning. Section 300.344 required that, "if the purpose of the meeting is the consideration of transition services for a student, the public agency (school) shall invite the student." If the student does not attend the IEP meeting in which transition is discussed (or the IEP/transition meeting), the IDEA required that the school "ensure that the student's preferences and interests are considered." Section 300.345 specified that the notice of the IEP/transition meeting must inform parents that the student will be invited to the meeting. The IDEA of 1997 strengthened the focus upon student self-determination by adding the requirement that the IEP include a statement that students and their parents have been notified in writing of the transfer of IDEA rights to students upon reaching the age of majority (section 615 (m)).

IDEA Regulations Pertaining to Outcome-Oriented Transition Planning

The IDEA of 1990 and 1997 regulations addressed outcome-oriented planning by strongly recommending provision of transition services in the area of "development of employment and other post-school adult living objectives." The IDEA described employment and postschool adult living objectives as including "post-secondary education, vocational training, integrated employment (including supported employment), continuing and adult education, adult services, independent living, or community participation" (section 602). By requiring

transition services in the area of development of employment and other postschool adult living objectives, the IDEA promoted both the *identification* of postsecondary goals through career exploration and the *development* of postsecondary goals through career development activities. Additionally, the IDEA's inclusion of independent living and community participation as possible postschool objectives suggested that transition services need to focus upon more than just school-to-work activities.

IDEA Regulations Pertaining to Developing a Coordinated Set of Activities

The IDEA mandated that each student's IEP/transition plan include, "if appropriate, a statement of each public agency's and each participating agency's responsibilities or linkages, or both, before the student leaves the school setting." It required that each meeting include, "the child's teacher, a regular education teacher (if the student is or might be in regular education) and . . . a representative of the public agency other than the child's teacher who is qualified to provide, or supervise the provision of, special education. . ." The IDEA also specified that, "the public agency shall invite . . . a representative of any other agency that is likely to be responsible for providing or paying for transition services" and went on to stipulate that, "if an agency invited to send a representative to a meeting does not do so, the public agency must take other steps to obtain the participation of the other agency in the planning of any transition services." The IDEA placed the responsibility for coordination of transition plans with schools and required that:

> If a participating agency fails to provide agreed upon transition services contained in the IEP of a student with a disability, the public agency responsible for the student's education shall, as soon as possible, initiate a meeting for the purpose of identifying alternative strategies to meet the transition objectives and, if necessary, revising the student's IEP.

IDEA Regulations Pertaining to Promoting Student Movement to Postschool Activities

The IDEA required that transition services be designed to move students toward their desired postschool activities and suggested that they should be initiated early enough to achieve the student's desired postschool outcomes. The IDEA of 1997 required that, *"beginning at age 14, and updated annually, a statement of the transition service needs of the child . . . that focuses on the child's courses of study (such as participation in advanced-placement courses or a vocational education program)"* be included in the IEP. The IDEA mandated *by no later than age 16* a statement of needed transition services in the IEP that addresses the need for transition services specified in the definition, including "instruction, related services, community experiences, the development of employment and other postschool objectives, and, when appropriate, acquisition of daily living skills and functional vocational evaluation" (section 602).

Common Myths in Regard to IDEA Transition Policy Implementation

Stowitschek and Kelso (1989) warned that making transition plans part of the IEP would cause them to take on many negative characteristics of the IEP, including lack of year-to-year continuity and low-quality objectives. Research indicates transition plans often lack vision, linkages, and methods for coordinating services (Gallivan-Fenlon, 1994; Grigal, Test, Beattie, & Wood, 1997; Lombard, Hazelkorn, & Neubert, 1992; Krom & Prater, 1993). Four common myths have become prevalent in schools where educators have focused upon transition "paper compliance" (Baer, Simmons, & Flexer, 1996).

Myth One: There Is One Transition Planning Process for All Students

Transition planning as a career planning process must be individualized and suited to the cognitive and career needs of individual students with disabilities. Some students may choose to participate in regular education career planning processes as part of transition planning (Clark & Kolstoe, 1995; Menchetti & Piland, 1998), whereas others may prefer person-centered planning approaches such as *Personal Futures Planning* (Mount, 1994; O'Brien, 1987). The principles of self-determination and appropriateness must be concurrently applied in the selection of transition planning approaches.

Students with disabilities should be able to take an active role in transition planning, but they also must be provided with planning that is sophisticated enough to address the complexity of school and adult service systems. Consequently, no one transition planning process fits all students. In fact, some students may need multiple planning approaches (e.g., person-centered planning and career planning).

Myth Two: Transition Planning Occurs Only in the IEP/Transition Meeting

Transition planning involves much more than a short meeting at the beginning of an IEP meeting. In a comfortable environment, students and families should be given time to discuss their needs and desired postsecondary outcomes, and to plan activities for several years at a time. This generally requires a discussion of these issues prior to the IEP/transition meeting since students with disabilities and their families have been shown to participate much less in larger meetings with many professionals in attendance (Pumpian, Campbell, & Hesche, 1992; Whitney-Thomas, Shaw, Honey, & Butterworth, 1998). The planning process, *Choosing Options and Accommodations for Children* (COACH), suggests that the initial interview limits participation to the teacher/facilitator, family members, and the student to assure meaningful student and family input (Giangreco, Cloninger, & Iverson, 1993).

Myth Three: Transition Plans Cover One Year

Transition plans are by definition long-term plans since they are focused upon postschool outcomes. The IDEA requires that these plans be reviewed annually but that they should not be discarded each year and started anew. Unfortunately, this presents a logistical problem when the transition plan is part of the IEP. As part of the IEP, transition services are subject to the same requirement as other IEP services, and it has been argued that multiyear transition plans obligate the school to provide services too far in the future to assure that they will be available when the time comes. Yet, without multiyear planning, the transition statement in the IEP becomes nothing more than a list of short-term functional activities. Many schools have addressed this dilemma by developing a long-term plan that is passed along from year to year.

Student participation in planning is necessary.

Myth Four: Transition Teams Meet Only Annually

The IDEA requires that the transition team be reconvened as soon as possible if transition services cannot be provided as planned. General principles of good planning require monitoring, evaluation, and revision of plans whenever major changes occur, including (1) change in student goals, (2) problems in student performance, (3) failure to obtain services as planned, or (4) new opportunities or programs that may benefit the student. Yet, research indicates that less than 25% of secondary schools have a mechanism for reconvening the IEP/transition team if services cannot be provided as planned (Baer et al., 1996).

Critical Point   Implementation of IDEA's transition mandates should not become a barrier to student choice and the use of transition practices that go beyond minimum or "paper compliance" requirements.

Preparing for the Transition Meeting

Choosing Transition Planning Processes

Transition planning must address the unique planning capabilities and needs of students with disabilities and their families. To some degree, all transition planning approaches should be (1) person-centered, (2) self-determined, and (3) career-oriented. Planning approaches that are developed for use with students with disabilities may focus upon one of these areas, but they should address all three. This often requires that more than one planning approach be used with a particular student (e.g., futures and career planning).

Planning approaches emphasizing *person-centered planning* have been used primarily for individuals who have difficulty developing career goals due to both the extent of their disability or a difficulty in expressing preferences (Menchetti & Piland, 1998). Although typically used with students with severe disabilities, these planning approaches also may benefit students with milder disabilities who have no postsecondary goals or direction to their IEPs (Rojewski, 1993). Person-centered planning approaches usually involve a facilitator, a recorder, the student, and various family, friends, classmates, and coworkers who work together to answer questions regarding the student's (1) history, (2) dreams, (3) nightmares, (4) relationships, (5) abilities, and (6) plan of action. Person-centered planning approaches include:

1. *Personal Futures Planning* (Mount & Zwernick, 1988). A type of person-centered planning that involves dreaming, describing, and doing with the family and their support system.
2. *McGill Action Planning System* (MAPs) (Vandercook, York, & Forest, 1989). A person-centered planning approach that focuses upon seven areas: (a) nonnegotiables, (b) strong preferences, (c) highly desirables, (d) personal characteristics, (e) personal concerns, (f) needed supports, and (g) action steps.
3. COACH (Giangreco et al., 1993). A form of person-centered planning that stands for choosing options and accommodations for children. Includes the family's values and dreams in IEP planning.
4. *Lifestyle Planning* (O'Brien, 1987). A form of person-centered planning that describes future goals and defines the steps needed to reach them.
5. *Transition Planning Inventory* (Clark & Patton, 1997). An inventory approach that focuses upon the student's skills and support needs in the areas of (a) employment,

(b) further education, (c) daily living, (d) leisure activities, (e) community participation, (f) health, (g) self-determination, (h) communication, and (i) interpersonal relationships.

Self-determination is an important focus of transition planning. Good person-centered and career-oriented planning processes address the need for students to make their own decisions, but self-determination models may enhance student participation by developing self-awareness and leadership skills. Self-determination approaches typically focus upon improving the student's ability (a) to self-advocate, (b) to make decisions, (c) to develop goals, (d) to demonstrate leadership, and (e) to take an active role in IEP/transition meetings. Self-determination approaches include:

1. *ChoiceMaker* (Martin, Huber Marshall, Maxson, & Jerman, 1996). A self-determination approach that focuses upon (a) choosing goals, (b) expressing goals, and (c) taking action.
2. *Group Action Planning* (Turnbull & Turnbull, 1993). A self-determination approach that helps students to take charge of personal futures planning.
3. *Whose Future Is It Anyway?* (Wehmeyer & Kelchner, 1995). A self-determination curriculum that is designed for persons with cognitive disabilities consisting of 36 lessons that address (a) having self-awareness, (b) making decisions, (c) obtaining supports and transition services, (d) writing and evaluating transition objectives, and (e) learning leadership skills.
4. *Next S.T.E.P.* (Halpern et al., 1997). A student-directed transition approach consisting of 16 lessons that address (a) getting started, (b) self-exploring and evaluating, (c) developing goals and activities, and (d) putting a plan into place.
5. IPLAN (Van Reusen & Bos, 1990). A form of person-centered planning that stands

for inventory, plan, listen, ask, and name your goals.

6. TAKE CHARGE (Powers et al., 1996). A student-directed collaborative approach that pairs youth with adults of the same gender with similar challenges, and uses four primary strategies: (a) skill facilitation, (b) mentoring, (c) peer support, and (d) parent support to develop student skills in achievement, partnership, and coping.

Career planning approaches can be effective for many students, especially students who plan to enter postsecondary education and technical careers. Career development approaches tend to be (1) systematic, (2) developmental, (3) focused on self-awareness, and (4) oriented to a wide range of occupations. Career planning approaches include:

1. *What Color Is My Parachute* (Bolles 1995). This publication provides an overview of career development and some useful exercises and examples related to identifying interests, researching jobs, developing résumés, and conducting interviews.

2. *Life-Centered Career Education* (LCCE) (Brolin & Schatzman, 1989). This career development approach delineates 22 major competencies that can be infused into primary, middle, and secondary curricula to address the major life domains of work, home, and academics.

3. *The Career Maturity Index* (Crites, 1978). This assessment, along with the *Career Development Inventory* (1990), can direct counseling (or the use of a computerized DISCOVER program) to address competencies in the areas of student, leisurite, citizen, worker, and homemaker.

4. *The Meyers/Briggs* (Myers & McCauley, 1985). This assessment identifies four personality temperaments that can be used to develop self- and career awareness (e.g., extroverted, intuitive, feeling, perceptive, or EIFP).

5. *Employability Life Skills Assessment* (Weaver & DeLuca, 1987). This criterion-referenced checklist may be used yearly to assess a student's level of performance in 24 critical employability skills areas in the domains of personal, social, and daily living habits.

6. *The Self-Directed Search* (Holland, 1985). This instrument identifies six personality types and matches them with six matching categories of jobs to help students make a career choice related to their needs and preferences.

The Self-Directed Search is particularly effective for transition planning since it provides information on student personality types and matches it with occupations that have a high probability of being a good career choice (Simmons & Baer, 1996). It is recommended that this and other instruments be used under the supervision of a person who is qualified to administer them.

Critical Point Transition planning approaches should be selected with the student and the family and should emphasize self-determination, person-centeredness, and career orientation.

Time Lines for Transition Planning

Like all people, persons with disabilities go through many transitions in their life (Brolin & Schatzman, 1989; Repetto & Correa, 1996). In the context of this book, transition planning is focused upon the transition from school to adulthood. However, it is important to view transition in the context of the student's total learning experience since transition planning at the secondary level must build upon the student's developmental experiences up to that time. Table 12–2 shows how transition choices should be developed and formed from primary school on.

Forming the Transition Planning Team

The composition of the transition planning team is a primary consideration in the development of

TABLE 12–2

Timelines for Transition Planning

Primary Level: Grades 1–4

Goals: Employability and independent living skills and attitudes

Objectives:

1. To develop positive work habits
2. To appreciate all types of work
3. To develop an understanding of how to cope with disability

Possible Activity Areas:

- Inclusion activities
- Responsibility activities
- Work sample activities
- Career field trips
- Discussions about work
- Discussions of interests and aptitudes
- Exploration of technology

Middle School: Grades 5–8

Goals: Career exploration and transition planning relative to course of study

Objectives:

1. To understand the relationship of school to work
2. To understand interest, aptitudes, and preferences
3. To understand work, education, independent living, and community options
4. To determine a general secondary course of study
5. To identify needed accommodations and supports for secondary education
6. To specify transition services needed to participate in a desired course of study by no later than age 14.

Possible Activity Areas:

- Visits to vocational and technical schools
- Visits to high school
- Complete interest inventories
- Functional vocational assessment
- Career fairs
- Survey transition needs and preferences
- Employability assessment
- Daily living skills classes
- Money and budgeting classes
- Community awareness classes
- Political awareness classes
- Job shadowing
- Career guidance
- Self-determination and advocacy training
- Training in use of disability technology and related services
- Computer training
- Mobility training
- Counseling
- Employability skills training

High School: Grades 9–10

Goals: Career exploration and transition planning
Objectives
1. To develop meaningful and realistic postsecondary goals
2. To develop work, education, residential, and community participation skills and supports relevant to goals
3. To learn to manage disability technology and request accommodations

Possible Activity Areas:
- Technology assessment
- Make agency referrals
- Update transition goals
- Self-determination training
- Develop IEP/transition plan
- Vocational education
- Placement in advanced classes
- Work experiences
- Job shadowing
- Job placement
- Job clubs
- Linkages with adult services

High School: Grades 11 and up

Goals: Transition and overlap into postsecondary environments desired by the student
Objectives:
1. To test goals through experiences and activities
2. To secure options for postsecondary education and/or employment
3. To develop residential and community participation supports and contacts
4. To develop linkages with adult services
5. To empower students and families to function in adult environments

Possible Activity Areas:
- Review and revise IEP/transition plans
- Involve adult services
- Self-determination training
- Apply for adult services
- Apply for postsecondary education
- Financial planning
- Visit relevant postsecondary environments
- Develop job seeking skills
- Job placements
- Community memberships
- Transfer transition coordination
- Develop follow up supports
- Transfer transition plan to family or adult services

Source: From *Transition planning: A guide for parents and professionals* (p. 9), by R. Baer, R. McMahan, and R. Flexer, 1999, Kent, Ohio: Kent State University. Copyright 1999 by Robert Baer. Reprinted with permission.

a transition plan. Selection of team members should be a collaborative effort with the student and the family integrally involved (O'Brien, 1987). This is important because research indicates that self-friend-family networks account for more than 80% of the jobs obtained by students after graduation (Hasazi, Gordon, & Roe, 1985; SRI International, 1992). The selection of the transition team also should include representatives from high school and postsecondary environments desired by students so that they can establish contacts and become familiar with the requirements of the programs they want to enter.

Critical Point   The transition team should be developed with the student and the family and should include core members, natural supporters, adult service providers, and representatives of postsecondary environments.

Core transition team members are persons who always should be involved in the IEP/transition planning meeting. According to the IDEA, core members include:

1. The student with a disability
2. Parents and guardians
3. The special education teacher
4. A representative of the local education agency who is knowledgeable about the general education curriculum
5. An individual who can interpret evaluation
6. A regular education teacher (if the student is or might be in regular or vocational education classes).

In addition to these core members, individual students may have specific needs or preferences that require the involvement of other transition stakeholders. These include but are not limited to (1) work-study coordinators and transition specialists, (2) related service providers, (3) vocational rehabilitation counselors, (4) adult service providers, (5) employers, (6) representatives of postsecondary education programs, and (7) community supporters and advocates. These

and other team members should be identified in the process of assessing the student's desired environments related to work, education, community participation, and residential living. The respective roles of transition team members are outlined in Table 12–3.

Transition Assessments

The IEP/transition coordinator should assure that students and their families have all the information they need to make informed choices regarding student postsecondary goals, course of study, and necessary transition services. Prior to the meeting, the educator should collect and obtain the assessments needed for the IEP/transition meeting. These may include a range of vocational and life skills assessments that can help students to identify their strengths, needs, interests, and preferences. It also can include student and family surveys that assess the student's career maturity and family-student agreement on postsecondary goals. The following list includes some types of assessments that may be useful for specific students (Clark & Patton, 1997):

- Interest inventories (computer and written)
- Transition surveys
- Employability skills inventories
- Personal futures planning
- Structured situational (i.e., home, community, and work) assessments
- Assessments of postschool environments desired by the student
- Curriculum-based assessment
- Structured interviews
- Social histories
- Adaptive behavior inventories
- Life skills inventories
- Assessment of prerequisite skills for vocational education
- Aptitude tests
- Personality scales
- Social skills inventories

TABLE 12-3

Responsibilities of Transition Team Members

Team Members	Responsibilities
Student*	Identifies needs, strengths, preferences, and interests
	Takes a leadership role in planning with supports
	Participates in all planning activities
	Identifies friends, family, and community members who can be part of the transition team
	Assumes IDEA rights at the age of majority
Parent/Guardian*	Provides information regarding student needs, strengths, preferences, and interests
Also:	Participates in referrals to transition programs and adult services
Siblings	Assists in procuring social security numbers, identification cards, and transportation passes
Friends	Plans for long-term financial support, social security, trust funds, or other supports
Advocates	Asks for assistance in obtaining community and residential services as needed
	Provides opportunities for the student to try out adult roles and responsibilities
	Identifies the person who will coordinate the transition plan
	Identifies friends, family, and community members who can be part of the transition team
Special education teacher*	Helps students to identify postsecondary goals and to obtain needed transition services
Collaborating with:	Identifies school or community agency personnel to be included in transition planning
Vocational education	Prepares the student and the family for participation in the IEP/transition team
Work study	Writes the statement of needed transition services in the IEP transition plan
Related services	Coordinates transition services and activities in the IEP/transition plan (may delegate)
Guidance counselor	Provides information and assists families in developing referrals for adult services
	Links the IEP to the student's course of study and required testing
	Collects and monitors information about student progress
	Provides or obtains accommodations and supports for all education services
Regular education teacher*	Connects the IEP to the general education curriculum
	Helps students to identify postsecondary goals and needed transition services
	Provides classroom instruction to support the student transition to adult environments
	Collects and monitors information about student progress
	Adapts curriculum and provides or obtains accommodation for regular education
	Obtains or provides accommodations for state and regional proficiency tests
An individual who can interpret evaluations*	Provides assessment information regarding student needs, interests, and preferences
	Provides assessment information regarding student strengths and aptitudes
	Interprets assessments and evaluations for the student and the family
	Identifies limitations of assessments and additional assessment needs
	Works with the student and family to identify assessment options

* Core Member

(Continued)

TABLE 12–3

Responsibilities of Transition Team Members (Concluded)

Representative of the local education agency familiar with the curriculum*	Provides information about programs offered throughout the school
	Identifies how the student with a disability can be included in general education programs
	Assists in obtaining technology, accommodations, and supports for inclusion and transition
	Helps to identify how to address general education curriculum and competencies
	Assists the transition team in obtaining accommodations and supports for student graduation, and for participation in state and regional proficiency tests
Adult service providers, including:	
VR services	May provide job training and placement before and after graduation
MR/DD services	May provide case management and service coordination services
Mental health	Determine eligibility for SSI and medicaid (generally VR and social security)
Bureau of employment	May provide independent living services
Social security	May provide functional vocational assessments and job counseling
Independent living center	May provide health services and supports
Employers	May provide technology and accommodations
Postsecondary educators	May help to fund postsecondary education or vocational training
Human services	May provide recreational and leisure opportunities
	May provide counseling and behavioral supports
	May assist in developing peer and coworker supports
	May provide opportunities to try out postsecondary environments
	May provide child support

*Core member.

Source: Transition planning: A guide for parents and professionals (p. 11), by R. Baer, R. McMahan, and R. Flexer, 1999, Kent, Ohio: Kent State University. Copyright 1999 by Robert Baer. Reprinted with permission.

- Vocational skills assessments
- Professional assessments (e.g., psychology, medical, vision, speech, and mobility)
- College entrance examinations
- Assessment of technology needs
- Career portfolios

Care must be used in selection of standardized assessment instruments and in presentation of their findings. Assessment information should be (1) valid for the type of student being tested, (2) related to actual and desired student environments, (3) understood by all members of the transition team, and (4) focused upon student strengths. Research indicates that standardized assessment procedures often lack validity for students with disabilities because they do not consider the effects of supports, technology, and training on student performance (Menchetti & Piland, 1998). Hagner and Dileo (1993) point out that standardized assessment procedures may have little use for students with severe disabilities since they lack the pressures, cues, sights, and sounds of the environments in which students will have to perform. These researchers advocate strongly for the use of situational assessments, or assessments that are conducted in the actual environments in which the student is expected to perform.

Critical Point   Transition assessments should be valid for the type of student tested, individualized, strength-focused, functional, and socially referenced.

Transition Service Options

According to the IDEA of 1997, transition services are a coordinated set of activities that generally should include (1) instruction, (2) community experiences, (3) development of employment and other postschool adult living objectives, and (4) related services. If appropriate, the IEP/transition plan also should include transition services in the areas of (1) daily living skills, (2) functional vocational evaluation, and (3) interagency link-

Varied transition services are required to meet mandates.

ages. The seven major categories of transition services outlined in the IDEA of 1997 can be described as follows:

1. *Instruction.* Includes tutoring, employability skills training, vocational education, social skills training, college entrance exam preparation, preparation for taking state and regional proficiency tests, and placement in advanced classes. Instruction may include teacher-developed accommodations, curriculum adaptations, and peer tutoring.
2. *Community experiences.* Includes job shadowing, community work experiences, tours of postsecondary education settings, and residential and community tours.
3. *Development of employment and other postschool adult living objectives.* Includes career planning,

FIGURE 12–1
Backward Planning Worksheet

Postsecondary Goal: Supported Employment in a Clerical Setting
Current Age: 18
Age to Graduate: 22

Needed transition service	Age 19	Age 20	Age 21	Age 22
1. Supported employment in a clerical setting			X	X
2 Follow-along support			X	X
3. Job placement services and job club		X	X	
4. Transportation training	X	X		
5. Develop social security work incentive plan		X		
6. Vocational education in clerical skills	X	X		
7. Community work experiences during the school year		X		
8. Summer jobs	X	X		
9. Job shadowing	X	X		
10. Guidance counseling	X			
11. Employability skills training	X	X		
12. Apply for social security benefits—done at age 18				
13. Referral to vocational rehabilitation—done at age 16				
14. Referral for MR/DD services—done at age 16				

Source: From *Transition planning: A guide for parents and professionals* (p. 17), by R. Baer, R. McMahan, and R. Flexer, 1999, Kent, Ohio: Kent State University. Copyright 1999 by Robert Baer. Reprinted with permission

guidance counseling, interest inventories, person-centered planning, futures planning, self-determination training, job placement, and job tryouts.

4. *Transition focus-related services.* Includes occupational and physical therapy, speech therapy, social services, psychology services, medical services, rehabilitation technology, and other professional supports to move the student toward postschool outcomes

5. *Daily living skills training.* Includes self-care training, home repair, health training, home economics, independent living training, and money management.

6. *Linkages with adult services.* Includes referrals or assignment of responsibility for services to vocational rehabilitation (VR), summer youth employment programs, mental retardation and developmental disability (MR/DD) services, mental health services, social security, independent living centers, and agency fairs involving a range of adult services.

7. *Functional vocational evaluation needs.* Includes situational work assessments, work samples, work-adjustment programs, aptitude tests, and a series of job tryouts.

Backward Planning

The transition coordinator should employ a technique known as "backward planning" in developing transition services and the IEP (Steere, Wood, Panscofar, & Butterworth. (1990). Figure 12–1 shows how backward planning would work for a student desiring supported employment in a clerical situation after graduation. Starting with the final year prior to graduation, the student is established in the environment of choice—in this case, supported employment—to assure that the necessary services and supports are in place prior to graduation so that he or she could be simply transferred to the adult service system. Two years before graduation, the student is moved toward transition into supported employment through job placement, job club, and follow-along services. Three years prior to graduation, transition services are focused upon community experiences and vocational education that lead to supported employment. Four years prior to graduation, the focus of activities is career exploration with a focus upon job shadowing, guidance counseling, and employability skills training. This backward planning approach should be used for each student's postsecondary goals, including postsecondary education, independent living, and community participation. A general rule of thumb for backward planning is, the more severe the disability, the more overlap that will be needed between school and postschool environments. Figure 12–1 shows a sample backward planning worksheet for a transition employment goal.

Critical Point The development and implementation of postsecondary goals should drive the student's educational experience each year until graduation.

Preparing for Student and Family Led IEP/Transition Meetings

Prior to the IEP/transition meeting, the transition coordinator should go over the summary of assessment-identified transition service needs with the student and the family in order to develop consensus on (1) general postsecondary goals, (2) the student's course of study, (3) the types of transition services needed, and (4) the student's self-determination needs. Backward planning can be done with the student and the family to test the feasibility of postsecondary goals and to help them understand the amount of effort that will be necessary to achieve those goals. The results of this

discussion should be summarized so that they can be used by the student and the family to drive the IEP/transition meeting. The student and the family also should be acquainted with the terms that may be used in the IEP meeting, and the use of ChoiceMaker or other student-led IEP curricula may aid in this process. A sample glossary is included in Appendix D.

An IEP/transition meeting agenda should be developed with time allotted for the student and the family to lead the discussion. The meeting agenda should specify meeting activities, the time allotted for each activity, and the desired outcomes. At the start of the IEP/transition meeting, there should be time for all transition team members to introduce themselves, to identify their role, and to state how they know the student. The following is a sample 2-hour IEP/transition team meeting agenda. Times and agenda items may vary depending on (1) the number of meeting participants, (2) the student transition service needs, and (3) the level of consensus among team members prior to the meeting. The team may want to appoint a timekeeper at the start of the meeting to notify members when the discussion is exceeding the allotted time. Figure 12–2 shows a sample agenda for an IEP/transition meeting.

Critical Point Educators must plan ahead to ensure student and family participation in the IEP meeting in which transition is discussed.

Implementing the Transition Plan

Writing the Statement of Needed Transition Services into the IEP

The way the statement of needed transition services is written into the IEP may vary according to both the organization of the IEP and the needs of individual students. Typically, an IEP transition statement (or transition plan) should include (1) the student's course of study and related transition needs, (2) the student's

FIGURE 12–2
Sample IEP/Transition Meeting Agenda

Cindy—Age 16		
Agenda Item	**Time—Presenter**	**Outcome**
I. Introductions	5 minutes—Teacher	Team sharing of names, relationship to student
II. Overview of agenda and meeting rules	5 minutes—Teacher	Team understanding of meeting purpose and process
III. Presentation of student/family postsecondary goals and course of study	10 minutes—Student and Family	Team understanding of student postsecondary goals and preferred couse of study
IV. Presentation of student transition service and activity preferences	10 minutes—Student and Family	Understanding of student transition service and activity preferences
V. Discussion of transition service needs/preferences	15 minutes—Team	Consensus on needed transition services
VI. Assignment of responsibilities and timelines	20 minutes—Team	Completed IEP/transition plan
VII. IEP development	60 minutes—Team	Completed IEP

Source: Adapted from *Transition planning: A guide for parents and professionals* (p. 19), by R. Baer, R. McMahan, and R. Flexer, 1999, Kent, Ohio: Kent State University. Copyright 1999 by Robert Baer. Reprinted with permission.

postsecondary goals in regard to work, post-secondary education, residential living, and community participation, and (3) needed transition services and the persons who are responsible for each. Figure 12–3 shows how a statement of needed transition services can be written into an IEP. It should be emphasized that the use of standard transition planning formats may impede the creativity of transition planning teams and should, therefore, only be used as a starting point for transition planning.

Assessing Transition Progress Using a Career Portfolio

The *career portfolio* is an important tool for assessing competencies, especially during the transition years. The career portfolio may serve several functions: It can provide a standardized form of assessment that can be used for all students, including those with the most severe disabilities. It also may help students to job match and to go

on job interviews by providing documentation of skills desired by employers (Sarkees-Wircenski & Wircenski, 1994).

The basis of a career portfolio is a set of competencies that can be applied to student high school experiences and activities. The student demonstrates these competencies in a number of environments, including the home, school, work, and community. Documentation of competencies may include examples of the student's work, photographs, supervisor's comments and evaluations, and even videotapes. The assessment of the career portfolio may be done by the teacher in collaboration with family members, other educators, related service providers, adult service providers, or employers.

The competency areas addressed by the career portfolio may be drawn from a number of sources. A widely recognized source of career competencies is the Secretary of Labor's Commission on Achieving Necessary Skills (commonly referred to as SCANS). An example of a

FIGURE 12–3
Sample Format for IEP/Transition Plan

Statement of Needed Transition Services			
Name: Date:			
Person responsible for coordinating transition:			
Postsecondary goals:			
Course of study and needed transition services:			
Transition area and related activities	Responsible Person	IEP Goal	Start End
1. *Instruction:*			
2. *Community experiences:*			
3. *Development of employment and adult living objectives:*			
4. *Related services:*			
5. *Daily living skills:*			
6. *Linkages with adult services:*			
7. *Functional vocational evaluation:*			
Comments:			

Source: From *Transition planning: A guide for parents and professionals* (p. 21), by R. Baer, R. McMahan, and R. Flexer, 1999, Kent, Ohio: Kent State University. Copyright 1999 by Robert Baer. Reprinted with permission.

SCANS career portfolio assessment appears in Figure 12–4.

A Case Study on Transition Planning

Cindy was a student who had autism with pervasive support needs relative to self-care, learning, self-direction, communication, and independent living. Her autism was often exhibited in the form of irrational fears, aggression, stereotypical behavior, and rituals. In middle and early high school , it was determined that Cindy was not responding to traditional educational approaches as evidenced by her distractiveness and aggression toward teachers and peers in this environment. At age 14, her parents determined that Cindy should pursue a course of study leading to employment after graduation with transition services in the areas of behavioral supports, direct instruction, and psychiatric consultation. This was written into Cindy's IEP at age 14.

Jill, Cindy's special education teacher, was charged with developing a new IEP/transition plan for her since she was turning 16 this year of school. After consultation with Cindy's parents and observation of Cindy's interests and preferences, it was determined that Cindy would benefit from personal futures planning, a psychology assessment, and a variety of situational assessments to determine her needs, interests, and preferences. These assessments were arranged with the help of the guidance counselor, the work-study coordinator, and a futures planning consultant from a local university.

Critical Point   Assessment approaches were developed in conjunction with Cindy and her family.

As a result of Personal Futures Planning (Mount & Zwernick, 1988), it was determined that Cindy and her parents wanted her to work in competitive employment and to live in a supported living situation after graduation. Jill had some concerns that these postsecondary goals may be rather ambitious since Cindy had such extensive behavioral concerns. However, Cindy's

parents pointed out that most of these behaviors were exhibited in the classroom and, therefore, could be controlled by the selection of a calm and nondistracting environment for employment after graduation. After some discussion, Jill agreed to support Cindy and her mother in presenting these postsecondary goals to the IEP/transition team.

Psychology assessments showed Cindy having considerable difficulty with changes in routine and a history of developing rituals that interfered with daily routines. A variety of situational assessments showed that Cindy preferred quiet and nondistracting environments and was quite interested in matching and organizing things. She did very well in the hospital records room filing records, although she had one outburst when maintenance workers had to work on the lights. She also did very well in delivering magazines and mail to patients. Transitional service needs were identified as follows:

1. *Instruction.* Cindy needed social skills training, behavioral supports, job skills training, and direct instruction approaches.
2. *Community experiences.* Cindy needed community work experiences related to working in nondistracting clerical settings, experiences in getting to and from the bus, and experiences in living away from her parents.
3. *Development of employment and other postschool adult living objectives.* Cindy needed extensive job placement services and a plan for ongoing behavioral supports in both supported employment and supported living.
4. *Related services.* Assessment showed that Cindy needed related services in the areas of psychology services and augmented communication technology.
5. *Daily living skills training.* As reported by her parents, Cindy needed help to use public transportation.
6. *Linkages with adult services.* Assessment showed that Cindy would benefit from

FIGURE 12–4
Sample Career Portfolio Assessment using SCANS Competencies

Student Name:	Code amount of support needed			
Date:	(C) Continuous, (H) Hourly, (D) Daily, (W) Weekly, (M) Monthly, (I) Independent (NO) No Opportunity.			
Evaluator(s):	Append photos, samples of work, videos, or comments			
SCANS Competencies	**Home**	**Work**	**Class**	**Leisure**
1. Organizing, Planning, and Resource Allocation				
1.1. Selects relevant activities				
1.2. Prioritizes activities				
1.3. Allocates time				
1.4. Follows schedule				
1.5. Handles money effectively				
1.6. Budgets money				
1.7. Uses materials effectively				
2. Working with Others				
2.1. Contributes to group effort				
2.2. Communicates with friends and coworkers				
2.3. Is courteous toward others				
2.4. Initiates activities and provides leadership				
2.5. Resolves conflicts				
2.6. Works with persons from diverse backgrounds				
3. Acquires and Uses Information				
3.1. Acquires new skills by reading or seeking help				
3.2. Organizes and maintains information				
3.3. Interprets directions or requests clarification				
3.4. Uses computers to process information				
4. Understanding Complex Interrelationships				
4.1. Understands tradition and culture of environment				
4.2. Understands role of self in environment				
4.3. Suggests ways to improve environment				

(Continued)

TABLE 12-4
(Concluded)

Student Name:	Code amount of support needed
Date:	(C) Continuous, (H) Hourly, (D) Daily, (W) Weekly, (M) Monthly, (I) Independent (NO) No Opportunity.
Evaluator(s):	Append photos, samples of work, videos, or comments

SCANS Competencies	Home	Work	Class	Leisure
5. Working with a Variety of Technologies				
5.1 Chooses proper tools or procedures				
5.2. Understands proper setup and operation of equipment				
5.3. Prevents, identifies, or solves problems with equipment				
6. Basic Skills				
6.1. Uses written information critical to environment				
6.2. Communicates ideas in writing				
6.3. Uses mathematics critical to environment				
6.4. Effectively listens and responds to verbal directions				
6.5. Effectively communicates verbally				
7. Thinking Skills				
7.1. Generates new ideas				
7.2. Uses good judgment				
7.3. Recognizes and solves problems				
7.4. Uses blueprints or drawings				
7.5. Knows how to find information				
7.6. Uses concepts and values in problem solving				
8. Personal Qualities				
8.1. Works hard and perseveres				
8.2. Maintains a positive view of self				
8.3. Is friendly, adaptable, and polite				
8.4. Exhibits self-control				
8.5. Is ethical and honest				

Source: From *Transition planning: A guide for parents and professionals* (p. 24–25), by R. Baer, R. McMahan, and R. Flexer, 1999, Kent, Ohio: Kent State University. Copyright 1999 by Robert Baer. Reprinted with permission.

supported employment through VR and DD services, and a social security PASS (plans for achieving self-support).

7. *Functional vocational evaluation.* Evaluations emphasized the need to do situational assessments in a variety of environments.

Critical Point   Assessments must be summarized in a manner that is understandable and focused upon student support needs and strengths rather than upon student deficits.

Jill, then, worked with Cindy and her parents to develop a list of whom should be invited to the IEP/transition team meeting. Cindy had shown preferences for Jeff Plant, an older friend who had taken her to many community activities and who was the facilitator of Cindy's futures planning meeting. Jill reported that Jeff Ringles, the work-study coordinator, had suggested involving VR services, social security, and MR/DD since these agencies would be needed to provide support for community work experiences and supported employment. Cindy's mother recommended Jackie Speaker, an occupational therapist who evaluated Cindy for augmented communication technology, and Leonard James, a behavioral specialist who had worked with Cindy. As required by IDEA, Jill also invited a district representative who was knowledgeable about the general education curriculum, Cindy's regular education teacher, and a vocational- education teacher who was able to interpret evaluations.

It was determined that Cindy's mother would start the meeting with a discussion of what she believed were Cindy's preferences in regard to employment, residential living, and community environments. She would also discuss transition services that she felt would address Cindy's needs and environmental preferences, including community work experiences, supported employment (before graduation), and vocational education. A meeting agenda was developed and a meeting was set for a time that was convenient for Cindy, her mother, and Jeff Plant, Cindy's friend.

Critical Point   Prepare the student and the family to participate in the IEP meeting and to lead parts of the discussion.

At the meeting, Jill asked team members to address themselves to Cindy and her mother and to identify themselves, their role, and how they knew Cindy. Jill emphasized that the purpose of the first part of this IEP meeting was to generate a plan that would lead to the types of postsecondary environments desired by Cindy. The rules for discussion were that the team must start with Cindy's environmental preferences and then brainstorm needed transition services to establish her in those postsecondary environments. These transition services, then, would be scheduled across the years leading up to graduation, beginning with the year just prior to graduation.

Jill appointed a recorder and led the IEP/transition team in brainstorming the types of transition services that Cindy would need to move into her preferred environments of a quiet nondistractive work setting, a small family-type residence, and leisure activities with her friends and family. To develop supported employment and independent living options, the adult service representatives suggested (1) the development of a PASS plan with social security, (2) job placement and training through VR, and (3) ongoing employment and residential supports from MR/DD. Fred Fryman, the MR/DD representative, suggested that their case managers could help to coordinate these services and to obtain residential services for Cindy.

The school representatives identified the need to involve Jill in applied mathematics, English, and vocational education since she showed interests and aptitudes in these areas. The regular education teacher agreed to give Cindy assignments that would help her to identify words and numbers that were critical to working in the clerical and library settings she seemed to prefer when she job shadowed at a number of locations. The vocational educator agreed to see about getting Cindy into their secretarial training program with supports and accommodations provided by her behavioral support specialist and occupational therapist. The work-study coordinator agreed to develop community work experiences and supported employment prior to graduation. The district representative agreed to obtain a waiver on some entry requirements for vocational education so that Cindy could attend.

The team suggested, and Cindy's mother concurred, that Cindy should stay in school as long as possible to assure that she had the needed training, technology, and supports to achieve her postsecondary goals. It was determined that she would remain in school until age 22. Using backward planning required transition services, which were planned as follows:

1. *Last year in school* (*age* 21). It was determined that Cindy would need to be established in supported employment with supports from both the school and adult service providers. Due to Cindy's concerns about changes in routine, it was decided that this placement should carry on into adulthood.
2. *Two years from graduation* (*age* 20). It was planned that this year should focus upon the development of the postschool objectives with needed transition services provided in the areas of job placement, development of ongoing supports including a PASS plan, and continued community and career exploration.
3. *Three years from graduation* (*age* 19). It was determined that this year should focus upon the development of community work experiences, situational assessments, and the use of technology and accommodations related to Cindy's desired postsecondary settings.
4. *Four years from graduation* (*age* 18). This year was focused upon completion of vocational education and academics with continued assessment of Cindy's performance

and preferences in regard to work and residential and community settings. Intake for all critical adult service program services also should have been completed.

5. *Five years from graduation* (*age* 17). It was decided that Cindy's transition service needs for the coming year would be mainly in the areas of academics, vocational education, development of employability skills, social skills training, daily living skills training, and mobility training. It also was determined that Cindy must be trained as soon as possible in order to identify technologies and accommodations that she would need for work.

As a result of this discussion, the following transition plan was developed. Each member was given a list of names, phone numbers, and addresses (including E-mail) to facilitate networking. Jill, then, took the time to address Cindy and her mother in order to explain the plan and to ask if they had any questions. The following IEP/transition plan (Figure 12–5) was developed as a result of this planning.

Writing IEP Goals for Transition Services

The IEP/transition meeting moved into planning the IEP for the coming year. IEP objectives were established for major transition services that required monitoring the student's performance. An IEP goal was established as follows for Cindy's community work experience in her transition plan (IEP goal 3.5 in Figure 12–5):

Critical Point   The transition goals should drive the development of the IEP goals and objectives.

   Transition Goal: Supported employment in a clerical or quiet nondistractive setting

1. **Present level of performance.** Cindy currently performs at 10% of the established rate for collating and sorting and is observed to be on-task 20% of the time when observed on the hour. She has tantrums on

FIGURE 12–5
Sample IEB/Transition Plan

Statement of Needed Transition Services

Name: Cindy Doe   Date: 5/1/00

Age: 16   Age to Graduate: 22

Person Responsible for Coordinating Transition: Jill Smith, Teacher

Postsecondary goals: Supported employment in clerical setting; supported living in hometown;
Involvement in integrated clubs and religious organizations; more friends

Course of study and needed transition services: Vocational education (clerical) with direct instruction and behavioral supports. Also classes in consumer sciences, applied academics

Transition Area and Related Activities	Responsible Person	IEP Goal	Start: End:
1. Instruction:			
1. Applied math and English	Pat Claire - math teacher	1.1, 1.2	9/00–6/01
2. Clerical vocational education	Joe Gonzalez - VOED teacher	3.3	9/00–6/01
3. Employability skills	Jill Smith - SPED teacher	3.2	9/00–6/01
4. Social skills training	Joe Lyon - teacher	4.1	9/00–6/01
2. Community Experiences:			
1. Job shadowing in clerical settings	Jeff Ringles - work study	3.4	9/00–6/01
2. Visits to clubs and church groups	Julie Doe - parent		9/00–6/01
3. Community work experiences	Jeff Ringles - work study	3.5	9/01–6/03
4. Supported employment	Jack Point - VR counselor		9/03–6/04
5. Summer camp	Julie Doe - parent		8/00–9/00
3. Development of Employment and Adult Living Objectives:			
1. Job placement and training	Jack Point - VR counselor		5/03–9/03
2. Development of a PASS plan	Sally Fort - social security		5/03–9/03
3. Development of residential plan	Fred Fryman - MR/DD		9/02–5/03
4. Development of ongoing supports	Fred Fryman - MR/DD		5/03–9/03
4. Related Services:			
1. Behavioral plan	Leonard James - Beh Spec.	4.2	By 9/00
2. Augmentative communication training	Jackie Speaker - O.T.		9/00–5/01
5. Daily Living Skills:			
1. Provide mobility training	Jeff Plant - Friend		4/01–5/01
2. Provide training in home safety	Jill Smith - SPED teacher	4.4	1/01–5/01
6. Linkages with Adult Services:			
1. Vocational rehabilitation services	Jack Point - VR counselor		Age 16
2. Developmental disability services	Fred Fryman - MR/DD		Age 16
3. Social security	Sally Fort - social security		Age 16
4. Residential services	Fred Fryman - MR/DD		Age 18
5. Case management services	Fred Fryman - MR/DD		Age 16
7. Functional Vocational Evaluation:			
1. Situational assessments in a variety of class, home, work, and leisure environments	Jeff Ringles - work study coordinator		9/00–5/01
2. Career portfolio	Sam Smith - guidance counselor		

Comments: Cindy will need a calm and nondistracting environment and ongoing supports.

Source: From *Transition planning: A guide for parents and professionals* (p. 30), by R. Baer, R. McMahan, and R. Flexer, 1999, Kent, Ohio: Kent State University. Copyright 1999 by Robert Baer. Reprinted with permission.

average once a day. Cindy shows preferences for quieter and less distractive settings and has shown aptitudes in the areas
of filing, matching, sorting, and collating,
in situational assessments.

2. **Needs.** Cindy would benefit from identifying job settings that meet her needs for
   quiet, her interests in clerical work, her
   preferences to be in an integrated setting,
   and her abilities in the areas of clerical
   work.

3. **Annual goal.** Cindy will show preferences
   and aptitudes for a job related to her clerical interests as evidenced by on-task behavior, social behavior acceptable to her
   employer, and work quantity.

4. **Objectives**
   a. Cindy will demonstrate preferences for
      at least two community jobs as evi-
      denced by on-task behavior and de-
      creased tantrum behavior.
   b. Cindy will demonstrate basic aptitudes
      for the jobs she prefers as evidenced
      by increased work quantity.

5. **Evaluation**
   a. *Procedure* Observational scale and work
      samples.
   b. *Criteria*
   • Cindy will remain on task at least 50% of the
     time when observed on the hour.
   • Cindy will perform essential job tasks at 25%
     of the established rate on average for the last
     week of the work experience.
   • Cindy will express preferences for job activi-
     ties through picture communication.
   c. *Schedule.* Cindy will be evaluated for
      on-task behavior at least once an hour.
      Cindy will be evaluated for work per-
      formance at the beginning, middle,
      and end of her community work expe-
      rience. Cindy's preferences will be sur-
      veyed before and after work.
   d. *The work-study coordinator will do evaluation*
      with the work-site supervisor in con-
      junction with Cindy.

   e. *Progress* will be reported every 2 weeks
6. **Services.** The work-study coordinator will
   develop job sites of interest to Cindy in the
   first semester of the year and involve her in
   choosing job sites through job shadowing.
   The work-study coordinator also will assist
   Cindy in work-site accommodations and in
   getting her to the job on the first day, in
   meeting coworkers, and in evaluating
   progress. Job training will be provided by VR.
7. **Duration.** Community work experiences
   will be arranged for 4 hours per day for 2
   days per week for 12 weeks.
8. **LRE.** Community work experiences will be
   provided in integrated settings within and
   outside the school.

Upon completion of the meeting, Cindy and
her parents were given a copy of the IEP/transi-
tion plan and the major points were explained to
them. They were informed that the IEP/transi-
tion team would be reconvened if any problems
emerged, and they were encouraged to communicate any questions or concerns to Jill as their
transition coordinator.

Critical Point   Plan to reconvene the transition
team, as needed.

In the following year, Jill monitored provision
of transition services and reconvened the team
as needed. She also called each transition service provider and Cindy's parents every 3 months
to determine how Cindy was progressing. At the
end of the year, Jill forwarded the IEP/transition
plan to Joe Lyon, who was to take over as Cindy's
special education teacher the following year.

As Cindy moved through high school, there
were a number of changes in the IEP transition
plan. Cindy was in a variety of work experiences
in a library setting, delivering mail, and photo-
copying for a bank. Despite her success in a couple of her work experiences, she continued to
need a great deal of supervision. Collectively,
the transition team had to advocate for provision of supported employment since Cindy's

MR/DD caseworker felt that she would be safer in a sheltered workshop.

However, after considerable work and support from her family, Cindy was able to obtain a supported employment placement at a government agency delivering mail in-house with ongoing supervision. Her ongoing need for a job coach was partially funded and deducted from her earnings as an impairment-related work expense (IRWE), thereby maintaining her eligibility for social security and Medicaid. Cindy's parents set up a PASS plan to help her purchase a computer for work. Cindy also was able to obtain a supported living situation and to participate in community activities with the help of medicaid funding.

Questions Families Frequently Ask

The educator who is responsible for coordinating the IEP/transition team meeting should be prepared to answer frequently asked questions of parents and students. Although it is impossible to know about all the agencies and services, the coordinator should have a basic working knowledge to assist the student and the family in determining who should be invited and involved in transition planning. The following are questions that are frequently asked by parents in regard to IEP/transition meetings.

1. What employment services are available in the community?

There are agencies in each community that provide youth and adults assistance in finding and maintaining employment. These include:

Vocational rehabilitation (VR) *services*: Provide or pay for vocational assessment, job placement, job training, postsecondary education, technology, and other time-limited services.

Mental retardation and developmental disabilities (MR/DD) *programs*: Provide ongoing supports for students with the most severe disabilities in the areas of sheltered employment, supported employment, residential services, and case management.

Summer youth employment programs: Provide time-limited summer youth employment programs and a variety of job programs, generally for economically disadvantaged students.

Mental health programs: Provide case management and occasionally supported employment for students with psychiatric disabilities.

Nonprofit agencies such as United Cerebral Palsy, the ARC, and Goodwill Industries: Provide sheltered employment, supported employment, and other services for youth and adults with disabilities, often through contract with VR.

Youth services programs: Generally provided to youth who have been in trouble with the law, often through contract with VR.

Employment agencies: Provide job placement, generally on a fee-for-service basis. Sometimes this service can be paid for by VR.

Postsecondary education programs: Often provide job placement and career services for their students. Vocational rehabilitation may pay part or all of the cost of these programs for eligible students.

2. What employment services do school districts provide students with disabilities?

School districts may provide a number of services that are available to students with disabilities. These are provided through general, special, and vocational education. Some examples of programs designed to provide work experience or vocational training are (a) work-study or transition coordinators, (b) occupational work-adjustment staff, (c) vocational educators, (d) school-to-work program staff, and (d) guidance counselors.

3. What should my child do to get into postsecondary education after high school?

There are four major types of postsecondary education: (a) vocational/technical schools, (b) community colleges (2-year), (c) liberal arts colleges, and (d) state universities. Every postsecondary program has academic requirements that must be met. However, state universities and community colleges often have remedial programs for students who have had difficulty in general areas of course work such as mathematics and English.

Postsecondary options should be explored early in high school to select the proper course work and to choose a postsecondary program that provides the services and supports that will be needed by the student after graduation. The student also should receive training in asking for needed accommodations and supports and visits and/or audit classes from desired schools (Turner, 1996). College and other entrance exams should be taken early and applications sent out in the final year of high school.

4. What can I do to help my son or daughter get a job?

Parents have a very important role to play in their child's getting and keeping a job. The expectation that their son or daughter will work is important to convey to their children as they grow. Supporting the school district's efforts to provide job preparation also is essential. Parents can assure that meaningful vocational goals are written into their child's IEP and transition plans and provide opportunities for their child to develop important work skills, habits, and attitudes by giving them chores and responsibilities. Parents also can assist job placement professionals by providing them with leads and introducing them to employers they may know.

5. How do I apply for adult services?

Generally, a student with an IEP will be eligible for vocational rehabilitation (VR) services and the school can initiate a referral at the parent's or student's request, but typically only students with the most severe disabilities obtain VR services. MR/DD programs usually serve only students with the most severe developmental disabilities and the family generally initiates referral. Summer youth employment programs usually serve students with milder disabilities who are economically disadvantaged, with referrals typically coming from the school. Mental health job programs are commonly accessed through the mental health counselor and generally reserved for students with the most severe psychiatric disabilities.

6. Is there an alternative to sheltered employment for students with severe disabilities?

Supported employment is designed to serve students who have traditionally gone into sheltered workshops and day activity centers. This is competitive paid work that is performed in an actual job site by individuals who, because of their disability, need ongoing support services to perform that work. Supported employment has four characteristics: (a) paid employment, (b) integration with nondisabled coworkers, (c) ongoing support after job training, and (d) drive initiated by student career goals. Supported employment models include:

- *Individual placement* approaches that include structured assistance in job placement and job training. A job developer develops a job of interest to the student and a job coach trains job skills and provides other training to maintain employment (e.g., social and travel skills). Once the job coach phases out, a professional, coworker, or family member provides follow-along services at the job site.
- *Mobile work crews* of three to eight persons are transported to perform contracted work such as janitorial and landscaping services at area businesses. These crews operate under the supervision of one or more employment specialists.
- *Cluster placements or enclaves* of three to eight persons are supervised by employment specialists and work in a business or industry doing the same job as other nondisabled workers.

7. Can a student have a job coach while still in high school?

Vocational rehabilitation or the school can provide job coaches for students with intense support needs while they are still in high school. School districts may choose to hire their own job coaches or to use VR services for eligible students. It is important to establish eligibility and to involve adult service providers in transition planning, if they are providing or paying for job coaches.

8. What are ongoing support services and follow-along services?

Ongoing support services or follow-along services are provided throughout the term of employment after the job coach is phased out. The purpose of these services is to enable the individual to continue to perform the work required by the employer. They may include services that occur at or away from the work site, such as transportation, personal care services, counseling, and behavioral supports. Typically, ongoing support services are provided through MR/DD programs or long-term mental health programs, but employers, family members, or other agencies also may provide them.

9. What is supplemental security income (SSI)?

Supplemental security income (SSI) is an income support program run by the Social Security Administration. Monthly benefits can be paid to youth or adults with disabilities if their individual or family income falls below a certain level, and if their disability is severe and expected to last at least 12 months. SSI can be helpful in supplementing student income while in post-secondary education or entry-level work. Generally, SSI is applied for at age 18 when family income is not considered.

10. What is the difference between SSI and social security benefits?

Social security disability insurance (SSDI) is a government insurance fund that is typically paid to a young person with a disability who has a retired, deceased, or disabled parent who paid into social security. Social security benefits are applied for in the same way as SSI; they may amount to more than SSI, or they may be supplemented by SSI if they are less than the SSI amount.

11. What information is needed to apply for SSI and SSDI?

Application should be made in person at the local social security office. The social security representative will need to see the following items:
- Social security number
- Birth certificate
- Information on income and resources: payroll slips, bank books, insurance policies, car registration, burial fund records, and other information about assets.
- Mortgage papers and lease arrangements
- Impairment-related information: name, address, and phone numbers of all doctors, hospital or medical facilities where the student has been treated or tested, and any medical reports in your possession.
- Work history (SSDI only).

12. When can SSI benefits be applied for?

SSI benefits may be applied for at any age if the child has a significant disability and if the income of the child and that of the family are very low. After age 18, students may be considered a family of one and receive SSI benefits if their income falls below SSI guidelines and if the total resources of the student amount to less than $2,000.

13. How can my son or daughter get medicaid benefits?

People who meet the eligibility requirements for SSI benefits are usually eligible for medicaid benefits as well. Medicaid benefits are applied for at the local office of the U.S. Department of Human Services. An individual may be eligible for medicaid and not receiving SSI if he or she is working and needs medicaid to maintain health benefits.

14. If students work, does this cause them to lose SSI?

SSI programs encourage recipients to work through a number of allowances and work incentives. Generally, SSI recipients only lose $1.00 for every $2.00 they earn and are allowed to exclude $85 of earned and unearned income and any impairment-related work expenses (IRWEs). A simple *estimate* of how much SSI payments drop due to work is to use the following formula:

$$\frac{\text{Net earnings} - \$85 - \text{IRWEs}}{2} = \text{SSI decrease}$$

For example, a person who earns $385 dollars a month will lose only $150 of SSI benefits. SSI has other work incentives, including deductions for (a) impairment-related work expenses (IR-WEs), (b) student earned income exclusion, (c) blind work expenses, (d) plans for achieving self-support (PASS), (e) property essential to self-support, and (f) continued payment under a VR program. These should be discussed with a social security representative.

15. What about medicaid and work?

Unless recipients earn more than double their SSI check plus $85, medicaid benefits will be continued automatically. Even if a recipient is no longer receiving an SSI payment, he or she can continue to receive medicaid if:

- The disabling condition continues.
- There is a need for medicaid to work.
- A person cannot afford medical coverage.

16. Why do I need to plan for residential living options?

Whether the student plans to remain at home or to move out, parents should assure that necessary residential supports are provided to ensure that the individual with a disability is cared for after the parents retire or become ill. Depending on eligibility, the student can maintain independence through family supports, medicaid waivers, low-income housing, personal care attendants, supported living services, or other residential programs. It should be emphasized that residential services often involve long waiting periods and, therefore, should be applied for many years before they are needed.

17. Why do I need to plan for community participation?

Research indicates that students with disabilities can become more isolated as they grow older. Due to lack of mobility, income, and social networks, students with disabilities may have dif-

ficulty making the right friends and meeting the right people to assure a good adult quality of life. Membership in religious/cultural affiliations (e.g., church or synagogue), clubs, and recreational programs provide natural and ongoing support networks that can assist persons with disabilities to maintain friendships throughout their life.

18. Can I have a transition plan without an IEP?

If a student has a substantial mental or physical impairment but does not qualify for special education, a transition plan can be developed under section 504 of the Rehabilitation Act, which requires access to appropriate education for all students with handicaps. Section 504 does not require an IEP, but it does require a plan for any area needed by the student to gain an appropriate education. This can include a transition plan.

Conclusion

Transition planning was developed in response to studies that showed poor postsecondary outcomes for graduates of special education programs. The IDEA of 1990 and 1997 developed a legal definition of transition planning that included four major criteria: (1) based on student needs, taking into account interests and preferences, (2) developed as part of an outcome-oriented process, (3) a coordinated set of activities, and (4) designed to promote movement into employment and other postschool environments. Common myths about transition plans have emerged as they have become part of the IEP, including the need to standardize the process for all students, to limit planning to a small part of the IEP meeting, to plan year to year, and to meet annually as part of the IEP meeting. At most schools, much of the transition planning process must occur outside the IEP meeting in order for the transition coordinator to individualize planning approaches, to conduct planning in a relaxed and creative atmosphere, to conduct multiyear planning, and to meet regularly.

The process of transition planning, therefore, extends far beyond the process of developing a transition statement as part of the IEP transition meeting. Preparation involves consideration of the method of planning and assessment, forming the transition planning team, exploring service options, and planning for student and family involvement. The implementation of the transition service plan starts with the IEP/transition meeting and continues through implementation of the IEP, assessment of progress, and coordination of transition services. There are many questions and problems that will arise as part of this process that will require the transition coordinator to update continuously knowledge about adult service options, supported employment, financial support, and postsecondary education.

Study Questions

1. There are four major criteria for transition planning. Discuss one in detail outlining IDEA's legal requirements and how schools should address this area.
2. Compare and contrast the transition requirements of the IDEA of 1997 and 1990.
3. Discuss how the transition plan has become part of the IEP, and how this has had unintended consequences for transition planning.
4. Discuss how a school can help students and families to become involved in the IEP transition planning process.
5. Discuss what a teacher should do to prepare for the IEP/transition meeting, and how this process might differ for students with mild and severe cognitive disabilities.

6. Discuss how transition progress can be assessed using standardized approaches.

Web Sites

SCANS Overview Site:
http://www.ed.gov/databases/ERIC_Digests/ed389879

School-to-Work Outreach Project:
http://www.ici.coled.umn.edu/schooltowork/default.html

All Means All School-to-Work Web Site:
http://www.ici.coled.umn.edu/all/

Transition to Work Program:
http://www.ici.coled.umn.edu/schooltowork/links.html

The Arc:
http://TheArc.org/

Disability Related Products and Services:
http://TheArc.org/related-links.htm#products-services

National Center on Educational Outcomes:
http://www.coled.umn.edu/nceo/

Alternate Assessments:
*http://www.coled.umn.edu/nceo/GrayAreaForum/Conference
    Report.htm*

Annual Report to Congress on the Implementation of IDEA
http://www.ed.gov/offices/OSERS/OSEP/OSEP98AnlRpt/

National Alliance of Business:
http://www.nab.com/

One-Stop Career Centers:
http://www.nab.com/workforcedevelopment/onestop.cfm

Workforce Investment Act:
*http://www.nab.com/workforcedevelopment/workforceinvestmentact/
    introduction/index.cfm*

School-to-Career:
http://www.nab.com/educationimprovement/schooltocareer/introduction/

Eric Database:
http://www.dssc.org/nta/html/index_2.htm

13

Coordinating Transition Services

Robert Baer
Phillip Rumrill

LEARNING OBJECTIVES

The objectives of this chapter are:

1. Identify two models of service coordination and their underlying philosophies.
2. Understand how student and family needs and preferences define service coordination.
3. Define five major goals of transition defined by Kohler.
4. Discuss ten major activities of the transition coordinator within these five goals.
5. Be able to apply these principles to a student with a disability and the family.

The last chapter covered best practices and the four essential elements of transition in the context of transition planning for individual students with disabilities. In this chapter, the authors examine these concepts within the framework of service coordination, starting with a discussion of two service delivery models—ecological and independent living—and how they relate to student needs, interests, and preferences. Determining student needs, interests, and preferences also is emphasized in the section on student involvement where the issue of informed consent is discussed. The essential transition element, outcome-oriented process, is emphasized in the section on developing program attributes and structures with a discussion of how to mobilize transition stakeholders through the development of a schoolwide interagency transition team. Development of a coordinated set of activities is discussed in the sections on student and family involvement and in the section on collaboration. Finally, promoting movement to employment and other postsecondary activities is considered in the section on student development and in the discussion of service coordination models. The chapter concludes with a case study that illustrates how the transition coordinator can apply these concepts.

Service Coordination: A Brief History

Service coordination has become a critical concern of disability advocates and policymakers due, in large part, to the growth of a staggeringly complex human service system (Paulson, 1993). In some states, persons with disabilities can receive services from 30 or more agencies, many with different eligibility requirements, intake procedures, service definitions, and philosophy (Szymanski, Hanley-Maxwell, & Asselin, 1990). When adding to this the challenges of entering a labor market demanding even higher levels of training and preparation, it is easy to understand the vital role that service coordination plays in achieving meaningful adult outcomes for youth with disabilities.

Along with the growing complexity of human services, educators and professionals have been faced with an increasingly aware disability community and an ever more diverse society (Mackelsprang & Salsgiver, 1996). Whereas early casework approaches focused mainly upon the "fit" between individuals and their environments, newer case management (or service coordination) models have had to recognize a larger role for consumers and a greater emphasis on adapting environments to their needs (Halpern, 1985; Mackelsprang & Salsgiver, 1996; Tower, 1994). Two models of service provision, ecological and independent living models, have emerged in response to these issues.

Ecological models of service delivery evolved from earlier casework models and changed the focus from adapting individuals to environments to adapting environments to meet the needs of individuals (Albin, Lucyshyn, Horner, & Flannery, 1996; Flexer et al., 1995). Ecological approaches emphasized the importance of assessing all the individual's environments, including future environments (Flexer et al., 1995). They were adopted by disability advocates who saw the futility of classroom programs focused upon "preparation" that did little to address training needs, services, and supports in the student's actual and future environments (Brown, Nietupski, & Hamre-Nietupski, 1976; Rainforth, York, & MacDonald, 1992; Tower, 1994). Vincent et al. (1980) described the "criteria of the next environment," an ecological model that focused training, services, and supports upon environments receiving individuals with disabilities. Brown et al. (1976) described "the criterion of ultimate function" as a means of focusing upon the environments ultimately desired by persons with disabilities.

Regardless of these efforts to make service delivery more sensitive to individual environments, the "helping" and formalized culture of the disability service system did not fit well with the emerging culture of disability advocates (Hanley-Maxwell, Pogoloff, & Whitney-Thomas, 1998; Shapiro, 1993). This led disability rights advocates, such as Ed Roberts and Judy Heumann, to champion the independent living model of disability service delivery (Shapiro, 1993). This model emerged at Berkeley in 1972 and defined dependence on professionals, and even relatives, as the primary problem faced by persons with disabilities (DeJong, 1984; Mackelsprang & Salsgiver, 1996; Tower, 1994). The independent living model stressed self-management of services through advocacy, self-help groups, generic support services, and elimination of barriers to access (DeJong, 1984; Tower, 1994). One of the primary goals of the independent living model was to wean individuals with disabilities from agency and professional control by providing them with a choice of providers and preferably cash benefits or vouchers for use at the individual's discretion. An example of this approach was the "American disabled for attendant programs today" (ADAPT), whose members rejected the use of agency-based professional services in favor of personal assistants who were hired by individuals with disabilities and paid for by vouchers or cash supports (Tower, 1994). The implications of the independent living model for service coordinators included the need (1) to emphasize self-determination, (2) to avoid unneeded intrusion of professionals, (3) to use natural supports networks, and (4) to emphasize generic rather than disability-specific services.

Despite the growth of independent living programs in the 1980s and 1990s, the disability service system maintained many constraints on the choice of service delivery approaches. A number of factors contributed to this. Many professionals were unwilling to leave the security of the classroom and the office to implement ecological approaches to service delivery. Typically, funding agencies and service providers were unwilling (or unable by law) to provide benefits or services without strings attached and were reluctant to adopt independent living approaches that "de-professionalized" the method of service provision (Holburn & Vietze, 1998; O'Brien , O'Brien, & Mount, 1997). Consequently, service providers continued to provide service-centered approaches while paying lip service to the need for ecological and independent living models. Hagner, Helm, and Butterworth (1996) noted that "it may be impossible to maintain the integrity of [person-centered] implementation on a large scale by a system that itself has not undergone fundamental change" (p. 169).

Critical Point Ecological and independent living models are preferred models of transition service coordination, but they are hard to implement in the current service system.

The Individual with Disabilities Education Act (IDEA) gave local education agencies the responsibility for transition service coordination and they faced many of the same problems in implementing person-centered planning approaches (deFur & Taymans, 1995; Racino, 1990). The responsibility for transition service coordination was assigned to educators who typically had inadequate training in coordinating agency services or in developing needed linkages with community supports (deFur & Taymans, 1995; Flexer, Simmons, & Tankersley, 1997; Kohler, 1998). Consequently, service coordination tended to be service-oriented and fragmented, resulting in frequent interruption of services and supports after graduation (Benz, Johnson, Mikkelsen, & Lindstrom, 1995; SRI International, 1992). This placed an even greater strain on the resources of persons with disabilities and their families in dealing with the stresses of adulthood (Baer, Simmons, & Flexer, 1996; Grigal, Test, Beattie, & Wood, 1997; Hayden & Goldman, 1996).

Educators have been struggling with the question of how to address both individual needs and preferences in transition service delivery and coordination. Traditional adult service delivery approaches may seem intrusive to students and families whose primary concern is independence and freedom from the disability system (Shapiro, 1993). On the other hand, independent living approaches that stress freedom from the service-centered adult service system may not work well for individuals who cannot manage their own services or who lack family and community supports. Hayden and Goldman (1996) suggest that the caregiver's marital status, the youth's level of cognitive disability, the frequency of maladaptive behaviors, and the health status of the adult family members are important considerations in determining support strategies. Often transition coordinators have been faced with the dilemma of providing inadequate transition supports or moving individuals with disabilities into an adult service system that promotes dependency and loss of control.

Cultural issues are a second consideration in the choice of service coordination models for a student with a disability. Discord and conflict frequently occur when the culture of a service delivery system differs significantly from the culture of the individual (Hanley-Maxwell, Pogoloff, & Whitney-Thomas, 1998). Some cultures depend more heavily on support from extended families, neighborhoods, and churches, whereas other cultures may reject the idea of social services altogether. For example, a transition coordinator in rural Ohio or Pennsylvania should know that many Amish communities will not accept "social services" but may use them if they are termed "educational services." Service coordinators in urban settings must be sensitive to extreme dissonance between social service agencies and minority cultures while recognizing the great potential of neighborhood and religious affiliations (Hornstein, 1997). Service coordinators need to understand the youth's culture, explore alternative service and support approaches, discuss individual needs and preferences, and provide choices regarding service providers and supporters.

Critical Point Individual needs, preferences, and cultural backgrounds are important considerations in service development and coordination.

Goals of Transition Service Coordination

Kohler (1998) conceptualized transition activities as falling into five categories: (1) student-focused planning, (2) student development, (3) family involvement, (4) collaboration, and (5) development of program structure and attributes. This structure relates to the four essential elements of transition in IDEA and can be used to organize the activities of the transition coordinator. Student-focused planning and family involvement primarily address IDEA's essential element of determining student needs, interests, and preferences. Collaboration addresses the IDEA element of developing a coordinated set of activities. Student development is highly related to promoting movement to postschool activities and development of program structure, and attributes primarily addresses the needs to develop an outcome-oriented process and to promote student movement to postsecondary settings.

Student-Focused Planning

Before the IEP/transition meeting, the transition coordinator should develop consensus among key transition stakeholders, including the youth, family, school, service providers, and natural supporters regarding what is to happen at the meeting. Typically, IEP/transition meetings do not allow time for extensive debate or disagreement and should not be held if a deadlock issue is imminent. If the transition coordinator disagrees with the goals and services selected by the youth and their families, the issue should be resolved prior to the meeting. At the IEP/transition meeting, the transition coordinator should *always* support the choices of the youth with disabilities and their families.

In some cases, the youth with disabilities may disagree with their families or guardians regarding career choices, services, or supports. In this situation, the transition coordinator should mediate by providing the youth and their families with additional information or experience in regard to career choices, or by scheduling follow-up meetings involving guidance counselors, employers, postsecondary educators, community members, or service providers. In the few instances where youth/families consensus cannot be reached, the transition coordinator generally should follow the wishes of the family while supporting the student before the age of majority, and vice versa, after the age of majority.

Prior to the IEP/transition meeting, the transition coordinator also should discuss the role of the youth and their families in the meeting itself. For youth and families with a high degree of career maturity, the transition coordinator may want to encourage them to assume the role of directing the IEP/transition meeting. This can be supported by using a survey of transition goals and service preferences such as the one presented in Figure 13–1 as an agenda for the meeting. The youth and/or the family can simply present and read their goals and service preferences to the team as a lead into the discussion. The transition coordinator can assist them in this role by serving as the timekeeper, notetaker, and prompter. In some cases, the transition coordinator needs to take a more direct role in the meeting. In this role, the coordinator should act as an advocate for the youth and the families by presenting goals, services, and support preferences, and by defending these choices in collaboration with the youth and the families.

Planning

Scheduling Meetings

The transition coordinator should work with special and general educators to schedule meetings in a way that maximizes student and family participation. Approaches include the use of personal invitations to students and family members, offering alternative times for meetings, holding meetings in alternative locations, and helping to arrange transportation for families. The transition coordinator also should develop strategies for maximizing participation of adult service providers by grouping IEP meetings that are to be attended by a given adult service provider and by arranging alternative ways for adult service providers to provide input.

The transition planning meeting needs to be scheduled and planned in a way that is family-friendly while assuring maximum participation of key educators and adult service providers. This may be difficult to do since adult service providers and educators may be reluctant to meet outside their regular schedules while families may find day meetings difficult to attend. This issue can be partially addressed by identifying those times that families are free during the day or times that educators and adult service providers are available on the weekends and in the evenings. These key times can be reserved for families that have difficulty meeting during regularly scheduled hours.

The invitation to the IEP/transition meeting should consist of a written invitation with an enclosed meeting agenda and a simple way to RSVP (e.g., phone call or self-addressed stamped envelope). The transition coordinator may need to make follow-up phone contacts to encourage key adult service providers, community members, and families to attend. Families, and even adult service providers, may avoid participation in IEP/transition planning as a result of previous experience where their input was not valued and IEPs were essentially developed outside the meeting. The coordinator needs to assure them that their role in the meeting will be critical. The meeting agenda should include items with times allotted for key members to present issues of concern to them.

FIGURE 13–1

Transition Needs and Preferences Survey

This survey is designed to help the school determine what type of experiences and education you will need to prepare for life after graduation from high school. It will be used to develop a long-range plan (or transition plan) that will be discussed at the next IEP meeting.

Please answer the following questions based on what you know about yourself (or the student, if filled out by a parent/guardian).

Student name:	Parent/Guardian:
Student age:	Today's date:

1. What kind of work or education do you hope to see yourself in after graduation from high school?

Full-Time   Part-Time

☐   ☐   University or College—*academically oriented four-year program*

☐   ☐   Community/Technical Colleges—*technical/paraprofessional training*

☐   ☐   Adult Vocational Education—*advanced job training (e.g., secretary)*

☐   ☐   Military Service—*Army, Navy, Air Force, Coast Guard, Marines, etc.*

☐   ☐   Competitive Employment—*a job trained by employer (or job coach)*

☐   ☐   Supported Employment—*a job with job coach training and then support*

☐   ☐   Sheltered Employment—*low pay work activities and training*

☐   ☐   Other _____

2. What age do you want to exit school?   18   19   20   21   22

3. Is there a particular kind of work or education that you are currently interested in or other comments? If so, specify:

4. Where do you hope to ultimately live as an adult?

☐   Independently in a home or apartment—*generally requires more than minimum wage*

☐   Independently in subsidized housing—*usually requires minimum wage or higher income*

☐   Wheelchair accessible housing—*ability to live on own or with personal care attendant*

☐   Supported living—*staff assist a few hours per day cooking , shopping, budgeting, etc.*

☐   Group home/foster care—*staff provide 24 hour care and help in self-care, health, etc.*

☐   With parents or relatives—*sometimes with help of support staff or Medicaid services.*

☐   Other _____

5. Is there a neighborhood, city, or locality you hope to live in?

6. What types of community participation do you hope will be available to you as an adult? (check all that apply)

☐   Clubs or groups that meet to talk about a common interest (e.g., computers, astronomy)
Specify, if possible _____

☐   Community recreational activities (e.g., YMCA, Community Centers, out with friends)
Specify, if possible _____

☐   Religious and cultural activities (e.g., church, synagogue, temple, study groups)
Specify, if possible _____

(continued)

FIGURE 13–1
(*Concluded*)

☐ Transportation for work and leisure activities (e.g., car, bus, friends, parents, bicycle)
Specify type(s) and for what purpose _____

☐ Continuing education (e.g., computers, cooking, sewing, home repair)
Specify, if possible_____

☐ Political participation (e.g., voting, involvement in political groups)
Specify type of participation if possible _____

☐ Other/Comments: _____

7. **Check any of the following services that you feel would be helpful to you in achieving your goals.**

☐ Interest Inventories (e.g., OASYS)	☐ Entrance Exam Training (e.g., SAT)
☐ In-School Job Placement	☐ Job Shadowing (i.e., observing a job)
☐ Work Adjustment Training	☐ Guidance Counseling
☐ Community Work Experience	☐ Vocational Education
☐ Summer Jobs	☐ College Experience
☐ Other/Comments:	

☐ Transportation and Driver Education	☐ Training in Handling Emergencies
☐ Consumer Sciences/Home Economics	☐ Training in Cooking and Nutrition
☐ Money Management Training	☐ Home Repair and Maintenance Training
☐ Sewing and Clothing Care Training	☐ First Aid Training
☐ Other/Comments:	

☐ Language and Hearing Services	☐ Occupational or Physical Therapy
☐ Accommodations and Technology	☐ Self-Advocacy Training
☐ Relationships and Marriage	☐ Vocational Rehabilitation
☐ Psychology, Social Work, Psychiatry	☐ Community Awareness Activities
☐ Other/Comments:	

☐ *Evaluation(s) (Specify Type Needed):*

☐ *Referrals (Specify to Whom):*

Source: From *Transition planning: A guide for parents and professionals* (p. 9), by R. Baer, R. McMahan, and R. Flexer, 1999, Kent, Ohio: Kent State University. Copyright 1999 by Robert Baer. Reprinted with permission.

Conducting IEP/Transition Meetings

The IEP/transition meeting should be conducted in a way that presents the youth with disabilities and their families in the best light. Starting with seating and introductions, the youth and their families should be given priority. The meeting should not start with a discussion of students' weaknesses or disabilities. If any student background is provided at the start of the meeting, it should focus upon positive experiences and strengths, exclusively. Otherwise, the meeting should start with a discussion of postsecondary goals that are developed with the students and their families, preferably with each student or the family presenting these themselves.

The second item on the agenda should be a discussion of what services and supports students will need to achieve their goals. This is another critical phase of the planning process since team members may revert to questioning the individual's goals at this stage. Unless students and families request input in this regard, discussion and reappraisal of goals should not be allowed to drag on. The coordinator may need to redirect the team from reappraisal of goals to noncritical brainstorming and generation of solutions at this stage (Koch & Rumrill, 1998b). This process may be aided by the use of lists of services and supports that are typically used with transition-age students or services that have been discussed previous to the meeting. At this stage, it also is useful to develop contingency plans for services and activities (such as summer programs) that may or may not be available due to eligibility, waiting lists, or lack of funding.

The transition coordinator should anticipate positive outcomes by asking questions such as, "When will this service be provided?" and "Who will provide this service or activity?" (Koch & Rumrill, 1998a). In addition, the transition coordinator should ask the question on how the transition plan will be connected to inclusive classroom activities and the student's particular course of study by asking questions such as,

"How will transition services and activities be supported by class work?" or "How will the student learn the math or spelling needed to participate in this program or activity?" The outcome of this stage of the meeting should be a list (or statement) of needed transition services and activities with time lines for their completion, contact persons, and reference to supportive classroom activities. The student, family, or transition coordinator may thank the team for their efforts at this stage and hand the meeting over to the student, family member, or teacher who is responsible for developing the remainder of the IEP.

Coordinating Referrals

The transition coordinator needs to develop linkages with adult service and vocational programs. The Social Security Administration and the rehabilitation services are the two most common providers of funding and services for youth with disabilities. Transition coordinators need to become familiar with social security and its work incentives programs, such as plans to achieve self-sufficiency (PASS), impairment-related work expenses (IRWEs), and student income exclusions. They must become familiar with the programs of the vocational rehabilitation (VR) services and with the services it funds, including postsecondary education, vocational school, assistive technology, computers, and job placement and training. Coordinators also should be aware of when students may apply for and begin receiving services since many adult service programs also serve youth and even children. The coordinator should be aware that adult services vary widely for different disability groups, from location to location, and from year to year.

The transition coordinator may want to sponsor an agency fair where students, teachers, and families can sign up for adult services at the school. As part of an agency fair, each agency representative and representatives of postsecondary environments can fill out a questionnaire. Figure 13–2 presents an example of such a questionnaire. These can be typed, alphabetized, and put together to make a directory that the school can give to students, families, community members, and families for easy reference.

Informed Choice and Self-Determination

Transition coordinators need to encourage and provide opportunities for self-determination and decision making in the transition process. Many youth with disabilities and their families will have had previous experiences with IEP planning that lead them to define their role as passive, uninvolved, or dependent. To promote self-determination, the transition coordinator should assess factors affecting the student's ability to make informed choices. Informed choice assumes that the youth with a disability is (1) free from coercion, (2) has the necessary information and experience, and (3) is able to make choices that have a reasonable expectation of positive outcome (Dinerstein, Herr, & O'Sullivan, 1999).

Assuring that youth are free from coercion is an important role of the transition coordinator. Coercion, unlike persuasion, is based on force rather than information. Coercion may be both covert and overt. Overt coercion may come from professionals or family members (Dinerstein, Herr, & O'Sullivan, 1999). Professionals may overtly threaten to discontinue services or approval if youth with disabilities do not accept services or programs they recommend. In some cases, family members may use their authority to pressure youth into accepting services that are more convenient for the family (e.g., the convenience of regular day activity programs versus supported employment). A greater concern for the transition coordinator is covert coercion. Covert coercion may include questions such as, "You want to work in a restaurant, yes?" Apart from leading questions such as this, research indicates that even "yes" and "no" questions can be coercive since many individuals with disabil-

ities have learned to answer yes to questions posed by persons in authority (Wehmeyer & Kelchner, 1995). Transition coordinators need to avoid yes and no questions in interviews, whenever possible. Open-ended questions are preferable, with comprehensive lists of well-defined choices provided as support.

Students need the necessary information and experience to make informed choices about their education program and the IEP planning process. Martin et al. (1996), Wehmeyer & Kelchner (1995), Van Reusen & Bos (1990), Powers et al. (1996), and Halpern et al. (1997) have developed self-determination curricula that may be useful in this regard. Transition coordinators should be aware of these self-determination curricula and encourage their use with students. Additionally, students should be aware of service, curriculum, and support options available in their school system.

Determining the reasonableness of the outcome of student decisions regarding the education program is perhaps the most difficult aspect of self-determination. A student that makes choices that do not have a reasonable chance of outcome may be considered unable to provide informed consent (Dinerstein, Herr, & O'Sullivan, 1999). However, a student who is not allowed to make some "unreasonable" decisions may never develop the maturity to give informed consent. The transition coordinator, therefore, must support the right of students and families to make unreasonable choices early in transition planning, while at the same time assuring that these choices do not result in substantial harm. For example, a failing student who chooses a college preparatory career path could meet with teachers of college preparatory high school courses, college admissions officers, and college disability services to discuss the reasonableness of their choice. If the student chooses to proceed with a well-informed but possibly unwise, decision, the transition coordinator should support this decision while minimizing the harm of failure. The IEP team should be re-

FIGURE 13–2
Outline for Panel Presentation

---

1. **Your name:** _____ **Title:** _____

2. **Your agency:** _____ **Phone:** _____

3. Please provide a brief overview of the purpose of your agency:

_____

_____

_____

_____

_____

4. Briefly, what transition services are available to students with disabilities before age 18?

_____

_____

_____

_____

5. Briefly, what transition services are available to students with disabilities after age 18?

_____

_____

_____

_____

_____

6. Generally, what types of students are eligible for your services and how should they be referred?

_____

_____

_____

_____

---

convened often for this purpose. In some cases, students may succeed against all odds. In other cases, students or families may need to revise their transition goals.

Critical Point The transition coordinator needs to assess student decisions relative to voluntariness, knowledge, and reasonableness of outcome and to provide self-determination training and opportunities to make choices.

Self-Advocacy and Self-Determination

Promoting student self-determination becomes a critical issue as the student approaches the age of majority under state law. The IDEA of 1997 requires transfer of IDEA rights and control of the IEP team at that age *unless the student has been determined incompetent or unable to give informed consent about the education program* (IEP). If the student has become increasingly self-determined and has had opportunities to demonstrate informed consent in the early years of transition planning, she or he is much more likely to be ready to be given IDEA rights at the age of majority. On the other hand, if this issue is not addressed, it is likely that the student will never have the opportunity to assume this role.

In keeping with the concept of self-determination, the transition coordinator should provide opportunities for students to practice advocacy skills in supported situations. Students should know about their disability, the accommodations they need, and how to communicate these needs with educators, employers, and community members. They should request accommodations and services on their own with the support of the transition coordinator. Self-advocacy is a critical skill that may make the difference between a student succeeding or failing in postsecondary education, employment, or social interactions.

Student Development

Siegel (1998) suggested that although there was no single transition program that serves all students with disabilities, all programs should

Support needs may vary over time.

maximize accessibility. According to Siegel (1998), youth with profound disabilities and extremely challenging behaviors should have access to supported employment services, day treatment, residential, and immersion programs and should have follow-along services that extend for up to 5 years. Youth with mild learning or emotional disabilities should be involved in job shadowing and have access to work experiences during the last 2 years of school. They also may need to have access to team teaching, vocational special education, community work experiences, participation in vocational service organizations, linkages with adult services, and support in accessing a community college program.

Critical Point Students with disabilities should have access to all educational and vocational programs with supports.

An important outcome of transition service coordination should be access to all secondary programs for students with disabilities. Transition coordinators must become familiar with school reform efforts, such as school to work, and collaborate with other groups that are interested in school reform. Siegel (1998) noted that all students need work experiences, career linkages, citizenship education, and leadership and diversity training. Kohler (1998) echoed this position by arguing that all school programs should provide academic, vocational, social, and personal development activities and should be flexible and responsive to individual students.

Linking Services and Instruction

Transition coordinators need to link services and instruction to support student postschool goals. They can do this at an individual level by assuring that students' courses of study relate to their postschool goals. The IDEA mandates that by age 14 or earlier, student IEPs should include a statement of transition services that students will need to pursue their desired course of study. The transition coordinator should assure that the necessary supports and services are in place for the student to succeed in the general or vocational education programs designed to promote movement of all students to postsecondary settings.

Identifying Opportunities and Competency Requirements

The transition coordinator must be aware of job and educational opportunities to direct the development of a coordinated set of activities for individual students. This awareness requires out-of-school activities such as touring area businesses and educational programs, meeting with employer groups, having students conduct informational interviews with employers and schools, and meeting with vocational educators. The coordinator also can invite employers to consult as part of individual IEP teams or as part of a schoolwide interagency transition team.

It is critical that the transition coordinator establish linkages with 2- and 4-year colleges, vocational and technical schools, employers, continuing education programs, residential programs, transportations, parks and recreation, YMCAs, independent living centers, neighborhood organizations, cultural centers, and a myriad of other community programs. Key contacts from each of these programs should be on file and easily accessible, and the coordinator should establish new contacts needed by individual students. Each contact should be cultivated and rewarded for participating in meetings or providing consults. Rewards can include thank you letters, invitations to school events, recognition dinners, or providing useful information of interest to the contact. It is important to understand that many of these contacts provide consultation on their own time, so their input should be used efficiently and effectively. The coordinator can use career fairs, group IEP/transition meetings, and conference calls to maximize the impact of their participation while minimizing time demands.

Developing Community Work Sites and Work Experience Programs

The development of community work sites and work experience programs for youth with disabilities requires the ability to use both the individual's and the school's network of contacts. Some common practices might include hosting an agency or business advisory committee, becoming a member of a business-oriented community group, maintaining a "job bank" with other agencies, or hosting a career fair (Baer, Martonyi, Simmons, Flexer, & Goebel, 1994). It is also important to survey staff, board members, former and current employers, and consumer supporters to develop job leads. The most efficient way to develop job leads is to be introduced to a prospective employer by someone these people may know.

Family Involvement

Families can provide critical insight into student interests, abilities, history, and preferences and may act as surrogate decisionmakers for students who are unable to give informed consent (Dinerstein, Herr, & O'Sullivan, 1999). They also play a critical role in improving student performance and attendance in school and in supporting the individual's transition after leaving school. Family involvement in transition planning and programs also can help the parents form realistic expectations for the students as they observe them performing competently in classroom and community environments with supports (Kohler, 1998).

The transition coordinator should be aware of the difficulties that families have in participating in the transition process. They may find transition planning ambiguous and confusing, be reluctant to discuss their child's disabilities in front of a group, and may lack clear, relevant, and timely information about transition services. The transition coordinator needs to address these issues by making families more knowledgeable, connected, and supported. The coordinator can support them in this regard through development of joint family-professional transition training, resource fairs, a single point of contact for all services, support groups, information materials, and networking activities (Kohler, 1998).

Critical Point The transition coordinator should develop a variety of options for families to participate in transition planning and the development of transition programs.

Research has found that family expectations of professionals typically fall into one of four general categories: (1) expectations for support and emotional guidance, (2) expectations for cognitive guidance and evaluation, (3) expectations for assuming personal initiative with professional feedback, and (4) expectations for collaboration (Koch & Rumrill, 1998b). It is important that transition coordinators negotiate, rather than impose, family roles in the transition process since congruence among youth, family, and professional expectations has been shown to be positively related to ratings of the working alliance (Al-Darmaki & Kivlighan, 1993). Additionally, families may have many other concerns and stressors that limit their ability to assume service coordination responsibilities (Hayden & Goldman, 1996).

The advocacy role of the transition coordinator should not be confused with the advocacy role of parents. Webster's dictionary defines *advocacy* as "speaking for or on behalf of a person." Advocacy in this sense can be empowering and disempowering. If the coordinator speaks on behalf of youth with disabilities and families who can speak for themselves, it is disempowering. On the other hand, the transition coordinator may be able to assist individuals and families in communicating with service providers whose culture and technical jargon may be foreign to the layperson. In this sense, advocacy by the transition coordinator may be seen as empowering.

Collaboration

The transition coordinator should promote collaboration in a way that minimizes the barriers among the student, family, and professionals; and that also improves collaboration among the professionals themselves (Baer, Goebel, & Flexer, 1993). In this regard, the transition coordinator must foster transition team processes that move team members from a multidisciplinary approach (where professional roles are rigid and specialized) to an interdisciplinary or transdisciplinary approach where professional, student, and family roles are less circumscribed. Multidisciplinary models of service delivery are more prevalent in medical programs where professionals typically work in a professional/patient relationship with only limited consultation with other disciplines. Interdisciplinary approaches are more prevalent in nonmedical disability programs where professionals typically work in a professional/consumer relationship as part of a team.

Independent living and some ecological models of service delivery imply the need for a transdisciplinary approach to service provision. In this approach, professionals work as consultants to individuals with disabilities and to other professionals on the team. Both services and planning are provided collaboratively. "Role release" is an important characteristic of the transdisciplinary model where team members work as part of an integrated program providing services and supports that are organized around individual needs rather than professional services (Baer, Goebel, & Flexer, 1993). In this approach, students, family members, and other professionals may participate in implementing physical therapy, behavior programming, and training as part of an integrated community program focused upon individual goals.

Critical Point   The transition coordinator should develop a team process that equalizes relationships between families and professionals and that minimizes barriers between the disciplines.

In directing collaboration, the transition coordinator should be familiar with laws pertaining to youth with disabilities. These include the IDEA, section 504 of the Rehabilitation Act, the Americans with Disabilities Act (ADA), and other civil rights legislation. Transition legislation and regulations can be difficult to read and interpret, so the coordinator should attend in-service programs and obtain publications by the National Association of Special Education Directors (NASDE) and other publications of professional and parent organizations.

A primary role of the transition coordinator is providing linkages to services and supports needed for the development of employment and other adult living objectives for youth with disabilities and their families. Prior to the IEP/transition meeting, the coordinator needs to develop linkages with postsecondary educators and adult service providers who can aid in the development of the transition plan, and natural supporters, employers, secondary educators, and service providers who can assist in its implementation. The transition coordinator should assist youth and their families in identifying and inviting potential IEP/transition meeting participants. Key linkages in this phase would include representatives from the student's desired postsecondary environments, school programs, adult service providers who can fund or provide services, and community supporters.

It is important to establish the right contacts for each program. It may be much more effective to use a representative of student disability services or learning centers from a 2- or 4-year college than an admissions officer who is unfamiliar with disability issues. For employers, it may be more effective to establish contact with their employee assistance programs than with personnel managers who are more inclined to screen than to welcome applicants with disabilities. The general rule for selecting contacts is that they should (1) be able to represent the postsecondary program, (2) be as knowledgeable of disability issues as possible, and (3) be supportive of persons with disabilities.

The transition coordinator is likely to encounter conflict in efforts to promote collaboration. A common myth about any collaborative process is that collaborators will agree, have shared values, and develop consensus without conflict (Koch & Rumrill, 1998b). Strong working relationships with transition team members should assure that conflict and disagreement can occur without destroying the relationship. Koch and Rumrill (1998b) define a four-step process for resolving conflicts: (1) accurately defining the conflict, (2) clarifying misconceptions, (3) generating options, and (4) implementing and evaluating resolutions. It is important to identify conflicts and resolve them as they arise to avoid breakdown in relationships and disruption of decision making and team process.

Transition coordinators should deal with conflicts discretely, preferably outside student or agency meetings. If a conflict threatens to disrupt an IEP/transition team meeting, the coordinator should recess or adjourn the meeting until the conflict is resolved. The coordinator should set up a meeting between the conflicting members, preferably in a relaxed neutral setting, and follow the four-step process for conflict resolution. In conflict resolution, the coordinator should assume the role of mediator and periodically reassure participants that conflict is normal in a good working alliance (Koch & Rumrill, 1998b). If the coordinator is directly involved in the conflict, he or she may bring in an outside person as an arbitrator.

Developing Communication Strategies and Methods to Release and Share Information

Communication among the many programs serving youth with disabilities can be challenging for transition coordinators who spend much of the time out of the office. Ohio's systems change project for transition explored this issue by funding a number of pilot sites to address shared intake, referral, and transition planning. Approaches varied among the sites and included:

- Sharing the IEP/transition plan with all agencies serving a given youth, who then used it as the base of all plans concerning the youth
- The development of a password protected the computer site where general information on students can be stored and released to agencies
- The development of common intake and referral sheet used as a single point of entry to all services by applying to any single agency (Baer, 1996).

Release of information restrictions can be a major impediment to communication. The transition coordinator may need to look into how information can be shared among transition providers without violating the privacy of youth with disabilities and their families. A blanket release of information that allows the sharing of information among all transition agencies for a limited time can facilitate information sharing. This can help students and families who often have to answer the same questions repeatedly to different transition service providers. Some considerations in the development of a blanket release of information form include the option for students and families to control:

1. What information is to be released: identifying information, case information, financial information, sensitive medical information (e.g., HIV and AIDS)
2. How long the release of information is in effect (e.g., 180 days, 360 days, etc.)
3. What agencies can receive student information (all agencies, specific agencies)
4. How information is protected by all agencies covered by the blanket release
5. How the student or family can revoke the release of information at any time
6. Assurances that refusal to sign the blanket release will not affect services (Baer, 1996)

In addition to the blanket release of information form, each participating agency will need to sign a member agreement for information sharing. This member agreement needs to specify: (1) how information will be used, (2) information will not be used in criminal manners, except as required by judicial order, and (3) members will maintain information in a secure manner. Both the blanket release of information and the member agreement should be shared with legal experts at each of the agencies to assure that they comply with the law and agency regulations. (See Appendix E for a sample blanket release of information and member agreement.)

Monitoring Fulfillment of Transition Team Member Responsibilities

The transition coordinator needs to develop mechanisms for monitoring services in IEP/transition plans. This is an area of particular concern since research indicates that less than 25% of

IEP/transition teams were reconvened when adult services could not be provided as planned (Baer et al., 1996). This lack of concern for maintaining planned transition services indicated to transition team participants that transition planning had little importance or relevance to what the student was actually doing in school.

The transition coordinator monitors service provision by establishing benchmarks and contacting service and support providers periodically to assure that they are on schedule. It is important that the transition coordinator make contacts with key service providers well in advance of transition service deadlines to allow time to correct problems or to revise time lines before they are missed. Additionally, periodic contact with members of a student's IEP/transition team allows the coordinator to gather information and to cement relationships. This investment in relationships with team members is a valuable resource when things go wrong or mistakes are made. If services cannot be provided as planned, the coordinator should reconvene the student's transition team. Reconvening the team offers the student and the family the opportunity to discuss alternative ways of addressing transition objectives.

Critical Point   The transition coordinator needs to assure that transition planning drives provision of student services and to reconvene the student's transition team if services cannot be provided as planned.

Development of Program Attributes and Structures

Often the transition system at a given school lacks the program structures to promote student-focused planning, student development, family involvement, or interagency collaboration (Kohler, 1998). Relative to the transition planning, this may be manifested in limited time for youth and family input in the development of the IEP/transition plan, use of technical language, inviting only preferred service providers to transition meetings, inconvenient meeting

times and places, and excessive bureaucracy. There also may be lack of critical transition programs, such as life skills instruction, career and vocational curricula, support services, and structured work experiences (Kohler, 1998).

To deal with these program issues, the transition coordinator must be able to mobilize transition stakeholders in adopting exemplary transition practices (Everson & Guillory, 1998). The transition coordinator may address these issues by forming a schoolwide interagency transition team. The membership of the school-level interagency transition team should include all transition stakeholders, including families, adult service providers, administrators, educators, employers, and transition specialists. The makeup of the team may vary from meeting to meeting, depending on the students or issues to be discussed, but it should generally address issues such as:

- Community supports
- Better access to vocational services
- Curriculum enhancement and life skills instruction
- Cross-training for students, parents, and professionals
- Development of work experiences
- Strategies to empower youth with disabilities and their families
- Strategies to empower minority youth with disabilities and their families

A number of surveys have been developed to self-assess transition policy compliance and the best practice (Baer, Simmons, & Flexer, 1996; Johnson, Sharpe, & Sinclair, 1998; Morgan, Moore, McSweyn, & Salzberg, 1992). Appendix F contains a survey that school-based interagency transition teams have used in Ohio to assess policy compliance and the best practice. This survey examines both current and the team members' perception of the best practice in relation to 36 criteria.

The school-level interagency transition team also can be an effective mechanism for maintaining current information on transition services by bringing school and adult service providers together to discuss the ever-changing system of services available to transition-age youth. Key representatives from major programs such as the rehabilitation services , developmental disabilities programs, JTPA (Job Training and Partnership Act), social security, mental health, and the U.S. Department of Human Services may be able to provide information pertaining to many other programs in the community.

Critical Point   The transition coordinator should support or develop a schoolwide interagency transition team to address systems issues, planning, and program development.

Generally, the transition coordinator needs to be familiar with group process skills to manage effectively the school-level transition team. Tuckman and Jensen (1977) suggest that groups go through five rather predictable stages of development: forming, storming, norming, performing, and adjourning. In the *forming* phase, the coordinator needs to recruit representatives of critical transition stakeholder groups and to convince them of the importance of addressing transition issues for youth with disabilities. In the *storming* phase, the coordinator needs to lead the group in a noncritical generation of ideas about desired transition outcomes and the best practices to achieve those outcomes. In the *norming* phase, the transition coordinator needs to develop an action plan that outlines who is to do what by when. In the *performing* stage, the transition coordinator as the leader needs to monitor performance, reward success, and problem solve failures. At the *adjourning* phase, the team members are given an option of leaving the team or renewing commitment. Often this is determined by the terms of membership.

Developing Methods to Identify Future Service Needs of Families and Students
The transition coordinator needs to develop a method of determining how many students and families need specific types of transition services prior to and after leaving high school. This information can be shared with programs and agencies that provide these services so that they can plan accordingly. The coordinator can use a number of approaches to identify these needs. These approaches include (1) a review of IEP/transition plans, (2) a survey of students, families, and professionals, or (3) focus groups.

Once the coordinator has obtained the information, it should be shared with all concerned providers and agencies. The school-based interagency transition team can assist the coordinator in this regard by providing a forum where the information can be discussed. The interagency transition team should address questions, including (1) Are services being utilized effectively? (2) Does the current service capacity meet the future needs of students? and (3) How can service capacity and service needs be addressed?

Coordinating Student Follow-Up Studies
Follow-up studies of students who have exited school provide information on the problems that students encounter after graduation and information on the effectiveness of transition services they received before graduation. Follow-up studies may be conducted for all students or for a random sample of students. Typically, follow-up studies look at student outcomes 1, 3, and 5 years after leaving school. Questions commonly addressed by follow-up studies include:

1. The person's age and date of leaving school (typically from school records)
2. The type of disability (typically from school records)
3. Ethnicity (typically from school records)
4. Employment information (e.g., duration, type, wages, benefits, hours, etc.)
5. Support information (e.g., adult services, financial supports, natural supports, etc.)
6. Community activities (civic, volunteer, recreation, etc.)

7. Transportation (e.g., car, bus, walking, family, etc.)
8. Living arrangements (e.g., family, independent, supported living, etc.)
9. Postsecondary education enrolled (2-year, 4-year, other) postsecondary education completed
10. Transition and school programs that were especially helpful
11. Transition and school programs that were unavailable or unhelpful

The coordinator may need to collaborate with persons with research experience to assure that those individuals who were sampled are truly representative of all students. Because follow-up studies are typically conducted by telephone interview, it may be necessary to develop alternative procedures for reaching students whom are difficult to find or contact. In addition, the coordinator may want to do focused follow-up studies for specific populations (e.g., persons with autism) that have unique concerns or barriers.

A Case Study in Transition Service Coordination

As a transition specialist at an urban school, Ellen and her mother came to me this June to discuss her educational program as she entered high school. Ellen's eighth grade teacher, Ms. Middleton, had informed them that since Ellen was 14 years old her IEP meeting would include a discussion of what she would be doing after graduation and how she would get there. The teacher also told them that we would be talking about other agencies and programs that might help Ellen to reach her goals. Ms. Middleton noted that they were very confused about what "transition" was and what this had to do with Ellen.

Ms. Middleton and I met Ellen and her mother outside the school and had coffee, soft drinks, and donuts while we discussed Ellen's transition to high school and what she would like to do after graduation. Ellen responded "yes" when her mother said "You want to go to college, don't you?" but it was clear that Ellen had no concept of what a nurse's aide did. Ellen clearly was looking for emotional support and guidance, so I surveyed both Ellen and her mother regarding what they saw Ellen doing both before and after graduation. Through this survey, it was clear that Ellen would need a lot more information and that her mother would need to give her more freedom in regard to her choices. We discussed the importance of self-determination and how it could be developed through functional and vocational evaluations, community experiences, informational interviews, and job shadowing. Ellen seemed to be interested, but her mother was concerned that she would miss out on class work. After some discussion, we suggested that Ellen and her mother meet with the guidance counselor and the work-study coordinator to explore this issue further.

Critical Point   Keep student-focused planning by scheduling meetings at alternative sites and by assuring the student is giving informed consent.

After meeting with the guidance counselor and the work-study coordinator, Ellen and her mother agreed to do the functional-vocational assessment which identified an interest in library work and a number of areas in which Ellen would need services and supports to pursue this course of study. Ellen had poor spelling skills and no typing skills. It also was clear that while Ellen expressed an interest in library work, she based this decision on the fact that she had no other experiences in this area. However, it was clear that Ellen liked that type of work environment and enjoyed books. The guidance counselor provided Ellen with a tentative list of classes and the work-study coordinator discussed some areas that might be explored through community work experiences and job shadowing.

Ellen and her mother preferred that I act on their behalf in the first IEP/transition meeting. In the meeting, we focused upon career exploration and the transition services and supports that Ellen would need to participate in her course of study. Since Ellen was only 14, and had unclear postsecondary goals, we did not try to develop a full transition plan with transition services in all the areas that would be required when Ellen was 16. The guidance counselor, the vocational evaluator, and the work-study coordinator were invited to the meeting. The guidance counselor agreed to enroll Ellen in business-related English, typing, and math classes. The vocational evaluator suggested a hand speller to help Ellen with her spelling problems. The work-study coordinator agreed to arrange some job-shadowing experiences around office work and related occupations. We discussed time lines and responsibilities for each service and I said that I would be calling monthly to check on Ellen's progress.

Critical Point   Promote student development by integrating academics and transition activities.

During the ensuing year, assessment information needed by other agencies was collected. Everyone involved with Ellen was encouraged to help her identify interests and needs, not only in regard to employment, but also in her home and the community. After a series of job-shadowing experiences and a very positive experience with her typing teacher, Ellen decided that she really wanted to do office work. However, Ellen was having extreme difficulty in English and math courses and it was feared that she would not be able to do the academic work to get into a 2-year business school. Ellen and her mother were becoming excited about her new goals, however, and agreed to present their vision at the second IEP/transition meeting. We went over postsecondary goals and needed transition services point by point and rehearsed how their plan would be presented at the meeting. After the discussion, it was decided that Ellen and her

mother would like to see her get a chance to try out a community work experience when she turned 16.

It now became clear that Ellen would need a full IEP/transition plan that addressed instruction, community experiences, and development of her employment objectives in the following year. She also would need linkages with adult service providers to provide the supports she needed to pursue a 2-year college degree. Also, the issue of Ellen's low English and math scores would need to be addressed in light of her postsecondary goals. Therefore, I contacted and discussed Ellen's upcoming IEP/transition meeting with the rehabilitation services, the work-study coordinator, local business schools, and Ellen's math and English teachers. Some difficulties were encountered with the math and English teachers who used a curriculum that focused upon preparation for a 4-year college. We defined the conflict as related to Ellen having to meet the same requirements as everyone else in the class and the misperception that we were trying to get Ellen out of demonstrating math and English competencies. We finally generated the option that Ellen's grade could be partially based on math and English competencies demonstrated on the job and that her class work focus upon applied math and English.

Critical Point   Promote collaboration and resolve conflict outside the IEP/transition meeting whenever possible.

All involved transition stakeholders were invited to Ellen's IEP/transition meeting. Due to a conflict, the counselor from the rehabilitation services could not make the meeting, but she provided written input and committed the agency to developing an individual work-related program (IPE) so that Ellen could receive accommodations and job coaching in her community work experience. Other members attending the meeting included the special education supervisor, the typing teacher, the work-study coordinator, the guidance counselor, Ellen, her mother, a reading resource teacher from a local business college, and the English teacher. At the start of the meeting, an agenda was distributed, as well as a copy of the survey that Ellen and her mother were going to present to the team. I explained to the team that each member should work toward Ellen's goals and share information and outcomes.

In her IEP/transition meeting Ellen and her mother enthusiastically presented a vision of Ellen working in an office setting and living in an apartment after attending a 2-year school. It was noted that Ellen had done very well in typing classes with the help of her speller and enjoyed her job-shadowing experiences in office settings. The English teacher was skeptical of this goal and suggested that a vocational program may be more appropriate. After a brief goal reappraisal, the team was brought back to a discussion of how to support Ellen's goal. The reading resource teacher from the business school suggested that they would consider Ellen's work experience in her admission and that they could provide notetakers and tutors to assist her in doing the academic work. The work-study coordinator volunteered to provide work experience. The English teacher brought up our previously discussed idea of allowing Ellen to receive credit for English and math skills that she demonstrated on the job and to incorporate these into instruction.

The family agreed to develop an individual plan for employment (IPE) with VR with business college and community work experience as vocational goals. The special education supervisor agreed to work with the principal on allowing the English and math teachers to revise their curricula. The IEP/transition plan reiterated the need for Ellen to have classroom accommodations in regard to spelling and note-taking. Needed transition services were also identified in regard to instruction (applied math and English), community experiences (work-study), development of postschool objectives (meeting

with the business college), and linkages to adult services (referral to VR). One concern was raised that it was school policy that Ellen would have to pass the state and regional proficiency tests in order to graduate. This issue could not be addressed by Ellen's transition team and was referred to the school-level interagency transition team.

The school-level interagency transition team consisted of parents, students, professionals, administrators, and adult service providers. When Ellen's issue regarding proficiency testing was brought to the team, several other parents agreed that this was a major concern of students with disabilities. It was noted that many students were dropping out of school due to frustration with proficiency tests. One administrator stated that this was a policy of the school that could not be changed. Using conflict management approaches, it became clear that school policy was based on a misperception of state guidelines on proficiency testing and that the school was not complying with the accommodation requirements outlined in the IDEA of 1997 and section 504 of the Rehabilitation Act. The administrators and parents worked together to generate options regarding accommodations and alternative ways that students with disabilities could demonstrate mastery. This resulted in the adoption of a career portfolio assessment as an alternative way of having students demonstrate skills required by the school. (This eventually helped Ellen to receive her degree and to go on to business school.)

Critical Point   Promote development of transition programs and structures through linkages with administration and other transition stakeholders.

The following year, Ellen was assigned a new transition coordinator. Ellen, her mother, the new coordinator, and I met over coffee, soft drinks, and donuts to discuss where to go from here. Ellen expressed interest in getting into a vocational program focused upon business, but she was experiencing difficulties in getting the required credits. Her expectations for her new transition coordinator would be that he would collaborate with her to address her educational needs. I bid farewell to Ellen and her mother and offered to keep in touch. I gave Ellen a self-addressed envelope and my phone number for her to contact me and let me know how she was doing. I was confident that Ellen was on the road to a meaningful future, regardless of the barriers that she would encounter along the way.

Critical Point   Develop ways of following up with students after graduation.

Conclusion

In this chapter, we have discussed two models of service provision: ecological and independent living. The ecological model of planning involves an array of professional and natural supports from the many environments that are or will be encountered by the person. The independent living model of planning attempts to minimize dependence on professionals and to limit intrusion into the lives of persons with disabilities. The transition coordinator needs to consider individual and family preferences, cultural concerns, and support options in determining which of these models to emphasize in service provision. The objectives of service coordination were identified as (1) student-focused planning, (2) student development (3) family involvement (4) collaboration, and (5) the development of transition programs and structures. Self-determination was defined as one of the major goals of service coordination.

Study Questions

1. Discuss two models of service provision that are considered state of the art for individuals with disabilities.
2. Discuss how student needs, preferences, and cultural background impact upon how services should be provided.

3. List and define the five major goals for transition programs and transition service coordination.
4. Describe why student self-determination is an important objective of transition service coordination.
5. List and define the five major functions of transition coordinators.
6. Describe two strategies for developing ongoing linkages and sharing information with adult service providers.
7. Describe how to prepare a student and the family for the IEP/transition meeting.
8. Describe how you would set up a schoolwide interagency transition team. Whom would you invite? What would you discuss? How would you involve families and students?

Web Sites

Transition Research Institute:
http://www.ed.uiuc.edu/sped/tri/institute.html

Heath Resource Center of the American Council on Education:
http://www.acenet.edu/about/programs/Access&Equity/HEATH/home.html

National Center for Learning Disabilities Inc.:
http://www.ncld.org/

National Center for Research in Vocational Education:
http://www.ncld.org/

The Office of Vocational and Adult Education:
http://www.ed.gov/offices/OVAE/

The National Center for Children and Youth with Disabilities (NICHCY):
http://www.nichcy.org/

The National Longitudinal Transition Study:
http://www.sri.com/policy/cehs/nlts/nltssum.html

National Institute on Disability and Rehabilitation Research (NIDRR):
http://www.ncddr.org/

National Network of Regional Education Laboratories:
http://www.nwrel.org/national/

Parent Advocacy Coalition for Educational Rights (PACER):
http://www.pacer.org/index.html

Research and Training Center on Independent Living at the University of Kansas:
http://www.lsi.ukans.edu/rtcil/rtcil.htm

National Institute for People with Disabilities:
http://www.yai.org/

Administration on Developmental Disabilities:
http://www.acf.dhhs.gov/programs/add/

IDEA practices:
http://www.ideapractices.org/

Office of Special Education Programs (OSEP):
http://www.ed.gov/offices/OSERS/OSEP/index.html

Model Transition Projects — The Transition Institute:
http://www.ed.uiuc.edu/sped/tri/projwebsites.html

Office of Special Education and Rehabilitative Services:
http://www.ed.gov/offices/OSERS/

Rehabilitation Services Commission:
http://www.ed.gov/offices/OSERS/RSA/rsa.html

Social Security Disability Information:
http://www.ssa.gov/odhome/odhome.htm

Presidential Task Force on Employment of Adults with Disabilities:
http://www.dol.gov/dol/sec/public/programs/ptfead/main.htm

Federal Resource Center for Special Education:
http://dssc.org/frc/

Great Lakes Area Regional Resource Center (GLARRC):
http://www.csnp.ohio-state.edu/glarrc.htm

Federal Register — Grants from U.S. Department of Education:
http://gcs.ed.gov/fedreg/announce.htm

14

Family Involvement

Lisa Turner

The objectives of this chapter are:

1. Provide an historical perspective of parent participation in IEP meetings.

2. Indicate the responsibilities of the school in enrolling parents in the IEP/ITP process.

3. Describe the conditions that lend themselves to encouraging and supporting parent participation in the IEP/ITP.

4. List the roles and functions of parents in raising their son or daughter with a disability.

5. Describe parental concerns and issues that prevent active parent involvement.

6. Identify contributions and attributes of parents with regard to the transition planning process.

7. Describe ways to demonstrate professional regard for parents.

The previous chapters have looked at the four essential elements of transition relative to the student, the school, and the transition coordinator. In this chapter, the author discusses the transition from the perspective of the family. Family involvement is a key element in determining student needs, interests, and preferences. They are not only the primary persons impacted by the results of the transition's outcome-oriented process, but they also are the major participants in that process. Without family involvement, much of the student's day-to-day activities would be uncoordinated with the activities of the school. In addition, of course, without family involvement much is lost in the effort to promote student movement to postsecondary environments.

The passage of the Education for All Handicapped Children Act of 1975 (P.L. 94-142) proved, in many ways, to be an asset to children with disabilities. In response to the law's mandates, special educators developed policies and procedures for both the provision of educational options and services and the determination of appropriate educational placements of students with disabilities. Also included in the law's mandates was the provision of opportunities for the inclusion of parents in the determination of their child's educational programming. The primary vehicle for parent participation has been the individualized education plan (IEP) meeting, in which parents are required participants. As stated in the clarifications of IEP requirements issued by the Office of Special Education, one of the major purposes of the IEP is as follows:

> the IEP meeting serves as a communication vehicle between parents and school personnel, and enables them as equal participants, to jointly decide what the child's needs are, what services will be provided to meet those needs, and what the anticipated outcomes may be . . . (Federal Register, 1981, p. 5462).

Therefore, the expectation for parents' involvement is not as passive recipients of information but rather as active decisionmakers. Unfortunately, parents still participate minimally and perform roles secondary to professional educators in the special education process (Dinnebeil & Rule, 1994; Gartner & Lipsky, 1987; Gilliam & Coleman, 1981; Pruitt & Wandry, 1998; Vaughn, Bos, Harrell, & Lasky, 1988). In the decision-making process for the education of their children, for many parents, their input is not significant nor are they part of a consensus process.

Although legal mandates provide opportunities for parents to participate in educational decision making, these opportunities have not been utilized. The literature repeatedly reflects the lack of parent involvement in the decision-making process. The following section provides an overview of the legal basis for parent participation and the rationale for such participation.

The literature over the past 20 years illustrates, with many examples, how parents function as passive participants in educational decision making (Turnbull & Morningstar, 1993). In one study (Gilmore, 1974), parent involvement in decision making was given a low priority rating by educators, with parental involvement perceived as desirable but not very important. Another early survey of professional members of school planning teams reported that most professionals felt that parent participation in IEP development should consist primarily of gathering and presenting relevant information rather than contributing to the planning process (Yoshida, Fenton, Kaufman, & Maxwell, 1978). Although many parents and professionals have supported the role of parents of children with disabilities as working partners in special education, the parent-professional relationship was described as still developing in early literature (e.g., Gerber, Banbury, Miller, & Griffin, 1986; Goldstein, Strickland, Turnbull, & Curry, 1980). Later reviews and analyses noted that professionals still do not employ suggested parent involvement practices to engage parents actively in their child's educational program (e.g., Hilton & Henderson, 1993), nor do educators consider parents to be equal partners in the decision-making process (Dinnebeil & Rule, 1994; Lynch & Stein, 1982; McNair & Rusch, 1987; Pruitt & Wandry, 1998; Repetto, White, & Snauwaert, 1990; Tilson & Neubert, 1988).

Updated legislation has provided additional opportunities for parents to participate in determining their children's educational program. In 1990, the Individuals with Disabilities Education Act (IDEA) (P.L. 101-476), was passed by federal legislators to amend the Education for All Handicapped Children Act. This legislation mandated transition services for all students with disabilities aged 16 or older, and 14 or younger, if appropriate. Also included was a section describing parent participation in IEPs. Section 300.346 (b) addressed the content of the IEP as follows:

> the IEP for each student, beginning no later than age 16 (and at a younger age, if appropriate) must include a statement of the needed transition services as defined in 300.18 including, if appropriate, a statement of each public agency's and each participating agency's responsibilities or linkages, or both, before the student leaves the school setting . . . (Individuals with Disabilities Education Act, 1990).

In 1997, the Individuals with Disabilities Education Act was amended further. It upheld the provisions inherent in the 1975 Education for All Handicapped Children Act and revised and expanded the provisions in the IDEA of 1990 with regard to the content of the IEP and parent participation. One of the new components to be included in the IEP is a new requirement for stating transition service needs beginning at age 14. Section 614(d)(1)(A)(vii)(I) is as follows:

> beginning at age 14, and updated annually, a statement of the transition service needs of the child under the applicable components of the child's IEP that focuses on the child's courses of study (such as participation in advanced-placement courses or a vocational education program) . . . (IDEA, 1997).

This new requirement expands the notion of parent participation from a minimum of 2 years to 4 years in transition planning. The IDEA of 1990 also required that parents be involved in transition planning. Section 300.345 required that:

> each public agency shall take steps to ensure that one or both of the parents of the child with a disability are present at each meeting or are afforded the opportunity to participate, including notifying parents of the meeting, scheduling the meeting at a mutually agreed on time and place, and the notice must indicate the purpose, time, and location of the meeting and who will be in attendance . . . (IDEA, 1990).

Section 300.345 continued to state that, "if neither parent can attend, the public agency shall use other methods to ensure parent participation, including individual or conference telephone calls" (IDEA, 1990).

Critical Point: The IDEA mandates that schools take multiple measures to involve parents in IEP and transition planning.

The IDEA regulations, therefore, mandate the inclusion of parents in the transition process through their invited participation in their child's IEP meeting. Additionally, because transition services must have an outcome orientation and be based on the student's needs and preferences, parent participation in the development of a transition plan for their child is strongly implied. The parents and student have intimate knowledge of their needs and preferences related to postschool outcomes and current and future environments in which they will have to function. For successful transitions to these identified outcomes and environments, the transition plan, and ultimately the IEP, must reflect the student and family's choices, and not those of the professionals. Because parents have an ongoing relationship with their child, they have a unique perspective on life planning that is difficult to match with periodic professional contact (Suelzle & Keenan, 1981). Parents can estimate the types of services their child will require and when those services will be needed

(McDonnell, Wilcox, Boles, & Bellamy, 1985). These services can then be oriented toward the identified outcomes and be provided in a timely manner to promote movement toward the attainment of those outcomes.

History of Family Involvement

Parent involvement in the educational planning of their children with disabilities is a difficult and arduous process. Due to litigation resulting in legislative mandates, parents are afforded increased opportunities to participate in their child's educational planning process. As indicated earlier, this is primarily the result of two major pieces of education-related legislation: the Education for All Handicapped Children Act of 1975 (EHA) and its amendments, the Individuals with Disabilities Education Act of 1990 and 1997 (IDEA). The EHA mandated parent participation in the IEP process, whereas IDEA included parents as participants in the legally mandated transition planning process. The following historical review examines the legislative mandates and the evolvement of parental participation over the past 20 years, organized into two major categories: (A) parent involvement in the IEP process and (B) parent involvement in transition planning. The first section examines the legal framework for parent participation in the IEP process and reviews traditional parental roles, levels of parental involvement, and professionals' perceptions of family involvement. The second section addresses current legislative mandates pertaining to parent involvement and examines parental participation in the transition planning process.

Parent Involvement in the IEP Process

Inherent in the intent of the EHA of 1975 was parent involvement. This was based on the premise that active parental participation in the educa-tional process has a positive effect on a child's learning experiences (Smith, 1990). Additionally, parent involvement promotes greater gains in school and enhances generalization of academic and social skills from school to home settings (Simpson, 1982; Turnbull & Turnbull, 1985).

Passive Participation

Early literature addressed various aspects of this issue, such as professionals' perceptions of parental roles (Gilliam & Coleman, 1981; Yoshida, Fenton, Kaufman, & Maxwell, 1978); parents' actual role (Goldstein, Strickland, Turnbull, & Curry, 1980); parents' perceptions of their roles (Lusthaus, Lusthaus, & Gibbs, 1981); and strategies for facilitating parental involvement (Cone, Delawyer, & Wolfe, 1985; Goldstein & Turnbull, 1982). Results of these studies and others indicated minimal participation during IEP meetings, with professionals perceiving parents as passive recipients of information.

Lack of Equal Status in Decision Making

Additionally, literature focusing upon the evaluation of the IEP process also noted the lack of opportunity for active parent involvement and equal status in decision making. Gartner and Lipsky (1987) reviewed available studies on parent participation in the IEP process and noted that many parents are minimally involved in providing information, making decisions, and advocating for their child's needs (e.g., Lusthaus, Lusthaus, & Gibbs, 1981; Vaughn, Bos, Harrell, & Lasky, 1988).

Lusthaus, Lusthaus, and Gibbs (1981) utilized a questionnaire to determine parental perceptions of their role in school decision making. The results indicated that parents most often found themselves in the role of giving and receiving information; the role of no involvement was second; and having decisional control was third, which appeared infrequently. Overall, parents indicated that they wanted to have more than an informational role in three areas: (1) the types of information they kept on their children, (2) medical services, and (3) school transfer. This may imply a change in the way parents perceive themselves and their role. As parents become educated regarding the educational system and increase their participation in planning for their children, Lusthaus et al. (1981) noted that parents may want their primary role to change to one of making and monitoring decisions.

Critical Point: Research indicates that parents lack the information and role status to participate as equal partners in the IEP planning process.

Types of Parent Participation/Interaction

A study by Vaughn, Bos, Harrell, and Lasky (1988) examined parent involvement in the initial placement/IEP process and described the conference as one of decision *telling*, not decision *making*. Twenty-six conferences for children referred for possible learning disabilities were observed. Results indicated that parents were engaged in verbal interaction on the average of only 14.8% of the conference time. On the average, parents asked only 4.5 questions during the conferences, with parents asking no questions at five conferences. Additionally, it was noted that despite their attendance at the conference, 23% of the parents interviewed did not know what was the meaning of the term "learning disability"; 23% felt nervous or cautious during the conference; 8% felt confused or overwhelmed; and 16% stated that they did not know how much time their child was supposed to receive special education. As a result of the study, the researchers concluded that parents continue to assume passive roles during IEP conferences. This is confounded by the fact that information required by parents to be active participants was not provided sufficiently, such as the nature of the disability or what special education services were. An example of this lack of parent information is indicated in the following case study.

CASE STUDY A

Mr. and Mrs. Brown have an 18-year-old son with mental retardation. Their son had been receiving special education services since age 6. They were participating in a transition educational program sponsored by their school district. The program presenter was discussing how transition activities could be incorporated into the students' IEPs. At that point, Mr. Brown raised his hand and asked what an IEP was.

Lack of IEP Efficacy

Smith (1990) completed a review of data-based research and position papers from 1975 to 1989 and found a history of IEP inadequacies and passive compliance. An overall assumption from the literature noted by Smith (1990) regarding IEP development suggested that although valid assessment, analysis, and diagnosis are essential to the IEP, it was questionable as to whether the available information facilitated IEP development. The following assumptions were generated: (1) generally, most teacher perception studies indicated that teachers felt that the IEP could be used as a general reference and contributed to an understanding of the child; (2) results of parent participation studies indicated minimal parental participation during IEP meetings, with parents perceived by professionals as recipients of information; (3) findings noted the lack of systematic training of professionals for participation in a multidisciplinary team process as well as the consistent absence of key personnel during IEP meetings; and (4) with regard to regular education teacher participation, it was noted that regular education teachers were ranked low in contributions and influence during IEP meetings and were minimally involved in IEP development. Additionally, Smith (1990) found that the research focus shifted from exemplary compliance with the spirit and intent of EHA to minimal compliance issues of cost and time reduction needed to compute IEPs by computer assistance.

Critical Point: Research suggests that schools, generally, have not complied with laws pertaining to IEP planning and have focused upon minimal rather than optimal compliance.

Smith (1990) noted that the IEP is supposed to provide (1) administrators with documentation of compliance, (2) teachers with formal instructional goals and objectives, (3) parents with a voice in decisions, and (4) students with an appropriate education. Implications based on the literature review include (1) IEPs were found to be questionable in complying with the law's intent, therefore, special education may also be questionable; (2) after more than a decade of research and recommendations, change regarding IEPs has not occurred; and (3) IEPs continued to be found deficient in a number of areas and are ineffective with regard to accountability, parent involvement, planning, and communication.

Minimal Roles in the Planning Process

Although practical suggestions were advocated at this time for the involvement of parents and students, they continue to have a minimal role in the planning process. Turnbull and Turnbull (1988) stated "the opportunity to express a preference or make a choice in special education is rare" (p. 338). This position is substantiated in the literature. Goldstein, Strickland, Turnbull, and Curry (1980) examined the dynamics of IEP conferences through naturalistic observational procedures. The observations were to determine the frequency of parent involvement in the conference and the nature of topics discussed. Results indicated that in the 14 observed conferences, only 5 of the 14 had full membership representation as mandated by the EHA rules and regulations. It was found that in 9 of the conferences the absentee member was the public agency representative (the person re-

sponsible for providing or supervising special education). Additionally, none of the observed conferences was attended by both parents. Although 14 topics were listed as required to be addressed, no one topic was recorded as being addressed during every conference. With regard to conference communication, the resource teacher was observed talking more than twice as much as the parent. The primary recipients of communication were parents (63% of statements), resource teachers (17% of statements), and classroom teachers (10% of statements).

The two consistent conference participants were the resource teacher and the parent. The IEP conference proceedings observed were characterized as the resource teacher reviewing the already developed IEP with the parent. Parents were provided the opportunity to present additional information that might have resulted in the modification of the IEP. This role is consistent with the findings of Yoshida, Fenton, Kaufman, and Maxwell (1978) regarding the responses of team members, who viewed appropriate parental involvement activities as giving and receiving information.

Need for Parent Training

The implications of this study (Yoshida et al., 1978) noted the need to train parents systematically to fulfill their roles and responsibilities in conjunction with IEP development and to train professionals to involve parents as full partners in the process. Competencies associated with shared decision making by parents and professionals should be specified and training models developed. Evaluation of the training programs should also be undertaken, with the ultimate outcome of a cooperative effort in the development of the most appropriate educational program for the child.

In another study, Gilliam and Coleman (1981) surveyed IEP conference participants to determine which IEP roles were perceived as (1) the most important to the IEP process, (2) the most influential in decision making, and

(3) contributing the most to the decisions made. Results noted that the ten highest ranked roles included special education teachers, psychologists, parents, and regular education teachers. However, parents, regular education teachers, social workers, and principals were ranked much higher in importance than in contribution and influence. These results indicated that although participants expected certain roles to be important in the IEP process, their expectations were only minimally fulfilled by the persons in these roles. Data revealed that parents were perceived as low in actual contribution and influence. The implications of this study suggested that although parents are expected to be influential, they have less actual influence in specific IEP functions than other participants. It could be assumed that parents either do not have expertise or are not perceived as having expertise regarding the planning process.

In summary, the literature reviewed suggests that the intent of the EHA of 1975 with regard to parent involvement in the IEP process has not been met. Despite the emphasis on parent participation mandated by EHA policy, the literature shows that many families are not actively involved in the IEP process and do not have equal status in decision making.

Parent Involvement in Transition Planning

The transition initiative of the 1980s evolved from the career education programs of the 1970s. The basic premise of both transition and career education requires interdisciplinary cooperation and collaboration among schools, adult service agencies, and employers as well as meaningful parent involvement. Because transition has as its foundation the basic tenets of career education, this section regarding parent involvement addresses both of these areas.

Career decisions made by youth with disabilities have an effect on every aspect of their lives (Kinnison, Jr., 1987). Super (1975) stated that the family shapes values and provides experiences, skills, and opportunities that are relevant to careers. Through parents' involvement during the educational planning process, the range and variety of occupational choices and placement options may be increased for their child (Brolin & Gysbers, 1979). However, it was noted by Ogusthorpe (1978) that most parents have minimal understanding regarding career development. Several authors suggested activities for parents to increase their knowledge of career education concepts in awareness, orientation, exploration, preparation, and placement (Brolin, 1976; Stowell, 1978; Vasa & Steckelberg, 1980), but there is little research to confirm the effectiveness of these activities.

Parents as Key Component in Transition Planning Process

During the last decade, one focus of literature and research in the field of special education was upon the identification of the components of effective transition planning. In order to facilitate successful transition for youth with disabilities from secondary school settings to adult life, several effective practices were identified throughout the literature. One of the most frequently noted effective practices was that of parent and family involvement in the transition process (e.g., Foss, 1990; Haring, Lovett, & Smith, 1990). However, research substantiating parent involvement as an effective practice is limited (Kohler, 1993).

Limited Research Substantiating Parent Involvement

Kohler (1993) reviewed and analyzed the transition literature concerning effective practices that are identified as having a positive impact on student outcomes. According to Kohler (1993), parent involvement was implied as effective practice in seven follow-up studies (Haring,

Lovett, & Smith, 1990; Humes & Brammer, 1985; Kranstover, Thurlow, & Bruininks, 1989; Mithaug, Horiuchi, & Fanning, 1985; Wehman, Kregel, & Seyfarth, 1985b; Wehman, Kregel, & Seyfarth, 1985c; Wise & Matthews, 1987), with only one study substantiating parent involvement as having a positive impact on student outcome (Schalock, Wolzen, Ross, Elliott, Werbel, & Peterson, 1986).

Empirically Substantiated Positive Parent Effect on Outcome

Schalock et al. (1986) evaluated the employment and living status of 108 individuals with moderate to severe disabilities who had graduated between 1979 and 1983 from rural schools utilizing a community-based job exploration and training model. The results showed that students whose families were moderately to highly involved with the students' programs were more successful on employment-related outcome variables. Family involvement was independently rated during the students' last year in school by two teachers and was found to be the only predictor variable to relate significantly to all nine major employment outcome variables. These variables included the present employment status, current living, primary income source, number of jobs held, number of months employed, total earnings, number of work hours per week, wages per hour, and weeks employed during the year. Thus, students whose families were rated as moderately to highly involved with their child's program did significantly better on each employment outcome variable. Schalock et al. (1986) noted that this finding was consistent with the literature indicating the significant influence of family support on both community integration and programmatic success.

In the theory-based and opinion literature, Kohler (1993) noted that all nine articles reviewed implied that parent involvement was a suggested practice without any substantiation (DeStefano, 1989; Halpern, 1985; Hardman &

McDonnell, 1987; Hoffman, 1988; McDonnell, Hardman, & Hightower, 1989; Stowitscheck & Kelso, 1989; Wehman, 1990; Wehman, Kregel, & Barcus, 1985; Will, 1984). Kohler (1993) also found that out of nine pseudoexperimental and quasi-experimental studies (D'Alonzo & Owen, 1985; Edwards, Kinneldorf, & Bradley, 1988; Halpern & Benz, 1987; Haynes & Justice, 1988; Heal, Gonzalez, Rusch, Copher, & DeStefano, 1990b; Hudson, Schwartz, Selander, Campbell, & Hensel, 1988; McDonnell, Wilcox, & Boles, 1986; Rusch & DeStefano, 1989; Tilson & Neubert, 1988), only the studies by Hudson et al. (1988) and Heal et al. (1990b) substantiated parent involvement as a recommended practice.

Empirically Substantiated Parent Involvement as Recommended Practice

In the study by Hudson et al. (1988), 50 successfully employed young adults with varying disabilities between the ages of 19 and 25 were interviewed regarding strategies or resources they felt had prepared them for employment. Support from school programs and staff, as well as from family and friends was considered important for 94% of the subjects in the completion of their education. In addition to being considered an educational strategy, family support also was perceived by 90% of the subjects as a personal resource for successful transition.

The researchers noted that a key influence in successful transition was the support network provided at school and at home. At school, this support was not only instructional, but it also included assistance with access to other resources and general advocacy. At home, the family contributed to a sense of competence and well-being. It was also noted that without this support, other resources are needed to compensate. Additionally, family support was cited as a successful strategy in all three areas analyzed.

The other substantiated study by Heal et al. (1990b) consisted of a comparison between a national sample of 54 matched pairs of high school students and young adults with learning disabilities or mental retardation who were successfully and unsuccessfully employed. Important elements that contributed to the success of competitively employed participants were identified through the completion of case study questionnaires that were completed by professionals. Results indicated that respondents noted home support, follow-up support, student ability, job match, social security disability income retention, employer incentives, and employer support as significantly more influential in ensuring placement success.

McDonnell, Wilcox, Boles, and Bellamy (1985) surveyed approximately 200 parents of high school students with severe disabilities in Oregon. With regard to projection of service needs, descriptive analyses noted that parents projected vocational, residential, and income support programs as the most important. Results regarding preferred features of adult service programs included (1) parent selection of vocational programs was the most influenced by the amount of job training and level of job security and (2) selection of residential programs was the most influenced by the amount of training their child would receive in the residence.

Based on the descriptive analyses, 65% of the parent respondents reported receiving information regarding available adult services in the community or information regarding how to access those services. Only 30% of the parents who had received some information about adult services reported that the classroom teacher was the source of that information. A significant number of parents received no information about available postschool services for their child.

Critical Point: Parent participation in IEP and transition planning is largely shaped by their training and their values.

Parents' Desire for More Involvement

Although parents have an important role in developing career goals and outcomes for their children, they continue to be mostly underinvolved in transition planning. McNair and Rusch (1991) completed a national study of 200 families having a child with disabilities between the ages of 14 and 25. Results indicated that parents were significantly less involved in transition programs than they desired, with 70% desiring involvement, whereas only 30% actually experienced involvement. Additionally, results indicated that more parents wanted an equal part in decision making and more involvement in finding job placements and residential arrangements than they were provided an opportunity to do.

Lack of Information Provided to Parents

Although these findings indicate a desire for more involvement, parents may not have adequate information to facilitate their involvement. In the study by McNair and Rusch (1991), results indicated that when asked to identify types of information that would help them plan for their child's postschool life, 40% of the parents noted that they wanted more information about their child's skills, 66% wanted more information about work options, 37% requested more information regarding residential options, and 56% desired more information about adult service agencies.

A follow-along project conducted by Malian and Love (1998) addressed transition issues from teacher, student, and parent perspectives. Survey and interview results indicated that (1) parents believed that their child had not received enough instruction in reading, math, writing, handling money, problem solving, exploring different types of jobs, and seeking jobs, whereas students believed that they had received sufficient instruction in reading, math, writing, problem solving, how to look for a job, and transportation; (2) parents felt that their children did not receive needed transition services; (3) parents believed that their children needed job training and placement services, but did not need help to secure a job; (4) teachers believed that students who remained in school received instruction in community-based settings; (5) course selection was determined predominantly by the schools; and (6) parent and student future expectations were similar. Implications from these results suggest focusing upon skill instruction, addressing high parental and student expectations, emphasizing the development of problem solving, providing extracurricular activities, and developing effective partnerships with families through communication.

From the preceding discussion, it is evident that parents have an important role in developing career goals and outcomes, have specific curricular concerns for their children, and continue to be mostly underinvolved in transition planning. Therefore, professional educators should not neglect their responsibility to actively involve the student's parents. Professionals have stated that parents and family members are the most important components in the transition from school to adult life because they have stable and continuous contact with their child throughout the entire process (Everson & Moon, 1987).

According to Benz and Halpern (1987), parent participation is an especially critical component in the transition planning process. Parents' participation is important because of the long-term effect parents have on their child's development. Parents impact their child through their own expectations and values (Benz & Halpern, 1987). Parental efforts are necessary to ensure continuity between school and adult services (Johnson, Bruininks, & Thurlow, 1987). Active family support and involvement were found to be consistent predictors of the employment and community living status of youth and adults with disabilities (Schalock, Wolzen, Ross, Elliott, Werbel, & Peterson, 1986). Kochany and Keller (1981) indicated that parents greatly influenced future career attitudes and options for their child by conveying the importance of different aspects

of career awareness, career exploration, and career preparation. Students with disabilities also have perceptions with regard to the importance of family involvement in determining and attaining postsecondary outcomes.

Halpern, Doren, and Benz (1993) reported the findings of a 3-year follow-along study of students with disabilities who by the transition process were able to go from school into their communities. Results indicated that most students found their jobs either on their own or with the help of family or friends. The potential for long-term effect on a child's development inherent in the parent-child relationship would be wasted if parents are not actively involved.

Critical Point: Parents play a key role in connecting the student to resources and supports.

Students' Perspectives

A qualitative study by Morningstar, Turnbull, & Turnbull (1995) examined the perspectives of students with disabilities on family involvement in the transition process. Results indicated that (1) the students' families highly influenced and shaped their career goals, (2) lack of systematic attention was given to the planning process, (3) the IEP process was reported to be irrelevant, and (4) self-determination training/support had not been part of the transition planning process. The findings suggest a collaborative effort to develop school-student-family partnerships, emphasizing self-determination.

The transition literature reviewed implies that it is necessary to educate and involve parents in taking an active role in the transition process. This would suggest a need to encourage and expect parents to take on a decision-making role with regard to the selection of outcomes, the selection of needed services, and the development and provision of those services. This also demands that parents be considered equal partners in the transition process with an equal voice in deciding and monitoring the delivery of services that will lead to successful adult outcomes for their children.

Although transition planning focuses upon the attainment of adult living outcomes, many parents do not have an understanding of how to plan for such outcomes for their children with disabilities (Brotherson, Berdine, & Sartini, 1993). Professionals need to assist parents in developing expectations related to employment, community living, and community participation through future forecasting and planning in order to prepare families for transitional change (Brotherson et al., 1993).

Parent Roles and Responsibilities

Parents and family members greatly influence the employment and community life adjustment of young adults with disabilities. The significant role of parents in the transitional adjustment of their children with disabilities working and living in the community implies that school programs must be structured to enlist parent input and involvement in the transition process.

Parental Expectations

Masino and Hodapp (1996) examined the effects of a visual impairment, hearing impairment, orthopedic impairment, and deafness on parental educational expectations. They found that parents had slightly higher expectations for college participation than did parents of students without disabilities. Implications suggest that parents should be included in discussions of their educational expectations for their children, and they should be involved earlier in their child's educational program.

Transition Team Membership

The primary means for interaction between parents and educational staff for the determination of delivery of transition services to children with disabilities is the transition team. The transition

Families play important transition education roles.

team members are crucial to the development of the student's transition plan. Because the transition plan must be based on the student's needs and preferences (IDEA, 1997), the parents and student must be considered an indispensable part of the transition team (Everson & Moon, 1987; Steere, Panscofar, Wood, & Hecimovic, 1990). Additionally, appropriate school personnel and adult services representatives should participate as team members to facilitate the attainment of the outcomes selected by the parents and student (Turnbull & Morningstar, 1993). The involvement of a team of skilled professionals with the active inclusion of the parents can result in meticulous attention to the child's individual needs and the selection of the most appropriate transition services which should lead to a more rewarding and productive life for the student with special needs.

The need for parent and professional partnerships in transition planning has long been recognized (Everson & Moon, 1987). Additionally, the need for parents to be involved as equal transition team members cannot be emphasized too strongly, particularly since it is legally mandated (IDEA, 1997). Both professionals and parents need to recognize this and develop strategies for ensuring fair and equitable participation in transition planning.

Transition Planning Roles and Responsibilities

Examples of the types of roles and responsibilities that parents should assume are found throughout the literature. McDonnell, Ferguson, and Mathot-Buckner (1992) noted that parental roles can range from daily care and financial support to serving as their child's primary case manager. Clark and Kolstoe (1995) listed the following parental roles and responsibilities:

1. Encourage student self-determination and independence at home.
2. Encourage and facilitate setting goals.
3. Teach, and assist in teaching, daily living and personal-social skills.
4. Encourage the student to work at home and at a neighborhood or community job.
5. Reinforce work-related behaviors at home (work habits, hygiene, grooming, etc.).
6. Explore and promote community resources for transition.
7. Assist in the student assessment process.
8. Assist the student in developing personal and social values, self-confidence, and self-esteem.
9. Work with legal and financial experts, as appropriate, to plan financial, legal, and residential alternatives (pp. 99–100).

Wehman, Moon, Everson, Wood, and Barcus (1988) defined professional and parent roles and responsibilities for transition from school to adult life as follows:

1. Attend ITP planning meetings.
2. Provide input to the team on family's needs, the young adult's needs, and the specific responsibilities the family is able and willing to assume.
3. Mobilize the team to develop a plan that integrates the young adult into the community and decreases his or her dependence on the family and on social service systems.
4. Focus the team's planning on the individual student's and family's needs.
5. Request information on the various issues that the family will need to address—for example, residential, recreational, guardianship, financial, medical, social, behavioral, or sexual issues.

6. Provide informal home and community skill training and provide behavioral intervention that compliments the secondary curricula (p. 208).

Wehman et al. (1988) suggested that the "optimal role that parents should assume during transition planning years is simply that of a participant" (p. 207).

Critical Point: There are many different roles that parents can play in transition and their roles will vary from parent to parent and from year to year.

Attributes of Parents

Parents typically attend IEP/ITP meetings as participants but are not actively involved. Individual transition planning teams need to encourage active parent participation. Active participation is more meaningful than passive attendance at meetings. As shown in Table 14–1, parents can make valuable contributions and bring many valuable attributes to the transition planning process.

Family Functions

In addition to the roles and responsibilities expected of parents during the transition planning process, they are also confronted with other functions. Turnbull, Summers, and Brotherson (1986) identified these family functions as:

1. The economic responsibility to generate income and to provide financial support for living costs and related payments and the domestic and health care responsibility to meet the daily needs of food, clothes, health and medical care, and safety
2. The recreational responsibility to provide leisure environments and activities
3. The responsibility for self-identity to increase each family member's sense of belonging
4. The affectionate responsibility to show and share love, care, emotional feelings, and companionship

TABLE 14–1

Parents' Attributes in Transition Planning

- Provide the most in-depth knowledge and insight regarding the child.
- Provide support of school participation.
- Reinforce and provide continuity of treatments over nonschool environments.
- Provide follow-up information after graduation.
- Express curricular concerns.
- Help to identify current and future environments for functioning to drive curriculum development.
- Make positive contributions to the transition team.
- Maintain high expectations and optimism for their child's future.
- Utilize strengths of the family.
- Provide family and friend support.
- Use the ability of making sound decisions regarding their child.
- Contribute novel solutions to problems.
- Take risks willingly.
- Keep the child's and family's best interests in mind.
- Make an intense commitment to their child.
- Remain as the only constant during years of changing services and professionals.
- Help to determine the child's interests and preferences.
- Display positive role models to develop values, morals, and positive work ethic in their child.
- Endeavor to network with other parents.

5. The responsibility for socialization to develop social skills and enhance interpersonal relationships

6. The educational and vocational responsibility to assist and support schooling and career selection and preparation.

It is beyond the scope of this chapter to expand on the different family subsystems, interactions, and functions. For a more complete description of family systems, please see Turnbull and Turnbull (1997).

Cultural and Linguistic Differences

Professionals must also appreciate the uniqueness and variation of each family. Haring, McCormick, and Haring (1994) note that families (1) vary in membership, (2) fulfill functions in a variety of ways, (3) differ in needs and resources, and (4) define events in different ways. Additionally, differing cultural, linguistic, and economic factors should be considered by professionals in the development and coordination of services for

families with exceptional children from culturally and linguistically diverse backgrounds.

Salend and Taylor (1993) noted a variety of areas in which professionals should develop an understanding to facilitate effective service delivery. These include (1) cultural considerations, (2) linguistic factors, and (3) socioeconomic factors. Cultural considerations include the family's acculturation levels, prior history with discrimination, expectations regarding behavior, family structure, disciplinary style, and disability etiology (Salend & Taylor, 1993). Linguistic factors include linguistic differences and patterns of communication, whereas socioeconomic factors address parent training programs (Salend & Taylor, 1993). Professionals should consider the previous factors in the development and delivery of appropriately designed services.

Professionals must be willing to work with parents and to respect them for what they contribute (Brotherson, Berdine, & Sartini, 1993). Professionals serving as members on transition teams should be aware of the family's needs and expectations for their child and focus upon these needs during the transition planning process (Everson & Moon, 1987). As parents become more educated regarding the issue of transition, they may begin to recognize their role in the transition process (Goodall & Bruder, 1986).

Strategies for Family Involvement

Throughout the literature on transition, active parent involvement has been implied as a necessary and critical component for successful transition planning (Benz & Halpern, 1987; Johnson, Bruininks, & Thurlow, 1987; Kohler, 1993; Lehmann, Deniston, & Grebenec, 1989; Turnbull, 1986). However, little research has been done to substantiate effective means by which parent involvement would actually be increased (Johnson & Rusch, 1993; Kohler, 1993; McNair & Rusch, 1991).

Although the literature advocates providing information to parents, the majority of transition-related information is typically made available to professionals, not to parents. Yet, professionals expect active involvement by parents in a process about which parents have been provided minimal information. Providing opportunities for parents to participate is different from providing actual means and methods needed for them to be effective participants (Van Reusen & Bos, 1990). Without an effective means to provide information and education to parents, it is highly unlikely that parents will become more actively involved in the process.

Guidelines for Parent Participation

Much of the literature supports and promotes parent participation in the planning process but does not emphasize the lead role that parents should assume (Nisbet, Covert, & Schuh, 1992). This role includes deciding upon the selection of outcomes, the selection of needed services, and the development and provision of those services, as well as the recognition of their expertise and advocation in the best in-

terest of their child. Guidelines for parent participation are noted throughout the literature (e.g., Benz & Halpern, 1986; Brotherson, Berdine, & Sartini, 1993; Everson & McNulty, 1992; Goldstein & Turnbull, 1982; McDonnell, Ferguson, & Mathot-Buckner, 1992). Table 14–2 lists suggested guidelines for parent participation found in the literature. Although many guidelines to enhance parent participation have been suggested, there is very little information regarding methods parents can utilize to determine the outcomes they desire for their son or daughter.

Need for Parent Education/Training

In order to become an effective member of the transition team, the informed participation of parents is a critical component of the transition process (Wehman, Kregel, & Barcus, 1985). Since active, informed parent involvement is necessary for joint decision making and a cooperative home/school partnership, it is the responsibility of the school system to find ways of encouraging families to participate (Lynch & Stein, 1987). The implications from the literature suggest the need for the provision of parent education/information programs to assist parents to become informed participants in their child's transition planning process. Education and information would provide parents with the knowledge and expertise necessary to make appropriate decisions regarding their child's individual transition plan (ITP). In order to empower families, education/training programs should be founded on the assumption that families are potentially capable and willing to make responsible decisions; that families want the best for their children; and that most family members who fail to show needed skills do so primarily due to an absence of sufficient opportunities to acquire needed competencies (Cohen, Agosta, Cohen, & Warren, 1989). This suggests that "enabling experiences" should be provided to parents and family members in order for confidence to be displayed or learned (Dunst, Trivette, &

TABLE 14–2

Suggested Guidelines for Parent Participation Found in the Literature

Suggested Guidelines	Literature Reference
• Encourage early expectations. • Help parents to recognize the importance of their contributions. • Support parents in honoring the choices of their child. • Increase the role of social support networks. • Address parent concerns regarding future employment issues for their child.	(Brotherson, Berdine, & Sartini, 1993, pp. 45–48)
• Adapt curriculum and training approaches that instill parent confidence in the child's abilities and skills. • Educate parents about adult service programs. • Provide parent-to-parent support. • Assist parents in understanding services, terminology, and regulations.	(McDonnell, Ferguson, & Mathot-Buckner, 1992, p. 45)
• Ensure that meetings are well planned and organized. • Schedule and structure meetings so all members contribute and participate. • Provide adequate notification of meetings. • Establish communication mechanisms so that parents are included in the loop.	(Everson & McNulty, 1992, p. 349)
• Include parents in all aspects of the planning process. • Send parents questions prior to the IEP conference with a follow-up telephone call. • Have a school counselor present as an advocate at the conference.	(Goldstein & Turnbull, 1982, p. 360)
• Orient students and families to local and regional agencies that provide postsecondary services. • Familiarize students and families with the specific responsibilities of the public schools (regular, special, and vocational education), vocational rehabilitation, and adult service programs. • Prepare students and families to work with various agencies in the transition process. • Train students in self-advocacy, beginning with participating actively in their own IEP meeting.	(Clark & Kolstoe, 1995, p. 350)

Sources: From Brotherson, Berdine, & Sartini, 1993, pp. 45–48; Clark & Kolstoe, 1995, p. 350; Everson & McNulty, 1992, p. 349; Goldstein & Turnbull, 1982, p. 360; McDonnell, Ferguson & Mathot-Buckner, 1992, p. 45.

Deal, 1988). Service providers should establish partnerships with parents to enable and empower consumers to the fullest extent possible. Programs should allow a variety of support options, develop and refine services for individual families, and encourage families to select those particular services that can appropriately meet their needs (Cohen et al., 1989). The following case study illustrates this point.

CASE STUDY B

Mrs. Jones is the parent of a 17-year-old young man with mild mental retardation. She attended a transition in-service program provided by a local university. Mrs. Jones admitted that she knew virtually nothing about transition and did not know how to advocate for her son's needs. During the in-service program, the transition process was explained. It was emphasized throughout the program that unless parents were proactive and advocated for their child's needs, they would have to live with the decisions made by the professionals. The program presenter emphasized the importance of the parents' role in helping their child to determine desired adult outcomes. Mrs. Jones received assistance in completing a preplanning document detailing what her child needed. By the end of the in-service, Mrs. Jones said she felt that she would be able to participate actively during her son's IEP/ITP meeting and would voice her son's needs and desired outcomes. She felt much more confident of her own abilities to advocate on behalf of her son with the knowledge and sense of empowerment that she had gained from the in-service program.

Need for Specific Knowledge Regarding Outcome Areas and Service Options

Wehman et al. (1985) indicated that parents should be provided opportunities to acquire knowledge and skills that are necessary for effective participation in transition planning through systematically planned parent education programs, which will "improve the effectiveness and durability of parent involvement in the transition process" (p. 30). Throughout the literature, parent education/information programs have been suggested as an effective practice to facilitate parent involvement (e.g., Anderson, Beckett, Chitwood, & Hayden, 1984; Bates, 1990; Everson, Barcus, Moon, & Morton, 1987; Wehman et al., 1985).

Additionally, because transition plans must be based on the student's needs and preferences, it is critical that parents be afforded informational opportunities in order to assist their child in the selection of adult outcomes/environments in the areas of employment, independent living, and community participation. Without knowledge regarding options and services in these key areas, parents' abilities to assist in identifying outcomes and needed services will be severely limited.

Critical Point: Parents need to be aware of postsecondary possibilities for persons with disabilities because they play a major role in shaping the student's career expectations.

Preplanning Opportunities

Professionals should go beyond simply inviting parents to attend transition planning meetings by providing preplanning opportunities for parents to receive information that will assist them in identifying and planning for their child's needs during the IEP/transition meeting. Although practical suggestions for increasing parent involvement are found throughout the literature (e.g., Brotherson et al., 1993; Everson & McNulty, 1992; McDonnell, Ferguson, & Mathot-Buckner, 1992), they are typically of a general nature, with little specificity as to content and method of delivery or empirical documentation of their effectiveness. In order to ensure the successful transition of youth with disabilities to postsecondary outcomes and environments, specific and effective means by which to involve parents actively in the process must be identified and implemented.

Effective Method to Increase Active Parent Participation

A study by Turner (1996) documented the effectiveness of a parent transition in-service program on the enhancement of active parent involvement. Thirty parents of students with disabilities from a five county area in northeast Ohio participated in a transition in-service program. The in-service program consisted of the provision of the following information: (1) the IDEA definition of transition services, (2) the four essential elements of the transition, (3) adult services information, (4) the parent involvement in transition planning, (5) the difference between IEP and ITP, (6) the completion of a needs and preferences survey to use during their sons or daughter's IEP meeting, and (7) examples of transition plans.

Subjects completed three surveys consisting of items utilizing a 5-point Likert scale and checklists. The first survey was completed prior to the in-service program to assess current levels of knowledge and involvement. The second survey was administered immediately following the in-service program to determine anticipated levels of involvement by the parents in the transition planning process. The third survey was completed by the participants following their sons or daughter's annual IEP/transition meeting to assess their actual level of involvement during the meeting.

Results indicated that as a result of their participation in the transition in-service program, respondents (1) increased their level of understanding regarding the transition, (2) recognized their importance and role in the process, (3) increased their confidence in their ability to participate in transition planning, (4) better understood adult services, and (5) reported that the program helped them to communicate and advocate for their child during the meeting. These results could be due to the fact that parents actually do desire more involvement in their child's transition planning process. When provided with the opportunity to gain more knowledge and information about transition, the parents take advantage of the opportunity in order to participate more actively in the planning process and to make informed decisions in the best interest of their child. Common sense dictates that acquiring specific and relevant information lends itself to the opportunity to become empowered to utilize such information. Without having an opportunity to acquire such information, however, involvement and participation cannot and should not be expected to occur.

Further, respondents noted that, after participating in the program, they (1) informed the IEP/transition team of their preferred goals and outcomes for employment, independent living, and community participation for their son or daughter; (2) increased the amount and type of their participation; (3) expressed more satisfaction with the planning process; (4) took a more active and directive role; and (5) obtained desired services for their child. These results suggest that as a result of the in-service program, participants realized the critical nature of their active involvement in determining and express-

ing postschool outcomes to professionals in order to convey their opinions and preferences regarding their child's future. They may have realized that if they were not actively involved in the decision-making process, professionals would make all the decisions regarding their child's future outcomes, and they would have to live with the consequences of those decisions. Their understanding of the value of their active participation and the critical role they needed to assume as an equal partner served to promote a proactive attitude regarding their involvement.

Additionally, respondents reported that they utilized the needs and preferences survey during the meeting as an organization tool, that is, having the survey helped them to discuss specific outcomes and services for their child, and was beneficial in that they felt better prepared and more organized during the meeting, thus enabling them to make decisions for their son or daughter.

Critical Point: Preplanning with parents using a needs and preferences survey (see Chapter 7) helped them to discuss specific outcomes and transition services with their child.

This study documented effective methods and procedures for actually increasing parent involvement and participation in the transition planning process. This research suggests that providing parents with this type of transition in-service program can positively affect their types and levels of participation and involvement and assist them in assuming a more proactive role in assisting their son or daughter to achieve a successful transition to adulthood.

Informing Parents Regarding Legal Rights

Another critical area of parent participation involves informing parents regarding their legal rights. Under current law, the parents of children with disabilities have substantial rights to be involved in their child's educational programming (EHA, 1975; IDEA, 1990, 1997). Table 14–3 provides a description of maintained and updated

TABLE 14–3

Parents' Rights and Responsibilities Under IDEA of 1997

Parents' Rights and Responsibilities from Previous Legislation Maintained under IDEA of 1997

- Public agencies must notify parents when they propose or refuse to initiate or change the identification, evaluation, or educational placement of the child, or the provision of a free appropriate public education to the child.
- Parents have the right to inspect and review all records relating to their child that the public agency collects, maintains, or uses regarding the identification, evaluation, or educational placement of the child, or the provision of a free appropriate public education to the child.
- Parental consent is required before a child may be evaluated for the first time.
- Parents have the right to obtain an independent educational evaluation of their child.
- Parents are part of the team that develops their child's IEP.
- Parental consent is required for a child's initial special education placement.

New Parent Rights and Responsibilities Added under IDEA 1997

- Parent input shall now be solicited during the evaluation process. As members of their child's IEP team, parents also are involved in the review of existing evaluation data during the initial evaluation and any reevaluation of their child.
- Parents are entitled to be part of the group that makes the decision regarding their child's eligibility.
- Parents are entitled to be part of the group that makes the decision regarding their child's educational placement.
- Parents need to provide consent for their child to be reevaluated.
- Parents must be given the opportunity to participate in meetings held with respect to the identification, evaluation, and educational placement of their child, and the provision of a free appropriate public education to their child.
- Parents have the right to receive regular reports on their child's progress.
- Parents must now notify the public agency if they intend to remove their child from the public school and place him or her in a private school at public expense.
- If parents intend to request a due process hearing, they must notify the public agency.

Source: From Individuals with Disabilities Education Act Amendments of 1997. Pub. L. No. 105-17, 105 U.S.C. 1st Sess (1997).

parent rights and responsibilities found in the legislation. Parents can be more effective if they are aware of the rights guaranteed by federal and state laws. These rights include procedural safeguards in the areas of identification, confidentiality, preevaluation activities, multifactored evaluation activities, IEP activities, and impartial due process hearings (Turnbull & Morningstar, 1993).

Legislative Guidelines for Parent Involvement in Shared Decision Making

Legislation has established guidelines for parent-professional interaction. Requirements for shared

decision making and responsibility in ensuring a free, appropriate public education (FAPE) for students with disabilities are associated with each of six major principles of the EHA, which include zero reject, nondiscriminatory evaluation, individualized education plans (IEPs), the least restrictive alternative, due process, and parent participation (Turnbull & Morningstar, 1993).

Zero Reject

The *zero reject principle* requires that all students with disabilities be provided a free, appropriate public education (EHA, 1975; IDEA, 1990, 1997). Zero rejection requirements created new relationships between professionals and parents based on the premise that appropriate educational services will be provided at no expense to the family (Turnbull & Morningstar, 1993). Turnbull and Morningstar (1993) reported that parent-professional interactions are initiated by determining the types of curriculum, services, and placement that determine an appropriate education instead of deciding whether or not the school will provide services to the student.

Nondiscriminatory Evaluation

The *principle* of *nondiscriminatory evaluation* ensures evaluation procedures that are broadly based, fairly administered, and given only with the parents' informed consent (EHA, 1975; IDEA, 1990, 1997). Broadly based testing must be validated for the test's specific purpose, be culturally sensitive, and utilize a minimum of two tests and information from nontest sources (EHA, 1975; IDEA, 1990, 1997). Turnbull & Morningstar (1993) noted that parents could provide information regarding their child's strengths, needs, and preferences, as well as actively participate in the evaluation process through interviews and the completion of functional evaluation measures.

Individualized Education Plan

The *Individualized Education Program* (IEP) is the primary means to ensure that students with disabilities receive an appropriate, meaningful education. The IEP is a property right belonging to the parent if the child is under the age of majority guaranteed by the Fifth and Fourteenth amendments to the U.S. Constitution. The notion of a mandatory IEP conference implies an expectation that parents have active decision-making opportunities before and during the conference (Turnbull & Morningstar, 1993). The IEP conference provides an opportunity for parents to state what they want for their child.

Least Restrictive Environment

The determination of the least restrictive environment for a student with a disability is made by the IEP team (EHA, 1975; IDEA, 1990, 1997).

Therefore, parents have the right to participate in the determination of the most appropriate environment for their child.

Due Process

The *due process principle* addresses consent, proper notification, independent evaluations, hearings, and surrogate parents (EHA, 1975; IDEA, 1990, 1997). Due process provides a system to protect the rights of the parents, students, and educators and ensures the right to protest the proposed actions of a school district (Turnbull & Morningstar, 1993). Through the principle of due process, school districts, as well as parents, are accountable for their actions.

Parent Participation

The principles previously discussed have implications for *parent participation* in the educational process. Regulations relevant to parent participation provide an opportunity for parents to have access to educationally relevant information and to be involved in educational decisions regarding their child. Increasing parents' knowledge of their rights guaranteed by federal and state laws, rules, and regulations will enable them to participate more fully in the educational process and to become more effective advocates for their children (Markel & Greenbaum, 1981).

Critical Point: Parents need to be aware of legal rights and responsibilities in order to play an effective role in transition planning with their child.

Parent as Advocate

Although parent involvement, participation, and education are critical to a child's success during postschool transition, the function of the parent as an advocate also is very important. Parents must organize and advocate effectively on their own behalf (Markel & Greenbaum, 1981; Massenzio, 1983; Rothschild & Bianchi, 1986). Professionals must think of themselves not only as service providers but also as partners and managers with parents in advocating for change within the system (Hamre-Nietupski, Krajewski, Nietupski, Ostercamp, Sensor, & Opheim, 1988). Parents and professionals are faced with the challenge of developing a partnership and using it to shape policy and programming. Parent-professional partnerships combine the strengths of each group in the advocacy process (Hamre-Nietupski et al., 1988). It was noted that parents are the most effective long-term advocates for their children with disabilities (Donellan & Mirenda, 1984). Hamre-Nietupski et al. (1988) noted that parents are strongly committed to their children and can instill a desire for a better life. Additionally, parents have knowledge of their children's needs and the ability to voice those needs to the community, and through networking with other parents, they influence leaders in the community through advocacy efforts (Hamre-Nietupski et al., 1988).

Professionals as Advocates

Parental efforts can be greatly enhanced through assistance from professionals committed to service provision. Hamre-Nietupski et al. (1988) noted that professionals provide experience and expertise in working with the educational system because they understand how the system works, know whom to contact, and provide strategies for overcoming obstacles within the system. Professionals have access to professional literature and research to support the feasibility of specific strategies. They also have knowledge of strategies to assist in educational planning and resources to implement such strategies (Hamre-Nietupski et al., 1988). The following case study illustrates this point.

CASE STUDY C

In one school district, the special education supervisor encouraged the parents to take a leadership role during a transition planning conference for their daughter with autism. The father, Mr. Smith,

was a CEO of a major corporation. He came to the meeting with a flip chart and a laser pointer. He stood at the head of the table during the meeting and directed the discussion. His points were well organized and clearly set forth on the flip chart. He asked relevant and well-thought-out questions of the professionals in attendance. He was very direct and forthright regarding his goals and expectations for his daughter. He did not slow up or back down until all of his questions had been answered and a coordinated service plan for his daughter was agreed upon. It was apparent that many professionals were uncomfortable with having Mr. Smith take such a directive role, because they were not accustomed to such roles being assumed by parents. The Smiths, however, expressed a high degree of satisfaction with the results of the meeting. They were appreciative of the fact that others had acknowledged their expertise and wisdom with regard to their daughter's needs and had given them the opportunity to voice their opinions and have some control over what happened to their family.

Various interventions were directed toward the enhancement of parental participation through professional interaction. One such example from the literature is a study completed by Goldstein and Turnbull (1982) that involved 45 parents of elementary-age children with learning disabilities. The school counselor, who functioned as a parent advocate, accompanied parents in the experimental group to the IEP meeting. The counselor's role as parent advocate included the introduction of the parents at the conference, the direction of questions to the parents, verbal reinforcement of their contributions, and a summarization of the discussion at the end of the conference. The researchers found that parents who were accompanied by advocates from the school made significantly more contributions during the meeting than did parents in the control group.

Critical Point: Professionals can support parents by supporting them at the IEP team meeting.

Social Support Mechanisms

In addition to the provision of support by professionals, parents need other forms of support. The successful transition of youth with disabilities from school to adulthood is perceived as a difficult and stressful experience for families and professionals (Brotherson et al., 1993). It is essential to provide support to parents in order for their child's transition to community-based programs and services to be successful. Brotherson et al. (1993) noted that a partial reason for the lack of success of many "model" transition programs may be due to their failure to provide sufficient support for parents. Direct involvement of family and friends has been noted as an effective practice (Wehman, 1990).

Family support is provided by an informal, personal system consisting of relatives, friends, neighbors, and acquaintances (Brotherson et al., 1993). This type of system provides emotional assistance, information, guidance, and substantive forms of assistance. Cohen et al. (1989) found that the natural support networks of some families may be limited. Brotherson et al. (1993) indicated that professionals need to assist parents in developing the support capacity of these informal social support networks and to examine their role in the transition process.

Social support networks of persons with disabilities assist with the transition to adulthood. Hasazi, Gordon, and Roe (1985) interviewed 301 young adults from nine Vermont school districts regarding current employment status after exiting high school. Individuals who were currently employed were questioned as to how they found their jobs. Results indicated that overall 84% of the working sample found employment through self, family, and friends. This type of network may represent promising, low-cost alternatives to traditional service approaches. These findings suggest the need for families to build their social support networks to increase employment outcomes for their children with disabilities.

School-Initiated Training for Parents

School programs should implement a variety of procedures and training programs to assist parents in developing more active roles in their child's transition to employment and community life. These include the adoption of curriculum and community training approaches to promote parent confidence (Brotherson et al., 1993; McDonnell, Ferguson, & Mathot-Buckner, 1992; Steere et al., 1990), initiating parent-to-parent support groups (McDonnell et al., 1992), educating parents about adult service programs (Bates, 1990; McDonnell et al., 1992), and educating parents regarding the laws and their legal rights in the educational process (Brotherson et al., 1993; Markel & Greenbaum, 1981).

Provision of Community Experiences

Schools can promote positive parental attitudes and support regarding community employment options by utilizing curriculum and training procedures to provide students with disabilities opportunities for community experiences. Successful community experiences assist in changing parents' attitudes and expectations regarding their child's participation in community employment settings (McDonnell, Ferguson, & Mathot-Buckner, 1992). In the Utah community employment placement project, it was shown that parents whose children had the opportunity to receive training in a variety of employment, personal management, and leisure activities were more open to job placements in the community than parents whose children were provided traditional classroom-based curriculum (McDonnell et al., 1992). Providing systematic training in community activities provides parents the opportunities to observe their child being successful in those settings. These types of experiences may facilitate a change in parents' attitudes regarding their child's participation in community-based employment settings (McDonnell et al., 1992). One major complaint heard from professionals is that parents' expectations for their child are unrealistic. One way to solve this problem is to provide parents the opportunity to observe their child in order to see what their child is capable of doing. This simple activity can have a tremendous impact upon a parent's perceptions. The following case study illustrates this point.

CASE STUDY D

Mr. Green was the father of a 20-year-old daughter with Down's syndrome. She was currently participating in a community-based transition program through her local high school. At that time, she was working in the food court at a local university, busing and cleaning tables. Mr. Green was planning for her to work in a sheltered workshop after she left high school and was not pleased with her current work placement.

The program coordinator convinced Mr. Green to stop by the food court one morning before he went to work to observe his daughter. He agreed to come but said he could only stay for a few minutes. The coordinator and Mr. Green stayed in the background watching his daughter perform her job duties. He saw her competently and cheerfully completing her job. He also saw her frequently interacting with the college students in the food court. The program coordinator turned to Mr. Green to say something and saw that he was in tears. When asked what was wrong, Mr. Green replied, "I never thought she would be able to do something like this. Just look at her— she's actually talking to other people. I've changed my mind. I want her working in the community." Mr. Green spent the rest of the morning with his daughter at the food court.

Critical Point: Involving parents in the student's community experiences can give them the opportunity to see the student perform competently in integrated work and in community settings.

Information Regarding Adult Service Programs

Parents also should be educated regarding available adult service programs. Most parents are concerned about their child's post high school

transition but have very little information about the adult service system (Johnson et al, 1987). School personnel can help to develop positive parental attitudes regarding supported and competitive employment and supported residential alternatives by sponsoring or providing programs for parents on employment, residential, and other community service programs (McDonnell et al., 1992). These types of educational training programs enable parents to become informed consumers, capable of making appropriate decisions that support their child's successful transition from school to community life (McDonnell et al., 1992).

Parent-to-Parent Support Groups

Another strategy to assist parents in their participation in their child's postschool transition includes providing opportunities for them to talk with other parents about significant issues with which they are confronted. Talking with other parents can lessen some of the anxiety that parents experience during this stressful transition phase (McDonnell et al., 1992). Having a child with a disability often can be very isolating. Parent support groups provide a means for parents to share their experiences with one another, receive and give advice, and offer support to one another. Many professionals do not encourage or support the organization of parent support groups because they are wary of parents talking to one another, gaining knowledge/information, and perhaps questioning their decisions. Considerable emotional and practical assistance can be attained from participation in a parent support group through discussing concerns and information sharing. The following case study illustrates this point.

CASE STUDY E

A new special education supervisor was hired by a small school district. The district had many parents who were dissatisfied and discontented with the current special education program and services being offered. The district also had been involved in a due process case, which the district had lost.

The special education supervisor decided to try to organize a parent support group. A survey was sent out to all the families asking which type of support group they would prefer—one run completely by the parents or one in which the professionals would be involved. Surprisingly, parents wanted to have the professionals involved with the group.

The special education supervisor organized monthly meetings at the local library. Each month an issue/topic selected by the parents was discussed. The supervisor arranged for speakers to be present to provide information and to answer parents' questions. Child care also was provided so that more parents could attend.

The response was overwhelmingly positive. As the word about the support group spread, more parents started to attend. An unexpected result was that, as parents gained more information and had their questions answered informally, they became more supportive of the special education program. Parents and educators collaborated together to work through issues and to solve problems. As a result of the group working together, perspectives were changed. People gained insight from one another and novel and creative solutions were devised, all within a united spirit of cooperation.

Critical Point: Parent support groups can play an important role in giving them practical and emotional support and can make them more supportive of special education.

In order to become active participants in the transitional decision-making process, parents need information, support, understanding, and involvement in the process (Brotherson et al., 1993; Steere et al., 1990). This involvement needs to go beyond sitting through an IEP/ITP meeting and signing forms giving directions to professionals involved in their child's educational program (Kinnison, Jr., 1987). The parents' role in the decision-making process should be emphasized routinely during every educational activity and/or meeting. Table 14–4 provides a listing of activities in which parents should have active involvement.

Professional Regard for Parents

In addition to parental rights in the decision-making process established by law, parents also have the right to be treated with dignity and respect during interactions with professionals. Professionals must allow parents to express openly their opinions, ideas, and suggestions with regard to their child's transition needs without fear of judgment or ridicule. Parents should be valued and treated as experts within their own right with regard to their knowledge and understanding of their child. The notion of equal decision-making power within the limits of the law requires respect and consideration being shown toward parents by professionals.

In order to promote active participation and equality in decision making, professional regard for parents must be demonstrated. This includes respect for and acknowledgment of (1) parents' abilities and expertise; (2) their capabilities to be advocates for their son or daughter; (3) their willingness to participate in the planning process; and (4) their aspirations for their child. Professional regard for parents may be demonstrated in a variety of ways; from extending basic courtesies, having good interpersonal skills, and treating parents as equals, to compliance with every aspect of federal and state rules and regulations. Professionals should comply with legal guidelines because it is professionally and ethically responsible behavior and protects the interests of the parent and child, not simply because it is legally mandated. Compliance can be equated with respect and consideration for parents. Specific ways to express professional regard for parents are provided in Table 14–5.

Professional respect and consideration for parents can have a profound impact upon their relationship and involvement. Here are some comments from parents regarding their interaction with professionals:

TABLE 14–4

Verbatim Text of the Individuals with Disabilities Education Act Amendments of 1997 Addressing Legally Mandated Activities Requiring Parent Involvement

---

Individualized Education Program

Section 614 (d) (1) (B)

"(B) INDIVIDUALIZED EDUCATION PROGRAM TEAM

The term 'individualized education program team' or 'IEP team' means a group of individuals composed of -

"(i) the parents of a child with a disability;"

Section 614 (d) (3)

"(3) DEVELOPMENT OF IEP

"(A) IN GENERAL. - In developing each child's IEP, the IEP team, subject to subparagraph (c), shall consider -

"(i) the strengths of the child and the concerns of the parents for enhancing the education of their child; and . . . "

Section 614 (d) (4)

"(4) REVIEW AND REVISION OF IEP

"(A) IN GENERAL. - The local education agency shall ensure that, subject to subparagraph (B), the IEP team -

"(ii) revises the IEP as appropriate to address -

"(III) information about the child provided to, or by, the parents, as described in subsection (c) (1) (B);"

Section 614 (d) (1) (A)

"(d) INDIVIDUALIZED EDUCATION PROGRAMS

"(viii) a statement of -

"(II) how the child's parents will be regularly informed (by such means as periodic report cards), at least as often as parents are informed of their nondisabled children's progress, of . . . "

Appropriate Evaluation

"(a) EVALUATIONS AND REEVALUATIONS

"(1) INITIAL EVALUATIONS.

"(C) PARENTAL CONSENT.

"(i) IN GENERAL. - The agency proposing to conduct an initial evaluation to determine if the child qualifies as a child with a disability as defined in section 602 (3) (A) or 602 (3) (B) shall obtain an informed consent from the parent of such child before the evaluation is conducted. Parental consent for evaluation shall not be construed as consent for placement for receipt of special education and related services."

"(2) REEVALUATIONS. - A LEA shall ensure that a reevaluation of each child with a disability is conducted -

"(A) if conditions warrant a reevaluation or if the child's parents or teacher requests a reevaluation, but at least once every 3 years; and . . . "

"(b) EVALUATION PROCEDURES

"(1) NOTICE. - The LEA shall provide notice to the parents of a child with a disability, in accordance with subsections (b) (3), (b) (4), and (c) of section 615, that describes any evaluation procedures such agency proposes to conduct.

"(4) DETERMINATION OF ELIGIBILITY. - Upon completion of administration of tests and other evaluation materials -

"(A) the determination of whether the child is a child with a disability as defined in section 602 (3) shall be made by a team of qualified professionals and the parent of the child in accordance with paragraph (5); and . . ."

"(B) a copy of the evaluation report and the documentation of determination of eligibility will be given to the parent."

"(c) ADDITIONAL REQUIREMENTS FOR EVALUATION AND REEVALUATIONS

"(1) REVIEW OF EXISTING EVALUATION DATA. - As part of an initial evaluation (if appropriate) and as part of any reevaluation under this section, the IEP Team described in subsection (d) (1) (B) and other qualified professionals, as appropriate, shall -   *(continued)*

TABLE 14–4

(*Concluded*)

"(A) review existing evaluation data on the child, including evaluations and information provided by the parents of the child, current classroom-based assessments and observations, and teacher and related services providers observation; and . . . "

"(B) on the basis of that review, and input from the child's parents, identify what additional data, if any, are needed to determine -

"(i) whether the child has a particular category of disability, as described in section 602 (3), or, in case of a reevaluation of a child, whether the child continues to have such a disability;

"(ii) the present levels of performance and educational needs of the child;

"(iii) whether the child needs special education and related services, or in the case of a reevaluation of a child, whether the child continues to need special education and related services; and

"(iv) whether any additions or modifications to the special education and related services are needed to enable the child to meet the measurable annual goals set out in the individualized education program of the child and to participate, as appropriate, in the general curriculum.

"(3) PARENTAL CONSENT. - Each local education agency shall obtain informed parental consent, in accordance with subsection (a) (1) (C), prior to conducting any reevaluation of a child with a disability . . . "

"(4) REQUIREMENTS IF ADDITIONAL DATA ARE NOT NEEDED. - If the IEP Team and other qualified professionals, as appropriate, determine that no additional data are needed to determine whether the child continues to be a child with a disability, the local educational agency -

"(A) shall notify the child's parents of -

"(i) that determination and the reasons for it; and

"(ii) the right of such parents to request an assessment to determine whether the child continues to be a child with a disability; and

"(iii) shall not be required to conduct such an assessment unless requested to by the child's parents.

Procedural Safeguards

Section 615 (b) (3) and (4): Prior Written Notice

"(b) TYPES OF PROCEDURES. - The procedures required by this section shall include -

"(3) written prior notice to the parents of the child whenever such agency -

"(A) proposes to initiate or change; or

"(B) refuses to initiate or change; the identification, evaluation, or educational placement of the child, in accordance with subsection (c), or the provision of a free appropriate public education to the child;

"(4) procedures designed to ensure that the notice required by paragraph (3) is in the native language of the parents, unless it clearly is not feasible to do so ..."

"(c) CONTENT OF PRIOR WRITTEN NOTICE. - The notice required by subsection (b) (3) shall include -

"(6) a statement that the parents of a child with a disability have protection under the procedural safeguards of this part and, if this notice is not an initial referral for evaluation, the means by which a copy of a description of the procedural safeguards can be obtained; and

"(7) sources for parents to contact to obtain assistance in understanding the provisions of this part."

Section 615 (d): Procedural Safeguards Notice

"(d) PROCEDURAL SAFEGUARDS NOTICE. -

"(1) IN GENERAL. - A copy of the procedural safeguards available to the parents of a child with a disability shall be given to parents, at a minimum -

"(A) upon initial referral for evaluation;

"(B) upon each notification of an individualized education program meeting and upon reevaluation of the child; and

"(C) upon registration of a complaint under subsection (b) (6).

Source: Individuals with Disabilities Education Act Amendments of 1997. Pub. L. No. 105-17, 105 U.S.C. 1st session. (1997).

TABLE 14–5

Professional Regard for Parents

Professional regard for parents can be exhibited in the following ways:
- Extend professional courtesy to parents.
- Utilize effective listening skills.
- Express appreciation for parents' involvement and contributions.
- Demonstrate appropriate verbal and nonverbal skills.
- Schedule meetings around parents' schedules.
- Seat parents at the head of the table (leadership position).
- Introduce everyone at the meeting, beginning with the parent.
- Express appreciation for the parents' attendance.
- Begin every meeting by talking positively about the child.
- Before presenting professionals/opinions, ask the parent to discuss their goals, wishes, and so on.
- Be sure the parent understands all aspects of the meeting and/or discussion by asking questions to ensure understanding.
- Use terms/language that parents will understand.
- Talk from a position of equal partnership, not of authority.
- Maintain a natural, relaxed demeanor.
- Use a friendly, warm, and courteous tone of voice.
- Maintain eye contact with the parent.
- Talk directly to the parent, not to other professionals.
- Allow opportunities for the parent to interact and interject their opinions and suggestions.
- If you do not know the answer to a parent's question, admit it and let him or her know you will get back to him or her. Do not try to bluff.
- During a parent-teacher conference, sit side by side, never across from a parent.
- Always sit at a table with the parent, never at your desk.
- Arrange for appropriately sized furniture and chairs.
- Maintain relaxed posture, face the parent, and lean slightly forward to demonstrate your interest.
- Always let parents know exactly who will be in attendance at meetings and why they will be there.
- Explain to parents what will be discussed prior to the meeting.
- Encourage parents to bring someone with them to provide support.
- Be sure parents have a clear understanding of their legal rights. It is the professional's responsibility to inform parents and to ensure their understanding.
- Extend invitations to parents to visit your classroom in order to observe their child.
- Utilize parents as volunteers in a variety of ways.
- Inform parents regularly about something their child has done well.
- Establish a preferred method for information exchange.
- Be able to assist parents in locating appropriate resources.
- Treat parents as experts regarding their child.
- Recognize parents' knowledge and expertise.
- Include all aspects of educational planning.
- Provide ways for parents to monitor their child's program/progress.
- Validate parent's opinions, suggestions, and ideas.
- Be open to creative planning and novel solutions to problems.
- Be sensitive to a parent's needs and feelings.

(continued)

TABLE 14–5

(Concluded)

- Invite parents to in-service programs available to teaching staff.
- Convey warmth and genuineness.
- Allow parents to make decisions regarding their child.
- Remember whose child he or she is—the parents', not the professionals'.
- Remember that the family has to live with the consequences of the decisions that are made for the child.
- Be aware of and sensitive to cultural differences.
- Always keep your word.
- Demonstrate acceptance of the family members as they are.
- Give parents your full attention while they are speaking.
- Be positive and sincere.

CASE STUDY E1

"This afternoon the guidance counselor called. He asked me to drop by to "catch up" with one another since we had not talked in a while. My son had been experiencing some behavior problems in school, so I was immediately concerned. He reassured me that everything was fine and he just wanted to chat. When I arrived at the school, the secretary escorted me down the hall to meet with him. As we walked by one room, I glanced in and saw a roomful of professionals. I kept going, knowing that wasn't where I was supposed to be. I was wrong. The guidance counselor was in that room and waved me in. I felt a wave of apprehension and fear swept over me, knowing that this was going to be bad. It was."

CASE STUDY E2

"During a conference for my son, one professional commented on my son's poor handwriting. I agreed, and said that we had been practicing his writing at home. The teacher replied in a condescending tone, 'In kindergarten we print, we don't write.' To which I replied, 'Would you prefer that I use the terms manuscript and cursive? If you want to use jargon, let's go.' The teacher blanched and never said another word during the rest of the conference."

CASE STUDY E3

"During a parent-teacher conference, my son's teacher complained about his behavior. When I asked for more specific information, she simply replied that she found his behavior unacceptable. I asked to see her data on the behaviors (e.g., duration, intensity, frequency, specific behaviors). When she couldn't provide any data, I said that behavior would not be addressed during the conference without specific data being supplied. She wasn't able to say anything else since without data there was no evidence of a problem."

CASE STUDY E4

"During a conference with the guidance counselor, the counselor recommended that I take my son in for a neurological evaluation. Since these types of evaluations are quite costly, I asked why she thought he needed that type of evaluation. She replied that he had poor handwriting. At that time, my son had been removed from first grade and placed into the second grade (without my permission). I told her that if she had bothered to review his school history, she would have seen that he had never been in the first grade. He was having difficulty learning cursive writing because he had never been taught manuscript. He never had the neurological evaluation and his handwriting today is very legible.

CASE STUDY E5

"One day when I was picking my children up from school, my son's teacher approached me and asked if she could speak to me for a minute. My heart started racing and the butterflies started to flutter in my stomach. Teachers only want to see you in order to tell you something bad about your child; they rarely pass on any good news. Imagine my surprise when she said that she wanted to tell me what a great son I had, that he was so intelligent, and that he had done something particularly clever in class that day. I was almost in tears as I thanked her for sharing that with me. It was just so unexpected."

Conclusion

Special education is the only field in which family participation in the educational process is mandated by law. As a result of litigation, the EHA of 1975 provided opportunities for the inclusion of parents in the determination of their child's educational programming. This was done to facilitate appropriate and successful educational programming for students with disabilities and to provide parents with an avenue to participate. However, the result of legally requiring parent participation has been that instead of being treated as valuable, equal, and active partners in the decision-making process, professionals have relegated families to a passive and acquiescent role, which often becomes adversarial in nature when parents do not agree with the professionals' decisions. Instead of equal partnerships, what has emerged has been one-sided decision making by "expert" professionals with an expectation of submissiveness and quiet acquiescence by parents.

Although professionals voice their concerns over the lack of parent involvement, it is questionable as to whether professionals actually want parents to become more proactive and involved in the educational process. Empowering parents to participate in the process as equal partners and advocates who request specific transition activities, services, and outcomes for their children may result in schools having to be more accountable for the provision of transition services, as well as for the attainment of selected postsecondary outcomes. Indeed, more active and knowledgeable involvement on the part of parents may result in increased compliance with legal mandates regarding the intent and spirit of the law established by the IDEA.

Educators must learn to comply with the legislative mandates in the spirit with which they were intended. This means that parents must be afforded the opportunities to participate in their child's educational process, not simply because they have a legal right to participate but, rather, because successful outcomes for youth with disabilities cannot be achieved without them.

Study Questions

1. Historically, how has parent participation in the IEP process occurred or been perceived?
2. What are the responsibilities of the school with regard to enrolling parents to participate actively in the IEP/ITP process?
3. What conditions lend themselves to encouraging and supporting active parent participation in the IEP/ITP process?
4. With regard to raising children with disabilities, what are the roles and functions of parents?
5. According to federal legislation, what are the requirements and guidelines with regard to parent involvement?
6. Maximizing active parent participation in the IEP/ITP process can be accomplished through what types of procedures?
7. What are the responsibilities of professionals in developing and maintaining relationships with parents?
8. What components of effective transition planning facilitate active parent involvement?
9. Historically, what has been the role of parents in the ITP process?
10. Why is it important for parents to be actively involved in their child's ITP process?
11. What kinds of barriers and issues have prevented active parent involvement?

12. How do parents contribute to the transition planning process?
13. What types of roles and responsibilities should be expected of parents during the ITP process?
14. For active parent involvement, what types of supports need to be provided to parents?
15. How can professionals demonstrate professional regard for parents?

Web Sites

The Arc
http://TheArc.org/

The National Association for Parents of the Visually Impaired (NAPVI)
http://www.spedex.com/napvi/mainstrm.html

NCLD, National Center for Learning Disabilities
http://www.ncld.org

NICD, National Information Center on Deafness
http://www.gallaudet.edu/~nicd

NICHCY, National Information Center for Children and Youth with Disabilities
http://nichcy.org

DB-Link, The National Clearinghouse on Children Who Are Deaf-Blind
http://www.tr.wosc.osshe.edu/dblink

Office for Civil Rights, U.S. Department of Education
http://www.ed.gov/offices/OCR

All Means All School-to-Work Website
http://www.ici.coled.umn.edu/all/

Transition to Work Program
http://www.ici.coled.umn.ed/schooltowork/links.html

Disability Related Products and Services
http://TheArc.org/related-links.htm#products-services

Heath Resource Center of the American Council on Education
http://www.acenet.edu/about/programs/Access&Equity/HEATH/home.html

UCP - Innovative Projects
http://www.ucpa.org

AHEAD, Association on Higher Education and Disability
http://www.ahead.org

Education Resources Directory (ERD)
http://www.ed.gov:8888/basisbwdocs/states/Directory.htm

Job Accommodation Network
http://janweb.icdi.wvu.edu/kinder./

National Clearinghouse of Rehabilitation Training Materials
http://www.nchrtm.okstate.edu

SECTION IV

Postschool and Community Environments

15   Transition to Employment

16   Postsecondary Education and Career Paths

17   Recreation and Leisure in the Community

18   My Home: Developing Skills and Supports for Adult Living

15

Transition to Employment

Thomas J. Simmons
Barry Whaley

LEARNING OBJECTIVES

The objectives of this chapter are:

1. Identify and indicate the services that are offered by state and local agencies that can provide employment-related services to persons with disabilities.

2. Describe how the persons with disabilities can gain access to services that those state and local agencies provide.

3. Understand the unique features of community-based vocational services for students with disabilities.

4. Understand the importance of developing valued cultural roles for people with disabilities.

5. Compare and contrast the effectiveness of supported employment and congregate/ segregated programming, including the elements of generic supports versus traditional placements.

6. Describe the elements of person-centered job selection, the formation of personal network in finding work, and the concept of target job development.

7. Identify job carving and job sharing as a concept in enabling people with disabilities to go to work.

8. Describe the importance of a career path for people with disabilities.

9. Describe the differences between social welfare and social entitlement programs along with two key social security incentive programs.

Chapter 15 is the initial chapter in a series that deals with postsecondary outcomes. It provides an overview of employment options and vocational factors that are links to financial independence. This chapter is particularly important because it deals with issues that most educators have not been prepared to teach.

The popular notion in American education is the belief that when students leave school, they will have the skills that are necessary to go to work. Although the public schools have done a good job in academic preparation, many students have fallen far short of attaining the mechanics needed to find a job that is right for them (Granger, 1996). Furthermore, schools, generally, have done a poor job of organizing and disseminating information on postschool resources to assist students in the transition from school to adult life. The training that students with disabilities have historically received has not provided them with strategies to cope with employment or postsecondary education (Blackorby & Wagner, 1996; Vogel & Adelman, 1992). Numerous students have been placed in regular education classes without the help of academic support services, such as tutors, study skills or test preparation classes, and learning labs (Blackorby & Wagner, 1996). Due to a paucity of choices, many students with disabilities have failed to develop educational and vocational aspirations that might positively impact postsecondary attendance or employment outcomes (Rojewski, 1996). Consequently, disabled students are not likely to be involved in postsecondary education and are more likely to reach a ceiling effect in their movement toward independence (Destafano & Wagner, 1992).

Employment is the ultimate in outcome orientation (Bolles, 1999; Dentzer, 1992). Rimmerman, Levy, and Botuck (1995) have noted that employment is the ultimate focus of much of our work in education. Halpern (1985) has indicated that even though work is a primary outcome, other aspects of one's life are still very predictive of postsecondary success. With the focus upon employment, one must assure that a broad range of experiences and interests have been explored. The authors of this chapter explore issues related to gaining employment for students with disabilities. This chapter explores how adult service agencies function and implement services. Further, a description of the programs and services appears to describe various types of strategies that have been found successful in the employment venue for persons with disabilities.

The information in this chapter identifies the types of community-based agencies that are essential to the success of the student in the transition process to adult services. The reader will gain knowledge of a person-centered approach to designing services and an understanding of the importance of a holistic effort in the transition process.

Four IDEA Principles and Relation to Employment

Obviously, to attain employment, a student's needs, interests, and preferences must be taken into consideration. These preferences are then matched with specific work conditions that will foster success. In finding a job with which an individual would be satisfied and able to grow in, one must find the job that is suited to the student's particular abilities and provide direct benefits to the individual performing the work. In finding the job of the best fit, one must take pains to delve into the work habits and history of experiences that are unique to each individual (Bolles, 1999). Mank, Cioffi, and Yovanoff (1997) have shown that personal differences have significant impacts upon outcomes of persons with disabilities. Consequently, to foster successful employment, significant emphasis must be made to gain a complete picture of the individual with a disability.

Multiple agencies must be involved in the transition process. It is apparent that interagency responsibilities or linkages need to be defined and clarified early in the transition process. To be successful in finding employment for persons with disabilities, multiple agencies should communicate and act in a spirit of cooperation (Everson & Guillory, 1998). There could be as many as four or five different agencies involved in the process. The school system must be the initiator of the process. Linkages need to be developed and appropriate goals should be set. Adult service agencies must be included, as early as possible, to facilitate the change in venue of the delivery of service. Assurances need to be gained to ensure that ongoing, comprehensive services will be provided far into adulthood.

To address the movement from school to postschool activities, schools must provide job shadowing, career exploration, work experience, and other related programs to facilitate appropriate outcomes (Siegel, 1998). The foundation of sound employment outcomes is the broad range of experiences offered by school programs (Bolles, 1999; Siegel, 1998). If a broad range of experiences is not offered, then the student will have to gain the missing knowledge and experience outside the school environment.

The research reported by Wagner and her associates coming from the National Longitudinal Study suggests that students with disabilities in general do not fare well when looking at postsecondary outcomes (Wagner, 1991). When looking at the data, one finds that broad inequities exist regarding postsecondary employment, education, independent living, and personal relationships (Wagner, 1991; Wagner, D'Amico, Marder, Newman, & Blackorby, 1992; Ward & Halloran, 1993). Indicative of this data is research provided by Funk (1992), who noted that only 32% of students with learning difficulties attended postsecondary education and only 15% of these stayed longer than one year. The remainder of the students with learning difficulties attended postsecondary programs intermittently. Of those students attending postsecondary training longer than one year, their focus

was business or technical training, with only 9 and 6% attending 2-year and 4-year colleges, respectively. Funk's data also indicated that only 28% of students with learning disabilities (LD) were employed and another 25% were looking for work. Of those students employed, 70% were working in the service industry and 25% in a technical/trade area. Funk (1992) also studied participation in postsecondary services and community involvement. The majority, 80%, of postsecondary students with LD never participated in community/adult services, with 50% reporting that they were unaware of community agencies or services. This suggests that school personnel are not providing the information that is necessary to make the transition to adulthood. This also may suggest that great confusion exists due to the diffuse nature of many adult service organizations.

Significant numbers of students are exiting special education and secondary education classrooms and, therefore, are unable to participate fully in our society. People with disabilities, with an overall unemployment rate of 71% (*Wall Street Journal*, May 17, 1999), represent an overlooked and untapped employment resource. Many students lack basic skills that are necessary to find a job or to know what resources and incentives are available to assist in the job search. Also, those students who do find work are employed in the competitive market or rely upon services provided by a supported employment provider.

Postschool Employment Agencies

To facilitate the development of postsecondary employment outcomes, the school personnel should be aware of the general structure and function of adult service agencies involved in facilitating employment outcomes. The agencies that are there to help in the process generally consist of approximately eight different but, in some cases, related agencies. Examples of the adult service agencies are vocational rehabilitation (VR) programs, developmental disabilities (DD) agencies, mental health (MH) programs, employment and training programs, and community and human service programs.

In general, no state offers or requires a postschool employment agency to provide services to all people that apply for services. In general, the agencies that help persons with disabilities to gain employment provide services through a selection or priority basis. One must either meet the agencies' criteria for providing services or the individual receives services once others who are higher on the agencies' priority list are served.

Critical Point   No individual is guaranteed access to adult services.

Programs such as the VR, DD, and MH are primary programs in that they fund or provide the basic resources to accomplish employment. Secondary programs, such as employment and training programs and community and human service programs, usually receive funding from the primary programs, so that the secondary programs can provide their services. In any case, all these agencies/programs should be involved in the development of employment services for the student that meets the respective agencies' criteria for providing services. Referral to these agencies should be discussed in the initial ITP team meeting, and a team representative should be given the responsibility to make the initial contact and referral.

Vocational Rehabilitation Agency

Each state and the U.S. territories have a vocational rehabilitation (VR) agency. Both state and federal money jointly fund the state's VR programs. The VR programs are operated by the state with rules that must meet federal guidelines regarding expenditure of money and resources. As described in Chapters 2 and 3 of this book, VR is a federally designed program. Vocational rehabilitation programs are authorized through the federal legislative process—the Rehabilitation Act amendments of 1992 (P.L. 102-569). This act authorizes federal funding of VR services throughout the states, with each state providing 25% of the operating costs and the federal government providing the remaining 75% of the match. The primary emphasis of VR programs is employment. Consequently, any individuals who are accepted for service must have a disability related to performing work.

To apply for services, one must either be referred or self-referred. Once referred, a potential client (a person with a disability) meets with the VR counselor and an application is taken and processed. The counselor must determine the potential client's needs and probable acceptance for receiving services. In order to qualify for services, the client must be of legal employable age and have the following characteristics:

> **You must have a physical or mental impairment.**
>
> **• Your impairment must result in a substantial impediment to employment.**
>
> **• If you meet the two criteria above, you will be determined eligible unless there is clear and convincing evidence that you cannot benefit from or do not require vocational rehabilitation services (Wehman, 1997).**

Additionally, most VR programs suggest that the potential client should be referred to them only 2 years before the student is projected to leave public schools. This, however, could change based on the individual needs of the student and the severity of the disability to employment (Wehman, 1997).

Critical Point   Direct referral to the VR agency should occur approximately 2 years before the student graduates.

To determine eligibility and to fulfill his or her part of the cooperative relationship, the client must provide evidence of disability, agree to be tested to ascertain employment support needs,

TABLE 15–1

Description of Vocational Rehabilitation Status Codes

Status 00. Represents referral to the rehabilitation program. The referral may be from another agency or individual or a self-referral to the state rehabilitation agency. Whether by personal contact, telephone, or letter, the referral information should include name and address of the individual, the nature of the disability, age and sex of the individual, the date of referral, and the source of referral.

Status 02. Represents application for rehabilitation services. This application can be made on an agency form or merely a letter signed by the individual. While the individual is in this status, the rehabilitation counselor acquires information to make a determination of eligibility or ineligibility for rehabilitation services. The rehabilitation counselor may decide to provide an extended evaluation period to make such a determination (status 06).

Status 06. Represents an extended evaluation period. In the event the rehabilitation counselor is unable to determine whether a client will vocationally benefit if provided rehabilitation services, he may authorize an extended period, not to exceed 18 months, in which to evaluate the person's rehabilitation potential and to determine eligibility or ineligibility for services.

Status 08. Is an ineligible closure status for all persons processed through referral application and/or extended evaluation and not accepted into the active caseload for rehabilitation services.

Status 10. Designates a person as eligible for rehabilitation services and permits individualized plan of employment (IPE) development. At this point the client becomes an active case. During this stage of the rehabilitation process, the counselor utilizes information from the diagnostic study and, with the client's involvement, prepares individualized plan of employment (IPE) of rehabilitation services for the client.

Status 12. Is an administrative code representing completion of the written program of services for the client. The client remains in this status until the necessary arrangements are made with service delivery agencies for implementing the individual plan for employment (IPE).

Status 14. Is intended as an in-service classification for cases that require counseling and guidance only, and possibly placement services for preparing the client for employment. It should be noted, however, that counseling and guidance occur throughout the rehabilitation process and support other services. If other services are unnecessary for achieving the rehabilitation objectives and goal, status 14 is an appropriate categorization.

Status 16. Represents physical and mental restoration services, including medical, surgical, psychiatric or therapeutic treatment, and/or fitting of a prosthetic.

---

participate in a rehabilitation planning process, and be actively involved in training/job seeking. Generally, the initial component of assessment and determination of acceptance should take no longer than 30 days. Once accepted, the client and the VR counselor jointly author and agree to an individual plan of employment (IPE). This plan should spell out exactly what the client's targeted employment goal is and what the counselor and client will do to help the client attain that goal.

The types of services that a VR agency offers are vocational and career counseling, employment training, job skill training, job coaching, money for employment-related expenses, and other employment-related services. All services are provided or purchased by the counselor based on the agreement formulated in the individual plan.

Whereas services are provided based on the individual plan, the cumulative success and rehabilitation of the client is based on the client's movement through the VR system and gaining employment. This movement is tracked by using a numerical system that indicates where the client is in the system of service provision. Table 15–1 provides an overall visual of the VR status system along with definitions of what is involved at each step. Counselors are evaluated based on the number of their clients that move through the system. Of course, the most

Table 15-1 Concluded

Status 18. Represents training. This status may be used to reflect almost any sort of learning situation, including school training, on-the-job training, tutoring, and training by correspondence. Many times physical or mental restoration services are also needed. In such cases the client is generally identified with the status which will represent the longest period of time.

Status 20. Like status 12, this is an administrative code indicating that the individual is ready for employment. The client has completed the preparation stages for employment and is either ready to accept a job or has been placed and has not yet begun employment.

Status 22. Signifies that the client is in employment. Federal legislation requires that the client remain in this status a minimum of 60 days before being closed as successfully rehabilitated (status 26).

Status 24. Is also an administrative classification that indicates service interruption in the rehabilitation process (statuses 14 to 22). The client remains in this status until he returns to one of the in-service statuses or his case is closed.

Status 26. Represents closed, rehabilitated. This status is the end result of the successful rehabilitation process. To be closed as successfully rehabilitated, the client must have been declared eligible for rehabilitation services, must have received appropriate diagnostic and related services, must have had an IPE, must have completed the program of services, and finally, must have been determined to be suitably employed for a minimum of 60 days.

Status 28. Indicates that the client's case is closed for other reasons after individualized plan of employment (IPE) program was initiated. Cases closed in this status have met the eligibility criteria for services and have been provided at least one of the services of the rehabilitation program, but the client has not become employed.

Status 30. Represents case closed for other reasons before the individualized plan of employment (IPE) was initiated. Such clients have been accepted for rehabilitation services but have not progressed to the point where any services were actually implemented under the IPE.

Status 32. Is a postemployment service phase for assisting rehabilitated clients in maintaining employment. Any rehabilitation services relates to the client's original goal and does not entail that a new comprehensive effort may be provided.

Source: Walls & Tseng, 1987, p. 185.

important level of achievement is that of status 26 (i.e., competitive employment).

Critical Point Individuals with disabilities are tracked through VR systems, and success for the individual, counselor, and agency is rated by the degree to which the individual is employed.

To achieve these outcomes, the counselor usually has a single pool of money to be spent for the caseload of their clients. The determination of the dollar amount that each counselor has is based on the number and severity of the clients in the caseload and the basic amount of dollars coming into the state. The counselor must use his or her best clinical judgment to de-

termine what services will be procured and at what cost for each client.

Visual Impairment Rehabilitation Program
Another agency that may or may not be part of the state VR system is a program that serves persons with visual impairment (VI). In some states, the VI agency is separate from the primary VR agency, and the agency uses a differentiated term such as the Department for the Blind or Rehabilitation Services for Visual Impairments. These VI agencies or services are authorized under the same VR Rehabilitation Act amendments, but the services are exclusively offered to persons with visual impairments. These services

may begin as early as elementary or middle school. In addition to having an employment focus, the VI agency also focuses upon providing services related to independent living and mobility. Otherwise, the services that are provided by the VI agency are essentially the same as those provided by the VR agency.

Developmental Disabilities Agencies

Developmental disabilities (DD) agencies are also found in all the United States and its territories. These agencies are supported by state and federal dollars, most of which come from federal sources such as the Developmental Disabilities and Assistance Act. Some states also add a significant amount of funding to the DD act funding. In states such as Ohio and Texas, additional funds are added at the local level through levies and other taxing methods. This increases the pool of money available for services.

The DD act and subsequent reauthorizations have provided the impetus for developing programs and services across the country for persons with more significant or developmental disabilities (Scheerenberger, 1983). The DD act generally provides proportional funding to each state based on the population size and the number of individuals with developmental disabilities. Each state develops differing methods for delivering these resources. In some states, there are separate entities that are sometimes called Mental Retardation and Developmental Disabilities (MR/DD) programs. Other states combine the DD agency with their mental health services. However, each state and territory has some mechanism for delivering services and providing supports to individuals with DD.

In general, each state has both state and local offices that are contact points for acquiring services. The state-level agency generally provides administrative and programmatic support. The DD act also provides for the operation of an advisory council (typically named a Developmental Disabilities Planning Council) and an ad-

vocacy agency (typically named protection and advocacy) to help in assuring appropriate service development throughout the state (Braddock, 1987). At the local level, there are agencies that either fund or provide funds for services to be developed. The local-level agencies distribute state flow-through dollars that meet the individual's needs. These local agencies generally have case managers, direct service staff, and/or counselors, who provide for assuring appropriate services to persons with DD (Braddock, 1987). The staff within these local agencies is required to develop individual habilitation plans (IHP) that meet the individual needs of the person with DD. Each IHP is developed in a similar manner as an IEP (individualized education plan) or an ITP (individual transition plan). There is a requirement to involve the individual with DD with a team of needed professionals, and to focus upon improving outcomes for the individual with DD in work and in other areas, such as living, recreation, relationships, communication, and personal skills. The programs that are provided to the individual vary depending on the plan.

To qualify for services under the DD act, the individual must have a disability that occurred before age 22 and significantly impairs three of seven major life activities. These life activities are language, capacity for independent living, economic self-sufficiency, self-direction, self-care, learning, and mobility (Wehman, 1997). Regarding the diagnosis, it is important to note that the DD agency serves individuals based on their capability as opposed to diagnostic labels.

Services that are provided by DD agencies vary according to the local and regional governing board that oversees the individual agencies. Each agency is either a not-for-profit self–administered program (with oversight provided by the state) or a state office directly representing the state. Services that can be provided include independent living programs, highly structured residences (institutions), supported living, various types of employment programs, a range of recreation and community experiences, counseling, and other community and institutional services. These services are again either offered or funded through the DD agency's resources. However, in either circumstance, the local and ultimately the state DD agencies are required to provide oversight and assurances that the delivery of services is appropriate.

Mental Health Agency

The mental health agency functions much like the DD agency/services that was explained earlier. There are state and local agencies: The local agencies can either be a private not-for-profit entity with an oversight board or the state may represent itself through offices and staff employed by the state. Mental health agencies are funded through a combination of funding options. Medicaid, social security, health insurance, and a variety of state and federal mental health funding mechanisms are used to support state MH services (Baer, Goebel, & Flexer, 1995; Cook & Hoffschmidt, 1995; Stroul, 1993).

Qualifying for MH services requires that an individual be diagnosed with a severe and persistent mental illness by a qualified clinician. Generally, the phrase "serious and persistent mental illness" is the term that is used to describe (SPMI) the disability. A diagnosis of SPMI is defined as:

> Certain mental or emotional disorders (organic brain syndrome, schizophrenia, recurrent depressive and manic depressive disorders, and paranoid and psychoses, plus other disorders that may become chronic) that erode or prevent the development of their functional capacities in relation to three of their primary aspects of daily life "personal hygiene, and self-care, self-direction, interpersonal relationships, social transactions, learning and recreation" (Goldman & Manderscheid, 1987, p. 13).

Other more specific criteria can be found in the American Psychiatric Association's DSM-IV codes for psychiatric diagnosis. However, key to diagnosis and differentiation from developmental disability is the fact that the delay in three major life activities should be due to a psychiatric cause (Lawn & Meyerson, 1995).

The services that one can receive also are similar to those one receives in the DD system. The key mechanism that guides the delivery of services is what Stroul (1995) calls a community support system (CSS). The CSS is designed to help maintain the individual with SPMI in the community. Consequently, services are determined based on the need of the individual to live successfully and independently in the community. The individual is able to receive the following services: mental health treatment, client identification and outreach, protection and advocacy, rehabilitation services, family and community supports, peer support, income support and entitlements, housing, health and dental care, and crisis response services (Stroul, 1995, p. 49).

In general, services from a MH program is offered at any time that a diagnosis is made. However, most mental health diagnoses are not made until later in the student's life, so it is uncertain when would be the most appropriate time to make a referral. However, if the individual is exhibiting significant problems and has an initial diagnosis, the student should be referred.

Mental Health Employment Service Delivery Options

The availability of training and employment programs and services can vary in different localities. As described earlier, the training and employment programs might be part of one of the primary service or program providers (VR, DD, or MH). Or independent programs may receive funding from those agencies to provide the placement and employment service. Employment and training programs are generally private not-for-profit agencies that have an executive director and an advisory board for administrative oversight. The programs are funded in part or on the whole with fee-for-service contracts with the primary providers. The employment and training programs are generally small organizations with small specialized staffs. The staff usually has special training in either community placement and employment or an expertise in a specific skill area. The employment service providers will perform the tasks of assisting the person with a disability in either gaining the skills to find a job or training the individual with a disability in a particular job. The employment and training staff also may perform a combination of the two components.

Another hybrid of the traditional employment and training agency is that of a business, such as a coffee shop or some other service or manufacturing business, that operates primarily to benefit the individual with a disability. Bond and Boyer (1988) have termed these employment agencies "client-employing programs." These operate as a service or manufacturing business and employ only persons with disabilities. Other similar organizations also may operate a business that employs a mixture of persons with and without disabilities. Additionally, still other employment and training programs will use the client-employing business as a training site for initial skill training. The site is used to facilitate future permanent placements in other similar settings. Although the client- employing business does perform a service and benefits to persons with disabilities, Bond (1991) and others (Simmons, Selleck, Steele, & Sepetauc, 1995) have criticized the model due to business and inclusionary factors.

Other community programs and human service agencies provide employment services that help persons with disabilities to gain access to employment; however, these programs are not only targeted to meet their unique needs. These programs include the state's agencies of employment services and job training partnership programs. Each of these programs offers employment and skill-related training to address the needs of individuals who are either not employed or in need of being reemployed.

State Bureau of Employment Services

The state's bureau or office of employment service is a workforce development program that has been in existence since the early 1900s (Droege, 1987). This program is funded through federal and state tax money. The primary focus of this agency is to meet the needs of each state's economic development and to match employers that are looking for employees with individuals looking for work. As with the VR, DD, and MH agencies, there are state and local offices. Local offices of employment services can be found in nearly every state and municipality. The services provided by the state employment agencies include computerized tracking of available jobs, centralized advertising, and referral of those jobs. Additionally, large special training programs are provided that meet individual employer needs, authorizing tax incentives to motivate employers to hire special classes of people and training programs that enable individuals to gain their high school equivalency diploma (GED, a general education diploma) and job-seeking skills classes. Although they are not the primary targets of the state offices of employment, persons with disabilities are one of the targeted populations that the agencies have a priority to serve. Consequently, state employment services will provide resources for special programs to meet the needs of the individual with disabilities. These special programs, however, differ in various localities.

Accessing services also is similar to the other primary service providers. In each locality, there are counselors, program specialists, employer liaisons, and training specialists. To gain access to the services, one must apply for services and go through some testing to determine the best job skill match. A referral will be provided if there is a match between the individual's skills and available jobs in the community. The tests that are provided have been developed by the U.S. employment services (USES) and are quite beneficial for individuals who assimilate well into the mainstream of individuals without disabilities. Some problems have been noted about the USES tests for persons with disabilities (Droege, 1987).

Workforce Investment Act

The Workforce Investment Act (WIA) (formerly the Job Training Partnership Act) programs have been in existence since the early 1980s (see Chapter 2). Originally named JTPA programs, the programs are authorized under the WIA (P.L. 105-220) and generally aligned with each state's one-stop-shop programs. With the passage of the WIA, JTPA and other programs were subsumed into Titles within the act. JTPA activities are now considered Title I of the act and for the purposes of this chapter the reference of Title I services will be used to distinguish these programs. Again, these Title I programs function similarly to the primary service pro-viders in that there are state and local offices. In fact, some Title I offices are jointly run by the state employment services. This law, authorized by the U.S. Congress, focuses Title I-provided services upon gaining employment outcomes for disadvantaged youth and adults. The services Title I offer are a bit more focused than the state's employment services. Those services generally are special training to gain job-seeking skills, GED training, vocational technical skills training, one-stop career center and job corps centers for disadvantaged youth who need additional education (Stodden, 1998). In many cases, the mechanism of service delivery for the Title I programs differ from that of the state's employment services. For Title I programs, services are contracted out to private providers. The providers may be any entity that can provide a special training program that meets the needs of qualified participants. The providers generally write competitive grant proposals to obtain the funds and must provide, within those proposals, specific measurable outcome objectives upon which the proposal will be evaluated. The outcomes that are linked to services are generally outcome goals. Examples of these goals would be 80% of the participants will gain employment, 90% of the participants will gain job readiness skills as measured by a "test," and 100% of the participants will interview for ten different jobs. These outcome goals are critical because each state and local municipality is evaluated based on its performance objectives. If the performance objectives do not match with state and federal guidelines, Title I funds may be reduced or rescinded (P.L. 105-220).

Again, to gain access to Title I services, the individual must apply. Information will be taken to determine financial background for eligibility purposes. In the case of Title I services, the individual and everyone he or she lives with must be at or below the poverty level. For individuals with disabilities, however, eligibility can be determined based on earnings of the individual only (with some exceptions), excluding others living with them. Once accepted, the individual can be referred to a service provider for appropriate programs. An example of a program funded by a Title I program is Jobs for (State's Name) Graduates. This program offers real-life experiences for students in businesses and job-seeking skills training. Other programs authorized under Title I include Native American programs, migrant and seasonal farm worker programs, veterans workforce investment, youth opportunity grants, along with numerous other programs.

Critical Point   The Workforce Investment Act is a comprehensive bill that consolidates a variety of federally funded programs.

Employment and Employer Involvement, Models and Practices

The evolution of school-to-work transition and competitive and supported employment is grounded in the basic assumption that people with disabilities should have the opportunity to demonstrate their competency in the general workforce. The emergence of competitive and supported employment for persons with disabilities is rooted in the programmatic and

Employer input is key to socially valid curriculum.

philosophical failings of segregated programs such as sheltered workshops and day activity centers. Historically, employment programs that attempted to meet the needs of persons with disabilities included specialized work training in what has been termed "sheltered employment" (Whitehead, 1977). The general underpinnings of the sheltered or special work process was to provide individualized environments to "habilitate" (habilitate, meaning to train versus the term "rehabilitate," meaning to retrain) individuals with disabilities, offering the individual a long-term, protective environment for learning work skills. The specialized sheltered employment genre, which included a three-step process to attain competitive employment, provided little in the way of relief for persons with disabilities (Bellamy, Rhodes, Barbeau & Mank, 1986). Although sheltered work settings represented a substantial leap forward in the design of early vocational programming for people with disabilities, these programs ultimately failed (Bellamy et al., 1986). Wages paid to participants of the programs are low compared to typical community jobs. There is, generally, no daily interaction with nondisabled people except for the paid staff who work at the facility (Bellamy et al,

1986). Ultimately, people with disabilities are not hired into these environments but are placed there for training. Sheltered employees can be dismissed or expelled from these programs but are not fired in the conventional manner. Generally, the work performed in these environments has little relevancy to preparing people for work in the general workforce (Bellamy et al., 1986). The greatest failing of segregated programming is that very few people move from segregated programs to real employment opportunities. Point of fact, Bellamy et al. (1986) suggested that 57 years was the average time an individual would need to move through the entire sheltered system and to gain competitive employment successfully.

Critical Point   Historically, persons with disabilities were placed in segregated agencies that did not offer adequate training to enable participants to gain competitive employment.

Why Real Jobs?

Work is one of several roles that define who we are in our community. We assign value to people based on the work they do. When we meet someone for the first time, after learning his or her name, we are curious as to the work the person does. Why is this? Perhaps we are exercising mental shorthand to assign value or the person's role in our culture. The more valued the job is, the more value and importance we assign to a person. For instance, someone with a professional background such as a physician or an attorney is afforded a greater social value than someone with less education or a nonprofessional job. Unfortunately, if one has a disability, one is seen as having little value to the culture. That person becomes labeled by the disability rather than by the other valued roles one possesses, such as worker, brother, uncle, parent, or wife. By going to work, one can demonstrate his or her competency and reduce the impact of the devaluing roles associated with the disability. By going to work, one realizes new, more valued roles that enable him or her to be more integrated in the community (Wolfensberger 1991).

Critical Point   Western culture tends to value people more if they work with the individual's value increasing or decreasing according to the value of the work. Persons with disabilities have traditionally been placed in lesser valued employment.

The promotion of valued roles is the essence of competitive and supported employment. To facilitate the outcome of competitive or supported employment, numerous structures can be developed to support persons with disabilities in the workforce (Hughes & Kim, 1998). Some examples of the strategies that have been used to provide such supports are business advisory councils, job clubs, mentoring programs, supported employment, and so on.

Business Advisory Councils

Business advisory councils (BACs) have been in use for over 20 years (Rusch, 1990). In fact, utilization of BACs has been mandated by programs funded through the projects with industry (PWI) programs of the Rehabilitation Services Administration since the early 1980s (P.L. 93-112). BACs are placement and employment programs that intricately involve employers in their development and oversight. Business advisory councils afford a close relationship with employers by engaging them in the actual implementation aspects of programs and services. Although BACs have been required within the PWI programs for numerous years, the degree of involvement of the BACs has varied quite significantly (Hagner & Vander-Sande, 1998).

Critical Point   Business advisory councils may be utilized to increase employment of persons with disabilities.

Baer, Simmons, and Flexer (1994), for example, implemented a BAC that was focused upon a specific program or services but utilized the employers to market services and as a provider of services to individuals with disabilities. Baer

et al. (1997) attended a systemic approach by enabling the employers to choose the amount of involvement in addressing the community's needs regarding employment of persons with disabilities. They used a traditional team process approach that focused upon stages of team development. The stages included forming, storming, norming, performing, and adjourning phases. These stages were used both to understand the processes and to facilitate the ongoing development. The authors (1997) found that their BAC was able to develop marketing and business connections that had a significant impact upon the employment of persons with disabilities. Further, Baer et al. (1994) found that the marketing activities cost the disability-related employment agencies far less to develop. In addition, the BAC became so involved that employers developed services that were not in existence before the BACs inception.

Critical Point   BACs, as with all committees or groups, follow certain developmental stages. The phases are forming, storming, norming, performing, and adjourning.

Job Clubs

A job club is another service program that has been around for numerous years (Malone, 1996). Azrin and Besalel (1979) developed a *job club approach* that focused upon training in job-seeking skills with the expectation that participants in the club also would be strongly involved in seeking and soliciting job leads (Azrin et al., 1979). In fact, the job club approach requires the participant to utilize these job-seeking efforts on a daily basis. Primary to this focus is the intensive nature of the job club approach (Azrin & Philip, 1980). Baer, Simmons, Flexer and Martonyi (1994) developed two job club programs meeting the needs of persons with both mental illness and physical disabilities. These respective programs fostered job-seeking skills and making contacts with friends, family members, and potential employers as usual daily routine. Further, the job clubs were continued beyond the point of individual placement to facilitate ongoing supports. Baer et al. (1994) determined that a higher percentage of placements and maintenance of that employment was attained as compared to other local community employment programs.

Critical Point   Job club programs have been found useful in developing and maintaining employment. The primary reasons seem to be the training of employability skills and ongoing group supports.

Mentoring

Mentoring has become a significant emphasized programmatic effort in recent years (Siegel, 1998). *Mentoring* is a process that involves matching an individual who is knowledgeable and skilled in work and job-getting strategies (Hagner & Vander-Sande, 1998). In fact, one can implement the mentoring role through several methods, by being a mentor who discusses and councils an individual, much like the "Big Brother" and "Big Sister" programs, or by being a mentor in the workplace (Hagner & Dileo, 1993; Smith & Rojewski, 1993). The coworker-mentoring role has been most extensively utilized with persons with disabilities (Mank, Oorthuys, Rhodes, Sandow, & Weyer, 1992). Hagner and Dileo (1993) suggest that selection of the mentor should be someone who has worked at the place of employment for at least several months, is well liked by his coworkers, is scheduled to work at the same time as the individual with a disability, and is a willing mentor.

Critical Point   Utilizing a mentor allows for a more typical approach to job training and an ongoing support for people with disabilities (Mank, Cioffi, & Yovanoff, 1997).

Supported Employment

A final area that promotes valued roles is *supported employment*. Supported employment is operationally defined as:

> Competitive work in integrated settings for individuals, (a) with severe disabilities for whom com-

The environment is a powerful teacher.

petitive employment has not traditionally occurred or (b) for individuals for whom competitive employment has been interrupted or intermittent as a result of a severe disability, and who, because of their disability, need ongoing support services to perform such work (Kiernan & Schalock, 1997).

Stated simply, "supported employment" is the provision of personalized job development, on-the-job training or consultation, and ongoing support services to enable someone who otherwise would be excluded from the workforce to go to work in a typical community job.

Critical Point   Supported employment is the provision of personalized job development, on-the-job training or consultation, and ongoing support services.

In the past 25 years, supported employment has proven to be an effective vocational service for people with a variety of disabilities. Early supported employment projects focused upon the needs of people with mental retardation. Over the years, supported employment was expanded to include other population groups, such as people with traumatic brain injury and people with pervasive mental illness.

A recent application of supported employment services addresses the needs of people with autism. Traditionally, vocational services for people with autism have been a rarity. Due to the elements of social withdrawal, sensory deficits, self-injury, and aggression, most people with autism never seek or are denied services. A 12-year longitudinal study of employment outcomes for people with autism was conducted by Community Services for Autistic Adults and Children (CSAAC). Seventy individuals with autism who were employed through CSAAC were studied. Nearly half of those people ($n = 35$) had previously been institutionalized. During the time span of the study, the 70 people worked at 381 jobs at 128 businesses in Maryland. Because autism is characterized by difficulty in initiating relationships, social interaction was limited to one or two people. Most people held jobs for at least 6 months and 11% remained employed for 3+ years (Smith, Belcher, Juhrs, & Nabors, 1994).

Four Features of Supported Employment

There are four features to supported employment services: individualized assessment, job development, on-the-job training, and ongoing support. *Individualized assessment* is a process by which the supported employment provider learns about the unique skills and abilities of the person for whom he or she is finding a job. There is a similarity between this process and the one described by Richard Nelson Bolles' *What Color Is Your Parachute* (1999). Bolles (1999) discusses five effective job-hunting methods. Among these is *the creative job-hunting approach*. This method urges the job seeker to figure out what his or her best skills and favorite "knowledges" are. This notion of learning what the job seeker has to offer is parallel to the idea of developing an individualized assessment or a person-centered approach to job selection. A person-centered approach begins with the premise that we all have unique skills and interests that define what a good job would be for us.

For people with disabilities, the disability can prevent us from getting to know who someone is and what their interests are. Knowing what someone is good at doing is the first step in creating a job match rather than "placing" someone at a job site.

Person-Centered Job Selection

Person-centered job selection relies upon the use of nontraditional assessment exercises for determining an appropriate job match. As opposed to standardized, norm-referenced testing that is designed to assign a diagnostic category, supported employment takes a personalized approach to learning about the individual. Where standardized tests describe what someone cannot do, person-centered activities allow the supported employment professional to learn the work preferences of the individual. By investing time in getting to know the individual's dreams, interests, and unique skills, the evaluator can look beyond the person's disability and develop the "right job" for the individual (adopted from Marc Gold and Associates). By investing the time to get to know a person's dreams, interests, and skills, the evaluator can perform an assessment in a balanced, trusting, and reciprocal way. By spending time in getting to know the person in typical environments, the evaluator can make an assessment of what considerations should be made in order for the person to be successful at his or her job. This type of assessment is different from finding a job and hoping the person will be successful. Too often, jobs for people with disabilities have centered on food service and cleaning jobs with little regard for matching skills and preferences with the requirements of a given job. In fact, the emerging criticism of supported employment is the overreliance on entry-level food service and janitorial jobs. These types of work are characterized by high turnover and low wages. Jobs of this type are an easy job placement for staff trainers who have not taken the time to assess what a "good job" would look like for the participant (Mank, 1997). When a person-centered approach is utilized, the job match is individualized and the job is more fulfilling for the participant.

Critical Point   Person-centered job placement can almost be defined as the opposite of norm-referenced assessment and placement.

The most important consideration in a person-centered approach to job selection is to ensure that the activities used for evaluation are meaningful and occur in everyday life. If the evaluation relies on artificial tasks or environments, then the individual will quickly realize the message that the task is not real or relevant. If there is no sense of purpose to the task, then what a sad message this must send to someone who, for their entire life, has always faced a life of lowered expectations. What message does this send to family members, employers, and the general public? Tasks used in evaluation should have a suitable level of challenge, offer the appropriate amount of decision making, and be appropriate for the age of the individual.

A person-centered approach to job selection leads to a job development approach that places faith in the power of friends and family of the job seeker. A group of friends and family have a personal stake and want to see good things happen for the person seeking work. As opposed to a formal group of therapists and paid professionals, the individuals who participate in a person-centered group are there voluntarily. Paid professionals will be involved in the planning but a balance of nonpaid people is preferred. This type of planning group places emphasis on the knowledge and resources of a job seeker's personal network. This is similar to Bolles (1999) who lists friends and family as the third and fourth most effective job-hunting method. Our friends and family form a personal network. Very few jobs in our culture are found by looking in the want ads or making phone calls to employers. Bolles (1999) lists classified ads as the least effective method of job seeking. According to Bolles (1999), answering blind ads in newspa-

pers leads to employment for only 5 to 24% of job seekers. Utilizing our network of friends, family, and acquaintances fills most jobs. In many circumstances, the axiom is true: "it's whom you know not what you know". For too long, human service professionals have discounted the power and efficacy of the job seeker's personal network in his or her job development efforts. See case study A, which presents a small experience of social network job seeking.

Critical Point   The most important consideration in a person-centered approach to job selection is to ensure that the activities used for evaluation are meaningful and occur in everyday life.

CASE STUDY A

Within the most recent year, a man with a disability was looking for work at a plastic factory. The staff of a local community employment agency made several contacts but after 2 months the man had no firm job offer. One Sunday night at a church service the congregation was encouraged to stand up and say whatever was on their minds. As Mark, the man with the disability, looked around the church he noticed the owner of the plastics molding company. Mark took this opportunity to stand up and tell the congregation that he had been unemployed for some time and needed a job. He stated "he always thought he'd like to work at a plastic formulating plant." Mark went to work the next week.

Once a job outcome has been targeted for the individual, the work of job development begins. As with any job seeker, an organized plan will be established for getting a job. As a means of preparation, a decision should be made early regarding how much the job seeker will do for him- or herself and how much representation will be required by the service provider. The key is to develop a job-seeking strategy where the individual is empowered in the process and takes an active role that is consistent with his or her ability. If too much assistance is provided, the job seeker may be stigmatized by the presence of the service provider. If too little support is provided, then the job search may not be successful. For instance, how much assistance will the job seeker need in contacting employers? Does the person represent him- or herself well enough so that the service provider should not sit in on the interview? Should the job seeker, due to the complexity of his or her disability, not attend the initial employer contacts? Can the job seeker participate in developing a résumé as part of the job search? Has the job seeker been adequately prepared for what to do and say in a job interview? For some job searches, the paid professional will take the lead in making job contacts and meeting with potential employers. For people who are more capable, the role of the staff person may be to organize the search and to provide advice and counseling to the job seeker.

Regardless of the amount of representation needed to get someone employed, it is essential that the staff person and the job seeker be aware of the accepted protocol for contacting an employer. The first question to consider is, "How would anyone contact this employer?" Is it better to send a letter with a résumé before a contact is made? Is it customary to walk in on an employer and make an unannounced "cold call"? Should a formal appointment be made, and to whom? Generally, the more typical the contact is to that of any job seeker, the greater is the likelihood of success.

Job Design

Creativity is essential in job design. One size does not fit all. Targeted job development requires considerably more flexibility and creativity than typical job acquisition activities. Targeted job development means that marketing activities are designed to benefit one person and not designed to sell the services offered by an agency. When an individual interviews for a job, that person is selling his or her skills and abilities. The same should be true for people who require a little extra attention in order to go

to work. Service professionals should be acutely aware of this fact when representing someone who is at risk of being seen in a devalued role by an employer or the community. The ultimate goal is, of course, to match the skills, preferences, and conditions for work with the setting, task, and decision-making complexity of a particular job. We all have individual requirements in regard to where we work, how we work, and when we work. Creativity in job design cannot be undersold when someone goes to work. Flexibility may include job carving or job sharing.

Job carving involves negotiating with an employer to construct a new job description from two or more standardized job descriptions at the business. An example of this process is provided in case study B. Within the job-carving process Dan's skills and interests are reviewed. Once the analysis was completed, employment was sought that allowed Dan to perform either a majority or separate components of presently available jobs. Employers, generally, are heavily involved in the development of job-carving practices. The employer is the one who knows his or her jobs, and with the assistance of a community employment specialist, a variety of jobs could be developed.

Critical Point   Creativity is essential in job design.

CASE STUDY B

Dan works at a laboratory run by the U.S. Geological Survey (USGS). His job is to sanitize sample bottles used by field-workers taking water samples from Maine to the Mississippi River. The bottle-sanitizing job is a time-consuming complex operation and involves dangerous chemicals. Prior to Dan's employment, this job was part of the chemist's job description. With Dan fulfilling these functions, the chemists have more time to devote to testing samples, preventing the typical spring and summer backlog of work. Dan is employed in a challenging job where he can demonstrate his competency. Additionally, Dan has taken on more complex tasks since he went to work at the lab. The staff of the community employment agency went to USGS with the purpose of designing a job that is specific to Dan's skills rather than trying to have Dan "fit" an existing job description. In developing a carved job, the community employment staff had to spend time in getting to know Dan and what his unique skills were. The community employment staff also had to get to know the employer and the business to learn what tasks would fit Dan's abilities. Close attention was paid to the environment, coworkers, tasks, and culture of the business.

Job-sharing arrangements are effective when individuals with disabilities are primarily interested in working part time (Granger, 1996). *Job-sharing arrangements*, as the name implies, allows for two people to share a single part-time job. Two people with disabilities or a person with a disability and a nondisabled person may share a job. This arrangement is most effective when the amount of earnings is restricted or when personal issues or responsibilities prevent someone from working full time.

Shared jobs or carved jobs can be effective for any job seeker. Job flexibility has found its place in our business culture. People work for a variety of reasons and have different requirements for what defines a good job for them. Salary alone is not the only factor that people consider in accepting a job. Issues such as child care, proximity to home, flexibility in scheduling, geographic area, and job satisfaction, all are issues that job seekers consider. This same flexibility is key to a quality job match and positively correlates with job satisfaction and job longevity (Dentzer, 1992).

In some instances, job seekers do fill an existing job description. At an early age, many people with disabilities have indicated that their expectations were high for having a career path. The role of the service provider in these situations is to work with the individual to develop a "road map" on what vocational steps should be taken to get the person to his or her ultimate job target. A career path involves competency building by working at a series of jobs that lead to the ultimate job target. See case studies C and D for two examples of how this can be accomplished.

CASE STUDY C

Jean is a good example of someone who has succeeded at her career path. Jean graduated from high school in 1969. For the next 11 years, she found herself working at a segregated sheltered workshop. In all those years, she never gave up her dream of working in an office setting. Jean began her career track volunteering at a local university library. At this job, she learned how to organize tasks, how to file, and how to conform to the culture of a business. After a short time, she went to work part time at a steel factory as a file clerk for the sales staff. Jean learned to organize and manage a complex filing system. She also was responsible for taking phone orders and making appointments for the sales staff. After several years, she left the factory to work for the local county clerk's office. This was a full-time position with comparable benefits and wages to her nondisabled coworkers. Jean is responsible for a variety of duties, including processing vehicle registrations, license plate renewals, and vehicle liens. Her present job is challenging and fits the requirements of her dream job of 15 years ago. She works in an office setting performing complex tasks. She works in a downtown office setting where she has contact with professional people. She has the opportunity to develop friendships with her coworkers and to attain respect for her job competency. After going to work at the clerk's office, Jean was able to move from the family home into her own apartment. She has an active social life and is making plans for her retirement.

CASE STUDY D

Another example of a career track has been the experiences of Trevor. Trevor experienced a brain injury while in college. After several years of rehabilitation services, Trevor was eager to enter the workforce. He worked for an industrial lighting company as a data entry operator. He later worked as an inventory control specialist for a major retail distribution warehouse. These clerical skills allowed Trevor to develop competencies that led to his ideal job, working as a runner for a large downtown law firm. Trevor has returned to school, pursuing an Associates Degree as a paralegal.

Natural Supports

The most significant development in the field of supported employment services is the way that people are trained to perform their job. In the early years of supported employment, the accepted method of job training was to provide a job coach to teach the new hire to do his or her job. The job trainer would begin at the job site several days before the new employee would begin. This would allow the job coach to develop a training strategy in preparation for the employee to go to work. As supported employment evolved, we have learned that there are distinct liabilities in having a job coach present at the job site. A job coach employed by a supported employment program, ultimately is artificial to the job environment. The presence of a job coach on site too often draws attention to the worker with a disability and can stigmatize the individual. Other employees notice the presence of the job coach and look upon the supported employee differently from a person who was trained in a more typical manner. The presence of a job coach sends a faulty message to other employees at the business that special skills and knowledge are required to work with and relate to the employee with a disability.

The focus of job training has shifted from external job training to the reliance of generic supports that naturally occur at the workplace (natural supports in the workplace). Many businesses have training programs in place for their employees (Nisbet & Hagner, 1988). All businesses have a unique culture that enables a new employee to learn his or her job and to become assimilated into the workplace. The strength of generic supports is to work within the accepted framework of the business in order to allow the person with a disability to be accepted into the workplace culture, as any other employee would be. The role of the supported employment staff, in these instances, is to act as a consultant or advisor to the business during the training period. Supported employment staff will act as advisors to the training staff providing information on teaching strategies, task organization, and other issues that may arise during job training. This role can be more difficult than the traditional job training role because the job trainer is not always present at the business. The results of this type of training are of tremendous benefit to the individual with a disability at the work site.

Critical Point The most significant development in the field of supported employment services is the way that people are trained to perform their job.

In a landmark study of supported employment, Mank, Cioffi, and Yovnoff (1997) investigated the relationship of employment features and outcomes for supported participants and the use of natural supports in the workplace. The analysis applied to the data in this research studied the relationship between the level of job-site integration and seven variables: the type of work, the level of disability, monthly wages, hourly wages, and the "typicalness" of the employees circumstances in relation to that of nondisabled coworkers. Mank et al. (1997) found that work-site interaction with nondisabled coworkers was positively correlated with higher wages and longer job retention. Most strikingly, it was found that the correlation holds regardless of the severity of the disability of the employee. Conversely, the study concluded that the more atypically someone's conditions are at the start of employment, the more atypical conditions continue regardless of time on the job or complexity of the task (Mank et al., 1997).

An example can be found in a central Kentucky employment agency through which a man named Terry gained a job. Terry has significant disabilities that prevented him from entering the workforce. His disabilities included total blindness, midrange deafness, and selective mutism, and he was presumed to have mental retardation. The central Kentucky agency's staff found that Terry had a tremendous interest in radio and music. His hobby was a music collection composed of thousands of recordings. When initially encountered, Terry worked 4 days per week at a day activity center putting toys in gumball machine eggs. Terry's ambition was to work in radio. It would have been impossible for the agency staff to learn to operate a radio station and to provide the training Terry needed. A radio station was located that employed a disc jockey, Edmund, who was also blind. He agreed to work with Terry in the role of a mentor. By utilizing Edmund's expertise, Terry went to work in an occupation that would have been impossible if traditional job-training techniques were utilized.

Managers change, coworkers move on, and benefit packages change. For these reasons, and many others, supported employment affords its participants something no other vocational service can provide—ongoing comprehensive support services. Early models for community-based vocational services, notably state VR programs, imposed service limits on their participants. Once someone was employed, services continued for a short period of time. Soon after that the individual was considered successfully employed and services ended. Although this arrangement may be suitable for people with some disabilities, time-limited services were not effective for people with severe disabilities. Supported employment makes a commitment to each person served that the individual will receive a level of support that is consistent with his or her needs. Supports are personally designed in order to enable the person to work with maximum independence. Too much support may further stigmatize the individual with a disability. Too little support may jeopardize the person's job. This balance is not

stagnant but fluid, allowing for support to change based on circumstances. The provision of long-term support is essential for both the employer and employee:

1. To address management and coworker changes at the business
2. To retrain, consult, and introduce a new task
3. To advocate for raises, benefits, and job advancement
4. To facilitate job changes as the result of termination, advancement, layoff, or business closure
5. To model appropriate work behavior
6. To develop appropriate social interaction skills

Without this valuable service, it would be unlikely that many people who are served in community-based vocational services would be successful. This is especially true for people with long-term mental illness, brain injury, mental retardation and autism.

Ongoing Supports

Ongoing support services should be individually designed rather than adhered to federal guidelines of two job-site visits per month. Some people require daily or weekly assistance on the job. Other people require visits away from the job rather than at their work site. Just as utilizing a job trainer can be stigmatizing for someone, the presence of a job coach appearing at the business can be equally damaging, if not more so. The goal for everyone served in supported employment is to design a support system that allows someone to work without the artificial encroachment of the service agency.

A key question that should be addressed even before the employee begins work is, "How is the job training gradually, but efficiently, withdrawn to get rid of artificial supports?" Far too often placements are attempted with no attention given to reducing artificial supports at the job site. By not addressing these questions, job trainers unwittingly "build their support" into the job site, resulting in the employee and the business becoming dependent on the artificial support offered by the job coach. Consequently, when supervision is withdrawn or transferred, the job site fails, regardless of the quality of the job or the competence of the employee.

Critical Point   A key question that should be addressed even before the employee begins work is, "How is the job training gradually, but quickly, withdrawn to get rid of artificial supports?"

Social Welfare, Social Entitlements, and Work Incentives

Most people with significant disabilities rely upon programs administered by the Social Security Administration to provide supplemental income and entitlement income. More importantly, these programs include medicaid and medicare benefits. Most people who attain employment through supported employment work part time. Parent (1996) found that 67% of supported employees received no employer-sponsored health benefit. Johnson, McGrew, Bloomburg, Bruininks, and Lin (1997) reported that nearly 75% of students exiting public school special education programs received supplemental security income (SSI) and, consequently, medicaid. Sixteen percent received social security disability income (SSDI) and medicare coverage.

Social Security/Disability Insurance

The SSDI program strictly limits income for disabled participants to $700.00 per month (effective July 1, 1999). Wages over this amount are considered trial work months. Social security allows for a 9-month trial work limit and an extended period of eligibility. At the end of this time, the Social Security Administration (SSA) makes a determination of substantial gainful work activity. This implies that the person with a disability is earning a wage for providing something of economic benefit to an employer. If it is determined that the individual can work in spite of his or her disability, then SSDI benefits are terminated.

Supplemental Security Insurance

The supplemental security insurance (SSI) program is a federal welfare subsidy and provides for work incentives to allow people to work. Under Pub. L. No. 99-643, SSI cash benefits to recipients are determined on a flexible scale based on countable income. As wages increase, cash benefits decrease. Under section 1619b, when the cash benefit reaches zero, recipients continue on the social security roles, allowing them to continue working. Medicaid benefits also continue under section 1619b (extended medicaid coverage). Medicaid benefits continue so long as wages fall below the federal threshold amounts for earnings. These incentives have allowed thousands of people to go to work. Unfortunately, there is considerable confusion as to how to use these benefits. Many people who can go to work do not due to ignorance of these work incentives or misinformation provided by service providers.

Additional Work Incentives

Two additional work incentives are emerging as effective work incentives: plans for achieving self-support (PASS) and impairment-related work expenses (IRWE). These programs are designed to set aside earned income in order to reduce "countable income" and to maintain social security eligibility. These programs enable people to purchase equipment or services that are necessary for individuals to work. Getzel, Emanual, Fesko, and Parent, (2000) determined that 57% of supported employment programs use PASS or IRWE to assist participants. The most frequently purchased services include transportation to work, job coach services, and work-site modifications.

Services and Agency Delivery Matrix

Table 15–2 provides an overview of services that, generally, are needed to support employment outcomes for students with disabilities. The row across the top of the table indicates agencies with the initial side column showing the potential services that could be provided. A legend is provided to describe the generic or usual categories of disabilities that one would refer to in delivering services. Although these categories do not match the categories delineated by IDEA, the terms, generally, are used across the country when referring to diagnostic categories.

The purpose of Table 15–2 is to provide the reader with a quick reference as to where an individual with a particular disability could acquire certain services. As was described in prior sections of this chapter and the book, all the services are available but all potential participants may not be able to qualify for access to the service. For instance, in row two, "Career Planning," one can look across and see that all the agencies would provide career services. However, each agency may have differing restrictions as to whom may receive the service. Further, case management, employer benefits (e.g., targeted job tax credits and reduced wage options) are limited to very few agencies. Other access issues include the particular agencies' conditions on providing services. To make the point, the VR agency may be required to offer various training and employment programs and the individual may qualify for receiving these services; however, the individual may not fit within the VR agencies' priority service categories. Consequently, the individual would not be able to access the service. One can use Table 15–2 as a guide for asking for services, but differences do exist in the practical application of those who might be able to receive the employment-related service.

Conclusion

Vocational services for people with disabilities, especially those who make use of natural supports and a wide variety of program resources, are effective in addressing the growing need of school-to-work transition services. Too often persons with disabilities still do not participate in adequate and beneficial work because of a lack of available community employment resources (Granger, 1995). Multiple programs exist that can have an impact upon employment outcomes for persons with a wide range of disability conditions. One must only seek them out to enable the services to find work for students with disabilities.

The accomplishments of supported employment, in particular, are significant. Over 200,000 people nationally, who previously were considered difficult to employ, are working in the general workforce. Incentives have been developed to assist people in reducing their dependency on social welfare programs. Early research has demonstrated that community-based vocational services offer participants higher earnings, an improved quality of life, and the opportunity to be more fully integrated in the community. Supported employment has also demonstrated that it can be a cost-effective model for delivering vocational services.

Study Questions

1. What services should one expect to access during the last few years of the student's life at school?
2. When accessing Vocational Rehabilitation Services, what services should one expect to receive?
3. What agencies provide life-long services to persons with disabilities?
4. Do all youth with disabilities qualify and receive services from their state's Vocational Rehabilitation Service?
5. What is the rationale for finding real jobs for persons with disabilities?
6. Define supported employment?

TABLE 15–2

Transition to Employment Service Providers

SERVICE ↓ / PROVIDERS →	Community Employment Agency	Public School	Vocational Education	Work-Study Voc. Sped Coord	Job/WIA /State Employment Agency	Voc. Rehab./ VI Agency	Mental Health Agency	MR/DD Agency	Post-secondary Education Agency	Adult Vo-Tech Agency
Functional vocational evaluation		All	All	All		All	PD	MD, OH		
Career planning	All	All	All	All	All	All	PD	MD, OH	All	All
Job shadowing	All	All	All	All		All	PD	MD, OH		All
Job search training	All	All	All	All	All	All	PD	MD, OH		All
Job placement	All	All	All	All	All	All	PD	MD, OH		All
Technology/AT		All		All		All	PD	MD, OH		
Transportation	All	All	All	All		All	PD	MD, OH		
Job training	All	All	All	All	All	All	PD	MD, OH		
Follow-along							PD	MD, OH		
Employer benefits					All	All	PD	MD, OH		
Case management						All	PD	MD, OH		
Independent living skills		All					PD	MD, OH		
Residential-home services							PD	MD, OH		
Financial supports							PD	MD, OH	All	All
Recreational services		All					PD	MD, OH	All	All

Legend: LD = learning disability, BD = behavior disorder, OH = orthopedic impairment, MD = multiple disability, PD = psychiatric disability, SI = sensory impairment.

Source: Adapted by permission: Baer, Simmons, & Flexer, 1996.

7. How is supported employment different from the historical method of employing persons with disabilities?
8. What legislative efforts have been passed to improve the employment options for students with disabilities?
9. What employment incentives can be used to facilitate the employment of persons with disabilities when they are on Welfare or Social Entitlements?
10. List and describe the programs and services that are available to youth with disabilities?

Web Sites

The Association of Persons in Supported Employment
http://www.apse.org/index.html

RSA - Rehabilitation Services Administration Office of Special Education and Rehabilitative Service
United States Department Of Education
http://www.apse.org/index.html

Commission on the Accreditation of Rehabilitation Facilities
http://www.carf.org/

The National Rehabilitation Information Center
http://www.naric.com/

Rehabilitation Research and Training Center on Blindness and Low Vision
http://www.blind.msstate.edu/irr/special.html

The West Virginia Research and Training Center
http://www.icdi.wvu.edu/

America's One-Stop Career Center System
http://www.ttrc.doleta.gov/onestop/

Employment and Training Administration
http://www.ttrc.doleta.gov/onestop/

The Vocational and Rehabilitation Research Institute
http://www.vrri.org/

Employment Support Institute
http://www.vcu.edu/busweb/esi/

Bureau of Labor Statistics
http://stats.bls.gov/

The U.S. Department of Labor.
http://www.dol.gov/

Links to State Vocational Rehabilitation web sites
http://www.ihdi.uky.edu/projects/dvr/websites.htm#dept

The National Alliance of The Disabled
http://www.naotd.org/home.html

Rehabilitation Research and Training Center on Workplace Supports
http://www.worksupport.com/

National Supported Employment Consortium (SEC)
http://www.vcu.edu/rrtcweb/sec/

National Center for Research in Vocational Education
http://vocserve.berkeley.edu/

Committee on Education and the Workforce
http://www.house.gov/eeo/

Cornell Youth and Work Program
http://www.human.cornell.edu/youthwork/

Training Resource Network, Inc.
http://www.trninc.com/seintlinks.html

Job Accommodation Network
http://www.jan.wvu.edu/

Job Corps
http://www.jobcorps.org/main.htm

Planning Your Future
http://safetynet.doleta.gov/

America's Job Bank
http://www.ajb.dni.us/

U.S.workforce.org
http://usworkforce.org

School to Work
http://www.stw.ed.gov/

Wage & Hour Information
http://www.interwork.sdsu.edu/wage hour/

16

Postsecondary Education and Career Paths

Deborah Durham Webster
Greg Clary
Penny L. Griffith

LEARNING OBJECTIVES

The objectives of this chapter are:

1. Understand the importance of incorporating postsecondary educational and training goals, when appropriate, in the transition planning process.

2. Recognize that succeeding in postsecondary programs means preparing students not only to meet academic requirements, but also to reach social and independent living goals as well, and to understand why planning ahead is an essential component in achieving postsecondary education goals.

3. Be aware of the various postsecondary education options; the demands of college life and the ways in which each individual institution differs (i.e., size, admission requirements, racial/gender makeup, cost, support services available, etc.); and ways in which to empower students and their families to choose the kinds of postsecondary option that best meets the student's individual interests, preferences, and needs.

4. Be aware of various ways to explore career interests and to understand the role career exploration activities play in matching potential

postsecondary schools to the individual student's interests, needs, and preferences.

5. Know and understand legislation that applies to the postsecondary sector (i.e., section 504 of the 1973 Vocational Rehabilitation Act and the Americans with Disabilities Act) and how it differs from IDEA and the importance of transmitting that knowledge to their students.

6. Begin to develop the skill necessary to empower their students through strategies that facilitate the students' self-awareness, including understanding their disability and the ability to self-advocate, and knowledge of their rights and responsibilities in postsecondary settings.

7. Be sensitive to the impact that cultural values, attitudes, and beliefs may have on the students and their families when promoting postsecondary educational goals, as well as issues that may arise for first-generation college students or those who come from a rural background.

8. Know and understand how postsecondary education and training goals relates to IDEA's four principles inherent in transition planning and services.

439

The last chapter addressed issues related to the transitioning process to employment settings. For many students, postsecondary education and training is an important step in reaching an employment goal. Therefore, this chapter provides an overview of the information needed to guide students and their transition team members in preparing for postsecondary environments. With the assumption of student participation in the IEP/ITP process as a basis, the four essential elements of the transition process are discussed in relation to secondary assessment, goal setting, and curriculum development. Various postsecondary options are described with a focus on matching these settings to essential element one—*determining student needs, interests, and preferences*. In addition, the authors provide specific methods to assess and explore career options based on cultural values and beliefs in the section on "students' needs, interests, and preferences." Essential element two is addressed under the section entitled, *"outcome-oriented process,"* which looks at the importance of identifying goals and preparing students for postsecondary outcomes through *backward* transition planning. Essential element three—*coordinated set of activities*—is discussed in the section on "interagency responsibilities and linkages," as well as being a theme that runs throughout the chapter. Lastly, essential element four—*promoting movement to postschool settings*—is examined in the section "movement from school to postsecondary environments." Here the authors discuss the role of academic as well as nonacademic preparation, including community-based experiences, which are vital for students' success in postsecondary education. The chapter concludes with an overview of issues that will enhance the participation of students with disabilities from a wide variety of environments in postsecondary education and training.

The transition from high school to adulthood tends to be a difficult time for all adolescents, but especially for many students with disabilities (Halpern, 1992; Rusch, DeStefano, Chadsey-Rusch, Phelps, & Szymanski, 1992). This process can be more difficult for students with disabilities because they may not have had the supports necessary to develop self-esteem, self-determination, social judgment, or self-management skills (Loewen & Iaquinto, 1990; Rosenthal, 1992), all of which are needed to succeed in postsecondary education. Continuing education after high school is only one option that a student might choose in the developmental process toward adulthood. This is a positive choice for obvious academic reasons and because a postsecondary degree enhances job opportunities. It also provides students with a potential postponement of adult obligations, such as complete financial independence, marriage and family, and job performance.

Why Go to College?

Ernest Boyer (1987), who conducted a nationwide interview of college students, found that the vast majority thought that going to college was necessary if an individual wished to earn good money in a satisfying career and to obtain the "good life." College graduates (including 2- and 4-year private and public colleges, as well as vocational and technical institutions) earn 20 to 40% more money over their working life span than persons who did not go to college; and they are more likely to be continuously employed and less likely to be laid off (Pascarella & Terenzini, 1991). In addition, when compared to high school graduates, graduates from higher education institutions enjoyed better health; had higher self-esteem, greater career mobility, and better interpersonal and problem-solving skills; were more tolerant in their views of others and more open to new ideas, more politically active, and more likely to participate in community affairs and to become leaders at work and in their communities (Knox, Lindsay, & Kolb, 1993; Pascarella & Terenzini, 1991).

Critical Point   Students with disabilities who earned a bachelor's degree in 1992 to 1993 had similar full-time starting salaries in 1994 as their peers in the general population (National Center for Education Statistics, 1999a).

If students with disabilities can access postsecondary education and be successful at maintaining their status, postsecondary environments can offer these students more developmental time in all areas of their lives. Actually, succeeding in college is hard work for anyone. For a student with a disability, it means that many things have had to fall into place. Most sources of information say that planning must begin "early," defined as late middle school or ninth grade, when high school course selection occurs (Cowen, 1993; Turner & Simmons, 1996). Ideally, though, it means that all support systems worked as intended prior to high school: (1) The disability was identified as early as possible. (2) Parents sought and received help. (3) Early preschool or school intervention took place. (4) The educational team collaborated well so that the IEP targeted the student's true needs. (5) The child was able to develop confidence and had opportunities to interact in positive social ways with peers. (6) The student was able to acquire basic academic skills needed to participate in and succeed at a secondary curriculum. To the degree that these conditions exist, the transition team, including the student, can devise an appropriate plan to assist the student in reaching his or her goal of postsecondary education.

This chapter provides an overview of the current literature regarding access to postsecondary environments for students with disabilities, postsecondary options and supports available to students with disabilities, and curricular planning and processes at the secondary level and beyond which adhere to the IDEA principles regarding transition services.

Secondary and Postsecondary Programs

Participation and Outcomes in Postsecondary Programs

Employment demands of the future will require further training beyond secondary school (de-Fur, Getzel, & Trossi, 1996). Sixty percent of jobs in 1950 were classified as unskilled but by the year 2000 that number will have dropped to 12 to 15% (Hoye, 1998; Lombard, Hazelkorn, & Miller, 1995). The high skill, high wage jobs of the future will demand a workforce with good critical thinking and academic skills, who also have good problem-solving and interpersonal skills and the ability to learn constantly on the job (Hoye, 1998). Therefore, access to and success in postsecondary education and training is a major factor in the transition from high school to adulthood (Fairweather & Shaver, 1991).

College graduates with disabilities appear to have higher employment rates than persons with disabilities who do not have a postsecondary degree (DeLoach, 1992; Harris & Associates, 1986). In fact, a Harris poll found that persons with disabilities who had a 4-year degree were four times more likely to be employed than persons with disabilities who never attend college (Harris & Associates, 1986). However, when compared to students without disabilities who have obtained a college degree, students with disabilities are still at a disadvantage in terms of securing employment (Rumrill, 1994). A more recent Harris poll found that although two-thirds of persons with disabilities between the ages of 16 and 64 are not working (and four out of five of those, or 79%, stated that they would prefer to be working), one-third indicated a need for further education or training (Harris & Associates, 1994).

Critical Point   The only students who began to approach the employment rates of their nondisabled counterparts were those with learning and speech impairments. The students in these categories were more likely to have taken a concentration of vocational education in high school (Wagner & Blackorby, 1996).

Specified Postschool Goals Lead to Better Outcomes

The National Longitudinal Transition Study (NLTS) found that postschool outcomes were better for students with disabilities who had a transition plan that included a specified postschool outcome, such as postsecondary education (Wagner, D'Amico, Marder, Newman, & Blackorby, 1992). However, a gap still exists between the postsecondary experiences of students with disabilities and their peers in the general population. The majority of high school seniors expect to attend some college, and almost half expect to complete at least a bachelor's degree (Gardner, 1987). Yet, the NLTS found that only 14% of youth with disabilities attended a postsecondary school 2 years after leaving high school, compared to 53% of the general population (Wagner et al., 1992). Three to five years after graduation from secondary school, the number of youth with disabilities who had attended a postsecondary school had increased to only 27% compared to 68% of the general population (Blackorby & Wagner, 1996). The national longitudinal follow-up data also revealed that retention rates in postsecondary programs were significantly lower for students with disabilities compared to their peers in the general population (Wagner et al., 1992). The issue of recruitment and retention becomes even more complex when a further look at the longitudinal data shows that students with disabilities were more likely to come from lower-income families and families with lower educational attainment (Fairweather & Shaver, 1991; National Center for Education Statistics, 1999a; Wagner & Blackorby, 1996).

Critical Point Postsecondary students with disabilities are more likely than the general population of college students to have family and financial obligations (such as dependents, other than a spouse) that may interfere with their schooling (National Center for Education Statistics, 1999a).

Students with Disabilities Attending Postsecondary Programs in Increasing Numbers

In spite of the obstacles numerous students with disabilities face in postsecondary programs, many of these students have demonstrated a resiliency that enabled them to succeed on their own. The number of students with disabilities enrolling in postsecondary institutions has continued to increase over the past few decades (Blackorby & Wagner, 1996; Henderson, 1992; U.S. Department of Education, 1996). For example, the number of full-time college freshmen reporting disabilities has tripled, from 2.6% in 1978 to 8.8% in 1991 (Henderson, 1992), increasing slightly to 9.2% in 1994 (Henderson, 1995). When students with disabilities who are enrolled part time or enrolled in graduate school are included, the figure rises to 10.3% (National Center for Educational Statistics, 1993). As shown in Table 16–1, the kinds of disabilities reported by freshmen also has changed over the years, with learning disabilities now accounting for nearly a third of all college students with disabilities in 2- and 4-year institutions, as opposed to 15% in 1985 (HEATH Resource Center, 1995).

Critical Point Compared with their nondisabled peers, college students with disabilities were more likely to be men, to be older, and to be white, non-Hispanic (National Center for Education Statistics, 1999a).

Hughes and Gajar (as cited in Gajar, 1998) attributed this increase to the following four factors: (1) compensatory services received in high school by students who are now enrolled in postsecondary education; (2) disability advocacy groups lobbying postsecondary institutions for increased services; (3) the impact of federal legislation, such as section 504 of the Rehabilitation Act (P.L. 93-112) of 1973 and the Americans with Disabilities Act (ADA) (P.L. 101-336) of 1990 (which requires postsecondary institutions to make reasonable accommodations and to provide access for persons with disabili-

TABLE 16–1

Percentage of Postsecondary Enrollment by
Disability Type, 1988 to 1994

Disability Type	1988	1991	1994
Health impairment	15.7	14.6	16.4
Hearing impairment	11.6	10.5	9.7
Learning disability	15.3	24.9	32.2
Orthopedic impairment	13.8	13.5	10.2
Other impairment	18.5	18.3	18.8
Speech impairment	3.8	5.4	3.5
Visual impairment	31.7	25.2	21.9

Source: Henderson, C. (1995). *College freshmen with
disabilities: A statistical profile.* HEATH Resource Center,
American Council on Education, U.S. Department of
Education.

ties); and (4) as enrollment of "traditional" students decline, postsecondary institutions are recruiting "nontraditional" students to keep their enrollment numbers up.

Although colleges and universities have made significant progress over the last 20 years to promote educational access and opportunities for students with disabilities (Rumrill, 1994), availability does not guarantee access to or success in a chosen program of study (Getzel & Kregal, 1996). The increase in the number of students with disabilities who actually graduate from college with a bachelor's degree or higher has been less dramatic than the increase in enrollment, rising only from 14% in 1986 to 16% in 1994 (Harris & Associates, 1994). Far too many students with disabilities enter postsecondary programs with little or no preparation and a number of qualified students do not attend at all (American Council on Education, 1996; Blackorby & Wagner, 1996; Marder, 1992; National Center for Education Statistics, 1999a; Newman & Cameto, 1993). For example, students and their families, teachers, and agency personnel may assume that because a high school student is academically prepared for a postsecondary education, little else is needed in terms of preparation for success in a postsecondary

institution (deFur et al., 1996). However, the higher standards imposed by colleges with less administrative and social supports, in addition to a greater emphasis on independent functioning (Siperstein, 1988), means that effective transition planning for many students must involve more than just focusing upon academics.

Critical Point Among the 1988 eighth graders who finished high school by 1994, the majority of students with disabilities (56%) were less likely to be even minimally qualified for admission to a 4-year college, compared with their peers in the general population (37%) (National Center for Education Statistics, 1999a).

Students and their transition teams need to become aware of factors which will hinder or enhance a student's postsecondary choices so that they can prepare accordingly. The topics presented in the following sections of this chapter provide the reader with information and skills which have been found to assist students in being successful. Transition teams need to access curriculum resources and to develop individualized intervention plans to focus preparations upon:

1. Dealing with a different legal status as a student with a disability
2. Choosing from the many postsecondary alternatives that are available
3. Spending time in activities that will be required later in college

Types of Postsecondary Programs

Students with disabilities and their transition teams should be aware of the differences among the types of colleges, universities, and vocational, technical, and proprietary schools. The purposes, programs of study, entrance criteria, requirements for licenses or certifications, and associates or baccalaureate degrees will all vary (HEATH Resource Center, 1995). Some differences among traditional postsecondary programs are shown in Table 16–2. In addition, the individual strengths, needs, and interests of the student also will vary and educational goals may change over time. An

TABLE 16–2

Postsecondary Educational Options

Four-Year Colleges and Universities

Colleges provide general academic programs leading to a bachelor's degree in the arts (BA) and sciences (BS). Universities offer the bachelor's degree in addition to professional and graduate programs leading to advanced degrees such as a master's degree or a doctorate. Tuition, room and board, and books are generally more expensive per year than at other types of postsecondary programs (HEATH Resource Center, 1995). Some have open admissions (i.e., anyone over the age of 18 and/or with a high school diploma or GED), but most have selective admissions based on high school GPA, class rank, SAT/ACT scores, letters of recommendation, personal interviews, and other evidence of achievement (HEATH Resource Center, 1995). Ninety-five percent of public and private colleges and universities offer "remedial" courses, taken by 40 to 70% of entering freshmen (Gray, 1996), which assist students in developing compensatory skills and strategies for learning, help them to identify necessary accommodations, and to gain confidence.

Community, Junior, Vocational, and Technical Colleges

Community colleges are nonresidential institutions which offer programs less than 4 years in length, generally 2 years or less. Programs can lead to a license, a certificate, an Associate of Arts (AA), Associate of Science (AS), or an Associate of Applied Science (AAS). The cost is generally thousands of dollars less than a 4-year college and allow students to take a few selected courses in an area of interest. Most of them are open admission, but they may require students to take a placement exam (i.e., ASSET). Students who are not academically prepared may be required to take some "developmental" course work. Usually this course work prepares students for the fastest growing jobs identified by the U.S. Bureau of Labor Statistics, such as computer engineers and technicians, dental hygienists, medical technicians, and paralegals (Kent, 1997).

Technical colleges have a special emphasis on training for specific careers in technical fields such as data processing or mechanical trades. Some offer programs leading to an AA or AS degree. They often operate in conjunction with local industry, business, and public and other service organizations (Mitchell, 1997). Some programs are formally linked to programs that students begin during their last 2 years of high school. Such partnerships are frequently referred to as tech-prep, school-to-career, or two plus two programs.

Proprietary schools are run-for-profit institutions that offer courses in such areas as secretarial, bookkeeping, or culinary training. Credits from these programs may or may not transfer to 2- or 4-year institutions.

---

important step toward a successful outcome is matching the individual's overall needs and goals to the appropriate learning institution.

Critical Point   Students need to have access to information regarding postsecondary options.

Consider the following. The majority of students from the academic middle of any high school graduating class who go on to attend a 4-year college or university will fail to receive a bachelor's degree; and of those who do graduate, one-third or more will end up employed in jobs they could have obtained without the degree (Gray, 1996). In a survey reported in the "Chronicle of Higher Education" (International Survey of Faculty Attitudes, 1994), 80% of the faculty thought that incoming freshmen were not academically prepared in written and oral communication, and 85% thought students were not adequately prepared in mathematics. Therefore, unless a student is academically and socially prepared, as well as highly motivated to succeed, a 4-year college or university may not be the appropriate choice after high school.

Critical Point   Only 12% of students with disabilities had taken any advanced math courses before graduating, which are often required for college entrance (Wagner & Blackorby, 1996).

Research has shown that earnings are not affected by whether a student attended a 2- or 4-year college (Pascarella & Terenzini, 1991). In fact, one of the fastest growing bodies of students in higher education are "reverse transfers" (i.e., students with a bachelor and/or graduate degree who enroll in 1- and 2-year certificate or associate degree programs) (Gray, 1996). Jobs in technical and occupational fields can lead to high-paying careers that equal or are greater than those earned by graduates from 4-year colleges and universities (Gray, 1996). "Nontraditional" students now account for over 60% of overall higher education enrollments (Aslanian, 1996).

Critical Point   Nearly one-half (45%) of all students with disabilities going on to a postsecondary education enrolled in 2-year institutions compared to one-third of students without disabilities. Students without disabilities were more likely to enroll in 4-year institutions (62%) compared to students with disabilities (42%).

The Carl D. Perkins Vocational and Applied Technology Education Act of 1990 (P.L. 101-392) mandates that students with disabilities have access to the full range of vocational and technical programs, such as tech-prep, which is described in Table 16–2 (Lombard, Hazelkorn, & Miller, 1995). However, in their national study on state policies and practices in tech-prep Lombard et al. (1995) found that few states had implemented the equal access provisions, even though 4 years had elapsed since the Perkins act had become law and funding was available.

High School versus Postsecondary Environments

Understanding Legal Rights and Responsibilities
Legally, postsecondary institutions must not discriminate in the recruitment, admissions, or treatment of students with disabilities. However, students with (and without) disabilities often lack knowledge regarding the civil rights of

students with disabilities (Pitman & Slate, 1994; Stageberg, Fischer, & Barbut, 1996). In order for students with disabilities to navigate and advocate successfully in postsecondary settings, they must be aware of their legal rights and responsibilities (Frank & Wade, 1993; HEATH Resource Center, 1995). Under the Individuals with Disabilities Education Act (IDEA), the school is responsible for identifying and assessing the student with a disability and for providing appropriate education instruction and related services. However, IDEA does not apply to students in postsecondary education, as the students themselves become responsible for many services that were once provided for them. The three pieces of legislation that impact postsecondary education are the Rehabilitation Act of 1973 (especially section 504), the Americans with Disabilities Act (ADA) of 1990, and the Family and Educational Rights and Privacy Act (FERPA) of 1974. (See Table 16–3.)

The Rehabilitation Act of 1973 was the first piece of civil rights legislation for persons with disabilities (Jarrow, 1992). Section 504 states that no *otherwise qualified* individual with disabilities be excluded from participation in, or denied the benefits of, or subjected to discrimination under any program receiving federally funded assistance. Although colleges and universities do not have to offer special education courses, subpart E, which focuses specifically upon higher education, further requires that both public and private institutions make appropriate academic adjustments and reasonable modifications to the colleges' procedures and policies. This is to ensure that students with disabilities can fully participate in the same programs and activities that are available to students without disabilities (Flexer, 1996).

Critical Point   Students must be aware of their legal rights, as well as their obligations.

Adjustments, Modifications, and Accommodations
The term *otherwise qualified* means that the person meets the requisite academic and/or technical

TABLE 16–3

Comparison of Federal Legislation Guiding Services for Persons with Disabilities

	The IDEA	Section 504	The ADA
Purpose of law	To provide a free, appropriate, public education (FAPE) in the least restrictive environment through federal funding to states, with substantive requirements attached to funding	A civil rights law which protects persons with disabilities from discrimination and requires reasonable accommodations to ensure nondiscrimination with no authorization for funding	A civil rights law which provides all persons with disabilities broader coverage than section 504 in all aspects of discrimination, with no authorization for funding
Scope and coverage	Applies to public schools and covers students ages 3 to 21 who have a disability that impacts their education	Applies to any program or activity that is receiving federal financial assistance and covers all qualified persons with disabilities regardless of whether special education services are required in elementary, secondary, or postsecondary settings	Applies to public or private employment, transportation, accommodations, and telecommunications regardless of whether federal funding is received and covers all qualified persons with disabilities, and qualified nondisabled persons related to or associated with a person with a disability
Disability defined	A listing of 13 disability categories is provided in the act, and all must adversely affect education performance	No listing of disabilities, but inclusionary criteria of any physical or mental impairment that substantially limits one or more major life activities, having a record of such an impairment, or being regarded as having an impairment	No listing of disabilities provided. Same criteria as found in section 504. HIV status and contagious and noncontagious diseases recently included

446

Indentification process	Responsibility of school district to identify through "child find" and evaluate at no expense to parent of individual	Responsibility of individual with disability to self-identify and provide documentation. Cost of evaluation must be assumed by the individual, not the institution	Same as section 504
Service delivery	Special education services and auxiliary aids mandated by child study team and stipulated in the IEP	Services, auxiliary aids, and academic adjustments may be provided in the regular education setting, arranged for by special education coordinator or student disability services	Services, auxiliary aids, and accommodations arranged for by the designated ADA coordinator. Requires that accommodations do not pose an "undue hardship" to employers
Enforcement agency	Office of Special Education and Rehabilitative Services in U.S. Department of Education	The Office for Civil Rights (OCR) in the U.S. Department of Education	Primarily the U.S. Department of Justice, in conjunction with the Equal Employment Opportunity Commission and Federal Communications Commission. May overlap with OCR
Remedies	Reimbursement by district of school-related expenses is available to parents of children with disabilities to ensure FAPE	A private individual may sue a recipient of federal financial assistance to ensure compliance with section 504	Same as section 504 with monetary damages up to $50,000 for the first violation; attorney fees and litigation expenses are also recoverable

Source: Adapted from: *Handicapped requirements handbook,* January, 1993, Washington, DC: Thompson Publishing Group.

standards required for admission to the post-secondary institution's programs and activities (Heyward, 1996). Section 504 also led to the promotion of disability resource programs in postsecondary institutions in order to provide appropriate academic adjustments such as the extension of time permitted to complete a degree (Flexer, 1996). Whereas reasonable modifications ensure that students with disabilities are not excluded or segregated from the general student population and apply to areas such as housing, financial and employment assistance, physical education and athletics, counseling, placement services, and social organizations (Flexer, 1996), the ADA upholds and extends the Rehabilitation Act's civil rights protection to all public and private colleges and universities, regardless of whether they receive federal funds (Flexer, 1996; Frank & Wade, 1993).

FERPA protects the confidentiality of student records at the postsecondary institution. Only persons with a legitimate reason can view the student's records or those given express permission by the student to do so. FERPA also gives the students the right to access their records and to challenge information contained in the record (HEATH Resource Center, 1995).

Although section 504 and the ADA require postsecondary institutions to provide equal access to their regular programs and prohibits the institution from making preadmission inquiry regarding a student's disability, once the student has been admitted, the student *alone* is responsible for self-identifying and providing the required documentation. Postsecondary institutions are not under any obligation to provide accommodations *until the student* contacts the college Office of Disability Services (ODS) (or the person on campus who is responsible for providing services) *and* provides the required documentation. This procedure must be followed at the start of each term/quarter/semester. Decisions concerning the exact accommodations to be provided are determined on an individual basis. Accommodations are then negotiated between the postsecondary

service provider and the student. The law states that the institution should provide effective accommodations based on the identified needs of the student, which means that the student's individual preference for a particular accommodation does not define the nature and level of services that should be provided (Heyward, 1996). However, students who are aware of the accommodations they need and who have the ability to self-advocate are in a better position to have their individual needs met.

Demands and Supports in Postsecondary Environments

Understanding legal foundations, rights and responsibilities, and the postsecondary options that are available to students provide the transition team with a basis for developing some transition goals leading to the outcome selected by the student (Webster, 1999). As the team studies the various options, they should help the student also become aware of the ways in which the various postsecondary environments differ from one another and from the high school environment. An example of differences between high school and college demands is shown in Table 16–4. In addition to assisting the student in understanding her or his own disability and knowing that she or he will have to self-identify and seek out support services in postsecondary settings, the team's understanding of the performance expectations of the individual in postsecondary environments forms the basis for additional transition goals. As the information provided under the legal rights and responsibilities section, as well as in this section suggest, students seeking postsecondary degrees will have to be much more independent, responsible, and self-motivated in college than they were in high school. Institutional support services are available, in accord with the federal requirements discussed, but students will have to know what each school offers and how to access the various resources. The students need to understand that they will no longer have a team guiding

TABLE 16–4

Differences Between High School and College

	High School	College
Responsibility	Teachers, counselors, and principals are responsible for providing students with support services.	The student is responsible for requesting assistance and advice when needed.
Class time	Students sit in class for 6 hours per day for 180 days, which totals 1,080 hours per year.	Students sit in class 12 to 15 hours per week, 15 weeks per semester. This totals about 450 hours per school year.
Tests	Tests are given weekly or at the end of a chapter, and quizzes are given frequently.	There will be fewer tests, 2 to 3 each semester per class and they will cover more material, perhaps 4 to 6 chapters.
Study time	Homework ranges between 1 to 3 hours per day.	A general rule of thumb is at least 2 hours of homework for every hour spent in class; 3 to 5 hours of homework daily.
Knowledge acquisition	Information is provided mostly through in-class resources, assigned reading, and classroom discussion. Out-of-class research is minimal.	Course work requires more library work and writing; longer papers are required as well as research.
Assignments	Assignments are broken down into step-by-step tasks.	Instructions may be less specific and some may only be given on the syllabus at the beginning of the semester. Students decide how they will complete the task.
Grades	Classroom attendance and participation contributes to grades with numerous quizzes, tests, and homework assignments. Class may be changed for some students with IEPs.	Grades are based on fewer tests and assignments. Attendance is not always a requirement. Students may need a certain GPA to move ahead. All students meet same class standards.
Teachers	Teachers often take attendance, check notebooks, put information on the chalkboard. They monitor progress and will offer assistance when needed. They directly impart knowledge and facts.	Instructors often lecture nonstop and do not always teach from the text. Students are expected to learn from outside readings and research. Students monitor their own progress and need for help.
Parent role	Parents are often advocates and work with teachers and counselors to assure the student is being supported academically.	Parent is a mentor and works with the student to offer support and guidance.
Freedom	Much of the student's time is structured by parents, teachers, and other adults.	Students structure their own time among academics, work, and extracurricular activities. They make their own decisions about schedules, class attendance, and studying.

Source: Adapted from: MacKillop, J. (1996). *Ladders to success: A student's guide to school after high school.* Puget Sound, WA: Puget Sound Educational Service District.

them; will probably not have an IEP (individualized education plan, although some colleges do provide these); may have to pay for extra help, such as tutoring services; and will need to understand all the other differences between their current environment and the various postsecondary settings available.

Critical Point Many college professors are unfamiliar with various types of accommodations. Therefore, a student who has the knowledge and ability to self-advocate will be more likely to get their needs met.

CASE STUDY

Succeeding in College Requires More Than Mere Academics—Michelle's Story

Due to my situation, which is a so-called disability known as cerebral palsy, my schedule and life have always been very structured. Therefore, I have been forced to develop time management skills. I need assistance with daily personal hygiene and eating. I am not able to take early classes or late night classes, unless I am enrolled in the same class as my attendant. To make it easier on both of us, they either work the shift before or after that class.

I have 11 personal attendants who assist me in my everyday life. It is very difficult to find people to work the early and late hour shifts, due to the fact that everyone needs sleep. We all have our own lives and I don't want to impede on other people's lives because the people who work for me most of the time are also my friends. I care about their lives as a friend and not only as an employer. Those special bonds that I form with assistants because I need so much help with personal things don't grow unless you are forced to work with them a lot or to take the time to spend quality time with one another. If that kind of friendship does not exist, I feel that it takes a toll on the working relationship, which leads me to my next point. I had to terminate someone's position today.

Lucky for me, I did not really consider her a close friend as of yet. It is very hard to reprimand my friends or to terminate their employment. I terminated her employment because this is the first se-

mester she had worked for me, and she had already asked for approximately 6 days off, only giving me 4 days' notice. They were all out-of-town trips, so she knew about them ahead of time. Normally, what we do when a person wants to take off is post a note in my room and then whoever chooses can sign up to take the shift. But for some reason, this person did not understand this concept. At the beginning of every semester, I give each attendant a phone list of all the other attendants' numbers. When they want to take off, they either post a sign or call each other.

The situation today affected my time management plan for the day. That is, because I had to take time out of my schedule to e-mail several attendants to explain the situation and to find someone to fill the shifts. The person whose employment was terminated works both Saturday and Sunday mornings. That shift is really important because I need to get out of bed. For the time being, I am going on a week-to-week basis with that shift. It may get a little harder to manage my time as I get further into my college career, due to class times. However, I made it this far, so I feel that with the help of all my friends and family, I can do pretty much anything.

I do most of my homework on my computers. I am able to type myself, but only six words per minute. In order to utilize my time in a better fashion, I normally dictate to my personal attendants, while they type for me. I also have all my textbooks on audiotapes through the Library for the Blind and Dyslexic. I have a visual perception problem, which means I cannot follow one line of text. It is caused by the cerebral palsy. The muscles in my eyes are weak, so they tend to stray off the line. Sometimes bigger print helps, but not always. It depends how close the lines are to each other.

As for my books on tape, my nightly attendant shift is from 7:00 to 11 P.M. During that shift I have to eat dinner, dictate any typing and take a shower. So, usually, when I have a chapter to listen to, I listen to it after my attendant leaves. I leave a little light on and over the 3 years I have been at Kent, I have programmed myself to stay awake. That is just another challenge that comes with cerebral palsy and having to manage my time. During the day, I'm able to spend up to 4 hours alone in my room, although there are always people in the hall. Those times when I'm alone in my room is another chance I get to listen to my books on tape.

During the day, I either take the vans from class to class or have my attendants walk with me. I don't like to walk by myself because of my visual perception problems. I also have trouble seeing curb cutouts and different elevations of land. Also, because I have been in an electric wheelchair since I was 7 years old and drive it so much, I have developed tendinitis. Therefore, when I have an attendant with me, I normally train her to drive for me. My tendinitis has gotten worse this semester, so having someone drive for me now is basically a requirement. We all have those instructions from my physical therapist at the health center. That is another thing that I am required to fit into my schedule. I go to therapy twice a week, for an hour each session. It helps me to assist my attendants when they are doing a transfer or helping to move me from one place to another. It also helps me with my stress level. A big part of cerebral palsy is something called "spasticity." It is the contraction and loosening of muscles. How tight my muscles are depends greatly on my mood or how much stress I'm under. My muscles also contract when I get excited or scared. They even contract when I just talk in general because my stomach diaphragm muscles don't work. So, it takes lots of effort to get air out. To get words out, I have to put every muscle into the effort of talking. Cerebral palsy is caused by a lack of oxygen to the brain, which occurred some time during the birthing process. There are several different variations of it, but in my case, of course, I am not affected cognitively.

There are a lot of people on campus affected with cerebral palsy and I just happen to be one of those who are the most affected physically. To go out with friends also is hard, if I don't go out with someone who works for me, during the normal time that person is scheduled to work, or with someone who's just a friend and doesn't work for me. I have to schedule people around times when I want to have fun. This is very maddening sometimes, but it's an everyday part of life! It's also part of life that some of my friends and I can't drive. All of these things I feel and know because I live my life, and it greatly affects the way I manage my time!

Another part of managing my time in my social life is something I do with a group of friends who are known as the GPC. It stands for gimp power coalition. A "gimp" is slang for someone with a physical challenge, to put it simply. I rely on this coalition throughout my everyday life at Kent to support me in any good times and bad that come along with the challenges that we have. Once a month, our GPC has a movie night; sometimes we end up watching the movies we rent and sometimes we don't because that is the one time in the month when we all get together and just talk or vent if we need to. I feel that I'm a very lucky person because I'm one of the few people whom I know is a part of two coalitions. I have a very strong GPC at home for all through school I was integrated with other people with physical challenges.

Some of my friends who are part of the Kent GPC come from different backgrounds and don't have a very strong GPC at home. That is why I feel very fortunate; otherwise, I would not be able to go through my everyday life anywhere at this time in my life without being a part of either one of my GPCs. As a result, being a part of these groups is so important in my life, which is just one more thing that affects my time management in everyday life.

(*Michelle Marcellus, Junior, Consumer Studies Major, Kent State University*)

Disability Support Services in Postsecondary Settings

Although legally all colleges and universities must provide access and reasonable accommodations, the ways in which the services are provided will vary among institutions (HEATH, 1997; Scott, 1996). These services range along a continuum from those where services are practically nonexistent to campuses that offer extensive, comprehensive services (Brinckerhoff, Shaw, & McGuire, 1993). Some colleges offer "college experience" summer programs for high school students with disabilities (Serebreni, Rumrill, Mullins, & Gordon, 1993) in addition to summer orientations for incoming freshmen (Scott, 1996). As postsecondary institutions and programs can differ in a variety of ways, as can the individual student's strengths, interests, and needs, the key lies in finding a good match between the two.

Critical Point   Research has shown that services and accommodations provided vary by type and size of the institution. Public 2- and 4-year institutions were more likely to provide a service or accommodation for students with disabilities than their counterparts in the private sector as were medium and larger sized institutions compared to smaller ones (National Center for Education Statistics, 1999b).

Students who are knowledgeable about their legal rights and aware of the mandated services available for them will have a more realistic expectation about what kinds of help they may expect in college. For transition planning purposes, it is important for prospective students to contact the Office for Students with Disabilities (OSD) at each school that they may be considering in order to determine the best fit. The Council for the Advancement of Standards in Higher Education (Miller, 1997) described the mission of disability support service programs as being twofold:

1. assurance that qualified students with disabilities have equal access to all institutional programs and services; and

2. advocate responsibly the needs of students with disabilities to the campus community.

Types of Services Offered

The array of services to students, staffing patterns, and the degree of administrative support varies widely among institutions of higher education. One issue common to all institutions is that their requirement to provide disability-related services begins when students request services. Types of services and accommodations specifically for students with disabilities cited in the literature include:

(a) summer or presemester specialized orientation programs; (b) individualized counseling and advising; (c) priority registration and/or reduced course-loads; (d) course substitutions, course waivers, and modified materials, program, or degree requirements; (e) taped textbooks, lectures, and the allowance of tape recorders in the classroom; (f) services of adjunct personnel such as notetak-

Many life-long skills are developed at college

ers, proofreaders, typists, readers, interpreters, mobility guides; (g) alternative testing accommodations such as untimed, individualized, or oral examinations; (h) assistance with study skills, self- and time management; (i) adaptive and regular technological assistance (e.g., calculators, Braille devices, reading machines, computer keyboard modifications, augmentative communication devices, modified word processors, modified telephones); and (j) accessibility adjustments, such as the removal of architectural barriers, designed parking areas, transportation assistance, and barrier guide sheets (Gajar, 1998, p. 391).

Institutional resources which are available to all students also may provide benefits to students with disabilities. Specific ways which generic services may be of special benefit to students with disabilities are shown in Table 16–5.

Critical Point   The range of support services differs among various postsecondary settings on a continuum from minimal to extensive.

College Climate

Colleges vary widely in terms of their missions, admission requirements, costs, accessibility,

TABLE 16–5

Postsecondary Institutional Resources and Their Benefits to Students with Disabilities

Resource	Function (Miller, 1997)	Benefits to Students with Disabilities
Academic advising (advising center, faculty advisor)	To assist students in developing meaningful education plans which are compatible with their life goals	1. Serve as either primary or supplemental source of academic advisement to students 2. May serve as other source for priority registration for students who are eligible 3. Source of information regarding academic policies, grading systems, and academic probation/suspension policies 4. May be resource to negotiate less than full-time status in order to provide full-time success 5. May be resource to discuss and negotiate course substitutions in particular content areas (e.g., foreign languages, math) 6. Good source of referral to other campus resources such as the tutoring center aimed at promoting student academic success
Admission/enrollment management office	Recruitment and evaluation of student applicants to the institution. In some instances, retention responsibilities also are involved	1. Serve as the initial contact point regarding information for students with disabilities (college forms, campus visitation days)
Adult learners/ commuter student services	To respond to the diverse needs of adult and commuting students in order to promote their full participation in the institution's total education process	1. May be source of seminar and programs on topics of interest to adult learners 2. May offer a campus facility such as a lounge/kitchen/study area for commuting students 3. Source of information and referral services and peer support. Since students with disabilities are typically older than other college students, this may be a good opportunity to interact with students who have similar concerns regarding child care, strategies for academic success, time management, and concerns about academic and social support
Career planning and placement	To assist students in defining and accomplishing personal and academic goals	1. Provision of career counseling, including analysis of interests, aptitude, abilities, desired lifestyle; and awareness of career choices 2. Source of occupational information regarding opportunities for co-op, internships, summer and part-time jobs 3. Provision of job placement counseling and referral 4. Assistance with résumé development, job search, strategies, and on-campus interviews 5. Source of graduate/professional school information as well as entrance exam preparation 6. Possible source of outreach programs and services specifically designed for students with disabilities

(*continued*)

TABLE 16–5

(Continued)

Resource	Function (Miller, 1997)	Benefits to Students with Disabilities
Counseling services	To assist students in defining and accomplishing personal and academic goals	1. Individual and/or group counseling in areas of personal, educational, career development/vocational choice, interpersonal relationship, family social problems 2. Possible source of psychological assessments and other assessments 3. Counseling support to help students access and overcome specific needs in education preparation
Health services	To provide health services which may include clinical services and health promotion/education (Clary, 1998)	1. Source of health education on such topics as wellness, drug/alcohol, self health, nutrition, and stress management 2. Possible resource for students with chronic health conditions to receive assistance for such specialized areas as medication management and monitoring, pain management, and liaison with primary home physician
Learning assistance center	To provide instruction and services that will support students in the development of skills necessary for their effective performance in the classroom	1. May serve as a resource for the provision of developmental services in the following areas: content tutoring, learning skills instruction, computer-assisted instruction, diagnosis of affective and cognitive skills, supplemental course instruction
Student activities office	To complement the academic program of studies and enhance the overall education experience of students through social, cultural, intellectual, recreational, and governance programs	1. Students may be exposed to various cultures and experiences, philosophy and political ideas, and diverse art and musical forums 2. Students may be aided in their awareness of the availability of campus facilities and other services 3. Students may be afforded opportunities to engage in workshop and public forums which raise awareness of issues affecting diverse populations, including individuals with disabilities 4. Students may be assisted with opportunities to enhance their leadership, decision making, and other skills 5. Student and campus organizations with direct ties to specific interests of students with disabilities may be available for participation and leadership opportunities (e.g., Organization for Students with Disabilities, Council for Exceptional Children, ADA Steering Committee)

TABLE 16–5

(*Concluded*)

Resource	Function (Miller, 1997)	Benefits to Students with Disabilities
Student financial aid office	Administers /coordinates institutional financial aid programs according to applicable federal and state guidelines and institutional policies that guarantee each student equal access to financial assistance	1. Provides detailed information and application forms for a variety of grants, loans, scholarships, and student employment 2. Source of student workshops on financial aid application procedures and scholarship opportunities 3. May serve as fiscal liaison with external sources of student financial assistance, such as the Office of Vocational Rehabilitation (OVR) in Blind and Visual Services (BVS) 4. Source of written notification to students regarding relevant eligibility policies, such as the academic progress requirement and grade-point average requirements 5. Source of financial aid information for students who are considering graduate and/or professional school 6. May be the office responsible for the assignment of student employment on campus, including such programs as the federal work-study program, employment programs, and off-campus job location and development programs 7. May offer emergency financial assistance (e.g., book loan programs, dire need fund)
Student orientation programs	To assist new students in making a successful transition into the institution with an emphasis on academic and social integration	1. Students receive information regarding relevant campus resources and programs such as the Office of Services for Students with Disabilities 2. Student retention is enhanced through referral to appropriate sources and academic advising 3. "External" orientation opportunities may be made available via credit-bearing orientation courses or "freshmen seminar," which offers an in-depth focus on such topics as study skills, basic career exploration, campus research, student roles and responsibilities, campus research, and student assessment opportunities

faculty and staff, student body, courses and programs offered, community and financial resources (including opportunities for financial aid), size, locations, athletics, and social activities (HEATH Resource Center, 1995; Kezar, 1997a; Scott, 1996). For example, research has

suggested that a student's cognitive and academic gains are enhanced in an institution where there is greater interaction between faculty and peers and where teaching, as opposed to research, is a priority (Astin, 1993). Traditionally, faculty with a research orientation tend to be in larger public universities, which often place less emphasis on student development and undergraduate education in general (Kezar, 1997b). However, according to Kezar (1997b), many of these institutions have recently begun to focus more upon undergraduate education and student development. More important than the actual size of the university or college is the degree to which a student participates in clubs, organizations, and activities and the ties they develop with a specific department (Pascarella & Terenzini, 1991). Research has also shown that one of the strongest predictors of a student's satisfaction with his or her postsecondary experience is leaving home to attend college (Astin, 1993), as students living away from home tend to be more involved in their campus activities. This correlation, however, does not apply to many students from ethnic minorities (Astin, 1993).

The racial and gender makeup of an institution also may impact upon the college experience. There is evidence to suggest, for example, that women's colleges enhance students' career attainment and socioecomic aspirations (Pascarella & Terenzini, 1991). Also, although historically black colleges and universities only enroll 16% of all African-American students, each year roughly one-third of all African Americans who get a college degree graduate from these colleges (Gray, 1996). In addition, the 31 tribal colleges in the United States and Canada provide academic, vocational, and technical programs (similar to those at mainstream institutions) to over 25,000 Americans from 250 federally recognized tribes (Monette, 1997). Attending these types of schools also may offer more mentors and role models and a greater likelihood of completing degrees (Kezar, 1997a). However, perseverance and social support can facilitate the success of minority students in institutions where the majority of students are from a different culture.

Critical Point   Students need to match their personal preferences and needs to the characteristics of the institution.

Finding the Right Fit

Research has shown that a student's motivation, interactions with faculty and other students, and involvement in campus activities have a greater impact upon educational outcomes than the type of institution one chooses (Kezar, 1997a; Tinto, 1993). Although selecting an institution depends on the student's interests, strengths, and needs, some institutions may better provide the types of environments in which an individual will thrive and succeed. Many high schools have college counselors who may assist the student and his or her team in choosing a postsecondary school. The key is finding a good match between the setting and the individual.

Awareness of the types of postsecondary options available, the student's rights and responsibilities, and the demands of college life is a first step toward providing an outcome-based transition program for students with disabilities. With this background knowledge in place, the transition team, including the student, can begin the process of devising a secondary curriculum that fits the chosen goal. Initially, selected goals may change or be modified along the way, but team members continue to have in mind what choices are available. The process of helping a student to reach her or his goal is grounded in the four principles of IDEA: *Transition services must* (1) *be based on students' needs, taking into account their preferences and interests;* (2) *be designed within an outcome-oriented process;* (3) *be a coordinated set of activities; and* (4) *promote movement from school to postschool activities.* These principles form the bases of assessment, curriculum, instructional methodology, experiential activities, and formative/summative evaluation of the transition student's secondary education.

Four Essential Elements of Transition

The transition planning process should be guided by the interests, needs, and preferences of students and their families. Family participation in this process is crucial as families not only influence career aspirations (Super, 1990; Symanski, 1994), but they also play a powerful role in developing future visions, which are related to career and lifestyle option (Morningstar, Turnbull, & Turnbull, 1996). Educators also must be aware of attitudes, values, and beliefs from the students' and families' cultural perspective in order to develop strategies to promote success in postsecondary educational settings (AHEAD, 1998). For example, some cultures may value collectivism or the group more strongly than individualism (Greenfield, 1994; Kim & Choi, 1994). Therefore, focusing upon how a postsecondary education could increase the status and standard of living for the extended family or group may increase the students' and families' motivation more than emphasizing the benefits to the individuals.

Determining Student Need and Interest

Interest Surveys and Needs Assessments

Determining the student's needs, interests, and preferences should begin early and continue throughout the student's school career. Teachers who effectively identify student's expectations, choices, and preferences through observations, conducting interviews and assessments with the students and significant others, are more successful in facilitating a positive transition to adulthood (Wehmeyer, Agran, & Hughes, 1998). Formal assessments such as the following provide an introduction to the idea of matching information about careers to an individual.

Critical Point   Identifying the student's needs, preferences, and interests is at the heart of good transition planning.

  The Self-directed Search (Holland, 1994). A self-rating instrument that aids the individual in determining career options that best match his or her personality, interests, values, skills, and abilities.

APTICOM (Vocational Research Institute). A desktop microcomputer that assists in assessing aptitudes, job interests, work-related language, and mathematical skill level. APTICOM creates a personal employment profile with recommendations.

Discover (ACT Test Administration). A computer program that assesses where the student is in personal career planning and includes Career Journey Inventory, Abilities Inventory, Uniact Interest Inventory, and Experience Inventory. The assessment process begins in the ninth grade and is completed by the twelfth grade.

S.A.G.E. (System of Assessment and Group Evaluation). A vocational assessment that includes four separate modules: Vocational Interests Inventory, Vocational Aptitude Battery, Cognitive and Conceptual Abilities Test, and Assessment of Work Attitudes.

Assessment of student needs and interests also can be incorporated into a student's academic performance by (1) using checklists based on subject areas and the strengths, needs, experiences, and skills needed to be successful in both high school and postsecondary education settings; (2) obtaining and recording information through observation of the student by teachers, family members, and others who are well acquainted with the student; and (3) recording information through interviews concerning academic, functional academics, and vocational and community experiences (Duffey et al., 1996); and (4) having student-teacher conferencing regarding ongoing classroom work as it applies to team-selected goals.

Student-Directed IEP/ITPs

The student's active participation in the team process is central to transition planning and decision making, especially if students' needs and interests are to be taken into account. By providing opportunities for students to make meaningful choices and to demonstrate preferences in what, how, and why they learn, the students' can acquire the skills of self-determination (Aune, 1991, Halpern, 1994; Sitlington & Frank, 1990) that are crucial for success in postsecondary education. For example, research has suggested that when learners are provided a rationale for why they are learning, student motivation and participation in activities increases (Deci & Chandler, 1986). Participation in meaningful transition planning and student satisfaction with school instruction is a strong predictor of participation in postsecondary education (Halpern, Yovanoff, Doren, & Benz, 1995). Although the mere physical presence of students at their IEP/ITP meetings may meet the statutory requirements of IDEA on its own, it fails to meet either the spirit or the intent of IDEA (Weymeyer & Ward, 1995), which calls for student participation to the greatest extent possible. Actively participating and having responsibility for developing transition goals will increase the opportunity for students (1) to become knowledgeable about the functional limitations of their disability, (2) to develop a sense of independence and perseverance, (3) to engage in problem solving and conflict resolution, (4) to develop self-advocacy and self-determination skills (deFur et al., 1996), and (5) to develop greater self-discipline and self-management skills (Shaw, Brinkerhoff, Kistler, & McGuire, 1991). Several examples of student-directed IEP programs are available and could be adapted as needed or used as guides in helping teams to learn how to empower students. (See Table 16–6.)

Critical Point Student participation is crucial for developing the skills that are necessary for postsecondary success.

Far too often students become the passive recipient of instructions and services and have no role in determining their learning needs and goals, or in evaluating their progress (Van Reusen & Bos, 1994). The disservice this does to students who will soon find themselves in a

postsecondary program cannot be overstated. At the postsecondary level, the students themselves bear a significant responsibility for the impact of their own college experience (Pascarella & Terernzini, 1991) and, therefore, students who have taken a more active role in their high school education will be in a better position to succeed in a postsecondary program. The different social, academic, and independent living expectations demanded in most postsecondary settings (Shaw et al., 1991) means that students who are college-bound, for example, will require more than just academic preparation to meet the challenges that lie ahead. Becoming actively involved in the transition process provides an ideal venue for students to become knowledgeable about the functional limitations of their disability; to develop a sense of independence and perseverance; and to engage in problem solving, which is essential in developing the crucial skills of self-determination and self-advocacy (deFur et al., 1996); as well as greater self-discipline and self-management (Shaw et al., 1991). If students are to succeed in postsecondary programs, they must be provided with the appropriate training that will enhance their skills in self-determination, identifying postschool goals, and choosing appropriate educational experiences (Aune, 1991; Halpern, 1994; Sitlington & Frank, 1990). Participation in meaningful transition planning and student satisfaction with school instruction is a strong predictor of participation in postsecondary education (Halpern, Yovanoff, Doren, & Benz, 1995).

Career Exploration and Planning
The School-to-Work Opportunities Act (STWOA) of 1994 calls upon schools to provide instructional programs and career guidance and planning that will result in assisting students in determining a career major that integrates academic and occupational content, with a view to enhancing the students' chances of succeeding in postsecondary programs and future employment

TABLE 16–6

Student-Directed IEP Programs

Program	Description
ChoiceMaker Self-Determination Transition Curriculum (Martin & Marshall, 1995)	Teaches self-determination through student self-management of the IEP process and includes three components: choosing goals, expressing goals, and taking action. Students learn to lead their IEP meetings to the greatest extent possible, based on their individual strengths. The materials were field-tested and revised with students with behavioral and learning disabilities from several school districts.
Whose Future Is It Anyway? (Wehmeyer & Kelchner, 1995)	Introduces the student to the concept of transition planning and enables them to take an active role in the planning process through a curriculum that focuses around the constructs involved in self-determination. A *Coach's Guide* (Wehmeyer & Lawrence, 1995a) is available to assist the person that the student has identified as the coach. The materials were field-tested on almost 60 students with mental retardation and other cognitive and developmental disabilities. The level of support required by students to complete the activities varies according to individual strengths and needs.
Next S.T.E.P.: Student Transition and Educational Planning (Halpern, Herr, Wolf, Lawson, Doren, & Johnson, 1997)	Teaches and engages students in the necessary skills involved in successful transition planning through four instructional modules (getting started, self-exploration and self-evaluation, developing goals and activities, and putting a plan into place). Includes videos and printed materials for teachers, students, and their families. The materials were field-tested and validated with more than 1,000 students with disabilities.
Self-Advocacy Strategy for Education and Transition Planning (Van Reusen, Bos, Schumaker, & Deshler, 1994)	Teaches both student-directed transition planning and self-advocacy skills. The program emphasizes the importance of self-advocacy in increasing student motivation and empowerment through seven instructional stages using the I-PLAN strategy (inventory your strengths, needs, goals, and needed accommodations; provide your inventory information; listen and respond; ask questions; and name your goals). The authors have demonstrated that students with disabilities who have used the I-PLAN strategy increased their motivation and participation in transition planning.
TAKE CHARGE for the Future (Powers, 1996)	A collaborative model that promotes student involvement in education and transition planning through: skill facilitation (i.e., achievement, partnership, and coping skills), mentoring with same-gender adults who have had similar experiences, peer support activities, and parent support in promoting their child's active involvement. The model was adapted from a validated approach (TAKE CHARGE) used to increase self-determination skills in both students with and without disabilities
Goal Action Planning (Turnbull, Blue-Banning, Anderson, Turnbull, Seaton, & Dinas, 1996)	Aimed at students with mental retardation and developmental disabilities who need extensive supports in order to participate actively in their education planning. Strategies used are adapted from future planning models and involve the student, their families, professionals, and other interested parties in identifying the student's dreams and hopes, resultant goals, and the resources needed to achieve those goals. An action plan is then devised across eight areas of daily life. The program has been field-tested and validated with students with significant disabilities.

Source: Adapted from: Wehmeyer, M. L., Agran, M., & Hughes, C. (1998). *Teaching self-determined students with disabilities: Basic skills for successful transition.* Baltimore: Paul H. Brookes.

(Benz & Kochhar, 1996). In addition to the various career interest inventories discussed earlier and strategies for career exploration in Table 16–7, a vocational assessment also can aid students in deciding upon an appropriate postsecondary program to facilitate their future employment goals.

Critical Point   Students need focused, structured instruction related to career guidance.

Although career development should begin as early as elementary school (Benz & Kochhar, 1996; Clark, Carlson, Fisher, Cook, & D'Alonzo, 1991), students should begin formally to explore the world of work no later than middle school, as they begin to discover their own talents and abilities, as well as career areas of interests or career majors. By exploring career options and reflecting upon career interests, students will be in a better position to understand what kinds of postsecondary programs can best meet their individual needs. In addition, students and their transition teams need to be aware of trends in the labor market and future employment opportunities in their areas of interest and strengths. In order for career planning to be effective, the transition team must develop partnerships among the student, educators (including career guidance services/school counselors), and community-based service providers, such as vocational rehabilitation personnel (deFur et al., 1996).

Career Plans and Portfolios

Like a transition plan, individual career plans (ICPs) (which should be developed no later than the eighth grade by all students) involve a backward planning process that should assist students, not only in selecting appropriate courses for the remainder of secondary school (Gray, 1996), but also allow the student and transition team to evaluate and make necessary adjustments continually in light of the student's performance. For example, is the student's GPA (grade-point average) (or another indicator of academic performance) com-

patible with the ICP and postsecondary program goals? If not, the transition team may need to consider other options, such as additional supports in class or a change in the postsecondary program goals. The ICP also should include both the academic, community supports and services needed by the students to succeed in their education programs (Getzel & Kregal, 1996). Activities outside school, such as hobbies, clubs, and organizations also can help the student to determine areas of interest (as well as what they do not like doing) that will impact their career planning.

Critical Point   Individual career plans allow for continual monitoring and adjustments of the secondary program.

Career portfolios can serve multiple purposes, including use of examples of schoolwork as an informal résumé to determine a student's likes and interests, a career counseling tool with student and families (Sarkees-Wircenski & Wircenski, 1994), and an expanded version of a résumé containing relevant information needed in applying for postsecondary programs.

Identifying Goals and Preparing Students for Postsecondary Outcomes

Since Will (1983) first defined transition as a bridge to adulthood, the main goal of the transition process has been achieving positive postschool outcomes (DeStefano & Wermuth, 1992; Halpern, 1992). In order to accomplish this successfully, goals must first be identified, along with the necessary instructional activities, supports, and services that will facilitate making those goals a reality. Once a student and family have identified a potential postsecondary program as a primary transition goal, and understand what demands and supports are available, the student and the transition team can begin to identify further the activities needed in order to reach that goal. The roles and responsibilities of students, teachers, and

TABLE 16–7

Career Exploration Activities

Activities for Enhancing Career Exploration

- Investigate the possibility of service learning programs which provide community service in nonpaid voluntary positions. These programs can increase the relevance of academic learning by giving the students opportunities to apply knowledge and skills while making a contribution to their local community. Academic credit may or may not be arranged depending on the student's field of study.
- Arrange for job shadowing where the student visits a professional at work to observe one or more positions. The student can get a more realistic view of the essential functions of occupational areas of interest. Experiences vary in time depending on the amount of time employers can provide, as well as the interest of the student.
- Investigate work experience opportunities (which are an expanded version of job shadowing) where the student works at a particular job for a set period of time, generally 2 to 6 weeks. These can be paid or nonpaid but provide an opportunity for the student to explore the demands of the job in greater depth.
- If appropriate, encourage the student to work a part-time or summer job which also can teach the student responsibility, reliability, and interpersonal skills, as well as provide a way to save and learn how to manage money for college.
- Arrange informational interviews where the student meets with people working in careers in which the student has expressed an interest. By asking questions about a particular occupation or companies, the students can gain a personal perspective on their career interests. Work with the career or guidance counselor and the student to generate possible questions before the interview.
- Establish mentors and networks in the local business community (all the preceding activities are a good way to begin the process).
- Work with the school guidance or career counselor who should have access to a variety of career interest inventories and vocational assessments.
- Schedule a career exploration class if available at your school.
- Use the school library, career or guidance center, and public library as a resource for books and pamphlets which provide information on a variety of careers and the latest trends in the labor market, as well as describe different types of college programs. Call or write to them directly to request a catalog.
- Link the student's hobbies or leisure activities to potential careers.
- Develop a career portfolio (see text for description and possible uses).
- Encourage the student to discuss career options with family and friends.
- Explore possible career options using the U.S. Department of Labor's *Dictionary of Occupational Titles* (1991) (which classifies jobs based on three primary types of activities; jobs that focus upon working with people, data skills, or machines and tools) and the *Occupational Outlook Handbook* (1994).
- Explore postsecondary programs that offer internships and/or cooperative education programs. An internship is a time-limited intensive learning experience outside the traditional classroom, where students are placed in supervised work-based learning situations with employers for planned learning activities. Academic credits may be given, depending on the student's academic program. Cooperative education programs work with students, faculty, and employers to help students clarify career and academic goals and expand classroom studies by participating in paid, practical work experiences. Academic credit can be arranged in schools offering this option.

461

TABLE 16–8

Roles and Responsibilities for Students Involved in Planning Postsecondary Outcomes

Student Roles and Responsibilities
Understand the nature of their disability, including its effect on learning and work.
Establish realistic goals after identifying strengths, needs, preferences, and interests.
Present a positive self-image by stressing strengths while understanding functional limitations due to the disability.
Know how, when, and where to discuss and request appropriate accommodations.
Develop personal qualities, such as self-assessment, risk-taking, and perseverance.
Develop and work on the use of appropriate social skills.
Develop and use effective studying, test preparation, test-taking, time management, and note-taking strategies.
Explore a range of postsecondary options and entrance requirements and deadlines for admission.
Select courses that will meet the necessary requirements.
Actively participate in and prepare for the postsecondary application process.
Maintain an ongoing personal file or portfolio that includes school and medical records, IEPs, résumés, and samples of academic work. Consider people to ask for recommendations, such as teachers, counselors, employers, and so on.
Identify and access resources that will provide needed support such as getting to know your career or guidance counselor and other college resources available at your school that can provide assistance.
Investigate different ways to save money for a postsecondary education.
Investigate the availability of financial aid from federal, state, local, and private sources, as well as scholarships.
Talk to adults in a variety of professions to see what they like and dislike about their jobs and what kind of education is needed for different kinds of jobs.
Get involved in school and/or community-based extracurricular activities that you find interesting or that enable you to explore career interests.
Practice self-advocacy in your classrooms and at your IEP meeting.

Source: Adapted from *Latest Developments* (1994) AHEAD.

parents shown in Tables 16–8, 16–9, and 16–10 suggest a coordinated curriculum which goes beyond course work and ensures that the student acquires skills in other developmental areas. Such a curriculum requires careful planning and ongoing communication among team members, and means that student learning and practicing skills must take place outside the school, as well as in the classroom. In addition, some role-release by teachers and parents must occur so that the student takes on more responsibility.

Critical Point   Postschool goals guide assessment and planning.

Backward Planning Based on Identified Postschool Goals

Once postschool goals have been identified, the student and his or her transition team must begin to ask questions, such as (1) What knowledge and skills are needed to make the transition successful to a postsecondary academic or technical/vocational program? (2) What knowledge and skills does the student have at present?

TABLE 16–9

Roles and Responsibilities for Families Involved in Planning Postsecondary Outcomes

Parent/Guardian Roles and Responsibilities
Encourage their child to develop independent decision making and self-advocacy skills.
Become involved in transition planning and ensure that their child is also involved and actively participating in the process.
Help their child to identify their strengths, needs, preferences, and interests and to develop realistic goals.
Encourage their child to develop future education plans and to explore realistic postsecondary options.
Help their child to select high school courses that meet postsecondary requirements.
Collaborate with secondary and postsecondary staff in making decisions concerning programs, services, and resources.
Help their child to collect and maintain their ongoing personal file or portfolio that includes school and medical records, IEPs, résumés, and samples of academic work.
Encourage their child to read independently, as well as to explore career interests through work or community service experiences.
Help their child to investigate the availability of financial aid from federal, state, local, and private sources, as well as scholarships.
Communicate confidence in their child's ability to be successful in a postsecondary environment.

Source: Adapted from *Latest Developments* (1994) AHEAD.

TABLE 16–10

Roles and Responsibilities for Educators Involved in Planning Postsecondary Outcomes

Secondary School Personnel Responsibilities
Encourage students to look beyond high school toward postsecondary education by initiating, designing, and evaluating effective transition plans and coordinating services that are consistent with federal and state laws, rules, and regulations.
Form a transition team consisting of a coordinator, the student, the parent(s) and/or other family members, administrators, teachers, counselors, and related service providers.
Develop an appropriate packet of materials to document the student's secondary school program and to facilitate service delivery in a postsecondary program.
Provide administrative support, information/resources, and time to foster collaboration among team members.
Inform the student about laws, rules, and regulations that ensure her or his rights.
Provide the appropriate course selection, counseling, and academic support services to meet the individual student's needs.
Ensure the student's competency in literacy and mathematics.
Ensure that the student learns effective studying, time management, test preparation, and test-taking strategies.
Ensure that the student has the skills to self-advocate effectively and to provide opportunities for practicing these skills.

Source: Adapted from *Latest Developments* (1994) AHEAD.

(and how will they be assessed?) and (3) What knowledge and skills does the student need to acquire? (NICHCY, 1993). As postsecondary programs build upon the skills and knowledge acquired in earlier years, planning the necessary strategies to achieve the student's ultimate goal must start early. For example, a student who does not plan ahead for a college education may have difficulty in completing all the required or recommended courses that are necessary to qualify for a 4-year college or university. In addition, students may need to work on acquiring more effective independent study skills or arranging accommodations that are needed for college board or SAT testing. The key lies in the student and transition team first determining the kind of postsecondary program that best fits the student's needs and then planning backward to incorporate activities that will facilitate the achievement of that goal.

Interagency Responsibility and Linkages

Making Linkages to Appropriate Service Providers
Many services and experiences that students with disabilities will need in order to make a successful transition to postsecondary education will require the input of persons beyond the immediate personnel in schools. Establishing interagency linkages may be one of the most integral components in developing successful transition services (Halpern, Benz, & Lindstrom, 1992). Therefore, it is imperative that the transition team draw upon the expertise of all relevant school, family, and community agencies (DeStefano & Wermuth, 1992) to ensure a seamless and successful transition to postsecondary programs. Depending on the individual student's interests, preferences, and needs, this could include VR personnel, transportation agencies, disability-specific agencies, personal care attendants; Job Training Partnership Act (JTPA) personnel and vocational and/or regular education teachers; career guidance counselors, recreational thera-

pists, employers, social workers, health (including mental health) care professionals; and representatives from the relevant postsecondary program. As a student's entitlement to education and related services end once the student has left the public school system, establishing needed linkages not only benefits the student during transition planning, but makes a smooth transition to adult life (NICHCY, 1993).

Critical Point Almost three-quarters of postsecondary institutions that enrolled students with disabilities, worked either formally or informally with their state VR agencies (National Center for Educational Statistics, 1999b).

It is especially important that transition teams network with relevant postsecondary personnel who may be able to provide a wealth of information on the kinds of preparations and requirements needed to make the transition to their particular programs. This could include persons, such as admission counselors, financial aid officers, and student disability service providers. Table 16–11 provides a list of resources and activities that postsecondary personnel may be able to provide.

Promoting Positive Postsecondary Outcomes

Appropriate instructional and other transition-related services always should be designed bearing in mind promoting movement from school to postsecondary activities (NICHCY, 1993). In order to achieve the desired postschool outcomes, the transition team must remember the nature and demands of the selected postsecondary program and setting and design appropriate experiences that may go beyond the mere academic (DeStefano & Wermuth, 1992).

Selecting Courses that Meet Postsecondary Requirements
Although effective transition planning for a postsecondary program involves a wide range of ac-

TABLE 16–11

Roles and Responsibilities of Postsecondary Personnel

- Provide linkages to high schools through outreach efforts.
- Inform secondary school personnel of the prerequisites necessary for the successful transition to postsecondary options.
- Disseminate information about college preparation and the expectations associated with various postsecondary environments.
- Provide opportunities for prospective students and their families to visit the campus and to provide information about the unique features of the specific postsecondary program.
- Help students to effectively negotiate postsecondary environments.
- Offer summer orientation programs on the admissions application process, admissions requirements, and general college survival skills.
- Clarify roles of the student and the service provider in a postsecondary setting.
- Offer comprehensive orientation programs to students who have chosen to attend a particular institution.
- Help the student to use a range of academic accommodations and technical aids, such as electronic advanced organizers, texts on tape, grammar and spell checkers, and other word processing programs.
- Assist the student in evaluating her or his dependence on external supports and adjust the level of assistance when appropriate.
- Work with the student to develop appropriate social and interpersonal communication skills.
- Facilitate the development of the student's self-advocacy skills, including a realistic understanding of the functional limitation due to the disability, and how to use this information for self-understanding and advocating in a postsecondary setting.
- Foster independence through increased responsibility and opportunity for self-management.
- Encourage the student to participate in the campus social life and extracurricular community and campus activities.
- Promote the student's self-esteem and self-confidence.
- Inform the student and their families about services that postsecondary institutions provide, such as student disability services, academic, and other specialized services.
- Ensure the timely development of documentation materials in keeping with application deadlines.
- Advocate, when appropriate, on behalf of students to ensure their rights under section 504 and ADA are safeguarded.
- Negotiate "reasonable academic adjustments" with faculty and administration that will maintain the integrity of the curriculum.
- Establish written policies and procedures concerning admissions, diagnoses, accommodations, curriculum requirements, and service delivery to students with disabilities.
- Work closely with admissions officers to ensure that students with disabilities are fairly considered.
- Act as a liaison to the greater college community and inform them about serving students with disabilities.
- Provide faculty and staff development on students with disabilities.

Source: Adapted from *Latest Developments* (1994) AHEAD.

tivities, such as facilitating the student's development in self-advocacy and socialization skills (Gartin, Rumrill, & Serebreni, 1996), the student also must be academically prepared for higher education programs. Individual programs and institutions vary in their specific entry require-

ments, which is why it is important to establish links early with the perspective institution's postsecondary personnel. (See Table 16–11.) Additionally, it is important to start planning for high school classes toward the end of middle school or junior high so that the student will have a greater opportunity to complete all the necessary courses needed to qualify for the postsecondary program of his or her choice. Therefore, the transition team should work with the school guidance counselor to ensure that the student takes the appropriate required and elective courses that are needed to meet the student's postschool goals. A typical college preparatory curriculum required for admission to most 4-year institutions follows (AHEAD, 1987; HEATH Resource Center, 1997; Turner & Simmons, 1996):

- Four years of English (e.g., English, American literature, English literature, English composition, world literature)
- Three years of mathematics (e.g., algebra I and II, geometry, precalculus, trigonometry, calculus, analytic geometry, probability)
- Three years of science (e.g., earth science, biology, chemistry, physics)
- Three years of social sciences (e.g., American history, world history, American government, state history, principles of democracy)
- Two years of a foreign language (e.g., Spanish, French, German, Latin, Russian, Japanese)
- One to two years of the arts (e.g., art/studio art, visual arts, photography, music, dance, drama, speech)
- One to three years of appropriate electives (e.g., economics, psychology, statistics, computer science, communications)

For students who are interested in attending 2-year postsecondary programs, some of the preceding courses could be substituted with vocational or technical courses in the student's field of interest. However, almost all 2-year programs require basic skill knowledge in science, mathematics, English, and computer awareness. Again, it is best to work with the school guidance counselor and personnel at the institution that the student wishes to attend.

Critical Point   The transition team is responsible for developing a coordinated set of school to post-

school activities, focusing upon curricula as well as community-based learning.

Most college instructors will not accept handwritten papers so that students who possess keyboard and word processing skills will be at an advantage when starting a postsecondary program. In addition, classes in study skills, time management, and assertiveness training may prove helpful because how a student's time is spent when in a postsecondary setting is the sole responsibility of the student, not of the institution.

Community-Based Experiences

For many students with disabilities, awareness of postsecondary options and the demands to succeed in those environments may not automatically enable the student to make valid judgments of preference (DeStefano & Wermuth, 1992). However, when linked to direct community-based activities, the students, their families, teachers, and other service providers will be in a better position to determine the needs, preferences, and interests. For example, in a postsecondary institution, the students will be faced not only with academic demands, but also with different social and independent living demands, such as managing finances, buying clothing, food, and other personal needs (deFur et al., 1996). Therefore, community-based activities might involve developing interests outside school, such as engaging in work or volunteer experiences, which can teach students responsibility, reliability, interpersonal skills, and team work. Connecting school-to-work activities (a cornerstone of the School-to-Work Opportunities Act [STWOA] of 1994) contributes to a more meaningful education experience for all students (Benz & Kochher, 1996), as well as facilitates the development of career interests and goals. Working part time, which also is a good way to earn money for a postsecondary education and extracurricular activities in and outside school, can help students to explore and develop their talents and interests (in addition to being an asset to a college application). Although too many students often are forced to choose between a traditional academic college-prep track or more functional community-based learning experiences, the restructuring of schools, implicit in STWOA's "concepts and principles, offers hope that this artificial dichotomy can be reduced, if not eliminated all together" (Benz & Kochhar, 1996, p. 43).

Inclusive School Environments

Postsecondary environments, although varying in the number of supports offered to students with disabilities, basically are inclusive environments. If students are to make a successful transition, it is important that they have experiences interacting with their peers in the general population. The NLTS found that 70% of students who participated in postsecondary academic programs spent 75% of their time in regular education high school classes (U.S. Department of Education, 1995). However, research, using the same database, found that more time spent in regular education also was associated with an increased likelihood of course failure (Hebbeler, 1993). Because course failure is one of the strongest predictors of dropping out of school, the relationship between inclusive school environments and positive postschool outcomes is complex. Therefore, students with disabilities in regular education settings must be given opportunities to succeed and the necessary supports if the results are to be positive. If instruction is based on student-determined interests, preferences, and needs, then the likelihood of success in inclusive settings is greatly enhanced (Halpern, 1994; Wehmeyer et al., 1998).

Although determining social integration outcomes for postsecondary environments is value-driven (Haring & Breen, 1989), many students who experience problems in the social/interpersonal domain in high school will continue to face similar types of problems in postsecondary settings (Chadsey & Sheldon, 1998). In a study of college students who were deaf, Brown and Foster (1991) concluded that natural existing opportunities were the most ideal settings in which social integration was more likely to occur. In other words, there is a greater probability of integration occurring if the social interactions are secondary to the task rather than artificially imposed. Students with disabilities who identify a need in this domain, therefore, may have to be encouraged to take advantage of these naturally occurring activities.

Critical Point   Students with disabilities may need access to instruction in social/interpersonal relationships in an inclusive environment.

Self-Advocacy

Self-determination also includes characteristics such as self-advocacy, creativity, and independence (Durlak, Rose, & Bursuck 1994). Although well meaning in intent, persons with disabilities often are encouraged to hide their disability (Field & Hoffman, 1994) by professionals and parents alike. In addition, a desire to conform and fit in with one's peers is natural for most adolescents and young adults, and the movement to a new postschool setting provides an opportunity to escape previous labels and the stigma associated with special education and being different (deFur et al., 1996). According to Ball-Brown and Frank (1993), the latter is a major reason that many students with disabilities of color do not access support services at postsecondary institutions. However, as the students alone are responsible for disclosing their disability at postsecondary institutions, they must learn to self-advocate effectively (Brinckeroff, Shaw, & McGuire, 1992; deFur et al., 1996; Lynch & Gussel, 1996; Scott, 1996) and to realize that it is to their advantage to "own" the diagnosis of their disability, especially "hidden disabilities," such as a learning disability (Brinckeroff et al., 1992).

Critical Point   Self-determination in adult life is based on skills related to self-knowledge, self-acceptance, and self-advocacy.

Research has shown that when the skills involved in self-advocacy are systematically taught and the students are given immediate and specific feedback, along with the opportunity to practice these skills in both training and natural environments, students with disabilities can acquire, maintain, and generalize these skills (Aune, 1991; Durlak et al., 1994). Again, active participation in transition planning is one of the best ways that students can develop their self-advocacy skills (deFur et al., 1996). For example, if the student and his or her transition team decides that the student needs extended time to complete tests, then he or she should request the required accommodation with the appropriate mainstream teacher.

Self-determination involves assuming responsibility for one's goals and accomplishments (Ward, 1988). Providing students with disabilities the opportunity to self-advocate and make choices is an empowering experience and enhances the student's perseverance (deFur et al., 1996). However, self-determination also involves assuming responsibility for one's setbacks (Ward, 1988). In their study of successful adults with learning disabilities, Gerber, Ginsberg, and Reiff (1992) found that the participants gained a sense of control over their professional lives by engaging in a process of "reframing" situations in which they recognized, accepted, and understood the impact of their learning disability and how to use their unique abilities to overcome potential obstacles. The participants in the study also had developed a strong desire to succeed, along with the ability to set realistic goals and to persevere in achieving them (Gerber et al., 1992).

Enhancing Participation in Postsecondary Education

Social Aspects of a Postsecondary Education

Although the institution may provide many supports for students with disabilities, students are more likely to persevere in working toward their degree when socially integrated into the community life of the college or university as well as when they are engaged in academics. (Astin, 1993; Tinto, 1993). Even though any programs or activities supported by the college, such as sporting events or artistic performances, must be accessible to students with disabilities, as must campus transportation systems (Scott, 1996), the onus is on the student to get involved. Involvement fosters integration (Astin, 1993), so it is important that students take advantage of the variety of activities that are available on campus and in the surrounding community. Research suggests that adult students with disabilities may have poor self-esteem and interpersonal and socialization skills (Brinckeroff et al., 1993; Vogel & Forness, 1992) that may result in social isolation. Studies of interactions between college students with various disabilities and their peers without disabilities (Fichten & Ansel, 1988; Fichten, Robillard, Tagalakis, & Ansel, 1991) found that whereas students with disabilities felt comfortable around their peers without disabilities, both students with and without disabilities had more negative thoughts about interacting with students with disabilities. Although there is a lack of research regarding effective interventions for the social integration of college students with disabilities, students who are persistent, yet adaptable (Gerber et al., 1992), and who are aware of their strengths and needs in social as well as academic areas (deFur et al., 1996), may find it easier to integrate socially in campus life. Personal and group counseling (Getzel & Kregal, 1996; Vogel & Forness, 1992) also may be effective social interventions as are involvement in student support groups (Getzel & Kregal, 1996).

Critical Point   College students with disabilities were equally likely to participate in cultural and recreational activities as their nondisabled college peers (13%) (National Center for Education Statistics, 1999a).

When students start college, their new independence, new environment, and new intellectual changes often will impact the student's sense of self (Fox, Zakely, Morris, & Jundt, 1993). The opportunity arises to question some values and norms that were accepted in their family and previous environments (Fox et al., 1993). For example, experimenting with drugs and alcohol is a reality at many colleges. Although risk-taking is an essential component of self-determination (Wehmeyer et al., 1998), research has shown that persons with mild disabilities are at greater risk for substance abuse than persons without disabilities (Gajar, Goodman, & McAffee, 1995). In addition, many students with disabilities do not receive awareness education in this area (Wehmeyer et al., 1998). Therefore, it is important that students with disabilities receive information on the potential problem of substance abuse so that they will be in a position when in college to make informed decisions.

Critical Point   Students with disabilities may need specific information regarding high-risk behaviors and choices.

First-Generation College Students

First-generation college students (i.e., the first person in the family to attend college) are growing in number (Mitchell, 1997) as the need for an education beyond high school is reflected in the current labor market. Many of these students come from ethnic minority and working-class families (Fox et al., 1993). For all students, making it through the first year is critical to college success and eventual graduation. Seventy-three percent of freshmen who entered a college or university in the fall of 1995 did not return to the same institution a year later (Geraghty, 1996). For students with disabilities who are the first-generation college students, the challenges are greater, as many are less academically and psychologically prepared for college than their peers from college-educated families (Mitchell, 1997). According to Michell (1997), some challenges facing the first-generation college students include effectively balancing their time between school and work (as many come from low-income families and must work out of ne-

cessity); lack of skills in time management, budgeting, and dealing with education bureaucracies; and the tension created between the student and his or her family and friends who may have difficulty in understanding the demands and rewards of college. In order to aid the transition of these students, parents need to become familiar with the academic, financial, and social demands of higher education. In addition, the transition team should investigate bridge programs (which involve partnerships among high schools, community colleges, and universities) and other services such as special tutoring, counseling, mentoring, and peer support programs that are designed to facilitate the success of first-generation college students. School guidance counselors, as well as colleges, will have information on programs offered to this population of students.

Critical Point   Additional barriers can exist for both first-generation and rural college students with disabilities.

Rural Students

Students from rural communities also may face similar types of challenges. The majority of jobs in rural areas are changing; as in most other jobs, they now require skills beyond those acquired by high school graduates (HEATH Resource Center, 1996). Too often rural high school students face limited access to information on postsecondary options. In addition, research has shown that students with disabilities in rural areas frequently must deal with fear, low aspirations, and attitudinal barriers; lack of counseling and information; lack of family support (and at times family opposition); and need for financial assistance (HEATH Resource Center, 1996). To overcome these barriers, the transition team should address the same principles of good transition planning previously discussed in this chapter, in addition to encouraging students and families to pursue postsecondary options. HEATH Resource Center (1996) recommends developing a parent network; holding parent/student transition planning events with appropriate guest speakers; sponsored field trips to postsecondary institutions for students with disabilities; and creating mentor programs that pair rural students with college students or college graduates (either in person, as pen pals, or through e-mail connections).

Specialized Programs

Postsecondary opportunities also exist outside the traditional academic college path. Many community colleges have a mission to promote opportunities for a diverse body of students. However, the NLTS found that of the 14% of all the students with disabilities who went on to a postsecondary education 2 years after leaving high school, only 5.8% were students classified as having mental retardation and 3.8% as having multiple disabilities (Wagner, 1989). In a study of students with mental retardation who attended a community college, Page and Chadsey-Rusch (1995) found that although the students had not made significant academic gains, they had achieved interpersonal and social benefits, such as enhanced self-esteem.

Some community, vocational, technical, and 4-year colleges offer specialized programs for students with disabilities. For example, Taft College and Monterey Peninsula College, both part of the California Community College system, offer a range of courses for students with developmental disabilities (Mertz, 1997). Taft's "Transition to Independent Living Program" offers a residential 22-month independent living skills curriculum (i.e., managing money, self–advocacy, and building and maintaining relationships) in conjunction with working on campus and participating in campus activities. Landmark College, a private coeducational institution in Putney, VT, specializes in serving students with dyslexia, attention deficit hyperactivity disorder (ADHD), or specific learning disabilities (SLD). It offers noncredit foundational courses along with an Associate of Arts (AA)

degree in General Studies and has articulation agreements with a variety of 4-year colleges (Mertz, 1997).

Some 4-year colleges also offer specialized programs for students with disabilities, such as Lesley Colleges' Threshold Program (a residential program in Cambridge, MA for students with severe learning disabilities and cognitive limitations). The nondegree program aims to develop the skills that are necessary for independent living through practical courses and field placements in the areas of early childhood and human and business services (Mertz, 1998). Others, such as Beacon College in Leesburg FL, offer students with learning disabilities the opportunity to earn AA and BA (Bachelor of Arts) degrees in Human Services and Liberal Studies (Mertz, 1998). In addition, although not commonplace, many colleges and universities have comprehensive programs designed for students with disabilities, such as Ohio State University, Southern Illinois University at Carbondale, Wright State University, OH, the University of Minnesota, and Ball State University, IN (HEATH Resource Center, 1995; Scott, 1996), and include services, such as independent tutoring in content areas or study and organizational and time management skills, which are beyond those the institution is required to provide under section 504 or ADA.

Critical Point Specialized programs in community, vocational and technical schools, and colleges are also available as postsecondary options for students with disabilities.

College guidebooks such as *Peterson's Colleges and Programs for Students with Learning Disabilities* (Mangrum & Strichart, 1997) and the K & W *Guide to Colleges for the Learning Disabled* (Kravets & Wax, 1995) can assist the transition team in finding specialized postsecondary programs. Understanding what each institution requires and has to offer, the student with his or her team can select among those environments that best fit the student's needs and goals.

Conclusion

Transition planning for college is really a subset of planning for adult life because postsecondary education is not an end in itself; it is one choice that a student might make in preparing her- or himself for adulthood. If students and their families are to make informed choices, they must be aware of the options and the pros and cons of the various options, and be given opportunities for making meaningful choices based on a self-knowledge of their strengths, interests, and needs. With appropriate preparation and continuing supports, postsecondary education provides an extended educational opportunity for developing social, interpersonal, and cognitive problem-solving skills, as well as academic and career skills that are becoming increasingly necessary in today's society for *all* our citizens.

CASE STUDY

Jim is a high school senior with a learning disability which is manifested primarily in the area of mathematics. According to Jim's IEP, he has difficulties with both his computation skills and remembering digits and number words. Except for his math classes, Jim has participated in an academic curriculum ("college prep") within the general educational environment since the ninth grade. He has utilized a resource room for individualized instruction and support in the area of mathematics throughout his high school career. His last standardized assessment was conducted when Jim was in the eighth grade, just prior to his entry into high school. At that time, he was found to be functioning at grade level in all areas of academic performance except for mathematics, for which it was determined he was achieving at a fifth grade level.

Jim is currently applying for admission at several public 4-year colleges and has made campus visits to two of them. He has indicated that he intends to major in psychology because he "wants to help people." A review of the various college catalogs indicates that psychology majors are required to take at least two math courses under the general education requirements (college algebra being the lowest level), and two statistics courses as part of the requirements of the major. Jim's high school transcript indicates that he has had "math/learning support" throughout his program but without any indication of the nature of the math courses.

During both campus visits his mother accompanied Jim, and he interviewed with an admissions representative and with the director of the Office for Students with Disabilities (OSD). One admissions representative indicated her concern that he did not meet the math requirement to be admitted into their university's psychology program but that he may qualify as a "special admit" under their developmental year program. Upon his satisfactory completion of this program's remedial math courses and the general education math requirements, Jim could then apply for acceptance into the psychology program. The other college admissions representative informed Jim that he did not meet the university's math requirement for admission nor did they offer any remedial courses. He recommended that Jim take the prerequisite math courses at a local community college and then reapply.

During his visits to the respective campus OSD offices, Jim was informed that all student requests for academic accommodations would be reviewed on a case-by-case basis. Requests that stem from the presence of a learning disability must be accompanied by a copy of a diagnostic battery, which was conducted by a licensed or certified professional who has specific training and expertise in the assessment of students with learning disabilities. This comprehensive report must not be more than 3 years old, in keeping with the best practice recommendations of the Association on Higher Education and Disability (AHEAD). During his OSD interviews, Jim had difficulty articulating the nature of his learning disability and the types of accommodative services that he might be interested in obtaining. In fact, Jim said very little during these interviews. His mother, however, would often speak for Jim when he was slow in responding to questions and was quick to point out that her son is a hard worker, would be great working with people, and simply needs one-on-one instruction in the area of math in order to succeed in college. She acknowledged that her son's diagnostic assessment did not meet the university's "recency" requirement but that Jim's IEP should suffice instead.

Case Study Discussion Questions

1. With regard to Jim's transition plan within his IEP, what issues have or have not been addressed pertaining to promoting movement from school to postschool activities:
   - Academic preparation for postsecondary education
   - Frequency and nature of standardized diagnostic assessments
   - Career exploration and choice
   - Investigation of postsecondary requirements and options
   - Self-determination skills
   - Student participation in the transition plan
2. If you were in the role as Jim's transition coordinator, what actions would you recommend should be taken as Jim completes his senior year in high school?
3. What are Jim's responsibilities as he continues to reach his postsecondary goals? His parents? His guidance counselor? His teachers?
4. What other long- and short-term options might the transition team, including Jim, identify?
5. What are the most pressing issues concerning Jim's postschool success?

Study Questions

1. Explain the reasons why it is important to incorporate postsecondary goals and objectives into the transition plans of students with disabilities?
2. Why should effective planning for a postsecondary education include more than just academic goals?
3. Discuss why each of the following is crucial to the student succeeding in a postsecondary environment:

   a. Self-awareness of one's interests, needs, and preferences, including understanding the functional limitations of one's disability
   b. Knowledge of the rights and responsibilities of students in a postsecondary environment and how they differ from IDEA
   c. The ability to self-advocate

4. How can teachers assist students and their families in finding the right fit between the student's interests, preferences, and needs and potential postsecondary institutions?
5. Discuss why it is important for students to have meaningful opportunities to take an active role in their transition planning, including leading IEP/ITP meetings.
6. Discuss how issues, such as cultural values of the students and their families, first-generation college students, and students from rural backgrounds, can impact the transition planning process.
7. Why are community-based experiences and appropriate linkages to other services providers (including adult services) necessary for a smooth transition to postsecondary education settings?
8. What should teachers be doing to ensure that the postsecondary education and training goals of their students meet the criteria of best transition planning and services, as defined by the four principles in IDEA?

Web Sites

College Is Possible:
http://www.CollegeIsPossible.org/index.html

Getting Ready for College Early: A Handbook for Parents of Students in the Middle and Junior High School Years:
http://www.ed.gov/pubs/GettingReadyCollegeEarly/#step1

Preparing Your Child for College:
http://www.ed.gov/pubs/Prepare/index.html
http://www.pedianet.com/news/eduannex/prepare.html

The Student Guide: Financial Aid from the U.S. Department of Education:
http://www.ed.gov/prog_info/SFA/StudentGuide/1998-9/index.html

College Board Online:
http://www.collegeboard.org/

The Education Testing Service Network:
http://www.ets.org/

Black Excel: The College Help Network:
http://cnct.com/home/ijblack/BlackExcel.shtml

NICHCY (National Information Center for Children with Disabilities):
http://www.nichcy.org/

The National Center for Learning Disabilities (NCLD):
http://www.ncld.org/

Gallaudet University:
http://www.gallaudet.edu/~nicd

AHEAD (Association on Higher Education and Disability):
http://ahead.org/

DO-IT (disabilities, opportunities, internetworking, and technology):
http://weber.u.washington.edu/~doit

National Clearinghouse on Postsecondary Education for Individuals with Disabilities [HEATH Resource Center]:
http://www.acenet.edu (then click on ACE programs for HEATH)

Education Resources Information Center Clearinghouse on Disability and Gifted Education:
http://ericec.org/ (then click on links to other information sources; also link to laws)

Disability Access Information and Support (DAIS):
http://www.janejarrow.com

Division on Career Development and Transition (DCDT):
http://www.ed.uiuc.edu/sped/dcdt

Job Accommodation Network (JAN)
http://www.janweb.icdi.wvu.edu

National Center for the Dissemination of Disability Research:
http://www.ncddr.org

The Center for Independent Living:
http://www.wenet.net/~cil/

17

Recreation and Leisure in the Community

Joyce Strand
Janice Kreiner

LEARNING OBJECTIVES

The objectives of this chapter are:

1. Discuss the purposes and advantages of leisure activities for individuals with disabilities.

2. Discuss the purpose and desired outcomes of community-based leisure activities for individuals with disabilities.

3. Characterize the four principles of IDEA in terms of the implications for leisure activities for individuals with disabilities.

4. Describe the procedures for the individualization of leisure activities.

5. Describe various perspectives of community-based leisure programming.

6. Identify and exemplify the benefits of community-based leisure programming.

7. Understand and characterize implementation of the four principles of IDEA in terms of leisure activities.

8. Describe and give examples of appropriate leisure activities for transition-age students.

9. Analyze the integrative framework of community-based leisure programming.

10. Implement assessment strategies used to aid student choices in leisure programming.

11. Implement techniques to facilitate participation in leisure activities for individuals with disabilities.

The previous chapter provided a description of the issues and strategies regarding accessing and planning a successful transition to postsecondary education. In this chapter, issues related to recreation and leisure are discussed. The importance of recreation and leisure pursuits cannot be overly emphasized. As one can see in reviewing Halpern's (1985) model, recreation and leisure activities are separate factors as they are related to employment and independent living. However, recreation and leisure experiences are intricately linked to overall success and satisfaction of the individual with a disability. To accomplish the ultimate independence, planning and programmatic efforts for students with disabilities should include a significant emphasis on recreation and leisure pursuits.

Of critical importance to the discussion of recreation and leisure and transition services is the inclusion of the way in which the four major elements of transition interweave into the recreation and leisure planning outcomes. In general, the emphasis of this chapter involves discussing recreation and leisure skills and training as they relate to the student's needs and preferences, the outcome-oriented process, interagency linkages, and movement activities from school to postschool environments. Other issues that are considered include implementation issues, leisure options, transportation, roles and responsibilities, community supports, safety, and various assessment methods and models.

What did you do last night? If you would ask this question to your friends and acquaintances in your community, you would probably have a variety of responses. These responses may include activities such as played softball, went bowling, went to a movie, went to a civic meeting, chauffeured kids, watched TV, worked in the garden, went biking, and so on. If you asked individuals with disabilities in your community, the responses would probably be quite different. For example, individuals with disabilities may go home from work, fix dinners with or without assistance from paid staff or family members, and then listen to radio or watch TV. If their residence is a group home, dinner may be made without their assistance or input, and the "group" may have a planned activity in the community. If the individual with a disability lives at home with older parents, it is common to go home and straight to his or her room, eat alone, talk on the phone or watch TV, again in his or her room, and then go to bed.

Critical Point There is no pleasure in having nothing to do; the fun is having lots to do and not doing it (Mary Wilson Little).

CASE STUDY A

For example, at Northern State University, the adapted physical education classes invite students from junior and senior high school transition classes to participate in a recreation program. The program has two primary purposes: (1) to expose preservice teachers to different disabilities in a positive environment and (2) to expose transition students to a variety of leisure lifelong activities (such as yoga, golf, and swimming).

Although acknowledged as a critical component to a person's well-being, leisure activities are not a priority in many transitional education programs. When leisure activities are available, they often are limited to segregated programs that occur during the regular school year. The problems are compounded when individuals have severe or developmental disabilities. Furthermore, individuals often are not encouraged or welcomed to participate in traditional community leisure and recreational activities.

On the other hand, in recent years, community recreational programs have become more accessible to persons with disabilities. Educators will generally accept that recreation programs and community-based leisure activities are an excellent way to provide the least restrictive environment as mandated by federal legislation. Recreation programs and leisure activities are excellent vehicles to provide students with opportunities to learn appropriate activities, communication, and social skills, important transition outcomes.

The purpose of this chapter is to provide an understanding of leisure programming in community-based settings. Leisure skills are a critical component of the transition process because it provides many connections and relationships for common participation. A key to enhancing the leisure component of the transition process is to provide administrators, parents, teachers, and individuals with disabilities resources and strategies to incorporate leisure in the transition plan.

Community Participation, Recreation and Leisure

Transition Needs

The inclusion of a chapter on leisure and recreation in the community for persons with disabilities is easily justified because of its importance. For example, individuals with disabilities can learn work skills and obtain and hold jobs (McDonnell, Wilcox, & Hardman, 1991; Rusch & Chadsey, 1998; Wehman, 1992). An individual with a disability can reside in an apartment, cook the dinner, shop, and perform most if not all the chores associated with living independently. However, individuals with disabilities have few, if any, friends, other than family, paid support staff, or other people with disabilities (Condeluci, 1995). The individual with a disability goes to work and then home. The importance of learning leisure skills should be a focus especially in the transitional years of adolescence.

Critical Point All people need to be involved in recreation and leisure.

We have only begun to sense the tragic wounds some mentally retarded persons may feel when it

dawns on them that the only people relating with them—outside of relatives—are paid to do so. If you or I came to such a sad realization about ourselves, it would rip at our souls to even talk about it. Chances are some of us would cover it up with one noisy, awkward bluff after another and chances are, some professionals seeing us act this way, would say we had "maladaptive" behavior. Think about what it would feel like to have even one person come to us and without pay, develop a reliable, long-term relationship with us because he or she wanted to literally accept us as we are. Then, think of the unspeakable feelings we might possess if—when others were "talking down" to us and "putting us in our place"—that kind person could be counted on to defend us and stick up for us as well. Most of us do have persons like that in our lives. But will the day ever come when retarded citizens will have them too? (Bob Perske, from *Listen People*.)

In his book, *Interdependence: The Route to Community* (1995), Condeluci refers to four basic themes that, in his experience, are the main thrust of rehabilitation and are vital to every person. In fact, these rehabilitation goals are the same as the major goals of most people. These goals are (1) a safe place to live, (2) meaningful things to do, (3) intimacy, and (4) rejuvenation. Although it is the intent of transition services to focus upon all these areas, the focus of this chapter is to look at the goal of rejuvenation. This is the time and opportunity to "refresh and recollect ourselves," something that is necessary for all individuals. Condeluci provided details on these issues:

In 1980, a survey was administered to persons with disabilities in Pittsburgh regarding the areas of service or programs that were essential to them. The typical list of vital services was listed on the poll. They included housing, transportation, jobs, accessibility issues, attitudes, and the like. Prior to this survey, some of us surmised which areas would be tops. We were certain that housing, jobs, or transportation would be first on the list. Top on the list, however, was recreation. Certainly, the others were important, but recreation far out-polled its closest competitor, housing.

Without question, recreation is a vital need of all people. Our 1980 survey was testimony to two important facts: (1) recreation was most important and (2) there were precious few recreational opportunities for people with disabilities. Today, we are seeing more recreational opportunities, but these efforts often are segregated, isolated, or terribly childlike (Condeluci, 1995, pp. 9–10).

What Condeluci (1995) was talking about is evident across the country. For example, while arenas and stadiums are beginning to think about people with disabilities and to make their facilities accessible, they often assume, incorrectly, that all people with disabilities want to sit together. This is without consideration that the designated sections are separate from their partners or family members without disabilities, in specialized handicapped sections. There are special "handicapped days" at attractions like Sea World, zoos, amusement parks, and county fairs. YMCAs as well as other local pools have set up special "handicapped swim nights." Service providers continue to fill the big yellow school buses with individuals who have disabilities to take them on outings en masse. Many programs such as city recreation programs, libraries, bowling lanes, shopping, and so on, only seem to address the issue of serving individuals with disabilities on an as-needed basis, if at all.

One might argue that participating in recreational activities with others that have commonalties is not such a "bad" thing. For example, it is quite common for senior citizens to travel together on organized bus tours. The difference is that they do this by choice, but they have other options from which to choose when they want to interact or socialize with diverse groups from their community. This often is *not* the case for people with disabilities. It is not that these segregated trips for individuals with disabilities are bad in themselves. What is "bad" is that, for individuals with disabilities, these segregated opportunities are all that they have available to them: They often have no other choices.

Opportunities for recreation are increasing for individuals with disabilities, but they may not always be appropriate. If the experiences do not afford the opportunity to meet new people and to develop relationships with others that do not have disabilities, then a vital link to rejuvenating interdependently in integrated community environments is missing.

Critical Point   Few recreation and leisure alternatives are available to individual with disabilities in either integrated or nonintegrated settings.

Health and Wellness

A report from the Surgeon General in 1996 emphasizes that:

> regular physical activity can help people with chronic, disabling conditions improve their stamina and muscle strength and can improve psychological well-being and quality of life by increasing the ability to perform activities of daily life.
>
> . . . People with disabilities are less likely to engage in regular moderate physical activity than people without disabilities, yet they have similar needs to promote their health and prevent unnecessary disease. Social support from family and friends has been consistently and positively related to regular physical activity.
>
> The recommendations of this report included (1) community-based programs, (2) environments and facilities that are accessible and safe, (3) persons with disabilities who are involved in planning physical activity programs, (4) provision of quality daily physical education for youth with disabilities, and (5) discussions with parents to make sure physical activity is included in their son's or daughter's life.

The rationale for any physical activity and health and wellness program is readily available. Individuals with disabilities have lower fitness than the general population as well as more health problems. These health problems could be reduced and fitness levels improved with a moderate increase in physical activity. The report recommended community-based programming. What better support is there for a community-based leisure activity program which focuses upon moderate exercise for students with disabilities than the Surgeon General's report from the U.S. government? With improvement in cardiovascular endurance, muscle strength, and flexibility, persons with disabilities would be better able to complete daily living activities, remain in more demanding employment positions, and recreate with a wider variety of options in their leisure activities.

Critical Point   Recreation and leisure is crucial in promoting health and wellness.

Community-Based Programs

Historically, individuals with disabilities have relied upon legislative mandate to secure their rights to education. However, the enactment of the Americans with Disabilities Act (ADA) signified more than the mere expansion of previous legislation for persons with disabilities. ADA spearheaded a major shift in the attitude toward individuals with disabilities. The physical and procedural alterations of the community environment to allow persons with disabilities access to community life equivalent to that of their peers who are not disabled was indicative of this major shift of attitude (Daniels, 1990). The special education initiative, particularly at the secondary level, mirrors this conceptual shift—also from focusing upon the inadequacies of the person with a disability to removing environmental barriers and providing experiences tied as closely as possible to those of their peers without disabilities (McDonnell, Wilcox, & Hardman, 1992).

In this same vein, and providing a philosophical foundation for the ADA provisions, the principle of normalization requires education approaches dictated by age-appropriate environments in contrast to traditional education, which alters the setting to fit the didactic techniques (Wolfensberger, 1972). McCord (1983) asserted that students learn appropriate skills most efficiently in settings that demand knowledge of those skills. An appropriate environment not only reinforces age-appropriate skills and social behavior, but it also provides a basis

for relevant goals and objectives for instructional planning. In addition, research indicates that persons without disabilities perceive persons with disabilities as more competent when interaction occurs in an integrated community setting (Voeltz, 1984). Studies investigating interaction between students with disabilities and their peers without disabilities document positive personal outcomes for persons without disabilities, such as enhanced self-esteem, social confidence, and acceptance of diversity (Peck, Donaldson, & Pessoli, 1990).

One basic premise of the community-based program is that when individuals have positive experiences with a group or an individual from a specific group, their attitude can change. Since many attitudes are based on hearsay and not on direct experience (Ajzen & Fishbein, 1982), providing direct experiences that are positive (Allport, 1954, 1960) for community members may be the best strategy a teacher can implement for a successful transition program. If a teacher can change the attitudes of community members, the consequences of the attitude change may be far reaching. An individual with a disability can learn leisure skills, but there must be an attitude of welcome from the community. In leisure pursuits. Even more than in vocational and residential settings, the community has to provide an attitude that all members of society have the right to participate. For in leisure, if this attitude is not present, individuals with disabilities are, indeed, excluded and segregated.

Critical Point   Inclusive community activities must be planned with appropriate supports in order to support leisure and recreation lifelong experiences.

Recognizing the implications of community inclusion, leaders in special education advocate for community-based curricula for secondary programs for persons with disabilities (Wehman, Moon, Everson, Wood, & Barcus, 1988). The ultimate goals for special education are adult interdependence and participation in community life, which can only be achieved by lifelong, true to life experiences. The current failure of special

Leisure and recreation skills are often neglected.

education graduates to achieve adult interdependence, especially in leisure and social settings, emphasizes the need for functional community-based programs. The education transition planning for adolescent students must establish linkages that will continue throughout a student's lifetime in order for a person with a disability to become a successful community member.

Essential Elements of Transition

Halpern's (1985) model of transition identified the secondary curriculum as the foundation for the three pillars of adult community adjustment: residential, employment, and social in-

terpersonal. In practice, the bulk of transition services have focused almost exclusively upon employment experiences in the community. Transitional work experiences in the community, following employment guidelines, provides on-the-job training and continued support on an individual basis to allow secondary students with disabilities to explore employment options and to develop marketable skills prior to graduation. At the same time, however, secondary special education curriculum must retain an academic focus fostered by characteristics of the high school setting (McDonnell et al., 1991). The resulting lack of coordination between school curriculum and transitional programs hampers job placements and restricts social interaction as well as residential options. By their nature and physical location, secondary schools do not bridge the gap to adult living and working or leisure activities. When the secondary school is located in rural or small towns, the options are even more restricted. For this reason it is imperative that community-based leisure programming begin in high school transition programs.

Critical Point Individuals with disabilities typically have had little input into decisions affecting their lives.

Individuals with disabilities generally have had little input into decisions affecting their lives. Current service delivery models, federal and state legislation, and individual programming have dramatically impacted the lives of individuals with disabilities by initiating a person-centered approach. Systems influence and maintain one another. For example, legislation is built upon the current best practices of service delivery; then, programming often is mandated and supervised. IDEA (Individuals with Disabilities Education Act) emphasizes four underlying essentials for transition planning that translate readily into a real person-centered approach to service delivery. The four underlying essentials will be examined in relation to leisure/recreational activities for adolescents with disabilities in the following sections of this chapter.

Students' Needs, Interests, and Preferences

What Does IDEA Say?

The language of IDEA states, "The coordinated set of activities must: (a) be based on individual student's needs; and (b) take into account student's preferences and interests." The intent of this section of IDEA is to reinforce the fact that students with disabilities and their families are to be afforded the right (and responsibility) to become actively involved in the planning, objective development, decision-making process, and service coordination for their future. Prior to this provision of the law, teachers and other professionals commonly made prescriptive choices for the student, often out of their own convenience (Martin, Marshall, & Maxon, 1993; Wehmeyer & Ward, 1995).

Why Is It Important?

The right to freely make choices and decisions regarding one's own life is something that most Americans take for granted. Making decisions regarding ordinary life choices, unfortunately, has not been afforded to individuals with disabilities. Too often, the need to "habilitate" overrides the provision of decision-making opportunities in the lives of individuals with disabilities. When choices are provided for individuals with disabilities, the choices are often ones that have no significant impact or control over an individual's daily routine.

Critical Point   Making decisions regarding ordinary life choices, unfortunately, has not been afforded to individuals with disabilities.

However, a review of the pertinent literature indicates several important factors:

1. Individuals with disabilities indeed have a preference for tasks or activities (Bambara, Ager, & Koger, 1994; Bambara, Koger, &

Katzer, 1995; Parsons, Reid, Reynolds, & Bumgarner, 1990).

2. Individuals with severe disabilities will attend to a task twice as much when they have chosen that task (Parsons, Reid, Reynolds, & Bumgarner, 1990).

3. Positive effects of choice making on increasing participation in activities were demonstrated (Bambara, Koger, Katzer, 1995; Dunlap, DePerczel, Clarke, Wilson, Wright, White, & Gomez, 1994).

4. Individuals provided with choices increased performance in activities and prevented or reduced problem behaviors (Bambara, Ager, & Koger, 1994; Bambara, Koger, & Katzer, 1995; Dyer, Dunlap, & Winterling, 1993; Parsons, Reid, Reynolds, & Bumgarner, 1990).

5. Preferences for a task may be an important determinant in the effectiveness of choice making in influencing task performance (Bambara, Ager, & Koger, 1994; Parsons, Reid, Reynolds, & Bumgarner, 1990).

6. The act of choosing may be preferred over being assigned, even when assigned a preferred task (Bambara, Ager, & Koger, 1994).

One of the simplest but frequently overlooked techniques of managing problem behavior is giving people choices . . . individuals in all kinds of social situations are likely to behave more constructively when they perceive that they have the power to make choices that are important to them. Conversely, people often behave badly when they feel "boxed in," perceiving [that] they have no choices (Kaufman et al., 1993, pp. 44–45).

These studies were conducted in a variety of settings, including work, residential, and classrooms. Regardless of the setting, it remains that individual students and their families have the right to be actively involved in the planning, the decision-making process, and in everyday choices that are afforded to individuals without disabilities. Educators are well practiced in determining employment needs, preferences, and desires. Ultimately, if educators desire that their students gain a level of interdependence in the area of leisure and recreation, these same skills and knowledge need to be applied to the world of leisure.

How Do We Do It?

First, students need to have exposure to many diverse leisure experiences. How can you ask any person to choose a leisure activity if the activity is not known or not available to him or her? Individuals need to be provided real-life, age-appropriate options, with many opportunities to experience the activities. Otherwise, informed choice is just an abstract concept. Students need to experience many activities, to try them out, and to evaluate what they like or dislike. They need to begin making decisions and choices early in life. Their opinions and choices should be respected so that they learn that it is important to express their opinions and choices. Individuals with disabilities have the right to learn that consequences occur from all choices. If they make a poor choice, they are not "bad" or "dumb" because all persons make poor choices or decisions at some time or another. However, in order to learn from the real-life experiences of making decisions, individuals with disabilities need to relish or suffer the consequences of their decisions. In a school environment, supports can be provided to help students learn to make informed choices. These supports also can be a protective mechanism to ensure that students, while learning to make decisions, are still safe. As an educator, safety of your students should be a primary consideration; but it should be assured that the educator's concern for safety is reasonable and prudent and not restrictive or handicapping.

Critical Point   Individuals need to be provided real-life, age-appropriate options, with many opportunities to experience the activities.

Although providing for individual choices is a must, and a best practice, we should not forget about the reasonableness of these choices. For example, depending on the part of the country you are from, surfing, downhill skiing, rock climbing, or beach combing are viable options for leisure activities. However, would you provide a choice of beach combing to one who is living in Kansas?

Another, yet often forgotten, factor when working with students with disabilities is that the students have the right to change their mind. Who among us does not have a tennis racquet, roller blades, or stationary bike in our basement collecting dust? After all, who has not changed his or her mind about participating or attending some leisure activity? Changing one's mind is a typical human behavior that all persons have the right to choose actively.

Critical Point   Students have the right to change their mind.

> Choice is also closely aligned with freedom—for choice, surely, is the essence of freedom (Warner, 1992, p. 58).

A leisure assessment should be conducted to find out interests and needs. Typically, the types of leisure assessments utilized by schools and agencies are (1) checklists of leisure activities and/or (2) pictorial representations of leisure activities. Another way to ascertain needs, interests, and preferences is to expose individuals with disabilities to a variety of leisure and recreational activities. Leisure assessment instruments will be discussed later in the chapter. However, the critical component of any assessment instrument is that it works for your students and your community. The important question that a teacher needs to ask is, "Does the information that one gets from this assessment help to provide activities for the students?" (See Table 17.1)

Outcome-Oriented Process

What Does IDEA Say?

Transition services must be "designed within an outcome-oriented process." The intent of this statement within the legislation is to get teachers, parents, and other professionals to start planning for what the student, parent, and

TABLE 17–1

Ideas for Elementary Education Teachers to Facilitate Transition into Leisure Activities

Concept	Example

Choice/decision making	• Provide many and continual opportunities for choice/decision making
	• Give the student an either/or choice in all aspects of the day:
	  Art medium: crayon or marker
	  Indoor or outdoor recess
	  Pen or pencil
	  Practice your work on paper or on the chalkboard
	  Playground ball or basketball and so on

Socialization	• Self-care classes • Interaction with peers who do not have disabilities during lunch, recess, and academic periods of the school day • Teach and encourage appropriate behavior during assemblies, movies, class changes in the hallway, and so on
Parental involvement	• At the annual IEP meeting, provide parents with a list of activities available in their community that are appropriate for the student • Encourage parents to enroll their child in a parks and recreation class • Ask parents to assist students with homework • Have parents fill out a questionnaire about how leisure time is spent at home • Keep a home-school journal
Initiation of activities	• Encourage students to play and interact with each other (limit number of teacher/student activities) • Leave time during the day for structured downtime, and leave desired activities in students' sight, so they can choose what to do • Accept student's choices without judgment (i.e., strategically providing options!)

Network of friends	• Provide many opportunities during the day for incidental interactions:
	  All neighborhood children should ride the same bus to school (no need for a "special ed." bus)
	  All students should enter/exit the same doors at school (no need to drop off student with disabilities closer to their classroom so they don't have to "walk *all* that way")
	  Encourage mingling in the hallways during class changes
	  Allow students to go to restroom, office, to run messages throughout school, and so on, independently
	  No need for separate recess or lunch periods
	  Integrate into regular activities of the school and classes as much as possible
	  Peer tutoring
	  Peer helpers

Community-based training	• Take small groups of two or three students to a variety of community outings • Schedule community outings weekly as a reinforcer • Enlist the help of room parents to assist with small group outings and/or transportation • Walk to community locations • Take public transportation to community outings • Let students help to shop for classroom supplies • Keep a classroom photo album of community outings

professionals want for this student over the long term. Instead of planning annual goals and short-term objectives, as educators are accustomed to doing with the Individualized Education Program. (IEP), educators are required to develop plans for longer periods (1 to 7 years). The student's desired product is supposed to be at the forefront of the process in the transition planning. This long-term planning, with the student's life after high school the focus, in turn should then drive the Individualized Education Program.

Why Is It Important?

Students in high school make plans on what they are going to do when they graduate. Sometimes these plans include college, technical school, getting a job, moving from the family home, or getting married. During the 1980s, professionals, families, and adults with disabilities began to realize that the current academic-based curriculum for students with disabilities was not adequate or appropriate for preparation for adulthood. Unemployment rates were extremely high, students with disabilities were dropping out of high school at higher numbers than their peers without disabilities, and students and parents were not equipped to navigate the multiple adult service agencies and did not understand the entitlement versus eligibility issue. Consequently, a change in focus from the academically based goals of the past to a functional long-term approach was propitious. With the student's long-term functional goals in mind, the academic program takes on a different perspective. To ensure successful integration into the community after graduation, the process of integration needs to occur while the student is still in high school.

Critical Point   During the 1980s, professionals, families, and adults with disabilities began to realize that the current academic-based curriculum for students with disabilities was not adequate or appropriate for preparation for adulthood.

Ideally, integration into the community happens naturally throughout the childhood of the individual with a disability. Often due to family concerns, medical restrictions, societal barriers or other life factors, individuals with disabilities have little "normal" life experiences. Therefore, educators have to assume that part of their role in the educational process of students with disabilities includes integration strategies and social skill development. Educators should be focusing upon building a support system, making community connections to assure that the process works. This is extremely important in community leisure and recreational programs. When dealing with residential and employment issues, one assumes that individuals have certain rights that go along with living and working in the community. However, this frequently is not extended to include recreational programs or leisure time activities. (I may work with you and even live in the same building as you, but I do not have to "play" with you.)

It is important to start making connections to the community while the student is still in secondary school. Ideally, of course, this should be a moot point. Students should have these connections to their community beginning in infancy. However, since educators are not dealing with the ideal situation, reality makes it critical that we start the process of connecting to community leisure activities and recreation programs while the student is still in school. This would provide the student with a support system in terms of school personnel and structure. The school personnel can assist the individual in learning how to make choices and to become self-confident in these choices. The school can provide the learning environment that is necessary for learning the social, psychomotor, and cognitive skills needed for learning the leisure activity. The student has the opportunity to practice appropriate social skills and to learn the nuances of social situations in leisure and recreational environments.

Critical Point   It is important to start making connections to the community while the student is still in school.

How Do We Do It?

The first issue is whether the student is prepared to make decisions and choices. Does the student realize his or her options for leisure activities? Has the student tried out these options? Does the student know what he or she likes and dislikes in leisure activities? Think of the fishing tackle that is sitting in garages because people thought they would like to fish. At what level does the student want to participate? Does he or she want to be competitive? Is this a recreational pursuit or an ongoing hobby? Only after some of these questions have been explored can outcome-based objectives be written.

Critical Point   Students must be provided training in choice making to be able to contribute in determining their needs and preferences.

After the students have an idea of what recreational and leisure activities they would like to pursue after graduation, then the educators should provide the skills for students and their families to initiate contacts within the community. It is important that the families and the students have these skills prior to graduation. They will be responsible for the continuation of the activities.

Another method in which the school can assist the student in connecting with the community is through instruction and advocating with community services. Community integration is not a one-way process. Educators have the responsibility of providing accurate information to the community regarding disability awareness issues. Community integration is no longer "getting the person ready" to meet the expectations of society; rather, it is a collaborative effort between the community and the students, where the community will accept the diversity of its citizens.

Critical Point   Educators have the responsibility of providing accurate information to the community regarding disability awareness issues.

In order for the outcome-oriented process to be successful, it is important that the teacher know the students' community, the leisure and recreational options for their students, and how to access these options. The teacher needs to know their local parks and recreation administrators, YMCA, YWCA, fitness centers, sport organizations, church groups, youth leagues, and other recreational organizations. If a university, college, or community college is located in their community, the university facilities may be available for usage by community members.

Community and school resources, and the teacher's imagination, are the only limitations to opportunities for transition teachers to implement creative and unique lessons. Special education teachers should remember that the underlying philosophy of special education is determining the students' needs and providing a program that appropriately meets those needs. Although this is a philosophy for all special education students, it is extremely important to follow through with these actions in the transition years.

Critical Point   Teachers need to know and communicate with the recreation and leisure settings in their community to assure that students are provided a broad array of experiences.

Interagency Responsibility or Linkages

What Does IDEA Say?

Section 614(d)(1)(vii)(II) of IDEA requires that the transition statement "include, when appropriate, a statement of the interagency responsibilities or any needed linkages." The intent is to get teachers, students, and parents thinking about what kind of support services might be needed once the student leaves high school, as well as providing adult service agencies information so that they can best serve the student's needs. In addition, the intent is to begin the eligibility process for a smooth transition from high school services into adult services.

Why Is It Important?

With the narrow focus on the goals of secondary education, it was recognized that the academic-based curriculum was not preparing students with disabilities for the adult world. This was especially true for families and students who had to navigate the adult service systems. The families may be surprised to learn that the adult service systems operate much differently from the school systems. The families in many cases have spent the last 12 to 15 years in learning about the school system in order to get what their son or daughter needs in an entitlement system. They will be leaving a system with which they possibly have become comfortable, and then suddenly they are thrust into systems that are based on eligibility and availability. There are many rules, procedures, and different agencies for families to learn about within the adult service systems. If not handled appropriately, this transition can lead to loss of valuable services and training time for the students. For example, a simple process of being put on a waiting list while the student is still in high school can facilitate movement up the list while the student is still in school rather than being placed on the bottom of the list upon graduation.

Critical Point   Academic-based curriculum, generally, does not prepare students with disabilities for the adult world.

Although these are important issues that families and students face, leisure and recreational pursuits are not always a priority for individuals with disabilities in adult service programs (Chadsey & Sheldon, 1999). In the individual planning process (e.g., IP, IHP, ISP, IPE, etc.),[1] leisure programming usually takes a back seat to issues of housing and employment. However, without leisure and appropriate social skills, individuals with disabilities lead a

lonely, isolated, mundane life. If the educators complete their recreational assessments, provide opportunities for leisure activities, and have a community base of support, then the transition to adult life is much easier. If a transition teacher has provided an appropriate leisure skills program, then the individual will choose to participate in leisure activities. Adult service agencies will have to respond to knowledgeable and skilled individuals with disabilities in the leisure domain.

Another important aspect to the development and planning of leisure activities collaboratively with adult service agencies is interagency linkage. By planning prior to graduation, these community and adult service agency linkages can lead to a more rewarding lifestyle for the individuals receiving services. When these linkages or connections are established, information regarding housing and employment needs can be shared to provide more opportunities for those who need it the most.

Critical Point   Prior to graduation, planning should focus upon developing these community and adult service agency linkages in order to facilitate a more rewarding lifestyle for the individuals who will be receiving services.

How Do We Do It?

What are the steps in setting up linkages with adult service systems? In terms of recreation and leisure, the student's needs, interests, and preferences should be shared with the adult agency. Educators need to find out what types of leisure activities are provided through the agency. Which types of leisure services are not provided? Who is the contact person (i.e., therapeutic recreation specialist)? Are there established procedures for participating in recreational programs or leisure activities? A good way to begin this process is to develop a database listing the adult service agencies, what services they provide, eligibility requirements, and specific contact information. The database can be as simple or as complex as desired. However,

---

[1]IP = individual plan; IHP = individual habilitation plan; ISP = individual service plan; and IWRP = individual written rehabilitation plan.

a simple card index with this information is all that is needed. It is important to keep the information updated, as contact personnel change. It requires educators to teach students and their families about the systems and how to make contacts independently.

Critical Point   Develop a database listing the adult service agencies, what services they provide, eligibility requirements, and specific contact information.

The educator can match agencies and services to fit the leisure needs of their students. A list of contact persons given to a student can mean the difference between success and failure in connecting and becoming actively involved with the recreational community. Since the transition planning meeting can include all persons that seem to be important in developing the transition plan, educators need to invite recreation representatives to the IEP meeting. When this occurs, there is a better understanding on both sides about individual needs and services to meet recreational needs.

Movement from School to Postschool Activities

What Does IDEA Say?
IDEA requires that the transition plan focus upon movement from school to postschool activities. This means that not only do educators need to help students and families identify the adult service agencies that they may need upon graduation but that the transition process must start prior to graduation. The students should be using these services before leaving school. This will assist with the intent of a smooth transition from school activities to adult activities.

Why Is It Important?
By having school personnel available while they are trying out various community-based leisure activities, and learning to navigate the adult service systems, the students have the support of the school as a safety net to regroup and try

again, in the event of a failed attempt at a community activity. It is important that the students have people around them with whom they are familiar as well. Remember, the more learning opportunities that can be provided for the students in the actual environment in which it is expected they will be performing, the more likely the students will make the transition to adult activities successfully. A smooth movement to postschool environments is facilitated by providing the student with practice in community-based leisure activities.

Critical Point   One of the most important factors that educators must consider when planning or developing leisure programming for individuals with disabilities is the students' developing interests and choices.

Another reason that it is important to focus upon movement from school to postschool activities in a community-based setting is the increase in the number of contacts that the student can make while participating in the community. These contacts can increase a student's potential for success. First, community-based leisure experiences can positively impact the community's attitudes toward individuals with disabilities. This will increase the potential for successful integration as well as the potential for natural supports. Second, the more students with disabilities get out in the community and make known their abilities, skills, interests, and goals, the more potential they have for making contacts that may later lead to a job or residential opportunity. Third, community members will discover that individuals with disabilities are more like them than different from them.

Critical Point   Community leisure skill practice and regular contacts with the community foster successful outcomes for students with disabilities.

How Do We Do It?
What does a teacher or administrator do to facilitate the movement from school to postschool activities? This is where the teaching strategy of

community-based activities takes on a greater meaning. Not only does community-based training work for residential and vocational training, it also is imperative for postschool successful leisure activities. The more opportunities the student gets out of the school environment and practice using the available community resources, the smoother the transition will be. Leisure and recreational activities lend themselves well to community-based programming.

Another factor to be considered, particularly for students with disabilities ages 18 to 22, is that juniors and seniors without disabilities are no longer considered "peers." Most high school activities are no longer the most appropriate kinds of activities for students nearing their twenties. While integrating transition-age students into regular extracurricular school activities is a great situation for practicing social skills related to leisure, it becomes less appropriate once the students' age-peers have graduated. It is more appropriate after the age of 18 to focus upon activities in the community with individuals of similar ages and interests. For example, older transition students may have access to university facilities where their age-peers also are recreating. So, would it not be more appropriate to practice their leisure skills in that setting?

Critical Point   Most high school activities are no longer the most appropriate kinds of activities for students nearing their twenties.

The four IDEA essentials in relation to leisure/recreation—(1) student's needs, interests, and preferences; (2) outcome-oriented process; (3) interagency responsibility or linkages; and (4) movement from school to postschool activities—can be implemented by special education teachers who know their school and community resources, develop innovative opportunities for their students, and believe that their students can be successful in their community. Successful transition programs are not necessarily the programs with the greatest financial resources. Successful transition programs are those that

have teachers who work hard and have administrative support and collaborate with community leaders. The four essential elements of IDEA, if followed, can be the guiding light to a transition leisure program that will impact your student's adult life.

Leisure Program Options

Numerous programs and agencies provide services to individuals with disabilities. Many of these agencies provide regular or therapeutic recreational programs for individuals with disabilities who are receiving services within their agencies. However, these programs may be segregated programs held at convenient times for staff. The following sections describe the types of programs and how, because of collaborative efforts, recreational opportunities should be available for individuals with disabilities.

Specific Programs

Independent Living
Independent living programs are designed to have persons with disabilities live outside their family home but in a less restrictive environment than that of a group home or other communal setting for persons with disabilities. The setting may be an apartment or house, with or without supervision from paid staff, and located in any type of community (see Chapter 18). Often there will be two individuals living in the same apartment or house. Options for leisure activities vary greatly from program to program. Some independent living programs provide many opportunities for recreation, whereas others provide only a minimal offering. Examples of leisure activities include parks and recreation regular programming, parks and recreation therapeutic programming, special "Boy or Girl" Scout troops, fitness centers, and other club organizations in the community. Communities sometimes provide individuals with disabilities free admission to high

school or university sporting events on a regular basis. Transportation is a major obstacle for individuals living in a community with limited supervision. Other alternatives include utilizing family members, paid staff, or public transportation to address commuting. Moving within a reasonable walking distance also may increase the likelihood of the individual gaining access to clubs and other organizations.

Critical Point   Transportation is a major obstacle for individuals living in a community with limited supervision.

Developmental Disability.

Developmental Disability (DD) programs are usually a single point of entry for individuals with mental retardation and developmental disabilities. These DD programs can be inclusive from birth to death. Their scope of service includes infant stimulation, parent training, case managers, preschool, K-12 segregated schools, resource special education teachers for regular schools, transition, work centers, job placement, supported employment, independent living, and group homes. Although leisure activities and recreational programs are considered important, they are generally not as great a priority as school, work, and residential issues. When leisure programs are offered for individuals receiving services from the DD programs, frequently they are self-contained or segregated–even when in a community setting. The DD programs often hire therapeutic recreation specialists to run their leisure programs. The programs consist of a variety of activities, including Special Olympic training, dances, ceramics, open gym nights, fitness activities, aquatics, and numerous others. Many times these programs could not be implemented without paid staff and/or volunteers. If the DD program is unable to fund the staff, then these programs are discontinued.

Critical Point   DD programs offer a wide variety of services that meet the needs of youth and adults with disabilities.

Mental Health

Mental health programs also vary in their approach to leisure activities and recreational programs. Many of these programs are emotionally therapeutic in nature. In other words, they focus upon cognitive and behavioral learning to deal with fears, anxieties, and phobias surrounding community interactions. The therapeutic approach is generally classroom-type counseling with "mock" interactions and practice, with a gradual reentry into community activities. Often leisure opportunities are limited for individuals with mental health problems because recreational activities are segregated: (1) by the agency and (2) by the community. Historically, individuals with mental health issues have had a more difficult time integrating into the community due to society's fear of "mental patients."

Parks and Recreation

City or county parks and recreation departments offer therapeutic recreation programs for individuals with disabilities as well. Depending on the park and recreation budgetary constraints, the programs offered can be extensive. However, unless a parent or individual with a disability enrolls specifically in regular recreational programs, the person will be steered to the therapeutic recreation programs, which are typically segregated. In one parks and recreation exemplary program, a parent wanted the 5-year-old daughter to be in the regular dance class offered for children ages 4 to 5. The parks and recreation department was aware of its obligation under the law, so the student enrolled in the dance class. The psychomotor and behavioral skills of the student with a disability were assessed as below age level.

The student's attendance in the program was impacting the dance class negatively in terms of behavior and teacher attention to the rest of the students. Rather than asking the student with a disability to withdraw from the dance class, the parks and recreation department hired an assistant for the dance instructor. This was a successful accommodation for a student and one that impacted all the students in the class. The student with a disability was impacted well into her transition years because she had the opportunity to participate with her peers in a regular community-based setting. The other nondisabled peers also benefited by having access to a wide range of associates with whom to interact.

Other

Other recreation program alternatives can be found in local resource guides, such as the yellow pages in phone books, which list youth organizations and centers, fitness centers, scouting organizations, church groups, park and recreation departments, and social service agencies. Depending on the organization, the mechanism for running these programs varies slightly. These programs are planned for the general populace and add or design specialized programs to fit the needs of individuals with disabilities. Sometimes the organization will permit staff from a school or agency that provides services for individuals with disabilities to use their facilities for free or for a nominal fee.

Each type of organization has its own staffing and funding systems in place. The staff education requirements vary within recreational programs. A few require a therapeutic recreation specialist degree from an accredited university. Many will accept any related degree that could include physical education, special education, or even social services. Other recreation programs will hire anyone that applies and is willing to work. Funding is a big issue for most cities, states, agencies, and schools. However, with the support from federal legislation, specifically the ADA, individuals with disabilities have the right to access and participate in leisure activities. Programs that are involved in leisure activities are typically aware of their obligation to provide access and services to individuals with disabilities. However, some of these programs still must be prodded into provision of those services.

Implementation of Leisure Programs

Transition Coordination for Recreation and Leisure

How does one go about obtaining the necessary leisure options and recreation programs for individuals with disabilities? One of the points of dispute in providing programming for students with disabilities is when teachers or administrators try to fit the student into existing programs. Special education philosophy and federal legislation promote individualization. It is essential for students in special education to get their education in the least restrictive environment that best fits their needs. Traditionally, segregated classrooms and/or resource rooms were utilized to get the student with disabilities ready for the all–inclusive classroom. As has been documented, the movement from segregated to integrated classrooms did not materialize. Students could be stuck in a "getting ready" mode for years. A different approach was needed. Start the student in the regular classroom, add supports as needed, and only when the student has documented evidence that it is not the least restrictive environment, then try another placement option. This is the approach that should be used for leisure activities and programming.

Critical Point   It is inappropriate to fit the student into available recreation and leisure services.

Community Awareness

In conjunction with determining and developing the leisure options for individuals with disabilities, community awareness has to be provided. The transition teacher requires a working knowledge not only of work and residential options, but also of the leisure activities and recreation programs that are available in their community. The program choices that are available may not be the problem; the problem may be societal acceptance. Emphasis on community awareness is extremely important. Your community may have a mayor's council for disability awareness or other similar programs. This is an appropriate avenue to get the school, community, and service organizations involved in disability awareness programs.

Teachers need to concentrate on the principles of generalization and durability (i.e., students learn best when they actually must use their skills) in least restrictive, most normal settings. Leisure skills and recreational programming can easily occur in the most normal setting when the foundations of community awareness have been established. Administrators in the public schools need to understand the transition provisions in IDEA, which require community instruction, the environment that is most normal and easily argued as the least restrictive.

Critical Point   Teachers need to concentrate on the principles of generalization and durability in the least restrictive, most normal settings.

Models of Service Delivery

There are three models of service delivery for leisure programs (Schleien, Green, & Heyne, 1993). The first is called *reverse mainstreaming*. The program is structured to meet the needs of individuals with disabilities. Individuals without disabilities are usually asked to participate. Reverse mainstreaming does provide opportunities for interactions with persons without disabilities but usually does not promote long-term types of interactions. One benefit of this type of program is the availability of professional staff to assist with programming. The second model for leisure programming is called *integrated generic mainstreaming*. This model is founded on the premise that the regular leisure program is provided for all individuals, with accommodations only being made for those that require some assistance. These programs have a larger menu with respect to all programs that are available to all community members. However, the cost of a single accommodation may limit the resources of the entire recreational program. Typically, staff trained in therapeutic recreation

or adapted physical education are not available for these types of programs. The third model for leisure programming is called *zero exclusion programs*.

Ideally, these programs are based on a collaborative effort between professionals in the regular recreation and therapeutic recreation departments. The focus is on an integrated, normalized setting with natural supports and accommodations as required. Again, there is little evidence of long-term alliances being forged between individuals with disabilities and individuals without disabilities. It would be wonderful to think that students with disabilities have a right to participate in all leisure activities in all possible situations; however, with rights there is responsibility.

Critical Point   The three models of service delivery for recreation and leisure are reverse mainstreaming, integrated generic mainstreaming, and zero exclusion programs.

CASE STUDY B

An example of a viable and inexpensive approach to providing students with opportunities to experience a variety of leisure activities that are typically not available was developed through a collaborative effort between a university and an agency. The agency had a therapeutic recreation program and the university had preservice university students and facilities. The problem for the therapeutic recreation program in their annual assessment of students and adults with disabilities was the limited knowledge and exposure to different types of leisure activities. Their primary exposure was through Special Olympics. It was decided that individuals with disabilities that were interested in participating would be provided an opportunity to experience three different leisure activities each week. The adapted physical education class was to develop three lesson plans each week to provide minimal instruction and opportunity for the individuals with disabilities to participate actively. The criteria were established that the activities had to be age-appropriate and could not be repeated within the semester time

frame. Some activities that the adapted physical education students provided were boccie, walleyball,
racquetball, ping pong, line dancing, miniature golf,
flying disc golf, and more traditional activities of
basketball, softball, and weight training. Overall, 30
activities were used to provide the individuals with
disabilities a foundation upon which to base preferences and choices. The collaborative effort also
provided opportunities for the university students to
work with individuals with disabilities in order to
find the commonalties rather than the differences.
This approach was extremely effective during discussions with the individuals with disabilities in the
determination of leisure activities within the therapeutic recreation department. The knowledge base
of the individuals with disabilities had been increased. They could make an informed choice
about what they did and did not want to do with
their leisure time based on actual experiences in a
fun and successful environment.

Finances

It is unfortunate, but a fact, that most leisure activities cost money. If the activities selected are
beyond the means of the student and family, then
the right to participate is outweighed by fiscal responsibility. Access to leisure activities may be
restricted due to the same fiscal constraints. Restricted accessibility because of physical barriers
is another matter. Under ADA, accessibility to
programs is mandated. Sometimes a teacher,
parent, student, or administrator will not act to
have a facility or agency accommodate the student's accessibility requirements. This is especially true in smaller rural communities. For
example, there could be a fear of repercussions to
a school, student, or teacher requesting accessibility (i.e., a fitness center not contributing any
further athletic fundraising to the school if the
center is forced to install a ramp or elevator).
There are no right or wrong answers to many situations. A teacher must weigh the factors and, in
collaboration with the transition planning team,
make decisions that are appropriate for the
student, the school, and the community.

Transportation

Transportation is one of the major issues for
leisure activities (or rather the lack of transportation). Instead of participating in leisure activities of choice, leisure participation may occur
because of proximity. Although this is a factor
for individuals without disabilities, the range is
more limited for individuals with disabilities.
Many leisure activities are restricted or not even
offered because of the distance from the residence, lack of transportation, or lack of access to
public transportation. As we move into the
twenty-first century, a factor that cannot be ignored is the safety of students using public
transportation. Teachers should be cognizant of
the student's needs for personal safety skills.

Roles and Responsibilities

School Responsibilities

Administrators of special education programs
are usually anxious about increased liability for
leisure programs, especially when they involve
community-based training. The community-
based programming must be part of the student's IEP. The individualized community-based
leisure program should be clear and concise regarding who, what, when, and where services are
delivered. If students have recreation and
leisure activities incorporated into their IEP, insurance will cover community-based training
(McDonnell et al., 1991).

Special education transition teachers should
receive ongoing training in the provision of community-based leisure programming. Training
must include methods to increase student
safety. For example, having a formal procedure
in place so that all students riding in a car or van
to a community outing must have their seat belt
buckled before starting the vehicle is a smart
practice. In most physical activities, there is an
inherent risk of injury that is not commonly associated with classroom tasks. Teachers need to
be aware about the added risk of movement activities in terms of student accidents. Teacher

training in procedures that must be followed in regard to any emergency should be documented and reviewed annually. Teachers should have a method to document student progress in the community-based leisure setting. Often, because it is a leisure activity, progress is not documented like other academically oriented tasks.

Critical Point   The school's insurance needs to cover any community-based instruction, especially if the activity is included in the IEP.

An extremely important component to community-based leisure training is transportation. How will the student get to the location? Will the teacher be required to drive? What vehicle is to be utilized? In many cases, the answer is simple. Educationally, the best mode of transportation would be one that the student can access and participate in learning how to use. Having the student use a municipality run bus or train system might be a preferred educational alternative. This could be accomplished by targeting utilization of the mass transit as a training program or an IEP objective to facilitate independence. Although this method of transportation might be one that allows for more potential problems, independence is more readily fostered when the student has learned to perform the activity on his or her own.

In another instance, the school may need to provide the transportation. In some school districts, teachers can drive (check with your school district policy) if they are properly licensed and in good standing. On the other hand, some school districts will only let their bus drivers transport students. This increases the cost of community-based programming dramatically. Sometimes a big yellow bus arrives with four students and one teacher. However, a teacher is under the constraints of their school policy. The vehicle that is to be used can vary with each school. We believe that it is prudent not to use a privately owned vehicle. Depending on the insurance company, liability and coverage can be rendered void in some instances if a teacher

transports students in his or her car. The bus, van, or car needs to have documented history of maintenance (usually a state requirement). Procedures for transporting any school-age students must be rigorously followed. This is a protection for the student, teacher, administrator, and school district.

Generally, teachers are protected when they drive students to community-based sites: If the teacher obeys the rules of the road and makes decisions based on what others would do in the same circumstance, then liability insurance will cover the teacher. However, if the teachers are negligent in their duties (i.e., running a stop sign or not having students buckled into their seats), then liability insurance will not provide the necessary protection. The bottom line for administrators is to make sure that (1) liability insurance coverage is adequate and current, (2) school personnel have the proper credentials and in-service training, and (3) transportation is appropriate and properly maintained.

Critical Point   Various methods can be utilized in gaining transportation access to recreation and leisure activities. The preferred method should be one that the student can perform independently.

Teacher Responsibility
The teacher who is providing a program in the community for the first time may be scared or inadequately prepared. The teacher may not want to take students with disabilities into the community nor to deal with community attitudes toward individuals with disabilities. It is uncomfortable for everyone when a manager, store owner, or agency asks you to leave a location. Sometimes this happens because a student is exhibiting inappropriate behavior, or other patrons feel uncomfortable, or because of society's ignorance of the law and/or disabilities. Like most new situations, the teacher will overcome this anxiety quickly. The teacher's responsibilities in leisure community-based training include teaching students appropriate leisure skills, expecting students to act and interact appropriately, supervising student safety, making

sure the student wants to do the activity, monitoring student progress, acting in a prudent manner in all situations, and ensuring positive interactions with the community members in order to change attitudes positively toward individuals with disabilities. A teacher needs to remember that a student should never be forced to participate in a leisure activity; encouraged, yes, but forced, no.

Critical Point   Teachers are the primary conduit for achieving recreational and leisure goals and they should be well-versed in operating community-based activities.

Student Responsibilities

The student with disabilities has a responsibility to learn the leisure skills, to participate, and to interact appropriately. In a community-based setting, it is important that the student wants to be there and to participate. The student also has the responsibility for saying "No" when he or she does not want to take part in the activity. For example, "Today, I do not want to go swimming." The student should be informed and understand the consequences of his or her choices.

> Supposing you have tried and failed again and again. You may have a fresh start any moment you choose, for this thing that we call "failure" is not the falling down, but the staying down (Mary Pickford, cited in Warner, 1992).

Individualized Leisure Planning and Supports

Generally, students with disabilities will be engaged enthusiastically in leisure activities when the student has had a choice in the activity. An important consideration for students with disabilities when making their choices is to remember whether that activity is a viable option for the student. For example, golf may be the activity of choice, but if greens fees are beyond the means of the student and their family, is it worth the time or is it fair to the student

and the teacher? However, this does not mean that you cannot experiment with activities in which your students are not normally engaged. Teachers should be aware of family resources, long-term participation opportunities, and availability of needed supports.

Planning

Preparation for recreation and leisure pursuits for everyone needs to start early in the student's life. This is a developed attitude toward attaining and maintaining a level of physical and psychological wellness. However, this is a difficult task for transition-age students with disabilities, who, due to numerous factors, have not been actively involved with leisure activities or recreational programming. Collaboration with families, friends, and community agencies is critical to developing a positive attitude toward leisure and recreational pursuits for this age group.

CASE STUDY C

One parent of an adult child with a severe disability was frustrated that her son only participated in leisure activities if she initiated the activity and participated with him. She realized that this was not "normal" for a 20-year-old young man. Plus, their interests did not always match—she was not much interested in attending drag races and monster truck rallies, and he was not amused by window shopping. So, as difficult as it was for her initially, she paid a male acquaintance, who was a college student around the same age as her son, to take him places. They went fishing and to gun shows, to movies, out to eat, and so on. Not only did this give her some respite from the caregiver role, but also her son was extremely pleased to participate in activities of his liking. The college student was happy to have some extra spending money. Much to everyone's pleasant surprise, the "paid friend" relationship developed into a true friendship. They now continue their relationship, doing things and going places together, and the "paid friend" even attends family functions such as Christmas and birthdays.

Prior to the individual planning meeting, assessments and conversations with the student and parent should focus on leisure activities. The student, through the combined efforts of the school and parents, should be exposed to a variety of age-appropriate community-based leisure activities. Exposure and opportunities to experience leisure activities give the student a knowledge base on which to determine preferences and choices. This is vital for attaining accurate and reliable information from the student. Many activities sound good or look good on paper, but being involved as an active participant can help to determine whether an activity is liked or disliked.

Taking a systematic approach best completes the development of leisure activities and recreational programs. The teacher and parents can survey the community to determine community-based options. This can begin by asking friends and relatives, looking in the yellow pages of the phone book, visiting the local parks and recreation department, YMCAs, YWCAs, and other social service agencies which focus upon leisure activities and recreational programming.

Community Leisure Supports

We believe that the principal reason that individuals with disabilities fail in the process of community integration is the lack of natural community supports. Teachers are primed to provide support systems in vocational placements. This typically does not carry over into residential placements or leisure activities. The lack of natural supports does not prevent residential placements because supports and linkages are discussed in the planning process. Parents often play an integral part in residential "supervision" or adult service agencies will pay staff to provide assistance. These essential individuals will assure that the student with a disability has his or her laundry done, groceries bought, and meals prepared. The same does not apply for recreational programming.

Memberships may be purchased to local health or fitness centers. A paid staff or family member may accompany the student for the first few times. Then, they expect the training or orientation to carry over because the student is independent in the setting. The student can perform all the needed skills to be successful in that setting. However, the student may refuse to go and the parents and the professionals feel defeated. The failure is not due to the training, the parents, or even the professionals. The failure occurs when the natural support network is not established for the individual with a disability. A collaborative effort of family, friends, and teachers needs to be established to support that individual in the community leisure setting. For the leisure program to be successful, the student should have fun and friends to accompany him or her in the leisure activity. The challenge for professionals is to develop a network that will sustain itself for the individual with a disability.

CASE STUDY D

A new high school special education teacher entered her classroom of profoundly retarded teenagers and was frustrated that her students did not know what to do with themselves during free time. They did not know how to initiate activities nor how to choose a desired activity when presented with choices. To make matters worse, there was very little in the way of things to choose from, and the school was on an extremely limited budget (and so was she!). But she wanted to teach the students that when they finished their work, they could be rewarded with free time, and she wanted to teach them how to fill their free time. So, she started by purchasing a deck of cards and a basketball. When the students finished their task, they were allowed to choose between playing cards or playing ball and were expected to follow through with their choice. The teacher gradually added equipment, materials, and supplies to the repertoire over the course of 2 years. They have options of playing cards, ball, board games, looking at photo albums, making crafts, writing, flying kites, going for walks outside, and so on. She made a wallet-sized notebook of pictures of each of the activity options. And now, after introducing activities one at a time in conjunction with the picture representation, the students not only can choose between two activities, but they can choose an activity from the laundry list of activities in the notebook. They are developing preferences for activities and are now learning to initiate filling their free time.

CASE STUDY E

A high school special education teacher has a unique use of homework in her class. The students are profoundly retarded, predominantly nonverbal, and require intensive work on socialization skills. The principal initiated a "homework for every student, everyday" rule, so the special education teacher decided to take him up on it. She now sends home homework with the students each night with simple questions about, "What did I do when I got home from school?" "What did I eat for dinner?" "What did I eat for breakfast?" The homework sheet encourages interaction between the students and their families; it provides continuity between home and school; it helps the students with memory recall; it assists with communication skills at school; and it helps with socialization skills at school. One student has even learned to use the questions to initiate interaction with nondisabled peers during class changes in the hallway—he will now go up to other students and ask them what they had for dinner last night.

Assessment

Assessment is a critical component to the special education process. Teachers need assessment information for individual education/ transition planning. Assessment is a critical component to the leisure or recreational area of transition of youth with disabilities. The problem, as outlined in the following paragraphs, is how to conduct the assessment with virtually little in the way of instrumentation and a lack of real-life experiences of individuals with disabilities. Other than limited, adapted physical education classes, where the focus is on motor skill development or team sports, individuals with disabilities do not know how to spend their leisure time.

Information that is important when trying to ascertain leisure skills and interests include leisure interests, leisure participation history, current activity patterns, family and friend involvement in leisure pursuits, medical considerations (i.e., limitations and precautions), and strengths and weaknesses in leisure and social skills.

Leisure Assessment Instruments

Leisure assessment instruments are either checklists, pictorial representations of checklists, and an observation or verbal report. The checklists can be lists of any known activity. The evaluator will sit with a student and quiz him or her on what he or she would like to do. For example, Do you like to play basketball? Do you like to fish? Do you like to play badminton? The student responds accordingly (usually with a "Yes") and often does not have any idea what the activity actually entails. After responding "Yes" to many of the items, the student realizes that he or she should say "No" to some; so, the student responds according to expectations with a few "nos." The diligent teacher will ask each student every item on the pages of the activities listed, whether or not it is appropriate. Another often used approach is termed the "menu approach." The school only has four leisure options available for students with disabilities. These are bowling, basketball, track and field, and aquatics. The students get to make a choice and the majority wins! However, typically, the school will only offer one option per semester.

Critical Point Leisure assessment instruments consist of checklists, pictorial representations of checklists, and an observation or verbal report.

CASE STUDY F

Home-school "journaling" is becoming more and more popular, and more and more beneficial, across the age span. A local preschool uses home-school "journaling" to keep parents informed of the child's day at school: What they enjoy doing? Whom they enjoy playing with? How they ate or napped? and so on. In addition, parents can communicate to the teachers' situations or events that are going on at home: special activities or events, illness, new puppies, special visitors, and so on. Knowing what is going on in a young child's day can give a parent or teacher valuable information about that child's behavior. It also helps to promote communication among children who are learning language (and many times difficult to understand).

A local second grade teacher uses home-school "journaling" to encourage communication between students and parents about the school day. Students practice their writing skills, sentence development, and idea sharing, by writing three to four sentences about the school day in a notebook that is then taken home to be shared with a parent(s). This helps to alleviate the following kind of interchange when the child gets home from school:

> *Mom:* "How was your day at school?"
> *Son:* "Fine."
> *Mom:* "What did you do today at school?"
> *Son:* "Nothing."

In another local situation, a high school special education teacher uses home-school "journaling" to communicate to parents the progress that is being made at school, as well as relating daily activities for those students who are nonverbal. The teacher also can communicate when more medication, or a change of clothes is needed at school, as well as to find out about things that are happening at home that might be affecting the student's behavior. While this teacher provides spiral steno notebooks for each student, one parent has purchased a diary-type journal to use so that they can save the memories.

Another method for assessment in the leisure area is asking parents what their child likes to do in his or her free time. Parents often are surprised about this question being asked. Teachers frequently are surprised by the activities that their students are involved in at home. For example, a 17-year-old female student colors in a coloring book and listens to records all evening. If the teacher probes, the parents might indicate that their daughter chooses to do this every evening. The next logical question to the parents should be "What are the other options from which she can choose?"

A method used frequently by teachers is direct observation. Through observation of students over a period of time, the watchful teacher can tell you what each student prefers to do in his or her leisure time (at school). Of course, this requires that the teacher allow free time and provide plenty of options from which the students can choose during this free time. It may even require that the teacher teach the student how to make a decision regarding the choices.

Of course, this seems to be the best guess method of assessing the leisure area. For the question to professionals is, "How can a student make a choice or respond to interest inventories with limited leisure experiences on which to base the choices?" If you remember the typical response from a student with a developmental disability to the question, "Where do you want to work?" The typical response is "McDonalds." Do all students with developmental disabilities want to work at McDonalds? Probably not, but based on their experiences of seeing an individual with a disability work at the local McDonalds; commercials on television suggesting individuals with disabilities can work there; questions from professionals asking if they want to work at a place like McDonalds; and the place where they probably eat the most often—their choice, based on their life experiences, is McDonalds. The authors believe (based on our experience) that limited exposure is the cause of many individuals with developmental disabilities selecting bowling as their preferred leisure activity. This lack of experience may be the reason that many leisure assessments, without some prior groundwork, are not valid. It may be reliable, though, because you may get the same response year after year.

To provide a more valid method of assessing leisure activity for your students and assessing their actual skill ability, select a variety of leisure activities for your students to try. Make each activity fun. After utilizing this leisure sampling technique, ask the student questions about preferences from the assortment of checklists and pictorial questionnaires.

Leisure Skills, Age Appropriateness, and Safety

Many students do not have leisure skills. This can be due to a variety of factors. Often individuals with disabilities have medical considerations that cause physicians and/or parents to reduce leisure options drastically. Individuals with disabilities may not have experienced success in any leisure pursuit, and, consequently, lack the motivation to try it again, or to try something new. Your students may not know how to throw a ball, listen during a movie, or interact appropriately in a game setting.

It is important to remember that the students are young adults. Teachers need to provide skills to students that they will carry over into adulthood. Although a big emphasis of segregated recreation programs, such as Special Olympics, appears to be competitive sports (i.e., basketball, softball, and track and field), the majority of individuals with disabilities will not be involved in these activities once they leave school. The same also is true for the majority of Americans without disabilities. The teacher's responsibility is to make certain that the students are learning functional leisure skills that can be exhibited in the communities where the youth will be living. Age-appropriate activities are critical to transition-age students. Integration into their community requires that the student should not be perceived as childlike. The final obligation of the teacher is to assure that the students learn skills

needed to be safe in his or her pursuit of leisure activities. Sometimes this includes personal safety skills as discussed earlier in the chapter or, more often, this includes safety equipment, for example, wearing a helmet when riding a bicycle or teaching pedestrian survival skills.

Critical Point   Teachers need to assure that students learn skills that are functional and beneficial in their own community and that the students do not exhibit behavior that would draw undo attention to themselves.

Conclusion

Meaningful leisure activities are a vital component in the balance of anyone's life. We know this not only because of the importance of leisure in our own personal lives, but also because IDEA has mandated that we consider this aspect in the lives of our students. When teachers seriously take their commitment to helping students reach their potential, in all areas of their lives, students with disabilities can only benefit. Since people with disabilities typically have more leisure time, it becomes even more important to consider the leisure aspect of the student's life. Teachers need to assess student's leisure interests and skills, teach appropriate leisure and social skills, and link students up with appropriate community activities and organizations. Remember, not only is it okay to have fun; it's necessary!

Study Questions

1. Why is it important to implement and/or access leisure activities for individuals with disabilities?
2. Why is it imperative that leisure activities for students with disabilities are implemented in the community?
3. What are the four principles of IDEA? What are the implications of these principles for leisure activities for individuals with disabilities?
4. What are the procedures for individualizing leisure activities for individuals with disabilities?

5. What are the various perspectives of community-based leisure programming? What are the implications of these perspectives?

Web Sites and Addresses

Check out the following web sites and addresses for a listing of leisure and therapeutic recreation assessments with individuals to contact for further information.

www.recreationtherapy.com/trnet/trnassess.htm

www.aahperd.org

One-Handed Keyboard
www.infogrip.com

Lifting Aids
www.blvd.com/blf

AbleInform Newsletter
www.sasquatch.com/ableinfo

Recreation Therapy
http://www.recreationtherapy.com

Canine Companions
http://caninecompanions.org/

Watchminder
www.watchminder.com/index.htm

Brain Injury Links
www.biawa.org/tbi.html

Communication Aids
http://peabody.vanderbilt.edu/projects/proposed/asttech/commaid/comaid.htm

Fishing Program
www.castforkids.org

Adaptive Equipment
www.achievableconcepts.com.au

Leisure Activity Profile
Total Leisure Counseling, Inc.
2730 Wilshire Boulevard, Suite 350
Santa Monica, CA 90403

Leisure Diagnostic Battery
Division of Recreation and Leisure Studies
Box 13875, NT Station
Denton, TX 76203

Leisurescope
Leisure Dynamics
1425 Timber Valley Road
Colorado Springs, CO 80919

18

My Home
Developing Skills and Supports for Adult Living

James A. Knoll
Carolyn Bardwell Wheeler

*No American should have to live in a
nursing home or state institution if
that individual can live in a
community with the right mix of
affordable supports.*
Donna Shalala, Secretary of Health
and Human Services
July 28, 1999, National Conference of
State Legislatures

LEARNING OBJECTIVES

The objectives of this chapter are:

1. Explain the factors that have contributed to the emergence of supported living and personal assistance services as the preferred organizing frameworks for residential services.

2. Explain the limitations inherent in the traditional services continuum as the organizing framework for residential services for people with mental retardation and developmental disabilities.

3. Define supported living and contrast it with group homes and other "facility-based" approaches.

4. Describe the emergence of the independent living movement.

5. Define personal assistance services and link increased demand for universal access to these services to the disabilities rights movement.

6. Describe legislative and legal developments that are contributing to increased access to supported living and personal assistance services.

7. Describe the use of vision, skills, resources, and supports as a framework for planning for successful transition to independent adult living.

Much of the literature on transition has preparation for employment as its primary focus. For the vast majority of people with disabilities, this is as it should be; just as for many other Americans, the principal determinant of the good life is a secure job that pays a decent salary. Historically, the education system and the adult services system have failed to emphasize paid employment as an expected outcome for people with disabilities. This was one of the factors that led to the mandates for transition planning being written into IDEA. However, it is a major mistake to limit discussions of transition to employment. For many people with disabilities, particularly individuals with severe disabilities, issues of employment must be linked with other aspects of adult life. The place of residence, access to transportation, a range of recreation opportunities, a network of relationships, and needed specialized supports and services are all connected to the opportunity to work, enjoy an acceptable quality of life, and contribute to the life of the community.

In this chapter, we conclude our discussion of what ultimately happens to students with disabilities. Whereas this chapter explores the issues of living independently, Chapter 17 provided a framework for developing and integrating recreation and leisure activities into an individual's life. Both chapters, as with Chapters 15 and 16, explore very real postsecondary issues. The importance of Chapter 18 is that, having lived independently, people with disabilities actually gain additional benefits of self-esteem and satisfaction.

This chapter examines some issues that are critical if students are preparing to live as independently as possible in *their own home* as adults. At the outset, it is important to emphasize that a focus on independent adult life is critical in the education of all students with disabilities. It is a serious error to assume that just because someone has a so-called mild disability, educators should not be concerned with assisting him or her to develop independent living skills. The question of independent community living becomes much more complex when the focus shifts to students with moderate to severe disabilities that need some form of assistance with activities of daily life. This chapter attempts to provide a reasonably balanced presentation of the multiple issues that must be addressed in this area of transition. We begin by examining the challenges that students with disabilities and their parents face as they focus upon independent adult life. We then explore the evolution in supports for home living for adults with severe disabilities that has occurred in the last several decades. This discussion presents the reader with some planning and service delivery issues that continue to confront people with disabilities in many areas today. This discussion is followed by an examination of the current best practice in community living for people with severe disabilities. The concluding section of the chapter presents catalogs of the range of concerns that should be addressed in planning for the transition to adult home life for all students with disabilities.

Certainly, most authors and teachers will contend that preparation for "independent living" is at the heart of the transition process. Unfortunately, the experience of parents and people with disabilities has been otherwise. This area is frequently one where there is a high degree of disconnect between what the schools do and the challenges people confront once they are no longer eligible for a free appropriate public education (FAPE).

The Parental Perspective: Life Is More Than a Job

Most parents of young adults with a disability see employment as an important consideration as they look to the future. However, for many parents, particularly those of students with moderate to severe disabilities, a job is a secondary consideration. Knowing their son or daughter as they do, parents are confronted with the question, "Who will look out for them when I am gone?" (Knoll, 1992). In this lies the critical question that all parents at some level ask the education system. "Are you preparing my child to make a smooth movement into adult life?" "Are you building a foundation for future security?" To the extent that the school system fails to have this real world focus upon transition, it fails to address this truly valued outcome; to that extent, the system is deficient. This is where the central meaning of transition becomes apparent.

For some parents, a narrow emphasis on employment can be at odds with their basic fears about lifelong security for their child. The promise of employment is a chimera—a wisp of smoke—that can vanish with the next economic downturn, corporate acquisition, or change of supervisors. Why should the relative security of social security disability be abandoned for the mere promise of a possibility?

Critical Point   Parents often define their hopes for their children with disabilities in terms of assurances of long term safety and security.

This sense of social insecurity is further intensified by the day-to-day battle which most families experience to obtain the most rudimentary services. Families are not looking for absolute certainty, but they are searching for a sense of stability and commitment to the long-term support of their son or daughter. Traditionally, this type of security often was tied to the bricks, mortar, and real estate of the old institutions and group homes. As we move into the twenty-first century, the fundamental challenge of transition for students with a disability is the need to develop the necessary skills and to mobilize the resources for the future so that the family can envision stability and security ahead for their child. Lack of knowledge about available resources, referrals to a waiting list, endless application forms to complete, complex interagency agreements, conflicts over responsibilities, and mere paperwork plans create anxieties, not assurance.

So, for many families, the centerpiece of the transition process and the foundation for all other outcomes, even the possibility of employment, is the development of a vision of a person's home as an adult. Home, "a place of safety and security, my place, the base of operations, where I'm in charge" is not usually on the top of the agenda for the typical young adult. This is something that takes on meaning and reality as the person becomes emancipated from his or her parents' home and forms an independent identity. In some ways, the establishment of our own household is the line of demarcation for true adulthood (Ferguson & Ferguson, 2000). We set up housekeeping; we define our place in the world. The absence of this vision for the future of their children with severe disabilities leads many parents not to see transition as a time to broaden horizons. Rather, they experience new limitations as the entitlement of free appropriate public education seems to be replaced by the uncertainty of adult life.

Thus, parents who often have struggled long and hard with the reality of a child's disability may view transition to adult life in a different light from that of the professional who is involved with the family. Not surprisingly, the young adult with a disability may have an experience and a perception of this whole process that differs from the perspective of both parents and professionals.

The Personal Perspective: Young and Restless

For 2 years, I (the senior author) spent every other Thursday evening at a community college meeting with a group of young adults from 18 to 30 years of age, who felt that their high school education had failed them. They called themselves "the young and the restless." They had come together to provide mutual support based on the common experience of having graduated from special education. They ranged in age from 18 to 35, with the vast majority of them in the late twenties. People in the group experienced a wide variety of disabilities although most of them had been labeled "mentally retarded" at some time during their education career. Most members lived at home with their parents or a family member. A few lived on their own or with friends. Some lived in group homes or other agency-run programs. There was one married couple with a child who owned their own home.

Critical Point   Young adults with disabilities have the same hopes and fears as their non-disabled peers.

In many ways, these folks were like their peers in this working-class suburb of Detroit, with one major difference. At a time in life when young Americans are usually striking out and establishing themselves in the world, these folks saw themselves confronting barriers, not possibilities. They were unanimous in the belief that their lives were being shaped and controlled by other people. That is why they were restless. For them, it was a time to stop waiting and to get moving with life. As the group matured and grew, they saw themselves moving beyond sharing experience and commiserating to advocating actively for something that most Americans take for granted: the right to make choices regarding their own lives.

On a personal level, my role as a resource and support person for this group was the most valuable learning experience in my professional career. After years as a teacher, researcher, and advocate I found myself confronting the essence of the values that lay at the heart of special education. The rhetoric about choice and self-determination, the assertions of the need to use people-first language, the need for education to provide people with the skills that are necessary to meet the challenges of the real world, and so much more took on new meaning

as I listened to and responded to the requests of the members of the young and the restless. What made this a powerful experience was the simple fact that for the first time in my career the tables were turned. They—people with cognitive disabilities—were really in charge. I was being called on to respond to what they *wanted*, not what we (parents, professionals, policymakers, etc.) felt they needed. The lessons of this experience are powerful and abiding. At the heart of the challenges confronting "the young and the restless," lay the essential failure of education and adult services to support meaningful transition into adult life.

Considering the standards of the 1980s and early 1990s, most of the members of the young and the restless had a reasonably good high school special education experience. However, they were largely segregated from their peers without disabilities, and the special school district that served most of them had a very strong focus on employment. Most of them had a wide variety of community job exploration and work experiences during their high school years. At the time, the group was meeting the director of the special high school program, who was able to boast that any of his graduates who wanted to work had a job when they finished high school. Many members of the group were the beneficiaries of this noteworthy effort. Yet, as mentioned earlier, they felt trapped, limited, and ill-served by their experience in special education. Why?

Almost universally, the members of the young and the restless had the following experiences. First, they were ill-prepared to face the challenges of life outside the workplace. The real fiscal and logistical demands of daily life were far more complex than what they learned in functional math, home economics, or life skill classes. Second, although they were prepared to be reliable and well-trained workers, they were not ready for the social complexities of the workplace. Third, the protective nature of their experience in special education had left them ill-prepared for the real world. They did not have the skill or experience to differentiate users and abusers from the decent people. Finally, they said that for the most part their parents, family members, service providers, and neighbors were not prepared to see them as young adults with the same needs and desires as others of their own age. Hence, the people with disabilities saw their options as restricted because of parental resistance, arbitrary limits on support services, and prejudice.

Critical Point   A commitment to self-determination requires a re-examination of professional roles.

Transition to a New Vision

The "story" in this chapter is not really about the young and the restless and their thousands of peers with a wide range of disability labels. The story here is about us—teachers, administrators, and adult service workers—and how we have learned to listen to all the young and restless people whom we encounter. We had to create the concept of transition to help us support people with disabilities as they face the challenge of growth and change that comes with movement toward becoming an adult in our society. The challenges were always present, but, for a long time, our preconception about what was possible for people with disabilities has limited our ability to act. So, this chapter is about "transition," not so much as mandated by IDEA, but as a fundamental reorientation in the thinking. The real story here is about how *we* learned to listen and see.

The evolution of a positive vision of the future does not emerge overnight. A vision of possibilities after high school for the young and the restless and their peers with disabilities comes from their life experience, just as it does for all young adults. The presence or absence of a vision of possibilities ultimately revolves around a series of questions that go to the heart of education quality:

- Are teachers and the school systems clear from the time a student enters school that the ultimate measure of education quality and success is how the individual does after graduation?
- Has the total education program been guided by a long-term vision of possibilities?
- Has transition toward a meaningful adult life been a facet of education from day one?
- Have teachers and administrators promoted values of independence, contribution, and community participation for all students?
- Or, has the focus of education for students with disabilities been one of low expectations and restricted opportunity that leads to a vision of life on public assistance, dependency, or providing employment for human service workers?

As every chapter in this text makes clear, a long-term systemic approach to transition is critical to shaping positive outcomes for all students with disabilities.

The reality is that a vision of possibilities is only partially dependent on opportunities provided by the school and the advocacy of parents and others. Unfortunately, the legitimate hopes and ambitions of people with disabilities in this country and throughout the world are, in fact, subject to societal and community forces that have little to do with personal motivation or vision. Generations of people with disabilities have seen their hopes and the hopes of their families shattered against the hard realities of service agencies and a public that has no vision of possibilities. Indeed, even today students who have received a free, appropriate public education in the least restrictive environment with an appropriate focus on transition toward meaningful adult outcomes can be frustrated. It is still true that even with a successful education experience, some students and their family members will experience the blank stare of an absent vision as they look to adult agencies to support them in their home, job, and community.

From Placements to People

To understand what is possible for young adults with disabilities today, we must review the evolution of residential services during this century. As ADAPT (Americans Disabled for Attendant Programs Today) points out:

> The 20th century began with eugenics taking a primary place in US and world history (it could be called the "Century of Eugenics"). But, it will end with a "qualified" victory for the integration of people with disabilities in all communities . . . [in] the 1920's and 30's when states not only sterilized and legally terminated the lives of people with disabilities, but their creation of institutions for people with disabilities became widespread; and as the century grew so did these institutions from nursing homes, to institutions for people with psychiatric or developmental disabilities. . . . Yesterday the question was should people with disabilities live in the community? Today it is how are we to provide services for people with disabilities in the community (ADAPT, 1999b, p. 1)?

The critical lessons that emerged from this movement from "special places for special people" to "an individualized system of support for home living" have relevance for all the young and the restless.

Relocation

By the late 1960s the rationale for segregation of people with disabilities based on the ideology of the eugenics movement was long dead. However, the professional practices and the facilities developed in the first half of the century loomed over people with disabilities and their families. Basically, the only publicly funded resources available for people with extensive disabilities existed in institutions, nursing homes, rehabilitation centers, and other long-term care facilities. A fundamental reorientation of services occurred in the United States during the late 1960s and 1970s. The most visible sign of this transformation has been the downsizing of publicly financed residential institutions for people with mental retardation and psychiatric illness into the 1970s. The exposé of life in these facilities and the associated lawsuits required states to begin the development of the so-called "community-based services." Although this relocation of services has had a far-reaching impact, it merely set the stage for what some have regarded as a true revolution. This revolution has changed both the modes of service delivery and the underlying philosophy that guides the thinking of providers. This essential reexamination of basic principles is at the heart of a new way of thinking about disability and the roles of the organization and the individuals that work with people with disabilities.

The profound nature of this change notwithstanding, in the public eye, the issue is simply "relocation." It continues to be controversial as the state department announces plans to close a large congregate care facility and to move the residents to smaller community homes. Indeed, this process of relocation provides a foundation for asking the basic questions that led to the transformation.

The controversies surrounding institutional closure and relocation have made the fundamental transformation largely invisible to the general public. For example, even today large segments of the general public continue to see people with developmental disabilities in terms of the prejudices and beliefs of the past. Indeed, the very idea that, in 1999, eight states (New Hampshire, Vermont, Rhode Island, Maine, New Mexico, West Virginia, Alaska, and Hawaii) and the District of Columbia no longer had an institution for people who were labeled as mentally retarded and that several other states had reduced their institutional population to the point that the one remaining facility has a total population equivalent to a large group home has come as an absolute revelation. Many in the general public still accept it as axiomatic that special people need special places.

Yet, this relocation of services that has gradually captured the public unaware is not the core of this chapter. What we want to explore is the next wave of this change that is even today challenging the "new" structure put in place by the previous generation's efforts at deinstitutionalization.

The public outcry at the abysmal conditions in the old institutions led to an effort to rectify the problem by developing smaller "homelike" settings in "typical neighborhoods." The group homes, board and care homes, adult foster care homes, and "independent living apartment programs" of the 1960s and the 1970s laid the foundation for the new community system of services. These networks of residential services were and often are still called "community alternatives," as an alternative to institutions. For the general public, the entire effort has, perhaps, been best captured under the rubric of "group homes." This is not surprising since group homes were and still are central to this effort. The last two decades have seen the emergence of a massive national system of small facilities housing 3 to 16 individuals. National chains of for-profit provider organizations that contract with states or local community mental health organization manage many of them.

Because a good part of this reform of services was paid for by federal money, under the medicaid program, much of the guidance was provided by federal regulations. It is important to realize that these regulations were initially designed to address the myriad of problems in the old large congregate care institutions. So-called "small ICF/MR" (intermediate care facility for the mentally retarded) regulations often were adopted by states to govern group homes that were not medicaid funded. This footnote on federal congregate care policy is an instructive artifact that helps to guide any student who wishes to understand the underlying tensions in the field of adult services today.

Essentially, the federal regulations took the guidance provided for the management of a facility that is designed for hundreds, if not thousands, of inmates and "simplified" them for facilities serving 16 or less and located in community settings. The underlying model that shaped these regulations was medical in focus and sought to provide quality care and treatment for "patients" who were defined by regulation as being dependent and "incompetent" to care for themselves. This gross simplification of a complex series of historical events serves to capture an important fact that goes to the heart of our central discussion in this chapter. *The "traditional" approach to community residential and vocational services for people with developmental disabilities is based on the largely uncritical translation of the institutional model into a community environment.* This reality notwithstanding, thousands of people in these community programs have a life experience significantly better than that of people who continue to reside in institutions. A generation of people had been the beneficiary of the "community-based model" of service.

Critical Point   Initial efforts to reform residential services for people with developmental disabilities focused on regulations for "cleaning up" institutions and using these new rules to guide the establishment of smaller facilities located in residential neighborhoods.

Perhaps, more importantly, the next phase in the conceptual revolution would have been impossible if the process of relocation had not occurred.

Renovation

Through the 1970s and into the 1980s, two currents intertwined to provide a critique of the rapidly developing system of community services for people with disabilities. As group homes, adult care facilities, and nursing homes proliferated, the principle of normalization and the independent living movement, emphasized that simply being smaller was not sufficient to be better. Together these two related philosophies of service pushed for a fundamental reexamination of practice in all organizations and agencies serving people with disabilities.

Normalization

Integral to the ongoing process of change was the vision of possibilities nurtured by the principle of *normalization*. First articulated in the late 1960s and early 1970s, normalization attempted to provide a coherent framework for planning services (Wolfensberger, 1972). It offered a positive response to the demeaning and dehumanizing conditions found in most institutions. At its core, normalization was premised on respect for the basic humanity of individuals with disabilities. It was based on the assumption that, like all human beings, people with cognitive disabilities would mature, develop, learn, and change based on their life experience. Further, it adopted an ecological perspective on human development by holding that the interaction between the person and the environment must be consciously examined in the design and management of human service organizations. In essence, "normalization" means making available patterns and activities of everyday life for people with disabilities that are as close as possible to those experienced by their same age peers. If you wanted people to grow, you could not provide them with narrowly constricted opportunities; you needed to provide them with the same range of possibilities as anyone else. The apparent simplicity of normalization led many critics to contend mistakenly that it denied the reality of disability. This did not mean, "making people normal." It acknowledged that a special set of guiding principles was required because people with disabilities often need extraordinary resources in order to achieve the most typical goals. Normalization provided a way for professionals to consider how they provided these extraordinary resources.

Thankfully, from a current vantage point in the twenty-first century some of these ideas seem self-evident. Yet, in the 1970s and 1980s, normalization had a revolutionary effect on services for people with developmental disabilities. It provided the generation of people coming into the field of human services in the decades with a critical framework from which to examine themselves and the agencies for which they worked. It was no longer acceptable to attribute less than optimal programming to the limitation of the "clients." Increasingly, there was a call for organizations to be accountable for assisting people to achieve meaningful quality-of-life outcomes.

Critical Point   Normalization provided a context for critical thinking about services for people with disabilities.

Only after relocation had occurred were advocates, parents, and progressive service providers able to confront the contradictions inherent in the "community-based services system." Eventually, the principle of normalization led many individuals who had built group homes to confront the structural problems inherent in these minifacilities. Increasingly, it became apparent that regulations and structures which were premised on the smooth running of large-scale congregate care facilities had little to do with assisting people to achieve their legitimate aspirations as a citizen. On a daily basis, service providers, advocates, and family members found themselves struggling to balance the tension inherent in the interplay of the individuals' hopes and fears, human relationships, and the bizarre requirements of state and federal regulations. All of this just so that people with disabilities could live a "normal life." It seemed so simple, yet, the implementation was quite complex.

Independent Living

As it evolved, the principle of normalization moved from being seen exclusively as a framework for services for people with mental retardation and developmental disabilities. Professionals in many other areas of disability service saw its value as a critical framework. Additionally, an emerging group of people with disabilities viewed it as a valuable tool to use in their challenge to the status quo. In the late 1960s and early 1970s, groups of people, primarily with physical disabilities, around the country (most notably in Berkley, CA, and in Denver, CO) began to organize to challenge the barriers they encountered in daily life. This beginning of the disability rights movement saw normalization as one tool that could assist people with disabilities in their struggle to gain control of their own lives.

This effort, which became known as the *independent living movement*, grew out of the social change of the 1960s. As racial and ethnic minorities and women came together in mutual support to challenge institutionalized discrimination, so did these pioneers with disabilities. They looked at the struggles of these other groups and saw that they too were the "victim" not of physical conditions but of societal prejudice. Historians of this movement (McDonald & Oxford, n.d.) point to its linkage to five social movements: (1) deinstitutionalization, (2) the African-American civil rights movement, (3) the "self-help" movement as seen in organizations such as Alcoholics Anonymous, (4) the demedicalization movement toward more holistic approaches to health care, and (5) the consumerism movement toward greater responsiveness on the part of providers and manufacturers. Central to this movement is the idea of control by consumers of goods and services over the choices and options that are available to them. People with disabilities were not to be seen as passive recipients of "care" or patients, but, rather, as self-directed individuals making the decisions that are needed to manage their own lives. This way of thinking quickly evolved beyond the management of one's own life to direct control and management of the services.

The development of independent living was synthesized in the late 1970s by Gerben DeJong (1979) when he presented independent living as a fully developed alternative to the medical model. Disability was neither abnormal nor a tragedy that transformed the person, but it was a natural part of the human experience. As DeJong articulated on independent living, the problems or deficits were found in the society, not the individual. Within this framework, people with disabilities were not sick or broken; they did not need to be "fixed." The real problems are the social and attitudinal barriers that they face. What was in need of repair was society, not the people with disabilities. Finally, and most importantly, control must be exercised by the individual and not by the medical or rehabilitation professional. From an independent living perspective, people with disabilities are self-determining individuals who are not passive victims, objects of charity, cripples, or incomplete people.

Critical Point   Consumer control is the centerpiece of the independent living movement.

The independent living movement found a focus for its philosophy in the programs of centers for independent living (CILs), which was established and funded by the Rehabilitation Act of 1973 (see Table 18–1). The legislation provides for a high degree of direct consumer control in these new centers. As might be anticipated, many of these new programs initially were found to be closely linked to traditional rehabilitation centers. As the network expanded and the mandate for true control by people with disabilities was underscored by subsequent reauthorization of the act, this ideal became a reality. Simultaneously, the "political wing" of the movement joined with other disability organizations to mobilize for federal passage of a civil rights act that recognized the reality of discrimination in the lives of Americans with disabilities. With the passage of the Americans with Disabilities Act in 1990, the movement was able to turn its attention to the reality of segregation of people with disabilities, specifically, the thousands of people with a wide variety of disabilities who were confined against their choice in nursing homes and other long-term

TABLE 18–1

Guiding Principle for Centers for Independent Living

As outlined in the Rehabilitation Act of 1973, as amended, Title VII, Chapter 1, Part C, Section 721, there are seven (7) standards for the center for independent living.

1. *Philosophy.* The center shall promote and practice the independent living philosophy of
   a. Consumer control of the center regarding decision making, service delivery, management, and establishment of the policy and direction of the center;
   b. Self-help and self-advocacy;
   c. Development of peer relationships and peer role models; and
   d. Equal access of individuals with severe disabilities to society and to all services, programs, activities, resources, and facilities, whether public or private and regardless of the funding source.

2. *Provision of services.* The center shall provide services to individuals with a range of severe disabilities. The center shall provide services on a cross-disability basis (for individuals with all different types of severe disabilities, including individuals with disabilities who are members of populations that are unserved or underserved by programs under this act). Eligibility for services at any center for independent living shall not be based on the presence of any one or more specific severe disabilities.

3. *Independent living goals.* The center shall facilitate development and achievement of independent living goals selected by individuals with severe disabilities who seek such assistance by the center.

4. *Community options.* The center shall work to increase the availability and to improve the quality of community options for independent living in order to facilitate the development and achievement of independent living goals by individuals with severe disabilities.

5. *Independent living core services.* The center shall provide independent living core services and, as appropriate, a combination of any other independent living services specified in section 7(30) (B).

6. *Activities to increase community capacity.* The center shall conduct activities to increase the capacity of communities within the service area of the center to meet the needs of individuals with severe disabilities.

7. *Resource development activities.* The center shall conduct resource development activities to obtain funding from sources other than this chapter.

Source: From the Rehabilitation Act of 1973 as amended, Title VII, Chap. 1, Pt. C, Section 721, Rehabilitation Services Administration, Office of Special Education and Rehabilitation Services, U.S. Department of Education.

care facilities. It became clear that the next target was the bias in favor of congregate care facilities that existed in professional practice and the federally funded program for people with significant disabilities (medicaid).

Initially, the independent living movement focused primarily upon its traditional core constituency of people with physical disabilities. With the growth of the movement, it became more inclusive involving people with conditions such as traumatic brain injury and psychiatric conditions. However, many individuals in the movement continued to see the issues of services for people with mental retardation and developmental disabilities as different. After all, these latter groups had a cognitive disability. Could they really manage their own lives? During the early 1990s, this changed as the self-advocacy movement and the emergence of "supported living" demonstrated that fundamentally all people with disabilities confronted the same barriers.

Revisioning

For people with developmental disabilities, the traditional approach to services was fairly successful at achieving deinstitutionalization. True community membership occurred less easily. By 1986, the majority of individuals who were receiving residential services were living in community facilities and residences (Lakin, Hill, White, & Write, 1988). However, it is important to note that although most individuals with developmental disabilities were living in communities, this did not mean that they actively participated in community life (Kregel, Wehman, Seyfarth, & Marshall, 1986). Programs and residences can easily be physically located in the community without being socially integrated (Biklen & Knoll, 1987a). The aforementioned medicaid regulations told providers to focus upon preparing staff to manage the facilities and failed to make community membership a clear priority (Knoll & Ford, 1987). These regulations led many traditional group homes to institute practices that actually erected barriers between the residents and the neighbors (Biklen & Knoll, 1987b).

These community-based group facilities were better than the old institutions. However, they continue to be *facilities and not homes*. The distinction between a home and a facility is an important one. Few people would choose to live in a facility. With few exceptions, persons living in housing provided by social service agencies did not choose where they live or with whom they live. Within this system, the type of facility determines the services. A change in service needs necessitates a move by the individual. Individuals are denied the opportunity to establish permanency or roots in their communities. Furthermore, with housing owned and controlled by service providers, residents develop neither a sense of ownership nor a feeling of "home" about where they live.

Critical Point   Supported living reflects a new way of thinking, which abandons the preconceptions of tra-

ditional facility-based approach, about how to meet the needs of people with severe disabilities.

In the mid-1980s, the new vision began to come into focus for the field of developmental disabilities. This did not occur in a university think tank, a state administrator's office, or a federal agency, but, rather, in small organizations that decided to "work around" the rules (Taylor, Racino, Knoll, & Lutifyya, 1987). Initially called the "nonfacility-based" approach to services, these local efforts challenged the typical way of doing business. They quickly helped to define a new state of the art in "community support" or just "support" rather than "community-based services."

The language used reflected "A new way of thinking" in the field of developmental disabilities (Minnesota Governor's Planning Council on Developmental Disabilities, 1987). "Support" as a new organizing framework in the mental retardation and developmental disabilities field was the engine of change in the late 1980s and early 1990s (Bradley, Ashbaugh, & Blaney, 1994). The inclusion of the concept in the 1992 revision of the definition of mental retardation published by the American Association on Mental Retardation (AAMR) has contributed to the continuing controversy surrounding that definition (Luckasson et al., 1992). It provided the basis for the authors of that definition contending that the 1992 document reflected a new paradigm for thinking about mental retardation (Luckasson & Spitalnik, 1994; Schalock et al., 1994).

Community "services," as developed during the era of deinstitutionalization, are based on the so-called "continuum" model. This continuum of residential services stretched from the traditional institution on one end to "independent living" at the other end. Along the way, the system offered various types of group living arrangements. These small facilities often are described as offering residents a range of "residential settings" that are "homelike" and "normalized," primarily because they are smaller and geographically less isolated than the large institutions of the past. The emphasis has been on the development of "programs," a predefined package of services, into which people can fit based on an assessment of their functioning level. The concept of community support offers an alternative to the continuum of services with its emphasis on program slots. Rather than focusing upon putting people into community programs, the attention is on building the "individual network" of formal and informal "supports" that a person needs in order to meet the day-to-day demands of his or her home and community (Ferguson & Olson, 1989; Taylor, 1988; Taylor, Racino, Knoll, & Lutifyya, 1987).

In effect, this approach emphasized the separation of housing from support services. Because initial efforts at the development of community programs for people with developmental disabilities usually were deinstitutionalization efforts, it was assumed that the two needs, housing and services, were linked. Experience showed that this was not so and was the reverse of innovation in cost-effective programs of in-home health and service to other "special" populations such as the dependent aged. In these other programs, people receive needed services by using community providers and/or specialized assistance on an "as needed" basis in their own homes. Changing needs did not necessitate a change of residence.

Closely connected to this conceptual breakthrough was another, still controversial, insight: the rejection of the continuum of services as a viable vehicle for organizing services for people with disabilities (Taylor, 1988). The concepts of the least restrictive environment and the continuum of services were useful for the transition of adults with disabilities into the community. As a result of focusing upon programs and a limited number of "options" rather than upon the individual, the services based on these concepts unduly limit the opportunities for people to achieve true membership. Membership is best served when supports are brought into a per-

son's home or other regular community setting, instead of configuring a "setting" around a predefined array of services.

In the area of policy and practices, supported living has moved from small local efforts to being touted as the "New Jerusalem." Many policy analyses see it as the cost-effective salvation for federal agencies, state departments, and local providers who are overwhelmed by demand for services. There has been widespread support for this movement by organizations and individuals confronting the demand for quality services (NAPRR, 1991, 1992; Smith, 1990). Additionally, the federal government explored supported living in eight medicaid community supported living arrangement (CSLA) demonstration projects (Lakin & Burwell, 1995).

Critical Point A supported living program delivers the individually needed services and supports to a person in their home rather than requiring them to move into a facility that provides a pre-established menu of services.

Living in My Own Home

As the preceding discussion makes quite clear, the current generation of students with moderate to severe cognitive disabilities, multiple disabilities, and physical disabilities is the first in the history of the United States that does not have to accept arbitrary limitation on the students' desire to live in their own home as adults. As we move into the twenty-first century, we at last see that the century we have left behind was the century of the institution. No longer is it necessary to use euphemisms such as "homelike setting" or "least restrictive residential alternative" to justify less than optimal living situations. People with significant needs for supports in daily living have the right to expect the same adult outcome as any other member of our society: life in a home of their own. This is really a new phenomenon. Achieving this outcome still requires substantial knowledge and action on the part of educators, parents, and advocates. The following is a discussion of the two related efforts that are increasingly making "a home of my own" a reality for people with varied types of disabilities. Supported living has emerged to provide the service framework for people with developmental disabilities. *Personal assistance services* (PAS) is emerging as the "umbrella" term that may eventually encompass supported living; but, historically, it has been seen as a service for individuals with physical disabilities.

CASE STUDY A

Supported Living in Our Own Words: Julie Allen

Supported living is one of the three greatest things that have happened in the lives of persons with disabilities! The other two are *personal futures planning* and *supported employment.* All three are person-centered supports, not services as defined by the social service system. They all set a person with disabilities free to make a life of his or her own, which is exactly what is happening to Julie and to us, her parents.

However, our life has not always been filled with such opportunity. When Julie graduated from public school at the age of 21, there were no adult services in our community that addressed Julie's needs and preferences. She sat home with mom and dad for a year, and the future looked bleak.

But now, with the help of supported living resources and a planning process, called personal futures planning, we are well on our way for Julie to have an independent life of her own (with support). Our initial intent has been for Julie to have opportunities to be integrated into the community where she lives and to learn new living skills. To accomplish this, our family has utilized supported living resources to employ an "attendant tutor." With the help of her attendant tutor, Julie does volunteer work at the local spouse abuse center and at her church. She is also learning basic housekeeping skills, such as dusting, sweeping, preparing meals, and more.

We are planning for Julie to live in an apartment of her own with a housemate in the near future. The funds to pay for a housemate have been approved. We have found an apartment, and we are in the process of interviewing potential housemates. Boy, are we excited (and a little anxious)! We also are looking for Julie to have a paid job in the community in the near future. We have learned that it is very important to find a good job match for Julie. Supported employment is helping in this area.

In our experience, the most challenging thing about supported living is putting your vision into practice. It is like recruiting the people who help to make the plan work and deal with the personnel problems that all small businesses have. That is really what a supported living plan is, the business of giving a person the support he or she needs to live in the community. You also have to define the dream in specific terms in order to put it in practice. Over time the dream becomes a reality through trial and error. If you make mistakes, or something doesn't work as you anticipated, you have the opportunity to keep adapting supports. There is no agency that decides whether you can have this service but not that one or that you are no longer eligible (or appropriate) for the program.

Supported Living

A careful review of the literature on supported living presents a clear perspective on some basic challenges in human services (see, e.g., Hall & Walker, 1998; Hulgin, Shoultz, Walker, & Drake, 1996; Klein, 1992; O'Brien & O'Brien, 1992; Racino, Walker, O'Connor, & Taylor, 1992; Taylor, Biklen, & Knoll, 1987; Taylor, Bogdan, & Racino, 1991). In particular, focus on people who are usually identified as the "most difficult to serve" or the "residual institutional population" requires an unambiguous examination of what it means to provide help. The common characteristic of programs that are successful at forging the bond between the person and the community is an absolute commitment to the individual and the belief in a common group of principles. Central to these principles is an uncompromising commitment to the community as the place where all people should live (Taylor,

TABLE 18–2

Key Concepts in Supported Living

- The majority of people with developmental disabilities have always lived at home with their families or on their own.
- People with disabilities need to be able to move out of the family home and to establish their own identity as adults.
- Control over your own life—particularly where and how you choose to live—is essential to the definition of adulthood in modern America.
- Despite great progress, reform efforts of the last 30 years continue to place control in the hands of human service organizations.
- Support of families and for adults requires a new role for human services built on a problem-solving partnership and recognition of the primacy of consumer control.
- The array of supports that an individual is provided for his and her needs in daily life is far different from a continuum of residential options or developing individualized service plans.
- "Supported living" has provided a useful framework for exploring how housing can be separated from supports.
- Individuals with the most severe disabilities can be supported in their own homes.
- Housing must be separated from supports.

Racino, Knoll, & Lutifyya, 1987). The central message of this literature is that the keys to developing an agency that supports community membership are conceptually very simple: It takes commitment, individualization, flexibility, and concern for human relationships. This vision is conceptually very simple but amazingly complex when it comes to instituting these values as the enduring basis of a publicly supported system of supports. (See Table 18–2.)

Real Life, Not "Programming"
Support personnel need to see the mutual interdependence of housemates and the demands of each individual's daily routine determining the needs for skill development or supports (Klein, 1992; Knoll & Ford, 1987).

Commitment
People with the greatest degree of disability and their families need reassurance that there are individuals who have made a long-term commitment to support them. The individuals and organizations that work with them must be willing to stick with them in good and bad times, and during periods of erratic behavior (Johnson, 1985, O'Brien & O'Brien, 1992).

Personal Advocacy
People with the most complex needs also are likely to be the ones with the greatest number of agencies involved in their lives. Everyone may have shuffled them around in the service system because no one was willing to make a commitment to provide them with what they need. This means that an agency that decides to accept a long-term responsibility to a person has to work both formally and informally to bring about change in other agencies. This also means advocating for new and innovative services that meet the specific need of the individual and for collaboration that crosses over agency lines of responsibility (Johnson, 1985; Lippert, 1987; O'Brien & O'Brien, 1991).

Choice
People with disabilities often have had few opportunities to experience making decisions, even small ones, throughout their lives. This indicates that support personnel must know how

to assist people in making real choices in areas of daily life and to be comfortable with balancing the risks involved. (Johnson, 1985; Klein, 1992; Knoll & Ford, 1987; O'Brien & O'Brien, 1991).

Flexibility

Supports must be developed to match the strengths and needs of the person, to build on natural community resources, and to attune to the realization that life can be chaotic at times. People change over time and the supports they need must adapt to match their changing life situation. (Johnson, 1985: Klein, 1992; Minnesota Governor's Planning Council on Developmental Disabilities, 1987; O'Brien & O'Brien, 1991, 1992).

Relationships

Being part of a community means that people have enduring relationships with people other than those paid to be with them. With real friendships come natural systems of support that often are able to forestall or prevent relatively minor problems from becoming insurmountable difficulties that escalate into a crisis. Most people have these systems, but people whose lives have been constrained within the human service system frequently have few natural networks. Often the most that the "formal" service system can do is to provide opportunities for people to develop relationships. For good or ill, friendships cannot be planned or controlled (Bartholmew, 1985; McKnight, 1987; O'Connell, 1988).

Current Challenges

The challenge becomes the clearest as providers and policymakers confront massive community waiting lists and thousands of students annually complete a "free, appropriate public education" only to discover that the adult system of services is not ready for them. Increasingly, adult providers determine that most people with disabilities and their parents find even the "best" of their group homes undesirable when compared with the ideal of a "home of your own."

The focus on "support" has led many organizations and individuals to change their vocabulary; yet, the actual operation of agencies and the style of individual professionals remain substantially the same. Much of this can be attributed to the well-established nature of the system of group homes and the strength of the existing provider network. As the failure of vocational services to convert rapidly to supported employment has demonstrated, it is very hard for a facility-based agency to give up its real estate and to redefine its mission. This confusion has been furthered by the seeming ease with which the term "support" can be appropriated to a wide range of activities that have little relationship to the conceptual underpinning of supported living. This phenomenon, similar to the myriad ways that "normalization" was distorted, has led some authors to develop lists of nonexamples (see Table 18–3, e.g.).

The belief in personal choice and control and full community participation for people with developmental disabilities requires the transformation of words and practice inherent in supported living. However, this promise will be lost if the field does not systematically reeducate itself. Professionals entering the field must be both imbued with this new way of thinking and have the skills needed to undertake the far-reaching changes that lie ahead. More than a decade ago Smull and Bellamy (1990) concluded that the supported services paradigm has primarily occurred as a result of the "creativity and effort of local service providers . . . the challenge for government is to sustain these gains, encourage further development, and make the benefits of the support paradigm more widely available. . . . Specific solutions to the policy challenges must be developed in the political context of existing state and federal programs" (p. 11).

TABLE 18–3

Supported Living is NOT . . .

- A "program" to fix or change people
- People forced to live the way we think is good for them
- A test to see if you can live with no problems, and if not, you get sent back to group living
- An incentive or reward for good behavior
- Being assigned roommate(s)
- Compatible with services that congregate and control people
- A way to avoid responsibility for careful decisions about threats to people's vulnerabilities
- Another stop on the service continuum
- A funding stream used to do more of the same kinds of services
- Having permission to live in an agency-controlled apartment
- Another name for "downsizing" existing facilities into smaller units; otherwise, renaming existing services
- Isolation and loneliness

Source: From "Supported living: What's the difference?" by John O'Brien, Responsive Systems Associates, Inc., 1993.

Access to Supported Living

As might be anticipated from the history of supported living, it takes many forms in states and communities around the country. What is consistent and unique about supported living is adherence to the key principles outlined earlier. Within the formal system of service, it is critical to appreciate the importance of these guiding principles as the vocabulary of support proliferates, sometimes in the absence of practices that fit the language. Nonetheless, a growing number of organizations are really implementing an individualized person-centered approach to supported living.

Critical Point　Recently some organizations and regional agencies have begun using the term "supported living" as the generic term for all residential services for people with disabilities. It is important to examine what an agency is doing to determine if it fits the definition of supported living.

Throughout the country, there are small local providers that exemplify the roots of supported living and use a variety of traditional funding mechanisms to assist people in their own homes. Although the supported living organization typically has been small, size no longer is an essential characteristic. A growing number of

fairly large organizations have begun to struggle with how to convert a well-established system of group homes into supported living.

Most states have a regionalized approach to adult services for people with developmental disabilities and this can contribute to significant within-state variation in the experience of people with disabilities and their families. Although they receive significant guidance from the state department, regional and county authorities enjoy considerable autonomy. This means that in one state neighboring communities may have very different access to supported living. Some regional entities have converted completely to supported living as a guiding philosophy. So, it is possible that a person in the next county may have no access to in-home supports. There, the experience of planning for transition may entail putting an individual's name on an endless waiting list for one of the rare slots in the region's six-person group homes.

As noted, early on federal medicaid had a significant impact upon the development of community services. This continues to be true in the area of supported living. As yet, the successful federal experiment with the community supported living arrangements (CSLA) has not led to a total revamping of the federal medicaid long-term care program. At present, a number of serious proposals for a fundamental reworking of "long-term care policy" have been proposed and are being debated (see the subsequent discussion of Mi-CASSA). Currently, individual states are given a great deal of flexibility under the home and community-based waiver (HCBW) options to use medicaid in a variety of flexible and individualized ways. This also has contributed to wide variation in what is available in a particular state. Some states have opted to use supported living as the guiding framework for all medicaid long-term care funds for people with developmental disabilities. In these states, the total system is moving toward supports for individuals. On the other hand, some states have made limited use of waiver programs or have developed plans that reflect a very traditional approach to service. In these locales, individuals who are dependent on medicaid to purchase their services will likely find the opportunities for supported living severely restricted.

Finally, it is important to remember that significant portions of services for people with developmental disabilities are funded exclusively by state funds. This means that some of the earliest innovations in supported living were financed with moneys that were not trapped in the complexities of the federal system. A variety of innovative efforts were designed and continue to be implemented using state funds. As with much information discussed in this chapter, it is important to keep in mind that, unlike access to public education at this time, there is no entitlement to supported living or most other adult services. It is true that if a person with a disability meets the criteria he or she is entitled to medicaid, but, as explained, that is hardly a guarantee of access to supported living.

In the typical state program, a procedure exists to restrict access to limited state dollars. Further, once the money is committed it is gone. This means that the next person who comes "through the door" requesting supported living will be told to come back during the next budget period.

The point of this discussion is to underscore that although supported living provides a framework for a basic reworking of the system of long-term care for people with developmental disabilities, we are a long way from seeing the promise of this change fully realized. Whereas the concept and descriptions of effective programs have been widely disseminated for over a decade, there are regions where supported living is still a totally novel concept. One can still hear the objection: "What are you talking about? He (or she) is too severely disabled to live outside a facility." It matters little that we can point to numerous examples that provide ample evidence of the efficiency, effectiveness, and quality that mark supported living. Until any person in need can gain local access to supported living that can be funded without a master's degree in public administration, the ideal is illusory.

In the case of supported living, like supported employment, long-term planning for transition is critical. The teacher must start early to build expectations for students with disabilities to have meaningful adult life. By shaping attitudes and expectations, educators also contribute to moving service systems toward becoming more responsive. Raising expectations early in life so that parents and family members of people with disabilities see what is possible and desirable is a critical tool in changing the look of adult services. On a certain level, transition planning that reaches back into the early grades is a form of marketing. It is about creating consumer demand for the best quality products. It is about helping parents to have the highest expectation for the person with a disability as an adult: "Yes, we expect he or she will work and live in his or her own home. The person will choose how to define home for him or herself."

One State's Approach to Supported Living

In Kentucky, supported living is a totally state-funded program that is established by state law.

Regional supported living councils made up of consumer representatives (e.g., people with disabilities, family members, and advocates) administer the program. Individuals seeking funding under supported living prepare a proposal that outlines the range of supports needed for the person with a disability to live as independently as possible in his or her own home. These proposals are reviewed and approved or disapproved and funded within the limits of available funds. The primary consideration in the review of the proposal is conformity to the guiding principles of supported living as outlined in the legislation.

A broad category of highly flexible, individualized services are designed and coordinated in such a manner as to provide the necessary assistance to do the following:

> Provide the support necessary to enable a person who is disabled to live in a home of the person's choice that is typical of those living arrangements in which persons without disabilities reside;
>
> Encourage the individual's integrated participation in the community with persons who are members of the general citizenry;
>
> Promote the individual's rights and autonomy;
>
> Enhance the individual's skills and competencies in living in the community; and
>
> Enable the individual's acceptance in the community by promoting home ownership or leasing arrangements in the name of the individual or the individual's family or guardian (House Bill No. 447, Kentucky's Supported Living Bill).

According to the law, supported living services can involve any form of personal assistance, environmental modification, or adaptive device that allows a person with a disability to live as independently as possible in his or her own home. These services can include, but are "not limited to," the following:

> *Adaptive and therapeutic equipment* assists in the purchase of specialized devices, such as TTY/TDD modules, communication devices, MedicAlert, fire alarm, canine companion, as-

sistive technology, and so forth, that are needed to help the person live in his or her own home or function more independently or securely.

Attendant care or personal assistance provides a person who assists with hygiene (i.e., grooming, bathing, etc.), fitness, personal appointments (i.e., dental and medical), appearance, or other personal needs that the person cannot perform without assistance.

Consultation provides for professional evaluation, assessment, and recommendations to enhance communication, accessibility, or assistive technology; assists in resolving difficult or unusual situations or challenges that the person faces, including behavioral challenges; and possibly includes person-centered planning by a trained and independent facilitator.

Home modifications cover the cost of architectural changes, such as ramps, widening doors, accessibility adaptations to bathrooms and kitchens, and so forth, that enable the person to live in the house. (Usually, there is a limitation on the amount that can be invested in rental property. In Kentucky, the current rental limitation is $2,500.00.)

Homemaker services help to maintain the household (i.e., cleaning, shopping, laundry, security, cooking, etc.) when a person or a roommate is not able to perform the task.

In-home training and home management provide for teaching and enhancing competencies or abilities and skills of the person's choice (i.e., laundry, cooking, budgeting, banking, etc.).

Recreation and leisure assistance provides for a person who will provide assistance in going places and doing things for fun. Respite provides for an alternative support provider to work with the person with a disability so that the primary provider or family members can have a break.

Roommates for live-in support or periodic assistance provides assistance in areas, such as personal care, supervision (if needed), and home management on a daily or periodic basis as needed. This paid support should not be confused with a housemate who shares the home with a person and with whom there may be a mutually agreed upon division of household responsibilities.

Start-up grants allow for the payment of a variety of one-time expenses, such as the security deposit, closing costs, purchase of furniture, and items that are not covered by other sources.

Support broker or personal agent is an individual who acts as the person's representative in coordinating plans, locating providers, negotiating with agencies, and providing oversight to ensure the implementation of plans and the quality of services (may also facilitate the person-centered planning process).

Supported living community resource developer is someone who coordinates and assists a person to develop relationships, opportunities, and networks in the community which might be sustained over time (e.g., facilitating participation in church activities, civic associations, community organizations, arts, recreation and fitness groups, personal hobbies, family activities, etc.).

Transportation may include transportation to work and community activities when other means are not available (would not include the purchase of a vehicle).

Perhaps the most critical component on this list is the phrase "not limited to" in the introduction. The essential skill in supported living is creativity and innovation in problem solving. It is important to have guidance from the top, in this case, state legislation that makes it clear that people are encouraged to think "outside the box." However, this permission to think creatively is of little avail if professionals in the field who can assist them in the process do not encourage the person with a disability and his or her supporters. In truth, though, when most

people are told that they have access to "anything they need," they only will be able to think in terms of what they already know. It is critical that someone works with the person and family to envision the future and to articulate the resources that are needed to achieve the goal. Helping people to decide what they need is not a passive process. This is a highly interactive, demanding process that calls on the best skills of someone who really understands people and the communities to which they belong.

CASE STUDY B

Supported Living in Our Own Words—Tim Scott

It was September 20, 1995, I was working in my office when the phone rang. I figured it to be another applicant or possibly an employer calling to make a job-related inquiry. But, instead, to my surprise, it was the Governor's Office asking if this was the Tim Scott who is doing such a fine job working with people with disabilities and advocating for supported living and supported employment in Kentucky.

After a few comments regarding the upcoming general assembly and briefly discussing my letters and my efforts to influence the members of Kentucky's Health and Welfare Committee to expand supported living, we hung up. I really didn't think about what had actually happened at the time of the call, but at the end of the day while driving home, it occurred to me that all the letters I had recently sent off may actually make a difference in some way, particularly the one to Governor Jones to thank him for supporting and setting up the regional councils for supported living.

I had been involved in an intense letter-writing campaign after graduating from UK (University of Kentucky). My purpose then was in regards to getting attendant care, or the means thereof, into western Kentucky due to my declining sense of self-worth and the overall well-being and mental health of myself and my mother who was providing the majority of my attendant care. I was a 29-year-old quadriplegic; how was I to get up daily and retain a job and attendants on $432 a month SSI? My family was my primary caregivers and main source of support for the last 12 years. To make things worse, my mother's arthritis was getting worse, which only added to the constant growing feelings of dependence. The aggravation and worry turned into depression and anger, and I started wondering about my self-esteem and my future due to the dissonance I was creating within my family.

With a strong religious conviction and a lot of patience, grace, and forgiveness, I fought on looking for answers. Vocational Rehabilitation (VR) and our local MH/MR (mental health/mental retardation) respite program had done all they could do pertaining to attendant care, and my situation was looking pretty bleak. In 1992, I had acquired a job but was still desperately exploring all avenues for attendants so that I could use my earnings to get out of my parents' home. Eventually, I was put with a gentleman who works for Kentucky MH/MR out of Western State Hospital, which is where I might end up if I didn't find help soon! But, anyway, this wonderful individual had some new and exciting news about a program called "supported living." He explained to me that if I would jump on board by making phone calls and writing letters to our state representatives, there was a good chance that help was on the way.

I didn't realize it at the time, but this man and his understanding and intentions would change my life forever. I was introduced to the "supported living" concept. Kentucky's MH/MR's intentions were to form a pilot program across Kentucky in its efforts to pass a bill in the general assembly to implement supported living. I didn't have anything to lose. I immediately thought it a wonderful idea and one that I wanted to be a part of. Supported living became a reality in early 1993. Since then, supported living has grown to become one of the best things this great state has done with its tax dollars. Supported living is a dream come true for those who might otherwise not have a chance to prove themselves.

I was one of the first to be awarded a small amount of supported living money due to my needs and my efforts on its part. Without it, I would not be able to retain my position as a Regional Placement Manager doing vocational counseling for Heartland Projects with Industry in Western Kentucky, which I have worked successfully for the last 4 years now.

Supported living has allowed me to hire adequate attendant care and even provides work-related assistance to help me perform my job duties, and it has helped with some assistive devices that are needed for both my job and daily living.

Although I work in a professional position, my income is not high enough to surpass the social security criteria for substantial and gainful activity due to impairment related work expenses (IRWE), that is, vehicle loan, medicine, and medical supplies and equipment that my insurance won't pay. Keeping your supported living plan and IWRE or PASS (plans for achieving self-support) expenses separate and distinguishable is important. Supported living funds are not considered as income and can be utilized with family members, a big plus over other programs, but participants must pay all applicable taxes.

Thanks to supported living, all my income isn't being taken for my primary care. In 1994, I was able to buy a computer, which I needed for my work. Also, I just built a nice ramp to access my residence and am now able to get in my bathtub due to a used overhead lift I was able to purchase. In addition, I have been blessed to have been married recently and have purchased a house which 3 years ago was only a dream. Although supported living moneys can't be used to purchase homes and automobiles directly, it has allowed me to save some of my income for the down payment toward the purchase of my house. Supported living is proof to me that God truly helps those who strive to help others and themselves. . . . Amen.

I witness first hand every day how supported living helps others because of my job responsibilities. I have seen it change family despair into delight. It has helped people to start and hold onto small businesses by building ramps and allowing tools to be purchased. It provides attendant care and security for countless individuals. And, most importantly, it allows individuals to get out of their houses and to become a part of a community.

Supported living is broad based in its ability to provide services and it works on a personal futures planning motto, which allows for personal choice. In my 16 years of dealing with disability issues, I personally believe that supported living is a true blessing and the wave of the future.

Personal Assistance Services

As the movement toward supported living was developing in the field of developmental disabilities, a consensus was developing around access to high-quality personal assistance as being critical to independent living for most other people with disabilities (Racino & Litvak, 1999). When these two movements are carefully reviewed, it becomes apparent that they are both sides of the same coin; that is, they are both built on the same foundations of self-determination, choice, and community participation. The two movements are offered as positive alternatives to restrictive congregate care placements. The primary difference lies in the fact that people with developmental disabilities often require a greater degree of support in problem solving and making choices. Once the advocates in the independent living centers saw this difference as a legitimate support need and not as characteristics that made people with developmental disabilities qualitatively different from other people with disabilities, the linkage of these two efforts was achieved (Racino & Litvak, 1999).

Critical Point   Access to PAS is seen by many people with disabilities as a civil rights issue. The ability to obtain a personal assistance can be the factor that enables many people to live and work in the community rather than face nursing home placement or isolation within the home.

According to a blue-ribbon panel assembled by independent living research utilization (ILRU) and the Robert Wood Johnson Foundation (Dautel & Frieden, 1999), personal assistance services (PAS) are the key to quality of life for the people with a wide range of disabilities. Racino (1999) outlines how PAS has moved from an almost exclusive focus on physical disability to provide an essential service to people with a very wide range of disabilities, including psychiatric conditions, brain injury, and mental retardation, in essence

merging with supported living. Reviewing the research on PAS, the blue-ribbon panel (Dautel & Frieden, 1999) found that access to these services is associated with maintenance of good health and functional capacity productivity (Richmond, Beatty, Tepper, & DeJong, 1997); employment (Nosek, 1990); independence in living arrangement (HSRI, 1991); and community integration (HSRI, 1991). The panel notes that the ability to manage one's own life has a profound impact on anyone's mental health status. It affects the ability to work, engage in family and social activities, and otherwise be actively involved in life. Although personal assistance is defined as a health care issue, ultimately access to this service can shape self-image.

According to Litvak, Zukas, and Heumann (1987):

> Personal assistance services (PAS) are tasks performed for a person who has a disability by another person that aim at maintaining well-being, personal appearance, comfort, safety, and interactions within community and society as a whole. In other words, personal assistance tasks are those tasks which the individual who has a disability would normally do for himself or herself if the person had no disability (p. 1).

The type of tasks that they are referring to include (1) assistance with personal care activities, such as dressing, grooming, feeding, toilet, and so forth; (2) assistance in moving around the home and the community; (3) assistance with home maintenance, including cleaning, shopping, cooking, laundry, and repairs; (4) help in caring for infants and children; (5) aid in cognitive life management, such as finances and decision making; (6) assurance of personal and home security; and (7) assistance in communication services, such as interpreting or reading.

In 1991, the Consortium of Citizens with Disabilities, a Washington-based coalition of the major disability organizations, developed a cross-disability statement of policy guidelines for personal assistance services. This list of principles presents a picture of PAS as critical for people with disabilities to attain "life, liberty, and the pursuit of happiness." The guidelines said that PAS should be designed:

- to be guided and directed by the choices, preferences, and expressed interests and desires of the individual;
- to increase the individual's control over life based on the choice of acceptable options that minimize reliance on others in making decisions and in performing everyday activities;
- to enable PAS users to select, direct, and employ their own paid personal assistants, if desired;
- to enable PAS users to contract with an agency for these services, if desired;
- to foster the increased independence, productivity, and integration of these individuals into the community; to be easily accessible and readily available to all eligible persons where and when desired and needed;
- to meet individual needs irrespective of labels;
- to allow payment to family members for the extraordinary personal assistance they provide;
- to be provided in any setting, including in or out of the person's home;
- to be based on an individual service plan; and
- to offer PAS users of all ages the opportunity and support needed to assume greater freedom, responsibility, and choice throughout life (Consortium of Citizens with Disabilities, 1991, p. 3).

Based on an extensive review of the PAS literature and interviews with PAS users, Connie Lyle O'Brien and John O'Brien (1992) have developed a checklist for evaluating personal assistance policies and programs. This checklist is structured around what they see as three essential qualities of effective personal assistance services: availability, comprehensiveness, and controllability. Table 18–4 provides a summary overview of the information provided in this instrument.

Access to Personal Assistance Services

The National Blue-Ribbon Panel on Personal Assistance Services (Dautel & Frieden, 1999) notes that, at present, access to PAS is just about as erratic as access to supported living. Litvak (1995) reports on the unduly complex and uncoordinated nature of the service system. With no coherent national policy, there continues to be a nationwide predisposition toward facility-based care and a catch-as-catch-can approach to delivering home and community services. Currently, in most locales, it is still easier for a person with a disability to obtain a bed in a nursing home than to obtain demonstrably more cost-effective personal assistance services. According to ADAPT (1999a), the average annual medicaid expenditure for a person using community-based services is $7,276.00, whereas expenditure for nursing home residents averages $23,225.00. At the present time, over 80% of our medicaid dollars ($40 billion) spent on long-term care are used for institutional services, leaving only 20% ($10 billion) for all community services (ADAPT, 1999a). In 1995, 22 states reported that they did not make use of the medicaid personal care optional services (Winterbottom, Liska, & Obermaier, 1995).

A year after the passage of the Americans with Disabilities Act, a group of leaders from the disabilities rights movement came together in Oakland, CA, under the sponsorship of the World Institute on Disability to begin the next phase in their campaign for full access. Out of this meeting came a resolution on personal assistance services, which said in part:

> People with disabilities are entitled to be enabled to achieve the highest possible level of personal functioning and independence through appropriate education, health care, social services and assistive technology, including, as necessary, the assistance of other people. . . . We consider independent living and the availability of services to be critical to the exercise of our full human and civil rights, responsibilities and privileges.

TABLE 18–4

Checklist for Evaluating Personal Assistance Services (PAS) Policies and Programs

Available

PAS are available to people:

"of all ages, based on functional need . . . regardless of incomes."

PAS do not create disincentives:

"to employment, to eligibility for other benefits and services, to marriage and child rearing."

PAS encourage and supplement natural supports.

PAS funding comes through a long-term, stable source.

PAS funding provides fair pay and benefits for assistants.

Comprehensive

PAS are negotiated based on individual needs, preferences, and circumstances.

The program does not arbitrarily limit what the assistants can agree to do.

Participants can get the assistance needed with:

"personal routines, household routines, travel, communication, cognitive assistance, raising children, assuring security."

The program provides emergency backup.

Participants can get assistance with no limits:

"Assistance is available . . . in the home . . . outside the home, at work, at school, to participate in community life, to travel."

The program offers as much assistance as needed when it is needed:

"up to 24 hours a day, 7 days a week, . . . The amount of assistance can change as the participant's needs change."

Controllable

Participants can decide how much control they want to exercise by choosing:

"to get cash or voucher to hire and supervise assistants."

"to hire a business agent or agency to manage personal assistance system for them."

"to use assistants employed, trained, and supervised by an agency."

The medical supervision is not required.

Assistants can perform any and all health care routines that the participant would perform if able.

Participants can provide all training if they desire.

Participants can be family members if they desire.

The program provides participants with access to information on how both to manage assistants and to perform daily routines and their personal assistance system.

The program provides mechanisms to mediate conflicts and disputes.

The program provides vehicles for participants to share information.

Source: Derived from O'Brien & O'Brien, 1992.

To this end, we condemn forced segregation and institutionalization as direct violations of our human rights. Government policies and funding should not perpetuate the forced segregation, isolation, or institutionalization of people with disabilities of any age. The Americans with Disabilities Act was passed into law to promote the equalization of opportunity. The passage of

TABLE 18–5

MiCASSA, the Medicaid Community Attendant Services and Supports Act

---

Purposes

The purposes of this Act are as follows:

(1) To provide that States shall offer community attendant services and supports for eligible individuals with disabilities, and

(2) to provide financial assistance to the States to support systems change initiatives designed to assist each State to develop and enhance a comprehensive consumer-responsive statewide system of long-term services and supports that provides real consumer choice and direction consistent with the principle that services and supports are provided in the most integrated setting appropriate to meeting the unique needs of the individual.

Policy

It is the policy of the United States that all programs, projects, and activities receiving assistance under this Act shall be carried out in a manner consistent with the following principles:

(1) Individuals with disabilities, or, as appropriate, their representatives, must be empowered to exercise real choice in selecting long-term services and supports that are of high quality, are cost-effective, and meet the unique needs of the individual in the most integrated setting appropriate;

(2) No person should be forced into an institution to receive services that can be effectively and efficiently delivered in the home or community;

(3) Federal and State policies, practices, and procedures should facilitate and be responsive to, not impede, an individual's choice; and

(4) Individuals and their families receiving long-term services and supports must be involved in decision making about their own care and be provided with sufficient information to make informed choices.

Source: S1935, 106th Congress, MiCASSA: The Medicaid Community Attendant Services and Supports Act, p. 2. (Introduced November 16, 1999.)

comprehensive federal personal assistance legislation is essential to realizing the historic promise of the Act (World Institute on Disability, 1991).

Critical Point   Legislation and litigation remain necessary to challenge the institutional bias that exists in federal and state long-term care policy for people with disabilities.

This effort culminated in the introduction of the Medicaid Community Attendant Services and Supports Act (MiCASSA, S1935) by Senators Harkin and Specter on November 16, 1999. This legislation provides a real basis for addressing the nationwide lack of access to personal assistance services and supported living. It reflects a consensus across the disability community of an effective vehicle for finally reversing the institutional bias that has dominated disability policy

in this country for the last century. Table 18–5 provides an excerpt from the introduction to MiCASSA that sets the tone of the entire act. By the time this text is in print, MiCASSA, or a very similar piece of legislation, will be a valuable tool for young adults with disabilities, their families, and teachers as they plan for the supports that are needed to live independently as an adult.

Additional impetus was given to MiCASSA and other efforts to improve access to individualized community supports for people with disabilities by an event that occurred a few months earlier. On June 22, 1999, the U.S. Supreme Court delivered an opinion in the case of *Olmstead v. L. C. and* E. W., 119 S.Ct. 2176 (1999). Two women with mental illness and mental retardation brought this lawsuit in a Georgia State psychiatric hospital. They requested services in the community so that they could live outside the state hospital. The professionals on their treatment team agreed with them. However, the state was very slow in developing community living arrangements and, as a result, the state had essentially an endless waiting list. Hence, the plaintiffs found themselves on the waiting list for years, so they sued Tommy Olmstead, the Commissioner of Georgia's Department of Human Resources. In their lawsuit, they charged that the state of Georgia violated the Americans with Disabilities Act (ADA) integration mandate by failing to provide services in the most integrated setting appropriate to meet their needs, which in their case was the community, not an institution.

In a "nutshell," the Supreme Court agreed with the plaintiffs. It stated clearly that denial of community placements to individuals with disabilities is precisely the kind of segregation that Congress sought to eliminate in passing the ADA. The Court noted that segregation and institutionalization, unless required because of a person's condition, constitute discrimination and violated the ADA's "integration mandate." There is much more to the decision as it outlines other considerations for the state. Nonetheless, it presents an important new lever to be used in expanding community supports for people with disabilities.

Within the context of this text, it is important to note that *Olmstead* has implications for students currently in school who will potentially be on a waiting list for community support services. The National Association of Protection and Advocacy Systems (NAPAS) (October 1999) feels that the decision extends to people who are or will be on a waiting list. In the decision, the Court states that one defense a state can offer against lawsuits such as *Olmstead* is that it has a comprehensive, effective working plan for placing qualified persons in less restrictive settings. In other words, the state can defend itself by showing that it is thinking and planning ahead to meet the needs of those at risk of institution-

alization. The implication currently for people who are not in facilities is that, "If an individual is on a waiting list to receive community supports, the state can presume that person is not currently receiving adequate community supports. If a person is not receiving appropriate community services, then they are at risk of institutionalization" (NAPAS, 1999).

Transition to Interdependent Life as an Adult

Increasing access to supported living and personal assistance services is breaking down barriers that historically have kept people with severe physical disabilities, cognitive disabilities, and multiple disabilities from living in their own homes. This transformation of adult services underscores the role of education in preparing *all students* for "assuming emergent adult roles in the community" (Halpern, 1994, p. 116). So, although the individual considerations may vary from person to person, public education has a responsibility to all children that begins when they walk through the door of a preschool program. It means all of education is about transition, that is, a lifelong process of growth as we learn to cope with an ever-changing world. The outcome of education is the development of lifelong learners who are prepared to live together and to contribute to the life of the community. This vision of *interdependent* living is the goal for all students.

The experience of the young and the restless and thousands of their peers who are receiving special education strongly suggest that this goal requires increased attention from the education system. Four items must be on the planning agenda as students, parents, educators, and service providers look to an adult life with maximal personal independence and community contribution for all students with disabilities. These items are not checkoffs on a form to be completed as the student has his or her fourteenth birthday. The preparation of lifelong learners starts the minute that the education system first meets the child and parents by addressing vision, skills, resources, and supports.

Vision

As we discussed at the beginning of this chapter, people with disabilities have long found their lives defined in terms of limitation. This makes it very difficult for the person and members of his or her family to think about meaningful adult outcomes when they reach transition age. Often they have been taught to avoid thinking about the future. Is it any wonder that discussion of employment or of home living are rejected as not making any sense? It is critical that from the beginning of a student's education career a long-term focus on adult outcomes should be nurtured. Families and people with disabilities must be encouraged to explore possibilities, just like every other student and family. This process begins, as it does with all students, with the earliest discussions of, "what do you want to be when you grow up?" This requires that professionals adopt a positive tone and demeanor in the interaction with even the youngest children. As the principal professionals, the disability experts, in the family's life for perhaps as long as 18 years, have a major responsibility to contribute to forming a positive vision.

Critical Point   Educators must start early to assist families to develop a positive long-term vision of adult life for children with disabilities. This should include informing them, even at the elementary level, about the "best practices" in adult services and the strengths and limitation of what is currently available in their locale.

Over the last 15 years, a number of strategies have been developed to assist in forming a long-range positive vision for people with significant disabilities. These techniques are known collectively as "person-centered planning." Over the last decade, they have contributed to the posi-

tive change described earlier in this chapter (O'Brien & Lovett, 1992; O'Brien, O'Brien, & Mount, 1997). The most commonly reported forms of person-centered planning are:

- Personal futures planning (Mount & Zwernik, 1988; O'Brien, 1987),
- MAPS/PATH (Forest & Lusthaus, 1989; Pearpoint, O'Brien, & Forest, 1993)
- Essential lifestyle planning (Smull, Sanderson, & Harrison, 1996)
- Circles of support (Ducharme, Beeman, DeMarasse, & Ludlum, 1994).

Although differing in some components or approaches, these all share a common focus and a consistent group of characteristics as outlined in Table 18–6. Central to this approach is the understanding that the meetings convened to develop a person-centered plan are not "owned" by the education system. The plan that emerges is not an Individualized Education Program (IEP), but a long-term vision that provides a context for the development of the education program. The education program is just one of several tools that are used to achieve a desirable future for the person.

Such planning, to be responsive, brings together the full array of friends, relatives, advocates, service providers, consultants, and others whose cooperation is essential for assuring the future quality of life of the individual of concern. O'Brien (1987) describes five quality-of-life outcomes: (1) community presence, (2) choice, (3) competence, (4) respect, and (5) community participation that set the tone for any person-centered forum. Within the framework of these themes, the participants, under the guidance of a trained facilitator, work together to respond to a series of targeted questions. The MAPs (originally McGill action planning system, now making action plans) is the approach that is most typically used with school-age children. The plan asks the participants to respond to the following eight questions (Vandercook, York, & Forest, 1989).

TABLE 18–6

Person-centered versus Traditional Planning

Traditional Planning	Person-Centered
Why:	
• To coordinate services across disciplinary lines.	• To establish and support a personal vision for an individual
• To clarify staff roles in the implementation of the program	• To build community support and action on behalf of the focus person
• To avoid punishment by regulators. Interest in coordination of organizational activities	• To make a voluntary commitment by people who are interested in helping someone they care for
Who?	
• Professionals and specialists	• Focus person and his or her spokesperson, family, friends, and associates. May include some human service workers
Where?	
• Human service setting, conference room: centralized site	• Community settings: living room, church room, library meeting room. Places close to where the members live
How?	
• Team leader initiates to meet requirements of regulations	• Focus person or spokesperson initiates to reach goals they are unable to accomplish working alone
What is produced?	
• Goals and objectives that fit within existing program options	• Vision that reflects desire of focus person and family
• Completed forms, paperwork, and specific goals and objectives to use to evaluate program effectiveness	• Commitments to action by community members and significant quality-of-life changes for the focus person
Roles?	
• Members have specific roles and clear boundaries for action. Plans do not change roles or boundaries. Members act with informal existing organizational channels of authority	• Participant's roles are constantly changing based on tasks. Boundaries for action are defined by personal vision and commitment. Members use informal networks and contacts to open doors
• Human service workers set all direction, organize all activities, and provide direct service	• Human service workers support direction set by group and have knowledge of resources
• Community members are usually not involved	• Community members are active contributors
• Person with disability is expected to comply with plan	• Person with disability directs plan and activities

Source: Derived in part from Mount, Beeman, & Ducharme, 1988.

1. "What is a MAP?" orients everyone to the process.
2. "What is the story?" explores the person's history.
3. "What is the dream?" invites everyone present to envision the optimal future for the focal person.

4. "What is the nightmare?" asks all to share their fears for the person's future.
5. "Who is the person?" uses brainstorming to develop a well-rounded picture of the diverse ways that people know the person.

Critical Point   Person-centered planning provides the blueprint for the development of IEPs and transition plans.

6. "What are the person's gifts?" asks all to develop a common picture of the person's personal assets.
7. "What are the needs?" explores areas in which the person needs supports.
8. "What is the plan of action?" engages all in developing a plan that will avoid the nightmares and help to realize the dreams.

The end result is a shared vision of the unique situation of a specific individual and a plan of action for moving toward that goal. By revisiting and periodically updating this vision and reexamining needs as the student progresses through school, the circle of support assures that the final goal of membership in an interdependent community does not fade from view.

As the person enters adolescence, the vision of the person-centered planning process of necessity must narrow. Table 18–7 outlines some considerations that should be addressed as the formal transition plan is being developed for a student with need for extensive supports. By starting early, problems can be identified, solutions decided upon, critical skills developed, and supports mobilized long before a student is scheduled to graduate.

Skills

Perhaps the principal lesson of the movement toward supported living has been a rejection of the "readiness model." This traditional approach to planning was based on a developmental approach and embedded in the traditional education, vocational, and residential services con-

tinuum. Under this model, there were certain specific skills that were a necessary prerequisite before a person could move on to the next less restrictive step in the continuum. Organizations that have used "support" as an organizing framework have demonstrated the fallacy in this logic. They have consistently demonstrated that an appropriate support can be mobilized to bridge the gap between a person's ability and the demands of a setting.

Does this mean that educators and adult providers should not worry about developing skills? Should we give up teaching? Is our only priority developing relationships with other people who will look out for people with disabilities who have not mastered daily living skills?

The response to these questions is a resounding no! Educators and others must continue to put as much (or more) energy into assisting people to develop the skills that are necessary to maximize their independence. Teaching, although not specifically highlighted in the taxonomy of supports outlined in the 1992 AAMR definition manual (Luckasson et al., 1992), continues to be a crucial support. Independent or at least partial mastery of a skill is a valuable asset to any person. Skill development is not an excuse for failing to support the development of relationships, but if appropriately focused, it can actually contribute to the nurturing connections.

Critical Point   Educators must have a longitudinal perspective on skill development, so that valuable instructional time is not wasted teaching and learning skills that have little or no long-term value or use to the student.

Usable Skills

The last 25 years of progress in the education of students with severe disabilities has taught all educators an important lesson about skill development. The skills we choose for targeting during our valuable and limited instruction time must have ecological validity. They must be responsive to the needs of the students' present

TABLE 18–7

Independent Living and Transition: What to Consider

Types and location of housing
- Adults with disabilities should have access to the kinds and location of housing as do nondisabled adults.
- Adults with disabilities should have access to neighborhoods that reflect their needs and wishes.
- What type of special consideration must be made in selecting a home?
- Access to transportation can be a factor in selecting a home

Choosing one's living companion(s)
- Disabled or nondisabled
- Paid or not paid
- Family member or helper

Promoting home ownership
- Home is where a person feels they belongs
- Ownership of deed or lease

Financing for housing
- Bank loan/housing subsidies
- Privately funded
- One-time start-up grant (supported living)
- SSI and medicaid

Individualized and flexible supports
- Family member
- Friend/neighbor
- Paid personal assistance
- Service coordinator
- Emergency call systems
- Back-up systems

Financing for supports
- Vocational rehabilitation
- Community-based services
- Private funding sources
- Developmental disabilities or social services offices

Hurdles to overcome
- Difficulties in separating housing and support in the minds of providers and administrators
- Label of the disability
- Lack of choices and control
- Program-centered versus person-centered ways of thinking

---

and future environments. It must be useful. It must contribute to achieving prioritized education outcomes. This lesson applies to all education, but it is particularly relevant to the education of student with disabilities.

This point needs to be emphasized: As *we think about the challenges confronting all students with disabilities, we need to examine what we teach to assure ecologi-* *cal validity.* This is as much a consideration for students with so-called mild disabilities and emotional and behavior disorders as it is for students with severe and multiple disabilities. Although this point refers to all areas of the curriculum, its greatest area of relevance is the preparation for independent living as an adult. Students with mild disabilities will not be eligible for support services such as their peers with more obvious disabilities. Therefore, it is critical that their teachers examine the curriculum and their IEPs in order to assure mastery of the skills that the students need to make it as an adult.

Teach Skills in Inclusive Settings

Some educators feel that there is an inherent tension between the need for students with disabilities to develop independent living skills and inclusive education (Fuchs & Fuchs, 1995). One of the rationales traditionally given for resource room and special class placement has been that these placements provide the opportunity to teach skills that are not part of the regular curriculum. Increasingly, this logic is being challenged on several fronts. First, the opportunity for positive social interaction and connections that have the potential to develop into sustained relationships outweighs the value of the separate placement (Strully & Strully, 1985). Second, the mainstream setting proves the opportunity to learn and master skills in an authentic setting, thereby providing ecological validity and increased likelihood of generalization (Brown et al., 1989). Third, efforts at reform in general education are providing increased opportunity for authentic instruction for all students (Baker, Wang, & Walberg, 1995). Fourth, differentiated instruction within the general education classroom can be effectively designed to assure that basic skills are addressed for students with disabilities (Kearns & Dryer, 1997). Finally, some systems are demonstrating how students with disabilities experience a high degree of inclusion in the early grades and then move into a program with a heavy emphasis on life skills when they are in the latter years of high school. At that point, the varied schedules of all students mean that the special education pull-out will be less obvious as many students engage in co-op and other out-of-school activities. Using this approach, some systems provide full-time community-based skills training for students with moderate to severe disabilities in the

post-18-year-age group, after their peers of the same age have graduated from the public school system. In this approach, the students with disabilities also graduate from the high school building and their program is based at a college campus or other community setting (Hall, Kleinert, & Kearns, 2000; Jorgensen, 1998).

Priority Skills

The hallmark of special education is the design of an instruction program that addresses the unique needs of each student. However, the multiple competing priorities within the school and the numerous skills for independent living found in resource manuals and curriculum guides mean educators must thoughtfully decide how to use limited instruction time (see, e.g., Cronin & Patton, 1993; Dever, 1988; Falvey, 1989; Ford, Schnorr, Meyer, Davern, Black, & Dempsey, 1989). Educators need to establish clear priorities for each student. This process requires careful assessment, effective communication with the student and family, and a clear picture of how the student's disability impacts upon participation and independence in the present and future environments. A major contribution to this decision-making process is the long-term vision of the future which each student and family have developed. Rather than attempting to provide a comprehensive community living curriculum guide, in Table 18–8 we have used the nine adaptive skills areas (other than "work") found in the 1992 AAMR definition manual (Luckasson et al., 1992) in order to generate a series of suggestive questions to assist in planning for student skill development.

Resources

Within the framework presented here, resources are potential sources of funding, services, informal supports, or equipment that will enable a person to maximize his or her independence. The organizations and agencies outlined subsequently should all be explored in

TABLE 18–8

Assessing Skills and Supports for Community Living

1. *Communication.* Does the student:
   Initiate the interaction with someone else?
   Use an alternative or augmentative communication system that is easily understood by a stranger?
   Engage in a reciprocal conversation?
   Communicate choices?
   Make requests?
   Ask for assistance?
   Make others aware of special communication needs?
   Effectively respond to complex directions?

2. *Self-care.* Does the student:
   Follow acceptable personal hygiene?
   Maintain personal appearance throughout the day?
   Carry and care for personal hygiene items?
   Care for hair?
   Wear clean clothing?
   Demonstrate acceptable dental hygiene?
   Dress appropriately for situation and weather?

3. *Home living.* Does the student:
   Take care of belongings?
   Pay bills?
   Use appliances and utensils safely?
   Keep household material organized?
   Perform simple repairs?
   Make shopping lists?
   Plan a nutritious diet?
   Prepare meals?
   Recognize household safety concerns?
   Demonstrate appropriate manners?
   Store perishables, appropriately?
   Clean up after meals?
   Perform household cleaning?

4. *Social skills.* Does the student:
   Share tasks with others?
   Take turns?
   Initiate interactions appropriately?
   Cope with negative feedback?
   Recognize social boundaries?
   Recognize and apologize for mistakes?
   Participate as a group member?
   Recognize varied social roles?
   Recognize site-specific rules or expectations?
   Follow rules?
   Help others?

5. *Community use.* Does the student:
   Drive an automobile?
   Have access to public transportation?
   Use public transportation?
   Understand a bus schedule?
   Call taxicabs or paratransit provider to arrange travel?
   Walk safely around the community?
   Find locations in the community?
   Give others directions?
   Cautiously interact with strangers?
   Ask for help if lost?
   Solve problems if lost?
   Use restaurants?
   Use stores?
   Use various community services?
   Use churches?
   Use health care facilities?
   Ask for help in a community setting?
   Locate desired items in stores and other settings?

6. *Self-direction.* Does the student:
   Manage a personal schedule for:
     a day?
     a week?
     a month?
   Consider alternatives in making personal decisions?
   Organize activities with others?
   Plan ahead?
   Regulate his or her behavior?
   Actively direct personal assistants?
   Understand his or her support needs?

(continued)

TABLE 18–8
(Concluded)

---

7. *Health and safety.* Does the student:
   Follow safety rules?
   Exit a building when hearing an alarm?
   Inform others when ill or injured?
   Take medicine as directed?
   Use the telephone to obtain help?

   Avoid alcohol, drugs, and tobacco?
   Know simple first aid?
   Avoid sexual abuse?
   Report abusive or threatened situations?
   Manage birth control?
   Inform others of plans?

8. *Functional academics.* Does the student:
   Maintain a checkbook?
   Manage a bank account?
   Maintain a monthly budget?
   Budget money for planned purchases?
   Effectively manage money when making a
   purchase?
   Use reading:
    to plan purchases?
    to shop?
    to obtain information?
    to communicate with others?
    to understand printed notices received in
    the mail?
    for recreation?

   Seek assistance when unable to understand
   written information?
   Use writing to:
    manage household?
    communicate with others?
    keep records?
    fill out forms?
   Seek assistance when a written document is
   required?
   Use computer technology to help with:
    financial management?
    written communication?
    accessing information?
   Telling time?

9. *Leisure.* Does the student engage in:
   A variety of recreational activities?
   Activities that enhance physical fitness
   and health?
   Provide an opportunity for developing
   relationships with other members of the
   community?

   Active recreation activities?
   Passive recreation activities?
   Recreation activities:
    alone?
    with a group?
    at home?
    in the community?

Source: Derived in part from Ford, A., Schnorr, R., Meyer, L., Davern, L., Block, J., & Dempsey, P. (1989). *The Syracuse community-referenced curriculum guide for students with moderate and severe disabilities.* Baltimore: Paul Brookes.

the planning for transition to independent living. In many cases, these potential sources of support can provide the lever needed to make things happen.

Income Maintenance

Unfortunately, it remains true that many people with disabilities are poor and thus are dependent on some form of public assistance. These programs are currently in a state of evolution with an increasing emphasis placed on providing incentives for recipients to go to work. For people with disabilities this has meant the gradual removal of actual disincentives to employment. Many people with disabilities will make some use of social security income (SSI) and social security disability insurance (SSDI) to contribute to their support as they establish themselves in their own home. Additionally, various traditional group living situations use social security funds to cover some of their residential cost. It is very important to make contact with the social security office to explore how these programs can most effectively sup-

TABLE 18–9

Housing Strategies

It is unfortunately true that many people with disabilities have very limited financial resources. So, as we increasingly delink the provision of services and supports from the provision of housing, we need to identify sources of funding to pay for housing. A report to the President's Committee on Mental Retardation identified the following strategies.
Federal programs:
- Section 8 housing certificate from HUD
- Public housing programs funded by HUD
- HUD's section 811 and PHA section 515 program provides capital housing grants to nonprofit organizations
- McKinney Act permanent housing funds develop housing for people at risk of becoming homeless
- HUD's community development block grants help local communities to develop urban areas including housing
- Low-income tax credits provide benefits for owners/investors in low-income housing
State/local efforts:
- Bridge subsidies for people on waiting lists
- Grants for closing costs, down payments, and setup costs
- Nonprofit housing corporations supported by state bond issues
- Programs of technical assistance and financial consultation
- Bank community reinvestment obligations
- Cooperative housing arrangements

Source: From Research and Training Center on Residential Services and Community Living, 1994. *Housing policy and persons with mental retardation.* Minneapolis, MN: Institute on Community Integration.

port the students desired future. It is important to obtain the most current information about opportunities like PASS (plans for achieving self-support), which allows for a certain degree of flexibility in these massive programs. The same office is also the source for information and applications for the food stamp program.

Critical Point   People with disabilities have an increasing array of options related to where and how they live as adults. Unfortunately, for them moving out of Mom and Dad's house still requires more than finding an affordable apartment. Transition planning must focus on identifying and accessing the resources and supports needed for students with disabilities and their families to have a life experience that parallels that of their nondisabled siblings and friends.

Resources for Home Ownership
Even with the reality of poverty, there are a number of ways for individuals with disabilities to

achieve the dream of home ownership. The range of programs and strategy that make this possible have expanded substantially in the last few years as supported living and PAS have gained increasing notice in the area of public policy. Several national projects have compiled resource guides for home ownership (Home of Your Own Project, 1995; Hulgin, Walker, Fisher, Handley, & Shoultz, 1995). Some of these strategies are summarized in Table 18–9. An important source of information and resources is the local or state office of the U.S. Department of Housing and Urban Development (HUD).

Community Mental Health
In many states, the entry to supported living and personal assistance services is found in the county or regional community mental health (CMH) center or regional developmental disabilities center. In some cases, these entities are

a branch of state government. In other cases, they are semiautonomous organizations that contract with the appropriate state agencies. In approaching these organizations, you must know what to look for since these organizations often are large and offer a variety of very different services. They may provide developmental disabilities and mental retardation services, child and adult mental health services, substance abuse services, and/or early intervention services. Depending on where you live, the CMH may be the principal or only provider of services for a particular population or provide no direct service other than service coordination (case management). Most CMHs are principal gatekeepers for adult services, and, thus, also are the place where you will encounter a large waiting list for services. All these factors mean that they are an early contact, and the development of good working relationships with representatives of these organizations will be able to help you and your students better prepare for moving into adult life.

Public/Home Health Services
Access to affordable health care is one of the major challenges confronting people with disabilities in the United States. This problem of access and the medical management of many residential programs have been, perhaps, the greatest barriers to independent community life for many people. As noted earlier, there are currently several initiatives that will reform the federal health care program for people with disabilities (medicaid). Many students with severe disabilities will already be eligible for and receiving medicaid. As other students become adults, they may become eligible for medicaid. This reality and the range of services provided under this program means that the local office of this agency should be on the planning agenda for most students. It should be noted that in some states people with developmental disabilities would access medicaid through the developmental disabilities program of the community mental health program. As in-

dicated in our discussion of MiCASSA, medicaid is an important potential source of personal assistance services. In this same area of planning, the local public health office, the Program for Children with Specialized Health Care Needs, the Visiting Nurse Association, home health agencies, and Durable Medical Equipment providers may all have a role to play in assisting students with physical disabilities to obtain assistants and services for their homes.

Centers for Independent Living
Traditionally, schools have not had many interactions with centers for independent living (CILS). This is unfortunate since these organizations, as shown in Table 18–10, have a wide array of services for individuals with all types of disabilities. This lack of connection has begun to change as CIL increasingly are dealing with people who have graduated from special education programs. Recently, the beginning of a discussion about the relationship of CILs to parent resource centers has started. This groundbreaking initiative follows on the CILs' increased opening to people with developmental disabilities. As educators increasingly deal with preparing their graduates with disabilities for independent and supported living and the use of PAS, the CILs should grow into an invaluable link for the students to maintain as they move out of the school system.

Community Living Organizations
Most communities have independent private for-profit and not-for-profit organizations that provide services for people with either developmental disabilities and/or mental health diagnoses. Most of these organizations trace their roots back to efforts at deinstitutionalization. Therefore, many of them are firmly "wedded" to the traditional continuum of service. However, it is important to note that the first examples of supported living were developed by small private organizations. Most of the "best" examples of supported living continue to be found in this

TABLE 18–10

Centers for Independent Living

As described by the Rehabilitation Services Administration (RSA) (1999) centers for independent living (CILs) are consumer-controlled, community-based, cross-disability, nonresidential private nonprofit organizations. They provide services for individuals or groups of individuals with significant disabilities that promote independence, productivity, and quality of life.

Currently, there are approximately 250 centers for independent living across the country, with at least one CIL in every state, the District of Columbia, U.S. Virgin Islands, Puerto Rico, and American Samoa. Annually, over 100,000 individuals with significant physical and mental disabilities receive direct services. Many additional individuals benefit from the centers' systems advocacy to increase the services of the communities to meet the needs of individuals with significant disabilities.

CILs provide a varied combination of services, including the core services of information and referral services; independent living skills training; peer counseling (including cross-disability peer counseling); and individual and systems advocacy. As appropriate, additional services also can include the following:

- Counseling
- Services related to securing housing or shelter
- Rehabilitation technology
- Mobility training
- Life skills training and interpreter and reader services for individuals with significant cognitive disabilities
- Personal assistance services
- Consumer information programs
- Education and training necessary for living in the community and participating in community activities
- Supported living
- Transportation
- Physical rehabilitation
- Therapeutic treatment; prostheses
- Individual and group recreation services
- Training to develop youth with disabilities to promote self-awareness and esteem
- Develop advocacy and self-empowerment skills, and develop career options
- Services to children
- Services to benefit individuals with significant disabilities in enhancing their independence, productivity, and quality of life
- Preventive services
- Community awareness programs to enhance the understanding and integration into the society of individuals with disabilities
- Other services that may be necessary and consistent with the provisions of the Rehabilitation Act of 1973, as amended

Source: From Rehabilitation Services Administration (RSA) Programs: Centers for Independent Living. Office of Special Education and Rehabilitation Services, U.S. Department of Education, 1999.

sector. Recently, though, an increasing number of larger private and public sector organizations have begun to implement a supported living approach. Many of these organizations also will provide other services and supports, such as supported employment and other day programming. Depending on the nature of the organization and the structure of your state service system, you may be able to involve these types of organizations directly in planning for an individual student. In other states, the community mental health agency or the state mental retardation/developmental disabilities services office is the only authorized entrée into these organizations.

Regional Transportation Authorities and Paratransit

In a world dominated by the automobile, people who do not drive are at a distinct disadvantage. The Americans with Disabilities Act has improved access by people with disabilities to public transportation, but transportation must remain a priority when planning for independent home living. For many students with a disability, access to public transportation will be the factor that ultimately determines where they can live. Regardless of the fact that regional transportation authorities are not on a state's interagency group on transition, the local school system should open a clear channel of communication with the transportation agency in its region.

Self-Advocacy

Throughout this book and especially in this chapter, the emphasis is on full membership and participation in the life of the community for all students with disabilities. The self-help movement and particularly the independent living movement have demonstrated that sometimes the best support for integration is taking time with people who share your experience of being treated "differently." The critical fact is that people choose to come together in mutual support. They are not placed into a self-advocacy group as part of their treatment plan. The opportunity to come together as a peer to learn from others, to assist others in problem solving, and to participate in group mobilization for change truly can assist a person to achieve that most elusive goal: empowerment. The role of the school is to support self-advocacy and to offer the students the opportunity to participate.

Supports

In essence, supports are a unique array of resources that are mobilized to bridge the gaps that exist between the skills and the abilities of the person and the demands of everyday life. Supports can include specialized services from agencies; assistive technology; personal assistants; service facilitation; adapted enviroments; and help from family, friends, roommates, and neighbors. As outlined previously, a philosophy of support is distinguished from a service mentality by the rejection of assuming that there is a prepackaged solution to addressing a person's needs. In fact, each network of supports will be uniquely tailored to each individual situation. The other distinguishing characteristic of this approach is the assumption that supports built on personal relationships are more reliable than those contracted from an anonymous public agency.

By its very nature, an effective system of supports will be tied into some form of person-centered planning. Individuals with disabilities and those who are the closest to them are actively engaged, with assistance from paid professionals, in creative problem solving. Ultimately, the individual with a disability manages the system of supports him- or herself. He or she has the final say in determining what is needed. This is a skill that must be developed for all students with disabilities throughout their education careers as they assume more and more responsibilities.

The simplest way to develop a support plan is to use a planning matrix similar to the one illustrated in Table 18–11. Here the adaptive skill areas outlined earlier form one axis with the possible sources of support along the other axis. Using this tool, the circle of support and the transition planning team can identify priority needs under each skill area. These priorities are critical skills that the student has not mastered or cannot perform because of the disability. The bulleted topics in Table 18–11 are specific skills that are problematic for many young adults with disabilities and are highlighted. After the critical skills, the ones that in another time would have been seen as requisite for independent living are identified and the appropriate source of support

TABLE 18-11

A Simplified Supports Planning Matrix

Adaptive Skill Areas	Sources of Support				
	People (family, friend, neighbors, housemate)	Technology	Environmental Modification	New Skill to Be Learned	Formal Service Agency
Communication					
Self-care					
Home living					
Social skills					
Community use: • Travel					
Self-direction • Managing supports					
Health and safety					
Functional academics: • Managing finances					
Leisure					

can be explored. The person and his or her supporters must ask a series of questions: Does a new skill need to be learned? Who in the network can offer assistance? Can the environment be modified or a more accessible setting found? Is there technology available that will make independent performance possible? Does a formal support need to be mobilized to meet this need? At this time, it can be determined which of the resources outlined earlier must be mobilized to provide additional assets to aid in achieving the student's independent living goals.

Conclusion

Transition is an interesting concept with multiple layers of meaning. Fundamentally, transition is about the ongoing process of change. It captures a sense of movement from one reality to another. This chapter has cataloged a transition in American society, not of people with disabilities into adult life. Today we are experiencing a fundamental transformation in which the assumptions and beliefs of just a few years ago are being left in the "dust of time." A new reality for Americans with disabilities, particularly those with the most severe disabilities, is on the horizon. Public policy and public opinion are both slowly but profoundly being transfigured by the tenacious advocacy of people with disabilities whose simple request is to have what everyone else wants—a home of his or her own. This transition as yet is hardly achieved and will reveal a new set of challenges to be confronted in assuring full citizenship to people with disabilities. Nonetheless, this is happening. The final point of this chapter for the reader to consider is the role you have to play in this larger transition as you assist in its occurrence in the life of individual students and in your home communities.

Critical Point In the final analysis, the ultimate measure of educational effectiveness is the extent to which the school system contributes to the quality of life of its graduates.

Study Questions

1. Why have schools often failed to adequately prepare students for transition to independent adult life?

2. During the last 25 years, what factors have moved the field of mental retardation from one dominated by institutional care to the emergence of supported living?

3. How are both supported living and personal assistance services radical departures form the traditional models of services for people with disabilities?

4. What factors currently limit access to supported living and personal assistance services?

5. What agencies and organizations should be involved in planning for transition to adult living for people with developmental disabilities?

6. Explain the linkage between the independent living movement, the disability rights movements, and personal assistance services.

7. What is person-centered planning? How does it contribute to effective transition planning?

8. What four factors are critical in planning for successful transition to adult living?

Web Sites

American Disabled for Attendant Programs Today (ADAPT)
http://www.adapt.org/

"There's no place like home, and we mean real homes, not nursing homes. We are fighting so people with disabilities can live in the community with real supports instead of being locked away in nursing homes and other institutions."

Center for Community Change Through Housing and Support
http://www.ccc-international.org/

The Center for Community Change, with over a decade of experience working with systems and agencies around the world, combines values of empowerment, community integration and recovery with planning, program development and training skills to help design consumer-directed, family-supporting, outcome-focused and cost-effective systems of care.

Center on Human Policy
http://soeweb.syr.edu/thechp/

A Syracuse University-based policy, research, and advocacy organization involved in the national movement to insure the rights of people with disabilities. Since its founding, the Center has been involved in the study and promotion of open settings (inclusive community opportunities) for people with disabilities. Through the National Resource Center on Supported Living and Choice and other funded projects, the Center distributes bulletins, research reports, articles, information packages, and other materials on a broad range of topics related to integration or inclusion for people with disabilities (http://soeweb.syr.edu/thechp/tchppub.htm).

These materials include detailed resources on housing, supported living, and community support.

Community Associates International
http://www.communityassociates.com/index.html

Community Associates International provides a valuable resource for people on the cutting edge of disability-related issues and shares a strong commitment to a common mission. Each of the community associates offers skills, knowledge, experience, and a strong desire to assist you or your organization in the development of innovative and effective services and supports that enable people to be fully included in communities around the world.

Freedom Clearinghouse
http://www.freedomclearinghouse.org/

How would you like to spend the rest of your life in a nursing home or other institution? Neither would we. Let's do something about it NOW. Activate your license to change the system! Sign up to be part of our team of advocates across the nation. Or browse this site to learn more about how people can stay in their own homes and out of nursing homes and other institutions. Become part of our network of friends who support our work.

ILRU (Independent Living Research Utilization)
http://www.bcm.tmc.edu/ilru/

This program is a national center for information, training, research, and technical assistance in independent living. Its goal is to expand the body of knowledge in independent living and to improve utilization of results of research programs and demonstration projects in this field. It is a program of TIRR (The Institute for Rehabilitation and Research), a nationally recognized medical rehabilitation facility for persons with disabilities.

ILRU-DIMENET Independent Living Library
http://www.dimenet.com/ilrulib/

Presents an on-line library of independent living-related resource materials that have been developed by staff at independent living centers and other organizations involved in the independent living and disability rights movements over the years. This on-line library is developed in response to numerous requests for resource materials on such subjects as board and staff training curricula and manuals, policies and procedures, by-laws, job descriptions, independent living history and philosophy, key state and federal statutes and regulations, for-profit initiatives, and so on. The library is intended to be super user-friendly, and this includes being searchable by subject and author.

Independent Living Resource Centre
http://www.ilrc.nf.ca/

Located in St. John's, Newfoundland, Canada, the Independent Living Resource Centre is a consumer controlled organization committed to providing supports, resources, and opportunities for empowerment, which enable persons with disabilities to make informed choices about their lives.

Individualized Funding Information Resources
http://members.home.net/bsalisbury/

This site provides comprehensive information about the development of ways that people with disabilities can gain control over the funds to pay for the supports they need—a crucial step towards self-determination and citizenship.

Institute on Community Integration
http://www.ici.coled.umn.edu/ici/

Believes that persons with developmental disabilities should live as valued members of our communities, receiving the services and supports they need to fully develop their potential. Research and Training Center on Community Living http://ici2.coled.umn.edu/rtc/ is part of the Institute and focuses on community supports for persons with developmental disabilities and their families; providing research, evaluation, training, and technical assistance activities in these areas: national data collection and analysis, personnel research and training, self-determination and self-advocacy, integrated recreation and leisure, quality assurance and quality enhancement, and positive behavior management and communication.

Institute on Disability
http://iod.unh.edu/

The Institute is a University Affiliated Program (UAP) located at the University of New Hampshire that promotes full inclusion of people with disabilities in their communities.

National Clearinghouse on Managed Care and Long-Term Supports and Services for People with Developmental Disabilities and Their Families
http://www.mcare.net/

The primary objective of the Clearinghouse is to meet the informational needs of individuals with disabilities, their families, policy makers, service providers, advocates, and others in the area of managed care and long-term supports and services.

National Home of Your Own Alliance
http://alliance.unh.edu/

The National Home of Your Own Alliance is a partnership between the federal government and nationally recognized advocates and lead-

ers whose goal is to create housing and support opportunities that people choose and control.

Oaks Group
http://oaksgroup.org/

The Oaks Group is a value-based stakeholder organization whose members believe persons with developmental disabilities should be fully included in the mainstream of community life, that children should have the opportunity to grow up in families, and adults should receive the help needed to live as close as possible to the way people without developmental disabilities live.

Opening Doors: A Housing Initiative for The Disability Community
http://www.c-c-d.org/intro_page.htm/

Opening Doors is a housing initiative designed to provide information and technical assistance on affordable housing issues to people with disabilities, their families, advocates, and service providers across the United States.

Options in Community Living
http://www.optionsmadison.com/

Options' mission is to provide support and coordinate services to enable adults with developmental disabilities to live in their own homes. The agency assists people to make informed choices and reach their own goals, with support available to the extent and for as long as it is needed. Options strives to help people with disabilities, their families, and the larger community learn from one another, in order to promote mutual understanding, personal satisfaction, and fulfillment of the potential of each individual.

Research Information on Independent Living (RIIL)
http://www.lsi.ukans.edu/rtcil/apps/riil/search.asp/

This database contains reviews of research materials concerning independent living issues. RIIL is a joint effort of the Research & Training Center on Independent Living (RTC/IL) at the University of Kansas and the Independent Living Research Utilization (ILRU) program of TIRR.

State of the States in Developmental Disabilities
http://www.uic.edu/depts/idhd/StateoftheStates/statehomepage.htm/

Established in 1982 to investigate the determinants of public spending for mental retardation/developmental disabilities (MR/DD) services, this project maintains a 20-year longitudinal record of revenue, spending, and programmatic trends in the 50 states and the District of Columbia. Analysis of the rich detail of the data base reveals the impact over time of federal and state fiscal policy, and illustrates important service delivery trends in the states in community living, public and private residential institutions, family support, supported employment, supported living, Medicaid Waivers, demographics, and related areas.

Supported Life Institute
http://www.supportedlife.org/

"A supported life is a life that is rich in qualities a person most desires, and one which shows how connected we all are to each other. It is a life which: grows from a person's own choices, desires and dreams; it is not controlled by what kind of services are currently available; goes beyond just meeting a person's basic needs, to reaching a rich quality of life; includes all areas of a person's life; is always changing throughout a person's life; is the kind of life we all want and is not unique to people who happen to have disabilities."

TASH (formerly The Association for Persons with Severe Handicaps)
http://www.tash.org/

An international advocacy association of people with disabilities, their family members, other advocates, and people who work in the disability field. TASH believes that no one with a disability should be forced to live, work, or learn in a segregated setting; that all individuals deserve the right to direct their own lives. TASH's mission is to eliminate physical and social obstacles that prevent equity, diversity, and quality of life.

World Institute on Disability (WID)
http://www.igc.apc.org/wid/

An international public policy center dedicated to carrying out cutting-edge research on disability issues and overcoming obstacles to independent living. The Research and Training Center on Personal Assistance Services is one of the institute's valuable projects.

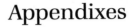

Appendixes

A   Self-Evaluation Strategies to Assist in Examining
    Cultural Beliefs and Multicultural Competence

B   Relationships with Minority Families

C   Life-Centered Career Education Transition
    Model and Competencies

D   Glossary of Terms Commonly Used in Transition Planning

E   Sample Blanket Release of Information and
    Member Agreement

F   Self-Survey of Transition Practices

Self-Evaluation Strategies to Assist in Examining Cultural Beliefs and Multicultural Competence

Questions and Considerations

1. Recognize that poverty does not mean dysfunction for families and that many families are able to provide strong, nurturing care. Take time to ask yourself how you might respond if your family was without income for several months or if it was cut in half for an extended period of time: What would you do without income? How would you protect your children?

2. What is your commitment to ongoing cultural learning? Are you focused, systematic, reflective, and evaluative in your approach? Do you use this systematic style to recognize culturally distinct modes of behavior (based on an understanding of one's own cultural values and behaviors) and interpret these differences within the community's context?

3. Do you use courses, seminars, and workshops as a starting point for personal follow-through? Do you use some level of sustained immersion in the various communities of your families? Do you go beyond being a "tourist" of each ethnic group, reading some novels, visiting ethnic sections of a large city, or visiting an ethnic festival?

4. Do you use your ongoing learnings to make continual and honest assessments of your own level of functioning with culturally different people, including a constant evaluation of the strength and nature of your own cultural beliefs? Do you continue to recognize that most professionals tend to overestimate their cross-cultural capabilities, and thereby underestimate their potentially negative impact? What steps do you take to address this tendency? (Green, 1999; McPhatter, 1997).

B

Relationships with Minority Families

Questions to Ask Yourself

1. Are there things that minority family members might say to a minority teacher that they probably would not say to a white teacher?
2. How do these family members describe these same things to you?
3. What might families expect a minority professional to understand intuitively about them and their needs?
4. What would families look for in a minority teacher or professional that they would not expect in a white teacher?
5. Are there distinctive advantages in being a minority professional with your families?
6. In the relations of white teachers with minority students and families, have you seen things or know of things that trouble you?

7. In relations between white and minority teachers and professionals, is there anything that troubles you? How could white professionals be more supportive of minority professionals? How could both groups be more mutually supportive?
8. What could white professionals do or what should they know if they want to work more effectively with minority students and families?
9. Can you describe instances where you felt that the needs of the minority students and families were in conflict with the kind of services offered by your organization or agency, or in conflict with its policies?
10. If you could restructure your office, program, or the personnel within it to better serve minority students and families, what would you do? (Green, 1999).

C

Life-Centered Career Education Transition Model and Competencies

FIGURE C–1
Curriculum/LCCE transition model

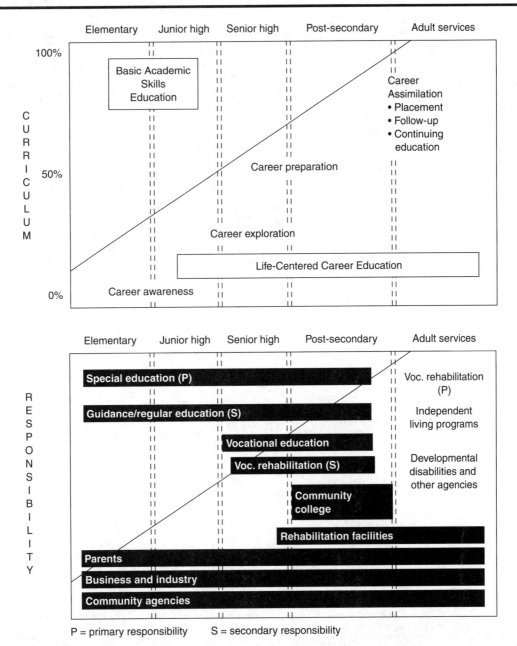

Source: From *Life centered career education: professional deveopment activity book* (p. 43) by the Council for Exceptional Children, 1993. Reston, VA: The Council for Exceptional Children. Copyright 1993 by the Council for Exceptional Children. Reprinted by permission.

FIGURE C–2
Life-centered career education competencies

Curriculum area	Competency	Subcompetency: The student will be able to:	
	1. Managing personal finances	1. Count money and make correct change	2. Make responsible expenditures
	2. Selecting and managing a household	7. Maintain home exterior/interior	8. Use basic appliances and tools
	3. Caring for personal needs	12. Demonstrate knowledge of physical fitness, nutrition and weight	13. Exhibit proper grooming and hygiene
	4. Raising children and meeting marriage responsibilities	17. Demonstrate physical care for raising children	18. Know psychological aspects of raising children
Daily Living Skills	5. Buying, preparing, and consuming food	20. Purchase food	21. Clean food and preparation areas
	6. Buying and caring for clothing	26. Wash/clean clothing	27. Purchase clothing
	7. Exhibiting responsible citizenship	29. Demonstrate knowledge of civil rights and responsibilities	30. Know nature of local, state, and federal governments
	8. Utilizing recreational facilities and engaging in leisure	33. Demonstrate knowledge of available community resources	34. Choose and plan activities
	9. Getting around the community	38. Demonstrate knowledge of traffic rules and safety	39. Demonstrate knowledge and use of various means of transportation
	10. Achieving self-awareness	42. Identify physical and psychological needs	43. Identify interests and abilities
	11. Acquiring self-confidence	46. Express feelings of self-worth	47. Describe others' perception of self
	12. Achieving socially responsible behavior—community	51. Develop respect for the rights and properties of others	52. Recognize authority and follow instructions
Personal-Social Skills	13. Maintaining good interpersonal skills	56. Demonstrate listening and responding skills	57. Establish and maintain close relationships
	14. Achieving independence	59. Strive toward self-actualization	60. Demonstrate self-organization
	15. Making adequate decisions	62. Locate and utilize sources of assistance	63. Anticipate consequences
	16. Communicating with others	67. Recognize and respond to emergency situations	68. Communicate with understanding
	17. Knowing and exploring occupational possibilities	70. Identify remunerative aspects of work	71. Locate sources of occupational and training information
	18. Selecting and planning occupational choices	76. Make realistic occupational choices	77. Identify requirements of appropriate and available jobs
Occupational Guidance and Preparation	19. Exhibiting appropriate work habits and behaviors	81. Follow directions and observe regulations	82. Recognize importance of attendance and punctuality
	20. Seeking, securing, and maintaining employment	88. Search for a job	89. Apply for a job
	21. Exhibiting sufficient physical-manual skills	94. Demonstrate stamina and endurance	95. Demonstrate satisfactory balance and coordination
	22. Obtaining specific occupational skills		

546

3. Keep basic financial records	4. Calculate and pay taxes	5. Use credit responsibly	6. Use banking services	
9. Select adequate housing	10. Set up household	11. Maintain home grounds		
14. Dress appropriately	15. Demonstrate knowledge of common illness, prevention and treatment	16. Practice personal safety		
19. Demonstrate marriage responsibilities				
22. Store food	23. Prepare meals	24. Demonstrate appropriate eating habits	25. Plan/eat balanced meals	
28. Iron, mend, and store clothing				
31. Demonstrate knowledge of the law and ability to follow the law	32. Demonstrate knowledge of citizen rights and responsibilities			
35. Demonstrate knowledge of the value of recreation	36. Engage in group and individual activities	37. Plan vacation time		
40. Find way around the community	41. Drive a car			
44. Identify emotions	45. Demonstrate knowledge of physical self			
48. Accept and give praise	49. Accept and give criticism	50. Develop confidence in oneself		
53. Demonstrate appropriate behavior in public places	54. Know important character traits	55. Recognize personal roles		
58. Make and maintain friendships				
61. Demonstrate awareness of how one's behavior affects others				
64. Develop and evaluate alternatives	65. Recognize nature of a problem	66. Develop goal-seeking behavior		
69. Know subtleties of communication				
72. Identify personal values met through work	73. Identify societal values met through work	74. Classify jobs into occupational categories	75. Investigate local occupational and training opportunities	
78. Identify occupational aptitudes	79. Identify major occupational interests	80. Identify major occupational needs		
83. Recognize importance of supervision	84. Demonstrate knowledge of occupational safety	85. Work with others	86. Meet demands for quality work	87. Work at a satisfactory rate
90. Interview for a job	91. Know how to maintain post-school occupational adjustment	92. Demonstrate knowledge of competitive standards	93. Know how to adjust to changes in employment	
96. Demonstrate manual dexterity	97. Demonstrate sensory discrimination			
There are no specific subcompetencies as they depend on skill being taught				

D

Glossary of Terms Commonly Used in Transition Planning

Accommodation Refers to any alteration of existing facilities or procedures to make them readily accessible to persons with disabilities.

Adult Services Refers to the many agencies and programs that are provided to adults with specific needs, such as disability, health, and income.

Advocacy Speaking on behalf of another person or group of persons.

Age of Majority The age that the state has determined a person is able to make decisions on his or her own (usually age 18) unless determined incompetent to do so by a court of law.

Agency Fairs A panel and/or exhibits designed to acquaint participants with the services, eligibility requirements, and referral procedures of adult service agencies.

Apprenticeships Periods of part-time work experience that may extend to a year or more that are usually associated with a specific occupation.

Aptitudes The particular strengths, knowledge, or skills that a person has that are generally related to an occupation or a career.

Audiologist A person who is qualified to assess a person's hearing and provide interventions to improve it.

Backward Planning A stepwise planning process that starts with desired goals and plans backward to the current level of functioning and support.

Bureau of Employment Services A program that helps individuals to find jobs through job listings, computer services, and counseling.

Career Development Index *See* Career Maturity Index.

Career Fairs Panels and/or exhibits designed to provide information on a range of careers.

Career Maturity Index This assessment, along with the Career Development Inventory (1990), can direct counseling (or the use of a computerized DISCOVER program) to address competencies in the areas of student, leisurite, citizen, worker, and homemaker.

Career Planning Refers to the general planning process related to helping the individual develop and achieve meaningful adult roles. Transition planning is a specific form of career planning.

Career Portfolio Assessment A standardized method of assessing the student's career portfolio activities by measuring mastery (e.g., novice, apprentice, expert) or level of independence.

Career Portfolios Organized samples (often a notebook) of student work and classroom activities that include writing samples, photographs, videos, and other demonstrations of student performance.

Case Manager A person from an agency who is responsible for seeing that services are obtained and coordinated for an individual. A transition coordinator is a form of case manager.

Choicemaker   A self-determination approach that focuses on (1) choosing goals, (2) expressing goals, and (3) taking action.

COACH   A form of person-centered planning that stands for choosing options and accommodations for children. Includes the family's values and dreams in IEP planning.

Community College   A postsecondary education program (generally 2 years) that leads to an occupation or entrance into a university.

Course of Study   Refers to the type of education program in which a student is enrolled, including vocational education, college preparation, and apprenticeships.

DD   *See* Developmental Disability.

Developmental Disability   A disability that is acquired during the period that the person is developing, generally before age 21 or at birth, and that significantly impacts several life activity areas, such as self-care, self-direction, learning, mobility, speech, and independent living.

Ecological Models   A model that focuses upon individuals and stresses working with the environments that affect their lives.

Education of All Handicapped Children Act   The landmark 1975 legislation that required education for all students with disabilities and introduced the terms IEP, least restrictive environment, free appropriate public education, and the multifactored evaluation to education.

Eligibility   A set of rules that determines whether students or families are qualified to receive services based on the nature and severity of the disability, income, or other characteristics.

Employability Life Skills Assessment   This criterion-referenced checklist may be used yearly to assess a student's level of performance in 24 critical employability skills areas in the domains of personal, social, and daily living habits.

Employment Specialist   In supported employment, a person who provides job placement,

training, and sometimes follow-along services to a worker with a disability. Sometimes used interchangeably with job coach.

Empowerment   Education and practices aimed at transferring power to or strengthening individuals and groups.

Enclave   A form of supported employment where a group of no more than eight persons with disabilities often work in an integrated employment setting with professional supervision.

Entitlements   Programs that must be provided to all eligible persons upon demand. Special education and social security are entitlements. Many adult services are not.

FAPE   *See* Free Appropriate Public Education.

Follow-Along Services   In supported employment, this term refers to services and supports that are provided to a worker with a disability after job training is completed.

Free Appropriate Public Education   The requirement, introduced by the EHA of 1975, that requires schools to provide an education relevant to the needs of students with disabilities. The courts have generally stated that appropriateness does not mean optimal, only that the student is progressing at a reasonable rate.

Functional Vocational Evaluation   An evaluation that focuses on identifying skills demonstrated by the student in actual vocational and life activities. Situational and work assessments are functional; IQ tests and tests of standardized reading levels are not.

Goals 2000: Educate America Act of 1993   Legislation that established eight education goals that state and local education agencies were to achieve by the year 2000.

Group Action Planning   A self-determination approach that helps students to take charge of personal futures planning.

Guardian   A person or agency that assumes limited or unlimited authority to make decisions for a minor or an adult who has been determined to be incompetent in a court of law.

Includes medical guardianships, guardianship of the person, and guardian of the estate.

Guidance Counselor A person who is qualified to assess an individual's career interests and provide counseling and support in making career decisions.

Housing and Urban Development A federal program that provides or funds subsidized housing for low-income persons.

HUD *See* Housing and Urban Development.

IDEA *See* Individuals with Disabilities Education Act.

IEP/Transition Meeting The meeting in which transition is discussed. This meeting should occur *no later than age* 14 to discuss the student's course of study and *no later than age* 16 to discuss services and supports needed to achieve the student's desired postschool outcomes.

IEP/Transition Plan *See* Transition Plan.

ILC *See* Independent Living Centers.

Impairment Related Work Expense Certain expenses for things that a person with a disability needs because of his or her impairment in order to work. May be deducted when determining eligibility for SSDI or SSI.

Inclusion The process of including students with disabilities in the environments, activities, and curricula of typical students and persons. Inclusion may mean different things to different people. Sometimes used interchangeably with the term "integration."

Independent Living Centers These are established by the Rehabilitation Act in response to consumer and people-first movements. ILCs are run predominately by consumers and can fund or support accommodations in vehicles and housing to make persons with disabilities more independent.

Individualized Education Program A statement of the programs and services that will be provided to a student with a disability who is eligible under the IDEA.

Individualized Service Plans Plans developed for specific individuals that describe services provided by an agency to help an individual achieve desired goals. These include individual habilitation plans (MR/DD), individual work-related plans (VR), and individual plans for employment (VR).

Individuals with Disabilities Education Act An updated version of the Education of All Handicapped Children's Act (EHA) that required the statement of needed transition services as part of the IEP in 1990.

Informational Interviews Interviews with employers to find out about their organization, jobs, and the types of people they employ.

Integration In the disability context, the process of including persons with disabilities in the environments, activities, and social networks of typical persons. Sometimes used interchangeably with the term "inclusion."

Internship *See* apprenticeships.

IPLAN A form of person-centered planning that stands for inventory, plan, listen, ask, and name your goals.

IRWE *See* Impairment Related Work Expense.

Job Analysis The process of analyzing a job in terms of essential elements, skills needed, and characteristics to aid in job matching and training.

Job Carving A technique used in advanced supported employment programs where a job is divided into components that can be done by a person with a severe disability.

Job Coach *See* Job Trainer.

Job Placement The process of helping an individual to find a job.

Job Shadowing The practice of allowing students to observe a real work setting to determine their interests and to acquaint them with the requirements of the job.

Job Sharing The practice of having two or more persons share a job to provide accommodations in work scheduling or job duties.

Job Trainer In supported employment, generally a paraprofessional who provides on-site job training and supports to a worker with a disability. Sometimes used interchangeably with an employment specialist or a job coach.

Language Specialist   *See* Speech Pathologist.

Least Restrictive Environment   A concept introduced to education by the EHA in 1975 that required a continuum of services for students with disabilities so that they could be educated in as integrated an environment as possible while still providing FAPE.

Life-Centered Career Education   This career development approach delineates 22 major competencies that can be infused into primary, middle, and secondary curricula to address the major life domains of work, home, and academics.

Lifestyle Planning   A form of person-centered planning that describes future goals and defines the steps needed to reach them.

LRE   *See* Least Restrictive Environment.

Mainstreaming   A term that was used widely in the 1970s to refer to the practice of placing students with disabilities in the regular education curriculum. This term lost favor when it was found that many students were being placed in regular classes without needed supports.

McGill Action Planning System   A person-centered planning approach that focuses on seven areas: (1) nonnegotiables, (2) strong preferences, (3) highly desirables, (4) personal characteristics, (5) personal concerns, (6) needed supports, and (7) action steps.

Medicaid   A health care program serving eligible low-income persons with disabilities whose income and assets are below specific levels. Generally, available to persons receiving SSI or SSI work incentives.

Medicare   An insurance program serving persons 65 and older and individuals with disabilities regardless of income if they are eligible for SSDI.

Mental Health Services   Services provided to persons with significant behavioral or mood disorders that are not related to mental retardation or developmental disabilities.

Mental Retardation and Development Disability Services   Services that are provided to persons with disabilities who were identified at birth or before age 21. In some states, they are referred to as developmental disability services.

Meyers-Briggs   This assessment identifies four personality temperaments that can be used to develop self- and career awareness (e.g., extroverted, intuitive, feeling, perceptive or ENFP).

MFE   *See* Multifactored Evaluation.

MH   *See* Mental Health Services.

MH/MR   In some states, mental health and mental retardation and developmental disability services are combined and referred to as MH/MR.

Mobile Work Crew   A supported employment placement where a group of no more than eight persons provide contract services to businesses (e.g., janitorial, landscaping), usually under the supervision of a professional.

MR/DD   *See* Mental Retardation and Development Disability Services.

Multifactored Evaluation   Introduced by the EHA of 1975. An evaluation by a variety of professionals to determine whether a student is in need of special education services. Originally, this was required before entering special education and every 3 years thereafter. With the IDEA of 1997, the MFE was changed to include assessment by nonprofessionals and parents.

Natural Supports   Refers to the use of persons, practices, and things that naturally occur in the environment to meet the support needs of an individual.

Next S.T.E.P.   A field-tested student-directed transition approach that consists of 16 lessons that address (1) getting started, (2) self-exploring and evaluating, (3) developing goals and activities, and (4) putting a plan into place.

Occupational Therapist   A person who is qualified to develop and implement programs to develop fine motor skills and skills and accommodations related to work and daily living.

Occupational Work Adjustment   A program that places a person in jobs or environments in order to develop appropriate work and social behaviors.

Occupational Work Experience   Refers to programs that allow a person to try one or more jobs for periods of a year or less in order to explore interests and to develop job skills.

PASS   *See* Plan for Achieving Self-Support.

People First   A movement of persons with disabilities that started in the late 1970s to take greater control of programs affecting them. The movement originated the concept of person-first language.

Person-Centered Planning   Refers to a number of planning approaches that tailor services and supports to meet the needs of the individual, as opposed to programs that try to fit individuals into available services.

Person-First Language   The practice of referring to persons with disabilities with the term denoting disability following and not supplanting terms referring to them as an individual (e.g., a person with a visual impairment, a person who uses a wheelchair). Person-first avoids impersonal, negative, and medical terminology (e.g., the disabled, cripples, retardates).

Personal Futures Planning   A type of person-centered planning that involves dreaming, describing, and doing with the family and their support system.

Physical Therapist   A person who is qualified to develop and implement programs to develop fine and gross motor skills and rehabilitation services to persons with physical disabilities.

Plan for Achieving Self-Support   A savings account that can be excluded from income and assets of persons with disabilities to allow them to save up for something that would make them self-sufficient (e.g., college fund).

Postsecondary Education   Education programs that follow high school, including colleges, universities, technical and vocational schools, and community colleges.

Postsecondary Programs   Programs that occur after high school (secondary education).

Proficiency Tests   Tests that are designed to determine if students are measuring up to education standards set by the state and/or district.

Psychiatrist   A medical doctor who can assess an individual's emotional, intellectual, and coping skills and typically provides medical interventions or medications to improve them.

Psychologist   A person who is qualified to assess an individual's emotional, intellectual, and coping skills and to provide counseling or interventions to improve them.

Referral   The process of notifying an agency to request services. A referral is often followed by an eligibility determination.

Rehabilitation Services Commission   A name for the agency that oversees the provision of vocational rehabilitation services in Ohio.

Rehabilitation Technologist   A person who is qualified to apply technology to meet the needs of persons with disabilities.

Related Services   Services that are not necessarily educational in nature but that are provided as part of an education program. Speech, language, hearing, social work, and psychology services are examples of related services.

SCANS Report   *See* Secretary's Commission on Achieving Necessary Skills Report.

School-to-Work Programs   Refers to general education secondary programs developed under the School-to-Work Opportunities Act of 1994 that include career education, work-based instruction experiences, and efforts to connect students with vocational and postschool programs.

Secretary's Commission on Achieving Necessary Skills Report   Competencies identified by employers that will be needed by workers of the future.

Section 8 Housing   Refers to housing subsidized by Housing and Urban Development (HUD).

Self-Advocacy   The ability and opportunity to speak on behalf of one's self.

Self-Determination   Refers to the ability and the opportunity for students to make decisions for themselves.

Self-Directed Search   This instrument identifies six personality types and matches them with six categories of jobs to help students make a career choice related to their needs and preferences.

SGA   *See* Substantial Gainful Employment.

Social Security Administration   The agency that oversees the provision of social security disability and supplemental security income and related work incentives.

Social Security Disability Insurance   In this context, a monthly check provided to children of parents who have retired or become disabled and have paid into social security. Only paid to individuals whose income falls below SGA after accounting for work incentives.

Social Worker   A person who is employed by a school or agency to help individuals, families, or groups in coping with their environments and obtaining needed services.

Speech Pathologist   A person who is qualified to assess a person's speech and provide interventions to improve it. Sometimes referred to as a language specialist.

SSA   *See* Social Security Administration. Sometimes used to refer to SSDI payments.

SSDI   *See* Social Security Disability Insurance.

SSI   *See* Supplemental Security Income.

Standards-Based Reform   Refers to school accountability efforts to assure that all students attain a level of proficiency defined by the state or district.

Statement of Needed Transition Services   *See* Transition Plan.

Student Earned Income Exclusion   An income that can be excluded for a student under age 22 in calculating SSI benefits.

STW   *See* School-to-Work Programs.

Subsidized Housing   Generally, HUD housing where a person pays rent based on income (e.g., 33% of income).

Substantial Gainful Employment   The amount of income a person can make after a trial work period and still receive SSDI payments.

Summer Youth Employment Programs   Subsidized summer employment for low-income youth, and sometimes youth with disabilities, through the local workforce investment board.

Supplemental Security Income   An income support payment administered by the Social Security Administration that is provided to children with disabilities and adults who are disabled and whose income and assets fall below a prescribed level after accounting for social security work incentives.

Supported Employment   A form of employment where training is done at the job site and ongoing supports are provided to maintain employment. Supported employment is intended for persons with the most severe disabilities. Supported employment jobs are in integrated settings and may consist of individual placements, mobile work crews, or enclaves.

Supports   Refers to accommodations, persons in the environment, or practices that help an individual in conducting life activities, including employment.

Take Charge   A student-directed collaborative approach that pairs youth with adults of the same gender with similar challenges and uses four primary strategies: (1) skill facilitation, (2) mentoring, (3) peer support, and (4) parent support to develop student skills in achievement, partnership, and coping.

Tech-Prep   A coordinated curriculum in the final 2 years of high school with a planned transition to a postsecondary institution, usually for an additional 2 years in a technical or health field.

Technical Schools   Refers to education programs that lead to certification in a highly specialized vocation such as electrical engineering.

Technology   Refers to machines, services, and adaptations that allow the individual to better control their environment.

Transition   The process of moving from adolescence to adult roles where the child reconciles his or her needs, interests, and preferences with adult norms and roles.

Transition Coordinator   A person or agency that is responsible for assuring that planned services are provided in a timely manner and in a way that complements other services provided to a student.

Transition Plan   Also known as the "statement of needed transition services" or individual transition plan (ITP). The IEP/transition plan states in the IEP what services, supports, and activities will be provided to students to help them reach their career goals.

Transition Planning   The process of helping students and their families to plan services to help them reach career goals and adult living objectives related to their needs, interests, and preferences. The IDEA requires transition planning activities documented in the IEP for students aged 14 and older.

Transition Planning Inventory   An inventory approach that focuses on student skill and support needs in the areas of (1) employment, (2) further education, (3) daily living, (4) leisure activities, (5) community participation, (6) health, (7) self-determination, (8) communication, and (9) interpersonal relationships.

Trial Work Period   The amount of time that an individual receiving SSDI can exceed SGA without losing benefits (currently up to nine nonconsecutive months in a 60-month period).

Vocational Education   Refers to secondary and postsecondary programs that teach skills related to specific occupations.

Vocational Rehabilitation Services   A federal and state program that provides a range of services to persons with disabilities, typically to achieve a particular career goal.

VR   *See* Vocational Rehabilitation Services.

Waiting List   A list of persons who have been determined eligible for services that are in short supply and cannot be provided until openings arise or services are expanded.

What Color Is Your Parachute?   This publication provides an overview of career development and some useful exercises and examples related to identifying interests, researching jobs, developing résumés, and conducting interviews.

Whose Future Is It Anyway?   A self-determination curriculum designed for persons with cognitive disabilities that consists of 36 lessons that address (1) self-awareness, (2) making decisions, (3) obtaining supports and transition services, (4) writing and evaluating transition objectives, and (5) leadership skills.

Work Adjustment   *See* Occupational Work Adjustment.

Work Experience   *See* Occupational Work Experience.

Work Incentives   A number of social security work incentives that allow a person to exclude part of his or her income to maintain eligibility for SSI or SSDI. Includes PASS, IRWEs, student earned income exclusion, and extended eligibility for medicaid.

Work Study   Jobs developed by the high school where the student receives credit toward graduation.

Workforce Investment Act   A 1998 act of Congress that brought a number of job service programs together as part of "one-stop shops." Covers the old job training partnership, rehabilitation services (which still maintains separate offices), and the Bureau of Employment Services.

E

Sample Blanket Release of Information and Member Agreement

SUMMIT COUNTY LOCAL INTERAGENCY TRANSITION TEAM
CONSENT FOR RELEASE OF INFORMATION

_____ Youth - Full Name	_____ Date of Birth
_____ Social Security Number (Optional)	_____ Student/Case Number

The following agencies have my permission to share information for the purpose of helping the student/youth move from school to adult services and to reduce paperwork:
*(Please check or cross-out any agencies you do **not** want to share information)*

- ☐ Akron Child Guidance Center
- ☐ The Summit County Health Department
- ☐ The Summit County Health Department
- ☐ County of Summit Board of Mental Retardation and Developmental Disabilities
- ☐ Summit County Children Services
- ☐ The Summit County Department of Human Services
- ☐ The Private Industry Council
- ☐ Rehabilitation Services Commission
- ☐ The Department of Youth Services
- ☐ Public School Systems (specify): _____
  _____

I authorize sharing of the following information: (circle yes or no and initial)

yes	no	_____	<u>Identifying Information</u>: name, birth date, sex, race, address, telephone number, social security number, disability, type of services being received and name of agency providing services to me or the individual named above.
yes	no	_____	<u>Case Information</u>: the above Identifying Information, plus medical and social history, treatment/service history, psychological evaluations, Individualized Education Plans (IEPs), transition plans, vocational assessments, grades and attendance, and other personal information regarding me or the individual named above. Information regarding the following shall not be released unless initialed below: _____ HIV and AIDS related diagnosis and treatment _____ Substance abuse diagnosis and treatment

I understand that the Consent for Release of Information expires 180 days from the date it is signed (*). I also understand that I may cancel this Consent For Release of Information at any time by stating so in writing with the date and my signature. This does not include any information which has been shared between the time that I gave permission to share information and the time that it was canceled.

This consent expires on,_____ 20 ___

_____ Signature of person authorized to consent	_____ Relationship to Youth
_____ Signature of Individual	_____ Date
_____ Witness/Agency Representative	_____ Date

* This release of information will expire in 90 days for information concerning substance and alcohol abuse diagnosis and treatment.

CONSENT FOR RELEASE OF INFORMATION

I understand that my signing or refusing to sign this consent will not affect public benefits or services that I am otherwise entitled to.

CASE INFORMATION:

If the release authorized the disclosure of **Case Information**, consent to such disclosure may include the following types of information, if they are in the files of the agency releasing the information.

      1. **Educational records**, including but not limited to the results of diagnostic evaluations, teacher observations, vocational assessments, grades, attendance, individualized education programs (IEPs) and transition plans.
      2. **Medical records**, including but not limited to the results of physical and mental examinations, diagnoses of physical and mental disorders, medication history, physical and mental health status and history, summary of treatment or services received, and summary of treatment plans and treatment needs.
      3. **Psychological and medical testing**, including but not limited to any IQ tests or other tests, of cognitive or emotional or mental status, and any reports of physical tests such as x-rays, CT scans, diagnostic blood testing, or other results.
      4. **HIV, AIDS, and AIDS related diagnoses and test results**, including information about treatment planned and received. (This information will be disclosed only if page 1 is initialed to permit it.)
      5. **Drug and alcohol abuse diagnoses and treatment**, including but not limited to results of evaluations, diagnoses, treatment and services received, treatment plans and treatment needs. (This information will be disclosed only if page 1 is initialed to permit it.)
      6. All records of services provided by Summit County Children Services except child abuse investigation reports.
      7. **Second-hand information** may require an additional release of information from the original source.

TO ALL AGENCIES RECEIVING INFORMATION DISCLOSED AS A RESULT OF THIS SIGNED CONSENT:

1.   If the records released include information of any diagnosis or treatment of drug or alcohol abuse, the following statement applies:

      Information disclosed pursuant to this consent has been disclosed to you from records whose confidentiality is protected by Federal law.

      Federal regulations (42 CFR Part 2) prohibit you from making any further disclosure of it without the specific written consent of the person to whom it pertains, or as otherwise permitted by such regulations. A general authorization for the release of medical or other information is NOT sufficient for this purpose.

2.   If the records released include information of an HIV-related diagnosis or test result, the following Statement applies:

            This information has been disclosed to you from confidential records protected from disclosure by state law. You shall make no further disclosure of this information without the specific, written, and informed release of the individual to whom it pertains, or as otherwise permitted by state law. A general authorization for the release of medical or other information is NOT sufficient for the purpose of the release of HIV test results or diagnoses.

Agencies and/or individuals added to the release will be apprised of the Summit County LITT "Member Agreement for Information Sharing"

SUMMIT COUNTY INTERAGENCY TRANSITION TEAM
Member Agreement for Information Sharing

Member Agencies:

      Alcohol, Drug Addiction, Mental Health Service Board (ADAMH)
      Summit County Health Department
      Akron Public Schools
      Stow City Schools
      Hudson Local Schools
      Nordonia Local Schools
      County of Summit Board of Mental Retardation and Developmental Disabilities
      Summit County of Children Services
      Department of Youth Services
      Department of Human Services
      Private Industry Council
      Rehabilitation Services Commission

This agreement is by and among the member agencies comprising the Summit Local Interagency Transition Team.

This agreement is entered into for the benefit of those who seek to share information without risk of liability from unauthorized release, and for the benefit of students and their families who wish to receive, without unreasonable diminution of their rights of privacy and avoidance of self-incrimination, the improved services which information sharing may produce. The Summit LITT agencies agree to:

1. Share information regarding students in compliance with the "Summit County Local Interagency Transition Team consent for Release of Information" (here in after "Consent") signed by each student and by his/her parent or guardian if under the age of 18, **unless greater release of information is otherwise required or authorized by law.**

2. Use information only for the purpose of improving the quality, efficiency or coordination of the delivery of transition services to the youth and his/her family. **No information first obtained from the consent may be used or transmitted by a member agency for the purpose of criminal investigation, prosecution, or sentencing, except as required by law or judicial order.**

3. Establish internal management systems to help assure that information-sharing activities will be limited to the terms of this agreement and of the student's Consent and will promptly cease upon expiration or revocation of the Consent.

4. Forward a copy of the signed Consent to all member agencies identified on the Consent.

5. Forward immediately to all member agencies any written notice of revocation of a student's Consent which it may receive.

6. Execute this agreement with all above-named member agencies. Member's information-sharing privileges under this agreement shall extend only to sharing agencies identified in the Consent.

This Agreement shall continue in force and effect for a period of one year, automatically renewed unless earlier terminated. This agreement may be terminated by any member agency, upon written notice. Any amendment to this agreement shall be executed in writing by all member agencies.

AGREED:

_____

_____

_____

_____

_____

_____

_____

_____

      Member Agency   Date

Self-Survey of Transition Practices

Survey on Transition Policy Compliance and Best Practices

Purpose. The goal of this survey is to obtain information on transition policy compliance and exemplary practices relating to the requirements of the Individuals with Disabilities Education Act (IDEA) Amendments of 1997. Additionally, this survey can be used as a self-assessment by families, educators, and adult service providers concerned with the transition of youth with disabilities.

Confidentiality. Answers to these questions are for research purposes and to report transition needs to the Division of Special Education – not monitoring. The responses of all survey participants will be aggregated for reporting purposes. Your identity and that of the school district and community will be kept confidential. Confidentiality will be maintained through the use of a number code for each survey. The coding key will be held by Rachel McMahan at Kent State University's Transition Center and will be used only for follow-up survey requests and response to training requests (if the *Additional Information* form on the last page is filled out).

*This survey was developed by Ohio's Cross-Training Committee of Project LIFE and Kent State University's Transition Center. Copy by permission - Transition Center, 308 White Hall, Kent State University, Kent, Ohio 44242 - (330) 672-3833.

* This survey has been adapted from the Report on the National Survey of the Implementation of the IDEA Transition Requirements by David R. Johnson, Michael Sharpe, and Mary Fox Sinclair - University of Minnesota, National Transition Network, Institute on Community Integration.

Directions: Students and parents - fill out numbers 1, 2, 3, 7, 8, and 9. Educators and adult service providers - fill out numbers 1-9.

Demographic Information

1. The person(s) completing this survey (CHECK ALL THAT APPLIES):

☐ superintendent ☐ administrator (other than supt.) ☐ special education coordinator ☐ VOSE coordinator	☐ work study coordinator ☐ special education teacher ☐ vocational education teacher ☐ regular education teacher	☐ school psychologist ☐ parent/guardian ☐ student ☐ other: _____

2. My school setting is: (CHECK ONE THAT BEST APPLIES):

☐ rural ☐ suburb of city of 100,000 or more	☐ small city up to 100,000 ☐ large city more than 100,000	

3. The county(s) I work with is (are): (LIST ALL IN THE SPACE PROVIDED BELOW):

4. What is the number of students you serve and their age breakdown? (GIVE BEST ESTIMATE FOR EACH CATEGORY):

☐ total served by you each year = _____ ☐ 19 - 22 years (_____ %)	☐ 17 - 18 years (_____ %) ☐ 15 - 16 years (_____ %)	☐ 13 - 14 years (_____ %) ☐ less than 13 years (_____ %)

5. What is the breakdown of disability categories for students you serve? (GIVE BEST ESTIMATES):

☐ specific learning disabilities-LD(____%) ☐ developmental disabilities-DH (____ %) ☐ multiple disabilities-MH (_____ %) ☐ orthopedic disabilities-OH (_____ %)	☐ severe behavior disabilities-SBH(____%) ☐ hearing impairments (_____ %) ☐ visual impairments (_____ %) ☐ traumatic brain injury (_____ %)	☐ autism (_____ %) ☐ other health impaired (_____ %) ☐ other _____ (_____ %)

6. The ethnic breakdown of students you serve (GIVE BEST ESTIMATES):

☐ White (_____ %) ☐ Hispanic (_____ %)	☐ African-American (_____ %) ☐ Native American (_____ %)	☐ Asian (_____ %) ☐ Other (_____ %)

7. How many hours of transition training have you received to date (CHECK BEST ESTIMATE):

☐ zero hours ☐ 1 - 2 hours	☐ 3 - 5 hours ☐ 6 - 8 hours	☐ 9 - 15 hours ☐ more than 15 hours

8. What kind of transition training have you had? (CHECK ALL THAT APPLY):

☐ no training ☐ in-house training	☐ SERRC training ☐ Project LIFE (Mazzoli, Izzo, Dennis)	☐ Transition Outreach Project (Izzo, Baer) ☐ Other _____

9. What role do you have in transition planning? (CHECK ALL THAT APPLY):

☐ no role in transition planning ☐ provide transition services	☐ attend IEP/transition meetings ☐ coordinate IEP/transition meetings	☐ supervise transition staff/planning ☐ other _____

Directions. The survey questions are divided into two sections. Section I is Policy Compliance and Section II is Best Practices. Section I is divided into four transition planning and service areas: (A) parent notification, (B) participation in meetings, (C) IEP content, and (D) agency responsibility. After each question in Section I is a number that correlates with the proposed IDEA regulations. Section II identifies best practices (exemplary practices) that have been shown to be effective - both in Ohio and nationally - but are not required by law. For each section, a range of strategies (e.g., 9a - 9e) are described that school districts might use to implement the transition component of IDEA. The response options, defined below, are based on the assumption that some strategies are used more often and others only in special circumstances.

> 1 = **Almost Never (used with less than 10% of the intended audience, i.e., students, parents, or agencies**
> 2 = **Sometimes (used with less than 50% but more than 10% of the intended audience)**
> 3 = **Frequently (used with 50% to 75% of the intended audience)**
> 4 = **Almost Always (used with more than 75% of the intended audience)**

When responding to the following questions, consider those students who are at least 14 years old or students who are younger and qualified for transition services.

SECTION I: POLICY COMPLIANCE

A: PARENT NOTIFICATION

1=Almost Never   2=Sometimes   3=Frequently   4=Almost Always

10. Parents are notified of the IEP meeting in which transition is discussed using the following strategies: 300.345 (b) (1)

(a) mailing a standard form letter or memo.	1	2	3	4
(b) mailing a personalized letter.	1	2	3	4
(c) contacting the parent at home or work over the telephone.	1	2	3	4
(d) asking the student to remind their parent of the upcoming transition IEP meeting.	1	2	3	4
(e) sending a notice of the meeting home with the student.	1	2	3	4

Information Needed? □ *Yes.* □ *No. Comments:* _____

11. If communication is not established through the first parent notice, what alternative steps are taken to inform parents of the upcoming meeting: 300.345 (d)

(a) mailing the notice to a different address.	1	2	3	4
(b) calling at varying times - weekdays, evening, or weekends.	1	2	3	4
(c) making a home visit.	1	2	3	4
(d) contacting a parent through a relative.	1	2	3	4
(e) contacting the parent through a community service agency provider.	1	2	3	4

Information Needed? □ *Yes.* □ *No. Comments:* _____

12. A mutually agreed upon time and location for the IEP meeting in which transition is discussed is determined by: 300.345 (a) (2)

(a) contacting the parent prior to sending out the parent notice.	1	2	3	4
(b) sending out a notice that offers the parent a choice of times.	1	2	3	4
(c) sending out a notice that offers the parent a choice of locations.	1	2	3	4
(d) records are kept of attempts to arrange a mutually agreed upon time and place by attaching personal notes, logs or standardized forms to the IEP or records folder.	1	2	3	4

Information Needed? □ *Yes.* □ *No. Comments:* _____

1=Almost Never   2=Sometimes   3=Frequently   4=Almost Always

13. If no parent can attend the IEP meeting in which transition is discussed, the methods used to involve parents in planning include: 300.345 (c)

(a) holding an individual meeting with the parent.	1	2	3	4
(b) a telephone conference call.	1	2	3	4
(c) an invitation to parents to submit their input in writing.	1	2	3	4
(d) mailing a draft of student transition goals and objectives to the parent for review and feedback.	1	2	3	4
(e) encouraging the parent to have a family friend or some other advocate attend in their absence.	1	2	3	4

Information Needed? ☐ *Yes.* ☐ *No.* *Comments:* _____

14. The district assures that parents understand the proceedings of the IEP meeting in which transition is discussed using the following strategies: 300.345 (e)

(a) notifying parents prior to the meeting by telephone or mail.	1	2	3	4
(b) disseminating information to parents on the transition planning process.	1	2	3	4
(c) providing formal workshops for parents of transition-age youth.	1	2	3	4
(d) providing informal consultation to parents upon request individually or in small groups.	1	2	3	4
(e) has "Whose IDEA Is It?" been given and explained to the student/parent?	1	2	3	4

Information Needed? ☐ *Yes.* ☐ *No.* *Comments:* _____

B: PARTICIPATION IN MEETINGS - student/agency participation

1=Almost Never   2=Sometimes   3=Frequently   4=Almost Always

15. Students are invited to participate in their IEP meetings in which transition is discussed using the following practices: 300.344 (b) (1)

(a) a verbal invitation from a staff member.	1	2	3	4
(b) a formal notice (e.g., memo or letter) sent directly to the student.	1	2	3	4

Information Needed? ☐ *Yes.* ☐ *No.* *Comments:* _____

16. Do the following school representatives attend the IEP meeting in which transition is discussed? 300.344 (a)

(a) regular education teacher (if student is or might be in regular education classes).	1	2	3	4
(b) at least one special education teacher.	1	2	3	4
(c) a representative from the local educational agency who is qualified and knowledgeable about the general curriculum and special education resources.	1	2	3	4
(d) an individual who can interpret evaluation.	1	2	3	4

Information Needed? ☐ *Yes.* ☐ *No.* *Comments:* _____

17. By no later than age 16, agencies (e.g., vocational rehabilitation, social security, mental retardation/developmental disabilities, mental health) are encouraged to participate in student IEP meetings in which transition is discussed using the following strategies: 300.344 (b) (3)

(a) parent or student request for agency representative to participate in IEP meeting in which transition is discussed.	1	2	3	4
(b) standard form letter or memo of invitation.	1	2	3	4
(c) unstandardized letter or memo drafted individually by a staff member.	1	2	3	4
(d) verbal invitation over the telephone or in person.	1	2	3	4
(e) maintaining regular contact with the service agencies over time.	1	2	3	4

Information Needed? ☐ *Yes.* ☐ *No.* *Comments:* _____

18. If an agency invited to send a representative does not do so, the following steps are taken to obtain their participation in the planning of transition services: 300.344 (b) (3)			
(a) a copy of the IEP/transition plan is forwarded to the agency.	1	2	3	4
(b) a subsequent meeting is arranged with the agency to discuss students' transition needs.	1	2	3	4
(c) the agency is contacted via telephone or mail to find out their agreement to provide services.	1	2	3	4

Information Needed? ☐*Yes.* ☐*No. Comments:* _____

_____

19. Preferences and interests of students are incorporated into the IEP using the following strategies: 300.344 (b) (2)				
(a) verifying with the student verbally that their preferences are incorporated in each transition goal.	1	2	3	4
(b) reviewing student survey results regarding their preferences as each goal is being drafted.	1	2	3	4
(c) obtaining feedback regarding IEP content from adults who are knowledgeable about the youths' preferences, needs and interests.	1	2	3	4
(d) student led IEP meeting where students describe and discuss their goals.	1	2	3	4
(e) formal surveys, interviews, or having someone represent the student if they cannot be at their meeting.	1	2	3	4
(f) other (specify): _____.	1	2	3	4

Information Needed? ☐*Yes.* ☐*No. Comments:* _____

_____

Reminder. This set of questions will address the extent to which current procedures and policies facilitate the development of the IEP. In this section, rate each strategy separately for students with mild to moderate educational needs and for students with moderate to intensive educational needs. **Circle the response that best describes how frequently each strategy (i.e., 20a, 21d, 23c) is used.**

C: CONTENT OF THE IEP

	Mild Moderate				Moderate Intensive			
20. By age 14, or earlier if determined appropriate by the IEP team, does the IEP/transition plan specify services needed (e.g., readers, instructional adaptations, more time to take tests) that focuses on the general course of study for individual students (e.g., such as participation in advanced-placement courses or a vocational education program)? 300.347 (b) (1)	1	2	3	4	1	2	3	4

Information Needed? ☐*Yes.* ☐*No. Comments:* _____

_____

	Mild Moderate				Moderate Intensive			
21. Starting at the age of 16, or earlier if determined by the IEP team, does the student have a statement of needed transition services that includes: 300.347 (b) (1); 300.27 (b)								
(a) instruction.	1	2	3	4	1	2	3	4
(b) related services.	1	2	3	4	1	2	3	4
(c) community experiences.	1	2	3	4	1	2	3	4
(d) development of employment or postsecondary education objectives.	1	2	3	4	1	2	3	4
(e) development of other postschool adult living objectives (e.g., community participation, residential).	1	2	3	4	1	2	3	4

Information Needed? ☐*Yes.* ☐*No. Comments:* _____

_____

1=Almost Never 2=Sometimes 3=Frequently 4=Almost Always	Mild Moderate				Moderate Intensive			

22. Starting at the age of 16, if appropriate, does the student have a statement of needed transition services that includes: 300.347 (b) (1)

	Mild Moderate				Moderate Intensive			
(a) acquisition of daily living skills.	1	2	3	4	1	2	3	4
(b) functional vocational evaluation.	1	2	3	4	1	2	3	4
(c) a statement of interagency responsibilities or any needed linkages.	1	2	3	4	1	2	3	4

Information Needed? Yes. No. *Comments:* _____

23. By the age of 17, does the IEP include a statement that the students and their parents have been notified in writing of the transfer of rights to students at the age of 18 in the areas of: 300.347 (c)

	Mild Moderate				Moderate Intensive			
(a) due process.	1	2	3	4	1	2	3	4
(b) IEP requirements.	1	2	3	4	1	2	3	4
(c) placement.	1	2	3	4	1	2	3	4
(d) eligibility.	1	2	3	4	1	2	3	4

Information Needed? Yes. No. *Comments:* _____

24. Do students with disabilities participate in general State and district-wide assessment programs (9th and 12th grade) with: 300.347 (a) (5)

	Mild Moderate				Moderate Intensive			
(a) no special training or accommodation.	1	2	3	4	1	2	3	4
(b) with tutoring to prepare for test.	1	2	3	4	1	2	3	4
(c) with additional time.	1	2	3	4	1	2	3	4
(d) with a reader.	1	2	3	4	1	2	3	4
(e) with use of technology.	1	2	3	4	1	2	3	4
(f) other (specify): _____.	1	2	3	4	1	2	3	4

Information Needed? Yes. No. *Comments:* _____

_____

D: AGENCY RESPONSIBILITY

1=Almost Never 2=Sometimes 3=Frequently 4=Almost Always	Mild Moderate				Moderate Intensive			

25. If a participation agency fails to provide agreed-upon transition services contained in the IEP: 300.348 (a)

	Mild Moderate				Moderate Intensive			
(a) the local education agency reconvenes the IEP team for the purpose of identifying alternative strategies to meet the transition objectives and, if necessary, revise the student's IEP.	1	2	3	4	1	2	3	4
(b) a different agency or agency representative is asked to deliver the services in question.	1	2	3	4	1	2	3	4
(c) an alternative plan for meeting the identified needs is developed with the same agency representative.	1	2	3	4	1	2	3	4
(d) the IEP goal or objective in question is modified or removed because no other agency is available to deliver the service.	1	2	3	4	1	2	3	4

Information Needed? Yes. No. *Comments:* _____

_____

SECTION II: BEST PRACTICE

1=Almost Never   2=Sometimes   3=Frequently   4=Almost Always

26. Students are provided opportunities to participate in activities designed to enhance their decision making skills and involvement in the transition process using the following strategies:

(a) offering classes specifically designed to enhance decision-making skills.   1 2 3 4

(b) interviewing or talking with students about their goals for the future.   1 2 3 4

(c) promoting self-determination and goal setting throughout the curriculum and instructional approaches.   1 2 3 4

(d) engaging students in the dialogue during their IEP meetings.   1 2 3 4

(e) sending information home to assist parents in preparing their child for participation.   1 2 3 4

(f) using person-centered planning strategies (e.g., MAPS (Making Action Plans); PATH (Planning Alternative Tomorrows and Hope); circle of friends).   1 2 3 4

(g) other (specify): _____   1 2 3 4

Information Needed? ☐*Yes.* ☐*No. Comments:* _____
_____

27. Strategies used to determine students' needs regarding the 4 transition areas (i.e., instruction, related services, community experiences, development of employment or other postschool adult living objectives) include:

(a) standardized tests regarding academic, social, behavioral skills.   1 2 3 4

(b) preference and interest inventories.   1 2 3 4

(c) functional vocational assessment.   1 2 3 4

(d) record review of past school performance, work experience, community living experiences.   1 2 3 4

(e) suggestions and recommendations from the student, family and other knowledgeable persons regarding youths' goals for the future.   1 2 3 4

(f) informal observations of student performance and behavior.   1 2 3 4

Information Needed? ☐*Yes.* ☐*No. Comments:* _____
_____

28. Programs or strategies used to develop employment and other post-school adult living objectives include:

(a) career vocational assessment.   1 2 3 4

(b) paid community employment experiences, including supported employment.   1 2 3 4

(c) instruction and experience in employability skills (e.g., filling out applications, interviewing).   1 2 3 4

(d) school-based vocational coursework (e.g., typing, computers, auto-mechanics).   1 2 3 4

(e) non-paid community-based work training.   1 2 3 4

(f) guidance counseling and instruction to prepare for entering postsecondary education.   1 2 3 4

Information Needed? ☐*Yes.* ☐*No. Comments:* _____
_____

29. Programs or strategies used to meet the needs of students with IEP/transition goals for the acquisition of daily living skills and functional vocational evaluation include:

(a) community-based assessment.   1 2 3 4

(b) daily living skills programs (e.g., dressing, cooking, personal hygiene).   1 2 3 4

(c) functional community living skills instruction and experience (e.g., money management, mobility).   1 2 3 4

Information Needed? ☐*Yes.* ☐*No. Comments:* _____
_____

1=Almost Never   2=Sometimes   3=Frequently   4=Almost Always

30. Programs or strategies used to meet the needs of students with IEP/transition goals relating to community experiences include:

	1	2	3	4
(a) community-based assessment.	1	2	3	4
(b) community-based instruction (e.g., riding bus routes, visiting a recreational center).	1	2	3	4
(c) accessing community service programs and informing students and families about their options.	1	2	3	4
(d) education and training on self-advocacy and use of accommodations.	1	2	3	4
(e) education and training regarding housing and support options (e.g., availability of low cost rental, Section 8 housing, types of support, how to choose a place to live).	1	2	3	4

Information Needed? ☐ *Yes.* ☐ *No.* *Comments:* _____

_____

31. Programs or strategies used to meet the transition instructional needs of students include:

	1	2	3	4
(a) instruction in regular education and college preparation coursework.	1	2	3	4
(b) instruction in general academic skills.	1	2	3	4
(c) instruction in vocational education.	1	2	3	4
(d) instruction in daily living skills (e.g., dressing, cooking, personal hygiene).	1	2	3	4
(e) instruction in functional community living skills (e.g., money management, mobility).	1	2	3	4

Information Needed? ☐ *Yes.* ☐ *No.* *Comments:* _____

_____

32. Agencies' active involvement and follow-through on responsibilities are fostered using the following strategies:

	1	2	3	4
(a) consulting participating agency representatives about the development of students' transition goals and objectives prior to the IEP meeting in which transition is discussed.	1	2	3	4
(b) routinely communicating with community agencies regarding transition services for youth.	1	2	3	4
(c) distributing to agencies a written description of the IDEA requirements that define agencies' responsibilities to provide and/or pay for agreed-upon transition services.	1	2	3	4
(d) routinely checking on the implementation status of agreed-upon transition services with the student, parent, and participating agencies.	1	2	3	4
(e) local interagency agreement delineating roles and responsibilities.	1	2	3	4

Information Needed? ☐ *Yes.* ☐ *No.* *Comments:* _____

_____

33. Overall, how frequently do students participate in their IEP meetings in which transition is discussed?
Information Needed? ☐ *Yes.* ☐ *No.* *Comments:* _____   1 2 3 4

_____

34. Overall, how frequently do families participate in the IEP meetings in which transition is discussed?
Information Needed? ☐ *Yes.* ☐ *No.* *Comments:* _____

   1 2 3 4

35. Overall, how frequently do recreational community service agencies participate in students' IEP meetings in which transition is discussed (e.g., informal support/supporters like Urban League, YMCA)?
Information Needed? ☐ *Yes.* ☐ *No.* *Comments:* _____

   1 2 3 4

_____

36. To what extent does your school district consider cultural or diversity issues in transition planning?
Information Needed? ☐ *Yes.* ☐ *No.* *Comments:* _____   1 2 3 4

_____

1=Almost Never   2=Sometimes   3=Frequently   4=Almost Always

37. Overall, how frequently do each of the following agency personnel participate in students' IEP meeting in which transition is discussed?

(a) vocational rehabilitation staff.	1	2	3	4
(b) mental health staff.	1	2	3	4
(c) mental retardation/developmental disabilities staff.	1	2	3	4
(d) department of human services staff.	1	2	3	4
(e) postsecondary education staff.	1	2	3	4
(f) social service agency staff/case manager.	1	2	3	4
(g) residential services staff.	1	2	3	4
(h) parent advocacy agency staff.	1	2	3	4

(i) other (specify): _____

Information Needed? ☐Yes. ☐No. Comments: _____

_____

38. Staff responsible for facilitating transition planning for students with disabilities have become knowledgeable about implementation strategies through:

(a) preservice training and education (e.g., college courses, licensure program).	1	2	3	4
(b) formal inservice training and education provided by the district and/or professional association.	1	2	3	4
(c) information shared informally by lead teachers or other knowledgeable school personnel.	1	2	3	4
(d) distribution of federal or state policy regarding transition planning and services.	1	2	3	4
(e) distribution of procedural guidelines outlining the steps of transition planning.	1	2	3	4
(f) staff are responsible for informing themselves.	1	2	3	4

Information Needed? ☐Yes. ☐No. Comments: _____

_____

39. Programs or strategies used to involve and empower families and students in transition planning include:

(a) offering trainings/workshops on transition planning and related areas (e.g., residential living options, work incentives). 1 2 3 4
(b) coordinating agency fairs where families can ask questions and gather information on transition services. 1 2 3 4
(c) use of parent mentors/volunteers to provide families assistance throughout the transition process (e.g., Connecting Advisory Program). 1 2 3 4
(d) develop transition resource kits to provide current information on transition resources and services available. 1 2 3 4

Information Needed? ☐Yes. ☐No. Comments: _____

_____

40. Programs or strategies used to develop partnerships between school-based and adult service professionals who provide transition services to students with disabilities include:

(a) a local interagency transition teams consisting of members from schools, agencies, and families to enhance networking and information sharing. 1 2 3 4
(b) interagency agreements for cooperative funding. 1 2 3 4
(c) interagency agreements for information sharing/release of information. 1 2 3 4
(d) interagency agreements for use of single referral document. 1 2 3 4
(e) use of computerized information sharing system. 1 2 3 4

Information Needed? ☐Yes. ☐No. Comments: _____

_____

41. Programs or strategies that agencies used to coordinate a single planning process include:

(a) use of school-based interagency transition teams. 1 2 3 4
(b) use of single release of information form. 1 2 3 4
(c) use of transition plan as the core plan for all cooperating agencies. 1 2 3 4
(d) use of computerized interagency information sharing of transition goals. 1 2 3 4

Information Needed? ☐Yes. ☐No. Comments: _____

_____

1=Almost Never   2=Sometimes   3=Frequently   4=Almost Always

42. Programs or strategies used to train students, families and professionals about transition planning and services include:

(a) use of local interagency transition teams to provide cross-training on transition planning and related areas (e.g., residential living options, work incentives). 1 2 3 4
(b) use of agency fair to provide the opportunity to gather information about agencies. 1 2 3 4
(c) use of agency services directory/video tape of multi-agency transition services. 1 2 3 4
(d) use of inter-agency panel presentations on multi-agency transition services. 1 2 3 4
(e) use of single-agency transition inservice provided by external agencies. 1 2 3 4

Information Needed? ☐ *Yes.* ☐ *No. Comments:* _____

43. Programs or strategies used to provide transition related services to students with disabilities include:

(a) use of community-based vocational training programs (e.g., transition enclaves). 1 2 3 4
(b) use of summer programs to enhance career awareness and employability skills (e.g., career camps). 1 2 3 4

Information Needed? ☐ *Yes.* ☐ *No. Comments:* _____

44. Does your school/district have an interagency transition team? ☐ Yes. ☐ No.
If yes, does your interagency transition team include representatives from the following areas?

(a) special education. 1 2 3 4
(b) general education. 1 2 3 4
(c) vocational education. 1 2 3 4
(d) special education administration. 1 2 3 4
(e) special education related services (e.g., occupational therapy, physical therapy, speech therapy). 1 2 3 4
(f) parents. 1 2 3 4
(g) students/consumers. 1 2 3 4
(h) adult service programs. 1 2 3 4
(i) school to work. 1 2 3 4
(j) employers. 1 2 3 4
(k) other (specify): _____ 1 2 3 4

Information Needed? ☐ *Yes.* ☐ *No. Comments:* _____

45. What types of services/activities are provided at your local educational agency for transition-aged youth with disabilities?

(a) activities designed to link students with employers. 1 2 3 4
(b) activities designed to link students with adult services. 1 2 3 4
(c) activities designed to link students with community service organizations. 1 2 3 4
(d) activities designed to link students with recreational organizations. 1 2 3 4
(e) general education services. 1 2 3 4
(f) vocational/technical education. 1 2 3 4
(g) work-based learning (paid). 1 2 3 4
(h) work-based learning (unpaid). 1 2 3 4
(I) career development activities. 1 2 3 4
(j) job shadowing/job try-outs. 1 2 3 4
(k) apprenticeships/mentorships/internships. 1 2 3 4
(l) other (specify): _____ 1 2 3 4

Information Needed? ☐ *Yes.* ☐ *No. Comments:* _____

46. Does your agency conduct follow-up studies of students who have exited school? 1 2 3 4
(a) talk to students informally 1 2 3 4
(b) survey students 1 year after graduation 1 2 3 4
(c) survey students 3 years after graduation 1 2 3 4
(d) survey students 5 years after graduation 1 2 3 4
(e) use surveys to continuously improve services

References

Adams, G., & Englemann, S. (1996). *Research on direct instruction: 20 years beyond DISTAR*. Seattle, WA: Educational Achievement Systems.

ADAPT (Americans Disabled for Attendant Programs Today). (1999a). *Senators Harkin and Specter introduce landmark legislation, S-1935 supports real choice in the new millennium*. Denver, CO. Author.

ADAPT (Americans Disabled for Attendant Programs Today). (1999b). *Summary of Olmstead Decision*. Denver, CO: Author.

Agran, M., Snow, K., & Swaner, J. (1999). Teacher perceptions of self-determination: Benefits, characteristics, strategies. *Education and Training in Mental Retardation and Developmental Disabilities*, 34, 293–301.

Airasian, P. W. (1994). *Classroom assessment*. New York: McGraw-Hill.

Ajzen, I., & Fishbein, M. (1982). Attitude-behavior relations: A theoretical analysis and review of empirical research. *Psychological Bulletin*, 84, 888–918.

Alberto, P. A., & Troutman, A. C. (1995). *Applied behavior analysis for teachers* (4th ed.). Upper Saddle River, NJ: Merril/Prentice Hall.

Albin, R. W., Lucyshyn, J. M., Horner, R. H., & Flannery, K. B. (1996). Contextual fit for behavioral support plans: A model for "goodness of fit." In L. K. Koegel, R. L. Koegel, & G. Dunlap (Eds.), *Positive behavioral support: Including people with difficult behavior in the community* (pp. 81–98). Baltimore: Paul H. Brookes.

Albright, L., & Cobb, R. B. (1988). Curriculum based vocational assessment. *Journal for Vocational Special Needs Education*, 10(2), 13–16.

Al-Darmarki, F., & Kivlighan, D. M. (1993). Congruence in client-counselor expectations and the working alliance, *Journal of Counseling Psychology*, 40(4), 379–384.

Allport, G. W. (1954). *The nature of prejudice*. Boston: Addison-Wesley Publishing.

Allport, G. W. (1960). *Personality and social encounter*. Boston: Beacon Press.

Althen, G. (1988). *American ways: A guide for foreigners in the United States*. Yarmouth, MD: Intercultural Press.

American Council on Education (1996). *Higher education and national affairs*. April 8, pp. 4, 6.

American Vocational Association. (1990). *The AVA guide to the Carl D. Perkins Vocational and Applied Technology Education Act of 1990*. Alexandria, VA: Author.

Americans with Disabilities Act of 1990, 42 U.S.C.A. § 12101 *et seq*.

Ammons, R. B., Butler, M. N., & Herzog, S. A. (1950). A projective test for vocational research and guidance at the college level. *Journal of Applied Psychology*, 34, 198–205.

Anderson, R. J., & Strathe, M. I. (1987). Career education for special needs youth. In G. D. Meers (Ed.), *Handbook of vocational special needs education* (2nd ed., pp. 259–274). Rockville, MD: Aspen Publishers.

Anderson, W., Beckett, C., Chitwood, S., & Hayden, D. (1984). *Next S.T.E.P.: Planning for employment*. Alexandria, VA: Parent Educational Advocacy Training Center.

Aslanian, C. B. (1996). *Adult learning in America: Why and how adults go back to school*. Washington, DC: Office of Adult Learning Services, the College Board.

Asselin, S. B., Hanley-Maxwell, C., & Syzmanski, E. (1992). Transdisciplinary personnel preparation. In F. R. Rusch, L. DeStefano, J. Chadsey-Rusch, L. A. Phelps, & E. Syzmanski (Eds.), *Transition from school to adult life* (pp. 265–284). Sycamore, IL: Sycamore Publishing.

Asselin, S. B., Todd-Allen, M, & deFur, S. (1998). Transition coordinators: Define yourselves. *Teaching Exceptional Children*, 30, 11–15.

Association on Higher Education and Disability (AHEAD). (1987). *Unlocking the doors: Making the transition from secondary to postsecondary education*. Columbus, OH: Author.

Association on Higher Education and Disability (AHEAD). (1998). *Expanding postsecondary options for minority students with disabilities*. Columbus, OH: Author.

Astin, A. (1993). *What matters in college: Four critical years revisited*. San Francisco: Jossey-Bass.

Aune, E. (1991). A transition model for postsecondary-bound students with learning disabilities. *Learning Disabilities Research & Practice, 6*, 177–187.

Azrin, N. H., & Besalel, V. B. (1979). *A behavioral approach to vocational counseling*. Baltimore: University Park Press.

Azrin, N. H., & Phillips, R. A. (1979). The job club method for handicapped: A comprehensive outcome model. *Rehabilitation Counseling Bulletin, 23*, 144–155.

Baer, R. (1996). *The Summit County L.I.F.E. Project: Linkages for individual and family empowerment* (Report) Kent, OH: Kent State University, Center for Innovation in Transition and Employment.

Baer, R., Goebel, G., & Flexer, R. W. (1993). An interdisciplinary team approach to rehabilitation. In R. W. Flexer & P. L. Solomon (Eds.), *Psychiatric rehabilitation in practice*. Boston: Andover Publishers.

Baer, R., Martonyi, E., Simmons, T., Flexer, R., & Goebel, G. (1994). Employer collaboration: A tri-lateral group process model. *Journal of Rehabilitation Administration, 18*(3), 151–163.

Baer, R., Simmons, T., & Flexer, R. (1996). Transition practice and policy compliance in Ohio: A survey of secondary special educators. *Career Development for Exceptional Individuals, 19*(1), 61–72.

Baker, E. T., Wang, M. C., & Walberg, H. J. (1995). The effects of inclusion on learning. *Education Leadership, 52*(4), 33–35.

Ball-Brown, B., & Frank, Z. L. (1993). Disabled students of color. *New Directions for Student Services, 64*, 79–88.

Bambara, L. M., Ager, C., & Koger, F. (1994). The effects of choice and task preference on the work performance of adults with severe disabilities. *Journal of Applied Behavior Analysis, 27*, 555–556.

Bambara, L. M., Koger, F., Katzer, T., & Davenport, T. A. (1995). Embedding choice in the context of daily routines: An experimental case study. *Journal of the Association for Persons with Severe Handicaps, 20*, 185–195.

Barrera, I., & Kramer, L. (1997). From monologues to skilled dialogues—Teaching the process of crafting culturally competent early childhood environments. In P. J. Winton, J. A. McCullum, & C. Catlett (Eds.), *Reforming personnel preparation in early intervention* (pp. 217–251). Baltimore: Paul H. Brookes.

Bartholomew, K. (1985, November). Options for individuals. *Institutions, Etc.*, pp. 2–3.

Bates, P. (1990). *Best practices in transition planning: Quality indicators*. Carbondale, IL: Illinois Transition Project.

Bauder, D. K, Lewis, P., & Whitlock, B. (1996). *Project future: Training personnel for the education of individuals with disabilities; Special projects* (CFDA 84.029K). Louisville, KY: enTECH.

Bauder, D. K, Lewis, P., Gobert, C., & Bearden, C. (1997). *Assistive technology guidelines for Kentucky schools*. Frankfort, KY: Kentucky Department of Education.

Becker, C. W., & Carnine, D. W. (1982). Direct instruction: A behavior theory model for comprehensive educational intervention with the disadvantaged. In S. W. Bijou & R. Ruiz (Eds.), *Behavior modification: Contributions to education* (pp. 145–210). Hillsdale, NJ: Erlbaum.

Bedore-Bideaux, K. A. (1998). *Engaging self-determination in the IEP through student participation*. Unpublished master's thesis. Ogden, UT: Weber State University.

Behrmann, M. (1995). Assistive technology training. In K. F. Flippo, K. J. Inge, & J. M. Barcus (Eds.), *Assistive technology: A resource for school, work, and community* (pp. 211–222). Baltimore, MD: Paul H. Brookes Publishing Co.

Behrmann, M. (Ed.). (1984). *Handbook of microcomputers in special education*. San Diego: College-Hill Press.

Behrmann, M., McCallen, M. H., & Morrissette, S. K. (1993). *Assistive technology issues for Virginia schools: Final report*. Submitted to the Virginia State Special Education Advisory Committee, Fairfax, VA: Virginia State Dept. of Education.

Behrmann, M. M. (1994). Assistive technology for students with mild disabilities. *Intervention in School and Clinic, 30*(2), 70–83.

Behrmann, M. M., & Schepis, M. (1994). Assistive technology assessment: A multiple case study review of three approaches with students with physical disabilities during the transition from school to work. *Journal of Vocational Rehabilitation, 4*(3), 202–210.

Bellamy, T. G., Rhodes, L. E., Bobeau, P. E., & Mank, D. M. (1986). Mental retardation services in sheltered workshops and day activity programs. In F. R. Rusch (Ed.), *Competitive employment: Issues and strategies* (pp. 257–271). Baltimore, MD: Paul H. Brookes.

Bender, M., Richmond, L., & Pinson-Millburn, N. (1985). *Careers, computers, and the handicapped*. Austin, TX: Pro-Ed.

Benz, M., Johnson, D. K., Mikkelsen, K. S., & Linstrom, L. E. (1995). Improving collaboration between school and vocation rehabilitation: Stakeholder identified barriers and strategies. *Career Development for Exceptional Individuals, 18*(2), 133–144.

Benz, M. R., & Halpern, A. S. (1986). Vocational preparation for high school students with mild disabilities: A statewide study of administrator, teacher, and parent perceptions. *Career Development for Exceptional Individuals, 9*(1), 3–33.

Benz, M. R., & Halpern, A. S. (1987). Transition services for secondary students with mild disabilities: A statewide perspective. *Exceptional Children, 53*(6), 507–514.

Benz, M. R., & Halpern, A. S. (1993). Vocational and transitional services needed and received by students with disabilities during their last year of high school. *Career Development for Exceptional Individuals, 16*(2), 197–212.

Benz, M. R., & Kochhar, C. A. (1996). School-to-work opportunities for all students: A position statement of the division on career development and transition. *Career Development for Exceptional Individuals, 19*(1), 31–48.

Benz, M. R., Johnson, D. K., Mikkelsen, K. S., & Lindstrom, L. E. (1995). Improving collaboration between school and vocational rehabilitation: Stakeholder-identified barriers and strategies. *Career Development for Exceptional Individuals, 18,* 133–144.

Benz, M. R., Yavonoff, P., & Doren, B. (1997). School-to-work components that predict postschool success for students with and without disabilities. *Exceptional Children, 63(2),* 151–166.

Berliss, J. R., Vanderheiden, G. C., & Borden, P. A. (1989). Campus/library information systems accessibility manual. *Journal of Rehabilitation Research & Development, 26(suppl.),* 170–171.

Berman, L. M., & Roderick, J. A. (1977). *Curriculum: Teaching what, how, and why of living.* Columbus, OH: Merrill.

Bickel, W. E., & Bickel, D. D. (1986). Effective schools, classrooms, and instruction: Implications for special education. *Exceptional Children, 52,* 489–500.

Biddle, B. J. (1979). *Role theory.* New York: Academic Press.

Biklen, D., & Knoll, J. (1987a). The disabled minority. In S. J. Taylor, D. Biklen, & J. A. Knoll (Eds.), *Community integration for people with severe disabilities* (pp. 3–24). New York: Teachers' College Press

Biklen, D., & Knoll, J. (1987b). The community imperative revisited. In J. A. Mulick & R. F. Antonak (Eds.), *Transitions in mental retardation* (Vol. 3, pp. 1–27), Norwood, NJ: Ablex.

Bisconer, S. W, Stodden, R. A., & Porter, M. (1993). A psychometric evaluation of curriculum-based vocational assessment rating instruments used with students in mainstream vocational courses. *Career Development for Exceptional Individuals, 16,* 19–26.

Blackhurst, A. E. (1997). Perspectives on technology in special education. *Teaching Exceptional Children, 29(5),* 41–48.

Blackhurst, A. E., & Cross, D. P. (1993). Technology in special education. In A. E. Blackhurst & W. H. Berdine (Eds.), *An introduction to special education* (3rd ed., pp. 77–103). New York: Harper Collins.

Blackhurst, A. E., & Hofmeister, A. M. (1980). Technology in special education. In L. Mann & D. Sabatino (Eds.), *Fourth review of special education* (pp. 199–228). New York: Grune and Stratton.

Blackhurst, A. E., & Morse, T. E. (1996). Using anchored instruction to teach about assistive technology. *Focus on Autism and Other Developmental Disabilities, 11(3),* 131–141.

Blackhurst, A. E., & Shuping, M. B. (1990). A philosophy for the use of technology in special education. *Technology and media back-to-school Guide.* Reston, VA: Council for Exceptional Children.

Blackhurst, A. E., Bausch, M. E., Bell, J. K., Burleson, R. B., Cooper, J. T., Cassaway, L. J., McCrary, N. E., & Zabala, J. S. (1999). *Assistive technology consideration form: The university of Kentucky assistive technology toolkit.* Lexington, KY: Department of Special Education and Rehabilitation Counseling, University of Kentucky.

Blackorby, J., & Wagner, M. (1996). Longitudinal postschool outcomes of youth with disabilities: Findings from the National Longitudinal Transition Study. *Exceptional Children, 62(5),* 399–414.

Blackstone, S. (1992). For consumers: Rethinking the basics. *Augmentative Communication News, 5,* 1–3.

Blackwell, T. L., Conrad, D. A., & Weed, R. O. (1992). *Job analysis and the ADA: A step by step guide.* Athens, GA: Elliot & Fitzpatrick.

Blatt, B. (1966). *Christmas in purgatory.* Boston: Allyn & Bacon.

Blick, D. W., & Test, D. W. (1987). Effects of self-recording on high-school students on-task behavior. *Learning Disability Quarterly, 10,* 203–213.

Blocher, D. (1974). *Developmental counseling* (2nd ed.). New York: Ronald Press.

Blustein, D. (1987). Integrating career counseling and psychotherapy: A comprehensive treatment strategy. *Psychotherapy, 24,* 794–799.

Blustein, D. L., & Spengler, P. M. (1995). Personal adjustment: Career counseling and psychotherapy. In W. B. Walsh & S. H. Osipow (Eds.), *Handbook of vocational psychology* (2nd ed., pp. 295–329). Hillsdale, NJ: Erlbaum.

Board of Trustees of the Council for Learning Disabilities. (1986). Measurement and training of perceptual and perceptual-motor functioning. *Learning Disabilities Quarterly, 9,* 247.

Bolles, R. N. (1995). *What color is my parachute? A practical manual for job hunters and career changers.* Berkeley, CA: Ten Speed Press.

Bolles, R. N. (1999). *What color is your parachute?* Berkeley, CA: Ten Speed Press.

Bond, G. R. (1991). Vocational rehabilitation for persons with severe mental illness: Past, present, and future. In R. Lieberman (Ed.), *Rehabilitation of the psychiatrically disabled.* New York: Pergamon.

Bond, G. R., & Boyer, S. L. (1988). Rehabilitation programs and outcomes. In J. A. Ciardiello & M. D. Bell (Eds.), *Vocational rehabilitation of persons with prolonged mental illness.* (pp. 231–263). Baltimore: Johns Hopkins University Press.

Bose, J. (1996). *Characteristics of the 100 largest public elementary and secondary school districts in the United States: 1993–94: Statistical analysis report.* Washington, DC: National Center for Educational Statistics.

Bowe, F. G. (1992). Employment: Dependence vs. independence. *OSERS News in Print, 5(2),* 4–7.

Bowser, G., & Reed, P. (1995). Educational TECH points for assistive technology planning. *Journal of Special Education Technology, 7(4),* 325–338.

Boyer, E. (1987). *College: The undergraduate experience in America.* New York: Harper & Row.

Braddock, D. (1987). *Federal policy toward mental retardation and developmental disabilities.* Baltimore: Paul H. Brookes.

Bradley, V. J., Ashbaugh, J. W., & Blaney, B. C. (1994). *Creating individual supports for people with developmental disabilities: A mandate for change at many levels.* Baltimore: Paul H. Brookes.

Brame, K. (1995). Strategies for recruiting family members from diverse backgrounds for roles in policy and program development. *Early Childhood Bulletin,* 5, 1–5. (ERIC Document Reproduction Service No. ED 398 721)

Brinckerhoff, L. C., Shaw, S. F., & McGuire, J. M. (1992). Promoting access, accommodations, and independence for college students with learning disabilities. *Journal of Learning Disabilities,* 25, 417–429.

Brinckerhoff, L. C., Shaw, S. F., & McGuire, J. M. (1993). *Promoting postsecondary education for students with learning disabilities.* Austin, TX: PRO-ED.

Brislin, R. (1993). *Understanding culture's influence on behavior.* Fort Worth, TX: Harcourt Brace.

Brolin, D. E. (1976). *Vocational preparation of retarded citizens.* Columbus, OH: Merrill.

Brolin, D. E. (1989). *Life centered career education: A competency-based approach.* Reston, VA: The Council for Exceptional Children.

Brolin, D. E. (1992a). *Competency assessment knowledge batteries: Life-centered career education,* Reston, VA: The Council for Exceptional Children.

Brolin, D. E. (1992b). *Competency assessment performance batteries: Life-centered career education,* Reston, VA: The Council for Exceptional Children.

Brolin, D. E. (1992c). *Life-centered career education: Competency units for occupational guidance and preparation.* Reston, VA: The Council for Exceptional Children.

Brolin, D. E. (1992d). *Life-centered career education: Competency units for personal-social skills.* Reston, VA: The Council for Exceptional Children.

Brolin, D. E. (1993). *Life-centered career education* [videorecording]. Reston, VA: The Council for Exceptional Children.

Brolin, D. E. (Ed.). (1995). *Career education: A functional life skills approach* (3rd. ed.). Upper Saddle River, NJ: Prentice Hall.

Brolin, D. E. (1996). Reflections on the beginning . . . and the future directions! *Career Development for Exceptional Individuals,* 19(2), 93–100.

Brolin, D. E. (1997). *Life-centered career education: A competency-based approach.* Reston, VA: The Council for Exceptional Children.

Brolin, D. E., & Gysbers, N. C. (1979). Career education for persons with handicaps. *The Personnel and Guidance Journal,* 58, 258–262.

Brolin, D. E., & Schatzman, B. (1989). Lifelong career development. In D. E. Berkell & J. M. Brown (Eds.), *Transition from school to work for persons with disabilities.* New York: Longman.

Brookhiser, R. (1991). *The way of the wasp.* New York: The Free Press.

Brophy, J. (1980). *Recent research on teaching.* East Lansing, MI: Institute for Research on Teaching, Michigan State University.

Brophy, J., & Good, T. L. (1986). Teacher behavior and student achievement. In M. C. Wittrock (Ed.), *Handbook of research on teaching* (3rd ed., pp. 328–375). New York: Macmillan.

Brotherson, M. J., Berdine, W. H., & Sartini, V. (1993). Transition to adult services: Support for ongoing parent participation. *Remedial and Special Education,* 14(4), 44–51.

Brown, C. (1992). Assistive technology, computers, and persons with disabilities. *Communications of the ACM,* 35(5), 36–45.

Brown, C., McDaniel, R., Couch, R., & McClanahan, M. (1994). *Vocational evaluation and software: A consumer's guide.* (Available from Materials Development Center, Stout Vocational Rehabilitation Institute, University of Wisconsin—Stout, Menomonie, WI 54751.)

Brown, D. (1990). Trait and factor theory. In D. Brown, L. Brooks, & Associates (Eds.), *Career choice and development: Applying contemporary theories to practice* (2nd ed., pp. 13–36). San Francisco: Jossey-Bass.

Brown, D. (1996). Status of career development theories. In D. Brown, L. Brooks, & Associates (Eds.), *Career choice and development: Applying contemporary theories to practice* (3rd ed., pp. 513–526). San Francisco: Jossey-Bass.

Brown, D., & Brooks, L. (1984). Preface. In D. Brown, L. Brooks, & Associates (Eds.), *Career choice and development: Applying contemporary theories to practice* (pp. ix–xii). San Francisco: Jossey-Bass.

Brown, D., & Brooks, L. (1990). Introduction to theories of career development: Origins, evolution, and current efforts. In D. Brown, L. Brooks, & Associates (Eds.), *Career choice and development: Applying contemporary theories to practice* (2nd ed., pp. 1–12). San Francisco: Jossey-Bass.

Brown, D., & Brooks, L. (1991). *Techniques of career counseling.* Boston: Allyn & Bacon.

Brown, D., & Brooks, L. (1996). Introduction to theories of career development and choice: Origins, evolution, and current efforts. In D. Brown, L. Brooks, & Associates (Eds.), *Career choice and development* (3rd ed., pp. 1–30). San Francisco: Jossey-Bass.

Brown, L., Branston, M. B., Hamre-Nietupski, S., Pumpian, I., Certo, N., & Gruenewald, L. (1979). A strategy for developing chronological age appropriate and functional curricular content for severely handicapped adolescents and young adults. *Journal of Special Education,* 13, 81–90.

Brown, L., Long, E., Udvari-Solner, A., Davis, L., VanDeventer, P., Ahlgren, C., Johnson, F., Gruenewald, L., & Jorgesen, J. (1989) The home school: Why students with severe intellectual disabilities must attend the schools of their brothers, sisters, friends, and neighbors. *Journal of the Association for Persons with Severe Handicaps,* 16, 39–47.

Brown, L., Nietupski, J,. & Hamre-Nietupski, S. (1976). The criterion of ultimate functioning and public school service for severely handicapped students. In M. A. Thomas (Ed.), *Please don't forget about me! Education's investment in the severely, profoundly, and multiple handicapped child.* (pp. 2–15). Reston, VA: The Council for Exceptional Children.

Brown, P. M., & Foster, S. B. (1991). Integrating hearing and deaf students on a college campus. *American Annals of the Deaf,* 136, 21–27.

Browning. P. L. (1997). *Transition in action for youth and young adults with disabilities.* Montgomery, AL: Auburn University, Wells Printing.

Bucher, D. E., & Brolin, D. E. (1987). The life-centered career education (LCCE) inventory: A curriculum-based, criterion-related assessment instrument. *Diagnostique, 12,* 131–141.

Bullis, M. D., Kosko, K., Waintrup, M., Kelley, P., & Issacson, A. (1994). Functional assessment services for transition, education, and rehabilitation: Project FASTER. *American Rehabilitation, 20*(2), 9.

Bureau of Labor Statistics. (1992). *Employee tenure and occupational mobility in the early 1990s.* Washington, DC: U.S. Department of Labor.

Burkhead, E. J., Sampson, J. P., & McMahon, B. T. (1986). The liberation of disabled persons in a technological society: Access to computer technology. *Rehabilitation Literature, 47*(7–8), 162–168.

Burnette, J. (1998). *Reducing the disproportionate representation of minority students in special education.* Reston, VA: ERIC Clearinghouse on Disabilities and Gifted Education, ERIC/OSEP Digest #E566.

Buschner, P. C., Watts, M. B., Siders, J. A., & Leonard, R. L. (1989). Career interest inventories: A need for analysis. *Career Development for Exceptional Individuals, 12*(2), 117–123.

Carden, A. (1990). Narrative as a paradigm for career research. In R. A. Young & W. A. Borgen (Eds.), *Methodological approaches to the study of career* (pp. 71–86). New York: Praeger.

Carey, L. M. (1994). *Measuring and evaluating school learning.* Boston: Allyn & Bacon.

Carl D. Perkins Vocational and Applied Technology Education Act. (1990). Pub. L. No. 101-392, 104, Stat. 756.

Carl D. Perkins Vocational Education Act. (1984). Pub. L. No. 98-524, 98, Stat. 2435.

Carney, I. H., & Orelove, F. P. (1988). Implementing transition programs for community participation. In B. L. Ludlow, A. P. Turnbull, & R. Luckasson (Eds.), *Transitions to adult life for persons with mental retardation: Principles and practices.* Baltimore: Paul H. Brookes.

Carnine, D. W. (1992). Expanding the notion of teachers' rights: Access to tools that work. *Journal of Applied Behavior Analysis, 25,* 13–19.

Cartledge, G., & Milburn, J. A. (1986). *Teaching social skills to children: Innovative approaches* (2nd ed.). Boston: Allyn & Bacon.

Cavalier, A. R., & Brown, C. C. (1998). From passivity to participation: The transformational possibilities of speech-recognition technology. *Teaching Exceptional Children, 30*(6), 60–65.

Chadsey, J., & Sheldon, D. (1998). Moving toward social inclusion in employment and postsecondary school settings. In F. R. Rusch & J. G. Chadsey (Eds.), *Beyond high school: Transition from school to work* (pp. 383–405). Belmont, CA: Wadsworth Publishing.

Chadsey-Rusch, J., Rusch, F. R., & O'Reilly, M. F. (1991). Transition from school to integrated communities. *Remedial and Special Education, 12*(6), 23–33.

Chambers, A. C. (1997). *Has technology been considered? A guide for IEP teams.* Albuquerque, NM: Council of Administrators in Special Education.

Chan, F., Reid, C., Kaskel, L., Roldan, G., Rahami, M., & Mpofu, E. (1997). Vocational assessment and evaluation of people with disabilities. *Physical Medicine and Rehabilitation Clinics of North America, 8,* 311–325.

Chan, S. (1998a). Families with Asian roots. In E. W. Lynch & M. H. Hanson (Eds.), *Developing cross-cultural competence: A guide for working with children and their families* (2nd ed., pp. 251–354). Baltimore: Paul H. Brookes.

Chan, S. (1998b). Families with Filipino roots. In E. W. Lynch & M. H. Hanson (Eds.), *Developing cross-cultural competence: A guide for working with children and their families* (2nd ed., pp. 355–408). Baltimore: Paul H. Brookes.

Clark, G. M. (1979). *Career education for the handicapped child in the elementary school.* Denver, CO: Love.

Clark, G. M. (1992, April). Providing transition services through a functional curriculum and functional instruction. Paper presented at The Council for Exceptional Children annual conference, Baltimore.

Clark, G. M. (1994). Is a functional curriculum approach compatible with an inclusive education model? *Teaching Exception Children, 26*(2), 36–39.

Clark, G. M. (1996). Transition planning assessment for secondary-level students with learning disabilities. *Journal of Learning Disabilities, 29*(1), 79–92.

Clark, G. M., & Kolstoe, O. P. (1995). *Career development and transition education for adolescents with disabilities* (2nd ed.). Needham, MA: Allyn & Bacon.

Clark, G. M., & Patton, J. R. (1997). *Transition planning inventory: Administration and resource guide.* Austin, TX: PRO-ED.

Clark, G. M., Carlson, B. C., Fisher, S., Cook, I. D., & D'Alonzo, B. J. (1991). Career development for students with disabilities in elementary schools: A position statement of the Division on Career Development. *Career Development for Exceptional Individuals, 14*(2), 109–120.

Clary, G. (1998, January). *Institutional and community resources for student support services and programs.* Paper presented at the Southeastern Association of Educational Opportunity Program Personnel Training Center Workshop. Memphis, TN.

Cobb, H. C. (1972). *The forecast of fulfillment.* New York: Teachers College Press.

Cobb, R. B., & Neubert, D. A. (1998). Vocational education: Emerging vocationalism. In F. R. Rusch & J. G. Chadsey (Eds.), *Beyond high school: Transition from school to work* (pp. 101–126). Belmont, CA: Wadsworth Publishing.

Cohen, S., Agosta, J., Cohen, J., & Warren, R. (1989). Supporting families of children with severe disabilities. *Journal of the Association for Persons with Severe Handicaps, 14*(2), 155–162.

Colorado Department of Education. (1998). *Teach access skills.* Denver, CO: Author.

Condeluci, A. (1995). *Interdependence: The route to community.* Winter Park, FL: GR Press.

Cone, J. D., Delawyer, D. D., & Wolfe, V. V. (1985). Assessing parent participation: The parent/family involvement index. *Exceptional Children, 51*(5), 417–424.

Consortium of Citizens with Disabilities (1991). *Recommended federal policy directions for personal assistance services for Americans with disabilities.* Washington, DC: Personal Assistance Task Force, Consortium of Citizens with Disabilities, p. 3.

Conyers, L., Koch, L., & Szymanski, E. (1998). Lifespan perspectives on disability and work: A qualitative study. *Rehabilitation Counseling Bulletin, 42,* 51–75.

Cook, A. M., & Hussey, S. M. (1995). *Assistive technologies: Principles and practice.* St. Louis: Mosby Publishing.

Cook, J. A., & Hoffschmidt, S. J. (1995). Comprehensive models of psychosocial rehabilitation. In R. W. Flexer and P. L. Solomon (Eds.), *Psychiatric rehabilitation in practice.* (pp. 81–98) Boston, MA: Andover Publishers.

Cooper, J. O., Heron, T. E., & Heward, W. L. (1987). *Applied behavior analysis.* New York: Macmillan.

Correa, V. I. (1989). Involving culturally diverse families in the educational process. In S. H. Fradd & M. H. Weismantel (Eds.), *Meeting the needs of culturally and linguistically different students: A handbook for educators* (pp. 130–144). Austin, TX: PRO-ED.

Coupe-O'Kane, J., Porter, J., & Taylor, A. (1994). Meaningful content and contexts for learning. In J. Coupe-O'Kane & B. Smith (Eds.), *Taking control* (pp. 14 B 30), London: David Fulton Publishers.

Cowen, S. (1993). Transition planning for LD college-bound students. In S. Vogel & P. Adelman (Eds.), *Success for college students with learning disabilities* (pp. 39–56). New York: Springer.

Crites, J. (1978). *The career maturity inventory.* Monterey, CA: CTB/McGraw-Hill.

Crites, J. (1978). *Theory and research handbook for the career maturity inventory.* Monterey, CA: McGraw Hill.

Crites, J. O. (1981). Integrative test interpretation. In D. H. Montross & D. J. Shinkman (Eds.), *Career development in the 1980s: Theory and practice* (pp. 161–168). Springfield, IL: Charles C. Thomas.

Cronin, M., & Patton, J. R. (1993). *Life skills across the curriculum for youths with special needs.* Austin, TX: PRO-ED.

Cronin, M., & Patton, J. R. (1993). *Life skills instruction for all students: A practical guide for integrating real-life content into the curriculum.* Austin, TX: PRO-ED.

Cross, D., Collins, B. C., & Boam-Wood, D. (1996). *Interdisciplinary preparation for physical disabilities: Education and related services.* Lexington, KY: Department of Special Education and Rehabilitation Counseling, University of Kentucky.

Cummins, J. (1986). Psychological assessment of minority students: Out of context, out of focus, out of control? In

A. C. Willing & H. F. Greenberg (Eds.), *Bilingualism and learning disabilities: Policy and practice for teachers and administrators* (pp. 3–11). New York: American Library Publishing.

Dalke, C. (1993). *Making a successful transition from high school to college: A model program.* In S. A. Vogel & P. B. Adelman (Eds.), *Success for college students with disabilities* (pp. 57–80). New York: Springer Verlag.

Dalke, C., & Schmitt, S. (1987). Meeting the transition needs of college-bound students with learning disabilities. *Journal of Learning Disabilities, 20*(3), 176–180.

D'Alonzo, B. J., & Owen, S. D. (1985). *Transition services for the disabled: A national survey.* Paper presented at the 63rd Annual Council for Exceptional Children Conference, Anaheim, CA.

Daniels, S. (1990). Disability in America: An evolving concept, a new paradigm. George Washington University. *Policy Network Newsletter, 3*(1), 1–3.

Dautel, P. J., & Frieden, L. (1999). *Consumer choice and control: Personal attendant services and supports in America, Report of the National Blue Ribbon Panel on Personal Assistance Services.* Houston, TX: Independent Living Research Utilization.

Dawis, R. V. (1996). The theory of work adjustment and person-environment-correspondence counseling. In D. Brown, L. Brooks, & Associates (Eds.), *Career choice and development* (3rd ed., pp. 75–120). San Francisco: Jossey-Bass.

Dawis, R. V., & Lofquist, L. H. (1984). *A psychological theory of work adjustment: An individual-differences model and its applications.* Minneapolis, MN: University of Minnesota Press.

Day, R. M., Powell, T. H., & Stowitschek, J. J. (1980). *SCIPPY: Social competence intervention package for preschool youngsters.* Nashville, TN: Vanderbilt University.

Deci, E. L., & Chandler, C. L. (1986). The importance of motivation for the future of the LD field. *Journal of Learning Disabilities, 19,* 587–594.

Deci, E. L., & Ryan, R. M. (1985). *Intrinsic motivation and self-determination in human behavior.* New York: Plenum.

Deci, E. L., & Ryan, R. M. (1994). Promoting self-determined education. *Scandinavian Journal of Educational Research* (38), 3 B 14.

deFur, S. H., & Patton, J. R. (1999). *Transition and school-based services: Interdisciplinary perspectives for enhancing the transition process.* Austin: PRO-ED.

deFur, S. H., & Taymans, J. M. (1995). Competencies needed for transition specialists in vocational rehabilitation, vocational education, and special education. *Career Development for Exceptional Individuals, 62*(1), 38–51.

deFur, S. H., Getzel, E. E., & Kregel, J. (1994). Individual transition plans: A work in progress. *Journal of Vocational Rehabilitation, 4*(2), 139–145.

deFur, S. H., Getzel, E. E., & Trossi, K. (1996). Making the postsecondary education match: A role for transition planning. *Journal of Vocational Rehabilitation, 6,* 231–240.

DeJong, G. (1979) Independent living: From social movement to analytic paradigm. *Archives of Physical Medicine and Rehabilitation, 60,* 435–446.

DeJong, G. (1984). Independent living: From social movement to analytic paradigm. In P. Marinelli & A. Dell Orto (Eds.), *The psychological and social impact of physical disability* (pp. 39–64). New York: Springer.

DeLoach, C. P. (1992). Career outcomes for college graduates with severe disabilities and sensory disabilities. *Journal of Rehabilitation*, 58(1), 57–63.

Dennis, R. E., & Giangreco, M. F. (1996). Creating conversation: Reflections on cultural sensitivity in family interviewing. *Exceptional Children*, 63, 103–116.

Deno, S. L. (1985). Curriculum-based measurement: The emerging alternative. *Exceptional Children*, 52, 219–232.

Dentzer, S. (1992). How to train workers for the 21st century. *U.S. News & World Report*, 21 September, pp. 72–78.

Derer, K., Polsgrove, L., & Rieth, H. (1996). A survey of assistive technology applications in schools and recommendations for practice. *Journal of Special Education Technology*, 13(2), 62–80.

DeStefano, L. (1989). Facilitating the transition from school to adult life for youth with disabilities. In W. E. Kiernan & R. L. Schalock (Eds.), *Economics, industry, and disability: A look ahead* (pp. 169–177). Baltimore: Paul H. Brookes.

DeStefano, L., & Snauwaert, D. (1989). A *value-critical approach to transition policy analysis* [Monograph]. Special Education Programs: Washington, DC.

DeStefano, L., & Wagner, M. (1992). Outcome assessment in special education: Implication for decision-making and long-term planning in vocational rehabilitation. *Career Development for Exceptional Individuals*, 16(2), 147–158.

DeStefano, L., & Wermuth, T. R. (1993). IDEA (P.L. 101–476): Defining a second generation of transition services. In F. R. Rusch. L. DeStefano, J. Chadsey-Rusch, L. A. Phelps, & E. Szymanski (Eds.), *Transition from school to adult life: Models, linkages, and policy* (pp. 537–549). Sycamore, IL: Sycamore.

Dever, R. (1988). *Community living skills: A taxonomy* (Monograph of the American Association on Mental Retardation). Washington, DC: American Association on Mental Retardation.

DeVillar, R. A. (1994). The rhetoric and practice of cultural diversity in U.S. schools: Socialization, resocialization, and quality schooling. In R. A. DeVillar, D. J. Faltis, & J. P. Cummins (Eds.), *Cultural diversity in schools: From rhetoric to practice* (pp. 25–56). Albany, NY: State University of New York.

DeVries, D. L., & Slavin, R. E. (1978). Teams-games-tournament (TGT): Review of ten classroom experiments. *Journal of Research and Development in Education*, 12, 28–38.

DiGangi, S. A., Maag, J. W., & Rutherford, R. B., Jr. (1991). Self-graphing of on-task behavior: Enhancing the reactive effects of self-monitoring of on-task behavior and academic productivity. *Learning Disability Quarterly*, 14, 221–230.

Dinerstein, R. D., Herr, S. S., & O'Sullivan, J. L. (1999). A *guide to consent*. Washington, DC: American Association on Mental Retardation.

Dinnebeil, L. A., & Rule, S. (1994). Congruence between parents' and professionals' judgment about the development of young children with disabilities: A review of the literature. *Topics in Early childhood Education*, 14, 1–26.

Dix, J. E., & Savickas, M. L. (1995). Establishing a career: Developmental tasks and coping responses. *Journal of Vocational Behavior*, 47, 93–107.

Doll, R. C. (1964). *Curriculum improvement: Decision-making and process*. Boston: Allyn & Bacon.

Donnellan, A., & Mirenda, P. (1984). Issues related to professional involvement with families of individuals with autism and other severe handicaps. *Journal of the Association for Persons with Severe Handicaps*, 9, 16–25.

Dowdy, C., & Smith, T. E. (1991). Future-based assessment and intervention. *Intervention in School and Clinic*, 27, 101–106.

Doyle, W. (1984). How order is achieved in classrooms: An interim report. *Journal of Curriculum Studies*, 16, 259–277.

Doyle, W. (1986). Classroom organization and management. In M. C. Wittrock (Ed.), *Handbook of research on teaching* (3rd ed., pp. 392–431). New York: Macmillan.

Droege, R. C. (1987). The USES testing program. In B. Bolton (Ed.), *Handbook of measurement and evaluation in rehabilitation*. (pp. 169–182). Baltimore: Paul H. Brookes.

DuBow, S., Geer, S., & Strauss, K. P. (1992). *Legal rights: The guide for deaf and hard of hearing people*. Washington, DC: Gallaudet University Press.

Ducharme, G., Beeman, P., DeMarasse, R., & Ludlum, C. (1994). Building community one person at a time: One candle power. In V. J. Bradley, J. W. Ashbaugh, & B. C. Blaney (Eds.), *Creating individual supports for people with developmental disabilities: A mandate for change at many levels* (pp. 347–360). Baltimore: Paul H. Brookes.

Duffey, J., Clark, D., Deitmen, K., Dellegrotto, J., Di Lullo, K., Di Martino, C., Laird, S., Oakes, K., & Rider, D. (1996). *Preparation for adult life: Adult life roles, post secondary education and training*. Harrisburg, PA: Pennsylvania Department of Education.

Dunham, M., Koller, J. R., & McIntosh, D. (1996). A preliminary comparison of successful and non-successful closure types among adults with specific learning disabilities in the vocational rehabilitation system. *The Journal of Rehabilitation*, 62(1), 42–47.

Dunlap, G., DePerczel, M., Clarke, S., Wilson, D., Wright, S., White, R., & Gomez, A. (1994). Choice-making to promote adaptive behavior for students with emotional and behavioral challenges. *Journal of Applied Behavior Analysis*, 27, 505–518.

Dunn, B. (1995). *The wild dream team*. University Park, PA: Pennsylvania State University, WPSX.

Dunn, R., & Griggs, S. A. (1995). *Multiculturalism and learning style: Teaching and counseling adolescents*. Westport, CN: Praeger.

Dunst, C., Trivette, C., & Deal, A. (1988). *Enabling and empowering families: Principles and guidelines for practice*. Cambridge, MA: Brookline Books.

Durlak, C. M., Rose, E., & Bursuck, W. D. (1994). Preparing high school students with learning disabilities for the transition to postsecondary education: Teaching the skills of self-determination. *Journal of Learning Disabilities*, 27(1), 51–59.

Dybwad, G. (1989). Self-determination: Influencing public policy. In R. Perske (Ed.), *National conference on self-determination*. Washington, DC: U.S. Department of Education, Office of Special Education and Rehabilitative Services.

Dyer, K., Dunlap, G., & Winterling, V. (1993). Effects of choice making in the serious problem behavior of students with severe handicaps. *Journal of Applied Behavior Analysis*, 23, 515–524.

Eber, L., Nelson, C. M., & Miles, P. (1997). School-based wraparound for students with emotional and behavior challenges. *Exceptional Children*, 63(4), 539–556.

Edelman, A., Schuyler, V., & White, P. (1998). *Maximizing success for young adults with chronic-related illnesses: Transition planning for education after high school*. Washington, DC: Heath.

Edgar, E. (1987). Secondary programs in special education: Are many of them justifiable? *Exceptional Parent*, 53(6), 555–561.

Edgar, E., & Polloway, E. A. (1994). Education for adolescents with disabilities: Curriculum and placement issues. *The Journal of Special Education*, 27(4), 438–452.

Education Amendments of 1972, 20 U.S.C. § 1681 *et seq*.

Education Amendments of 1974, Pub. L. No. 93-380, 88 Stat. 580.

Education for All Handicapped Children Act of 1975, 20 U.S.C. § 1401 *et seq*.

Education for All Handicapped Children Act, Pub. L. No. 94-142, 20 U.S.C. 1412 (1975).

Education of the Handicapped Act of 1970, Pub. L. No. 91-230, § 601–662, 84 Stat. 175.

Education of the Handicapped Amendments of 1986, 20 U.S.C. § 1401 *et seq*.

Edwards, J. P., Kinneldorf, M., & Bradley, C. (1988). *Final report of the Portland State University secondary school-to-work transition projects emphasizing transition to work and leisure roles*. Portland, OR: Portland State University.

Elbaum, B., Vaughn, S., Hughes, M., & Moody, S. W. (1999). Grouping practices and reading outcomes for students with disabilities. *Exceptional Children*, 65, 399–415.

Elder, J. (1988). Transition from school to work: Changing attitudes and opportunities. *Exceptional Parent*, 18(1), 27–29.

Elementary and Secondary Education Act of 1965, Pub. L. No. 89-10, 79 Stat. 27.

Elementary and Secondary Education Act, amended by Pub. L. No. 89-750. § 161 [Title VI], 80 Stat. 1204 (1966).

Ellis, A. K., & Fouts, J. T. (1997). *Research on educational innovations* (2nd ed.). Larchmont, NY: Eye on Education.

Ellis, E. S. (1997). Watering up the curriculum for adolescents with learning disabilities: Goals of the knowledge dimension. *Remedial & Special Education*, 18.(6) 326–346.

Elrod, G. F., Sorgenfrei, T. B., & Gibson, A. P. (1989). The degree of agreement between the expressed and scale-determined career interests of adolescents with mild

handicaps. *Career Development for Exceptional Individuals*, 12(2), 107–116.

Emmer, E., Evertson, C., & Anderson, L. (1980). Effective classroom management at the beginning of the school year. *Elementary School Journal*, 80, 219–231.

Engleman, S., Becker, W. C., Carnine, D., & Gersten, R. (1988). The direct instruction follow through model: Design and outcomes. *Education and Treatment of Children*, 11(4), 303–317.

Englert, C. S. (1983). Measuring special education teacher effectiveness. *Exceptional Children*, 50, 247–254.

Englert, C. S., Mariage, T. V., & Tarrant, K. L. (1992). Defining and redefining instructional practice in special education: Perspectives on good teaching. *Teacher Education and Special Education*, 15, 62–86.

Esposito, L., & Campbell, P. H. (1993). Computers and severely and physically handicapped individuals. In J. D. Lindsey (Ed.), *Computers and exceptional individuals* (2nd Ed., pp. 159–171). Austin, TX: PRO-ED.

Eubanks, S. C. (1996). *The urban teacher challenge: A report on teacher recruitment and demand in selected great city schools*. Belmont, MA: Recruiting New Teachers.

Everson, J. M. (1990). A local team approach. *Teaching Exceptional Children*, 23(1), 44–46.

Everson, J. M., & Guillory, J. D. (1998). Building statewide transition services through collaborative interagency teamwork. In F. Rusch & J. Chadsey (Eds.), *Beyond high school: Transition from school to work* (pp. 299–317). Belmont, CA: Wadsworth Press.

Everson, J. M., & McNulty, K. (1992). Interagency teams: Building local transition programs through parental and professional partnerships. In F. R. Rusch, L. DeStefano, J. Chadsey-Rusch, L. A. Phelps, & E. Szymanski (Eds.), *Transition from school to adult life: Models, linkages, and policy* (pp. 341–352). Sycamore, IL: Sycamore Publishing.

Everson, J. M., & Moon, M. S. (1987). Transition services for young adults with severe disabilities: Defining professional and parental roles and responsibilities. *Journal of the Association for Persons with Severe Handicaps*, 12(2), 87–95.

Everson, J. M., & Rachal, P. (1996). *What are we learning about state and local interagency partnerships? An analysis of state and interagency activities for students who are deaf-blind in seventeen states*. Sands Point, NY: Helen Keller National Center—Technical Assistance Center.

Everson, J. M., Barcus, M., Moon, M. S., & Morton, M. V. (1987). *Achieving outcomes: A guide to interagency training in transition and supported employment*. Richmond, VA: Virginia Commonwealth University, Project Transition into Employment.

Evertson, C. (1982). Differences in instructional activities in higher and lower achieving junior high English and mathematics classrooms. *Elementary School Journal*, 82, 329–351.

Evertson, C., Anderson, C., Anderson, L., & Brophy, J. (1980). Relationship between classroom behavior and student outcomes in junior high math and English classes. *American Elementary Research Journal*, 17, 43–60.

Evertson, C., & Emmer, E. (1982). Effective management at the beginning of the year in junior high classes. *Journal of Educational Psychology*, 74, 485–498.

Evertson, C., Emmer, E., Clements, B., Sanford, J., Worsham, M., & Williams, E. (1980). Predictors of effective teaching in junior high mathematics classrooms. *Journal of Research in Mathematics Education*, 11, 167–178.

Experience-based career education: Basic procedures manual. (1976). Fort Dodge, IA: Iowa Central Community College.

Fairweather, J. S., & Shaver, D. M. (1991). Making the transition to postsecondary education and training. *Exceptional Children*, 57(3), 264–270.

Falvey, M. (1989). *Community-based curriculum: Instructional strategies for students with severe handicaps*. Baltimore: Paul H. Brookes.

Falvey, M., Brown, L., Lyon, S., Baumgart, D., & Schroeder, J. (1980). Strategies for using cues and correction procedures. In W. Sailor, B. Wilcox, & L. Brown (Eds.), *Methods of instruction for severely handicapped students* (pp. 109–133). Baltimore: Paul H. Brookes.

Falvey, M. A. (1989). *Community-based curriculum: Instructional strategies for students with severe disabilities* (2nd ed.,). Baltimore: Paul H. Brookes.

Farren, C., Gray, J. D., & Kaye, B. (1984). Mentoring: A boon to career development. *Personnel*, 61, 20–24.

Federal Register. (1981, January 19). Washington, DC: U.S. Government Printing Office.

Ferguson, P. M., & Ferguson, D. L. (2000). The promise of adulthood. In M. E. Snell & F. Brown, *Instruction of students with severe disabilities* (5th ed., pp. 629–656). Upper Saddle River, NJ: Merill/Prentive Hall.

Ferguson, P. M., & Olsen, D. (Eds.). (1989). *Supported community life: Connecting policy to practice in disability research*. Eugene, OR: Specialized Training Program.

Fichten, C. S., & Ansel, R. (1988). Thoughts concerning interactions between college students who have a physical disability and their nondisabled peers. *Rehabilitation Counseling Bulletin*, 32, 23–40.

Fichten, C. S., Robillard, K., Tagalakis, V., & Ansel, R. (1991). Casual interaction between college students with various disabilities and their nondisabled peers: The internal dialogue. *Rehabilitation Psychology*, 36(1), 3–20.

Field, S., & Hoffman, A. (1994). Development of a model for self-determination. *Career Development for Exceptional Individuals*, 17(2), 159–169.

Field, S., & Hoffman, A. (1995). *Steps to self-determination*. Austin, TX: PRO-ED.

Field, S., Martin, J, Miller, R., Ward, M., & Wehmeyer, M. (1998). *A practical guide for teaching self-determination*. Reston, VA: The Council for Exceptional Children.

Fielder, I. (1996). Assistive devices: Empowerment issues. *American Rehabilitation*, 22(4), 26–29.

Finch, C. R., & Crunkilton. S. R. (1993). *Curriculum development in vocational and technical education* (4th ed.). Boston: Allyn & Bacon.

Fisher, S. K., & Gardner, J. E. (1999). Introduction to technology in transition. *Career Development for Exceptional Individuals*, 22(2), 131–152.

Flexer, R. (1996). Federal laws and program acdcessibility. In C. Flexer, D. Wray, R. Leavitt, & R. Flexer (Eds.), *How the student with hearing loss can succeed in college: A handbook for students, families, and professional* (2nd ed., pp. 13–27). Washington, DC: Alexander Graham Bell Association for the Deaf.

Flexer, R. W., Goebel, G. W., Simmons, T. J., Baer, R., Shell, D., Steele, R., & Sabousky, R., (1994). Participant, employer, and rehabilitation resources in supported employment: A collaborative approach. *Journal of Applied Rehabilitation Counseling*, 25(4), 9–15.

Flexer, R., Simmons, T., & Tankersly, M. (1997). Graduate interdisciplinary training at Kent State University. *Journal of Vocational Rehabilitation*, 8, 183-195.

Foley, R. M., & Munschenck, N. A. (1997). Collaboration activities and competencies of secondary school special educators: A national survey. *Teacher Education and Special Education*, 20, 47–60.

Ford, A., Schnorr, R., Meyer, L., Davern, L., Black, J., & Dempsey, P. (1989). *The Syracuse community-referenced curriculum guide for students with moderate and severe disabilities*. Baltimore: Paul Brookes.

Ford, B. A. (1992). Multicultural education training for special educators working with African-American youth. *Exceptional Children*, 59, 107–114.

Forest, M., & Lusthaus, E. (1989). Promoting educational equality for all students: Circles and MAPS. In S. Stainback, W. Stainback, & M. Forest (Eds.), *Educating all students in the mainstream of regular education* (pp. 43–57). Baltimore, MD: Paul H. Brookes.

Forest, M., & Lusthaus, E. (1989). Promoting educational equality for all students: Circles and MAPS. In S. Stainback, W. Stainback, & M. Forest (Eds.), Educating all students in the mainstream of regular education (pp. 43–57). Baltimore, MD: Paul H. Brookes.

Forest, M., Pearpoint, J., & Snow, J. (1993). Natural support systems: Families, friends, and circles. In J. Pearpoint, M. Forest, & J. Snow (Eds.), *The inclusion papers: Strategies to make inclusion work* (pp. 116–132). Toronto: Inclusion Press.

Forness, S. R., Kavale, K. A., Blum, I. M., & Lloyd, J. W. (1997). Mega-analysis of meta-analyses: What works in special education and related services. *Teaching Exceptional Children*, 29(6), 4–9.

Foss, G., & Vilhauer, D. A. (1986). *Working II: Interpersonal skills assessment and training for employment: Teachers guide*. Santa Monica, CA: James Stanfield.

Foss, G., Bullis, M. D., & Vilhauer, D. A. (1984). Assessment and training of job-related social competence for mentally retarded adolescents and adults. In A. S. Halpern & M. J. Fuhrer (Eds.), *Functional assessment in rehabilitation* (pp. 145–157). Baltimore: Paul H. Brookes.

Foss, G., Cheney, D., & Bullis, M. D. (1986). TICE: *Test of interpersonal competence for employment*. Santa Monica, CA: James Stanfield.

Foss, P. D. (1990). *Transition from school to community: What works for students with disabilities?* Unpublished master's thesis, University of Central Florida.

Fox, L., Zakely, J., Morris, R., & Jundt, M. (1993). Orientation as a catalyst: Effective retention through academic and social integration. In M. L. Upcraft, R. H. Mullendore, B. O. Barefoot, & D. S. Fidler (Eds.), *Designing successful transitions: A guide for orienting students to college* [Monograph Series No. 13] 49–59. Columbia, SC: University of South Carolina.

Fradd, S. H., & Weismantel, M. J. (1989). Developing and evaluating goals. In S. H. Fradd & M. H. Weismantel (Eds.), *Meeting the needs of culturally and linguistically different students: A handbook for educators* (pp. 34–62). Austin, TX: PRO-ED.

Franca, V. M., Kerr, M. M., Reitz, A. L., & Lambert, D. (1990). Peer tutoring among behaviorally disordered students: Academic and social benefits to tutor and tutee. *Educational Treatment of Children*, 13, 109–128.

Frank, K., & Wade, P. (1993). Disabled student services in postsecondary education: Who's responsible for what? *Journal of College Student Development*, 34, 26–30.

Frey, R. M., & Kolstoe, O. P. (1965). *A high school work-study program for mentally subnormal students*. Carbondale, IL: Southern Illinois University Press.

Friend, M., & Cook, L. (1990). Collaboration as a predictor for success in school reform. *Journal of Educational and Psychological Consultation*, 1, 69–86.

Fuchs, D., & Fuchs, L. S. (1995). Sometimes separate is better. *Education Leadership*, 52(4), 22–26.

Fuchs, L. S. (1993). Enhancing instructional programming and student achievement with curriculum-based measurement. In J. J. Kramer (Ed.), *Curriculum-based assessment: Examining old problems, evaluating new solutions* (pp. 65–103). Lincoln, NE: Buros Institute of Mental Measurements.

Fujiura, G. T., & Yamaki, K. (1997). Analysis of ethnic variations in developmental disability prevalence and household economic status. *Mental Retardation*, 35, 286–294.

Funk, D. (1992). *Transitional services for handicapped youth: Follow-up and follow along*. Final report submitted to the U.S. Department of Education, Office of Special Education and Rehabilitation Services. (ID# 15R80062-91), Washington, DC.

Gajar, A. (1998). Post-secondary education. In F. R. Rusch & J. G. Chadsey (Eds.), *Beyond high school: Transition from school to work* (pp. 383–405). Belmont, CA: Wadsworth Publishing.

Gajar, A., Goodman, L., & McAfee, J. (1993). *Secondary schools and beyond: Transition of individuals with mild disabilities*. Upper Saddle River, NJ: Merrill/Prentice Hall.

Gajar, A. H. (1998). Postsecondary education. In F. R. Rusch & J. G. Chadsey (Eds.), *Beyond high school: Transition from school to work* (pp. 383–405). Belmont, CA: Wadsworth Publishing.

Gallivan-Fenlon, A. (1994). "Their senior year": Family and service provider perspectives on the transition from school to adult life for young adults with disabilities. *Journal of the Association for Persons with Severe Handicaps*, 19(1), 11–23.

Garcia, S. B., & Yates, J. R. (1986). Policy issues associated with serving bilingual exceptional children. In A. C. Willing & H. F. Greenberg (Eds.), *Bilingualism and learning disabilities: Policy and practice for teachers and administrators* (pp. 113–134). New York: American Library Publishing.

Gardner, J. A. (1987). *Transition from high school to postsecondary education: Analytical studies*. Washington, DC: Center for Educational Statistics (ERIC Reproduction Service No. ED280 370).

Gartin, B. C., Rumrill, P., & Serebreni, R. (1996). The higher education transition model: Guidelines for facilitating college transition among college-bound students with disabilities. *Teaching Exceptional Children*, 29(1), 30–33.

Gartner, A., & Lipsky, D. K. (1987). Beyond special education: Toward a quality system for all students. *Harvard Educational Review*, 57, 367–395.

Gault, A. (1989). *Mexican immigrant parents and the education of their handicapped children: Factors that influence parent involvement*. Unpublished doctoral dissertation, University of Illinois at Urbana-Champaign, Urbana, IL.

Gaylord-Ross, R., & Browder, D. (1991). Functional assessment: Dynamic and domain properties. In L. Meyer, C. Peck, & L. Brown (Eds.), *Critical issues in the lives of people with severe disabilities* (pp. 45–66). Baltimore: Paul H. Brookes.

Geraghty, M. (1996, July 19). More students quitting college before sophomore year, data show. *The Chronicle of Higher Education*, pp. A35–A36.

Gerber, P. J., Banbury, M. M., Miller, J. H., Griffin, H. D. (1986). Special educators' perceptions of parental participation in the individual education plan process. *Psychology in the Schools*, 23, 158–163.

Gerber, P. J., Ginsberg, R., & Reiff, H. B. (1992). Identifying alterable patterns in employment success for highly successful adults with learning disabilities. *Journal of Learning Disabilities*, 25, 475–487.

Gerber, P. J., Reiff, H. B., & Ginsberg, R. (1994). Critical incidents of highly successful adults with learning disabilities. *The Journal of Vocational Rehabilitation*, 4(2), 105–112.

German, S., Martin, J. E., Huber Marshall, L., & Sale, R. P. (2000). Promoting self-determination: Teaching goal attainment with the *Take Action* process. *Career Development for Exceptional Individuals*, 23, 27–38.

Gersten, R. Carnine, D., & White, W. A. T. (1984). The pursuit of clarity: Direct instruction and applied behavior analysis. In W. L. Heward, T. E. Heron, D. S. Hill, & J. Trapp-Porter (Eds.), *Focus on behavior analysis in education* (pp. 38–57). Columbus, OH: Merrill.

Gersten, R., Carnine, D., & Woodward, J. (1987). Direct instruction research: The third decade. *Remedial and Special Education, 8*(6), 48–56.

Gersten, R., Woodward, J., & Darch, C. (1986). Direct instruction: A research-based approach to curriculum design and teaching. *Exceptional Children, 53,* 17–31.

Getzel, E., Emanuel, E. J., Fesko, S., & Parent, W. (2000). *Factors that inhibit and facilitate transition-age youth in accessing and using SSI work Incentives: Implications for policy, research, and practice.* Paper presented at Annual Project Directors' Meeting, National Transition Alliance for Youth with Disabilities, Washington, DC.

Getzel, E. E., & Kregel, J. (1996). Transitioning from the academic to the employment setting: The employment connection program. *Journal of Vocational Rehabilitation, 6,* 273–287.

Giangreco, M. F., Cloninger, C. J., & Iverson, V. S. (1993). *Choosing options and accommodations for children: A guide to planning inclusive education.* Baltimore: Paul H. Brookes.

Gill, D., & Edgar, E. (1990). Outcomes of vocational programs designed for students with mild disabilities: The Pierce County Vocational Special Education Cooperative. *Journal for Vocational Special Needs Education, 12*(3), 17–22.

Gilliam, J. E., & Coleman, M. C. (1981). Who influences IEP committee decisions? *Exceptional Children, 47*(8), 642–644.

Gilmore, G. (1974). School psychologist-parent contact: An alternative model. *Psychology in the Schools, 11,* 170–173.

Gliedman, J., & Roth, W. (1980). *The unexpected minority: Handicapped children in America.* New York: Carnegie Council on Children.

Goals 2000: Educate America Act of 1994, 20 U.S.C.S. § 5801 *et seq.*

Goldman, Esq., C. D. (1991). *Disability Rights Guide* (2nd ed.). Lincoln, NE: Media Publishing.

Goldman, H. H., & Mandershied, R. W. (1987). The epidemiology of psychiatric disabilities. In A. T. Meyerson & T. Fine (Eds.), *Psychiatric disability: Clinical, legal, and administrative dimensions* (pp. 13–21). Washington, DC: American Psychiatric Association Press.

Goldstein, A. P., Sprafkin, R. P., Gershaw, N. J., & Klein, P. (1980). *Skillstreaming the adolescent.* Champaign, IL: Research Press.

Goldstein, S., Strickland, B., Turnbull, A. P., & Curry, L. (1980). An observational analysis of the IEP conference. *Exceptional Children, 46*(4), 278–286.

Goldstein, S., & Turnbull, A. P. (1982). Strategies to increase parent participation in IEP conferences. *Exceptional Children, 48*(4), 360–361.

Goodall, P., & Bruder, M. B. (1986, April). Parents and the transition process. *The Exceptional Parent,* 22–28.

Goode, D. (1990). Thinking about and discussing quality of life. In R. Schalock & M. Begab (Eds.), *Quality of life: Perspectives and issues* (pp. 41–58). Washington, DC: American Association on Mental Retardation.

Granger, M. (1996, March 22). Accommodating employees with disabilities: A matter of attitude. *Journal of Managerial Issues, 8* (14) 78.

Gray, K. (1996). The baccalaureate game: Is it right for all teens? *Phi Delta Kappan, 77*(8), 528–534.

Green, J. W. (1999). *Cultural awareness in the human services: A multi-ethnic approach.* Boston: Allyn & Bacon.

Greenberg, H. F. (1986). Preface. In A. C. Willing & H. F. Greenberg (Eds.), *Bilingualism and learning disabilities: Policy and practice for teachers and administrators* (pp. xv–xvi). New York: American Library Publishing.

Greenfield, P. M. (1994). Independence and interdependence as developmental scripts: Implications for theory, research, and practice. In P. M. Greenfield & R. R. Cocking (Eds.), *Cross-cultural roots of minority child development* (pp. 1–37). Hillsdale, NJ: Erlbaum.

Greenwood, C. R. (1991). Longitudinal analysis of time, engagement, and achievement in at-risk versus nonrisk students. *Exceptional Children, 57,* 521–534.

Gresham, F. M. (1986). Conceptual issues in the assessment of social competence in children. In P. S. Strain, M. J. Guralnick, & H. M. Walker (Eds.), *Children's social behavior: Development assessment and modification* (pp. 143–179). New York: Academic Press.

Gresham, F. M., & Nagle, R. J. (1980). Social skills training with children: Responsiveness to modeling and coaching as a function of peer orientation. *Journal of Consulting and Clinical Psychology, 48,* 718–729.

Grigal, M., Test, D. W., Beattie, J., & Wood, W. M. (1997). An evaluation of transition components of individualized education programs, *Exceptional Children, 63*(3), 357–372.

Hagner, D., & Dileo, D. (1993). *Working together: Workplace culture, supported employment, and persons with disabilities.* Cambridge, MA: Brookline Books.

Hagner, D., & Sande, J. (1998). School sponsored work experience and vocational instruction. In F. R. Rusch & J. G. Chadsey (Eds.), *Beyond high school: Transition from school to work* (pp. 340–366). Belmont, CA: Wadsworth Publishing.

Hagner, D., Fesko, S., Cadigan, M., Kiernan, W., & Butterworth, J. (1996). Securing employment: Job search and employer negotiation strategies in rehabilitation. In E. M. Szymanski & R. M. Parker (Eds.), *Work and disability: Issues and strategies in career development and job placement* (pp. 309–340). Austin, TX: PRO-ED.

Hagner, D., Helm, D., & Butterworth, J. (1996). "This is your meeting": A qualitative study of person-centered planning. *Mental Retardation, 34,* 159–171.

Hagner, D., Rogan, P., & Murphy, S. (1992). Facilitating natural supports in the workplace: Strategies for support consultants. *Journal of Rehabilitation, 58,* 29–34.

Hall, D. T. (Ed.). (1987). *Career development in organizations.* San Francisco: Jossey-Bass.

Hall, M., Kleinert, H., & Kearns, J. F. (2000). Going to college: Post-secondary programs for students with moderate and severe disabilities. *Teaching Exceptional Children, 32*(3), 58–65.

Hall, M., & Walker, P. (Eds.) (1998). *Annotated bibliography on community integration* (3rd ed.). Syracuse, NY: Syracuse University, Center on Human Policy.

Hallahan, D. P., Lloyd, J. W., Kosiewicz, M. M., Kauffman, J. M., & Graves, A. W. (1979). Self-monitoring of attention as a treatment for a learning disabled boy's off-task behavior. *Learning Disability Quarterly, 2,* 24–32.

Hallenbeck, B. A., & Kauffman, J. M. (1995). How does observational learning affect the behavior of students with emotional or behavioral disorders? A review of research. *Journal of Special Education, 29,* 45–71.

Halloran, W. D. (1993). Transition services requirement: Issues, implications, challenge. In R. C. Eaves & P. J. McLaughlin (Eds.), *Recent advances in special education and rehabilitation* (pp. 210–224). Boston: Andover Medical Publishers.

Halpern, A. S. (1985). Transition: A look at the foundations. *Exceptional Children, 51,* 479–502.

Halpern, A. S. (1992). Transition: Old wine in new bottles. *Exceptional Children, 58*(3), 202–211.

Halpern, A. S. (1994). The transition of youth with disabilities to adult life: A position statement of the Division on Career Development and Transition, The Council for Exceptional Children. *Career Development of Exceptional Individuals, 17*(2), 115–124.

Halpern, A. S. (1996). *Transition skills inventory.* Eugene, OR: Secondary Transition Program College of Education, University of Oregon.

Halpern, A. S., & Benz, M. R. (1987). A statewide examination of secondary special education for students with mild disabilities: Implications for the high school curriculum. *Exceptional Children, 54*(2), 122–129.

Halpern, A. S., Benz, M. R., & Lindstrom, L. E. (1992). A systems change approach to improving secondary special education and transition programs at the community level. *Career Development for Exceptional Individuals, 15*(1), 109–120.

Halpern, A. S., Doren, B., & Benz, M. R. (1993). Job experiences of students with disabilities during their last two years in school. *Career Development for Exceptional Individuals, 16*(1), 63-73.

Halpern, A. S., & Fuhrer, M. J. (Eds.). (1984). *Functional assessment in rehabilitation.* Baltimore: Paul H. Brookes.

Halpern, A. S., Herr, C. M., Wolf, N. K., Lawson, J. D., Doren, B., & Johnson, M. D. (1997). *Next S.T.E.P.: Student transition and education.* Austin, TX: PRO-ED.

Halpern, A. S., & Irvin, L. (1986). *Social and prevocational information battery-revised.* Monterey, CA: CTB McGraw-Hill.

Halpern, A. S., Irvin, L., & Landman, J. (n.d.). *Tests for everyday living.* Monterey, CA: CTB/McGraw Hill.

Halpern, A. S., Lehmann, J., Irvin, L., & Heiry, T. (1982). *Contemporary assessment for mentally retarded adolescents and adults.* Baltimore: University Park.

Halpern, A. S., Yavonoff, P., Doren, B., & Benz, M. R. (1995). Predicting participation in postsecondary education for school leavers with disabilities. *Career Development for Exceptional Individuals, 62*(2), 151–164.

Hammond, J., & Morrison, J. (1996). *The stuff Americans are made of.* New York: Macmillan.

Hamre-Nietupski, S., Krajewski, L., Nietupski, J., Ostercamp, D., Sensor, K., & Opheim, B. (1988). Parent/professional partnerships in advocacy: Developing integrated options within resistive systems. *Journal of the Association for Persons with Severe Handicaps, 13*(4), 251–259.

Hanley-Maxwell, C., & Collet-Klingenberg, L. (1994). *Synthesis in design of effective curricular practices in transition from school to the community* on-line]. Available:http://darkwing.uoregan.edu/~ncite/otherRsc/research. html.

Hanley-Maxwell, C., & Szymanski, E. M. (1992). School-to-work transition and supported employment. In R. M. Parker & E. M. Szymanski (Eds.), *Rehabilitation counseling: Basics and beyond* (pp. 135–164). Austin, TX: PRO-ED.

Hanley-Maxwell, C. Pogoloff, S. M. & Whitney-Thomas J. (1998). Families: The heart of transition. In F. R. Rusch & J. G. Chadsey (Eds.), *Beyond high school: Transition from school to work* (pp. 234–264). New York: Wadsworth Publishing.

Hanley-Maxwell, C., Szymanski, E., & Owens-Johnson, L. (1998). School-to-adult life transition and supported employment. In E. M. Szymanski & R. M. Parker (Eds.), *Rehabilitation counseling: Basics and beyond* (3rd ed., pp. 143–179). Austin, TX: PRO-ED.

Hanson, M. J. (1998a). Ethnic, cultural, and language diversity in intervention settings. In E. W. Lynch & M. H. Hanson (Eds.), *Developing cross-cultural competence: A guide for working with children and their families* (2nd ed., pp. 3–22). Baltimore: Paul H. Brookes.

Hanson, M. J. (1998b). Families with Native American roots. In E. W. Lynch & M. H. Hanson (Eds.), *Developing cross-cultural competence: A guide for working with children and their families* (2nd ed., pp. 93–126). Baltimore: Paul H. Brookes.

Hanson, M. J., & Carta, J. J. (1996). Addressing the challenges of families with multiple risks. *Exceptional Children, 62,* 201–212.

Hardman, M., & McDonnell, J. (1987). Implementing federal transition initiatives for youths with severe handicaps: The Utah community-based transition project. *Exceptional Children, 53,* 493–498.

Haring, K. A., Lovett, D. L., & Smith, D. D. (1990). A follow-up study of recent special education graduates of learning disabilities programs. *Journal of Learning Disabilities, 23*(2), 108–113.

Haring, N. G., McCormick, L., & Haring, T. G. (1994). *Exceptional children and youth: An introduction to special education.* New York: Macmillan.

Haring, T. G., & Breen, C. (1989). Units of analysis of social interaction outcomes in supported education. *The Journal of the Association for Persons with Severe Handicaps, 14,* 255–262.

Harmon, L. W., Hansen, J. C., Borgen, F. H., & Hammer, A. L. (1994). *Applications and technical guide for the Strong Interest Inventory.* Palo Alto, CA: Consulting Psychologists Press.

Harper, D. (1996). Emerging needs of adults with developmental disabilities. *The Journal of Rehabilitation*, 62(1), 7–10.

Harris, L., & Associates, Inc. (1986). *The ICD survey of disabled Americans: Bringing disabled Americans into the mainstream.* New York: Author.

Harris, L. & Associates, Inc. (1994). *N.O.D./Harris survey of Americans with disabilities* (Study No. 942003). New York: Author.

Harry, B. (1992a). *Cultural diversity, families, and the special education system: Communication and empowerment.* New York: Teachers College Press.

Harry, B. (1992b). Making sense of disability: Low-income, Puerto Rican parents' theories of the problem. *Exceptional Children*, 59, 27–40.

Harry, B. (1992c). Restructuring the participation of African-American parents in special education. *Exceptional Children*, 59, 123–131.

Hasazi, S. B., Gordon, L. R., & Roe, C. A. (1985). Factors associated with the employment status of handicapped youth exiting high school from 1979 to 1983. *Exceptional Children*, 51, 455–469.

Haskew, P., & Donnellan, A. M. (1992) *Emotional maturity and well-being: Psychological lessons of facilitated communion.* Danbury, CT: DRT Press.

Hayden, M. F., & Goldman, J. (1996). Families of adults with mental retardation: Stress levels and need for services. *Social Work*, 41(6), 657–667.

Haynes, J., & Justice, T. (1988). *Organizational barriers to transition: Summary.* Sacramento, CA: California Department of Education, Special Education Division.

Hazel, J. S., Schumaker, J. B., Sherman, J. A., & Sheldon-Wildgen, J. (1982). *Asset: A social skills program for adolescents.* Champaign, IL: Research Press.

Heal, L. W., Copher, J. I., & Rusch, F. R. (1990). Interagency agreements (IAA's) among agencies responsible for the transition education of students with handicaps from secondary schools to post-school setting. *Career Development for Exceptional Children*, 13(2), 121–127.

Heal, L. W., Copher, J. I., Destefano, L. D., & Rusch, F. R.(1989). A comparison of successful and unsuccessful placements of secondary students with mental handicaps into competitive employment, *Career Development for Exceptional Individuals*, 12(2), 167–177.

Heal, L. W., Gonzalez, P., Rusch, F. R., Copher, J. I., & DeStefano, L. (1990). A comparison of successful and unsuccessful placements of youths with mental handicaps into competitive employment. *Exceptionality*, 1(3), 181–196.

HEATH Resource Center (1995). *Getting ready for college: Advising high school students with learning disabilities.* Washington, DC: American Council on Education, U.S. Department of Education.

HEATH Resource Center (1996). Vast spaces and stone walls: Overcoming barriers to postsecondary education for rural students with disabilities. *Information from HEATH*, 15(2–3), 1–4.

HEATH Resource Center (1997). *How to choose a college: Guide for the student with a disability.* Washington, DC: American Council on Education, U.S. Department of Education.

Hebbeler, K. (1993). Overview of the high school experience of students with disabilities. In M. Wagner (Ed.), *The secondary programs of students with disabilities.* Menlo Park, CA: SRI International.

Hecklinger, F., & Black, B. (1991). *Training for life: A practical guide for career and life planning.* Dubuque, IA: Kendall Hunt Publishing.

Heins, E. D., Lloyd, J. W., & Hallahan, D. P. (1986). Cued and noncued self-recording of attention to task. *Behavior Modification*, 10, 235–254.

Henderson, C. (1992). *College freshman with disabilities: A statistical profile.* Washington, DC: HEATH Resource Center, American Council on Education, U. S. Department of Education.

Henderson, C. (1995). *College freshman with disabilities: A statistical profile.* Washington, DC: HEATH Resource Center, American Council on Education, U. S. Department of Education.

Hendricks, D. J., & Hirsh, A. E. (1991). The Job accommodation network: A vital resource for the 90's. *Rehabilitation Education*, 5, 261–264.

Herr, E. L., & Cramer, S. H. (1992). *Career guidance and counseling through the lifespan: Systematic approaches* (4th ed.). New York: Harper Collins.

Herr, E. L., Rayman, J. R., & Garis, J. W. (1993). *Handbook for the college and university career center.* Westport, CT: Greenwood Press.

Hershenson, D. B., & Szymanski, E. M. (1992). Career development of people with disabilities. In R. M. Parker & E. M. Szymanski (Eds.), *Rehabilitation counseling: Basics and beyond* (2nd ed., pp. 273–303). Austin, TX: PRO-ED.

Heyward, S. M. (1996). *Frequently asked questions: Postsecondary education and disability.* Cambridge, MA: Heyward, Lawton & Associates.

Hilton, A., & Henderson, C. J. (1993, September). Parent involvement: A best practice or forgotten practice? *Education and Training in Mental Retardation*, 199–211.

Hobbs, N. (1975). *The futures of children: Categories, labels, and their consequences: Report of the project on classification of exceptional children.* San Francisco: Jossey-Bass.

Hoffman, A., Field, S., & Sawilowsky, S. (1996). *Self-determination knowledge scale.* Austin, TX: PRO-ED.

Hoffman, R. C. (1988). Transition. In G. A. Robinson (Ed.), *Best practices in mental disabilities* (Vol. 2, pp. 114–126). (ERIC Document Reproduction Service No. ED 304 834).

Holburn, S., & Vietze, P. (1998). Has person-centered planning become the alchemy of developmental disabilities? *Mental Retardation*, 36(6), 485–488.

Holder-Brown, L., & Parette, H. P. (1992). Children with disabilities who use assistive technology: Ethical considerations. *Young Children* 47(6), 73–77.

Holland, J. L. (1985a). *Making vocational choices: A theory of vocational personalities and work environments.* Upper Saddle River, NJ: Prentice Hall.

Holland, J. L. (1985)b. *Manual for vocational preference inventory.* Odessa, FL: Psychological Assessment Resources.

Holland, J. L. (1992). *Making vocational choices: A theory of vocational personalities and work environments* (3rd ed.). Odessa, FL: Psychological Assessment Resources.

Holland, J. L., Fritzche, B. A., & Powell, A. B. (1994). *Self-directed search technical manual.* Odessa, FL: Psychological Assessment Resources.

Holtzman, W. H., Jr. (1986). Issues in the implementation of master's level training programs for bilingual special education. In A. C. Willing & H. F. Greenberg (Eds.), *Bilingualism and learning disabilities: Policy and practice for teachers and administrators* (pp. 137–146). New York: American Library Publishing.

Home of Your Own Project (1995). *Extending the American dream: Home ownership through creative financing.* Durham, NH: University of New Hampshire, Institute on Disability.

Hops, H., Fleishman, D. H., Guild, J., Paine, S., Street A., Walker, H. M., & Greenwood, C. R. (1978). *Program for establishing effective relationship skills* (PEERS). Eugene, OR: University of Oregon, Center at Oregon for Research in the Behavioral Education of the Handicapped.

Hops, H., & Walker, H. M. (1988). CLASS: *Contingency for learning academic and social skills.* Delray Beach, FL: Educational Achievement Systems.

Horne, M. D. (1985). *Attitudes towards handicapped students.* Hillsdale, NJ: Erlbaum.

Hoye, J. D. (1998, July). *Integrating school-to-work into preservice teacher education.* Paper presented at Conference for Professors of Education in Ohio, Kent, OH.

Hoyt, K. B. (1975). *Career education: Contributions to an evolving concept.* Salt Lake City, UT: Olympus.

Hoyt, K. B. (1977). *A primer for career education.* Washington, DC: U.S. Government Printing Office.

HSRI (Human Services Research Institute). (1991). *New models for the provision of personal assistance services: Final report.* Bethesda, MD: Human Services Research Institute.

Huber Marshall, L. H., Martin, J. E., Hughes, C., Jerman, P., & Maxson, L. (1999). *Choosing personal goals.* Longmont, CO: Sopris West.

Huber Marshall, L. H., Martin, J. E., Maxson, L., & Jerman, P. (1996). *Choosing employment goals.* Longmont, CO: Sopris West.

Huber Marshall, L. H., Martin, J. E., Maxson, L., Hughes, W., Miller, T. L., McGill, T., & Jerman, P. (1996). *Take action: Making goals happen.* Longmont, CO: Sopris West.

Hudson, P. J., Schwartz, S. E., Sealander, K. A., Campbell, P., & Hensel, J. W. (1988). Successfully employed adults with handicaps: Characteristics and transition strategies. *Career Development for Exceptional Individuals, 11*(1), 7–14.

Hughes, C., & Kim, J., (1998). Supporting the transition from school to adult life. In F. Rusch & J. Chadsey, *Beyond high school: Transition from school to work* (pp. 367–380). Belmont, CA: Wadsworth Press.

Hulgin, K., Shoultz, B., Walker, P., & Drake, S. (1996). *Innovative practices in supported living: An overview of organizations, issues, and resource materials.* Syracuse, NY: Syracuse University, Center on Human Policy

Hulgin, K., Walker, P., Fisher, E., Handley, M., & Shoultz, B. (1995). *Housing for people with severe disabilities: A collection of resource materials.* Syracuse, NY: Syracuse University, Center on Human Policy.

Humes, C. W., & Brammer, G. (1985). LD career success after high school. *Academic Therapy, 21*(2), 171–177.

Individuals with Disabilities Education Act Amendments of 1997, 20 U.S.C. §1400 *et seq.*

Individuals with Disabilities Education Act Amendments of 1997, Pub. L. No. 105-17, 105th Cong., 1st sess.

Individuals with Disabilities Education Act of 1990, 20 U.S.C. §1400 et seq.

Individuals with Disabilities Education Act Regulations, 34 C.F.R. § 300.533 *et seq.* (1997).

Inge, K. J., & Shepherd, J. (1995). Assistive technology applications and strategies for school system personnel. In K. F. Flippo, K. J. Inge, & J. M. Barcus (Eds.), *Assistive technology: A resource for school, work, and community* (pp. 133–166). Baltimore, MD: Paul H. Brookes.

International Survey of Faculty Attitudes. (1994, June 9). *The Chronicle of Higher Education,* pp. A35–A38.

Iowa Department of Education. (1998). *School to adult life: Working together towards successful transition.* Des Moines, IA: Author.

Iowa Department of Education, Division of Early Childhood, Elementary, and Secondary Education. (1998). *Working together towards successful transition: School to adult life.* Des Moines, IA: Author.

Ippoliti, C., Peppey, B., & Depoy, E. (1994). Promoting self-determination for persons with developmental disabilities. *Disability & Society* (9), 453 B 460.

Ivey, A. (1986). *Developmental therapy: Theory into practice.* San Francisco: Jossey-Bass.

Jackson, N. F., Jackson, D. A., & Morroe, C. (1983). *Getting along with others: Teaching social effectiveness to children.* Champaign, IL: Research Press.

James, S. D., & Egel, A. L. (1986). A direct prompting strategy for increasing reciprocal interactions between handicapped and nonhandicapped siblings. *Journal of Applied Behavior Analysis, 19,*173–186.

Janesick, V. J. (1995). Our multicultural society. In E. L. Meyen & T. M. Skrtic (Eds.), *Special education and student disability, an introduction: Traditional, emerging, and alternative perspectives* (4th ed., pp. 713–728). Denver, CO: Love Publishing.

Jarrow, J. (1992). *Title by title: The ADA's impact on postsecondary education.* Columbus, OH: Association on Higher Education and Disability (AHEAD).

Job Accommodation Network. (1987). *The President's Committee on Employment of People with Disabilities' Job Accommodation Network Evaluation Report.* West Virginia University, Morgantown, WV: Author.

Job Accommodation Network. (1995). *Accommodation benefit/cost data summary.* West Virginia University, Morgantown, WV: Author.

Joe, J. R., & Malach, R. S. (1998). Families with Native American roots. In E. W. Lynch & M. H. Hanson (Eds.), *Developing cross-*

cultural competence: A guide for working with children and their families (2nd ed., pp. 127–164). Baltimore: Paul H. Brookes.

Johnson, D. & Guy, B. (1997). Implications of lessons learned from a state systems change initiative on transition for youth with disabilities. *Career Development for Exceptional Individuals, 20* (2), 191–200.

Johnson, D., Bruininks, R., & Thurlow, M. (1987). Meeting the challenge of transition service planning through improved interagency cooperation. *Exceptional Children, 53*(6), 522–530.

Johnson, D. R., McGrew, K. S., Bloomberg, L., Bruininks, R. H., & Lin, H. C. (1997). Results of a national follow-up study of young adults with severe disabilities. *Journal of Vocational Rehabilitation, 8,* 119–133.

Johnson, D. R., Sharpe, M., & Sinclair, M. F. (1997). *Report on the national survey of the implementation of the IDEA transition requirements.* Minneapolis: National Transition Network, Institute on Community Integration, University of Minnesota.

Johnson, D. W., & Johnson, R. T. (1986). Mainstreaming and cooperative learning strategies. *Exceptional Children, 52,* 553–561.

Johnson, D. W., Maruyama, G., Johnson, R. T., Nelson, D., & Skon, L. (1981). The effects of cooperative, competitive, and individualistic goal structures on achievement: A meta-analysis. *Psychological Bulletin, 89,* 47–62.

Johnson, J. & Rusch, F. (1993). Secondary special education and transition services: Identification and recommendations for future research and demonstration. *Career Development for Exceptional Individuals, 16*(1), 1–18.

Johnson, T. Z. (1985). *Belonging to the community.* Madison, WI: Options in Community Living.

Jones, R. T., Kazdin, A. E., & Haney, J. I. (1981). Social validation and training of emergency fire safety skills for potential injury prevention and life saving. *Journal of Applied Behavior Analysis, 14,* 249–260.

Jorgensen, C. M. (1998). Restructuring high school for all students: Taking inclusion to the next level. Baltimore: Paul H. Brookes.

June, J., & Kelley, Y. (1998). *Quality indicators handbook,* [Monograph]. Louisville, KY: Jefferson County Public Schools.

Katz, M. R. (1993). *Computer-assisted career decision making: The guide in the machine.* Hillsdale, NJ: Erlbaum.

Kauffman, J. M. (1987). Research in special education: A commentary. *Remedial and Special Education, 8*(6), 57–62.

Kauffman, J. M. (1997). *Characteristics of emotional and behavioral disorders of children and youth* (6th ed.). Upper Saddle River, NJ: Merrill/Prentice Hall.

Kauffman, J. M. (1998). Are we all postmodernists now? *Behavioral Disorders, 23,* 149–152.

Kauffman, J. M. (1999). The role of science in behavioral disorders. *Behavioral Disorders, 24,* 265–272.

Kauffman, J. M., Hallahan, D. P., Mostert, M. P., Trent, S. C., & Nuttycombe, D. G. (1993). *Managing classroom behavior: A reflective case-based approach.* Boston: Allyn & Bacon.

Kazdin, A. E. (1989). *Behavior modification in applied settings* (4th ed.). Pacific Grove, CA: Brookes/Cole Publishing.

Kearns, J. & Dryer, L. (1997) *Teaching all students in Kentucky schools* (TASKS). Lexington, KY: University of Kentucky, Human Development Institute.

Keitel, M. A., Kopala, M., & Adamson, W. S. (1996). Ethical issues in multicultural assessment. In L. A. Suzuki, P. J. Meller, & J. G. Ponterotto (Eds.), *Handbook of multicultural assessment* (pp. 29–48). San Francisco: Jossey-Bass.

Kelly, W. J., Salzberg, C. L., Levy, S. M., Warrenfeltz, R. B., Adams, T. W., Crouse, T. R., & Beegle, G. P. (1983). The effects of role-playing and self-monitoring on the generalization of vocational skills by behaviorally disordered adolescents. *Behavioral Disorders, 9,* 27–35.

Kentucky Council on Postsecondary Education. (1998). *Futures: Your guide to life after high school* Frankfort, KY: The Kentucky Council on Postsecondary Education.

Kern, L., Childs, K. E., Dunlap, G., Clarke, S., & Falk, G. D. (1994). Using assessment-based curricular intervention to improve the classroom behavior of a student with emotional and behavioral challenges. *Journal of Applied Behavior Analysis, 27,* 7–19.

Kerr, M. M., & Nelson, C. M. (1998). *Strategies for managing behavior in the classroom* (3rd ed.). Upper Saddle, NJ: Merrill/Prentice Hall.

Kezar, A. (1997a). At the fork in the path: Some guidance from the research. *The ERIC review: The path to college, 5*(3), 26–29.

Kezar, A. (1997b). How colleges are changing. *The ERIC review: The path to college, 5*(3), 29–32.

Kiburz, C. S., Miller, S. R., & Morrow, L. W. (1985). Structured learning using self-monitoring to promote maintenance and generalization of social skills across settings for a behaviorally disordered adolescent. *Behavior Disorders, 11,* 47–55.

Kim, V., & Choi, S. H. (1994). Individualism, collectivism, and child development. In P. M. Greenfield & R. R. Cocking (Eds.), *Cross-cultural roots of minority child development* (pp. 226–257). Hillsdale, NJ: Erlbaum.

King-Sears, M. E. (1997). Best academic practices for inclusive classrooms. *Focus on Exceptional Children, 29,* 1–22.

Kinnison, L. R., Jr. (1987). Do parents know best? *The Journal for Vocational Special Needs Education, 10*(1), 13–16.

Klein, J. (1992). Get me the hell out of here: Supporting people with disabilities to live in their own homes. In J. Nisbet (Ed.), *Natural supports in school, at work, and in the community for people with severe disabilities* (pp. 277–339). Baltimore: Paul H. Brookes.

Kleinert, H. L., Kearns, F. K., & Kennedy, S. (1997). Accountability for all students: Kentucky's alternate portfolio assessment for students with moderate and severe cognitive disabilities. *Journal of Association for Persons with Severe Disabilities, 22*(2), 88–101.

Knoll, J. (1992). Being a family: The experience of raising a child with a disability or chronic illness. In V. J. Bradley,

J. Knoll, & J. M. Agosta (Eds.), *Emerging issues in family supports* (American Association on Mental Retardation Monograph Series No 18, pp. 9–56). Washington, DC: American Association on Mental Retardation.

Knoll, J. & Ford, A. (1987) Beyond caregiving: A reconceptualization of the role of the residential service provider. In S. J. Taylor, D. Biklen, & J. A. Knoll (Eds.), *Community integration for people with severe disabilities* (pp. 129–146). New York: Teachers' College Press.

Knopp, L., & Otuya, E. (1995). Who is teaching America's school children? *Research Briefs, 6,* 1–13.

Knowlton, H., Turnbull, D. R., Backus, L., & Turnbull, H. R. (1988). Letting go: Consent and the yes but . . . "problem in transition." In B. L. Ludlow, A. P. Turnbull, & R. Luckasson (Eds.), *Transitions to adult life for people with mental retardation* (pp. 45–66). Baltimore: Paul H. Brookes.

Knox, W., Lindsay, P., & Kolb, N. (1993). *Does college make a difference? Long-term changes in activities and attitudes.* Westport, CT: Greenwood Press.

Koch, L., & Johnston-Rodriguez, S. (1997). The career portfolio: A vocational rehabilitation tool for assessment, planning, and placement. *Journal of Job Placement, 13*(1), 19–22.

Koch, L. C., & Rumrill, P. D. (1998a). Interpersonal communication skills for case managers. *Healthcare and rehabilitation managers' desk reference.* Lake Zurich, IL: Vocational Consultants Press.

Koch, L. C., & Rumrill, P. D. (1998b). The working alliance: An interdisciplinary case management strategy for health professionals. *Work, 10,* 55–62.

Kochany, L., & Keller, J. (1981). An analysis and evaluation of the failures of severely disabled individuals in competitive employment. In P. Wehman (Ed.), *Competitive employment: New horizons for severely disabled individuals* (pp. 181–198). Baltimore: Paul H. Brookes.

Kochar, C. A., & Deschamps, A. B. (1992). Policy crossroads in preserving the right of passage to independence for learners with special needs: Implications of current change in national vocational and special education policies. *Journal for Vocational Special Needs Education, 14*(2–3), 9–19.

Kochar, C. A., & West, L. L. (1995). Future directions for federal legislation affecting transition services for individuals with special needs. *Journal for Vocational Special Needs Education, 17*(3), 85–93.

Kohler, P. D. (1993). Best practices in transition: Substantiated or implied? *Career Development for Exceptional Individuals, 16,* 107–121.

Kohler, P. D. (1996). Preparing youths with disabilities for future challenges: A taxonomy for transition planning. In P. D. Kohler (Ed.), *Taxonomy for transition planning: Linking research and practice* (pp. 1–62). Champaign, IL: Transition Research Institute at Illinois, University of Illinois at Urbana-Champaign [Monograph].

Kohler, P. D. (1998). Implementing a transition perspective of education: A comprehensive approach to planning

and delivering secondary education and transition services. In F. R. Rusch & J. G. Chadsey (Eds.), *Beyond high school: Transition from school to work* (pp. 179–205). New York: Wadsworth Publishing.

Kohler, P. D., DeStefano, L., Wermuth, T., Grayson, T., & McGinty, S. (1994). An analysis of exemplary transition programs: How and why are they selected? *Career Development for Exceptional Individuals, 17*(2), 187–202.

Kokaska, C., & Brolin, D. E. (1985). *Career education for handicapped individuals* (2nd ed.). Columbus, OH: Charles E. Merrill Publishing.

Kolstoe, O. P., & Frey, R. M. (1965). *A high school work study program for mentally subnormal students.* Carbondale, IL: Southern Illinois University Press.

Kortering, L. J., & Edgar, E. B. (1988). Vocational rehabilitation and special education: A need for cooperation. *Rehabilitation Counseling Bulletin, 3*(3), 178–184.

Kounin, J. S. (1970). *Discipline and group management in classrooms.* New York: Holt, Rinehart and Winston.

Kounin, J. S. (1983). *Classrooms: Individuals or behavior settings?* [Monographs] in Teaching and Learning. (ERIC Document # ED 240 070).

Kranstover, L. L., Thurlow, M. L., & Bruininks, R. H. (1989). Special education graduates versus non-graduates: A longitudinal study of outcomes. *Career Development for Exceptional Individuals, 12,* 153–166.

Kravets, M., & Wax, I. F. (Eds.). (1995). *The K & W guide to colleges for the learning disabled* (3rd ed.). Cambridge, MA: Educators Publishing Service.

Kregel, J., Wehman, P., Seyfarth, J., & Marshall, K. (1986). Community integration of young adults with mental retardation: Transition from school to adulthood. *Education and Training of the Mentally Retarded, 21,* 35–42.

Krom, D. M. & Prater, M. A. (1993). IEP goals for intermediate-aged students with mild mental retardation. *Career Development for Exceptional Individuals, 16*(1), 87–95.

Krouse, J., Gerber, M. M., & Kauffman. J. M. (1981). Peer tutoring: Procedures, promises, and unresolved issues. *Exceptional Education Quarterly, 1*(4), 107–115.

Krumboltz, J. (1988). *The Career Beliefs Inventory.* Palo Alto, CA: Consulting Psychologists Press.

LaGreca, A. M., & Santogrossi, A. A. (1980). Social skills training with elementary school students. *Journal of Consulting and Clinical Psychology, 48,* 220–227.

LaGreca, A. M., Stone, W. L., & Bell, C. R. (1982a). *Vocational problem behavior inventory.* Miami, FL: Department of Psychology, University of Miami, Coral Gables.

LaGreca, A. M., Stone, W. L., & Bell, C. R. (1982b). Assessing the problematic interpersonal skills of mentally retarded workers in a vocational setting. *Applied Research in Mental Retardation, 3,* 37–53.

Lahm, E., & Morrissette, S. (1994) *Zap'em with assistive technology.* Paper presented at the annual meeting of the Council for Exceptional Children, April, 1994, Denver, CO.

Lahm, E. A. (Ed.). (1989). *Technology with low incidence populations: Promoting access to education and learning*. Reston, VA: Council for Exceptional Children.

Lakin, C., & Burwell, B. (1995) Medicaid community supported living arrangements: Five-year "pilot projects" with lasting effects. IMPACT 8(4), 4–5, 27.

Lakin, K., Hill, B., White, C., & Write, E. (1988). *Longitudinal change and interstate variability in the size of residential facilities for persons with mental retardation*. Minneapolis, MN: Center on Residential and Community Services, University of Minnesota.

Langone, J. (2000). Technology for individuals with severe and physical disabilities. In J.D. Lindsey (Ed.), *Technology and exceptional individuals* (3rd ed.) (pp. 327–350). Austin TX: PRO ED.

LaPlante, M. P., Kennedy, J., Kaye, S. H., & Wenger, B. L. (1997). Disability and employment. *Disability statistics abstract*, 11, San Francisco: Disability Statistics Rehabilitation Research and Training Center, University of California.

Lareau, A. (1989). *Home advantage: Social class and parental intervention in elementary education*. London: The Falmer Press.

Larrivee, B. (1986). Effective teaching for mainstreamed students is effective teaching for all students. *Teacher Education and Special Education*, 9, 173–179.

Larson, C. (1981). *State of Iowa dissemination model for MD and LD students*. Fort Dodge: IA: Iowa Central Community College.

Lawn, B., & Meyerson, A. T. (1995). A modern perspective on psychiatry in rehabilitation. In R. W. Flexer and P. L. Solomon (Eds.), *Psychiatric rehabilitation in practice*. (pp. 31–44). Boston, MA: Andover Publishers.

Lazzaro, J. J. (1996). Toward software both seen and heard. *Technology Review*, 99(7), 66–67.

Leake, D., & Stodden, B. (1994). Getting to the core of transition: A re-assessment of old wine in new bottles. *Career Development for Exceptional Individuals*, 17(1), 65–76.

LeConte, P. (1986). Vocational assessment of special needs learners: A vocational education perspective. Paper presented at Annual meeting of American Vocational Association in Atlanta, GA.

LeConte, P. J., & Kochhar, C. A. (1983). Agents for success in job training partnerships. *Journal for Vocational Special Needs Education*, 6(1), 24–28.

LeConte, P. J., & Neubert, D. (1987). Vocational education for special needs students: Linking vocational assessment and support. *Diagnostique*, 12, 156–167.

Lee, J. (1995). *A survey of regional special education assistive technology practices in North Dakota*. Cavalier, ND: Interagency Project for Assistive Technology.

Lehmann, J. P., Deniston, T., & Grebenc, R. (1989). Counseling parents to facilitate transition: The difference parents make. *The Journal for Vocational Special Needs Education*, 11(3), 15–18.

Leventhal, J. D. (1996). Assistive devices for people who are blind or have visual impairments. In J. C. Galvin & M. J. Scherer (Eds.), *Evaluating, selecting, and using appropriate assistive technology* (pp. 125–143). Gaithersburg, MD: Aspen Publishers, Inc.

Lewis, R. D. (1997). *When cultures collide: Managing successfully across cultures*. London: Nicholas Brealey Publishing.

Lewis, W. C. (1972). *Why people change*. New York: Holt, Rinehart and Winston.

Lindstrom, L., Benz, M., & Johnson, M. (1996). Developing job clubs for students in transition. *Teaching Exceptional Children*, 29(2), 18–21.

Linn, R., & DeStefano, L. (1986). *Review of student assessment instruments and practices in use in the secondary/transition project*. Champaign, IL: Secondary Transition Intervention Effectiveness Institute, University of Illinois at Urbana-Champaign. (ERIC Document Reproduction Service No. ED 279 123).

Lippert, T. (1987). *The case management team: Building community connections*. St. Paul, MN: Metropolitan Council.

Litvak, S., Zukas, H., & Heumann, J. (1987). *Attending to America: Personal assistance for independent living*. Berkeley, CA: World Institute on Disability.

Lloyd, J. W., & Landrum, T. J. (1990). Self-recording of attending to task: Treatment components and generalization of effects. In T. E. Scruggs & B. Y. Wong (Eds.), *Intervention research in learning disabilities* (pp. 235–262). New York: Springer-Verlag.

Lloyd, J. W., Landrum, T. J., & Hallahan, D. P. (1991). Self-monitoring applications for classroom intervention. In G. Stoner, M. R. Shinn, & H. M. Walker (Eds.), *Interventions for achievement and behavior problems*. Harrisonburg, VA: NASP.

Loewen, G., & Iaquinto, M. (1990). Rebuilding a career plan: Issues for head injured students. In J. J. Vander Putten (Ed.), *Reaching new heights: Proceedings of the 1989 AHSSPPE Conference*. Columbus, OH: Association on Handicapped Student Service Programs in Postsecondary Education.

Lofquist, L., & Dawis, R. (1991). *Essentials of person-environment correspondence counseling*. Minneapolis, MN: University of Minnesota Press.

Lofquist, L. H., & Dawis, R. V. (1969). *Adjustment to work: A psychological view of man's problems in a work-oriented society*. New York: Appleton-Century-Crofts, Education Division, Meredith Corporation.

Lombard, R. C., Hazelkorn, M. N., & Miller, R. J. (1995). Special populations and tech prep. A national study of state policy and practice. *Career Development for Exceptional Individuals*, 18(2), 145–156.

Lombard, R. C., Hazelkorn, M. N., & Neubert, D. A. (1992). A survey of accessibility to secondary vocational education programs and transition services for students with disabilities in Wisconsin. *Career Development for Exceptional Individuals*, 15(2), 179–188.

Lovejoy, M. C., & Routh, D. K. (1988). Behavior disordered children's social skills: Increased by training, but not sustained or reciprocated. *Child and Family Behavior Therapy*, 10, 15–27.

Lubin, R., Jacobson, J. W., & Kiely, M. (1982). Projected impact of the functional definition of developmental disabilities: The categorically disabled population and service eligibility. *American Journal of Mental Deficiency*, 87, 73–79.

Luckasson, R., Coulter, D., Pollaway, E., Reiss, S., Schalock, R., Snell, M., Spitalnik, D., & Stark, J. (1992). *Mental retardation: Definition, classification, and systems of supports* (9th ed.), Washington, DC: American Association on Mental Retardation.

Luckasson, R., & Spitalnik, D. (1994). Political and programmatic shifts of the 1992 AAMR definition of mental retardation. In V. J. Bradley, J. W. Ashbaugh, & B. C. Blaney (Eds.), *Creating individual supports for people with developmental disabilities: A mandate for change at many levels.* (pp. 81–95). Baltimore: Paul H. Brookes.

Luft, P. (1995, April). *Addressing minority overrepresentation in special education: Cultural barriers to effective collaboration.* Presentation at the annual convention of the Council for Exceptional Children, Indianapolis, IN.

Luft, P. (1999). Assessment and collaboration: Key elements in comprehensive and cohesive transition planning. *Work*, 13, 31–41.

Luft, P., & Koch, L. (1998). Transition of adolescents with chronic illness: Overlooked needs and rehabilitation considerations. *Journal of Vocational Rehabilitation*, 10, 205–217.

Luft, P., Rumrill, P., & Snyder-Marks, J. L. (in press). Transition strategies for youths with sensory impairments. *Journal of Job Placement*.

Lusthaus, C. S., Lusthaus, E. W., & Gibbs, H. (1981). Parents' role in the decision process. *Exceptional Children*, 48(3), 256–257.

Lynch, E. C., & Beare, P. L. (1990). The quality of IEP objectives and their relevance to instruction for students with mental retardation and behavioral disorders. *Remedial and Special Education*, 11(2), 48–55.

Lynch, E. W. (1998a). Conceptual framework: From culture shock to cultural learning. In E. W. Lynch & M. H. Hanson (Eds.), *Developing cross-cultural competence: A guide for working with children and their families* (2nd ed., pp. 23–46). Baltimore: Paul H. Brookes.

Lynch, E. W. (1998b). Developing cross-cultural competence. In E. W. Lynch & M. H. Hanson (Eds.), *Developing cross-cultural competence: A guide for working with children and their families* (2nd ed., pp. 47–90). Baltimore: Paul H. Brookes.

Lynch, E. W., & Stein, R. C. (1982). Perspectives on parent participation in special education. *Exceptional Education Quarterly*, 3, 56–63.

Lynch, E. W., & Stein, R. C. (1987). Parent participation by ethnicity: A comparison of Hispanic, Black, and Anglo families. *Exceptional Children*, 54, 105–111.

Lynch, R. T., & Gussel, L. (1996). Disclosure and self-advocacy regarding disability-related needs: Strategies to maximize integration in postsecondary education. *Journal of Counseling & Development*, 74, 352–357.

Maag, J. W. (1989). Assessment in social skills training: Methodological and conceptual issues for research and practice. *Remedial and Special Education*, 10(4), 6–17.

Maag, J. W., Reid, R., & DiGangi, S. A. (1993). Differential effects of self-monitoring attention, accuracy, and productivity. *Journal of Applied Behavior Analysis*, 26, 329–344.

Mackelsprang, R. W., & Salsgiver, R. O. (1996). People with disabilities and social work: Historical and contemporary issues. *Social Work*, 41(1), 7–14.

Maddy-Bernstein, C. (1997). Vocational preparation for students with disabilities. In H. M. Wallace, R. F. Bieh, J. C. MacQueen, & J. A. Blackman (Eds.), *Mosby's resource guide to children with disabilities and chronic illness* (pp. 381–392). St. Louis, MO: Mosby-Year Book.

Malian, I. M., & Love, L. L. (1998). Leaving high school: An ongoing transition study. *Teaching Exceptional Children*, 30(1), 4–10.

Malone, B. L. (1996). Job clubs: Providing an empathetic ear, moral support, and a built-in EEO procedure. *Equal Employment Opportunity Career Journal*, 31 October, Vol. 30 (pp. 20–32).

Mangrum, C. T., & Strichart, S. S. (Eds.). (1997). *Peterson's colleges with programs for students with learning disabilities or attention deficit disorders* (5th ed.). Princeton, NJ: Peterson's Guides.

Mank, D., Cioffi, A. & Yovanoff, P. (1997). An analysis of the typicalness of supported employment jobs, natural supports, and wage and integration outcomes. *Mental Retardation*, 35(3), 185–197.

Mank, D., Oorthuys, J., Rhodes, L., Sandow, D., & Weyer, T. (1992). Accommodating workers with mental disabilities. *Training and Development Journal*, 46, 49–52.

Marder, C. (1992). *How well are youth with disabilities really doing? A comparison of youth with disabilities and youth in general.* Menlo Park, CA: SRI International.

Markel, G., & Greenbaum, J. (1981). Assertiveness training for parents of disabled children. *The Exceptional Parent*, 11(4), 17–22.

Markowitz, J. (1996, May). *Strategies that address the disproportionate number of students from racial/ethnic minority groups receiving special education services: Case studies of selected states and school districts, final report.* Paper presented at the National Association of State Directors of Special Education, Alexandria, VA.

Martin, J. E., & Huber Marshall, L. H. (1995). ChoiceMaker: A comprehensive self-determination transition program. *Intervention in School and Clinic*, 30(3), 147–156.

Martin, J. E., & Huber Marshall, L. H. (1996a). ChoiceMaker: Infusing self-determination instruction into the IEP and transition process. In D. J. Sands & M. L. Wehmeyer (Eds.), *Self-determination across the life span* (pp. 215–236). Baltimore: Paul H. Brookes.

Martin, J. E., & Huber Marshall, L. H. (1996b). *ChoiceMaker self-determination transition assessment.* Longmont, CO: Sopris West, Inc.

Martin, J. E., Huber-Marshall, L., Maxson, L. L., & Jerman, P. (1996). *Self-directed.* IEP. Longmont, CO: Sopris West.

Martin, J. E., Huber Marshall, L., & Sale, R. P. (1999). IEP *Team Tells All!* Manuscript submitted for publication.

Martin, J. E., Huber Marshall, L., Wray, D., O'Brien, J., & Snyder, L. (1999). *Choose and Take Action.* Software and lesson package submitted for publication.

Martin, J. E., Hughes, W., Huber Marshall, L. H., Jerman, P., & Maxson, L. (1999). *Choosing education goals.* Longmont, CO: Sopris West.

Martin, J. E., Marshall, L. H., & Maxson, L. L. (1993). Transition policy: Infusing self-determination and self-advocacy into transition programs. *Career Development for Exceptional Individuals,* 16(1), 53–61.

Martin, J. E., Mithaug, D. E., Oliphint, J., & Husch, J. V. (in press). *ChoiceMaker employment: A self-determination transition and supported employment handbook.* Baltimore: Paul H. Brookes.

Masino, L. L., & Hodapp, R. M. (1996). Parental educational expectations for adolescents with disabilities. *Exceptional Children,* 62(6), 515–524.

Maslow, A. H. (1970). Motivation and personality (2nd ed.). New York: Harper & Row.

Massenzio, S. (1983). Legal resource networks for parents of individuals with special needs. *Exceptional Children,* 50(3), 273–275.

Mastropieri, M. A., & Scruggs, T. E. (1987). *Effective instruction for special education.* Boston: Little, Brown.

Mastropieri, M. A., & Scruggs, T. E. (1994). *Effective instruction for special education* (2nd ed.). Austin, TX: PRO-ED.

Mattessich, B. W., & Monsey, B. R. (1992). *Collaboration: What makes it work.* St. Paul, MN: Amherst H. Wilder Foundation Publishing Center.

McCord, W. (1983). The outcomes of normalization: strengthened bonds between handicapped persons and their communities. *Education and Training of the Mentally Retarded,* 18(3), 153–157.

McDonald, G., & Oxford, M. (n.d.). *History of independent living.* Dayton, OH: Access Center for Independent Living.

McDonnell, J., Ferguson, B., & Mathot-Buckner, C. (1992). Transition from school to work for students with severe disabilities: The Utah community employment placement project. In F. R. Rusch, L. DeStefano, J. Chadsey-Rusch, L. A. Phelps, & E. Szymanski (Eds.), *Transition from school to adult life: Models, linkages, and policy* (pp. 33–50). Sycamore, IL: Sycamore Publishing.

McDonnell, J., Hardman, M. L., & Hightower, J. (1989). Employment preparation for high school students with severe handicaps. *Mental Retardation,* 27(6), 396–405.

McDonnell, J., Wilcox, B., & Boles, S. M. (1986). Do we know enough to plan for transition? A national survey of state agencies responsible for services to persons with severe handicaps. *Journal of The Association for Persons with Severe Handicaps,* 11(1), 53–60.

McDonnell, J. J., Wilcox, B., Boles, S. M., Bellamy, G. T. (1985). Issues in transition from school to adult services: A survey of parents of secondary students with severe handi-caps. *The Journal of the Association for Persons with Severe Handicaps,* 10(1), 61–65.

McDonnell, J., Wilcox, B., & Hardman, M. L. (1991). *Secondary programs for students with developmental disabilities.* Boston: Allyn & Bacon.

McFall, R. (1982). A review and reformulation of the concept of social skills. *Behavioral Assessment,* 4, 1–33.

McGahee-Kovac, M. (1995). *A student's guide to the IEP.* Washington, DC: National Information Center for Children and Youth with Disabilities

McGinnis, E., Goldstein, A. P., Sprafkin, R. P., & Gershaw, N. J. (1984). *Skillstreaming the elementary school child.* Champaign, IL: Research Press.

McKnight, J. (1987). Regenerating community. *Social Policy,* Winter, 54–58.

McLaughlin, T. F. (1983). Effects of self-recording for on-task and academic responding: A long term analysis. *Journal of Special Education Technology,* 6(3), 5–12.

McMahan, R. K., & Baer, R. (1999). *Survey on transition policy compliance and best practices: Final report.* Kent, OH: Transition Center, Kent State University.

McNair, J., & Rusch, F. R. (1987). Parent survey: Identification and validation of transition issues. *Interchange,* 7(4), Urbana-Champaign, IL: University of Illinois, Transition Institute.

McNair, J., & Rusch, F. R. (1991). Parent involvement in transition programs. *Mental Retardation,* 29(2), 93–101.

McPhatter, A. R. (1997). Cultural competence in child welfare: What is it? How do we achieve it? What happens without it? *Child Welfare,* 50, 85–106.

McPherson, A., & Brackett, J. D. (1994). Postsecondary school transition issues affecting the vocational rehabilitation of young adults with LD. *The Journal of Vocational Rehabilitation,* 4(2), 131–138.

Meara, N. M., & Patton, M. J. (1994). Contribution of the working alliance in the practice of career counseling. *Career Development Quarterly,* 43, 161–178.

Meers, G. C. (1987). An introduction to vocational special needs education. In G. D. Meers (Ed.), *Handbook of vocational special needs education* (2nd ed., pp. 3–28). Rockville, MD: Aspen Publishers.

Meers, G. D. (1992). Getting ready for the next century: vocational preparation of students with disabilities. *Teaching Exceptional Children,* 24, 36–39.

Mehan, J., Hertweck, A., & Meihls, J. L. (1986). *Handicapping the handicapped: Decision-making in students' educational careers.* Palo Alto, CA: Stanford University.

Menchetti, B. M., & Piland, V. C. (1998). A person-centered approach to vocational evaluation and career planning. In F. R. Rusch & J. Chadsey (Eds.), *Beyond high school: Transition from school to work.* New York: Wadsworth Publishing.

Menchetti, B. M., Rusch, F. R., & Owens, D. M. (1983). Vocational training. In J. Matson & S. Breuing (Eds.), *Assessing the mentally retarded* (pp. 247–285). New York: Grune & Stratton.

Mercer, C. D., & Mercer, A. R. (1998). *Teaching students with learning problems* (5th ed.). Upper Saddle River, NJ: Merrill/Prentice Hall.

Merrill, K. W. (1994). *Assessment of behavioral, social, and emotional problems.* New York: Longman.

Mertz, M. K. (1997). After inclusion: Next S.T.E.P.s for high-school graduates. *Exceptional Parent, 27*(9), 44–49.

Miller, S. M., & Roby, P. (1970). Poverty: Changing social stratification. In P. Townsend (Ed.), *The concept of poverty: Working papers on methods of investigation and life-styles of the poor in different countries* (pp. 124–145). New York: American Elsevier Publishing.

Miller, T. (Ed.). (1997). *The book of professional standards for higher education.* Washington, DC: Council for the Advancement of Standards in Higher Education (CAS).

Minnesota Governor's Planning Council on Developmental Disabilities. (1987). *A new way of thinking.* St. Paul, MN: Author.

Mitchell, K. (1997). Making the grade: Help and hope for the first-generation college student. *The ERIC Review: The Path to College, 5*(3), 13–15.

Mitchell, L. K., & Krumboltz, J. D. (1996). Krumboltz's learning theory of career choice and counseling. In D. Brown, L. Brooks, & Associates (Eds.), *Career choice and development* (3rd ed., pp. 233–280). San Francisco: Jossey-Bass.

Mithaug, D. E. (1993). *Self-regulation theory: How optimal adjustment maximizes gain.* Westport, CT: Praeger.

Mithaug, D. E., Horiuchi, C. N., & Fanning, P. N. (1985). A report on the Colorado statewide follow-up survey of special education students. *Exceptional Children, 51,* 397–404.

Mithaug, D. E., & Mar, D. K. (1980). The relation between choosing and working prevocational tasks in two severely retarded young adults. *Journal of Applied Behavior Analysis* (13), 177B–182.

Mithaug, D. E., Wehmeyer, M. L., Agran, M., Martin, J. E., & Palmer, S. (1998). The self-determined learning model of instruction. In M. L. Wehmeyer & D. J. Sands (Eds.), *Making it happen: Student involvement in education planning, decision making, and instruction* (pp. 299–328). Baltimore: Paul H. Brookes.

Mokuau, N., & Tauili'ili, P. (1998). Families with native Hawaiian and Samoan roots. In E. W. Lynch & M. H. Hanson (Eds.), *Developing cross-cultural competence: A guide for working with children and their families* (2nd ed., pp. 409–440). Baltimore: Paul H. Brookes.

Monette, G. C. (1997). Tribal colleges: Tradition, heritage, and community. *The ERIC Review: The Path to College, 5*(3), 24–25.

Moon, M. S., Hart, D., Komissar, C., & Friedlander, R. (1995). Making sports and recreation activities accessible. In K. F. Flippo, K. J. Inge, & J. M. Barcus (Eds.), *Assistive technology: A resource for school, work, and community* (pp. 187–197). Baltimore, MD: Paul H. Brookes Publishing Co

Moores, D. (1996). *Educating the deaf: Psychology, principles, and practices* (4th ed.). Boston: Houghton Mifflin.

Morgan, D. P., & Jemson, W. R. (1988). *Teaching behaviorally disordered students: Preferred practices.* Columbus, OH: Merrill.

Morgan, R. L., Moore, S. C., McSweyn, C. A., & Salzberg, C. L. (1992). Transition from school to work: Views of secondary special educators. *Education and Training in Mental Retardation, 27*(4), 315–323.

Morningstar, M. E., Turnbull, A. P., & Turnbull, H. R. (1996). What do students with disabilities tell us about the importance of family involvement in the transition from school to adult life? *Exceptional Children, 62,* 249–260.

Mount, B. (1989). *Making futures happen: A manual for facilitators of personal futures planning.* St. Paul, MN: Governor's Council on Developmental Disabilities.

Mount, B. (1992). *Personal futures planning: Promises and precautions.* New York, NY: Graphic Futures.

Mount, B. (1994). Benefits and limitations of personal futures planning. In J. Bradley, J. W. Ashbaugh, & B. C. Blaney (Eds.), *Creating individual supports for people with developmental disabilities* (pp. 97–98). Baltimore: Paul H. Brookes.

Mount, B., Beeman, P., & Ducharme, G. (1988). What are we learning about circles of support? Manchester, CT: Communitas.

Mount, B., & Zwernick. (1988). *It's never too early, it's never too late: A booklet about personal futures planning.* St. Paul, MN: Governor's Planning Council on Developmental Disabilities. Publication No. 421, 88–109.

Munk, D. D., & Repp, A. C. (1994). The relationship between instructional variables and problem behavior: A review. *Exceptional Children, 60,* 390–401.

Myers, L. B., & McCauley M. H. (1985). *Manual: A guide to the development and use of the Myers-Briggs type indicator.* Palo Alto, CA: Consulting Psychologists Press.

National Association of Private Residential Resources (NAPRR). (1991). *Supported living.* Annandale, VA: Author.

National Association of Private Residential Resources (NAPRR), (1992) *Supported living,* Vol. II. Annandale, VA: Author.

National Association of Protection and Advocacy Systems. (1999, October). *Questions and answers about the Olmstead v. L. C. and E. W. decision.* Washington, DC: Author.

National Center for Education Statistics. (1993). *Education of the Handicapped Act Amendment of 1990 (PL 101-476): Summary of major changes in parts A through H of the Act.* Washington, DC: U.S. Department of Education.

National Center for Education Statistics. (1999a). *Students with disabilities in postsecondary education: A profile of preparation, participation, and outcomes.* NCES 1999-187. Washington, DC: U.S. Department of Education.

National Center for Education Statistics. (1999b). *An institutional perspective on students with disabilities in postsecondary education.* NCES 1999-046. Washington, DC: U.S. Department of Education.

National Information Center for Children and Youth with Disabilities. (1993). *Transition services in the IEP: Transition summary,* 3(1), Washington, DC: Office of Special

Education Programs of the U.S. Department of Education.

Neel, R. S., & Billingsley, F. F. (1989). Impact: A functional curriculum handbook for students with moderate to severe disabilities. Baltimore: Paul H. Brookes.

Neubert, D. (1985). Use of vocational evaluation recommendations in selected public school settings. Career Development for Exceptional Individuals, 9, 98–105.

Neubert, D. A. (1997). Time to grow: The history and future of preparing youth for adult roles in society. Teaching Exceptional Children, 29(5), 5–17.

Neubert, D. A., & Repetto, J. B. (1992). Serving individuals with special needs through professional development: Meeting the intent of the Act. Journal for Vocational Special Needs Education, 2–3(14), 37–41.

Newman, L., & Cameto, R. (1993). What makes a difference? Factors related to postsecondary school attendance for young people with disabilities. Paper presented at the Division J: Postsecondary Education of the American Educational Research Association annual meeting, Atlanta, GA.

NICHCY News Digest. (1993). 2(2), 1–7. Washington, DC: The National Information Center for Children and Youth with Disabilities. Author.

NICHCY Transition Summary. (1990, December). Vocational assessment: A guide for parents and professionals. Washington DC: The National Information Center for Children and Youth with Disabilities. Author.

NICHCY. (1988). Individualized education programs. (2–17), Washington DC: The National Information Center for Children and Youth with Disabilities. Author.

NICHCY. (1993, March). Transition services defined by IDEA. 3(1), 2–19. Washington DC: The National Information Center for Children and Youth with Disabilities. Author.

Ninness, H. A. C., Fuerst, J., Rutherford, R. D., & Glenn, S. S. (1991). Effects of self-management training and reinforcement on the transfer of improved conduct in the absence of supervision. Journal of Applied Behavior Analysis, 24, 499–508.

Nirje, B. (1972). The right to self-determination. In W. Wolfensberger (Ed.). The principle of normalization in human services (pp. 176–193). Toronto: National Institute on Mental Retardation.

Nisbet, J., Covert, S., & Schuh, M. (1992). Family involvement in the transition from school to adult life. In F. R. Rusch, L. DeStefano, J. Chadsey-Rusch, L. A. Phelps, & E. Szymanski (Eds.), Transition from school to adult life: Models, linkages, and policy (pp. 407–424). Sycamore, IL: Sycamore Publishing.

Nisbet, J., & Hagner, D. (1988). Natural supports in the workplace: A reexamination of supported employment. Journal of the Association for Persons with Severe Handicaps, 13, 260–267.

Norman, M. E., & Bourexis, P. S. (1995). Including students with disabilities in school-to-work opportunities. Washington, DC: Council of Chief State School Officers.

Nosek, M. A. (1990). Personal assistance: Key to employability of persons with physical disabilities. Journal of Applied Rehabilitation Counseling, 21(4), 3–8.

Obiakor, F. E., & Utley, C. A. (1996). Rethinking preservice and inservice training programs for teachers in the learning disabilities field: Workable multicultural models. (ERIC Document Reproduction Service No. ED 397 594).

O'Brien, C., & O'Brien, J. (1992). Checklist for evaluating personal assistance services (PAS) policies and programs. Livonia, GA: Responsive Systems Associates.

O'Brien, J. (1987). A guide to life-style planning: Using the activities catalogue to integrate services and natural support system. In G. T. Bellamy & B. Wilcox (Eds.), A comprehensive guide to the activities catalogue: An alternative curriculum for youth and adults with severe disabilities (pp. 175–190). Baltimore: Paul H. Brookes.

O'Brien, J. (1993). Supported living: What's the difference? Livonia, GA: Responsive Systems Associates.

O'Brien, J., & Lovett, H. (1992). Finding a way toward everyday lives: The contribution of person-centered planning. Harrisburg, PA: Pennsylvania Office of Mental Retardation.

O'Brien, J., & O'Brien, C. (1991). More than just a new address: Images of organizations for supported living agencies Syracuse, NY: Center on Human Policy, Syracuse University.

O'Brien, J., & O'Brien, C. (1992). Remembering the soul of our work: Stories by staff of Options in Community Living Madison, Wisconsin. Madison, WI: Options in Community Living.

O'Brien, J., O'Brien, L., & Mount, B. (1997). Person-centered planning has arrived . . . or has it? Mental Retardation, 35(6), 480–484.

O'Connell, M. (1988). Community building in Logan Square: How a community grew stronger with the contribution of people with disabilities. Evanston, IL: Center for Urban Affairs and Policy Research, Northwestern University.

Odens, S., & Asher, S. R. (1977). Coaching children in social skills for friendship making. Child Development, 48, 495–506.

Office of Special Education Programs, U. S. Department of Education. (1997). The Individuals with Disabilities Education Act Amendments of 1997: Curriculum. Washington, DC.

Ogusthorpe, M. R. (1978). The career conversation: Training parents to help their children make career decisions. (ERIC Document Reproduction Service No. ED 159 584).

Ohio Department of Education, Division of Special Education. (1999). District self-study for the 1999–2000 school improvement review. Worthington, OH: Author.

Ohio Department of Education. (1990). Ohio speaks. Columbus, OH: Author.

Ohio Rehabilitation Services Commission (1997). Transition guidelines and best practices. Columbus, OH: RSC Office of Public Information.

Olson, W. (1999). Under the ADA, we may all be disabled. The Wall Street Journal, May 17, A27.

O'Neill, R. E., Horner, R. H., Albin, R. W., Sprague, J. R., Storey, K., & Newton, J. S. (1997). Functional assessment and *program development for problem behavior: A practical handbook* (2nd ed.). Pacific Grove, CA: Brooks/Cole Publishing.

Page, B., & Chadsey-Rusch, J. (1995). The community college experience for students with and without disabilities: A viable transition outcome? *Career Development for Exceptional Individuals,* 18(2), 85–96.

Pancsofar, E. L. (1986). Assessing work behavior. In F. R. Rusch (Ed.), *Competitive employment issues and strategies* (pp. 93–102). Baltimore: Paul H. Brookes.

Pancsofar, E. L., & Steere, D. E. (1997). The C.A.P.A.B.L.E. process: Critical dimensions of community-based assessment. *Journal of Vocational Rehabilitation,* 8, 99–108.

Parent, W. (1996). Consumer choice and satisfaction in supported employment. Paper presented at International Symposium on Supported Employment, Norfolk Virginia, *The Journal of Vocational Rehabilitation,* 6(1), 15–22.

Parent, W. Sherron, P., Stallard, D., & Booth, M. (1993). Job development and placement: Strategies for success. *Journal of Vocational Rehabilitation,* 3(3), 17–26.

Parette, H. P. (1999). Transition and assistive technology planning with families across cultures. *Career Development for Exceptional Individuals,* 22(2), 213–231.

Parette, H. P., Brotherson, M. J., Hourcade, J. J., & Bradley, R. H. (1996). Family-centered assistive technology assessment. *Intervention in School and Clinic,* 32(2), 104–112.

Parette, H. P., & Hourcade, J. J. (1997). Family issues and assistive technology needs: A sampling of state practices. *Journal of Special Education Technology,* 13, 27–43.

Parette, H. P., Jr., Hourcade, J. J., & VanBiervliet, A. (1993). Selection of appropriate technology for children with disabilities. *Teaching Exceptional Children,* 25(3), 18–22.

Parette, H. P., Jr., Hourcade, J. J., & VanBiervliet, A. (1996). Family-centered assistive technology assessment. *Intervention in School and Clinic,* 32(2), 104–112.

Parette, H. P., & VanBiervliet, A. (1990). A prospective inquiry into technology needs and practices of school-age children with disabilities. *Journal of Special Education Technology,* 10, 198–206.

Parette, H. P., & VanBiervliet, A. (1991). School-age children with disabilities: Technology implications for counselors. *Elementary School Guidance & Counseling,* 25, 182–194.

Parker, R. M., & Schaller, J. L. (1996). Issues in vocational assessment and disability. In E. M. Szymanski & R. M. Parker (Eds.), *Work and disability: Issues and strategies in career development and job placement* (pp. 127–164). Austin, TX: PRO-ED.

Parsons, M. B., Reid, D. H., Reynolds, J., & Bumgarner, M. (1990). Effects of chosen versus assigned jobs on the work performance of persons with severe handicaps. *Journal of Applied Behavior Analysis,* 23, 253–258.

Pascarella, E., & Terenzini, P. (1991). *How college affects students: Findings and insights from twenty years of research.* San Francisco: Jossey-Bass.

PA-TASH. (1994). PA-TASH supports the right to communicate. *PA-TASH Newsletter,* 4(2), 1–4.

Pati, G., & Morrison, G. (1982). Enabling the disabled. *Harvard Business Review,* 60, 152–168.

Patterson, J. (1996). Occupational and labor market information and analysis. In E. M. Szymanski & R. M. Parker (Eds.), *Work and disability: Issues and strategies in career development and job placement* (pp. 209–254). Austin, TX: PRO-ED.

Patton, J. R., Cronin, M. E., Bassett, D. S., & Koppel, A. E. (1997). A life skills approach to mathematics instruction: Preparing students with learning disabilities for the real-life math demands of adulthood. *Journal of Learning Disabilities,* 30(2), 178–187.

Patton, J. R., & Polloway, E. A. (1990). Mild mental retardation. In N. G. Haring, L. McCormick, & T. G. Haring (Eds.), *Exceptional children and youth* (6th ed., pp. 212–256). Upper Saddle River, NJ: Merrill/Prentice Hall.

Patton, J. R., Smith, T. E. C., Clark, G. M., Polloway, E. A., Edgar, E., & Lee, S. (1996). Individuals with mild mental retardation: Postsecondary outcomes and implications for educational policy. *Education and Training in Mental Retardation and Developmental Disabilities,* 31(2), 75–85.

Pearpoint, J. (1990). *From behind the piano: The building of Judith Snow's unique circle of friends.* Toronto, CA: Inclusion Press.

Pearpoint, J. (1993). Kick 'em out or keep 'em in: Exclusion or inclusion. In J. Pearpoint, M. Forest, & J. Snow (Eds.), *The inclusion papers: Strategies to make inclusion work* (pp. 80–88). Toronto: Inclusion Press.

Pearpoint, J., O'Brien, J., & Forest, M. (1993). PATH: A workbook for planning positive possible futures. Toronto Inclusion Press.

Peck, C., Donaldson, J., & Pezzoli, M. (1990). Some benefits some nonhandicapped adolescents perceive for themselves from their social relationships with peers who have severe handicaps. *The Journal of the Association for Persons with Severe Handicaps,* 15(4), 241–149.

Pennsylvania Association of Retarded Citizens v. Commonwealth of Pennsylvania, 343 F. Suppl. 279 (E.D. Pa. 1972).

Perske, R. (1973). *New hope for the families.* Nashville, TN: Abingdon.

Phelps, L. A., & Hanley-Maxwell, C. (1997). School-to-work transitions for youth with disabilities: A review of outcomes and practices. *Review of Educational Research,* 67(2), 197–226.

Phelps, L. A., & Maddy-Bernstein, C. (1992). Developing effective partnerships for special populations: The challenge of partnerships and alliances. *The Journal for Vocational Special Needs Education,* 14(2–3), 33–36.

Phillips, B. (1991). *Technology abandonment: From the consumer point of view.* Washington, DC: Request Publication.

Phillips, B. (1992). *Perspectives on assistive technology services in vocational rehabilitation: Client and counselors.* Washington, DC: National Rehabilitation Hospital, Assistive Technology/Rehabilitation Engineering Program.

Phillips, J. F., Reid, D. H., Korabek, C. A., & Hursh, D. E. (1988). Community-based instruction with profoundly mentally retarded persons: Client and public responsiveness. *Research in Developmental Disabilities, 9*, 3–21.

Pierce, K., & Scheibman, L. (1995). Increasing complex social behaviors in children with autism: Effects of peer-implemented pivotal response training. *Journal of Applied Behavior Analysis, 28*, 285–295.

Pinderhughes, E. (1995). Empowering diverse populations: Family practice in the 21st century. *Families in Society, 76*, 131–140.

Pitman, J. A., & Slate, J. R. (1994). Students' familiarity with and attitudes toward the rights of students who are disabled. *Journal of Applied Rehabilitation Counseling, 25*(2), 38–40.

Polirstok, S. R. (1986). Training problematic adolescents as peer tutors: Benefits for the tutor and the school at large. *Techniques: A Journal for Remedial Education and Counseling, 2*, 204–210.

Pollitzer, W. S. (1994). Ethnicity and human biology. *American Journal of Human Biology, 6*, 3–11.

Pomplun, M. (1997). When students with disabilities participate in cooperative groups. *Exceptional Children, 64*, 49–58.

Powell, T., Pancsofar, E. L., Steere, D., Butterworth, J., Itzkowitz, J., & Rainforth, B. (1991). *Supported employment: Providing integrated employment opportunities for person with disabilities.* New York: Longman.

Power, P. (1991). *A guide to vocational assessment* (2nd ed.). Austin, TX: PRO-ED.

Powers, L. E. (1997). *Self-determination research results.* Colorado Springs, CO: Presentation at University of Colorado Self-Determination Meeting.

Powers, L. E., Sowers, J., Turner, A., Nesbitt, M., Knowles, E., & Ellison, R. (1996). TAKE CHARGE: A model for promoting self-determination among adolescents with challenges. In L. E. Powers, G. H. S. Singer, & J. Sowers (Eds.), *On the road to autonomy: Promoting self-competence for children and youth with disabilities* (pp. 291–322). Baltimore: Paul H. Brookes.

Presidents Panel on Mental Retardation. (1962). *A proposed program for national action to combat mental retardation.* Washington, DC: U.S. Government Printing Office.

Pruitt, P., & Wandry, D. (1998). Listen to us! Parents speak out about their interactions with special educators. *Preventing School Failure, 42*, 161–167.

Pumpian, I., Campbell, C., & Hesche, S. (1992). Making person-centered dreams come true. *Resources, 4*(4), 1–6.

Pumpian, I., & Fisher, D. (1993). *Job placement: The final frontier?* Washington, DC: National Institute on Disabilities and Rehabilitation Research [NIDRR].

Pumpian, I., Fisher, D., Certo, N. J., & Smalley, K. A. (1997). Changing jobs: An essential part of career development. *Career Development for Exceptional Individuals, 35*, 39–48.

Putnam, J. W. (Ed.). (1998). *Cooperative learning and strategies for inclusion: Celebrating diversity in the classroom.* Baltimore: Paul H. Brookes.

Qin, Z., Johnson, D. W., & Johnson, R. T. (1995). Cooperative versus competitive efforts and problem solving. *Review of Educational Research, 65*(2), 129–143.

Racino, J. A. (1990). Preparing personnel to work in community support services. In A. P. Kaiser & C. M. McWhorter (Eds.), *Preparing personnel to work with persons with severe disabilities* (203–226). Baltimore: Paul H. Brookes.

Racino, J. A. (1999). *Policy, program evaluation, and research in disability: Community support for all.* Binghamton, NY: Haworth Press.

Racino, J. A., & Litvak, S. (1999). Moving toward universal access to support—policy is personal: Introduction. In J. A. Racino (Ed.), *Policy, program evaluation, and research in disability: Community support for all.* Binghamton, NY: Haworth Press.

Racino, J. A., O'Connor, S., & Walker, P. (1992). Conclusion. In J. A. Racino, P. Walker, S. O'Connor, & S. J. Taylor (Eds.), *Housing, support, and community: Choices and strategies for adults with disabilities.* Baltimore: Paul H. Brookes.

Racino, J. A., Walker, P., O'Connor S., & Taylor, S. J. (Eds.). (1992). *Housing, support, and community: Choices and strategies for adults with disabilities.* Baltimore: Paul H. Brookes.

Rae, S., Martin, G., & Smyk, B. (1990). A self-management package versus a group exercise contingency for increasing on-task behavior of developmentally handicapped workers. *Canadian Journal of Behavioral Science, 22*, 45–58.

Ragland, E. U., Kerr, M. M., & Strain, P. S. (1978). Effects of social initiations on the behavior of withdrawn autistic children. *Topics in Early Childhood Special Education, 13*, 565–578.

Rainforth, B., York, J., & MacDonald, C. (1992). *Collaborative teams for students with severe disabilities.* Baltimore: Paul H. Brookes.

Raskind, M. H. (1997/1998). A guide to assistive technology. *Their World*, 72–74.

Reed, C., & Rumrill, P. (1997). Supported employment: Principles and practices for interdisciplinary collaboration. *Work: A Journal of Prevention, Assessment, and Rehabilitation, 9*, 237–244.

Reed, P. (1997). *Assessing students' need for assistive technology.* Oshkosh, WI: Wisconsin Assistive Technology Initiative.

Rehabilitation Act Amendments of 1992, 29 U.S.C. § 794 *et seq.*

Rehabilitation Act of 1973, Section 504, 29 U.S.C. § 794.

Rehabilitation, Comprehensive Services, and Developmental Disabilities Act of 1978, Pub. L. No. 95-062.

Rehabilitation Services Administration, Office of Special Education and Rehabilitation Services, U.S. Department of Education. (1999). Rehabilitation Services Administration (RSA) Programs: Centers for Independent Living. Retrieved January 15, 2000 from the World Wide Web: http://www.ed.gov/offices/OSERS/RSA/rsa.html

Repetto, J. B., & Correa, V. I. (1996). Expanding views on transition. *Exceptional Children 62*(6), 551–563.

Repetto, J. B., White, W. J., & Snauwaert, D. T. (1990). Individualized transition plans (ITP): A national perspective. *Career Development for Exceptional Individuals, 13*(2), 109–119.

Reschly, D. J. (1997). *Disproportionate minority representation in general and special education: Patterns, issues, and alternatives.* Washington, DC: Office of Special Education and Rehabilitative Services, and Mountain Plains Regional Resource Center.

Research and Training Center on Residential Services and Community Living. (1994). *Housing policy and persons with mental retardation.* Minneapolis, MN: Institute on Community Integration.

Rhodes, L., Sandow, D., Mank, D., Buckley, J., & Albin, J. (1991). Expanding the role of employers in supported employment. *The Journal of the Association for Persons with Severe Handicaps, 16*(4), 213–217.

Richmond, G., Beatty, P., Tepper, S., & DeJong, G. (1997). The effect of consumer-directed personal assistance services on the productivity outcomes of people with disabilities. *Journal of Rehabilitation Outcomes Measurement, 1*(4), 48–51.

Rimmerman, A., Levy, J. M., & Botuck, S. (1995). Predicting the likelihood of job placement: A short-term perspective. *The Journal of Rehabilitation, 61* (1) 50–54, 50.

Rivera, D. P., & Smith, D. D. (1997). *Teaching students with learning and behavior problems* (3rd ed.). Boston: Allyn & Bacon.

Rodriquez, R. F. (1994). Administrators' perceptions of teaching competencies for rural minority group children with exceptionalities. *Rural Special Education Quarterly, 13,* 40–44.

Roessler, R., & Bolton, B. (1985). Employment patterns of former vocational rehabilitation clients and implications for rehabilitation practice. *Rehabilitation Counseling Bulletin, 28*(3), 179–187.

Roessler, R., & Rumrill, P. (1995). Promoting reasonable accommodations: An essential postemployment service. *Journal of Applied Rehabilitation Counseling, 26*(4), 3–7.

Rojewski, J. W. (1993). Theoretical structure of career maturity for rural adolescents with learning disabilities. *Career Development for Exceptional Individuals, 16*(1), 39–52.

Rojewski, J. W. (1996). Educational and occupational aspirations of high school seniors with learning difficulties. *Exceptional Children, 62*(5), 463–476.

Rokeach, M. (1975). *Beliefs, attitudes, and values: A theory of organization and change.* San Francisco: Jossey-Bass.

Rose, S. M. (1972). *The betrayal of the poor: The transformation of community action.* Cambridge, MA: Schenkman Publishing.

Rosenberg, M. S., Wilson, R., Maheady, L., & Sindelar, P. T. (1997). *Educating students with behavior disorders* (2nd ed.). Needham Heights, MA: Allyn & Bacon.

Rosenshine, B. V. (1986). Synthesis of research on explicit teaching. *Educational Leadership, 43*(7), 60–69.

Rosenshine, B. V., & Stevens, R. (1986). Teaching functions. In M. C. Wittrock (Ed.), *Handbook of research on teaching* (3rd ed., pp. 376–391). New York: Macmillan.

Rothschild, I., & Bianchi, J. (1986). Parent/educator meetings can work for your child. *Annual Education Issue of the Exceptional Parent, 16*(5) 23–28.

Rudrud, E. H., Ziarnik, J. P., Berstein, G. S., & Ferrara, J. M. (1984). *Proactive vocational habilitation.* Baltimore: Paul H. Brookes.

Rumrill, P., & Koch, L. (1998). The career maintenance specialist: Broadening the scope of successful rehabilitation. *Journal of Rehabilitation Administration, 22*(2), 111–121.

Rumrill, P. D. (1994). The "win-win" approach to Title I of the Americans with Disabilities Act: Preparing college students with disabilities for career-entry placements after graduation. *Journal of Postsecondary Education and Disability, 11*(1), 15–19.

Rusch, F. R. (1979). Toward the validation of social/vocational survival skills. *Mental Retardation, 17,* 143–145.

Rusch, F. R. (1990). *Supported employment: Models, methods and issues.* Sycamore, IL: Sycamore Publishing.

Rusch, F. R., & Chadsey, J. G. (1998). *Beyond high school: Transition from school to work.* The Wadsworth Special Education Series.

Rusch, F. R., & DeStefano, L. (1989). Transition from school to work: Strategies for young adults with disabilities. *Interchange, 9*(3), 1–2. Urbana-Champaign, IL: University of Illinois, Secondary Transition Intervention Effectiveness Institute.

Rusch, F. R., DeStefano, L., Chadsey-Rusch, J., Phelps, L. A., & Szymanski, E. (1992). *Transition from school to adult life: Models, linkages, and policy.* Sycamore, IL: Sycamore Publishing.

Rusch, F. R., McKee, M., Chadsey-Rusch, J., & Renzaglia, A. (1988). Teaching a student with severe handicaps to self-instruct: A brief report. *Education and Training in Mental Retardation, 23,* 51–58.

Rusch, F. R., & Millar, D. M. (1998). Emerging transition best practices. In F. R. Rusch & J. G. Chadsey (Eds.), *Beyond high school: Transition from school to work* (pp. 36–60). New York: Wadsworth Publishing.

Rusch, F. R., Mithaug, D. E., & Flexer, R. W. (1986). Obstacles to competitive employment and traditional program options for overcoming them. In F. R. Rusch (Ed.), *Competitive employment: Issues and strategies* (pp. 7–21). Baltimore: Paul H. Brookes.

Rusch, F. R., Morgan, T. K., Martin, J. E., Riva, M., & Agran, M. (1985). Competitive employment: Teaching mentally retarded employees self-instructional strategies. *Applied Research in Mental Retardation, 6,* 389–407.

Rusch, F. R., Schultz, R. P., Mithaug, D. E., Stewart, J. E., & Mar, D. E. (1982). *Vocational assessment and curriculum guide.* Seattle, WA: Exceptional Education.

Rusch, F. R., Szymanski, E. M., & Chadsey-Rusch, J. (1992). The emerging field of transition services. In F. R. Rusch, L. Destefano, J. Chadsey-Rusch, L. A. Phelps, & E. Szymanski (Eds.), *Transition from school to adult life: Models, linkages, and policy.* Sycamore, IL: Sycamore Publishing.

Russo, C. J., & Talbert-Johnson, C. (1997). The overrepresentation of African American children in special education: The resegregation of educational programming? *Education and Urban Society, 29,* 136–148.

Ryan, C. (1995). Work isn't what it used to be: Implications, recommendations, and strategies for vocational rehabilitation. *Journal of Rehabilitation, 61*(4), 7–15.

Ryan, R. B., Connell, J. P., & Plant, R. W. (1990). Emotions in non-directed test learning. *Learning and Individual Differences*, 2, 736B–750.

Rylance, B. J. (1997). Predictors of high school graduation or dropping out for youth with severe emotional disturbances. *Behavior Disorders*, 23(1), 5–17.

Ryndak, D. L., & Alper, S. (1996). *Curriculum content for students with moderate and severe disabilities in inclusive settings*. Boston: Allyn & Bacon.

Sale, P., & Martin, J. E. (1997). Self-determination. In P. Wehman & J. Kregel (Eds.), *Functional curriculum for elementary, middle, and secondary age students with special needs* (pp. 43–67). Austin, TX: PRO-ED.

Salembier, G., & Furney, K. S. (1997). Facilitating participation: Parents' perceptions of their involvement in the IEP/transition planning process. *Career Development for Exceptional Children*, 20, 29–42.

Salend, S. J. (1994). *Effective mainstreaming: Creating inclusive classrooms* (2nd ed.). Upper Saddle River, NJ: Merrill/Prentice Hall.

Salend, S. T., & Taylor, L. (1993). Working with families: A cross-cultural perspective. *Remedial and Special Education*, 14(5), 25–32.

Salzberg, C. L., & Morgan, J. (1995). Preparing teachers to work with paraeducators. *Teacher Education and Special Education*, 18(1), 49–55.

Sands, D. S., Adams, L., & Stout, D. M. (1995). A statewide exploration of the nature and use of curriculum in special education. *Exceptional Children*, 62(1), 68–83.

Sarason, S. B., & Doris, J. (1979). *Educational handicap, public policy, and social history: A broadened perspective on mental retardation*. New York: The Free Press.

Sarkees-Wincenski, M., & Scott, J. L. (1995). *Vocational special needs* (3rd ed.). Homewood, IL: American Technical Publishers.

Sarkees-Wircenski, M., & Wircenski, J. (1994). Transition planning: Developing a career portfolio for students with disabilities. *Career Development for Exceptional Individuals*, 17, 203–214.

Savickas, M. L. (1989). Career-style assessment and counseling. In T. Sweeney (Ed.), *Adlerian counseling: A practical approach for a new decade* (3rd ed., pp. 289–320). Muncie, IN: Accelerated Development Press.

Savickas, M. L. (1996). A framework for linking career theory and practice. In M. L. Savickas & W. B. Walsh (Eds.), *Handbook of career counseling theory and practice* (pp. 191–208). Palo Alto, CA: Davies-Black.

Sax, C., Pumpian, I., & Fisher, D. (March, 1997). Assistive technology and inclusion. *CISP Issue Briefs*, 1–5.

SCANS: The Secretary's Commission on Achieving Necessary Skills (1992, June). *SCANS in the schools*. Washington, DC: SCANS, U.S. Dept. of Labor, Pelavin Assoc.

Schalock, R., Stark, J., Snell, M., Coulter, D., Pollaway, E., Luckasson, R., Reiss, S., & Spitalnik, D. (1994). The changing conception of mental retardation: Implications for the field. *Mental Retardation*, 32(3), 181–193.

Schalock, R. L., Wolzen, B., Ross, I., Elliott, B., Werbel, G., & Peterson, K. (1986). Post-secondary community placement of handicapped students: A five-year follow-up. *Learning Disability Quarterly*, 9(4), 295–303.

Scheerenberger, R. C. (1983). *A history of mental retardation*. Baltimore, Paul H. Brookes.

Scherer, M. (1991). Assistive technology use, avoidance and abandonment: What we know so far. In *Proceedings of the 6th annual technology and persons with disabilities conference* (pp. 815–826). Washington, DC: Rehabilitation Engineering Center, National Rehabilitation Hospital.

Scherer, M. J. (1997). Assessing individuals' predispositions to the use, avoidance, or abandonment of assistive technologies. *Journal of Rehabilitation Research & Development*, 31, 135–136.

Scherer, M. J., & Galvin, J.C. (1996). An outcomes perspective of quality pathways to the most appropriate technology. In J. C. Galvin & M. J. Scherer (Eds.), *Evaluating, selecting, and using appropriate assistive technology*. Gaithersburg, MD: Aspen Publishers, Inc.

Schleien, S. J., Green, F. P., & Heyne, L. A. (1993). Integrated community recreation. In M. E. Snell (Ed.), *Instruction of students with severe disabilities*, (4th ed., p. 530). Upper Saddle River, NJ: Merrill/Prentice Hall.

Schloss, P. J., & Smith, M. A. (1998). *Applied behavior analysis in the classroom* (2nd ed.). Boston: Allyn & Bacon.

Schloss, P. J., Smith, M. A., & Schloss, C. N. (1995). *Instructional methods for adolescents with learning and behavior problems* (2nd ed.). Boston: Allyn & Bacon.

Schniedewind, N., & Salend, S. J. (1987). Cooperative learning works. *Teaching Exceptional Children*, 19, 22–25.

School to Work Opportunity Act of 1994, Pub. L. No. 103-239, 20 U.S.C. § 6101 et seq.

Scott, S. B. (1997). Comparison of service delivery models influencing teacher's use of assistive technology for students with severe disabilities. *Occupational Therapy in Health Care*, 11(11), 61–70.

Scott, S. S. (1996). Understanding colleges: An overview of college support services and programs available to clients from transition planning through graduation. *Journal of Vocational Rehabilitation*, 6, 217–230.

Scruggs, T. E., Mastropieri, M. A., & Richter, L. (1985). Peer tutoring among behaviorally disordered students: Social and academic benefits. *Behavioral Disorders*, 11, 283–294.

Scruggs, T. E., Mastropieri, M., Veit, D. T., & Osguthorpe, R. T. (1986). Behaviorally disorders students as tutors: Effects on social behavior. *Behavioral Disorders*, 12(1), 36–44.

Scuccimarra, D., & Speece, D. (1990). Employment outcomes and social integration of students with mild handicaps: The quality of life two years after high school. *Journal of Learning Disabilities*, 23(4), 213–219.

Section 504 of the Rehabilitation Act of 1973, 29 U.S.C. § 794 et seq.

Senge, P. M. (1990). *The fifth discipline: The art and practice of learning organization*. New York: Doubleday/Currency—Dell Publishing Group.

Serebreni, R., Rumrill, P. D., Mullins, J. A., & Gordon, S. E., (1993). Project Excel: A demonstration of the higher education transition model for high-achieving students with disabilities. *Journal of Postsecondary Education and Disability*, 10, 15–23.

Sexton, D., Lobman, M., Constans, T., Snyder, P., & Ernest, J. (1997). Early interventionists' perspectives of multicultural practices with African-American families. *Exceptional Children*, 63, 313–328.

Shapiro, E. S., McGonigle, J. J., & Ollendick, T. H. (1980). An analysis of self-assessment and self-reinforcement in a self-managed token economy with mentally retarded children. *Applied Research in Mental Retardation*, 1, 227–240.

Shapiro, J. P. (1993). *No Pity*. New York: Times Books.

Sharifzadeh, V. S. (1998). Families with middle eastern roots. In E. W. Lynch & M. H. Hanson (Eds.), *Developing cross-cultural competence: A guide for working with children and their families* (2nd ed., pp. 441–482). Baltimore: Paul H. Brookes.

Sharon, S. (1980). Cooperative learning in small groups: Recent methods and effects on achievement, attitudes and ethnic relations. *Review of Educational Research*, 50, 241–249.

Shaw, S., Brinckerhoff, L. C., Kistler, J. K., & McGuire, J. M. (1991). Preparing students with learning disabilities for postsecondary education: Issues and future needs. *Learning Disabilities: A Multidisciplinary Journal*, 2(1), 21–26.

Sherif, C. W., Sherif, M., & Nebergall, R. E. (1965). *Attitude and attitude change*. Philadelphia: W. B. Saunders.

Shingleton, J. D., & Fitzpatrick, E. B. (1985). *Dynamics of placement: How to develop a successful career planning and placement program*. Bethlehem, PA: College Placement Council Foundation.

Siegel, S. (1998). Foundations for a school-to-work system that serves all students. In F. R. Rusch & J. G. Chadsey (Eds.), *Beyond high school: Transition from school to work* (pp. 146–178). New York: Wadsworth Publishing.

Siegel, S., Robert, M., Greener, K., Meyer, G., Halloran, W., & Gaylord-Ross, R. (1993). *Career ladders for challenged youths in transition from school to adult life*. Austin, TX: PRO-ED.

Siegel, S., & Sleeter, C. S. (1991). Transforming transition: Next stages for the school-to-work transition movement. *Career Development for Exceptional Individuals*, 14(2), 27–41.

Silbert, J., Carnine, D., & Stein, M. (1990). *Direct instruction mathematics* (2nd ed.). Columbus, OH: Merrill.

Simich-Dudgeon, C. (1986). A multidisciplinary model to educate minority language students with handicapping conditions. In A. C. Willing & H. F. Greenberg (Eds.), *Bilingualism and learning disabilities: Policy and practice for teachers and administrators* (pp. 95–110). New York: American Library Publishing.

Simmons, T., & Baer, R. (1996). What I want to be when I grow up: Career planning. In C. Flexer, D. Wray, R. Leavitt &

R. Flexer (Eds.), *How the student with hearing loss can succeed in college: A handbook for students, families, and professionals* (2nd ed., pp. 117–130). Washington, DC: Alexander Graham Bell Association for the Deaf.

Simmons, T. J. (1996). *Postsecondary higher educational settings: Model environment for the delivery of secondary special education services*. Model demonstration Grant funded by the Office of Special Education. Washington, DC: S. Department of Education.

Simmons, T. J., & Flexer, R. W. (1992). Community based job training for persons with mental retardation: An acquisition and performance replication. *Education and Training in Mental Retardation*, 15, 261–272.

Simmons, T. J., Selleck, V., Steele, R. B., & Sepetauc, F. (1993). Supports and rehabilitation for employment. In R. W. Flexer and P. L. Solomon (Eds.), *Psychiatric rehabilitation in practice*, (pp. 119–136), Boston, MA: Andover Medical Publishers.

Simon, M., Cobb, B., Halloran, W., Norman, M., & Bourexis. (1994). *Meeting the needs of youth with disabilities: Handbook for implementing community-based vocational education programs according to the Fair Labor Standards Act*. Minneapolis, MN: National Transition Network.

Simpson, G. W. (1997). To grow a teacher. *American School Board Journal*, 184, 42–43.

Simpson, R. L. (1982). *Conferencing parents of exceptional children*. Rockville, MD: Aspen Publications.

Sindelar, P. T., Smith, M. A., Harriman, N. E., Hale, R. L., & Wilson, R. J. (1986). Teacher effectiveness in special education programs. *The Journal of Special Education*, 20, 195–207.

Siperstein, G. N. (1988). Students with learning disabilities in college: The need for a programmatic approach to critical transitions. *Journal of Learning Disabilities*, 21, 431–436.

Sitlington, P. L. (1996a). Transition assessment: Where have we been and where should we be going? *Career Development for Exceptional Individuals*, 19, 159–168.

Sitlington, P. L. (1996). Transition assessment—Where have we been and where should we be going? *Career Development for Exceptional Children*, 19, 159–168.

Sitlington, P. L. (1996b). Transition to living: The neglected component of transition programming for individuals with learning disabilities. *Journal of Learning Disabilities*, 29(1), 31–41.

Sitlington, P. L., & Frank, A. R. (1990). Are adolescents with learning disabilities successfully crossing the bridge into adult life? *Learning Disabilities Quarterly*, 13(2), 97–111.

Sitlington, P. L., Neubert, D., Begun, W., Le Conte, W., & Lombard, R. (1996). *Assess for success: Handbook for transition assessment*. Reston, VA: The Council for Exceptional Children.

Sitlington, P. L., Neubert, D. A., & Le Conte, P. J. (1997). Transition assessment: The position of the Division on Career Development and Transition. *Career Development for Exceptional Individuals*, 20(1), 69–79.

Skinner, D., Bailey, D. B., Jr., Correa, V., & Rodriguez, P. (1999). Narrating self and disability: Latino mothers' construction of identities vis-à-vis their child with special needs. *Exceptional Children*, 65, 481–495.

Slaney, R. B., & McKinnon-Slaney, F. (1990). The use of vocational card sorts in career counseling. In C. E. Watkins, Jr., & V. L. Campbell (Eds.), *Testing in counseling practice* (pp. 317–371). Hillsdale, NJ: Erlbaum.

Slavin, R. E. (1978). Student teams and achievement divisions. *Journal of Research and Development in Education*, 12, 39–49.

Slavin, R. E. (1991). Synthesis of research on cooperative learning. *Educational Leadership*, 48(5), 71–82.

Slavin, R. E., Madden, N. A., & Stevens, R. J. (1990). Cooperative learning models for the 3 R's. *Educational Leadership*, 47(4), 22–28.

Slavin, R. E., Stevens, R. J., & Madden, N. A. (1988). Accommodating student diversity in reading and writing instruction: A cooperative learning approach. *Remedial and Special Education*, 9(1), 60–66.

Smith, B. (1994). Handing over control to people with learning difficulties. In J. Coupe-O'Kane & B. Smith (Eds.), *Taking Control* (pp. 4–13). London: David Fulton Publishers.

Smith, F., Lombard, R., Neubert, D., Le Conte, P., Rothenbacher, C., & Sitlington, P. (1996). The position statement of the interdisciplinary council on vocational evaluation and assessment. *Career Development for Exceptional Individuals*, 19, 73–76.

Smith, G. (1990). *Supported living: New directions in services for people with developmental disabilities*. Alexandria, VA: National Association of State Mental Retardation Program Directors.

Smith, M. D., Belcher, R. G., & Juhrs, P. D. (1995). *A guide to successful employment for individuals with autism*. Baltimore: Paul H. Brookes.

Smith, M. D., Belcher, R. G., Juhrs, P. D., & Nabors, K. (1994). Where people with autism work. *Journal of Vocational Rehabilitation*, 4(1), 10–17.

Smith, S. W. (1990). Individualized education programs (IEPs) in special education: From intent to acquiescence. *Exceptional Children*, 57(1), 6–14.

Smull, M., & Bellamy, T. (1990). Community services for adults with disabilities: Policy challenges in the emerging support paradigm. In L. H. Meyer, C. A. Peck, & L. Brown (Eds.), *Critical issues in the lives of people with severe disabilities* (pp. 527–536). Baltimore: Paul H. Brookes.

Smull, M. W., Sanderson, H., & Harrison, S. B. (1996). *Reviewing essential lifestyle plans: Criteria for best plans*. Kensington, MD: Support Development Associates.

Snell, M. E. (1981). Daily living skills. In J. M. Kauffman & D. P. Hallahan (Eds.), *Handbook of special education* (pp. 530–551). Upper Saddle River, NJ: Prentice Hall.

Snell, M. E. (1983). Developing the IEP: Selecting and assessing skills. In M. E. Snell (Ed.), *Systematic instruction of the moderately and severely handicapped* (2nd ed., pp. 76–112). Upper Saddle River, NJ: Merrill/Prentice Hall.

Snell, M. E. (1987). *Systematic instruction of the moderately to severely handicapped* (3rd ed.). Columbus, OH: Merrill.

Snell, M. E. (1993). *Instruction of students with severe disabilities* (4th ed.). New York: Merrill.

Snell, M. E., & Browder, D. M. (1986). Community-referenced instruction: Research and issues. *Journal of the Association for Persons with Severe handicaps*, 11, 1–11.

Snyder, E. P., & Shapiro, E. D. (1997). Teaching students with emotional/behavioral disorders the skills to participate in the development of their own IEPs. *Behavioral Disorders*, 22, 246B–259.

Sowers, J. (1991). Employment for persons with physical disabilities and related technology, *Journal of Vocational Rehabilitation*, 1(2) 55–64.

Sowers, J. (1995). Adaptive environments in the workplace. In K. F. Flippo, K. J. Inge, & J. M. Barcus (Eds.), *Assistive technology: A resource for school, work, and community* (pp. 167–185). Baltimore, MD: Paul H. Brookes.

Sowers, J. & Powers, L. (1991). *Vocational preparation and employment of students with physical and multiple disabilities*. Baltimore: Paul H. Brookes.

Sowers, J., & Powers, L. (1995). Enhancing the participation and independence of students with severe physical and multiple disabilities in performing community activities. *Mental Retardation*, 33(4), 209–220.

Speigel-McGill, P., Bambara, L. M., Shores, R. E., & Fox, J. J. (1984). The effects of proximity on socially oriented behaviors of severely multiple handicapped children. *Education and Treatment of Children*, 7, 365–378.

Spokane, A. R. (1996). Holland's theory. In D. Brown, L. Brooks, & Associates (Eds.), *Career choice and development* (3rd ed., pp. 33–74). San Francisco: Jossey-Bass.

Stageberg, D., Fischer, J., & Barbut, A. (1996). University students' knowledge of civil rights laws pertaining to people with disabilities. *Journal of Applied Rehabilitation Counseling*, 27(4), 25–29.

Stainback, W., Stainback, S., Nietupski, J., & Hamre-Neitupski, S. (1986). Establishing effective community work stations. In F. R. Rusch (Ed.),*Competitive employment: Issues and strategies* (pp. 93–102). Baltimore: Paul H. Brookes.

Stanford Research Institute (SRI) International. (1990). *National longitudinal transition study of special education students*. Washington, DC: The Office of Special Education Programs.

Stanford Research Institute (SRI) International. (1992). *What happens next? Trends in postschool outcomes of youth with disabilities*. Washington, DC: The Office of Special Education Programs.

State Agency Exchange. (1969). *The rehabilitation agency focus*. Washington, DC: U.S. Government Printing Office.

Steere, D. E., Panscofar, E., Wood, R., & Hecimovic, A. (1990). Principals of shared responsibility. *Career Development for Exceptional Individuals*, 13(2), 143–153.

Steere, D. E., Wood, R., Panscofar, E. L., & Butterworth, J. (1990). Outcome-based school-to-work transition planning for students with severe disabilities. *Career Development for Exceptional Individuals*, 13(1), 57–70.

Stevens, N. B. (1973). Job-seeking behavior: A segment of vocational development. *Journal of Vocational Behavior*, 3, 209–219.

Stevens, R. J., & Slavin, R. (1995). The cooperative elementary school: Effects on students' achievement, attitudes, and social relations. *American Educational Research Journal*, 32, 321–351.

Stewart, E. D., Danielian, J., & Festes, R. J. (1969). *Simulating intercultural communication through role playing*. Alexandria, VA: Human Resources Research Organization.

Stodden, R. A. (1998). School-to-work transition: Overview of disability legislation. In F. R. Rusch & J. G. Chadsey (Eds.), *Beyond high school: Transition from school to work* (pp. 60–76). Belmont, CA: Wadsworth Publishing.

Stodden, R. A. (1986). Vocational assessment: An introduction [Special issue]. *Career Development for Exceptional Individuals*, 9, 67–68.

Stodden, R. A., Ianacone, R. N., Boone, R., & Bisconer, S. W. (1987). *Curriculum-based vocational assessment: A guide for addressing youth with special needs*. Honolulu, HI: Center Publications, International Education.

Stodden, R. A., & Leake, D. W. (1994). Getting to the core of transition: A re-assessment of old wine in new bottles. *Career Development for Exceptional Individuals*, 17(1), 65–76.

Storey, K., & Mank, D. (1989). Vocational education of students with moderate and severe disabilities: Implications for service delivery and teacher preparation. *Career Development for Exceptional Individuals*, 12(1), 11–24.

Stowell, M. A. (1978). *Handicapped learner participation in vocational education: A report on student, parent, and teacher interviews.* (ERIC Document Reproduction Service No. ED 162 479).

Stowitschek, J. J., & Kelso, C. A. (1989). Are we in danger of making the same mistakes with ITPs as were made with IEPs? *Career Development for Exceptional Individuals*, 12(2), 139–151.

Strain, P. S., Kerr, M. M., & Ragland, E. U. (1979). Effects of peer-mediated social initiations and prompt reinforcement procedures on the social behavior of autistic children. *Journal of Autism and Developmental Disorders*, 9, 41–54.

Strain, P. S., Odom, S. L., & McConnell, S. (1984). Promoting social reciprocity of exceptional children: Identification, target behavior selection, and intervention. *Remedial and Special Education*, 5(1), 21–28.

Strain, P. S., Shores, R. E., & Timm, M. A. (1977). Effects of peer initiations on the social behavior of withdrawn preschool children. *Journal of Applied Behavior Analysis*, 10, 289–298.

Strong, S. R., & Claiborn, C. D. (1982). *Change through interaction*. New York: John Wiley.

Stroul, B. A., (1989) Rehabilitation in community support systems. In R. W. Flexer and P. L. Solomon (Eds.), *Psychiatric rehabilitation in practice.* (pp. 45–61). Boston, MA: Andover Publishers.

Strully, J., & Strully, C. (1985). Friendship and our children. *Journal of the Association for Persons with Severe Handicaps*, 10, 224–227.

Subich, L. (Ed.). (1993). How personal is career counseling? *Career Development Quarterly*, 42, 129–191.

Suelzle, M., & Keenan, V. (1981). Changes in family support networks over the life cycle of mentally retarded persons. *American Journal of Mental Deficiency*, 86(3), 267–274.

Sugai, G., & Rowe, P. (1984). The effect of self-recording on out-of-seat behavior of an EMR student. *Education and Treatment of the Mentally Retarded*, 19, 23–34.

Summers, J. A. (1981). The definition of developmental disabilities: A concept in transition. *Mental Retardation*, 19, 259–265.

Sumner, S., & Fritts, M. (1997). *The IEP planner [computer file]: LCCE transition skills program*. Highland Park, IL: Rodan Associates.

Super, D. E. (1954). Career patterns as a basis for vocational counseling. *Journal of Counseling Psychology*, 1, 12–20.

Super, D. E. (Ed.). (1974). *Measuring vocational maturity for counseling and evaluation*. Washington, DC: National Career Development Association.

Super, D. E. (1975). *The psychology of careers*. New York: Harper & Row.

Super, D. E. (1984). Career and life development. In D. Brown, L. Brooks, & Associates (Eds.), *Career choice and development: Applying contemporary theories to practice* (pp. 192–234). San Francisco: Jossey-Bass.

Super, D. E. (1990). A life-span, life-space approach to career development. In D. Brown, L. Brooks, & Associates (Eds.), *Career choice and development: Applying contemporary theories to practice* (2nd ed., pp. 197–261). San Francisco: Jossey-Bass.

Super, D. E., Savickas, M. L., & Super, C. M. (1996). The life-span, life-space approach to careers. In D. Brown, L. Brooks, & Associates (Eds.), *Career choice and development* (3rd ed., pp. 121–178). San Francisco: Jossey-Bass.

Super, D. E., Thompson, A. S., Lindeman, R. H., Joordan, J., & Myers, R. A. (1981). *Career development inventory*. Palo Alto, CA: Consulting Psychologists Press.

Sweeney, M. (1996). *The effects of self-determination training on student involvement in the IEP process*. Unpublished doctoral dissertation., Tallahassee, FL: Florida State University.

Szymanski, E. M. (1994). Transition: life-span, life-space considerations for empowerment. *Exceptional Children*, 60, 402–410.

Szymanski, E., & Hershenson, D. (1998). Career development of people with disabilities: An ecological model. In E. M. Szymanski & R. M. Parker (Eds.), *Rehabilitation counseling: Basics and beyond* (3rd ed., pp. 327–378). Austin, TX: PRO-ED.

Szymanski, E., Fernandez, D., Koch, L., & Merz, M. (1996). *Career development: Planning for placement*. Madison, WI: University of Wisconsin, Rehabilitation Research and Training Center on Career Development and Advancement.

Szymanski, E. M., & Hanley-Maxwell, C. (1997). Career development of people with developmental disabilities: An ecological model. *The Journal of Rehabilitation*, 62(1), 48–55.

Szymanski, E. M., & Parker, R. M. (1996). Work and disability: Introduction. In E. M. Szymanski & R. M. Parker (Eds.), *Work and disability: Issues and strategies in career development and job placement* (pp. 1–7). Austin, TX: PRO-ED.

Szymanski, E. M., Hanley-Maxwell, C., & Asselin, S. B. (1992). Systems interface: Vocational rehabilitation, special education, and vocational education. In F. R. Rusch, L. Destefano, J. Chadsey-Rusch, L. A. Phelps, & E. Szymanski (Eds.), *Transition from school to adult life: Models, linkages, and policy.* (pp. 153–172). Sycamore, IL: Sycamore Publishing.

Szymanski, E. M., Hanley-Maxwell, C., & Asselin, S. (1990). Rehabilitation counseling, special education, and vocational special needs education: Three transitional disciplines. *Career Development for Exceptional Individuals, 13*(1), 29–38.

Szymanski, E. M., Hershenson, D. B., Enright, M. S., & Ettinger, J. M. (1996). Career development theories, constructs, and research: Implications for people with disabilities. In E. M. Szymanski & R. M. Parker (Eds.), *Work and disability: Issues and strategies in career development and job development* (pp. 79–126). Austin, TX: PRO-ED.

Szymanski, E. M., Turner, K. D., & Herschenson, D. B. (1992). Career development and work adjustment of persons with disabilities: Theoretical perspectives and implications for transition. In F. R. Rusch, L. Destefano, J. Chadsey-Rusch, L. A. Phelps, & E. Szymanski (Eds.), *Transition from school to adult life: Models, linkages, and policy* (pp. 391–406). Sycamore, IL: Sycamore Publishing.

Talbert-Johnson, C. (1998). Why [are] so many African-American children in special ed? *School Business Affairs, 64,* 30–35.

Taylor, R. (1997). *Assessment of exceptional students: Educational and psychological procedures* (4th ed.). Boston: Allyn & Bacon.

Taylor, S., & Bogden, R. (1990). Quality of life and the individual perspective. In R. L. Schalock & M. Bogale (Eds.), *Quality of life: Perspectives and issues* (pp. 27–40). Washington, DC: American Association of Mental Retardation.

Taylor, S. J. (1988). Caught in the continuum: A critical analysis of the principle of the least restrictive environment. *Journal of the Association for Persons with Severe Handicaps, 13,* 41–53.

Taylor, S. J., Biklen, D., & Knoll, J. A. (Eds.) (1987). *Community integration for people with severe disabilities.* New York: Teachers' College Press.

Taylor, S. J., Bogdan, R., & Racino, J. A. (Eds.) (1991). *Life in the community: Case studies of organizations supporting people with disabilities.* Baltimore: Paul H. Brookes.

Taylor, S. J., Racino, J., Knoll, J., & Lutfiyya, Z. (1987). *The nonrestrictive environment: A resource manual on community integration for people with the most severe disabilities.* Syracuse, NY: Human Policy Press.

Technology-Related Assistance for Individuals with Disabilities Act of 1988, 29 U.S.C § 2201 et seq.

Thorkildsen, R. (1994). *Research synthesis on quality and availability of assistive technology devices. Executive summary.* Technical report No. 8. (ERIC Document Reproduction Service No. ED 386 856)

Thurlow, M., & Elliott, J. (1998). Student assessment and evaluation. In J. R. Rusch & J. G. Chadsey (Eds.), *Beyond high school: Transition from school to work* (pp. 265–296). New York: Wadsworth Publishing Company.

Tilson, G. P., Jr., & Neubert, D. A. (1988). School-to-work transition of mildly disabled young adults: Parental perceptions of vocational needs. *The Journal for Vocational Special Needs Education, 11*(1), 33–37.

Tilson, G. P., Lueking, R. G., & Donavan, M. R. (1994). Involving employers in transition: The BRIDGES from school to work model. *Career Development for Exceptional Individuals, 17*(1), 77–89.

Tinto, V. (1993). *Leaving college: Rethinking the causes and cures of student attrition* (2nd ed.). Chicago: University of Chicago Press.

Todis, B., & Walker, H. (1993). User perspective on assistive technology in educational settings. *Focus on Exceptional Children, 26,* 1–16.

Tower, K. D. (1994). Consumer-centered social work practice: Restoring client self-determination. *Social Work, 39*(2), 191–196.

Trace Center (1996). CO-Net, HyperAbleDATA [CD-Rom program]. Madison: University of Wisconsin, Author.

Trivette, C. M., Dunst, C. J., Boyd, K., & Hamby, D. W. (1996). Family-orientated program models, helping practices and parental control appraisals. *Exceptional Children, 62*(3), 237–248.

Tucker, J. A. (1985). Curriculum-based assessment: An introduction. *Exceptional Children, 52,* 199–204.

Tuckman, B. W., & Jensen, M. A. C. (1977). States in small group development revisited. *Group and Organizational Studies, 2,* 419–442.

Turnbull, A. P., & Turnbull, H. R. (1990). *Families, professionals, and exceptionality: A special partnership* (2nd ed.). Columbus, OH: Charles H. Merrill Publishing.

Turnbull, A. P., & Morningstar, M. E. (1993). Family and professional interaction. In M. E. Snell (Ed.), *Instruction of students with severe disabilities* (4th ed., pp. 31–60). Upper Saddle River, NJ: Merrill-Prentice Hall.

Turnbull, A. P., & Turnbull, H. R. (1985). Developing independence. *Journal of Adolescent Health Care, 6*(2), 108–119.

Turnbull, A. P., & Turnbull, H. R. (1988). Toward great expectations for vocational opportunities: Family-professional partnerships. *Mental Retardation, 26*(6), 337–342.

Turnbull, A. P., & Turnbull, H. R. (1993). Empowerment and decision-making through Group Action Planning. In *Lifelong transitions: Proceedings of the third annual parent/family conference.* Washington, DC: U.S. Department of Education.

Turnbull, A. P., Barber, P., Kerns, G. M., & Behr, S. K. (1995). The family of children and youth with exceptionalities. In E. L. Meyen & T. M. Skrtic (Eds.), *Special education and student disability, an introduction: Traditional, emerging, and alternative perspectives* (4th ed., pp. 141–170). Denver, CO: Love Publishing.

Turnbull, A. P., Summers, J. A., & Brotherson, M. J. (1984). *Working with families with disabled members: A family systems approach.* Lawrence, KS: University of Kansas, Kansas University Afffiliated Facility.

Turnbull, A. P., Summers, J. A., & Brotherson, M. J. (1986). Family life cycle. In J. J. Gallagher & P. M. Vietz (Eds.), *Families of handicapped persons* (pp. 45–65). Baltimore: Paul H. Brookes.

Turnbull, H. Rutherford, III. (1993). *Free appropriate public education: The law and children with disabilities* (4th ed.). Denver, CO: Love Publishing.

Turnbull, H. R., Turnbull, A. P., Bronicki, G. J., Summers, J. A., & Roeder-Gordon, C. (1989). *Disability and the family: A guide to decisions for adulthood.* Baltimore: Paul H. Brookes.

Turner, L. (1996). Selecting a college option: Determining the best fit. In C. Flexer, D. Wray, R. Leavitt, & R. Flexer (Eds.), *How the student with hearing loss can succeed in college: A handbook for students, families, and professionals* (pp. 142–164). Washington, DC: Alexander Graham Bell Association for the Deaf.

Turner, L. P. (1996). *Parent involvement in transition planning.* Unpublished doctoral dissertation, Kent State University, Kent, OH.

Turner, L. P., & Simmons, T. J. (1996). Getting ready for transition to college. In C. Flexer, D. Wray, R. Leavitt, & R. Flexer (Eds.), *How the student with hearing loss can succeed in college: A handbook for students, families, and professionals* (2nd ed., pp.131–145). Washington, DC: Alexander Graham Bell Association for the Deaf.

U.S. Department of Education (1995). *Seventeenth annual report to Congress on the implementation of the Individuals with Disabilities Education Act.* Washington, DC: Author.

U.S. Department of Education (1996). *Eighteenth annual report to Congress on the implementation of the Individuals with Disabilities Education Act.* Washington, DC: Author.

U.S. Department of Education. (1997). *Nineteenth annual report to Congress on the implementation of the Individuals with Disabilities Education Act.* Washington DC: Author.

U.S. Department of Education. (1997). *The implementation of the Individuals with Disabilities Education Act: Section 618. Nineteenth Annual Report to Congress.* Washington, DC: Author.

U.S. Department of Education, Office for Civil Rights (1987). *1986 elementary and secondary school civil rights survey: National summaries.* Arlington, VA: DBS Corporation, subcontract from Opportunity Systems, Inc.

U.S. Department of Education, Office for Civil Rights. (1994). *1992 elementary and secondary school civil rights compliance report (draft).* Washington, DC: Author.

U.S. Department of Labor (1991). *The revised handbook for analyzing jobs.* Washington, DC: Employment and Training Administration.

Vallentutti, P. S., Bender, M., & Sims-Tucker, B. (1996). *A functional curriculum for teaching students with disabilities: Functional academics* (2nd ed.). Austin, TX: PRO-ED.

van Keulen, J. E., Weddington, G. T., & DeBose, C. E. (1998). *Speech, language, learning, and the African American child.* Boston: Allyn & Bacon.

Van Reusen, A. K., & Bos, C. S. (1990). I Plan: Helping students communicate in planning conferences. *Teaching Exceptional Children* 22(4), 30–32.

Van Reusen, A. K., & Bos, C. (1994). Facilitating student participation in individual educational programs through motivation strategy instruction. *Exceptional Children,* 60(5), 466–475.

Van Reusen, A. K., Bos, C. S., Schumaker, J. B., & Deshler, D. D. (1994). *Self-advocacy strategy for education and transition planning.* Lawrence, KS: Edge Enterprises.

Vandercook, T., York, J., & Forest, M. (1989). The McGill action planning system (MAPS): A strategy for building the vision. *Journal of the Association for Persons with Severe Handicaps,* 14(3), 205–215.

Varney, G. H. (1989). *Building productive teams: An action guide and resource book.* San Francisco: Jossey-Bass.

Vasa, S. F., & Steckelberg, A. L. (1980). Parent programs in career education for the handicapped. *Career Development for Exceptional Individuals,* 3, 74–82.

Vaughn, S., Bos, C. S., Harrell, J. E., & Lasky, B. A. (1988). Parent participation in the initial placement/IEP conference: Ten years after mandated involvement. *Journal of Learning Disabilities,* 21, 82–89.

VEWAA glossary. (1988). (Available from Materials Development Center, Stout Vocational Rehabilitation Institute, University of Wisconsin–Stout, Menomonie, WI 54751). Author.

Vincent, L., Salisbury, C., Walter, G., Brown, P., Gruenwald, L., & Powers, M. (1980). Criteria of the next environment. In W. Sailor, B. Wilcox, & L. Brown (Eds.), *Methods of instruction for severely handicapped students* (pp. 303–328). Baltimore: Paul H. Brookes.

Voeltz, L. (1984). Program and curriculum innovations to prepare children for integration. In N. Certo, N. Haring, & R. York (Eds.) Public school integration of severely handicapped students: Rational issues and progressive alternative. (pp. 155–181). Baltimore: Paul H. Brookes.

Vogel, S. A., & Adelman, P. B. (1992). The success of college students with learning disabilities: Factors related to educational attainment. *Journal of Learning Disabilities,* 25(7), 430–441.

Vogel, S. A., & Forness, S. R. (1992). Social functioning in adults with learning disabilities. *School Psychology Review,* 21(3), 375–386.

Wagner, M. (1989). *Youth with disabilities during transition: An overview of descriptive findings from the national longitudinal transition study.* Menlo Park, CA: SRI International.

Wagner, M. (1991). *Dropouts with disabilities: What do we know? What can we do?* (A report from the National Longitudinal Transition Study of Special Education Students). Menlo Park, CA: SRI International.

Wagner, M., & Blackorby, J. (1996). Transition from high school to work or college: How special education students fare. The Future of Children: Special Education for Students with Disabilities, 6(1), 103–110.

Wagner, M., D'Amico, R., Marder, C., Newman, I., & Blackorby, J. (1992). What happens next? Trends in postschool outcomes of youth with disabilities. Menlo Park, CA: SRI International.

Wagner, M., Newman, L., & Shaver, D. M. (1989). The National Longitudinal Transition Study of Special Education Students: Report on procedures for the first wave of data collection (1987). Menlo Park, CA: SRI International.

Wald, J. L. (1996). Culturally and linguistically diverse professionals in special education: A demographic analysis. Reston, VA: National Clearinghouse for Professions in Special Education and OSERS.

Walker, H. M., Colvin, G., & Ramsey, E. (1995). Antisocial behavior in schools: Strategies and best practices. Pacific Grove, CA: Brooks/Cole Publishing.

Walker, H. M., Hops, H., & Greenwood, C. (1993). RECESS: A program for reducing negative-aggressive behavior. Seattle, WA: Educational Achievement Systems.

Walker, H. M., Hops, H., Greenwood, C. R., & Todd, N. (1979). Differential effects of reinforcing topographic components of free play and social interaction: Analysis and direct replication. Behavior Modification, 3, 291–320.

Walker, H. M., McConnell, S. R., Holmes, D., Todis, B., Walker, J., & Golden N. (1983). ACCEPTS: A children's curriculum for effective peer and teacher skills. Austin, TX: PRO-ED.

Walls, R. T., & Tseng, M. S. (1987). Measurement of client outcomes in rehabilitation, In B. Bolton (Ed.), Handbook of measurement and evaluation in rehabilitation (pp. 183–201). Baltimore: Paul H. Brookes.

Ward, M. J. (1988). The many facets of self-determination. National Information Center for Children and Youth with Handicaps: Transition Summary, 5, 2–3. Washington, DC: Office of Special Education Programs of the U.S. Department of Education.

Ward, M. J. (1994, Winter). Self-determination: A means to an end. Impact, 6, 8.

Ward, M. J. (1996). Coming of age in the age of self-determination: An historical and personal perspective. In D. J. Sands & M. L. Wehmeyer (Eds.), Self-determination across the life span (pp. 1–14). Baltimore: Paul H. Brookes.

Ward, M. J., & Halloran, W. J. (1989). Transition to uncertainty: Status of many school leavers with severe disabilities. Career Development for Exceptional Individuals, 12(2), 71–78.

Ward, M. J., & Halloran, W. (1993, Fall). Transition issues for the 1990s. OSERS News in Print, 6, (1) 4–5. (ERIC Document Reproduction Service No. ED 364035)

Warner, C. (1992). Treasury of women's quotations. Upper Saddle River, NJ: Prentice-Hall.

Warrenfeltz, R. B., Kelly, W. J., Salzberb, C. L., Beegle, C. P., Levy, S. M., Adams, T. A., & Crouse, T. R. (1981). Social skills training of behavior disordered adolescents with self-monitoring to promote generalization to a vocational setting. Behavioral Disorders, 7, 18–27.

Weaver, R., & DeLuca, J. R. (1987). Employability life skills assessment: Ages 14–21. Dayton, OH: Miami Valley Special Education Center.

Webb, N. (1985). Student interaction and learning in small groups: A research summary. In R. Slavin, S. Sharon, R. Hertz-Lazarowitz, C. Webb, & R. Schmuck (Eds.), Learning to cooperate, cooperating to learn. New York: Plenum.

Weber, D., & Demchak, M. A. (1996). Using assistive technology with individuals with severe disabilities. Computers in the Schools, 12(3), 43–57.

Weber, J. (1988). Dropout rates for students in different high school curricula: another look. Journal of Vocational Education Research, 13(1), 35–39.

Webster, D. D. (1999, July). Developing the leadership potential of postsecondary students with disabilities. Paper presented at AHEAD Conference, Atlanta, GA.

Wehman, P. (1990). School-to-work: Elements of successful programs. Teaching Exceptional Children, 23(1), 40–43.

Wehman, P. (1992). Transition for young people with disabilities: Challenges for the 1990's. Education and Training in Mental Retardation; 27, 112–118.

Wehman, P. (1996). Life beyond the classroom: Transition strategies for young people with disabilities (2nd ed.). Baltimore: Paul H. Brookes.

Wehman, P. (1997). Editorial. Journal of Vocational Rehabilitation, 8(1), 1–3.

Wehman, P. (1997). Exceptional individuals in school, community, and work. Austin Texas: PRO-ED.

Wehman, P., & Kregel, J. (1985). A supported work approach to competitive employment of individuals with moderate and severe handicaps. Journal of the Association for Persons with Severe Handicaps, 10, 3–11.

Wehman, P., Kregel, J., & Barcus, J. M. (1985). From school to work: A vocational transition model for handicapped students. Exceptional Children, 52(1), 25–37.

Wehman, P., Kregel, J., & Seyfarth, J. (1985a). Transition from school to work for individuals with severe handicaps: A follow-up study. Journal of the Association for Persons with Severe Handicaps, 10(3), 132–136.

Wehman, P., Kregel, J., & Seyfarth, J. (1985b). Employment outlook for young adults with mental retardation. Rehabilitation Counseling Bulletin, 29, 90–99.

Wehman, P., Moon, M. S., Everson, J. M., Wood, W., & Barcus, J. M. (1988). Transition from school to work: New challenges for youth with severe disabilities. Baltimore: Paul H. Brookes.

Wehmeyer, M., & Schwartz, M. (1997). Self-determination and positive adult outcomes: A follow-up of youth with mental retardation or learning disabilities. Exceptional Children, 63(2), 245–255.

Wehmeyer, M., & Lawrence, M. (1996). Whose future is it anyway? Promoting student involvement in transition planning. *Career Development for Exceptional Individuals,* 18(2), 69–84.

Wehmeyer, M. L. (1992). Self-determination: Critical skills for outcome-oriented transition services. *The Journal for Vocational Special Needs Education,* 15, 3–9.

Wehmeyer, M. L. (1993). Perceptual and psychological factors in career decision-making of adolescents with and without cognitive disabilities. *Career Development for Exceptional Individuals,* 16 (2), 135–146.

Wehmeyer, M. L. (1994). Perceptions of self-determination and psychological empowerment of adolescents with mental retardation. *Education and Training in Mental Retardation and Developmental Disabilities,* 29, 9–21.

Wehmeyer, M. L. (1995). *The ARC's self-determination scale: Procedural guidelines.* (Available from The ARC of the United States, 500 E. Border Street, Suite 300, Arlington, TX 76010.)

Wehmeyer, M. L. (1997). Student-directed learning and self-determination. In M. Agran (Ed.), *Student directed learning: teaching self-determination skills* (pp. 28–59). Pacific Grove, CA: Brooks/Cole Publishers.

Wehmeyer, M. L. (1998). National survey of the use of assistive technology by adults with mental retardation. *Mental Retardation,* 36, 44–51.

Wehmeyer, M. L. (1998). Student involvement in transition-planning and transition-program implementation. In F. R. Rusch & J. G. Chadsey (Eds.), *Beyond high school: Transition from school to work.* (pp. 206–233). Belmont CA: Wadsworth Publishing.

Wehmeyer, M. L., Agran, M., & Hughes, C. (1998). *Teaching self-determination to students with disabilities: Basic skills for successful transition.* Baltimore: Paul H. Brookes.

Wehmeyer, M. L., Palmer, S. B., Agran, M., Mithaug, D. E., & Martin, J. E. (in press). *Exceptional Children.*

Wehmeyer, M. L., & Kelchner, K. (1995). *The ARC's self-determination scale.* Arlington, TX: ARC.

Wehmeyer, M. L., & Kelchner, K. (1995b). *Whose future is it anyway?* Arlington, TX: ARC.

Wehmeyer, M. L., & Ward, M. J. (1995). The spirit of IDEA mandate: Student involvement in transition planning. *Journal of the Association for Vocational Special Needs Education,* 17, 108–111.

Welsh Office, Department of Education. (1994). *Code of practice on the identification and assessment of special education needs.* Cardiff, Wales, UK: Author.

Wermuth, T. (1991). Impact of educational legislation on transition and supported employment programs. *The Advance,* 3, 3–4. Richmond, VA: Association for Persons in Supported Employment [APSE].

West, J. (1991). *The Americans with Disabilities Act: From policy to practice.* New York: Milbank Fund.

Westling, D. L., & Fox, L. (2000). *Teaching students with severe disabilities* (2nd ed.). Upper Saddle River, NJ: Merrill/Prentice Hall.

White, W. A. T. (1988). A meta-analysis of effects of direct instruction in special education. *Education and Treatment of Children,* 11, 364–374.

Whitehead, C. W. (1977). *Sheltered workshop study: A nationwide report on sheltered workshops and their employment of handicapped individuals* (Workshop Survey, Vol. I, U.S. Department of Labor Services Publications). Washington, DC: U.S. Government Printing Office.

Whitney-Thomas, J., & Hanley-Maxwell, C. (1996). Packing the parachute: Parents experiences as their children prepare to leave high school. *Exceptional Children,* 63(1), 75–88.

Whitney-Thomas, J., Shaw, D., Honey, K., & Butterworth, J. (1998). Building a future: A study of student participation in person-centered planning, *The Journal of the Association for Persons with Severe Handicaps,* (23)2, 119–133.

Wilcox, B., & Bellamy, G. T. (1987). *The activities catalog: An alternative curriculum for youth and adults with severe disabilities.* Baltimore: Paul H. Brookes.

Will, M. (1983). OSERS *programming for the transition of youth with disabilities: Bridges from school to working life.* Washington, DC: U.S. Department of Education, Office of Special Education and Rehabilitative Services. (ERIC Document Reproduction Service No. ED 256 132)

Williams, B. (1991). Assistive technology in the eye of the beholder. *Journal of Vocational Rehabilitation,* 1(2)9–12.

Willig, A. C. (1986). Special education and the culturally and linguistically different child: An overview of issues and challenges. In A. C. Willing & H. F. Greenberg (Eds.), *Bilingualism and learning disabilities: Policy and practice for teachers and administrators* (pp. 191–209). New York: American Library Publishing.

Willis, W. (1998). Families with African American roots. In E. W. Lynch & M. H. Hanson (Eds.), *Developing cross-cultural competence: A guide for working with children and their families* (2nd ed., pp. 165–208). Baltimore: Paul H. Brookes.

Winterbottom, C., Liska, D. W., & Obermaier, K. M. (1995). *State-level databook on health care access and financing.* Washington, DC: The Urban Institute.

Winup, K. (1994). The role of a student committee in promotion of independence among school leavers. In J. Coupe-O'Kane & B. Smith (Eds.), *Taking control* (pp. 103 B 116). London: David Fulton Publishers.

Wise, W. E., & Matthews, C. L. (1987). A *study of the relationship of education and transition factors to the job status of mildly and moderately handicapped students.* (Rep. No. 95-01/87/06/04). Dover, DE: Delaware State Department of Public Instruction.

Wisniewski, L., & Sedlak, R. (1992). Assistive devices for students with disabilities: Integrating learners with disabilities in regular education programs. *Elementary School Journal,* 92, 297–314.

Wolfe, V. V., Boyd, L. A., & Wolfe, D. A. (1983). Teaching cooperative play to behavior-problem preschool children. *Education and Treatment of Children,* 6, 1–9.

Wolfensberger, W. (1972). *The principal normalization in human services.* Toronto: National Institute on Mental Retardation.

Wolfensberger, W. (1991). *A brief introduction to SRV as a high-order concept for structuring human services*. Syracuse, NY: Training Institute for Human Service Planning, Leadership and Change Agency.

Wolffe, K. (1997). *Career counseling for people with disabilities: A practical guide to finding employment*. Austin, TX: PRO-ED.

Wolman, J. M., Campeau, P. L., DuBois, P. A., Mithaug, D. E., & Stolarski, V. S. (1994). *AIR self-determination scale and user guide*. Palo Alto, CA: American Institutes for Research.

Woolcock, W. W., Stodden, R. A., & Bisconer, S. W. Process and outcome-focused decision making. In F. R. Rusch, L. DeStefano, J. Chadsey-Rusch, L. A. Phelps & E. Szymanski (Eds.), *Transition from school to adult life: Models, linkages, and policy* (pp. 219–244). Sycamore, IL: Sycamore Publishing.

Workman, E. A., Helton, G. B., & Watson, P. J. (1982). Self-monitoring effects in a four-year-old child: An ecological behavior analysis. *Journal of School Psychology*, 20, 57–64.

World Institute on Disability. (1991). *Personal assistance services: A new millennium. Resolution on personal assistance services passed by participants of the international personal assistance services symposium*. Oakland, CA: World Institute on Disability.

Yoshida, R. K., Fenton, K. S., Maxwell, J. P., & Kaufman, N. J. (1978). Ripple effect: Communication of planning team decisions to program implementation. *Journal of School Psychology*, 16, 178–183.

Young, C. C., & Kerr, M. M. (1979). The effects of a retarded child's social initiations on the behavior of severely retarded school-aged peers. *Education and Training of the Mentally Retarded*, 14, 185–190.

Ysseldyke, J. E., & Algozzine, B. (1995). *Special education: A practical approach for teachers* (3rd ed.). Boston: Houghton Mifflin.

Ysseldyke, J. E., Algozzine, B., & Thurlow, M. L. (1992). *Critical issues in special education* (2nd ed.). Boston: Houghton Mifflin.

Ysseldyke, J. E., & Thurlow, M. L. (1994). *Educational outcomes for students with disabilities*. New York: Haworth Press.

Zabala, J. (1994).The SETT *framework: Critical questions to ask when making informed assistive technology decisions*. Paper presented at Closing the Gap Conference, Oct, 1994, Minneapolis, MN.

Zigmond, N., & Miller, S. E. (1992). Improving high school programs for students with learning disabilities: A matter of substance as well as form. In F. R. Rusch, L. Destefano, J. Chadsey-Rusch, L. A. Phelps, & E. Symanski (Eds.), *Transition from school to adult life: Mafels, linkages, and policy* (pp. 17–31). Sycamore, IL: Sycamore Publishing.

Zuniga, M. E. (1998). Families with Latino roots. In E. W. Lynch & M. H. Hanson (Eds.), *Developing cross-cultural competence: A guide for working with children and their families* (2nd ed., pp. 209–250). Baltimore: Paul H. Brookes.

Name Index

Adams, G., 232
Adams, L., 230
Adamson, W. S., 128
Adelman, P. D., 417
Agosta, J., 399
Agran, M., 307, 308, 311, 312, 457
Airasion, P. W., 215
Al-Darmarki, F., 376
Alberto, P. A., 255
Albin, J., 62
Albin, R. W., 365
Algozzine, B., 133, 256
Alper, S., 242, 243, 244
Althen, G., 123, 124
Anderson, C., 251
Anderson, L., 251, 253
Anderson, R. J., 166, 170, 191
Anderson, W., 401
Ansel, R., 468
Ashbaugh, J. W., 509
Aslanian, C. B., 445
Asselin, S., 44, 97, 102, 104, 365
Astin, A., 455, 456, 468
Aune, E., 458, 468
Azrin, N. H., 190, 427

Backus, L., 58
Baer, R., 54, 55, 92, 114, 115, 116,
    179, 191, 338, 339, 341, 366, 375,
    376, 377, 379, 423, 427, 428
Baker, E. T., 528
Bambara, L. M., 480
Banbury, M. M., 387
Barbeau, P. E., 426
Barber, P., 125
Barbut, A., 445
Barcus, J., 20, 45, 61, 63, 224, 240,
    393, 397, 399, 478
Barcus, M., 401

Barrera, I., 124
Bartholomew, K., 513
Bates, P., 401, 406
Bauder, D. K., 276, 286, 287, 288, 289
Baumgart, D., 295
Bausch, M. E., 275
Beare, P. L., 63
Beattie, J., 118, 230, 338, 366
Beatty, P., 519
Becker, C. W., 232
Becker, W. C., 232
Beckett, C., 401
Bedore-Bideaux, K. A., 324
Beeman, P., 524
Begun, W., 199
Behr, S. K., 125
Behrmann, M., 64, 273, 286, 292
Belcher, R. G., 114, 429
Bell, J. K., 275
Bellamy, G. T., 66, 389, 394, 426
Bender, M., 64, 239, 292
Benz, M., 36, 48, 58, 67, 190, 244,
    366, 393, 395, 399, 458, 460,
    464, 466, 467
Berdine, W. H., 396, 398, 399
Berliss, J. R., 273
Berman, L. M., 229
Bernstein, G. S., 291
Besalel, V. B., 427
Bianchi, J., 404
Bickel, D. D., 256
Bickel, W. E., 256
Biklen, D., 509, 511
Billingsley, F. F., 239
Bisconer, S. W., 58
Black, B., 190
Black, J., 528
Blackhurst, A. E., 64, 273, 275,
    276, 286, 289

Blackorby, J., 7, 28, 417, 418, 442,
    443, 444
Blackstone, S., 274, 287
Blaney, B. C., 509
Blatt, B., 9
Blick, D. W., 263
Bloomberg, L., 435
Bogdan, R., 511
Boles, S. M., 66, 389, 393, 394
Bolles, R. N., 341, 417, 418,
    429, 430
Bolton, B., 75
Bond, G. R., 424
Borden, P. A., 273
Borgen, F. H.
Bos, C., 323, 340, 372, 387, 389,
    390, 399, 458
Bose, J., 127
Botuck, S., 417
Bourexis, P. S., 28
Bowe, F. G., 48
Bowser, G., 273
Boyer, E., 440
Boyer, S. L., 424
Braddock, D., 422
Bradley, C., 393
Bradley, R. H., 287, 288
Bradley, V. J., 509
Brame, K., 156, 157, 158
Brammer, G., 393
Branston, M. B., 239
Brinckerhoff, L. C., 451, 467, 468
Brislin, R., 121, 122, 123, 129
Brolin, D. E., 164, 166, 167, 168,
    171, 175, 178, 208, 209, 210,
    214, 224, 239, 240, 341, 392
Bronicki, G. J., 44
Brookhiser, R., 123, 138
Brooks, L., 70, 76, 79

Brophy, J., 248, 249, 250, 251, 252, 253
Brotherson, M. J., 287, 288, 396, 397, 398, 399, 401, 406, 408
Browder, D., 205, 244
Brown, C., 64, 220, 274
Brown, D., 70, 73, 76, 79
Brown, L., 41, 59, 239, 295, 365, 528
Brown, P., 467
Browning, P. L., 55, 57, 220
Bruder, M. B., 399
Bruininks, R., 393, 395, 399, 435
Bucher, D. E., 214
Buckley, J., 62
Bullis, M. D., 210
Bumgarner, M., 480
Burkhead, E. J., 279
Burleson, R. B., 275
Burnette, J., 127, 129, 154, 158
Bursuck, W. D., 229, 467
Burwell, B., 510
Butterworth, J., 60, 338, 348, 366

Cameto, R., 443
Campbell, C., 338
Campbell, P., 393
Campbell, P. H., 289
Campeau, P. L., 307
Carey, L. M., 215
Carlson, B. C., 460
Carney, I. H., 66
Carnine, D., 232
Carta, J. J., 136
Cartledge, G., 236
Cavalier, A. R., 64
Certo, N., 77, 164, 239
Chadsey, J., 467, 476, 485
Chadsey-Rusch, J., 440
Chambers, A. C., 276, 289
Chan, F., 184, 185
Chan, S., 124, 144, 146
Chandler, C. L., 458
Cheney, D., 210
Childs, K. E., 331
Chitwood, S., 401
Choi, S. H., 457
Cioffi, A., 417, 428, 433

Clark, G. M., 16, 39, 49, 70, 71, 163, 164, 165, 166, 167, 168, 171, 173, 175, 176, 182, 208, 209, 210, 212, 245, 338, 340, 344, 397, 460
Clarke, S., 331, 480
Clements, B., 251
Cloninger, C. J., 338
Cobb, R. B., 165, 186
Cohen, S., 399, 400, 406
Coleman, M. C., 387, 389, 391
Collet-Klingenberg, L., 228, 239
Colvin, G., 236
Condeluci, A., 476, 477
Cone, J. D., 389
Connell, J. P., 307
Conrad, D. A., 183
Constans, T., 129
Conyers, L., 76
Cook, A. M., 299
Cook, I. D., 460
Cook, J. A., 423
Cook, L., 131, 148
Cooper, J., 262, 275
Copher, J. I., 44, 54, 393
Correa, V., 58, 157, 341
Couch, R., 220
Coupe-O'Kane, J., 306
Covert, S., 399
Cowen, S., 441
Cramer, S. H., 76
Crites, J., 79, 89, 341
Cronin, M., 240, 528
Cross, D., 275, 276, 286, 289
Crunkilton, S. R., 229, 230
Cummins, J., 127
Curry, L., 387, 389, 391

D'Alonzo, B. J., 393, 460
D'Amico, R., 418, 442
Dalke, C., 58, 65
Danielian, J., 138
Daniels, S., 478
Darch, C., 231
Dautel, P. J., 519, 520
Davern, L., 528
Dawis, R., 80
Day, R. M., 238
Deal, A., 400

DeBose, C. E., 127
Deci, E. L., 305, 458
DeFur, S., 96, 104
DeJong, G., 366, 507, 519
Delawyer, D. D., 389
DeLoach, C. P., 441
DeLuca, J. R., 341
DeMarasse, R., 524
Demchak, M. A., 274
Dempsey, P., 528
Deniston, T., 399
Dennis, R. E., 132, 136
Deno, S. L., 253
Dentzer, S., 417
DePerczel, M., 480
Depoy, E., 305
Derer, K., 273, 291
Deschamps, A. B., 61
Deshler, D. D., 49, 323
DeStefano, L., 10, 42, 44, 393, 417, 440, 460, 464, 466
Dever, R., 528
DeVillar, R. A., 121
DiGangi, S. A., 263
Dileo, D., 63, 347, 428
Dinerstein, R. D., 372, 376
Dinnebeil, L. A., 387, 388
Doll, R. C., 228
Donaldson, J., 478
Donnellan, A., 231
Doren, B., 48, 58, 244, 323, 395, 458
Doris, J., 126, 127, 129
Doyle, W., 248, 253, 254, 255, 256
Drake, S., 511
Droege, R. C., 424
Dryer, L., 528
DuBois, P. A., 307
DuBow, S., 17
Ducharme, G., 524
Dunlap, G., 331, 480
Dunn, R., 123, 124, 138, 144
Dunst, C., 399
Durlak, C. M., 229, 467, 468
Dybwad, G., 157
Dyer, K., 480

Eber, 96
Edelman, A., 194

Edgar, E., 42, 43, 61, 63, 239, 243
Edwards, J. P., 393
Elbaum, B., 261
Elliott, B., 393, 395
Elliott, J., 211, 214
Ellis, A. K., 232
Ellis, E. S., 292
Emmer, E., 251, 253, 255, 256
Englemann, S., 232
Englert, C. S., 248, 256, 257
Enright, M. S., 78, 182
Ernest, J., 129
Esposito, L., 289
Ettinger, J. M., 78, 182
Eubanks, S. C., 129
Everson, J., 61, 96, 100, 114, 115,
    116, 224, 240, 379, 395, 396,
    397, 399, 401, 418, 478
Evertson, C., 251, 253, 255, 256

Fairweather, J. S., 441, 442
Falvey, M., 295, 528
Fanning, P. N., 393
Farren, C., 170, 191
Fenton, K. S., 387, 389, 391
Ferguson, B., 397, 399, 401, 406
Ferguson, D. L., 501
Ferguson, P. M., 501, 510
Fernandez, D., 78
Ferrara, J. M., 291
Fesko, S., 435
Festes, R. J., 138
Fichten, C. S., 468
Field, S., 307, 308, 312, 316,
    326, 467
Fielder, I., 274
Finch, C. R., 229, 230
Fischer, J., 445
Fisher, D., 77, 164, 177, 279
Fisher, E., 531
Fisher, S., 460
Fisher, S. K., 295
Flannery, K. B., 365
Flexer, R., 54, 100, 114, 115, 118,
    178, 191, 192, 229, 244, 338,
    365, 366, 375, 376, 377, 379,
    423, 427, 445, 448
Foley, R. M., 104
Ford, A., 509, 512, 513, 528

Ford, B. A., 158
Forest, M., 190, 224, 340, 524
Forness, S. R., 468
Foss, G., 210
Foss, P. D., 392
Foster, S. B., 467
Fouts, J. T., 232
Fox, L., 132, 175, 177, 469
Fradd, S. H., 136, 157
Frank, A. R., 458
Frank, K., 445, 448
Frey, R. M., 39
Frieden, L., 519, 520
Friedlander, R., 297
Friend, M., 131, 148
Fritts, M., 168
Fuchs, D., 528
Fuchs, L. S., 253, 528
Fuhrer, M. J., 211
Fujiura, G. T., 132
Funk, D., 418
Furney, K. S., 126

Gajar, A., 65, 74, 113, 182, 208,
    209, 210, 223, 442, 452, 469
Gallivan-Fenlon, A., 60, 338
Galvin, 276
Garcia, S. B., 127
Gardner, J., 295, 442
Gartin, B. C., 465
Gartner, A., 387, 389
Gault, A., 132
Gaylord-Ross, R., 205
Geer, S., 17
Geraghty, M., 469
Gerber, P. J., 310, 387, 468
German, S., 325
Gershaw, N. J., 238
Gersten, R., 231, 232
Getzel, E., 435, 441, 443, 460, 468
Giangreco, M. F., 132, 136, 338, 340
Gibbs, H., 389
Gill, D., 63
Gilliam, J. E., 387, 389, 391
Gilmore, G., 387
Ginsberg, R., 310, 468
Gliedman, J., 157
Goebel, G., 115, 191, 375, 376,
    377, 423

Goldman, H. H., 423
Goldman, J., 366, 367, 376
Goldstein, A. P., 238, 389, 399, 405
Goldstein, S., 387, 391
Gomez, A., 480
Gonzalez, P., 393
Good, T. L., 248, 249, 250, 251,
    252, 253
Goodall, P., 399
Goode, D., 48
Goodman, L., 74, 182, 469
Gordon, L. R., 334, 344, 406
Gordon, S. E., 20, 41, 42, 451
Granger, M., 417
Graves, A. W., 262
Gray, J. D., 170
Gray, K., 444, 445, 446
Green, F. P., 490
Green, J. W., 121, 123, 124, 130,
    131, 132, 137, 138, 155, 156
Greenbaum, J., 404, 406
Greenberg, H. F., 127
Greenfield, P. M., 457
Greenwood, C., 238
Gresham, F. M., 236
Griffin, H. D., 387
Grigal, M., 60, 118, 230, 338, 366
Griggs, S. A., 123, 124, 138, 144
Gruenewald, L., 239
Guillory, J. D., 96, 100, 114, 115,
    379, 418
Gussel, L., 467
Guy, B., 291
Gysbers, N. C., 392

Hagner, D., 63, 264, 347, 366,
    427, 428
Hale, R. L., 257
Hall, M., 511, 528
Hallahan, D. P., 262
Halloran, W., 44, 55, 61, 305, 418
Halpern, A. S., 5, 39, 40, 41, 43, 44,
    48, 49, 58, 61, 63, 67, 200, 208, 211,
    244, 245, 323, 340, 365, 372, 393,
    395, 399, 417, 440, 458, 460, 464,
    467, 475, 479, 523
Hammond, J., 123, 124, 138
Hamre-Neitupski, S., 239, 264,
    365, 405

Handley, M., 531
Hanley-Maxwell, C., 44, 54, 57, 66,
    74, 75, 76, 97, 104, 193, 228,
    239, 365, 366, 367
Hanson, M. J., 121, 123, 124, 130,
    136, 138, 140, 156
Hardman, M., 230, 393, 476, 478
Haring, K. A., 58, 392
Haring, N. G., 398
Haring, T. G., 398
Harrell, J. E., 387, 389, 390
Harriman, N. E., 257
Harris, L., 441, 443
Harrison, S. B., 524
Harry, B., 123, 124, 125, 127, 132,
    133, 136, 138, 156, 157
Hart, D., 297
Hasazi, S. B., 20, 41, 42, 58, 334,
    344, 406
Haskew, P., 231
Hayden, D., 3401
Hayden, M. F., 366, 376
Haynes, J., 393
Hazel, J. S., 49, 238
Hazelkorn, M. N., 44, 48, 338,
    441, 445
Heal, L. W., 44, 54, 61, 393
Hebbeler, K., 467
Hecimovic, A., 396
Hecklinger, F., 190
Heins, E. D., 262
Helm, D., 366
Helton, G. B., 262
Henderson, C., 387, 442
Hendricks, D. J., 296
Hensel, J. W., 393
Heron, T. E., 262
Herr, C. M., 323
Herr, E. L., 76
Herr, S. S., 372, 376
Hershenson, D., 70, 71, 73, 75, 77,
    78, 80, 81, 83, 84, 166, 173, 174,
    181
Hertweck, A., 123
Hesche, S., 338
Heward, W. L., 262
Heyne, L. A., 490
Heyward, S. M., 448
Hightower, J., 393

Hill, B., 509
Hilton, A., 387
Hirsh, A. E., 296
Hobbs, N., 123, 124, 126, 138
Hodapp, R. M., 396
Hoffman, A., 307, 308, 312, 467
Hoffman, R. C., 393
Hoffschmidt, S. J., 423
Hofmeister, A. M., 273
Holburn, S., 366
Holder-Brown, L., 276
Holland, J. L., 79, 83, 89, 341, 457
Honey, K., 338
Hops, H., 238
Horiuchi, C. N., 393
Horner, R. H., 365
Hourcade, J. J., 276, 287, 288
Hoyt, K. B., 15
Huber Marshall, L., 307, 308, 310,
    312, 316, 323, 325, 340
Hudson, P. J., 393
Hughes, C., 115, 307, 427, 442, 457
Hughes, M., 261
Hughes, W., 316
Hulgin, K., 511, 531
Humes, C. W., 393
Husch, J. V., 326
Hussey, S. M., 299

Inge, K. J., 289
Ippoliti, C., 305
Irvin, L., 208
Iverson, V. S., 338

Jackson, D. A., 238
Jackson, N. F., 238
Jacobson, J. W., 18
Janesick, V. J., 132
Jensen, M. A., 115, 380
Jerman, P., 316, 323, 340
Joe, J. R., 124, 130, 140
Johnson, D., 291, 395, 399, 407
Johnson, D. K., 366
Johnson, D. R., 379
Johnson, J., 49, 54, 63
Johnson, J. R., 44
Johnson, M., 190
Johnson, M. D., 323
Johnson, T. Z., 512, 513

Johnston-Rodriguez, S., 180, 195
Joordan, J., 80
Jorgensen, C. M., 528
Juhrs, P. D., 114, 429
Jundt, M., 469
June, J., 104, 108
Justice, T., 393

Katzer, T., 480
Kauffman, J. M., 236, 262, 480
Kaufman, N. J., 387, 389, 391
Kaye, B., 170
Kaye, S. H., 75
Kazdin, A. E., 241
Kearns, F. K., 233
Kearns, J., 528
Keitel, M. A., 128
Kelchner, K., 209, 312, 323,
    340, 372
Keller, J., 395
Kelley, Y., 104, 108
Kelso, C. A., 56, 60, 63, 228,
    338, 393
Kennedy, J., 75
Kennedy, S., 233
Kern, L., 331
Kerns, G. M., 125
Kezar, A., 455, 456
Kiburz, C. S., 263
Kiely, M., 18
Kiernan, W., 428
Kim, J., 427
Kim, V., 457
King-Sears, M. E., 258
Kinneldorf, M., 393
Kinnison, L. R., Jr., 392, 408
Kistler, J. K., 458
Kivlighan, D. M., 376
Klein, J., 511, 512, 513
Klein, P., 238
Kleinert, H., 233, 528
Knoll, J., 501, 509, 510, 512, 513
Knoll, J. A., 511
Knopp, L., 127, 129
Knowlton, H., 58
Knox, W., 441
Koch, L., 76, 78, 83, 180, 183, 194,
    195, 371, 376, 377, 378
Kochany, L., 395

Kochhar, C. A., 36, 61, 460, 467
Koger, F., 480
Kohler, P., 49, 51, 54, 55, 56, 57, 68, 102, 224, 366, 375, 376, 379, 392, 393, 399
Kokaska, C., 164, 166, 208, 209, 210
Kolb, N., 441
Kolstoe, O. P., 39, 49, 70, 71, 163, 164, 165, 166, 167, 168, 171, 173, 175, 176, 182, 208, 209, 210, 338, 397
Komissar, C., 297
Korabek, C. A., 244
Kortering, L. J., 61
Kosiewicz, M. M., 262
Kounin, J. S., 253, 255
Krajewski, L., 405
Kramer, L., 124
Kranstover, L. L., 393
Kravetz, M., 470
Kregel, J., 20, 63, 70, 393, 399, 509
Krom, D. M., 48, 338
Krumboltz, J., 81, 82, 83, 89

Lahm, E., 289
Lakin, C., 510
Lakin, K., 509
Landrum, T. J., 263
Langone, J., 298
LaPlante, M. P., 75
Lareau, A., 123
Larrivee, B., 257
Lasky, B. A., 387, 389, 390
Lawn, B., 423
Lawson, J. D., 323
Lazzaro, J. J., 274
Le Conte, W., 201
Leake, D., 55, 56
LeConte, P., 201
Lee, J., 279
Lehmann, J., 399
Levy, J. M., 417
Lewis, P., 289
Lewis, R. D., 122, 149
Lin, H. C., 435
Lindeman, R. H., 80
Lindsay, P., 441
Lindstrom, L., 67, 190, 366, 464
Linn, R., 208, 209, 210

Lippert, T., 512
Lipsky, D. K., 387, 389
Liska, D. W., 520
Litvak, S., 519, 520
Lloyd, J. W., 262, 263
Lobman, M., 129
Loewen, G., 440
Lofquist, L., 80
Lombard, R., 44, 48, 60, 63, 199, 201, 338, 441, 445
Love, L. L., 242, 394
Lovett, D. L., 392, 393
Lovett, H., 524
Lubin, R., 18, 19
Luckasson, R., 509, 526, 528
Lucyshyn, J. M., 365
Ludlum, C., 524
Luft, P., 76, 124, 156, 164, 182, 194, 200, 208, 209, 224
Lusthaus, C. S., 389, 390
Lusthaus, E., 190, 224, 524
Lusthaus, E. W., 389, 390
Lynch, E. C., 63
Lynch, E. W., 123, 124, 130, 131, 133, 136, 157, 388, 399
Lynch, R. T., 467
Lyon, S., 295

Maag, J. W., 263
MacDonald, C., 365
Mackelsprang, R. W., 365, 366
Maddy-Bernstein, C., 61, 62, 165
Malach, R. S., 124, 130
Malian, I. M., 394
Malone, B. L., 427
Mandershied, R. W., 423
Mangrum, C. T., 470
Mank, D., 62, 63, 417, 426, 428, 429, 433
Mar, D., 307
Marder, C., 418, 442, 443
Mariage, T. V., 248
Markel, G., 404, 406
Markowitz, J., 127, 130, 154, 157
Marshall, K., 509
Marshall, L. H., 480
Martin, J. E., 307, 308, 310, 311, 312, 316, 323, 325, 326, 340, 372, 480

Martonyi, E., 114, 191, 375, 427
Masino, L. L., 396
Massenzio, S., 404
Mastropieri, M., 237, 238, 248, 256
Mathot-Buckner, C., 397, 399, 401, 406
Mattessich, B. W., 100
Matthews, C. L., 393
Maxson, L., 307, 316, 323, 340
Maxwell, J. P., 387, 389, 391
McAfee, J., 74, 182
McCallen, M. H., 286, 341
McClanahan, M., 220
McConnell, S., 236
McCord, W., 478
McCormick, L., 398
McCrary, N. E., 275
McDaniel, R., 220
McDonald, G., 507
McDonnell, J., 66, 230, 243, 389, 393, 394, 397, 399, 401, 406, 407, 476, 478, 479, 491
McFall, R., 236
McGahee-Kovac, M., 323
McGill, T., 316
McGinnis, E., 238
McGonigle, J. J., 262
McGrew, K. S., 435
McGuire, J. M., 451, 458, 467
McKnight, J., 513
McLaughlin, T. F., 263
McMahan, R. K., 55, 279
McNair, J., 66, 388, 394
McNulty, K., 399, 401
McPhatter, A. R., 123, 124
McSweyn, C. A., 379
Meers, G., 164, 188, 291
Mehan, J., 123, 136
Meihls, J. L., 123
Menchetti, B., 63, 209, 338, 340, 347
Mercer, A. R., 233
Mercer, C. D., 233
Mertz, M. K., 470
Merz, M., 78
Meyer, L., 528
Meyerson, A. T., 423
Mikkelsen, K. S., 366
Milburn, J. A., 236
Miles, 96

Miller, J. H., 387
Miller, R., 312
Miller, R. J., 441, 445
Miller, S. E., 245
Miller, S. M., 132
Miller, S. R., 263
Miller, T., 452
Miller, T. L., 316
Mitchell, K., 469
Mitchell, L. K., 81, 82
Mithaug, D. E., 229, 307, 308,
    326, 393
Mokuau, N., 146
Monette, G. C., 456
Moody, S. W., 261
Moon, M., 61, 224, 240, 297, 298,
    395, 396, 397, 399, 401, 478
Moore, S. C., 379
Moores, D., 129
Morgan, J., 64
Morgan, R. L., 379
Morningstar, M. E., 66, 387, 395,
    396, 403, 404, 457
Morris, R., 469
Morrison, G., 296
Morrison, J., 123, 124, 138
Morrissette, S., 286
Morrow, L. W., 263
Morse, T. E., 286
Morton, M. V., 401
Mount, B., 49, 224, 338, 340, 352,
    366, 524
Mullins, J. A., 451
Munk, D. D., 306
Myers, L. B., 341
Myers, R. A., 80

Nabors, K., 429
Neel, R. S., 239
Nelson, 96
Neubert, D., 39, 44, 48, 165, 186,
    199, 201, 245, 338, 388, 393
Newman, I., 418, 442
Newman, L., 186, 443
Nietupski, J., 264, 365, 405
Nirje, B., 57, 305
Nisbet, J., 399
Norman, M., 28
Nosek, M. A., 519

O'Brien, C., 511, 512, 513
O'Brien, J., 224, 316, 338, 340, 344,
    366, 511, 512, 513, 524
O'Brien, L., 366
O'Connor, S., 511
O'Neill, R. E., 331
O'Sullivan, J. L., 372, 376
Obermaier, K. M., 520
Obiakor, F. E., 127, 154, 156, 157
Odom, S. L., 236
Ogusthorpe, M. R., 392
Oliphint, J., 326
Ollendick, T. H., 262
Olson, W., 510
Oorthuys, J., 428
Opheim, B., 405
Orelove, F. P., 66
Ostercamp, D., 405
Otuya, E., 127, 129
Owen, S. D., 393
Owens, D. M., 209
Owens-Johnson, L., 75, 193
Oxford, M., 507

Palmer, S., 307, 308
Panscofar, E., 60, 348, 396
Parent, W., 435
Parette, H. P., 276, 286, 287, 288
Parker, R. M., 83, 185
Parsons, M. B., 480
Pascarella, E., 440, 441, 445,
    456, 458
Pati, G., 296
Patterson, J., 183
Patton, J. R., 104, 112, 186, 208,
    240, 243, 340, 344, 528
Pearpoint, J., 190, 224, 524
Peck, C., 478
Peppey, B., 305
Perske, R., 14, 476
Peterson, K., 393, 395
Phelps, L. A., 54, 57, 61, 62, 440
Phillips, B., 287
Phillips, J. F., 244
Piland, V. C., 63, 338, 340, 347
Pinderhughes, E., 123, 124, 155
Pinson-Millburn, N., 64
Pitman, J. A., 445
Plant, R. W., 307

Pogoloff, S. M., 66, 366, 367
Pollitzer, W. S., 131, 132
Polloway, E. A., 239, 243
Polsgrove, L., 273, 291
Porter, J., 306
Powell, T., 79, 221, 238
Power, P., 184
Powers, L., 64, 295, 322
Powers, L. E., 341, 372
Prater, M. A., 48, 338
Pruitt, P., 387, 388
Pumpian, I., 60, 77, 164, 177, 239,
    277, 338
Putnam, J. W., 258

Rachal, P., 115, 116
Racino, J., 366, 509, 510, 511,
    512, 519
Rainforth, B., 365
Ramsey, E., 236
Raskind, M. H., 273
Reed, C., 193
Reed, P., 273, 276, 289
Reid, D. H., 244, 480
Reid, R., 263
Reiff, H. B., 310, 468
Repetto, J. B., 58, 341, 388
Repp, A. C., 306
Reschly, D. J., 127
Reynolds, J., 480
Rhodes, L., 62, 426, 428
Richmond, G., 519
Richmond, L., 64
Rieth, H., 273, 291
Rimmerman, A., 417
Rivera, D. P., 233
Robillard, K., 468
Roby, P., 132
Roderick, J. A., 229
Rodriquez, R. F., 155
Roe, C. A., 20, 41, 42, 334, 344, 406
Roeder-Gordon, C., 44
Roessler, R., 75, 194
Rojewski, J. W., 63, 340, 417, 428
Rose, E., 229, 467
Rose, S. M., 132
Rosenshine, B., 232, 248, 250, 251,
    252, 256, 258
Ross, I., 393, 395

Roth, W., 157
Rothenbacher, C., 201
Rothschild, I., 404
Rowe, P., 263
Rudrud, E. H., 291
Rule, S., 387, 388
Rumrill, P., 183, 193, 194, 195, 200, 224, 371, 376, 377, 378, 441, 443, 451, 465
Rusch, F., 49, 54, 63, 399
Rusch, F. R., 44, 66, 209, 229, 388, 393, 394, 427, 440, 476
Russo, C. J., 127
Rutherford, R. B., Jr., 263
Ryan, C., 193
Ryan, R. B., 307
Ryan, R. M., 305
Rylance, B. J., 244, 245
Ryndak, D. L., 242, 243, 244

Sale, P., 312
Sale, R. P., 323, 325
Salembier, G., 126
Salend, S., 260, 265, 398
Salsgiver, R. O., 8, 365, 366
Salzberg, C. L., 64, 379
Sampson, J. P., 279
Sande, J., 264
Sanderson, H., 524
Sandow, D., 62, 428
Sands, D. S., 230, 231
Sanford, J., 251
Sarason, S. B., 126, 127, 129
Sarkees-Wincenski, M., 72, 180, 215, 350, 460
Sartini, V., 396, 398, 399
Savickas, M. L., 71, 72, 80, 83, 85, 88, 89
Sawilowsky, S., 312
Sax, C., 279
Schaller, J. L., 185
Schalock, R., 393, 395, 428, 509
Schatzman, B., 341
Scheerenberger, R. C., 422
Schepis, M., 292
Scherer, M., 276, 287, 289
Schleien, S. J., 490
Schloss, C. N., 236
Schloss, P. J., 236

Schmitt, S., 65
Schniedewind, N., 260
Schnorr, R., 528
Schroeder, J., 295
Schuh, M., 399
Schumaker, J. B., 49, 238, 323
Schuyler, V., 194
Schwartz, M., 310
Schwartz, S. E., 393
Scott, S. B., 286
Scott, S. S., 451, 455, 467, 468
Scruggs, T. E., 237, 238, 248, 256
Scuccimarra, D., 58, 66
Sedlak, R., 289
Selleck, V., 424
Senge, P. M., 108
Sensor, K., 405
Sepetauc, F., 424
Serebreni, R., 451, 465
Sexton, D., 129, 130
Seyfarth, J., 393, 509
Shapiro, E. D., 324
Shapiro, E. S., 262
Shapiro, J. P., 366, 367
Sharon, S., 258
Sharpe, M., 54, 379
Shaver, D. M., 186, 441, 442
Shaw, D., 338
Shaw, S., 458
Shaw, S. F., 451, 467
Sheldon, D., 200, 467, 485
Sheldon-Wildgen, J., 238
Sherman, J. A., 238
Shoultz, B., 511, 531
Shuping, M. B., 273
Siegel, S., 51, 53, 74, 165, 374, 375, 418, 428
Simich-Dudgeon, C., 127
Simmons, T., 54, 92, 100, 113, 114, 118, 178, 179, 191, 244, 338, 341, 366, 375, 379, 424, 427, 441, 466
Simpson, G. W., 129
Simpson, R. L., 389
Sims-Tucker, B., 239
Sinclair, M. F., 54, 379
Sindelar, P. T., 257
Siperstein, G. N., 443
Sitlington, P., 72, 74, 182, 199, 200,

201, 204, 205, 208, 209, 210, 221, 244, 458
Slate, J. R., 445
Slavin, R., 258
Smalley, K. A., 77, 164
Smith, B., 305
Smith, D. D., 58, 233, 393
Smith, F., 201
Smith, G., 389, 390, 391, 392, 510
Smith, M. A., 236, 257
Smith, M. D., 114, 429
Smull, M., 524
Snauwaert, D., 10, 42, 44, 388
Snell, M., 58, 238, 244, 265, 268
Snow, J., 190, 224
Snow, K., 307
Snyder, E. P., 324
Snyder, L., 316
Snyder, P., 129
Snyder-Marks, J. L., 200, 224
Sowers, J., 64, 292, 295, 296
Speece, D., 58, 66
Spitalnik, D., 509
Spokane, A. R., 79
Sprafkin, R. P., 238
Stageberg, D., 445
Stainback, S., 264
Stainback, W., 264
Steckelberg, A. L., 392
Steele, R., 424
Steere, D., 58, 348, 396, 406, 408
Stein, R. C., 123, 136, 157, 388, 399
Stevens, R., 248, 250, 251, 252, 256, 258
Stewart, E. D., 138
Stodden, R., 31, 36, 48, 55, 56, 109, 165, 425
Stolarski, V. S., 307
Storey, K., 63
Stout, D. M., 230
Stowell, M. A., 392
Stowitschek, J. J., 56, 60, 63, 228, 238, 338, 393
Strain, P. S., 236
Strathe, M. I., 166, 170, 191
Strauss, K. P., 17
Strichart, S. S., 470
Strickland, B., 387, 389, 391

Stroul, B. A., 423
Strully, C., 528
Strully, J., 528
Sugai, G., 263
Summers, J. A., 44, 397
Sumner, S., 168
Super, D. E., 70, 79, 80, 83, 89, 164, 457
Swaner, J., 307
Szymanski, E., 44, 58, 59, 61, 70, 71, 73, 74, 75, 76, 77, 78, 79, 80, 81, 82, 83, 84, 97, 104, 166, 173, 174, 181, 193, 365, 440

Tagalakis, V., 468
Talbert-Johnson, C., 127
Tankersley, M., 178, 366
Tarrant, K. L., 248
Tauili'ili, P., 146
Taylor, A., 306
Taylor, L., 398
Taylor, R., 184
Taylor, R. L., 199
Taylor, S. J., 509, 510, 511
Taymans, J. M., 96, 104, 243, 366
Tepper, S., 519
Terenzini, P., 440, 441, 445, 456, 458
Test, D. W., 60, 118, 230, 263, 338, 366
Thompson, A. S., 80
Thorkildsen, R., 276, 289
Thurlow, M., 133, 211, 214, 224, 393, 395, 399
Tilson, G. P., 388, 393
Tinto, V., 456, 468
Todd-Allen, M., 102
Todis, B., 288
Tower, K. D., 365, 366
Trivette, C., 399
Trossi, K., 441
Troutman, A. C., 255
Tuckman, B. W., 115, 380
Turnbull, A. P., 10, 44, 66, 125, 340, 387, 389, 391, 395, 396, 397, 398, 399, 403, 404, 405, 457
Turnbull, H. R., 10, 44, 58, 66, 125, 127, 129, 132, 203, 340,

389, 391, 395, 398, 399, 457
Turner, L., 66, 360, 401
Turner, L. P., 441, 466

Utley, C. A., 127, 154, 156, 157

Vallentutti, P. S., 239
van Keulen, J. E., 127, 128, 129, 131
Van Reusen, A. K., 323, 340, 372, 399, 458
VanBiervliet, A., 276, 286
Vander-Sande, J., 427, 428
Vandercook, T., 340, 524
Vanderheiden, G. C., 273
Varney, G. H., 100
Vasa, S. F., 392
Vaughn, S., 261, 387, 389, 390
Vietze, P., 366
Voeltz, L., 478
Vogel, S. A., 417, 468

Wade, P., 445, 448
Wagner, M., 7, 28, 186, 417, 418, 442, 443, 444, 470
Walberg, H. J., 528
Wald, J. L., 129
Walker, H., 288
Walker, H. M., 236, 238
Walker, P., 511, 531
Wandry, D., 387, 388
Wang, M. C., 528
Ward, M., 44, 58, 61, 307, 312, 418, 458, 468, 480
Warren, R., 399
Warrenfeltz, R. B., 263
Watson, P. J., 262
Wax, I. F., 470
Weaver, R., 341
Webb, N., 259
Weber, D., 274
Webster, D. D., 448
Weddington, G. T., 127
Weed, R. O., 183
Wehman, P., 20, 45, 48, 55, 56, 61, 62, 63, 67, 70, 104, 108, 166, 168, 177, 178, 224, 240, 241, 265, 268, 393, 397, 399, 401, 406, 419, 422, 476, 478, 509
Wehmeyer, M., 57, 58, 106, 164,

209, 274, 305, 307, 308, 310, 311, 312, 323, 340, 372, 457, 467, 469, 480
Weismantel, M. J., 136, 157
Wenger, B. L., 75
Werbel, G., 393, 395
Wermuth, T., 165, 460, 464, 466
West, J., 23, 48
Westling, D. L., 132, 175, 177
Weyer, T., 428
Weymeyer, M. L., 458
White, C., 509
White, P., 194
White, R., 480
White, W. A. T., 232
White, W. J., 388
Whitehead, C. W., 426
Whitlock, B., 289
Whitney-Thomas, J., 66, 338, 366, 367
Wilcox, B., 66, 230, 389, 393, 394, 476, 478
Will, M., 42, 68, 70, 337, 393, 460
Williams, B., 293
Williams, E., 251
Willig, A. C., 127
Willis, W., 131, 132
Wilson, D., 480
Wilson, R. J., 257
Winterbottom, C., 520
Winterling, V., 480
Winup, K., 306
Wircenski, J., 72, 180, 182, 215, 350, 460
Wise, W. E., 393
Wisniewski, L., 289
Wolf, N. K., 323
Wolfe, V. V., 389
Wolfensberger, W., 8, 427, 478
Wolffe, K., 76, 78, 79, 82, 183
Wolman, J. M., 307, 311
Wolzen, B., 393, 395
Wood, R., 348, 396
Wood, W., 61, 224, 240, 397, 478
Wood, W. M., 60, 118, 230, 338, 366
Woodward, J., 231, 232
Woolcock, W. W., 48
Workman, E. A., 262

Worsham, M., 251
Wray, D., 316
Wright, S., 480
Write, E., 509

Yamaki, K., 132

Yates, J. R., 127
York, J., 340, 365, 524
Yoshida, R. K., 387, 389, 391
Yovanoff, P., 244, 417, 428, 458
Ysseldyke, J. E., 133, 211, 224, 256

Zabala, J., 275, 276, 289
Zakely, J., 469
Ziarnik, J. P., 291
Zigmond, N., 245
Zuniga, M. E., 124, 133
Zwernick, 49, 340, 352, 524

⇌ Subject Index ⇌

Note: The italicized letter *f* following a page number indicate a figure. The italicized letter *t* following a page number indicate a table.

A *Student's Guide to the* IEP, 323
AAMR *Adaptive Behavior Scales*, 207
Academic assessments,
    210–211, 212*t*
Academic skills, 174–176
    content teachers, collaboration
      and consultation, 107–108
    curriculum development, 230,
      231–236
ACCEPTS, *A Children's Curriculum*
    for Effective Peer and Teacher
    Skills, 238
Access and accommodation,
    25–26
    accommodations planning, 194
    ADA, 23–25, 445–448
    best practices, 64–65
    postsecondary education, 448
Acculturation of American values,
    130–131, 138
Acts, legal. *See* Legislation and
    policy.
ADA, 23–25, 445–448
    Job Analysis and the ADA: *A Step-*
      by-Step Guide, 183
Adult Basic Literacy Assessment, 210
Advocacy organizations:
    See specific names of organizations
    historical development, 10–11
African-American values and
    beliefs, 140–142, 142*t*–143*t*
Agencies, public:
    See also specific names of agencies
    coordinating referrals with,
      371–372
    cultural values and, 128–129
    employment. *See* Employment
      agencies/programs.
    fairs, 371–372, 373*f*

interagency assessment
    processes, 223–225
interagency responsibilities
    and linkages, 118, 163,
    293–294, 417–418, 464,
    484–486
school-level interagency
    transition team, forming,
    379–380
Agricultural fields, 188*t*
American Association on Mental
    Retardation (AAMR) *Adaptive*
    Behavior Scales, 207
"American" values:
    assimilation and acculturation,
      130–131, 138
    key differences from other
      cultures, 134*t*–135*t*
    typical, 123, 138, 139*t*
American Vocational Association
    (AVA), 188–189
Americans with Disabilities Act
    (ADA) of 1990, 23–25,
    445–448
    Job Analysis and the ADA: *A Step-*
      by-Step Guide, 183
APTICOM, 209, 457
Aptitude tests, 182
ARC, 10
Asian-American values and
    beliefs, 143–145, 146*t*–147*t*
Assessments, 197–226
    academic, 210–211, 212*t*
    appropriate use of tests,
      221–222
    aptitude tests, 182
    assistive technology (AT), 276,
      279–285
    behavioral, 220–221

characteristics, 199–201
clearly specified purpose(s), 200
collaborative processes, 223
college student needs, 457
comprehensive profile, 200
comprehensive transition
    planning, 224–225
criterion-referenced, 214
cultural diversity and, 127–128
curriculum-based, 182,
    213–214
defined, 199
defining transition domains,
    200–203
ecological, 74, 184–185
effective teaching strategies, 253
formal, 206–211, 222, 223*t*
functional, 205–206, 330–331
general skills tests, 207–208
IDEA requirements, 203–204
IEPs/transition planning, 334,
    347, 350, 352, 353–354*f*
import aspects, 200–201
importance, 198–199
individualized aspect, 200
informal, 211–222, 223*t*
interdisciplinary, processes,
    223–225
living environments, 201, 209
ongoing and continuous, 200
personal-social environments,
    202–203, 209–210
portfolios, 182, 214–215, 350,
    352, 353–354*f*
purposes for, 198, 202–203
recreation and leisure, 495–497
results, 198, 222
self-determination, 312–315
situational, 184–185, 216

special education compared to transition, 198
student school records, 213
surveys and interviews, 215–216, 217–219
utility, 198–199
work samples, 182, 208–209, 220
working environments, 201–202, 208–209
ASSET, A *Social Skills Program for Adolescents*, 238
Assimilation of American values, 130–131, 138
Assistive technology (AT), 273–301
   barriers and solutions, 281, 286–288, 289t
   community environments, 297
   consideration guide, 282t–285t
   definitions, 273–274
   evaluation of effectiveness, 287, 289t
   examples of, 274–276, 277–278
   follow-up services, 287, 289t
   by functional category, 275t
   by functional domain, 277–278
   home environments, 299
   IDEA principles, 290–294
   importance of, 273
   interagency responsibilities, 293–294
   legislation, 273–274
   leisure environments, 297–298
   misconceptions and realities, 281t
   outcome-oriented process, 291–292
   parent knowledge, 287–288, 289t
   postschool environments, 292–293, 294–299
   recreational environments, 297–298
   selection of, 276, 279–285
   student's needs, interests, and preferences, 290–291
   support services, 286–287, 289t
   training barriers and solutions, 286, 288t
   transition issues, 288–290

travel considerations, 298–299
unifying functional model, 276, 280–281f
videoconferencing, 286–287, 289t
work environments, 294–296
AT. *See* Assistive technology (AT).
Automation forces, 186
AVA, 188–189

Backward chaining, 268
Backward planning, 60–61, 348–349
   based on postsecondary goals, 462, 464
BACs, 427
Barden-LaFollette Act, 10, 13t, 16
Becker Reading-Free Interest Survey, 208
Behavior management, 253–256
   clarity and directness, 255
   "overlapping," 254
   pacing and accountability, 255–256
   responding to behavior, 254–255
   school year, beginning of, 256
   transitions, 256
   "withitness," 253–254
Behavioral assessments, 220–221
Bennett Hand-Tool Dexterity Test, 208
Best practices, 54–67
   access and accommodation, 64–65
   community experiences, 62–64
   defining, problems, 54–56
   ecological approaches, 59–60
   family involvement, 66–67
   general principles, 56
   individualized backward planning, 60–61
   postsecondary education, 65–66
   service coordination, 61–62
   student self-determination, 57–59
   systems change strategies, 67
"Bridges" model, 42–43
   Halpern's alternative, 43–44
Brigance Diagnostic Inventory of Essential Skills, 210
Bureau for Education of Handicapped Children, 11

Business advisory councils (BACs), 427
Business fields, 188t

Career and vocational education, 162–196
   academic skill development, 174–176
   agricultural fields, 188t
   aptitude tests, 182
   assessments, 197–226. *See* Assessments.
   business fields, 188t
   classroom-based development, 176–177
   community-based experiences, 177–178, 179t
   community-based instruction (CBI). *See* Community-based instruction (CBI).
   community linkages, 190–192
   consumer fields, 188t
   curriculum development, 227–246. *See* Curriculum development.
   definitions of, 163–165
   early learning experiences, 166
   early transition models, 41
   employer linkages, 191–192
   Experience-Based Career Education (EBCE) model, 170
   experienced-based programs, 187
   foundational skills and attitudes, 173–174
   health fields, 188t
   historical development, 165–166
   homemaking fields, 188t
   identifying student's needs, interests, and preferences, 163
   importance of, 163
   Individualized Placement Plans (IPPs), 191–192
   industrial fields, 188t
   informational interviews, 183–184
   instructional strategies, 247–271. *See* Instructional strategies.
   interest inventories, 182

Career and vocational
    education (*cont*.):
  interfacing with transition
    planning, 188–189
  job analyses, 183, 265, 266–267*f*
  job matching, 184–185, 265, 417
  job-opportunity resources,
    182–183
  job placement, 189–192,
    193–194. *See* Job placement.
  job seeking interventions,
    189–190
  job shadowing, 184, 418
  labor market trends, 186–187
  Life-Centered Career Education
    (LCCE) model, 166–168,
    171–172, 176–177, 214,
    239–240. *See* Life-Centered
    Career Education (LCCE)
    model.
  life-span perspective, 164
  long-term job tenure, 177
  maintaining and advancing in
    careers, 192–195
  marketing fields, 188*t*
  mentoring model/programs,
    170, 191, 428
  models, 166–171
  monetary support, 165
  monitoring processes, 181–185
  occupational specific
    programs, 187
  planning, 163
  planning strategies, 179–181
  portfolios, 180–181, 182, 195,
    214–215, 350, 352, 353–354*f*, 460
  professional linkages, 191
  program options and
    adaptations, 166
  "real world focus" programs, 187
  School-Based Career
    Development and Transition
    Education Model,
    168–170, 173
  situational assessments,
    184–185, 216
  stages of, 171–172
  structure of vocational
    education, 187

  student and potential work and
    learning environments,
    monitoring congruence, 184–185
  student monitoring, 182
  supported employment,
    193–194, 428–435. *See*
    Supported employment.
  task analyses, 183, 265, 268,
    269–270*f*
  Tech-Prep programs, 175
  technology fields, 188*t*
  three dimensional learning
    programs, 187
  trade fields, 188*t*
  2 + 2 programs, 175
  types of programs, 187–188
  vocation-specific preparation,
    185–189
  work and learning
    environments (potential),
    monitoring, 182–184
Career development, 69–94
  See also Career and vocational
    education
  collaboration among team
    members, 74–75
  coordinating agency
    relationships, 73
  developmental theories, 78, 79–80
  ecological assessments, 74,
    184–185
  ecological model, 83–85, 86*t*
  exposure to work
    environments, 71
  family involvement, 74
  Hershenson's theory of work
    adjustment, 80–81
  individualized career plan, 89,
    92, 93*t*
  Krumboltz's social learning
    theory, 81–82
  life-span perspective, 70
  linking theory and practice,
    Savickas's framework, 85,
    88–89, 90*t*–91*t*
  Minnesota theory of work
    adjustment, 80
  models for applying theories,
    82–89

  obstacles, 75–76
  occupational choice theories,
    77–78
  planning for future
    environments, 72–73
  quality-of-life focus, 73
  relationship to transition
    planning, 71–75
  self-advocacy, 73–74
  self-determination, 73–74
  structural theories, 78, 79
  student's needs, interests, and
    preferences, 72
  theories of, 76–82
  work adjustment theories,
    77–78, 80–81
Career Development Inventory (CDI), 208
Career Education
    Implementation Incentive
    Act of 1977, 16, 41
Career Information Delivery
    Systems (CIDS), 183
Career maintenance, 192–195
Career maintenance clubs, 194
Career Maturity Index, The, 341
Career Maturity Inventory (CMI), 208
Career opportunity resources,
    182–183
Career portfolios, 180–181
  assessments, 182, 214–215,
    350, 352, 353–354*f*
  as career maintenance
    strategy, 195
  college students, 460
Carl D. Perkins Vocational
    Education Act of 1984, 20,
    21–22, 23*t*
  1990 amendments, 29, 445
  1998 amendments, 3, 29–30
CBI. *See* Community-based
    instruction (CBI).
CDI, 208
Centers for independent living
    (CILs), 507–508, 532, 533*t*
CETA, 19*t*, 22
Chambers of Commerce, 183, 191
ChoiceMaker curriculum, 340
  assessments, 312, 313*t*, 314
  attaining goals, 324–325

Characteristics I Like Versus Here,
Form-B, 327f
choose and take action software,
326–330
choosing education goals
lessons, 320–321
choosing employment goals
lessons, 319–320, 321, 322f
choosing general goals lessons,
318, 319f
choosing goals process
lessons, 318–319
choosing personal goals
lessons, 321–322
constructs, 308t
curriculum matrix, 317t
development of, 316, 318
dream job lessons, 320
expressing goals, 322–324
Job Characteristics I Like Graph, 322f
Job Characteristics I Like
Worksheet, 320f
lesson matrix, 315t
lesson packages, 316–330
matrix, 317t
self-directed IEPs, 323–324
students with severe needs,
326–330
take action lessons, 325–326
Take Action Review, 326f
use of, 318
Work, Social and Personal Skills
Supervisor Worksheet, 321f
Choose and take action software,
326–330
Christmas in Purgatory, 9
CIDS, 183
CILs, 507–508, 532, 533t
"Circles of Friends," 190
"Circles of Support," 190, 191
City parks and recreation
programs, 488–489
CLASS, *Contingencies for Learning*
Academic and Social Skills, 238
Classroom-based instruction:
career development, 176–177
functional curriculum, 243
Clubs, career maintenance, 194
Clubs, job, 190, 427–428

Clustered placement, 193
CMH, 531–532
CMI, 208
COACH, 340
Collaboration and consultation,
95–119
academic and technical content
teachers, 107–108
career development
opportunities, 74–75
community-based education
(CBE), 105–107
community linkages, 190–192
"coordinated set of activities," 96
delivery of services, 97
dynamics of, 96–97
employer linkages, 191–192
family participation,
supporting, 148–150,
152t–154t, 405
federal/state vocational
rehabilitation programs,
109–113
goal development, 96
group dynamics, 114–117
IDEA requirement, 96
interagency assessment
processes, 223–225
interagency responsibilities
and linkages, 118, 163,
293–294, 417–418, 464,
484–486
interdisciplinary approach, 100
interdisciplinary team
functioning, 96–97
interface of, 97–98
JTPA agencies and programs,
111, 425
mental health and
developmental disability
(MH/DD) agencies, 111–113
movement from school to
postschool activities, 118
multidisciplinary approach, 100
outcome-oriented process,
117–118
preschool education and
training collaborators, 113
professional linkages, 191

rehabilitation counseling,
scope of practice, 99
role expansion and role release,
101–102
school administrators, 108–109
school-based programs and
services, 104–109
school collaborator
responsibilities, 102, 104
service delivery systems,
98–100
special education, scope of
practice, 99–100
special education teachers,
104–105, 105–106
STEP case study, 113–114
student participation,
supporting, 150–154
students' needs, interests, and
preferences, 117
team models, 100–101
transdisciplinary approach,
100–101
transition coordinator's role,
102, 103t, 376–379
transition team decision
making, 116
transition team development,
114–116
transition team processes,
117–119
vocational education, scope of
practice, 99
College education, 439–473. *See*
Postsecondary education.
Colorado standard-referenced
IEPs, 315–316
Community-based education
(CBE), 105–107
drop-out prevention
activities, 105
family involvement, 106
related service providers, 107
special education teacher's
responsibility, 105–106
student involvement, 106–107
Community-based instruction
(CBI), 177–178, 179t, 263–271
benefits, 263–264

Community-based instruction
    (CBI) (cont.):
  functional curriculum and,
      243, 244
  job matching, 265
  job-skills training, 268–271
  locations of, 264
  preparation for, 264–268
  purpose of, 263
  rationale for, 264
  staffing, 265
  student transportation, 265
  task analyses, 265, 268, 269–270f
Community
      experiences/environments:
  assistive technology (AT), 297
  best practices, 62–64
  career and vocational
      education, 177–178, 179t
  family involvement, 406
  postsecondary education,
      466–467
Community linkages, 190–192
Community living organizations,
    532–534
Community mental health (CMH),
    531–532
Community recreation programs,
    478–479
Community services for autistic
    adults and children
    (CSAAC), 429
Community support systems
    (CSSs), 423
Community work sites, 375
Comprehensive Employment and
    Training Act (CETA) of 1973,
    19t, 22
Consultation. See Collaboration
    and consultation.
Consumer fields, 188t
Consumer's Guide, 220
Cooperative learning, 258–261
  description of, 258
  group goals, 258–259
  group project format, 260
  importance, 258
  individual accountability, 259
  jigsaw format, 260

peer teaching format, 260–261
positive outcomes, 258
role assignments, 259–260
suitability, 258
Cooperative Transitional Program
    (CTSP), Kent State
    University, 178
Coordinating services, 364–385
  See also Collaboration and
      consultation
  balancing individual needs and
      preferences, 366–367
  case study, 381–384
  casework approaches, 365
  collaborative efforts,
      promoting, 376–379
  community work sites,
      developing, 375
  cultural issues, 367
  ecological model, 365, 366
  family involvement, 376
  future needs, identifying, 380
  goals of, 367–381
  historical development, 365–367
  IEP/transition coordinator/
      specialist. See IEP/transition
      coordinator/specialist.
  IEP/transition meetings, 367–371
  IEP/transition plans, monitoring
      services in, 378–379
  independent living model, 365
  job opportunities and
      competency requirements,
      identifying, 375
  program attributes and
      structures, developing, 379–381
  recreation and leisure, 489–491
  referrals, 371–372
  school-level interagency
      transition team, forming,
      379–380
  self-advocacy, promotion of, 373
  self-determination, promotion
      of, 372–373
  student development, 374–376
  student-focused planning,
      367–374
  student follow-up studies,
      380–381

work experience programs,
    developing, 375
Coordinator/specialist role. See
    IEP/transition
    coordinator/specialist.
County parks and recreation
    programs, 488–489
Criterion-referenced
    assessments, 214
CTSP, Kent State University, 178
Cultural competence:
  achieving, 154–156
  comprehensive cultural
      training, 157–158
  defining, 124
  family participation,
      supporting, 148–150,
      152t–154t, 405
  family status issues,
      understanding, 131–132
  family values, understanding
      differences, 136–137
  IDEA's essential elements and,
      124–126
  ITP legislative mandates and
      practices, 137t, 147–154
  models of, 155–156
  negotiating multicultural
      differences, 137–147
  negotiating transition
      mandates, 147–154
  personal and professional
      power, understanding, 131
  professional and in-service
      training, 156–157
  special education teachers,
      126–130
  strategies for supporting
      minority parents, 157
  student participation,
      supporting, 150–154
Cultural diversity, 120–160
  African-American values and
      beliefs, 140–142, 142t–143t
  "American values," assimilation
      and acculturation, 130–131, 138
  "American values," key
      differences from other
      cultures, 134t–135t

"American values," typical, 123, 138, 139t
Asian-American values and beliefs, 143–145, 146t–147t
assessment processes and, 127–128
cooperation *versus* competition, 134t
disability, contrasting views of, 133–135
economic status, 123, 132
educational status, 132
equality and, 123
family participation, supporting, 148–150, 152t–154t, 398–399, 405
family relationships, contrasting values for, 135–137
fate *versus* self-determinism, 135t
gender roles and responsibilities, 134t
homogeneity, preference for, 121
impact on transition mandates, 132–154
individual *versus* family or group orientation, 133, 134t
institutionalized values, 128–129
interaction styles, 129, 135t
Latino Peoples' values and belief, 142–143, 144t–145t
learning about differences, difficulties, 121–122
legislation and policy, 124–126
Native American values and beliefs, 138, 140, 140t–141t
Pacific-American values and beliefs, 146–147, 148t–149t
participatory decision making and, 133
pluralism and tolerance, difficulties, 121–122
professional effectiveness and. *See generally* Cultural competence.
service delivery and, 367
in special education, 126–130
status differences, 122–123, 131–132

student participation, supporting, 150–154
time orientation, 134t
in the United States, 121–124
Curriculum-based assessments, 182, 213–214
Curriculum development, 227–246
academic skills, 230, 231–236
areas of, 229f
barriers to, 245
ChoiceMaker curriculum. *See ChoiceMaker* curriculum.
definition of "curriculum," 228–229
Direct Instruction, 232
essential transition elements and, 228
functional skills, 230, 238–234
general education curriculum, 231–236
Kentucky State learner objectives, 233, 234t–235t
outcome-oriented approach, 230
professional competence, 228
social skills, 236–238
special education, 230
state academic standards and curriculum, 232–236
vocational, 230

Day centers, 426
DCDT, 4–5
DD services, 111–113, 422–423
leisure activities, 488
Definitions:
assessment, 199
career development, 70, 76–77
career education, 163–164
career maintenance, 192
curriculum, 228–229
developmental disability, 18–19
AT device, 273
essential elements, 4
functional approach, 238
instruction, 248
occupational choice, 77
rehabilitation technology, 274
self-determination, 305
AT service, 274

social skills, 236
supported employment, 428
transition services, 3–4
vocational education, 164
work adjustment, 77
Demographic changes, 186–187
Developmental (career development) theories, 78, 79–80
Developmental Disabilities and Bill of Rights Act of 1970, 19t
1984 amendments, 23t
Developmental disabilities (DD) services, 111–113, 422–423
leisure activities, 488
Developmental Disabilities Services Facilities Construction Act of 1970, 18
Dictionary of Occupational Titles, 183
Differential Aptitude Test (DAT), 208
Direct instruction, 232
self-monitoring, 262
Discover (ACT Test Administration), 457
Discrimination. *See* Access and accommodation; Integration; Nondiscrimination rights.
Diversity, cultural, 120–160. *See* Cultural diversity.
Division of Career Development and Transition (DCDT) of the Council of Exceptional Children, 4–5
DOL, 111
resources, 183
"trainee" status criteria, 178, 179t
Dream job lessons, 320
Drop-out prevention activities (CBE), 105
Duration recording, 221

EBCE model, 170
Ecological approaches:
best practices, 59–60
career development, 74, 83–85, 86t
service delivery, 365, 366
Ecological assessments, 74, 184–185

Ecological Inventory (functional model), 239
Education for All Handicapped Children Act of 1975, 12, 15, 19t, 387, 403, 404
  1983 amendments, 20, 23t
Elementary and Secondary Education Act (ESEA) amendments, 11, 13t
Elizabethan Poor Laws, 8
Employability Life Skills Assessment, 341
Employer linkages, 191–192
Employment:
  agencies/programs, 418–425. *See* Employment agencies/programs.
  ChoiceMaker curriculum, 319–320, 321f, 322f
  day centers, 426
  dream job lessons, 320
  Employability Life Skills Assessment, 341
  historical development, 425–426
  inequities, 418
  Job Analysis and the ADA: *A Step-by-Step Guide*, 183
  job opportunities, 182–183, 375
  Kent State University Cooperative Transitional Services Program, Job Analysis/Requirements, 266–267
  long-term job tenure, 177
  quick reference table, 436, 437t
  real jobs, rationale for, 426–427
  The Revised Handbook for Analyzing Jobs, 183
  School-Based Career Development and Transition Education Model, 169f, 173
  sheltered workshops, 426
  supported employment, 193–194, 428–435. *See* Supported employment.
  Test of Interpersonal Competency for Employment (TICE), 210
  underemployment, 75, 441
    unemployment rate, 75, 418, 441
Employment agencies/programs, 418–425
  business advisory councils (BACs), 427
  community support systems (CSSs), 423
  Comprehensive Employment and Training Act (CETA) of 1973, 19t, 22
  developmental disabilities (DD) agencies, 111–113, 422–423
  impairment-related work expenses (IRWE), 435
  interagency responsibilities and linkages, 417–418
  job banks, 265, 375
  job carving, 190, 431
  job clubs, 190, 427–428
  job development, 189–190
  job fairs, 371–372, 373f
  job matching, 184–185, 265, 417
  job placement, 189–192, 193–194
  job shadowing, 184, 418
  job sharing arrangements, 432
  job-skills training, 268–271
  Job Training and Partnership Act (JTPA) of 1982, 20, 23t
  JTPA agencies and programs, 111, 425
  mental health agencies, 423–424
  mentoring model/programs, 170, 191, 428
  plans for achieving self-support (PASS), 435
  quick reference table, 436, 437t
  social welfare and entitlements, 435
  state employment agencies, 424
  state employment and training programs (ETPs), 110–111
  supported employment, 193–194, 428–435. *See* Supported employment.
  visual impairment (VI) rehabilitation programs, 421–422
  vocational rehabilitation (VR) agencies/programs, 419–422
    work incentives, 435
    Work Opportunity Investment Act (WIA), 26–27, 425
Entrepreneurial approaches to placement, 193–194
ESEA amendments, 11, 13t
Essential transition elements, 5–7
  assistive technology (AT), 290–294
  curriculum development, 228
  defined, 4
  instructional strategies, 248
  models and best practices, 54–67. *See* Best practices; Models, transition.
  multicultural issues, 124–126
  postsecondary education, 440, 456–468
  recreation and leisure, 479–487
  service coordination, 367
  transition planning and the IDEA of 1990 and 1997, 334, 337–338
ETPs, 110–111
Eugenics movement, 504
Event recording, 220–221
Experience-Based Career Education (EBCE) model, 170
Experienced-based programs, 187

Fads in special education, 231
Family and Educational Rights and Privacy Act (FERPA) of 1974, 445, 448
Family functions, 397–398
Family involvement, 386–414
  best practices, 66–67
  career development, 74
  community-based education (CBE), 106
  community experiences, 406
  cultural/linguistic differences, 398–399. *See generally* Cultural diversity.
  decision making, legislative guidelines, 403–404
  decision making, unequal status, 389–390

due process principle, 404
guidelines for, 399, 400t, 403–404
history of, 389–396
IDEAs and regulations, 388,
    403, 404, 409t–410t
IEP conferences, 404
IEP efficacy, lack of, 390–391
IEPs/transition planning, 376,
    392, 397
information programs for
    parents, 399–401
information regarding adult
    service programs, 407
information regarding legal
    rights, 402–403, 404
information to parents, lack of,
    394–395
least restrictive environment
    determination, 404
legal rights and
    responsibilities, 387–388,
    402–404, 409t–410t
minimal roles and passive
    participation, 387, 389, 391,
    392
nondiscriminatory evaluation
    principle, 404
parent as advocate, 404–405
parent information programs,
    399–401
parent-to-parent support
    groups, 407–408
parent training/education
    programs, 399–401, 406
parent transition in-service
    program, 401–402
parents' attributes, 397, 398t
parents' desire for more
    involvement, 394
parents' expectations, 396
parents' perceptions, 389
positive effect on outcome,
    393
postsecondary education,
    456–457, 463t
premises favoring, 389
preplanning opportunities, 401
professional regard for parents,
    408, 411t–412t

professional support, 405
professionals, training, 391
professionals' perceptions,
    388, 389
as recommended practice, 393
research substantiating,
    392–394
roles and responsibilities,
    396–399
social support mechanisms, 406
strategies for, 399–412
students' perspectives, 395–396
transition coordinator's role, 376
transition team membership, 396
transition team support,
    148–150, 152t–154t,
    398–399, 405
types of, 390
zero reject principle, 403–404
FAPE, 15, 40
Federal grant competitions since
    1983, 21t
Federal vocational rehabilitation
    services, 109–110
FERPA, 445, 448
Forward chaining, 268
Free appropriate public education
    (FAPE), 15, 40
Functional assessments, 205–206
    EBD students, 330–331
Functional curriculum, 230,
    238–234
    classroom-based instruction, 243
    community-based instruction
        (CBI), 243, 244
    content areas, overlapping
        impacts, 239
    decision to use, 239
    identifying activities, 240–241
    instructional setting, 243–244
    major components, 240–244
    models of, 239–240
    negotiating goals, 242–243
    organizing information/skills
        content, 241t
    prioritizing activities, 241–242
    transition, 244
Functional Curriculum for Teaching
    Students with Disabilities, 239

General Equivalency Diploma
    (GED) training, 111
Getting Along with Others, 238
Goals 2000: Educate America Act
    of 1994, 3, 27–28
Grant competitions since 1983,
    federal, 21t
Group Action Planning, 340
Group dynamics of collaboration,
    114–117
Guide for Occupational Exploration,
    The, 183

Handicapped Children Early
    Education Assistance Act, 11
Health fields, 188t
Hershenson's theory of work
    adjustment, 80–81
Historical development:
    advocacy organizations, 10–11
    career and vocational
        education programs,
        165–166
    coordinating services, 365–367
    disability rights movement,
        precursors, 12–14
    early values and cultural
        approaches, 8–9
    employment, 425–426
    family involvement, 389–396
    independent living movement,
        12–14, 366, 506–508
    legislation. See generally
        Legislation and policy.
    PARC v. Commonwealth of
        Pennsylvania, 12
    people first movement, 14
    residential services, 504–510
    transition models. See generally
        Models, transition.
    work-study programs, 39–41
Home environments, 510–511
    See also Residential services
    assistive technology (AT), 299
    "facility" distinguished, 509
    home ownership resources, 531
    personal assistance services
        (PAS), 519–523. See Personal
        assistance services (PAS).

Home environments (*cont.*):
    resources for home
        ownership, 531
    supported living, 511–518. *See*
        Supported living.
Home health services, 532
Homemaking fields, 188*t*
HyperAble DATA, 279

ICPs, 89, 92, 93*t*, 179–180, 460
IDEA:
    See generally specific topics
        throughout this index
    1990 act, 3, 23, 30–31, 33*t*–35*t*,
        334–339
    1997 amendments, 3, 31–32,
        33*t*–35*t*, 334–339
    essential elements of transition
        services. *See* Essential
        transition elements.
IEP/transition
        coordinator/specialist, 102,
        103*t*, 344
    agency fairs, 371–372, 373*f*
    collaboration responsibilities,
        102, 103*t*, 376–379
    communication strategies,
        developing, 378
    community work sites,
        developing, 375
    conducting meetings, 371
    conflict resolution, 377
    family participation
        responsibilities, 376
    future needs, identifying, 380
    group process skills, 380
    IEP/transition plans, monitoring
        services in, 378–379
    information sharing methods,
        developing, 378
    job opportunities and
        competency requirements,
        identifying, 375
    linking services and
        instruction, 375
    preparation for meetings, 367–368
    program attributes and
        structures, developing, 379–381
    referrals, 371–372

    scheduling meetings, 368
    school-level interagency
        transition team, forming,
        379–380
    self-advocacy, promotion of, 373
    self-determination, promotion
        of, 372–373
    student development
        responsibilities, 374–376
    student-focused planning,
        367–374
    student follow-up studies,
        coordinating, 380–381
    transition team member
        responsibilities, monitoring
        fulfillment of, 378–379
    work experience programs,
        developing, 375
IEP/transition meetings, 322–323
    agenda, 349, 350*f*, 368, 369–370*f*
    college student participation, 458
    conducting, 371
    conflicts, 378
    family involvement. *See generally*
        Family involvement.
    frequently asked questions,
        359–362
    invitation to, 368
    planning, 368
    preparation for, 367–368,
        369–370*f*
    scheduling, 368
    student/family led, 349
    student-focus, 367–368
IEP/transition teams:
    See also Collaboration and
        consultation
    composition, 341, 344
    decision making, 116
    development, 114–116
    family membership, 396
    family participation,
        supporting, 148–150,
        152*t*–154*t*, 405
    interagency assessment
        processes, 223–225
    interagency responsibilities
        and linkages, 118, 163,

        293–294, 417–418, 464,
        484–486
    interdisciplinary team
        functioning, 96–97
    models, 100–101
    monitoring fulfillment of
        responsibilities, 378–379
    movement from school to
        postschool activities, 118
    outcome-oriented process,
        117–118
    processes, 117–119
    roles and responsibilities, 344,
        345*t*, 346*t*
    school-level interagency
        transition team, 379–380
    student participation,
        supporting, 150–154
    students' needs, interests, and
        preferences, 117
IEPs/transition planning, 3, 15
    approaches to, 339–341
    assessments, 334, 347, 350,
        352, 353–354*f*
    backward planning, 60–61,
        348–349, 462, 464
    career development and, 71–75
    career planning approaches, 341
    career portfolios, 350, 352,
        353–354*f*
    case study, 352, 355–356, 357*f*
    college student-directed IEPs,
        457–458, 459*t*
    coordinated set of activities,
        334, 337–338
    family involvement, 376, 392, 397.
        See generally Family involvement.
    goals for services, writing, 356,
        358–359
    high school, 343*t*
    IDEA of 1990 and 1997, 334–339
    implementing, 349–359
    interdisciplinary assessments,
        224–225
    legislative mandates and
        practices, 137*t*
    middle school, 342*t*
    minimal school compliance,
        390–391

monitoring services in, 378–379

myths, 338–339

negotiating transition mandates, 147–154

outcome-oriented process, 334, 337

person-centered approach, 340, 524–526

primary school, 342t

sample plan, 357f

self-determination approach, 340–341

self-directed IEPs, 311–316, 323–324, 457–458, 459t

service options, 347–348

standard-referenced IEPs, 315–316

statement of needed services, writing, 349–350, 351f

student movement to postschool activities, 334, 337, 338

student needs, interests, and preferences, 334, 337, 369–370f

timelines for, 341, 342t–343t

vocational education and, 188–189

IMPACT: A Functional Curriculum Handbook for Students with Moderate to Severe Disabilities, 239

Impairment-related work expenses (IRWE), 435

Income maintenance, 530–531

Independent Living Behavior Checklist, 209

Independent living services:

centers for independent living (CILs), 507–508, 532, 533t

historical movement, 12–14, 366, 506–508

leisure options, 487–488

model, 365

Rehabilitation Act of 1973, 16

Individual education programs (IEPs). See IEPs/transition planning.

Individual placement, 193

Individualized backward planning, 60–61, 348–349

based on postsecondary goals, 462, 464

Individualized career plans (ICPs), 89, 92, 93t, 179–180, 460

Individualized leisure planning, 493–494

Individualized Placement Plans (IPPs), 191–192

Individualized Transition Plans (ITPs):

See also IEPs/transition planning

college student-directed IEPs, 457–458, 459t

legislative mandates and practices, 137t

negotiating transition mandates, 147–154

Individuals with Disabilities Education Acts (IDEA). See IDEA.

Industrial fields, 188t

Industrialization forces, 186

Informational interviews, 183–184

Institutionalized cultural values, 128–129

Instruction:

See generally Career and vocational education classroom. See Classroom-based instruction.

community-based. See Community-based instruction (CBI).

direct instruction, 232, 262

"on-the-spot," for social skills, 238

strategies, 247–271. See Instructional strategies.

Instructional strategies, 247–271

application to students with disabilities, 256–257

application to transition curricula, 257–258

clarity and directness, 255

community-based instruction (CBI). See Community-based instruction (CBI).

complementary techniques, 258–271

cooperative learning, 258–261

defining "instruction," 248

demonstration, 251

disruptive behavior, responding to, 254–255

effective teaching, 248–258

essential transition elements, 248

guided practice, 251–253

importance of instruction, 248

learning time, 249–250

"overlapping" activities, 254

pacing of instruction, 255

review and preview, 250–251

school year, importance of beginning of, 256

self-monitoring, 261–263

student accountability, 253, 255–256

student assessment, 253

student behavior, 253–256

summary of effective techniques, 249t

transitions, 256

"withitness," 253–254

Integration:

community housing, 522–523

integrated generic mainstreaming, 490

nondiscrimination rights. See Integration.

students with nondisabled peers, 104–105

Interdependence: The Route to Community, 476–477

Interdependent adult life, 523–536

community living organizations, 532–534

community mental health (CMH), 531–532

home health services, 532

home ownership resources, 531

income maintenance, 530–531

paratransit, 534

person-centered planning, 524–526, 527t

Interdependent adult life (*cont.*):
   public health services, 532
   regional development disability
      centers, 531–532
   regional transportation
      authorities, 534
   resources, 528, 530–534
   self-advocacy, 534
   skills, 526–528, 529*t*
   supports, 529*t*, 534–536
Interdisciplinary assessments:
   collaborative processes, 223
   comprehensive transition
      planning, 224–225
Interdisciplinary collaborative
      approach, 100
Interdisciplinary team
      functioning, 96–97
Interest inventories, 182
Interviews:
   informational interviews, career
      education, 183–184
   transition assessments,
      215–216, 217–219*f*
IPLAN, 340–341
IPPs, 191–192
IRWE, 435
ITPs. *See* Individualized transition
   plans (ITPs).

Job analyses, 183, 265
   Kent State University Cooperative
      Transitional Services Program
      Job Analysis/Requirements,
      266–267
Job Analysis and the ADA: *A Step-by-*
   Step Guide, 183
Job banks, 265, 375
Job carving, 190, 431
Job clubs, 190, 427–428
Job development, 189–190
   supported employment,
      193–194, 428–435. *See*
      Supported employment.
Job fairs, 371–372, 373*f*
Job matching, 184–185, 265, 417
Job opportunities:
   identifying, 375
   resources, 182–183

Job placement, 189–192
   clustered placement, 193
   community linkages, 190–192
   employer linkages, 191–192
   entrepreneurial approaches,
      193–194
   individual placement, 193
   job seeking interventions,
      189–190
   mobile work crews, 193
   professional linkages, 191
   supported employment,
      193–194, 428–435. *See*
      Supported employment.
Job shadowing, 184, 418
Job sharing arrangements, 432
Job-skills training, 268–271
   backward chaining, 268
   baseline, 268
   employer/coworker input,
      270–271
   forward chaining, 268
   ongoing task analyses, 268,
      269–270*f*
   prompts, 268
   task-specific, 270
   whole sequence instruction, 268
Job Training and Partnership Act
      (JTPA) of 1982, 20, 23*t*
   agencies and programs, 111, 425

K & W *Guide to Colleges for the*
   Learning Disabled, 470
Kent State University Cooperative
      Transitional Services
      Program Job
      Analysis/Requirements,
      266–267*f*
Kentucky State learner objectives,
      233, 234*t*–235*t*
Knowledge of the World of Work
   Scale, 208
Kohler's model, 49–51
Krumboltz's social learning
      theory, 81–82
Kuder Vocational Preference Record, 208

Labor Department, U.S. (DOL), 111
   resources, 183

"trainee" status criteria, 178, 179*t*
Labor market trends, 186–187
Latino Peoples' values and belief,
      142–143, 144*t*–145*t*
Laws. *See* Legislation and policy.
LCCE model, 166–168, 171–172,
      176–177, 214, 239–240
Learning time, 249–250
Least restrictive environment
      (LRE), 15
   determination, family
      involvement, 404
Legislation and policy:
   See also specific names of legislation
   career and vocational
      education programs, 165–166
   cultural influences, 124–126
   early values and cultural
      approaches, 8–9
   family involvement, 387–388,
      402–404, 409*t*–410*t*
   1917 to 1943, 9–10, 13*t*
   1943 to 1954, 10, 13*t*
   1960s, 10–12, 13*t*
   1970s, 14–19
   1980s, 19–22, 23*t*
   1990s, 23–36
   ongoing supports, 8
   postsecondary education,
      445–448
   rehabilitation-related, 7–8
   self-determination, 310–311
   technology-related, 273–274
   understanding relationship
      among, 7
   vocational-related, 7, 165–166
Leisure, 474–498. *See* Recreation
   and leisure.
Leisure Time Activities Scale, 210
Life-Centered Career Education
      (LCCE) model, 166–168, 341
   assessment program, 214
   career assimilation, 172, 177
   career awareness, 171, 172*t*, 176
   career exploration, 171,
      172*t*, 176
   career preparation, 172,
      176–177
   functional curricula, 239–240

Lifestyle Planning, 340
Linkages:
See generally Collaboration and
consultation
community, 190–192
employer, 191–192
interagency responsibilities
and linkages, 118, 163,
293–294, 417–418, 464,
484–486
professional, 191
school-level interagency
transition team, 379–380
transition coordinator's role,
375, 377
transition systems, 44–45
Living environments, assessment,
201, 209
Local career resources, 183
LRE, 15

Macquarrie Test for Mechanical
Ability, 208
Making action plans (MAPS), 340,
524–526
Marketing fields, 188t
Mccarron-Dial Work Evaluation
System, 209
McDonalds restaurant, 496
McGill Action Planning System
(MAPS), 340, 524
Medicaid Community Attendant
Services and Supports Act
(MiCASSA, S1935), 522–523
Mental health and developmental
disability (MH/DD) services,
111–113, 422–423
leisure programs, 488
Mental Retardation and Facilities
and Construction Act of 1963,
12, 13t
Mentoring model/programs, 170,
191, 428
MFEs, 15
MH/DD services, 111–113,
422–423
leisure programs, 488
MiCASSA (S1935), 522–523
Minnesota Spatial Relations Test, 208

Minnesota theory of work
adjustment, 80
Mobile work crews, 193
Models, career and vocational
education, 166–171
Experience-Based Career
Education (EBCE) model, 170
Life-Centered Career Education
(LCCE) model. See Life-
Centered Career Education
(LCCE) model.
mentoring model, 170, 191, 428
School-Based Career
Development and Transition
Education Model, 168–170, 173
Models, career development,
82–89
ecological model, 83–85, 86t
linking theory and practice,
Savickas's framework, 85,
88–89, 90t–91t
Models, cultural competence,
155–156
Models, functional curricula,
239–240
Models, self-determination, 309t
Models, service delivery for
leisure programs, 490
Models, team, 100–101
Models, transition, 38–54
best practices, 54–67. See Best
practices.
career education initiative, 41
early, 39–41
Halpern's alternative to the
bridges model, 43–44
Kohler's model, 49–51
life skills approach, 39
linkages, 44–45
1930s, 39
1950s, 39
1980s, 42–48
1990s, 48–54
OSERS transition model, 42f
quality-of-life focus, 43–44,
48–49
Siegel's model, 51–54
Wehman's model, 45, 48
Will's bridges model, 42–43

work preparation models,
45–48
work-study programs, 39–41
Monitoring students, 182
congruence between student
and potential work and
learning environments,
184–185
self-monitoring technique,
261–263
Multicultural aspects, 120–160.
See Cultural diversity.
Multifactored evaluations
(MFE), 15
Myers/Briggs, 341

National Association for
Vocational Education Special
Needs Personnel
(NAVESNP), 188–189
National Association of Retarded
Children (now ARC), 10
National Longitudinal Transition
Study (NLTS), 20, 48
Native American values and
beliefs, 138, 140, 140t–141t
NAVESNP, 188–189
Next S.T.E.P., 323, 340
NLTS, 20, 48
Nondiscrimination rights:
access and accommodation. See
Access and accommodation.
ADA of 1990, 16–18, 445–448
community housing, 522–523
evaluation procedures, 404
Rehabilitation Act of 1973,
16–18, 445
students integrated with
nondisabled peers, 104–105

Occupational choice theories,
77–78
Occupational Outlook Handbook, 183
Occupational specific
programs, 187
On-the-job training:
supported employment,
193–194, 428–435. See
Supported employment.

"On-the-spot" instruction for social skills, 238
"Opportunistic teaching" of social skills, 238
OSERS transition model, 42f

Pacific-American values and beliefs, 146–147, 148t–149t
Paratransit, 534
PARC v. Commonwealth of Pennsylvania, 12
Parental involvement. See Family involvement.
Participatory decision making:
  See generally Self-determination
  ChoiceMaker curriculum. See ChoiceMaker curriculum.
  cultural diversity and, 133
  EBD students, 330–331
  family involvement. See generally Family involvement.
PASS, 435
Peer teaching, 260–261
PEERS, Program for Establishing Effective Relationship Skills, 238
People first movement, 14
  language suggestions, 15t
Person-centered job selection, 429–431
Person-centered planning, 340, 524–526, 527t
Personal assistance services (PAS), 519–523
  access to, 520–523
  checklist for evaluating, 521
  guidelines, 520
  Medicaid Community Attendant Services and Supports Act (MiCASSA, S1935), 522–523
Personal Futures Planning, 340
Personal-social environments, assessment, 202–203, 209–210
Personalized job development, 193–194, 428–435. See Supported employment.
Peterson's Colleges and Programs for Students with Learning Disabilities, 470

Plans for achieving self-support (PASS), 435
Portfolios, career, 180–181
  assessments, 182, 214–215, 350, 352, 353–354f
  as career maintenance strategy, 195
  college students, 460
Postsecondary education, 439–473
  academic preparation, 175
  access and accommodation, 448
  backward planning, 462, 464
  benefits of, 440–441
  best practices, 65–66
  career exploration and planning, 458, 460, 461t–462t
  career plans and portfolios, 460
  case study, 450–451
  climate, 452, 455–456
  community-based experiences, 466–467
  course selection, 464–466
  demands and supports, 448–451
  educators' role and responsibilities, 463t
  enrollment rates, 442–443
  essential transition elements and, 440, 456–468
  family involvement, 456–457, 463t
  finding the right fit, 456
  first-generation students, 469
  high school demands, differences from, 449t
  inclusive school environments, 467
  legal rights and responsibilities, 445–448
  movement to postsecondary environments, 464–468
  personnel role and responsibilities, 465t
  planning postsecondary outcomes, 460, 462–464
  promoting positive postsecondary outcomes, 464–468
  recruitment and retention, 442

  rural students, 469–470
  self-advocacy, 467–468
  service provider linkages, 464
  social aspects, 468–469
  specialized programs, 470
  student-directed IEP/ITPs, 457–458, 459t
  student interest surveys, 457
  student records, confidentiality, 448
  student roles and responsibilities, 462t
  student's needs, interests, and preferences, 456–460
  student's needs assessments, 457
  support services offered, 451–452, 453t–455t
  types of institutions, 443–445
Practices, best, 54–67. See Best practices.
Preschool education and training collaborators, 113
President's Panel on Mental Retardation, 10–11
Private Industry Councils, 191
Professional linkages, 191
Progress Assessment Chart of Social and Personal Development, 210
Prompts:
  job-skills training, 268
  self-monitoring, 262
Public agencies:
  See also specific names of agencies
  coordinating referrals with, 371–372
  cultural values and, 128–129
  employment. See Employment agencies/programs.
  fairs, 371–372, 373
  interagency assessment processes, 223–225
  interagency responsibilities and linkages, 118, 163, 293–294, 417–418, 464, 484–486
  school-level interagency transition team, forming, 379–380

Public health services, 532
Public sector support services
    collaborators, 109–113
Purdue Pegboard Test, 208

Quality-of-life focus:
    career development, 73
    models, 43–44, 48–49

*Reading-Free Vocational Interest
    Inventory*, 208
"Real world focus" programs, 187
RECESS, A *Program for Reducing
    Negative-Aggressive Behavior*, 238
Recreation and leisure, 474–498
    age appropriateness, 497
    assessments, 495–497
    assistive technology (AT),
        297–298
    city/county parks and recreation
        programs, 488–489
    community awareness, 489–490
    community-based programs,
        478–479
    community leisure
        supports, 494
    coordinating services, 489–491
    Developmental Disability (DD)
        programs, 488
    elementary students, 481–484
    essential transition elements,
        479–487
    financing, 491
    group outings, 477
    health and wellness, 477–478
    implementation of programs,
        489–495
    independent living program
        options, 487–488
    individualized leisure planning,
        493–494
    integrated generic
        mainstreaming, 490
    interagency responsibilities or
        linkages, 484–486
    leisure program options,
        487–489
    Leisure Time Activities Scale, 210
    local resource guides, 489

movement from school to
    postschool activities,
    486–487
outcome-oriented planning,
    481–484
planning, 493–494
rejuvenation, 476–477
reverse mainstreaming, 490
safety, 497
school responsibilities,
    491–492
service delivery models,
    490–491
skills, 497
student responsibilities, 493
student's needs, interests, and
    preferences, 480–481
teacher responsibilities,
    492–493
transition needs, 476–477
transportation issues, 491
zero exclusion programs, 490
"Reforms" in special education, 231
Regional development disability
    centers, 531–532
Regional transportation
    authorities, 534
Rehabilitation, Comprehensive
    Services, and Developmental
    Disability amendments of
    1978, 18
Rehabilitation Act:
    1973 Act, 13, 16, 19t, 445,
        446t, 447t
    1986 amendments, 20, 23t
    1992 amendments, 26, 274
    1998 amendments, 26–27
    Section 504, nondiscrimination
        rights, 16–18
Residential services, 499–539
    continuum model, 509–510
    historical development,
        504–510
    independent living. *See*
        Independent living services.
    interdependent adult life,
        523–536
    new vision and possibilities, 503
    normalization, 506

parental perspective, 500–501
personal assistance services
    (PAS), 519–523. *See* Personal
    assistance services (PAS).
personal perspective, 501–503
from placements to people,
    504–510
relocation of, 504–505
revisioning, 509–510
supported living, 511–518. *See*
    Supported living.
Reverse mainstreaming, 490
*Revised Handbook for Analyzing Jobs,
    The*, 183

S.A.G.E. (System of Assessment
    and Group Evaluation), 457
Savickas's framework for linking
    career theory and practice,
    85, 88–89, 90t–91t
School administrator
    collaboration, 108–109
School-Based Career
    Development and Transition
    Education Model, 168–170
    human relationships, 169f, 173
    job and daily living skills,
        169f, 173
    occupational information,
        169f, 173
    values, attitudes, and habits,
        169f, 173
School-based programs and
    services, 104–109
School collaborator
    responsibilities, 102, 104
School to Work Opportunity Act
    (STWOA) of 1994, 3, 16, 28–29
SCIPPY, *Social Competence
    Intervention Package for Preschool
    Youngsters*, 238
Self-advocacy, 534
    career development, 73–74
    postsecondary education,
        467–468
    transition coordinator's
        responsibilities, 373
*Self-Advocacy Strategy for Education
    and Transition Planning*, 323

Self-determination, 303–332
  assessments, 312–315
  attaining goals, 324–325
  best practices, 57–59
  career development, 73–74
  case scenarios, 306t
  choice strand, 305–307
  ChoiceMaker curriculum. *See*
    ChoiceMaker curriculum.
  choosing education goals,
    320–321
  choosing employment goals,
    319–320, 321f, 322f
  choosing general goals, 318,
    319f
  choosing goals process,
    318–319
  choosing personal goals,
    321–322
  components, 308
  curriculum matrix, 317t
  expressing goals, 322–324
  federal laws, 310
  goal setting and attainment
    strand, 307, 308
  IDEA and, 310
  importance of, 310
  individual education programs
    (IEPs), 311–316, 323–324
  learning model, 309t
  state laws, 310–311
  students with severe needs,
    326–330
  take action lessons, 325–326
  teaching, 316–330
  transition coordinator's
    responsibilities, 372–373
Self-Determination Knowledge Scale, 312
Self-Determination Scale, 209, 312
Self-Directed IEP, 323
Self-Directed Search, The, 208, 341, 457
Self-monitoring, 261–263
  applications, 263
  benefits, 263
  components of, 262–263
  cueing, 262
  description of, 261
  direct instruction, 262
  matching, 262–263

  rationale for, 262
  self-management
    techniques, 262
Service coordination, 61–62,
  364–385. *See* Coordinating
  services.
Sheltered workshops, 426
Siegel's model, 51–54
*Singer Vocational Evaluation
  System*, 209
Situational assessments,
  184–185, 216
Skill Streaming the Adolescent, 238
*Skill Streaming the Elementary
  Child*, 238
Smith-Fess Act, 9, 13t
Smith-Hughes Act, 9, 13t
Smith-Sears Act, 9, 13t
*Social and Prevocational Information
  Battery* (SPIB), 208, 210
Social learning theory
  (Krumboltz), 81–82
Social policy. *See* Legislation
  and policy.
Social security/disability
  insurance (SSDI), 435, 530
Social skills, 236–238
Social welfare and entitlements, 435
Special education teachers:
  AT training issues, 286, 288t
  collaboration and consultation,
    104–105, 105–106
  community-based education
    (CBE), 105–106
  cultural competence, 126–130
  curriculum development, 228, 230
  fads and "reforms," 231
Special Olympics, 497
SPIB, 208, 210
SSDI, 435, 530
SSI, 435, 530
State academic standards and
  curriculum, 232–236
State career resources, 183
State employment agencies, 424
State employment and training
  programs (ETPs), 110–111
State vocational rehabilitation
  services, 109–110

Statutes. *See* Legislation and
  policy.
Steps toward educational
  progress (STEP), 113–114
*Street Survival Skills Questionnaire,
  The*, 209
Structural career development
  theories, 78, 79
Student monitoring, 182
  congruence between student
    and potential work and
    learning environments,
    184–185
  self-monitoring technique,
    261–263
Student school records, 213
  confidentiality of college
    records, 448
Student self-determination:
  See generally Self-determination
  ChoiceMaker curriculum. *See*
    ChoiceMaker curriculum.
Student transportation. *See*
  Transportation.
  recreation programs and leisure
    activities, 491
Student work samples,
  assessment, 182, 208–209, 220
Student's Guide to the IEP, 323
STWOA, 3, 16, 28–29
Supplemental security insurance
  (SSI), 435, 530
Supported employment, 193–194,
  428–435
  autism, 429
  definitions, 428
  features of, 429–435
  job design, 431–433
  natural supports, 433–434
  ongoing supports, 434–435
  person-centered job selection,
    429–431
Supported living, 511–518
  access to, 514–515
  case study, 517–518
  current challenges, 513
  Kentucky's approach, 515–517
  key concepts, 512–513
Surveys and interviews, 215–216

informational interviews, career
education, 183–184
needs and preferences survey,
217–219f, 369–370f
Systems change strategies, 67

TAKE CHARGE, 341
Task analyses, 183
community-based instruction
(CBI), 265, 268, 269–270f
Teachers:
AT training issues, 286, 288t
collaboration and consultation,
107–108
cultural competence. See
generally Cultural
competence.
special education. See Special
education teachers.
Teaching. See Instruction.
Tech Act, 273
Tech-Prep programs, 175
Technical content teachers,
collaboration, 107–108
Technology:
assistive, 273–301. See Assistive
technology (AT).
fields, 188t
forces of, 186
importance of, 273
Technology-Related Assistance
for Individuals with
Disabilities Act, 273
Test for Everyday Living, 209
Test of Interpersonal Competency for
Employment (TICE), 210
The Career Maturity Index, 341
The Guide for Occupational
Exploration, 183
The Myers/Briggs, 341
The Revised Handbook for Analyzing
Jobs, 183
The Self-Directed Search, 208, 341, 457
The Street Survival Skills
Questionnaire, 209
The Wide-Range Interest and Opinion
Test (WRIOT), 208
Three dimensional learning
programs, 187

TICE, 210
"Time-outs," 220
Time sampling, 221
Trade fields, 188t
Transition coordinator/specialist.
See IEP/transition
coordinator/specialist.
Transition models, 38–54. See
Models, transition.
Transition planning, 333–363
See generally IEPs/transition
planning
ChoiceMaker curriculum. See
ChoiceMaker curriculum.
collaboration and consultation,
95–119. See Collaboration
and consultation.
coordinating transition
services, 364–385. See
Coordinating services.
family involvement, 386–414.
See Family involvement.
new vision and possibilities, 503
parental perspective, 500–501
personal perspective, 501–503
self-determination, 57–59,
303–332. See Self-
determination.
Transition Planning Inventory, 208,
340
Transition Skills Inventory, 208
Transition teams. See
IEP/transition teams.
Transportation:
community-based instruction
(CBI), 265
paratransit, 534
recreation programs and leisure
activities, 491
regional transportation
authorities, 534
Travel AT considerations, 298–299
2 + 2 programs, 175

Underemployment, 75, 441
Unemployment rate, 75, 418, 441
Unifying functional model (AT
selection), 276, 280–281f
United Cerebral Palsy, 10

University education, 439–473. See
Postsecondary education.
U.S. Department of Labor
(DOL), 111
resources, 183
"trainee" status criteria, 178, 179t

Valpar Work Sample, 209
VI rehabilitation programs,
421–422
Videoconferencing, 286–287, 289t
Vineland Adaptive Behavior Scales, 207
Visual impairment (VI)
rehabilitation programs,
421–422
Vocational education, 162–196.
See Career and vocational
education.
Vocational Education Act of 1963,
11, 13t
1968 amendments, 11, 13t
1976 amendments, 19t
Vocational Rehabilitation
amendments:
1954 amendments, 10, 13t
1967 amendments, 11, 13t
1973 amendments, 40
Vocational rehabilitation (VR)
agencies/programs, 419–422

Waksman Social Skills Rating
Form, 210
Wehman's model, 45, 48
What Color is My Parachute?, 341
Whole sequence instruction, 268
Whose Future Is It Anyway?,
323, 340
WIA, 26–27, 425
Wide Range Achievement Test
(WRAT), 210
Wide-Range Interest and Opinion Test
(WRIOT), The, 208
Will's bridges model, 42–43
Halpern's alternative,
43–44
"With-it" teachers, 253–254
Wolfensberger models, 8, 9t
Work adjustment theories, 77–78,
80–81

Work and learning environments
    (potential):
  congruence between student
    and, 184–185
  monitoring, 182–184
Work experience programs,
    developing, 375
Work Force Investment Act (WIA)
    of 1998, 26–27

Work incentives, 435
Work Opportunity Investment Act
    (WIA), 26–27, 425
Work preparation models, 45–48
Work process changes, 187
Work samples, 182, 208–209, 220
Work-study programs, 39–41
  early transition models, 39–41

Working environments,
    assessment, 201–202,
    208–209
WRIOT, 208

Zero exclusion programs, 490
Zero reject principle, 403–404